- **Illustrations** have been selected to reinforce main points. They include numerous maps, artwork and photographs, figures, and tables. Frequently a map or a picture is more effective than words alone in explaining or emphasizing a particular development.

STUDY TIP Primary sources are the raw materials of history. Each feature includes Analyzing the Evidence questions designed to help you interpret each source as a historian would.

STUDY TIP Consider the illustrations as you read to help see the story unfold. For a quick review later, flip through the chapter, look at the illustrations, and read the captions. This will help jog your memory.

- **Boxed features** are a central element of each chapter. They present primary sources as a way to experience the immediacy of the past through the words and perspectives of those who lived it. The features — Comparing American Voices, Reading American Pictures, and Voices from Abroad — emphasize important developments in the narrative.

Review at the end of the chapter

- **A summary** concludes each chapter and highlights the main chapter themes.

- **Connections** immediately following the summary link the chapter's main themes back to the part introduction and provide a bridge to the next chapter.

- **Chapter review questions** ask you to relate the themes presented in the different sections of the chapter. They model the types of broad questions your instructor might ask on an exam.

- **Timelines** help you keep the chronology of events straight.

STUDY TIP Visit the book companion Web site at bedfordstmartins.com/henretta to find practice quizzes and numerous other opportunities to check your progress as you master the material in each chapter.

America's History
Volume Two: Since 1865

America's History

Volume Two: Since 1865

Sixth Edition

James A. Henretta
University of Maryland

David Brody
University of California, Davis

Lynn Dumenil
Occidental College

Bedford / St. Martin's
Boston • New York

For Bedford/St. Martin's
Executive Editor for History: Mary Dougherty
Director of Development for History: Jane Knetzger
Senior Developmental Editor: William J. Lombardo
Senior Production Editor: Bridget Leahy
Senior Production Supervisor: Joe Ford
Executive Marketing Manager: Jenna Bookin Barry
Editorial Assistants: Holly Dye and Amy Leathe
Production Assistants: Amy Derjue and Lidia MacDonald-Carr
Copyeditors: Barbara Bell and Lisa Wehrle
Text Design: Catherine Hawkes, Cat and Mouse Design
Indexer: EdIndex
Photo Research: Pembroke Herbert and Sandi Rygiel/Picture Research Consultants & Archives
Cover Design: Donna Lee Dennison
Cover Art: Expansive view of newly built houses jammed side-by-side, divided by a never-ending street clogged with moving vans unloading families' possessions on moving day. © J R Eyerman. Getty Images / Time & Life Pictures; Levittown, PA, detailed map. © State Museum of Pennsylvania, Pennsylvania Historical and Museum Commission, and The Historical Society of Washington, DC.
Cartography: Mapping Specialists Limited
Composition: TechBooks
Printing and Binding: R.R. Donnelley & Sons Company

President: Joan E. Feinberg
Editorial Director: Denise B. Wydra
Director of Marketing: Karen Melton Soeltz
Director of Editing, Design, and Production: Marcia Cohen
Managing Editor: Elizabeth M. Schaaf

Library of Congress Control Number: 2006940141

Copyright © 2008 by Bedford/St. Martin's

All rights reserved. No part of this book may be reproduced, stored in a retrieval system, or transmitted in any form or by any means, electronic, mechanical, photocopying, recording, or otherwise, except as may be expressly permitted by the applicable copyright statutes or in writing by the Publisher.

Manufactured in the United States of America.

1 0 9 8 7
f e d c b a

For information, write: Bedford/St. Martin's, 75 Arlington Street, Boston, MA 02116 (617-399-4000)

ISBN-10: 0–312–44350–1   ISBN-13: 978–0–312–44350–4 (combined edition)
ISBN-10: 0–312–45285–3   ISBN-13: 978–0–312–45285–8 (Vol. 1)
ISBN-10: 0–312–45286–1   ISBN-13: 978–0–312–45286–5 (Vol. 2)
ISBN-10: 0–312–46548–3   ISBN-13: 978–0–312–46548–3 (high school edition)

Acknowledgments

Acknowledgments and copyrights can be found at the back of the book on pages C-1–C-2, which constitute an extension of the copyright page.

PREFACE FOR INSTRUCTORS

ONE OF THE GIFTS OF textbook writing is the second and third chances it affords. Where else, after all, does the historian have the opportunity to revisit work and strive, on a regular basis, to make it better? Relishing the opportunity, we have, with each edition, sharpened the narrative, refined arguments, restructured chapters, and incorporated fresh scholarship. In this, the sixth edition, we pick up that task again, only this time with a more ambitious goal. We want to bring *America's History* into the twenty-first century. *America's History* was conceived nearly thirty years ago and built into it were assumptions — both intellectual and pedagogical — that, for this edition, we have reconsidered. On the intellectual side, this has led us to a thorough rethinking and recasting of our post-1945 chapters. On the pedagogical side, it has led us to a back-to-basics approach, utilizing an array of learning tools that we are confident will engage and instruct today's students. On both counts, *America's History* will strike instructors as quite new. But we have not departed from the core idea with which we began — to write a comprehensive text that has explanatory power and yet is immediately accessible to every student who enrolls in the survey course.

From the very inception of *America's History*, we set out to write a *democratic* history, one that would convey the experiences of ordinary people even as it recorded the accomplishments of the great and powerful. We focus not only on the marvelous diversity of peoples who became American but also on the institutions — political, economic, cultural, and social — that forged a common national identity. And we present these historical trajectories in an integrated way, using each perspective to make better sense of the others. In our discussion of government and politics, diplomacy and war, we show how they affected — and were affected by — ethnic groups and economic conditions, intellectual beliefs and social changes, and the religious and moral values of the times. Just as important, we place the American experience in a global context. We trace aspects of American society to their origins in European and African cultures, consider the American Industrial Revolution within the framework of the world economy, and plot the foreign relations of the United States as part of an ever-shifting international system of imperial expansion, financial exchange, and diplomatic alliances. In emphasizing the global context, we want to remind students that America never existed alone in the world; that other nations experienced developments comparable to our own; and that, knowing this, we can better understand, through comparative discussions at opportune moments, what was distinctive and particular to the American experience.

In these eventful times, college students — even those who don't think much about America's past or today's news — have to wonder about 9/11 or the Iraq war or the furor over illegal immigration: How did that happen? This question is at the heart of historical inquiry. And in asking it, the student is thinking historically. In *America's History* we aspire to satisfy that student's curiosity. We try to ask the right questions — the big ones and the not-so-big — and then write history that illuminates the answers. We are writing narrative history, but harnessed to historical argument, not simply a retelling of "this happened, then that happened."

Structure

One way of overcoming the student's sense that history is just one-damn-thing-after-another is to show her that American history is constituted of distinct periods or eras that give it shape and meaning. Accordingly, we devised early on a six-part structure, corresponding to what we understood to be the major phases of American development. Part Six, carrying the story from 1945 to the present, stood somewhat apart because it was, by definition, unfinished. In earlier editions, that made sense, but as we move into the twenty-first century, it becomes increasingly clear that we have entered a new phase of American history, and that the era that began in 1945 has ended. So now we have a fully realized Part Six, which we call the Age of Cold War Liberalism, 1945–1980, and a new Part Seven, with the breaking point at 1980 signaling the advent of a conservative America in an emerging post–Cold War world. Students who know only this new age will find in Part Six a coherent narrative history of the times of their parents and grandparents. In Part Seven, they will find an account of an era truly their own, carried to the present with a full chapter on the post-2000 years.

Given the importance of the part structure in the text's scheme, we have taken pains to provide students with the aids to comprehension they need to benefit fully from this organization. Each part begins with a two-page overview. First, a **thematic timeline** highlights the key developments in politics, the economy, society, culture, and foreign affairs; then these themes are fleshed out in a corresponding **part essay**. Each part essay focuses on the crucial engines of historical change—in some eras primarily economic, in others political or diplomatic—that created new conditions of life and transformed social relations. The part organization, encapsulated in the thematic timelines and opening essays, helps students understand the major themes and periods of American history, to see how bits and pieces of historical data acquire significance as part of a larger pattern of development.

The individual chapters are similarly constructed with student comprehension in mind. A **chapter outline** gives readers an overview of the text discussion, followed by a **thematic introduction** that orients them to the central issues and ideas of the chapter. Then, at the end of the chapter, we remind students of important events in a **chapter timeline** and reiterate the themes in an **analytic summary**. The summaries have been thoroughly revised, with the aim of underlining as concretely as possible the main points of the chapter. In addition, we have added a new feature, **Connections**, that enables students to take a longer view, to see how the chapter relates to prior and forthcoming chapters. We are also more attentive to the need of students for effective study aids. Within each chapter, we now append focus questions to each section, and at the chapter's end, a set of study questions. And where students are likely to stumble, we provide a **glossary** that defines the **key concepts** bold faced in the text where first mentioned.

Features: Back to Basics

In keeping with our back-to-basics approach, *America's History* has rebuilt its features program around primary sources, providing students with an opportunity to experience the past through the words and perspectives of those who lived it and, equally important, to encounter historical evidence and learn how to extract meaning from it. The cornerstone of this program is the two-page **Comparing American Voices** feature that appears in every chapter. Each contains several primary sources—excerpts from letters, diaries, autobiographies, and public testimony—offering varying, often conflicting, views on a single event or theme discussed in the chapter. An introduction establishes the historical context, generally with reference to the chapter, and headnotes identify and explain the provenance of the individual documents. These are followed by a series of questions—under the heading Analyzing the Evidence—that focus the student's attention on revealing aspects of the documents and show her how historians—herself included—can draw meaning from contemporary evidence. Instructors will find in Comparing American Voices a major resource for inducting beginning students into the processes of historical analysis. Carried over from the previous edition is **Voices from Abroad,** featuring first-person testimony by foreign visitors and observers, but now also equipped with questions like those in Comparing American Voices, and with a similar pedagogical intent.

America's History has always been noted for its rich offering of maps, figures, and pictures that help students visualize the past. Over 120 **full-color maps** encourage a geographic perspective, many of them with annotations that call out key points. All the maps are cross-referenced in the narrative text, as are the tables and figures. Nearly 40 percent of the **art** and **photographs** are new to this edition, selected to reflect changes in the text and to underscore chapter themes. Most appear in full color, with unusually **substantive captions** that actively engage students with the image and encourage them to analyze visuals as primary documents. To advance further this pedagogical aim, we have developed a new feature that we call **Reading American Pictures**, a full page in each chapter devoted to the visual study of one or more carefully selected contemporary paintings, cartoons, or photographs. These are introduced by a discussion of the context in which they were produced and followed by questions designed to prompt students to treat them as another form of historical evidence. We anticipate that the exercise will provoke lively classroom discussion. In our pedagogical program focusing on primary sources, Reading American Pictures is offered as the visual counterpart to Comparing American Voices and Voices from Abroad.

Textual Changes

Of all the reasons for a new edition, of course, the most compelling is to improve the text itself. Good narrative history is primarily a product of good sentences and good paragraphs. So our labors have been mostly in the trenches, so to speak, in a line-by-line striving for the vividness and human presence that are hallmarks of narrative history. We are also partisans of economical writing, by necessity if we are to incorporate what's new in the field and in contemporary affairs while holding *America's History* to a manageable length. This is a challenge we welcome, believing as we do that brevity is the best antidote to imprecise language and murky argument. Of the more substantive changes, a notable one arose from the refocusing of our features program on primary sources. Whereas previous editions contained boxed essays on American lives, we have now integrated those stories of ordinary and notable Americans into the narrative, much expanding and enlivening its people-centered approach.

Within chapters we have been especially attentive to chronology, which sometimes involved a significant reordering of material. In Part Two (1776–1820), chapters 6 and 7 now provide a continuous political narrative from the Declaration of Independence to the Era of Good Feelings. In Part Three (1820–1877), feedback from instructors persuaded us to consolidate our treatment of the pre–Civil War South into a single, integrated chapter. In Part Four (1877–1914), our chapter on Gilded Age politics has been reorganized to improve chronology and placed after the chapter on the city so as to provide students with a seamless transition to the Progressive era. In Part Five (1914–1945), the three chapters on the 1920s, the Great Depression, and the New Deal have been melded into two crisper, more integrated chapters. All of the chapters in Part Six (1945–1980) and the new Part Seven (1980–2006) have been thoroughly reworked as part of our rethinking of the post-1945 era. In the companion Chapters 26 and 27, we now offer a thematic treatment of the 1950s, while Chapters 28 and 29 provide a coherent narrative account of liberalism's triumph under Kennedy and Johnson and its dramatic decline after 1968. Part Seven represents a much expanded coverage of the post-1980 years, with new chapters devoted to social and economic developments and America since 2000. Altogether, these organizational changes represent the biggest shake-up of *America's History* since its inception.

The revising process also affords us a welcome opportunity to incorporate fresh scholarship. In Part One, we have added new material on life in Africa, the slave trade, the emergence of an African American ethnicity, and on such non-English ethnic colonial groups as the Scots Irish and the Germans. In Chapter 11, we have a completely new section on urban popular culture (masculinity, sexuality, minstrel shows, and racism) drawing on recent advances in cultural history, inventive scholarship that also informs Chapter 18 (on the late-nineteenth-century city) and several twentieth-century chapters, including in Chapter 27 our treatment of consumer culture in the 1950s. Chapter 16 contains fresh information about the impact of farming on the ecosystem of the Great Plains. In Chapter 20, the opening section has been recast to incorporate recent insights into the middle-class impulse behind progressivism, and a new section treats the industrial strife that reoriented progressivism toward the problem of the nation's labor relations. Of the many revisions in the post-1945 chapters, perhaps the most notable derive from the opening of Soviet archives, which allows us at last to see the Cold War from both sides of the Iron Curtain, and also to amend our assessment of the impact of communism on American life. In addition, Part Six contains fresh material on the civil rights movement, on the Vietnam War, and on the revival of American conservatism. Even richer are the additions to Part Seven, "Entering a New Era: Conservatism, Globalization, Terrorism, 1980–2006," especially in the treatment of social movements and the information technology revolution in Chapter 31, and a completely new post-2000 Chapter 32, which, unlike all the preceding chapters, relies not on secondary sources, but primarily on a reading of the contemporary press and the public record.

Supplements

For Students

***Documents to Accompany* America's History, Sixth Edition.** Edited by Melvin Yazawa, University of New Mexico (Volume 1), and Kevin Fernlund, University of Missouri, St. Louis (Volume 2), this primary source reader is designed to accompany *America's History*, Sixth Edition, and offers a chorus of voices from the past to enrich the study of U.S. history. Both celebrated figures and ordinary people, from Frederick Douglass to mill workers, demonstrate the diversity of America's history while putting a human face on historical experience. A wealth of speeches, petitions, advertisements, and posters paint a vivid picture of the social and political life of the time, providing depth and breadth to the textbook discussion. Brief introductions set each document in context, while questions for analysis help link the individual source to larger historical themes.

NEW *E-Documents to Accompany* **America's History, Sixth Edition.** The most robust gathering of primary sources to accompany any U.S. history survey text is now available online. *E-Documents to Accompany* America's History, *Sixth Edition* is perfect for adding an electronic dimension to your class or integrating with your existing online course.

Online Study Guide at bedfordstmartins.com/ henretta. The popular Online Study Guide for *America's History* is a free and uniquely personalized learning tool to help students master themes and information presented in the textbook and improve their historical skills. Assessment quizzes let students evaluate their comprehension and provide them with customized plans for further study through a variety of activities. Instructors can monitor students' progress through the online Quiz Gradebook or receive e-mail updates.

Maps in Context: A Workbook for American History. Written by historical cartography expert Gerald A. Danzer (University of Illinois, Chicago), this skill-building workbook helps students comprehend essential connections between geographic literacy and historical understanding. Organized to correspond to the typical U.S. history survey course, *Maps in Context* presents a wealth of map-centered projects and convenient pop quizzes that give students hands-on experience working with maps. Available free when packaged with the text.

NEW *The Bedford Glossary for U.S. History.* This handy supplement for the survey course gives students clear, concise definitions of the political, economic, social, and cultural terms used by historians and contemporary media alike. The terms are historically contextualized to aid comprehension. Available free when packaged with the text.

NEW *History Matters: A Student Guide to U.S. History Online.* This new resource, written by Alan Gevinson, Kelly Schrum, and Roy Rosenzweig (all of George Mason University), provides an illustrated and annotated guide to 250 of the most useful Web sites for student research in U.S. history as well as advice on evaluating and using Internet sources. This essential guide is based on the acclaimed "History Matters" Web site developed by the American Social History Project and the Center for History and New Media. Available free when packaged with the text.

Bedford Series in History and Culture. Over 100 titles in this highly praised series combine first-rate scholarship, historical narrative, and important primary documents for undergraduate courses. Each book is brief, inexpensive, and focused on a specific topic or period. Package discounts are available.

Historians at Work Series. Brief enough for a single assignment yet meaty enough to provoke thoughtful discussion, each volume in this series examines a single historical question by combining unabridged selections by distinguished historians, each with a different perspective on the issue, with helpful learning aids. Package discounts are available.

Trade Books. Titles published by sister companies Farrar, Straus and Giroux; Henry Holt and Company; Hill and Wang; Picador; and St. Martin's Press are available at deep discounts when packaged with Bedford/St. Martin's textbooks. For more information, visit bedfordstmartins.com/tradeup.

Critical Thinking Modules at bedfordstmartins.com/ historymodules. This Web site offers over two dozen online modules for interpreting maps, audio, visual, and textual sources, centered on events covered in the U.S. history survey. An online guide correlates modules to textbook chapters.

Research and Documentation Online at **bedfordstmartins.com/resdoc.** This Web site provides clear advice on how to integrate primary and secondary sources into research papers, how to cite sources correctly, and how to format in MLA, APA, *Chicago,* or CBE style.

The St. Martin's Tutorial on Avoiding Plagiarism at **bedfordstmartins.com/plagiarismtutorial.** This online tutorial reviews the consequences of plagiarism and explains what sources to acknowledge, how to keep good notes, how to organize research, and how to integrate sources appropriately. This tutorial includes exercises to help students practice integrating sources and recognize acceptable summaries.

Bedford Research Room at **bedfordstmartins.com/ researchroom.** The Research Room, drawn from Mike Palmquist's *The Bedford Researcher,* offers a wealth of resources — including interactive tutorials, research activities, student writing samples, and links to hundreds of other places online — to support students in courses across the disciplines. The site also offers instructors a library of helpful instructional tools.

For Instructors

Instructor's Resource Manual. Written by Jason Newman (Cosumnes River College, Los Rios Community College District), the *Instructor's Resource Manual for AMERICA'S HISTORY,* Sixth Edition, provides both first-time and experienced instructors with valuable teaching tools — annotated chapter outlines, lecture strategies, in-class activities, discussion questions, suggested writing assignments, and related readings and media — to structure and customize their American history course. The manual also offers a convenient, chapter-by-chapter guide to the wealth of supplementary materials available to instructors teaching *America's History.*

Computerized Test Bank. A fully updated Test Bank CD-ROM offers over 80 exercises for each chapter, allowing instructors to pick and choose from a collection of multiple-choice, fill-in, map, and short and long essay questions. To aid instructors in tailoring their tests to suit their classes, every question includes a textbook page number so instructors can direct students to a particular page for correct answers. Also, the software allows instructors to edit both questions and answers to further customize their texts. Correct answers and model responses are included.

Transparencies. This set of over 160 full-color acetate transparencies of all maps and selected images in the text helps instructors present lectures and teach students important map-reading skills.

Book Companion Site at **bedfordstmartins.com/ henretta.** The companion Web site gathers all the electronic resources for *America's History,* including the Online Study Guide and related Quiz Gradebook, at a single Web address, providing convenient links to lecture, assignment, and research materials such as PowerPoint chapter outlines and the digital libraries at Make History.

NEW Make History at **bedfordstmartins.com/ makehistory.** Comprising the content of our five acclaimed online libraries — Map Central, the U.S. History Image Library, DocLinks, HistoryLinks, and PlaceLinks — Make History provides one-stop access to relevant digital content including maps, images, documents, and Web links. Students and instructors alike can search this free, easy-to-use database by keyword, topic, date, or specific chapter of *America's History* and can download any content they find. Instructors using *America's History* can also create entire collections of content and store them online for later use or post their collections to the Web to share with students.

Instructor's Resource CD-ROM. This disc provides instructors with ready-made and customizable PowerPoint multimedia presentations built around chapter outlines, maps, figures, and selected images from the textbook. The disc also includes all maps and selected images from the textbook in jpeg format, the *Instructor's Resource Manual* in pdf format, and a quick-start guide to the Online Study Guide.

Course Management Content. E-content is available for *America's History* in Blackboard, WebCT, and other platforms. This e-content includes nearly all of the offerings from the book's Online Study Center as well as the book's test bank.

Videos and Multimedia. A wide assortment of videos and multimedia CD-ROMs on various topics in American history is available to qualified adopters.

NEW *The AP U.S. History Teaching Toolkit for* **America's History,** *Sixth Edition.* Written by AP experts Jonathan Chu (University of Massachusetts, Boston) and Ellen W. Parisi (Williamsville East High School and D'Youville College), this entirely new AP resource is the first comprehensive history resource for AP teachers. The *AP U.S. History Teaching ToolKit* provides materials to teach the basics of and preparation for the AP U.S. history examination, including entire DBQs. The *ToolKit* also includes a wealth of materials that address the course's main challenges, especially coverage, pacing, and methods for conveying the critical knowledge and skills that AP students need.

NEW *AP U.S. History Testbank for* **America's History,** *Sixth Edition.* Written by Ellen W. Parisi (Williamsville East High School and D'Youville College) specifically for AP teachers and students, the *AP U.S. History Test Bank* is designed to help students recall their textbook reading and prepare for the format and difficulty level of the AP exam. Each chapter of *America's History*, Sixth Edition, has a twenty-question multiple-choice quiz and five AP-style questions that mimic the exam questions. Each major part of *America's History* has a corresponding test containing fifty AP-style questions, which can be used for both student self-testing and in-class practice exams. All multiple-choice questions include five distracters.

Acknowledgments

We are very grateful to the following scholars and teachers who reported on their experiences with the fifth edition or reviewed chapters of the sixth edition. Their comments often challenged us to rethink or justify our interpretations and always provided a check on accuracy down to the smallest detail.

Elizabeth Alexander, *Texas Wesleyan University*
Marjorie Berman, *Red Rocks Community College*
Rebecca Boone, *Lamar University*
Michael L. Cox, *Barton County Community College*
Glen Gendzel, *Indiana University-Perdue*
Jessica Gerard, *Ozarks Technical Community College*
Martin Halpern, *Henderson State University*
Yvonne Johnson, *Central Missouri State University*
Sanford B. Kanter, *San Jacinto College South*
Anthony Kaye, *Penn State University*
William J. Lipkin, *Union County College*
Daniel Littlefield, *University of South Carolina*
James Meriwether, *California State University, Bakersfield*
William Moore, *University of Wyoming*
Allison Parker, *SUNY Brockport*
Phillip Payne, *St. Bonaventure University*
Louis W. Potts, *University of Missouri, Kansas City*
Yasmin Rahman, *University of Colorado at Boulder*
Kim Richardson, *Community College at Jacksonville*
Howard Rock, *Florida International University*
Donald W. Rogers, *Central Connecticut State University*
Jason Scott Smith, *University of New Mexico*
David Steigerwald, *The Ohio State University, Marion*
David G. Thompson, *Illinois Central College*
Christine S. White, *San Jacinto College South*

We also extend our thanks and gratitude to our high school colleagues and college instructors associated with the College Board who commented on *America's History* and reviewed the new AP supplements tailored specifically for our textbook.

Tom Alleman, *Carbon High School*
Margaret Bramlett, *St. Paul's Episcopal School*
Cameron Flint, *Cloverleaf High School*
Tim Greene, *Jersey Shore Senior High School*
Jonathan Lurie, *Rutgers University*
Jackie McHargue, *Duncanville High School*
Christine Madsen, *Flintridge Prep School*
Louisa Moffitt, *Marist School*
Joseph J. O'Neill, *Mount Saint Charles Academy*
La Juana J. Reban Coleman, *NMHU Center at Rio Rancho*
Rex Sanders, *A & M Consolidated High School*
Mary van Weezel, *Lakeland Regional High School*
Joe Villano, *Marist College (retired)*

As the authors of *America's History*, we know better than anyone else how much this book is the work of other hands and minds. We are grateful to Mary Dougherty and Jane Knetzger, who oversaw the project, and William Lombardo, who used his extensive knowledge and critical skills as a well-trained historian to edit our text and suggest a multitude of improvements. As usual, Joan E. Feinberg has been generous in providing the resources we needed to produce the sixth edition. Bridget Leahy did more than we had a right to expect in producing an outstanding volume. Karen Melton Soeltz and Jenna Bookin Barry in the marketing department have been instrumental in helping this book reach the classroom. We also thank the rest of our editorial and production team for their dedicated efforts: Amy Leathe, Holly Dye, Amy Derjue, and Lidia MacDonald-Carr; Pembroke Herbert and Sandi Rygiel at Picture Research Consultants and Archives; and Sandy Schechter. Finally, we want to express our appreciation for the invaluable assistance of Patricia Deveneau and Jason Newman, whose work contributed in many ways to the intellectual vitality of this new edition of *America's History*.

James A. Henretta
David Brody
Lynn Dumenil

BRIEF CONTENTS

PART FOUR
A Maturing Industrial Society, 1877–1914   484

- **16** The American West   487
- **17** Capital and Labor in the Age of Enterprise, 1877–1900   519
- **18** The Industrial City: Building It, Living In It   551
- **19** Politics in the Age of Enterprise, 1877–1896   583
- **20** The Progressive Era, 1900–1914   611
- **21** An Emerging World Power, 1877–1914   641

PART FIVE
The Modern State and Society, 1914–1945   670

- **22** War and the American State, 1914–1920   673
- **23** Modern Times, 1920–1932   705
- **24** Redefining Liberalism: The New Deal, 1933–1939   737
- **25** The World at War, 1939–1945   767

PART SIX
The Age of Cold War Liberalism, 1945–1980   798

- **26** Cold War America, 1945–1960   801
- **27** The Age of Affluence, 1945–1960   831
- **28** The Liberal Consensus: Flaming Out, 1960–1968   861
- **29** Towards a Conservative America: The 1970s   895

PART SEVEN
Entering a New Era: Conservatism, Globalization, Terrorism, 1980–2006   924

- **30** The Reagan Revolution and the End of the Cold War, 1980–2001   927
- **31** A Dynamic Economy, A Divided People, 1980–2000   957
- **32** Into the Twenty-First Century   989

DOCUMENTS   D–1
APPENDIX   A–1
GLOSSARY   G–1
CREDITS   C–1
INDEX   I–1

CONTENTS

Preface *v*
Brief Contents *xi*
Maps *xix*
Figures and Tables *xxi*
Special Features *xxii*
About the Authors *xxiii*

15 Reconstruction, 1865–1877 *457*

Presidential Reconstruction *458*
    Presidential Initiatives 458
    Acting on Freedom 461
    Congress versus President 464

Radical Reconstruction *466*
    Congress Takes Command 466
    Woman Suffrage Denied 469
    Republican Rule in the South 469
    The Quest for Land 472

The Undoing of Reconstruction *476*
    Counterrevolution 476
    The Acquiescent North 478
    The Political Crisis of 1877 480

Summary *481*
    Connections: Sectionalism 482

Timeline *483*

For Further Exploration *483*

■ **VOICES FROM ABROAD**
David Macrae: The Devastated South *460*

■ **COMPARING AMERICAN VOICES**
Freedom *462*

■ **READING AMERICAN PICTURES**
Why Sharecropping? *475*

PART FOUR
A Maturing Industrial Society, 1877–1914 *484*

16 The American West *487*

The Great Plains *488*
    Indians of the Great Plains 489
    Wagon Trains, Railroads, and Ranchers 489
    Homesteaders 495
    The Fate of the Indians 498

The Far West *505*
    The Mining Frontier 505
    Hispanics, Chinese, Anglos 508
    Golden California 512

Summary *515*
    Connections: The American West 515

Timeline *517*

For Further Exploration *517*

■ **READING AMERICAN PICTURES**
Uncovering the Culture of the Plains Indians *490*

■ **COMPARING AMERICAN VOICES**
Becoming White *500*

■ **VOICES FROM ABROAD**
Baron Joseph Alexander von Hübner: A Western Boom Town *507*

17 Capital and Labor in the Age of Enterprise, 1877–1900 *519*

Industrial Capitalism Triumphant *520*
    The Age of Steel 520
    The Railroad Boom 522
    Large-Scale Enterprise 524

The World of Work 528
    Labor Recruits 528
    Autonomous Labor 536
    Systems of Control 537

The Labor Movement 538
    Reformers and Unionists 540
    The Emergence of the AFL 542
    Industrial War 543
    American Radicalism in the Making 544

Summary 547
    Connections: Economy 548

Timeline 549

For Further Exploration 549

■ **VOICES FROM ABROAD**
Count Vay de Vaya und Luskod: Pittsburgh Inferno 532

■ **COMPARING AMERICAN VOICES**
Working Women 534

■ **READING AMERICAN PICTURES**
The Killing Floor: Site of America's Mass-Production Revolution? 539

18 The Industrial City: Building It, Living in It 551

Urbanization 552
    City Innovation 552
    Private City, Public City 555

Upper Class/Middle Class 558
    The Urban Elite 558
    The Suburban World 559
    Middle-Class Families 561

City Life 566
    Newcomers 566
    Ward Politics 568
    Religion in the City 572
    City Amusements 574
    The Higher Culture 578

Summary 579
    Connections: Society 580

Timeline 581

For Further Exploration 581

■ **READING AMERICAN PICTURES**
Challenging Female Delicacy: The New Woman 565

■ **COMPARING AMERICAN VOICES**
Coming to America: The Downside 570

■ **VOICES FROM ABROAD**
José Martí: Coney Island, 1881 575

19 Politics in the Age of Enterprise, 1877–1896 583

The Politics of the Status Quo, 1877–1893 584
    The Washington Scene 584
    The Ideology of Individualism 587
    The Supremacy of the Courts 588

Politics and the People 589
    Cultural Politics: Party, Religion, and Ethnicity 589
    Organizational Politics 592
    Women's Political Culture 594

Race and Politics in the New South 595
    Biracial Politics 596
    One-Party Rule Triumphant 597

The Crisis of American Politics: The 1890s 599
    The Populist Revolt 602
    Money and Politics 604
    Climax: The Election of 1896 605

Summary 608
    Connections: Politics 608

Timeline 609

For Further Exploration 609

■ **READING AMERICAN PICTURES**
Parties and People: How Democratic Was American Politics? 591

■ **VOICES FROM ABROAD**
Ernst Below: Beer and German American Politics 593

■ **COMPARING AMERICAN VOICES**
"Negro Domination!" 600

20 The Progressive Era, 1900–1914 611

The Course of Reform 612
    The Middle-Class Impulse 612
    Progressive Ideas 612

Women Progressives *614*
Urban Liberalism *618*
Reforming Politics *623*
Racism and Reform *624*

Progressivism and National Politics *627*
The Making of a Progressive President *627*
Regulating the Marketplace *627*
The Fracturing of Republican Progressivism *632*
Woodrow Wilson and the New Freedom *633*

Summary *638*
Connections: Politic *638*

Timeline *639*

For Further Exploration *639*

■ **COMPARING AMERICAN VOICES**
The Triangle Fire *620*

■ **VOICES FROM ABROAD**
James Bryce: America in 1905: "Business Is King" *628*

■ **READING AMERICAN PICTURES**
Reining in Big Business? Cartoonists Join the Battle *630*

21 An Emerging World Power, 1877–1914 *641*

The Roots of Expansion *642*
Diplomacy in the Gilded Age *642*
The Economy of Expansionism *644*
The Making of a "Large" Foreign Policy *646*
The Ideology of Expansionism *647*

An American Empire *648*
The Cuban Crisis *648*
The Spoils of War *650*
The Imperial Experiment *652*

Onto the World Stage *655*
A Power among Powers *659*
The Open Door in Asia *662*
Wilson and Mexico *664*
The Gathering Storm in Europe *666*

Summary *668*
Connections: Diplomacy *668*

Timeline *669*

For Further Exploration *669*

■ **COMPARING AMERICAN VOICES**
Debating the Philippines *656*

■ **READING AMERICAN PICTURES**
Imperial Dilemmas *658*

■ **VOICES FROM ABROAD**
Jean Hess, Émile Zola, and Ruben Dario: American Goliath *660*

PART FIVE
The Modern State and Society, 1914–1945 *670*

22 War and the American State, 1914–1920 *673*

Great War, 1914–1918 *674*
War in Europe *674*
The Perils of Neutrality *675*
"Over There" *678*
The American Fighting Force *680*

War on the Home Front *683*
Mobilizing Industry and the Economy *683*
Mobilizing American Workers *685*
Wartime Reform: Woman Suffrage and Prohibition *688*
Promoting National Unity *692*

An Unsettled Peace, 1919–1920 *694*
The Treaty of Versailles *694*
Racial Strife, Labor Unrest, and the Red Scare *698*

Summary *702*
Connections: Diplomacy *702*

Timeline *703*

For Further Exploration *703*

■ **VOICES FROM ABROAD**
A German Propaganda Appeal to Black Soldiers *682*

■ **COMPARING AMERICAN VOICES**
The Great Migration *686*

■ **READING AMERICAN PICTURES**
"Over Here": Women's Wartime Opportunities *689*

23 Modern Times, 1920–1932 *705*

The Business-Government Partnership of the 1920s *706*
    Politics in the Republican "New Era" *706*
    Corporate Capitalism *709*
    Economic Expansion Abroad *711*
    Foreign Policy in the 1920s *712*

A New National Culture *713*
    A Consumer Society *713*
    The World of the Automobile *714*
    The Movies and Mass Culture *714*

Redefining American Identity *718*
    The Rise of Nativism *718*
    Legislating Values: Evolution and Prohibition *721*
    Intellectual Crosscurrents *723*
    Cultural Wars: The Election of 1928 *726*

The Onset of the Great Depression, 1929–1932 *727*
    Causes and Consequences *727*
    Herbert Hoover Responds *728*
    Rising Discontent *730*
    The 1932 Election *731*

Summary *734*
    Connections: Society *734*

Timeline *735*

For Further Exploration *735*

■ **READING AMERICAN PICTURES**
Patrolling the Texas Border *720*

■ **COMPARING AMERICAN VOICES**
The Scopes Trial *724*

■ **VOICES FROM ABROAD**
Mary Agnes Hamilton: Breadlines and Beggars *732*

24 Redefining Liberalism: The New Deal, 1933–1939 *737*

The New Deal Takes Over, 1933–1935 *738*
    Roosevelt's Leadership *738*
    The Hundred Days *739*
    The New Deal under Attack *744*

The Second New Deal, 1935–1938 *746*
    Legislative Accomplishments *746*
    The 1936 Election *747*
    Stalemate *748*

The New Deal's Impact on Society *749*
    The Rise of Labor *749*
    Women and Blacks in the New Deal *750*
    Migrants and Minorities in the West *755*
    A New Deal for the Environment *759*
    The New Deal and the Arts *760*
    The Legacies of the New Deal *762*

Summary *764*
    Connections: Economy *764*

Timeline *765*

For Further Exploration *765*

■ **COMPARING AMERICAN VOICES**
Ordinary People Respond to the New Deal *740*

■ **VOICES FROM ABROAD**
Odette Keun: A Foreigner Looks at the Tennessee Valley Authority *758*

■ **READING AMERICAN PICTURES**
Interpreting the Public Art of the New Deal *761*

25 The World at War, 1939–1945 *767*

The Road to War *768*
    The Rise of Fascism *768*
    Isolationists versus Interventionists *769*
    Retreat from Isolationism *770*
    The Attack on Pearl Harbor *771*

Organizing for Victory *774*
    Financing the War *774*
    Mobilizing the American Fighting Force *775*
    Workers and the War Effort *777*
    Politics in Wartime *781*

Life on the Home Front *782*
    "For the Duration" *782*
    Migration and Social Conflict *783*
    Civil Rights during Wartime *784*

Fighting and Winning the War *787*
    Wartime Aims and Tensions *787*
    The War in Europe *788*
    The War in the Pacific *791*
    Planning the Postwar World *791*

Summary 796
    Connections: Government 796

Timeline 797

For Further Exploration 797

- **READING AMERICAN PICTURES**
  U.S. Political Propaganda on the Homefront during World War II 776
- **COMPARING AMERICAN VOICES**
  Women in the Wartime Workplace 778
- **VOICES FROM ABROAD**
  Monica Itoi Sone: Japanese Relocation 786

PART SIX
The Age of Cold War Liberalism, 1945–1980 798

26 Cold War America, 1945–1960 801

The Cold War 802
    Descent into Cold War, 1945–1946 802
    George Kennan and the Containment Strategy 803
    Containment in Asia 810

The Truman Era 813
    Reconversion 813
    The Fair Deal 815
    The Great Fear 815

Modern Republicanism 818
    They Liked Ike 818
    The Hidden-Hand Presidency 819
    Eisenhower and the Cold War 819
    Containment in the Post-Colonial World 822
    Eisenhower's Farewell Address 827

Summary 828
    Connections: Diplomacy and Politics 828

Timeline 829

For Further Exploration 829

- **VOICES FROM ABROAD**
  Jean Monnet: Truman's Generous Proposal 807
- **COMPARING AMERICAN VOICES**
  Hunting Communists and Liberals 820

- **READING AMERICAN PICTURES**
  Why a Cold War Space Race? 823

27 The Age of Affluence, 1945–1960 831

Economic Powerhouse 832
    Engines of Economic Growth 832
    The Corporate Order 834
    Labor-Mangement Accord 835

The Affluent Society 837
    The Suburban Explosion 837
    The Search for Security 841
    Consumer Culture 842
    The Baby Boom 844
    Contradictions in Women's Lives 846
    Youth Culture 847
    Cultural Dissenters 847

The Other America 849
    Immigrants and Migrants 849
    The Urban Crisis 850
    The Emerging Civil Rights Struggle 852

Summary 858
    Connections: Economy 858

Timeline 859

For Further Exploration 859

- **VOICES FROM ABROAD**
  Hanoch Bartov: Everyone Has a Car 840
- **READING AMERICAN PICTURES**
  The Cold War and the Civil Rights Movement 854
- **COMPARING AMERICAN VOICES**
  Challenging White Supremacy 856

28 The Liberal Consensus: Flaming Out, 1960–1968 861

John F. Kennedy and the Politics of Expectation 862
    The New Politics 862
    The Kennedy Administration 863
    The Civil Rights Movement Stirs 864
    Kennedy, Cold Warrior 868
    The Kennedy Assassination 870

Lyndon B. Johnson and the Great Society 871
    The Momentum for Civil Rights 871
    Enacting the Liberal Agenda 872

Into the Quagmire, 1963–1968 877
    Escalation 877
    Public Opinion on Vietnam 879
    Student Activism 879

Coming Apart 884
    The Counterculture 884
    Beyond Civil Rights 885

1968: A Year of Shocks 888
    The Politics of Vietnam 888
    Backlash 891

Summary 892
    Connections: Diplomacy and Politics 892

Timeline 893

For Further Exploration 893

■ **COMPARING AMERICAN VOICES**
The Toll of War 880

■ **VOICES FROM ABROAD**
Che Guevara: Vietnam and the World Freedom Struggle 883

■ **READING AMERICAN PICTURES**
War and its Aftermath: Images of the Vietnam Conflict, 1968 and 1982 890

29 The 1970s: Towards a Conservative America 895

The Nixon Years 896
    Nixon's Domestic Agenda 896
    Détente 896
    Nixon's War 898
    The 1972 Election 901
    Watergate 901

Battling for Civil Rights: The Second State 902
    The Revival of Feminism 903
    Enforcing Civil Rights 906

Lean Years 911
    Energy Crisis 911
    Environmentalism 912
    Economic Woes 913

Politics in the Wake of Watergate 917
    Jimmy Carter: The Outsider as President 917
    Carter and the World 920

Summary 922
    Connections: Society 922

Timeline 923

For Further Exploration 923

■ **COMPARING AMERICAN VOICES**
Debating the Equal Rights Amendment 908

■ **READING AMERICAN PICTURES**
A Near Meltdown at Three Mile Island, 1979 914

■ **VOICES FROM ABROAD**
Fei Xiaotong: America's Crisis of Faith 919

PART SEVEN
Entering a New Era: Conservatism, Globalization, Terrorism, 1980–2006 924

30 The Reagan Revolution and the End of the Cold War, 1980–2001 927

The Rise of Conservatism 928
    Reagan and the Emergence of the New Right 928
    The Election of 1980 929

The Reagan Presidency, 1981–1989 933
    Reaganomics 933
    Reagan's Second Term 936

Defeating Communism and Creating a New World Order 938
    The End of the Cold War 939
    The Presidency of George H. W. Bush 943
    Reagan, Bush, and the Middle East, 1980–1991 944

The Clinton Presidency, 1993–2001 946
    Clinton's Early Record 946
    The Republican Resurgence 948
    Clinton's Impeachment 950
    Foreign Policy at the End of the Twentieth Century 951

Summary 954
    Connections: Government and Politics 954

Timeline 955

For Further Exploration 955

■ **COMPARING AMERICAN VOICES**
Christianity and Public Life 930

READING AMERICAN PICTURES
Image Warfare: Fighting to Define the Reagan Presidency *934*

VOICES FROM ABROAD
Zhu Shida: China and the United States: A Unique Relationship *940*

31 A Dynamic Economy, A Divided People, 1980–2000 *957*

America in the Global Economy and Society *958*
   The Economic Challenge *958*
   The Turn to Prosperity *961*
   Globalization *963*

The New Technology *970*
   The Computer Revolution *970*
   Technology and the Control of Popular Culture *973*

Culture Wars *975*
   An Increasingly Pluralistic Society *976*
   Conflicting Values: Women's and Gay Rights *983*

Summary *986*
   Connections: Society and Technology *986*

Timeline *987*

For Further Exploration *987*

COMPARING AMERICAN VOICES
Cheap Labor: Immigration and Globalization *978*

VOICES FROM ABROAD
Janet Daley: A U.S. Epidemic *981*

READING AMERICAN PICTURES
The Abortion Debate Hits the Streets *985*

32 Into the Twenty-First Century *989*

The Advent of George W. Bush *990*
   The Contested Election of 2000 *990*
   The Bush Agenda *991*

American Hegemony Challenged *996*
   September 11, 2001 *998*
   The War on Terror: Iraq *999*
   The Election of 2004 *1002*

Unfinished Business 1005
   The President's Travails *1005*
   What Kind of America? *1007*
   What Kind of World? *1012*

Timeline *1017*

For Further Exploration *1017*

READING AMERICAN PICTURES
Conservatism at a Crossroads *997*

VOICES FROM ABROAD
Abu Musab al-Zarqawi: A Strategy for the Iraq Insurgency *1003*

COMPARING AMERICAN VOICES
The Stem-Cell Research Controversy *1010*

Documents *D-1*
   The Declaration of Independence *D-1*
   The Articles of Confederation and Perpetual Union *D-3*
   The Constitution of the United States of America *D-7*
   Amendments to the Constitution with Annotations (Including the Six Unratified Amendments) *D-13*

Appendix *A-1*

Glossary *G-1*

Credits *C-1*

Index *I-1*

MAPS

15 Reconstruction, 1865–1877

Reconstruction 467
The Barrow Plantation, 1860 473
The Barrow Plantation, 1881 473

16 The American West

The Natural Environment of the West, 1860s 488
Western Trunk Lines, 1887 491
The Indian Frontier, to 1890 499
The Sioux Reservations in South Dakota, 1868–1899 502
The Mining Frontier, 1848–1890 506
The Settlement of the Pacific Slope, 1860–1890 509

17 Capital and Labor in the Age of Enterprise, 1877–1900

The Expansion of the Railroad System, 1870–1890 524
The Dressed Meat Industry, 1900 525
The New South, 1900 529

18 The Industrial City: Building It, Living In It

The Expansion of Chicago, 1865–1902 554
Sources of European Immigration to the United States, 1871–1910 567
The Lower East Side, New York City, 1900 568

19 Politics in the Age of Enterprise, 1877–1896

Presidential Elections of 1880, 1884, and 1888 586
Disfranchisement in the New South 597
The Heyday of Western Populism, 1892 602
Presidential Elections of 1892 and 1896 607

20 The Progressive Era, 1900–1914

Woman Suffrage, 1890–1919 618
National Parks and Forests, 1872–1980 631
Presidential Election of 1912 635

21 An Emerging World Power, 1877–1914

The Spanish-American War of 1898 651
The American Empire, 1917 655
The Panama Canal: The Design 662
Policeman of the Caribbean 662
The Great Powers in East Asia, 1898–1910 663

22 War and the American State, 1914–1920

European Alliances in 1914 *675*
U.S. Participation on the Western Front, 1918 *679*
The Great Migration and Beyond *690*
Prohibition on the Eve of the Eighteenth Amendment, 1919 *693*
Europe and the Middle East after World War I *696*

23 Modern Times, 1920–1932

Ku Klux Klan Politics and Violence in the 1920s *708*
The Spread of Radio, to 1939 *717*
Presidential Election of 1928 *727*
The Great Depression: Families on Relief, to 1933 *729*
The Presidential Election of 1932 *733*

24 Redefining Liberalism: The New Deal, 1933–1939

Popular Protest in the Great Depression, 1933–1939 *751*
The Dust Bowl and Federal Building Projects in the West, 1930–1941 *756*
The Tennessee Valley Authority, 1933–1952 *760*

25 The World at War, 1939–1945

World War II in the North Atlantic, 1939–1943 *772*
Japanese Relocation Camps *785*
World War II in Europe, 1941–1943 *788*
World War II in Europe, 1944–1945 *789*
World War II in the Pacific, 1941–1942 *792*
World War II in the Pacific, 1943–1945 *793*

26 Cold War America, 1945–1960

Cold War in Europe, 1955 *806*
The Korean War, 1950–1953 *811*
Presidential Election of 1948 *815*
American Global Defense Treaties in the Cold War Era *824*
The Military-Industrial Complex *826*

27 The Age of Affluence, 1945–1960

Shifting Population Patterns, 1950–1980 *838*
Connecting the Nation: The Interstate Highway System, 1930 and 1970 *839*

28 The Liberal Consensus: Flaming Out, 1960–1968

Decolonization and the Third World, 1943–1990 *865*
The Civil Rights Struggle, 1954–1965 *866*
The United States and Cuba, 1961–1962 *869*
Black Voter Registration in the South, 1964 and 1975 *873*
Presidential Election of 1964 *873*
The Vietnam War, 1968 *877*
Presidential Election of 1968 *892*

29 The 1970s: Toward a Conservative America

States Ratifying the Equal Rights Amendment, 1972–1977 *906*
From Rust Belt to Sun Belt, 1940–2000 *916*

30 The Reagan Revolution and the End of the Cold War: 1980–2001

Presidential Election of 1980 *932*
U.S. Involvement in Latin America and the Caribbean, 1954–2000 *937*
The Collapse of the Soviet Union and the Creation of Independent States, 1989–1991 *942*
Presidential Election of 1992 *947*
Ethnic Conflict in the Balkans: The Breakup of Yugoslavia, 1991–1992 *952*

31 A Dynamic Economy, A Divided People, 1980–2000

Growth of the European Community, 1951–2005 *965*
Hispanic and Asian Populations, 2000 *977*

32 Into the Twenty-First Century

Proposed Oil Development in the Arctic National Wildlife Refuge (ANWR) *994*
U.S. Involvement in the Middle East, 1979–2006 *1001*
Ethnoreligious Groups in Iraq, 2006 *1016*

FIGURES AND TABLES

Figures

Business Activity and Wholesale Prices, 1869–1900   *520*

Changes in the Labor Force, 1870–1910   *528*

American Immigration, 1870–1914   *531*

Floor Plan of a Dumbbell Tenement   *556*

Ethnocultural Voting Patterns in the Midwest, 1870–1892   *590*

The Federal Bureaucracy, 1890–1917   *637*

Balance of U.S. Imports, 1870–1914   *645*

A Statistical Index of Boom and Bust   *728*

Unemployment, 1915–1945   *729*

Government Military and Civilian Spending as a Percentage of GDP, 1920–1980   *774*

National Defense Spending, 1940–1965   *813*

Gross Domestic Product, 1930–1972   *833*

Labor Union Strength, 1900–1997   *836*

The American Birthrate, 1860–1980   *845*

Legal Immigration to the United States by Region, 1931–1984   *849*

Americans in Poverty, 1959–2000   *876*

U.S. Troops in Vietnam, 1960–1973   *878*

U.S. Energy Consumption, 1900–2000   *911*

The Inflation Rate, 1960–2000   *915*

The Annual Federal Budget Deficit (or Surplus), 1940–2005   *935*

Productivity, Family Income, and Wages, 1970–2004   *958*

The Increase in Two-Worker Families   *960*

Boom and Bust in the Stock Market   *964*

American Immigration, 1920–2000   *976*

Tables

Primary Reconstruction Laws and Constitutional Amendments   *468*

Ten Largest Cities by Population, 1870 and 1900   *552*

High School Graduates, 1870–1910   *564*

Newspaper Circulation   *577*

Progressive Legislation and Supreme Court Decisions   *616*

Exports to Canada and Europe Compared with Exports to Asia and Latin America, 1875–1900   *645*

American Banks and Bank Failures, 1920–1940   *739*

Major New Deal Legislation   *747*

Major Great Society Legislation   *874*

Impact of the Bush Tax Cuts, 2001–2003   *996*

SPECIAL FEATURES

■ Comparing American Voices

Freedom 462
Becoming White 500
Working Women 534
Coming to America: The Downside 570
"Negro Domination!" 600
The Triangle Fire 620
Debating the Philippines 656
The Great Migration 686
The Scopes Trial 724
Ordinary People Respond to the New Deal 740
Women in the Wartime Workplace 778
Hunting Communists and Liberals 820
Challenging White Supremacy 856
The Toll of War 880
Debating the Equal Rights Amendment 908
Christianity and Public Life 930
Cheap Labor: Immigration and Globalization 978
The Stem-Cell Research Controversy 1010

■ Reading American Pictures

Why Sharecropping? 475
Uncovering the Culture of the Plains Indians 490
The Killing Floor: Site of America's Mass-Production Revolution? 539
Challenging Female Delicacy: The New Woman 565
Parties and People: How Democratic Was American Politics? 591
Reining in Big Business? Cartoonists Join the Battle 630
Imperial Dilemmas 658
"Over Here": Women's Wartime Opportunities 689
Patrolling the Texas Border 720
Interpreting the Public Art of the New Deal 761
U.S. Political Propaganda on the Homefront during World War II 776

Why a Cold War Space Race? 823
The Cold War and the Civil Rights Movement 854
War and its Aftermath: Images of the Vietnam Conflict, 1968 and 1982 890
A Near-Meltdown at Three Mile Island, 1979 914
Image Warfare: Fighting to Define the Reagan Presidency 934
The Abortion Debate Hits the Streets 985
Conservatism at a Crossroads 997

■ Voices From Abroad

David Macrae: The Devastated South 460
Baron Joseph Alexander von Hübner: A Western Boom Town 507
Count Vay de Vaya und Luskod: Pittsburgh Inferno 532
José Martí: Coney Island, 1881 575
Ernst Below: Beer and German American Politics 593
James Bryce: America in 1905: "Business Is King" 628
Jean Hess, Émile Zola, and Ruben Dario: American Goliath 660
A German Propaganda Appeal to Black Soldiers 682
Mary Agnes Hamilton: Breadlines and Beggars 732
Odette Keun: A Foreigner Looks at the Tennessee Valley Authority 758
Monica Itoi Sone: Japanese Relocation 786
Jean Monnet: Truman's Generous Proposal 807
Hanoch Bartov: Everyone Has a Car 840
Che Guevara: Vietnam and the World Freedom Struggle 883
Fei Xiaotong: America's Crisis of Faith 919
Zhu Shida: China and the United States: A Unique Relationship 940
A U.S. Epidemic 981
Abu Musab al-Zarqawi: A Strategy for the Iraq Insurgency 1003

ABOUT THE AUTHORS

JAMES A. HENRETTA is Priscilla Alden Burke Professor of American History at the University of Maryland, College Park. He received his undergraduate education at Swarthmore College and his Ph.D. from Harvard University. He has taught at the University of Sussex, England; Princeton University; UCLA; Boston University; as a Fulbright lecturer in Australia at the University of New England; and at Oxford University as the Harmsworth Professor of American History. His publications include *The Evolution of American Society, 1700–1815: An Interdisciplinary Analysis;* "*Salutary Neglect": Colonial Administration under the Duke of Newcastle; Evolution and Revolution: American Society, 1600–1820; The Origins of American Capitalism;* and an edited volume, *Republicanism and Liberalism in America and the German States, 1750–1850*. His most recent publication is a long article, "Charles Evans Hughes and the Strange Death of Liberal America," (*Law and History Review*, 2006), derived from his ongoing research on The Liberal State in New York, 1820–1975.

DAVID BRODY is Professor Emeritus of History at the University of California, Davis. He received his B.A., M.A., and Ph.D. from Harvard University. He has taught at the University of Warwick in England, at Moscow State University in the former Soviet Union, and at Sydney University in Australia. He is the author of *Steelworkers in America; Workers in Industrial America: Essays on the 20th Century Struggle;* and *In Labor's Cause: Main Themes on the History of the American Worker*. His most recent book is *Labor Embattled: History, Power, Rights* (2005). He has been awarded fellowships from the Social Science Research Council, the Guggenheim Foundation, and the National Endowment for the Humanities. He is past president (1991–1992) of the Pacific Coast branch of the American Historical Association.

LYNN DUMENIL is Robert Glass Cleland Professor of American History at Occidental College in Los Angeles. She is a graduate of the University of Southern California and received her Ph.D. from the University of California, Berkeley. She has written *The Modern Temper: American Culture and Society in the 1920s* and *Freemasonry and American Culture: 1880–1930*. Her articles and reviews have appeared in the *Journal of American History;* the *Journal of American Ethnic History: Reviews in American History;* and the *American Historical Review*. She has been a historical consultant to several documentary film projects and is on the Pelzer Prize Committee of the Organization of American Historians. Her current work, for which she received a National Endowment for the Humanities Fellowship, is on World War I, citizenship, and the state. In 2001–2002 she was the Bicentennial Fulbright Chair in American Studies at the University of Helsinki.

America's History

Volume Two: Since 1865

15 Reconstruction
1865–1877

Presidential Reconstruction
Presidential Initiatives
Acting on Freedom
Congress versus President

Radical Reconstruction
Congress Takes Command
Woman Suffrage Denied
Republican Rule in the South
The Quest for Land

The Undoing of Reconstruction
Counterrevolution
The Acquiescent North
The Political Crisis of 1877

Summary
Connections: Sectionalism

IN HIS SECOND INAUGURAL ADDRESS, President Lincoln spoke of the need to "bind up the nation's wounds." No one knew better than Lincoln how daunting a task that would be. Slavery was finished. That much was certain. But what system of labor should replace plantation slavery? What rights should the freedmen be accorded beyond emancipation? How far should the federal government go to settle these questions? And, most immediately pressing, on what terms should the rebellious states be restored to the Union?

The last speech Lincoln delivered, on April 11, 1865, demonstrated his grasp of these issues. Reconstruction, he said, had to be regarded as a practical, not a theoretical, problem. It could be solved only if Republicans remained united, even if that meant compromising on principled differences dividing them, and only if the defeated South gave its consent, even if that meant forgiveness of the South's transgressions. The speech revealed the middle ground, at once magnanimous and open-minded, on which Lincoln hoped to reunite a wounded nation.

What course Reconstruction might have taken had Lincoln lived is one of the unanswerable questions of American history. On April 14, 1865 — five days after Lee's surrender at Appomattox — Lincoln was shot in the head at Ford's Theatre in Washington by John Wilkes Booth, a

◀ **Chloe and Sam (1882)**

After the Civil War the country went through the wrenching peacemaking process known as Reconstruction. The struggle between the victorious North and the vanquished South was fought out on a political landscape, but Thomas Hovenden's heartwarming painting reminds us of the deeper meaning of Reconstruction: that Chloe and Sam, after lives spent in slavery, might end their days in the dignity of freedom. Thomas Colville Fine Art.

prominent Shakespearean actor and Confederate sympathizer who had been plotting to abduct Lincoln and rescue the South. After Lee's surrender, Booth became bent on revenge. Without regaining consciousness, Lincoln died on April 15, 1865.

With one stroke John Wilkes Booth sent Lincoln to martyrdom, hardened many Northerners against the South, and handed the presidency to a man utterly lacking in Lincoln's moral sense and political judgment, Vice President Andrew Johnson.

Presidential Reconstruction

The problem of Reconstruction—how to restore rebellious states to the Union—was not addressed by the Founding Fathers. The Constitution does not say which branch of government handles the readmission of rebellious states or, for that matter, even contemplates the possibility of secession. It was an open question whether, upon seceding, the Confederate states had legally left the Union. If so, their reentry surely required legislative action by Congress. If not, if even in defeat they retained their constitutional status, then the terms for restoring them to the Union might be treated as an administrative matter best left to the president. In a constitutional system based on the **separation of powers**, the absence of clarity on so fundamental a matter made for explosive politics. The ensuing battle between the White House and Capitol Hill over who was in charge became one of the fault lines in Reconstruction's stormy history.

Presidential Initiatives

Lincoln, as wartime president, had the elbow room to take the lead, offering in December 1863 a general amnesty to all but high-ranking Confederates willing to pledge loyalty to the Union. When 10 percent of a state's 1860 voters had taken this oath, the state would be restored to the Union, provided that it accepted the Thirteenth Amendment abolishing slavery (see Chapter 14). The Confederate states did not bite, however, and congressional Republicans proposed a harsher substitute for Lincoln's Ten Percent Plan. The Wade-Davis Bill, passed on July 2, 1864, laid down, as conditions on the rebellious states, an oath of allegiance to the Union by a majority of each state's adult white men; new governments formed only by those who had never borne arms against the North; and permanent disfranchisement of Confederate leaders. The Wade-Davis bill served notice that the congressional Republicans were not about to hand over Reconstruction policy to the president.

Lincoln executed a **pocket veto** of the Wade-Davis bill by not signing it before Congress adjourned. At the same time he initiated informal talks with congressional leaders aimed at a compromise. It was this stalemate that Lincoln was addressing when he appealed for Republican flexibility in the last speech of his life. Lincoln's successor, however, had no such inclinations. Andrew Johnson believed that Reconstruction was the president's prerogative, and by an accident of timing, he was free to act on his convictions. Under leisurely rules that went back to the early republic, the 39th Congress elected in November 1864 was not scheduled to convene until December 1865.

Andrew Johnson and Reconstruction. Johnson was a self-made man from the hills of eastern Tennessee. Born in 1808, he was apprenticed as a boy to a tailor and set up shop in Greeneville. Despite his lack of formal schooling—his wife was his teacher—Johnson prospered. His tailor shop became a political meeting place, and, natural leader that he was, he soon entered local politics with the backing of Greeneville's small farmers and laborers. In 1857, after a relentless climb up the political ranks, he became a U.S. Senator. A Jacksonian

Andrew Johnson

The president was not an easy man. This photograph of Andrew Johnson (1808–1875) conveys some of the prickly qualities that contributed so centrally to his failure to reach an agreement with Republicans on a moderate Reconstruction program. Library of Congress.

Democrat, Johnson despised equally the "bloated, corrupt aristocracy" of the Northeast and the Tennessee planter elite that dominated Memphis and its environs. It was the poor whites that Johnson championed, however, not the enslaved blacks nor, for that matter, emancipation.

Loyal to the Union, Johnson refused to leave the Senate when his state seceded. In this, he was utterly alone; no southern colleague stayed with him. When federal forces captured Nashville in 1862, Lincoln appointed Johnson Tennessee's military governor. Tennessee, one of the war's bloodiest battlefields, was bitterly divided along geographical lines: Unionist in the east and Rebel in the west. Johnson's assignment was to hold the state together, and he did so, with an iron hand. He was rewarded by being named Lincoln's running mate in 1864. Choosing this war Democrat seemed a smart move, designed to promote wartime unity and court the support of southern Unionists.

In May 1865, just a month after Lincoln's death, Johnson advanced his version of Reconstruction. He offered amnesty to all Southerners who took an oath of allegiance to the Constitution, except for high-ranking Confederate officials and wealthy planters, the elite whom Johnson blamed for secession. Johnson appointed provisional governors for the southern states, requiring as conditions for their restoration only that they revoke their ordinances of secession, repudiate their Confederate debts, and ratify the Thirteenth Amendment. Within months all the former Confederate states had met Johnson's terms and enjoyed functioning, elected governments.

At first Republicans responded favorably. The moderates among them were sympathetic to Johnson's argument that it was up to the states, not the federal government, to define the civil and political rights of the freedmen. Even the Radicals — the Republicans bent on a hard line toward the South — held their fire. They liked the stern treatment of Confederate leaders, and hoped that the new southern governments would show good faith by generous treatment of the freed slaves.

Nothing of the sort happened. The South lay in ruins (see Voices from Abroad, "David Macrae: The Devastated South," p. 460). But Southerners held fast to the old order. The newly seated legislatures moved to restore slavery in all but name. They enacted laws — known as **Black Codes** — designed to drive the former slaves back to the plantations. The new governments had been formed mostly by southern Unionists, but when it came to racial attitudes, little distinguished these loyalists from the Confederates. Despite his hard words against them, moreover, Johnson forgave ex-Confederate leaders easily, so long as he got the satisfaction of humbling them when they appealed for pardons. Soon the ex-Confederates, emboldened by Johnson's indulgence, were filtering back into the halls of power. Old comrades packed the delegations to the new Congress: nine members of the Confederate Congress, seven former officials of Confederate state governments, four generals and four colonels, and even the vice president of the Confederacy, Alexander Stephens. This was the last straw for the Republicans.

The Battle Joined. Under the Constitution, Congress is "the judge of the Elections, Returns and Qualifications of its own Members" (Article 1, Section 5). With this power the Republican majorities in both houses refused to admit the southern delegations when Congress convened in early December 1865, effectively blocking Johnson's Reconstruction program. In response the southern states backed away from the Black Codes, replacing them with regulatory ordinances silent on race yet, in practice, applying only to blacks, not to whites. On top of that, a wave of violence erupted across the South. In Tennessee a Nashville paper reported that white gangs "are riding about whipping, maiming and killing all negroes who do not obey the orders of their former masters, just as if slavery existed." Congressional Republicans concluded that the South had embarked on a concerted effort to circumvent the Thirteenth Amendment. They decided that the federal government had to intervene.

Back in March 1865, before adjourning, the 38th Congress had established the Freedmen's Bureau to aid ex-slaves during the transition from war to peace. Now in early 1866, under the leadership of the moderate Republican Senator Lyman Trumbull, Congress voted to extend the Freedmen's Bureau's life, gave it direct funding for the first time, and authorized its agents to investigate mistreatment of blacks.

More extraordinary was Trumbull's civil rights bill, declaring the ex-slaves to be citizens and granting them, along with every other citizen, equal rights of contract, access to the courts, and protection of person and property. Trumbull's bill nullified all state laws infringing on citizens' equal protection under the law, authorized U.S. attorneys to bring enforcement suits in the federal courts, and provided for fines and imprisonment for violators. Provoked by an unrepentant South, even the most moderate Republicans demanded that the federal government assume responsibility for the civil rights of the freedmen.

VOICES FROM ABROAD

David Macrae
The Devastated South

In this excerpt from The Americans at Home *(1870), an account of his tour of the United States, the Scottish clergyman David Macrae describes the war-stricken South as he found it in 1867–1868, at a time when the crisis over Reconstruction was boiling over.*

I was struck with a remark made by a Southern gentleman in answer to the assertion that Jefferson Davis [the president of the Confederacy] had culpably continued the war for six months after all hope had been abandoned.

"Sir," he said, "Mr. Davis knew the temper of the South as well as any man in it. He knew if there was to be anything worth calling peace, the South must win; or, if she couldn't win, she wanted to be whipped—well whipped—thoroughly whipped."

The further south I went, the oftener these remarks came back upon me. Evidence was everywhere that the South had maintained the desperate conflict until she was utterly exhausted. . . . Almost every man I met at the South, especially in North Carolina, Georgia, and Virginia, seemed to have been in the army; and it was painful to find many who had returned were mutilated, maimed, or broken in health by exposure. When I remarked this to a young Confederate officer in North Carolina, and said I was glad to see that he had escaped unhurt, he said, "Wait till we get to the office, sir, and I will tell you more about that." When we got there, he pulled up one leg of his trousers, and showed me that he had an iron rod there to strengthen his limb, and enable him to walk without limping, half of his foot being off. He showed me on the other leg a deep scar made by a fragment of a shell; and these were but two of seven wounds which had left their marks upon his body. When he heard me speak of relics, he said, "Try to find a North Carolina gentleman without a Yankee mark on him."

Nearly three years had passed when I traveled through the country, and yet we have seen what traces the war had left in such cities as Richmond, Petersburg, and Columbia. The same spectacle met me at Charleston. Churches and houses had been battered down by heavy shot and shell hurled into the city from Federal batteries at a distance of five miles. Even the valley of desolation made by a great fire in 1861, through the very heart of the city, remained unbuilt. There, after the lapse of seven years, stood the blackened ruins of streets and houses waiting for the coming of a better day. . . . Over the country districts the prostration was equally marked. Along the track of Sherman's army—especially, the devastation was fearful—farms laid waste, fences burned, bridges destroyed, houses left in ruins, plantations in many cases turned into wilderness again.

The people had shared in the general wreck, and looked poverty-stricken, careworn, and dejected. Ladies who before the war had lived in affluence, with black servants round them to attend to their every wish, were boarding together in half-furnished houses, cooking their own food and washing their own linen, some of them, I was told, so utterly destitute that they did not know when they finished one meal where they were to find the next. . . . Men who had held commanding positions during the war had fallen out of sight and were filling humble situations—struggling, many of them, to earn a bare subsistence. . . . I remember dining with three cultured Southern gentlemen, one a general, the other, I think, a captain, and the third a lieutenant. They were all living together in a plain little wooden house, such as they would formerly have provided for their servants. Two of them were engaged in a railway office, the third was seeking a situation, frequently, in his vain search, passing the large blinded house where he had lived in luxurious ease before the war.

SOURCE: Allan Nevins, ed., *America through British Eyes* (Gloucester, MA: Peter Smith, 1968), 345–347.

ANALYZING THE EVIDENCE

▶ In general, we value accounts by foreigners for insights they provide into America that might not be visible to its own citizens. Do you find any such insights in the Reverend Macrae's account of the postwar South?

▶ The South proved remarkably resistant to northern efforts at reconstruction. Can we find explanations for that resistance in Macrae's account?

▶ The North quickly became disillusioned with radical Reconstruction (see p. 466). Is there anything in Macrae's sympathetic interviews with wounded southern gentlemen and destitute ladies that sheds light on the susceptibility of many Northerners to propaganda depicting a South in the grip of "a mass of black barbarism"?

Acting on Freedom

While Congress debated, emancipated slaves acted on their own ideas about freedom. News that their bondage was over left them exultant and hopeful (see Comparing American Voices, "Freedom," pp. 462–463). Freedom meant many things — the end of punishment by the lash; the ability to move around; the reuniting of families; and the opportunity to begin schools, to form churches and social clubs, and, not least, to engage in politics. Across the South blacks held mass meetings, paraded, and formed organizations. Topmost among their demands was the right to vote — "an essential and inseparable element of self-government." No less than their former masters, ex-slaves intended to be actors in the savage drama of Reconstruction.

Struggling for Economic Independence. Ownership of land, emancipated blacks believed, was the basis for true freedom. In the chaotic final months of the war, freedmen seized control of plantations where they could. In Georgia and South Carolina, General William T. Sherman reserved large coastal tracts for liberated slaves and settled them on 40-acre plots. Sherman just didn't want to be bothered with the refugees as his army drove across the Lower South, but the freedmen assumed that Sherman's order meant that the land would be theirs. When the war ended, resettlement became the responsibility of the Freedmen's Bureau, which was charged with distributing confiscated land to "loyal refugees and freedmen" and regulating labor contracts between freedmen and planters. Many black families stayed on their old plantations, awaiting redistribution of the land to them. When the South Carolina planter Thomas Pinckney returned home, his freed slaves told him: "We ain't going nowhere. We are going to work right here on the land where we were born and what belongs to us."

Johnson's amnesty plan, entitling pardoned Confederates to recover property seized during the war, blasted these hopes. In October 1865 Johnson ordered General Oliver O. Howard, head of the Freedmen's Bureau, to restore the plantations on the Sea Islands off the South Carolina coast to their white owners. When Howard reluctantly obeyed, the dispossessed blacks protested: "Why do you take away our lands? You take them from us who have always been true, always true to the Government! You give them to our all-time enemies! That is not right!"

In the Sea Islands and elsewhere, former slaves resisted efforts to evict them. Led by black veterans of the Union army, they fought pitched battles with plantation owners and bands of ex-Confederate soldiers. Landowners struck back hard. One black veteran wrote from Maryland: "The returned colard Solgers are in Many cases beten, and their guns taken from them, we darcent walk out of an evening.... They beat us badly and Sumtime Shoot us." Often aided by federal troops, the local whites generally prevailed in this land war.

Resisting Wage Labor. As planters prepared for a new growing season, a great battle took shape over the labor system that would replace slavery. Convinced that blacks needed supervision, planters wanted to retain the gang labor of the past, only now with wages replacing the food, clothing, and shelter their slaves had once received. The Freedmen's Bureau, although watchful against exploitative labor contracts, sided with the planters. The main thing, its reform founders believed, was not to encourage dependency under "the guise of guardianship." Rely on your "own efforts and exertions," an agent told a large crowd of freedmen in North Carolina, "make contracts with the planters" and "respect the rights of property."

This was advice given with little regard for the world in which those North Carolina freedmen lived. It was not only their unequal bargaining power they worried about or even that their ex-masters' real desire was to re-enslave them under the guise of "free" contracts. In their eyes the condition of wage labor was, by definition, debasing. The rural South was not like the North, where working for wages was by now the norm and qualified a man as independent. In the South, selling one's labor to another—and in particular, selling one's labor to work another's land—implied not freedom, but dependency. "I mean to own my own manhood," responded one South Carolina freedman to an offer of wage work. "I'm going to own my own land."

The wage issue cut to the very core of the former slaves' struggle for freedom. Nothing had been more horrifying than that as slaves their persons had been the property of others. When a master cast his eye on a slave woman, her husband had no recourse; nor, for that matter, was rape of a slave a crime. In a famous oration celebrating the anniversary of emancipation, the Reverend Henry M. Turner spoke bitterly of the time when his people had "no security for domestic happiness" and "our wives were sold and husbands bought, children were begotten and enslaved by their fathers." That was why formalizing marriage was so urgent a matter and why, when hard-pressed planters demanded that freedwomen go back into the fields, they resisted so resolutely. If the ex-slaves were to be free as white folk, then their wives could not, any

COMPARING AMERICAN VOICES

Freedom

In the annals of America, probably no human relationship was so conducive to mutual incomprehension as enslavement. Slavery meant one thing to the masters, something altogether different to the slaves. And when freedom came, there was no bridging this bottomless gulf. That, more than anything, explains the racial strife over land, over equal rights, and over political power that engulfed the Reconstruction South. The following documents offer vivid testimony to this bitter legacy of slavery.

EDWARD BARNELL HEYWARD

This letter is from the son of a (formerly) wealthy plantation owner, to his friend Jim, evidently a Northerner. Heyward has not quite gotten over the fact that he — and his northern friend — has survived the war, nor that he is now poor. And, in defeat, he feels deeply alienated from America; he is thinking of migrating to England. What is most telling about his letter, however, is his despair over the future of his ex-slaves. He is afraid, remarkably, that emancipation means "their best days are over."

E. B. Heyward
Gadsden P.O.
South Carolina
22 January 1866

My dear Jim

   Your letter of date July 1865, has just reached me and you will be relieved by my answer, to find, that I am still alive, and extremely glad to hear from you....
   I have served in the Army, my brother died in the Army, and every family has lost members. No one can know how reduced we are, particularly the refined & educated....
   Our losses have been frightful, and we have now, scarcely a support. My Father had five plantations on the coast, and all the buildings were burnt, and the negroes, now left to themselves, are roaming in a starving condition ... like lost sheep, with no one to care for them.
   They find the Yankee only a speculator, and they have no confidence in anyone. They very naturally, poor things, think that freedom means doing nothing, and this they are determined to do. They look to the government, to take care of them, and it will be many years, before this once productive country will be able to support itself. The former kind and just treatment of the slaves, and their docile and generous temper, makes them now disposed to be [quiet] and obedient: but the determination of your Northern people to give them a place in the councils of the Country and make them the equal of the white man, will at last, bear its fruit, and we may *then* expect them, to rise against the whites, and in the end, be exterminated themselves.
   I am now interested in a school for the negroes, who are around me, and will endeavor to do my duty, to them, as ever before, but I am afraid their best days are past.
   As soon as able, I shall quit the Country, and leave others to stand the storm, which I now see making up, at the North, which must soon burst upon *the whole* country, and break up everything which we have so long boasted of.
   I feel now that I have *no country*, I *obey* like a subject, but I cannot love such a government. Perhaps the next letter, you get from me, will be from England.
   I have, thank God! A house over my head & something to eat & am as ever always

your friend,
E. B. Heyward

JOURDON ANDERSON

This is a letter by Jourdan Anderson, a Tennessee slave who escaped with his family during the war and settled in Dayton, Ohio, to his former master. Folklorists have recorded the sly ways that slaves found, even in bondage, for "puttin' down" their masters. But only in freedom — and beyond reach in a northern state at that — could Anderson's sarcasm be expressed so openly, with the jest that his family might consider returning if they first received the wages due them, calculated to the dollar, for all those years in slavery. Anderson's letter, although probably written or edited by a white friend in Dayton, surely is faithful to what the ex-slave wanted to say.

Dayton, Ohio
August 7, 1865.

To My Old Master, Colonel P. H. Anderson, Big Spring, Tennessee.

Sir:

I got your letter, and was glad to find that you had not forgotten Jourdon.... I thought the Yankees would have hung you long before this, for harboring Rebs they found at your house. I suppose they never heard about your going to Colonel Martin's house to kill the union soldier that was left by his company in their stable. Although you shot at me twice before I left you, I did not want to hear of your being hurt, and am glad you are still living. It would do me good to go back to the dear old home again, and see Miss Mary and Miss Martha and Allen, Esther, Green, and Lee. Give my love to them all, and tell them I hope we will meet in the better world, if not in this....

I want to know particularly what the good chance is you propose to give me. I am doing tolerably well here. I get twenty-five dollars a month, with victuals and clothing; have a comfortable home for Mandy,—the folks call her Mrs. Anderson,—and the children—Milly, Jane, and Grundy—go to school and are learning well.... We are kindly treated. Sometimes we overhear others saying, "Them colored people were slaves" down in Tennessee. The children feel hurt when they hear such remarks; but I tell them it was no disgrace in Tennessee to belong to Colonel Anderson. Many darkeys would have been proud, as I used to be, to call you master....

Mandy says she would be afraid to go back without some proof that you were disposed to treat us justly and kindly; and we have concluded to test your sincerity by asking you to send us our wages for the time we served you. This will make us forget and forgive old scores, and rely on your justice and friendship in the future. I served you faithfully for thirty-two years, and Mandy twenty years. At twenty-five dollars a month for me and two dollars a week for Mandy, our earnings would amount to eleven thousand six hundred and eighty dollars. Add to this the interest for the time our wages have been kept back, and deduct what you paid for our clothing, and three doctor's visits to me, and pulling a tooth for Mandy, and the balance will show what we are in justice entitled to....

In answering this letter, please state if there would be any safety for my Milly and Jane, who are now grown up, and both good-looking girls.... I would rather stay here and starve—and die, if it come to that—than have my girls brought to shame by the violence and wickedness of their young masters. You will also please state if there has been any schools opened for the colored children in your neighborhood. The great desire of my life now is to give my children an education, and have them form virtuous habits.

Say howdy to George Carter, and thank him for taking the pistol from you when you were shooting at me.

From your old servant,
Jourdon Anderson.

SOURCE: Stanley I. Kutler, ed., *Looking for America: The People's History,* 2nd ed., 2 vols. (New York: W. W. Norton, 1979), 2: 4–6, 24–27.

ANALYZING THE EVIDENCE

- The South proved fiercely resistant to accepting the ex-slaves as citizens with equal rights. In what ways does Heyward's letter provide insight into that resistance and (despite Heyward's professed sympathy) help explain why so many blacks were beaten and killed when they tried to exercise their rights?

- In what ways does Anderson's letter suggest that, despite Heyward's dire prediction, the best days of the freed slaves were not "behind them" and that, on the contrary, they were hungry for the benefits of freedom?

- Once emancipated, ex-slaves were free to go wherever they wanted. Yet they mostly stayed put and, despite the bitterness of their enslavement, often became sharecroppers for their former masters, as, for example, on the Barrow plantation (see Map 15.2, p. 473). Does Anderson's letter suggest why they might have made that choice? Does it matter that his former master is also named Anderson?

Wage Labor of Former Slaves

This photograph, taken in South Carolina shortly after the Civil War, shows former slaves leaving the cotton fields. Ex-slaves were organized into work crews probably not that different from earlier slave gangs, although they now labored for wages and their plug-hatted boss bore little resemblance to the slave drivers of the past. New-York Historical Society.

more than white wives, labor for others. "I seen on some plantations," one freedman recounted, "where the white men would . . . tell colored men that their wives and children could not live on their places unless they work in the fields. The colored men [answered that] whenever they wanted their wives to work they would tell them themselves; and if he could not rule his own domestic affairs on that place he would leave it and go someplace else."

The reader will see the irony in this definition of freedom: It assumed the wife's subordinate role and designated her labor the husband's property. But if that was the price of freedom, freedwomen were prepared to pay it. Far better to take a chance with their own men than with their ex-masters.

Many former slaves voted with their feet, abandoning their old plantations and seeking better lives in the towns and cities of the South. Those who remained in the countryside refused to work the cotton fields under the hated **gang-labor system** or negotiated tenaciously over the terms of their labor contracts. Whatever system of labor finally might emerge, it was clear that the freedmen would never settle for anything resembling the old plantation system.

The efforts of former slaves to control their own lives challenged deeply entrenched white attitudes. "The destiny of the black race," asserted one Texan, could be summarized "in one sentence — subordination to the white race." Southern whites, a Freedmen's Bureau official observed, could not "conceive of the negro having any rights at all." And when freedmen resisted, white retribution was swift and often terrible. In Pine Bluff, Arkansas, "after some kind of dispute with some freedmen," whites set fire to their cabins and hanged twenty-four of the inhabitants — men, women, and children. The toll of murdered and beaten blacks mounted into untold thousands. The governments established under Johnson's plan only put the stamp of legality on the pervasive efforts to enforce white supremacy. Blacks "would be *just as well* off with no law at all or no Government," concluded a Freedmen's Bureau agent, as with the justice they got under the restored white rule.

In this unequal struggle, blacks turned to Washington. "We stood by the government when it wanted help," a black Mississippian wrote President Johnson. "Now . . . will it stand by us?"

Congress versus President

Andrew Johnson was not the man to ask. In February 1866 he vetoed the Freedmen's Bureau bill. The bureau, Johnson charged, was an "immense patronage," showering benefits on blacks never granted to "our own people." Republicans could not muster enough votes to override his veto. A month later, again rebuffing his critics, Johnson vetoed Trumbull's civil rights bill, arguing that federal protection of black rights constituted "a stride toward centralization." His racism, hitherto muted, now blazed forth: "This is a country for white men, and by God, as long as I am president, it shall be government for white men."

Galvanized by Johnson's attack on their legislation, the Republicans went into action. In early April they got the necessary two-thirds majorities in both houses and enacted the Civil Rights Act. Republican resolve was reinforced by news of mounting violence in the South, culminating in three days of rioting in Memphis. Forty-six blacks were left dead, and hundreds of homes, churches, and schools were burned. In July an angry Congress renewed the Freedmen's Bureau over a second Johnson veto.

The Fourteenth Amendment. Anxious to consolidate their gains, Republicans moved to enshrine black civil rights in an amendment to the Constitution. The heart of the Fourteenth Amendment was Section 1, which declared that "all persons born or naturalized in the United States" were citizens. No state could abridge "the privileges or immunities of citizens of the United States," deprive "any person of life, liberty, or property, without due process of law," or deny anyone "the equal protection of the laws." These phrases were vague, intentionally so, but they established the constitutionality of the Civil Rights Act and, at the least, laid the groundwork for a federally enforced standard of equality before the law in the states.

For the moment, however, the Fourteenth Amendment was most important as a factor in partisan politics. With the 1866 congressional elections approaching, Johnson somehow figured he could turn the Fourteenth Amendment to his advantage. He urged the states not to ratify it. Months earlier, Johnson had begun maneuvering against the Republicans. He aimed at building a coalition of white Southerners, northern Democrats, and conservative Republicans under the banner of a new party, National Union. Any hope of launching it, however, was shattered by Johnson's intemperate behavior and by escalating violence in the South. A dissension-ridden National Union convention in July ended inconclusively, and Johnson's campaign against the Fourteenth Amendment became, effectively, a campaign for the Democratic Party.

"The First Vote"

This lithograph appeared in *Harper's Weekly* in November 1867. The voters represent elements of African American political leadership: an artisan with tools, a well-dressed member of the middle class, and a Union soldier. Corbis-Bettmann.

Republicans responded furiously, unveiling a practice that would become known as "waving the bloody shirt." The Democrats were traitors, charged Indiana governor Oliver Morton. Their party was "a common sewer and loathsome receptacle, into which is emptied every element of treason North and South." In late August Johnson embarked on a disastrous "swing around the circle"—a railroad tour from Washington to Chicago and St. Louis and back—that violated the custom against personal campaigning by presidents. Johnson made matters worse by engaging in shouting matches with hecklers and insulting the hostile crowds.

The 1866 congressional elections inflicted a humiliating defeat on Johnson. The Republicans won a three-to-one majority in Congress. They considered themselves "masters of the situation" and free to proceed "entirely regardless of [Johnson's] opinions or wishes." As a referendum on the Fourteenth Amendment, moreover, the election was a striking victory, demonstrating vast popular support for the civil rights of the former slaves. The Republican Party emerged with a new sense of unity—a unity coalescing not at the center, but on the left, around the unbending program of the Radical minority.

Radical Republicans. The Radicals represented the abolitionist strain within the Republican Party. Most of them hailed from New England or from the upper Midwest, which was heavily settled by New Englanders. In the Senate they were led by Charles Sumner of Massachusetts and in the House by Thaddeus Stevens of Pennsylvania. For them Reconstruction was never primarily about restoring the Union but about remaking southern society. "The foundations of their institutions . . . must be broken up and relaid," declared Stevens, "or all our blood and treasure will have been spent in vain."

Only a handful went as far as Stevens in demanding that the plantations be treated as "forfeited estates of the enemy" and broken up into small farms for the former slaves. About securing the freedmen's civil and political rights, however, there was agreement. In this endeavor Radicals had no qualms about expanding the powers of the national government. "The power of the great landed aristocracy in those regions, if unrestrained by power from without, would inevitably reassert itself," warned Congressman George W. Julian of Indiana. Radicals were aggressively partisan. They regarded the Republican Party as God's instrument for regenerating the South.

At first, in the months after Appomattox, few but the Radicals themselves imagined that so extreme a program had any chance of enactment. Black **suffrage** especially seemed beyond reach, since the northern states themselves (except in New England) denied blacks the vote. And yet, as fury mounted against the intransigent South, Republicans became ever more radicalized until, in the wake of the smashing congressional victory of 1866, they embraced the Radicals' vision of a reconstructed South.

> - Why can the enactment of southern Black Codes in 1865 be considered a turning point in the course of Reconstruction?
> - Why was working for wages resisted by ex-slaves struggling for freedom after emancipation?
> - To what extent was President Johnson responsible for the radicalization of the Republican Party in 1866?

Radical Reconstruction

Afterward, thoughtful Southerners admitted that the South had brought radical Reconstruction on itself. "We had, in 1865, a white man's government in Alabama," remarked the man who had been Johnson's provisional governor, "but we lost it." The state's "great blunder" was not to "have at once taken the negro right under the protection of the laws." Remarkably, the South remained defiant even after the 1866 elections. Every state legislature but Tennessee's rejected the Fourteenth Amendment. It was as if they could not imagine that governments installed under the presidential imprimatur and fully functioning might be swept away. But that, in fact, is just what the Republicans intended to do.

Congress Takes Command

The Reconstruction Act of 1867, enacted in March by the Republican Congress, organized the South as a conquered land, dividing it into five military districts, each under the command of a Union general (Map 15.1). The price for reentering the Union was granting the vote to the freedmen and disfranchising those of the South's prewar leadership class who had participated in the rebellion. Each military commander was ordered to register all eligible adult males (black as well as white), supervise the election of state conventions, and make certain that

Map 15.1 Reconstruction

The federal government organized the Confederate states into five military districts during radical Reconstruction. For each state the first date indicates when that state was readmitted to the Union; the second date shows when Radical Republicans lost control of the state government. All the ex-Confederate states rejoined the Union from 1868 to 1870, but the periods of radical rule varied widely. Republicans lasted only a few months in Virginia; they held on until the end of Reconstruction in Louisiana, Florida, and South Carolina.

the new constitutions contained guarantees of black suffrage. Congress would readmit a state to the Union if its voters ratified the constitution, if that document proved acceptable to Congress, and if the new state legislature approved the Fourteenth Amendment (thus ensuring the needed ratification by three-fourths of the states). Johnson vetoed the Reconstruction Act, but Congress overrode the veto (Table 15.1).

Impeachment. The Tenure of Office Act, a companion to the Reconstruction Act, required Senate consent for the removal of any official whose appointment had required Senate confirmation. Congress chiefly wanted to protect Secretary of War Edwin M. Stanton, a Lincoln holdover and the only member of Johnson's cabinet who favored radical Reconstruction. In his position Stanton could do much to frustrate Johnson's anticipated efforts to undermine Reconstruction. The law also required the president to issue all orders to the army through its commanding general, Ulysses S. Grant. In effect, Congress was attempting to reconstruct the presidency as well as the South.

Seemingly defeated, Johnson appointed generals recommended by Stanton and Grant to command the five military districts in the South. But he was just biding his time. In August 1867, after Congress had adjourned, he "suspended" Stanton and replaced him with Grant, believing that the general would be a good soldier and follow orders. Next Johnson replaced four of the commanding generals. Johnson, however, had misjudged Grant, who publicly objected to the president's machinations. When the Senate reconvened in the fall, it overruled Stanton's suspension. Grant, now an open enemy of Johnson's, resigned so that Stanton could resume his office.

On February 21, 1868, Johnson formally dismissed Stanton. The feisty secretary of war, however, barricaded the door of his office and refused to admit Johnson's appointee. Three days later, for the

Table 15.1 Primary Reconstruction Laws and Constitutional Amendments

Law (Date of Congressional Passage)	Key Provisions
Thirteenth Amendment (December 1865*)	Prohibited slavery
Civil Rights Act of 1866 (April 1866)	Defined citizenship rights of freedmen
	Authorized federal authorities to bring suit against those who violated those rights
Fourteenth Amendment (June 1866†)	Established national citizenship for persons born or naturalized in the United States
	Prohibited the states from depriving citizens of their civil rights or equal protection under the law
	Reduced state representation in House of Representatives by the percentage of adult male citizens denied the vote
Reconstruction Act of 1867 (March 1867)	Divided the South into five military districts, each under the command of a Union general
	Established requirements for readmission of ex-Confederate states to the Union
Tenure of Office Act (March 1867)	Required Senate consent for removal of any federal official whose appointment had required Senate confirmation
Fifteenth Amendment (February 1869‡)	Forbade states to deny citizens the right to vote on the grounds of race, color, or "previous condition of servitude"
Ku Klux Klan Act (April 1871)	Authorized the president to use federal prosecutions and military force to suppress conspiracies to deprive citizens of the right to vote and enjoy the equal protection of the law

*Ratified by three-fourths of all states in December 1865.
†Ratified by three-fourths of all states in July 1868.
‡Ratified by three-fourths of all states in March 1870.

first time in U.S. history, House Republicans introduced articles of **impeachment** against a sitting president, employing the power granted the House of Representatives by the Constitution to charge high federal officials with "Treason, Bribery, or other high Crimes and Misdemeanors." The House serves in effect as the prosecutor in such cases. Eleven counts of presidential misconduct were brought, nine of them violations of the Tenure of Office Act.

The case went to the Senate, which acts as the court in impeachment cases, with Chief Justice Salmon P. Chase presiding. After an eleven-week trial, thirty-five senators on May 15 voted for conviction, one vote short of the two-thirds majority required. Seven moderate Republicans broke ranks, voting for acquittal along with twelve Democrats. The dissenting Republicans felt that the Tenure of Office Act was of dubious validity (in fact, the Supreme Court subsequently declared it unconstitutional) and that removing a president for defying Congress was too extreme, too damaging to the constitutional system of checks and balances, even for the sake of punishing Johnson. And they were wary of the alternative, the Radical Republican Benjamin F. Wade, the president pro tem of the Senate, who, since there was no vice president, stood next in line for the presidency.

Despite his acquittal, however, Johnson had been defanged. For the remainder of his term he was powerless to alter the course of Reconstruction.

The Election of 1868. The impeachment controversy made Grant, already the North's war hero, a Republican hero as well, and he easily won the party's presidential nomination in 1868. In the fall campaign he supported radical Reconstruction, but he also urged reconciliation between the sections. His Democratic opponent, Horatio Seymour, a former governor of New York, almost declined the nomination because he doubted that the Democrats could overcome the stain of disloyalty.

As Seymour feared, the Republicans "waved the bloody shirt," stirring up old wartime emotions against the Democrats to great effect. Grant did about as well in the North (55 percent) as had

Lincoln in 1864. Overall, he won by a margin of 52.7 percent and received 214 of 294 electoral votes. The Republicans also retained two-thirds majorities in both houses of Congress.

The Fifteenth Amendment. In the wake of their victory, the Republicans quickly produced the last major piece of Reconstruction legislation—the Fifteenth Amendment, which forbade either the federal government or the states from denying citizens the right to vote on the basis of race, color, or "previous condition of servitude." The amendment left room for **poll taxes** and property requirements or literacy tests that might be used to discourage blacks from voting, a necessary concession to northern and western states that already relied on such provisions to keep immigrants and the "unworthy" poor from the polls. A California senator warned that in his state, with its rabidly anti-Chinese sentiment (see Chapter 16), any restriction on that power would "kill our party as dead as a stone."

Despite grumbling by Radical Republicans, the amendment passed without modification in February 1869. Congress required the states still under federal control—Virginia, Mississippi, Texas, and Georgia—to ratify it as a condition for being readmitted to the Union. A year later the Fifteenth Amendment became part of the Constitution.

Woman Suffrage Denied

If the Fifteenth Amendment troubled some proponents of black suffrage, this was nothing compared to the outrage felt by women's rights advocates. They had fought the good fight for the abolition of slavery for so many years, only to be abandoned when the chance finally came to get the vote for women. All it would have taken was one more word in the Fifteenth Amendment, so that the protected categories for voting would have read "race, color, *sex,* or previous condition." Leading suffragists such as Susan B. Anthony and Elizabeth Cady Stanton did not want to hear from Radical Republicans that this was "the Negro's hour" and that women should wait for another day. How could suffrage be granted to former slaves, Stanton demanded, but not to them?

In a decisive debate in May 1869 at the Equal Rights Association, the champion of universal suffrage, the black abolitionist Frederick Douglass, pleaded for understanding. "When women, because they are women, are hunted down . . . dragged from their homes and hung upon lamp posts . . . when their children are not allowed to enter schools; then they will have an urgency to obtain the ballot equal to our own." Not even all his black sisters agreed. "If colored men get their rights, and not colored women theirs," protested Sojourner Truth, "you see the colored men will be masters over the women, and it will be just as bad as it was before." As for white women in the audience, remarked Frances Harper in support of Douglass, they "all go for sex, letting race occupy a minor position," or worse. In her despair, Elizabeth Cady Stanton lashed out in ugly racist terms against "Patrick and Sambo and Hans and Ung Tung," aliens ignorant of the Declaration of Independence and yet entitled to vote while the most accomplished of American women remained voteless. Douglass's resolution in support of the Fifteenth Amendment failed, and the Equal Rights convention broke up in acrimony.

At this searing moment a rift opened in the ranks of the women's movement. The majority, led by Lucy Stone and Julia Ward Howe, reconciled themselves to disappointment and accepted the priority of black suffrage. Organized into the American Woman Suffrage Association, these moderates remained allied to the Republican Party, in hopes that once Reconstruction had been settled it would be time for the woman's vote. The Stanton-Anthony group, however, struck out in a new direction. The embittered Stanton declared that woman "must not put her trust in man." The new organization she headed, the New York–based National Woman Suffrage Association, accepted only women, focused exclusively on women's rights, and resolutely took up the battle for a federal woman suffrage amendment.

The fracturing of the women's movement obscured the common ground the two sides shared. Both appealed to constituencies beyond the narrow confines of abolitionism and evangelical reform. Both elevated suffrage into the preeminent women's issue. And both were energized for the battles that lay ahead. "If I were to give vent to all my pent-up wrath concerning the subordination of woman," Lydia Maria Child wrote the Republican warhorse Charles Sumner in 1872, "I might frighten *you*. . . . Suffice it, therefore, to say, either the theory of our government is *false,* or women have a right to vote." If radical Reconstruction seemed a barren time for women's rights, in fact it had planted the seeds of the modern feminist movement.

Republican Rule in the South

Between 1868 and 1871 all the southern states met the congressional stipulations and rejoined the Union. Protected by federal troops, state Republican organizations took hold across the South. The Reconstruction administrations they set up remained in power for periods ranging from a few months in Virginia to nine years in South Carolina, Louisiana, and Florida. Their core support came

Women's Rights, 1870s

This 1870s engraving reveals a distinguishing feature of the woman suffrage movement as it emerged after Reconstruction, which was that it became exclusively a movement of women (although there are a couple of men in the audience). Bettmann/Corbis.

from African Americans, who constituted a majority of registered voters in Alabama, Florida, South Carolina, and Mississippi.

Carpetbaggers and Scalawags. Ex-Confederates had a name for Southern whites who supported Reconstruction: **scalawags,** an ancient Scots-Irish term for runty, worthless animals. Whites who had come from the North they denounced as **carpetbaggers**—self-seeking interlopers who carried all their property in cheap suitcases called carpetbags. Such labels glossed over the actual diversity of these white Republicans.

Some carpetbaggers, while motivated by personal profit, also brought capital and skills. Others were Union army veterans taken with the South—its climate, people, and economic opportunities. And interspersed with the self-seekers were many idealists anxious to advance the cause of emancipation.

The scalawags were even more diverse. Some were former slave owners, ex-Whigs and even ex-Democrats, drawn to Republicanism as the best way to attract northern capital to southern railroads, mines, and factories. But most were yeomen farmers from the backcountry districts who wanted to rid the South of its slaveholding aristocracy. They had generally fought against, or at least refused to support, the Confederacy, believing that slavery had victimized whites as well as blacks. "Now is the time," a Georgia scalawag wrote, "for every man to come out and speak his principles publickly [sic] and vote for liberty as we have been in bondage long enough."

African American Leadership. The Democrats' scorn for black leaders as ignorant field hands was just as false as stereotypes about white Republicans. The first African American leaders in the South came from an elite of free blacks. They were joined by northern blacks who moved south heartened by the arrival of radical Reconstruction. Like their white allies, many were Union army veterans. Some had participated in the antislavery crusade; a number were employed by the Freedmen's Bureau or northern missionary societies. Others had escaped from slavery and were returning home. One of these was Blanche K. Bruce, who had been tutored on the Virginia plantation of his white father. During the war Bruce escaped and established a school for ex-slaves in Missouri. In 1869 he moved to Mississippi, became active in politics, and in 1874 became Mississippi's second black U.S. senator.

As the reconstructed Republican governments of 1867 began to function, this diverse group of ministers, artisans, shopkeepers, and former soldiers reached out to the freedmen. African American speakers, some financed by the Republican Party, fanned out into the old plantation districts and recruited ex-slaves for political roles. Still, few of the new leaders were field hands; most had been preachers or artisans. The literacy of one ex-slave, Thomas Allen, who was a Baptist minister and shoemaker, helped him win election to the Georgia legislature. "In my county," he recalled, "the colored people came to me for instructions, and I gave them the best instructions I could. I took the *New York Tribune* and other papers, and in that way I found out a great deal, and I told them whatever I thought was right."

Although never proportionate to their numbers in the population, black officeholders were prominent across the South. In South Carolina African Americans constituted a majority in the lower house of the legislature in 1868. Three were elected to Congress; another joined the state supreme court. Over the entire course of Reconstruction, twenty African Americans served in state administrations as governor, lieutenant governor, secretary of state, treasurer, or superintendent of education; more than six hundred served as state legislators; and sixteen were U.S. congressmen.

The Radical Program. The Republicans had ambitious plans for a reconstructed South. They wanted to end its dependence on cotton agriculture, build an entrepreneurial economy like the North's, and make a better life for all southerners. Although they fell short, they accomplished more than their critics gave them credit for.

The Republicans modernized state constitutions, eliminated property qualifications for the vote, and swept out the Black Codes restricting the lives of the freedmen. Women also benefited from the Republican defense of personal liberty. The new constitutions expanded the rights of married women, enabling them to hold property and earnings independent of their husbands—"a wonderful reform," a Georgia woman wrote, for "the cause of Women's Rights." Republican social programs called for the establishment of hospitals, more humane penitentiaries, and asylums for orphans and the mentally ill. Money poured into road-building projects and the region's shattered railroad network.

To pay for their ambitious programs the Republican governments copied taxes that Jacksonian reformers had earlier introduced in the North—in particular, property taxes on both real estate and personal wealth (see Chapter 10). The goal was to make planters pay their fair shares and to broaden the tax base. In many plantation counties, former slaves served as tax assessors and collectors, administering the taxation of their one-time owners.

Higher tax revenues never managed to overtake the huge obligations assumed by the Reconstruction governments. State debts mounted rapidly, and, as crushing interest on bonds fell due, public credit collapsed. On top of that, much spending was wasted or ended up in the pockets of public officials. Corruption was ingrained in American politics, rampant everywhere in this era, not least in the Grant administration itself. Still, in the free-spending atmosphere of the southern Republican regimes, corruption was especially luxuriant and damaging to the cause of radical Reconstruction.

Schools and Churches. Nothing, however, could dim the achievement in public education. Here the South had lagged woefully; only Tennessee had a system of public schooling before the Civil War. Republican state governments vowed to make up for lost time, viewing education as the foundation for a democratic order. African Americans of all ages rushed to the newly established schools, even when they had to pay tuition. An elderly man in Mississippi explained his hunger for education: "Ole missus used to read the good book [the Bible] to us . . . on Sunday evenin's, but she mostly read dem places where it says, 'Servants obey your masters.' . . . Now we is free, there's heaps of tings in that old book we is just suffering to learn."

Hiram R. Revels

In 1870 Hiram R. Revels (1822–1901) was elected to the U.S. Senate from Mississippi to fill Jefferson Davis's former seat. Revels was a free black from North Carolina who had migrated to the North and attended Knox College in Illinois. He recruited blacks for the Union army and, as an ordained Methodist minister, served as chaplain of a black regiment in Mississippi, where he settled after the war. Library of Congress.

Freedmen's School, c. 1870
This rare photograph shows the interior of one of the three thousand freedmen's schools established across the South after the Civil War. Although many of these schools were staffed by white missionaries, a main objective of northern educators was to prepare blacks to take over the classrooms. The teacher shown here is surely one of the first. Library of Congress.

The building of schools was part of a larger effort by African Americans to fortify the institutions that had sustained their spirits in the slave days, most especially, Christianity. Now, in freedom, the African Americans left the white-dominated congregations, where they had been relegated to segregated balconies and denied any voice in church governance, and built churches of their own. These churches joined together to form African American versions of the Southern Methodist and Baptist denominations, including, most prominently, the National Baptist Convention and the African Methodist Episcopal Church. Everywhere the black churches served not only as places of worship but also as schools, social centers, and political meeting halls.

Black clerics were community leaders and often political leaders as well. As Charles H. Pearce, a Methodist minister in Florida, declared, "A man in this State cannot do his whole duty as a minister except he looks out for the political interests of his people." Calling forth the special destiny of the ex-slaves as the new "Children of Israel," black ministers provided a powerful religious underpinning for the Republican politics of their congregations.

The Quest for Land

In the meantime the freedmen were locked in a great economic struggle with their former owners. In 1869 the Republican government of South Carolina had established a land commission empowered to buy property and resell it on easy terms to the landless. In this way about 14,000 black families acquired farms. South Carolina's land distribution plan showed what was possible, but it was the exception and not the rule. Despite a lot of rhetoric, Republican regimes elsewhere did little to help the freedmen fulfill their dreams of becoming independent farmers. Federal efforts proved equally feeble. The Southern Homestead Act of 1866 offered 80-acre grants to settlers, limited for the first year to freedmen and southern Unionists. The advantage was mostly symbolic, however, since only marginal land was made available, off the beaten track in swampy, infertile parts of the Lower South. Few of the homesteaders succeeded.

There was no reversing President Johnson's order restoring confiscated lands to ex-Confederates. Property rights, it seemed, trumped everything else, even for most Radical Republicans. The Freedman's Bureau, which had earlier championed the land claims of the ex-slaves, now devoted itself to teaching them how to be good agricultural laborers.

Sharecropping. While they yearned for farms of their own, most freedmen started out landless, with no option but to work for their former owners — but not, they vowed, under the conditions of slavery — no gang work, no supervision by overseers, no fines or punishments, no regulation of their private lives. In certain parts of the agricultural South wage work became the norm — for example, on the great sugar plantations of Louisiana financed by northern capital. The problem was that cotton planters lacked the money to pay wages, at least not until the crop came in, and sometimes, in lieu of a straight wage, they offered a share of the crop. As a wage, this was a bad deal for the freedmen, but if they could be paid in shares for their work, why could they not pay in shares to rent the land they worked?

This form of land tenancy was already familiar in parts of the white South, and the freedmen now seized on it for the independence it offered them. Planters resisted, believing, as one wrote, that "wages are the only successful system of controlling hands." But, in a battle of wills that broke out all across the cotton South, the planters yielded to "the inveterate prejudices of the freedmen, who desire to be masters of their own time."

Thus there sprang up the distinctive laboring system of cotton agriculture called **sharecropping**, in which the freedmen worked as renters, exchanging their labor for the use of land, house, implements, seed, and fertilizer, and typically turning over one-half to two-thirds of their crops to the landlord (Map 15.2). The sharecropping system joined laborers and the owners of land and capital in a common sharing of risks and returns. But it

Map 15.2   The Barrow Plantation, 1860 and 1881

Comparing the 1860 map of this central Georgia plantation with the 1881 map reveals the impact of sharecropping on patterns of black residence. In 1860 the slave quarters were clustered near the planter's house. In contrast, by 1881 the sharecroppers scattered across the plantation's 2,000 acres, building cabins on the ridges between the low-lying streams. The name Barrow was common among the sharecropping families, which means almost certainly that they had been slaves on the Barrow plantation who, years after emancipation, still had not moved on. For all the croppers freedom surely meant not only their individual lots and cabins, but also the school and church shown on the map.

was a very unequal relationship, given the force of southern law and custom on the white landowner's side and the sharecroppers' dire economic circumstances. Starting out penniless, they had no way of making it through the first growing season without borrowing for food and supplies.

Country storekeepers stepped in. Bankrolled by their northern suppliers, they "furnished" the sharecropper and took as collateral a **lien** on the crop, effectively assuming ownership of the cropper's share and leaving him only the proceeds that remained after his debts had been paid. Once indebted at one store, sharecroppers were no longer free to shop around. They became an easy target for exorbitant prices, unfair interest rates, and crooked bookkeeping. As cotton prices declined during the 1870s, more and more sharecroppers failed to settle accounts and fell into permanent debt. And if the merchant was also the landowner, or conspired with the landowner, the debt became a pretext for forced labor, or **peonage,** although evidence now suggests that sharecroppers generally managed to pull up stakes and move on once things became hopeless. Sharecroppers always thought twice about moving, however, because part of their "capital" was being known and well reputed in their home communities. Freedmen who lacked that local standing generally found sharecropping hard going and ended up in the ranks of agricultural laborers.

In the face of so much adversity, black families struggled to better themselves. That it enabled family struggle was, in truth, the saving advantage of sharecropping because it mobilized husbands and wives in common enterprise while shielding both from personal subordination to whites. Wives were doubly blessed. Neither field hands for their ex-masters nor dependent housewives, they became partners laboring side by side with their husbands. The trouble with sharecropping, one planter grumbled, was that "it makes the laborer too independent; he becomes a partner, and has to be consulted." By the end of Reconstruction, about a quarter of sharecropping families had managed to save enough to rent with cash payments, and eventually black farmers owned about a third of the land they cultivated (see Reading American Pictures, "Why Sharecropping?," p. 475).

A Comparative Perspective. The battle between planters and freedmen over the land was by no means unique to the American South. Whenever slavery ended — in Haiti after the slave revolt of 1791, in the British Caribbean by abolition in 1833, in Cuba and Brazil by gradual emancipation during the 1880s — a fierce struggle ensued between planters bent on restoring a gang-labor system and ex-slaves bent on gaining economic autonomy. The outcome of this universal conflict depended on the ex-slaves' access to land. Where vacant land existed, as in British Guiana, or where plantations could be seized, as in Haiti, the ex-slaves became subsistence farmers, and insofar as the Caribbean plantation economy survived without the ex-slaves, it did so by the importation of indentured servants from India and China. Where land could not be had, as in British Barbados or Antigua, the ex-slaves returned to plantation labor as wage workers, although often in some combination with customary rights to housing and garden plots. The cotton South fit neither of these broad patterns. The freedmen did not get the land, but neither did the planters get field hands. What both got was sharecropping.

There are two ways of explaining this outcome. One is political. Outside the American South, emancipated slaves rarely got civil or political equality. Even in the British islands, where substantial self-government existed, high property qualifications effectively disfranchised the ex-slaves. In the United States, however, hard on the heels of emancipation came civil rights, manhood suffrage, and, for a brief era, a real measure of political power for the freedmen. Sharecropping took shape during Reconstruction, and there was no going back afterward.

That there was no going back suggests a second explanation for the triumph of sharecropping, namely, that it was a good fit for cotton agriculture. We can see this in the experience of other countries that became major producers in response to the global cotton famine set off by the Civil War. In all these places, in India, Egypt, Brazil and West Africa, some variant of the sharecropping system emerged. Most striking was the adoption everywhere of crop-lien laws, at the behest of the international merchants and bankers putting up the capital. Indian and Egyptian villagers got the advances they needed to shift from subsistence agriculture to cotton, but at the price of being placed, as in America, permanently under the thumb of the furnishing merchants. Implicit in advancing that money, of course, was the realization that cotton, unlike sugar cane, could be raised efficiently by small farmers (provided they had the lash of indebtedness always on their backs). American planters resisted sharecropping because they started at a different place: not traditional, subsistence economies that had to be converted to cotton but a proven plantation system over which they had been absolute masters.

READING AMERICAN PICTURES

Why Sharecropping?

Sharecroppers in Georgia. Brown Brothers.

The account of sharecropping on the neighboring pages describes the experience of hundreds of thousands of ex-slaves and plantation owners. How do we know that our generalizations are true? Or, more concretely, that a sharecropper reading our account would nod and say, "Yes, that's the way it was." One sliver of evidence is this photograph depicting a family of ex-slaves standing proudly by their new cabin and young cotton crop. In what ways does this contemporary photograph confirm or amplify our account of sharecropping?

ANALYZING THE EVIDENCE

▶ The cotton rows go right up to the house. Why would this family not have set aside land for a garden and for some livestock? And what does this suggest about the historians' claim that sharecropping doomed the South to a cash-crop monoculture?

▶ Note the gent in the background — most likely the landowner — with his handsome horse and carriage. The family is posing for the photograph, yet he pays no heed and breaks into the frame. And he seems to feel, although he has rented it out, that he still has the run of the place. What does this suggest about the limits of sharecropping as a means of achieving independence by the freedmen?

▶ In that struggle, of course, everything was relative. What elements in the photograph suggest that, compared to what they had known as slaves or, after emancipation, would have faced as day laborers, this family might have thought they had not fared so badly? (Students are urged to consult Map 15.2 on p. 473, bearing in mind of course that this family did not actually live on the Barrow plantation.)

For America's ex-slaves sharecropping was not the worst choice; it certainly beat laboring for their former owners. But for southern agriculture the costs were devastating. Sharecropping committed the South inflexibly to cotton because, as a market crop, it generated the cash required by landlords and furnishing merchants. Neither soil depletion nor low prices ever enabled sharecroppers to shift away from cotton. With farms leased year to year, neither tenant nor owner had much incentive to improve the property. And the crop-lien system lined merchants' pockets with unearned profits that might otherwise have gone into agricultural improvement. The result was a stagnant farm economy, blighting the South's future and condemning it to economic backwardness—a kind of retribution, in fact, for the fresh injustices visited on the people it had once enslaved.

> - Do you think it was predictable in 1865 that five years later the ex-slaves would receive the constitutional right to vote? Or that, having gone that far, the nation would deny the vote to women?
> - What do you regard as the principal achievements of radical Reconstruction in the South? Do you think the achievements outweigh the failures?
> - Why did the ex-slaves' struggle for land end in the sharecropping system?

The Undoing of Reconstruction

Ex-Confederates were blind to the achievements of radical Reconstruction. Indeed, no amount of success could have persuaded them that it was anything but an abomination, undertaken without their consent and denying them their rightful place in southern society. Led by the planters, ex-Confederates staged a massive counterrevolution—one designed to "redeem" the South and restore them to political power under the banner of the Democratic Party. But the Redeemers could not have succeeded on their own. They needed the complicity of the North. The undoing of Reconstruction is as much about northern acquiescence as it is about southern resistance.

Counterrevolution

Insofar as they could win at the ballot box, southern Democrats took that route. They worked hard to get ex-Confederates restored to the voting rolls, they appealed to southern patriotism, and they campaigned against black rule. But force was equally acceptable. Throughout the Deep South, especially where black voters were heavily concentrated, ex-Confederate planters and their supporters organized secretly and terrorized blacks and their white allies.

Nathan Bedford Forrest and the Politics of Terror. No one looms larger in this bloody story than Nathan Bedford Forrest, the Confederacy's most decorated cavalry general. Born in poverty in 1821, he scrambled up the booming cotton economy and became a big-time Memphis slaver trader and Mississippi plantation owner. A man of fiery temper, he championed secession. When the war broke out, Forrest immediately formed a Tennessee cavalry regiment, fought bravely (and was badly wounded) at the battle of Shiloh, and won fame as a daring cavalry raider. On April 12, 1864, his troopers perpetrated one of the war's worst atrocities, the slaughter of black troops at Fort Pillow, Tennessee, acting on rumors that they had harassed local whites. The Fort Pillow massacre foreshadowed the civil strife that would consume Tennessee during Reconstruction.

Nathan Bedford Forrest in Uniform, c. 1865
Before he became Grand Wizard of the Ku Klux Klan, Forrest had been a celebrated cavalry general in the Confederate army. This photograph shows him in uniform before he was mustered out. Library of Congress.

Although nominally in control since 1862, Union authorities never managed to subdue Tennessee's irreconcilable Confederate sympathizers. The Republican-elected governor in 1865, William G. Brownlow, was a tough man, a former Confederate prisoner not shy about calling his enemies to account. They struck back with a campaign of terror, targeting especially Brownlow's black supporters. It was amidst this general mayhem that the first den of the Ku Klux Klan emerged in Pulaski, Tennessee, in late 1865 or early 1866. As it proliferated across the state, the Klan turned to General Forrest, who had been trying, unsuccessfully, to rebuild his prewar fortunes. Late in 1866, at a clandestine meeting in Nashville, Forrest donned the robes of Grand Wizard. His activities are mostly cloaked in mystery, but there is no mystery about why Forrest gravitated to the Klan. For him, the Klan was politics by other means, the instrument by which disfranchised former Confederates like himself might strike a blow against the despised Republicans who ran Tennessee.

In many towns the Klan became virtually identical to the Democratic clubs. In fact, Klan members — including Forrest — dominated Tennessee's delegation to the Democratic national convention of 1868. The Klan unleashed a murderous campaign of terror against Republican sympathizers. Governor Brownlow responded resolutely, threatening to mobilize the state militia and root out the Klan. If Brownlow tried, answered Forrest, "There will be war, and a bloodier one than we have ever witnessed." In the end, it was the Republicans, not the Klan, who cracked. In March 1869 Brownlow retreated to the U.S. Senate. The Democrats were on their way back to power, and the Klan, having served its purpose, was officially disbanded in Tennessee.

Elsewhere, the Klan raged on, murdering Republican politicians, burning black schools and churches, and attacking party gatherings, with more or less the same results as in Tennessee. By 1870, the Democrats had seized power in Georgia and North Carolina and were making headway across the South.

The Federal Reaction. Congress responded by passing legislation, including the Ku Klux Klan Act of 1871, designed to enforce the rights of ex-slaves under the Fourteenth and Fifteenth Amendments. These so-called enforcement laws authorized federal prosecutions, military intervention, and martial

"Worse than Slavery," 1874
This cartoon by Thomas Nast registers the despair felt by advocates of racial equality at the failure of Reconstruction. The Klan ruffians and White Leaguers have prevailed, Nast is saying, and white terrorism has reduced the oppressed black family to conditions worse than slavery. Granger Collection.

law to suppress terrorist activities that deprived citizens of their civil and political rights. In South Carolina, where the Klan became most deeply entrenched, federal troops occupied nine counties, made hundreds of arrests, and drove as many as two thousand Klansmen from the state.

The Grant administration's assault on the Klan raised the spirits of southern Republicans, but also revealed how dependent they were on the federal government. The potency of the Ku Klux Klan Act, a Mississippi Republican wrote, "derived alone from its source" in the federal government. "No such law could be enforced by state authority, the local power being too weak." If they were to prevail over antiblack terrorism, Republicans needed what one carpetbagger described as "steady, unswerving power from without."

But northern Republicans grew weary of Reconstruction and the endless bloodshed it seemed to produce. Prosecuting Klansmen was an uphill battle. U.S. attorneys usually faced all-white juries and unsympathetic federal judges, with scant resources for handling the cases. After 1872 prosecutions began to drop off; many Klansmen received hasty pardons. And then the constitutional underpinnings of the antiterrorist campaign came into question, culminating in the Supreme Court's decision in *United States v. Cruikshank* (1876) that the federal government had exceeded its authority under the Fourteenth Amendment. If the rights of the ex-slaves were being violated by individuals or private groups (like the KKK), that was a state responsibility and beyond the federal jurisdiction.

In a kind of self-fulfilling prophecy, the reluctance of the Grant administration to shore up Reconstruction guaranteed that it would fail. Republican governments that were denied federal help one by one fell victim to the massive resistance of their ex-Confederate enemies: Texas in 1873, Alabama and Arkansas in 1874, Mississippi in 1875.

The Mississippi campaign showed all too clearly what the Republicans were up against. As elections neared in 1875, paramilitary groups such as the Rifle Clubs and Red Shirts operated openly. Mississippi's Republican governor, Adelbert Ames, a Congressional Medal of Honor winner from Maine, appealed to President Grant for federal troops, but Grant refused. Brandishing their guns and stuffing the ballot boxes, the Redeemers swept the 1875 elections and took control of Mississippi. Facing impeachment, Governor Ames resigned his office and returned to the North.

By 1876 Republican governments, backed by token U.S. military units, remained in only three states—Louisiana, South Carolina, and Florida. Elsewhere, the former Confederates were back in power.

The Acquiescent North

The faltering of Reconstruction stemmed from more than discouragement about prosecuting the Klan, however. Sympathy for the freedman began to wane. The North was flooded with one-sided, often racist reports, such as James M. Pike's *The Prostrate State* (1873), describing South Carolina in the grip of "a mass of black barbarism." The impact of this propaganda could be seen in the fate of the Civil Rights bill, which Charles Sumner introduced in 1870 in an attempt to apply federal power against the discriminatory treatment of African Americans, guaranteeing them, among other things, equal access to public accommodation, schools, and jury service. By the time the bill passed in 1875, it had been stripped of its key provisions. The Supreme Court finished the demolition job when in 1883 it declared the remnant Civil Rights Act unconstitutional.

The political cynicism that overtook the Civil Rights Act signaled the Republican Party's reversion to the practical politics of earlier days. In many states a second generation took over the party—men like Roscoe Conkling of New York, who treated the Manhattan Customs House, with its regiment of political appointees, as an auxiliary of his organization. Conkling and similarly minded politicos had little enthusiasm for Reconstruction, except when it benefited the Republican Party. As the party lost headway in the South, Republicans lost interest in the battle for black rights. In Washington President Grant presided benignly over this transformation of his party, turning a blind eye on corruption even as its waters began to lap against the White House.

Not all Republicans embraced Grant's politics as usual. Yet even the high-minded, the heirs of antislavery Christian reform, turned against Reconstruction. The touchstone for them was "free labor," the idea of America as a land of self-reliant, industrious property owners. They had framed the Civil War as a battle between "free labor" and its antithesis, the plantation society of masters and slaves. And now, with the South defeated, the question became: Would the emancipated slaves embrace "free labor"? No, asserted Pike's *The Prostrate South* and similarly inflammatory reports. Instead of choosing self-reliance, the freedmen were running riot, demanding patronage, becoming dependents of the corrupt Reconstruction regimes they had voted into power. With this tragic misreading of the former slaves — and of their uphill struggle for land and self-rule — Republican allies drifted away and turned against radical Reconstruction.

More was at work, however, than disillusionment with the freedmen. In the aftermath of war, a broader loss of nerve gripped northern reformers. The meaning of "free labor" had not been uncontested. If middle-class Republicans juxtaposed it against black slavery, labor leaders juxtaposed it also against *wage* slavery, and suddenly, when peace arrived, there was a burst of trade-union activity, calls for sweeping labor reform, and a formidable new organization on the scene, the National Labor Union. Radical proposals came forth, most famously, Ira Steward's demand for the eight-hour day, which, by his cock-eyed theory, would close the gap between rich and poor "until the capitalist and laborer are one" — a true "free labor" society. The labor reform movement lacked staying power, however. The eight-hour drive failed, and so did campaigns for cooperative industry and currency reform. After an abortive effort at launching a labor party in 1872, the National Labor Union collapsed.

If the surge of labor agitation died, not so the fear it inspired among middle-class reformers. Intent on a "harmony of interests," they got instead a strong whiff of class conflict. These advocates of "free labor," once zealous for black freedom and equal rights, clambered to the safer ground of civil-service reform. Henceforth it was the evils of corrupt politics that would claim their attention. They repudiated the wartime expansion of federal power and refashioned themselves as **liberals** — believers in free trade, market competition, and limited government. And, with unabashed elitism, they denounced universal suffrage, which "can only mean in plain English the government of ignorance and vice." American reform had arrived at a dispiriting watershed. The grand impulse that had driven the antislavery struggle, insofar as it survived the trauma of Reconstruction, now took the form of pallid efforts at purifying American politics, with Grant as the first target.

The Liberal Republicans and the Election of 1872. As Grant's administration lapsed into cronyism, a revolt took shape inside the Republican Party, led by an influential collection of intellectuals, journalists, and reform-minded businessmen. Unable to deny Grant renomination, the dissidents broke away and formed a new party under the name Liberal Republican. Their candidate was Horace Greeley, longtime editor and publisher of the *New York Tribune* and veteran of American reform in all its variety, including antislavery. The Democrats, still in disarray, also nominated Greeley, notwithstanding his editorial diatribes against them. A poor campaigner, Greeley was assailed so bitterly that, as he said, "I hardly knew whether I was running for the Presidency or the penitentiary."

Grant won overwhelmingly, capturing 56 percent of the popular vote and every electoral vote. Yet the Liberal Republicans had managed to shift the terms of political debate in the country. The agenda they had established — civil service reform, limited government, reconciliation with the South — was adopted by the Democrats as they shed their disloyal reputation and reclaimed their place as a legitimate national party.

Scandal and Depression. Charges of Republican corruption, mounting ever since Grant's reelection, came to a head in 1875. The scandal involved the Whiskey Ring, a network of liquor distillers and treasury agents who defrauded the government of millions of dollars of excise taxes on whiskey. The ringleader was a Grant appointee, and Grant's own private secretary, Orville Babcock, had a hand in the thievery. The others went to prison, but Grant stood by Babcock, possibly perjuring himself to save his secretary from jail. The stench of scandal, however, had engulfed the White House.

On top of this, a financial panic struck in 1873, triggered by the bankruptcy of the Northern Pacific Railroad and its main investor, Jay Cooke. Both Cooke's privileged role as financier of the Civil War and the generous federal subsidies to the Northern Pacific caused many economically pressed Americans to blame Republican financial mismanagement and thievery. Grant's administration responded ineffectually, rebuffing the pleas of debtors for relief by increasing the money supply (see Chapter 19).

Among the casualties of the bad economy was the Freedman's Savings and Trust Company, which held the small deposits of thousands of ex-slaves. When the bank failed in 1874, Congress refused to compensate the depositors, and many lost their life savings. In denying their pathetic pleas, Congress was signaling also that Reconstruction had lost its moral claim on the country. National politics had moved on; concerns about the economy and political fraud, not the plight of the ex-slaves, absorbed the northern voter as another presidential election approached in 1876.

"Grantism"

Grant was lampooned on both sides of the Atlantic for the behavior of his scandal-ridden administration. The British magazine *Puck* shows Grant only barely defying gravity to keep his corrupt subordinates aloft and out of jail. Despite the scandals, the British public welcomed Grant with admiration on his triumphant foreign tour in 1877. Stock Montage.

The Political Crisis of 1877

Abandoning Grant, the Republicans nominated Rutherford B. Hayes, governor of Ohio, a colorless figure but untainted by corruption or by strong convictions — in a word, a safe man. His Democratic opponent was Samuel J. Tilden, governor of New York, a wealthy lawyer with ties to Wall Street and a reform reputation for his role in cleaning up New York City politics. The Democrat Tilden, of course, favored **home rule** for the South, but so, more discreetly, did the Republican Hayes. Reconstruction actually did not figure prominently in the campaign and was mostly subsumed under broader Democratic charges of "corrupt centralism" and "incapacity, waste, and fraud." By now Republicans had essentially written off the South. Not a lot was said about the states still ruled by Reconstruction governments — Florida, South Carolina, and Louisiana.

Once the returns started coming in on election night, however, those three states began to loom very large indeed. Tilden led in the popular vote and, victorious in key northern states, he seemed headed for the White House until sleepless politicians at Republican headquarters realized that if they kept Florida, South Carolina, and Louisiana, Hayes would win by a single electoral vote. Republicans still controlled the state election machinery and, citing Democratic fraud and intimidation, they certified Republican victories. The audacious announcement came forth from Republican headquarters: Hayes had carried Florida, South Carolina, and Louisiana and won the election. Newly elected Democratic officials also sent in electoral votes for Tilden, and, when Congress met in early 1877, it faced two sets of electoral votes from those states.

The Constitution does not provide for this contingency. All it says is that the president of the Senate (in 1877, a Republican) opens the electoral certificates before the House (Democratic) and the Senate (Republican) and that "the Votes shall then be counted" (Article 2, Section 1). Suspense gripped the country. There was talk of inside deals, of a new election, even of a violent coup. Just in case, the commander of the army, General William T. Sherman, deployed four artillery companies in Washington. Finally, Congress appointed an electoral commission to settle the question. The commission included seven Republicans, seven Democrats, and, as the deciding member, David Davis, a Supreme Court justice not known to have fixed party loyalties. Davis, however, disqualified himself by accepting an Illinois seat in the Senate. He was replaced by Republican justice Joseph P. Bradley, and by 8 to 7 the commission awarded the disputed votes to Hayes.

Outraged Democrats had one more trick up their sleeves. They controlled the House, and they stalled a final count of the electoral votes so as to prevent Hayes's inauguration on March 4. But a week before, secret Washington talks had begun between southern Democrats and Ohio Republicans representing Hayes. Everything turned on South Carolina and Louisiana, where rival governments were encamped at the state capitols, with federal soldiers holding the Democrats at bay. Exactly what deal was struck or how involved Hayes himself was will probably never be known, but on March 1 the House Democrats suddenly ended their delaying tactics, the ceremonial counting of votes went forward, and Hayes was inaugurated on schedule. He soon ordered the Union troops back to their barracks, the Republican governors in South Carolina and Louisiana fled the unprotected statehouses, and Democratic claimants took control. Reconstruction had ended.

In 1877 political leaders on all sides seemed ready to say that what Lincoln had called "the work" was complete. But for the former slaves, the work had only begun. Reconstruction turned out to have been a magnificent aberration, a leap beyond what most white Americans actually felt was due their black fellow citizens. Still, something real had been achieved—three rights-defining amendments to the Constitution, some elbow room to advance economically, and, not least, a stubborn confidence among blacks that, by their own efforts, they could lift themselves up. Things would get worse, in fact, before they got better, but the work of Reconstruction was imperishable and could never be erased.

> ➤ Why did the Redeemers resort to terror in their campaign to regain political control of the South?

> ➤ What changes in the North explain why the Republicans abandoned the battle for Reconstruction?

> ➤ Explain how the contested presidential election of 1876–1877 brought an end to Reconstruction.

SUMMARY

By any measure—in lives, treasure, or national amity—the Civil War was the most shattering event in American history. In this chapter we describe how the nation picked up the pieces. Reconstruction confronted two great tasks: first, restoring the rebellious states to the union, and second, incorporating the emancipated slaves into the national citizenry. Separable perhaps in theory, the two tasks were inseparably part of a single grand struggle.

Reconstruction went through three phases. In what has been called the presidential phase, Lincoln's successor Andrew Johnson unilaterally offered the South easy terms for reentering the Union. This might have succeeded had Southerners responded with restraint, but instead they adopted oppressive Black Codes and welcomed ex-Confederates back into power. Infuriated by southern arrogance, congressional Republicans closed ranks behind the Radicals, embraced the freedmen's demand for full equality, placed the South under military rule in 1867, and inaugurated radical Reconstruction.

In this second phase, the new Republican state governments tried to transform the South's decrepit economic and social structures, while on the plantations ex-slaves battled for economic independence. No amount of accomplishment, however, could reconcile the ex-Confederates to Republican rule, and they staged a violent counterrevolution in the name of white supremacy and "redemption."

Distracted by Republican scandals and economic problems, the Grant administration had little stomach for a protracted guerrilla war in the

South. Left on their own, the Reconstruction governments fell one by one to Redeemer intimidation and violence. In this third phase, as Reconstruction wound down, the concluding event was the contested election of 1876, which the Republicans resolved by trading their last remaining southern strongholds, South Carolina and Louisiana, for retention of the White House. On that unsavory note, Reconstruction ended.

Connections: Sectionalism

In many ways, Reconstruction marked the final stage in a titanic sectional struggle whose origins went back to the early nineteenth century. As we noted in the essay opening Part Three (p. 269):

> The North developed into an urbanizing and industrializing society based on free labor, whereas the South remained a rural, agricultural society dependent on slavery.

In Chapter 13 we described how the sectional crisis arising from these differences broke apart the Union in 1861. The Civil War (Chapter 14) tested the war-making capacities of the rival systems. At first the advantage lay with the military prowess of the agrarian South, but in the end the superior resources of the industrial North prevailed. Even in defeat, however, the South could not be forced into a national mold. That was the ultimate lesson of Reconstruction. In the aftermath, the South persisted on its own path, as we will see in Chapter 17, which discusses the emergence of its distinctive low-wage labor system, and Chapter 19, which describes the development of its one-party, whites-only politics. The gradual, if partial, dissolution of southern uniqueness in the twentieth century is a theme of later chapters of this book.

CHAPTER REVIEW QUESTIONS

- Why did the debate over restoring the South to the Union devolve into an institutional struggle between the presidency and the Congress?

- Do you believe that the failure of Reconstruction was primarily a failure of leadership? Or, to put it more concretely, that the outcome might have been different had Lincoln lived? Or chosen a different vice president?

- Was there any way of reconciling the Republican desire for equality for the ex-slaves with the ex-Confederate desire for self-rule in the South?

TIMELINE

1863	Lincoln announces his Ten Percent Plan
1864	Wade-Davis Bill passed by Congress
	Lincoln "pocket" vetoes Wade-Davis Bill
1865	Freedmen's Bureau established
	Lincoln assassinated; Andrew Johnson succeeds as president
	Johnson implements his restoration plan
1866	Civil Rights Act passes over Johnson's veto
	Johnson makes disastrous "swing around the circle"; defeated in congressional elections
1867	Reconstruction Act
	Tenure of Office Act
1868	Impeachment crisis
	Fourteenth Amendment ratified
	Ulysses S. Grant elected president
1870	Ku Klux Klan at peak of power
	Fifteenth Amendment ratified
1872	Grant's reelection
1873	Panic of 1873 ushers in depression of 1873–1877
1875	Whiskey Ring scandal undermines Grant administration
1877	Compromise of 1877; Rutherford B. Hayes becomes president
	Reconstruction ends

FOR FURTHER EXPLORATION

The best current book on Reconstruction is Eric Foner's major synthesis, *Reconstruction: America's Unfinished Revolution, 1863–1877* (1988), available also in a shorter version. *Black Reconstruction in America* (1935), by the African American activist and scholar W. E. B. Du Bois, deserves attention as the first book on Reconstruction that stressed the role of blacks in their own emancipation. For the presidential phase of Reconstruction, see Dan T. Carter, *When the War Was Over: The Failure of Self-Reconstruction in the South, 1865–1867* (1985). On the freedmen, Leon F. Litwack, *Been in the Storm So Long: The Aftermath of Slavery* (1979), provides a stirring account. More recent emancipation studies emphasize slavery as a labor system: Julie Saville, *The Work of Reconstruction: From Slave to Wage Laborer in South Carolina, 1860–1870* (1994), and Amy Dru Stanley, *From Bondage to Contract* (1999), which expands the discussion to show what the onset of wage labor meant for freedwomen. In *Gendered Strife & Confusion: The Political Culture of Reconstruction* (1997), Laura F. Edwards explores via a local study the impact of "peripheral" people — the ordinary folk of both races — on Reconstruction politics. Eric Foner, *Nothing But Freedom: Emancipation and Its Legacy* (1983), helpfully places emancipation in a comparative context. William S. McFeely, *Grant: A Biography* (1981), deftly explains the politics of Reconstruction. The emergence of the sharecropping system is explored in Gavin Wright, *Old South, New South* (1986), and Edward Royce, *The Origins of Southern Sharecropping* (1993). On the Compromise of 1877, see C. Vann Woodward's classic *Reunion and Reaction* (1956). A helpful Web site on Reconstruction, with documents and illustrations, can be found at **www.pbs.org/wgbh/amex/reconstruction/index.html**, which derives from the PBS documentary in the *American Experience* series.

TEST YOUR KNOWLEDGE

To assess your command of the material in this chapter, see the Online Study Guide at **bedfordstmartins.com/henretta**.

For Web sites, images, and documents related to topics and places in this chapter, visit **bedfordstmartins.com/makehistory**.

PART FOUR: A Maturing Industrial Society
1877–1914

	ECONOMY	SOCIETY	CULTURE	POLITICS	DIPLOMACY
	The Triumph of Industrialization	**The West**	**The Industrial City**	**From Inaction to Progressive Reform**	**An Emerging World Power**
1877	▸ Andrew Carnegie launches modern steel industry ▸ Knights of Labor becomes national movement (1878)	▸ Nomadic Indian life ends	▸ National League founded (1876) ▸ Dwight L. Moody pioneers urban revivalism	▸ Election of Rutherford B. Hayes ends Reconstruction	▸ United States becomes net exporter
1880	▸ Gustavus Swift pioneers vertically integrated firm ▸ American Federation of Labor (1886)	▸ Chinese Exclusion Act (1882) ▸ Dawes Act divides tribal lands (1887)	▸ Electrification brightens city life ▸ First Social Register defines high society (1888)	▸ Ethnocultural issues dominate state and local politics ▸ Civil service reform (1883)	▸ Diplomacy of inaction ▸ Naval buildup begins
1890	▸ United States surpasses Britain in iron and steel output ▸ Economic depression (1893–1897) ▸ Industrial merger movement begins	▸ U.S. Census declares westward movement over ▸ Wounded Knee Massacre; Indian resistance ends ▸ California national parks established	▸ Immigration from southeastern Europe rises sharply ▸ William Randolph Hearst's *New York Journal* pioneers yellow journalism	▸ Black disfranchisement in South ▸ Populist Party founded (1892) ▸ William McKinley wins presidency; defeats Bryan's freesilver crusade (1896)	▸ Social Darwinism and Anglo-Saxonism promote expansion ▸ Spanish-American War (1898–1899); conquest of the Philippines
1900	▸ Immigrants dominate factory work ▸ Industrial Workers of the World (1905)	▸ California farmers rely on Japanese labor ▸ "Gentlemen's Agreement" (1908) excludes Japanese workers	▸ Social progressivism comes to the city ▸ Movies begin to overtake vaudeville	▸ McKinley assassinated; Roosevelt inaugurates progressivism in national politics ▸ Hepburn Act regulates railroads (1906)	▸ Panama cedes Canal Zone to United States (1903) ▸ Roosevelt Corollary to Monroe Doctrine (1904)
1910	▸ Henry Ford builds first automobile assembly line	▸ Women vote in western states ▸ U.S. government approves Hetch Hetchy reservoir	▸ Urban liberalism ▸ World War I halts European immigration	▸ NAACP (1910) ▸ Woodrow Wilson elected (1912) ▸ New Freedom legislation creates Federal Reserve, FTC	▸ Taft's diplomacy promotes U.S. business ▸ Wilson proclaims U.S. neutrality in World War I

The year 1876 marked the hundredth anniversary of the Declaration of Independence. In celebration the nation mounted a Centennial Exposition where it all began, in Philadelphia. Observing the hectic preparations, the German journalist Ernst Otto Hopp anticipated the impact that this grand world's fair would have on his European compatriots. "Foreigners will be astounded at the vision of American production.... The pits of Nevada will display their enormous stores of silver, Michigan its copper, California its gold and quicksilver, Missouri its lead and tin, Pennsylvania its coal and iron.... And from a thousand factories will come the evidences of the wonders of American mechanical skill." Herr Hopp got it right. In 1876 the country Hopp described as a "young giant" was on the cusp of becoming, for better or worse, the economic powerhouse of the world. In Part Four we undertake to explain how it happened and what it meant for American life.

THE WEST In his catalogue of achievements, Ernst Hopp emphasized the mining pits of Nevada and California's gold and quicksilver. He might also have mentioned the corn, wheat, and livestock flowing cityward from the Great Plains. For it was the eastern demand for new sources of food and mineral resources that drove the final surge of western settlement and integrated the Great Plains and Far West into the nation's industrializing economy. Defending their way of life, western Indians were ultimately defeated not so much by army rifles as by the encroachment of railroads, mines, ranches, and proliferating farms. These same forces disrupted the old established Hispanic communities of the Southwest but spurred Asian, Mexican, and European migrations that made for a multiethnic western society.

INDUSTRY Equally as momentous as the final settlement of the West was the fact that for the first time, as the decade of the 1870s passed, farmers no longer constituted a majority of working Americans. Henceforth, America's future would be linked to its development as an industrializing society. In the manufacturing sector, production became increasingly mechanized and increasingly directed at making the capital goods that undergirded economic growth. As the railroad system was completed, the vertically integrated model began to dominate American enterprise. The labor movement became firmly established, and as immigration surged, the foreign-born and their children became America's workers. What had been partial and limited now became general and widespread; America turned into a land of factories, corporate enterprise, and industrial workers.

THE CITY Industrialization also transformed the nation's urban life. By 1900 one in five Americans lived in cities. That was where the jobs were — as workers in the factories; as clerks and salespeople; as members of a new, salaried middle class of managers, engineers, and professionals; and, at the apex, as a wealthy elite of investors and entrepreneurs. The city was more than just a place to make a living, however. It provided a setting for an urban lifestyle unlike anything seen before in America.

POLITICS The unfettered, booming economy of the Gilded Age at first marginalized political life, or rather, the role of government, which, for most Americans, was very nearly invisible. The major parties remained robust because they exploited a culture of popular participation and embraced the ethnic and religious identities of their constituencies. The depression of the 1890s triggered a major challenge to the political status quo, with the rise of the agrarian Populist Party and its radical demand for free silver. The election of 1896 turned back that challenge and established the Republicans as the dominant national party.

Still unresolved was the threat that corporate power posed to the marketplace and democratic politics. How to curb the trusts dominated national debate during the Progressive era. From different angles political reformers, women progressives, and urban liberals went about the business of cleaning up machine politics and making life better for America's urban masses. African Americans, victimized by disfranchisement and segregation, found allies among white progressives and launched a new drive for racial equality.

DIPLOMACY Finally, the dynamism of America's economic development altered the country's foreign relations. In the decades after the Civil War, America had been inward-looking, neglectful of its navy and inactive diplomatically. The business crisis of the 1890s brought home the need for a more aggressive foreign policy that would advance the nation's overseas economic interests. In short order, the United States went to war with Spain, acquired an overseas empire, and became actively engaged in Latin America and Asia. There was no mistaking America's standing as a Great Power and, as World War I approached, no evading the entanglements that came with that status.

16 The American West

IN THE WANING DECADES OF the nineteenth century, America seemed like two nations. One was an advanced industrial society—the America of factories and sprawling cities. But another America remained frontier country, with pioneers streaming onto the Great Plains, repeating the old dramas of "settlement" they had been performing ever since Europeans had first set foot on the continent. Not until 1890 did the U.S. census declare that a "frontier of settlement" no longer existed: The country's "unsettled area has been so broken into . . . that there can hardly be said to be a frontier line."

Eighteen-ninety also marked the year the country surpassed Great Britain in the production of iron and steel. Newspapers carried reports of Indian wars and industrial strikes in the same edition. The last tragic episode in the suppression of the Plains Indians, the massacre at Wounded Knee, South Dakota, occurred only eighteen months before the great Homestead steel strike of 1892. This alignment of events from the distant worlds of factory and frontier was not accidental. The final surge of settlement across the Great Plains and the Far West was powered primarily by the energy of American industrialism.

The Great Plains
Indians of the Great Plains
Wagon Trains, Railroads, and Ranchers
Homesteaders
The Fate of the Indians

The Far West
The Mining Frontier
Hispanics, Chinese, Anglos
Golden California

Summary
Connections: The American West

◀ **The Yo-Hamite Falls, 1855**

This is one of the earliest artistic renderings of Yosemite Valley, drawn, in fact, before the place came to be called Yosemite. The scale of the waterfall, which drops 2,300 feet to the valley below, is dramatized by artist Thomas A. Ayres's companions in the foreground. In this romantic lithograph one can already see the grandeur of the West that Yosemite came to represent for **Americans.** University of California at Berkeley, Bancroft Library, Honeyman Collection.

The Great Plains

During the 1860s agricultural settlement reached the western margins of the tall-grass prairie. Beyond, roughly at the ninety-eighth meridian (Map 16.1), stretched a vast, dry country, uninviting to farmers accustomed to woodlands and ample rainfall. They saw it much as did the New York publisher Horace Greeley on his way to California in 1859: "a land of starvation," "a treeless desert," baking in heat in the daytime and "chill and piercing" cold at night.

Greeley was describing the Great Plains. The geologic event creating the Great Plains occurred sixty million years ago when the Rocky Mountains arose out of the ocean covering western North America. With no outlet, the shallow inland sea to the east dried up, forming a hard pan on which sediment washing down from the mountains built up a loose, featureless surface. Because the moisture-laden winds from the Pacific spent themselves on the western slopes of the Sierras, the climate was dry, but variable, interspersing cycles of rainfall and drought. The prevailing notion of a **Great American Desert** was not fanciful: Much of the Great Plains had been drought-stricken and desert-like when American explorers first traversed it in the early nineteenth century. Only vegetation resistant to the harsh climate could take hold on the plains. Bunch grasses like blue grama, the linchpins of this

Map 16.1   The Natural Environment of the West, 1860s

As settlers pushed into the Great Plains and beyond the line of semiaridity, they sensed the overwhelming power of the natural environment. In a landscape without trees for fences and barns, and without adequate rainfall, ranchers and farmers had to relearn their business. The Native Americans peopling the plains and mountains had learned to live in this environment, but this knowledge counted for little against the ruthless pressure of the settlers to domesticate the West.

fragile ecosystem, matted the easily blown soil into place and sustained a rich wildlife dominated by grazing antelope and buffalo. What the dry short-grass country had not permanently sustained, until the past few centuries, was human settlement.

Indians of the Great Plains

Probably 100,000 Native Americans lived on the Great Plains at mid-nineteenth century. They were a diverse people, divided into six linguistic families and at least thirty tribal groupings. On the eastern margins and along the Missouri River, the Mandans, Arikaras, and Pawnees planted corn and beans and lived in permanent villages. Smallpox and measles introduced by Europeans ravaged these settled tribes. Less vulnerable to epidemics because they were dispersed were the hunting tribes that had first arrived on the Great Plains in the seventeenth century: Kiowas and Comanches in the southwest; Arapahos and Cheyennes on the central plains; and, to the north, Blackfeet, Crows, and the great Sioux nation.

The Sioux. Originally the Sioux had been eastern prairie people, occupying settlements in the lake country of northern Minnesota. With fish and game dwindling, some tribes drifted westward and around 1760 began to cross the Missouri River. These Sioux, or Lakota (meaning "allies"), became nomadic, living in portable skin tepees and hunting buffalo, or, more properly, bison. From tribes to the southwest, they acquired horses. Once mounted, the Sioux became splendid hunters and formidable fighters, claiming the entire Great Plains north of the Arkansas River as their hunting grounds and driving out or subjugating longer-settled tribes.

A society that celebrates the heroic virtues of hunting and war — men's work — is likely to define gender roles sharply. But before the Sioux had horses, buffalo hunting could not be an exclusively male enterprise. It took the efforts of both men and women to construct the "pounds" into which, beating the brush side by side, they endeavored to stampede the herds. Once on horseback, however, the men rode off to the hunt while the women stayed behind to prepare the mounting piles of buffalo skins. Subordination to the men was not how Sioux women understood their unrelenting labor; this was their allotted share in a partnership on which the proud, nomadic life of the Sioux depended.

Sioux Religion. Living so close to nature, depending on its bounty for survival, the Sioux endowed every manifestation of the natural world with sacred meaning. Unlike Europeans, they conceived of God not as a supreme being but, in the words of the pioneering ethnologist Clark Wissler, as a "series of powers pervading the universe" — Wi, the sun; Skan, the sky; Maka, the earth; Inyan, the rock. Below these came the moon, wind, and buffalo down through a hierarchy embodying the entire natural order.

By prayer and fasting Sioux prepared themselves to commune with these mysterious powers. Medicine men provided instruction, but the religious experience was personal and open to both sexes. The vision, when a supplicant achieved it, attached itself to some object — a feather, an animal skin, or a shell — that was tied into a sacred bundle and became the person's lifelong talisman. In the Sun Dance the entire tribe celebrated the rites of coming of age, fertility, the hunt, and combat, followed by fasting and dancing in supplication to Wi, the sun.

The world of the Lakota Sioux was not self-contained. From their earliest days as nomadic hunters, they had exchanged pelts and buffalo robes for the produce of agriculturalist Pawnees and Mandans. When white traders appeared on the upper Missouri River during the eighteenth century, the Sioux began to trade with them. Although the buffalo remained their staff of life, the Sioux came to rely as well on the traders' kettles, blankets, knives, and guns. The trade system they entered was linked to the Euro-American market economy, yet it was also integrated into the Sioux way of life. Everything depended on the survival of the Great Plains as the Sioux had found it — wild grassland on which the antelope and buffalo ranged free (see Reading American Pictures, "Uncovering the Culture of the Plains Indians," p. 490).

Wagon Trains, Railroads, and Ranchers

On first encountering the Great Plains, Euro-Americans thought these unforested lands best left to the Indians. After exploring a drought-stricken stretch in 1820, Major Stephen H. Long declared it "almost wholly unfit for cultivation, and of course uninhabitable by a people depending upon agriculture for their subsistence."

For years thereafter maps marked the plains as the Great American Desert. In 1834 Congress formally designated the Great Plains as permanent Indian country. The army wanted the border forts, stretching from Lake Superior to Fort Worth, Texas, constructed of stone because they would be there forever. Trade with the Indians would continue but now closely supervised and licensed by the federal government, with the Indian country otherwise off limits to whites.

Events swiftly overtook the nation's solemn commitment as Americans began to eye Oregon and California; Indian country became a bridge to the Pacific. The first wagon train headed west for

READING AMERICAN PICTURES

Uncovering the Culture of the Plains Indians

Tepee Liner. American Hurrah, New York City.

Preliterate peoples, by definition, do not leave written records, which are the staff of life for historians. For ancient civilizations, all historians have to go on are archeological ruins, surviving artifacts, and artwork. In the case of the Plains Indians, who also had no written language, historians are more fortunate because white contemporaries observed, interviewed, and even painted the Plains Indians. The drawback is that this evidence is secondhand, filtered through the preconceptions and prejudices of white Americans. So surviving artifacts that speak directly about the Indian way of life are highly prized. One such artifact is this artfully decorated dewcloth, which hung inside a tepee to shield the privacy of the occupants and keep out the cold.

ANALYZING THE EVIDENCE

- By looking at the dewcloth, can you explain why the Plains Indians developed a sharply divided sexual division of labor, with the women relegated to the laborious domestic tasks?

- Although the dewcloth celebrates fighting prowess, the Plains Indians were ultimately defeated by the U.S. Army. Do the images you see give you any clues about why they lost?

- The dewcloth depicts both battle scenes and buffalo hunting. Although visually they appear seamless, in reality, of course, fighting and hunting were entirely separate activities. By inspecting the images, can you see why the artist chose to depict them as a single phenomenon? Does your answer offer any insight into the culture of the Plains Indians?

Oregon from Missouri in 1842. Soon thousands of emigrants traveled the Oregon Trail to the Willamette Valley or cut south beyond Fort Hall into California. Approaching Fort Hall in 1859, Horace Greeley thought "the white coverings of the many emigrant and transport wagons dott[ing] the landscape" gave "the trail the appearance of a river running through great meadows, with many ships sailing on its bosom." Only these "ships" left behind not a trailing wake of foam but a rutted landscape littered with abandoned wagons and rotting garbage.

The Railroads. Talk about the need for a railroad to the Pacific soon surfaced in Washington. How else could the Pacific territories acquired from Mexico and Britain in 1848 (see Chapter 13) be linked to the Union or the ordeal of the overland journey by wagon train be alleviated? The project languished while North and South argued over the terminus for the route. Meanwhile, the Indian country was crisscrossed by overland freight lines, and Pony Express riders delivered mail between Missouri and California. In 1861 telegraph lines brought San Francisco into instant communication with the East. The next year, with the South in rebellion, the federal government finally moved forward with the transcontinental rail project.

No private company could be expected to foot the bill by itself. The construction costs were staggering, and in the short run not much traffic could be expected along the thinly populated route. So the federal government awarded generous land grants plus millions of dollars in loans to the two companies that undertook the transcontinental project (Map 16.2).

Map 16.2 Western Trunk Lines, 1887

In the 1850s the talk in Washington had been about the need for a transcontinental railroad to bind the West to the Union. This map shows vividly how fully that talk had turned into reality in a matter of three decades. By 1887 no portion of the Pacific Coast lacked a rail connection to the East.

The Union Pacific, building westward from Omaha, made little headway until the Civil War ended but then advanced rapidly across Indian country, reaching Cheyenne, Wyoming, in November 1867. It took the Central Pacific nearly that long moving eastward from Sacramento, California, to cross the crest of the Sierra Nevada. Both then worked furiously — since the government subsidy was based on miles of track laid — until, to great fanfare, the tracks met at Promontory, Utah, in 1869. None of the other railroads following other westward routes made it as far as the Rockies before Jay Cooke's Northern Pacific failed, triggering the Panic of 1873 and bringing work on all the western roads to an abrupt halt (see Chapter 17).

By then, however, railroad tycoons had changed their minds about the Great Plains. No longer did they see it through the eyes of the Oregon-bound settlers traveling on foot and in wagons — as a place to be gotten through en route to the Pacific. They realized that railroads were laying the basis for the economic exploitation of the Great Plains. With economic recovery in 1878, construction soared. During the 1880s, 40,000 miles of track were laid west of the Mississippi, including links from southern California, via the Southern Pacific to New Orleans and via the Santa Fe to Kansas City, and from the Northwest, via the Northern Pacific to St. Paul, Minnesota (see Map 17.1, p. 524).

The Cattle Kingdom. Of all the opportunities beckoning, the most obvious was cattle raising. Grazing buffalo made it easy to imagine the plains as cow country. But first the buffalo had to go. All that it would take was the right commercial incentives. A small market for buffalo robes had existed for years, and hunters made good livings provisioning army posts and leading sporting parties. Then in the early 1870s, as the arriving railroads lowered transportation costs and eastern tanneries learned how to cure the hides, the demand for buffalo skins skyrocketed. Parties of professional hunters with high-powered rifles began a systematic slaughter of the buffalo. Already diminished by disease and shrinking pasturage, the great herds almost vanished within ten years. Many people spoke out against this mass killing, but no way existed to stop people bent on making a quick dollar. Besides, as General Philip H. Sheridan pointed out, exterminating the buffalo would starve the Indians into submission.

In south Texas about five million head of longhorn cattle already grazed on Anglo ranches, hardly worth bothering about because they could not be profitably marketed. In 1865, however, the Missouri Pacific Railroad reached Sedalia, Missouri, far enough west to be accessible to Texas ranchers and their herds. At the Sedalia terminus, a longhorn worth $3 in Texas might command $40. With this incentive Texas ranchers inaugurated the famous Long Drive, hiring cowboys to herd the longhorn cattle hundreds of miles north to the railroads that were pushing west across Kansas.

At Abilene, Ellsworth, and Dodge City, ranchers sold their cattle, and trail-weary cowboys went on binges. These cattle towns captured the nation's

Killing the Buffalo

This woodcut shows passengers shooting buffalo from a Kansas Pacific Railroad train — a small thrill added to the modern convenience of traveling west by rail. North Wind Picture Archives.

Cowboys on the Open Range

In open-range ranching, cattle from different ranches grazed together. At the roundup, cowboys separated the cattle by owner and branded the calves. Cowboys, celebrated in dime novels, were really farmhands on horseback, with the skills to work on the range. An ethnically diverse group, including blacks and Hispanics, they earned $25 a month, plus meals and a bed in the bunkhouse, in return for long hours of grueling, lonesome work. Library of Congress.

imagination as symbols of the Wild West. The reality was much more ordinary. The cowboys, many of them African Americans and Hispanics, were in fact farmhands on horseback who worked long hours under harsh conditions for small pay. Colorful though it seemed, the Long Drive was actually a makeshift method of bridging a gap in the developing transportation system. As soon as railroads reached the Texas range country during the 1870s, ranchers abandoned the Long Drive.

The Texas ranchers owned or leased the land they used, sometimes in huge tracts. North of Texas, where the land was in the public domain, cattlemen simply helped themselves. Hopeful ranchers would spot a likely area along a creek and claim as much land as they could qualify for as settlers under federal homesteading laws, plus what might be added by the fraudulent claims taken out by one or two ranch hands. By a common usage that quickly became established, ranchers had a "range right" to all the adjacent land rising up to the divide — the point where the land sloped down to the next creek.

News of easy money traveled fast. Calves cost $5; steers sold for maybe $60 on the Chicago market. Rail connections were in place or coming in. The grass was free. The rush was on, drawing from as far away as Europe both hardheaded investors and romantics (like the recent Harvard graduate Teddy Roosevelt) eager for a taste of the Wild West. By the early 1880s the plains overflowed with cattle — as many as 7.5 million head ravaging the grass and trampling the water holes.

A cycle of good weather only postponed the inevitable disaster. When it came — a hard winter in 1885, a severe drought the following summer, then record blizzards and bitter cold — cattle died by the hundreds of thousands. An awful scene of rotting carcasses greeted the cowhands riding out onto the range the following spring. Beef prices plunged when hard-pressed ranchers dumped the surviving cattle on the market. The boom collapsed and investors fled, leaving behind a more enduring ecological catastrophe: the destruction of native grasses from the relentless overgrazing by the cattle herds.

Open-range ranching came to an end. Ranchers fenced their land and planted hay. Instead of merely exploiting the plains ecosystem, they now managed and shaped it to their own purposes. And with cattle no longer fending for themselves over the winters, it became feasible to cross-breed the hardy longhorns with white-faced Herefords and get a meatier and tastier animal. Ranching entered a more placid, domesticated era. In the meantime, Hispanic shepherds from New Mexico brought sheep in to feed on the mesquite and prickly pear that supplanted the native grasses. Sheep raising, previously scorned by ranchers as unmanly and resisted as a threat to cattle, became a major enterprise in the sparser high country. Some ranchers even sold out to the despised "nesters" — those who wanted to try farming the Great Plains.

Buffalo Bill and the Mythic West. As the romance faded on the ground, it flowered in the American imagination. The grand perpetrator of a mythic West, William F. Cody, was an unlikely candidate for that role, a barely educated, hard-drinking ex-guerrilla fighter (and occasional horse thief). At loose ends after the Civil War, Cody got a lucky break in 1867 when he was hired to provide buffalo meat for work crews laying railroad track through Indian country in Kansas. A crack shot

"A Close Call"

One of the charms of Buffalo Bill's Wild West Show was that it reenacted exploits of his that actually happened or, at any rate, that Buffalo Bill claimed to have happened. In this poster advertising the 1894 season, U.S. troopers are rescuing him in the nick of time from a scalping.
Granger Collection, New York.

and excellent horseman, Cody's skills as a buffalo hunter soon won him the name "Buffalo Bill." In 1868 Indian war broke out, and Cody got his second claim to fame as an intrepid army scout.

Out of these promising materials, a legendary figure emerged. In July 1869 the dime novelist Ned Buntline came through Kansas, met Cody, and immediately wrote *Buffalo Bill, the King of the Border Men*—the first of some 1,700 potboilers featuring Cody and his exploits. Then there were the buffalo-hunting parties for the rich and famous that Cody led, and his appearance in 1872 on the New York stage in a Buntline creation, playing himself. The line between reality and make-believe began to blur. In the Sioux wars of 1875–1876, serving again as an army scout, Cody rode into battle in his stage vaquero outfit—black velvet and scarlet with lace—so that when he reenacted the mayhem on stage he could wear the very clothes in which he had seen action.

Cody's mythic West became full blown in his Wild West Show, first staged in 1883, that offered displays of horsemanship, sharp-shooting by Little Annie Oakley, and real Indians (in one season Chief Sitting Bull toured with the company). Buffalo Bill traded on his talents as showman, but he also knew the authentic world that lay behind the make-believe. Long after that world was gone, his Wild West Show kept it alive in legend, where it still remains in the cowboys and Indians that populate our movies and television screens.

Homesteaders

No westerners had less in common with Buffalo Bill's world than the settlers who followed the cattlemen on to the Great Plains. Before coming, of course, they needed to be persuaded that crops would grow in that dry country. Powerful interests worked hard to overcome the popular notion that the plains were the Great American Desert. Foremost were the railroads, eager to sell off the public land they had been granted — 180 million acres of it — and to develop traffic for their routes. They aggressively advertised, offered cut-rate tickets, and sold off their land at bargain prices. Land speculators, transatlantic steamship lines, and the western states and territories did all they could to encourage settlers. And so did the federal government, which offered 160 acres of public land to all comers under the Homestead Act (1862).

"Why emigrate to Kansas?" asked a testimonial in *Western Trail*, the Rock Island Railroad's gazette. "Because it is the garden spot of the world. Because it will grow anything that any other country will grow, and with less work. Because it rains here more than any other place, and at just the right time."

As if to confirm the optimists, an exceptionally wet cycle occurred between 1878 and 1886. Some settlers attributed the increased rainfall to soil cultivation and tree planting. Others credited

Drouthy Kansas

This tongue-in-cheek sketch, with its humongous pumpkins and melon-sized grapes, was drawn in 1868 by Henry Worrall, a local Topeka artist, as humorous reassurance to friends thinking about settling in Kansas but worried about its dry climate. The sketch then developed a life of its own. It was widely reproduced and used by the railroads and land agents to encourage people to come to Kansas. The illustration above, dated 1875, is one such reproduction, sent around by a Manhattan, Kansas, dealer offering land and farms for sale. By that time, "drouthy" weather — a sharp dry spell — had set in and hard-pressed farmers were cursing "that damn sketch of Henry Worrall's." Kansas State Historical Society.

The Shores Family, Custer County, Nebraska, 1887
Whether the Shores family came west as Exodusters, we do not know. But in 1887, when this photograph was taken, they were well settled on their Nebraska farm, although still living in sod houses. The patriarch of the family, Jerry Shores, an ex-slave, is second from the right.
Nebraska State Historical Society.

God. As a settler on the southern plains remarked, "The Lord just knew we needed more land an' He's gone and changed the climate."

No amount of optimism, however, could dispel the pain of migration. "That last separating word of *Farewell!* sinks deeply into the heart," one pioneer woman recorded in her diary, thinking of family and friends left behind. But then came the treeless plains. "Such an air of desolation," wrote a Nebraska-bound woman; from another woman in Texas, "such a lonely country."

Some women were liberated by this hard experience. Prescribed gender roles broke down as women shouldered men's work on new farms and became self-reliant in the face of danger and hardship. When husbands died or gave up, wives operated farms on their own. Under the Homestead Act, which accorded widows and single women the same rights as men, women filed 10 percent of the claims. Even with a man around, women contributed crucially to the farm enterprise. Farming might be thought of as a dual economy in which men's labor brought in the big wage at harvest time, while women provisioned the family day by day and produced a steady bit of money for groceries by selling eggs or butter. If the crop failed, it was women's labor that carried the family through. No wonder farming placed a high premium on marriage: a mere 2.4 percent of Nebraska women in 1900 had never married.

Male or female, the vision of new land beckoned people onto the plains. By the 1870s the older agricultural states had filled up, and farmers looked hungrily westward. "Hardly anything else was talked about," recalled the short-story writer Hamlin Garland about his Iowa neighbors. "Every man who could sell out had gone west or was going.... Farmer after farmer joined the march to Kansas, Nebraska, and Dakota.... The movement ... had ... become an exodus, a stampede."

The same excitement took hold in northern Europe, as Norwegians and Swedes for the first time joined the older German migration. At the peak of the "American fever" in 1882, over 105,000 Scandinavians emigrated to the United States. Swedish and Norwegian became the primary languages in parts of Minnesota and the Dakotas. Roughly a third of the farmers on the northern plains were foreign-born.

The motivation for most settlers, American or European, was to better themselves economically. But for some southern blacks, Kansas briefly represented something more precious — the Promised Land of racial freedom. In the spring of 1879, with Reconstruction over and federal protection withdrawn, black communities fearful of white vengeance were swept by enthusiasm for Kansas. Within a month or so, some 6,000 blacks left Mississippi and Louisiana, most of them with nothing more than the clothes on their backs and faith in the Lord. They called themselves Exodusters, participants in the exodus to the dry prairie. How many of them remained is hard to say, but the 1880 census reported 40,000 blacks in Kansas — by far the largest African American concentration in the West aside from Texas, whose expanding cotton frontier attracted hundreds of thousands of black migrants during the 1870s and 1880s.

Taming the Land. No matter where they came from, homesteaders found the plains an alien place. A

ZITKALA-ŠA (GERTRUDE SIMMONS BONNIN)

How Commissioner Morgan's ideas about Indian education was actually experienced by one of its "beneficiaries" is vividly described by Zitkala-Ša, known later as the author Gertrude Simmons Bonnin, who recalled in 1900 her painful transformation from Sioux child to pupil at a Quaker missionary school in Indiana.

The first day . . . a paleface woman, with white hair, came up after us. We were placed in a line of girls who were marching into the dining room. These were Indian girls, in stiff shoes and closely clinging dresses. The small girls wore sleeved aprons and shingled hair. As I walked noiselessly in my soft moccasins, I felt like sinking into the floor, for my blanket had been stripped from my shoulders. . . . Late in the morning, my friend Judewin gave me a terrible warning. Judewin knew a few words of English; and she had overheard the paleface woman talk about cutting our long, heavy hair. Our mothers had taught us that only unskilled warriors who were captured had their hair shingled by the enemy. Among our people, short hair was worn by mourners, and shingled hair by cowards! . . . In spite of myself, I was carried downstairs and tied fast in a chair. I cried aloud, shaking my head all the while until I felt the cold blades of the scissors against my neck, and heard them gnaw off one of my thick black braids. Then I lost my spirit. . . .

Now, as I look back upon the recent past, I see it from a distance, as a whole. I remember how, from morning till evening, many specimens of civilized peoples visited the Indian school. The city folks with canes and eyeglass, the countrymen with sunburned cheeks and clumsy feet. . . . Both sorts of these Christian palefaces were alike astounded at seeing the children of savage warriors so docile and industrious.

As answers to their shallow inquiries they received the students' sample work to look upon. Examining the neatly figured pages, and gazing upon the Indian girls and boys bending over their books, the white visitors walked out of the schoolhouse well-satisfied: they were educating the children of the red man! . . .

In this fashion many have passed idly through the Indian schools during the last decade, afterward to boast of their charity to the North American Indian. But few there are who have paused to question whether real life or long lasting death lies beneath this semblance of civilization.

SOURCE: Linda K. Kerber and Jane De-Hart Mathews, eds., *Women's America: Refocusing the Past*, 2nd ed. (New York: Oxford University Press, 1987), 254–257.

ANALYZING THE EVIDENCE

- Why, in Commissioner Morgan's conception of Indian education, was it necessary to cut off Zitkala-Ša's beautiful black braids?

- Zitkala-Ša went on to become a well-known author and reformer; indeed, she took an Anglo-American name. Commissioner Morgan would surely have regarded her as a triumph of his system of Indian education. So why is she not more appreciative of his efforts on her behalf?

- Commissioner Morgan's report is concerned strictly with education. Can it also be read as a primer of American values? If so, in what ways?

Map 16.4 The Sioux Reservations in South Dakota, 1868–1889

In 1868, when they bent to the demand that they move onto the reservation, the Sioux thought they had gained secure rights to a substantial part of their ancestral hunting grounds. But as they learned to their sorrow, fixed boundary lines only increased their vulnerability to the land hunger of the whites and sped up the process of expropriation.

But these were veteran troops, including 2,000 black cavalrymen of the Ninth and Tenth Regiments, whom Indians called, with grim respect, "buffalo soldiers." Technology also favored the army. Telegraph communications and railroads enabled the troops to be quickly concentrated; repeating rifles and Gatling machine guns increased their firepower. As fighting intensified in the mid-1870s, a reluctant Congress appropriated funds for more western troops. Because of tribal rivalries, the army could always find Indian allies. Worst of all, however, beyond the U.S. Army's advantages or the Indians' disunity, was the overwhelming impact of white settlement.

Resisting the reservation solution, the Indians fought on for years — in Kansas in 1868 and 1869, in the Red River Valley of Texas in 1874, and sporadically among the fierce Apaches, who made life miserable for white settlers in the Southwest until their wily chief Geronimo was finally captured in 1886. On the northern plains the crisis came in 1875, when the Office of Indian Affairs — despite an 1868 treaty — ordered the Sioux to vacate their Powder River hunting grounds and withdraw to the reservation.

Led by Sitting Bull, Sioux and Cheyenne warriors gathered on the Little Big Horn River west of the Powder River country. In a typical concentrating maneuver, army columns from widely separated forts converged on the Little Big Horn. The Seventh Cavalry, commanded by famous Civil War hero George A. Custer, came upon the Sioux encampment on June 25, 1876. Disregarding orders, the reckless Custer sought out battle on his own. He attacked from three sides, hoping to capitalize on the element of surprise. But his forces were spread too thin. The other two contingents fell back with heavy losses to defensive positions, but Custer's own force of 256 men was surrounded and annihilated by Crazy Horse's warriors. It was a great victory but not a decisive one. The day of reckoning was merely postponed.

Pursued by the military, physically exhausted Sioux bands one by one gave up and moved to the reservation. Last to come in were Sitting Bull's followers. They had retreated to Canada, but in 1881, after five hard years, they recrossed the border and surrendered at Fort Buford, Montana.

Not Indian resistance, but white greed wrecked the reservation solution. In the mid-1870s prospectors began to dig for gold in the Black Hills, land sacred to the Sioux and entirely inside their Dakota reservation. Unable to hold back the prospectors or to buy out the Sioux, the government opened up the Black Hills to gold seekers at their own risk. In 1877, after Sioux resistance had crumbled, federal agents forced the tribes to cede the western third of their Dakota reservation (Map 16.4).

That the Plains Indians would resist was inevitable. "You might as well expect the rivers to run backward as that any man who was born a free man should be contented when penned up and denied liberty to go where he pleases," said Chief Joseph of the Nez Percé, who led his people in 1877, including women and children, on an epic 1,500-mile march from eastern Oregon to escape confinement in a small reservation. In a series of heroic engagements, the Nez Percé fought off the pursuing U.S. Army until, after four months of extraordinary hardship, the remnants of the tribe were finally cornered and forced to surrender in Montana near the Canadian border.

The U.S. Army was thinly spread, having been cut back after the Civil War to a total force of 27,000.

Indian School

In this photograph taken at the Riverside Indian School in Anadarko, Oklahoma Territory, the pupils have been shorn of their braids and dressed in laced shoes, Mother Hubbard dresses, and shirts and trousers — one step on the journey into the mainstream of white American society. Children as young as five were separated from their families and sent to Indian schools like this one that taught them new skills while encouraging them to abandon traditional Indian ways. University of Oklahoma, Western History Collections.

The Indian Territory of Oklahoma met a similar fate. Two million acres in the heart of the territory had not been assigned, and white homesteaders coveted that fertile land. The "boomer" movement, stirred up initially by railroads operating in the Indian Territory, agitated for an opening of this so-called Oklahoma District to settlers. In 1889 the government reluctantly placed the Oklahoma District under the Homestead Act. On April 22, 1889, a horde of claimants rushed in and staked out the entire district within a few hours. Two tent cities — Guthrie with 15,000 people and Oklahoma City with 10,000 — were in full swing by nightfall.

Undermining Tribal Culture. In the meantime the campaign to move the Indians onto "the white man's road" relentlessly went forward. During the 1870s the Office of Indian Affairs developed a program to train Indian children for farm work and prepare them for citizenship. Some attended reservation schools, while the less lucky were sent to distant boarding schools. Mother Hubbard dresses and shirts and trousers visibly demonstrated that these bewildered children were being inducted into white society (see Comparing American Voices, "Becoming White," pp. 500–501).

And not a moment too soon, believed many avowed friends of the Native Americans. The Indians had never lacked sympathizers — especially in the East, where reformers created the Indian Rights Association after the Civil War. The movement got a boost from Helen Hunt Jackson's influential book *A Century of Dishonor* (1881), which told the story of the unjust treatment of the Indians. What would save them, the reformers believed, was assimilation into white society, starting with the children. The reformers also favored efforts by the Office of Indian Affairs to undermine tribal authority. Above all, they esteemed private property as a "civilizing force" and hence advocated **severalty**, land ownership by individuals.

The result was the Dawes Severalty Act (1887), authorizing the president to carve up tribal lands, with each family head receiving an allotment of 160 acres and individuals receiving smaller parcels. The land would be held in trust for twenty-five years, and the Indians would be granted U.S. citizenship. Remaining reservation lands would be sold off, with the proceeds placed in an Indian education fund.

The Last Battle: Wounded Knee. The Sioux were among the first to bear the brunt of the Dawes Act. The federal government, announcing it had gained tribal approval, opened their "surplus" land to white settlement on February 10, 1890. But no surveys had been made nor had any provision been made for land allotments for the Indians living in the ceded areas. On top of these signs of bad faith, drought wiped out the Indians' crops that summer. It seemed beyond endurance. They had lost their ancestral lands. They faced a future as farmers, which was alien to their traditions. And immediately confronting them was a winter of starvation.

But news of salvation had also come. An Indian messiah, a holy man who called himself Wovoka, was preaching a new religion on a Paiute reservation in Nevada. In a vision Wovoka had gone to heaven and received God's word that the world would be regenerated. The whites would disappear, all the Indians of past generations would return to Earth, and life on the Great Plains would be as it was before the white man appeared. All this would come to pass in the spring of 1891. Awaiting that great day the Indians should practice the Ghost Dance, a day-long ritual that sent the spirits of the dancers rising to heaven. As the frenzy of the Ghost Dance swept through some Sioux encampments in the fall of 1890, resident whites became alarmed and called for army intervention.

Wovoka had an especially fervent following among the Minneconjous, where the medicine man Yellow Bird held sway. But their chief, Big Foot, had fallen desperately ill with pneumonia, and the Minneconjous agreed to come in under military escort to an encampment at Wounded Knee Creek on December 28. The next morning, when the soldiers attempted to disarm the Indians, a battle exploded in the encampment. Among the U.S. troopers, 25 died; among the Indians, 146 men, women, and children perished, many of them shot down as they fled.

Wounded Knee was the final episode in the war against the Plains Indians but not the end of their story. The division of tribal lands now proceeded without hindrance. The Lakota Sioux fared relatively well, and many of the younger generation settled down as small farmers and stock grazers. Ironically, the more fortunate tribes were probably those occupying infertile land that settlers did not want. The flood of whites into South Dakota and Oklahoma, on the other hand, left the Indians as small minorities in lands once wholly theirs — 20,000 Sioux in a South Dakotan population of 400,000 in 1900; 70,000 of various tribes in a population of a million when Oklahoma became a state in 1907.

Even so, tribal life survived until, with the restoration of the reservation policy in 1934, it once again rested on a communal territorial basis. All along, Native American cultures had been adaptive, changing in the face of adversity and even absorbing features of white society. This cultural resilience persisted — in religion, in tribal structure, in crafts — but the fostering pre-conquest world was gone, swept away, as an Oklahoma editor put it in the year of statehood, by "the onward march of empire."

➤ What was the role of the railroads in the settlement of the Great West?

➤ How would you characterize the agricultural settlers' relationship to the natural environment of the Great Plains?

➤ What was the new Indian reservation policy, and why was it a failure?

The Dead at Wounded Knee

In December 1890 U.S. soldiers massacred 146 Sioux men, women, and children in the Battle of Wounded Knee in South Dakota. It was the last big fight on the northern plains between the Indians and the whites. Black Elk, a Sioux holy man, related that "after the soldiers marched away from their dirty work, a heavy snow began to fall ... and it grew very cold." The body of Yellow Bird lay frozen where it had fallen. National Anthropological Archives, Smithsonian Institution, Washington, DC.

The Far West

On the western edge of the Great Plains, the Rocky Mountains rise up to form a great barrier between the mostly flat eastern two-thirds of the country and the rugged Far West. Beyond the Rockies lie two vast highlands: in the north the Columbia plateau, extending into eastern Oregon and Washington, and, flanking the southern Rockies, the Colorado plateau. Where the plateaus break off, the desertlike Great Basin begins, covering western Utah and all of Nevada. Separating this arid interior from the Pacific Ocean are two great mountain ranges — the Sierra Nevada and, to the north, the Cascades — beyond which lies a coastal region that is cool and rainy in the north but increasingly dry southward, until in southern California rainfall becomes almost as sparse as in the interior.

Clearly the trans-mountain West could not be occupied in standard American fashion — that is, by a multitude of settlers moving along a broad front and, homestead by homestead, bringing it under cultivation. The wagon trains heading to Oregon's Willamette Valley adopted an entirely different strategy — the planting of an island of settlement in a vast, often barren landscape.

New Spain had pioneered this strategy when in 1598 it had sent the first wagon trains 700 miles northward from Mexico into the upper Rio Grande Valley and established Santa Fe. When the United States seized the Southwest 250 years later, major Hispanic settlements existed in New Mexico and California, with lesser settlements scattered along the borderlands into south Texas. At that time, aside from Oregon, the only significant Anglo settlement was around the Great Salt Lake in Utah, where persecuted Mormons had planted a New Zion. Fewer than 100,000 Euro-Americans — roughly 25,000 of them Anglo, the rest Hispanic — lived in the entire Far West when it became U.S. territory in 1848.

The Mining Frontier

More emigrants would be coming, certainly, but the Far West seemed unlikely to be much of a magnet. California was "hilly and mountainous," noted a U.S. naval officer in 1849, too dry for farming and surely not "susceptible of supporting a very large population." He had not taken account of the recent discovery of gold in the Sierra foothills. California would indeed support a very large population, drawn not by arable land but by dreams of gold.

Extraction of mineral wealth became the basis for the Far West's development (Map 16.5). By 1860, when the Great Plains was still Indian country, California was a booming state with 300,000 residents. In a burst of city building, San Francisco became a bustling metropolis — it had 57,000 residents in 1860 — and was the hub of a mining empire that stretched to the Rockies.

In its swift urbanization the Far West resembled southeastern Australia, whose gold rush began in 1851, much more than the American Midwest. Like San Francisco, Melbourne was a city incongruously grand amid the empty spaces and rough mining camps of the Australian "outback." The distinctive pattern of isolated settlement persisted in the Far West, driven now, however, by a proliferation of mining sites and by people moving not east to west but west to east, coming mainly from California.

By the mid-1850s, as easy pickings in the California gold country diminished, prospectors began to pull out and spread across the West in hopes of striking it rich elsewhere. Gold was discovered on the Nevada side of the Sierra Nevada, in the Colorado Rockies, and along the Fraser River in British Columbia. New strikes occurred in Montana and Wyoming during the 1860s, a decade later in the Black Hills of South Dakota, and in the Coeur d'Alene region of Idaho during the 1880s.

As the news of each gold strike spread, a wild, remote area turned almost overnight into a mob scene of prospectors, traders, gamblers, prostitutes, and saloon keepers (see Voices from Abroad, "Baron Joseph Alexander von Hübner: A Western Boom Town," p. 507). At least 100,000 fortune seekers flocked to the Pike's Peak area of Colorado in the spring of 1859. Trespassers on government or Indian land, the prospectors made their own law. The mining codes devised at community meetings limited the size of a mining claim to what a person could reasonably work. This kind of informal lawmaking also became an instrument for excluding or discriminating against Mexicans, Chinese, and African Americans in the gold fields. It turned into hangman's justice for the many outlaws who infested the mining camps.

The heyday of the prospectors was always brief. They were equipped only to skim gold from the surface outcroppings and stream beds. Extracting the metal locked in underground lodes required mine shafts and crushing mills — hence capital, technology, and business organization. The original claim holders quickly sold out when a generous

Map 16.5 The Mining Frontier, 1848–1890

The Far West was America's gold country because of its geological history. Veins of gold and silver form when molten material from the earth's core is forced up into fissures caused by the tectonic movements that create mountain ranges, such as the ones that dominate the far western landscape. It was these veins, the product of mountain-forming activity many thousands of years earlier, that prospectors began to discover after 1848 and furiously exploit. Although widely dispersed across the Far West, the lodes that they found followed the mountain ranges bisecting the region and bypassing the great plateaus not shaped by the ancient tectonic activity.

bidder came along. At every gold-rush site the prospector soon gave way to entrepreneurial development and large-scale mining. Rough mining camps turned into big towns.

Consider Nevada's Virginia City, which started out as a bawdy, ramshackle mining camp, but then, with the opening of the Comstock silver lode in 1859, acquired a stock exchange, fancy hotels, even Shakespearean theater. The rough edges were never quite smoothed out. In 1870 a hundred saloons operated day and night, brothels lined D Street, and men outnumbered women two to one. But in its booming heyday Virginia City seemed a place that would last forever. In the 1880s, however, as the Comstock lode played out, Virginia City declined and, in a fate all too familiar in bonanza mining, became a ghost town. What remained, likewise entirely familiar, was a ravaged landscape, with mountains of debris, poisoned water sources, and woods denuded by the mines' insatiable need for timbering. Comstock, one critic remarked, was "the tomb of the forests of the Sierras."

In its final stage the mining frontier entered the industrial world. At some sites gold and silver proved less important than the more common metals—copper, lead, and zinc—for which there was a huge demand by eastern industry. Entrepreneurs raised capital, built rail connections, financed the technology for treating the lower-grade copper deposits, constructed smelting facilities, and recruited a labor force. Like other workers, western miners organized trade unions (see Chapter 17). As elsewhere in corporate America, the western mining industries went through a process of consolidation, culminating by the turn of the century in near-monopoly control of western copper and lead production.

The Pacific Slope. Without its mineral wealth, Far West history would have been very different. Oregon's Willamette Valley, not dry California, had mostly attracted westward-bound settlers before the gold strike at Sutter's Mill in 1848. And, but for that, California would likely have remained like the Willamette Valley—an agricultural backwater with no markets for its products and a slow-growing population. In 1860, although already a state, Oregon had scarcely 25,000 inhabitants, and its principal city, Portland, was little more than a village. Booming California and its tributary mining country pulled Oregon from the doldrums by creating a market for the state's produce and timber. During the 1880s Oregon and Washington (which became a state in 1889) grew prodigiously. Where scarcely 100,000 settlers had lived twenty years earlier, there were nearly 750,000 by 1890 (Map 16.6). Portland and Seattle blossomed into important commercial centers, both prospering from a mixed economy of farming, ranching, logging, and fishing.

At a certain point, especially as railroads gave access to eastern markets, this diversified growth became self-sustaining. But what had triggered it—what had provided the first markets and underwritten the economic infrastructure—was the bonanza mining economy, at the hub of which

VOICES FROM ABROAD

Baron Joseph Alexander von Hübner

A Western Boom Town

During a leisurely trip around the world in 1871, Baron von Hübner, a distinguished Austrian diplomat, traveled across the United States, taking advantage of the newly completed transcontinental railroad to see the Wild West. After observing Mormon life in Salt Lake City, he went northward to Corinne, Utah, near the juncture where the Central Pacific and Union Pacific railroads met (see Map 16.2, p. 491). The baron might have arrived with romantic notions of the Wild West popular among Europeans of his class. That was not, however, how he departed.

Corinne has only existed for four years. Sprung out of the earth as if by enchantment, this town now contains upwards of 2,000 inhabitants, and every day increases in importance. It is a victualing center for the advanced posts of the [miners] in Idaho and Montana. A coach runs twice a week to Virginia City and to Helena, 350 and 500 miles to the north. Despite the serious dangers and the terrible fatigue of the journeys, these diligences are always full of passengers. Various articles of consumption and dry goods of all sorts are sent in wagons. The "high road" is but a rough track in the soil left by the wheels of the previous vehicles.

The streets of Corinne are full of white men armed to the teeth, miserable looking Indians dressed in the ragged shirts and trousers furnished by the federal government, and yellow Chinese with a business-like air and hard, intelligent faces. No town in the Far West gave me so good an idea as this little place of what is meant by "border life," the struggle between civilization and savage men and things. . . .

All commercial business centers in Main Street. The houses on both sides are nothing but boarded huts. I have seen some with only canvas partitions. . . . The lanes alongside of the huts, which are generally the resort of Chinese women of bad character, lead into the desert, which begins at the doors of the last houses. . . .

To have on your conscience a number of man-slaughters committed in full day, under the eyes of your fellow citizens; to have escaped the reach of justice by craft, audacity, or bribery; to have earned a reputation for being "sharp," that is, for knowing how to cheat all the world without being caught — those are the attributes of the true rowdy in the Far West. . . . Endowed as they often are with really fine qualities — courage, energy, and intellectual and physical strength — they might in another sphere and with the moral sense which they now lack, have become valuable members of society. But such as they are, these adventurers have a reason for being, a providential mission to fulfill. The qualities needed to struggle with and conquer savage nature have naturally their corresponding defects. Look back, and you will see the cradles of all civilization surrounded with giants of Herculean strength ready to run every risk and to shrink from neither danger nor crime to attain their ends. It is only by the peculiar temper of the time and place that we can distinguish them from the backwoodsman and rowdy of the United States.

SOURCE: Oscar Handlin, ed., *This Was America* (Cambridge, MA: Harvard University Press, 1949), 313–315.

ANALYZING THE EVIDENCE

- We read foreign impressions of America because we hope to find in them insights that Americans themselves might not have. In what ways, if any, do you find such insights in Baron von Hübner's account of Corinne?

- The baron describes Corinne as a booming supply center for the hard-rock mining industry of Montana and Idaho. Yet his explanation of Corinne is more romantic. He sees in its activities a "struggle between civilization and savage men and things." Is that a helpful insight for us? Would it have been shared or seen as helpful, say, by a Boston businessman looking to invest in real estate in Corinne?

- The baron is unsparing in his description of the prostitutes, "miserable looking" Indians, and other low-life inhabiting Corinne. But he makes an exception for the gunmen roaming the streets. Despite their "defects," they have "a providential mission to fulfill." What does he mean by that? Would his view have made sense to the hypothetical Boston businessman mentioned above? Or to other Americans who saw in the West the economic opportunity of a lifetime?

Hydraulic Mining

When surface veins of gold were played out, miners turned to hydraulic mining, which was invented in California in 1853. The technology was simple, using high-pressure streams of water to wash away hillsides of gold-bearing soil. Although building the reservoirs, piping systems, and sluices cost money, the profits from hydraulic mining helped transform western mining into big business. But, as this daguerreotype suggests, hydraulic mining wreaked havoc on the environment. Collection of Matthew Isenburg.

stood San Francisco, the metropolis for the entire Far West.

Hispanics, Chinese, Anglos

California was the anchor of two distinct far western regions. First, it joined with Oregon and Washington to form the Pacific slope. Second, by climate and Hispanic heritage, California was linked to the Southwest, which today includes Arizona, New Mexico, and Texas.

The Hispanic Southwest. The first Europeans to enter the Far West — two centuries before the earliest Anglos — were Hispanics moving northward out of Mexico. There, along a 1,500-mile borderland, outposts had been planted over many years by the viceroys of New Spain. Most populous were the settlements along New Mexico's upper Rio Grande Valley; the main town, Santa Fe, was over 200 years old and contained 4,635 residents in 1860. Farther down the Rio Grande was El Paso, nearly as old but much smaller, and, to the west in present-day

Map 16.6 The Settlement of the Pacific Slope, 1860–1890

In 1860 the settlement of the Pacific slope was remarkably uneven — fully underway in northern California and scarcely begun anywhere else. By 1890 a new pattern had begun to emerge, with the swift growth of southern California foreshadowed and the settlement of the Pacific Northwest well launched.

Arizona, Tucson, an old presidio, or garrison, town. At the western end of this Hispanic crescent, in California, a Spanish-speaking population was spread thinly in the old presidio towns along the coast and on a patchwork of great ranches.

The economy of this Hispanic crescent was pastoral, consisting primarily of cattle and sheep ranching. In south Texas there were family-run ranches. Everywhere else the social order was highly stratified. At the top stood an elite — the dons occupying royal land grants — who were proudly Spanish and devoted to the traditional life of a landed aristocracy. Below them, with little in between, was a laboring class of servants, artisans, vaqueros (cowboys), and farm hands. New Mexico also contained a large mestizo population — people of mixed Hispanic and Indian blood, a Spanish-speaking and Catholic peasantry, but still faithful to the village life and farming methods of their Pueblo heritage.

Pueblo Indians, although their dominance over the Rio Grande Valley had long passed, still occupied much of the region, living in the old ways in adobe villages, rendering the New Mexico countryside a patchwork of Hispanic and Pueblo settlements. To the north a vibrant new tribe, the Navajos, had taken shape, warriors like the Apaches from whom they descended but also skilled at crafts and sheep raising.

New Mexico was one place where European and Native American cultures managed a successful, if uneasy, coexistence and where the Indian inhabitants were equipped to hold their own against the Anglo challenge. In California, by contrast, the Hispanic occupation had been harder on the indigenous hunter-gatherer peoples, undermining their tribal structure, reducing them to forced labor, and making them easy prey for the aggressive Anglo miners and settlers, who, in short order, nearly wiped out California's once numerous Indian population.

Anglo-Hispanic Conflict. The fate of the Hispanic Southwest after its incorporation into the United States in 1848 depended on the rate of Anglo immigration. In New Mexico, which remained off the beaten track even after the railroads arrived in the 1880s, the Santa Fe elite more than held its own, incorporating the Anglo newcomers into Hispanic society through intermarriage and business partnerships. In California, however, expropriation of the great ranches was relentless, even though the 1848 treaty with Mexico had recognized the property rights of the *Californios* and had made them U.S. citizens. Around San Francisco the great ranches disappeared almost in a puff of smoke. Farther south, where Anglos were slow to arrive, the dons held on longer, but by the 1880s just a handful of the original Hispanic families still retained their Mexican land grants.

The New Mexico peasants found themselves equally embattled. Crucial to their livelihood was the grazing of livestock on communal lands. But these were customary rights that could not withstand legal challenge when Anglo ranchers established title and began putting up fences. The peasants responded as best they could. Their subsistence economy relied on a division of labor that gave women a productive role in the village economy. Women tended the small gardens, engaged in village bartering, and maintained the households. With the loss of the communal lands, the men began migrating seasonally to the Colorado mines and sugar-beet fields, earning dollars while leaving the village economy in their wives' hands.

Elsewhere, hard-pressed Hispanics struck back for what they considered rightfully theirs. When Anglo ranchers began to fence in communal lands in San Miguel County, the New Mexicans long settled there, *los pobres* (the poor ones), organized themselves into masked night-riding raiders and in 1889 mounted an effective campaign of harassment against the interlopers. After 1900, when Anglo farmers swarmed into south Texas, the displaced Tejanos (Hispanic residents of Texas) responded with sporadic but persistent night-riding attacks. Much of the raiding by Mexican "bandits" from across the border in the years before World War I was really more in the nature of a civil war by embittered Hispanics who had lived north of the Rio Grande for generations (see Chapter 21).

But they, like the New Mexico villagers who became seasonal wage laborers, could not avoid being driven into the ranks of a Mexican American working class as the Anglo economy developed. This same development also began to attract increasing numbers of immigrants from Mexico itself.

Mexican Migrants. All along the Southwest borderlands, economic activity picked up in the late nineteenth century. Railroads were being built, copper mines opening in Arizona, cotton and vegetable agriculture spreading in south Texas, and orchards being planted in southern California. In Texas the Hispanic population increased from about 20,000 in 1850 to 165,000 in 1900. Some came as contract workers for railway gangs and harvest crews; virtually all were relegated to the lowest-paying and most back-breaking work; and everywhere they were discriminated against by Anglo employers and workers.

The galloping economic development that drew Mexican migrants also accounted for the exceptionally high rate of European immigration to the West. One-third of California's population was foreign-born, more than twice the level for the country as a whole. Most numerous were the Irish, followed by the Germans and British. But there was another group unique to the West — the Chinese.

The Chinese Migration. Attracted initially by the California gold rush, 200,000 Chinese came to the United States between 1850 and 1880. In those years they constituted a considerable minority of

Mexican Miners

When large-scale mining began to develop in Arizona and New Mexico in the late nineteenth century, Mexicans crossed the border to earn Yankee dollars. In this unidentified photograph from the 1890s, the men are wearing traditional clothing, indicating perhaps that they are recent arrivals at the mine. Division of Cultural Resource, Wyoming Department of Commerce.

California's population — around 9 percent — but because virtually all were actively employed, they represented probably a quarter of the state's labor force. Elsewhere in the West, at the crest of mining activity, their numbers could surge remarkably, to over 25 percent of Idaho's population in 1870, for example.

The arrival of the Chinese was part of a worldwide Asian migration that had begun in the mid-nineteenth century. Driven by poverty, the Chinese went to Australia, Hawaii, and Latin America; Indians to Fiji and South Africa; and Javanese to Dutch colonies in the Caribbean. Most of these Asians migrated as **indentured servants**, which in effect made them the property of others. In America, however, indentured servitude was no longer lawful — by the 1820s state courts were banning it as involuntary servitude — so the Chinese came as free workers, going into debt for their passage money but not surrendering their personal freedom or right to choose their employers.

Once in America, Chinese immigrants normally entered the orbit of the Six Companies, a powerful confederation of Chinese merchants in San Francisco's Chinatown. Most of the arrivals were young men eager to earn a stake and return to their native Cantonese villages. The few Chinese women — the male-female ratio was thirteen to one — worked mostly as servants and prostitutes, sad victims of the desperate poverty that drove the Chinese to America. Some were sold by impoverished parents; others were enticed or kidnapped by procurers and transported to America.

Until the early 1860s, when surface mining played out, Chinese men labored mainly in the California gold fields — as prospectors where white miners permitted it and as laborers and cooks where they did not. Then, when construction began on the transcontinental railroad, the Central Pacific hired Chinese workers. Eventually they constituted four-fifths of the railroad's labor force, doing most of the pick-and-shovel work laying the track across the Sierra Nevada. Many were recruited by labor agents and worked in labor gangs run by "China bosses," who not only supervised but fed, housed, paid, and often cheated them.

When the transcontinental railroad was completed in 1869, the Chinese scattered. Some stayed in railroad construction gangs, while others labored in California's Central Valley as agricultural workers or, if they were lucky, became small farmers and orchardists. The mining districts of Idaho, Montana, and Colorado also attracted large numbers of Chinese, but according to the 1880 census, nearly three-quarters remained in California. "Wherever we put them, we found them good," remarked Charles Crocker, one of the promoters of the Central Pacific. "Their orderly and industrious habits make them a very desirable class of immigrants."

Anti-Chinese Agitation. White workers did not share Crocker's enthusiasm. Elsewhere in the country, racism was directed against African Americans; in California, where there were few blacks, it found a target in the Chinese. "They practice all the unnameable vices of the East," wrote the young journalist Henry George. "They are utter heathens, treacherous, sensual, cowardly and cruel." Sadly, this vicious racism was intertwined with labor's republican ideals. The Chinese, argued George, would "make nabobs and princes of our capitalists, and crush our working classes into the dust . . . substitut[ing] . . . a population of serfs and their masters for that population of intelligent freemen who are our glory and our strength."

The anti-Chinese frenzy climaxed in San Francisco in the late 1870s when mobs ruled the streets, at one point threatening to burn the docks of the Pacific Mail Steamship Company where the Chinese immigrants debarked. The fiercest agitator, an Irish teamster named Denis Kearney, quickly became a dominant figure in the California labor movement. Under the slogan "The Chinese Must Go!" Kearney led a Workingmen's Party against the state's major parties. Democrats and Republicans jumped on the bandwagon, joining together in 1879 to write a new state constitution replete with anti-Chinese provisions and pressuring Washington to take up the issue. In 1882 Congress passed the Chinese Exclusion Act, which barred further entry of Chinese laborers into the country.

The injustice of this law — no other nationality was similarly targeted — rankled the Chinese. Why us, protested one woman to a federal agent, and not the Irish, "who were always drunk and fighting?" Merchants and American-born Chinese, who were free to come and go, routinely registered a newly born son after each trip, enabling many an unrelated "paper son" to enter the country. Even so, resourceful as the Chinese were at evading the exclusion law, the flow of immigrants slowed to a trickle.

But the job opportunities that had attracted the Chinese to America did not subside. If anything, the West's agricultural development intensified the demand for cheap labor, especially in California, which was shifting from wheat, the state's first great cash crop, to fruits and vegetables.

Building the Central Pacific

Chinese laborers in 1867 at work on the great trestle spanning the canyon at Secrettown in the Sierra Nevada. University of California at Berkeley, Bancroft Library.

Such intensive agriculture required lots of workers—stoop labor, meagerly paid, and mostly seasonal. This was not, as one San Francisco journalist put it, "white men's work." That ugly phrase serves as a touchstone for California agricultural labor as it would thereafter develop—a kind of caste labor system, always drawing some downtrodden, footloose whites, yet basically defined along color lines.

But if not the Chinese, then who? First, Japanese immigrants, who came in increasing numbers and by the early twentieth century constituted half of the state's agricultural labor force. Then, when anti-Japanese agitation closed off that population flow in 1908, Mexico became the next, essentially permanent, source of migratory workers for California's booming commercial agriculture.

The irony of the state's social evolution is painful to behold. Here was California, a land of limitless opportunity, boastful of its democratic egalitarianism, and yet simultaneously, and from its very birth, a racially torn society, at once exploiting and despising the Hispanic and Asian minorities whose hard labor helped make California the enviable land it was.

Golden California

Life in California contained all that the modern world of 1890 had to offer—cosmopolitan San Francisco, comfortable travel, colleges and universities, even resident painters and writers. Yet California was still remote from the rest of America, a long journey away and, of course, differently and spectacularly endowed by nature. Location, environment, and history all conspired to set California somewhat apart from the American nation. In certain ways so did the Californians.

Creating a California Culture. What Californians yearned for was a cultural tradition of their own. Closest to hand was the bonanza era of the forty-niners, captured on paper by Samuel Clemens. Clemens left his native Missouri for Nevada in 1861. He did a bit of prospecting, worked as a reporter, and adopted the pen name Mark Twain. In 1864 he arrived in San Francisco, where he became a newspaper columnist writing about what he pronounced "the livest, heartiest community on our continent."

Listening to the old miners in Angel's Camp in 1865, Twain jotted down one tale in his notebook, as follows:

> Coleman with his jumping frog—bet stranger $50—stranger had no frog, and C. got him one:—in the meantime stranger filled C's frog full of shot and he couldn't jump. The stranger's frog won.

In Twain's hands, this fragment was transformed into a tall tale that caught the imagination of the country and made his reputation as a humorist. "The Celebrated Jumping Frog of Calaveras County" somehow encapsulated the entire world of make-or-break optimism in the mining camps.

In such short stories as "The Luck of Roaring Camp" and "The Outcasts of Poker Flat," Twain's fellow San Franciscan Bret Harte developed this theme in a more literary fashion and firmly implanted it in California's memory. But this past was too raw, too suggestive of the tattered beginnings of so many of the state's leading citizens—in short too disreputable—for an up-and-coming society.

Then in 1884 Helen Hunt Jackson published her novel *Ramona*. In this story of a half-Indian girl caught between two cultures, Jackson intended to advance the cause of the Native Americans, but she placed her tale in the evocative context of early California, and that rang a bell. By then the missions planted by the Catholic Church had been long abandoned. The padres were wholly forgotten, their Indian converts scattered and in dire poverty. Now that lost world of "sun, silence and adobe" became all the rage. Sentimental novels and histories appeared in abundance. There was a movement to restore the missions. Many communities began to stage Spanish fiestas, and the mission style of architecture enjoyed a great vogue among developers.

In its Spanish past California found the cultural traditions it needed. The same kind of discovery was taking place elsewhere in the Southwest, although in the case of Santa Fe and Taos there really were live Hispanic roots to celebrate.

Land of Sunshine. All this enthusiasm was strongly tinged with commercialism. And so was a second distinctive feature of California's development—the exploitation of its climate. While northern California boomed, the southern part of the state remained thinly populated, too dry for anything but grazing and some chancy wheat growing. What it did have, however, was an abundance of sunshine. At the beginning of the 1880s there burst upon the country amazing news of the charms of southern California. "There is not any malaria, hay fever, loss of appetite, or languor in the air; nor any thunder, lightning, mad dogs . . . or cold snaps." This publicity was mostly the work of the Southern Pacific Railroad, which had reached Los Angeles in 1876 and was eager for business.

When the Santa Fe Railroad arrived in 1885, a furious rate war broke out. One-way fares from Chicago or St. Louis to Los Angeles dropped to $25 or less. Thousands of people, mostly midwesterners, poured in. A dizzying real estate boom developed, along with the frantic building of such resort hotels as San Diego's opulent Hotel del Coronado. Los Angeles County, which had less than 3 percent of the state's population in 1870, had 12 percent by 1900. By then southern California had firmly established itself as the land of sunshine. It had found a way to translate climate into riches.

That was what California wheat farmers discovered when they began to convert to "specialty" crops. Some of these, like the peaches and pears grown in the Sierra foothills, competed with crops elsewhere in the country, but others—oranges, almonds, raisins—required California's Mediterranean climate. By 1910, the state had essentially abandoned wheat, its original money crop, and was shipping vast quantities of fruit across the country. Although heavily dependent on migrant labor—hence its reputation as an "industrial" form of agriculture—California fruit farming was actually carried on in mostly small-scale units because it required intensive, hands-on cultivation. Indeed, the vineyards around Fresno, from whence came virtually all the nation's raisins, began as a planned community, sold off in 20-acre units. What perhaps came closer to an industrial model were the big cooperatives set up by these modest-sized producers to market and brand

John Muir

John Muir spent a lifetime studying, glorying in, and defending the California wilderness. This arresting photograph (c. 1902) catches him as he would have wanted to be remembered — a man at home with nature. Library of Congress.

their crops. For most Americans, the taste of California came via Sunkist oranges, Sun Maid raisins, and Blue Diamond almonds. And, as an added dividend, it was this same clever marketing that persuaded Americans that fruit was an everyday food, not a luxury saved for birthdays and Christmas.

John Muir and the Great Outdoors. That California was specially favored by nature some Californians knew even as the great stands of redwoods were being hacked down, the streams polluted, and the hills torn apart by reckless hydraulic mining. Back in 1864 influential Americans who had visited it prevailed on Congress to grant to the state of California "the Cleft, or Gorge in the granite peak of the Sierra Nevada Mountain, known as Yosemite Valley," which would be reserved "for public pleasuring, resort, and recreation." When the young naturalist John Muir arrived in California four years later, he headed straight for Yosemite. Its "grandeur . . . comes as an endless revelation," he wrote.

Muir's environmentalism was at once scientific and romantic. An exacting researcher, he demonstrated for the first time that Yosemite was the product of glacial action (and went on to study glaciers around the world). California scientists who accepted Muir's thesis were persuaded also by his concept of wilderness as a laboratory and joined him against "despoiling gain-seekers . . . eagerly trying to make everything immediately and selfishly commercial." Married to Muir's scientific appeal, however, was a powerful dose of romanticism, sanctifying nature as sacred space and elevating its defense into a kind of religious crusade, a battle "between landscape righteousness and the devil." One result of Muir's zeal was the creation of California's national parks in 1890 — Yosemite, Sequoia, and General Grant (later part of King's Canyon). Another was a campaign launched immediately afterward to mandate a system of national forest reserves. And a third was the formation in 1892 of the Sierra Club, which became a powerful voice for the defenders of California's wilderness.

They won some and lost some. Advocates of water-resource development insisted that California's irrigated agriculture and thirsty cities could not grow without tapping the abundant snow pack of the Sierra Nevada. By the turn of the century, Los Angeles faced a water crisis that threatened its growth. The answer was a 238-mile aqueduct to the Owens River in the southern Sierra. A bitter controversy blew up over this immense project, driven by the resistance of local residents to the flooding of the beautiful Owens Valley. More painful for John Muir and his preservationist allies was their failure to save the Hetch Hetchy Valley — "one of nature's rarest and most precious mountain temples," in Muir's words — on the northern edge of Yosemite National Park. After years of controversy the federal government in 1913 approved the damming of Hetch Hetchy's Tuolumne River to serve the water needs of San Francisco.

When the stakes became high enough, nature preservationists like John Muir generally came out on the short end. Even so, something original and distinctive had been added to California's heritage — the linking of a society's well-being with the protection of its natural environment. This realization, in turn, said something important about the nation's relationship to the West. If the urge to conquer and exploit persisted, at least it was now tempered by a sense that nature's bounty was not limitless. And this, more than any announcement by the U.S. census that a "frontier line" no longer existed, registered the country's acceptance that the age of heedless westward expansion had ended.

> Why is mining the key to understanding the settlement of the Far West?

> In what ways are the experiences of Hispanics and Chinese in the Far West similar? In what ways different?

> Why can we speak of a distinctly California history in the late nineteenth century?

SUMMARY

In this chapter, we trace the final stages of the Euro-American occupation of the continental United States, now strongly driven by the nation's industrial development. Factories needed the West's mineral resources; urbanites depended on its agricultural products; and, from railroads to barbed wire, the implements of industrialism accelerated the pace of conquest. The patterns of settlement, however, differed in the two great ecological regions that make up the trans-Mississippi West.

East of the Rockies, the semiarid Great Plains remained in 1860 the ancestral home to nomadic Indian tribes, still living in a vibrant society based on the horse and the buffalo. With the U.S. military leading the way, cattle ranchers and homesteaders in short order displaced the Indians and domesticated the Great Plains. Despite fierce resistance, by 1890 the Indians had been crowded onto reservations and forced to abandon their tribal ways of life.

Beyond the Rockies, where the terrain was largely arid and uninhabitable, occupation took the form of islands of settlement rather than progressive occupation along a broad frontier that had prevailed on the Great Plains. And while arable land had been the lure for settlers up to that point, what drove settlement in the Far West was the discovery of mineral wealth.

Also distinctive of Far Western development was its dominance by a single state, California, which anchored both the crescent of Hispanic settlement across the Southwest and the Pacific slope region stretching to the Canadian border. The discovery of gold set off a huge migration that overwhelmed the thinly spread Hispanic population and transformed California into a populous state with a large urban sector centered in San Francisco. California developed a distinctive culture that capitalized on its rediscovered Hispanic heritage and its climate and natural environment. California also capitalized on the Chinese, Japanese, and Mexicans who provided the state's cheap labor, infusing a dark streak of racism into its otherwise sunny culture.

Connections: The American West

As readers of earlier chapters of this text know, there were many "Wests" in American history. Colonists considered the Appalachians the West; for Jeffersonians, it was the Ohio Valley; for Jacksonians, the Mississippi Valley. The land beyond the Mississippi Valley — the Great Plains, the Rockies, and the Pacific slope discussed in this chapter — constitutes the last American West, the region that remains, even to readers of this text, the country's West. What distinguishes the settlement of this last American West is that it coincided with, and was driven by, America's industrial revolution. As we observe in the part opener (p. 485):

It was eastern demand for new sources of food and mineral resources that drove the final surge of western settlement and integrated the Great Plains and Far West into the nation's industrializing economy.

Integration, of course, worked in both directions, so that students should bear in mind as they read Chapters 17 and 18 the West's role in fostering the nation's industrializing economy and urban growth. The West also had a distinctive impact on American politics, driving the Populist movement in the 1890s (Chapter 19) and strongly influencing progressivism after 1900 (Chapter 20). In the twentieth century the West becomes increasingly absorbed in the national narrative, but students should be watchful for where its distinctive role pops up, as, for example, Hollywood in the 1920s (Chapter 23) and as a site for the defense industry during World War II (Chapter 25).

CHAPTER REVIEW QUESTIONS

- Do you think this chapter successfully makes the case that the final phases of the frontier movement should be seen as an extension of American industrialization?

- Would it be possible to write an account of the settlement of the Great Plains and Far West without taking account of the natural environment?

- Although frontier history is generally treated as an Anglo-American story, in the Far West it is much more about ethnic diversity. Why is that?

TIMELINE

1849	California gold rush
	Chinese migration begins
1862	Homestead Act
1864	Yosemite Valley reserved as public park
1865	Long Drive of Texas longhorns begins
1867	Patrons of Husbandry (the Grange) founded
	U.S. government adopts reservation policy for Plains Indians
1868	Indian treaty confirms Sioux rights to Powder River hunting grounds
1869	Union Pacific–Central Pacific transcontinental railroad completed
1875	Sioux ordered to vacate Powder River hunting grounds; war breaks out
1876	Battle of Little Big Horn
1877	San Francisco anti-Chinese riots
1879	Exoduster migration to Kansas
1882	Chinese Exclusion Act
1884	Helen Hunt Jackson's novel *Ramona* published
1886	Dry cycle begins on the Great Plains
1887	Dawes Severalty Act
1889	Oklahoma opened to white settlement
1890	Indian massacre at Wounded Knee, South Dakota
	U.S. census declares end of the frontier

FOR FURTHER EXPLORATION

The starting point for western history is Frederick Jackson Turner's famous essay, "The Significance of the Frontier in American History" (1893), reprinted in Ray A. Billington, ed., *Frontier and Section: Selected Essays of Frederick Jackson Turner* (1961). In recent years there has been a reaction against Turnerian scholarship for being Eurocentric—for seeing western history only through the eyes of frontiersmen and settlers—and for masking the rapacious and environmentally destructive underside of western settlement. Patricia N. Limerick's skillfully argued *The Legacy of Conquest* (1987) opened the debate. Richard White's *"It's Your Misfortune and None of My Own": A New History of the American West* (1991) provides the fullest synthesis. For some of the most debated issues, see the essays in Clyde A. Milner, ed., *A New Significance: Re-envisioning the History of the American West* (1996). On women's experiences—another primary concern of the new scholarship—a useful introduction is Susan Armitage and Elizabeth Jameson, eds., *The Women's West* (1987). On the Plains Indians, a lively account is Robert M. Utley, *The Indian Frontier of the American West* (1984). The ecological impact of Plains settlement is subtly probed in Frieda Knobloch, *The Culture of Wilderness: Agriculture as Colonization in the American West* (1996). One facet of this subject is reconsidered in Andrew C. Isenberg, *The Destruction of the Bison: An Environmental History* (2000). On the integration of the Plains economy with the wider world, an especially rich book is William Cronon, *Nature's Metropolis: Chicago and the Great West* (1991). Sarah Deutsch, *No Separate Refuge* (1987), offers an imaginative treatment of the New Mexican peasantry. On the Asian migration to America, the best introduction is Ron Takaki, *Strangers from a Different Shore* (1989). David Vaught, *Cultivating California: Growers, Specialty Crops, and Labor, 1875–1920* (1999), offers a fresh interpretation of California's agricultural development, especially debunking the widely held view that California farms were "factories in the field." Kevin Starr, *California and the American Dream, 1850–1915* (1973), provides a full account of the emergence of a distinctive California culture. A comprehensive Web site with many links is **www.americanwest.com**.

TEST YOUR KNOWLEDGE

To assess your command of the material in this chapter, see the Online Study Guide at **bedfordstmartins.com/henretta**.

For Web sites, images, and documents related to topics and places in this chapter, visit **bedfordstmartins.com/makehistory**.

17 Capital and Labor in the Age of Enterprise

1877–1900

THE YEAR THAT RECONSTRUCTION ENDED, 1877, also marked the first great labor crisis of American industrial history. Much like the dot.com bust of our own time, the post–Civil War railroad boom collapsed after the Panic of 1873. Railroad building ground to a halt, workers lost their jobs, and wages fell. On July 16, 1877, railroad workers went on strike to protest a wage cut at the Baltimore and Ohio Railroad. In towns along the B&O tracks, crowds cheered as the strikers attacked company property and prevented trains from running. The strike rippled across the country, reaching as far as the Pacific Coast and provoking rioting in San Francisco. The Pennsylvania Railroad's roundhouse in Pittsburgh went up in flames on July 21, and at many rail centers rioters and looters roamed freely. Only the arrival of federal troops restored order. On August 15 President Rutherford B. Hayes wrote in his diary, "The strikers have been put down *by force*." The Great Strike of 1877 had been crushed, but only after raising the specter of social revolution.

And then recovery came. Within months railroad building resumed. The economy boomed. In the next fifteen years, the output of manufactured goods increased by over 150 percent. Confidence in the nation's industrial future rebounded. "Upon [material progress] is founded all other progress," asserted a railroad president in 1888. "Can there be any

Industrial Capitalism Triumphant
The Age of Steel
The Railroad Boom
Large-Scale Enterprise

The World of Work
Labor Recruits
Autonomous Labor
Systems of Control

The Labor Movement
Reformers and Unionists
The Emergence of the AFL
Industrial War
American Radicalism in the Making

Summary
Connections: Economy

◀ **Homestead at Twilight**

In this evocative painting Aaron Henry Gorson (1872–1933) looks across the Monongahela River at Andrew Carnegie's great steel mill, a symbol of America's industrial prowess but also, as the clouds of smoke lighting the sky suggest, a major source of the Pittsburgh district's polluted air. Westmorland Museum of Art.

doubt that cheapening the cost of necessaries and conveniences of life is the most powerful agent of civilization and progress?"

The rail magnate's boast represents the confident face of America's industrial revolution. President Hayes's anxious diary entries suggest a darker side. After 1877 armories appeared in cities across the country. They were fortresses designed to withstand assault by future strikers and rioters. It was a paradox of the nation's industrial history that an economy celebrated for its dynamism and inventiveness was also brutally indifferent to the many who fell by the wayside and hence an economy never secure, never free of social conflict.

Industrial Capitalism Triumphant

Economic historians speak of the late nineteenth century as the age of the Great Deflation, an era when worldwide prices fell steadily. Falling prices normally signal economic stagnation; there is not enough demand for available goods and services. In England, a mature industrial power, the Great Deflation did indeed signal economic decline. That was not the case in the United States. In fact, industrial expansion here went into high gear during the Great Deflation. Manufacturing efficiencies enabled American firms to cut prices and yet earn profits and afford still better equipment. Real income for Americans went up dramatically, increasing by nearly 50 percent (from $388 to $573 per year) between 1877 and 1900. The industrializing economy was a wealth-creating machine beyond anything the world had ever seen (Figure 17.1).

The Age of Steel

By the 1870s, factories were a familiar sight in America. But the goods they produced — textiles, shoes, paper, and furniture — mainly replaced articles made at home or by individual artisans. Early manufacturing was really an extension of the pre-industrial economy. Gradually, however, a different kind of demand developed as the country's economy surged. Railroads needed locomotives; new factories needed machinery; cities needed trolley lines, sanitation systems, and commercial buildings. Railroad equipment, machinery, and construction materials were *capital goods*, that is, goods that added to the nation's productive capacity.

Central to the capital-goods sector was a technological revolution in steel making. The country already had a large iron industry, turning out a product called wrought iron, a malleable metal easily worked by blacksmiths and farmers. But wrought iron was ill suited for industrial uses; in particular, it did not stand up under heavy use as railway track. Additionally, wrought iron was expensive because it could be produced only in small batches by skilled puddlers. In 1856 the British inventor Henry Bessemer designed a furnace — the Bessemer converter — that refined raw pig iron into an essentially new product: steel, a metal more durable than wrought iron and, on top of that, much cheaper to produce because the process required virtually no hands-on labor. Bessemer's invention attracted many users, but it was Andrew Carnegie who fully exploited its potential.

Andrew Carnegie and American Steel. Carnegie's was the great American success story. He arrived from Scotland in 1848 at the age of twelve with his

FIGURE 17.1 Business Activity and Wholesale Prices, 1869–1900

This graph shows the key feature of the performance of the late-nineteenth-century economy: While output was booming, the price of goods was falling.

Bessemer Converter, Bethlehem Works, Steelton, Pennsylvania, 1885

Workers for Bethlehem Steel in Steelton, Pennsylvania, posed for this 1885 photograph with a Bessemer converter. The late nineteenth century in America came to be known as "America's Age of Steel," thanks to the increased steel production that the Bessemer converter helped generate. Hagley Museum and Library.

poverty-stricken family. He became a telegraph operator, and then went to work for the Pennsylvania Railroad and rapidly scaled the managerial ladder. In 1865, having amassed a fortune in wartime speculation, Carnegie struck out on his own as an iron manufacturer. His main customers were his network of former associates in the railroad business.

In 1872 Carnegie erected a massive steel mill outside Pittsburgh, with the Bessemer converter as its centerpiece. Ferrous metallurgy involves three steps: blast furnaces smelt ore into pig iron; the pig iron is refined into useable metal, either wrought iron or steel; finally, the refined metal is stamped or rolled into desired shapes for purchasers. The Bessemer converter broke a bottleneck at the refining stage, enabling Carnegie's engineers to construct larger blast furnaces and faster rolling mills, and design an integrated plant that achieved continuous operation: Iron ore entered the blast furnaces at one end and came out the other end as finished steel rails. Carnegie's new plant became a model for the industry, setting in motion the replacement of the iron mills that had once dotted western Pennsylvania by giant steel mills.

The United States was blessed with rich mineral resources that enabled the steel industry to capitalize on Carnegie's technological breakthroughs. From the great Mesabi range in northern Minnesota, iron ore came down the Great Lakes by ship in vast quantities. The other key ingredient, coal, arrived from the great Appalachian field that stretched from Pennsylvania to Alabama. A minor enterprise before the Civil War, coal production doubled every decade after 1870, exceeding 400 million tons a year by 1910.

As steam engines became the nation's energy workhorses, prodigious amounts of coal began to

Andrew Carnegie

Carnegie was born in poverty in Scotland. He clawed his way up in America, via his Pittsburgh steel mills, to fabulous wealth. Once he got there, Carnegie liked to think of himself as a lord of the manor or, in his case, "laird" of a grand estate in Scotland. In this photograph, taken in his retirement, he is properly attired for that role and properly attended by a handsome collie. Bettmann/Corbis.

be consumed by railroads and factories. Industries previously dependent on waterpower rapidly converted to steam. The turbine, utilizing continuous rotation rather than the steam engine's back-and-forth piston motion, marked another major advance during the 1880s. With the coupling of the steam turbine to the electric generator, the nation's energy revolution was completed, and after 1900 America's factories began a massive conversion to electric power.

The Railroad Boom

Although water transportation was perfectly adequate for the country's needs before the Civil War, it was love at first sight when locomotives arrived from Britain in the early 1830s. Americans were impatient for the year-round, on-time service not achievable by canal barges and riverboats. By 1860, as a network of tracks crisscrossed the eastern half of the country, the railroad clearly was on the way to being industrial America's mode of transportation.

Constructing the Railroads. The question was, who would pay for it? Railroads could be state enterprises, like the canals, or they could be financed by private investors. Unlike most European countries, the United States chose free enterprise. Even so, government played a big role. Eager for the economic benefits, many states and localities lured railroads with offers of financial aid, mainly by buying railroad bonds. Land grants were the principal means by which the federal government encouraged interregional rail construction.

The most important boost, however, was not money or land but a legal form of organization — the corporation — that enabled private capital to be raised in prodigious amounts. Investors who bought stock in the railroads enjoyed *limited liability:* They risked only the money they had invested; they were not personally liable for the railroad's debts. A corporation could also borrow money by issuing interest-bearing bonds, which was how the railroads actually raised most of the money they needed.

Railroad building generally was handed over to construction companies, which, despite the name, were primarily financial structures. Hiring contractors and suppliers often involved persuading them to accept the railroad's bonds as payment and, when that failed, wheeling and dealing to raise cash by selling or borrowing on the bonds. The construction companies were notoriously corrupt. In the worst case, the Union Pacific's Credit Mobilier, probably half the construction funds was the pocketed by the promoters.

The railroad business was not for the faint of heart. Most successful were promoters with the best access to capital, such as John Murray Forbes, a great Boston merchant in the China trade who developed the Chicago, Burlington, and Quincy Railroad in the Midwest; or Cornelius Vanderbilt, who started with the fortune he had made in the steamboat business. Vanderbilt was primarily a consolidator, linking previously independent lines and ultimately, via his New York Central, providing unified railroad service between New York City and Chicago. James J. Hill, who without federal subsidy made the Great Northern into the best of the

Wall Street: Gould's Private Bowling Alley

This 1882 cartoon testifies vividly to Jay Gould's unsavory reputation as a financial manipulator, bowling over his adversaries with Trickery and False Reports and keeping score of his ill-gotten gains on the slate at lower right. Granger Collection.

transcontinental railroads, was certainly the nation's champion railroad builder. In contrast Jay Gould, who at various times controlled the Erie, Wabash, Union Pacific, and Missouri Pacific railroads, always remained a stock market speculator at heart. But even Gould, although he rigged stock prices and looted his properties, made a positive contribution. By throwing his weak railroads against better-established operators (in hopes of being bought out), he forced down rates and benefited shippers. A gifted strategist, Gould was an early promoter of integrated railroads, the catalyst prompting Vanderbilt's creation of the New York Central.

Railroad development in the United States was often sordid, fiercely competitive, and subject to boom and bust. Yet promoters raised vast sums of capital and built a network bigger than that of the rest of the world combined. By 1900 virtually no corner of the country lacked rail service.

The Railway System. Along with this prodigious growth came increasing efficiency. The early railroads, built by competing local companies, had been a jumble of discontinuous segments. Gauges of track—the width between the rails—varied widely, and at terminal points railroads were not connected. As late as 1880, goods could not be shipped through from Massachusetts to South Carolina. Eight times along the way, freight cars had to be emptied and their contents transferred to other cars across a river or at a different terminal.

In 1883 the railroads rebelled against the jumble of local times that made scheduling a nightmare and, acting on their own, divided the country into the standard time zones still in use (Map 17.1). By the end of the 1880s, a standard track gauge (4 feet, 8½ inches) had been adopted everywhere. Fast-freight firms and standard accounting procedures enabled shippers to move goods without breaks in transit, transfers between cars, or the other delays that had once bedeviled them.

At the same time railroad technology was advancing. Durable steel rails permitted heavier traffic. Locomotives became more powerful and capable of pulling more freight cars. To control the greater mass being hauled, the inventor George Westinghouse perfected the automatic coupler, the air brake, and the friction gear for starting and stopping a long line of cars. Costs per ton-mile fell by 50 percent between 1870 and 1890, resulting in a steady drop in freight rates for shippers.

The railroads fully met the transportation needs of the maturing industrial economy. For investors, however, the costs of freewheeling competition and unrestrained growth were painfully high. Many railroads were saddled with huge debts from the extravagant construction era; about a fifth of railroad bonds failed to pay interest even in a good year like 1889. When the economy turned bad, as it did in 1893, a third of the industry went into bankruptcy.

Out of the rubble came a massive railroad reorganization. This was primarily the handiwork of

MAP 17.1 The Expansion of the Railroad System, 1870–1890

In 1870 the nation had 53,000 miles of rail track; in 1890 it had 167,000 miles. That burst of construction essentially completed the nation's rail network, although there would be additional expansion for the next two decades. The main areas of growth were in the South and west of the Mississippi. The time zones introduced in 1883 are marked by the gray lines.

Wall Street investment banks such as J. P. Morgan & Co. and Kuhn, Loeb & Co., whose main role had been to market railroad stocks and bonds. When railroads failed, the investment bankers stepped in to pick up the pieces. They persuaded investors to accept lower interest rates or put up more money. They eased competitive pressures by consolidating rivals. By the early twentieth century, half a dozen great regional systems had emerged, and the nerve center of American railroading had shifted to Wall Street.

Large-Scale Enterprise

Until well into the industrial age, all but a few manufacturers operated on a small scale, producing mostly for nearby markets. Then, after the Civil War, big business arrived. "Combinations of capital on a scale hitherto wholly unprecedented constitute one of the remarkable features of modern business methods," the economist David A. Wells wrote in 1889. He could see "no other way in which the work of production and distribution can be prosecuted." What was there about the nation's economy that led to Wells's sense that big business was inevitable?

Most of all, the American market. Unlike Europe, the United States was not carved up by national borders that impeded the flow of goods. The population, swelled by immigration and a high birthrate, jumped from 40 million in 1870 to over 60 million in 1890. People flocked to the cities, and the railroads brought these expanding markets within the reach of distant producers. Nowhere else did manufacturers have so vast and receptive a market for standardized products.

Gustavus Swift and Vertical Integration. How they seized that opportunity is perhaps best revealed in the meatpacking industry. With the opening of the Union Stock Yards in 1865, Chicago became the cattle market for the country. Livestock came in by rail from the Great Plains, was auctioned off at the Chicago stockyards, and then shipped to eastern cities, where, as in the past, the cattle were slaughtered in local "butchertowns". Such an arrangement—a national livestock market but localized processing—adequately met the needs of an exploding urban population and could have done so indefinitely, as was the case, in fact, in Europe.

Gustavus F. Swift, a shrewd Chicago cattle dealer from Massachusetts, saw the future differently. He recognized that livestock lost weight en route to the East and that local slaughterhouses lacked the scale to utilize waste by-products or cut labor costs. If he could keep it fresh in transit, however, dressed beef could be processed in bulk at the Chicago stockyards. Other packers, like Armour & Co., already did that for smoked and salted pork products that did not require refrigeration. Once his engineers figured out a cooling system, Swift invested in a fleet of refrigerator cars and constructed a central packing plant next to the Chicago stockyards. This was only the beginning of Swift's innovations. In the cities receiving his chilled meat, Swift built his own network of branch houses and a fleet of delivery wagons. He constructed facilities to process the fertilizer, chemicals, and other usable by-products (wasting, it was said, only the pig's squeal). As demand grew, Swift expanded to other stockyard centers, including Kansas City, Fort Worth, and Omaha (Map 17.2).

MAP 17.2 The Dressed Meat Industry, 1900

The meatpacking industry clearly shows how transportation, supply, and demand combined to foster the growth of the American industrial economy. The main centers of beef production in 1900—Chicago, Omaha, Kansas City, and St. Louis—were rail hubs with connections westward to the cattle regions and eastward to cities hungry for cheap supplies of meat. Vertically integrated enterprises sprang from these elements, linked together by an efficient and comprehensive railroad network.

Step by step Swift created a new kind of enterprise—a *vertically integrated firm* capable of handling within its own structure all the functions of an industry. Swift's lead was followed by several big Chicago pork packers. By 1900 five firms, all of them nationally organized and vertically integrated, produced nearly 90 percent of the meat shipped in interstate commerce.

The term that describes this condition is *oligopoly*—market dominance by the few. In meatpacking, that was mostly the result of a radically new form of business. As the vertically integrated firms emerged, the livestock dealers and small slaughterhouses that populated the earlier industry were simply squeezed out or bypassed. But at the consuming end, where competition had to be met, Swift and fellow Chicago packers ruthlessly cut prices and drove independent distributors to the wall. And that brings into focus the second reason for large-scale enterprise—not greater efficiency, but market control. The impulse to drive out the competition, although universally felt, was strongest in bonanza industries, where (a) no player started with any particular advantage and (b) the market was especially chaotic, as, for example, petroleum.

John D. Rockefeller and Monopoly Power. Rural Americans had long been aware of scattered pools of petroleum oozing up mysteriously from the bowels of the earth. Snake-oil salesmen sometimes added the black stuff to their concoctions. Farmers used it to grease their wagons. Mostly, it was just a nuisance. Then in the 1850s experimenters figured out how to extract kerosene, a clean-burning fuel excellent for domestic heating and lighting. The potential market was vast. All that was needed was the crude oil. One likely place was Titusville, Pennsylvania, where the air stunk from pools of petroleum. In 1859, Edwin L. Drake drilled down and at 69 feet struck oil. Overnight a forest of derricks and makeshift refineries sprung up around Titusville. Much of the refining, however, soon shifted to population centers with better transshipping facilities. Chief among these, once it got a rail connection to the Pennsylvania fields in 1863, was Cleveland, Ohio.

At that time, John D. Rockefeller was an up-and-coming Cleveland grain dealer, twenty-four years old, and doing nicely thanks to the Civil War (which he, like Carnegie and virtually all the budding tycoons of his time, sat out). Rockefeller liked to boast of his humble origins, but in fact he grew up comfortably, even if it was tainted money from his father's escapades as an itinerant quack doctor. Initially skeptical of the wild oil business, Rockefeller soon plunged in. He had a sharp eye for able partners, a genius for finance, and strong nerves. Betting on the industry's future, he borrowed heavily to expand capacity. Within a few years his firm—Standard Oil of Ohio—was Cleveland's leading refiner, and Rockefeller was casting his eyes on the entire industry.

His natural allies were the railroads, who, like him, hated the boom-and-bust of the oil business. What they wanted was predictable, high-volume traffic, and for a good customer like Rockefeller, they offered secret rebates that gave him a leg up on competitors. Then in 1870, hit by another oil bust, the railroads concocted a remarkable scheme. Operating under cloak of the innocent-sounding South Improvement Company, they invited key refiners, including Rockefeller, to join a conspiracy to take over the industry. The participants would cease competing and instead divide up traffic and production. And for the cooperating refiners there was this delicious bonus: rebates not only on their own shipments, but on those of their *rivals*. With this deal in his pocket, Rockefeller offered his Cleveland competitors a stark choice: sell out or die. News of the conspiracy leaked out, and the South Improvement Company collapsed under a hail of denunciations, but not before Rockefeller had taken over the Cleveland industry. With his power-play tactics perfected, he was on his way to national dominance. By the early 1880s Standard Oil controlled 95 percent of the nation's refining capacity. In Washington, outraged politicians began to consider legislation intended to rein in Rockefeller's monopoly.

If countless critics reviled him, Rockefeller didn't seem to mind. A church-going Baptist, Rockefeller was invincibly convinced of his own rectitude; he was doing the Lord's work by bringing order out of industrial chaos. The small fry his company swallowed, he once remarked, should regard Standard Oil as "an angel of mercy."

Rockefeller was not satisfied, in fact, merely to milk his monopoly advantage in refining. Obsessed from the outset with efficiency, he was quick to see the advantages of vertical integration. In this, Rockefeller was like Gustavus Swift, bent on designing a business structure capable of serving a national (and, in Rockefeller's case, international) market. Starting with refining, Standard Oil rapidly added a vast distribution network, oil pipe lines and tankers, and even, despite Rockefeller's distaste for speculative ventures, a big stake in the oil fields.

The Birth of Consumer Marketing. In retailing, the lure of a mass market brought comparable

Kellogg's Toasted Corn Flakes

Like crackers, sugar, and other nonperishable products, cereal had been traditionally sold in bulk from barrels. In the 1880s the Quaker Oats Company hit on the idea of selling oatmeal in boxes of standard size and weight. A further wrinkle was to process the cereal so that it could be consumed right from the box (with milk) for breakfast. And lo and behold: Kellogg's Corn Flakes! This is one of Kellogg's earliest advertisements. Picture Research Consultants & Archives.

changes. For rural consumers, Montgomery Ward and Sears, Roebuck developed huge mail-order enterprises. From Vermont to California, farm families selected identical goods from catalogues and became part of a nationwide consumer market. In the cities, retailers followed different strategies. The department store, pioneered by John Wanamaker in Philadelphia in 1875, soon became a fixture in downtowns across the country. Alternatively, retailers could reach consumers efficiently by opening a chain of stores, which was the strategy of the Great Atlantic and Pacific Tea Company (A&P) and F. W. Woolworth.

Americans were ready consumers of standardized, mass-marketed goods. Their geographic mobility tended to erase the preference for local products that shaped European tastes. Moreover, social class in America, though by no means absent, was blurred at the edges and did not call, for example, for class-specific ways of dressing. Foreign visitors often noted that ready-made clothing made it difficult to tell salesgirls from debutantes on city streets.

It was not, however, always smooth going for the innovative national marketers. Shop owners put up stiff resistance, appealing to local pride and sometimes agitating for ordinances to keep Swift and A&P at bay. Nor were standardized goods universally welcomed. Many people were leery, for example, of Swift's Chicago beef. How could it be wholesome weeks later in Boston or Philadelphia? Cheap prices helped, but advertising mattered more.

Modern advertising was born in the late nineteenth century, bringing brand names and a billboard-cluttered urban landscape. By 1900 companies were spending over $90 million a year for space in newspapers and magazines. Advertisements urged readers to bathe with Pears' soap, eat Uneeda biscuits, sew on a Singer machine, and snap pictures with a Kodak camera. The active molding of demand became a major challenge for the managers of America's national firms.

The Managerial Revolution. And so, even more urgently, did the task of controlling such far-flung enterprises. Nothing in the world of small business prepared Swift and other industrial pioneers for this challenge. Fortunately for them, railroaders had already paved the way. A managerial crisis had overtaken the trunk lines as they thrust westward before the Civil War. On a 50-mile road, remarked the Erie executive Daniel C. McCallum in a classic statement of the problem, the superintendent could personally attend to every detail, "and any system, however imperfect, may prove comparatively successful." But 500-mile trunk lines were too big for even the most energetic superintendent to oversee directly. It was in "the want of a system" that lay "the true secret of their failure." Acknowledging that he was working in the dark — "we have no precedent or experience upon which we can fully rely" — McCallum urged that the railroads begin devising the structures, the *system*, that would enable them to control their widespread activities. Step by step, always under the prod of necessity, the trunk lines separated overall management from day-to-day operations, departmentalized operations by function (maintenance of way, rolling stock, traffic), defined lines of communication, and perfected cost-accounting methods enabling industrial society to another. In the United States workers were especially torn about how to proceed, and only in the 1880s did they settle on a labor movement that was distinctively American, like no other. While European movements embraced some variant of politically engaged socialism, American unionists rejected politics and emphasized **collective bargaining** with employers.

Reformers and Unionists

Thomas B. McGuire, a New York wagon driver, was ambitious. He had saved $300 from his wages "so that I might become something of a capitalist eventually." But his venture as a cab driver in the early 1880s soon failed:

> Corporations usually take that business themselves. They can manage to get men, at starvation wages, and put them on a hack, and put a livery on them with a gold band and brass buttons, to show that they are slaves—I beg pardon; I did not intend to use the word slaves; there are no slaves in this country now—to show that they are merely servants.

Slave or liveried servant, the symbolic meaning was the same to McGuire. He was speaking of the crushed aspirations of the independent American worker.

The Knights of Labor. What would satisfy the Thomas McGuires of the nineteenth century? Only the establishment of an egalitarian society in which every citizen might become economically independent. This republican goal resembled Jefferson's yeoman society, but labor reformers had no interest in returning to an agrarian past. They accepted industrialism, but not the accompanying unjust wage system that distinguished between capitalists and workers. In the future, all would be "producers," laboring together in what labor reformers commonly called the "cooperative commonwealth." This was the ideal that inspired the Noble and Holy Order of the Knights of Labor.

Founded in 1869 as a secret society of garment workers in Philadelphia, the Knights of Labor spread to other cities and, by 1878, emerged as a national movement. The Knights boasted an elaborate ritual that appealed to the fraternal spirit of nineteenth-century workers. The local assemblies of the Knights engendered a spirit of comradeship, very much like the Masons or Odd Fellows. For the Knights, however, fraternalism was harnessed to labor reform. The goal was to "give voice to that grand undercurrent of mighty thought, which is today [1880] crystallizing in the hearts of men, and urging them on to perfect organization through which to gain the power to make labor emancipation possible."

But how was "emancipation" to be achieved? Through cooperation, the Knights argued. They intended to set up factories and shops that would be owned and run by the employees. As these cooperatives flourished, American society would be transformed into a cooperative commonwealth. But little was actually done. Instead the Knights devoted themselves to "education." Their leader, Grand Master Workman Terence V. Powderly, regarded the organization as a vast labor college open to all but lawyers and saloonkeepers. The cooperative commonwealth would arrive in some mysterious way as more and more "producers" became members and learned the group's message from lectures, discussions, and publications. Social evil would not end in a day but "must await the gradual development of educational enlightenment."

Trade Unionism. The labor reformers, exemplified by the Knights, expressed the grander aspirations of American workers. Another kind of organization—the trade union—tended to their everyday needs. Ever since they had first appeared early in the century, trade unions had been at the center of the lives of craft workers. Apprenticeship rules regulated entry into a trade, and the **closed shop**—reserving all jobs for union members—kept out lower-wage and incompetent workers. Union rules specified the terms of work, sometimes in minute detail. Above all, trade unionism defended the craft worker's traditional skills and rights.

The trade union also expressed the craft's social identity. Hatters took pride in their alcohol consumption, an on-the-job privilege that was jealously guarded. More often craft unions had an uplifting character. A Birmingham ironworker claimed that his union's "main object was to educate mechanics up to a standard of morality and temperance, and good workmanship." Some unions emphasized mutual aid. Because operating trains was a high-risk occupation, the railroad brotherhoods provided accident and death benefits and encouraged members to assist one another. On and off the job, the unions played a big part in the lives of craft workers.

The earliest unions were local craft organizations, sometimes limited to a single ethnic group, especially among German workers. As expanding markets intruded, breaking down their ability to control local conditions, unions formed national organizations, beginning with the International

The Knights of Labor

The caption on this union card — "By Industry We Thrive" — expresses the core principle of the Knights of Labor that everything of value is the product of honest labor. The two figures are ideal representations of that "producerist" belief — handsome workers, respectably attired, doing productive labor. A picture of the Grand Master Workman, Terence V. Powderly, hangs on the wall, benignly watching them. Picture Research Consultants & Archives.

Typographical Union in 1852. By the 1870s molders, ironworkers, bricklayers, and about thirty other trades had done likewise. The national union, uniting local unions of the same trade, was becoming the dominant organizational form in America.

The practical job interests that trade unions espoused might have seemed a far cry from the idealism of the Knights of Labor. But both kinds of motives arose from a single worker's culture. Seeing no conflict, many workers carried membership cards in both the Knights and a trade union. And because the Knights, once established in a town or city, tended to become politically active and to field independent slates of candidates, that too became a magnet attracting trade unionists interested in local politics.

Trade unions generally barred women, and so did the Knights until 1881, when women shoe workers in Philadelphia struck in support of their male coworkers and won the right to form their own local assembly. By 1886 probably 50,000 women belonged to the Knights of Labor. Their courage on the picket line prompted Powderly's rueful remark that women "are the best men in the Order." For a handful of women, such as the hosiery worker Leonora M. Barry, the Knights provided a rare chance to take up leadership roles as organizers and officials.

Similarly, the Knights of Labor grudgingly opened the door for black workers, out of the need for solidarity and, just as important, in deference to the Order's egalitarian principles. The Knights could rightly boast that their "great work has been to organize labor which was previously unorganized."

The Emergence of the AFL

In the early 1880s the Knights began to act more like trade unions, negotiating over wages and hours and going on strike to win their demands. They made especially effective the use of boycotts against "unfair" employers. And with the economy booming, the Knights began to win strikes, including a major victory against Jay Gould's Southwestern railway system in 1885. Workers flocked to the organization, and its membership jumped from 100,000 to perhaps 700,000.

The rapid growth of the Knights frightened the national trade unions. They began to insist on a clear separation of roles, with the Knights confined to labor reform activities. This was partly a battle over turf, but it also reflected a deepening divergence of labor philosophies.

Samuel Gompers and Pure-and-Simple Unionism. On the union side, the key figure was Samuel Gompers, a Dutch-Jewish cigar maker whose family had emigrated, via London, to New York in 1863. Gompers was a worker-intellectual, a familiar type in the craft trades, little educated, but widely read and engaged by ideas. Gompers always contended that what he missed at school (he had gone to work at ten) he more than made up for in the shop, where cigar makers commonly paid one of their number to read to them while they worked.

Worker-intellectuals like Gompers gravitated to New York's radical circles, where during the 1870s the right course for bringing about the revolution was being fiercely debated. Partly out of these debates, partly from his experience in the Cigar Makers Union, Gompers hammered out a doctrine that he called "pure-and-simple" unionism. "Pure" referred to membership: strictly limited to workers, organized by craft and occupation, with no participation by middle-class reformers. "Simple" referred to goals: only what immediately benefited

Samuel Gompers

This is a photograph of the labor leader in his forties taken when he was visiting striking miners in West Virginia, an area where mine operators resisted unions with special fierceness. The photograph was taken by a company detective. George Meany Memorial Archives.

workers — wages, hours, and working conditions. Pure-and-simple unionism focused on the workplace, where workers had some power, and was suspicious of politics. What it aimed at was collective bargaining with employers. For Gompers, the keyword was *power*. "No matter how just," he said, "unless the cause is backed up with power to enforce it, it is going to be crushed and annihilated." This was at the crux of the dispute with the Knights: that they were innocent, with their grand schemes, of American power realities, and, on top of that, by mucking around on union turf, harmful to power-building unions.

In December 1886, having failed to persuade the Knights of Labor to desist, the national trade unions formed the American Federation of Labor (AFL), with Gompers as president. The AFL in effect locked into place the trade-union structure as it had evolved by the 1880s. Underlying this structure was the conviction that workers had to take the world as it was, not as they dreamed it might be.

Haymarket. The issue that crystallized the rupture between the rival movements was the eight-hour workday. Nothing, the trade unions believed, would do more to improve the everyday lives of American workers. The Knights leaders, although sympathetic, regarded shorter hours as a secondary issue and a distraction from higher goals. They demurred when the trade unions set May 1, 1886, as the deadline for achieving the eight-hour workday. But many Knights, ignoring the leadership, responded enthusiastically, and as the deadline approached, a wave of strikes and demonstrations broke out across the country.

At one such eight-hour-day strike, at the McCormick reaper works in Chicago, a battle erupted on May 3, leaving four strikers dead. Chicago was a hotbed of **anarchism**—the revolutionary advocacy of a stateless society—and local anarchists, most of them German immigrants, called a protest meeting the next evening at Haymarket Square. When police began to disperse the crowd, someone threw a bomb that killed or wounded several of the police, who responded with wild gunfire. Most of the casualties, including some policemen, came from police bullets. Despite the lack of evidence, the anarchists were found guilty of murder and criminal conspiracy. Four were executed, one committed suicide, and the others received long prison sentences—victims of one of the great miscarriages of American justice.

Seizing on the antiunion hysteria set off by the Haymarket affair, employers took the offensive. They broke strikes violently, compiled blacklists of strikers, and forced workers to sign **yellow-dog contracts**, in which, as a condition of employment, workers pledged not to join labor organizations. If trade unionists needed any confirmation of the tough world in which they lived, they found it in Haymarket and its aftermath.

The Knights of Labor, hard-hit despite its official opposition to the eight-hour strikes, never recovered from Haymarket. In the meantime the more resilient AFL took firm root, justifying Gompers's confidence that he had found the correct formula for the American labor movement. What he overlooked was the generous inclusiveness of the Knights of Labor. The AFL was far less welcoming to women and blacks, confining them, where they were admitted, to separate, second-class organizations. It was a flaw that would come back to haunt the labor movement.

Industrial War

Radical as were its intellectual origins, pure-and-simple unionism was conservative in effect. American trade unions did not challenge the economic order. All they wanted was a larger share for working people. But it was precisely that claim against company profits that made American employers so opposed to collective bargaining. In the 1890s they unleashed a fierce counterattack on the trade-union movement.

The Homestead Strike. The skilled workers of Homestead, Pennsylvania, the site of one of Carnegie's steel mills, imagined themselves safe from that threat. They earned good wages, lived comfortably, and generally owned their own homes. The mayor of the town was one of their own. And they had faith in Andrew Carnegie—for had not Good Old Andy said in a famous magazine article that workers had as sacred a right to combine as did capitalists?

Espousing high-toned principles made Carnegie feel good, but a healthy profit made him feel even better. He decided that collective bargaining had become too expensive, and he was confident that his skilled workers could be replaced by the advanced machinery he was installing. Lacking the stomach for the hard battle, Carnegie fled to a remote estate in Scotland, leaving behind a second-in-command well qualified to do the dirty work. This was Henry Clay Frick, a former coal baron and a veteran of labor wars in the coal fields.

After a brief pretense at bargaining, Frick announced that effective July 1, 1892, the company would no longer deal with the Amalgamated Association of Iron and Steel Workers. If the employees wanted to work, they would have to come back on an individual basis. The mill had already been fortified so that strikebreakers could be brought in to resume operations. At stake for Carnegie's employees now were not just wage cuts but the defense of a way of life. The town mayor, a union man, turned away the county sheriff when he tried to take possession of the plant. The entire community mobilized in defense of the union.

At dawn on July 6, barges were seen approaching Homestead up the Monongahela River. On board were armed guards hired by the Pinkerton Detective Agency to take possession of the steel works. Behind hastily erected barricades the strikers opened fire, and a bloody battle ensued. When the Pinkertons surrendered they were mercilessly pummeled by the enraged women of Homestead as they retreated to the railway station. Frick appealed to the governor of Pennsylvania, who called out the state militia and placed Homestead under martial law. The great steel works was taken over and opened to strikebreakers, while union leaders and town officials were arrested on charges of riot, murder, and treason.

The defeat at Homestead marked the beginning of the end for trade unions in the steel industry. Ended too were any lingering illusions about the sanctity of workers' communities like Homestead. "Men talk like anarchists or lunatics when they insist that the workmen of Homestead have done right," asserted one conservative journal. Nothing could be permitted to interfere with Carnegie's property rights or threaten law and order.

The Homestead strike ushered in a decade of strife, pitting working people against the formidable power of corporate industry and the even more formidable power of their own government. That hard reality was driven home to workers at a place that seemed an even less likely site for class warfare than Homestead.

The Great Pullman Boycott. Pullman, Illinois, was a model factory town, famous for its landscaping and city plan. The town's builder and sole employer was George M. Pullman, inventor of the sleeping car that brought comfort and luxury to railway travel. When business fell off during the economic depression in 1893, Pullman cut wages but not the rents for company housing. Confronted by a workers' committee in May 1894, Pullman denied any connection between his roles as employer and landlord. He then fired the workers' committee.

The strike that ensued would have warranted only a footnote in American history but for the fact that the Pullman workers belonged to the American Railway Union (ARU), a rapidly growing, new union of railroad workers. Its leader, Eugene V. Debs, directed ARU members not to handle Pullman sleeping cars, which, although operated by the railroads, were owned and serviced by the Pullman Company. This was a **secondary labor boycott**: force was applied on a second party (the railroads) to bring pressure on the primary target (Pullman). Since the railroads insisted on running the Pullman cars, a far-flung strike soon spread across the country, threatening the entire economy.

The railroads maneuvered quietly to bring the federal government into the dispute. Their hook was the U.S. mail cars, which they attached to every train hauling Pullman cars. When strikers stopped these trains, the railroads appealed to President Cleveland to protect the U.S. mail. Cleveland's Attorney General Richard Olney, a former railroad lawyer, unabashedly sided with his former employers. When federal troops failed to get the trains running again, Olney obtained court injunctions prohibiting the ARU leaders from conducting the strike. Debs and his associates refused, were charged with contempt of court, and jailed. Leaderless and uncoordinated, the strike quickly disintegrated.

No one could doubt why the great Pullman boycott had failed: It had been crushed by the naked use of government power on behalf of the railroad companies.

American Radicalism in the Making

Oppression does not radicalize every victim, but some it does radicalize. And when social injustice is most painfully felt, when the underlying power realities stand openly revealed, the process of radicalization speeds up. Such was the case during the depression of the 1890s. Out of the industrial strife of that decade emerged the main forces of twentieth-century American radicalism.

Eugene V. Debs and American Socialism. Very little in Eugene Debs's background would have suggested that he would one day become the nation's leading Socialist. A native of Terre Haute, Indiana, a prosperous railroad town, Debs grew up believing in the essential goodness of American society. A popular young man-about-town, Debs considered a career in politics or business but instead became involved in the local labor movement. In 1880, at the age of twenty-five, he was elected national secretary-treasurer of the Brotherhood of Locomotive Firemen, one of the craft unions that represented the skilled operating trades on the railroads. Troubled by his union's indifference to the low-paid track and yard laborers, Debs left his comfortable post to devote himself to the American Railway Union, an **industrial union**, that is, a union open to all railroad workers, regardless of skill. That was why the Pullman workers were eligible for ARU membership.

The Pullman strike visibly changed Debs. Sentenced to six months in a federal prison, he emerged an avowed radical, committed to a lifelong struggle against a system that enabled employers to enlist the powers of government to beat down working people. Initially, Debs identified himself as

The Pullman Strike

Chicago was the hub of the railway network and the strategic center of the battle between the Pullman boycotters and the trunk line railroads. For the strikers, the crucial thing was to prevent those trains with Pullman cars attached from running; for the railroads, it was to get the trains through at any cost. The arrival of federal troops meant that the trains would move and that the strikers would be defeated. *Harper's Weekly*, July 21, 1894.

a Populist (see Chapter 19), but he quickly gravitated to the Socialist camp.

German refugees had brought the ideas of Karl Marx, the radical German theorist, to America after the failed revolutions of 1848 in Europe. Marx postulated a class struggle between capitalists and workers, ending in a revolution that would abolish private ownership of the means of production and bring about a classless society. Little noticed by most Americans, Marxist socialism struck deep roots in the German American communities of Chicago and New York. With the formation of the Socialist Labor Party in 1877, Marxist socialism established itself as a permanent, if narrowly based, presence in American politics.

When Eugene Debs appeared in their midst in 1897, the Socialists were in disarray. American capitalism had just gone through its worst crisis, yet their party had failed to make much headway.

Many blamed the party head, Daniel De Leon, who considered ideological purity more important than winning elections. Debs joined in the revolt against the dogmatic De Leon and helped launch the rival Socialist Party of America in 1901.

A spellbinding campaigner, Debs talked socialism in an American idiom, making Marxism understandable and persuasive to many ordinary citizens. Under him the new party began to break out of its immigrant base and attract American-born voters. In Texas, Oklahoma, and Minnesota, socialism exerted a powerful appeal among distressed farmers. The party was also highly successful at attracting women activists. Inside of a decade, with a national network of branches and state organizations, the Socialist Party had become a force to be reckoned with in American politics.

King Debs

In this cartoon, *Harper's Weekly* depicts Eugene Debs as a tyrant, capable by his rule over the American Railway Union of halting all railway traffic and bringing the nation's economy to its knees. It was this conception of "King Debs" that, for many middle-class Americans, justified the extraordinary intervention by the federal government that crushed the Pullman boycott and landed Debs in prison. Library of Congress.

Western Radicalism. Farther west a different brand of American radicalism was taking shape. After many years of mostly friendly relations, the atmosphere in the western mining camps turned ugly during the 1890s. The powerful new corporations that were taking over wanted to be rid of the miners' union, the Western Federation of Miners (WFM). Moreover, silver and copper prices began to drop, bringing pressure to cut miners' wages. When strikes resulted, they took an especially violent turn.

In 1892 striking miners at Coeur d'Alene, a silver-mining district in northern Idaho, engaged in gun battles with company guards, sent a car of explosive powder careering into the Frisco mine, and threatened to blow up the smelters. Martial law was declared, the strikers were imprisoned in stockades, and the strike was broken. In subsequent miners' strikes, government intervention was equally naked and unrestrained. By 1897 the WFM president, Ed Boyce, was calling on all union members to arm themselves, and his rhetoric — he called the wage system "slavery in its worst form" — developed a hard edge.

Led by the fiery Boyce and "Big Bill" Haywood, the WFM joined in 1905 with left-wing Socialists to create a new movement, the Industrial Workers of the World (IWW). The Wobblies, as IWW members were called, fervently supported the Marxist class struggle — but at the workplace rather than in politics. By resistance at the point of production and ultimately by means of a **general strike**, they believed that the workers would bring about a revolution. A new society would emerge, run directly by the workers through their industrial unions. The term **syndicalism** describes this brand of workers' radicalism.

Industrial Violence

Strikes in the western mining districts were generally bloody affairs. On management's side, the mayhem was often perpetrated by the forces of law and order. In this photograph, we see a line of mounted troopers during the 1894 strike at Cripple Creek, Colorado. Our view is from the rear. From the front, the sight would have been more fearsome because the formation of the troopers suggests they might be about to charge and begin breaking heads. Denver Public Library, Western History Division.

In both its major forms — politically-oriented Socialism and the syndicalist IWW — American radicalism flourished after the crisis of the 1890s, but only on a limited basis and never with the possibility of seizing national power. Nevertheless, Socialists and Wobblies served a real purpose. American radicalism, by its sheer vitality, bore witness to what was exploitative and unjust in the new industrial order.

▶ How would you distinguish between labor reform and trade unionism?

▶ Why did the AFL prevail over the Knights of Labor?

▶ Why are the 1890s the critical period in the rise of American radicalism?

SUMMARY

In this chapter, we trace the emergence of modern American industrialism during the late nineteenth century. We show how an unrivaled capacity for supplying the capital goods and energy fueled an expanding manufacturing economy. On the demand side, the key development was an efficient railway network that provided manufacturers with easy access to national markets. We show how entrepreneurs like Swift and Rockefeller, eager to exploit this opportunity, built vertically integrated firms and developed functions for shaping consumer demand and managing far-flung, complex business activities entirely new to American enterprise. Also new, and troubling, was the market power suddenly in the hands of great firms like Rockefeller's Standard Oil.

On the labor side, the biggest challenge was finding enough workers for America's burgeoning industries. The South recruited local populations, of both races, while the industrial North relied on immigrants from Europe; both regions drew on young and single women. Race, ethnicity, and gender became defining features of the American working class. Mass production — the high-volume output of standardized products — accelerated the productivity of industry but also de-skilled workers and mechanized their jobs, as did the systematizing methods of Frederick W. Taylor's scientific management.

In these years, after much trial and error, the American labor movement took shape. The Knights of Labor enjoyed one final surge in the mid-1880 and succumbed to the AFL. Although accepting of the economic order, the AFL's insistence on a larger share for workers evoked fierce opposition from employers. The resulting industrial warfare of the 1890s stirred new radical impulses, leading both to the political socialism of Eugene V. Debs and to the industrial radicalism of the IWW.

Connections: Economy

The economic developments described in this chapter originated far back in the nineteenth century, when the factory system first emerged in the Northeast and roads, canals, and the early railroads launched a market revolution (Chapter 9). The industrial power that resulted gave the North the upper hand in the Civil War, while in turn the war effort further stimulated the North's industrial development (Chapter 14). Only afterward, however, in the years covered by this chapter, was that development fully consolidated. As we observed in the part opener (p. 485):

What had been partial and limited now became general and widespread; America turned into a land of factories, corporate enterprise, and industrial workers.

Virtually every aspect of America's subsequent history is shaped by its consolidation as an industry power. That was the condition, as we shall see in Chapter 21, for the nation's foray into imperial politics in the 1890s. It was the condition for the dramatic rise in living standards in the 1920s (Chapter 23), when mass-produced automobiles and other consumer durables began to flow to the American masses, and by its failure after 1929, for the social upheaval that led to the New Deal (Chapter 24). In these and other ways, American industrialism is a central fact of our modern history. Because it is, in fact, so central a condition, students should be attentive to the impact of American industrialism as they read beyond Chapter 17.

CHAPTER REVIEW QUESTIONS

➤ Why is growth of capital goods important to the development of American industry after 1877?

➤ Why is it that the late nineteenth century became the age of big business?

➤ Does it matter that the United States had to rely on Europe to meet the nation's need for workers?

➤ Why did American workers find it hard to choose between labor reform and trade unionism? And why, when they did choose, did it take the form of the AFL's "pure-and-simple" unionism?

TIMELINE

1869	Knights of Labor founded in Philadelphia
1872	Andrew Carnegie starts construction of Edgar Thomson steelworks near Pittsburgh
1873	Panic of 1873 ends railroad boom
1875	John Wanamaker establishes first department store in Philadelphia
1877	Baltimore and Ohio workers initiate nationwide railroad strike
1878	Gustavus Swift introduces refrigerator car
1883	Railroads establish national time zones
1886	Haymarket Square bombing in Chicago
	American Federation of Labor (AFL) founded
1892	Homestead steel strike crushed
	Wave of western miners' strikes begins
1893	Panic of 1893 leads to national depression
	Surge of railroad bankruptcies; reorganization by investment bankers begins
1894	President Cleveland sends troops to break Pullman boycott
1895	Southeastern European immigration exceeds northern European immigration for first time
	Frederick W. Taylor formulates scientific management
1901	Eugene V. Debs helps found Socialist Party of America
1905	Industrial Workers of the World (IWW) launched

FOR FURTHER EXPLORATION

For students new to economic history, biography offers an accessible entry point into what can be a dauntingly technical subject. The biographical literature is especially rich in American history because of this country's fascination with its great magnates and because of a long-standing debate among historians over what contribution (if any) the business moguls made to America's industrializing economy. The initiating book was Matthew Josephson's classic *The Robber Barons* (1934), which, as the title implies, argued that America's great fortunes were built on the wealth that others had created. The contrary view was taken by the financial historian Julius Grodinsky, whose *Jay Gould: His Business Career, 1867–1892* (1957) explained masterfully how this railroad buccaneer helped shape the transportation system. Since then, there have been superb, mostly sympathetic, business biographies, including Joseph F. Wall, *Andrew Carnegie* (1970); Ron Chernow, *Titan: The Life of John D. Rockefeller* (1998); Jean Strause, *Morgan: American Financier* (1999), and, for the man who revolutionized the newspaper business, David Nasaw, *The Chief: The Life of William Randolph Hearst* (2002). The founder of scientific management has also recently been the subject of a robust biography: Robert Kanigel, *The One Best Way: Frederick W. Taylor and the Enigma of Efficiency* (1997). On labor's side, the biographical literature is nearly as rich. The founder of the AFL is the subject of a lively brief biography by Harold Livesay, *Samuel Gompers and Organized Labor in America* (1978); Gompers's autobiography, *Seventy Years of Life and Labor* (2 vols., 1925), also makes rewarding reading. His main critic is treated with great insight in Nick Salvatore, *Eugene V. Debs: Citizen and Socialist* (1982). The IWW leader William D. Haywood left a colorful autobiography, *Bill Haywood's Book* (1929), and Haywood is also the subject of Peter Carlson's biography, *Roughneck* (1982). Biography, of course, tends to overlook the foot soldiers of history, but social historians have striven mightily in recent years to tell their stories. An excellent example is Paul Krause, *The Battle for Homestead, 1880–1892* (1992), which rescues from obscurity the working people who led that decisive steel strike. There is an excellent Web site on Andrew Carnegie at **http://andrewcarnegie.tripod.com/**.

TEST YOUR KNOWLEDGE

To assess your command of the material in this chapter, see the Online Study Guide at **bedfordstmartins.com/henretta**.

For Web sites, images, and documents related to topics and places in this chapter, visit **bedfordstmartins.com/makehistory**.

18 The Industrial City: Building It, Living in It

V‍ISITING HIS FIANCÉE'S MISSOURI HOMESTEAD in 1894, Theodore Dreiser was struck by "the spirit of rural America, its idealism, its dreams." But this was an "American tradition in which I, alas, could not share," Dreiser wrote. "I had seen Pittsburgh. I had seen Lithuanians and Hungarians in their [alleys] and hovels. I had seen the girls of the city — walking the streets at night." Only twenty-three at the time, Dreiser would go on to write one of the great American urban novels, *Sister Carrie* (1900), about one young woman in the army of small-town Americans flocking to the Big City. But Dreiser, part of that army, already knew that between rural America and Pittsburgh an unbridgeable chasm had opened up.

In 1820, after two hundred years of settlement, fewer than one in twenty Americans lived in a city of 10,000 people or more. After that, decade by decade, the urban population swelled until, by 1900, one of every five Americans was a city dweller. Nearly 6.5 million inhabited just three great cities: New York, Chicago, and Philadelphia (Table 18.1).

The city was the arena of the nation's vibrant economic life. Here the factories went up, and here the new immigrants settled, constituting in 1900 a third of the residents of the major American cities. Here, too, lived the millionaires and a growing white-collar middle class. For all these

Urbanization
City Innovation
Private City, Public City

Upper Class/Middle Class
The Urban Elite
The Suburban World
Middle-Class Families

City Life
Newcomers
Ward Politics
Religion in the City
City Amusements
The Higher Culture

Summary
Connections: Society

◀ **Mulberry Street, New York City, c. 1900**

The influx of southern and eastern Europeans created teeming ghettos in the heart of New York City and other major American cities. The view is of Mulberry Street, with its pushcarts, street peddlers, and bustling traffic. The inhabitants are mostly Italians, and some of them, noticing the photographer preparing his camera, have gathered to be in the picture. Library of Congress.

TABLE 18.1 Ten Largest Cities by Population, 1870 and 1900

1870		1900	
City	Population	City	Population
1. New York	942,292	New York	3,437,202
2. Philadelphia	674,022	Chicago	1,698,575
3. Brooklyn*	419,921	Philadelphia	1,293,697
4. St. Louis	310,864	St. Louis	575,238
5. Chicago	298,977	Boston	560,892
6. Baltimore	267,354	Baltimore	508,957
7. Boston	250,526	Cleveland	381,768
8. Cincinnati	216,239	Buffalo	352,387
9. New Orleans	191,418	San Francisco	342,782
10. San Francisco	149,473	Cincinnati	325,902

*Brooklyn was consolidated with New York in 1898.
Source: U.S. Census data.

people the city was more than a place to make a living. It provided the setting for an urban culture unlike anything seen before in the United States. City people, although differing vastly among themselves, became distinctively and recognizably urban.

Urbanization

The march to the cities seemed irresistible to nineteenth-century Americans. "The greater part of our population must live in cities," declared the Congregational minister Josiah Strong. And from another writer: "There was no resisting the trend." Urbanization became inevitable because of another inevitability of American life — industrialism.

Until the Civil War, cities lived on commerce, not industry. They were the places where goods were bought and sold for distribution into the interior or out to world markets. Early industry, on the other hand, sprang up mostly in the countryside, where factories had access to water power from streams, nearby fuel and raw materials, and workers recruited from farms and villages.

As industrialization proceeded, city and factory began to merge. Once steam engines came along, mill operators no longer depended on water-driven power. Railroads enabled entrepreneurs to locate factories at places best situated in relation to suppliers and markets. Iron makers gravitated to Pittsburgh because of its superior access to coal and ore fields. Chicago, midway between western livestock suppliers and eastern markets, became a great meatpacking center. Geographic concentration of industry meant urban growth. And so did the rising scale of production. A plant that employed thousands of workers instantly created a small city in its vicinity, sometimes in the form of a company town like Aliquippa, Pennsylvania, which became body and soul the property of the Jones and Laughlin Steel Company. Other firms built big plants at the edge of large cities so that they could draw on the available labor supply and transportation facilities. As the metropolis spread, the lines between industrial towns sometimes blurred and, as in northern New Jersey or along Lake Michigan south of Chicago, extended urban-industrial areas emerged.

Older commercial cities meanwhile became more industrial. Warehouse districts could readily be converted to small-scale manufacturing; a distribution network was right at hand. In addition, as gateways for immigrants, port cities offered abundant cheap labor. Boston, Philadelphia, Baltimore, and San Francisco became hives of small-scale, labor-intensive industrial activity. New York's enormous pool of immigrant workers made that city a magnet for the garment trades, cigar making, and diversified light industry. Preeminent as a city of trade and finance, New York also ranked as the nation's largest manufacturing center.

City Innovation

As cities expanded, so did the problems confronting them. How would so many people move around, communicate, have their physical needs met? The city demanded innovation no less than did industry itself and, in the end, compiled just as impressive a record of technological achievement.

The older commercial cities had been compact places, densely settled around harbors or riverfronts. As late as 1850, when it had 565,000 people, Philadelphia covered only ten square miles. From the foot of Chestnut Street on the Delaware River, a person could walk almost anywhere in the city within forty-five minutes. Thereafter, as it developed, Philadelphia spilled out and, like American cities everywhere, engulfed the surrounding countryside.

Nothing like this happened in continental Europe, where even rapidly growing cities remained physically compact, with built-up neighborhoods abruptly giving way to countryside. In America cities grew beyond their boundaries, forming what the federal census in 1910 began to designate as metropolitan areas. While highly congested at the center, American cities were actually thinly populated compared to German cities, which counted 158 people per acre as against 22 per acre in the United States.

"The only trouble about this town," wrote Mark Twain on arriving in New York in 1867, "is that it is too large. You cannot accomplish anything in the way of business, you cannot even pay a friendly call without devoting a whole day to it.... [The] distances are too great." Moving nearly a million New Yorkers around was not as hopeless as Twain thought, but it did challenge the ingenuity of city builders.

Mass Transit. The first innovation, dating back to the 1820s, was the omnibus, an elongated version of the horse-drawn carriage. More efficient was the horsecar, whose key advantage was that it ran on iron tracks so that the horses could pull more passengers at a faster clip through congested city streets. The chief objection to tracks was resolved by a modest but crucial refinement in 1852—a grooved rail that was flush with the pavement. Then came the electric trolley car, the brainchild primarily of Frank J. Sprague, an engineer once employed by the great inventor Thomas A. Edison. In 1887 Sprague designed an electric-driven system for Richmond, Virginia: A "trolley" carriage running along an overhead power line was attached by cable to streetcars equipped with an electric motor—hence the name "trolley car." After Sprague's success, the trolley swiftly displaced the horsecar and became the primary mode of transportation in most American cities.

In America's greatest metropolises, however, the streetcar itself was no solution. Congestion led to demands that transit lines be moved off the streets. In 1879 the first elevated railroads went into operation on Sixth and Ninth Avenues in New York City. Powered at first by steam engines, the "els" converted to electricity following Sprague's success with the trolley. Chicago developed elevated transit most fully (Map 18.1). Others looked below ground. Boston opened a short underground line in 1897, but it was the completion in 1904 of a subway running the length of Manhattan that demonstrated the full potential of the high-speed underground train. Mass transit had become *rapid* transit.

Skyscrapers. Equally remarkable was the architectural revolution sweeping metropolitan business districts. With steel girders, durable plate glass, and the passenger elevator available by the 1880s, a

The Chicago Elevated, 1900

This is Wabash Avenue, looking north from Adams Street. For Americans from farms and small towns, this photograph by William Henry Jackson captured something of the peculiarity of the urban scene. What could be stranger than a railroad suspended above the streets in the midst of people's lives? KEA Publishing Services, Ltd.

MAP 18.1 The Expansion of Chicago, 1865–1902

In 1865 Chicagoans depended on horsecar lines to get around town. By 1900 the city limits had expanded enormously and so had the streetcar service, which was by then electrified. Elevated trains eased the congestion on downtown streets. And the continuing extension of the streetcar lines, some beyond the city limits, assured that suburban development would be continuing as well.

Map annotations:
- The residential areas of the city tended to spread out along elevated (light-rail) railroad lines and streetcar tracks. These new forms of mass transit enabled people living in distant neighborhoods to reach the central business district and other places of employment.
- Note that the number of square miles within Chicago's city limits increased more than 300 percent between 1865 and 1902.
- Note that some areas of the old city were not used for either residence or industry. Most of these were large regional parks or undeveloped land.

Map legend: Central Business District; Industrial area; Residential area; Parks and undeveloped land; Elevated lines, 1902; Streetcar lines, 1902.

---

wholly new way of construction opened up. A steel skeleton supported the building, while the walls, previously weight bearing, served as curtains enclosing the structure. The sky, so to speak, became the limit.

The first "skyscraper" to be built on this principle was William Le Baron Jenney's ten-story Home Insurance Building (1885) in Chicago. Although unremarkable in appearance—it looked just like the other downtown buildings—the steel-girder technology Jenney's building contained liberated the aesthetic perceptions of American architects. A Chicago school sprang up, dedicated to the design of buildings whose form expressed, rather than masked, their structure and function. The presiding genius was the architect Louis Sullivan, who developed a "vertical aesthetic" of set-back windows and strong columns that gave skyscrapers a "proud and soaring" presence. Chicago pioneered sky-

scraper construction, but New York, with its unrelenting demand for prime downtown space, took the lead after the mid-1890s. The fifty-five-story Woolworth Building, completed in 1913, marked the beginning of the modern Manhattan skyline.

The Electric City. For ordinary citizens the electric lights that dispelled the gloom at night offered the most dramatic evidence that times had changed. Gaslight—illuminating gas produced from coal—had been in use since the early nineteenth century but, at 12 candlepower, the lamps were too dim to brighten the city's downtown streets and public spaces. The first use of electricity, once generating technology made it commercially feasible in the 1870s, was for better city lighting. Charles F. Brush's electric arc lamps, installed in Wanamaker's department store in Philadelphia in 1878, threw a brilliant light and soon replaced

Lighting Up Minneapolis, 1883

Like other American cities, Minneapolis at night had been a dim place until the advent of Charles F. Brush's electric arc lamps. This photograph marks the opening day, February 28, 1883, of Minneapolis's new era, the installation of a 257-foot tower topped by a ring of electric arc lamps. The electric poles on the right, connecting the tower to a power station, would soon proliferate into a blizzard of poles and overhead wires, as Minneapolis, like every late nineteenth-century city, became an electric city. © Minnesota Historical Society/CORBIS.

gaslight on city streets across the country. Electric lighting then entered the American home, thanks to Thomas Edison's invention of a serviceable incandescent bulb in 1879. Edison's motto — "Let there be light!" — truly described the experience of the modern city.

Before it had any significant effect on industry, electricity gave the city its modern tempo, lifting elevators, powering streetcars and subway trains, turning night into day. Meanwhile, Alexander Graham Bell's telephone (1876) sped communication beyond anything imagined previously. Twain's complaint of 1867, that it was impossible to carry on business in New York, had been answered: All he needed to do was pick up the phone.

Private City, Public City

City building was mostly an exercise in private enterprise. The lure of profit spurred the great innovations—the trolley car, electric lighting, the skyscraper, the elevator, the telephone—and drove urban real estate development. The investment opportunities looked so tempting that new cities sprang up almost overnight from the ruins of the Chicago fire of 1871 and the San Francisco earthquake of 1906. Real estate interests, eager to develop subdivisions, often were instrumental in pushing streetcar lines outward from the central districts of cities. The subway, predicted the *New York Times*, would open the outer suburbs to "a population of ten millions... housed comfortably, healthfully and relatively cheaply" — a gold mine for developers.

America gave birth to what one urban historian has called the "private city" — shaped primarily by the actions of many individuals, all pursuing their own goals and bent on making money. The prevailing belief was that the sum of such private activity would far exceed what the community might accomplish through public effort.

Yet constitutionally it was up to city governments to draw the line between public and private. New York City was entirely within its rights to operate a municipally owned subway, the State Supreme Court ruled in 1897. Even the use of private land was subject to whatever regulations the city might impose. Moreover, city governance improved impressively in the late nineteenth century. Though by no means free of the corruption of earlier days, municipal agencies became far better organized and staffed and, above all, more expansive in the functions they undertook. Nowhere in the world, indeed, were there more massive public projects — aqueducts, sewage systems, bridges, and spacious parks.

The Urban Environment. In the space between public and private, however, was an environmental no-man's land. City streets were often filthy and poorly maintained. "Three or four days of warm spring weather," remarked a New York journalist, would turn Manhattan's garbage-strewn, snow-clogged streets into "veritable mud rivers." Air quality likewise suffered. A visitor to Pittsburgh noted "the heavy pall of smoke which constantly overhangs her... until the very sun looks coppery through the sooty haze." As for the lovely hills rising from the rivers, "They have been leveled down, cut into, sliced off, and ruthlessly marred and mutilated." Pittsburgh presented "all that is unsightly and forbidding in appearance, the original beauties of nature having been ruthlessly sacrificed to utility."

Hardest hit by urban growth were the poor. In earlier times they had mainly lived in makeshift wooden structures in alleys and back streets and then, as more prosperous families moved away, in the subdivided homes left behind. As land values climbed after the Civil War, speculators tore down these houses and began to erect buildings specifically designed for the urban masses. In New York City the dreadful result was five- or six-story tenements, structures housing twenty or more families in cramped, airless apartments (Figure 18.1). In New York's Eleventh Ward, an average of 986 persons occupied each acre, a density only to be exceeded in Bombay, India.

Reformers recognized the problem but seemed unable to solve it. Some favored model tenements financed by public-spirited citizens willing to accept a limited return on their investment. When private philanthropy failed to make much of a dent, cities turned to housing codes. The most advanced code was New York's Tenement House Law of 1901,

Figure 18.1 Floor Plan of a Dumbbell Tenement

In a contest for a design that met an 1879 requirement that every room have a window, the dumbbell tenement won. The interior indentation, which created an airshaft between adjoining buildings, gave the tenement its "dumbbell" shape. What was touted as a "model" tenement demonstrated instead the futility of trying to reconcile maximum land usage with decent housing. Each floor contained four apartments of three or four rooms, the largest only 10 by 11 feet. The two toilets in the hall became filthy or broke down under daily use by forty or more people. The narrow airshaft provided almost no light for the interior rooms and served mainly as a dumping ground for garbage. So deplorable were these tenements that they became the stimulus for the next wave of New York housing reform.

which required interior courts, indoor toilets, and fire safeguards for new structures, but did little for existing housing stock. Commercial development had pushed up land values in downtown areas. Only high-density, cheaply built housing could earn a sufficient profit for the landlords of the poor. This economic fact defied nineteenth-century solutions.

It was not that America lacked an urban vision. On the contrary, an abiding **rural ideal** had influenced American cities for many years. Frederick Law Olmsted, who designed New York City's Central Park, wanted cities that exposed people to the beauties of nature. One of Olmsted's projects, the Chicago Columbian Exposition of 1893, gave rise to the influential "City Beautiful" movement. The results included larger park systems, broad boulevards and parkways, and, after the turn of the century, zoning laws and planned suburbs.

Cities usually heeded urban planners too little and too late. "Fifteen or twenty years ago a plan might have been adopted that would have made this one of the most beautiful cities in the world," Kansas City's park commissioners reported in 1893.

City Garbage

"How to get rid of the garbage?" was a question that bedeviled every American city. The difficulties of keeping up are all too clear in this ground-level photograph by the great urban investigator, Jacob Riis, looking down Tammany Street in New York City circa 1890.

Museum of the City of New York.

At that time "such a policy could not be fully appreciated." Nor, even if Kansas City had foreseen its future, would it have shouldered the "heavy burden" of trying to shape its development. The American city had placed its faith in the dynamics of the marketplace, not the restraints of a planned future. The pluses and minuses are perhaps best revealed by the following comparison.

A Balance Sheet: Chicago and Berlin. Chicago, Illinois, and Berlin, Germany, had virtually equal populations in 1900. But they had very different histories. Seventy years earlier, when Chicago had been a muddy frontier outpost, Berlin was already a city of 250,000 and the royal seat of the Hohenzollerns of Prussia.

With German unification in 1871, the imperial authorities rebuilt Berlin on a grander scale. "A capital city is essential for the state, to act as a pivot for its culture," proclaimed the Prussian historian Heinrich von Treitschke. Berlin served that national purpose — "a center where Germany's political, intellectual, and material life is concentrated, and its people can feel united." Chicago had no such pretensions. It was strictly a place of business, made great by virtue of its strategic grip on the commerce of America's heartland. Nothing in Chicago approached the grandeur of Berlin's boulevards or its monumental palaces and public buildings, nor were Chicagoans witness to the pomp and ceremony of the imperial parades up broad, tree-lined Unter den Linden to the national cathedral.

Yet as a functioning city, Chicago was in many ways superior to Berlin. Chicago's waterworks pumped 500 million gallons of water a day, or 139 gallons of water per person, while Berliners had to make do with 18 gallons. Flush toilets, a rarity in Berlin in 1900, could be found in 60 percent of Chicago's homes. Chicago's streets were lit by electricity, while Berlin still relied mostly on gaslight. Chicago had a much bigger streetcar system, twice as much acreage devoted to parks, and a public library containing many more volumes. And Chicago had just completed an amazing sanitation project that reversed the course of the Chicago River so that its waters — and the city's sewage — would flow away from Lake Michigan and southward down into the Illinois and Mississippi rivers.

Giant sanitation projects were one thing; an inspiring urban environment was something else. For well-traveled Americans admiring of things European, the sense of inferiority was palpable. "We are enormously rich," admitted the journalist Edwin L. Godkin, "but . . . what have we got to show? Almost nothing. Ugliness from an artistic point of view is the mark of all our cities." Thus the urban balance sheet: a utilitarian infrastructure that was superb by nineteenth-century standards, but "no municipal splendors of any description, nothing but population and hotels."

> ▶ Why can we say that technological innovation was just as significant in building American cities as it was in driving American industrialization?
> ▶ Why was the American city not capable of doing a better job of protecting the environment and providing adequate housing for the poor?
> ▶ If we count the degraded environment and poor housing as failures, why does Chicago come off so well in comparison to Berlin?

Upper Class/Middle Class

In the compact city of the early republic, class distinctions had been embedded in the way men and women dressed and by the deference they demanded from or granted others. As the industrial city grew, these marks of class weakened. In the anonymity of a big city, recognition and deference no longer served as mechanisms for conferring status. Instead, people began to rely on conspicuous display of wealth, membership in exclusive clubs, and above all, residence in exclusive neighborhoods.

For the poor, place of residence depended, as always, on being close to their jobs. But for higher-income urbanites, where to live became a matter of personal means and social preference.

The Urban Elite

As early as the 1840s, Boston merchants had taken advantage of the new railway service to escape the congested city. Fine rural estates appeared in Milton, Newton, and other outlying towns. By 1848 roughly 20 percent of Boston's businessmen were making the trip by train to their downtown offices. Ferries that plied the harbor between Manhattan and Brooklyn or New Jersey served the same purpose for well-to-do New Yorkers.

Lifestyles of the Rich. As commercial development engulfed downtown residential areas, the exodus by the elite quickened. In Cincinnati, wealthy families settled on the scenic hills rimming the crowded, humid tableland that ran down to the

Ohio River. On those hillsides, a traveler noted in 1883, "The homes of Cincinnati's merchant princes and millionaires are found . . . elegant cottages, tasteful villas, and substantial mansions, surrounded by a paradise of grass, gardens, lawns, and tree-shaded roads." Residents of the area, called Hilltop, founded country clubs, downtown gentlemen's clubs, and a round of social activities for the pleasure of Cincinnati's elite.

Despite the attractions of country life, many of the very richest preferred the heart of the city. Chicago boasted its Gold Coast; San Francisco, Nob Hill; Denver, Quality Hill; and Manhattan, Fifth Avenue. New York novelist Edith Wharton recalled how the comfortable midcentury brownstones gave way to the "'new' millionaire houses," which spread northward on Fifth Avenue along Central Park. Great mansions, emulating the aristocratic houses of Europe, lined Fifth Avenue at the turn of the century.

But great wealth did not automatically confer social standing. An established elite dominated the social heights, even in such relatively raw cities as San Francisco and Denver. It had taken only a generation — sometimes less — for money made in commerce or real estate to shed its tarnish and become "old" and genteel. In long-settled Boston, wealth passed intact through several generations, creating a closely knit tribe of elite families that kept moneyed newcomers at bay. Elsewhere urban elites tended to be more open, but only to the socially ambitious who were prepared to make visible and energetic use of their money.

New York City became the home of a national elite as the most ambitious gravitated to this preeminent capital of American finance and culture. Manhattan's extraordinary vitality in turn kept the city's high society fluid and relatively open. In Theodore Dreiser's novel *The Titan* (1914), the tycoon Frank Cowperwood reassures his unhappy wife that if Chicago society will not accept them, "there are other cities. Money will arrange matters in New York — that I know. We can build a real place there, and go in on equal terms, if we have money enough." New York thus came to be a magnet for millionaires. The city attracted them not only as a business center but for the opportunities it offered for display and social recognition.

This infusion of wealth shattered the older elite society of New York. Seeking to be assimilated into the upper class, the flood of moneyed newcomers simply overwhelmed it. There followed a curious process of reconstruction, a deliberate effort to define the rules of conduct and identify those who properly "belonged" in New York society.

Ward McAllister and "High Society." The key figure was Ward McAllister, a southern-born lawyer who had made a quick fortune in gold-rush San Francisco and then took up a second career as the arbiter of New York society. In 1888 McAllister compiled the first *Social Register*, which announced that it would serve as a "record of society, comprising an accurate and careful list" of all those deemed eligible for New York society. McAllister instructed the socially ambitious on how to select guests, set a proper table, arrange a party, and launch a young lady into society. He presided over a round of assemblies, balls, and dinners that defined the boundaries of an elite society. At the apex stood "The Four Hundred" — the true cream of New York society. McAllister's list corresponded to those invited to Mrs. William Astor's gala ball of February 1, 1892.

From Manhattan an extravagant life of leisure radiated out to such favored resorts as Saratoga Springs, New York, and Palm Beach, Florida. In Rhode Island, Newport featured a grand array of summer "cottages," crowned by the Vanderbilts' Marble House and The Breakers. Visitors arrived via private railway car or aboard yachts and amused themselves at the races and gambling casinos. In the city, the rich dined extravagantly at Delmonico's, on one famous occasion while mounted on horseback. The underside to this excess — scandalous affairs, rowdy feasts that ended in police court, the notoriously opulent costume ball thrown at the Waldorf-Astoria by the Bradley Martins at the peak of economic depression in 1897 — was avidly followed in the press and awarded the celebrity we now accord to rock singers and Hollywood stars.

Americans were adept at making money, remarked the journalist Edwin L. Godkin in 1896, but they lacked the European aristocratic traditions for spending it. "Great wealth has not yet entered our manners," Godkin remarked. In their struggle to find the way and establish the manners, the moneyed elite made an indelible mark on urban life. If there was magnificence in the American city, that was mainly their handiwork. And if there was conspicuous waste and display, that too was their doing.

The Suburban World

The middle class left a smaller imprint on the public face of the city. Many of its members, unlike the rich, preferred privacy, retreating into a suburban world that insulated them from the hurly-burly of urban life.

Since colonial times, self-employed lawyers, doctors, merchants, and proprietors had been the backbone of a robust American middle class.

Going to the Opera, 1873

In this painting by Seymour J. Guy, William H. Vanderbilt, eldest son and successor of the railroad tycoon Cornelius Vanderbilt, has gathered with his family and friends preparatory to attending the opera. It was the sponsorship of New York's Metropolitan Opera that helped the Vanderbilts achieve social recognition among the older, more established moneyed families of New York City. Courtesy, Biltmore Estate, Asheville, NC.

While independent careers remained important, in the age of industrialism spawned a new middle class of salaried employees. Corporate organizations required managers, accountants, and clerks. Industrial technology called for engineers, chemists, and designers, while the distribution system needed salesmen, advertising executives, and store managers. These salaried ranks increased sevenfold between 1870 and 1910—much faster than any other occupational group. Nearly 9 million people held white-collar jobs in 1910, more than a fourth of all employed Americans.

Some members of this white-collar class lived in the row houses of Baltimore and Boston or the comfortable apartment buildings of New York City. More preferred to escape the clamor and congestion of the city. They were attracted by a persisting rural ideal, agreeing with the landscape architect Andrew Jackson Downing that "nature and domestic life are better than the society and manners of town." As trolley service pushed out from the city center, middle-class Americans followed the wealthy into the countryside. All sought what one Chicago developer promised for his North Shore subdivision in 1875—"qualities of which the city is in a large degree bereft, namely, its pure air, peacefulness, quietude, and natural scenery."

No major American city escaped **suburbanization** during the late nineteenth century. City limits everywhere expanded rapidly, but even so, much of the suburban growth took place in outlying towns. By 1900 more than half of Boston's people lived in "streetcar suburbs" outside Boston proper; nationwide, according to the 1910 census, about 25 percent of the urban population lived in such autonomous suburbs.

The geography of the suburbs was truly a map of class structure; where a family lived told where it ranked socially. As one proceeded out from the city center, the houses became finer, the lots larger, the inhabitants wealthier. Affluent businessmen and professionals had the time and flexibility for a long commute into town. Closer in, people wanted transit lines that carried them quickly between home and office. Lower-income commuters generally had more than one wage earner in the family, less secure employment, and jobs requiring movement around the city. It was better for them to be closer to the city center because crosstown lines afforded the mobility they needed for their work.

Suburban boundaries shifted constantly, as working-class city residents who wanted to better their lives moved to the cheapest suburbs, prompting an exodus of older residents, who in turn pushed the next higher group farther out in search of space and greenery. Suburbanization was the sum of countless individual decisions. Each family's move represented an advance in living standards—not only more light, air, and quiet but better accommodation than the city afforded. Suburban houses were typically larger for the same money and came equipped with flush toilets, hot water, central heating, and, by the turn of the century, electricity.

The suburbs also restored an opportunity that Americans thought they had lost when they moved to the city. In the suburbs home ownership again became the norm. "A man is not really a true man until he owns his own home," propounded the Reverend Russell H. Conwell in his famous sermon on the virtues of moneymaking, "Acres of Diamonds."

The small towns of rural America had fostered community life. Not so the suburbs. The grid street pattern, while efficient for laying out lots, offered no natural focus for group life, nor did the shops and services that lay scattered along the trolley-car streets. Suburban development conformed to the economics of real estate and transportation, and so did the thinking of middle-class home seekers entering the suburbs. They wanted a house that gave them good value and convenience to the trolley line.

The need for community had lost some of its force for middle-class Americans. Two other attachments assumed greater importance: one was work; the other, family.

Middle-Class Families

In the pre-industrial economy, work and family life were intertwined. Farmers, merchants, and artisans generally worked at home. The household, as the unit of production, encompassed not only blood relatives, but everyone living and working there. As industrialism progressed, family life and economic activity parted company. The father departed every morning for the office, and children spent more years in school. Clothing was bought ready made; food came increasingly in cans and packages. Middle-class families became smaller, excluding all but nuclear members and consisting typically by 1900 of husband, wife, and three children.

Within this family circle relationships became intense and affectionate. "Home was the most expressive experience in life," recalled the literary critic Henry Seidel Canby of his growing up in the 1890s. "Though the family might quarrel and nag, the home held them all, protecting them against the outside world." The suburb provided a fit setting for such middle-class families. The quiet, tree-lined streets created a domestic space insulated from the harshness of commerce and enterprise.

The Wife's Role. The burdens of this domesticity fell heavily on the wife. It was nearly unheard of for her to seek an outside career—that was her husband's role. Her job was to manage the household. "The woman who could not make a home, like the man who could not support one, was condemned," Canby remembered. As the physical burdens of household work eased, higher-quality homemaking became the new ideal—a message propagated by Catharine Beecher's best-selling book *The American Woman's Home* (1869) and by such magazines as the *Ladies' Home Journal* and *Good Housekeeping*, which first appeared during the 1880s. This advice literature instructed wives that, in addition to their domestic duties, they had the responsibility for bringing sensibility, beauty, and love to the household. "We owe to women the charm and beauty of life," wrote one educator. "For the love that rests, strengthens and inspires, we look to women." In this idealized view the wife made the home a refuge for her husband and a place of nurture for their children.

Womanly virtue, even if much glorified, by no means put wives on equal terms with their husbands. Although the legal status of married women—their right to own property, control separate earnings, make contracts, and get a divorce—improved markedly during the nineteenth century, law and custom still dictated a wife's submission to her husband. She relied on his ability as the family breadwinner, and despite her superior virtues and graces she was thought to be below him in vigor and intellect. Her mind could be employed "but little and in trivial matters," wrote one prominent physician, and her proper place was as "the companion or ornamental appendage to man."

Not surprisingly, many bright, independent-minded women rebelled against marriage. The marriage rate fell to a low point during the last

Middle-Class Domesticity

For middle-class Americans the home was a place of nurture, a refuge from the world of competitive commerce. Perhaps that explains why their residences were so heavily draped and cluttered with bric-a-brac. All of it emphasized privacy and pride of possession. Culver Pictures.

forty years of the nineteenth century. More than 10 percent of women of marriageable age remained single, and the rate was much higher among college graduates and professionals. Only half the Mount Holyoke College class of 1902, for example, married. "I know that something perhaps, humanly speaking, supremely precious has passed me by," remarked the writer Vida Scudder. "But how much it would have excluded!" Married life "looks to me often as I watch it terribly impoverished, for women."

The Cult of Masculinity. If fewer women were marrying, of course, so were fewer men. We can, thanks to the census, trace the tardy progression into marriage of the male cohort born just after the Civil War: In 1890, when they were in their early thirties, two-fifths were unmarried; a decade later, in their early forties, a quarter still had not married; and ultimately, a hard-core, over 10 percent, never married. One historian has labeled the late nineteenth century the Age of the Bachelor, a time when being an unattached male lost its social stigma and, especially in large cities, became a happy alternative for many men of marriageable age. A bachelor's counterpart to Vida Scudder's dim view of marriage was this ditty making the rounds in the early 1880s:

> No wife to scold me
> No children to squall
> God bless the happy man
> Who keeps bachelor's hall.

With its residential hotels, restaurants, and abundant personal services, the urban scene afforded bachelors all the comforts of home and, on top of that, a happy array of men's clubs, saloons, and sporting events.

The appeal of the manly life was not, however, confined to confirmed bachelors. American males inherited a pride in independence — achieved above all by being one's own boss — but the salaried jobs they increasingly held left them distinctly not their own bosses. Nor, once work and household had been severed, could they enjoy the patriarchal hold over family life that had empowered their fathers and grandfathers. A palpable anxiety arose that the American male was becoming, as one magazine editor warned, "weak, effeminate, decaying." There was a telling shift in language. While people had once spoken of *manhood*, which meant leaving *childhood* behind, they now spoke of *masculinity*, the opposite of *femininity*: Being a man meant surmounting the feminizing influences of modern life.

And how was this to be accomplished? By engaging in competitive sports like football, which became hugely popular in this era. By working out and becoming fit because, as the psychologist G. Stanley Hall put it, "you can't have a firm will without firm muscles." By resorting to the great outdoors — preferably out west — and engaging in Theodore Roosevelt's "strenuous life." Or vicariously, by reading Owen Wister's best-selling cowboy novel, *The Virginian* (1902), or that celebration of primitive man, Edgar Rice Burroughs's *Tarzan of the Apes* (1912). The surging popularity of westerns and adventure novels was surely a marker of the fears by urban dwellers that theirs was not a life for real men.

Changing Views of Women's Sexuality. Women perhaps had an easier time of it because they were in the process of being liberated from a repressive past — from the medical judgment that, as one popular text put it, "the majority of women (happily for society) are not very much troubled by sexual feeling of any kind." Middle-class women had bought into

Manliness

A maxim of modern advertising states: Link your product to what the public admires. At the turn of the century, Americans admired real men, like the Graeco-Roman wrestlers in this 1911 advertisement. If you want to be like them, eat Grape-Nuts. An advertisement in *The All-Story*, December 1911.

this dreary view of them because it eased a painful family dilemma. They wanted fewer children, but, other than abstinence, were often at a loss about what to do. Contraceptive devices, although heavily marketed, were either unreliable or, as in the case of condoms, stigmatized by association with the brothel.

On top of that, advocates of birth control had to contend with Anthony Comstock, an agent of the post office who was also secretary of the Society for the Suppression of Vice. In that capacity he campaigned relentlessly to uplift the nation's morals. The vehicle he chose was a federal law passed at his behest in 1873 prohibiting the sending of obscene materials through the U.S. mails. Comstock defined obscenity to include any information about birth control or, for that matter, any open discussion of sex. So powerful was Comstock's influence that the suppression of vice became a national obsession during the 1870s. Among the victims were women who wanted some release from the burden of unwanted pregnancies.

Many doctors disapproved of contraception, fearing that uncoupling sex from procreation would release the sexual appetites of men, to the detriment of their health and the moral fiber of society. It is this official writing (along with Comstock's antivice campaign) that has given us the notion of a Victorian age of sexual repression. Letters and diaries suggest that in the privacy of their homes husbands and wives acted otherwise. Yet they must have done so in constant fear of unwanted pregnancies. A fulfilling sexual relationship was not easily squared with desires to limit and space childbearing.

Around 1890 a change set in. Despite Comstock, contraception became more acceptable and reliable. Experts began to abandon the notion that women "are not very much troubled by sexual feelings of any kind." In succeeding editions of his book *Plain Home Talk on Love, Marriage, and Parentage*, for example, the physician Edward Bliss Foote began to favor a healthy sexuality that gave pleasure to women as well as men. It was the beginning of a sexual revolution.

During the 1890s the artist Charles Dana Gibson created the image of the "new woman." In his drawings the Gibson girl was tall, spirited, athletic, and chastely sexual. She rejected bustles, hoop skirts, and tightly laced corsets, preferring shirtwaists and other natural styles that did not disguise her female form (see Reading American Pictures, "Challenging Female Delicacy: The New Woman," p. 565). In the city, women's sphere began to take on a more public character. Among the new urban institutions catering to women, the most important was the department store, which became a temple for their emerging role as consumers.

Attitudes toward Children. The offspring of the middle class experienced their own revolution. In the past children had been regarded as an economic asset — added hands for the family farm, shop, or countinghouse. Especially for the urban middle class, this no longer held true. Parents stopped expecting their children to be working members of the family. In the old days Ralph Waldo Emerson remarked in 1880, "Children had been repressed and kept in the background; now they are considered, cosseted, and pampered." There was such a thing as "the juvenile mind," lectured Jacob Abbott in his book *Gentle Measures in the Management and Training of the Young* (1871). The family was responsible for providing a nurturing environment in which the young personality could grow and mature.

Preparation for adulthood became increasingly linked to formal education. School enrollment went up 150 percent between 1870 and 1900. As the years before adulthood began to stretch out, a new stage of life — adolescence — emerged. While rooted in longer years of family dependency, adolescence shifted much of the socializing role from parents to peer group. The impact was most marked on the daughters of the middle class, who, freed from the chores of housework, were now encouraged to devote themselves to self-development, including for many the chance to go to high school (Table 18.2). The liberating consequences surely went beyond their parents' expectations. In a revealing shift in terminology, "young lady" gave way to "school girl," and the daughterly submissiveness of earlier times gave way

TABLE 18.2 High School Graduates, 1870–1910

Year	Numbers	Percent 17-Year-Olds	Male	Female
1870	16,000	2.0	7,000	9,000
1890	44,000	3.0	19,000	25,000
1910	156,000	8.6	64,000	93,000

SOURCE: *Historical Statistics of the United States*, 2 vols. (Washington, DC: U.S. Bureau of the Census, 1975), 1: 386.

READING AMERICAN PICTURES

Challenging Female Delicacy: The New Woman

Recalling her Baltimore girlhood, the president of Bryn Mawr College remembered "the awful doubt, felt by women themselves as well as by men, as to whether women as a sex were physically and mentally fit for" higher education. To male readers of this text, that might sound silly, what with the female classmates they see working out at the gym or that formidable woman professor they've encountered in a course (maybe this one). But it wasn't silly in the late nineteenth-century. On the neighboring page, we claim that the notion of female delicacy expired during the 1890s, but saying it is one thing, capturing so elusive a change is another, and for that we turn to an unexpected historical source — the fine art of the period. This wonderful painting (1897) is by John Singer Sargent, the greatest portraitist of the age, depicting a wealthy socialite couple, Mr. and Mrs. Isaac Newton Phelps Stokes.

Mr. and Mrs. Isaac Phelps Stokes, John Singer Sargent (1897). The Metropolitan Museum of Art, Bequest of Edith Minturn Phelps Stokes (Mrs. I.N.), 1938. Photo copyright 1992, The Metropolitan Museum of Art.

ANALYZING THE EVIDENCE

▶ Sargent presents Mrs. Phelps Stokes in a shirtwaist and long skirt, the uniform of the "New Woman." Does anything else about her appearance convey independence and strength? How do these qualities contrast with older views of women? Does she strike you as someone likely to suffer a nervous collapse?

▶ Implicit in the New Woman was a repudiation of the idea of wives as "the companion or ornamental appendage of man." Is there anything about the way Mr. and Mrs. Phelps Stokes are presented as a couple that suggests this marital revolution?

▶ Sargent was a high-society painter. His subjects were almost exclusively elite women, decked out in their finest. Wealthy patrons prized his portraits partly because they enjoyed having their women depicted as the objects of conspicuous consumption. But in this portrait, Sargent dispenses with the evening gown and jewels and shows Mrs. Phelps Stokes in everyday dress. Can the fact that she is not depicted as an object of conspicuous consumption be explained by her portrayal as a New Woman? Or throw any light on the changing relations between men and women in this period?

to self-expressive independence. On achieving adulthood, it was not so big a step for the daughters of the middle class to become Gibson's "new women."

> - Why is Ward McAllister so significant a figure in the annals of the rich?
> - Why did the suburbs become so prominent a feature of the late-nineteenth-century city?
> - In the middle-class family of this era, how might the wife's position have been more stressful than that of her husband? Why was this so?

City Life

With its soaring skyscrapers, jostling traffic, and hum of business, the city symbolized energy and enterprise. When the budding writer Hamlin Garland and his brother arrived in Chicago from Iowa in 1881, they knew immediately that they had entered a new world: "Everything interested us.... Nothing was commonplace, nothing was ugly to us." In one way or another every city-bound migrant, whether fresh from the American countryside or from a foreign land, experienced something of this sense of wonder.

The city was utterly unlike the rural world. In the countryside every person had been known to his or her neighbors. Mark Twain found New York "a splendid desert, where a stranger is lonely in the midst of a million of his race.... Every man rushes, rushes, rushes, and never has time to be companionable [or] to fool away on matters which do not involve dollars and duty and business."

Migrants could never recreate in the city the communities they had left behind. But they found ways of belonging, they built new institutions, and they learned how to function in an impersonal, heterogeneous environment. An urban culture emerged, and through it there developed a new breed of American who was entirely at home in the modern city.

Newcomers

The explosive growth of America's big-city population — the numbers living in places of 100,000 people or more jumped from about 6 million to 14 million between 1880 and 1900 — meant that cities were very much a world of newcomers (Map 18.2). Many came from the nation's countryside; half of rural families on the move in these years were city bound. But it was newcomers further marked off by skin color or ethnicity who found entry into city life most daunting. At the turn of the century, upwards of 30 percent of the residents of New York, Chicago, Boston, Cleveland, Minneapolis, and San Francisco were foreign-born. The biggest ethnic group in Boston was Irish; in Minneapolis, Swedish; in most other northern cities, German. But by 1910 the influx from southern and eastern Europe had changed the ethnic complexion of many of these cities. In Chicago, Poles took the lead; in New York, eastern European Jews; in San Francisco, Italians.

As the earlier "walking cities" disappeared, so did the opportunities for intermingling with older populations. The later arrivals from southern and eastern Europe had little choice about where they lived; they needed to find cheap housing near their jobs. Some gravitated to the outlying factory districts; others settled in the congested downtown **ghettos.** In New York Italians crowded into the Irish neighborhoods west of Broadway, and Russian and Polish Jews pushed the Germans out of the Lower East Side (Map 18.3). A colony of Hungarians lived around Houston Street, and Bohemians occupied the poorer stretches of the Upper East Side between Fiftieth and Seventy-sixth streets. Virtually every city with a large immigrant population experienced this kind of ethnic sorting-out, as, for example, San Francisco, with its Chinatown, Italian North Beach, and Jewish Hayes Valley.

Capitalizing on fellow feeling, immigrant institutions of many kinds sprang up. Newspapers appeared wherever substantial numbers lived. In 1911 the 20,000 Poles in Buffalo supported two Polish-language daily papers. Immigrants throughout the country avidly read *Il Progresso Italo-Americano* and the Yiddish-language *Jewish Daily Forward*, both published in New York City. Companionship could always be found on street corners, in barbershops and club rooms, and in saloons. Italians marched in saint's day parades, Bohemians gathered in singing societies, and New York Jews patronized a lively Yiddish theater. To provide help in times of sickness and death, the immigrants organized mutual-aid societies. The Italians of Chicago had sixty-six of these organizations in 1903, mostly composed of people from particular provinces or towns. Immigrants built a rich and functional institutional life in urban America to an extent unimagined in their native places (see Comparing American Voices, "Coming to America: The Downside," pp. 570–571).

MAP 18.2   Sources of European Immigration to the United States, 1871–1910

Around 1900 Americans began to speak of the "new" immigration. They meant the large numbers of immigrants arriving from eastern and southern Europe — Poles, Slovaks and other Slavic groups, Yiddish-speaking Jews, Italians — and overwhelming the still substantial and more familiar immigrants from the British Isles and northern Europe (see also Figure 17.3, American Immigration, 1870–1914, on p. 531).

Urban Blacks. The African American migration from the rural South to northern cities was just beginning at the turn of the century. The black population of New York increased by 30,000 between 1900 and 1910, making New York second only to Washington, D.C., as a black urban center, but the 91,000 African Americans in New York in 1910 represented fewer than 2 percent of the population, and that was true of Chicago and Cleveland as well.

Urban blacks retreated from the scattered neighborhoods of older times into concentrated ghettos — Chicago's Black Belt on the South Side, for example, or the early outlines of New York's Harlem. Race prejudice cut down job opportunities. Twenty-six percent of Cleveland's blacks had been skilled workers in 1870; only 12 percent were skilled by 1890. Entire occupations such as barbering (except for a black clientele) became exclusively white. Cleveland's blacks in 1910 mainly worked as domestics and day laborers, with little hope of moving up the job ladder.

In the face of pervasive discrimination, urban blacks built their own communities. They created a flourishing press, fraternal orders, a vast array of women's organizations, and a middle class of doctors, lawyers, and small entrepreneurs. Above all, there were the black churches — twenty-five in Chicago in 1905, mainly Methodist and Baptist. More than any other institution, remarked one scholar in 1913, it was the church "which the

MAP 18.3 The Lower East Side, New York City, 1900

As this map shows, the Jewish immigrants dominating Manhattan's Lower East Side preferred living in neighborhoods populated by those from their home regions of eastern Europe. Their sense of a common identity made for a remarkable flowering of educational, cultural, and social institutions on the Jewish East Side.

Jewish Ethnic Concentrations
- Hungarian
- Galician (Polish)
- Russian
- Romanian
- Mixed Middle Eastern and Romanian

Negro may call his own. . . . A new church may be built . . . and . . . all the machinery set in motion without ever consulting any white person. . . . [Religion] more than anything else represents the real life of the race." As in the southern countryside, the church was the central institution for city blacks, and the preacher was the most important local citizen. Manhattan's Union Baptist Church, housed like many others in a storefront, attracted the "very recent residents of this new, disturbing city" and, ringing with spirituals and prayer, made Christianity come "alive Sunday mornings."

Ward Politics

Race and ethnicity divided newcomers. Politics, by contrast, integrated them into the wider urban society. Migrants to American cities automatically became ward residents and acquired a spokesman at city hall. Their alderman got streets paved, or water mains extended, or permits granted — so that, for example, in 1888 Vito Fortounescere could "place and keep a stand for the sale of fruit, inside the stoop-line, in front of the northeast corner of Twenty-eighth Street and Fourth Avenue" in Manhattan, or the

The Cherry Family Tree, 1906

Wiley and Fannie Cherry migrated in 1893 from North Carolina to Chicago, settling in the small African American community on the West Side. The Cherrys apparently prospered and by 1906, when this family portrait was taken, had entered the black middle class. When migration intensified after 1900, longer-settled urban blacks like the Cherrys became uncomfortable, and relations with the needy rural newcomers were often tense. Courtesy, Lorraine Heflin / Chicago Historical Society.

parishioners of Saint Maria of Mount Carmel could set off fireworks at their Fourth of July picnic.

These favors came via a system of boss control that, although present at every level of party politics, flourished most luxuriantly in the big cities. Urban **political machines** like Tammany Hall in New York depended on a grassroots constituency, so they recruited layers of functionaries — precinct captains, ward bosses, aldermen — whose main job was to be accessible and, as best they could, serve the needs of the party faithful.

The machine acted as a rough-and-ready social service agency, providing jobs for the jobless, a helping hand for a bereaved family, and intercession against an unfeeling city bureaucracy. The Tammany ward boss George Washington Plunkitt had a "regular system" when fires broke out in his district. He arranged for housing for burned-out families, "fix[ing] them up till they get things runnin' again. It's philanthropy, but it's politics, too — mighty good politics."

The business community was similarly served. Contractors sought city business, gas companies and streetcar lines wanted licenses, manufacturers needed services and not-too-nosy inspectors, and the liquor trade and numbers rackets relied on a tolerant police force. All of them turned to the machine boss and his lieutenants.

Of course, the machine exacted a price for these services. The tenement dweller gave his vote. The businessman wrote a check. Naturally, some of the money that changed hands leaked into the pockets

COMPARING AMERICAN VOICES

Coming to America: The Downside

At the height of the eastern European immigration, sociologists became concerned about the problem of "anomie," the breakdown of codes of behavior under conditions of stress and social disorder. The classic study was William I. Thomas and Florian Znaniecki's *The Polish Peasant in Europe and America* (1918). Among the evidences of anomie, none were more heart-rending than the abandonment of families by their fathers. In Jewish communities of eastern Europe, desertion was nearly unheard of, although rabbis generally countenanced divorce in childless marriages. In America, however, desertion became a serious problem, so much so that the leading Yiddish-language newspaper in New York, the *Jewish Daily Forward*, ran a regular feature seeking information about wayward husbands.

DESERTED WIFE

The Daily Forward *also boasted a famous page entitled* Bintel Brief, *which in Yiddish means "bundle of letters." The letters from immigrant readers about their trials and tribulations in America are a unique documentary source, offering a window into the lives of obscure people who rarely left personal records for historians to study. Nothing, indeed, could have been more personal than the stories and pleas for advice from "Dear Editor." The document below, written in 1908 by a Deserted Wife, made use of Bintel Brief to appeal directly to her missing husband.*

Worthy Editor
Have pity on me and my two small children and print my letter in the *Forward*.

Max! The children and I now say farewell to you. You left us in such a terrible state. You had no compassion for us. For six years I loved you faithfully, took care of you like a loyal servant, never had a happy day with you. Yet I forgive you for everything.

Have you ever asked yourself why you left us? Max, where is your conscience: you used to have sympathy for the forsaken women and used to say their terrible plight was due to the men who left them in dire need. And how did you act? I was a young, educated, decent girl when you took me. You lived with me for six years, during which time I bore you four children. And then you left me.

Of the four children, only two remain, but you have made them living orphans. Who will bring them up? Who will support us? Have you no pity for your own flesh and blood? Consider what you are doing. My tears choke me and I cannot write any more.

Be advised that in several days I am leaving with my two living orphans for Russia. We say farewell to you and beg you to take pity on us and send us enough to live on.

Your Deserted Wife and Children

WAYWARD HUSBANDS

The letter below, written in 1910, offers the husbands' side of the story. Students should read both letters with this question in mind: What was there about the immigrant experience in America that might account for so profound a breakdown of traditional values and marital obligations?

Dear Editor:
This is the voice of thirty-seven miserable men who are buried but not covered over by earth, tied down but not in chains, silent but not mute, whose hearts beat like humans, yet are not like other human beings.

When we look at our striped clothes, at our dirty narrow cots, at our fellow companions in the cells, the beaten, lowest members of society, who long ago lost their human dignity, the blood freezes in our veins. We feel degraded and miserable here. And why are we confined here? For the horrible crime of being poor, not being able to satisfy the mad whims of our wives. That's why we pine away here, stamped with the name "convict." That's why we are despised, robbed of our freedom, and treated like dogs.

We ask you, worthy Editor, to publish our letter so your readers, especially the women, will know how we live here. This letter is written not with ink but with our hearts' blood. We are coughing from the polluted air that we breathe in the cells. Our bones ache from lying on the hard cots and we get stomach aches from the food they give us.

The non-support "plague" is the worst plague of all. For the merest nonsense, a man is caught and committed to the workhouse. He doesn't even get a chance to defend himself. Even during the worst times of the Russian reaction people didn't suffer as the men suffer here in America because of their wives. For a Jewish wife it's as easy here to condemn her husband to imprisonment as it is for her to try on a pair of gloves. In all the world there isn't such legal injustice as here in the alimony courts.

What do they think, these women! If they believe that the imprisoned husbands, after the six months, will become purified and come out good, sweet and loving, they're making a big mistake.

The worst offense is committed by the Jewish charity organizations. They sympathize with the wife when her husband is in jail. They forget, however, that they "manufacture" the grass widows and living orphans when they help the woman. As soon as the wife tastes an easy and a free dollar, as soon as she discovers that the "charities" won't let her starve, she doesn't care that her husband is condemned. She lives a gay life, enjoys herself, and doesn't think of her husband.

Therefore it is your duty as editor of the *Forward*, the news paper that is read mainly by the working class, the class that furnishes more than all others the candidates for the workhouse and for grass widowhood, to warn all the Jewish women not to take such revenge on their husbands. They do more harm to themselves than to their men. They drive away their husbands for life that way, and make themselves and their children miserable. The women must learn that sending their husbands to prison is a poor method of improving them. It is a double-edged sword that slashes one side as deeply as the other.

Finally, I appeal to all the women whose husbands are imprisoned for non-support in the workhouse on Blackwell's Island Prison, and I write to them as follows: Their husbands have sworn here that if they, the women, do not have them released in time for *Pesach* [Passover], they will never again return and the women will remain grass widows forever.

We ask you to publish this letter immediately.
Respectfully,
[The letter is signed by thirty-seven men]

SOURCE: Isaac Metzker, ed., *A Bintel Brief: Sixty Years of Letters from the Lower East Side* (Schocken: New York, 1971), 85–86, 110–112.

ANALYZING THE EVIDENCE

▶ In the first letter, the deserted wife seems bewildered by her situation. She has no idea why Max has abandoned her. How would you explain her incomprehension?

▶ In the second letter, the incarcerated husbands seem equally bewildered. They can't understand why refusing to support their wives would be regarded as a crime. Can you explain their irresponsibility? Or why they would resent the assistance given to their families by Jewish charity organizations? What part of their confusion would you ascribe to their traditional role as patriarchal heads of families? And what part to their American experience?

▶ In his response to their letter, the Editor acknowledged that among the thirty-seven "there must be some who weren't in a position to support their families, but it's nothing new to find innocent men suffering along with the guilty." Is that a distinction you would accept? And what does it suggest about the economic causes of family instability in the ghettoes?

▶ Deadbeat husbands, of course, are not a problem only of the past. They're still very much with us. Would you regard the sentence meted out to them a hundred years ago — six months in jail — an appropriate punishment today?

Italian Bread Peddlers, New York City
Because of crowded conditions in East Side tenements, immigrant life spilled out onto the streets, which offered a bit of fresh air, a chance to socialize with neighbors, and a place to shop for food, including bread. KEA Publishing Services Ltd.

of machine politicians. This "boodle" could be blatantly corrupt — kickbacks by contractors; protection money from gamblers, saloonkeepers, and prostitutes; payoffs from gas and trolley companies. In the 1860s boss William Marcy Tweed had made Tammany a byword for corruption, until he was brought down in 1871 by his extravagant graft in the building of a lavish city courthouse. Thereafter, machine corruption became less blatant. The turn-of-the-century Tammanyite George Plunkitt declared that he had no need for kickbacks and bribes. He favored what he called "honest graft," the easy profits that came to savvy insiders. Plunkitt made most of his money building wharves on Manhattan's waterfront. One way or another, legally or otherwise, machine politics rewarded its supporters.

Plunkitt was an Irishman, and so were most of the machine politicians controlling Tammany Hall. But by the 1890s Plunkitt's Fifteenth District was filling up with Italians and Russian Jews. In general, the Irish had no love for these newer immigrants, but Plunkitt played no favorites. On any given day (as recorded in a diary) he might attend an Italian funeral in the afternoon and a Jewish wedding in the evening, and at each he probably paid his respects with a few Italian words or a choice bit of Yiddish.

In an era when so many forces acted to isolate ghetto communities, politics served an *integrating* function, cutting across ethnic lines and giving immigrants and blacks a stake in the larger urban order.

Religion in the City

For urban blacks, as we have seen, the church was a mainstay of their lives. So it was for many other city dwellers. But cities were not easy ground for religious practice. All the great faiths — Judaism, Catholicism, and Protestantism — had to scramble to reconcile religious belief with the secular urban world.

Judaism: The Challenge to Orthodoxy. About 250,000 Jews, mostly of German origin, inhabited America when the eastern European Jews began arriving in the 1880s. Well established and prosperous, the German Jews embraced Reform Judaism, abandoning religious practices — from keeping a kosher kitchen to conducting services in Hebrew — "not adapted to the views and habits of modern civilization." This was not the way of the Yiddish-speaking Jews from eastern Europe. Eager to preserve their traditional piety, they founded their own Orthodox synagogues, often in vacant stores and ramshackle buildings, and practiced Judaism as they had at home.

In the villages of eastern Europe, however, Judaism had involved not only worship but an entire way of life. Insular though it might be, ghetto life in the American city could not recreate the communal environment on which strict religious observance depended. "The very clothes I wore and the very food I ate had a fatal effect on my religious habits," confessed the hero of Abraham Cahan's novel *The Rise of David Levinsky* (1917). "If you . . . attempt to bend your religion to the spirit of your surroundings, it breaks. It falls to pieces." Levinsky shaved off his beard and plunged into the Manhattan clothing business. Orthodox Judaism survived this shattering of faith but only by reducing its claims on the lives of the faithful.

"Americanism" and the Catholic Church. Catholics faced much the same problem, defined as "Americanism" by the church. To what degree should congregants adapt to American society? Should children attend parochial or public schools? Should they intermarry with non-Catholics? Should the traditional education for the clergy be changed? Bishop John Ireland of St. Paul, Minnesota, felt that "the principles of the Church are in harmony with the interests of the Republic." But traditionalists, led by Archbishop Michael A. Corrigan of New York, denied the possibility of such harmony and argued for insulating the church from the pluralistic American environment.

Immigrant Catholics, anxious to preserve what they had known in Europe, generally supported the church's conservative wing. But they also desired that church life express their ethnic identities. Newly arrived Catholics wanted their own parishes, where they could celebrate their customs, speak their languages, and establish their own parochial schools. When they became numerous enough, they also demanded their own bishops. The Catholic hierarchy, which was dominated by Irish Catholics, felt that the integrity of the church itself was at stake. The demand for ethnic parishes implied local control of church property. And if there were bishops for specific ethnic groups, this would mean disrupting the diocesan structure that unified the church.

With some strain, the Catholic Church managed to satisfy the immigrant faithful. It met the demand for representation by appointing immigrant priests as auxiliary bishops within existing dioceses. Ethnic parishes also flourished. By World War I, there were more than two thousand foreign-language churches and many others that were bilingual. Not without strain the Catholic Church accommodated itself to the demands of ethnic identity in urban America.

Protestantism: Regaining Lost Ground. For Protestant denominations the city posed different but not easier challenges. Every major city retained great downtown churches where wealthy Protestants worshiped. Some of these churches, richly endowed, took pride in nationally prominent pastors, such as Henry Ward Beecher of Plymouth Congregational Church in Brooklyn or Phillips Brooks of Trinity Episcopal Church in Boston. But the eminence of these churches, with their fashionable congregations and imposing edifices, could not disguise the growing remoteness of traditional Protestantism from much of its urban constituency. "Where is the city in which the Sabbath day is not losing ground?" lamented a minister in 1887. The families of businessmen, lawyers, and doctors could be seen in any church on Sunday morning, he noted, "but the workingmen and their families are not there."

To counter this decline the Protestant churches responded by evangelizing among the unchurched and indifferent. Starting in the 1880s they also began providing reading rooms, day nurseries, clubhouses, vocational classes, and other services. The Salvation Army, which arrived from Great Britain in 1879, spread the gospel of repentance among the urban poor and built an assistance program that ranged from soup kitchens to shelters for former prostitutes. When all else failed, the down-and-outers of American cities knew they could count on the Salvation Army.

For single people, there were the Young Men's and Women's Christian Associations, which had arrived from Britain before the Civil War. Housing for single women was an especially important mission of the YWCAs. The gymnasiums that made the YMCAs synonymous with "muscular Christianity" were equally important for young men. No other organizations so effectively combined activities for

Immaculate Heart of Mary Church, 1908
In crowded immigrant neighborhoods the church rose from undistinguished surroundings to assert the centrality of religious belief in the life of the community. This photograph is a view of Immaculate Heart of Mary Church, taken from Polish Hill in Pittsburgh in 1908. Pittsburgh City Photographer Collection, Archives Service Center, University of Pittsburgh.

young people with an evangelizing appeal through Bible classes, nondenominational worship, and a religious atmosphere.

The social meaning that people sought in religion explained the enormous popularity of a book called *In His Steps* (1896). The author, a Congregational minister named Charles M. Sheldon, told the story of a congregation that resolved to live by Christ's precepts for one year. "If the church members were all doing as Jesus would do," Sheldon asked, "could it remain true that armies of men would walk the streets for jobs, and hundreds of them curse the church, and thousands of them find in the saloon their best friend?"

The most potent form of urban evangelism—revivalism—said little about social uplift. From their origins in the eighteenth century, revival movements had steadfastly focused on individual redemption. The resolution of earthly problems, revivalists believed, would follow the conversion of the people to Christ. Beginning in the mid-1870s, revival meetings swept through the cities.

The pioneering figure was Dwight L. Moody, a former Chicago shoe salesman and YMCA official. After preaching in Britain for two years, Moody returned to America in 1875 and began staging revival meetings that drew thousands. He preached an optimistic, uncomplicated, nondenominational message. Eternal life could be had for the asking, Moody shouted as he held up his Bible. His listeners needed only "to come forward and take, TAKE!"

Many other preachers followed in Moody's path. The most colorful was Billy Sunday, a hard-drinking former outfielder for the Chicago White Stockings who mended his ways and found religion. Like Moody and other city revivalists, Sunday was a farm boy. His rip-snorting attacks on fashionable ministers and the "booze traffic" carried the ring of rustic America. By realizing that many people remained villagers at heart, revivalists found a key for bringing city dwellers back to the church.

City Amusements

City people compartmentalized life's activities, setting workplace apart from home and working time apart from free time. "Going out" became a necessity, demanded not only as solace for a hard day's work but proof that life was better in the New World than in the Old. "He who can enjoy and does not enjoy commits a sin," a Yiddish-language paper told its readers. And enjoyment now meant buying a ticket and being entertained (see Voices from Abroad, "José Martí: Coney Island, 1881," p. 575).

Music halls attracted huge audiences. Chicago had six **vaudeville** houses in 1896, twenty-two in 1910. Evolving from tawdry variety and minstrel shows, vaudeville cleaned up its routines, making them suitable for the entire family, and turned into professional entertainment handled by national booking agencies. With its standard program of nine singing, dancing, and comedy acts, vaudeville attained enormous popularity just as the movies arrived. The first primitive films, a minute or so of humor or glimpses of famous people, appeared in 1896 in penny arcades and as filler in vaudeville shows. Within a decade, millions of city people were watching films of increasing length and artistry at nickelodeons (named after the five-cent admission charge) across the country.

For young unmarried workers the cheap amusements of the city created a new social space. "I want a good time," a New York clothing operator told an investigator. "And there is no . . . way a

Amusement Park, Long Beach, California

The origins of the roller coaster go back to LaMarcus Thompson's Switchback Railway, installed at Coney Island in 1884 and featuring gentle dips and curves. By 1900, when Long Beach's Jack Rabbit Race was constructed, the goal was to create the biggest possible thrill. Angelenos journeyed out by trolley to Long Beach not only to take a dip in the ocean but also to ride the new roller coaster. The airplane ride in the foreground is a further wrinkle on the peculiarly modern notion that the way to have fun is to be scared to death. Curt Teich Postcard Archives.

VOICES FROM ABROAD

José Martí
Coney Island, 1881

José Martí, a Cuban patriot and revolutionary (see p. 648), was a journalist by profession. In exile from 1880 to 1895, he spent most of his time in New York City, reporting to his Latin American readers on the customs of the Yankees. Martí took special—one might say perverse—pleasure in observing Americans at play. Bear in mind, as you read his account of Coney Island, that Martí is writing from a self-consciously different cultural perspective.

From all parts of the United States, legions of intrepid ladies and Sunday-best farmers arrive to admire the splendid sights, the unexampled wealth, the dizzying variety, the herculean surge, the striking appearance of Coney Island, the now famous island, four years ago an abandoned sand bank, that today is a spacious amusement area providing relaxation and recreation for hundreds of thousands of New Yorkers who throng to its pleasant beaches every day....

Other nations—ourselves among them—live devoured by a sublime demon within that drives us to the tireless pursuit of an ideal of love or glory.... Not so with these tranquil souls, stimulated only by a desire for gain. One scans those shimmering beaches... one views the throngs seated in comfortable chairs along the seashore, filling their lungs with the fresh, invigorating air. But it is said that those from our lands who remain here long are overcome with melancholy... because this great nation is void of spirit.

But what coming and going! What torrents of money! What facilities for every pleasure! What absolute absence of any outward sadness or poverty! Everything in the open air: the animated groups, the immense dining rooms, the peculiar courtship of North Americans, which is virtually devoid of the elements that compose the shy, tender, elevated love in our lands, the theatre, the photographers' booth, the bathhouses! Some weigh themselves, for North Americans are greatly elated, or really concerned, if they find they have gained or lost a pound....

This spending, this uproar, these crowds, the activity of this amazing ant hill never slackens from June to October, from morning 'til night.... Then, like a monster that vomits its contents into the hungry maw of another monster, that colossal crowd, that straining, crushing mass, forces its way onto the trains, which speed across wastes, groaning under their burden, until they surrender it to the tremendous steamers, enlivened by the sound of harps and violins, convey it to the piers, and debouch the weary merrymakers into the thousand trolleys that pursue the thousand tracks that spread through slumbering New York like veins of steel.

SOURCE: Juan de Onís, trans., *The America of José Martí: Selected Writings* (New York: Noonday Press, 1954), 103–10.

ANALYZING THE EVIDENCE

- When Martí says America is "devoid of spirit," what does he mean? Why would such a thought be prompted by his observation of people having fun at Coney Island?

- In the final paragraph, Martí describes what might be considered a technological marvel—the capacity of New York's transportation system to move many thousands of revelers from Coney Island back to their homes in a few hours. But consider how Martí characterizes this—"a monster that vomits its contents into the angry maw of another monster"—with this question in mind: Does Martí's distaste negate the value of his account as a historical source about city mass transit?

- Let's put the above question in a larger context. Suppose you hadn't read the text's treatment of urban leisure. Would you profit from reading Martí's account? Having read the text's discussion, do you find it amplified—are new insights added—by Martí's account?

girl can get it on $8 a week. I guess if anyone wants to take me to a dance he won't have to ask me twice." Hence the widespread ritual among the urban working class of "treating." The girls spent what money they had dressing up; their boyfriends were expected to pay for the fun. Parental control over courtship broke down, and amid the bright lights and lively music of the dance hall and amusement park, working-class youth forged a more easygoing culture of sexual interaction and pleasure seeking.

The geography of the big city carved out ample space for commercialized sex. Prostitution was not new to urban life, but in the late nineteenth century it became more open and more intermingled with other forms of public entertainment. Opium and cocaine were widely available and not yet illegal. In New York the red-light district was the Tenderloin, running northward from Twenty-third Street between Fifth and Eighth Avenues.

The Tenderloin and the Bowery farther downtown were also the sites of a robust gay subculture. The long-held notion that homosexual life was covert, in the closet, in late-nineteenth-century America appears not to be true, at least not in the country's premier city. In certain corners of the city, a gay world flourished, with a full array of saloons, meeting places, and drag balls, which were widely known and patronized by uptown "slummers."

Of all forms of (mostly) male diversion, none was more specific to the city, or so spectacularly successful, as professional baseball. The game's promoters decreed that baseball had been created in 1839 by Abner Doubleday in the village of Cooperstown, New York. Actually, baseball was neither of American origin — stick-and-ball games go far back into the European Middle Ages — nor particularly a product of rural life. Under a variety of names, team sports resembling baseball proliferated in early nineteenth-century America. In an effort to regularize the game, the New Yorker Alexander Cartwright codified the rules in 1845, only to see his Knickerbockers defeated the next year at Hoboken by the New York Baseball Club in what is regarded as the first modern baseball game. Over the next twenty years, clubs sprang up across the country, and inter-city competition developed on a scheduled basis. In 1868 baseball became openly professional, following the lead of the Cincinnati Red Stockings in signing players to contracts for the season.

Big-time baseball came into its own with the launching of the National League in 1876. The team owners were profit-minded businessmen who shaped the sport to please the fans. Wooden grandstands gave way to the concrete and steel stadiums of the early twentieth century, such as Fenway Park in Boston, Forbes Field in Pittsburgh, and Shibe Park in Philadelphia. For the urban multitudes baseball grew into something more than an afternoon at the ballpark. By rooting for the home team, fans found a way of identifying with the city in which they lived. Amid the diversity and anonymity of urban life, the common experience and language of baseball acted as a bridge among strangers.

Most efficient at this task, however, was the newspaper. James Gordon Bennett, founder of the *New York Herald* in 1835, wanted "to record the facts . . . for the great masses of the community." The news was whatever interested city readers, starting with crime, scandal, and sensational

The Bowery at Night, 1895

The Bowery (a name dating back to the original Dutch settlement) is a major thoroughfare in lower Manhattan. This painting by W. Louis Sonntag, Jr., shows the street in all its glory, crowded with shoppers and pleasure seekers. It was during this time that the Bowery gained its raffish reputation. Museum of the City of New York.

The National Pastime

In 1897, as today, the end-of-season games filled the bleachers. Here the Boston Beaneaters are playing the Baltimore Orioles. Boston won. The Baltimore stadium would soon be replaced by a bigger concrete and steel structure, but what is happening on the field needs no updating. The scene is virtually identical to today's game. Library of Congress.

events. After the Civil War the *New York Sun* added the human-interest story, which made news of ordinary happenings. Newspapers also targeted specific audiences. A women's page offered recipes and fashion news, separate sections covered sports and high society, and the Sunday supplement helped fill the weekend hours. In the competition for readers, the champion newsman was Joseph Pulitzer, the owner of the *St. Louis Post-Dispatch* and, after 1883, the *New York World* (Table 18.3).

TABLE 18.3 Newspaper Circulation

Year	Total Circulation
1870	2,602,000
1880	3,566,000
1890	8,387,000
1900	15,102,000
1909	24,212,000

SOURCE: *Historical Statistics of the United States*, 2 vols. (Washington, DC: U.S. Bureau of the Census, 1975), 2:810.

William Randolph Hearst and Yellow Journalism. Pulitzer was in turn challenged by William Randolph Hearst. Hearst was an unlikely press magnate, the pampered son of a California silver king who, while at Harvard (on the way to being expelled) got interested in Pulitzer's newspaper game. He took over his father's dull *San Francisco Examiner* and rebuilt it into a highly profitable, sensationalist paper. For example: Were any grizzly bears left in California? Hearst dispatched a newsman to the Tehachapi Mountains, where after three months of arduous trapping he caught a grizzly. All this the *Examiner* reported in exhaustive detail, building suspense as the search progressed and ending triumphantly with the carnival display of the unfortunate beast. There was much more of the same — rescues, murders, scandals, sob stories, anything that might arouse in readers what Hearst's editor called "the gee-whiz emotion." Hearst's brand of sensationalism was was dubbed **yellow journalism,** after *The Yellow Kid* (1895), the first comic strip to appear in color.

"He who is without a newspaper," said the great showman P. T. Barnum, "is cut off from his species." Barnum was speaking of city people and their hunger for information. Hearst understood this. That's why he made barrels of money.

The Higher Culture

In the midst of this popular ferment, new institutions of higher culture were taking shape in America's cities. A desire for the cultivated life was not, of course, specifically urban. Before the Civil War the lyceum movement had sent lecturers to the remotest towns, bearing messages of culture and learning. Chautauqua, founded in upstate New York in 1874, carried on this work of cultural dissemination. However, great institutions such as museums, public libraries, opera companies, and symphony orchestras could flourish only in metropolitan centers.

Cultural Institutions. The nation's first major art museum, the Corcoran Gallery of Art, opened in Washington, D.C., in 1869. New York's Metropolitan Museum of Art started in rented quarters two years later, then moved in 1880 to its permanent site in Central Park and launched an ambitious program of art acquisition. When financier J. P. Morgan became chairman of the board in 1905, the Metropolitan's preeminence was assured. The Boston Museum of Fine Arts was founded in 1876 and Chicago's Art Institute in 1879.

Symphony orchestras also appeared, first in New York under the conductors Theodore Thomas and Leopold Damrosch in the 1870s and then in Boston and Chicago during the next decade. National tours by these leading orchestras planted the seeds for orchestral societies in many other cities. Public libraries grew from modest collections (in 1870 only seven had as many as fifty thousand books) into major urban institutions. The greatest library benefactor was Andrew Carnegie, who announced in 1881 that he would build a library in any town or city that was prepared to maintain it.

William Randolph Hearst

In this photograph, dated 1904, Hearst is forty-one and past his glory days as the child prodigy of American journalism. He had managed to get himself elected to Congress from New York City and at the time was maneuvering, unsuccessfully, for the Democratic nomination for president. Brown Brothers.

By 1907 Carnegie had spent more than $32.7 million to establish about a thousand libraries throughout the country.

The late nineteenth century was the great age not only of moneymaking, but also of money *giving*. Generous with their surplus wealth, new millionaires patronized the arts partly as a civic duty, partly to promote themselves socially, but also out of a sense of national pride.

"In America there is no culture," pronounced the English critic G. Lowes Dickinson in 1909. Science and the practical arts, yes—"every possible application of life to purposes and ends"—but "no life for life's sake." Such condescending remarks received a respectful American hearing out of a sense of cultural inferiority to the Old World. In 1873 Mark Twain and Charles Dudley Warner published a novel, *The Gilded Age*, satirizing America as a land of money grubbers and speculators. This enormously popular book touched a nerve in the American psyche. Its title has since been appropriated by historians to characterize the late nineteenth century—America's "Gilded Age"—as an era of materialism and cultural shallowness.

Some members of the upper class, such as the novelist Henry James, despaired of the country and moved to Europe. But the more common response was to try to raise the nation's cultural level. The newly rich had a hard time of it. They did not have much opportunity to cultivate a taste for art, and a great deal of what they collected was junk. On the other hand George W. Vanderbilt, grandson of the rough-hewn Cornelius Vanderbilt, championed French Impressionism, and the coal and steel baron Henry Clay Frick built a brilliant art collection that is still housed as a public museum in his mansion in New York City. The enthusiasm of moneyed Americans largely fueled the great cultural institutions that sprang up during the Gilded Age.

The Literary Scene. A deeply conservative idea of culture sustained this generous patronage. The aim was to embellish life, not to probe or reveal its meaning. "Art," says the hero of the Reverend Henry Ward Beecher's sentimental novel *Norwood* (1867), "attempts to work out its end solely by the use of the beautiful, and the artist is to select out only such things as are beautiful." The idea of culture also took on an elitist cast: Shakespeare, once a staple of popular entertainment (in various bowdlerized versions), was appropriated into the domain of "serious" theater. And simultaneously the world of culture became feminized. "Husbands or sons rarely share those interests," noted one observer. In American life, remarked the clergyman Horace Bushnell, men represented the "force principle," women the "beauty principle."

The depiction of life, the eminent editor and novelist William Dean Howells wrote, "must be tinged with sufficient idealism to make it all of a truly uplifting character. We cannot admit stories which deal with false or immoral relations. . . . The finer side of things—the idealistic—is the answer for us." The "genteel tradition," as this literary school came to be known, dominated the nation's purveyors of elite culture—its journals, publishers, and college professors—from the 1860s onward.

But the urban world could not finally be kept at bay. Howells himself resigned in 1881 from the *Atlantic Monthly,* a stronghold of the genteel tradition, and called for a literature that sought "to picture the daily life in the most exact terms possible." In a series of realistic novels—*A Modern Instance* (1882), *The Rise of Silas Lapham* (1885), and *A Hazard of New Fortunes* (1890)—Howells captured the urban middle class. Stephen Crane's *Maggie: Girl of the Streets* (1893), privately printed because no publisher would touch it, unflinchingly described the destruction of a slum girl.

The city had entered the American imagination and become, by the early 1900s, a main theme of American art and literature. And because it challenged so many assumptions of an older, republican America, the city also became an overriding concern of reformers and, after the run of the century, a main theater in the drama of the Progressive era.

▶ In both politics and religion, established institutions had to find ways of incorporating a flood of newcomers to the city. But the politicians seemed to have an easier time of it. Why was that?

▶ American cities housed a great many people struggling to get by. Yet they always seemed ready to dig into their pockets for a newspaper or a ticket to the ball game. Why was that?

▶ Why is it that we date the arrival of institutions of higher culture with the rise of the industrial city?

SUMMARY

In this chapter, we explore the emergence of a distinctively urban American society. The chapter is concerned, first of all, with how the great nineteenth-century cities came to be built. Urban growth was driven by industrialization—by the geographic concentration of industries, by the increasing scale of production, and by industry's need for city-based financial and administrative services. A burst of innovation brought forth mass transit, skyscrapers, electricity, and much else that made the big city livable. Although not constrained constitutionally, the public sector left city building as much as possible to private initiative and private capital. The result was dramatic growth, with an infrastructure superior to Europe's, but at the price of a degraded environment and nasty living conditions for the poor.

Our second concern is with an urban class structure defined most visibly by geography. The poor inhabited the inner cities and factory districts. The middle class spread out into the suburbs, while the rich lived insulated in fancy neighborhoods or beyond the suburbs. For the wealthy an elite society emerged, stressing an opulent lifestyle and exclusive social organizations. The middle class withdrew into the private world of the family. Intersecting with family were issues of gender identity, with white-collar husbands embracing a cult of masculinity, and wives emboldened by the liberating prospects of the "new woman."

Finally, this chapter describes the components of a distinctive urban culture. City life was strongly flavored by the ways that newcomers—European immigrants, southern blacks, small-town whites—adapted to an alien urban environment. In politics and religion, we see most vividly how American institutions adapted to the newcomers. City life was also distinguished by an explosion of leisure activities, ranging from vaudeville to the yellow press and, at a more elevated level, by the institutions of art, music, and literature that sustain a nation's higher culture.

Connections: Society

The first cities—Boston, New York, Philadelphia, New Orleans—go far back in American history, back indeed, in their origins to the earliest days of colonial settlement. Spurred by the market revolution, they and their counterparts in the interior grew prodigiously in the first half of the nineteenth century. As readers of earlier chapters will know, cities always played a disproportionate part in the nation's economic, political, and cultural life. But only in the late-nineteenth-century years, as the United States became an industrial power, did the rural/urban balance shift and the cities develop a distinctly urban culture. As we say in the part opener (p. 485), the city became

> more than just a place to make a living. . . . It provided a setting for an urban lifestyle unlike anything seen before in America.

The consequences of that development loom large in the nation's later history, for example, as the primary site for reform during the Progressive era (Chapter 20) and as the spark for cultural conflict in the 1920s (Chapter 23). In succeeding decades, we can still distinguish what is distinctively urban in American development, but in truth urban history and American history increasingly merge as the United States becomes in our own time ever more a nation of urban and suburban dwellers, and farmers the tiniest of fractions of the American labor force.

CHAPTER REVIEW QUESTIONS

▶ In what ways does the city growth we study in this chapter intersect with the industrial developments treated in the preceding chapter?

▶ Why did the rich and the middle class develop such different lifestyles in the late-nineteenth-century city?

▶ How did newcomers of deeply rooted, diverse rural backgrounds all become "city people"?

TIMELINE

1869	Corcoran Gallery of Art, nation's first major art museum, opens in Washington, D.C.
1871	Chicago fire
1873	Mark Twain and Charles Dudley Warner publish *The Gilded Age*
1875	Dwight L. Moody launches urban revivalist movement
1876	Alexander Graham Bell patents telephone National Baseball League founded
1879	Thomas Edison creates practical incandescent light bulb Salvation Army, originally formed in Britain, is established in the United States
1881	Andrew Carnegie offers to build a library for every American city
1883	New York City's Metropolitan Opera founded Joseph Pulitzer purchases *New York World*
1885	William Jenney builds first steel-framed structure, Chicago's Home Insurance Building
1887	First electric trolley line constructed in Richmond, Virginia
1893	Chicago Columbian Exposition "City Beautiful" movement
1895	William Randolph Hearst enters New York journalism
1897	Boston builds first American subway
1900	Theodore Dreiser publishes *Sister Carrie*
1901	New York Tenement House Law
1904	New York subway system opens
1906	San Francisco earthquake
1913	Fifty-five-story Woolworth Building opens in New York City

FOR FURTHER EXPLORATION

The starting point for modern urban historiography is Sam Bass Warner's pioneering book on Boston, *Streetcar Suburbs, 1870–1900* (1962). In a subsequent work, *The Private City: Philadelphia in Three Periods* (1968), Warner broadened his analysis to show how private decision making shaped the character of the American city. Innovations in urban construction are treated in Carl Condit, *Rise of the New York Skyscraper, 1865–1913* (1996); Harold L. Platt, *The Electric City: Energy and the Growth of the Chicago Area, 1880–1930* (1991); and Alan Trachtenberg, *The Brooklyn Bridge* (1965). On the social elite, see Frederic C. Jaher, *The Urban Establishment* (1982). Aspects of middle-class life are revealed in Howard B. Chudacoff, *The Age of the Bachelor* (1999); Michael A. Ebner, *Creating Chicago's North Shore: A Suburban History* (1988); Jane Hunter, *How Young Ladies Became Girls: The Victorian Origins of American Girlhood* (2003); John F. Kasson, *Rudeness and Civility: Manners in Nineteenth-Century America* (1990); Andrea Tone, *Devices and Desires: A History of Contraception in America* (2001). On urban life, see especially Gunther Barth, *City People: The Rise of Modern City Culture* (1982); David Block, *Baseball Before We Knew It* (2004); Timothy J. Gilfoyle, *City of Eros: New York City, Prostitution and the Commercialization of Sex, 1790–1920* (1991); John F. Kasson, *Amusing the Million: Coney Island at the Turn of the Century* (1978); and Kathy Peiss, *Cheap Amusements: Working Women and Leisure in Turn-of-the-Century New York* (1986). The best introduction to Gilded Age intellectual currents is Alan Trachtenberg, *The Incorporation of America: Culture and Society, 1865–1893* (1983). On the Columbian Exposition of 1893, an excellent Web site is "The World's Columbian Exposition: Idea, Experience, Aftermath" at **xroads.virginia.edu/~ma96/WCE/title.html**, including detailed guides to every site at the fair and analysis of its lasting impact.

TEST YOUR KNOWLEDGE

To assess your command of the material in this chapter, see the Online Study Guide at **bedfordstmartins.com/henretta**.

For Web sites, images, and documents related to topics and places in this chapter, visit **bedfordstmartins.com/makehistory**.

FOR PRESIDENT — GROVER CLEVELAND

LET THE EAGLE SCREAM!

FOR VICE-PRESIDENT — A.G. THURMAN

19 Politics in the Age of Enterprise, 1877–1896

Ever since the founding of the republic, foreign visitors had been coming to America to observe the political goings-on of a democratic society. Most celebrated was the French aristocrat Alexis de Tocqueville, the author of *Democracy in America* (1832). When an equally brilliant visitor, the Englishman James Bryce, sat down to write his own account fifty years later, he decided that Tocqueville's great book could not be his model. For Tocqueville, Bryce noted, "America was primarily a democracy, the ideal democracy, fraught with lessons for Europe." In his own book, *The American Commonwealth* (1888), Bryce was much less rhapsodic. The robust democracy hailed by Tocqueville had descended into the barren politics of post–Civil War America.

Bryce was anxious, however, not to be misunderstood. Europeans would find in his book "much that is sordid, much that will provoke unfavorable comment." But they needed to be aware of "a reserve of force and patriotism more than sufficient to sweep away all the evils now tolerated, and to make a politics of the country worthy of its material grandeur and of the private virtues of its inhabitants." Bryce was ultimately an optimist: "A hundred times in writing this book have I been disheartened by the facts I was stating; a hundred times has the recollection of the abounding strength and vitality of the nation chased away these tremors."

The Politics of the Status Quo, 1877–1893
The Washington Scene
The Ideology of Individualism
The Supremacy of the Courts

Politics and the People
Cultural Politics: Party, Religion, and Ethnicity
Organizational Politics
Women's Political Culture

Race and Politics in the New South
Biracial Politics
One-Party Rule Triumphant

The Crisis of American Politics: The 1890s
The Populist Revolt
Money and Politics
Climax: The Election of 1896

Summary
Connections: Politics

◀ **Bandanna, 1888 Election**

During the late nineteenth century, politics was a vibrant part of America's culture. Party paraphernalia, such as this colorful bandanna depicting the Democratic presidential nominee Grover Cleveland and his running mate, A. G. Thurman, flooded the country. Collection of Janice L. and David J. Frent.

"Where Is He?"

This *Puck* cartoon, which appeared two weeks after Benjamin Harrison's defeat for reelection at Grover Cleveland's hands in 1892, is a commentary on Harrison's insignificance as president. The hat in Uncle Sam's hands belonged to Benjamin Harrison's grandfather, President William Henry Harrison. *Puck* started using the hat as a trademark for Benjamin Harrison after he had been elected in 1888. As his term progressed, the hat grew increasingly larger and the president successively smaller. By the time of his defeat, just the hat was left and Harrison had disappeared altogether. Bancroft Library, University of California at Berkeley. *Puck,* November 16, 1892.

What was it that Bryce found so disheartening in the practice of American politics? That is this chapter's first subject. The second is about the underlying vitality that Bryce sensed, and how it reemerged and reinvigorated the nation's politics by the century's end.

The Politics of the Status Quo, 1877–1893

In times of national ferment, as a rule, public life becomes magnified. Leaders emerge. Great issues are debated. The powers of government expand. All this had been true of the Civil War era, when the nation's political structure had been severely tested, not least by the contested presidential election of 1876. In 1877, with Rutherford B. Hayes safely settled in the White House, the era of sectional strife finally ended.

Political life went on, but drained of its earlier drama. The 1880s heralded no Lincolns, no great national debates. While Republican defenders of the Union had envisioned a social and economic order reshaped by an activist state, now, in the 1880s, political leaders retreated to a more modest conception of national power. An irreducible core of public functions remained and even, as on the question of railroad regulation, grudging acceptance of new federal responsibilities. But the dominant rhetoric celebrated that government which governed least, and as compared to the Civil War era, American government did govern less.

The Washington Scene

There were five presidents from 1877 to 1893: Rutherford B. Hayes (Republican, 1877–1881), James A. Garfield (Republican, 1881), Chester A. Arthur (Republican, 1881–1885), Grover Cleveland (Democrat, 1885–1889), and Benjamin Harrison (Republican, 1889–1893). All were estimable men. Hayes had served effectively as governor of Ohio for three terms, and Garfield had done well as a congressional leader. Arthur, despite his reputation as a hack politician, had shown fine administrative skills as head of the New York Customs house. Cleveland enjoyed an enviable reputation as reform mayor of Buffalo and governor of New York. None was a charismatic leader, but circumstances, more than personal qualities, explain why these presidents did not make a larger mark on history.

The president's most demanding task was dispensing **patronage** to the faithful. Under the **spoils system**, government appointments were treated as rewards for those who had served the victorious party. Reform of this practice became urgent after President Garfield was shot and killed in 1881. The motives of his assassin, Charles Guiteau, were murky, but civil service reformers blamed the poisonous atmosphere of a spoils system that left many disappointed in the scramble for office. The resulting Pendleton Act (1883) established a nonpartisan Civil Service Commission authorized to fill federal jobs by examination. The original list covered only 10 percent of the jobs, however, and the White House still staggered (as Cleveland grumbled) under the "damned, everlasting clatter for office." Though standards of public administration did rise, there was no American counterpart to the professional civil services being trained in these years at France's *grand ecoles* and Germany's universities.

The duties of the executive branch were, in any event, modest. The White House staff consisted of a half dozen assistants plus a few clerks, doorkeepers, and messengers. Budgetary matters were not the president's province, but Congress's; federal agencies accordingly paid more heed to the key money-dispensing committees on Capitol Hill than to the White House. Of the 100,000 federal employees in 1880, 56 percent worked for the post office. Even the important cabinet offices — Treasury, State, War, Navy, Interior — were sleepy places carrying on largely routine duties. Virtually all federal funding came from customs duties and excise taxes on liquor and tobacco, which produced more money than the government spent. How to reduce the federal surplus ranked as one of the most nettlesome issues of the 1880s.

On matters of national policy, the presidents took a back seat to Capitol Hill. This was partly because — unlike in Lincoln's day — they took a modest view of their powers. "The office of President is essentially executive in nature," Cleveland conceded. On the congressional side, party leaders like Roscoe Conkling, Republican senator from New York, considered themselves coequal with the president. Conkling did not hesitate to take on Rutherford B. Hayes over the latter's lenient policy toward the South — hence the name of Conkling's faction, the Stalwarts. Even more incendiary was any tampering with the patronage prerogatives of congressional barons, as Hayes's successor James Garfield learned when he challenged Conkling over the New York Customs House. James G. Blaine, Conkling's rival and successor as Senate boss — Blaine's faction called itself the Half-Breeds — was equally imperious in dealing with Chester Arthur's administration.

This was the era, in Woodrow Wilson's scathing words, of "congressional government." But Congress was, in fact, not well set up to take command. It was regularly bogged down by arcane procedures and by unruly factions. Nor did either party have a strong agenda. Historically, the Democrats favored **states' rights**, while the Republicans were heirs to the Whig enthusiasm for federally assisted economic development. After Reconstruction, however, the Republicans backed away from state interventionism and, in truth, party differences became muddy. On most leading issues of the day — civil service reform, the currency, regulation of the railroads — divisions occurred within the parties and not between them.

Only the **tariff** remained a fighting issue. From Lincoln's administration onward, high duties had protected American industry from imported goods. It was an article of Republican faith, as President Harrison said in 1892, that "the protective system . . . has been a mighty instrument for the development of the national wealth." The Democrats, free traders by tradition, regularly attacked Republican protectionism. The tariff was a genuine issue, with real economic consequences. And on both sides, it stirred strong partisan feelings. Yet, in practice, the tariff was a negotiable issue like any other. Congressmen voted their constituents' interests regardless of party rhetoric. As a result, tariff bills were generally a patchwork of bargains among special interests.

Late in the decade, after a string of inconclusive revisions, the tariff debate suddenly heated up. An ardent free trader, Cleveland cast off his reluctance to lead the nation and campaigned in 1888 on a platform of thorough-going tariff reduction. His narrow defeat emboldened the Republicans, who in 1890 pushed through the McKinley tariff (after its author William McKinley), raising average rates to a record 49.5 percent, with even higher duties called for if other nations retaliated against American goods. The issue was by no means laid to rest, however. The McKinley tariff, coinciding with a surge of economic troubles in the country, proved unpopular and threw the Republicans very much on the defensive as the 1892 elections approached.

Campaign Politics. Taking a stand on big issues, like the tariff, was risky because the parties were so evenly balanced. By the end of Reconstruction, with the South solidly in their corner, the Democrats stood on equal terms with the Republicans. Every presidential election from 1876 to 1892 was decided by a thin margin (Map 19.1), and Congress regularly changed hands. Under these circumstances, when any false move might tip the scales, caution seemed the best policy.

That did not stop Republican orators from "waving the bloody shirt" against the Democrats. The tactic was not wholly cynical. In various ways, Civil War issues persisted. Pensions for disabled veterans and their widows was a perennial question, favored by Republicans as a matter of honor, resisted by Democrats as extravagant and fraud-ridden. In his first term, President Cleveland vetoed a record number of private pension bills, as well as general legislation for indigent veterans.

MAP 19.1 Presidential Elections of 1880, 1884, and 1888

The anatomy of political stalemate is evident in this trio of electoral maps of the 1880s. First, note the equal division of the popular vote between Republicans and Democrats. Second, note the remarkable persistence in the pattern of electoral votes, in which overwhelmingly states went to the same party in all three elections. Finally, we can identify who determined the outcomes — the two "swing" states, New York and Indiana, whose vote shifted every four years and always in favor of the winning candidate.

1880

Candidate	Electoral Vote	Popular Vote	Percent of Popular Vote
James A. Garfield (Republican)	214	4,453,295	48.5
Winfield Hancock (Democrat)	155	4,414,082	48.1
James B. Weaver (Greenback-Labor)	—	308,578	3.4

1884

Candidate	Electoral Vote	Popular Vote	Percent of Popular Vote
Grover Cleveland (Democrat)	219	4,879,507	48.5
James G. Blaine (Republican)	182	4,850,293	48.2

1888

Candidate	Electoral Vote	Popular Vote	Percent of Popular Vote
Benjamin Harrison (Republican)	233	5,447,129	47.9
Grover Cleveland (Democrat)	168	5,537,857	48.6

Cleveland's electoral success — he was the first Democrat in the White House since the 1850s — only hardened Republican determination not to let go of the Civil War legacy. And so did anxiety about their own party's future. Keeping alive the sectional crisis that had given it birth was a form of party building, a way of cementing Republican solidarity. So "waving the bloody shirt" expressed concerns of real substance. Yet on Reconstruction's real unfinished business — the fate of ex-slaves — the Republicans backed away, never fulfilling their pledge to provide federal funding to combat illiteracy or effective protections for black voters. Nor was there denying the demagogic uses of "waiving the bloody shirt" during elections. Lord Bryce had grounds for criticizing the Republicans for "clinging too long to outworn issues and neglecting the problems . . . which now perplex the country."

Alternatively, campaigns could descend into comedy. In the hard-fought election of 1884, for example, the Democrat Cleveland burst on the scene as a reformer, fresh from his victories over corrupt machine politics in New York State. But years earlier Cleveland, a bachelor, had fathered an illegitimate child, and throughout the campaign he was dogged by the ditty, "Maw, Maw, where's my Paw?" (After his victory Cleveland's supporters gleefully responded, "He's in the White House, haw-haw-haw.") Cleveland's opponent, James G. Blaine, already on the defensive for taking favors from the railroads, was weakened by the unthinking charge of a too ardent Republican clergyman that the Democrats were the party of "Rum, Romanism and Rebellion." In a twinkling he had insulted Catholic voters and, so some believed, lost the election for Blaine. In the midst of all the mudslinging, the issues got lost.

The characteristics of public life in the 1880s — the passivity of the federal government, the evasiveness of the political parties, the absorption in politics for its own sake — derived ultimately from the underlying conviction that little was at stake in national affairs. In 1887 Cleveland vetoed a small appropriation for drought-stricken Texas farmers with the remark that "though the people support the Government, the Government should not support the people." Governmental activity was itself considered a bad thing. All the state could do, said Senator Conkling, was "to clear the way of impediments and dangers, and leave every class and every individual free and safe in the exertions and pursuits of life." Conkling was expressing the political corollary to the economic doctrine of **laissez-faire**—the belief, already well-rooted in the Jeffersonian-Jacksonian politics of the antebellum era—that the less government interfered, the better.

The Ideology of Individualism

At the peak of the labor strife of the 1880s, the cotton manufacturer Edward Atkinson gave a talk to the textile workers of Providence, Rhode Island. They had, he told them, no cause for discontent. "There is always plenty of room on the front seats in every profession, every trade. . . . There are men in this audience who will fill some of those seats, but they won't be boosted into them from behind." (There were certainly women in the audience—at least half the textile industry's labor force was female—but, as was the norm for the times, Atkinson assumed that economic advancement mattered only to men.) Atkinson's homely talk went to roots of conservative American thought: any man, however humble, could rise as far as his talents would carry him; every person received his just reward, great or small; and the success of the individual, so encouraged, contributed to the progress of the whole. How persuasive the workers listening to Atkinson found his message we have no way of knowing. But the confidence with which he presented his case is evidence of the continuing appeal of the **ideology** of individualism in the age of enterprise.

A flood of popular writings trumpeted the creed of individualism, from the rags-to-riches tales of Horatio Alger to innumerable success manuals with such titles as *Thoughts for the Young Men of America, or a Few Practical Words of Advice to Those Born in Poverty and Destined to be Reared in Orphanages* (1871). Self-made men such as Andrew Carnegie became cultural heroes. A best seller was Carnegie's *Triumphant Democracy* (1886), which paid homage to a country that enabled a penniless Scottish child to rise from bobbin boy to steel magnate.

Facing the World
The cover of this Horatio Alger novel (1893) captures the American myth of opportunity. Our hero, Harry Vane, is a poor but earnest lad, ready to make his way in the world and, despite the many obstacles thrown in his path, sure to succeed. In some 135 books Horatio Alger repeated this story, with minor variations, for an eager reading public that numbered in the millions. Frank and Marie-Therese Wood Print Collections, Alexandria, VA.

From the pulpit came the assurances of the Episcopal bishop William Lawrence of Massachusetts that "godliness is in league with riches." Bishop Lawrence was voicing a familiar theme of American Protestantism: Success in one's earthly calling revealed the promise of eternal salvation. It was all too easy for a conservative ministry to bless the furious acquisitiveness of industrial America. "To secure wealth is an honorable ambition," intoned the Baptist minister Russell H. Conwell.

Social Darwinism. The celebration of individualism drew strong support from social theorizing drawn from biology. Evolution itself—the idea that the species are not fixed but change over time—was not new. It had been gathering scientific support ever since the early nineteenth century. But evolutionary science lacked an explanatory mechanism. This was what the British naturalist Charles Darwin provided in *On the Origin of Species* (1859), which advanced the concept of *natural selection*. In nature, Darwin wrote, all living things struggle to survive. Individual members of a species are born with genetic mutations that better fit them for their particular environment — camouflage coloring for a bird or butterfly, for example. These survival characteristics, since they are genetically transmissible, become dominant in future generations, and the species evolves.

Darwin himself disapproved of the term *evolution* (the word doesn't appear in his book) because it implied an upward progression. In his view, natural selection was blind — there was no intelligent design behind it. Since environments changed randomly, so did the adaptation of species. For Darwin, evolutionary progress was meaningless. But he had given evolution the stamp of scientific legitimacy and others, less scrupulous than he about drawing larger conclusions, moved confidently to apply evolution to social development.

Foremost was the British philosopher Herbert Spencer, who spun out an elaborate analysis of how human society had advanced through competition and "survival of the fittest." **Social Darwinism**, as Spencer's ideas became known, was championed in America by William Graham Sumner, a sociology professor at Yale. Competition, said Sumner, is a law of nature that "can no more be done away with than gravitation." And who are the fittest? "The millionaires. . . . They may fairly be regarded as the naturally selected agents of society. They get high wages and live in luxury, but the bargain is a good one for society."

Social Darwinists regarded with horror any interference with social processes. "The great stream of time and earthly things will sweep on just the same in spite of us," Sumner wrote in a famous essay, "The Absurd Attempt to Make the World Over" (1894). As for the government, it had "at bottom . . . two chief things . . . with which to deal. They are the property of men and the honor of women. These it has to defend against crime." And beyond that, it had to leave people alone.

The Supremacy of the Courts

Suspicion of government not only paralyzed political initiative; it also shifted power away from the executive and legislative branches. "The task of constitutional government," declared Sumner, "is to devise institutions which shall come into play at critical periods to prevent the abusive control of the powers of a state by the controlling classes in it." Sumner meant the judiciary. From the 1870s onward the courts increasingly accepted the role that he assigned to them, becoming the guardians of the rights of private property against the grasping tentacles of government.

The main target of the courts was not Washington, but the states. This was because, under the federal system as it was understood in the late nineteenth century, the **residual powers** — those not delegated by the Constitution to the federal government — left the states with primary authority over social welfare and economic regulation. The great question in American law was how to balance the states' police powers to defend the general welfare against the liberty of individuals to pursue their private interests. Most states, caught up in the conservative ethos of the day, were cutting back on expenditures and public services. Even so, there were more than enough state initiatives to alarm vigilant judges. Thus, in the landmark case *In re Jacobs* (1885), the New York State Court of Appeals struck down a law prohibiting cigar manufacturing in tenements on the grounds that such regulation exceeded the police powers of the state.

As the federal courts took up the battle against state activism, they found their strongest weapon in the Fourteenth Amendment (1868), the Reconstruction amendment that prohibited the states from depriving "any person of life, liberty, or property, without due process of law." The due process clause had been introduced to protect the civil rights of the former slaves. But due process protected the property rights and liberty of any "person," and legally, corporations counted as persons. So interpreted, the Fourteenth Amendment became by the turn of the century a powerful restraint on the power of the states to regulate private business.

The Supreme Court similarly hamstrung the federal government. In 1895 the Court ruled that the federal power to regulate interstate commerce did not cover manufacturing and struck down a federal income tax law. And in areas where federal power was undeniable — such as the regulation of railroads — the Supreme Court scrutinized every measure for undue interference with the rights of property.

The preeminent jurist of the day, Stephen J. Field, made no bones about the dangers he saw in the nation's headlong industrial development. "As the inequalities in the conditions of men become more and more marked and . . . angry menaces against order find vent in loud denunciations — it becomes more and more the imperative duty of the court to enforce with a firm hand every guarantee of the Constitution."

Power conferred status. The law, not politics, attracted the ablest people and held the public's esteem. A Wisconsin judge boasted, "The bench symbolizes on earth the throne of divine justice.... Law in its highest sense is the will of God." Judicial supremacy revealed how entrenched the ideology of individualism had become in industrial America and also how low American politicians had fallen in the esteem of their countrymen.

▶ A novel published in 1880 speaks derisively of American democracy as being "of the people, by the people, for the benefit of Senators." What was there about the political scene that would have prompted the author to say that?

▶ Why was Darwin's *Origins of Species,* which was strictly about biology, important in the development of the ideology of conservatism?

▶ How do you explain the reverence accorded to the judiciary in the late nineteenth century?

Politics and the People

The country may have felt, as Kansas editor William Allen White wrote, "sick with politics" and "nauseated at all politicians," but somehow this did not curb the popular appetite for politics. Proportionately more voters turned out in presidential elections from 1876 to 1892 than at any other time in American history. People voted Democratic or Republican loyally for a lifetime. National conventions attracted huge crowds. "The excitement, the mental and physical strains," remarked an Indiana Republican after the 1888 convention, "are surpassed only by prolonged battle in actual warfare, as I have been told by officers of the Civil War who latter engaged in convention struggles." The convention he described had nominated the colorless Benjamin Harrison on a routine platform. What was all the excitement about?

Cultural Politics: Party, Religion, and Ethnicity

In the late nineteenth century, politics was a vibrant part of the nation's culture. America "is a land of conventions and assemblies," a journalist noted,

The Presidential B.B. Club (1888)
On the left Grover Cleveland is the baseman; at center Benjamin Harrison is at bat; and on the right Cleveland tags Harrison out — not, alas, the right prediction, since Harrison won the 1888 election. Collection of Janice L. and David J. Frent.

"where it is the most natural thing in the world for people to get together in meetings, where almost every event is the occasion for speechmaking." During the election season the party faithful marched in torchlight parades. Party paraphernalia flooded the country — handkerchiefs, mugs, posters, and buttons emblazoned with the Democratic donkey or the Republican elephant, symbols that had been adopted in the 1870s. In the 1888 campaign the candidates were featured on cards, like baseball players, tucked into packets of Honest Long Cut tobacco. In an age before movies and radio, politics ranked as one of the great American forms of entertainment (see Reading American Pictures, "Parties and People," p. 591).

Party loyalty was a deadly serious matter, however. Long after the killing ended, Civil War emotions ran high. Among family friends in Cleveland, recalled the urban reformer Brand Whitlock, the Republican Party was "a synonym for patriotism, another name for the nation. It was inconceivable that any self-respecting person should be a Democrat" — or, among ex-Confederates in the South, that any self-respecting person could be a Republican.

Beyond these sectional differences the most important determinants of party loyalty were religion and ethnicity (Figure 19.1). Statistically, northern Democrats tended to be foreign-born and Catholic, while Republicans tended to be native-born and Protestant. Among Protestants, the more *pietistic* a person's faith — that is, the more personal and direct the believer's relationship to God — the more likely he or she was to be a Republican and to favor using the powers of the state to uphold moral values and regulate personal behavior.

During the 1880s, as ethnic tensions built up in many cities, education became an arena of bitter conflict. One issue was whether instruction in the public schools should be in English. Immigrant groups often wanted their children taught in their own languages. In St. Louis, a heavily German city, the long-standing policy of teaching German to all students was overturned after a heated campaign. Religion was an even more explosive educational issue. Catholics fought a losing battle over public aid for parochial schools, which by 1900 was prohibited by twenty-three states. In Boston a furious controversy broke out in 1888 over the use of an anti-Catholic history textbook. When the school board withdrew the offending book, angry Protestants elected a new board and returned the text to the curriculum.

Then there was the regulation of public morals. In many states, so-called *blue laws* restricted activity on Sundays. When Nebraska banned Sunday baseball, the state's courts approved the law as a blow struck in

FIGURE 19.1 Ethnocultural Voting Patterns in the Midwest, 1870–1892

	Democrat	Republican
Immigrants		
Irish Catholic	95	5
Polish Catholic	95	5
German Catholic	85	15
German Lutheran	55	45
Dutch Reformed	30	70
Swedish Lutheran	10	90
Irish Protestant	5	95
Native-born		
Free Will Baptist	5	95
Methodist	10	90
Congregational	10	90
Presbyterian	30	70
Disciples	60	40

These figures demonstrate how voting patterns among midwesterners reflected ethnicity and religion in the late nineteenth century. Especially striking is the overwhelming preference by immigrant Catholics for the Democratic Party. Among Protestants there was an equally strong preference for the Republican Party by certain groups of immigrants (Swedish Lutherans and Irish Protestants) and native born (Free Will Baptists, Methodists, and Congregationalists), but other Protestant groups were more evenly divided in their party preferences.

"the contest between Christianity and wrong." But German and Irish Catholics, who saw nothing evil in a bit of fun on Sunday, considered blue laws a violation of their personal freedom. **Ethnocultural** conflict also flared over the liquor question. In many states, evangelical Christians pushed for strict licensing and local-option laws governing the sale of alcoholic beverages. Indiana permitted drinking but only joylessly in rooms containing "no devices for amusement or music . . . of any kind."

Because the hottest social issues of the day — education, the liquor question, and observance of the Sabbath — were also party issues, they lent deep significance to party affiliation (see Voices from Abroad, "Ernst Below: Beer and German American Politics," p. 593). And because these issues were fought out mostly at the state and local levels, they hit very close to home. Crusading Methodists thought of Republicans as the party of morality.

READING AMERICAN PICTURES

Parties and People: How Democratic Was American Politics?

In the text we say that the late nineteenth century was a great age of popular participation in politics. As indicators, we offer voter turnout, persisting voting patterns, and party participation. The photographs below provide an additional indicator, evidence of citizens as party activists. The upper photo shows the members of the local Republican Party organization of Newport, Rhode Island, named in honor of Levi P. Morton, vice president in the Benjamin Harrison administration (1889-1893). The lower photo shows farm families en route to a Populist rally in Dickinson County, Kansas, sometime in the 1890s.

The Levi P. Morton Association (1888). Newport Historical Society.

En Route to a Populist Rally, Dickinson County, Kansas (1890s). Kansas State Historical Society.

ANALYZING THE EVIDENCE

- Compare the people in the two photographs. Do the differences you see suggest anything about the class composition of American political parties in the late nineteenth century?

- Giving women the vote, as the text says, was a highly divisive and unresolved issue in the late nineteenth century. Do these photographs throw any light on that issue? Or on how Republicans and Populists aligned themselves on it?

- A hallmark of the nineteenth-century parties was their capacity to organize at the grassroots level. That is apparent in both photographs. But Populists regarded their brand of grassroots activism to be different — and far more democratic — from main-line parties. Do the photographs reveal any evidence that helps us understand why they might have felt that way?

For embattled Irish and German Catholics, who favored "the largest individual liberty consistent with public order," the Democratic Party was the defender of their freedoms.

It would have been easy enough to invoke these divisions in national politics as, for example, Senator Blaine did in 1875 when, angling for the Republican presidential nomination, he proposed a federal amendment banning public funding of parochial schools. But Republicans generally held back, and for good reason. They could never be sure, given the parity of the parties nationally, that more would be lost than gained by playing the values card. That was a lesson brought bitterly home to Republicans by the loose talk about "Rum, Romanism, and Rebellion" in the 1884 campaign. It is in this particular respect that the politics of morality has changed since the 1880s — not that it is any more potent today, but that it functions on a bigger stage. While battles over Demon Rum and the Sabbath played out locally, the equivalent battles over abortion and gay rights have become national issues and help define presidential politics.

Organizational Politics

Late nineteenth-century politics was robust also because of the organizational activity it generated. By the 1870s both major parties had evolved formal, well-organized structures. At the base lay the precinct or ward, where party meetings were open to all members. County, state, and national committees ran the ongoing business of the parties. Conventions determined party rules, adopted platforms, and selected the party's candidates. At election time the party's main job was to get out the vote. Wherever elections were close and hard fought, the parties mounted intensive efforts organized down to the individual voter. In Indiana, for example, the Republicans appointed ten thousand "district men," each responsible for turning out a designated group of voters.

Party governance seemed, on its face, highly democratic, since in theory all power derived from the party members. In practice, however, the parties were run by unofficial internal organizations — political machines — which consisted of insiders willing to do party work in exchange for public jobs or the sundry advantages of being connected. Although most evident in city politics (see Chapter 18), the machine system was integral to political life at every level, right up to the national parties. The machines tended toward one-man rule, although the "boss" ruled more by the consent of the secondary leaders than by his own absolute power. The high stakes of office, jobs, and influence made for intense intra-party factionalism. Absorbed in the tasks of power brokerage, machine bosses treated public issues as somewhat irrelevant. And the spoils system they managed unquestionably fouled the public realm with the stench of corruption.

Yet the record of machine politics was not wholly negative. In certain ways the standards of governance got better. Disciplined professionals, veterans of machine politics, proved effective as state legislators and congressmen because they were more experienced in the give-and-take of politics. More important, party machines filled a void in the nation's public life. They did informally much of what the governmental system left undone, especially in the cities.

The Mugwumps. Even so, machine politics never managed to become respectable. Many of the nation's social elite — intellectuals, well-to-do businessmen, and old-line families — resented a politics that excluded people like themselves, the "best men." There was, too, a genuine clash of values. Political reformers called for "disinterestedness" and "independence" — the opposite of the self-serving careerism fostered by the machine system. James Bryce, whose comments open this chapter, was wined and dined by this circle when he came to the United States. His writings were colored by the prejudices of the political reformers, and, like them, he discounted the cultural and organizational contributions of American party politics.

Many of them had earned their spurs as Liberal Republicans who dissented against President Grant's reelection in 1872. In 1884, led by Carl Schurz and Charles Francis Adams Jr., they again left the Republican Party because they could not stomach its tainted presidential candidate, James G. Blaine. Mainly from New York and Massachusetts, these reform Republicans became known as Mugwumps — a derisive bit of contemporary slang, supposedly of Indian origin, referring to pompous or self-important persons. The Mugwumps threw their support to Democrat Grover Cleveland and may have ensured his election by giving him the winning margin in New York State.

After the 1884 election the enthusiasm for reform spilled over into local politics, spawning good-government campaigns across the country. Although they won some municipal victories, the Mugwumps were more adept at molding public opinion than at running government. Controlling the newspapers and journals read by the educated middle class, the Mugwumps defined the terms of political debate, denying the machine system legitimacy and injecting an elitist bias into political opinion.

Mark Twain was not alone in proclaiming "an honest and saving loathing for universal suffrage."

VOICES FROM ABROAD

Ernst Below

Beer and German American Politics

Ernst Below (1845–1910) toured the United States in the early 1890s, enjoying the hospitality of the prosperous German American communities he encountered along the way. Following is an excerpt from the book he published on his return to Germany, Bilder aus dem Westen (1894). The reader will note that the action takes place at a Turner festival. Turner is the German word for "gymnast." In the nineteenth century the gymnastic movement had an enormous vogue in Germany, helping to weld a spirit of German nationalism in that fragmented country before unification in 1871.

In Kansas City we sat on the veranda, taking coffee with Mr. Held, the attorney.... The men spoke of the chances of our host's election to Congress. Our friend, Karl, had the latest precise news from the battlefield and told of the stratagems used by one party or another in the attempt to make sure of victory. I showed my surprise that an educated, honest, thoughtful man, under such conditions, could bring himself to be concerned with politics....

The next night the great *Turnverein* [Gymnastic Association] hall was brightly lighted.... When I entered the hall the gymnastic exercises had already begun.... On the walls hung ... pictures of Washington, Lincoln and Grant; side by side with William I, Bismarck and Moltke.... At one end of the hall sat old Kumpf, the former mayor. Speaking to him from either side with great seriousness were two German Democrats, city officials. Kumpf was, like most of the old German turners, once a solid Republican.... Yet even he was displeased with the flirtation of his party with the temperance and prohibition forces in recent times. Nevertheless, he could not bring himself publicly to go over to the Democrats, and he laughingly parried the attacks of the two city officials.... A little later one of them tried a different assault.... He pointed to the adjoining room, in which a great many men surrounded the refreshment table. In their midst stood Joe Davenport, the Republican candidate for mayor, who was ordering a round of drinks and cigars for everyone.

"Listen to what he says," went on the Democrat. "... I know for a fact that he wrote yesterday to the Young Men's Christian Association promising in return for their votes a complete closing of all saloons on Sundays. Either here or there he must break his word.... Go up to the scamp and expose his game!"

... Now the mayoralty candidate climbed onto a barrel and praised Germany and the Germans, the Rhine and the "Fatherland." ... After Davenport finished there was no end of *hochs* and *hurrays*. Only with difficulty did Old Kumpf succeed in getting the floor and drawing the attention of the crowd.... Pointing to Mr. Holmes the rival Democratic candidate who had, unnoticed, come into the hall during the concluding exercises [Kumpf said]: "Although I do not fight for exactly the same principles as this man, still I must acknowledge that he offers a true guarantee against the hypocritical attempts of the prohibitionists.... With this in mind, I say, 'long live our next mayor, Mister Holmes!'"

Loud applause arose from all sides; men, women, and children jostled about trying to shake the hand of the future mayor. The band struck up the "Star Spangled Banner" while the whole assemblage rose to its feet and loudly sang the words....

Soon a loud uproar reigned in the refreshment room. One group yelled ridicule against another, as the satellites of Davenport sought to ridicule the sudden change in sentiment. After the beer had been poured out in streams on both sides for some time no one really knew what was going on; not a man could tell exactly who belonged to which party....

As I left the hall I was greeted by Rothmann, the director of the German school. He was indignant at the scenes which had so unworthily closed a meeting that had begun so well. "This time at least," he said, "the Germans should have held together to show that they could unitedly support Held, our [Republican] candidate for Congress. But when it comes to the most vital interest of the Germans in America, they are only concerned with their little appetites...."

SOURCE: Oscar Handlin, ed., *This Was America* (Cambridge, MA: Harvard University Press, 1949), 383–89.

ANALYZING THE EVIDENCE

- In his speech, the Republican candidate Joe Davenport, himself no German, sings the praises of Germany, the "Fatherland." Why does he do that?

- In the Civil War era, German Americans were solidly Republican, loyal supporters of Lincoln. The former mayor, Old Kumpf, is of that generation. So why does he stand up and denounce the Republican candidate Davenport?

- The goings-on at the Turnverein hall are about the campaign for mayor. Yet when the school principal Rothman leaves, he is complaining about the injury done to Held, the Republican candidate for Congress. Does that call into question our claim in the text that national politics in the late nineteenth century was insulated — unlike in our own time — from ethnocultural politics?

This democratic triumph of the early republic—a beacon for other nations to follow—now went into reverse, as northern states began to impose **literacy tests** and limit the voting rights of immigrants. The **secret ballot**, an import from Australia widely adopted around 1890, abetted the Mugwump antidemocratic campaign. Traditionally, voters had submitted party-supplied tickets in public view at the polling place. With the Australian reform, citizens cast their ballots in voting booths, freed from party surveillance, but for the uneducated and foreign-speaking, navigating a lengthy official ballot could be intimidating. And so could new voter registration procedures that registrars commonly used to bar those considered unfit for the suffrage.

The Mugwumps were reformers, but not on behalf of social justice. The travails of working people meant little to them, while keeping the state out of the welfare business meant a great deal. As far as the Mugwumps were concerned, the government that was best was the government that governed least. Theirs was the brand of "reform" perfectly in keeping with the conservative ethos of the time. In this respect, they and their critics—conservative judges and party leaders who otherwise disdained Mugwumpery—were in agreement.

Women's Political Culture

The young Theodore Roosevelt, an up-and-coming Republican state politician in 1884, spoke contemptuously of the Mugwumps as "man-milliners" (makers of ladies' hats). The sexual slur was not accidental. In attacking organizational politics, the Mugwumps were challenging a bastion of male society. At party meetings and conventions, men carried on not only the business of politics but also the rituals of male sociability amid cigar smoke and whiskey. Politics was identified with manliness. It was competitive. It dealt in the commerce of power. It was frankly self-aggrandizing. Party politics, in short, was no place for a woman.

So, naturally, the woman suffrage movement met fierce opposition. Acknowledging the uphill battle that lay ahead, suffragists overcame the bitter divisions of the Reconstruction era (see Chapter 15), reuniting in 1890 in the National American Woman Suffrage Association. In that same spirit of realism, suffragists abandoned efforts to get a constitutional amendment and concentrated on state campaigns. Except out West—in Wyoming, Idaho, Colorado, and Utah—the most they could win was the right to vote for school boards or on tax issues. "Men are ordained to govern in all forceful and material things, because they are men," asserted an anti-suffrage resolution, "while women, by the same decree of God and nature, are equally fitted to bear rule in a higher and more spiritual realm, where the strong frame and the weighty brain count for less"—that is to say, not in politics.

Yet this invocation of the doctrine of **"separate spheres"**—that men and women had different natures, and that women's nature fitted them for "a higher and more spiritual realm"—did open a channel for women into public life. "Women's place is Home," acknowledged the journalist Retha Childe Dorr. "But Home is not contained within the four walls of an individual house. Home is the community. The city full of people is the Family.... And badly do the Home and Family need their mother." Indeed, in antebellum times women had long engaged in uplifting activities—fighting prostitution, assisting the poor, agitating for prison reform, and demanding better educational and job opportunities (see Chapter 9). Since many of these goals required state action, women's organizations of necessity turned to politics, but they had to find a way in, and that meant first of all creating their own political sphere.

Just before Christmas in 1873 the women of Hillsboro, Ohio, began to hold prayer meetings in front of the town's saloons, appealing to owners to close their doors and end the misery of families of hard-drinking fathers. Thus began a spontaneous uprising—the "Woman's Crusade"—that spread across the country. From this agitation came the Woman's Christian Temperance Union (WCTU), which, under the guidance of Frances Willard, blossomed into the leading women's organization in the country.

Frances Willard and Women's Politics. Willard was a suffragist, but no admirer of Susan B. Anthony or Lucy Stone. "The clamor for 'rights,'" she felt, was the wrong approach. Better to offer "only prayerful, persistent pleas for the opportunity of duty"—that is, to link the vote to women's concerns as wives and mothers. Willard's political motto was "Home Protection." In 1879, after carefully laying the groundwork, she defeated the antisuffragist incumbent and became national president of the WCTU.

The liquor evil, while genuinely felt by Willard, was not why she abandoned a promising career as an educator; she had been president of the Evanston College for Ladies, and when it was folded into Northwestern, the first dean of women there. She regarded the WCTU essentially in political terms, a vehicle uniquely suited for converting womanly virtue into political power. Willard understood her middle-class members. Like herself, they were "literary-minded," evangelical Christian, with a

Wanted, Sober Men

This drawing appeared in a magazine in 1899, twenty-five years after the women of Hillsboro, Ohio, rose in revolt against the town's saloonkeepers and launched the Woman's Christian Temperance Union (WCTU). But the emotion it expresses had not changed — that the saloon was the enemy of the family. Culver Pictures.

vocation for service. She intended to mold them into a political force. With men excluded, the WCTU gave the natural leaders among the women space to hone their skills. And for the others, there was Willard's "Do-Everything" program, an ever-widening array of issues — labor conditions, prostitution, public health, international peace — that introduced these sheltered women to the ills of the world.

On the liquor front, the WCTU made some headway, mainly by local-option ordinances but also, as in Iowa, by statewide prohibition. Finding a way into men's political realm, however, was more challenging. Willard's own preference was for third-party politics. In the early 1880s, she led the WCTU into the Prohibition Party, a pretty moribund operation until the women came in, but even then, significant only in a handful of midwestern states. Willard had her reasons. In a small pond, she could be a big fish, as indeed she quickly became in the Prohibition Party. She was also something of a maverick, disdainful of the mainstream parties and supportive of the Knights of Labor. Finally, Willard got the coveted endorsement of woman suffrage by the Prohibition Party. But of course that did nothing to advance the suffrage cause. And, in truth, the third-party gambit was a misstep, causing friction in the WCTU and mostly failing to wean members from their traditional party loyalties.

The major parties, in fact, were not as antifemale as their manly facades might have suggested. Understanding all too well that womenfolk influenced their men, both parties in their different ways campaigned for the women's "vote." In this competition, the Republicans had the advantage of their ideological roots in antebellum evangelical reform. Willard's motto "Home Protection" was not hers alone. Republicans had used the term, or a variant, against slavery, and in Willard's time they even used it to defend the tariff: Protection from cheap foreign goods meant higher American wages and hence "protection" for the family. In advancing this pro-family line, the Republicans recruited female party operatives and found a pool of them in, of all places, the WCTU. So, despite herself, Willard contributed to the expanding role of women in mainstream politics.

Not much changed in the short run. At the national level Republicans remained against prohibition and against woman suffrage. For its part, the WCTU abandoned Willard's political activism and dropped out of the suffrage struggle. But the link it established between women's social concerns and political participation helped lay the groundwork for fresh attacks on male electoral politics. In the meantime, even without the vote, the WCTU demonstrated how potent a force women might be in the public arena and how vibrant a political culture they could build.

➤ Who were the Mugwumps? Do you regard them as important players in post-Reconstruction politics? If so, why?

➤ What do we mean by "ethnocultural" politics, and why is it important for an understanding of late-nineteenth-century American politics?

➤ Why was it that women, although they mostly couldn't vote, nevertheless became important political actors in this era?

Race and Politics in the New South

When Reconstruction ended in 1877, so did the hopes of African Americans that they would enjoy the equal rights promised them by the Fourteenth and Fifteenth Amendments. Southern schools were segregated. Access to jobs, the courts, and social services was racially determined and unequal. No laws segregated public accommodation, however, and practices varied across the South. Only on the railroads, as rail travel became common, did whites demand that blacks be excluded from first-class cars, with the result that southern railroads became, after 1887, the first public accommodation legally segregated.

In politics the situation was still more fluid. Redemption had not driven blacks out of politics (see Chapter 15). On the contrary, their turnout at elections in the post-Reconstruction years was not far behind the turnout by whites. But blacks did not participate on equal terms with whites. In the black belt areas, where African Americans sometimes outnumbered whites, **gerrymandered** voting districts ensured that, while blacks got some offices, political control remained in white hands. Blacks were routinely intimidated during political campaigns. Even so, an impressive majority remained staunchly Republican, refusing, as the last black congressman from Mississippi told his House colleagues in 1882, "to surrender their honest convictions, even upon the altar of their personal necessities."

Whatever hopes blacks entertained for better days, however, faded during the 1880s and then, in the next decade, expired in a terrible burst of racial terrorism.

Biracial Politics

No democratic society can survive if it does not allow competing economic and social interests to be heard. In the United States the two-party system performs that role. The sectional crisis severely tested the two-party system because, in both the North and the South, opposing the dominant party came to be seen as treasonable. In the victorious North, despite the best efforts of the Republicans, the Democrats shed their disgrace after the war and reclaimed their status as a major party. In the defeated South, however, the scars of war cut deep, and Reconstruction cut even deeper. The struggle for "**home rule**" empowered southern Democrats. They had "redeemed" the South from Republican domination — hence the name they adopted: Redeemers. Cloaked in the mantle of the Lost Cause, the Redeemers claimed a monopoly on political legitimacy.

The Republican Party in the South did not fold up, however. On the contrary, it soldiered on, sustained by tenacious black loyalty, by a hard core of white support, by patronage from Republican national administrations, and by a key Democratic vulnerability. This was the gap between the universality the Democrats claimed as the party of Redemption and its actual domination by a single interest — the South's economic elite.

Class antagonism, though masked by sectional patriotism, was never absent from southern society. The Civil War had brought out long-smoldering differences between planters and hill-country farmers, who felt called on to shed blood for a slaveholding system in which they had no part. Afterward, class tensions were exacerbated by the spread of farm tenancy and by the emergence of low-wage industrial labor. Unable to make their grievances heard, economically distressed southerners broke with the Democratic Party in the early 1880s and mounted insurgent movements across the region. Most notable were the Readjusters, who briefly gained power in Virginia over the issue of Reconstruction debt: They opposed repayment to bond-holding speculators that would have left the state destitute. After subsiding briefly, this agrarian discontent revived mightily in the late 1880s, as tenant farmers joined farmers' alliances and helped create the Populist Party (see p. 602).

As this insurgency accelerated, the question of black participation became critical. Racism cut through southern society and, so some thought, most infected the lowest rungs. "The white laboring classes here," wrote an Alabamian in 1886, "are separated from the Negroes, working all day side by side with them, by an innate consciousness of race superiority," which "excites a sentiment of sympathy and equality with the classes above them." Yet when times got bad enough, hard-pressed whites could also see blacks as fellow victims. "They are in the ditch just like we are," asserted one white Texan. Southern Populists never fully reconciled these contradictory impulses. They did not question the racist conventions of social inequality. Nor were the interests of white farmers and black tenants always in concert. But once agrarian protest turned political, the logic of interracial solidarity became hard to deny.

In the meantime, black farmers had developed a political structure of their own. The Colored Farmers' Alliance operated much less openly than its white counterparts — it could be worth a black man's life to make too open a show of his independence — but nevertheless gave black voters a voice at the table with white Populists. The demands of partisan politics, once the break with the Democrats came, clinched the argument for interracial unity. Where the Populists fused with the Republican Party, as in North Carolina and Tennessee, they automatically became allies of black leaders. Where the Populists fielded separate third-party tickets, they needed to appeal directly to black voters. "The accident of

Map 19.2 Disfranchisement in the New South

In the midst of the Populist challenge to Democratic one-party rule in the South, a movement to deprive blacks of the right to vote spread from Mississippi across the South. By 1910 every state in the region except Tennessee, Arkansas, Texas, and Florida had made constitutional changes designed to prevent blacks from voting, and these four states accomplished much the same result through poll taxes and other exclusionary methods. For the next half century, the political process in the South would be for whites only.

color can make no difference in the interest of farmers, croppers, and laborers," argued the Georgian Tom Watson. "You are kept apart that you may be separately fleeced of your earnings." This interracial appeal, even if not always wholehearted, put at risk the foundations of elite southern politics.

One-Party Rule Triumphant

The Democrats struck back with all their might. They played the race card, parading as the "white man's party" while denouncing the Populists for promoting "Negro rule." Yet they shamelessly competed for the black vote. In this they had many advantages: money, control of the local power structures, and a paternalistic relationship to the black community. When all else failed, mischief at the polls enabled the Democrats to beat back the Populists. Across the South in the 1892 elections, the Democrats snatched victory from defeat by a miraculous vote count—including the votes of many long dead or gone. Thus the Mississippian Frank Burkitt's bitter attack on the conservatives: They were "a class of corrupt office-seekers" who had "hypocritically raised the howl of white supremacy while they debauched the ballot boxes . . . disregarded the rights of the blacks . . . and actually dominated the will of the white people through the instrumentality of the stolen negro vote."

Black Disfranchisement. In the midst of these deadly struggles, the Democrats decided to settle matters once and for all. The movement to disfranchise the blacks, hitherto tentative, swiftly gathered steam (Map 19.2). In 1890 Mississippi adopted a literacy test that effectively drove the state's blacks out of politics. The motives behind it were cynical, but the literacy test could be dressed up as a reform for white Mississippians tired of electoral fraud and violence. Their children and grandchildren, argued one influential figure, should not be left "with shotguns in their hands, a lie in their mouths and perjury on their lips in order to defeat the negroes." Better, a Mississippi journalist wrote, to devise "some legal defensible substitute for the abhorrent and evil methods on which white supremacy lies." This logic even persuaded some weary Populists: Frank Burkitt, for example, was arguing *for* the Mississippi literacy test in the words quoted in the previous paragraph.

The race question had helped bring down the Populists; now it helped reconcile them to defeat. Embittered whites, ambivalent all along about interracial cooperation, turned their fury on the blacks. Insofar as disfranchising measures asserted militant white supremacy, poor whites approved. Of course, it was important that their own vulnerability—their own lack of education—be partially offset by lenient enforcement of the literacy test. Thus, to take a blatant instance, Louisiana's grandfather clause exempted from the test those entitled to vote on January 1, 1867 (before the Fifteenth Amendment gave freedmen that right), together with their sons and grandsons. But poor whites were not protected from property and poll-tax requirements, and many stopped voting.

Poor whites might have objected more had their spokesmen not been conceded a voice in southern politics. A new brand of demagogic politician came forward to speak for them, appealing not to their economic interests but to their racial prejudices. Tom Watson, the Georgia Populist, rebuilt his political career as a spellbinding

Disfranchisement

This political drawing that appeared in *Judge* magazine on July 30, 1892, shows members of the Ku Klux Klan barring black voters from the polls. By 1892, in fact, this drawing was behind the times. Literacy tests and poll taxes were beginning to disfranchise blacks with less menace and more likelihood of evading the constitutional requirement (note the sign behind the Klansmen) under the Fifteenth Amendment that the right to vote not be denied "on account of race, color, or previous condition of servitude." Museum of American Political Life.

race-baiter (see Comparing American Voices, "'Negro Domination!'" pp. 600–601). In South Carolina "Pitchfork" Ben Tillman, more of a mainstream Democratic politician, adeptly manipulated images of white manhood. What bound southerners together, no matter their class, was their sturdy independence, their defense of the virtue of white womanhood, and their resistance to outside meddling in southern affairs. A U.S. senator for many years, Tillman was as fiery as Tom Watson at condemning blacks as "an ignorant and debased and debauched race."

The Ascendancy of Jim Crow. A brand of white supremacy emerged that was more virulent than anything blacks had faced since Reconstruction. The color line, hitherto incomplete, became rigid and comprehensive. Segregated seating in trains, first adopted in the late 1880s, provided a precedent for the legal separation of the races. The enforcing legislation, known as **Jim Crow** laws, soon applied to every type of public facility — restaurants, hotels, streetcars, even cemeteries. In the 1890s the South became a region fully segregated by law for the first time.

The U.S. Supreme Court soon ratified the South's decision. In *Plessy v. Ferguson* (1896), the Court ruled that segregation was not discriminatory — that is, it did not violate the Fourteenth Amendment — provided that blacks received accommodations equal to those of whites. The "separate but equal" doctrine ignored the realities of southern life. Segregated facilities were rarely if ever "equal" in any material sense, and segregation was itself intended to underscore the inferiority of blacks (as was also the case in the Southwest, where Hispanics and Asian were segregated under cover of *Plessy v. Ferguson*). With a similar disregard for reality, the Supreme Court in *Williams v. Mississippi* (1898) validated the disfranchising devices of the southern states on the grounds that, if race was not a specified criterion for disfranchisement, the rights of blacks to vote under the Fifteenth Amendment were not being violated.

The Case of Grimes County. What this counterrevolution meant is perhaps best captured locally by the events in Grimes County, a cotton-growing area in east Texas, where African Americans composed more

Miss Ida B. Wells

In 1887 Ida Wells (Wells-Barnett after she married in 1895) was thrown bodily from a train in Tennessee for refusing to vacate her seat in a section reserved for whites, launching her into a lifelong crusade for racial justice. Her mission was to expose the evil of lynching in the South. This portrait is from the title page of a pamphlet she published in 1892 entitled, "Southern Horrors. Lynch Law in All Its Phases."
Miriam and Ira D. Wallach Division of Art, Prints and Photographs, The New York Public Library. Astor, Lenox and Tilden Foundations.

than half of the population. They kept the local Republican Party going after Reconstruction and regularly sent black representatives to the Texas legislature during the 1870s and 1880s. More remarkably, the local Populist Party that appeared among white farmers proved immune to Democrats' taunts of "black rule." A Populist-Republican coalition swept the county elections in 1896 and 1898, a surprising remnant of the southern Populist movement.

In 1899 defeated Democratic candidates and prominent citizens organized the secret White Man's Union. Blacks were forcibly prevented from voting in town elections that year. The two most important black leaders were shot down in cold blood. Night riders terrorized both white Populists and black Republicans. When the Populist sheriff proved incapable of enforcing the law, the game was up. Reconstituted as the White Man's Party, the Union became the local Democratic Party in a new guise. The Democrats carried Grimes County by an overwhelming vote in 1900. The day after the election, gunmen laid siege to the sheriff's office. They killed his brother and a friend and drove him, badly wounded, out of the county forever.

The White Man's Party ruled Grimes County for the next fifty years. The whole episode was the handiwork of the county's "best citizens," suggesting how respectable terror had become in the service of white supremacy. Grimes County, as a leading citizen grimly said, intended to "force the African to keep his place." After Populism was crushed in that corner of Texas, blacks could survive only if they stayed out of politics and avoided trouble with whites.

Like the blacks of Grimes County, southern blacks in many places resisted as best they could. When Georgia adopted the first Jim Crow law applying to streetcars in 1891, Atlanta blacks declared a boycott, and over the next fifteen years blacks boycotted segregated streetcars in at least twenty-five cities. "Do not trample on our pride by being 'jim crowed,'" the Savannah *Tribune* urged its readers: "Walk!" Ida Wells-Barnett emerged as the most outspoken black crusader against lynching, so enraging the Memphis white community by the editorials in her newspaper, *Free Speech*, that she was forced in 1892 to leave the city.

Some blacks were drawn to the Back-to-Africa movement, abandoning all hope that they would ever find justice in America. But for most Africa was not a real choice. They were Americans, and they had to bend to the raging forces of racism and find a way to survive.

▶ The Redeemers imposed a system of one-party rule on the South after Reconstruction. Why was this system initially vulnerable to attack?

▶ How do you explain the disfranchisement of southern blacks during the 1890s? What measures did whites enact to prevent blacks from voting?

▶ What was "Jim Crow"? Would the answer to question 1 serve also to explain Jim Crow's establishment in the South?

The Crisis of American Politics: The 1890s

Populism was a catalyst for political crisis not only in the South but also across the entire nation. But while in the South the result was preservation of

COMPARING AMERICAN VOICES

"Negro Domination!"

The title of this feature—Comparing American Voices—does not always mean comparing what different Americans have said. It's also possible, taking a chronological approach, to compare what a single individual said at different times. In the two documents that follow, the author is Tom Watson, the fiery Georgia Populist. In both, he was addressing the "everlasting and overshadowing Negro Question" that he thought distinguished the South and obstructed the radical, class-based politics he advocated. The two documents offer diametrically opposite answers and thereby illuminate how it came to be that the race-obsessed South disfranchised its black population.

TOM WATSON: 1892

In 1892, when Watson wrote the essay below, he had recently been elected to Congress on a third-party ticket and had high hopes that Populism would break the grip of the conservative Democrats and bring a new day for the South's oppressed tenant farmers, black and white.

The white tenant lives adjoining the colored tenant. Their houses are almost equally destitute of comforts. Their living is confined to bare necessities.... They pay the same enormous prices for farm supplies. Christmas finds them both without any satisfactory return for a year's toil. Dull and heavy and unhappy, they both start the plows again when "New Year's" passes.

Now the People's Party says to these two men, "You are kept apart that you may be separately fleeced of your earnings. You are made to hate each other because upon that hatred is rested the keystone of the arch of financial despotism which enslaves you both. You are deceived and blinded that you may not see how this race antagonism perpetuates a monetary system which beggars both."

This is so obviously true it is no wonder both these unhappy laborers stop to listen. No wonder they begin to realize that no change of law can benefit the white tenant which does not benefit the black one likewise; that no system which now does injustice to one of them can fail to injure both. Their every material interest is identical. The moment this becomes a conviction, mere selfishness, the mere desire to better their conditions, escape onerous taxes, avoid usurious charges, lighten their rents, or change their precarious tenements into smiling, happy homes, will drive these two men together, just as their mutual inflamed prejudices now drive them apart.

... Why should the colored man always be taught that the white man of his neighborhood hates him, while a Northern man, who taxes every rag on his back, loves him? Why should not my tenant come to regard me as his friend rather than the manufacturer who plunders us both? Why should we perpetuate a policy which drives the black man into the arms of the Northern politician?

... To the emasculated individual who cries "Negro supremacy!" there is little to be said.... Not being prepared to make any such admission in favor of any race the sun ever shone on, I have no words which can portray my contempt for the white men, Anglo-Saxons, who can knock their knees together, and through their chattering teeth and pale lips admit they are afraid the Negroes will "dominate us." The question of social equality does not enter into the calculation at all. That is a thing each citizen decides for himself. No statute ever yet drew the latch of the humblest home—or ever will. Each citizen regulates his visiting list—and always will.

The conclusion, then, seems to me this: They will become political allies, and neither can injure the one without weakening both. It will be in the interest of both that each should have justice. And on these broad lines of mutual interest, mutual forbearance, and mutual support the present will be made the stepping-stone to future peace and prosperity.

SOURCE: "The Negro Question in the South," *Arena*, vol. VI (1892), in *A More Perfect Union: Documents in U.S. History*, 2 vols., ed. Paul F. Boller and Ronald Story (Boston: Houghton Mifflin, 1984), 2: 83–85.

TOM WATSON: 1904

After the 1896 election and the collapse of Populism, Watson withdrew from politics. In 1904, however, he returned to head a Populist presidential ticket, in part as a protest against the rightward drift of the national Democratic Party. Although he had no illusions about how he would do nationwide (he got a total of 117,000 votes), he was chagrined by his poor showing in his native state, which he attributed to the race-baiting of the conservative Democratic machine. Two weeks later, on November 19, 1904, he delivered the following address to a partisan crowd at the courthouse in Thomson, Georgia.*

There never was a time when the greedy corporations, the soulless combinations of sordid wealth, has so nearly got the industrial world by the throat.... There never was a time when the avarice of the few so monopolized the wealth created by the laborers of this republic as to-day....

The time has come when we must act for the best interests for our homes and firesides. Negroes may call themselves Republicans, or call themselves Democrats, or call themselves Methodists, or call themselves Baptists, but when you touch them on any subject that concerns their color they are all just negroes. They run together, they stand as one man representing the colored race. So with the whites in the South.... When any question comes up in the South that concerns us as a race then every distinction falls down and we stand together. ... Every man ought to know that; every man does know it.

And yet we allow these small politicians [to frighten] us, year after year, into voting for men whom we know nothing about and for a platform we utterly detest.... Our task from the beginning has been peculiarly difficult in the South because of the belief if the white people divide the negro would be the balance of power and would rule the South. That has been our stumbling block.... Now, no Southern man wanted negro domination ... no Anglo-Saxon man anywhere ever wanted it. No. The white race has made civilization what it is, and the white race intends to keep it what it is. We told those colored people whenever we spoke to them that "when we took hold of you, you were savages from Africa; we taught you everything you know.... You have had the best example of civilization and to the extent that you have copied it you have become good citizens, farmers, carpenters, black-smiths — Christians, because our God has become your God." And we said to those people, "Follow us and we will guarantee you" — what? Social equality? No. Political equality? — No. We said, "We will give you equality as a citizen, under the law that will protect your life, your limb, your property, your home and your fire-side, just as it protects ours." That is as far as we ever went, and I am willing to go that far to-day. [Applause.] And the man who does not believe in going that far is not a man who believes in Jeffersonian democracy. [Applause.]

But the Democrats said, "You will divide the white people and the negro will have the balance of power. We will have negro domination." ... We wept; and bowed down in sack-cloth and ashes. That is all we could do. Our Party was swept out of existence. Then what? The Southern states began to disfranchise the negro, and in almost every state the negro has been taken out of politics. And why hasn't he been taken out of politics in Georgia? ... [The Democrats] were using the fear of negro domination to hold your votes.... Now what? What! They were afraid of the negro, weren't they? They were afraid of the negro and negro domination (They say) and here they had had almost a generation to put him out but he is in as big as life. The negro is an old sinner 364 days of the year, but the 365th, which is on election day, he is "sugar in the gourd." [Applause, laughter and cheers.]

At the very opening of this campaign, I threw at their feet the challenge — "If you are earnest in what you say, if you are afraid of the negro, if you are really afraid of the negro, you miserable coward [applause], if you really mean it, then we are ready to help you out of your scrape, you pusillanimous political coward, we will come up and help you pass any kind of law that you yourself say was necessary to keep the white man on top." [Applause and cheers.]

*NOTE: In 1907, with Watson's backing, the Georgia legislature passed a law disfranchising blacks.

SOURCE: "Speech of Hon. Thomas E. Watson, Delivered at Thomson, Ga., November 19th, 1904," unpublished ms., Watson Papers, University of North Carolina. Printed by permission.

ANALYZING THE EVIDENCE

- In his 1904 speech, Watson claimed that his views on black participation in politics had not changed. Is that correct?

- Do you think Watson became more of a racist between 1892 and 1904? In what ways?

- The "Negro Question" had to do with the relations between the races. In what ways did Watson redefine those relations between 1892 and 1904?

one-party rule, in national politics the result was a revitalized two-party system.

Ever since Reconstruction, national politics had been stalemated by the even balance between the parties. In the late 1880s the equilibrium began to break down. Benjamin Harrison's election to the presidency in 1888 was the last close election of the era (Democrat Grover Cleveland actually got a larger popular vote). Thereafter, the tide turned against the Republicans, saddled by the lackluster Harrison administration and by Democratic charges that the protectionist McKinley Tariff of 1890 was a giveaway to the business interests. That year Democrats took the House of Representatives decisively and won a number of governorships in normally Republican states. In 1892 Cleveland regained the presidency by the largest margin in twenty years (the only president to be elected to two nonconsecutive terms).

Had everything else remained equal, the events of 1890 and 1892 might have initiated an era of Democratic supremacy. But everything else did not remain equal. By the time of Cleveland's inauguration, farm foreclosures and railroad bankruptcies signaled economic trouble. On May 3, 1893, the stock market crashed. In Chicago 100,000 jobless workers walked the streets; nationwide the unemployment rate soared above 20 percent.

As depression set in, which party would prevail—and on what platform—became an open question. The first challenge to the status quo arrived from the West and South, where falling grain and cotton prices were devastating farmers.

The Populist Revolt

Farmers were of necessity joiners. They needed organization to overcome their social isolation and provide economic services—hence the appeal of the Granger movement, which had spread across the Midwest after 1867 (see Chapter 16), and after the Grange's decline, the emergence of a new movement of farmers' alliances in many rural districts. From diffuse organizational beginnings, two dominant groups emerged. One was the Farmers' Alliance of the Northwest, which was confined mainly to the midwestern states. More dynamic was the National (or Southern) Farmers' Alliance, which in the mid-1880s spread rapidly from Texas onto the Great Plains and eastward into the cotton South as "traveling lecturers" extolled the virtues of cooperative activity and reminded farmers of "their obligation to stand as a great conservative body against the encroachments of monopolies and . . . the growing corruption of wealth and power." While thus recapitulating Granger resentment against railroads and merchants, the alliances initially resisted the temptation of third-party politics, preferring instead self-help and institution-building.

A prime example was the Texas Exchange, a huge cooperative that marketed the crops of cotton farmers and provided them with cheap loans. When cotton prices fell in 1891, the Texas Exchange failed. The Texas Alliance then proposed a new scheme—a **"subtreasury" system**, which would enable farmers to store their crops in public warehouses and borrow against the unsold crops from a public fund until the cotton could be profitably sold. The subtreasury plan provided the same credit and marketing functions as the defunct Texas Exchange, but with a crucial difference: The federal government would be the underwriter. When the Democratic Party declared the scheme too radical, the Texas Alliance decided to strike out in politics independently.

These events in Texas revealed, with special clarity, a process of politicization that rippled through the Alliance movement. Rebuffed by the major parties, Alliance men more or less reluctantly abandoned their Democratic and Republican allegiances, and as state Alliances grew stronger and more impatient, they began to field independent slates. The confidence gained at the state level led to the formation of the national People's (Populist) Party in 1892. In the elections that year, with the veteran antimonopoly campaigner James B. Weaver as their presidential candidate, the Populists captured a million votes and carried four western states (Map 19.3). For the first

Map 19.3 The Heyday of Western Populism, 1892

This map shows the percentage of the popular vote won by James B. Weaver, the People's Party candidate, in the presidential election of 1892. Except in California and Montana, the Populists won broad support across the West and genuinely threatened the established parties in that region.

Mary Elizabeth Lease

As a political movement the Populists were short on cash and organization but long on rank-and-file zeal and tub-thumping oratory. No one was more rousing on the stump than Mary Elizabeth Lease, who came from a Kansas homestead and pulled no punches. "What you farmers need to do," she proclaimed in her speeches, "is to raise less corn and more Hell!" The photograph shows her as a nineteenth-century lady. The cartoonist's drawings show her in action. Kansas Historical Society.

MRS. MARY ELIZABETH LEASE AS SHE APPEARED IN 1895 WHEN SHE WAS AT THE HEIGHT OF HER POLITICAL ACTIVITIES IN KANSAS.

time agrarian protest truly challenged the national two-party system.

One Populist advantage was the many women in the movement. They had gotten in on the ground floor, when the alliances were just networks of local clubs that had formed for largely social purposes. The women had come along with their men. Although prominent as speakers and lecturers, women rarely became alliance leaders, and their role diminished with the shift into politics. In deference to the southern wing, the Populist platform was silent on woman suffrage. Still, neither Democrats nor Republicans would have countenanced a spokeswoman such as the fiery Mary Elizabeth Lease, who became famous for calling on farmers "to raise less corn and more hell." The profanity might have been a reporter's invention, but the passion was all hers. Mrs. Lease insisted just as strenuously on Populism's "grand and holy mission . . . to place the mothers of this nation on an equality with the fathers."

Populist Ideology. "There are but two sides," proclaimed a Populist manifesto. "On the one side are the allied hosts of monopolies, the money power, great trusts and railroad corporations. . . . On the other are the farmers, laborers, merchants and all the people who produce wealth. . . . Between these two there is no middle ground."

By this reasoning farmers and workers formed a single producer class. The claim was not merely rhetorical. The national platform contained strong labor planks, and party leaders earnestly sought union support. Texas railroad workers and Colorado miners cooperated with the farmers' alliances, got their support in strikes, and actively participated in forming state Populist parties. The attraction of Populism, in fact, pulled the labor movement to the left. Inside the American Federation of Labor Samuel Gompers briefly lost control to a faction that advocated independent labor politics in alliance with the Populists. The center of this agitation was Chicago, where the radical reformer Henry Demarest Lloyd envisioned a farmer-labor movement that might actually prevail in America.

In its explicit class appeal — in recognizing that "the irrepressible conflict between capital and labor is upon us" — Populism parted company from the two mainstream parties. Indeed, it had the makings of an American version — a farmer-labor version — of the social democratic parties emerging in Europe at this time, although Populism lacked the Marxist component. But, like the European parties, it favored a strong state. In the words of the Populist platform: "We believe that the power of government — in other words, of the people — should be expanded as rapidly and as far as the good sense of an intelligent people and the teachings of experience shall justify, to the end that oppression, injustice and poverty should eventually cease in the land." Spokesmen such as Lorenzo Dow

Lewelling, Populist governor of Kansas, considered it to be "the business of the government to make it possible to live and sustain the life of my family."

At the founding Omaha convention in 1892, Populists called for nationalization of the railroads and communications; protection of the land, including natural resources, from monopoly and foreign ownership; a graduated income tax; and the free and unlimited coinage of silver. From this array of issues, the last—free silver—emerged as the cardinal demand of the Populist Party.

Free Silver. Reeling from rock-bottom prices, embattled farmers gravitated in the early 1890s to the unlimited coinage of silver because they hoped that an increase in the money supply would raise farm prices and give them some relief. In addition, the party's slim resources would be fattened by hefty contributions from silver-mining interests. Wealthy mine operators, scornful though they might be of Populist radicalism, yearned for the day when the government would buy at a premium all the silver they could produce.

Free silver triggered a debate for the soul of the Populist Party. Henry Demarest Lloyd voiced labor's objection. He called free silver the "cowbird of reform," stealing in and taking over the nest that others had built. Free silver, if it became the defining party issue, would undercut the broader Populist program and alienate wage earners, who had no enthusiasm for inflationary measures. The bread-and-butter appeal of free silver, however, was simply too great.

But once Populists made that choice, they fatally compromised their party's identity as an independent movement. For free silver was not an issue over which Populists held a monopoly. It was, on the contrary, a question at the very center of mainstream American politics.

Money and Politics

In a rapidly developing economy, the money supply is bound to be a hotly contested issue. The volume of money has to increase rapidly enough to meet the economy's needs or growth will be stifled. How fast the money supply should grow, however, is a divisive question. More money in circulation inflates prices and reduces the real cost of borrowing, to the benefit of debtors and commodity producers. The "sound money" people—creditors, individuals on fixed incomes, established businessmen—have an opposite interest.

Before the Civil War the main source of the nation's money supply had been state-chartered banks, several thousand of them, all issuing banknotes to borrowers that then circulated as money. The economy's need for money was amply met by the state banks, although the soundness of the banknotes—the ability of the issuing banks to stand behind their notes and redeem them at face value—was always uncertain. This freewheeling activity was sharply curtailed by the U.S. Banking Act of 1863, which prohibited state banks from issuing banknotes not backed by U.S. government bonds. However, because the Lincoln administration was printing paper money—**greenbacks**—to pay for the Civil War, in effect the U.S. Treasury replaced the state banks as the source of easy money.

Once the war ended, the question became: Should the federal government continue in that role? No, argued the sound money interests. Washington had no business printing paper money and should restore the traditional practice of limiting the national currency to the amount of *specie*—gold and silver—held by the U.S. Treasury. The issue was hotly contested for a decade, but in 1875 the sound money interests prevailed, and the circulation of greenbacks as legal tender—that is, backed by nothing more than the good faith of the federal government—came to an end. With state banknotes also in short supply, the country entered an era of chronic **deflation**.

This was the context out of which the silver question emerged. Since the colonial era, both gold and silver had served as specie, but as the supply of silver tightened, it became more valuable as metal than as money and in 1873 was officially dropped as a medium of exchange. Soon silver mining in the West surged, and the price of silver suddenly fell. The greenback supporters began agitating for a resumption of the bimetallic policy. If the federal government resumed buying at the fixed ratio prevailing before 1873—16 ounces of silver equaling 1 ounce of gold—silver would flow into the treasury and greatly expand the volume of money.

With so much at stake for so many people, the currency question became one of the staples of post-Reconstruction politics. Twice the pro-silver coalition in Congress won modest victories. First, the Bland-Allison Act of 1878 required the U.S. Treasury to purchase and coin between $2 million and $4 million worth of silver each month. Then, in the more sweeping Sherman Silver Purchase Act of 1890, an additional 4.5 million ounces of silver bullion was to be purchased monthly, to serve as the basis for new issues of U.S. Treasury notes.

These legislative battles, although hard fought, cut across party lines, in the familiar fashion of post-Reconstruction politics. But in the early 1890s, as hard times set in, silver suddenly became a defining issue between the parties; in particular, it radicalized the Democrats.

Climax: The Election of 1896

As the party in power, the Democrats bore the brunt of responsibility for the economic crisis. Any Democratic president would have been hard pressed, but the man who actually held the job, Grover Cleveland, could hardly have made a bigger hash of it. When jobless marchers — the so-called Coxey's army — arrived in Washington in 1894 to demand federal relief, Cleveland dispersed them forcibly and arrested their leader, Jacob S. Coxey, for trespassing on the Capitol grounds. Cleveland's brutal handling of the Pullman strike (see Chapter 17) further alienated the labor vote. Nor did he live up to his reputation as a tariff reformer. Cleveland lost control of the battle when the protectionist McKinley Tariff of 1890 came up for revision in Congress. The resulting Wilson-Gorman Tariff of 1894, which Cleveland allowed to pass into law without his signature, caved in to special interests and left many rates unchanged.

Cleveland and Free Silver. Most disastrous, however, was Cleveland's stand on the silver question. Cleveland was a committed sound-money man. Nothing that happened after the depression set in — not collapsing prices, not the suffering of farmers, not the groundswell of support for free silver within his own party — budged Cleveland. Economic pressures, in fact, soon forced him to abandon a silver-based currency altogether. With the government's gold reserves dwindling, Cleveland persuaded Congress in 1893 to repeal the Sherman Silver Purchase Act, in effect sacrificing the country's painfully crafted program for maintaining a limited bimetallic policy. Then, as his administration's problems deepened, Cleveland turned in 1895 to a syndicate of private bankers led by J. P. Morgan to arrange the gold purchases needed to replenish the treasury's depleted reserves. The administration's secret negotiations with Wall Street, once discovered, enraged Democrats and completed Cleveland's isolation from his party.

William Jennings Bryan and the Cross of Gold. At their Chicago convention in 1896, the Democrats repudiated Cleveland and turned left. The leader of the triumphant silver Democrats was William Jennings Bryan of Nebraska. Bryan was a political phenomenon. Only thirty-six years old, he had already served two terms in Congress and had become a passionate advocate of free silver. Bryan, remarked the journalist Frederic Howe, was "preeminently an evangelist," whose zeal sprang from "the Western self-righteous missionary mind." With biblical fervor Bryan swept up his audiences when he joined the debate on free silver at the

The Candidates, 1896

The 1896 presidential campaign marked one small step in the technology of electioneering — the introduction of the celluloid campaign button, which a party supporter could pin on his lapel. It is doubtful, however, that this innovation made any difference in the outcome of the election. Collection of Janice L. and David J. Frent.

Democratic convention. He locked up the presidential nomination with a stirring attack on the gold standard: "You shall not press down upon the brow of labor this crown of thorns, you shall not crucify mankind on a cross of gold."

Bryan's nomination meant that the Democrats had become the party of free silver; his "cross of gold" speech meant that the money question would be a national crusade. No one could be neutral on this defining issue. Silver Republicans bolted their party; gold Democrats went for a splinter Democratic ticket or supported the Republican Party; even the Prohibition Party split into gold and silver wings. The Populists, meeting after the Democratic convention, accepted Bryan as their candidate. The free-silver issue had become so vital that they could not do otherwise. Although they nominated their own vice presidential candidate, Tom Watson of Georgia, the Populists found themselves for all practical purposes absorbed into the Democratic silver campaign.

The Republicans took up the challenge. Their party leader was the wealthy Cleveland iron maker Mark Hanna, a brilliant political manager and an exponent of the new industrial capitalism. Hanna orchestrated an unprecedented money-raising campaign among America's corporate interests. His candidate, William McKinley of Ohio, personified the virtues of Republicanism, standing solidly for high tariffs, sound money, and prosperity. While Bryan broke with tradition and crisscrossed the country by railroad in a furious whistle-stop campaign, the dignified McKinley received delegations at his home in Canton, Ohio. Bryan orated with moral fervor; McKinley talked of economic progress and a full dinner pail.

Not since 1860 had the United States witnessed so hard-fought an election over such high stakes. For

The Cross of Gold

Bryan's Cross of Gold speech was one of the great orations in American political history. Republican critics, however, were not so keen on it and did their best to puncture its Christian aura. In this cartoon by Grant Hamilton, Bryan is accused of cynically using the cross and crown of thorns for political purposes. What Bryan's really up to, the cartoon suggests, is revolution, hence in the background a pillaged city and the little man, right out of the French revolution. Library of Congress/Picture Research Consultants & Archives.

THE SACRILEGIOUS CANDIDATE.
No man who drags into the dust the most sacred symbols of the Christian world is fit to be president of the United States.

misfits who have almost nothing in common but opposition to the existing order and institutions."

Though little noticed at the time, ethnocultural influences figured strongly in the campaign. In their bid for electoral dominance in 1890 and 1892, the Democrats had turned to their advantage the Republican reputation as the party of temperance and religious intolerance. Now, in 1896, the Republicans beat a strategic retreat from the politics of morality. McKinley himself had represented an ethnically mixed district of northeastern Ohio. In appealing to his immigrant and working-class constituents, he had learned the art of easy tolerance, expressed in his words, "Live and let live." Of the two candidates, the prairie orator Bryan, with his biblical language and moral righteousness, presented the more alien image to traditional Democratic voters in the big cities.

McKinley won handily, with 271 electoral votes to Bryan's 176. He kept the ground Republicans had regained in the 1894 midterm elections and pushed into Democratic strongholds, especially in the cities. Boston, New York, Chicago, and Minneapolis, all taken by Cleveland in 1892, went for McKinley in 1896. Bryan ran strongly only in the South, in silver-mining states, and in the Populist West (Map 19.4). But the gains his evangelical style brought him in some Republican rural areas did not compensate for his losses in traditionally Democratic urban districts.

The paralyzing equilibrium in American politics ended in 1896. The Republicans skillfully turned both economic and cultural challenges to their advantage. They persuaded the nation that they were the party of prosperity, and they persuaded many traditionally Democratic urban voters that they were sympathetic to ethnic diversity. In so doing the Republicans became the nation's majority party, notwithstanding the Demcratic lock on the South. In 1896, too, electoral politics regained its place as an arena for national debate, setting the stage for the reform politics of the Progressive era.

Map 19.4 Presidential Elections of 1892 and 1896

In the 1890s the age of political stalemate came to an end. Students should compare the 1892 map with Map 19.1 (p. 586) and note especially Cleveland's breakthrough in the normally Republican states of the upper Midwest. In 1896 the pendulum swung in the opposite direction, with McKinley's consolidation of Republican control over the Northeast and Midwest far overbalancing the Democratic advances in the thinly populated western states. The 1896 election marked the beginning of forty years of Republican dominance in national politics.

Candidate	Electoral Vote	Popular Vote	Percent of Popular Vote
Grover Cleveland (Democrat)	277	5,555,426	46.1
Benjamin Harrison (Republican)	145	5,182,690	43.0
James B. Weaver (Populist)	22	1,029,846	8.5
Minor parties	—	285,297	2.3

Candidate	Electoral Vote	Popular Vote	Percent of Popular Vote
William McKinley (Republican)	271	7,102,246	51.1
William J. Bryan (Democrat)	176	6,492,559	47.7

the middle class, sound money stood symbolically for the soundness of the social order. With jobless workers tramping the streets and bankrupt farmers up in arms, Bryan's fervent assault on the gold standard struck fear in many hearts. Republicans denounced the Democratic platform as "revolutionary and anarchistic" and Bryan's supporters as "social

▶ Farmers, like other Americans, had strong ties to the established parties, yet many of them became Populists anyway. Why was that?

▶ Cleveland is rated as a pretty good president for his first term and a bad one for his second term. How do you explain that reversal?

▶ It would be hard to imagine American voters today getting excited about the money supply (and hard, no doubt, for students to get excited about it in this chapter). So how do you account for the fact that free silver was the hot topic of the 1896 election?

SUMMARY

This chapter is about late nineteenth-century politics. We start with the period 1877–1892, when the great politics of sectional crisis gave way to an age of political quiescence. Except for the judicial branch, governmental institutions were weak, the national parties avoided big issues, and laissez-faire was the prevailing philosophy. And yet, while little seemed at stake, politics engendered extraordinarily high levels of popular participation. This was partly because of the entertainment value, but more importantly because politics was the arena in which the nation's ethnic and religious conflicts were fought out and because organizationally the parties were strongly developed and highly active. Finally, while still lacking voting rights, women carved out for themselves, in their guise as defenders of the family, an increasingly prominent place in politics.

In the South, post-Reconstruction politics followed a different, less settled course because the emergent one-party system was resisted by poor whites and Republican blacks. Biracial southern Populism flared briefly in the late 1880s and then failed, triggering a grim reaction that disfranchised African Americans, completed a rigid segregation system, and let loose a terrible cycle of racial hatred and violence. Blacks resisted, but had to bend to overwhelming power of white supremacy.

In this chapter's final section, we return to national politics, which in the 1890s again became an arena of principled debate. Galvanized by the rise of Populism, the Democratic Party committed itself to free silver, sidetracking the last great third-party challenge to mainstream politics and making the election of 1896 a moment of truth for the major parties. The Republicans won decisively, ending a paralyzing stalemate and assuring themselves of political dominance for the next thirty years.

Connections: Politics

The immediate antecedents of the political history covered by this chapter are in the sectional crisis of the 1850s (Chapter 13) and the Reconstruction era (Chapter 15), when fundamental questions of Union and slavery were resolved. In the aftermath, politics took a breather and, as we say in the part opener (p. 485):

> The major parties remained robust only because they exploited a culture of popular participation and embraced the ethnic and religious identities of their constituencies.

When the Populist revolt broke out in the early 1890s, the Democrats took the opportunity to drive African Americans out of politics and consolidate their grip on the South, while the Republicans carried the 1896 election and became the dominant national party. It seemed as if politics would then revert to the holding pattern of the 1880s, but instead, as we will see in Chapter 20, the demand for reform took hold and the two parties—first the Republicans, then the Democrats—embraced progressive politics. Although that impulse seemed exhausted after World War I (Chapter 23), in fact the Progressives had set the stage for the New Deal (Chapter 24).

CHAPTER REVIEW QUESTIONS

➤ In light of James Bryce's complaint about the triviality of American politics (see chapter opener), how do you account for the fact that the voter turnout in the 1880s was the highest in our history?

➤ How important do you think race was in explaining the failure of southern Populism?

➤ Why do historians regard the election of 1896 as one of the decisive elections in American history?

TIMELINE

1874	Woman's Christian Temperance Union founded
1877	Rutherford B. Hayes inaugurated as president, marking end of Reconstruction
1881	President James A. Garfield assassinated
1883	Pendleton Civil Service Act
1884	Mugwump reformers leave Republican Party to support Grover Cleveland, first Democrat-elected president since 1856
1887	Florida adopts first law segregating railroad travel
1888	James Bryce's *The American Commonwealth*
1890	McKinley Tariff
	Democrats sweep congressional elections, inaugurating brief era of Democratic Party dominance
	Mississippi becomes first state to adopt literacy test to disfranchise blacks
1892	People's (Populist) Party founded
1893	Panic of 1893 leads to national depression
	Repeal of Sherman Silver Purchase Act (1890)
1894	"Coxey's army" of unemployed fails to win federal relief
1896	Election of Republican president William McKinley; free-silver campaign crushed
	Plessy v. Ferguson upholds constitutionality of "separate but equal" segregation

FOR FURTHER EXPLORATION

The literature on late-nineteenth-century politics is a topic on which historians have had a field day. On the ideological underpinnings, an older book by Robert G. McCloskey, *American Conservatism in the Age of Enterprise* (1951), still retains its freshness. Mark Wahlgren, *Rum, Romanism & Rebellion: The Making of a President, 1884* (2000), is a fresh analysis of the first phase of post-Reconstruction national politics. The mass appeal of Gilded Age politics is incisively explored in Michael E. McGerr, *The Decline of Popular Politics: The American North, 1865–1928* (1986). Alexander Keyssar, *The Right to Vote: The Contested History of Democracy in the United States* (2000), is illuminating on the conservative assault on voting rights in this period. Kathryn Kish Sklar, *Florence Kelley and the Nation's Work* (1995), traces the emergence of women's political culture through the life of a leading reformer. Rebecca Edwards, *Angels in the Machinery: Gender in American Party Politics* (1997), reveals women's unexpectedly large role within the main parties. On southern politics the seminal book is C. Vann Woodward, *Origins of the New South, 1877–1913* (1951), which still defines the terms of discussion among historians. The most far-reaching revision is Edward L. Ayers, *The Promise of the New South* (1992). The process of sectional reconciliation is imaginatively treated in David W. Blight, *Race and Reunion: The Civil War in Memory* (2001). The most recent treatment of disfranchisement is Michael Perman, *Struggle for Mastery: Disfranchisement in the South, 1888–1908* (2001). Richard D. Hofstadter, *The Age of Reform* (1955), stresses the darker side of Populism, in which intolerance and paranoia figure heavily. Hofstadter's thesis, which once dominated debate among historians, has given way to a more positive assessment. The key book here is Lawrence Goodwyn, *Democratic Promise: The Populist Moment* (1976), which argues that Populism was a broadly based response to industrial capitalism. Peter H. Argesinger, *The Limits of Agrarian Radicalism* (1995), stresses the effectiveness of the party status quo to frustrate western Populism. Michael Kazin, *The Populist Persuasion* (1995), describes how the language of Populism entered the discourse of mainstream American politics. Much information on Gilded Age presidents can be found at the Web site **americanpresident.org/presidentialresources.htm**.

TEST YOUR KNOWLEDGE

To assess your command of the material in this chapter, see the Online Study Guide at **bedfordstmartins.com/henretta**.

For Web sites, images, and documents related to topics and places in this chapter, visit **bedfordstmartins.com/makehistory**.

20 The Progressive Era
1900–1914

On the face of it, the political tumult of the 1890s ended with William McKinley's election in 1896. After the bitter struggle over free silver, the victorious Republicans had no stomach for crusades. The main thing, as party chief Mark Hanna said, was to "stand pat and continue Republican prosperity."

Yet beneath the surface a deep unease had set in. Hard times had unveiled truths not acknowledged in better days—that a frightening chasm, for example, had opened between America's social classes. In Richard Olney's view the great Pullman strike of 1894 had brought the country "to the ragged edge of anarchy." As Cleveland's attorney general, it had been Olney's job to crush the strike (see Chapter 17). But he took little joy from his success. He asked himself, rather, how such repressive actions might be avoided in the future. His answer was that the government should regulate labor relations on the railroads so that crippling rail strikes would not happen. As a first step toward Olney's goal, Congress adopted the Erdman Railway Mediation Act in 1898. In such ways did the crisis of the 1890s turn the nation's thinking to reform.

The problems themselves, however, were of much older origin. For many decades Americans had been absorbed in building the world's most advanced industrial economy. At the beginning of the twentieth century, they paused, looked around, and began to add up the costs—a frightening concentration of corporate power, a rebellious working class, misery in the cities, and the corruption of machine politics.

The Course of Reform
The Middle-Class Impulse
Progressive Ideas
Women Progressives
Urban Liberalism
Reforming Politics
Racism and Reform

Progressivism and National Politics
The Making of a Progressive President
Regulating the Marketplace
The Fracturing of Republican Progressivism
Woodrow Wilson and the New Freedom

Summary
Connections: Politics

◀ **Reba Owen, Settlement-House Worker**

The settlement house was a hallmark of progressive America. Columbus, Ohio, had five, including Godman Guild House, where Reba Owen served as a visiting nurse, tending the pregnant mothers and children of the neighborhood. LifeCare Alliance/Courtesy, Ohio Historical Society.

Now, with the strife-torn 1890s behind them, reform became an absorbing concern of many Americans. It was as if social awareness reached a critical mass around 1900 and set reform activity going as a major, self-sustaining phenomenon. For this reason the years from 1900 to World War I have come to be known as the Progressive era.

The Course of Reform

Historians have sometimes spoken of a progressive "movement." But progressivism was not a movement in any meaningful sense. There was no agreed-upon agenda, no unifying organization. Both the Republican and Democratic parties had progressive wings. And, at different times and places, different social groups became active. The term *progressivism* describes a widespread, many-sided effort after 1900 to build a better society. And yet, if progressivism was many-sided, it did have a center, and that was the urban middle class.

The Middle-Class Impulse

In 1889 Jane Addams and Ellen Gates Starr established Hull House on Chicago's West Side after visiting Toynbee Hall in the London slums. Flanked by saloons and "horrid little houses," in a neighborhood of mainly Italian immigrants, the dilapidated mansion that they called Hull House was the model for scores of settlement houses that sprang up in the ghettos of the nation's cities, serving as community centers and spark plugs for neighborhood betterment. At the Henry Street Settlement in New York City, Lillian Wald made visiting nurses a major service. Mary McDowell, head of the University of Chicago Settlement, installed a bathhouse, a children's playground, and a citizenship school for immigrants.

The settlement house was a hallmark of social progressivism, and for Jane Addams it meant a lifetime in ugly surroundings, endlessly battling for garbage removal, playgrounds, better street lighting, and police protection.

Why would she have made that choice? Addams was a daughter of the middle class. She might have lived a life of ease and personal cultivation, and that indeed was what her prosperous parents had intended for her when they sent her off to Rockford College. But Addams came home in 1881 sad and unfulfilled, feeling "simply smothered and sickened by advantages." Hull House became her salvation, enabling her to "begin with however small a group to accomplish and to live." In retrospect, she realized that hers was not an individual crisis, but a crisis that afflicted her entire generation. In a famous essay, she spoke of the "subjective necessity" of the settlement house. Addams meant that it was as much for the young middle-class residents eager to serve as it was a response to the needs of slum dwellers.

The generational crisis was also a crisis of faith. Progressives like Jane Addams characteristically grew up in homes imbued with Christian piety, then found themselves incapable of sustaining the faith of their parents. Many went through a religious crisis, ultimately settling on careers in social work, education, or politics, where religious striving might be translated into secular action. Jane Addams, for one, took up settlement-house work believing that by uplifting the poor, she would herself be uplifted: She would experience "the joy of finding Christ" by acting "in fellowship" with the needy.

The Protestant clergy itself struggled with these issues, translating a long-felt concern for the plight of the poor into a major theological doctrine — the Social Gospel. The leading exponent was the Baptist cleric Walter Rauschenbusch, whose ideas had been forged by his ministry in the squalid Hell's Kitchen section of New York City. The churches must not wall themselves off from the misery and despair in their midst, said the Reverend Rauschenbusch. They had to embrace the "social aims of Jesus." The Kingdom of God on Earth would be achieved not by striving for personal salvation but in the cause of social justice.

What lent urgency to these inner callings was the discovery that there was no insulating middle-class Americans from the ills of industrial society. That was a truth borne painfully home to Jane Addams when her eldest sister lay ill in a hospital during the Pullman strike. Held up by the turmoil, her sister's distraught family failed to reach her bedside before she died. Addams feared that such painful episodes, inescapable whenever labor and capital came to blows, would inculcate "lasting bitterness" in middle-class homes. There was no denying that "the present industrial system is in a state of profound disorder," and no denying the stake of the middle class in "right[ing] it." It was up to reformers like herself, products of the middle class, to take up that task.

Progressive Ideas

Finding solutions, however, was easier said than done. Jane Addams wrote poignantly of her uncertainty, having launched Hull House, about just how to proceed. She "longed for . . . an explanation of the social chaos and the logical steps toward its better ordering." The answers that were forthcoming depended first of all on the emergence of a new intellectual style that we can call *progressive*.

If the facts could be known, everything else was possible. That was the starting point for progressive thinking. Hence the burst of enthusiasm for scientific investigation — statistical studies by the federal government of immigration, child labor, and economic practices; social research by privately funded foundations delving into industrial conditions; vice commissions in many cities looking into prostitution, gambling, and other moral ills of an urban society. Great faith was also placed in academic expertise. In Wisconsin the state university became a key resource for Governor Robert La Follette's reform administration — the reason, one supporter boasted, for "the democracy, the thoroughness, and the accuracy of the state in its legislation."

Similarly, progressives were strongly attracted to scientific management, which had originally been intended to rationalize work in factories (see Chapter 17). But its founder, Frederick W. Taylor, argued that his basic approach — the "scientific" analysis of human activity — offered solutions to waste and inefficiency in municipal government, schools and hospitals, even at home. Scientific management, said Taylor, could solve all the social ills that arise from "such of our acts as are blundering, ill-directed, or inefficient."

Scientific management was an American invention, but progressive intellectuals also felt themselves part of a transatlantic world. Ideas flowed in both directions, with the Americans, in fact, very much on the receiving end. Since the 1870s, they had flocked to German universities, absorbing the economics and political science that became key tools of progressive reform. On many fronts, social politics overseas seemed far in advance of the United States. The sense of having fallen behind — that "the tables are turned," as the young progressive Walter Weyl wrote, and that "America no longer teaches democracy to an expectant world, but herself goes to school in Europe and Australia" — was a spur to fresh ideas.

The main thing was to resist ways of thinking that discouraged purposeful action. Social Darwinists who had so dominated Gilded Age thought (see Chapter 19) were wrong in their belief that society developed according to fixed and unchanging laws. "It is folly," pronounced the Harvard philosopher William James, "to speak of the 'laws of history,' as of something inevitable, which science only has to discover, and which anyone can then foretell and observe, but do nothing to alter or avert." James denied the existence of absolute truths and advocated instead a philosophy he called **pragmatism**, which judged ideas by their consequences. Philosophy should be concerned with solving problems, James insisted, and not with contemplating ultimate ends.

Nowhere were the battle lines more sharply drawn than in the courts, where judges treated the law as if it had arisen from eternal principles. One such principle was liberty of contract, which the Supreme Court invoked in *Lochner v. New York* (1905) to strike down a state law limiting the hours of bakers. The Court contended it was protecting the contractual liberty of the bakers (as well as their employers). Nonsense, responded the dissenting Justice Oliver Wendell Holmes. If the choice was between working and starving, could it be said that bakers freely chose to work 14 hours a day?

Legal realism, as Justice Holmes's reasoning came to be known, rested on his conviction that "the life of the law has not been logic; it has been experience." Dean Roscoe Pound of the Harvard Law School called for "the adjustment of principles and doctrines to the human conditions they are to govern rather than assumed first principles." Nor should the law claim to be above the struggle, added Pound's student Felix Frankfurter; its proper role was to be "a vital agency for human betterment."

No practitioner of legal realism took this advice more to heart than the brilliant Boston lawyer Louis D. Brandeis, the son of Jewish emigrants from Austria-Hungary. He became known as "the people's lawyer" because, on behalf of the little guy, he regularly took on and beat the mightiest vested interests in town. An admirer of Frederick W. Taylor, Brandeis won a famous railroad rate case by demonstrating that the railroads operated inefficiently and didn't deserve to charge their customers more money. In fact, it was Brandeis who coined the term *scientific management*. Always ready to enlist in a good cause, Brandeis embodied progressivism's greatest strength — its capacity for uniting the brainpower of progressive intellectuals with the high-mindedness of social reformers.

The Muckrakers. The progressive mode of action — idealistic in intent, tough-minded in practice — nurtured a new kind of reform journalism. During the 1890s bright new magazines like *Collier's* and *McClure's* began to find an urban audience for lively, fact-filled reporting. Almost by accident, editors discovered that what most interested middle-class readers was the exposure of mischief in American life. Investigative reporters fanned out on the trail of evildoers.

Who Said Muck Rake?

A popular biographer in the 1890s, Ida Tarbell turned her journalistic talents to muckraking. Her first installment of "The History of the Standard Oil Company," which appeared in *McClure's Magazine* in November 1902, was a bombshell, with its exposure of John D. Rockefeller's chicanery on the way to fabulous wealth. In this cartoon, Miss Tarbell seems a mild enough lady, but there's her muck rake, and further in the background, a cowering President Roosevelt. That he was paying attention, the cartoon suggests, is apparent in the headline of the newspaper she is reading. Drake Oil Well Museum.

Lincoln Steffens's article "Tweed Days in St. Louis" in the October 1902 issue of *McClure's* is credited with starting the trend. In a riveting series Steffens wrote about "the shame of the cities"—the corrupt ties between business and political machines. Ida M. Tarbell attacked the Standard Oil monopoly, and David Graham Phillips told how money controlled the Senate. William Hard exposed industrial accidents in "Making Steel and Killing Men" (1907) and child labor in "De Kid Wot Works at Night" (1908). Hardly a sordid corner of American life escaped the scrutiny of these tireless reporters.

Theodore Roosevelt, among many others, thought they went too far. In a 1906 speech, he compared them to the man with a muckrake in *Pilgrim's Progress* (by the seventeenth-century English preacher John Bunyan) who was too absorbed with raking the filth on the floor to look up and accept a celestial crown. Thus the term **muckraker** became attached to journalists who exposed the underside of American life. Their efforts were in fact health-giving. More than any other group, the muckrakers called the people to arms.

Women Progressives

When she started out, Jane Addams did not regard Hull House as a specifically woman's enterprise. But of course, in her personal odyssey, it had mattered that she was a daughter, not a son. And while men were welcome, the settlement houses were overwhelmingly led and staffed by women. Over time, as the reform impulse quickened, the settlement-house movement became a nodal point for the distinctively feminine cast of social progressivism.

This was in keeping with women's long-established role as the nation's "social housekeepers," those who traditionally shouldered the burden of humanitarian work in American cities. Middle-class women were the foot soldiers for charity organizations, visiting needy families, assessing their problems, and referring them to relief agencies. After many years of such dedicated labor, Josephine Shaw Lowell of New York City concluded that giving assistance to the poor was not enough. "If the working people had all they ought to have, we should not have the paupers and criminals," she declared. "It is better to save them before they go

Saving the Children

In the early years at Hull House, Jane Addams recalled, toddlers sometimes arrived for kindergarten tipsy from a breakfast of bread soaked in wine. To settlement-house workers, the answer to such ignorance was in child-care education, and so began the program to send visiting nurses into immigrant homes. They taught mothers the proper methods of caring for children — including, as this photograph shows, the daily infant bath, given in a dishpan if necessary. Chicago Historical Society.

under, than to spend your life fishing them out afterward." Lowell founded the New York Consumers' League in 1890. Her goal was to improve the wages and working conditions of female clerks in the city's stores by issuing a "White List" — a very short list at first — of cooperating shops.

From these modest beginnings Lowell's organization spread to other cities and blossomed into the National Consumers' League in 1899. At its head stood a feisty, outspoken woman, Florence Kelley, an early resident of Hull House and then chief factory inspector of Illinois. Investigating the sweated trades of Chicago, Kelley and Jane Addams quickly lost faith in voluntary reform: The exploited garment workers could be rescued only by state factory legislation. When she joined the National Consumers' League, Kelley brought that focus to its work. Under her crusading leadership, the Consumers' League became a powerful advocate for protective legislation for women and children.

Among its achievements, none was more important than the Supreme Court's *Muller v. Oregon* decision in 1908, which upheld an Oregon law limiting the workday for women to ten hours. The Consumers' League recruited Louis Brandeis, whose brief before the Court devoted a scant two pages to the narrow constitutional issue — whether, under its police powers, Oregon had the right to regulate women's working hours. Instead, Brandeis rested his case on data gathered by the Consumers' League describing the toll that long hours took on women's health and family duties. The *Muller* decision was a triumph for legal realism and, by approving an expansive welfare role for the states, cleared the way for a mighty lobbying effort by women's organizations, whose victories included the first law providing public assistance for mothers with dependent children in Illinois in 1911; the first minimum wage law for women in Massachusetts in 1912; more effective child-labor laws in many states; and, at the federal level, the Children's and Women's bureaus in the Labor Department in 1912 and 1920, respectively (Table 20.1). The **welfare state**, insofar as it arrived in America in these years, was what women progressives had made of it; they erected a "maternalist" welfare system.

Revival of Woman's Suffrage. Women reformers like Jane Addams and Florence Kelley breathed new life into the suffrage movement. Why, they asked, should a woman who was capable of running a settlement house or lobbying a bill be denied the right to vote? And why should only women like themselves be making that fight? By asking that question, they opened the way for working-class women to join the suffrage struggle and, just as important, revealed the capacity of social reformers to expand beyond their middle-class base.

Believing that working women should be encouraged to help themselves, New York reformers in 1903 founded the National Women's Trade Union League. Financed by wealthy supporters, the league organized women workers, played a considerable role in their strikes, and trained working-class leaders. One such leader was Rose Schneiderman, who became a union organizer among New York's

TABLE 20.1	Progressive Legislation and Supreme Court Decisions
State Laws	
1903	Wisconsin primary law
	Oregon ten-hour law for women
1910	New York Bureau of Industries and Immigration
	Washington State adopts woman suffrage
1911	Illinois law providing aid for mothers with dependent children
	New York State Factory Commission
1912	Massachusetts minimum-wage law for women and children
Federal Laws	
1898	Erdman Railway Mediation Act
1902	Newlands Reclamation Act
1903	U.S. Bureau of Corporations
	Elkins Act
1906	Hepburn Railway Act
	Pure Food and Drug Act
	Meat Inspection Act
1909	Payne-Aldrich Tariff Act
1913	Underwood Tariff Act
	Federal Reserve Act
1914	Federal Trade Commission Act
	Clayton Antitrust Act
1916	Seamen's Act
	Federal Farm Loan Act
Supreme Court Decisions	
1895	*U.S. v. E. C. Knight* shelters manufacturing from antitrust law
1897	*U.S. v. Trans-Missouri* quashes "rule of reason" in antitrust suits
1904	*U.S. v. Northern Securities* orders dissolution of a company ruled a monopoly under Sherman Act
1905	*Lochner v. New York* invalidates a state law limiting hours of bakers
1908	*Muller v. Oregon* approves a state law limiting working hours of women
	Loewe v. Lawlor (Danbury Hatters case) finds a labor boycott to be a conspiracy in restraint of trade
1911	*U.S. v. Standard Oil* restores rule of reason as guiding principle in antitrust cases

garment workers; another was Agnes Nestor, who led Illinois glove workers. Although often resenting the patronizing ways of their well-to-do sponsors, such trade-union women identified their cause with the broader struggle for women's rights. When New York State held suffrage referenda in 1915 and 1917, strong support came from Jewish and Italian precincts inhabited by unionized garment workers.

Around 1910, suffrage activity began to quicken, and tactics shifted. In Britain suffragists had begun to picket Parliament, assault politicians, and stage hunger strikes while in jail. Inspired by their example, Alice Paul, a young Quaker once a resident of

Suffragists on Parade, 1913

After 1910 the suffrage movement went into high gear. Suffragist leaders decided that a constitutional amendment was a more effective route than battling for the vote state by state. The impressive women's parade in Washington, D.C., at Woodrow Wilson's inauguration served notice on the incoming administration that the suffragists meant business. The new president was not pleased with his uninvited guests. Brown Brothers.

Britain, applied similar confrontational tactics to the American struggle. Although woman suffrage had been won in six western states since 1910, Paul rejected the state-by-state route as too slow (Map 20.1). She advocated a constitutional amendment that in one stroke would grant women everywhere the right to vote. In 1916 Paul organized the militant National Woman's Party.

The mainstream National American Woman Suffrage Association (NAWSA), from which Paul had split off, was also rejuvenated. Carrie Chapman Catt, a skilled organizer from the New York movement, took over as national leader in 1915. Under her guidance NAWSA brought a broad-based organization to the campaign for a federal amendment.

Feminism. In the midst of this suffrage struggle, something new and more fundamental began to happen. A younger generation — college-educated, self-supporting women — refused to be hemmed in by the social constraints of women's "separate sphere." "Breaking into the Human Race" was the aspiration they proclaimed at a mass meeting in New York in 1914. "We intend simply to be ourselves," declared the chair Marie Jenny Howe, "not just our little female selves, but our whole big human selves."

The women at this meeting called themselves **feminists**, a term that was just coming into use. In this, its first incarnation, *feminism* meant freedom for full personal development. Thus did Charlotte Perkins Gilman, famous for her advocacy of communal kitchens as a means of liberating women from homemaking, imagine the new woman: "Here she comes, running, out of prison and off the pedestal; chains off, crown off, halo off, just a live woman."

Feminists were militantly pro-suffrage, but unlike their more traditional suffragist sisters, not on the basis that women would uplift American politics. Rather, they demanded the right to vote because they considered themselves just as good as men. At the moment the reviving suffrage movement was about to triumph, it was overtaken by a larger revolution that redefined the struggle for women's rights as a battle against all the constraints that prevented women from achieving their potential as human beings.

This feminist revolution also challenged women's social progressivism, which was premised on the belief that women were the weaker sex. It was just this argument, at the very heart of Brandeis's brief in the landmark *Muller* case, that rang true with the Supreme Court. "The two sexes differ in structure of body, in the functions to be performed by each, in the amount of physical strength," the Court agreed. "This difference justifies . . . legislation . . . designed to compensate for some of the burdens which rest upon her." But feminists wanted no such

MAP 20.1 Woman Suffrage, 1890–1919

By 1909, after more than sixty years of agitation, only four lightly populated western states had granted women full voting rights. A number of other states offered partial suffrage, limited mostly to voting for school boards and such issues as taxes. Between 1910 and 1918, as the effort shifted to the struggle for a constitutional amendment, eleven states joined the list granting full suffrage. The most stubborn resistance was in the South.

compensation. Thus, to the surprise of Maryland's progressive governor Charles J. Bonaparte, some feminists objected to his 1914 women's minimum wage bill because it implied that "women need some special care, protection and privilege." A wedge was surfacing that would ultimately fracture the women's movement, dividing an older generation of progressives from feminists who prized gender equality more highly than any social benefit.

Urban Liberalism

The evolution of the women's movement — in particular, the recruitment of working-class women to what had been a middle-class struggle — was entirely characteristic of how progressivism evolved more generally.

When the Republican Hiram Johnson ran for California governor in 1910, he was the reform candidate of the state's middle class. Famous as prosecutor of the corrupt San Francisco boss Abe Ruef, Johnson pledged to purify California politics and curb the Southern Pacific Railroad — the dominating economic power in the state. By his second term, Johnson was championing social and labor legislation. His original base in the middle class had eroded, and he had become the champion of California's working class.

Johnson's career reflected a shift in the center of gravity of progressivism, which had begun as a movement of the middle class but then took on board America's working people. A new strain of progressive reform emerged that historians have labeled *urban liberalism*. To understand this phenomenon, we have to begin with city machine politics.

Thirty minutes before quitting time on Saturday afternoon, March 25, 1911, fire broke out at the

The Triangle Tragedy

This drawing, by the artist John Sloan, captures better than any photograph the horror of the Triangle fire. The image of the two women clinging to each other as they fell is accurate. According to observers, a number of young workers, with no other way to escape the flames, chose to fall to their deaths in each other's arms. The fireman who can't bear to watch is probably a product of Sloan's imagination, but the anguish he felt is true enough, because when the fire trucks arrived, they didn't have the equipment to save anyone. The ladders were too short, and the nets the firemen spread too weak. The bodies simply shot right through to the ground. *Harper's Weekly*, May 8, 1915.

Triangle Shirtwaist Company in downtown New York. The flames trapped the workers, who were mostly young immigrant women. Many leapt to their deaths; the rest never reached the windows. The dead, 146 of them, averaged nineteen years of age.

In the wake of the tragedy, the New York State Factory Commission developed a remarkable program of labor reform: fifty-six laws dealing with fire hazards, unsafe machines, industrial homework, and wages and hours for women and children. The chairman of the commission was Robert F. Wagner; the vice chairman was Alfred E. Smith. Both were Tammany Hall politicians, serving at the time as leaders in the state legislature. They established the commission, participated fully in its work, and marshaled the party regulars to pass the proposals into law — all with the approval of the Tammany machine. The labor code that resulted was the most advanced in the country.

Tammany's response to the Triangle fire meant that it was conceding that social problems had outgrown the powers of party machines. Only the state could bar industrial firetraps or alleviate sweatshop work and slum life. And if that meant weakening grass-roots loyalty to Tammany, so be it. Al Smith and Robert Wagner absorbed the lessons of the Triangle investigation. They formed durable ties with such progressives as the social worker Frances Perkins, who sat on the commission as the representative of the New York Consumers' League, and became urban liberals — advocates of active intervention by the state in uplifting the laboring masses of America's cities (see Comparing American Voices, "The Triangle Fire," pp. 620–621).

It was not only altruism that converted seasoned politicians like Smith and Wagner. The city machines faced strong competition from a new breed of middle-class, skilled urban reformers such as Mayor Brand Whitlock of Toledo, Ohio, whose administration not only attacked city-hall corruption but also provided better schools, cleaner streets, and more social services for Toledo's needy. Combining campaign magic and popular programs, Whitlock and similarly progressive mayors in Cleveland, Jersey City, and elsewhere won over the urban masses and challenged the rule of the machines.

Also confronting the bosses was a challenge from the left. The Socialist Party was making headway in the cities, electing Milwaukee's Victor Berger as the nation's first Socialist congressman in 1910 and winning municipal elections across the country. In the 1912 presidential election, the Socialist candidate Eugene Debs (see Chapter 17) garnered a record 6 percent of the vote. The political universe of the urban machines had changed, and they had to pay closer attention to opinion in the precincts.

Cultural Pluralism Embattled. Urban liberalism was driven not only by the plight of the economically downtrodden but by a sharpening nativist attack on immigrants. Old-stock evangelical Christians had long agitated for laws that would reinforce

COMPARING AMERICAN VOICES

The Triangle Fire

Entire books have been written about the tragic Triangle Shirtwaist Company fire, which was a defining event of the Progressive era. On the previous page, we can offer only a brief account. In the space below, however, we offer documents by four contemporaries who in one way or another played some part in the Triangle tragedy and its aftermath. In reading these documents, ask yourself in what ways they tell you things you didn't learn or couldn't have learned from the text.

WILLIAM G. SHEPARD, REPORTER

Following is an eyewitness account that appeared in newspapers across the country. It was filed by a reporter for the United Press, who phoned it in to his editor as he watched the unfolding tragedy.

I was walking through Washington Square when a puff of smoke issuing from a factory building caught my eye. I reached the building before the alarm was turned in. I saw every feature of the tragedy visible from outside the building. I learned a new sound — a more horrible sound than description can picture. It was the thud of a speeding, living body on a stone sidewalk.... I looked up — saw that there were scores of girls at the windows. The flames from the floor below were beating in their faces. Somehow I knew that they, too, must come down, and something within me — something I didn't know was there — steeled me.

I even watched one girl falling. Waving her arms, trying to keep her body upright until the very instant she struck the sidewalk, she was trying to balance herself. Then came the thud — then a silent, unmoving pile of clothing and twisted, broken limbs....

On the sidewalk lay heaps of broken bodies. A policeman later went about with tags, which he fastened with wire to the wrists of the dead girls, and I saw him fasten no. 54 to the wrist of a girl who wore an engagement ring....

The floods of water from the firemen's hose that ran into the gutter were actually stained red with blood. I looked upon the heap of dead bodies and I remembered these girls were shirtwaist makers. I remembered their great strike of last year in which these same girls had demanded more sanitary conditions and more safety precautions in the shops. These dead bodies were the answer.

STEPHEN S. WISE, RABBI

A week after the fire, on April 2, 1911, a memorial meeting was held at the Metropolitan Opera House. One of the speakers was Rabbi Stephen S. Wise, a prominent figure in New York reform circles. Following is what he said.

This was not an inevitable disaster which man could neither foresee nor control. We might have foreseen it, and some of us did; we might have controlled it, but we chose not to do so.... It is not a question of enforcement of law nor of inadequacy of law. We have the wrong kind of laws and the wrong kind of enforcement. Before insisting upon inspection and enforcement, let us lift up the industrial standards so as to make conditions worth inspecting, and, if inspected, certain to afford security to workers.... And when we go before the legislature of the state, and demand increased appropriations in order to ensure the possibility of a sufficient number of inspectors, we will not forever be put off with the answer: We have no money.

The lesson of the hour is that while property is good, life is better; that while possessions are valuable, life is priceless. The meaning of the hour is that the life of the lowliest worker in the nation is sacred and inviolable, and, if that sacred human right be violated, we shall stand adjudged and condemned before the tribunal of God and history.

ROSE SCHNEIDERMAN, TRADE UNIONIST

Rose Schneiderman was another speaker at the Opera House meeting. At age thirteen, she had gone to work in a garment factory like Triangle Shirtwaist's and, under the tutelage of the Women's Trade Union League, had become a labor organizer. The strike she mentions in her speech was popularly known as the Uprising of the 30,000, a nearly spontaneous walkout in 1909 that launched the union movement in the women's garment trades.

I would be a traitor to these poor burned bodies if I came here to talk good fellowship. We have tried you good people of the public and we have found you wanting. The old Inquisition had its rack and its thumbscrews and its instruments of torture with iron teeth. We know what these things are today; the iron teeth are our necessities, the thumbscrews are the high-powered and swift machinery close to which we must work, and the rack is here in the firetrap structures that will destroy us the minute they catch on fire.

This is not the first time girls have been burned alive in the city. . . . Every year thousands of us are maimed. The life of men and women is so cheap and property is so sacred. There are so many of us for one job it matters little if 146 of us are burned to death.

We have tried you citizens; we are trying you now, and you have a couple of dollars for the sorrowing mothers, brothers, and sisters by way of a charity gift. But every time the workers come out in the only way they know to protest against conditions which are unbearable the strong hand of the law is allowed to press down heavily upon us . . . [and] beats us back, when we rise, into the conditions that make life unbearable.

I can't talk fellowship to you who are gathered here. Too much blood has been spilled. I know from my experience it is up to the working people to save themselves. The only way they can save themselves is by a strong working-class movement.

MAX D. STEUER, LAWYER

After finding physical evidence of the locked door that had blocked escape from the fire, the district attorney brought manslaughter charges against the Triangle proprietors, Max Blanck and Isaac Harris, who hired in their defense the best, highest-priced trial attorney in town, Max D. Steuer. In this talk, delivered some time later to a rapt audience of lawyers, Steuer described how he undermined the testimony of the key witness for the prosecution.

There are many times, many times when a witness has given evidence very hurtful to your cause and you say, "No questions," and dismiss him or her in the hope that the jury will dismiss the evidence too. [*Laughter.*] But can you do that when the jury is weeping, and the little girl witness is weeping too? [*Laughter.*] . . . There is one [rule] that commands what not to do. Do not attack the witness. Suavely, politely, genially, toy with the story.

In the instant case, about half an hour was consumed by the examiner [Steuer]. . . . Very little progress was made; but the tears had stopped. And then she was asked, "Now, Rose, in your own words, and in your own way will you tell the jury everything you did, everything you said, and everything you saw from the moment you first saw flames."

The question was put in precisely the same words that the District Attorney had put it, and little Rose started her answer with exactly the same word that she had started it to the District Attorney . . . and the only change in her recital was that Rose left out one word. And then Rose was asked, "Didn't you leave out a word that you put it in when you answered it before?" . . . So Rose started to repeat to herself the answer [*laughter*], and as she came to the missing word she said, Oh, yes!" and supplied it; and thereupon the examiner went on to an entirely different subject . . . when again he [asked her to repeat her story]. . . . And Rose started with the same word and finished with the same word, her recital being identical with her first reply to the same question.

The jurymen were not weeping. Rose had not hurt the case, and the defendants were acquitted; there was not word of reflection at any time during that trial upon poor little Rose.

SOURCE: Leon Stein, ed., *Out of the Sweatshop* (New York: Quadrangle Books, 1977), 188–98.

ANALYZING THE EVIDENCE

▶ The hardest task of the historian is to conjure up the reality of the past — "this is what it was really like." That's where eye-witness evidence like the reporter Shepard's comes in. What is there in his account that you could not reasonably expect a historian to capture?

▶ Both Rabbi Wise and Rose Schneiderman are incensed at the Triangle carnage. Yet their speeches are quite different. In what ways? And with what implications for alternate paths to progressive reform?

▶ Max Steuer and Rose Schneiderman came from remarkably similar backgrounds. They were roughly the same age, grew up in poverty on the Lower East Side, and started out as child workers in the garment factories. So consider how differently they ended up! That of course speaks to the varieties of immigrant experience in America. But is there anything in their statements that helps account for their differing life paths? Would Steuer have been as effective had he been questioning Schneiderman?

their cultural and moral norms. After 1900 this movement strongly revived, cloaking itself now in the mantle of progressive reform. The Anti-Saloon League — "the Protestant church in action" — became a formidable advocate for prohibition in many states, skillfully attaching Demon Rum to other reform targets: The saloon made for dirty politics, poverty, and bad labor conditions.

The moral reform agenda expanded to include a new goal: restricting the immigration of southern and eastern Europeans into the United States. Edward A. Ross of the University of Wisconsin denounced "the pigsty mode of life" of Italian and Polish immigrants. The danger, respected social scientists said, was that America's Anglo-Saxon population would be "mongrelized" and its civilization swamped by "inferior" Mediterranean and Slavic cultures. Feeding on this fear, the Immigration Restriction League spearheaded a campaign to end America's historic open-door policy. Like prohibition, immigration restriction was considered by its proponents to be a progressive reform.

Urban liberals thought otherwise. They denounced prohibition and immigration restriction as attacks on the personal liberty and worthiness of urban immigrants. The Tammany politician Martin McCue accused the Protestant ministry "of seeking to substitute the policeman's nightstick for the Bible."

Organized Labor. City machines, always pragmatic, adopted urban liberalism without much ideological struggle. The same could not be said of the trade unions, the other institution that spoke for American working people. In its early years the American Federation of Labor (AFL) had strongly opposed state interference in labor's affairs. Samuel Gompers preached that workers should not seek from government what they could accomplish by their own economic power and self-help. **Voluntarism**, as trade unionists called this doctrine, did not die out, but it weakened substantially during the progressive years.

The AFL, after all, claimed to speak for the entire working class. When muckrakers exposed exploitation of workers and middle-class progressives came forward with solutions, how could the labor movement fail to respond? Thus began a retreat from labor's commitment to voluntarism. In state after state, organized labor joined the battle for progressive legislation and increasingly became its strongest advocate, including most particularly workers' compensation for industrial accidents.

Maimed Factory Worker
Lewis Hine, a great photographer of immigrant life, took this undated picture of a disabled factory worker. Two of his four children are in the background. How was he to support them? If his accident occurred before the passage of workers' compensation laws, they were probably out of luck. George Eastman House.

Industrial hazards took an awful toll at the workplace. Two thousand coal miners were killed every year, dying from cave-ins and explosions at a rate 50 percent higher than in German mines. Liability rules, based on **common law**, so heavily favored employers that victims of industrial accidents rarely got more than token compensation. The tide turned quickly once the labor movement got on board; between 1910 and 1917 all the industrial states enacted insurance laws covering on-the-job accidents.

Social Insurance Deferred. The United States hesitated, however, to broaden the attack on the hazards of modern industrial life. Health insurance and unemployment compensation, although popular in Europe, scarcely made it onto the American political agenda. Old-age pensions, which Britain adopted in 1908, got a serious hearing, only to come up against an odd barrier: The United States already had a pension system of a kind, for Civil War veterans. Easy access — as many as half of all native-born men over sixty-four or their survivors were collecting veterans' benefits in the early twentieth century — reinforced fears of state-induced dependency. Clarence J. Hicks, an industrial-relations expert, recalled Civil War pensioners idling away the hours around the wood stove in the grocery store in his Wisconsin town. They had decided "that the country owed them a living," lost their initiative, and "retreated from the battle of life."

Not until a later generation experienced the ravages of the Great Depression (see Chapter 23) would the country be ready for social insurance. A secure old age, unemployment insurance, health benefits — these human needs of a modern industrial order were beyond the reach of urban liberals in the Progressive era.

Reforming Politics

Like the Mugwumps of the Gilded Age (see Chapter 19), progressive reformers attacked corrupt party rule, but more adeptly and aggressively. Indeed, what distinguished political reform after 1900 was that it was no longer an amateurs' project. In the Progressive era, political reformers understood the levers of power as well as did the scoundrels they were trying to throw out, and that was why, once the smoke cleared, the political reforms of this era proved enduring. In this, as in other realms, progressivism was a potent mix of idealism and tough-mindedness.

Robert M. La Follette and the Wisconsin Idea. Born in 1855, Robert M. La Follette started as a conventional politician, rising from the Republican ranks in Wisconsin to serve in Congress for three terms. He was a party regular, never doubting that he was in honorable company until, by his own account, a Republican boss offered him a bribe to fix a judge in a railroad case. Awakened by this "awful ordeal," La Follette broke with the Wisconsin machine in 1891 and became a tireless advocate of political reform, which for him meant restoring America's democratic ideals. "Go back to the first principles of democracy; go back to the people," he told his audience when he launched his campaign against the state Republican machine. In 1900, after

Robert M. La Follette

La Follette was transformed into a political reformer when a Wisconsin Republican boss attempted to bribe him in 1891 to influence a judge in a railway case. As he described it in his *Autobiography*, "Out of this awful ordeal came understanding; and out of understanding came resolution. I determined that the power of this corrupt influence ... should be broken." This photograph captures him at the top of his form, expounding his progressive vision to a rapt audience of Wisconsin citizens at an impromptu street gathering. Library of Congress.

battling for a decade, La Follette won the Wisconsin governorship on a platform of higher taxes for corporations, stricter utility and railroad regulation, and political reform.

The key to party reform, La Follette felt, was denying bosses the power to choose the party's candidates. This could be achieved by state legislation requiring that nominations be decided not in party conventions but by popular vote. Enacted in 1903, the **direct primary** expressed La Follette's democratic idealism, but it also suited his particular political talents. The party regulars opposing him were insiders, more comfortable in the caucus room than out on the stump. But that was where La Follette, a superb campaigner, excelled. The direct primary gave La Follette an iron grip on Republican politics in Wisconsin that lasted until his death twenty-five years later.

What was true of La Follette was more or less true of all successful progressive politicians. They typically described their work as political restoration, frequently confessing that they had converted to reform after discovering how far party politics had drifted from the ideals of representative government. Like La Follette, Albert B. Cummins of Iowa, William S. U'Ren of Oregon, and Hiram Johnson of California all espoused democratic ideals and all skillfully used the direct primary as the stepping stone to political power. They practiced a new kind of popular politics, which in a reform age could be a more effective way to power than the backroom techniques of the old-fashioned machine politicians.

Even the most democratizing of reforms espoused by the progressives—the initiative and recall—were really exercises in power politics. The *initiative* enabled citizens to have issues placed on the ballot; *recall* empowered them to remove officeholders who had lost the public's confidence. It soon became clear, however, that direct democracy did not supplant organized politics. Initiative and recall campaigns required organization, money, and expertise, and these were attributes not of the people at large but of well-financed interests. Like the direct primary, the initiative and recall had as much to do with power relations as with political reform.

Racism and Reform

The direct primary was the flagship of progressive politics—the crucial reform, as La Follette said, for defeating the party bosses and returning politics to "the people." The primary originated not in Wisconsin, however, but in the South, and by the time La Follette got his primary law in 1903, primaries were already operating in seven southern states. In the South, however, the primary was a *white* primary. Since by 1900 the Democratic nomination in the South was tantamount to election, barring African Americans from the party primary effectively barred them from political participation.

How could this exercise in white supremacy be justified as democratic reform? By the racism that pervaded even the progressive ranks. In a 1902 book on Reconstruction, Professor John W. Burgess of Columbia University pronounced the Fifteenth Amendment "a monstrous thing" for granting blacks the vote after the Civil War. Burgess was southern born, but he was confident that his northern audience saw the "vast differences in political capacity" between blacks and whites. Even the Republican Party offered no rebuttal. Indeed, as president-elect in 1908, William Howard Taft applauded southern disfranchising laws as necessary to "prevent entirely the possibility of domination by . . . an ignorant electorate." Taft assured southerners that "the federal government has nothing to do with social equality." Taft's successor, Woodrow Wilson, was prepared to go even further, signaling after he entered the White House in 1913 that he favored segregation of the U.S. civil service.

Booker T. Washington and Black Accommodation. The black leader of the day was Booker T. Washington, who in a famous speech in Atlanta in 1895 had retreated from the defiant stand of an older generation of black abolitionists such as Frederick Douglass. Conciliatory toward the South, Washington considered "the agitation of the question of social equality the extremest folly." The Atlanta Compromise, as his stance became known, was "accommodationist," in the sense that it avoided a direct assault on white supremacy. Despite the conciliatory face he put on before white audiences, however, Washington did not concede the struggle. Behind the scenes he lobbied hard against Jim Crow laws and disfranchisement. In an age of severe racial oppression, no black dealt more skillfully with the elite of white America or wielded greater influence inside the Republican Party. What Washington banked on was black economic progress. When they had grown dependent on black labor and black enterprise, white men of property would recognize the justice of black rights. As Washington put it, "There is little race prejudice in the American dollar."

Black leaders knew Washington as a hard taskmaster, jealous of his authority and not disposed to regard opposition kindly. Even so, opposition surfaced, especially among younger, educated

Booker T. Washington

In an age of severe racial oppression, Washington emerged as the acknowledged leader of black people in the United States. He was remarkable both for his ability as spokesman to white Americans and for his deep understanding of the aspirations of black Americans. Born a slave, Washington suffered the indignities experienced by all blacks after emancipation. But having been befriended by several whites as he grew to manhood, he also understood what it took to gain white support — and maneuver around white hostility — in the black struggle for equality. Library of Congress.

blacks. They thought Washington was conceding too much. He instilled black pride, but of a narrowly middle-class and utilitarian kind. What about the special genius of blacks that W. E. B. Du Bois, a Harvard-educated African American sociologist, celebrated in his collection of essays, *The Souls of Black Folk* (1903)? And what of the "talented tenth" of the black population, whose promise could be stifled by manual education? Moreover, the situation for blacks was deteriorating, even in the North. Over 200,000 blacks migrated from the South between 1900 and 1910, sparking white resentment in northern cities. Attacks on blacks became widespread, capped by a bloody race riot in Springfield, Illinois, in 1908. In the face of all this, many black activists lost patience with Booker T. Washington's silence.

The Civil Rights Struggle Revived. The key figure was William Monroe Trotter, the pugnacious editor of the *Boston Guardian*. "The policy of compromise has failed," Trotter argued. "The policy of resistance and aggression deserves a trial." In 1906, after breaking with Washington, Trotter and Du Bois called a meeting at Niagara Falls — but on the Canadian side because no hotel on the U.S. side would admit blacks. The Niagara Movement that resulted had an impact far beyond the scattering of members and local bodies it organized. The principles it affirmed would define the struggle for the rights of African Americans: first, encouragement of black pride; second, an uncompromising demand for full political and civil equality; and above all, the resolute denial "that the Negro-American assents to inferiority, is submissive under oppression and apologetic before insults."

Going against the grain, a handful of white reformers rallied to the African American cause. Among the most devoted was Mary White Ovington, who grew up in an abolitionist family. Like Jane Addams, Ovington became a settlement-house worker, but among urban blacks in New York rather than in immigrant Chicago. News of the Springfield race riot of 1908 changed her life. Convinced that her duty was to fight racism, Ovington called a meeting of sympathetic white progressives, which led to the formation of the National Association for the Advancement of Colored People (NAACP) in 1909. Most of the members of the strife-torn Niagara Movement moved over to the NAACP. The organization's national leadership was dominated by whites, with one crucial exception. Du Bois became the editor of the NAACP's journal, *The Crisis*. With a passion that only a black voice could provide, Du Bois used that platform to demand equal rights. The NAACP scored its first success in helping beat back the Wilson administration's effort at segregating the federal civil service.

On social welfare the National Urban League took the lead, uniting in 1911 the many agencies serving black migrants arriving in northern cities. Like the NAACP, the Urban League was interracial, including both white reformers such as Ovington and black welfare activists such as William Lewis Bulkley, a New York school principal who was the league's main architect. In the South welfare work was very much the province of black women, who to some extent filled the vacuum left by black disfranchisement. Mostly working in the churches and schools, they also utilized the southern branches of the National Association of Colored Women's Clubs, which had started in 1896. And because their

Colored Women's League of Washington, D.C.

At a time when black men were being driven from politics in the South, their wives and sisters organized themselves and became an alternative voice of black conscience. Sara Iredell Fleetwood, superintendent of the Freedman's Hospital Training School for Nurses, founded the Colored Women's League of Washington, D.C., in 1892 for purposes of "racial uplift." This picture of the league was taken on the steps of Frederick Douglass's home in Anacostia, Washington. Mrs. Fleetwood is seated at the far right, third row from the bottom. The notations are by someone seeking to identify the other members, a modest effort to save for posterity these women, mostly teachers, who did their best for the good of the race. Library of Congress.

activities seemed unthreatening to white supremacy, black women were able to reach across the color line and find allies among white southern women.

Progressivism was a house of many chambers. Most were infected by the racism of the age, but not all. A saving remnant of white progressives rallied to the cause of racial justice. In alliance with black civil-rights advocates, they defined the issues and established the organizations that would spur the struggle for a better life for African Americans over the next half century.

- How do you account for the revival of the woman's suffrage movement during the Progressive era?

- In what ways did political reformers of the Progressive era (like Robert La Follette) differ from the Mugwump reformers of the late nineteenth century?

- What is the relationship between progressive reform and the struggle for racial equality?

Progressivism and National Politics

In its origins, progressivism was a local phenomenon, spurred by immediate and visible problems. But reformers soon realized that many social problems, like child labor and industrial safety, were best handled by Washington and that, so far as concerned the overweening power of big business, there was no place else to turn. Seasoned reformers like Robert La Follette, ambitious for a wider stage, migrated to Washington and ultimately formed a progressive bloc on Capitol Hill. Progressivism burst on the national stage, however, not via Congress, but by way of the presidency. This was partly because the White House provided a "bully pulpit"—to use Theodore Roosevelt's phrase. But just as important was the twist of fate that brought Roosevelt to the White House on September 14, 1901.

The Making of a Progressive President

Like many other budding progressives, Theodore Roosevelt was motivated by a high-minded, Christian upbringing. Born in 1858, he always identified himself—loudly—with the cause of righteousness. But Roosevelt did not scorn power and its uses. To the amazement of his socially prominent family, he plunged into Republican politics after Harvard and maneuvered himself into the New York State legislature. Contemptuous of the gentlemen Mugwumps, he much preferred the company of party professionals. Roosevelt rose in the New York party because he skillfully developed broad popular support and thus forced himself on reluctant state Republican bosses.

Safely back from the Spanish-American War as the hero of San Juan Hill (see Chapter 21), Roosevelt won the New York governorship in 1898. During his term in office he signaled his progressivism by pushing through civil service reform and a tax on corporations. He discharged the corrupt superintendent of insurance over the Republican Party's objections and asserted his confidence in the government's capacity to improve the life of the people.

Hoping to neutralize him, the party chieftains chose Roosevelt in 1900 for what seemed a dead-end job as William McKinley's running mate. Roosevelt accepted reluctantly. But on September 6, 1901, an anarchist named Leon F. Czolgosz shot the president. When McKinley died eight days later, Roosevelt became president, to the dismay of party regulars.

Roosevelt in fact moved cautiously, attending first to politics. Anxious to rein in the formidable conservative bloc in Congress, he adroitly used the patronage powers of his office to gain control of the Republican Party. But Roosevelt was also uncertain about how to proceed. At first the new president might have been described as a progressive without a cause.

Regulating the Marketplace

Most troubling to Roosevelt was the threat posed by big business to competitive markets. The drift toward large-scale enterprise was itself not new; for many years industrialists had been expanding their operations because of the efficiencies that vertical integration offered (see Chapter 17). But the bigger the business, the greater the power over markets. And when, in the aftermath of the depression of the 1890s, promoters scrambled to merge rival firms, the primary motive was not lower costs but the elimination of competition. These mergers—**trusts**, as they were called—greatly increased business concentration. By 1910, 1 percent of the nation's manufacturers accounted for 44 percent of the nation's industrial output (see Voices from Abroad, "James Bryce: America in 1905: 'Business Is King,' " p. 628).

J. Pierpont Morgan

J. P. Morgan was a giant among American financiers. He had served an apprenticeship in investment banking under his father, a leading Anglo-American banker in London. A gruff man of few words, Morgan had a genius for instilling trust and the strength of will to persuade others to follow his lead and do his bidding—qualities the great photographer Edward Steichen captured in this portrait. Courtesy, George Eastman House, reprinted with permission of Joanna T. Steichen.

VOICES FROM ABROAD

James Bryce
America in 1905: "Business Is King"

James Bryce, British author of The American Commonwealth *(1888), a great treatise on American politics, visited the United States regularly over many years. In an essay published in 1905, Lord Bryce took stock of the changes he had seen during the previous quarter century. What most impressed him, beyond the sheer growth of material wealth, was the loss of individualism and the intensifying concentration of corporate power. In this he was at one with his old friend Theodore Roosevelt, who at that very time was gearing up to do battle with the trusts.*

That which most strikes the visitor to America today is its prodigious material development. Industrial growth, swift thirty or forty years ago, advances more swiftly now. The rural districts are being studded with villages, the villages are growing into cities, the cities are stretching out long arms of suburbs, which follow the lines of road and railway in every direction. The increase of wealth, even more remarkable than the increase of population, impresses the European more than ever before because the contrast with Europe is greater. The huge fortunes, the fortunes of those whose income reaches or exceeds a million dollars a year, are of course far more numerous than in any other country.... With this extraordinary material development it is natural that in the United States, business, that is to say, industry, commerce, and finance, should have more and more come to overshadow and dwarf all other interests, all other occupations.... Business is king.

Commerce and industry themselves have developed new features. Twenty-two years ago there were no trusts.... Even then, however, corporations had covered a larger proportion of the whole field of industry and commerce in America than in Europe, and their structure was more flexible and efficient. Today this is still more the case; while as for trusts, they have become one of the most salient phenomena of the country. They fix the attention, they excite the alarm of economists and politicians as well as of traders in the Old World, while they exercise and baffle the ingenuity of American legislators. Workingmen follow, though hitherto with unequal steps, the efforts at combination which the lords of production and distribution have been making. The consumer stands, if not with folded hands, yet so far with no clear view of the steps he may make for his own protection. Perhaps his prosperity—for he is prosperous—helps him to be quiescent.

The example of the United States, the land in which individualism has been most conspicuously vigorous, may seem to suggest that the world is passing out of the stage of individualism and returning to that earlier stage in which groups of men formed the units of society. The bond of association was, in those early days, kinship, real or supposed, and a servile or quasi-servile dependence of the weak upon the strong. Now it is the power of wealth which enables the few to combine so as to gain command of the sources of wealth.... Is it a paradox to observe that it is because the Americans have been the most individualistic of peoples that they are now the people among whom the art of combination has reached its maximum? The amazing keenness and energy, which were stimulated by the commercial conditions of the country, have evoked and ripened a brilliant talent for organization. This talent has applied new methods to production and distribution and has enabled wealth, gathered into a small number of hands, to dominate even the enormous market of America.

SOURCE: Allan Nevins, ed., *America through British Eyes* (Gloucester, MA: Peter Smith, 1968), 384–87.

ANALYZING THE EVIDENCE

- In what ways does it seem to Bryce that America's economic development stands in contrast to Europe's?

- How does he explain the "paradox" that the Americans — "the most individualistic of peoples" — should be leaders in developing business forms that will stifle individualism?

- Do Bryce's observations as a foreigner shed any special light on why an antitrust movement was building up in the country?

As early as his first annual message, Roosevelt acknowledged the nation's uneasiness with the "real and grave evils" of economic concentration. But what weapons could the president use in response?

Under long-established common law, anyone injured by monopoly or illegal restraint of trade could sue for damages. With the passage of the Sherman Antitrust Act of 1890, these common-law rights entered the U.S. statute books and could be enforced by the federal government when offenses involved interstate commerce. Neither Presidents Cleveland nor McKinley showed much interest, but the Sherman Act was there waiting to be deployed against abusive economic power.

Trust-Busting. Roosevelt's opening move was to create a Bureau of Corporations (1903) empowered to investigate business practices and bolster the Justice Department's capacity to mount antitrust suits. The department had already filed such a suit against the Northern Securities Company, a combine of the railroad systems of the Northwest. In a landmark decision the Supreme Court ordered Northern Securities dissolved in 1904.

That year Roosevelt handily defeated a weak conservative Democratic candidate, Judge Alton B. Parker. Now president in his own right, Roosevelt stepped up the attack on the trusts. He took on many of the nation's giant firms, including Standard Oil, American Tobacco, and DuPont. His rhetoric rising, Roosevelt became the nation's trust-buster, a crusader against "predatory wealth" (see Reading American Pictures, "Reining in Big Business? Cartoonists Join the Battle," p. 630).

But Roosevelt was not antibusiness. He regarded large-scale enterprise as a natural tendency of modern industrialism. Only firms that abused their power deserved punishment. But how to identify those companies? Under the Sherman Act, following common-law practice, the courts decided whether an act in restraint of trade was "unreasonable"—that is, harmful of the public interest—on a case-by-case basis. In the *Trans-Missouri* decision (1897), however, the Supreme Court abandoned this discretionary "rule of reason," holding now that actions that restrained or monopolized trade, regardless of the public impact, automatically violated the Sherman Act.

Little noticed at first, *Trans-Missouri* placed Roosevelt in a quandary. He had no desire to hamstring legitimate business activity, but he could not rely on the courts to distinguish between "good" and "bad" trusts. So Roosevelt assumed this task himself, which he could do because as chief executive it was up to him to initiate—or not initiate—antitrust prosecutions by the Justice Department.

In November 1904, with a government suit looming, the United States Steel Corporation's chairman Elbert H. Gary approached Roosevelt with a deal—cooperation in exchange for preferential treatment. The company would open its books to the Bureau of Corporations; if it found evidence of wrongdoing, the company would be warned privately and given a chance to set matters right. Roosevelt accepted this "gentlemen's agreement" because it met his interest in accommodating the modern industrial order while maintaining his public image as slayer of the trusts.

Railroad Regulation. The railroads posed a different problem. As quasi-public enterprises, they had never been free of oversight by the states; in 1887 they became subject to federal regulation by the Interstate Commerce Commission (ICC). As with the Sherman Act, this assertion of federal authority was mostly symbolic at first. Then Roosevelt got started, pushing through in 1903 the Elkins Act that prohibited discriminatory railway rates unfairly favoring preferred or powerful customers—a practice, Ida Tarbell reminded Americans with her muckraking articles on Standard Oil, that had given Rockefeller a leg-up in building his oil monopoly. With the 1904 election behind him, Roosevelt launched a drive for real railroad regulation. In 1906, after nearly two years of wrangling, Congress passed the Hepburn Railway Act, which empowered the ICC to set maximum shipping rates and prescribe uniform methods of bookkeeping. As a concession to the conservative Republican bloc, however, the courts retained broad powers to review the ICC's rate decisions.

Passage of the Hepburn Act was a triumph of Roosevelt's skills as a political operator. Despite grumbling by Senate progressives, Roosevelt was satisfied. He had achieved a landmark expansion of the government's regulatory powers over business.

The Environment. Another target was the West's natural resources. Although an ardent outdoorsman, Roosevelt was not a wilderness **preservationist** in the mold of John Muir (see Chapter 16). Having shaken off the illusions of his youthful days as a tenderfoot rancher, Roosevelt accepted the grim reality that the West's abundance, far from being limitless, was a finite and rapidly disappearing resource. Roosevelt was a **conservationist**. He believed in efficient use and sustainability, so that "we will hand . . . the water, the wood, the grasses . . . on to our children . . . in better and not worse shape than we got them."

READING AMERICAN PICTURES

Reining in Big Business? Cartoonists Join the Battle

For many years Americans had been troubled by the increasing scale of business enterprise. But after 1900 that concern boiled over with amazing and unexpected force. Almost overnight, curbing the trusts became the dominating political issue of the Progressive era. In the text we ascribe that development to a sudden speeding up of merger activity and a President uniquely gifted at crystallizing national sentiment. Is anything more to be learned abut this political phenomenon from scrutinizing the political cartoon below that appeared in humor magazine *Puck*?

ANALYZING THE EVIDENCE

- Historians value political cartoons in part because they are a gauge of what the public knows; the cartoonist's assumption is that readers will understand the content without being told. If that's so, what does the *Puck* cartoon reveal about the public's familiarity with the great tycoons of the time?

- Why is the location important? If the issue is business power, why are we being shown Wall Street rather than, say, the headquarters of U.S. Steel in Pittsburgh?

- Cartoons are also a kind of shorthand, stripping an issue to its barest elements and saying: "This is what it's really about." So in this cartoon, with Jack (Theodore Roosevelt) confronting the Wall Street Giants (Morgan, Rockefeller, the railroad tycoon James J. Hill), what's regulating big business really about?

"Jack and the Wall Street Giants," *Puck,* January 13, 1904. Library of Congress.

MAP 20.2 National Parks and Forests, 1872–1980

Close inspection of this map reveals that the national park system did not begin with the Progressive era. Indeed, Yellowstone, the first park, dates from 1872. In 1893, the federal government began the protection of national forests. Without Roosevelt, however, the national forest program might have languished, and during his presidency he added 125 million acres to the forest system plus six national parks. More importantly, Roosevelt endowed these systems with a progressive, public-spirited stamp that has remained a principle resource of environmentalists striving to preserve the nation's natural heritage. In the list of progressive triumphs, a robust national park and forest system is one of the most enduring.

In this endeavor, Roosevelt's guiding principle was, as his Public Lands Commission (1903) stated it, "public ownership"—the primacy of federal authority over the public domain for purposes of efficient management. This meant, first of all, vigorously deploying Roosevelt's executive powers, which he did by tripling the number of national forests, removing additional millions of acres of coal lands from private development, and adding national parks and (a new category authorized in 1906) many national monuments (Map 20.2). Equally significant were advances in federal administration, most importantly in an expanded Forest Service headed by an expert forester, Gifford Pinchot. That this ambitious program did not mean opposition to development was evident in Roosevelt's support for the Newland Reclamation Act (1902), which authorized irrigation projects for reclaiming and settling arid western lands.

Although mindful of western interests, federal bureaucrats like Pinchot infuriated ranchers and loggers unaccustomed to interference from Washington. They rebelled against grazing fees and logging restrictions, and their representatives in Washington eventually fought Roosevelt to a draw. Nowhere, in fact, did progressivism face fiercer resistance. Even so, there was no turning back. Roosevelt had reversed a century of heedless exploitation and imprinted conservation on the nation's public agenda (Map 20.2).

Consumer Protection. The protection of consumers, another signature issue for progressives, was very much the handiwork of muckraking journalism. What sparked the issue was a riveting series of articles in *Collier's* by Samuel Hopkins Adams exposing the patent-medicine business as "undiluted fraud," dangerous to the nation's health.

Then, in 1906, Upton Sinclair's novel *The Jungle* appeared. Sinclair thought he was writing about the exploitation of workers in Chicago meatpacking plants, but what caught the nation's attention were his descriptions of rotten meat and filthy conditions. President Roosevelt, weighing into the legislative battle, authorized a federal investigation of the stockyards. Within months the Pure Food and Drug and the Meat Inspection Acts passed, and another administrative agency joined the expanding federal bureaucracy — the Food and Drug Administration.

The Square Deal. During the 1904 presidential campaign, Roosevelt had taken to calling his program the Square Deal. This kind of labeling was new and would become a hallmark of American politics in the twentieth century, emblematic of a political style that dramatized issues, mobilized public opinion, and asserted presidential leadership. But the label meant something of substance as well. After many years of passivity and weakness, the federal government was reclaiming the role it had abandoned after the Civil War. Now, however, the target was the business economy. When companies abused their powers, the government would intercede to assure ordinary Americans a "square deal."

Campaigning for the Square Deal

When William McKinley ran for president in 1896, he sat on his front porch in Canton, Ohio, and received delegations of voters. That was not Theodore Roosevelt's way. He considered the presidency a "bully pulpit," and he used the office brilliantly to mobilize public opinion and to assert his leadership. The preeminence of the presidency in American public life begins with Roosevelt's administration. Here, at the height of his crusading power, Roosevelt stumps for the Square Deal in the 1904 election. Library of Congress.

Roosevelt was well aware, however, that his Square Deal was built on nineteenth-century foundations. In particular, antitrust doctrine seemed inadequate in an age of industrial concentration. Better, Roosevelt felt, for the federal government to regulate big business than try to break it up. In his final presidential speeches, Roosevelt dwelled on the need for a reform agenda for the twentieth century. Having chosen to retire after two terms, this was the task he bequeathed to his chosen successor, William Howard Taft.

The Fracturing of Republican Progressivism

William Howard Taft was an estimable man in many ways. An able jurist and a superb administrator, he had served Roosevelt well as governor-general of the Philippines after the Spanish-American War (see Chapter 21). But he was not by nature a progressive politician. He disliked the give-and-take of politics, he distrusted power, and, unlike Roosevelt, he was not one to cut corners. He revered the processes of law and was, in fundamental ways, a conservative.

Taft's Democratic opponent in the 1908 campaign was William Jennings Bryan. This was Bryan's last hurrah, his third attempt at the presidency, and he made the most of it. Eloquent as ever, Bryan attacked the Republicans as the party of the "plutocrats" and outdid them in urging tougher antitrust legislation, stricter railway regulation, and advanced labor legislation. Almost single-handedly, Bryan moved the Democratic Party into the mainstream of national progressive politics. But his robust campaign was not enough to offset Taft's advantages as Roosevelt's candidate. Taft won comfortably, entering the White House with a mandate to pick up where Roosevelt left off.

Taft's Troubles. By 1909 reform politics had unsettled the Republican Party. On the right, conservatives were girding themselves against further losses. Led by the formidable Senator Nelson W. Aldrich of Rhode Island, they were still a force to be reckoned with. On the left, progressive Republicans were rebellious. They felt that Roosevelt had been too easy on business, and with him gone from the White House, they intended to make up for lost time. Reconciling these conflicting forces within the Republican Party would have been a daunting task for a master politician. For Taft it spelled disaster.

First there was the tariff. Progressives considered protective tariffs a major reason why competition had declined and the trusts had taken hold. Although Taft had campaigned for tariff reform, he was won over by the conservative Republican bloc and ended up approving the protectionist Payne-Aldrich Tariff Act of 1909, which critics charged sheltered eastern industry from foreign competition.

Next came the Pinchot-Ballinger affair, which pitted Chief Forester Gifford Pinchot against Secretary of the Interior Richard A. Ballinger. Pinchot, a chum of Roosevelt's, accused Ballinger of plotting to transfer resource-rich Alaskan land to a private business group. When Pinchot aired these charges, Taft fired him for insubordination. Despite Taft's strong conservationist credentials, the Pinchot-Ballinger affair marked him among progressives as a friend of the "interests," bent on plundering the nation's resources.

Taft found himself propelled into the conservative Republican camp, an ally of "Uncle Joe" Cannon, the dictatorial Speaker of the House of Representatives. When a House revolt finally broke Cannon's power in 1910, it was regarded as a defeat for the president as well. Galvanized by Taft's defection, the reformers in the Republican Party became a dissident faction, calling themselves "Insurgents."

The Taft-Roosevelt Split. Home from a year-long safari in Africa, Roosevelt yearned to reenter the political fray. Taft's dispute with the Insurgents gave Roosevelt the cause he needed. But Roosevelt was a loyal party man, too astute a politician not to recognize that a party split would benefit the Democrats. He could be spurred into rebellion only by a true clash of principles. On the question of the trusts, just such a clash materialized.

Taft's legalistic mind rebelled at Roosevelt's practice of choosing among trusts when it came to antitrust prosecutions. The Sherman Act was on the books. "We are going to enforce that law or die in the attempt," Taft promised grimly. But he was held back until the Supreme Court reasserted the rule of reason in the *Standard Oil* decision (1911), which meant that, once again, the courts themselves undertook to distinguish between good and bad trusts. With that burden lifted, Taft's attorney general George W. Wickersham stepped up the pace of antitrust actions, immediately targeting the United States Steel Corporation. One of the charges was that the steel trust had illegally acquired the Tennessee Coal and Iron Company in 1907. Roosevelt had personally approved the transaction, believing it was necessary — so U.S. Steel representatives had told him — to prevent a financial collapse on Wall Street. Taft's suit against U.S. Steel thus amounted to a personal attack that Roosevelt could not, without dishonor, ignore.

The New Nationalism. Ever since leaving the White House, Roosevelt had been pondering the trust problem. Between breaking up big business and submitting to corporate rule, lay another alternative. The federal government could be empowered to oversee the nation's industrial corporations to make sure they acted in the public interest. They would be regulated by a federal trade commission as if they were natural monopolies or public utilities.

In a speech in Osawatomie, Kansas, in August 1910, Roosevelt made the case for what he called the New Nationalism. The central issue, he argued, was human welfare versus property rights. In modern society, property had to be controlled "to whatever degree the public welfare may require it." The government would become "the steward of the public welfare."

This formulation unleashed Roosevelt. He took up the cause of social justice, adding to his program a federal child labor law, regulation of labor relations, and a national minimum wage for women. Most radical, perhaps, was Roosevelt's attack on the legal system. Insisting that the courts stood in the way of reform, Roosevelt proposed sharp curbs on their powers, even raising the possibility of popular recall of court decisions.

Early in 1912 Roosevelt announced his candidacy for the presidency, immediately sweeping the Insurgent faction into his camp. A bitter party battle ensued. Roosevelt won the states that held primary elections, but Taft controlled the party caucuses elsewhere. Dominated by party regulars, the Republican convention chose Taft. Considering himself cheated out of the nomination, Roosevelt led his followers into a new Progressive Party, soon nicknamed the "Bull Moose" Party. In a crusading campaign Roosevelt offered the New Nationalism to the people.

Woodrow Wilson and the New Freedom

While the Republicans battled among themselves, the Democrats were on the move. The scars caused by the free-silver battle had faded, and William Jennings Bryan's 1908 campaign established the party's progressive credentials. The Democrats made dramatic electoral gains in 1910. And Bryan, after fourteen years as the party's standard-bearer, made way for a new generation of leaders.

The ablest was Woodrow Wilson of New Jersey, a noted political scientist who, as university president, had brought Princeton into the front rank of

On to the White House

At the Democratic convention of 1912, Woodrow Wilson only narrowly defeated the front-runner, Champ Clark of Missouri. *Harper's Weekly* triumphantly depicted Wilson immediately after his nomination — the scholar turned politician riding off on the Democratic donkey, with his running mate, Thomas R. Marshall, hanging on behind. The magazine's editor, George Harvey, had identified Wilson as presidential timber back in 1906, long before the Princeton president had thought of politics, and had worked on his behalf from then on. Newbury Library.

American universities. In 1910, with no political experience, he accepted the Democratic nomination for governor of New Jersey and won. Wilson compiled a sterling reform record, including the direct primary, workers' compensation, and utility regulation. Wilson went on to win the Democratic presidential nomination in 1912 in a bruising battle.

Wilson possessed, to a fault, the moral certainty that was common among progressive leaders. The product of a family of Presbyterian clerics, he instinctively assumed the mantle of righteousness. Only gradually, however, did Wilson hammer out, in reaction to Roosevelt's New Nationalism, a coherent reform program, which he called the New Freedom. As he warmed to the debate, Wilson cast his differences with Roosevelt in fundamental terms of slavery and freedom. "This is a struggle for emancipation," he proclaimed in October 1912. "If America is not to have free enterprise, then she can have freedom of no sort whatever." The New Nationalism represented a future of collectivism, Wilson warned, whereas the New Freedom would preserve political and economic liberty.

Wilson actually had much in common with Roosevelt. "The old time of individual competition is probably gone by," Wilson admitted. He even agreed that preventing the abuse of private power required a strong federal government. He parted company from Roosevelt over means, not ends, confident that the government's existing powers were adequate, with some tinkering, to the task of restraining big business.

Despite all the rhetoric, the 1912 election fell short as a referendum on the New Nationalism

MAP 20.3 Presidential Election of 1912

Candidate	Electoral Vote	Popular Vote	Percent of Popular Vote
Woodrow Wilson (Democrat)	435	6,296,547	41.9
Theodore Roosevelt (Progressive)	88	4,118,571	27.4
William H. Taft (Republican)	8	3,486,720	23.2
Eugene V. Debs (Socialist)	0	900,672	6.0
Other minor parties	—	—	1.5

The 1912 election reveals why the two-party system is so strongly rooted in American politics. The Democrats, though a minority party, won an electoral landslide because the Republicans divided their vote between Roosevelt and Taft. This result indicates what is at stake when major parties splinter. The Socialists, despite a record vote of 900,000, received no electoral votes. To vote Socialist in 1912 meant in effect to throw away one's vote.

versus the New Freedom. The outcome turned on a more humdrum reality: Wilson won because he kept the Democratic vote, while the Republicans split between Roosevelt and Taft. Despite a landslide in the electoral college, Wilson received only 42 percent of the popular vote (Map 20.3).

Yet the 1912 election proved a turning point for economic reform. The debate between Roosevelt and Wilson had brought forth, in the New Freedom, a program capable of finally resolving the decade-long crisis over corporate power. Just as important, the election created a rare legislative opportunity. With Congress in Democratic hands, the time was ripe to act on the New Freedom.

The First Phase: Tariffs and the Federal Reserve. Long out of power, the Democrats were hungry for tariff reform. The Underwood Tariff Act of 1913 pared rates down to 25 percent, targeting especially the trust-dominated industries. Democrats confidently expected the Underwood Tariff to spur competition and reduce prices for consumers.

Wilson then turned to the nation's banking system, whose key weakness was the absence of a central bank, or federal reserve. The main function of central banks at that time was to regulate commercial banks and back them up in case they could not meet their obligations to depositors. In the past this backup role had been assumed by the great New York banks that handled the accounts of outlying banks. If the New York banks weakened, the entire system could collapse. This had nearly happened in 1907, when the Knickerbocker Trust Company failed and panic swept the nation's financial markets.

But if the need for a central bank was clear, the form it should take was hotly disputed. President Wilson, initially no expert, learned quickly and reconciled the reformers and bankers. The resulting Federal Reserve Act of 1913 gave the nation a banking system that was resistant to financial panic. The act delegated operational functions to twelve district reserve banks funded and controlled by their member banks. The Federal Reserve Board imposed public regulation on this regional structure. One crucial new power granted the Federal Reserve was authority to issue currency—federal reserve notes based on assets within the system—that resolved the paralyzing cash shortages experienced during runs on the banks. Another was authority by the Federal Reserve Board to set the discount rate (the interest rate) charged by the district reserve banks to the member banks and thereby the flow of credit to the general public. In one stroke the act strengthened the banking system and reined in Wall Street.

Settling the Trust Problem. Wilson now turned to the big question of the trusts. He relied heavily on a new advisor, Louis D. Brandeis, the celebrated "people's lawyer." Brandeis denied that bigness meant efficiency. On the contrary, he argued, firms that vigorously competed in a free market ran most efficiently. The main thing was to prevent the trusts from unfairly using their power to curb free competition.

Strengthening the Sherman Act, the obvious course, proved hard to do. Was it feasible to say exactly when company practices like overlapping boards of directors, discriminatory pricing, or exclusive contracts became illegal? Brandeis decided that it was not, and Wilson assented. In the Clayton Antitrust Act of 1914, amending the Sherman Act, the definition of illegal practices was left flexible, subject to the test of whether an action "substantially lessen[ed] competition or tend[ed] to create a monopoly."

This retreat from a definitive antitrust prescription meant that a federal trade commission would be needed to back up the Sherman and Clayton Acts. Wilson was understandably hesitant, given his opposition during the campaign to Roosevelt's powerful trade commission. At first Wilson favored an advisory, information-gathering agency. But ultimately, under the 1914 law establishing it, the Federal Trade Commission (FTC) received broad powers to investigate companies and issue "cease and desist" orders against unfair trade practices that violated antitrust law.

Despite a good deal of commotion, this arduous legislative process was actually an exercise in consensus building. Wilson opened the debate in a conciliatory way. "The antagonism between business and government is over," he said, and the time ripe for a program representing the "best business judgment in America." Afterward, Wilson felt he had brought the long controversy to a successful conclusion, and in fact he had. Steering a course between Taft's conservatism and Roosevelt's radical New Nationalism, Wilson carved out a middle way. He brought to bear the powers of government without shattering the constitutional order and curbed corporate abuses without threatening the capitalist system.

The Labor Question. In the meantime, as one crisis over economic power was being resolved, another boiled up. After midnight on October 1, 1910, an explosion ripped through the Los Angeles *Times* headquarters, killing twenty employees and wrecking the building. It turned out that John J. McNamara, a high official of the AFL's Bridge and Structural Iron Workers Union, was behind the dynamiting, and that his brother and another union member had done the deed. Lincoln Steffens gave voice to a question that, in the midst of the national outrage over the bombing, people kept asking. Why would

The Ludlow Massacre, 1914

Like John Sloan's drawing on page 619, this is one in a series expressing Sloan's outrage at social injustice in progressive America. It appears on the cover of *The Masses,* a popular socialist magazine. The drawing memorializes a tragic episode during a miners' strike at Ludlow, Colorado — the asphyxiation of many women and children when the state militia torched the tent city of evicted miners — and the aftermath, an armed revolt by enraged miners. University of Michigan Library.

"healthy, good-tempered boys like these McNamara boys . . . believe . . . that the only recourse they have for improving the conditions of the wage earner is to use dynamite against property and life?"

Steffens's question resonated ever more urgently as a wave of violent strikes swept the country—New York garment workers in 1910; railroad workers on the Illinois Central and Harriman lines in 1911; and textile workers, led by the Industrial Workers of the World (see Chapter 17), in Lawrence, Massachusetts, in 1912, and Paterson, New Jersey, in 1913. The IWW presence compounded middle-class anxieties that the country was in the grip of class war because the Wobblies did indeed invoke the violent language of class war. Finally, in a ghastly climactic episode in 1914, state militia during a bitter Colorado coal miners' strike torched a tent city at Ludlow and asphyxiated many strikers' wives and children. Infuriated miners took up arms and plunged Colorado into a civil war that ended only with arrival of the U.S. Army.

The "labor question" was suddenly on the progressive agenda. President Wilson appointed a blue ribbon U.S. Commission on Industrial Relations, whose job it would be, as the youthful journalist Walter Lippmann wrote, to explain "why America, supposed to become the land of promise, has become the land of disappointment and deep-seated discontent." In its majority report, the Commission took note that workers earning $10 or less a week lived at poverty levels, that they were ground down by repeated spells of unemployment, and that "an almost universal conviction [prevailed] that they, both as individuals and as a class, are denied justice." The core reason for industrial violence, including the McNamara bombing, was the fierce anti-unionism of American employers, which left workers with no voice and no hope for justice at the workplace. In its most important recommendation, the majority report called for federal legislation to protect the right of workers to organize and engage in collective bargaining. If this seemed, in 1915, too radical a proposal, it was in fact the opening shot in a battle for labor rights that would end triumphantly in the New Deal (see Chapter 24).

The immediate effect was to push President Wilson to the left. Having denounced Roosevelt's paternalism, he had at first been unreceptive to what he saw as special-interest demands by organized labor. On the leading issue—that unions be exempt from antitrust prosecutions that spiked their boycott weapon—the most Wilson was willing to accept was cosmetic language in the Clayton Act that did not grant them the immunity they

FIGURE 20.1 The Federal Bureaucracy, 1890–1917

The surge in federal employment after 1900 mirrored the surge in government authority under Theodore Roosevelt's progressive leadership. Not even Wilson, although he ran on a platform of limited government, could stem the tide.

sought. But now, instructed by the revelations of his Commission on Industrial Relations—and by labor's increasing clout at the polls—Wilson warmed up to the AFL. As his second presidential campaign drew near, Wilson lost some of his scruples about the paternalism of pro-labor legislation. In 1915 and 1916 he championed a host of bills beneficial to American workers: a federal child-labor law; the Adamson eight-hour law for railroad workers; and the landmark Seamen's Act, which eliminated age-old abuses of sailors aboard ship. Nor was it lost on observers that, his New Freedom rhetoric notwithstanding, Wilson presided over an ever more active federal government and an ever-expanding federal bureaucracy (Figure 20.1).

Wilson encountered the same dilemma that confronted all successful progressives—the clash of moral principle against the unyielding realities of political life. Progressives were high-minded but not radical. They saw evils in the system, but they did not consider the system itself to be evil. They also prided themselves on being realists as well as moralists. So it stood to reason that Wilson, like other progressives who achieved power, would find his place at the center.

But it would be wrong to underestimate their achievement. Progressives made presidential leadership important again, they brought government back into the nation's life, they laid the foundation for twentieth-century social and economic policy. And, as we shall see, they put an enduring stamp on America's self-definition as a world power.

21 An Emerging World Power, 1877–1914

IN 1881 GREAT BRITAIN SENT a new envoy to Washington. He was Sir Lionel Sackville-West, son of an earl and brother-in-law of the Tory leader Lord Denby, but otherwise distinguished only as the lover of a celebrated Spanish dancer. His well-connected friends wanted to park Sir Lionel somewhere comfortable, but out of harm's way. So they made him minister to the United States.

Twenty years later such an appointment would have been unthinkable. All the European powers staffed their missions in Washington with top-of-the-line ambassadors. And they treated the United States, without question, as a fellow Great Power.

In Sir Lionel's day the United States scarcely cast a shadow on world affairs. America's army was smaller than Bulgaria's; its navy ranked thirteenth in the world and was a threat mainly to the crews manning its rickety ships. By 1900, however, the United States was flexing its muscles. It had just made short work of Spain in a brief but decisive war and acquired an empire stretching from Puerto Rico to the Philippines. America's standing as a rising naval power was manifest, and so was its muscular assertion of national interest in the Caribbean and the Pacific.

The Europeans could not be sure what America's role would be, since the United States retained its traditional policy against entangling alliances.

The Roots of Expansion
Diplomacy in the Gilded Age
The Economy of Expansionism
The Making of a "Large" Foreign Policy
The Ideology of Expansionism

An American Empire
The Cuban Crisis
The Spoils of War
The Imperial Experiment

Onto the World Stage
A Power among Powers
The Open Door in Asia
Wilson and Mexico
The Gathering Storm in Europe

Summary
Connections: Diplomacy

◀ **Battle of Santiago de Cuba, 1898**
James G. Tyler's dramatic painting of the final sea battle of the Spanish-American War showcased America's newest weapon of war, the battleship. Franklin D. Roosevelt Library.

But foreign offices across the Continent acknowledged the importance of the United States and carefully assessed its likely response to every event.

The Roots of Expansion

With a population of fifty million, the United States already ranked with the great European powers in 1880. In industrial production the nation stood second only to Britain and was rapidly closing the gap. Anyone who doubted the military prowess of Americans needed only to recall the ferocity with which they had fought one another in the Civil War. The great campaigns of Lee, Sherman, and Grant had entered the military textbooks and were closely studied by army strategists everywhere, as was evident in the skirmishing lines and massed charges employed by the German infantry against the French in the Franco-Prussian War of 1870.

And when vital interests were at stake, the United States had not shown itself lacking in diplomatic vigor. The Civil War had put the United States at odds with both France and Britain. The dispute with France involved Mexico. The United States regarded a French-sponsored regime set up there under Archduke Maximilian in 1863 as threatening to the security of the Southwest, whose seizure in 1848 still rankled Mexico. Once the Civil War ended, the United States responded forcefully. In 1867, as American troops under General Philip Sheridan massed on the border, the French military withdrew, abandoning Maximilian to a Mexican firing squad.

With Britain, the thorny issue involved damages to Union shipping by the *Alabama* and other Confederate sea raiders operating from English ports. American hopes of taking Canada as compensation were dashed by Britain's grant of dominion status to Canada in 1867. But four years later, after lengthy negotiations, Britain expressed regret and agreed to the arbitration of the *Alabama* claims, settling to America's satisfaction the last outstanding diplomatic issue of the Civil War.

Diplomacy in the Gilded Age

In the years that followed, the United States lapsed into diplomatic inactivity, not out of weakness but for lack of any clear national purpose in world affairs. The business of building the nation's industrial economy absorbed Americans and turned their attention inward. And while telegraphic cables provided the country with swift overseas communication after the 1860s, wide oceans still kept the world at a distance and gave Americans a sense of isolation and security.

European affairs, which centered on Franco-German rivalry and on bewildering Balkan enmities, hardly concerned the United States. As far as President Cleveland's secretary of state, Thomas F. Bayard, was concerned, "we have not the slightest share or interest [in] the small politics and backstage intrigues of Europe."

In these circumstances, why maintain a big navy? After the Civil War, the fleet gradually deteriorated. Of the 125 ships on the navy's active list, only about 25 were seaworthy at any one time, mainly sailing ships and obsolete ironclads modeled on the *Monitor* of Civil War fame. The administration of Chester A. Arthur (1881–1885) began a modest upgrading program, commissioning new ships, raising the standards for the officer corps, and founding the Naval War College. But the fleet remained small, without a unified naval command, and deployed mainly for coastal defense.

The conduct of diplomacy was likewise of little account. Appointment to the Foreign Service was mostly through the spoils system. American envoys and consular officers were a mixed lot, with many idlers and drunkards among the hardworking and competent. For its part the State Department tended to be inactive, exerting little control over either policy or its missions abroad. In Asia, Africa, and the Pacific islands the American presence was likely to be Christian missionaries, many of them women, and as women's social activism intensified at home, that too made itself felt in distant lands. As part of its do-everything program, the Woman's Christian Temperance Union began sending emissaries abroad to proselytize among the natives and convey the message that women's rights were an American cause.

Latin American Diplomacy. In the Caribbean, the expansionist enthusiasms of the Civil War era subsided. William H. Seward, Lincoln and Andrew Johnson's secretary of state, had dreamed of an American empire extending from the Caribbean across Mexico to Hawaii. Nothing came of his grandiose plans, nor of President Grant's efforts to purchase Santo Domingo (the future Dominican Republic) in 1870. The Senate regularly blocked later moves to acquire bases in Haiti, Cuba, and Venezuela. The long-cherished interest in a canal across Central America also faded. Despite its claim to exclusive rights, the United States stood by when a French company headed by the builder of Egypt's Suez Canal, Ferdinand de Lesseps, started to dig across the Panama isthmus in 1880. That project failed after a decade, but because of bankruptcy, not American opposition.

Diplomatic activity quickened when the energetic James G. Blaine became secretary of state in 1881. He got involved in a border dispute between Mexico and Guatemala, tried to settle a war Chile was waging against Peru and Bolivia, and called the first Pan-American conference. Blaine's interventions in Latin American disputes went badly, however, and his successor canceled the Pan-American conference after Blaine left office in late 1881. This was a characteristic example of Gilded Age diplomacy, driven largely by partisan politics and carried out without any clear sense of national purpose.

Pan-Americanism — the notion of a community of states of the Western Hemisphere — took root, however, and Blaine, returning in 1889 for a second stint at the State Department, approved the plans of the outgoing Cleveland administration for a new Pan-American conference. But little came of it, except for an agency in Washington that became the Pan-American Union. Any South American goodwill won by Blaine's efforts was soon blasted by the humiliation the United States visited upon Chile because of a riot against American sailors in the port of Valparaiso in 1891. Threatened with war, Chile apologized to the United States and paid an indemnity of $75,000. It was not lost upon South Americans that the United States, for all its fine talk about a community of nations, regarded itself as the hemisphere's dominating power, and acted accordingly.

Pacific Episodes. In the Pacific, American interest centered on Hawaii, where sugarcane had attracted a horde of American planters. Nominally an independent nation, Hawaii fell under American dominance. An 1875 treaty gave Hawaiian sugar duty-free entry into the American market and declared the islands off limits to other powers. A second treaty in 1887 granted the United States naval rights at Pearl Harbor.

When Hawaii's favored access to the American market was abruptly canceled by the McKinley Tariff of 1890, sugar planters began to plot an American takeover of the islands so that Hawaiian sugar would be treated as a domestic product. They organized a revolt in January 1893 against Queen Liliuokalani and quickly negotiated a treaty of annexation with the Harrison administration. Before the Senate could approve it, however, Grover Cleveland returned to the presidency and withdrew the treaty. To annex Hawaii, he declared, would violate America's "honor and morality" and an "unbroken tradition" against acquiring territory far from the nation's shores.

Meanwhile, the American presence elsewhere in the Pacific was growing. In 1867 the United States purchased Alaska from Imperial Russia for 7.2 million dollars. The initiative had come from St. Petersburg, which was anxious to unload an indefensible, treasury-draining possession. Secretary of State Seward, ever the expansionist, was happy to oblige, although it took some doing to persuade a dubious Congress. Alaska gave the United States not only a windfall of vast natural resources but also an un-looked-for presence stretching across the northern Pacific. Far to the south, in the Samoan Islands, the United States secured rights in 1878 to a coaling station for its steamships at Pago Pago harbor — a key link on the route to Australia — and established an informal protectorate there. In 1889, after some jostling with Germany and Britain, the rivalry over Samoa ended in a tripartite protectorate, with America retaining its rights in Pago Pago.

Sugarcane Plantation, Hawaii

Over 300,000 Asians from China, Japan, Korea, and the Philippines came to work in the Hawaiian cane fields between 1850 and 1920. The hardships they endured are reflected in plantation work songs, such as this one by Japanese laborers:

But when I came what I saw was Hell
The boss was Satan
The lunas [overseers] his helpers.

© Curt Teich Postcard Archives, Lake County Museum.

American diplomacy in these years has been characterized as a series of incidents, not the pursuit of a foreign policy. Many things happened, but intermittently and without any well-founded conception of national objectives. This was possible because, as the Englishman James Bryce remarked in 1888, America still sailed "upon a summer sea." In the stormier waters that lay ahead, a different kind of diplomacy would be required.

The Economy of Expansionism

"A policy of isolation did well enough when we were an embryo nation," remarked Senator Orville Platt of Connecticut in 1893. "But today things are different.... We are 65 million people, the most advanced and powerful on earth, and regard to our future welfare demands an abandonment of the doctrines of isolation." What especially demanded that Americans look outward was their prodigious economy.

The Search for Foreign Markets. America's gross domestic product (GDP) — the total value of goods and services — quadrupled between 1870 and 1900. But was American demand big enough to absorb this multiplying output? Over 90 percent was consumed at home. Even so, foreign markets mattered. Roughly a fifth of the nation's agricultural output was exported, and as the industrial economy expanded, so did the export of manufactured goods. Between 1880 and 1900, the industrial share of total exports jumped from 15 percent to over 30 percent.

American firms began to plant themselves overseas. As early as 1868 the Singer Sewing Machine Company established a factory in Glasgow, Scotland. The giant among American firms doing business abroad was Rockefeller's Standard Oil, with European branches operating tankers and marketing kerosene across the Continent. In Asia, Standard Oil cans, converted into utensils and roofing tin, became a visible sign of American market penetration. Brand names like Kodak (cameras), McCormick (agricultural equipment) and Ford (the Model T) became household words around the world.

Foreign trade was important partly for reasons of international finance. As a developing economy the United States attracted a lot of foreign capital. The result was a heavy outflow of dollars to pay interest and dividends to foreign investors. To balance this account, the United States needed to export more goods than it imported. In fact, a favorable

The Singer Sewing Machine

The sewing machine was an American invention that swiftly found markets abroad. The Singer Company, the dominant firm, not only exported large quantities but also produced 200,000 machines annually at a Scottish plant that employed 6,000 workers. Singer's advertising rightly boasted of its prowess as an international company and of a product that was "The Universal Machine." New-York Historical Society.

FIGURE 21.1 Balance of U.S. Imports, 1870–1914

By 1876 the United States had become a net exporting nation. The brief reversal after 1888 aroused fears that the United States was losing its foreign markets and helped fuel the expansionist drive of the 1890s.

import-export balance was achieved in 1876 (Figure 21.1). But because of its dependence on foreign capital, America had to be constantly vigilant about its export trade.

Even more important, however, was the relationship that many Americans perceived between foreign markets and the nation's social stability. Hard times always sparked agrarian unrest and labor strife. The problem, many thought, was that the nation's capacity to produce was outrunning its capacity to consume. When the economy slowed, cutbacks in domestic demand drove down farm prices and caused layoffs across the country. The answer was to make sure there would always be enough buyers for America's surplus products, and this meant buyers in foreign markets.

Trade and Diplomacy. How did these concerns about overseas trade relate to America's foreign policy? The bulk of American exports in the late nineteenth century — over 80 percent — went to Europe and Canada (Table 21.1). In these countries the normal practice of diplomacy sufficed to protect the nation's economic interests, although normal practice included close cooperation with big international players like Standard Oil. Rockefeller was thankful for the "ambassadors and ministers and consuls [who] have aided to push our way into new markets to the utmost corners of the world." In these places — in Asia, Latin America, and other regions that Americans considered "backward" — a tougher brand of intervention was required because there the United States was competing with other industrial powers.

Asia and Latin America represented only a modest part of America's export trade. Still, this trade was growing — it was worth $200 million in 1900 — and parts of it mattered a great deal to specific industries — for example, the Chinese market for American textiles. The real importance of these non-Western markets, however, was not so much their current value as their future promise. China especially exerted a powerful grip on the American mercantile imagination. Many felt that the China trade, although quite small at the time, would one day be the key to American prosperity. Therefore, China and other beckoning markets must not be closed to the United States.

In the mid-1880s the pace of European imperialism picked up. After the Berlin Conference of 1884, Africa was rapidly carved up by the European powers. In a burst of modernizing energy, Japan transformed itself into a major power and began to

TABLE 21.1 Exports to Canada and Europe Compared with Exports to Asia and Latin America, 1875–1900

Year	Exports to Canada and Europe ($)	Percentage of Total	Exports to Asia and Latin America ($)	Percentage of Total
1875	494,000,000	86.1	72,000,000	12.5
1885	637,000,000	85.8	87,000,000	11.7
1895	681,000,000	84.3	108,000,000	13.4
1900	1,135,000,000	81.4	200,000,000	14.3

SOURCE: Compiled from information in *Historical Statistics of the United States* (1960); U.S. Department of Commerce, *Long Term Growth, 1860–1965* (1966); National Bureau of Economic Research, *Trends in the American Economy in the Nineteenth Century* (1960).

challenge China's claims to Korea. In the Sino-Japanese War (1894–1895), Japan won an easy victory and started a scramble among the Great Powers, including Russia, to divide China into spheres of influence. In Latin America, U.S. interests began to be challenged more aggressively by Britain, France, and Germany.

On top of all this came the Panic of 1893, setting in motion industrial strikes and agrarian protests that Cleveland's secretary of state, Walter Q. Gresham, like many other Americans, took to be "symptoms of revolution." With the nation's social stability seemingly at risk, securing the markets of Latin America and Asia became an urgent matter.

The Making of a "Large" Foreign Policy

"Whether they will or no, Americans must now begin to look outward. The growing production of the country requires it." So wrote Captain Alfred T. Mahan, voicing an opinion many others held by 1890. What he added, however, was uniquely his — a strategy of American expansionism. Mahan's argument was that control of the seas was the key to imperial power, and from this insight emerged an American expansionist strategy.

Alfred T. Mahan and the Strategy of Naval Power. Mahan was a naval officer in an age when the navy was no place for an ambitious young man. Posted to a rickety ship cruising Latin America, he spent his spare time reading history. In a library in Lima, Peru, he hit upon the idea that great empires — Rome in ancient times, Britain in his own day — had derived their power from control of the seas. This insight became the basis for his *The Influence of Seapower upon History* (1890), the celebrated book that shaped America's strategic thinking about its role in the world.

The United States should regard the oceans not as barriers, Mahan wrote, but as "a great highway... over which men pass in all directions." Traversing that highway required a robust merchant marine (America's had fallen on hard times since its heyday in the 1850s), a powerful navy to protect American commerce, and overseas bases. Having converted from sail to steam, navies required coaling stations far from home. Without such stations, Mahan warned, warships were "like land birds, unable to fly far from their own shores."

Mahan advocated the construction of a canal across Central America connecting the Atlantic and Pacific Oceans. Such a canal would enable the eastern United States to "compete with Europe, on equal terms as to distance, for the markets of East Asia." The canal's approaches would need to be guarded by bases in the Caribbean Sea. Hawaii would have to be annexed to extend American power into the Pacific. What Mahan envisioned was a form of colonialism different from Europe's — not rule over territories and populations, but control of strategic points around the globe in defense of America's trading interests.

Other enthusiasts of a powerful America flocked to Mahan, including such up-and-coming politicians as Theodore Roosevelt and Henry Cabot Lodge. The influence of these men, few in number but well connected, increased during the 1890s. Lodge became a senator, while Roosevelt became McKinley's assistant secretary of the navy. They pushed steadily for what Lodge called a "large policy."

Alfred T. Mahan
Mahan's theory about the influence of sea power on history came to him while he was killing time on a tour of naval duty, reading Roman history in a library in Lima, Peru, in 1885. His insight was personal as well as intellectual: Embarrassed by the decrepit ships on which he served, Mahan thought the United States should have a modern fleet in which officers like himself could serve with pride (and with some hope of professional advancement). U.S. Naval Historical Foundation.

Rebuilding the Navy. Mahan proposed a battleship fleet capable of striking a decisive blow against an enemy far from America's shores. In 1890 Congress appropriated funds for three battleships as the first installment on a two-ocean navy. Battleships might be expensive, said Benjamin F. Tracy, Harrison's ambitious secretary of the navy, but they were "the premium paid by the United States for the insurance of its acquired wealth and its growing industries." The battleship took on a special aura for those — like the young Roosevelt — who had grand dreams for the United States. "Oh, Lord! If only the people who are ignorant about our Navy could see those great warships in all their majesty and beauty, and could realize how [well fitted they are] to uphold the honor of America!"

The incoming Cleveland administration was less spread-eagled and, by canceling Harrison's scheme for annexing Hawaii, established its antiexpansionist credentials. But after hesitating briefly Cleveland picked up the naval program of his Republican predecessor, pressing Congress just as forcefully for more battleships (five were authorized) and making the same basic argument. The nation's commercial vitality — "free access to all markets," in the words of Cleveland's second secretary of state, Richard Olney — depended on its naval power.

While rejecting the territorial aspects of Mahan's thinking, Cleveland absorbed the underlying strategic arguments about where America's vital interests lay. This explains the remarkable crisis that suddenly blew up in 1895 over Venezuela.

The Venezuela Crisis. For years a border dispute simmered between Venezuela and British Guiana. Now the United States demanded that the dispute be resolved. The European powers were carving up Africa and Asia. How could the United States be sure that Europe did not have similar designs on Latin America? Secretary of State Olney made that point in a bristling note to London on July 25, 1895, insisting that Britain accept arbitration or face the consequences. Invoking the Monroe Doctrine, Olney warned that the United States would brook no challenge to its vital interests in the Caribbean. These vital interests were America's, not Venezuela's; Venezuela was not consulted during the entire dispute.

Once the British realized that Cleveland meant business, they backed off and agreed to arbitration of the boundary dispute. Afterward, Olney remarked with satisfaction that, as a great industrial nation, the United States needed "to accept [a] commanding position" and take its place "among the Powers of the earth." Other countries would have to accommodate America's need for access to "more markets and larger markets for the consumption and products of the industry and inventive genius of the American people."

The Ideology of Expansionism

As policymakers hammered out a new foreign policy, a sustaining ideology took shape. One source of expansionist dogma was the Social Darwinist theory that dominated the political thought of this era (see Chapter 19). If, as Charles Darwin had shown, animals and plants evolved through the survival of the fittest, so did nations. "Nothing under the sun is stationary," warned the American social theorist Brooks Adams in *The Law of Civilization and Decay* (1895). "Not to advance is to recede." By this criterion the United States had no choice; if it wanted to survive, it had to expand.

Linked to Social Darwinism was a spreading belief in the inherent superiority of the Anglo-Saxon "race." In the late nineteenth century, Great Britain basked in the glory of its representative institutions, industrial prosperity, and far-flung empire — all ascribed to the supposed racial superiority of its people and, by extension, of their American cousins as well. On both sides of the Atlantic, **Anglo-Saxonism** was in vogue. Thus did John Fiske, an American philosopher and historian, lecture the nation on its future responsibilities: "The work which the English race began when it colonized North America is destined to go on until every land on the earth's surface that is not already the seat of an old civilization shall become English in its language, in its religion, in its political habits, and to a predominant extent in the blood of its people."

Fiske entitled his lecture "Manifest Destiny." A half century earlier this term had expressed the sense of national mission — America's "manifest destiny" — to sweep aside the Native American peoples and occupy the continent. In his widely read book *The Winning of the West* (1896), Theodore Roosevelt drew a parallel between the expansionism of his own time and the assault on the Indians. To Roosevelt, what happened to "backward peoples" mattered little because their conquest was "for the benefit of civilization and in the interests of mankind." More than historical parallels, however, linked the Manifest Destiny of past and present.

In 1890 the U.S. Census reported the end of the continental movement westward: there was no longer a frontier beyond which land remained to be conquered. The psychological impact of that news was profound, spawning among other things a new historical interpretation that said the nation's character was shaped by the frontier. In a landmark essay setting out this thesis — "The Significance of the Frontier in American History" (1893) — the young historian Frederick Jackson Turner suggested a link between the closing of the frontier and overseas expansion. "He would be a rash prophet who should assert that the expansive character of American life has now entirely ceased," Turner wrote. "Movement has been its dominant fact, and, unless this training has no effect upon a people, the American energy will continually demand a wider field for its exercise." As Turner predicted, Manifest Destiny did turn outward.

Thus a strong current of ideas, deeply rooted in American experience and traditions, justified the new diplomacy of expansionism. The United States was eager to step onto the world stage. All it needed was the right occasion.

- ▶ What is the relationship between America's economic interests abroad and the expansionist impulse of the late nineteenth century?
- ▶ Describe Alfred T. Mahan's impact on American strategic thinking in the late nineteenth century.
- ▶ What were the intellectual currents that encouraged Americans to believe that their country should be an imperial power?

An American Empire

Ever since Spain had lost most of its American empire in the early nineteenth century, Cubans had yearned to join their mainland brothers and sisters in freedom. Movements for independence had sprung up repeatedly, most recently in a rebellion in the late 1860s. In February 1895, inspired by the poet José Martí, Cuban patriots rebelled again. Although Martí died in an early skirmish, his followers persisted and mounted a stubborn guerrilla war. The Spaniards controlled the towns, the insurgents much of the countryside. In early 1896 the newly appointed Spanish commander, Valeriano Weyler, adopted a harsh policy of *reconcentration*, forcing entire populations into guarded camps. Because no aggressive pursuit followed, this ruthless strategy only inconvenienced the guerrilla fighters. The toll on civilians, however, was devastating. Out of a population of 1,600,000, as many as 200,000 died of starvation, exposure, or dysentery.

The Cuban Crisis

Rebel leaders shrewdly saw that they could tip the balance by drawing the United States into their struggle. A key group of exiles, the Junta, set up shop in New York to make the case for *Cuba Libre*. By itself, their cause might not have attracted much interest. The Spaniards were behaving no more dishonorably than any other colonial power; nor were atrocities in short supply elsewhere in the world. The Cuban exiles, however, arrived at a lucky moment.

William Randolph Hearst had just purchased the *New York Journal*, and he was in a hurry to build readership. Locked in a circulation war with Joseph Pulitzer's *New York World*, Hearst elevated Cuba's agony into flaming front-page headlines. Not much actual news could be extracted from Cuba, for the sporadic fighting took place in the remote interior, beyond the reach of Hearst's correspondents in Havana. It did not matter. Rebel claims were good enough for Hearst, and a drumbeat of superheated articles began to appear about mostly nonexistent battles and about Spanish atrocities.

Across the country powerful sentiments stirred: humanitarian concern for the suffering Cubans, sympathy with their aspirations for freedom, and, as anger against Spain rose, a fiery patriotism soon tagged **jingoism**. These sentiments were often entwined with American anxieties over the perceived effeminacy of modern life (see Chapter 18). A gendered language infused much of the debate, with rebels portrayed as chivalric defenders of Cuban women against the "lustful bondage" of the Spaniards. It would be good for the nation's character, jingoists argued, for Americans to ride to the rescue. The government should not pass up this opportunity, said Senator Albert J. Beveridge, to "manufacture manhood." In this emotion-laden atmosphere, Congress began calling for Cuban independence.

Presidential Politics. Grover Cleveland, still in office when the rebellion broke out, took a cooler view of the situation. His concern was with America's vital interests, which, he told Congress, were "by no means of a wholly sentimental or philanthropic character." The Cuban civil war was disrupting trade and destroying American property, especially Cuban sugar plantations. Cleveland also was worried that Spain's troubles might draw in other European powers. A chronically unstable Cuba was incompatible with America's strategic interests, in particular, the planned inter-oceanic canal whose Caribbean approaches would have to be safeguarded.

If Spain could put down the rebellion, that was fine with Cleveland. But there was a limit, he felt, to how long the United States could tolerate Spain's impotence.

The McKinley administration, on taking office in March 1897, adopted much the same pragmatic line. Like Cleveland, McKinley was motivated by a conception of the United States as the dominant Caribbean power, with vital interests that had to be protected. McKinley, however, was inclined to be tougher on the Spaniards. He was upset by their "uncivilized and inhumane conduct" in Cuba. And he had to contend with rising jingoism in the Senate. But the notion, long held by historians, that McKinley was swept along against his better judgment by popular opinion and by congressional pressure was wrong. McKinley was very much his own man — a skilled politician and a canny, if undramatic, president. In particular, McKinley was sensitive to business fears of any rash action that might disrupt an economy just recovering from depression.

The Road to War. On September 18, 1897, the American minister in Madrid informed the Spanish government that it was time to "put a stop to this destructive war." Either ensure an "early and certain peace" or the United States would step in. At first America's hard line seemed to work. The conservative regime fell, and a liberal government, upon taking office in October 1897, moderated its Cuban policy. Spain recalled General Weyler, backed away from reconcentration, and offered Cuba a degree of self-rule but not independence. Madrid's incapacity soon became clear, however. In January 1898 Spanish loyalists in Havana rioted against the offer of autonomy. The Cuban rebels, encouraged by the prospect of American intervention, demanded full independence.

On February 9, 1898, Hearst's *New York Journal* published a private letter by Dupuy de Lôme, the Spanish minister to the United States. In it de Lôme called President McKinley "weak" and "a bidder for the admiration of the crowd." Worse, his letter suggested that the Spanish government was not taking the American demands seriously. De Lôme immediately resigned, but the damage had been done.

A week later the U.S. battle cruiser *Maine* blew up and sank in Havana harbor, with the loss of 260 seamen. "Whole Country Thrills with the War Fever," proclaimed the *New York Journal*. From that moment onward popular passions against Spain became a major factor in the march toward war.

"Remember the *Maine*!"

In late January 1898 the *Maine* entered Havana harbor on a courtesy call. On the evening of February 15, a mysterious blast sent the U.S. warship to the bottom. This dramatic lithograph conveys something of the impact of that event on American public opinion. Although no evidence ever linked the Spanish authorities to the explosion, the sinking of the *Maine* fed the emotional fires that prepared the nation for war with Spain. Granger Collection.

McKinley kept his head. He assumed that the sinking had been accidental. A naval board of inquiry, however, issued a damaging report. Disagreeing with a Spanish investigation, the American board concluded improbably that the sinking had been caused by a mine. (A 1976 naval inquiry disagreed: The more likely cause was faulty ship design that placed explosive munitions too close to coal bunkers prone to spontaneous fires.) No evidence linked the Spanish to the purported mine. But if a mine did sink the ship, then the Spanish were responsible for not protecting a peaceful American vessel within their jurisdiction.

President McKinley had no stomach for the martial spirit engulfing the country. He was not swept along by the calls for blood to avenge the *Maine*. But he could not ignore an aroused public opinion. Hesitant business leaders now also became impatient for the dispute with Spain to end. War was preferable to the unresolved Cuban crisis. On March 27, McKinley cabled to Madrid what was in effect an ultimatum: an immediate armistice for six months, abandonment of the practice of reconcentration, and, with the United States as mediator, peace negotiations with the rebels. Desperate to avoid war, the Spanish government was prepared to concede on all these points, but balked at McKinley's added demand that mediation had to result in Cuban independence. That would have meant the Madrid regime's downfall and, indeed, might have jeopardized the Crown itself.

On April 11, McKinley informed Congress that further negotiation was useless and asked for authority to intervene in Cuba. His motives were as he described them: "In the name of humanity, in the name of civilization, in behalf of endangered American interests which give us the right and the duty to speak and to act, the war in Cuba must stop." The War Hawks in Congress—a mixture of empire-minded Republicans like Henry Cabot Lodge and western Democrats espousing Cuban self-determination—chafed under McKinley's cautious progress. But the president did not lose control, and he defeated their demand for recognition of the rebel republican government, which would have reduced the administration's freedom of action in dealing with Spain.

The resolutions authorizing intervention in Cuba contained an amendment by Senator Henry M. Teller of Colorado disclaiming any intention by the United States to take possession of Cuba. No European government should say that "when we go out to make battle for the liberty and freedom of Cuban patriots, that we are doing it for the purpose of aggrandizement." This had to be made clear with regard to Cuba, "whatever," Senator Teller added, "we may do as to some other islands."

Did McKinley have in mind "some other islands"? Was this really a war of aggression, secretly motivated by a desire to seize strategic territory from Spain? In a strict sense, almost certainly no. It was not *because* of expansionist ambitions that McKinley forced Spain into a corner. But once war came McKinley saw it as an opportunity. As he wrote privately after hostilities began: "While we are conducting war and until its conclusion, we must keep all we get; when the war is over we must keep what we want." Precisely what would be forthcoming, of course, depended on the fortunes of battle.

The Spoils of War

Hostilities formally began when Spain declared war on the United States on April 24, 1898. Across the country regiments began to form. Theodore Roosevelt immediately resigned as assistant secretary of the navy, ordered a fancy uniform, and accepted a commission as lieutenant colonel of a volunteer cavalry regiment soon to become famous as the Rough Riders. Raw recruits poured into makeshift bases around Tampa, Florida. Confusion reigned. Tropical uniforms did not arrive; the food was bad, the sanitation worse; and rifles were in short supply. No provision had been made for getting the troops to Cuba; the government hastily began to collect a miscellaneous fleet of yachts, lake steamers, and commercial boats. Fortunately, the small regular army was a disciplined, highly professional force: Its 28,000 seasoned troops provided a nucleus for the 200,000 civilians who had to be turned into soldiers inside of a few weeks.

The navy was in better shape. Spain had nothing to match America's seven battleships and armored cruisers, and the ships it did have were undermanned and ill-prepared for battle. The Spanish admiral, Pascual Cervera, gloomily expected that his fleet would "like Don Quixote go out to fight windmills and come back with a broken head."

The Pacific Campaign. The decisive engagement of the war took place in the far Pacific, not in Cuba. This was the handiwork of Theodore Roosevelt, who, while still in the Navy Department, had gotten the intrepid Commodore George Dewey appointed commander of the Pacific fleet, with instructions that, in the event of war, he was to set sail immediately against the Spanish fleet in the Philippines. When hostilities began, Roosevelt confronted his surprised superior, John Long, and pressured him into validating the instructions to Dewey. On May 1, American ships cornered the Spanish fleet in Manila Bay and destroyed it. The victory produced euphoria in the United States. Immediately, part of the army being trained for the Cuban campaign was diverted to the Philippines. Manila, the Philippine capital, fell on August 13, 1898.

With Dewey's naval victory, American strategic thinking clicked into place. "We hold the other side of the Pacific and the value to this country is almost beyond imagination," declared Senator Lodge. "We must on no account let the [Philippine] Islands go." President McKinley agreed, and so did his key advisors. Naval strategists had long coveted an anchor in the western Pacific. At this time, too, the Great Powers were carving up China into spheres of influence. If American merchants wanted a crack at that glittering market, the United States would have to project its power into Asia.

Once the decision for a Philippine base had been made, other decisions followed almost automatically. The question of Hawaii was quickly resolved. After stalling the previous year, Hawaiian annexation went through Congress by joint resolution in July 1898. Hawaii had suddenly acquired a crucial strategic value: It was a halfway station on the way to the Philippines. The navy pressed for a coaling base in the central Pacific; that meant Guam, a Spanish island in the Marianas. There was need also for a strategically located base in the Caribbean; that meant Puerto Rico. By July, before the assault on Cuba, the full scope of McKinley's war aims had crystallized.

The Cuban Front. And so had the strategic objective in the Cuban campaign: a quick and decisive victory forcing Spain to fulfill America's imperial requirements. The Spanish forces were already depleted by the long guerrilla war. Tied down by the rebels, they permitted the landings at Daiquiri to go uncontested. Santiago, where the Spanish fleet was anchored, became the key to the military campaign (Map 21.1). Half-trained and ill-equipped, the American forces moving on the city might have been checked by a determined opponent. The Spaniards fought to maintain their honor, but they had no stomach for a real war against the Americans.

MAP 21.1 The Spanish-American War of 1898

The swift American victory in the Spanish-American War resulted from overwhelming naval superiority. Dewey's destruction of the Spanish fleet in Manila harbor doomed the Spaniards in the Philippines. In Cuba, American ground forces won a hard victory on San Juan Hill, for they were ill equipped and poorly supplied. With the United States in control of the seas, the Spaniards saw no choice but to give up the battle for Cuba.

The Battle of San Juan Hill

On July 1, 1898, the key battle for Cuba took place on heights overlooking Santiago. African American troops bore the brunt of the fighting. Although generally overlooked, the black role in the San Juan battle is done justice in this contemporary lithograph, without the demeaning stereotypes by which blacks were normally depicted in an age of intensifying racism. Even so, the racial hierarchy is maintained. The blacks are the foot soldiers; their officers are white. Library of Congress.

The main battle, on July 1, occurred near Santiago on the heights commanded by San Juan Hill. Roosevelt's dismounted Rough Riders (there had been no room for horses on the transports) seized Kettle Hill. Then the frontal assault against the San Juan heights began. Four black regiments took the brunt of the fighting. White observers grudgingly credited much of the victory to the "superb gallantry" of the black soldiers. In fact it was not quite a victory. The Spaniards, driven from their forward positions, retreated to a well-fortified second line. The exhausted Americans had suffered heavy casualties; whether they could have mounted a second assault was questionable. They were spared this test, however, by the Spanish. On July 3 Cervera's fleet in Santiago harbor made a daylight attempt to run the American blockade and was destroyed. A few days later, convinced that Santiago could not be saved, the Spanish forces surrendered.

The two nations signed an armistice in which Spain agreed to liberate Cuba and cede Puerto Rico and Guam to the United States. American forces occupied Manila pending a peace treaty.

The Imperial Experiment

The big question was the Philippines, an archipelago of 7,000 islands populated — as William R. Day,

McKinley's secretary of state, put it in the racist language of that era — by "eight or nine millions of absolutely ignorant and many degraded people." Not even avid American expansionists advocated colonial rule over subject peoples — that was European-style imperialism, not the strategic bases that Mahan and his followers had in mind. Mahan and Lodge initially advocated keeping only Manila. It gradually became clear, however, that Manila was not defensible without the whole of Luzon, the large island on which the city was located.

Taking the Philippines. McKinley and his advisors surveyed the options. One possibility was to return most of the islands to Spain, but the reputed evils of Spanish rule made that a "cowardly and dishonorable" solution. Another possibility was to partition the Philippines with one or more of the Great Powers. But, as McKinley observed, to turn over valuable territory to "our commercial rivals in the Orient — that would have been bad business and discreditable."

Most plausible was Philippine independence. As in Cuba, Spanish rule had already stirred up a rebellion, led by the ardent patriot Emilio Aguinaldo. An arrangement might have been possible like the one being extracted from the Cubans over Guantanamo Bay: the lease of a naval base to the Americans as the price of freedom. But after some hesitation McKinley concluded that "we could not leave [the Filipinos] to themselves — they were unfit for self-rule — and they would soon have anarchy and misrule over there worse than Spain's was."

Emilio Aguinaldo

At the start of the war with Spain, U.S. military leaders brought the Filipino patriot Emilio Aguinaldo back from Singapore because they thought he would stir up a popular uprising that would help defeat the Spaniards. Aguinaldo came because he thought the Americans favored an independent Philippines. These differing intentions — it has remained a matter of dispute what assurances Aguinaldo received — were the root cause of the Filipino insurrection that proved far costlier in American and Filipino lives than the war with Spain that preceded it. Corbis-Bettmann.

As for the Spaniards, they had little choice against what they considered "the immoderate demands of a conqueror." In the Treaty of Paris they ceded the Philippines to the United States for a payment of $20 million. The treaty encountered harder going at home and was ratified by the Senate (requiring a two-thirds majority) on February 6, 1899, with only a single vote to spare.

The Anti-Imperialists. The administration's narrow margin signaled the revival of an antiexpansionist tradition that had been briefly silenced by the passions of a nation at war. In the Senate opponents of the treaty invoked the country's republican principles. Under the Constitution, argued the conservative Republican George F. Hoar, "no power is given to the Federal Government to acquire territory to be held and governed permanently as colonies" or "to conquer alien people and hold them in subjugation." The alternative — making eight million Filipinos American citizens — was equally unpalatable to the anti-imperialists, who were no more champions of "these savage people" than were the expansionists.

Leading citizens enlisted in the anti-imperialist cause, including the steel king Andrew Carnegie, who offered a check for $20 million to purchase the independence of the Philippines; the labor leader Samuel Gompers, who feared the competition of cheap Filipino labor; and Jane Addams, who believed that women should stand for peace. The key group was a social elite of old-line Mugwumps, reformers such as Carl Schurz, Charles Eliot Norton, and Charles Francis Adams. In November 1898 a Boston group formed the first of the Anti-Imperialist Leagues that began to spring up around the country.

Although skillful at publicizing their cause, the anti-imperialists never became a popular movement. They shared little but their anti-imperialism and, within the Mugwump core, lacked the common touch. Moreover the Democrats, their natural allies, waffled on the issue. Although an outspoken anti-imperialist, William Jennings Bryan, the Democratic standard-bearer, confounded his friends by favoring ratification of the treaty. He hesitated to stake his party's future on a crusade against a national policy he privately believed to be irreversible. Still, if it was an accomplished fact, Philippine annexation exacted a higher moral cost than anyone had expected.

War in the Philippines. On February 4, 1899, two days before the Senate ratified the treaty, fighting broke out between American and Filipino patrols on the edge of Manila. Confronted by American annexation, the rebel leader Aguinaldo asserted his nation's independence and turned his guns on the occupying American forces.

The ensuing conflict far exceeded in ferocity the war just concluded with Spain. Fighting tenacious guerrillas, the U.S. Army resorted to the same tactics the Spaniards had employed in Cuba, moving people into towns, carrying out indiscriminate attacks beyond the perimeters, and burning crops and villages. Atrocities became commonplace on both sides. In three years of warfare, 4,200 Americans and many thousands of Filipinos died. The fighting ended in 1902, and William Howard Taft, who had been appointed governor-general, set up a civilian administration. He intended to make the Philippines a model of American road-building and sanitary engineering.

McKinley's convincing victory over William Jennings Bryan in the 1900 election, though by no means a referendum on American expansionism, suggested popular satisfaction with America's overseas adventure. Yet a strong undercurrent of misgivings was evident (see Comparing American Voices, "Debating the Philippines," pp. 656–657). Americans had not anticipated the brutal methods needed to subdue the Filipino guerrillas. "We are destroying these islanders by the thousands, their villages and cities," protested the philosopher William James. "No life shall you have, we say, except as a gift from our philanthropy after your unconditional surrender to our will. . . . Could there be any more damning indictment of that whole bloated ideal termed 'modern civilization'?"

There were, moreover, disturbing constitutional issues to be resolved. The Treaty of Paris, while guaranteeing them freedom of religion, specifically withheld from the inhabitants of the ceded Spanish territories any promise of citizenship. It would be up to Congress to decide their "civil rights and political status." Did this treatment conform to the Constitution? In 1901 the Supreme Court said that it did. The Constitution did not automatically extend citizenship to the acquired territories. Whether the inhabitants would be granted citizenship, or even the constitutional protections available to aliens in the United States, was up to Congress. A line was thus drawn between overseas expansion and the nation's continental expansion, marking the new territories as colonies, not future states, and marking the United States irrefutably as a colonial power. In 1916, in accordance with a recommendation by a special commission set up by McKinley, the Jones Act committed the United States to Philippine independence but set no date (the Philippines formally achieved independence in 1946).

The brutal war in the Philippines rubbed off some of the moralizing gloss but left undeflected America's global aspirations. In a few years the United States had assembled an overseas empire: Hawaii, Puerto Rico, Guam, the Philippines, and finally, in 1900, several of the Samoan islands that had been jointly administered with Germany and Britain (Map 21.2). The United States, remarked the legal scholar John Bassett Moore in 1899, had moved "from a position of comparative freedom from entanglements into a position of what is commonly called a world power" (see Reading American Pictures, "Imperial Dilemmas," p. 658)."

▸ Why should a rebellion in Cuba — after all, an internal affair of Spain's — have become a cause for war with the United States?

▸ If America's quarrel with Spain was over Cuba, why was the most important engagement of the Spanish-American War Dewey's naval victory in the Philippines?

▸ If, as Americans repeatedly said, they had fought Spain to help the Cuban people gain independence, how did the United States find itself fighting the Filipino people for just the opposite reason, that is, to prevent them from having independence?

Onto the World Stage

In Europe the flexing of America's muscles against Spain caused a certain amount of consternation. The major powers had tried before war broke out to intercede on Spain's behalf — but tentatively, because no one was looking for trouble with the Americans. President McKinley had listened politely to their envoys and then proceeded with his war.

The decisive outcome confirmed what the Europeans already suspected. After Dewey's naval victory, the semiofficial French paper *Le Temps*

MAP 21.2   The American Empire, 1917

In 1890 Alfred T. Mahan wrote that the United States should regard the oceans as "a great highway" across which America would carry on world trade. That was precisely what resulted from the empire the United States acquired after the Spanish-American War. The Caribbean possessions, the strategically located Pacific islands, and, in 1903, the Panama Canal Zone, gave the United States commercial and naval access to a wider world.

COMPARING AMERICAN VOICES

Debating the Philippines

As we know from President McKinley's musings, seizing the Philippines was an act of national self-interest. Of the alternatives, it was the one that seemed best calculated to serve America's strategic aims in Asia. But McKinley's geopolitical decision had unintended consequences. For one, it provoked a bloody insurrection. For another, it rubbed up against the nation's democratic principles. As these consequences hit home, a divided Senate set up a special committee and held closed hearings. Congressional testimony is a source much prized by historians. Some of it, of course, is prepared testimony. But once the questioning begins, the testimony becomes unscripted and can be especially revealing. The documents below are taken from the 1902 testimony before the Senate Committee on the Philippines.

IDEALS

General Arthur MacArthur was in on the action in the Philippines almost from the start. He commanded one of the first units to arrive there in 1898 and in 1900 was reassigned back as military governor and general commander of the troops. His standing as a military man—holder of the Congressional Medal of Honor from the Civil War—was on a par with his more famous son, Douglas MacArthur. Here he explains in prepared testimony his vision of America's mission to the Philippines.

At the time I returned to Manila [May 1900] to assume the supreme command it seemed to me that . . . our occupation of the island was simply one of the necessary consequences in logical sequence of our great prosperity, and to doubt the wisdom of [occupation] was simply to doubt the stability of our own institutions and in effect to declare that a self-governing nation was incapable of successfully resisting strains arising naturally from its own productive energy. It seemed to me that our conception of right, justice, freedom, and personal liberty was the precious fruit of centuries of strife . . . [and that] we must regard ourselves simply as the custodians of imperishable ideas held in trust for the general benefit of mankind. In other words, I felt that we had attained a moral and intellectual height from which we were bound to proclaim to all as the occasion arose the true message of humanity as embodied in the principles of our own institutions. . . .

All other governments that have gone to the East have simply planted trading establishments; they have not materially affected the conditions of the people. . . . There is not a single establishment, in my judgment, in Asia to-day that would survive five years if the original power which planted it was withdrawn therefrom.

The contrasting idea with our idea is this: In planting our ideas we plant something that can not be destroyed. To my mind the archipelago is a fertile soil upon which to plant republicanism. . . . We are planting the best traditions, the best characteristics of Americanism in such a way that they can never be removed from that soil. That in itself seems to me a most inspiring thought. It encouraged me during all my efforts in those lands, even when conditions seemed most disappointing, when the people themselves, not appreciating precisely what the remote consequences of our efforts were going to be, mistrusted us; but that fact was always before me—that going deep down into that fertile soil were the indispensable ideas of Americanism.

SKEPTICISM

At this point, the general was interrupted by Colorado Senator Thomas Patterson, a Populist-Democrat and a vocal anti-imperialist.

Sen. Patterson: Do you mean that imperishable idea of which you speak is the right of self-government?

Gen. MacArthur: Precisely so; self-government regulated by law as I understand it in this Republic.

Sen. Patterson: Of course you do not mean self-government regulated by some foreign and superior power?

Gen. MacArthur: Well, that is a matter of evolution, Senator. We are putting these institutions there so they will evolve themselves just as here and everywhere else where freedom has flourished. . . .

Sen. Patterson: [after the General had concluded his formal statement] Do I understand your claim of right and duty to retain the Philippine Islands is based upon the proposition that they have come to us upon the basis of our morals, honorable dealing, and unassailable international integrity?

Gen. MacArthur: That proposition is not questioned by

anybody in the world, excepting a few people in the United States.... We will be benefited, and the Filipino people will be benefited, and that is what I meant by the original proposition—

Sen. Patterson: Do you mean the Filipino people that are left alive?

Gen. MacArthur: I mean the Filipino people....

Sen. Patterson: You mean those left alive after they have been subjugated?

Gen. MacArthur: I do not admit that there has been any unusual destruction of life in the Philippine Islands. The destruction is simply the incident of war, and of course it embraces only a very small percentage of the total population.... I doubt if any war—either international or civil, any war on earth—has been conducted with as much humanity, with as much careful consideration, with as much self-restraint, as have been the American operations in the Philippine Archipelago....

REALITIES

Brigadier General Robert P. Hughes, a military district commander, testified as follows:

Q: In burning towns, what would you do? Would the entire town be destroyed by fire or would only the offending portions of the town be burned?—A. I do not know that we have ever had a case of burning what you would call a town in this country, but probably a barrio or a sitio; probably half a dozen houses, native shacks, where the insurrectos would go in and be concealed, and if they caught a detachment passing they would kill some of them.

Q: What did I understand you to say would be the consequences of that?—A. They usually burned the village.

Q: All the houses in the village?—A. Yes, every one of them.

Q: What would become of the inhabitants?—A. That was their lookout....

Q: If these shacks were of no consequence what was the utility of their destruction?—A. The destruction was a punishment. They permitted these people to come in there and they gave no sign. It is always—

Q: The punishment in that case would fall, not upon the men, who could go elsewhere, but mainly upon the women and the little children.—A. The women and children are part of the family, and where you wish to inflict punishment you can punish the man probably worse in that way than in any other.

Q: But is that within the ordinary rules of civilized warfare?...—A. These people are not civilized.

Daniel J. Evans, Twelfth Infantry, describes the "water cure"

Q: The committee would like to hear... whether you were the witness to any cruelties inflicted upon the natives of the Philippine Islands; and if so, under what circumstances.—A. The case I had reference to was where they gave the water cure to a native in the Ilicano Province at Ilocos Norte... about the month of August 1900. There were two native scouts with the American forces. They went out and brought in a couple of insurgents.... They tried to get from this insurgent... where the rest of the insurgents were at that time.... The first thing one of the Americans—I mean one of the scouts for the Americans—grabbed one of the men by the head and jerked his head back, and then they took a tomato can and poured water down his throat until he could hold no more.... Then they forced a gag into his mouth; they stood him up... against a post and fastened him so that he could not move. Then one man, an American soldier, who was over six feet tall, and who was very strong, too, struck this native in the pit of the stomach as hard as he could.... They kept that operation up for quite a time, and finally I thought the fellow was about to die, but I don't believe he was as bad as that, because finally he told them he would tell, and from that on he was taken away, and I saw no more of him.

SOURCE: Henry F. Graff, ed., *American Imperialism and the Philippine Insurrection* (Boston: Little, Brown, 1969), 64–65, 80–81, 137–39, 144–45.

ANALYZING THE EVIDENCE

- In the text we offer an account of the reasons the United States decided to hold the Philippines. In what ways does General MacArthur's testimony add to our account? Confirm it? Contradict it?

- In the same vein: The text tells you about the anti-imperialist movement. In what ways does Senator Patterson's cross-examination of General MacArthur provide you with a better sense of what was eating the anti-imperialists?

- Does the clash of ideas in the documents you have just read strike you as dated, in the sense, for example, that the Model T or the nickelodeon are dated? Or does that debate remain relevant for our own time, reminding you of what you today might read about in a paper or hear in a newscast?

READING AMERICAN PICTURES

Imperial Dilemmas

When nations go to war, patriotic fervor — jingoism — takes hold and critics speak out at their peril. That's a moment when political cartoonists really earn their pay, because criticism is their stock in trade. It's in their clever drawings, if anywhere, that the historian will spy second thoughts as the nation marches on to war and glory. Here we have two examples of cartoonists at work just as the United States was plunging into what Senator Lodge called our "Splendid Little War," the Spanish-American War of 1898.

ANALYZING THE EVIDENCE

- The date on the *Life* magazine cover — June 16, 1898 — is significant. Commodore Dewey has won his smashing victory in Manila Bay, opening the path to an overseas empire, and U.S. troops are preparing for the assault on Cuba. At this important moment, what is the *Life* cartoon's message?

- The United States went to war with Spain ostensibly to secure Cuban independence. What second thoughts about that objective are raised in the cartoon "Free Cuba?" Does it give you an inkling of the policy the United States would pursue with Cuba and the Philippines once their independence from Spain had been secured?

- In recent years, historians have become sensitive to the role of gender in many aspects of American life, even aspects seemingly remote — like international relations. Can you find any evidence in either of these cartoons that gendered thinking helped shape America's imperial adventure? In what ways?

Free Cuba? 1898, Granger Collection.

Hurrah for Imperialism! *Life,* 1898. Newbury Library.

observed that "what passes before our eyes is the appearance of a new power of the first order." And the *London Times* concluded: "This war must . . . effect a profound change in the whole attitude and policy of the United States. In the future America will play a part in the general affairs of the world such as she has never played before" (see Voices from Abroad, "Jean Hess, Émile Zola, and Ruben Dario: American Goliath," p. 660).

A Power among Powers

The politician most ardently agreeing with the *London Times*' vision of America's future was the man who, with the assassination of William McKinley, became president on September 14, 1901. Unlike his predecessors in the White House, Theodore Roosevelt was an avid student of world affairs, widely traveled and acquainted with many European leaders. He had no doubt about America's role in the world.

It was important, first of all, to uphold the country's honor in the community of nations. The country should never shrink from righteous battle. "All the great masterful races have been fighting races," Roosevelt declared. But when he spoke of war, Roosevelt had in mind actions by the "civilized" nations against "backward peoples." Roosevelt felt "it incumbent on all the civilized and orderly powers to insist on the proper policing of the world." That was why Roosevelt sympathized with European imperialism and how he justified American dominance in the Caribbean.

As for the "civilized and orderly" policemen of the world, the worst thing that could happen was for them to fall to fighting among themselves. Roosevelt had an acute sense of the fragility of world peace, and he was farsighted about the likelihood—in this he was truly exceptional among Americans—of a catastrophic world war. He believed in American responsibility for helping to maintain the balance of power.

Anglo-American Friendship. After the Spanish-American War, the European powers had been uncertain about how to deal with the victor. Only Great Britain had a clear view of what it wanted, as its position in Europe steadily worsened in the face of a rising challenge from Germany and soured relations with France and Russia over clashing imperial interests. In its growing isolation Britain turned increasingly to the United States. In the Hay-Pauncefote Agreement (1901), Britain gave up its treaty rights to participate in any Central American canal project, clearing the way for a canal under exclusive U.S. control. And two years later the last of the vexing U.S.-Canadian border disputes—this one involving British Columbia and Alaska—was settled, again to American satisfaction.

No formal alliance was forthcoming, but Anglo-American friendship had been placed on such a firm basis that after 1901 the British admiralty designed its war plans on the assumption that America was "a kindred state with whom we shall never have a parricidal war." Roosevelt heartily agreed. "England and United States, beyond any other two powers, should be friendly." In his unflagging efforts to maintain a global balance of power, the cornerstone of Roosevelt's policy was the English relationship.

The Big Stick. Among nations, however, what counted was strength, not merely goodwill. Roosevelt wanted "to make all foreign powers understand that when we have adopted a line of policy we have adopted it definitely, and with the intention of backing it up with deeds as well as words." As Roosevelt famously said, "Speak softly and carry a big stick." By a "big stick" he meant, above all, naval power.

The battleship program went on apace under Roosevelt. In 1904 the U.S. Navy stood fifth in the world; by 1907 it was third. At the top of Roosevelt's agenda, however, was a canal across Central America. The Spanish-American War had graphically demonstrated the strategic need: The entire country had waited anxiously while the battleship *Oregon* steamed at full speed from the Pacific around the tip of South America to join the final action against the Spanish fleet in Cuba.

The Panama Canal. Freed by Britain's surrender of its joint canal rights in 1901, Roosevelt turned to the delicate task of leasing from Colombia the needed strip of land across Panama, a Colombian province. Furious when the Colombian legislature voted down the proposed treaty, Roosevelt contemplated outright seizure of Panama but settled on a more devious solution. With an independence movement brewing in Panama, the United States lent covert assistance that ensured the success of a bloodless revolution against Colombia. On November 6, 1903, the United States recognized Panama and two weeks later got a perpetually renewable lease on a canal zone. Roosevelt never regretted the victimization of Colombia, although the United States, as a kind of conscience money, paid Colombia $25 million in 1922.

VOICES FROM ABROAD

Jean Hess, Émile Zola, and Ruben Dario
American Goliath

Until the 1890s, foreign commentary was mostly about the strange habits of Americans. It was, one might say, an anthropological approach to America. But once the United States flexed its muscles internationally, a different kind of foreign commentary emerged, as is evident in the three documents below. None of them resulted from a visit to the United States. There was plenty to say from afar. Moreover, the commentary now mirrored the commentators as much as what they commented on. America was no longer merely an object of curiosity. What the Goliath did mattered. That's what came from being a Great Power.

Jean Hess, a Frenchman well traveled in East Asia, questioned American motives for intervening in the Philippines (1899).

Nowhere, in my opinion, better than in the Philippines, has it been shown that modern wars are simply "deals." The American intervention in the struggle engaged in by the revolutionary Tagals against the Spanish government has turned out to be nothing but a speculation of "business men," and not the generous effort of a people paying a debt in procuring for others the liberty that it concedes belongs to all. . . . Back of all these battles, this devastation and mourning, in spite of the newly-born Yankee imperialism, there was only, there is only, what the people of the Bourse [stock market] call a deal.

Émile Zola, the great French novelist, feared that America's military adventurism was dealing a blow to the cause of world peace (1900).

I know that, for belief in peace and future disarmament, the time is scarcely auspicious, as we are now beholding an alarming recrudescence of militarism. Nations which till now seem to have held aloof from the contagion, to have escaped this madness so prevalent in Europe, now appear to be attacked. Thus, since the Spanish war, the United States seems to have become a victim of the war fever. . . . I can see in that great nation a dangerous inclination toward war. I can detect the generation of vague ideas of future conquest. Until the present time that country wisely occupied itself with its domestic affairs and let Europe severely alone, but now it is donning plumes and epaulets, and will be dreaming of possible campaigns and be carried away with the idea of military glory — notions so perilous as to have been responsible for the downfall of nations.

In 1905, a year after the promulgation of the Roosevelt Corollary, the acclaimed Nicaraguan poet Ruben Dario issued an impassioned challenge from a small Central American country under the shadow of the Goliath. (Nicaragua was in fact occupied by U.S. Marines four years later.) Dario addressed his poem "To Roosevelt."

You are primitive and modern, simple and complex;
you are one part George Washington and one
part Nimrod.
You are the United States,
future invader of our naive America
with its Indian blood, an America
that still prays to Christ and still speaks Spanish.
. . . .
The United States is grand and powerful.
. . . A wealthy country,
joining the cult of Mammon to the cult of Hercules;
while Liberty, lighting the path to easy conflict, raises her torch in New York.

But our own America . . .
has lived, since the earliest moments of its life,
in light, in fire, in fragrance, and in love—
the America of Moctezuma and Atahuelpa. . . .
O men with Saxon eyes and barbarous souls,
our America lives. And dreams. And loves.
And it is the daughter of the Sun. Be Careful.
Long live Spanish America!

SOURCES: Philip S. Foner and Robert C. Winchester, eds., *The Anti-Imperialist Reader: A Documentary History of Anti-Imperialism in the United States*, 2 vols. (New York: Holmes and Meier, 1984), 1: 98–99, 417–18; Thomas G. Paterson and Dennis Merrill, eds., *Major Problems in American Foreign Relations*, 2 vols. (Lexington, MA: D. C. Heath, 1995), 1: 508–9; *Selected Poems of Ruben Dario*, trans. Lysander Kemp (Austin: University of Texas Press, 1965).

ANALYZING THE EVIDENCE

- The theme of this chapter is the emergence of the United States as a Great Power. What evidence is there in these documents that foreigners actually saw the United States that way?

- In world affairs Americans generally had a pretty good opinion of themselves — better, certainly, than of the corrupt Europeans. Do these documents suggest that Europeans took the Americans at their own word?

- Ruben Dario says that Americans have "barbarous souls." Does his poem suggest why he might say a mean thing like that? Does the fact that he's a Nicaraguan matter? Is his judgment shared by the Frenchmen Hess and Zola?

The Panama Canal: Excavating the Culebra Cut
The Canal Zone was acquired through devious means from which Americans could take little pride (and which led in 1978 to the U.S. Senate's decision to restore the property to Panama). But the building of the Panama Canal itself was a triumph of American ingenuity and drive. Dr. William C. Gorgas cleaned out the malarial mosquitoes that had earlier stymied the French. Under Colonel George W. Goethals, the U.S. Army overcame formidable obstacles in a mighty feat of engineering. This photograph shows the massive effort under way in December 1904 to excavate the Culebra Cut so that oceangoing ships would be able to pass through. Corbis-Bettmann.

Building the canal, one of the heroic engineering feats of the century, involved a vast swamp-clearing project, the construction of a series of great locks, and the excavation of 240 million cubic yards of earth. It took the U.S. Army Corps of Engineers and the digging by thousands of hired laborers eight years to finish the huge project. When the Panama Canal opened in 1914, it gave the United States a commanding commercial and strategic position in the Western Hemisphere (Map 21.3).

Policeman of the Caribbean. Next came the task of making the Caribbean basin secure. The countries there, said Secretary of State Elihu Root, had been placed "in the front yard of the United States" by the Panama Canal. Therefore, as Roosevelt put it, they had to "behave themselves."

In the case of Cuba, good behavior was readily managed by the settlement following the Spanish-American War. Before withdrawing in 1902 the United States reorganized Cuban public finances and concluded a swamp-clearing program that eliminated yellow fever, a disease that had ravaged Cuba for many years. As a condition for gaining independence, Cuba accepted a proviso in its constitution called the Platt Amendment, which gave the United States the right to intervene if Cuban independence was threatened or if internal order broke down. Cuba also granted the United States a lease on Guantanamo (which is still in effect), where the U.S. Navy built a large base. It was a bitter pill for the Cubans, who thought they had made their own revolution, only to find their hard-won independence poisoned at birth. Mutual incomprehension — Americans expected gratitude, Cubans felt mainly

MAP 21.3   The Panama Canal: The Design

The forty-mile-long canal route zigzags to take maximum advantage of the regional topography, including an existing internal waterway via Gatun Lake. The lake is situated 85 feet above sea level, necessitating the use of locks to raise and lower ships as they approach the lake and the section known as the Culebra Cut, pictured on the previous page.

resentment — sowed the seeds of a new revolutionary movement and Fidel Castro's future triumph in 1959. Of that, of course, Theodore Roosevelt was oblivious.

Claiming that instability in the Caribbean invited the intervention of European powers, he announced in 1904 that the United States would act as "policeman" of the region, stepping in, "however reluctantly, in flagrant cases . . . of wrong-doing or impotence" (Map 21.4). This so-called Roosevelt Corollary to the Monroe Doctrine transformed its broad principle against European interference in Latin America into an unrestricted American right to regulate Caribbean affairs. The Roosevelt Corollary was not a treaty with other states; it was a unilateral declaration sanctioned only by American power and national interest.

Citing the Roosevelt Corollary, the United States intervened regularly in the internal affairs of Caribbean states. In 1905 American personnel took over the customs and debt management of the Dominican Republic and, similarly, the finances of Nicaragua in 1911 and Haiti in 1916. When domestic order broke down, the U.S. Marines occupied Cuba in 1906, Nicaragua in 1909, and Haiti and the Dominican Republic in later years.

The Open Door in Asia

Commercial interest dominated American policy in East Asia, especially the prospect of the huge China market. By the late 1890s Japan, Russia,

MAP 21.4   Policeman of the Caribbean

After the Spanish-American War, the United States vigorously asserted its interest in the affairs of its neighbors to the south. As the record of interventions shows, the United States truly became the "policeman" of the Caribbean.

Germany, France, and Britain had all carved out spheres of influence in China. Fearful of being frozen out, U.S. Secretary of State John Hay in 1899 sent them an Open Door note claiming the right of equal trade access—an open door—for all nations that wanted to do business in China. Despite its Philippine bases, the United States lacked real leverage in East Asia and elicited only noncommittal responses from the occupying powers. But Hay chose to interpret them as accepting the American open-door position.

When a secret society of Chinese nationalists, the Boxers, rebelled against the foreigners in 1900, the United States sent 5,000 troops from the Philippines and joined the multinational campaign to break the Boxers' siege of the diplomatic missions in Peking (Beijing). America took this opportunity to assert a second principle of the Open Door: that China would be preserved as a "territorial and administrative entity." As long as the legal fiction of an independent China survived, so would American claims to equal access to the China market.

In the Caribbean the European powers had acceded to American dominance. But Britain, Germany, France, and Russia were strongly entrenched in East Asia and not inclined to defer to American interests (Map 21.5). The United States also confronted a powerful Asian nation—Japan—that had its own vital interests. Although the open-door policy was important to him, Roosevelt sensed that higher stakes were at risk in the Pacific.

Japan had unveiled its military strength in the Sino-Japanese War of 1894–1895, which began the division of China into spheres of influence—not colonies, but regions marked off by the Great Powers over which they asserted informal dominance. A decade later, provoked by Russian rivalry in Manchuria and Korea, Japan suddenly attacked the tsar's fleet at Port Arthur, Russia's leased port in China. In a series of brilliant victories, the Japanese smashed the Russian forces in Asia. Anxious to restore a balance of power, Roosevelt mediated a settlement of the Russo-Japanese War at Portsmouth, New Hampshire, in 1905. Japan emerged as the dominant power in East Asia.

Contemptuous of other Asian nations, Roosevelt respected the Japanese—"a wonderful and civilized people . . . entitled to stand in absolute equality with all the other peoples of the civilized world." He conceded that Japan had "a paramount interest in what surrounds the Yellow Sea, just as

MAP 21.5 The Great Powers in East Asia, 1898–1910

The pattern of foreign dominance over China was via "treaty ports," where the powers based their naval forces, and "spheres of influence" extending from the ports into the hinterland. This map reveals why the United States had a weak hand; it lacked a presence on this colonized terrain. The Boxer rebellion in 1900, by bringing an American expeditionary force to Peking, gave the United States a chance to insert itself onto the Chinese mainland, and American diplomats made the most of the opportunity to defend U.S. commercial interest in China.

the United States has a paramount interest in what surrounds the Caribbean." But American strategic and commercial interests in the Pacific had to be accommodated. The United States approved of Japan's protectorate over Korea in 1905, and then of its declaration of full sovereignty six years later. However, a surge of anti-Asian feeling in California complicated Roosevelt's efforts. In 1906 San Francisco's school board placed all Asian students in a segregated school, infuriating Japan. The "Gentlemen's Agreement" of 1907, in which Japan agreed to restrict immigration to the United States, smoothed matters over, but periodic racist slights by Americans made for continuing tensions with the Japanese.

Roosevelt meanwhile moved to balance Japan's military power by increasing American naval strength in the Pacific. American battleships visited Japan in 1908 on a global tour that impressively displayed U.S. sea power. Late that year, near the end of his administration, Roosevelt achieved a formal accommodation with Japan. The Root-Takahira Agreement confirmed the status quo in the Pacific, as well as the principles of free oceanic commerce and equal trade opportunity in China.

William Howard Taft, however, entered the White House in 1909 convinced that the United States had been short-changed. He pressed for a larger role for American investors, especially in the railroad construction going on in China. An exponent of **dollar diplomacy**—the aggressive coupling of American political and economic interests abroad—Taft hoped that American capital would counterbalance Japanese power and pave the way for increased commercial opportunities. When the Chinese Revolution of 1911 toppled the ruling Manchu dynasty, Taft supported the victorious Chinese Nationalists, who wanted to modernize their country and liberate it from Japanese domination. The United States thus entered a long-term rivalry with Japan that would end in war thirty years later.

The United States had become embroiled in a distant struggle heavy with future liabilities but little by way of the fabulous profits that had lured Americans to Asia.

Wilson and Mexico

When Woodrow Wilson became president in 1913, he was bent on reform in American foreign policy no less than in domestic politics. Wilson did not really differ with his predecessors on the importance of America's economic interests overseas. He applauded the "tides of commerce" that would arise from the Panama Canal. But he opposed dollar diplomacy, which he believed bullied weaker countries financially and gave undue advantage to American business. It seemed to Wilson "a very perilous thing to determine the foreign policy of a nation in terms of material interest."

The United States, Wilson insisted, should conduct its foreign policy in conformity with its democratic principles. He intended to foster "constitutional liberty in the world," especially among the nation's neighbors in Latin America. In a major foreign-policy speech in 1913, Wilson promised that the United States would "never again seek one additional foot of territory by conquest." He was committed to advancing "human rights, national integrity, and opportunity" abroad. To do otherwise would make "ourselves untrue to our own traditions."

Mexico became the primary object of Wilson's ministrations. A cycle of revolution had begun there in 1911. The dictator Porfirio Díaz was overthrown by Francisco Madero, who spoke much as Wilson did about liberty and constitutionalism. But before Madero got very far with his reforms, he was deposed and murdered in February 1913 by one of his generals, Victoriano Huerta. Other powers recognized Huerta's provisional government but not the United States, despite a long-standing tradition of granting quick recognition to new governments. Wilson abhorred Huerta, called him a murderer, and pledged "to force him out."

By intervening in this way, Wilson insisted, "we act in the interest of Mexico alone.... We are seeking to counsel Mexico for its own good." Wilson meant that he intended to put the Mexican Revolution back on the constitutional path started by Madero. Wilson was not deterred by the fact that American business interests, with big investments in Mexico, favored Huerta.

The emergence of armed opposition in northern Mexico under Venustiano Carranza strengthened Wilson's hand. But Carranza's Constitutionalist movement was ardently nationalist and had no desire for American intervention. Carranza angrily rebuffed Wilson's efforts at bringing about elections by means of a compromise with the Huerta regime. He also vowed to fight any intrusion of U.S. troops in his country. All he wanted from Wilson, Carranza asserted, was recognition of the Constitutionalists' belligerent status, so that they could purchase arms in the United States. In exchange for vague promises to respect property rights and "fair" foreign concessions, Carranza finally got his way in 1914. American weapons began to flow to his troops.

When it became clear that Huerta was not about to fall, the United States threw its own forces into the conflict. On the pretext of a minor insult to the U.S. Navy at Tampico, Wilson ordered the occupation of the port of Veracruz on April 21, 1914, at the cost of 19 American and 126 Mexican lives. At that point the Huerta regime began to crumble. Carranza nevertheless condemned the United States, and his forces came close to engaging the Americans. When he entered Mexico City in triumph in August 1914, Carranza had some cause to thank the Yankees. But if any sense of gratitude existed, it was overshadowed by the anti-Americanism inspired by Wilson's insensitivity to Mexican pride and revolutionary zeal.

No sooner had the Constitutionalists triumphed than Carranza was challenged by his northern general, Pancho Villa, with some encouragement by American interests in Mexico. Defeated and driven northward, Villa began to stir up

Pancho Villa, 1914
This photograph captures General Villa at the height of his powers, at the head of Carranza's northern army in 1914. The next year, he broke with Carranza and, among other desperate tactics, began to attack Americans. Much admired in the United States, Villa overnight became Public Enemy No. 1. He evaded General Pershing's punitive expedition of 1916, however, demonstrating the difficulties even modern armies have against a guerilla foe who knows the terrain and can melt away into a sympathetic population. Brown Brothers.

trouble along the border, killing sixteen American civilians taken from a train in January 1916 and two months later raiding the town of Columbus, New Mexico. Wilson sent 11,000 troops under General John J. Pershing across the border after the elusive Villa. Soon Pershing's force resembled an army of occupation more than a punitive expedition. Mexican public opinion demanded that Pershing withdraw, and armed clashes with Mexican troops began. At the brink of war, the two governments backed off, and U.S. forces began to withdraw in early 1917. Soon after, with a new constitution ratified and elections completed, the Carranza government finally received official recognition from Washington.

The Gathering Storm in Europe

In the meantime Europe had begun a drift toward war. There were two main sources of tension. One was the rivalry between Germany, the new superpower of Europe, and the European states threatened by its might—above all France, which had been humiliated in the Franco-Prussian War of 1870. The second danger zone was the Balkans, where the Ottoman Empire was disintegrating and where, in the midst of explosive ethnic rivalries, Austria-Hungary and Russia were maneuvering for dominance. Out of these conflicts an alliance system had emerged, with Germany, Austria-Hungary, and Italy (the Triple Alliance) on one side and France and Russia (the Dual Alliance) on the other.

The tensions in Europe were partially released by European imperial adventures, especially by France in Africa and by Russia in Asia. These activities put France and Russia at odds with imperial Britain, effectively excluding Britain from the European alliance system. Fearful of Germany, however, Britain in 1904 resolved its differences with France, and the two countries reached a friendly understanding, or *entente*. When Britain came to a similar understanding with Russia in 1907, the basis was laid for the Triple Entente. A deadly confrontation between two great European power blocs became possible.

In these European quarrels Americans had no obvious stake nor any inclination, in the words of a cautionary Senate resolution, "to depart from the traditional American foreign policy which forbids participation . . . [in] political questions which are entirely European in scope." But on becoming president, Theodore Roosevelt took a lively interest in European affairs and was eager, as the head of a Great Power, to make a contribution to the cause of peace. In 1905 he got his chance.

The Anglo-French entente of the previous year was based partly on a deal about territory in North Africa: The Sudan went to Britain, Morocco to France. Then Germany suddenly challenged France over Morocco—a disastrous move, conflicting with Germany's self-interest in keeping France's attention diverted from Europe. The German ruler, Kaiser Wilhelm II, turned to Roosevelt for help. Roosevelt arranged an international conference, which was held in January 1906 at Algeciras, Spain. With U.S. diplomats playing a key role, the crisis was defused. Germany got a few token concessions, but France's dominance over Morocco was sustained.

Algeciras marked an ominous turning point—the first time the power blocs fated to come to blows in 1914 squared off against one another. But in 1906 the outcome of the conference seemed a diplomatic triumph. Roosevelt's secretary of state, Elihu Root, boasted of America's success in "preserv[ing] world peace because of the power of our detachment." Root's words prefigured how the United States would define its role among the Great Powers. It would be the apostle of peace, distinguished by its "detachment," by its lack of selfish interest in European affairs.

Opposing this internationalist impulse, however, was America's traditional suspicion of foreign entanglements. In principle, Americans were all in favor of world peace; organizations like the American Peace Society flourished during the Progressive era. But the country grew nervous when it came to translating principle into practice. Thus Americans embraced the international movement for the peaceful resolution of disputes among nations. They enthusiastically greeted the Hague Peace Conference of 1899, which established the International Court of Arbitration. Making use of the Court, however, required bilateral treaties with other nations defining the arbitration ground rules. Roosevelt carefully excepted all matters affecting "the vital interests, the independence, or the honor" of the United States. Even so, the Senate shot down Roosevelt's arbitration treaties. Taft's efforts met a similar fate.

So, when he became Wilson's secretary of state, William Jennings Bryan took a milder route. An apostle of world peace, Bryan devoted himself to negotiating a series of "cooling off" treaties with other countries—so called because the parties agreed to wait for one year while disputed issues were submitted to a conciliation process.

Algeciras, 1906

When President Roosevelt intervened in the Moroccan crisis, he was intent only on resolving a dangerous dispute between European powers. That Morocco, a formally independent Muslim nation with its own king, was also a party to the dispute was of little interest to him. In this photograph, El-Hadj el-Mokri, the Moroccan ambassador to Spain, signs an agreement at Algeciras on April 7, 1906, allowing France to police his country's borders. In so doing, he helped resolve France's dispute with Germany, but of course at his own country's expense. Unnoticed in the general congratulations was the humiliation visited upon Morocco, one among innumerable such humiliations that seeded the bitterness the Muslim world today feels against the West. Copyright Hulton-Deutsch Collection/CORBIS.

Although admirable, these bilateral agreements had no bearing on the explosive power politics of Europe. As tensions there reached the breaking point in 1914, the United States remained effectively on the sidelines.

Yet at Algeciras Roosevelt had correctly anticipated what the future would demand of America. So did the French journalist Andre Tardieu, who remarked in 1908:

> The United States is ... a world power.... Its power creates for it ... a duty—to pronounce upon all those questions that hitherto have been arranged by agreement only among European powers.... The United States intervenes thus in the affairs of the universe.... It is seated at the table where the great game is played, and it cannot leave it.

▶ What did Roosevelt mean when he said the United States had to be the "policeman" of the Caribbean?

▶ Why did the United States find it so much more difficult to work its will in the Far East than in the Caribbean?

▶ Woodrow Wilson believed the United States should be true to its democratic principles in dealing with Latin America. How would you rate Wilson's approach when he applied it to the Mexican Revolution?

SUMMARY

In this chapter, we explore how the United States emerged as a Great Power in the late nineteenth century. By any economic or population standard, the country already ranked with the major European powers. But America's orientation was inward-looking, and that was reflected in the lax conduct of its foreign policy and the neglect of its navy. America's swift economic growth, however, and the resulting need for outlets for its surplus products, forced the country to look outward. By the early 1890s strategists like Alfred T. Mahan were calling for a battleship navy, an inter-ocean canal, and overseas bases. Accompanying this expansionist thinking were legitimating ideas drawn from Social Darwinism, Anglo-Saxon racism, and America's tradition of Manifest Destiny.

The Spanish-American War provided the opportunity for acting on these imperialist inclinations. Swift victory enabled the United States to seize from Spain the key possessions it wanted. In taking the Philippines, however, the United States overstepped the colonialism palatable to the country — strategic bases, not control over alien populations. The result was a bitter Filipino insurrection, and a resurgence of anti-imperialist sentiment at home. Even so, the McKinley administration realized the strategic goals it had set, and the United States entered the twentieth century poised to take its place as a Great Power.

In Europe, the immediate consequences were few. Only in its growing ties with Britain and by Roosevelt's involvement in the Moroccan crisis did the United States depart from its traditional avoidance of European entanglements. In the Caribbean and Asia, however, the United States moved aggressively, building the Panama Canal, asserting its dominance over the nearby states, and pressing for the Open Door in China. When Woodrow Wilson became president, he tried to bring the conduct of foreign policy more into conformity with the nation's political ideals, only to have the limitations of that approach revealed by his intervention in the Mexican Revolution. Although world peace was an increasingly popular cause in America, that sentiment did not translate into diplomatic action. The United States stood on the sidelines as a great war engulfed Europe in 1914.

Connections: Diplomacy

The events related in this chapter mark a turning point in the nation's relations with the larger world. For nearly a century, American diplomacy had dealt mostly with the lingering effects of its colonial origins (Chapter 8) and with the territorial claims arising from Manifest Destiny (Chapter 13). Even as its population and economy grew prodigiously, America was content to remain on the diplomatic sidelines until it finally burst onto the world stage at the end of the 1890s. As we say in the part opener (p. 485):

> In short order, the United States went to war with Spain, acquired an overseas empire, and became actively engaged in Latin America and Asia. There was no mistaking America's standing as a Great Power....

In the next chapter we will see how the United States handled that challenge as a participant in World War I, and, again, in Chapter 25, how it learned from its mistakes and tried to do better in World War II. From then on, American diplomacy becomes a dominant theme in this text, but the dilemma the country first faced in 1900 — how to define its role as a Great Power — remains as current and unresolved today as it was a hundred years ago.

CHAPTER REVIEW QUESTIONS

➤ Why did it become untenable for the United States to adhere to its traditional isolation from world affairs?

➤ By 1899 the United States had acquired an overseas empire. How did that happen?

➤ How did Roosevelt, Taft, and Wilson differ as architects of American imperialism?

TIMELINE

1875	Treaty brings Hawaii within U.S. orbit
1876	United States achieves favorable balance of trade
1881	Secretary of State James G. Blaine inaugurates Pan-Americanism
1889	Conflict with Germany in Samoa
1890	Alfred Thayer Mahan's *The Influence of Seapower upon History*
1893	Annexation of Hawaii fails
	Frederick Jackson Turner's "The Significance of the Frontier in American History"
1894	Sino-Japanese War begins breakup of China into spheres of influence
1895	Venezuela crisis
	Cuban civil war
1898	Spanish-American War
	Hawaii annexed
	Anti-imperialist movement launched
1899	Treaty of Paris
	Guerrilla war in the Philippines
	Open-door policy in China
1901	Theodore Roosevelt becomes president; diplomacy of the "big stick"
1902	United States withdraws from Cuba; Platt Amendment gives United States right of intervention
1903	United States recognizes Panama and receives grant of Canal Zone
1904	Roosevelt Corollary to the Monroe Doctrine
1906	United States mediates Franco-German crisis over Morocco at Algeciras
1907	Gentlemen's Agreement with Japan
1908	Root-Takahira Agreement
1913	Intervention in the Mexican Revolution
1914	Panama Canal opens
	World War I begins

FOR FURTHER EXPLORATION

Walter LaFeber, *The American Search for Opportunity, 1865–1913* (1993), is an excellent, up-to-date synthesis. LaFeber emphasizes economic interest—the need for overseas markets—as the source of American expansionism. His immensely influential *The New Empire, 1860–1898* (1963) initiated the scholarly debate on this issue. A robust counterpoint is Fareed Zakaria's *From Wealth to Power* (1998), which asks why the United States was so slow (compared to other imperial nations) to translate its economic power into international muscle. The debate can be explored at greater depth in Michael Hunt, *Ideology and U.S. Foreign Policy* (1987); Thomas J. McCormick, *China Market: America's Quest for Informal Empire, 1893–1901* (1967); and Mark R. Shulman, *Navalism and the Emergence of American Sea Power, 1882–1893* (1995). On the war with Spain the liveliest narrative is still Frank Freidel, *A Splendid Little War* (1958). Ivan Musicant, *Empire by Default* (1998), offers a fuller, up-to-date treatment. The overlooked role of the Cuban rebels is brought to light by Louis S. Perez, *The War of 1898: The United States and Cuba* (1998). Lewis Gould, *The Spanish-American War and President McKinley* (1982), emphasizes McKinley's strong leadership. Ernest R. May, *Imperial Democracy: The Emergence of America as a Great Power* (1961), exemplifies the earlier view that McKinley was a weak figure driven to war by jingoistic pressures. One source of the raging jingoism of this era is uncovered in Kristin L. Hoganson, *Fighting for American Manhood: How Gender Provoked the Spanish-American and Philippine-American Wars* (1998). On the Mexican involvement see John S. D. Eisenhower, *Intervention! The United States and the Mexican Revolution* (1993). The revolution as experienced by the Mexicans is brilliantly depicted in John Womack, *Zapata and the Mexican Revolution* (1968). Michael J. Hogan and Thomas G. Patterson, eds., *Explaining the History of American Foreign Relations*, 2d ed. (2004) is a useful collection of new essays on historical writings on American diplomacy, much of it pertinent to the period covered by this chapter.

The Library of Congress maintains an excellent Web site, "The World of 1898: The Spanish-American War," at **www.loc.gov/rr/hispanic/1898/**, with separate sections on the war in Cuba, the Philippines, Puerto Rico, and Spain. "American Imperialism" at **www.boondocksnet.com** includes an extensive collection of stereoscopic images, political cartoons, maps, photographs, and documents from the period.

TEST YOUR KNOWLEDGE

To assess your command of the material in this chapter, see the Online Study Guide at **bedfordstmartins.com/henretta**.

For Web sites, images, and documents related to topics and places in this chapter, visit **bedfordstmartins.com/makehistory**.

PART FIVE: The Modern State and Society
1914–1945

	GOVERNMENT	DIPLOMACY	ECONOMY	SOCIETY	CULTURE
	The Rise of the State	**From Isolation to World Leadership**	**Prosperity, Depression, and War**	**Nativism, Migration, and Social Change**	**The Emergence of a Mass National Culture**
1914	▸ Wartime agencies expand power of federal government ▸ High taxes on the wealthy and on corporations	▸ United States enters World War I (1917) ▸ Wilson's Fourteen Points (1918)	▸ Shift from debtor to creditor nation ▸ Agricultural prosperity	▸ Southern blacks migrate to factory work in North ▸ Attacks against German Americans ▸ "Red Scare" (1919–1920)	▸ Wartime promotion of national unity ▸ Americanization campaign ▸ Silent screen; Hollywood becomes movie capital of the world
1920	▸ Republican ascendancy ▸ Prohibition (1920–1933) ▸ Business-government partnership ▸ Nineteenth Amendment gives women the vote	▸ Treaty of Versailles rejected by U.S. Senate (1920) ▸ Washington Conference sets naval limits (1922) ▸ Dawes Plan (1924)	▸ Economic recession (1920–1921) ▸ Booming prosperity (1922–1929) ▸ Automobile age begins ▸ Rise of welfare capitalism	▸ Rise of nativism and revival of KKK ▸ National Origins Act (1924) ▸ Mexican American immigration grows ▸ Harlem Renaissance	▸ Advertising promotes consumer culture ▸ New media — radio, movies — create national popular culture ▸ Image of "Roaring Twenties"
1930	▸ Franklin Roosevelt becomes president (1933) ▸ The New Deal: vast government intervention in economy ▸ Social welfare liberalism	▸ Good Neighbor Policy toward Latin America (1933) ▸ Isolationism grows ▸ U.S. neutrality proclaimed (1939)	▸ Great Depression (1929–1941) ▸ TVA aids development ▸ Rise of CIO and organized labor	▸ Farming families migrate from dust bowl states to California ▸ Indian New Deal ▸ Reverse migration to Asia and Mexico	▸ Documentary impulse in arts ▸ Works Project Administration assists artists
1940	▸ Government mobilizes industry for war output ▸ Massive war budgets and debt ▸ Universal income tax system	▸ United States enters World War II (1941) ▸ Allies defeat fascist powers ▸ Atomic bombing of Japan (1945) ▸ United Nations created (1945)	▸ War spending ends depression ▸ Business executives join government ▸ Labor unions prosper ▸ Married women enter workforce	▸ Internment of Japanese Americans ▸ Segregation in armed forces ▸ Rural whites and blacks migrate to war jobs in cities	▸ Movie industry expands and aids war effort ▸ Rationing limits consumer culture

In the 1930s journalist Mark Sullivan described World War I as a "fundamental alteration, from which we would never go back." Sullivan was correct in viewing the war as a pivotal point in world history, but many of the important factors that were transforming America were in place before the war. By 1914 industrialization, massive immigration, and the growth of cities had set the foundations for distinctly *modern* American society: diverse, prosperous, and urban. This new society was also more organized, more bureaucratic, and more complex. And by 1945, after having mobilized its resources to fight two world wars and the Great Depression, it was more wealthy and powerful, with a much larger national government. The edifice of the new society was largely complete.

GOVERNMENT An essential feature of modern American society was a strong national state. This state came late and haltingly to the United States compared with those of the industrialized countries of western Europe. American participation in World War I called forth an unprecedented mobilization of the domestic economy, but policymakers quickly dismantled the centralized wartime bureaucracies in 1919. During the 1920s the Harding and Coolidge administrations embraced a philosophy of business-government partnership, believing that corporate capitalism would provide for the welfare of the American people. It took the Great Depression, with its countless business failures and unprecedented levels of unemployment, to overthrow that long-cherished idea. Franklin D. Roosevelt's New Deal dramatically expanded federal responsibility for the economy and the welfare of ordinary citizens. An even greater expansion of the national state resulted from the massive mobilization following America's entry into World War II. Unlike the experience after World War I, the new state apparatus remained in place when the war ended.

DIPLOMACY A second defining feature of modern America was its slow but steady movement toward a position of world political leadership, which it continues to hold today. World War I provided the first major impetus: Before 1914 the world had been dominated by European nations, but from that point on the United States grew increasingly influential in international economic and political affairs. In 1918 American troops provided the margin of victory for the Allies, and President Wilson helped to shape the treaties that ended the war. Although the United States refused to join the League of Nations, its dominant economic position meant that it played an active role in world affairs in the 1920s and 1930s. America's global presence accelerated in 1941, when the nation threw all its energies into a second world war waged against fascist nations in Europe and Asia. Of all the major powers, only the United States emerged physically unscathed from that devastating global conflagration. The country was also the only one to possess a dangerous new weapon—the atomic bomb. Within wartime decisions and strategies lay the roots of the Cold War that followed.

ECONOMY The dominant world position of modern America was the result of a robust domestic economy. Between 1914 and 1945 the nation boasted the world's most productive economic system. Even the Great Depression, which hit the United States harder than any other industrialized nation, did not permanently undermine America's global economic standing. American businesses successfully competed in world markets, and American financial institutions played the leading role in international economic affairs. Large-scale corporate organizations replaced smaller family-run businesses. The automobile industry symbolized the ascendancy of mass-production techniques. Many workers shared in the general prosperity but also bore the brunt of economic downturns. These uncertainties fueled the dramatic growth of the labor movement in the 1930s.

SOCIETY The character of modern American society was shaped by the great wave of European immigration between 1880 and 1914 and the movement of native-born Americans from farms to cities. The growth of metropolitan areas gave the nation an increasingly urban tone, and geographical mobility broke down regional differences. Many old-stock white Americans viewed these processes with alarm; in 1924 they secured legislation limiting immigration to countries in the Western Hemisphere. Migration across the border from Mexico continued to shape the West and Southwest. And the internal movement of people continued: African Americans moved north and west to take factory jobs, dust bowl farmers migrated to the Far West, and Applachian whites took jobs in World War II defense plants around the country.

CULTURE Finally, modern America saw the emergence of a mass national culture. By the 1920s advertising and the new entertainment media—movies, radio, and magazines—disseminated the new values of consumerism, and the Hollywood movie industry exported this vision of the American experience worldwide. Not even the Great Depression could divert Americans from their desire for leisure, self-fulfillment, and consumer goods. The emphasis on consumption and a quest for a rising standard of living would define the American experience for the rest of the twentieth century.

SEPT 29th 1917

Leslie's
Illustrated Weekly Newspaper

Price 10 Cents
In Canada, 15 Cents

Notice to Reader
When you finish reading this magazine place a one cent stamp alongside of this notice, hand same to any postal employe and it will be placed in the hands of our soldiers or sailors at the front.
No wrapping—no address.
A. S. BURLESON,
Postmaster-General.

Paul Stahr

Be Patriotic
sign your country's pledge to save the food

22 War and the American State
1914–1920

WHEN THE UNITED STATES ENTERED the Great War in 1917, President Wilson and his administration led the country with the same idealistic rhetoric they had brought to domestic concerns during the Progressive era. "It's Up to You—Protect the Nation's Honor—Enlist Now." "Rivets Are Bayonets—Drive Them Home!" "Women! Help America's Sons Win the War: Buy U.S. Government Bonds." "Food Is Ammunition—Don't Waste It." At every turn during the eighteen months of U.S. participation in the Great War—at the movies, in schools and libraries, in shop windows and post offices, at train stations and factories—Americans encountered dramatic posters urging them to do their share. These posters, although now often displayed as colorful reminders of a bygone era, had the serious goal of unifying the American people in voluntary, self-sacrificing service to the nation.

As symbols of the increased presence of the federal government in the lives of Americans, the posters had an even broader significance. The new federal bureaucracies created to coordinate the war effort began the process that led to the emergence, during the New Deal of the 1930s, of a national administrative state. Finally, these patriotic placards underlined the fact that modern warfare was waged by citizens as well as armies. The war effort required a mobilization of the entire population and opened

The Great War, 1914–1918
War in Europe
The Perils of Neutrality
"Over There"
The American Fighting Force

War on the Home Front
Mobilizing Industry and the Economy
Mobilizing American Workers
Wartime Reform: Woman Suffrage and Prohibition
Promoting National Unity

An Unsettled Peace, 1919–1920
The Treaty of Versailles
Racial Strife, Labor Unrest, and the Red Scare

Summary
Connections: Diplomacy

◀ **American Women and the War Effort**

Popular magazines like *Leslie's Illustrated Weekly Newspaper* teamed up with the federal government to promote food conservation. Here an idealized woman draped in the Stars and Stripes encourages voluntary sacrifice on her fellow citizens. Eager to avoid food rationing, government officials mobilized 500,000 volunteers to go door to door to secure housewives' signatures on cards that pledged them to follow food conservation guidelines. *Leslie's,* September 29, 1917 / Picture Research Consultants & Archives.

up new employment opportunities for white women and for members of ethnic minorities. The passions of war also sharpened old ethnic and ideological differences and turned them into crusades of hate, first against those of German origin or descent and then of "Bolshevik" Reds or communists. In aggravating latent class, racial, and ethnic divisions among the American people, the war on the home "front" foreshadowed the social confrontations of the 1920s and 1960s.

The Great War likewise transformed the nation's position in the world. Before the conflict began in 1914, European nations had dominated international politics and trade. Four years of costly and bloody warfare shattered European supremacy. When the war ended, the United States was no longer a regional power — it was now seated at the table of the "great game" of international politics and committed, in Woodrow Wilson's words, to making the world "safe for democracy." Even as American leaders ceased to pursue this idealistic goal during the 1920s, the nation spread its political, economic, and cultural influence across the globe.

The Great War, 1914–1918

When war erupted in August 1914, most Americans saw no reason to involve themselves in the struggle among Europe's imperialistic powers. No vital U.S. interests were at stake. Indeed, the United States had good economic relationships with both the Allied Powers of Great Britain, France, and Russia and the Central Powers of Germany and Austria-Hungary. For many citizens, the war confirmed their faith in what historians call *American exceptionalism* — the belief that their democratic values and institutions allowed the country to avoid corrupting foreign alliances and warfare. But a combination of factors — economic interests, neutrality rights, cultural ties with Great Britain, and German miscalculations — would finally draw the United States into the war on the Allied side in 1917.

War in Europe

Almost from the moment France, Russia, and Britain formed the Triple Entente in 1907 to counter the Triple Alliance of Germany, Austria-Hungary, and Italy (see Chapter 21), European leaders began to prepare for what they saw as an inevitable conflict. The spark that ignited the war came in Europe's perennial tinderbox, the Balkans, where Austria-Hungary and Russia were competing for power and influence as the Ottoman Empire slowly disintegrated. Austria's seizure in 1908 of the Ottoman provinces of Bosnia and Herzegovina, with their substantial Slavic populations, had enraged Slavic ideologues in Russia and its ally, the independent Slavic state of Serbia. In response, Serbian terrorists recruited Bosnians to resist Austrian rule. In June 1914 in the town of Sarajevo, a nineteen-year-old Bosnian student, Gavrilo Princip, assassinated Franz Ferdinand, the heir to the Austro-Hungarian throne, and his wife, the Duchess of Hohenberg.

The complex system of European diplomatic alliances, which for years had maintained a fragile peace, now quickly pulled all the major powers into war. Blaming Serbia for the assassination, Austria-Hungary declared war on Serbia on July 28. Russia, which had a secret treaty with Serbia, mobilized its armies; Germany responded by declaring war on Russia and its French ally. To attack France, the Germans launched a brutal invasion of the neutral country of Belgium, which prompted Great Britain to declare war on Germany on August 4. In less than a week, nearly all of Europe was at war.

The combatants formed two large rival blocs. The Allied Powers — Great Britain, France, Russia — were pitted against the Central Powers — Germany and Austria-Hungary, joined by Turkey in 1914 (Map 22.1). Two major battle zones emerged. The British and French (and later the Americans) battled on the Western Front against the Germans, who also fought against the Russians on the Eastern Front. Because most of the warring nations held colonial empires, the conflict spread to parts of the world far beyond Europe, including the Middle East, Africa, and China. Indeed, by 1915, Italy and Japan had joined the Allied side and Bulgaria linked up with the Central Powers — hoping to use the war to secure valuable colonies or adjacent territories. Because of its worldwide scope, the conflict soon became known as the Great War and, following a second global conflict during the 1940s, as World War I.

The term *Great War* also suggested its terrible devastation, both to armies and civilians. New military technology, much of it from the United States, made warfare more deadly than ever before. Every soldier carried a long-range, high-velocity rifle that could hit a target at 1,000 yards — a vast technical improvement over the 300-yard range of the rifle-musket used in the American Civil War. The machine gun was an even more deadly technological innovation. Its American-born inventor, Hiram Maxim, moved to Great Britain in the 1880s to follow a friend's advice: "If you want to make your

MAP 22.1 European Alliances in 1914

In early August 1914 a complex set of interlocking alliances drew all of the major European powers into war. At first the United States avoided the conflict, which did not directly threaten its national interests. Not until April 1917 did America enter the war on the Allied side.

Map annotations:
- Wars often change boundary lines as a result of peace treaties. World War I ended by breaking up Germany as well as the Russian, Austro-Hungarian, and Ottoman empires, creating new nations and reconfiguring the entire map. Compare this map with Map 22.5 on page 696.
- Romania was aligned with the Central Powers in 1914 but later entered the war on the side of the Allies.
- In 1914, Italy switched sides from the Central Powers to the Allied cause.
- Bulgaria was not officially part of the alliance system in 1914 but joined the fighting in 1915 as one of the Central Powers.

fortune, invent something which will allow those fool Europeans to kill each other more quickly." The concentrated fire of rifles, machine guns, and artillery gave a tremendous advantage to defensive positions. For four bloody years, the Allies and the Central Powers fought over a narrow swath of territory that cut across Belgium and northern France. Millions of soldiers lived for months in 25,000 miles of heavily fortified trenches. One side and then the other would mount an attack across "no man's land," only to be caught in a sea of barbed wire or mowed down by machine guns and artillery fire. Trying to break the stalemate, the Germans launched an attack at Ypres in April 1915 that used deadly poison gas, yet another technological nightmare that inflated the number of casualties. As the Germans tried to break through the French lines at Verdun between February and December 1916, they suffered 450,000 casualties; the French fared even worse, with 550,000 dead or wounded soldiers. All to no avail. From 1914 to 1918, the Western Front barely moved.

The Perils of Neutrality

As the stalemate continued, the United States grappled with its role in the international conflagration. Two weeks after the outbreak of war in Europe, President Wilson called on Americans to be "neutral in fact as well as in name, impartial in thought as well as in action." If he kept America out of the European conflict, Wilson reasoned, he could arbitrate — and influence — its ultimate settlement, much as Theodore Roosevelt had helped to end the Russo-Japanese War of 1905.

Domestic Divisions. The nation's divided loyalties also influenced Wilson's policy. Many Americans, including Wilson, felt deep cultural ties to the Allies, especially Britain and France. Yet most Irish Americans resented Britain's centuries-long occupation of their homeland and the cancellation of Irish Home Rule in 1914. Moreover, more than ten million immigrants had come to the United States from Germany and Austria-Hungary, and many of

Trench Warfare

Millions of soldiers lived for months at a time in trenches that stretched for hundreds of miles across northern France. This photograph captures a moment of peace, when an exhausted soldier could catch some sleep or scribble a letter to his wife or family. Life in the trenches profoundly scarred many men and created a raft of new psychological ailments: "gas neurosis," "burial-alive neurosis," and "soldier's heart" — all symptoms of shell shock. Imperial War Museum, London.

them lived in German-speaking rural communities or belonged to German cultural organizations. Whatever his personal sympathies, Wilson could not easily have rallied the nation to the Allied side in 1914.

Many politically active Americans refused to support either side. Progressive Republican senators, such as Robert La Follette of Wisconsin and George Norris of Nebraska, vehemently opposed American participation in the European conflict. Virtually the entire political left, led principally by Eugene Debs and the Socialist Party, condemned the war as a conflict among greedy capitalist and imperialist nations. A. Philip Randolph and other African American leaders wanted no part in a struggle among white nations. Newly formed pacifist groups, among them the American Union against Militarism and the Women's Peace Party, both founded in 1915, mobilized popular opposition to the war. So too did two giants of American industry, Andrew Carnegie and Henry Ford. In December 1915 Ford spent half a million dollars to send one hundred men and women to Europe on a "peace ship" in an attempt to negotiate an end to the war.

Conflict on the High Seas. Such sentiments might have kept the nation neutral if the conflict had not spread to the high seas. The United States wished to trade peacefully with all the warring nations, but the combatants would not grant America this luxury. By September 1914, the British had imposed a naval blockade on the Central Powers in the hope of cutting off vital supplies of food, raw materials, and military armaments. The United States complained strongly at this infringement of its rights as a "neutral carrier" but did not take punitive action. The war had produced a spectacular increase in trade with the Allies that more than made up for the lost commerce with the Central Powers. American trade with Britain and France grew from $824 million in 1914 to $3.2 billion in 1916. By 1917, U.S. banks had lent the Allies $2.5 billion. In contrast, American trade and loans to Germany totaled only $29 million and $27 million, respectively, by 1917. This imbalance in commerce and credit translated into closer U.S. ties with the Allies, despite the nation's official posture of neutrality.

To challenge British control of the seas, the German navy launched a devastating new weapon, the U-boat (short for *Unterseeboot*, the "undersea" boat or submarine). In April 1915 the German embassy in the United States issued a warning to civilians that all ships flying the flags of Britain or its allies were liable to destruction. A few weeks later, a German U-boat off the coast of Ireland torpedoed the British luxury liner *Lusitania*, killing 1,198 people, 128 of them Americans. The attack on the unarmed passenger vessel (which was later revealed to have been carrying munitions) incensed Americans — newspapers branded it a "mass murder" — and prompted President Wilson to send a series of strongly worded protests to Germany. Mounting tension between the two nations temporarily subsided in September 1915, when Germany announced its U-boats would no longer attack passenger ships without warning.

The *Lusitania* crisis prompted Wilson to rethink his opposition to military preparedness. The president was further discouraged by the failure of his repeated attempts in 1915 and 1916 to mediate an end to the European conflict through his aide, Colonel Edward House. With neither side apparently interested in serious peace negotiations, in the fall of 1915 Wilson endorsed a $1 billion buildup of the army and the navy.

Nonetheless, American public opinion still ran strongly against entering the war, a factor that profoundly shaped the election of 1916. The reunited Republican Party passed over the belligerently prowar Theodore Roosevelt in favor of Supreme Court Justice Charles Evans Hughes, a former progressive governor of New York. The Democrats renominated Wilson, who campaigned both on his record

The 1916 Campaign

The Women's Bureau of the Democratic National Committee sponsored this campaign van. It reminded Americans of President Woodrow Wilson's progressive program of reform and his recent support for the eight-hour workday and a farm loan program. To clinch the case for reelection, it asked: "WHO KEEPS US OUT OF WAR?" Corbis-Bettmann.

as a progressive (see Chapter 20) and as the president who "kept us out of war." Wilson eked out a narrow victory; winning California by 4,000 votes, he secured a slim majority in the Electoral College.

Moving Toward War. Whatever Wilson's campaign slogan, the events of early 1917 diminished his lingering hopes of staying out of the conflict. On January 31 Germany announced the resumption of unrestricted submarine warfare, a decision dictated by the impasse in the land war. In response, Wilson broke off diplomatic relations with Germany on February 3. A few weeks later, newspapers published an intercepted communication from Germany's foreign secretary, Arthur Zimmermann, to the German minister in Mexico City. Zimmermann urged Mexico to join the Central Powers and, in the event the United States entered the war, promised to help Mexico recover "the lost territory of Texas, New Mexico, and Arizona." This threat to the territorial integrity of the United States jolted both congressional and public opinion. During 1916, the civil warfare sparked by the Mexican Revolution had spilled over the border. When raids led by Pancho Villa resulted in the deaths of sixteen U.S. citizens, a U.S. army force commanded by General John J. Pershing occupied parts of northern Mexico (see Chapter 21) and the two nations edged toward war. Given these tensions along the border, American policymakers took the German threat seriously.

The resumption of unrestricted submarine warfare and the Zimmermann telegram inflamed anti-German sentiment throughout the nation. German U-boats were now attacking American ships without warning, sinking three on March 18 alone. On April 2, 1917, Wilson appeared before a special session of Congress to ask for a declaration of war. The rights of the nation had been trampled, and its trade and citizens' lives imperiled, he told the legislators, but America should not enter the war for selfish or material motives. Rather, reflecting his Christian zeal and progressive idealism, Wilson justified the war as a moral crusade: "We desire no conquest, no dominion. We seek no indemnities for ourselves, no material compensation for the sacrifices we shall freely make. We are but one of the champions of the rights of mankind." In a memorable phrase intended to ennoble the nation's role, Wilson proposed that U.S. participation in the war would make the world "safe for democracy."

Four days later, on April 6, 1917, the United States declared war on Germany. Reflecting the divided feelings of the country, the vote was far from unanimous. Six senators and fifty members of the House voted against the action, including Representative Jeannette Rankin of Montana, the first woman elected to Congress. "I want to stand by my country," she declared, "but I cannot vote for war."

"Over There"

To native-born Americans, Europe seemed a great distance away—literally "over there," as the lyrics of George M. Cohan's popular song described it. After the declaration of war, many citizens were surprised to learn that the United States planned to send troops to Europe—they had assumed that the nation's participation would be limited to military and economic aid. In May 1917, General John J. Pershing traveled to London and Paris to determine how the United States could best support the war effort. The answer was clear; as Marshal Joseph Joffre of France put it: "Men, men, and more men."

Conscription. The problem was that the United States had never maintained a large standing army; in 1917, the U.S. army consisted of fewer than 200,000 men. To field a fighting force, the government turned to conscription—a compulsory military draft. The Selective Service Act in May 1917 underlined the increasing power of the state over ordinary citizens. Unlike the Civil War, when resistance to the military draft was common, conscription went smoothly. By combining central direction by military authorities in Washington with local civilian-run draft boards, the Selective Service System respected the nation's tradition of individual freedom and local autonomy. Still, the process of draft registration demonstrated the bureaucratic potential of the American state. On a single day, June 5, 1917, more than 9.5 million men between the ages of twenty-one and thirty were processed for military service in their local voting precincts. By the end of the war, almost 4 million men, popularly known as "doughboys," plus a few thousand female navy clerks and army nurses, were in uniform. Another 300,000 men (labeled as "slackers") evaded the draft, and another 4,000 received classification as conscientious objectors.

President Wilson chose General Pershing to head the American Expeditionary Force (AEF). Before the new army could fight, it had to be trained and outfitted and transported across the submarine-infested Atlantic. The nation's first significant contribution to the Allied war effort was to secure the safety of the seas. When the U.S. entered the war, German U-boats were sinking 900,000 tons of Allied ships each month. By sending merchant and troop ships in armed convoys, the U.S. Navy cut that rate to

400,000 tons by the end of 1917. More important, no American soldiers were killed on the way to Europe.

Allied Victory on the Western Front. Meanwhile, trench warfare on the Western Front continued its deadly grind. Allied commanders pleaded for American reinforcements, but Pershing was reluctant to put his soldiers under foreign commanders, preferring to delay introducing American troops until the AEF could be brought up to full strength. Thus, until May 1918, the brunt of the fighting continued to fall on the French and British. Their burden increased when the Eastern Front collapsed following the Bolshevik (Communist) Revolution in Russia in November 1917. To consolidate its power at home, the Bolshevik regime, led by Vladimir Ilych Lenin, sought peace with the Central Powers. In the Treaty of Brest-Litovsk in March 1918, the new Russian government surrendered its sovereignty over vast territories in central Europe, including Russian Poland, the Ukraine, and the Baltic provinces. Freed from warfare with Germany, Lenin's Communist government emerged victorious after a three-year civil war against supporters of the ousted tsar, Nicholas II, and other counterrevolutionaries.

When the war with Russia ended in March 1918, the Germans launched a major offensive on the Western Front. By May the German army had advanced to within 50 miles of Paris and was bombarding the city with long-range artillery. As Allied leaders intensified their calls for American troops, Pershing committed about 60,000 Americans to help the French repel the Germans in the battles of Château-Thierry and Belleau Wood (Map 22.2). Augmented by American troops, who now began to arrive in massive numbers, the Allied forces brought the German offensive to a halt in mid-July. By mid-September 1918 American and French troops, led by General Pershing, had forced the Germans to retreat at St. Mihiel. The last major assault of the war began on September 26, when Pershing pitted over a million American soldiers against vastly outnumbered and exhausted German troops. The Meuse-Argonne campaign pushed the enemy back across the Selle River near Verdun and broke the German defenses, at a cost of over 26,000 American lives.

World War I ended on November 11, 1918, when German and Allied representatives signed an **armistice** in the railway car of Marshal Ferdinand Foch of France. The flood of American troops and supplies during the last six months of the war had helped secure the Allied victory. The nation's decisive contribution signaled a shift in international power as European diplomatic and economic dominance declined, and the United States emerged as a world leader.

MAP 22.2   U.S. Participation on the Western Front, 1918

When American troops reached the European front in significant numbers in 1918, the Allied and Central Powers had been fighting a deadly **war of attrition** for almost four years. The influx of American troops and supplies helped to break the stalemate. Successful offensive maneuvers by the American Expeditionary Force included those at Belleau Wood and Château-Thierry and the Meuse-Argonne campaign.

The American Fighting Force

About 2 million American soldiers were in France at the war's end. Two-thirds of them had seen some military action, but most American soldiers escaped the horrors of sustained trench warfare. Still, during the eighteen months that the United States was at war, 53,000 American servicemen were killed in action, and another 203,000 suffered wounds. Another 63,000 died from other causes, mainly the devastating influenza pandemic that swept the world in 1918 and 1919 and killed at least 50 million people. However, the nation's military casualties were a mere speck as compared with the 8 million soldiers lost by the Allies and the Central Powers and the 500,000 American civilians who died in the influenza epidemic.

Eddie Rickenbacker: Flying Ace. Although individual bravery was increasingly anachronistic in modern warfare, the war generated its share of American heroes. The best known were Sergeant Alvin York, who single-handedly killed 25 Germans and took 132 prisoners in the battle of Châtel-Chéhéry in the Meuse-Argonne campaign, and Edward Vernon Rickenbacker, a former professional racecar driver. When the war began in 1914, Rickenbacker added an English-sounding middle name to disguise his German ancestry and enlisted immediately once the United States entered the war. Sent to France as a driver, he quickly learned to fly and, in March 1918, joined the 94th Aero Pursuit Squadron. Eddie soon demonstrated his skills, dueling in the skies with the German "Flying

Fighting the Flu

The influenza epidemic of 1918 to 1919 traversed the globe, making it a pandemic that killed as many as 50 million people. According to recent research, the flu began as a virus native to wild birds and then mutated into a form that passed easily from one human to another. In the United States, one-fifth of the population was infected and more than 500,000 civilians died — ten times the number of American soldiers who died in combat during World War I. The epidemic spread with frightening speed and strained the resources of a public-health system already fully mobilized for the war effort. In October 1918 alone, 200,000 Americans died. Here doctors, army officers, and reporters don surgical masks and gowns before touring hospitals that treat influenza patients. Corbis-Bettmann.

Flying Aces
As millions of men suffered and died in the trenches, a few hundred pilots did battle in the sky. America's best-known fighting pilot was Eddie Rickenbacker (middle) of the Ninety-fourth Aero Pursuit Squadron, who was credited with twenty-six "victories" over enemy aircraft. The Ninety-fourth was known as the hat-in-the-ring squadron for the American custom of throwing a hat into the ring as an invitation to fight. Note the hat insignia on the plane. Corbis-Bettmann.

Circus" led by Manfred von Richthofen, the famous "Red Baron." By the war's end, Rickenbacker had fought in 134 air battles, downed 26 German planes, and become a national hero. Although air pilots played only a minor role in the war, they captivated the popular imagination — as their daredevil aerial exploits provided a vivid contrast to the monotony of deadly trench warfare.

Rickenbacker's more important contribution to history came later. In 1935 he joined Eastern Airlines, one of the pioneering flagships of commercial aviation, and soon became its president. Until his death in 1973, Rickenbacker was a leading figure in the development of commercial aviation, which in the years after World War II revolutionized world travel.

Diversity and Racism in the Armed Forces. Most American soldiers were not heroes like York and Rickenbacker, but rather ordinary men from rural farms and crowded cities. The army taught them about venereal disease, issued them condoms, and gave them safety razors — changing the sexual outlook and shaving habits of a generation. The recruits reflected the heterogeneity of the nation's population. About one-fifth of the American soldiers had been born in another country, leading some people to call the AEF the American Foreign Legion. Army censors had to be able to read forty-nine languages to check letters written home by American servicemen. Although this diversity worried some observers, most predicted that service in the armed forces would promote the Americanization of the nation's immigrants.

The "Americanization" of the army remained imperfect at best, with African American soldiers receiving the worst treatment. Over 400,000 black men served in the military, accounting for 13 percent of the armed forces; 92 percent were draftees, a far higher rate than that of whites. Blacks were organized into rigidly segregated units, almost always under the control of white officers. In addition, blacks were assigned to the most menial tasks, such as kitchen and clean-up details. Although the policy of segregation minimized contact between black and white recruits, racial violence erupted at several camps. The worst incident occurred in Houston in August 1917, when black members of the Twenty-fourth Infantry's Third Battalion killed fifteen white soldiers and police officers in retaliation for a string of racial incidents. Sixty-four soldiers were tried in military courts, and nineteen were hanged. The army quickly disbanded the battalion, but the legacy of racial mistrust lingered throughout the rest of the war (see Voices from Abroad, "A German Propaganda Appeal to Black Soldiers," p. 682).

In contrast to the segregation of African Americans, Native Americans served in integrated combat units. Ironically, racial stereotypes about the natural abilities of Native American men as warriors, adroit tacticians, and camouflage experts enhanced their military reputations and meant that officers gave them hazardous duties as advance scouts, messengers, and snipers. Approximately 13,000, or 25 percent, of the adult male Native American population served in the military, often with distinction. Roughly 5 percent died, compared to 2 percent for the military as a whole.

After the armistice, American troops came home and quickly readjusted to civilian life. Spared the trauma of sustained battle, many members of the AEF had experienced the war "over there"

VOICES FROM ABROAD

A German Propaganda Appeal to Black Soldiers

In an effort to undermine morale, both the Allied Powers and the Central Powers distributed propaganda tracts among the opposing troops. This piece of German propaganda was directed toward black soldiers in France. According to Charles Williams — who, with the cooperation of the secretary of war, the Federal Council of Churches, and the Phelps-Stokes Fund, investigated conditions for black recruits — the reaction of African American soldiers who read the propaganda was clear: "We know what they say is true, but don't worry; we're not going over."

To the Colored Soldiers of the U.S. Army,

September, 1918, Vosges Mountains.

Hello, boys, what are you doing over there? Fighting the Germans? Why? Have they ever done you any harm? Of course, some white folks and the lying English-American papers told you that the Germans ought to be wiped out for the sake of humanity and democracy. What is democracy? Personal freedom, all citizens enjoying the same rights socially and before the law. Do you enjoy the same rights as the white people do in America, the land of freedom and democracy? Or aren't you rather rated over there as second class citizens? Can you go to a restaurant where white people dine, can you get a seat in a theatre where white people sit, can you get a pullman seat or berth in a railroad car, or can you ride in the South in the same street car with white people? And how about the law? Is lynching and the most horrible cruelties connected therewith a lawful proceeding in a democratic country?

Now all of this is entirely different in Germany, where they do like colored people, where they do treat them as gentlemen and not as second class citizens. They enjoy exactly the same social privileges as every white man, and quite a number of colored people have mighty fine positions in Berlin and other big German cities.

Why, then, fight the Germans only for the benefit of the Wall Street robbers to protect the millions they have lent to the English, French, and Italians? You have been made the tool of the egotistic and rapacious rich in England and America, and there is nothing in the whole game for you but broken bones, horrible wounds, broken health or — death. No satisfaction whatever will you get out of this unjust war. You have never seen Germany; so you are fools if you allow people to teach you to hate it. Come over and see for yourself. Let those do the fighting who make profit out of this war; don't allow them to use you as cannon food. To carry the gun in their defense is not an honor but a shame. Throw it away and come over to the German lines. You will find friends who will help you along.

SOURCE: Charles H. Williams, *Sidelights on Negro Soldiers* (Boston: B. J. Brimmer Co., 1923), 70–71.

ANALYZING THE EVIDENCE

- Are there any statements in this tract that are not true? If it makes truthful claims, is it accurate to call it "propaganda"?

- According to Williams, black soldiers accepted the validity of this harsh description of African American life in the United States. How do you explain their decision to remain loyal to a country that oppressed them and their people?

more as tourists than as soldiers. Before joining the army, most recruits had barely traveled beyond their hometowns, and for them the journey across the ocean to Europe was a once-in-a-lifetime event. Their letters described "old cathedrals, chateaux and ancient towns ... quite wonderful ... to eyes so accustomed to the look of the New World." In 1919, a group of former AEF officers formed the American Legion "to preserve the memories and incidents of our association in the great war." The word *legion* perfectly captured the romantic, almost chivalric memories that many veterans held of their wartime service. Only later did disillusionment set in over the contested legacy of World War I.

> What were the causes of World War I? Why is the conflict considered a "world" war?

> Why did America become involved in the war? How did President Wilson justify his decision to enter the war in 1917? How did Americans respond?

> How did the fighting in Europe differ from previous wars? What was the experience like for soldiers on the front lines?

"Remember Your First Thrill of American Liberty"
U.S. government officials were eager to enlist all Americans in the battle against the Central Powers. They carefully crafted patriotic advertising campaigns that urged Americans to buy bonds, conserve food, enlist in the military, and join in the war effort in countless other ways. This poster targeted recent immigrants to the United States, reminding them that "American Liberty" carried with it the "Duty" to buy war bonds. Library of Congress.

War on the Home Front

Fighting World War I required an extraordinary economic effort on the home front. At the height of mobilization, one-fourth of the gross national product went for war production. Although the federal government expanded its power and presence during the emergency, the watchword was voluntarism—and it worked. Corporations, workers, and the general public did their part to win the war. Business and government proved especially congenial partners, a collaboration that typified the pattern of state building in America. Similarly, the rapid dismantling of the federal bureaucracy after the war reflected the longstanding preference for limited government. Still, during the war many progressives continued their efforts to use governmental policies to improve American society.

Mobilizing Industry and the Economy

Even before the formal declaration of war, the United States had become the arsenal of the Allied Powers. As hundreds of tons of American supplies—grain, guns, and manufactured goods—crossed the Atlantic and the Allies paid for them in gold, the United States became a leading creditor nation. Moreover, as the cost of the war drained British economic reserves, U.S. financial institutions began to provide capital for investments around the globe. America's shift from debtor to creditor status, which would last until the 1980s, guaranteed the nation a major role in the international financial affairs and world politics.

Paying for the War. Wars are expensive, and World War I was no exception. The Wilson administration spent $33 billion fighting the war—about eight times more than Union government expended during the Civil War. Because the disruption of international trade reduced tariff revenues, a major source of federal income, Treasury Secretary William McAdoo turned for revenue to the income taxes permitted by the Sixteenth Amendment (1913). Working with Democrats in Congress, he secured passage of War Revenue Bills in 1917 and 1918 that embodied progressive principles of economic justice. Rather than taxing the wages and salaries of working-class and middle-class Americans, this legislation imposed substantial levies on the income of wealthier individuals and the excess-profits of business corporations. Because of this unprecedented intrusion of the state into the workings of corporate capitalism, by 1918 U.S. corporations were paying over $2.5 billion in taxes per year—more than half of all federal taxes.

In all, the United States raised about one-third of the cost of the war from taxes. The rest came from loans, especially the popular Liberty Loans that encouraged public support for the war effort. Because of these loans, the federal debt increased from $1 billion in 1915 to $20 billion in 1920.

Wartime Economic Regulation: Bernard Baruch. Mobilization required the coordination of economic production. To the dismay of many progressives who had hoped that the war emergency would increase federal regulation of business, the Wilson administration suspended antitrust laws to encourage output and turned to nation's business executives for economic expertise. Corporate officials flocked to Washington, where they served with federal officials on the boards of war-related agencies. The agencies usually sought a middle ground between state control of the economy and total freedom for business, a compromise that had mixed results.

The central agency for directing military production was the War Industries Board (WIB), established in July 1917. After a fumbling start that showed the limits of voluntarism, the Wilson administration reorganized the board under the direction of Bernard Baruch, a Wall Street financier. Born in 1870 to a family of German Jewish immigrants, Baruch began as an office boy in a Wall Street firm and quickly achieved success as a stockbroker, speculator, and member of the New York Stock Exchange. An immensely wealthy man, he supported Wilson's bid for the presidency in 1912 and came to his aid in 1917. (He also served President Franklin D. Roosevelt as a member of his "Brain Trust"; see Chapter 24). Baruch was a superb administrator. Under his direction, the War Industries Board greatly expanded the federal government's economic powers: It gathered economic data and statistics, allocated scarce resources among industries, ordered factories to convert to war production, set prices, and standardized procedures. Although the WIB had the authority to compel compliance, Baruch preferred to win voluntary cooperation from industry. A man of immense charm, he usually succeeded—helped along by the lucrative military contracts at his disposal. Despite higher taxes, corporate profits soared because of guaranteed profits on military production and the war-driven economic boom that continued without interruption until 1920.

In some instances, the new federal agencies took dramatic, decisive action. When the severe winter of 1917–1918 led to coal shortages in northeastern cities, the Fuel Administration ordered all factories east of the Mississippi River to shut down for four days; then it artificially raised the price of coal to increase production. The Railroad War Board, which coordinated the nation's sprawling transportation system, took even more aggressive action. To ensure the rapid movement of troops and equipment, in December 1917 it seized control of private railroads. The Board guaranteed railroad shareholders a "standard return" equal to their average earnings between 1915 and 1917 and promised to return the carriers to private control following the end of the war. Although progressive reformers wanted to assist railroad workers and shippers by continuing federal control, the government fulfilled its pledge.

Perhaps the most successful wartime agency was the Food Administration, created in August 1917 and led by Herbert Hoover, an engineer who had managed major projects around the world. Using the slogan "Food will win the war," Hoover convinced farmers to expand production of wheat and other grains from 45 million acres in 1917 to 75 million in 1919. The increased output not only supplied Americans with food but also allowed a threefold rise in food exports to war-torn Europe. Rather than ration items in short supply, the Food Administration mobilized "the spirit of self-denial and self-sacrifice." Hoover sent women volunteers from door to door to persuade housewives to observe "Wheatless" Mondays, "Meatless" Tuesdays, and "Porkless" Thursdays and Saturdays. Hoover, a Republican in politics, emerged from the war as one of the nation's most admired public figures.

With the signing of the armistice in November 1918, the United States scrambled to dismantle

Bernard Baruch in 1919 When this photograph was taken, Baruch was forty-nine years old and had just served as chairman of the War Industries Board and as an advisor to President Woodrow Wilson at the Versailles Peace Conference. Copyright Bettmann/Corbis.

wartime controls. Wilson disbanded the WIB on January 1, 1919, resisting suggestions that the board would stabilize the economy during demobilization. Like most Americans, Wilson could tolerate government planning during an emergency but not as a permanent feature of the economy.

Although the nation's participation in the war lasted just eighteen months, it left an enduring legacy: the modern bureaucratic state. Entire industries were organized as never before, linked to a maze of government agencies and executive departments. A modern and progressive system of income taxation was established, with the potential for vastly increasing federal revenue. Finally, the collaboration between business and government was mutually beneficial, a lesson both partners would put to use in state building in the 1920s and afterward.

Mobilizing American Workers

Modern wars are never won solely by armies and business and government leaders. Farmers, factory workers, and other civilians played crucial roles in the America's World War I victory, thanks in part to government propaganda posters that constantly exhorted citizens "to do their bit for Uncle Sam." However, World War I produced fewer rewards for workers than for owners and managers.

Organized Labor. The position of labor unions improved during the war, although they remained junior partners to business and government. Samuel Gompers, leader of the American Federation of Labor (AFL), traded the union's support for the war for a voice on government policy; he sat on the National Defense Advisory Commission. The National War Labor Board (NWLB), formed in April 1918, also improved the working lives of laboring men and women. Composed of representatives of labor, management, and the public, the NWLB established an eight-hour day for war workers, with time and a half for overtime, and endorsed equal pay for women workers. In return for a no-strike pledge, the NWLB supported the workers' right to organize unions and required employers to deal with shop committees. When executives at a Smith and Wesson arms plant in Springfield, Massachusetts, discriminated against union employees, the NWLB took over the firm.

After years of federal hostility toward labor, the NWLB's actions brought a dramatic change in labor's status and power. From 1916 to 1919 AFL membership grew by almost one million workers, reaching over three million at the end of the war. Few of the wartime gains lasted, however. Like other agencies, the NWLB was quickly disbanded at war's end. Wartime inflation ate up most of the wage hikes, and a virulent postwar antiunion movement caused a decline in union membership that lasted into the 1930s.

Black and Mexican American Workers. The war emergency created job opportunities for ethnic and racial minorities. For the first time northern factories actively recruited African Americans, spawning a "Great Migration" from southern farms to the nation's industrial heartland (Map 22.3). During the war, more than 400,000 African Americans moved northward to St. Louis, Chicago, New York, and Detroit. The rewards were great. Black workers in Henry Ford's Detroit auto works took home $5 day, the same high pay as white workers. Other African Americans looked forward to working in northern meatpacking plants; as one migrant from Mississippi recalled, "You could not rest in your bed at night for thoughts of Chicago." African Americans encountered discrimination in the North — in jobs, housing, and education — but most celebrated their escape from the repressive racism and low pay of the southern agricultural system (see Comparing American Voices, "The Great Migration," pp. 686–687).

Mexican Americans in California, Texas, New Mexico, and Arizona also found new opportunities. Wartime labor shortages prompted many Mexican Americans to leave farm labor for industrial jobs in rapidly growing southwestern cities, where they mostly settled in segregated neighborhoods (barrios). Continuing political instability in Mexico combined with a demand for agricultural laborers in the U.S. encouraged more Mexicans to move across the border. Between 1917 and 1920 at least 100,000 Mexicans entered the United States, and, despite meeting discrimination because of their dark skins and Catholic religion, many of them stayed.

Women and the War Effort. Women were the largest group to take advantage of new wartime opportunities. White women and, to a lesser degree, black and Mexican American women, took factory jobs usually filled by men. About one million women joined the labor force for the first time, and another eight million women gave up low-wage jobs as teachers and domestic servants for higher-paying industrial work. Americans soon got used to the sight of female streetcar conductors, train engineers, and defense workers. But everyone — including most working women — believed that those jobs would return to men after the war (see Reading American Pictures, " 'Over Here': Women's Wartime Opportunities," p. 689).

COMPARING AMERICAN VOICES

The Great Migration

The Great Migration of African Americans from the rural South to the cities of the North marked a pivotal point in twentieth-century African American history and one that scholars have explored extensively. To capture this black experience, historians have drawn on a variety of primary sources, including black newspapers such as the *Chicago Defender* and the *Atlanta Journal*; records of the Chicago Urban League, an organization that helped southern migrants adjust to their new environment; and the report of the Chicago Commission on Race Relations, which interviewed many African Americans following the devastating race riot of 1919 (see p. 698). Other newspaper and magazine articles reveal the responses of southern whites to the departure of their agricultural labor force and of northern whites to the influx of African Americans.

ANONYMOUS AFRICAN AMERICAN MIGRANTS
Letters Home to the South

Particularly evocative sources on the Great Migration are the letters written by the migrants. African American historian Emmett J. Scott recognized their historical value as early as 1919 and published a collection of "letters from Negroes of all conditions in almost all parts of the South," in the Journal of Negro History. *Given that many migrants spoke "black English," Scott may have edited these letters for grammar and style. As you read these letters, consider why they were important to the migrants and their families. What insights do they offer as to the reasons for African American migration? When Scott published these letters, he omitted the names of writers and recipients. What factors might have influenced his decision?*

CHICAGO, ILLINOIS.

My dear Sister: I was agreeably surprised to hear from you and to hear from home. I am well and thankful to say I am doing well. The weather and everything else was a surprise to me when I came. I got here in time to attend one of the greatest revivals in the history of my life — over 500 people joined the church. We had a Holy Ghost shower. You know I like to have run wild. It was snowing some nights and if you didnt hurry you could not get standing room. Please remember me kindly to any who ask of me. The people are rushing here by the thousands and I know if you come and rent a big house you can get all the roomers you want. You write me exactly when you are coming. I am not keeping house yet I am living with my brother and his wife. My sone is in California but will be home soon. He spends his winter in California. I can get a nice place for you to stop until you can look around and see what you want. I am quite busy. I work in Swifts packing Co. in the sausage department. My daughter and I work for the same company — We get $1.50 a day and we pack so many sausages we dont have much time to play but it is a matter of a dollar with me and I feel that God made the path and I am walking therein.

Tell your husband work is plentiful here and he wont have to loaf if he want to work.... Well goodbye from your sister in Christ.

CHICAGO, ILLINOIS, 11/13/17.
Mr. H———
Hattiesburg, Miss.

Dear M———: Yours received sometime ago and found all well and doing well. hope you and family are well.

I got my things alright the other day and they were in good condition. I am all fixed now and living well. I certainly appreciate what you done for us and I will remember you in the near future.

M, old boy, I was promoted on the first of the month I was made first assistant to the head carpenter when he is out of the place I take everything in charge and was raised to $95. a month. You know I know my stuff.

Whats the news generally around H'burg? I should have been here 20 years ago. I just begin to feel like a man. It's a great deal of pleasure in knowing that you have got some privilege My children are going to the same school with the whites and I dont have to umble to no one. I have registered—Will vote the next election and there isnt any "yes sir" and "no sir"—its all yes and no and Sam and Bill.

Florine says hello and would like very much to see you.

All joins me in sending love to you and family. How is times there now? Answer soon, from your friend and bro.

SOURCE: *Journal of Negro History* 4, no. 4 (1919): 457, 458–459.

DWIGHT THOMPSON FARNHAM
Making Efficient Use of Migrant Black Workers

As the migrants' letters suggest, African Americans felt optimistic about the opportunities available in the North. But the "promised land" often fell short of expectations. In Chicago and other cities, African Americans lived in run-down houses and often had to take the roughest and most dangerous jobs. As the following excerpt from an Industrial Management *article of 1918 indicates, blacks did not escape racism when they moved north. As you read Dwight Thompson Farnham's advice to factory employers, consider the significance of his reference to the "ancestor's environment" of the black workers. What other clues does this document provide as to the racist underpinnings of Farnham's approach to managing black workers?*

Last year some of our more progressive corporations awoke to the fact that there was a vast reservoir of labor—amounting to over 10,000,000 souls—nearly 11 per cent of the country's population—as yet practically untapped for manufacturing purposes. With true American initiative these corporations sent agents into the South. Negro settlements were placarded with notices setting forth the high wages and the ideal living conditions prevailing in the North. Trainloads of negro mammies, pickaninnies and all that miscellaneous and pathetic paraphernalia of mysterious bundles and protesting household pets which accompanies our colored citizen on his pilgrimages moved into St. Louis, Kansas City and Chicago, and from there were distributed to the industrial centers of the country....

The really serious problem which confronts the would-be user of negro labor is that of handling his negroes in such a way as to avoid disastrous loss of operating efficiency.... The mistake most foremen make is that they use the same method with the negro that they use with white labor....

Once the plant executives, the foremen who come in contact with the workmen, realize that the negro is different physically, temperamentally and psychologically from any of the white races, the battle is half won.... The man who hates the negro very seldom ever gets on with him. The darky is as quick to feel dislike as a child and resents it accordingly. The man who regards his antics at first with amused toleration is much more likely to eventually control him, although there will be a great many periods of discouragement when the amateur overseer will feel very much as did A. B. Frost's dominie who rescued the bull calf and undertook to lead him to safety with the latter tied about his waist. Sympathy and understanding are necessary but sentimentality is fatal, as experience demonstrates....

The rank and file of negroes require more supervision than the rank and file of whites. By this I do not mean more "driving" nor more "watching," I mean constructive supervision in the sense of thinking for and looking ahead for. We must provide the negro with the foresight of which his ancestor's environment has largely deprived him....

A certain amount of segregation is necessary at times to preserve the peace. This is especially true when negroes are first introduced into a plant. It is a question if it is not always best to have separate wash rooms and the like. In places where different races necessarily come into close contact and in places where inherited characteristics are especially accentuated, it is better to keep their respective folkways from clashing wherever possible....

SOURCE: Dwight Thompson Farnham, "Negroes a Source of Industrial Labor," *Industrial Management* 56, no. 2 (August 1918): 123–128, from Eric Arnesen, *Black Protest and the Great Migration: A Brief History with Documents* (Boston: Bedford/St. Martin's, 2003), 74–78.

ANALYZING THE EVIDENCE

- When historians analyze historical events, they seek to uncover their causes. What explanation do the migrants' letters give for the Great Migration? Is it the same as that given by Farnham? How do you explain the difference?

- In addition to the violence of the postwar race riots discussed on page 698, urban African Americans suffered from unemployment as factories cut back production. After reading Farnham's selection, suggest several reasons why southern black migrants were often "the last hired and the first fired."

- Do the migrants' letters give any clues as to why migration out of the South continued after World War I, despite the problems blacks encountered in the North?

German Beer, Mexican Workers

Immigrants from Germany owned and managed most of the breweries in the United States. But the workers at the Maier and Zoblein Brewery in Los Angeles circa 1900 came from many nations, including Mexico. About four thousand Mexicans lived in Los Angeles County in 1900 (about 4 percent of the population); by 1930, there were 150,000 Mexicans in Los Angeles, about 7 percent of the rapidly growing city. Los Angeles Public Library.

Wartime Reform: Woman Suffrage and Prohibition

Many progressive reformers used the war effort to push for improvements in women's lives. Mary Van Kleek, an industrial sociologist, joined the Department of Labor to lobby for equal pay for women workers, and Pauline Goldmark, a social reformer from the National Consumer's League, advocated more employment opportunities for women in her role as a railroad administrator. More important, women's groups used the war effort to secure two constitutional amendments: woman suffrage and **Prohibition.**

Suffrage Victory: Alice Paul. When the war began, the National American Woman Suffrage Association (NAWSA) threw the support of its two million members behind the Wilson administration. Its president, Carrie Chapman Catt, argued that women had to prove their patriotism to advance the cause of the suffrage movement. In response, NAWSA women in communities all over the country labored exhaustively to promote food

READING AMERICAN PICTURES

"Over Here": Women's Wartime Opportunities

Working Women at the Puget Sound Navy Yard, Washington, 1919. National Archives.

Women took on new jobs during World War I by working as mail carriers, police officers, heavy machinery operators, and farm laborers attached to the Women's Land Army. Black women, who were customarily limited to employment as domestic servants or agricultural laborers, found that the war opened up new opportunities and better wages in industry. When the war ended, black and white women alike usually lost jobs deemed to be men's work. However, in 1919, when an anonymous photographer took this picture, these women riveters were still hard at work at the Puget Sound Navy Yard near Seattle, Washington.

ANALYZING THE EVIDENCE

- Look carefully at the picture. What had the women been doing when asked by the photographer to pose for this shot? What clues indicate the work activities of the women?

- Why do you imagine that the photograph was taken? If this photograph had been published in a Seattle newspaper, how might viewers have responded to it?

- Although the women are posed, the men in the background seem to acting in a spontaneous fashion. How might we interpret their behavior?

- What does the photograph suggest about the women's attitude about their work as ship-builders?

- The presence of black women indicates diversity in the wartime Seattle workforce. Does anything in the photo tell us about the relationship between white and black women in the shipyards?

MAP 22.3 The Great Migration and Beyond

Employment opportunities that opened up during World War I and World War II served as catalysts for the Great Migration of African Americans out of the rural South. In the first migration, which began in 1915, blacks headed primarily to industrial cities of the North and Midwest, such as Chicago, New York, and Pittsburgh (see Comparing American Voices, "The Great Migration," pp. 686–687). During World War II, blacks' destinations expanded to include the West, especially Los Angeles, the San Francisco Bay Area, and Seattle. This map simplifies a complex process of movement by individuals and families, who often moved several times and retained close ties with kinfolk in the South.

conservation, to protect children and women workers, and to distribute emergency relief through organizations like the Red Cross.

Alice Paul and the National Woman's Party (NWP) took a more militant tack to win the vote. Born and raised as a Quaker, whose ranks had produced some of the leading women reformers of the nineteenth century, Paul graduated from Swarthmore College, worked in the settlement house movement, and in 1912 earned a Ph.D. in political science at the University of Pennsylvania. Inspired by the militant British suffragist Christabel Pankhurst, Paul became a congressional lobbyist for NAWSA. Increasingly frustrated by the refusal of political leaders to support woman suffrage, in 1916 she founded the NWP, which immediately undertook an activist campaign of mass meetings and parades. In July 1917, Paul and other NWP militants began picketing the White House, standing as "Silent Sentinels" and holding woman suffrage banners—perhaps the first instance of group nonviolent civil disobedience in American history. Arrested for "obstructing traffic" and sentenced to seven months in jail, Paul and the women protesters went on a hunger strike, which prison authorities met with forced feeding. Public shock at the women's treatment drew renewed attention to the issue of woman suffrage and put new pressure on the Wilson administration.

Alice Paul, Suffragist and Politician

Taking advantage of the newest technology, Alice Paul goes on the radio in 1922 to announce plans for the dedication of the Washington headquarters of the National Women's Party. Despite her success in winning the vote for women, Paul was unable to mobilize support for a separate political party to represent their interests. Copyright Bettmann/Corbis.

Impressed by the patriotism of the NAWSA and worried by the militancy of Paul and the NWP, President Wilson sensed that his campaign to make the world safe for democracy had to begin at home. In January 1918, he urged support for woman suffrage as a "war measure." The constitutional amendment quickly passed the House of Representatives but took eighteen months to get through the Senate and another year to win ratification by the states. Finally, on August 26, 1920, Tennessee gave the Nineteenth Amendment the last vote it needed. The goal that had first been declared publicly at the Seneca Falls convention in 1848 was finally achieved seventy-two years later, thanks in part to the war emergency.

Moral Reform, Family Welfare, and Prohibition. Other activists used the war to advance their agendas. Moral reformers concerned with vice and prostitution joined with military officials to keep the army "fit to fight." They encouraged the government to educate soldiers about sexually transmitted diseases and to shut down "red-light" districts near military training camps. With the assistance of two Protestant Christian organizations, the Young Men's Christian Association and the Young Women's Christian Association, government officials warned young men and women about the dangers of sexual activity and celebrated the value of "social purity."

Other reformers pressed for measures to protect the families of army recruits. Responding to reports of economic hardship among working-class military families, Congress enacted the War Risk Insurance Act in 1917. The act required enlisted men and noncommissioned officers to allot $15 of their monthly military pay to their dependents; the federal government contributed an additional allowance to the dependents of servicemen, disbursing almost $570 million between 1917 and 1921. This program of federal regulation and assistance was unprecedented; although short-lived, these wartime family assistance programs would shape the welfare programs established in the New Deal era (see Chapter 24).

An even more dramatic intrusion of the federal government into people's private lives resulted from the efforts of prohibitionists. On the eve of World War I, nineteen states had passed prohibition laws, and many other states allowed local communities to regulate liquor sales. Generally, only industrial states with large immigrant populations, such as Massachusetts, New York, Rhode Island, Illinois, and California, had resisted the trend toward restricting the sale and consumption of alcoholic beverages.

Many progressives supported prohibition. Urban reformers, worried about alcoholic husbands, impoverished families, and public morality, considered a ban on drinking as a benefit to society rather than a repressive denial of individual freedom. In rural communities many people equated liquor with the sins of the city: prostitution, crime, immigration, machine politics, and public disorder. The churches with the greatest

Safe Sex, Vintage 1919

To teach young American men how to avoid venereal diseases, the War Department used posters, pep talks, and films. There were no effective treatments for venereal infections until 1928, when Alexander Fleming discovered penicillin, and so the army urged soldiers to avoid prostitutes or use condoms. *Fit to Fight* starred handsome Ray McKee, who had already appeared in eighty films, and was directed by E. H. Griffith, who would go on to direct sixty Hollywood films between 1920 and 1946. Social Welfare History Archives Center, University of Minnesota / Picture Research Consultants & Archives.

strength in rural areas, including Methodists, Baptists, and Mormons, also strongly condemned drinking. Protestants from rural areas dominated the membership of the Anti-Saloon League, which had supplanted the Woman's Christian Temperance Union as the leading proponent of prohibition.

Temperance advocates knew their enemies. The liquor industry flourished in cities, especially among recent immigrants from Europe and citizens of German and Irish descent. Most saloons were located in working-class neighborhoods and served as gathering places for workers. Machine politicians conducted much of their business in bars. Consequently, many immigrants and working-class people opposed prohibition; they demanded the freedom to drink what they pleased and resented the attempt of progressive reformers and religious zealots to destroy their ethnic cultures.

However, the fervor of World War I gave political momentum to the prohibitionist cause. Intense anti-German hysteria was one spur to action. Because many major breweries—Pabst, Busch, Schlitz—had been founded by German immigrants, many Americans felt that it was unpatriotic to drink beer. Beer consumption also declined because Congress undertook to conserve scarce food supplies by prohibiting the use of barley, hops, and other grains in breweries and distilleries. The national prohibition campaign culminated in December 1917, when Congress passed the Eighteenth Amendment. Ratified by nearly every state by 1919 and effective on January 16, 1920, the amendment prohibited the "manufacture, sale, or transportation of intoxicating liquors" anywhere in the United States (Map 22.4).

The Eighteenth Amendment was the most striking example of the wartime success of a progressive reform. It also stood as yet another example of the widening influence of the national state on matters of economic policy and personal behavior. Unlike woman suffrage, the other constitutional amendment that won wartime passage, Prohibition never gained general acceptance and was repealed with the Twenty-first Amendment in 1933.

Promoting National Unity

The progressive educator and philosopher John Dewey, a staunch supporter of American involvement in World War I, argued that wars represented a "plastic juncture" when societies became open to reason and new ideas. Rudolph Bourne, a one-time pupil of Dewey's and an outspoken pacifist, strongly disagreed. "If the war is too strong for you to prevent," Bourne asked, how can you "control and mold [it] to your liberal purposes?"

MAP 22.4 Prohibition on the Eve of the Eighteenth Amendment, 1919

Well before the adoption of the Eighteenth Amendment in 1919, the temperance crusade had won bans on the legal sale of alcoholic beverages in many states. Maine, North Dakota, and Kansas had been dry since the nineteenth century; a few southern states joined the movement during the Progressive era; but the rush to prohibition came only during World War I, when it became unpatriotic to distill scarce grain into alcohol or to buy beer from German American brewers. Most states that resisted prohibition were heavily urban and industrial or had large numbers of immigrants and German Americans.

President Wilson shared Bourne's pessimism about the effect of wartime passions: "Once lead this people into war, and they'll forget there ever was such a thing as tolerance." But the president also recognized the need to create support for the war. "It is not an army we must shape and train for war, it is a nation." By backing the campaign to promote "One Hundred Percent Americanism," Wilson undermined the spirit of reform that had elevated him to the highest office in the land.

George Creel and Wartime Propaganda. In April 1917 Wilson formed the Committee on Public Information (CPI) to promote public support for the war. This government propaganda agency, headed by the journalist George Creel, attracted progressive reformers and muckraking journalists such as Ida Tarbell and Ray Stannard Baker. Professing lofty goals—educating citizens about democracy, promoting national unity, assimilating immigrants, and breaking down the isolation of rural life—the committee acted as a nationalizing force by promoting the development of a common ideology.

The CPI touched the lives of practically every American. It distributed seventy-five million pieces of patriotic literature and, by enlisting thousands of volunteers—"four-minute men"—to deliver short pro-war speeches at local movie theaters, reached a huge audience. Creel called the CPI "the world's greatest adventure in advertising" and hoped it would "inspire" patriotism without inflaming passions. However, by 1918 the committee was encouraging its speakers to use inflammatory stories of alleged German atrocities to build support for the war effort.

Curbing Dissent. As a spirit of conformity pervaded the home front, many Americans found themselves the targets of suspicion. Businesses took out newspaper ads instructing citizens to report to the Justice Department "the man who spreads pessimistic stories, cries for peace, or belittles our efforts to win the war." Posters warned Americans to look out for German spies. A quasi-vigilante group, the American Protective League, mobilized about 250,000 self-appointed "agents," furnished them with badges issued by the Justice Department, and told them to spy on neighbors and coworkers. In 1918, the members of the League staged violent raids against draft evaders and opponents of the war.

The CPI urged recent immigrants and long-established ethnic groups to become "One Hundred Percent Americans" by giving up their Old World customs and ties. German Americans bore the brunt of this Americanization campaign. German music and operas—Beethoven, Bach, Wagner—were banished from the concert halls, and many communities prohibited the teaching of the German language in their schools. Sauerkraut was renamed "liberty cabbage," and hamburgers became "liberty sandwiches" or Salisbury steaks. When the influenza epidemic struck down thousands of

Americans, rumor had it that German scientists were spreading germs in the aspirin distributed by Bayer, a German drug company. Although anti-German hysteria dissipated when the war ended, hostility toward "hyphenated" Americans — the Irish-, Polish-, or Italian-American — survived into the 1920s.

During the war, law enforcement officials tolerated little criticism of established values and institutions. The main legal tools for curbing dissent were the Espionage Act of 1917 and the Sedition Act of 1918. The Sedition Act focused on disloyal speech, writing, and behavior that might "incite, provoke, or encourage resistance to the United States, or promote the cause of its enemies." The Espionage Act imposed stiff penalties for antiwar activities and allowed the federal government to ban treasonous materials from the mails. The postmaster general revoked the mailing privileges of groups considered to be radical, virtually shutting down their publications.

Individuals also felt the long arm of the state. Because the Espionage and Sedition acts defined treason and sedition loosely, they led to the conviction of more than a thousand people. The Justice Department focused particularly on Socialists, who criticized the war and the draft, and on radicals like the Industrial Workers of the World (the IWW, see Chapter 17), whose attacks on militarism threatened to disrupt war production in the western lumber and copper industries. In September 1917 the Justice Department arrested 113 IWW leaders and charged them with interfering with the war effort. Socialist Party leader Eugene Debs was sentenced to ten years in jail for stating that the master classes declared war while the subject classes fought the battles. Victor Berger, a Milwaukee Socialist who had been jailed under the Espionage Act, was twice prevented from taking the seat to which he had been elected in the U.S. House of Representatives.

The courts rarely resisted these wartime excesses. In *Schenck v. United States* (1919), the Supreme Court upheld the conviction of Charles T. Schenck, the general secretary of the Socialist Party. Schenck had not been jailed for violent acts but for mailing pamphlets urging draftees to resist induction into the army. Writing for a unanimous court, Justice Oliver Wendell Holmes declared that the freedom of speech guaranteed by the First Amendment did not extend to words that constituted "a clear and present danger to the safety of the country." The legal restrictions on free speech imposed during World War I became a permanent feature of American life. Well into the twentieth century, the courts used Holmes's "clear and present danger" test to curb individual freedom in the name of national security.

> - How did the nation mobilize its industrial base and manpower to fight World War I? What were the main challenges?
> - What was the impact of World War I on racial and ethnic minorities? On women?
> - In what ways did the government limit civil liberties during the war, and with what justification?

An Unsettled Peace, 1919–1920

The end of the war created a new set of problems. The Wilson administration had to demobilize the troops, return war plants to civilian use, and, most important, negotiate a peace treaty. President Wilson made peacemaking his highest goal and, from December 1918 to June 1919, went to Europe to achieve it. As Wilson bargained and fought with Allied leaders to achieve a moral international order, he ignored urgent domestic issues. Ethnic and racial tensions that had smoldered during the war erupted in controversy and strife. And fears of domestic radicalism boiled over in America's first Red Scare.

The Treaty of Versailles

In January 1917 Woodrow Wilson had proposed a "peace without victory" on the grounds that only a peace among equals could last. His goal was not a "balance of power, but a community of power; not organized rivalries, but an organized common peace." The keystone of Wilson's postwar plan was a permanent League of Nations that would prevent future wars.

The Fourteen Points. President Wilson approached the peace negotiations in France with the zeal of a missionary. Determined to win approval for his vision of a new world order, he was prepared to appeal to "the peoples of Europe over the heads of their rulers." And well he might. Wildly enthusiastic European crowds greeted the American president as a hero; in Paris two million people lined the Champs-Élysées to pay tribute to "Wilson the Just." The president scored a diplomatic victory in January 1919 when the Allies accepted his **Fourteen Points** as the basis for the peace negotiations. In this blueprint for the postwar world, the president called for open diplomacy, "absolute freedom of navigation upon the seas," arms reduction, the removal of trade barriers, and an international commitment to **national self-determination** for the peoples of the Austro-Hungarian, Russian, and German empires. Essential to Wilson's vision was the creation of a multinational organization "for the purpose of affording mutual guarantees of political independence and territorial integrity to great and small States alike." The League of Nations became Wilson's obsession.

The Fourteen Points expressed the spirit of progressivism. Widely distributed as propaganda during the final months of the war, Wilson's plan would extend American ideals — democracy, freedom, and peaceful economic expansion — to the rest of the world. The League of Nations, acting as an international regulatory body (akin to the Federal Trade Commission in the United States), would mediate disputes among nations, supervise arms reduction, and — according to the crucial Article X of its covenant — curb aggressor nations through collective military action. Wilson hoped that the presence of the League would prevent future wars and thus ensure that the Great War would be "the war to end all wars." By emphasizing these lofty goals, the American president set the stage for disappointment: His ideals for world reformation proved too far-reaching to be practical or attainable.

Negotiating the Treaty. Twenty-seven countries and peoples sent representatives to the peace conference at Versailles, near Paris, many of them hoping the Allied Powers would recognize their claims to national sovereignty. Distrustful of the new Bolshevik regime in Russia and its call for a worker-led revolution against capitalism and imperialism, the Allies deliberately excluded its representatives. That action was hardly surprising; in 1918, the United States, Britain, and Japan had

The Peace at Versailles
This painting by Sir William Orpen of the signing of the peace treaty in the Hall of Mirrors at Versailles in June 1919 captures the solemnity and grandeur of the occasion. Wilson holds a copy of the treaty, with British Prime Minister David Lloyd George to his right and French Premier Georges Clemenceau to his left. The president was justifiably proud of his role in the peace negotiations, but his refusal to compromise doomed the treaty in the U.S. Senate. Imperial War Museum, London.

MAP 22.5 Europe and the Middle East after World War I

World War I and its aftermath dramatically altered the landscape of Europe and the Middle East. In central Europe, the collapse of the German, Russian, and Austro-Hungarian empires brought the reconstitution of Poland and the creation of a string of new states based on the principle of national (ethnic) self-determination. The demise of the Ottoman Empire resulted in the appearance of the quasi-independent territories of Iraq, Syria, Lebanon, and Palestine, whose affairs were supervised by one of the Allied Powers under a mandate of the League of Nations.

deployed thousands of troops in Russia to support anti-Bolshevik forces. The victorious Allies also barred Germany from the peace conference, choosing instead to work out the details and impose the completed treaty on their defeated foe.

The Big Four — Wilson, Prime Minister David Lloyd George of Great Britain, Premier Georges Clemenceau of France, and Prime Minister Vittorio Orlando of Italy — did most of the negotiating. The three European leaders sought a peace that differed radically from Wilson's plan. They wanted to punish Germany by demanding heavy reparations and treat themselves to the spoils of war. Indeed, Britain, France, and Italy had already made secret agreements to divide up German colonies in Africa.

Given the existence of such schemes, it is a tribute to Wilson that he managed to influence the peace settlement as much as he did. The president intervened repeatedly to soften harsh demands for reprisal against Germany. Moreover, he won support for national self-determination, a fundamental principle of the Fourteen Points. In accord with that precept, the Big Four fashioned the independent states of Austria, Hungary, Poland, Yugoslavia, and Czechoslovakia in central Europe and established four new nations along the Baltic Sea: Finland, Estonia, Lithuania, and Latvia (Map 22.5). This string of states, which stretched from the Baltic to the Mediterranean, not only embodied the Wilsonian principle of national self-determination but also served as a *cordon sanitaire*—a sanitary zone protecting the peoples of western Europe from direct exposure to the Communist ideology of Soviet Russia.

Wilson had less success in achieving other goals. The diplomats at Versailles dismantled the empires of the Central Powers but, instead of creating independent states, assigned the colonies to the victorious Allied nations to administer as mandates. France and England received parts of the old Turkish and German empires in the Middle East and Africa, and Japan assumed responsibility for the former German colonies and spheres of influence in the Far East. Still, some of the Allied Powers received less than they wanted. Japan lost face when it failed to win a treaty provision that affirmed racial equality, and Italy protested bitterly when it was denied lands along its border with Yugoslavia and a colony in Africa. Moreover, representatives of colonized peoples, such as Ho Chi Minh, the future revolutionary leader of Vietnam, were generally ignored when they sought freedom for their nations—a decision that had grave consequences for France and the United States in the second half of the twentieth century (see Chapter 29). The resistance of Allied leaders likewise meant that important issues, such as freedom of the seas and free trade, never even appeared on the agenda. Most important, Wilson was unable to deter French and British demands that Germany accept a "war guilt" clause and pay enormous war reparations. In a draconian settlement that left lasting resentment, the Allies forced Germany to give up valuable territories, coal supplies, merchant ships, and valuable patents—and to pay $33 billion in monetary reparations.

The Fate of the Treaty. In the face of these disappointments, Wilson consoled himself with the hope that the League of Nations, which was authorized by the peace treaty, would moderate the terms of the settlement and secure a peaceful resolution of other international disputes. For the United States to participate in the League, he would have to persuade the Senate to ratify the Treaty of Versailles. The outlook was not promising. Although major newspapers and the important religious denominations supported the treaty, the Republican Party had a majority in the Senate and was openly hostile to the agreement.

Opposition to the treaty and the League came from several sources. One group, called the "irreconcilables," consisted of western Republican progressives such as William Borah of Idaho, Hiram Johnson of California, and Robert La Follette of Wisconsin. Isolationist in outlook, they opposed U.S. involvement in European affairs and membership in the League of Nations. Less dogmatic, but more influential, was a group of Republicans led by Senator Henry Cabot Lodge of Massachusetts. Lodge and his allies wanted amendments to Article X of the treaty—the provision for collective security—to ensure that the treaty would not infringe on Congress's constitutional authority to declare war. Beyond that, they worried that Article X would prevent the United States from pursuing an independent foreign policy. Wilson refused to compromise, especially to placate Lodge, a hated political rival. "I shall consent to nothing," he told the French ambassador. "The Senate must take its medicine."

To mobilize popular and political support for the treaty, the president embarked on an extensive and exhausting speaking tour. His impassioned defense of the League of Nations brought large audiences to tears, but the strain proved too much for the sixty-two-year-old president. In late September 1919 in Pueblo, Colorado, Wilson collapsed; a week later, back in Washington, he suffered a severe stroke that left him paralyzed on one side of his body. Wilson still refused to compromise. From his sickbed, the president ordered Democratic senators to vote against all Republican amendments. Brought up for a vote in November 1919, the treaty failed to win the required two-thirds majority; a second attempt, in March 1920, fell seven votes short.

The treaty was dead and so was Wilson's leadership of the nation. Although the president slowly recovered from his stroke, he was never the same. When Wilson died in 1924, David Lloyd George remarked, he was "as much a victim of the war as any soldier who died in the trenches." During the final eighteen months of the Wilson administration, the president's wife, Edith Bolling Galt Wilson, his physician, and the various cabinet heads oversaw the routine business of government.

The United States never ratified the Versailles treaty or joined the League of Nations. Many wartime issues remained partially resolved, notably the enormous reparations demanded from Germany and the fate of Europe's colonial empires amidst rising demands for national self-determination.

These problems played a major role in the coming of World War II; some, like the competing ethnic nationalisms in the Balkans, remain unresolved today (see Chapters 25 and 30).

Racial Strife, Labor Unrest, and the Red Scare

"The World War has accentuated all our differences," a journalist in the popular periodical *World's Work* acutely observed. "It has not created those differences, but it has revealed and emphasized them." In the aftermath of the war, race riots revealed white resistance to the rising expectations of African Americans. Thousands of strikes exposed class tensions, and an obsessive government-led hunt for foreign radicals reflected deep-seated anxieties about social order and the nation's ethnic pluralism.

Race Riots. Many African Americans emerged from the war determined to insist on their rights as American citizens. Thousands had fought for their country; millions of others had loyally supported the war effort. Black demands for equal treatment simply exacerbated white racism and violence. In the South, the number of lynchings rose from forty-eight in 1917 to seventy-eight in 1919, including several of African American soldiers in their military uniforms. In the northern states, now home to tens of thousands of southern-born blacks, race riots broke out in more than twenty-five cities. One of the first and most deadly riots occurred in 1917 in East St. Louis, Illinois; nine whites and more than forty blacks died in a conflict sparked by competition over jobs at a defense plant. In Chicago, five days of rioting in July 1919 left twenty-three blacks and fifteen whites dead. By the end of that summer, the death toll from racial violence had reached 120.

The causes of the Chicago riot were similar to those in other cities. The arrival of fifty thousand African American newcomers during the war years had strained the city's social fabric and increased racial tensions. Blacks competed with whites—many of them recent arrivals from central Europe—for scarce housing and jobs. Unionized white workers

Chicago Race Riot

Racial violence exploded in Chicago during the summer of 1919, and photographer Jun Fujita was on the scene to capture it. As one of the few Japanese immigrants in Chicago at the time, Fujita was probably no stranger to racism, and it took personal courage to put himself in the midst of the escalating violence. When the riot finally ended, thirty-eight people were dead and more than five hundred were injured. Chicago Historical Society / Photo by Jun Fujita.

General Strike in Seattle

Seattle was a strong union town, and 110 local unions took part in the 1919 general strike that paralyzed the city. Although the strike was peaceful, city officials deputized local citizens for police duty, such as this ragtag group of volunteers being issued guns. Museum of History and Industry, Seattle, WA.

deeply resented blacks who served as strikebreakers; indeed, in some stockyards and packing plants, white workers considered the words *Negro* and *scab* to be synonymous. In close elections, black voters often held the balance of power, which allowed their leaders to demand political favors and patronage positions.

Ethnic conflicts over jobs and patronage had long been part of the urban scene, but racism turned them into violent confrontations. When gangs of young white men bombed or burned houses in African American neighborhoods or attacked their residents, blacks fought back in self-defense and for their rights as citizens. Wilson's rhetoric about democracy and self-determination had raised their expectations, too.

A Year of Strikes, 1919. Workers also had higher expectations. The economic prosperity and government regulations of the war years had brought them higher pay, shorter hours, and better working conditions. As workers tried to maintain and advance these gains, employers tried to cut high wartime wages and root out unions. Consumers and native-born Americans generally sided with management. They blamed workers for the rapidly rising cost of living, which jumped nearly 80 percent between 1917 and 1919, and remained suspicious of unions, which they identified with radicalism and foreigners.

These developments set the stage for a massive confrontation between employers and workers. In 1919 more than four million wage laborers — one in every five — went on strike, a proportion never since equaled. The year began with a walkout by shipyard workers in Seattle, a strong union town, and spread into a general strike that crippled the city. Another major strike disrupted the steel industry; 350,000 workers demanded union recognition and an end to twelve-hour shifts and the seven-day workweek. Elbert H. Gary, the head of the United States Steel Corporation, refused to negotiate; he hired Mexican and African American strikebreakers, maintained substantial production, and eventually broke the strike. Public employees fared no better. Late in the year, the Boston police force shocked many Americans by demanding union representation and going on strike to get it. Governor Calvin Coolidge of Massachusetts propelled himself into the political spotlight by declaring, "There is no right to strike against the public safety by anybody, anywhere, any time." Coolidge fired the entire police force, and the strike failed. The public supported the governor's decisive action, and the Republican Party rewarded Coolidge by nominating him in 1920 as its vice presidential candidate. The impressive gains made by workers and unions during the war swiftly melted away. Inflation cut workers' purchasing power, corporate managers attacked workers' unions, and judges issued coercive injunctions against picketers and strikers. Lacking public support, unions declined in numbers and strength throughout the 1920s.

The Red Scare and the Palmer Raids. A majority of white Americans opposed unions because they feared radicalism. The socialist outlook of many recent immigrants frightened native-born citizens, and the communist ideology of the Russian Bolsheviks terrified them. President Wilson shared these concerns. Embarking for Europe in 1919, he warned of "a flood of ultraradicalism, that will swamp the world." When the Bolsheviks founded the Third International (or Comintern) in 1919, an organization intended to export Communist ideology and foster revolutions throughout the world, Americans began to see radicals everywhere. Hatred of the German "Huns" was quickly replaced by hostility toward the Bolshevik "Reds."

Ironically, as public concern about domestic Bolshevism increased, radicals were rapidly losing members and political power. Of the fifty million adults in the United States in 1920, no more than 70,000 belonged to either the fledgling U.S. Communist Party or the Communist Labor Party in 1919. Both the International Workers of the World and the Socialist Party had been weakened by wartime repression and internal dissent. Yet the public and the press continued to blame almost every disturbance, especially labor conflicts, on alien radicals. "REDS DIRECTING SEATTLE STRIKE—TO TEST CHANCE FOR REVOLUTION," warned a typical newspaper headline.

Political tensions mounted amid a series of terrorist threats and bombings in the spring of 1919. In April, alert postal workers discovered and defused thirty-four mail bombs addressed to prominent government officials. In June a bomb detonated outside the Washington townhouse of the recently appointed attorney general, A. Mitchell Palmer. Palmer and his family escaped unharmed, but the bomber was blown to bits. Angling for the presidential nomination, Palmer capitalized on the event by fanning fears of domestic radicalism.

With President Wilson virtually incapacitated, Palmer had a free hand. He set up an antiradicalism division in the Justice Department and appointed J. Edgar Hoover to direct it. Hoover's division shortly became the Federal Bureau of Investigation (FBI). Then the attorney general staged the first of what became known as "Palmer raids." In November 1919, on the second anniversary of the Russian Revolution, Palmer's agents stormed the headquarters of radical organizations. The dragnet pulled in thousands of aliens who had committed no crime but were suspect because of their anarchist or revolutionary beliefs or their immigrant backgrounds. Lacking the protection of U.S. citizenship, they could be deported without a formal indictment or trial. In December 1919 the USS *Buford*, nicknamed the "Soviet Ark," sailed to Russia with a cargo of 294 deported radicals—including the famous anarchists Emma Goldman and Alexander Berkman.

The peak of Palmer's power came with his New Year's raids in January 1920. In one night, with the greatest possible publicity, federal agents rounded up six thousand radicals. They invaded private homes, union headquarters, and meeting halls—arresting citizens and aliens alike and denying them access to legal counsel. Palmer was riding high in his ambitions for the presidency, but then he overstepped himself. He predicted that on May Day 1920 an unnamed radical conspiracy would attempt to overthrow the U.S. government. State militia units and police went on twenty-four-hour alert to guard the nation against the threat of revolutionary violence, but not a single incident occurred. As the summer of 1920 passed without major labor strikes or renewed bombings, the hysteria of the Red Scare began to abate, and Palmer faded from view.

The Sacco and Vanzetti Case. The wartime legacy of antiradicalism and anti-immigrant sentiment persisted well into the next decade. At the height of the Red Scare in May 1920, police in South Braintree, Massachusetts, arrested Nicola Sacco, a shoemaker, and Bartolomeo Vanzetti, a fish peddler, for the robbery and murder of a shoe company's paymaster. Sacco and Vanzetti were self-proclaimed anarchists and Italian aliens who had evaded the draft; both were armed at the time of their arrest. Convicted of the paymaster's murder and sentenced to death in 1921, Sacco and Vanzetti sat on death row for six years while supporters appealed their verdicts. Although evidence suggesting their innocence surfaced, Judge Webster Thayer denied a motion for a new trial. Scholars still debate the question of their guilt, but most agree that the two anarchist immigrants did not receive fair handling by the judicial system. As the future Supreme Court justice Felix Frankfurter said at the time, "The District Attorney invoked against them a riot of political passion and patriotic sentiment."

The war—with its nationalistic emphasis on patriotism and traditional cultural values—left ugly racial, ethnic, and class tensions in its wake. Still, the United States emerged from World War I as a much stronger nation than when it entered. Unlike its European allies and enemies, it had suffered relatively few casualties and no physical destruction to its lands or cities. Indeed, thanks to the war, the

The Passion of Sacco and Vanzetti **by Ben Shahn (1931–1932)**

Ben Shahn (1898–1969) came to the United States from Lithuania as a child and achieved fame as a social realist painter and photographer. Shahn used his art to advance his belief in social justice. In this painting, Sacco and Vanzetti lie dead and pale, hovered over by four distinguished Massachusetts citizens. Judge Webster Thayer, who presided at their trial in 1921, stands in a window in the background; the grim-faced men holding lilies, a symbol of death, are President A. Lawrence Lowell of Harvard and the two other members of a commission appointed by the governor in 1927 to review the case. The commission concluded that the men were guilty, a finding that led to their execution. Copyright Geoffrey Clements / CORBIS, Copyright Estate of Ben Shahn/VAGA, New York.

United States had become a major international power, both economically and politically.

- Describe the peace conference at Versailles. What nations attended? What nations did not? Who became the primary decision makers?

- What was President Wilson's vision of the postwar world, and how specifically did he propose to achieve it? How did other participants at the peace conference react to Wilson's ideas?

- What were the main components of the final treaty, and how do you explain the refusal of the United States to ratify it?

- What were the main causes and results of postwar social conflicts within the United States?

SUMMARY

In this chapter, we saw that the United States entered the war in 1917 for a variety of reasons: German violations of American neutral rights at sea, cultural and economic ties to the Allied powers, and Wilson's progressive goal of using the power and influence of the United States to end the conflict and create a just world order.

In tracing mobilization on the home front, we explored the problems facing the federal government as it created an army from scratch, boosted agricultural and industrial production, and recruited workers and raw materials for the defense industry. Some reformers — women suffragists, labor organizers, and prohibitionists — successfully used the war emergency to advance their goals. But we also saw how the passions and disruptions of wartime undercut the spirit of progressive reform and increased social tensions. As the fighting in Europe ended, race riots, strikes, and police raids brought violence to American factories and cities.

We also explored the challenges facing Wilson as he sought a just and lasting peace. The Versailles treaty embodied only some of the president's Fourteen Points, and his postwar hopes suffered another blow when the U.S. Senate refused to ratify the treaty, which would have authorized American participation in the League of Nations. Nonetheless, American participation in World War I — first economically and then militarily — set in motion a major shift in international power. The United States emerged from the war as a dominant world power, a position it would retain throughout the twentieth century.

Connections: Diplomacy

As noted in the Summary, during and after World War I the United States was in a position to play a powerful role in international affairs. But the nation lacked both a strong diplomatic tradition and a respected foreign policy bureaucracy. Moreover, the American public and many members of Congress were unwilling to support active engagement in international politics. As a result, during the 1920s and 1930s the United States retreated from diplomatic involvement in European and Asian affairs, except with respect to financial matters. As we stated in the essay that opened Part Five (p. 671), the "dominant economic position" of privately owned American banks and corporations pulled the nation into the world economy.

Our discussion in Chapter 23 will show how American bankers financed the international economic system during the 1920s, assisting Germany to pay war reparations and the Allied Powers to pay their war debts. Chapter 24 will then explain how the collapse of international economy during the Great Depression prompted Americans to question the wisdom of the nation's intervention in World War I and encouraged a further retreat into political isolationism. Only the threat to democracy posed by fascist governments in Germany, Japan, and Italy in the late 1930s allowed President Franklin Roosevelt to persuade a reluctant nation to prepare for a new war. The story of Roosevelt's political and diplomatic initiatives appears in Chapter 25, which also charts the crucial contribution of the United States to the war against the Axis Powers. Coming in quick succession, the First and Second World Wars thrust the United States into world affairs. This diplomatic revolution is one of the central themes of Part Five.

CHAPTER REVIEW QUESTIONS

➤ How did World War I change America — both its standing in the world and at home? Why is the war important enough for the authors of this textbook to give it a full chapter?

➤ Is it fair to say that progressivism shaped America's involvement in World War I — why the United States entered the war, how the nation fought, and Wilson's plan for peace? Why or why not?

➤ In what ways did World War I contribute to the growth of the American state?

TIMELINE

1914	Outbreak of war in Europe
	United States declares neutrality
1915	German submarine sinks *Lusitania*
1916	Woodrow Wilson reelected president
	Revenue Act of 1916 raises taxes
1916–1919	Great Migration of African Americans to North
1917	United States enters World War I
	Selective Service Act initiates draft
	War Risk Insurance Act protects soldiers' families
	War Industries Board established
	Militant demands for woman suffrage
	East St. Louis race riot
	Espionage Act
	Bolsheviks come to power in Russia
	Committee on Public Information established
1918	Wilson proposes Fourteen Points peace plan
	Meuse-Argonne campaign tests U.S. soldiers
	Eugene Debs imprisoned under Sedition Act
	Armistice ends war
	U.S. and Allied troops intervene in Russia
1919	Treaty of Versailles
	Chicago race riot
	Major wave of labor strikes
	Red Scare and Palmer raids
	Schenck v. United States limits free speech
	League of Nations defeated in Senate
	Eighteenth Amendment (Prohibition) ratified
	War Industries Board disbanded
1920	Nineteenth Amendment (woman suffrage) ratified
	Sacco and Vanzetti arrested

FOR FURTHER EXPLORATION

A recent definitive military history of World War I is Hew Strachan, *The First World War* (2004). "The Great War and the Shaping of the 20th Century" at **www.pbs.org/greatwar/index.html** accompanies the PBS documentary series of the same name. The BBC site on World War I contains excellent memoirs, animations, and maps at **www.bbc.co.uk/history/war/wwone**. "The World War I Document Archive" at **www.lib.byu.edu/~rdh/wwi** provides extensive primary documents and Web links. Frank Freidel, *Over There: The Story of America's First Great Overseas Crusade* (1990), offers soldiers' vivid firsthand accounts. Meirion and Susie Harries, *The Last Days of Innocence: America at War, 1917–1918* (1997), captures America's war experience at home and abroad. "Newspaper Pictorials: World War I Rotogravures" at **memory.loc.gov/ammem/collections/rotogravures** uses the Sunday sections of two prominent New York newspapers to chronicle American life and attitudes toward the war. For the war in fiction, begin with William March, *Company K* (1993), and Ernest Hemingway's *In Our Time* (1925) and *A Farewell to Arms* (1929). For the home front, see *Pale Horse, Pale Rider* (1939) by Katherine Anne Porter.

"The Deadly Virus: The Influenza Epidemic of 1918" at **www.archives.gov/exhibits/influenza-epidemic/index.html** describes the outbreak that infected one-fifth of the world's population. See also "Influenza 1918," the PBS companion site at **www.pbs.org/wgbh/amex/influenza**. Leo Robert Klein's "Red Scare" at **newman.baruch.cuny.edu/digital/redscare** explores strikes, race riots, deportations, and various social movements from 1918 to 1920. The Authentic History Center at **www.authentichistory.com/1900s.html** documents racial stereotypes and the movements for suffrage and prohibition. On prohibition, see "Alcohol, Temperance, and Prohibition" at **dl.lib.brown.edu/temperance**. For the Anti-Saloon League, go to the collection of documents, fliers, cartoons, and songs at the Westerville (Ohio) Public Library, **www.wpl.lib.oh.us/AntiSaloon/index.html**. William M. Tuttle Jr., *Race Riot: Chicago in the Red Summer of 1919* (1970), provides analysis of that devastating riot, as well as a summary of the Great Migration of African Americans.

The Library of Congress Web site "American Leaders Speak: Recordings from World War I and the 1920 Election" at **memory.loc.gov/ammem/nfhtml**, offers voice recordings of key figures of the World War I era. "The South Texas Border, 1900–1920" at **memory.loc.gov/ammem/award97/txuhtml/runyhome.html** is a collection of over eight thousand items pertaining to the Lower Rio Grande Valley. Of particular interest is the material on the years surrounding World War I.

TEST YOUR KNOWLEDGE

To assess your command of the material in this chapter, see the Online Study Guide at **bedfordstmartins.com/henretta**.

For Web sites, images, and documents related to topics and places in this chapter, visit **bedfordstmartins.com/makehistory**.

SAN DIEGO to NEW YORK

NEW YORK to PARIS →

GOOD WILL FLIGHT in UNITED STATES

PAN-AMERICAN FLIGHT

MILES
50 150 250   400
0 100 200 300   500

FORTY THOUSAND MILES THROUGH THE AIR

In a single year. This is the unblemished record of Col. Charles A. Lindbergh, who returned to St. Louis from his tour of Central America on February 13. During that time, he was in the air a total of 468 hours.

23 Modern Times
1920–1932

THE 1920S WAS A DECADE filled with sharp contrasts—between Prohibition laws and speakeasy nightclubs, modern science and fundamentalist religion, economic boom and financial bust, popular heroes and social villains. Charles Lindbergh was one of the heroes. In May 1927, Lindbergh flew his small plane, *The Spirit of St. Louis,* from New York to Paris, a distance of 3,620 miles. He did it alone and without stopping—a tense journey that stretched over 33 hours. Nobody had ever done this before. Returning home to tickertape parades, Lindbergh became *Time* magazine's first Man of the Year in 1928. The handsome young aviator captivated the nation by blending a mastery of modern technological expertise with the middle-class virtues of hard work and individualism. Amidst the grinding routine of life in a modern industrial society, Lindbergh showed that an adventurous individual could make a difference.

The life of Samuel Insull taught Americans the same lesson—with a twist. A financial entrepreneur who was more important than Lindbergh and almost as well known, Insull began the decade as a hero and ended it as a villain. Insull was born in England and came to New York to work as the personal secretary to the great inventor Thomas Edison. In 1892, he moved to Chicago, where he built a small electrical power company into

The Business-Government Partnership of the 1920s
Politics in the Republican "New Era"
Corporate Capitalism
Economic Expansion Abroad
Foreign Policy in the 1920s

A New National Culture
A Consumer Society
The World of the Automobile
The Movies and Mass Culture

Redefining American Identity
The Rise of Nativism
Legislating Values: Evolution and Prohibition
Intellectual Crosscurrents
Culture Wars: The Election of 1928

The Onset of the Great Depression, 1929–1932
Causes and Consequences
Herbert Hoover Responds
Rising Discontent
The 1932 Election

Summary
Connections: Society

◀ **Charles Lindbergh (1902–1974), Famous Aviator**
Lindbergh's trans-Atlantic flight instantly made him a celebrity with the catchy nicknames of "Lucky Lindy" and "The Lone Eagle." Financed by Harry Guggenheim, scion of a wealthy mining family interested in promoting aviation, Lindbergh flew the *Spirit of St. Louis* on a goodwill tour in 1928. He touched down in all 48 states, stopped in 92 cities, delivered 147 speeches, and was feted in dozens of parades. Granger Collection.

a giant enterprise. By 1907, Insull's Commonwealth Edison Company was providing electrical power for the entire city; by 1924 his Chicago Rapid Transit Company was offering transportation to many of its residents as well. At the peak of his power in 1929, Insull controlled electric utility companies in five thousand communities in thirty-two states. To finance this utility empire, Insull used the tools of modern capitalism: He created a pyramid of holding companies that allowed him to manage companies valued at $500 million with a personal investment of only $27 million. He funded much of the rest by issuing low-priced stocks and bonds, which nearly one million Americans eagerly snapped up.

As Insull's career shows, many characteristics of modern America were in place by the end of World War I. The war had made the United States a major player in the world and solidified the foundations of the modern American corporate economy. But it was the 1920s that saw the coming of a mass national culture. Thanks to entrepreneurs like Insull and automobile manufacturer Henry Ford, millions of Americans could embrace the new consumer culture with its plethora of assembly-line-produced goods: cars, refrigerators, phonographs, and radios. The economic innovations and prosperity of the 1920s gave Americans the highest standard of living in the world. The values of the nineteenth-century middle classes — the Protestant ethic of hard work, self-denial, and frugality — gave way to a fascination with consumption, leisure, and self-realization, some of the essential features of modern life.

Then, suddenly and unexpectedly, the collapse of the stock market in 1929 and the coming of the Great Depression threw the nation and its political and business leaders into disarray. By 1932, the holding company pyramid built by Samuel Insull had collapsed in bankruptcy, and 600,000 investors had lost their life savings. The Chicago financier fled to Greece and then to Paris, not — like Lindbergh — in triumph but in disgrace. At home, Americans faced silent factories and massive unemployment; the optimism of the 1920s about the promise of American life would now be put to a severe test.

The Business-Government Partnership of the 1920s

The business-government partnership fostered by World War I expanded throughout the 1920s. As the *Wall Street Journal* enthusiastically proclaimed, "Never before, here or anywhere else, has a government been so completely fused with business." And, the *Journal* might have added, so successfully fused. The nation's prosperity from 1922 to 1929 seemed to confirm the wisdom of allowing corporate interests to manage economic life. Gone, or at least submerged, was the reform impulse of the Progressive era (see Chapter 20). Middle-class Americans no longer viewed business leaders as rapacious robber barons; they were now respected — even sacred — public figures. President Calvin Coolidge captured the prevailing public mood when he solemnly declared, "The man who builds a factory builds a temple. The man who works there worships there."

Politics in the Republican "New Era"

With the ailing Woodrow Wilson out of the presidential picture in 1920, the Democrats nominated Governor James M. Cox of Ohio for president and Assistant Secretary of the Navy Franklin D. Roosevelt as vice president. The Democratic platform called for U.S. participation in the League of Nations and a continuation of Wilson's progressivism. The Republicans, now led by the conservative, pro-business wing of the party, selected Ohio Senator Warren G. Harding and Vermont Governor Calvin Coolidge as their candidates. Sensing the desire of many Americans to put the war and the stresses of 1919 behind them, Harding promised "not heroics but healing, not nostrums but normalcy." On election day, he won in a landslide, beginning a Republican dominance that would last until 1932.

Warren Harding had been neither an outstanding state politician in Ohio nor an influential figure in the U.S. Senate. But with victory nearly certain in 1920, Republican Party leaders wanted a candidate they could dominate. Genial, loyal, and mediocre, "Uncle Warren" fit the bill. Harding knew his limitations and assembled a strong cabinet, composed of progressives as well as conservatives, to help him guide the government. Charles Evans Hughes, former reform governor, Supreme Court justice, and presidential candidate, took firm control of the State Department. As secretary of agriculture, Henry C. Wallace created new links with farm organizations while Attorney General Harlan Fiske Stone, a future chief justice, cleaned up the mess at the Department of Justice left by the Palmer Raids. Financier Andrew W. Mellon ran the Treasury Department and quickly reduced the high wartime tax rates, freeing up money for private investment.

The "Associated State." The most active member of the Harding administration was Secretary of Commerce Herbert Hoover, who had successfully headed the Food Administration during the war.

Under Hoover's direction, the Commerce Department fostered the creation of two thousand trade associations representing companies in almost every major industry. Government officials worked closely with the associations, providing them with statistical research, assisting them to devise industry-wide standards, and urging them to stabilize prices and wages. By creating informal governmental ties between government and industry—an "associated state"—Hoover hoped to promote the public interest. His goal was to achieve through voluntary cooperation what Progressive era reformers had sought through governmental regulation.

Unfortunately, not all government-business cooperation served all of the interests of the public. The Republican-dominated Federal Trade Commission (FTC) ignored antitrust laws that forbade restraints on trade, such as collusion among companies on prices. Similarly the Supreme Court, now headed by the former conservative Republican president William Howard Taft, refused to break up the mammoth United States Steel Corporation; as long as there was some competition in the steel industry, the Court ruled, the company's dominant position and ability to set prices were within the law.

The same could not be said about many of President Harding's political associates, who turned out to be dishonest and corrupt. When Harding died suddenly of a heart attack in San Francisco in August 1923, evidence of widespread fraud and corruption in his administration was just coming to light. The worst scandal concerned the secret leasing to private companies of government oil reserves in Teapot Dome, Wyoming, and in Elk Hills, California. Secretary of the Interior Albert Fall was eventually convicted of taking $300,000 in bribes and became the first cabinet officer in American history to serve a prison sentence.

The 1924 Election. Following Harding's death, Vice President Calvin Coolidge moved to the White House. In contrast to his predecessor's political cronyism and outgoing style, Coolidge personified the austere rectitude of a Vermont Yankee. Coolidge's taciturn personality and unimpeachable morality reassured Republican voters, who were drawn primarily from the native-born Protestant middle classes, small business owners, skilled workers, farmers, northern blacks, and wealthy industrialists. To win their backing, Coolidge affirmed his support for business and limited government and announced his candidacy for the presidency in 1924.

When the Democrats gathered to nominate a candidate, they were even more divided than usual. Traditionally the party drew its strength from white voters in the Jim Crow South and immigrant-dominated urban political machines in the North, two constituencies whose interests often collided. Throughout the 1920s, the two groups of Democrats disagreed mightily over Prohibition, immigration restriction, and, most seriously, the mounting power of the racist and anti-immigrant Ku Klux Klan (Map 23.1). These conflicts produced a hopeless

Warren Harding and Calvin Coolidge

The political careers of New Era political leaders Warren G. Harding (1865–1923) and Calvin Coolidge (1872–1933) present a study in contrasts. Harding (left), a small-town politician from Marion, Ohio, was prone to cronyism and mediocrity. Calvin Coolidge (right), of Vermont, was cut from a different cloth: taciturn, upright, stern, and capable. In the wake of the Harding scandals, Coolidge reassured citizens' faith in Republican government by his unimpeachable ethics. © Bettmann/Corbis.

MAP 23.1 Ku Klux Klan Politics and Violence in the 1920s

Unlike the Reconstruction-era Klan, the Klan of the 1920s was geographically dispersed and had substantial strength in the West and Midwest as well as the South. Although the Klan is often thought of as a rural movement, some of its strongest "klaverns" were in Chicago, Los Angeles, Atlanta, Detroit, and other large cities. The organization's members operated as vigilantes in areas where they were strong; elsewhere, their aggressive tactics triggered riots between Klansmen and their ethnic and religious targets.

deadlock between northern supporters of Governor Al Smith of New York and southern and western advocates of former Treasury Secretary William A. McAdoo of California. After 103 ballots, the delegates compromised on John W. Davis, a wealthy and influential Wall Street lawyer who hailed from West Virginia.

The 1924 campaign also featured a third-party challenge by Senator Robert M. La Follette of Wisconsin, who ran on the Progressive Party ticket. La Follette's candidacy mobilized reformers and labor leaders as well as disgruntled farmers. His progressive-minded platform called for nationalization of railroads, public ownership of utilities, and the right of Congress to overrule Supreme Court decisions.

The Republicans won an impressive victory, with Coolidge receiving 15.7 million votes to Davis's 8.4 million and La Follette's 4.9 million. Perhaps the most significant aspect of the election was the low voter turnout. Only 52 percent of the electorate cast ballots in 1924, compared to more than 70 percent in presidential elections of the late nineteenth century. Newly enfranchised women voters were only partially to blame; a long-term drop in voting by men, rather than apathy among women, caused most of the decline.

Women in Politics. After achieving the suffrage in 1920, women expanded their political activism. Partisan women tried to break into party politics, but Democrats and Republicans granted them only token positions. African American women were equally unsuccessful as they struggled for voting rights in the South and a federal antilynching law. Women were more influential as lobbyists. The Women's Joint Congressional Committee, a Washington-based coalition of ten major white women's organizations, including the newly formed League of Women Voters, lobbied actively for reform legislation. Its major accomplishment was the passage in 1921 of the them out of office. By the late 1920s, when it became clear that women did not vote as a bloc, Congress cut off appropriations for the program.

As support for progressive reform languished on the national level, some state leaders pursued ambitious agendas. In New York, where urban social-welfare liberalism was coalescing under the leadership of Al Smith and Robert Wagner (see Chapter 20), new legislation expanded aid to public schools, added benefits to workers' compensation programs, and created new state forests, scenic parks, and automobile parkways. However, the dominant motif of the 1920s was limited government. Responsibility for the well-being of the country lay increasingly in the hands of its corporate business leaders.

Corporate Capitalism

The revolution in business management that began in the 1890s finally triumphed in the 1920s. Large-scale corporate bureaucracies headed by chief executive officers (CEOs) replaced individual- or family-run enterprises as the major form of business organization. Few CEOs owned a significant part of their enterprises; the owners—thousands of stock shareholders—no longer controlled daily operations. Moreover, many corporations were so large that they dominated their markets; what the famous eighteenth-century economist Adam Smith had called the "invisible hand" of market forces gave way to the "visible hand" of managers who controlled output and prices.

Business Consolidation. Indeed, by 1930 a handful of managers stood at the center of American economic life. As a result of a vigorous pattern of consolidation, the two hundred largest corporations controlled almost half the nonbanking corporate wealth in the United States. During the 1920s businesses combined at a rapid rate, with the largest number of mergers occurring in rapidly growing industries such as chemicals (Dupont), electrical appliances and machinery (Westinghouse and General Electric), and automobiles (General Motors). Rarely did any single corporation monopolize an entire industry; rather, an **oligopoly** of a few major producers dominated the market and controlled prices. The nation's financial institutions expanded and consolidated along with its corporations. Total banking assets rose from $48 billion in 1919 to $72 billion in 1929. Mergers between Wall Street banks enhanced the role of New York as the financial center of the United States and, increasingly, the world. In 1929 almost half the

The League of Women Voters

The League was the brainchild of Carrie Chapman Catt, the president of the National American Woman Suffrage Association. Formed in 1920, as the Nineteenth Amendment was about to give women the vote, the League undertook to educate Americans to be responsible citizens and to win enactment of legislation favorable to women. The League helped to secure passage of the Sheppard-Towner Act of 1921, which provided federal aid for maternal and child-care programs. In the 1930s, members campaigned for the enactment of the Social Security and other social welfare legislation. Library of Congress.

Sheppard-Towner Federal Maternity and Infancy Act. The first federally funded health-care legislation, the act aimed to lower high rates of infant mortality by funding medical clinics, prenatal educational programs, and visiting nurse projects. The act was controversial. Conservatives charged that it was both a Communist plot to socialize American medicine and an attack on the rights of the states, which traditionally handled public health measures. Indeed, many men in Congress voted for the Sheppard-Towner Act only because they feared that otherwise newly enfranchised women would vote nation's banking resources were controlled by 1 percent of American banks, a mere 250 depositories.

The Economy during the 1920s. Many Americans benefited from the success of corporate enterprise, particularly after 1921. Immediately after World War I, the nation experienced a series of economic shocks. In 1919, Americans spent their wartime savings, causing rampant inflation: Prices jumped by a third in a single year. Then came a sharp two-year recession that raised unemployment to 10 percent and cut prices more than 20 percent. Finally, in 1922 the economy began to grow smoothly and almost continuously. Between 1922 and 1929 the gross domestic product grew from $74.1 billion to $103.1 billion, approximately 40 percent, and per capita income rose impressively from $641 to $847.

An abundance of new consumer products, particularly the automobile, sparked economic growth during the 1920s. Manufacturing output expanded 64 percent during the decade, as factories churned out millions of cars, refrigerators, stoves, and radios. To produce these goods, basic industries supplied huge quantities of raw materials: steel, copper, chemicals, natural gas, electrical power, oil and gasoline. More efficient machinery and new methods of mass production increased workers' productivity by 40 percent. Scientific management, first introduced in 1895 by Frederick W. Taylor (see Chapter 20), also boosted productivity. Widely implemented in the 1920s, these techniques allowed managers to extract greater output from workers.

The economy had some weaknesses. Agriculture—which still employed one-fourth of all workers—never fully recovered from the postwar recession. During the war, American farmers had borrowed heavily to expand production, but as European farmers returned to their fields, the world market was glutted with goods. Prices for wheat dropped by 40 percent, corn by 32 percent, and hogs by 50 percent. As their income plunged, farmers looked to Congress for help. The McNary-Haugen bills of 1927 and 1928 proposed a system of federal price supports for a slew of agricultural products—wheat, corn, cotton, rice, and tobacco. President Coolidge opposed the bills as "class" (special-interest) legislation and vetoed both of them. Between 1919 and 1929, the farmers' share of the national income plummeted from 16 percent to 8.8 percent.

Other "sick industries," particularly coal and textiles, also missed out on the prosperity of the 1920s. Like farmers, these businesses had expanded output during the war and now faced overcapacity and falling prices. This underside of American economic life foreshadowed the Great Depression of the 1930s.

Modern Industry/Modern Art

This dramatic poster, executed by artist Norman Erickson in 1928, promotes the United States Steel Company's mills of Gary, Indiana, as a tourist attraction on a par with Yellowstone National Park. And it reflects a new interest in industrial landscapes by serious artists. The Gary experienced by steelworkers had less beauty than Erickson's poster and more soot, grime, and hard work. Yet the artist's eerie orange background captured the color of the heavily polluted sky around Gary's steel mills. Chicago Historical Society.

Welfare Capitalism. Unlike farmers and miners, industrial workers and white-collar employees shared in the prosperity of the 1920s. Henry Ford and other major corporate employers paid their workers well to increase their buying power as consumers. Many industries went to a shorter workweek (five full days and a half day on Saturday), giving their employees more leisure time. Profitable firms, such as International Harvester, offered workers two weeks of paid vacation every year.

The 1920s were also the heyday of **welfare capitalism**, a system of labor relations that stressed management's responsibility for employees' well-being. At a time when unemployment compensation and government-sponsored pensions did not exist, General Electric, U.S. Steel, and other large corporations offered workers health insurance, old-age pension plans, and the opportunity to buy stock in the company at below-market prices. Other firms subsidized mortgages or contributed to employee savings plans. Their goal was to create a loyal and long-serving workforce, particularly among salaried employees, mostly managers and office workers, and important wage workers, such as shop foremen.

Welfare capitalism had a second goal of deterring production-line workers from joining labor unions. In addition to providing ample benefits, some companies set up employee committees to voice workers' complaints and to consult regularly with managers over working conditions. Other corporations attacked unions as un-American because they forced workers to become members; they celebrated the "American Plan" of an open, nonunion shop. Decisions by the conservative-minded Supreme Court undercut union activism and government regulation of the labor market. In *Colorado Coal Company v. United Mine Workers*, the Court ruled that a striking union could be penalized for illegal restraint of trade. The Court also stuck down federal legislation regulating child labor, and in *Atkins v. Children's Hospital*, it voided a minimum wage for women workers in the District of Columbia. Such decisions and aggressive anti-union campaigns caused membership in labor unions to fall from 5.1 million in 1920 to 3.6 million in 1929 — about 10 percent of the nonagricultural workforce. Welfare capitalism seemed to represent the wave of the future in industrial relations.

Economic Expansion Abroad

The growing power of U.S. corporations was clearly apparent in the international arena. American manufacturers actively promoted foreign sales of consumer products: radios, telephones, automobiles, and sewing machines. To supply these markets, firms built factories in foreign countries and bought up existing businesses. General Electric set up production facilities in Latin America, China, Japan, and Australia; General Motors expanded its sales in Europe by taking over the Vauxhall Motor Company in Britain and Opel in Germany. Other American firms invested abroad in new sources of supply. Attracted by lower livestock prices, three major American meatpackers — Swift, Armour, and Wilson — built plants in Argentina. The United Fruit Company developed plantations in Costa Rica, Honduras, and Guatemala; other American companies set up sugar plantations in Cuba and rubber plantations in the Philippines and Malaya. Standard Oil of New Jersey acquired oil reserves in Mexico and Venezuela (a precursor to American oil investments in the Middle East after World War II). During the 1920s foreign investments by U.S. corporations more than doubled, to a total of $15.2 billion.

American banks were equally active in providing funds to European countries that were rebuilding their war-torn economies. American banks also emerged as key players in the postwar debt system. The banks lent money to Germany, enabling it to pay reparations to the Allied Powers. Britain and France then used these funds to pay off their wartime loans from the United States. While American political leaders insisted on payment of these debts ("They hired the money, didn't they?" scoffed President Coolidge), they made it very difficult to do. The Fordney-McCumber Tariff of 1922 followed the long-standing Republican policy of using high tariffs to exclude foreign-made goods. Unable to sell their goods in the United States, European nations could not easily earn the dollars needed to pay their debts.

In 1924, U.S. diplomats and bankers met with their counterparts from France, Great Britain, and Germany to address the debt situation and to promote European financial stability. The meeting produced the Dawes Plan, named for Charles G. Dawes, the Chicago banker who negotiated the agreement; it reduced the reparations that Germany owed to the Allies and provided substantial American bank loans to assist the Germans to keep up with the payments. The success of the Dawes Plan depended on the continuing flow of American capital to Germany and the ability of the Allies to pay their debts to the United States.

This fragile and unstable system of international finance collapsed in the wake of the American stock market crash in October 1929. The outflow of capital from the United States to Europe slowed and then stopped, undermining the flow of reparation payments. The stock market crisis also increased congressional support for a policy of economic nationalism; the Hawley-Smoot Act of 1930 raised tariffs on imports to an all-time high and made it nearly impossible for the Allied Powers to pay off the remaining $4.3 billion in war loans. Even as American corporations successfully extended their sales and investments to the corners of the earth, American politicians and bankers failed to create a stable structure of international finance.

American Companies Abroad

United Fruit was one of the many American companies that found opportunities for investment in South America in the 1920s and introduced "new" tropical foods to the United States. The company used elaborate and informative color advertisements to sell these new products. Bananas were sufficiently exotic that the ads explained to consumers how to tell when bananas were ripe and never to put them in the ice-box. Duke University Library, Special Collections.

Foreign Policy in the 1920s

American foreign policy during the 1920s and 1930s was both **isolationist** and internationalist. By refusing to join the League of Nations or the Court of International Justice (the World Court), the United States declined to play an active role in international politics; in this regard, the nation's stance was clearly isolationist. However, as the efforts of American diplomats to shore up the international financial system suggest, the United States pursued a vigorous, internationalist economic policy. Moreover, officials in the Department of State and the Department of Commerce worked constantly to open up new foreign markets for American manufacturers and bankers and to protect existing American interests in other countries.

These initiatives were particularly important in the Caribbean and Latin America, where the United States had a long history of economic activity and military intervention. Both continued during the 1920s. To quell civil unrest and exclude European intervention, the U.S. government dispatched troops to the Dominican Republic from 1916 and 1924. American military forces likewise remained in Nicaragua almost continuously from 1912 to 1933 and in Haiti from 1915 to 1934. Relations with Mexico remained tense, a legacy of U.S. intervention during the Mexican Revolution (see Chapter 21) and of the Mexican government's efforts to **nationalize** its oil and mineral deposits — a policy that alarmed Standard Oil of New Jersey (owned primarily by the Rockefeller family) and other U.S. petroleum companies with investments in Mexico.

The Washington Conference and the Kellogg-Briand Pact. As the United States continued to seek a dominant position in the Western Hemisphere, it sought to reduce its political and military commitments in East Asia and in Europe. The Washington Naval Arms Conference of 1921 revealed American strategy in the Pacific. Secretary of State Charles Evans Hughes won acceptance of a bold plan that placed strict limits on naval expansion. His goal was to deter both excessive expenditures on arms and the buildup of Japanese naval power, which would give Japan a dominant position in East Asia. The major naval powers agreed to scrap some warships, to halt the construction of large battleships for ten years, and to maintain the tonnage of naval vessels among Britain, the United States, Japan, France, and Italy at a fixed ratio. As one commentator quipped, in a short speech Hughes had sunk "more ships than all the admirals of the world have sunk in a cycle of centuries."

Seven years later, American Secretary of State Frank Kellogg devised another low-cost solution to a European problem. Rather than sign an agreement committing the United States to guarantee the territorial integrity of France, Kellogg persuaded French foreign minister Aristide Briand to support a broader pact condemning militarism. Fifteen nations signed the pact in Paris in 1928; forty-eight more approved it later. The signatories agreed to "condemn recourse to war for the solution of international controversies, and renounce it as an instrument of national policy." U.S. peace groups enthusiastically supported the pact, and the U.S. Senate ratified it eighty-five to one. Critics correctly pointed out that the agreement lacked mechanisms for enforcement and was little more than an "international kiss."

In the end, fervent hopes and pious declarations were no cure for the massive economic, political, and territorial problems created by World War I. U.S. policymakers vacillated, as they would in the 1930s, between wanting to play a larger role in world events and fearing that treaties and responsibilities would limit their ability to act unilaterally. Their diplomatic efforts would ultimately prove inadequate to the mounting international crises of the 1930s that led to World War II.

➤ How do you explain the resurgent popularity of business leaders during the 1920s? What changed from the Progressive era, when corporate executives were held in contempt?

➤ In what ways did government and business work together during the "new era"? What were the sources of this relationship?

➤ Describe American foreign policy — both political and economic — during the 1920s. Is it best characterized as "isolationist" or "internationalist"?

A New National Culture

The 1920s represented an important watershed in the development of a mass national culture. A new emphasis on leisure, consumption, and amusement characterized the era. Automobiles, paved roads, the parcel post service, movies, radios, telephones, mass-circulation magazines, brand names, and chain stores linked Americans — in the mill towns in the southern Piedmont, outposts on the Oklahoma plains, and ethnic enclaves in states along the Atlantic and Pacific coasts — in an expanding web of national experience. In fact, as consumerism spread around the world, American products and culture achieved global influence.

A Consumer Society

In homes across the country during the 1920s, Americans sat down to breakfasts of Kellogg's corn flakes and toast from a General Electric toaster. Then they got into Ford Model Ts to go to work or go shopping at Safeway, A&P, or Woolworths, one of the chain stores that had sprung up across the country. In the evening the family gathered to listen to radio programs like *Great Moments in History,* to catch up on events in the latest issue of *Reader's Digest,* or to enjoy the melodramatic tales in *True Story;* on weekends they might see the newest Charlie Chaplin film at the local theater. Millions of Americans now shared similar daily experiences.

Yet many Americans — blacks, working-class families, and many farmers — did not participate fully in the new commercial culture or accept its middle-class values. As one historian puts it, "Buying an electric vacuum cleaner did not turn Josef Dobrowolski into *True Story*'s Jim Smith." Moreover, the unequal distribution of income limited many consumers' ability to buy the enticing new products. At the height of prosperity in the 1920s, the average annual income for the bottom 40 percent of American families was only $725 (about $8,200 today); after meeting the cost of food, housing, and clothing, they had only $135 to spend on everything else. Many Americans stretched their incomes by buying on the newly devised installment plan that allowed people to purchase cars, radios, refrigerators, and sewing machines "on time." "Buy now, Pay later," said the ads, and millions did. By 1927, two-thirds of American cars were financed through monthly payments, and consumer lending grew to $7 billion a year — the tenth-largest business in the United States.

Electric appliances — refrigerators, radios, fans, irons, vacuum cleaners — were among the most important of the new products and had a dramatic impact on women's lives. While unmarried women increased their participation in the workforce, the primary roles for most married women remained those of housewives and mothers. Electric appliances made housewives' chores less arduous but did not greatly increase their leisure time. More middle-class housewives began to do their own housework and laundry, replacing human servants with electric ones. The new gadgets also raised standards of cleanliness, encouraging women to spend more time doing household chores.

To encourage consumers to view the new products as "necessities" rather than "luxuries," manufacturers were spending no less than $2.6 billion a year on advertising by 1929. A new advertising industry (centered on New York City's Madison Avenue) devised sophisticated ways to spur sales, often aided by experts in the growing academic field of psychology. Some ads featured white-coated doctors to imply scientific approval of their products. Others appealed to people's social aspirations by depicting elegant men and women who smoked certain brands of cigarettes or drove recognizable makes of cars. Ad writers also preyed on people's insecurities, coming up with a variety of socially unacceptable "diseases," such as the dreaded "B.O." (body odor).

Most consumers were not the passive victims of manipulative advertising agencies but willing participants in a new culture. For many middle-class Americans, the traditional criteria for judging self-worth — personal character, religious commitment, and social standing — now had a powerful rival: the gratification of personal desires through the acquisition of more and better possessions.

The World of the Automobile

No possession typified the new consumer culture better than the automobile. "Why on earth do you need to study what's changing this country?" a Muncie, Indiana, resident asked sociologists Robert and Helen Lynd. "I can tell you what's happening in just four letters: A-U-T-O!" The showpiece of modern capitalism, the automobile revolutionized American economic and social life.

Mass production of cars stimulated the prosperity of the 1920s. Before the introduction of the moving assembly line in 1913, Ford workers took twelve and a half hours to put together an auto; on an assembly line they took only ninety-three minutes. By 1927 Ford was producing a car every twenty-four seconds. Auto sales climbed from 1.5 million in 1921 to 5 million in 1929, a year in which Americans spent $2.58 billion on cars. By the end of the decade, Americans owned 23 million cars — about 80 percent of the world's automobiles — an average of one car for every five people.

The expansion of the auto industry had a ripple effect on the American economy. It stimulated the steel, petroleum, chemical, rubber, and glass industries and, directly or indirectly, provided jobs for 3.7 million workers. Highway construction became a billion-dollar-a-year enterprise, financed by federal subsidies and state gasoline taxes. Car ownership broke down the isolation of rural life, spurred the growth of suburbs, and, in 1924, spawned the first suburban shopping center, Country Club Plaza outside Kansas City.

The auto also changed the way Americans spent their leisure time. Although gasoline was not cheap (about $2.30 a gallon in 2006 prices), they took to the roads, becoming a nation of tourists. The American Automobile Association, founded in 1902, reported that in 1929 about 45 million people — almost a third of the population — took vacations by automobile, patronizing the "autocamps" and tourist cabins that were the forerunners of post–World War II motels. Like the movies, cars changed the dating patterns of young Americans. Contrary to many parents' views, premarital sex was not invented in the backseat of a Ford, but a Model T offered more privacy than did the family living room or the front porch and contributed to increased sexual experimentation among the young.

The Movies and Mass Culture

The new mass media — glossy magazines, radio, and especially movies — did more than anything else to involve Americans in a common national culture. American movies had their roots in turn-of-the-century nickelodeons, where for a nickel a mostly working-class audience could see one-reel silent films such as *The Great Train Robbery*. By 1910 the moviemaking industry had concentrated in southern California, which had cheap land, plenty of sunshine, and varied scenery — mountains, deserts, cities, and the Pacific Ocean — within easy reach. By the end of World War I, the United States was producing 90 percent of all films, and Hollywood reigned as the movie capital of the world.

As directors turned to feature films and began exhibiting them in large, ornate theaters, movies drew their audiences from the middle class as well as the working class. Early movie stars, including Buster Keaton, Charlie Chaplin, Mary Pickford, and Douglas Fairbanks, became idols who helped to set national trends in clothing and hairstyles. Then a new cultural icon, the flapper, burst on the scene to represent emancipated womanhood.

Clara Bow: The "It" Girl. Clara Bow was Hollywood's favorite flapper, a bobbed-hair "jazz baby" who rose to stardom almost overnight. Born into an extremely poor family in Brooklyn, New York, in 1905, Bow dropped out of school in the eighth grade and set her sights on a career as an actress. At the age of eighteen she won a Hollywood contract; three years later she was a star — the lead character in *It,* one of the first movies to gross $1 million. Whatever "It" was, Clara had it. With her boyish figure and shock of red hair, she had a strikingly sensual presence; "she could

Twenties Sex Symbol
Clara Bow was not the girl next door, as this seductive film still from *Her Wedding Night* (1930) confirms. "I've never taken dope," gushed one seventeen-year-old boy, "but it was like a shot of dope when you looked at this girl." Bow's career was cut short by several nervous breakdowns, some unhappy love affairs, and the arrival of "talkies," which did not suit her style. She left Hollywood in 1931 to marry a Nevada rancher and made her last film in 1932. Culver Pictures.

flirt with the grizzly bear," wrote one reviewer. Thousands of young women took Bow as their model. Decked out in short skirts and rolled-down silk stockings, flappers wore makeup, smoked, danced to jazz, and flaunted their liberated lifestyle. Like so many cultural icons, the flappers represented only a tiny minority of women but, thanks to the movies and advertising industry, they become the symbol of women's sexual and social emancipation.

The movies were big business, grossing $1.6 billion in 1926. The large studios—United Artists, Paramount, and Metro-Goldwyn-Mayer—dominated the industry and were run mainly by eastern European Jewish immigrants such as Samuel Goldfish (later Goldwyn). Movies became even more profitable and culturally powerful with the advent of the "talkies." Warner Brothers' *The Jazz Singer* (1927), starring Al Jolson, was the first feature-length film to offer sound. Despite the enormous expense—some $300 million—all the major studios quickly made the transition to "talkies." By 1929, the nation's 23,000 movie theaters were selling 90 million tickets a year.

Jazz. That the first talkie was *The Jazz Singer* was not a coincidence. Jazz music captured important aspects of the culture of the 1920s, especially its creative excitement and sensual character. As a word, *jazz* was originally a vulgar term for the sex act; as music, it was (and is) an improvisational form whose notes are rarely written down. Jazz began in the dance halls and bordellos of turn-of-the century New Orleans and was a thoroughly American—indeed, African American—art form. Most of the early jazz musicians were black, and they carried its rhythms to Chicago, New York, Kansas City, and Los Angeles. The best-known performers were

All That Jazz

The phonograph machine dramatically expanded the popularity of jazz music, which now could be heard at home as well as in a city jazz joint. The success of "Crazy Blues" by Mamie Smith and her Jazz Hounds, which sold a million records in 1920, convinced record companies that there was an African American market for what were called "race records." Composer Perry Bradford plays the piano; Bradford was also the composer of "Keep A Knockin," which Little Richard made into a major rock 'n' roll hit in 1957. Division of Political History, Smithsonian Institution, Washington, D.C.

composer-pianist Ferdinand "Jelly Roll" Morton, trumpeter Louis "Satchmo" Armstrong, composer-bandleader Edward "Duke" Ellington, and singer Bessie Smith, "the empress of the Blues."

Phonograph records increased the appeal of jazz and the blues by capturing their spontaneity and distributing it to a wide audience; jazz, in turn, boosted the infant recording industry. Soon this uniquely American art form had caught on in Europe, especially in France. Because jazz often expressed black dissent to the straightforward, optimistic rhythms of white music, it became popular among certain groups of American whites — young people, intellectuals, social outcasts — who felt stifled by middle-class culture. Later in the century, other African American musical forms — notably rhythm-and-blues and hip-hop — would again subvert middle-class values and inject themes of sex and violence into American popular culture.

Journalism and Radio. Mass-circulation magazines and the radio were also key factors in the creation of a national culture. In 1922 ten magazines claimed a circulation of at least 2.5 million, including the *Saturday Evening Post,* the *Ladies' Home Journal,* and *Good Housekeeping.* Tabloid newspapers, which highlighted crime, sports, comics, and scandals, also became part of the national scene, as did news services such as the Associated Press. Thanks to the AP, people across the United States read the same articles.

The newest instrument of mass culture, professional radio broadcasting, was truly a child of the 1920s. It began in November 1920 when station KDKA in Pittsburgh carried the presidential election returns; a mere nine years later, eight hundred stations, most affiliated with the Columbia Broadcasting Service (CBS) or the National Broadcasting Company (NBC), were on the air and nearly ten million American households (40 percent of the total) owned a radio (Map 23.2). Unlike Europe, where radio was a government monopoly, American radio stations were government licensed but privately owned; they drew their revenue from advertisers and corporate sponsors. One of the most

MAP 23.2 The Spread of Radio, to 1939

In 1938 about three-quarters of the U.S. population — approximately 26 million households — owned radios. Four national networks dominated broadcasting, transmitting news and entertainment programs on local stations across the country. Powerful clear-channel stations located in major cities reached listeners hundreds of miles away. By 1939, only sparsely populated areas were beyond radio's reach.

popular radio shows of all time, *Amos 'n' Andy*, which premiered on the NBC network in 1928, featured two white actors playing stereotypical black characters. Stock phrases from the weekly show, like "Check and double check," quickly became part of everyday speech. So many people "tuned in" (a new phrase of the 1920s, similar to "log in" today) to *Amos 'n' Andy* that other activities came to a halt during the show's airtime.

Leisure and Sports. As the workweek shrank and paid vacations increased, Americans had more time and energy to expend on recreation. Cities and suburbs built baseball diamonds, tennis courts, swimming pools, and golf courses. Sports became a big business as private entrepreneurs built huge football and baseball stadiums and formed professional teams to play in them. Fans could attend games, listen to them on the radio, or catch highlights in the movie newsreels. Star athletes — boxer Jack Dempsey, golfer Bobby Jones, baseball slugger Babe Ruth — became national celebrities. Excluded from the white teams, outstanding black athletes like baseball pitcher Satchel Paige played on teams in the Negro National League and the Southern Negro League.

> How do we explain the rise of a new national culture in the 1920s? In what ways did Americans across the nation begin to share common experiences?

> How did the automobile epitomize the new values of mass consumption and the changing patterns of leisure in America?

> What facets of cultural change does the example of Clara Bow help us to understand?

Redefining American Identity

As movies, radio, advertising, and mass-production industries began to transform the country into a modern, cosmopolitan nation, many Americans welcomed these changes as exciting evidence of progress. Others were uneasy. Flappers dancing to jazz, youthful sexual experimentation in Model Ts, hints of a decline in religious values: These harbingers of a new era worried rural folk and city dwellers who had been born and raised in small towns. They were also troubled by the powerful presence in American cities of millions of Catholic and Jewish immigrants from Europe and African American migrants from the South. Beneath the clichés of the Jazz Age and the Roaring Twenties were deeply felt tensions that surfaced in conflicts over immigration, religion, Prohibition, and race relations. At stake was no less than the definition of what it meant to be an American.

The Rise of Nativism

Tensions between city dwellers and rural folk escalated sharply during the 1920s. For the first time in the nation's history, more people lived in urban areas — ranging from small towns of 2,500 people to large cities — than in rural areas. And there was no mistaking the trend. During the 1920s about 6 million American left farms for the cities. By 1929, ninety-three cities had populations over 100,000. New York City exceeded 7 million; Chicago boasted almost 3 million, and the population of Los Angeles exploded to 1.2 million. Because political districts did not reflect this population shift, rural areas still controlled most state legislatures. Sharp battles over the use of tax dollars, especially for city services, intensified the growing cultural conflict between the two regions.

Immigration Restriction. Racial and ethnic pluralism lay at the heart of this conflict. When native-born white Protestants — both farmers and city dwellers — looked at their society in 1920, they saw a nation of 105 million people that had changed dramatically in only forty years. During that time, more than 23 million immigrants had come to America, many of them Jews or Catholics from southern and eastern Europe and many of peasant stock. Senator William Bruce of Maryland branded them "indigestible lumps" in the "national stomach," implying that they might never be absorbed into the dominant culture. Such **nativist** sentiments, which recalled the reaction to migrants from Ireland and German in the 1840s and 1850s, were widely shared.

Nativist animosity fueled a new drive against immigration. "America must be kept American," President Coolidge declared in 1924. Congress had banned Chinese immigration in 1882, and Theodore Roosevelt had negotiated a "Gentleman's Agreement" that limited Japanese immigration in 1907 (see Chapter 21). Now nativists charged that there were too many European migrants and certainly too many who were anarchists, socialists, and radical labor organizers. Responding to these concerns, Congress passed an emergency immigration act in 1921 and a more restrictive measure, the

National Origins Act, in 1924. The act cut immigration quotas to 2 percent of each nationality, as reflected in the 1890 census — which had included few people from southeastern Europe and Russia. In 1929 an even more restrictive quota went into effect, setting a cap of 150,000 immigrants per year from Europe and continuing to ban most migrants from Asia.

The new laws continued to permit unrestricted immigration from countries in the Western Hemisphere, and Latin Americans arrived in increasing numbers. Over a million Mexicans entered the United States between 1900 and 1930. Some fled the chaos of the Mexican Revolution of 1910; many more Mexicans migrated in response to American labor shortages during World War I. Nativists lobbied Congress to cut this flow, and so too did the leaders of labor unions, who pointed out that a flood of impoverished migrants would lower wages for all American workers. But Congress heeded the pleas of American employers, especially large-scale farmers in Texas and California, who wanted cheap labor. Only the coming of the Great Depression cut off migration from Mexico (see Reading American Pictures, "Patrolling the Texas Border," p. 720).

Ku Klux Klan Women Parade in Washington, D.C.
During the 1920s the antiblack and anti-Catholic Ku Klux Klan was a powerful force in American life. Perhaps as many as 500,000 women joined the Women of the Ku Klux Klan (WKKK), including these women who paraded down Pennsylvania Avenue in Washington, D.C., in 1928. The organization was so deeply rooted in the daily lives of many southern and midwestern white Protestants that one woman from rural Indiana remembered her time in the KKK as "just a celebration . . . a way of growing up." National Archives at College Park, MD.

READING AMERICAN PICTURES

Patrolling the Texas Border

The United States Border Patrol, Laredo, Texas, 1926. University of Texas at Austin.

In 1926, San Antonio photographer Eugene Omar Goldbeck took this photograph of Border Patrol officers in Laredo, Texas. Since 1917, Mexicans, like other immigrants, had been subject to a head tax and a literacy test. However, because of pressure from southwestern employers eager for cheap Mexican labor, the U.S. government had not enforced these provisions and migrant laborers moved back and forth across the border. Following the passage of the National Origins Act of 1924, the federal government established the Border Patrol to prevent Europeans from entering the United States illegally through Canada and Mexico. The Border Patrol focused its enforcements efforts on the Southwest and then mainly to stem the tide of Mexican immigration. In addition to the Border Patrol, new procedures, including bathing, delousing, and medical inspections at key points of entry, "hardened" the border and ended the casual movement of Mexican workers in and out of the United States.

ANALYZING THE EVIDENCE

➤ Goldbeck's photograph is clearly a posed one. What do you suppose was the intent of presenting the Border Patrol in this fashion?

➤ What is the significance of the type of uniforms the officers are wearing?

➤ What aspects of their methods might potentially exacerbate the illegal immigrant problem?

➤ If you were an immigrant worker, how might you read this image?

The New Klan. Another expression of nativism in the 1920s was the revival of the Ku Klux Klan (see Chapter 15). Shortly after the premiere in 1915 of *Birth of a Nation,* a popular film glorifying the Reconstruction-era Ku Klux Klan, a group of southerners gathered on Stone Mountain outside Atlanta to revive the racist organization. Taking as its motto "Native, white, Protestant supremacy," the modern Klan appealed to both urban and rural folk, though its largest "klaverns" were in urban areas. The KKK found significant support in the Far West, the Southwest, and the Midwest, especially Oregon, Indiana, and Oklahoma. The Klan of the 1920s did not limit its harassment to blacks but targeted Catholics and Jews as well. Its tactics remained the same: arson, physical intimidation, and economic boycotts. The new Klan also turned to politics; hundreds of Klansmen won election to local offices and state legislatures (see Map 23.1, p. 708). At the height of its power in 1925, the Klan had over three million members—including a strong contingent of women who pursued a political agenda that combined racism, nativism, and equal rights for white Protestant women.

After 1925 the Klan declined rapidly, undermined by internal rivalries and rampant corruption. Especially damaging was the revelation that Grand Dragon David Stephenson, the Klan's national leader, had kidnapped and sexually assaulted his former secretary, driving her to suicide. In addition, the passage of the National Origins Act in 1924 robbed the Klan of a potent issue. Nonetheless, the Klan remained strong in the Jim Crow South, and during the 1930s, some northern Klansmen supported the American Nazi movement, which shared its antiblack and anti-Jewish beliefs.

Legislating Values: Evolution and Prohibition

Other cultural conflicts erupted over religion and alcoholic beverages. The debate between modernist and revivalist Protestants, which had been simmering since the 1890s (see Chapter 18), came to a boil in the 1920s. Modernists, or liberal Protestants, found ways to reconcile their religious beliefs with Charles Darwin's theory of evolution and other scientific principles. Revivalist Protestants, who were strongly rooted in **fundamentalist** Baptist and Methodist churches, insisted on a literal reading of the Bible. So too did popular evangelical preachers such as Billy Sunday and Aimee Semple McPherson, who used storefront churches and open air revivals to popularize their own blends of charismatic fundamentalism.

The Scopes Trial. Religious controversy entered the political arena when fundamentalists wrote their beliefs into law. In 1925 the Tennessee state legislature made it "unlawful . . . to teach any theory that denies the story of the Divine creation of man as taught in the Bible, and to teach instead that man has descended from a lower order of animals." The American Civil Liberties Union (ACLU), which had been formed during the Red Scare to protect free speech rights, challenged the constitutionality of the law. It intervened in the trial of John T. Scopes, a high school biology teacher, who had taught the principles of evolution to his class and faced a jail sentence

The First Modern Evangelist: Aimee Semple McPherson (1890–1944)

Aimee McPherson founded the Four Square Gospel Church, which now claims a worldwide membership of two million. Born as Beth Kennedy in Ontario, Canada, she married missionary Robert Semple in 1907. After his death in China, she married Harold McPherson and eventually settled in Los Angeles. By 1923, she was preaching to a radio audience and to crowds of 5,000 at her massive Angelus Temple. In 1926 McPherson attracted national attention by disappearing for a month and claiming she was kidnapped. Many suspected she was at a romantic hideaway with the Temple's radio operator, but her preaching career flourished into the 1930s. She died of an overdose of sedatives in 1944.

Copyright Bettmann / Corbis.

for doing so. The case attracted national attention because Clarence Darrow, a famous criminal lawyer, defended Scopes, and William Jennings Bryan, three-time presidential candidate and ardent fundamentalist, spoke for the prosecution.

The press dubbed the Scopes trial the "monkey trial." The label referred both to Darwin's argument that human beings and primates share a common ancestor and to the circus atmosphere at the trial, which was broadcast live over Chicago radio station WGN. The jury took only eight minutes to deliver its verdict: guilty. Though the Tennessee Supreme Court overturned Scopes's conviction, the controversial law remained on the books for more than thirty years (see Comparing American Voices, "The Scopes Trial," pp. 724–725). As the 1920s ended, science and religion were locked in a standoff; beginning in the 1980s, fundamentalists would launch a new attack against Darwin and modern science (see Chapter 32).

The "Noble Experiment." Like the dispute over evolution, Prohibition—the "noble experiment," as it was called—involved the power of the state to enforce social values (see Chapter 22). Americans drank less after the Eighteenth Amendment took effect in January 1920, but those who continued to drink gave the decade its reputation as the Roaring Twenties. Urban ethnic groups—German, Irish, Italian—had long opposed restrictions on drinking and refused to comply with the new law. Some brewed their own beer or distilled "bathtub gin." Many others patronized illegal saloons and clubs, called speakeasies, that sprang up everywhere; there were more than 30,000 speakeasies in New York City alone. Liquor smugglers operated with ease

Defining Beer

The Eighteenth (Prohibition) Amendment banned "intoxicating liquors." Over the strong objections of the beer industry, the Volstead Act of 1919 outlawed beverages with an alcoholic content of more than 0.5 percent. As support for Prohibition declined in the early 1930s, former brewery owners and workers campaigned for the legalization of beer, as in this march. In March 1933, nine months before the repeal of the Prohibition amendment, Congress amended the Volstead Act to allow the manufacture of beer with an alcoholic content of 3.2 percent. Library of Congress.

along Canadian and Mexican borders and used speedboats to land cargoes of wine, gin, and liquor along the Atlantic Coast. Organized crime (the "Mob"), which already had a presence among Italians and Jews in major cities, took over the bootleg trade and grew wealthy from its profits. The "noble experiment" turned out to be a dismal failure.

Those Americans who favored repeal of the Eighteenth Amendment — the "wets" — slowly built support for their cause in Congress and the state legislatures. The coming of the Great Depression hastened the process, as politicians looked for ways to create jobs and raise tax revenue. With the ratification of the Twenty-first Amendment on December 5, 1933, nationwide Prohibition came to an inglorious end.

Intellectual Crosscurrents

As millions of Americans celebrated the military victory in World War I and their peacetime prosperity, influential writers and intellectuals rendered bitter dissents. The novelist John Dos Passos railed at the obscenity of "Mr. Wilson's war" in *The Three Soldiers* (1921) and again in *1919* (1932). Ernest Hemingway's novels *In Our Time* (1924), *The Sun Also Rises* (1926), and *A Farewell to Arms* (1929) also powerfully described the dehumanizing consequences and the futility of war. In his despairing poem *The Waste Land* (1922), T. S. Eliot portrayed a fragmented civilization in ruins.

Influenced by Eliot's dark vision, writers offered stinging critiques of what they saw as the complacent, moralistic, and anti-intellectual tone of American life. In *Babbitt* (1922), the novelist Sinclair Lewis satirized the stifling conformity of a middle-class businessman. In 1925 Theodore Dreiser wrote his naturalistic masterpiece *An American Tragedy* and F. Scott Fitzgerald published *The Great Gatsby*, both probing indictments of the mindless pursuit of material goods and wealth.

Harlem Renaissance. More affirmative works of art and literature emanated from Harlem, the center of African American life in New York City. During the 1920s, Harlem stood as "the symbol of liberty and the Promised Land to Negroes everywhere," as an influential black minister put it. Talented African American artists and writers flocked to Harlem, where they broke with older genteel traditions of black literature to reclaim a cultural identity with their African roots.

The Harlem Renaissance championed racial pride. Authors such as Claude McKay, Jean Toomer, and Jessie Fauset explored the black experience and represented the "New Negro" in fiction. Countee Cullen and Langston Hughes turned to poetry, and Augusta Savage used sculpture to draw attention to black accomplishments. Zora Neale Hurston spent a decade collecting folklore in the South and the Caribbean and incorporated that material into her short stories and novels. This creative work embodied the ongoing African American struggle to find a way, as the influential black intellectual W. E. B. Du Bois explained, "to be both a Negro and an American."

The poet Langston Hughes, who became a leading exponent of the Harlem Renaissance, captured its affirmative spirit when he asserted, "I am a Negro — and beautiful." Hughes drew on the black artistic forms of blues and jazz in *The Weary Blues* (1926), a groundbreaking collection of poems. Considered the most original black poet and the most representative African American writer of the time, Hughes also wrote novels, plays, and essays.

The Harlem Renaissance

The Crisis, edited by the leading black intellectual W. E. B. Du Bois, was the magazine of the National Association for the Advancement of Colored People (NAACP). With its dramatic use of modern architecture and art, this cover from 1929 suggests the cultural and political awakenings associated with the Harlem Renaissance. Henry Lee Moon Library and Civil Rights Archive, NAACP, Washington, DC.

COMPARING AMERICAN VOICES

The Scopes Trial

In 1925, the Tennessee legislature passed a law prohibiting the teaching of the scientific theory of evolution in the state's public schools. The law resulted in the trial of John Scopes in Dayton, Tennessee, and triggered a much broader debate about science and religion, free speech and government power. As the following passages suggest, the participants in these debates began from different premises and came to different conclusions.

JOHN ROACH STRATON
Preserving a Christian Worldview

John Roach Straton was a prominent Protestant minister who, for religious reasons, strongly supported the Tennessee law. He published these remarks in the American Fundamentalist *in 1925.*

The real issue at Dayton and everywhere today is: "Whether the religion of the Bible shall be ruled out of the schools and the religion of evolution, with its ruinous results shall be ruled into the schools by law." The issue is whether the taxpayers—the mothers and fathers of the children—shall be made to support the false and materialistic religion, namely evolution, in the schools, while Christianity is ruled out, and thereby denied their children.

That is the exact issue in this country today. And that it is a very real and urgent issue is proved by the recent invasion of the sovereign state of Tennessee by a group of outside agnostics, atheists, Unitarian preachers, skeptical scientists, and political revolutionists.... They left New York and Chicago, where real religion is being most neglected, and ... went to save from itself a community ... where man is still regarded, not as a descendant of the slime and beasts of the jungle, but as a child of God....

THE AMERICAN CIVIL LIBERTIES UNION (ACLU)
Defending Free Inquiry in the Classroom

The American Civil Liberties Union (ACLU) was founded during World War I to oppose governmental suppression of free speech and individual rights. The ACLU assisted Scopes's defense and, in a later pamphlet entitled The Gag on Teaching *(1931), condemned the attempts by various private interest groups to use state power to control the content of education.*

The great essential to education is freedom—freedom in presenting and studying all the facts, and freedom of teachers to believe as they see fit and to express their beliefs like other citizens. It holds that, when for any reason this freedom is curtailed, real education itself is crippled.

The professed objects of our educational system have always been freedom from propaganda for private interests, liberty for teachers outside their classrooms, and the training of children without reference to any economic dogma....

During the hysteria of war [World War I], the pattern for interference with education was set, and majority dogmas became firmly entrenched. The dogmas of conventional patriotism developed first as part of the war propaganda, evidenced in the laws for the teaching of the Constitution, flag-saluting, special oaths of loyalty from teachers, and the revision of history textbooks. Then came the efforts of the Ku Klux Klan and the Fundamentalists in the name of Protestantism to outlaw evolution, compel the reading of the Bible (Protestant version) and, in one state [Oregon], to ban all private (meaning Catholic) schools....

The tendencies to restrict freedom of teaching can be fought only by constant agitation, repeal of the present restrictive laws, opposition to specific measures and cases of discrimination and by the growth of teachers' unions to protect teachers' liberties.

THE AMERICAN FEDERATION OF TEACHERS
Freedom: The Key to Knowledge

The American Federation of Teachers joined the ACLU in criticizing political interference and censorship in education. In this Resolution of 1925, the AFT defends the professional expertise of American educators.

In certain states of the union teaching as a constructive social function has been menaced, and may be menaced again, by misguided legislative authority that fears to trust the intelligence, the public spirit and the devotion to duty of the profession whose obligation it is, and whose desire it is, to serve the people by training the children for intelligent citizenship. The reactionary Lusk school laws in the state of New York [which required that teachers subscribe to loyalty oaths] . . . as well as the numerous bills in several states that have been designed to censor the writing and the teaching of history in the schools all reflect the same unfortunate suspicion and mistrust of educational intelligence which the Tennessee anti-evolution law betrays. . . .

Without freedom in the intellectual life, and without the inspiration of uncensored discovery and discussion, there could ultimately be no scholarship, no schools at all and no education. . . .

WILLIAM JENNINGS BRYAN
Let the Sovereign People Decide

William Jennings Bryan endorsed the biblical story of creation, but his defense of the Tennessee law reflected his deep belief in democratic government and the legitimacy of majority rule. In "Who Shall Control" (1925), Bryan offers a robust defense of the law and of his political philosophy.

The first question to be decided is: Who shall control our public schools? . . . Four sources of control have been suggested. The first is the people, speaking through their legislatures. That would seem to be the natural source of control. The people are sovereigns and governments derive their just powers from the consent of the governed. . . . Legislatures regulate marriage and divorce, property rights, descent of property, care of children, and all other matters between citizens. Why are our legislatures not competent to decide what kind of schools are needed, the requirements of teachers, and the kind of instruction that shall be given?

If not the legislatures, then who shall control? Boards of Education? It is the legislature that authorizes the election of boards and defines their duties, and boards are elected by the people or appointed by officials elected by the people. All authority goes back at last to the people; they are the final source of authority.

Some have suggested that the scientists should decide what shall be taught. How many scientists are there? . . . The American Society for the Advancement of Science has about eleven thousand members. . . . [That] makes about one scientist for every ten thousand people — a pretty little oligarchy to put in control of the education of all the children. . . .

The fourth source suggested is the teacher. Some say, let the teacher be supreme and teach anything that seems best to him. The proposition needs only to be stated to be rejected as absurd. The teacher is an employee and receives a salary; employees take directions from their employers. . . . [A] teacher must respect the wishes of his employers on all subjects upon which the employers have a deep-seated conviction. . . .

The Tennessee case is represented by some as an attempt to stifle freedom of conscience and freedom of speech, but the charge is seen to be absurd when the case is analyzed. Professor Scopes, the defendant in the Tennessee case, has a right to think as he pleases — the law does not attempt to regulate his thinking. . . .

Professor Scopes was not arrested for doing anything as an individual. He was arrested for violating a law as a representative of the state and as an employee in a school. . . . The right of free speech cannot be stretched as far as Professor Scopes is trying to stretch it. A man cannot demand a salary for saying what his employers do not want said.

SOURCE: Jeffrey P. Moran, *The Scopes Trial: A Brief History with Documents* (Boston: Bedford/St. Martins, 2002), 211–212, 192–194, 189–191.

ANALYZING THE EVIDENCE

▶ Was the Tennessee battle really a conflict between modern urban values and traditional rural beliefs?

▶ Are there any limits to legislative power? What constitutional provisions might restrict political censorship or the suppression of scientific knowledge?

▶ Does the prescribed teaching of the Christian Bible violate the First Amendment to the Constitution, which forbids the "establishment" of religion?

▶ Is there an inherent conflict between a democratic polity and freedom of intellectual and scientific inquiry?

▶ In recent years, the Japanese government has censored textbooks to exclude information about the "rape of Nanking" in the 1930s (see Chapter 25). How might that controversy be used in debates over the Scopes trial?

SUMMARY

By the 1920s the United States was on its way to becoming a modern, urban society based on corporate business enterprises and mass consumption. As we have seen, the Republican Party controlled the national government and fostered a close partnership between business and government. At home, Secretary of Commerce Herbert Hoover promoted industry-wide trade associations to coordinate economic policy; abroad, American diplomats encouraged economic expansion while avoiding direct involvement in international politics.

We also explored the ways in which movies, radio, and other mass media encouraged the development of a national culture. This emergent culture placed a new emphasis on leisure, consumption, and amusement. However, only a minority of Americans could take full advantage of the comfortable, even elegant, lifestyles promoted by the new advertising industry. Families needed a middle-class income to buy all of the conveniences of modern life: cars, radios, vacuum cleaners, and toasters. Most farmers were left outside the charmed circle of prosperity, as were most African Americans and many working-class immigrants from Europe and Mexico.

Not everyone welcomed the new secular values of the 1920s. Cultural disputes over drinking alcoholic beverages, teaching science, and forming immigration policies spilled over into politics, bringing the new Ku Klux Klan to prominence and disrupting the already fractured Democratic Party. Republican political ascendancy continued under President Herbert Hoover, who expected to extend the prosperity of the Twenties and lessen poverty.

Instead, Hoover had to deal with the worst depression in American history. As we have seen, the Great Depression had many causes: speculation in stocks, long-term weaknesses in major industries, and fragile international finances. When Hoover's policies proved unavailing, voters turned to Democrat Franklin D. Roosevelt. The new president entered office faced with massive unemployment, a banking crisis, and a citizenry on the verge of despair.

Connections: Society

As we noted in the essay that began Part Five (p. 671), two central themes of the years between 1914 and 1945 are the migration of people within the United States and the expression of intolerance against immigrants and racial minorities. Both of these themes were clearly apparent in Chapter 22. There we described the migration during World War I of African Americans from the rural South to urban jobs in the North and the postwar race riots that shook Chicago, East St. Louis, and other cities. That chapter also detailed wartime attacks and prejudice directed against American citizens of German ancestry. As we have just seen in Chapter 23, nativist sentiment reached a peak in the mid-1920s in the "new" Ku Klux Klan, which conducted a campaign of intimidation against Catholics and Jews as well as blacks. This sentiment also prompted the passage of new immigration legislation, which limited entry into the United States to residents of the Western Hemisphere. Chapter 24 will continue that story by explaining how the Great Depression of the 1930s prompted the "reverse" migration of people back to Mexico, Asia, and Europe. It will also discuss the movement of hundreds of thousands of farmers from the "dust bowl" states of the Great Plains to California and explain how New Deal agricultural programs prompted a new migration of African Americans from the rural South. Finally, in Chapter 25, we will see that in World War II, as in World War I, internal migration and wartime passions triggered race riots and, in an extreme example of racial prejudice, the internment of more than 100,000 Japanese Americans.

CHAPTER REVIEW QUESTIONS

▶ What were the main cultural conflicts of the 1920s? Are they the same or different from the "culture wars" of the present?

▶ This chapter is titled "Modern Times." What was especially "modern" about the 1920s that made the decade stand out from previous years?

▶ Describe the continuing process of state building in the 1920s. In what ways did the government become more or less active in society, the economy, and American culture?

▶ What problems in the American economy were exposed by the crisis of the Great Depression? To what extent did those economic problems reflect social problems, especially social inequality?

TIMELINE

1920	Eighteenth Amendment outlaws alcoholic beverages
	First commercial radio broadcast
	Warren G. Harding elected president
	Census reveals shift in population from farms to cities
1920–1921	Economic recession cuts jobs
1921	Sheppard-Towner Act assists maternal care
	Washington Conference supports naval disarmament
1922–1929	Record economic growth expands consumption
	Automobile Age begins
1922	T. S. Eliot, *The Waste Land*
1923	President Harding dies in office; succeeded by Calvin Coolidge
	Time magazine founded
1924	Dawes Plan reduces German reparation payments
	Teapot Dome scandal
	U.S. troops withdrawn from Dominican Republic
	National Origins Act limits immigration
1925	F. Scott Fitzgerald, *The Great Gatsby*
	Height of Ku Klux Klan's power
	Scopes trial over free speech and the teaching of science
1927	First "talkies" in movie industry
	Charles Lindbergh's solo flight
1928	Herbert Hoover elected president
	Kellogg-Briand Pact condemning militarism signed
1929	Ernest Hemingway, *A Farewell to Arms*
	Stock market crash
1930	Hawley-Smoot Tariff cuts imports
1931	Miners strike in Harlan County, Kentucky
1932	Reconstruction Finance Corporation created
	Bonus Army rebuffed in Washington
	Communist-led hunger marches in cities
	Farm Holiday Association dumps produce
	Franklin D. Roosevelt elected president

FOR FURTHER EXPLORATION

Lynn Dumenil, *The Modern Temper: American Culture and Society in the 1920s* (1995), offers an overview, while Loren Baritz, ed., *The Culture of the Twenties* (1970), provides a collection of documents. For politics and the state, consult Ellis W. Hawley, *The Great War and the Search for a Modern Order: A History of the American People and Their Institutions, 1917–1933* (1979), and Lee Nash, ed., *Understanding Herbert Hoover: Ten Perspectives* (1987). For fiction, see Sinclair Lewis's classics, *Main Street* (1920) and *Babbitt* (1922), and Sherwood Anderson's *Winesburg, Ohio* (1919). The Library of Congress's "Prosperity and Thrift: The Coolidge Era and the Consumer Economy, 1921–1929" at **memory.loc.gov/ammem/coolhtml/coolhome.html** contains original documents, film footage, and scholarly insights.

Harlem Renaissance authors appear in Alain Locke, ed., *The New Negro* (1925). See also the Circle Association's "Web Links to the Harlem Renaissance" at **www.math.buffalo.edu/~sww/circle/harlem-ren-sites.html**. "Marcus Garvey: Look for Me in the Whirlwind" at **www.pbs.org/wgbh/amex/garvey** contains images and materials on other African American leaders. Kevin Boyle, *Arc of Justice: A Saga of Race, Civil Rights, and Murder in the Jazz Age* (2004), and David Levering Lewis, *W. E. B. Du Bois: The Fight for Equality and the American Century 1919–1963* (2000), describe the racial tensions beneath the surface of the Roaring Twenties.

The SUNY-Binghamton's Web site, "Women and Social Movements in the United States, 1830–1930," at **womhist.binghamton.edu**, is especially rich on the 1920s. "Flapper Station" at **home.earthlink.net/~rbotti** details the youth culture of the 1920s. See also "Music of the Roaring Twenties" at **www.authentichistory.com/audio/1920s/1920smusic01.html**. For an exhaustive history of jazz from 1880 to 1930, see "Jazz Roots" at **www.jass.com** and "The Red Hot Jazz Archive: A History of Jazz Before 1930" at **www.redhotjazz.com**. "Ad Access" at **scriptorium.lib.duke.edu/adaccess** contains images of a wide variety of U.S. advertisements between 1911 and 1955. To gain insight into America's first media superstar, see "Charles Lindbergh: An American Aviator" at **www.charleslindbergh.com**. The conflict over creationism and evolution during the 1920s is detailed in "Tennessee vs. John Scopes: The 'Monkey Trial'" at **www.law.umkc.edu/faculty/projects/ftrials/scopes/scopes.htm**.

See the Web site accompanying "The Crash of 1929," an American Experience production for PBS, at **www.pbs.org/wgbh/amex/crash**.

TEST YOUR KNOWLEDGE

To assess your command of the material in this chapter, see the Online Study Guide at **bedfordstmartins.com/henretta**.

For Web sites, images, and documents related to topics and places in this chapter, visit **bedfordstmartins.com/makehistory**.

RADIO

RURAL ELECTRIFICATION ADMINISTRATION

24 Redefining Liberalism: The New Deal

1933–1939

"WHAT IS GOING TO BECOME OF US?" asked an Arizona man. "You can't sleep, you know. You wake up at 2 A.M. and you lie and think." Many Americans went sleepless in 1933, as the nation entered the fourth year of the worst economic contraction in its history. Times were hard — very hard — and there was no end in sight.

In his inaugural address in March 1933, President Franklin Delano Roosevelt tried to dispel the gloom and despondency that gripped the nation. "The only thing we have to fear is fear itself," Roosevelt declared. His demeanor grim and purposeful, Roosevelt issued a ringing call "for action, and action now," and promised strong presidential leadership. He would ask Congress for "broad Executive power to wage a war against the emergency, as great as the power that would be given to me if we were in fact invaded by a foreign foe." With these words, Roosevelt launched a program of federal activism — which he called the *New Deal* — that would change the nature of American government.

The New Deal represented a new form of liberalism, the ideology of individual rights that had long shaped the character of American society and politics. To protect those rights, "classical" nineteenth-century liberals had sought to keep governments small and relatively powerless. Their successors, the "regulatory" liberals of the Progressive era, had

The New Deal Takes Over, 1933–1935
Roosevelt's Leadership
The Hundred Days
The New Deal under Attack

The Second New Deal, 1935–1938
Legislative Accomplishments
The 1936 Election
Stalemate

The New Deal's Impact on Society
The Rise of Labor
Women and Blacks in the New Deal
Migrants and Minorities in the West
A New Deal for the Environment
The New Deal and the Arts
The Legacies of the New Deal

Summary
Connections: Economy

◀ **New Deal Art**

The Rural Electrification Administration used this poster, designed by Lester Beall in 1937, to celebrate the power of radio and to encourage farmers to form cooperatives to bring electric power to their localities. The radio gave rural folk immediate access to news of farm prices and world events, soap operas, and advertising — making them part of modern American life.
The Wolfsonian-Florida International University, Miami Beach, Florida, The Mitchell Wolfson, Jr. Collection.

safeguarded the liberty of individuals by bolstering the authority of the state and federal governments to oversee and, if necessary, to control large business corporations. The New Deal activists went much further — their **"social welfare" liberalism** expanded individual rights. Beginning in the 1930s and continuing until the 1970s, they increased the amount and scope of national legislation; created an increasingly centralized federal administrative system; and instituted new programs, such as Social Security, that gave the national government responsibility for the welfare of every American citizen. Their efforts did not go unchallenged. Critics of the New Deal charged that its program of "big government" and "social welfare" directly repudiated traditional **classical liberal** principles and, beginning with the "Reagan Revolution" of the 1980s, would seek to undo many of its programs.

The New Deal Takes Over, 1933–1935

The Great Depression destroyed Herbert Hoover's political reputation and boosted that of Franklin Delano Roosevelt. Although some Americans, especially wealthy conservatives, hated the new Democratic president, he was immensely popular; millions called him by his initials — FDR — which became his nickname. Ironically, the ideological differences between Hoover and Roosevelt were not vast. Both were committed to maintaining the nation's basic social and institutional structures. Both believed in the morality of a balanced budget and extolled the values of hard work, cooperation, and sacrifice. But Roosevelt's personal charm, his political savvy, and his willingness to experiment made all the difference. Above all, his New Deal programs put people to work, instilling hope for the nation's future.

Roosevelt's Leadership

Roosevelt immediately established a close rapport with the American people. More than 450,000 letters poured into the White House in the week after his inauguration, and they continued to come at a rate of 5,000 a week throughout the 1930s. Whereas one person had handled public correspondence under Hoover, a staff of fifty was required by the new administration. Roosevelt's masterful use of the new medium of radio, especially the "fireside chats" during his first two terms, bolstered his relationship with the people. Many citizens thanked him personally for their successes, saying "He gave me a job" or "He saved my home" (see Comparing American Voices, "Ordinary People Respond to the New Deal," pp. 740–741).

FDR
Franklin Delano Roosevelt was a successful politician partly because he loved to mix with a crowd. Despite Roosevelt's upper-class background, he had a knack for relating easily to those from all occupations. Although a well-dressed crowd turned out to greet him in Elm Grove, West Virginia, as he campaigned for the presidency in 1932, Roosevelt took care to be photographed shaking hands with coal miner Zeno Santanella. Courtesy of the Franklin D. Roosevelt Library.

Roosevelt's charisma allowed him to continue the expansion of presidential powers begun in the administrations of Theodore Roosevelt and Woodrow Wilson. He dramatically enlarged the role of the executive branch in setting the budget and initiating legislation. For policy formulation, he relied heavily on his "Brain Trust" of professors from Columbia and Harvard universities: Raymond Moley, Rexford Tugwell, Adolph A. Berle, and Felix Frankfurter. He turned as well to his talented cabinet, which included Secretary of the Interior Harold L. Ickes, Frances Perkins at Labor, Henry A. Wallace at Agriculture, and Henry Morgenthau, Jr., the secretary of the Treasury. Financier Bernard Baruch was also influential. This array of intellectual and administrative talent attracted hundreds of highly qualified recruits to Washington. Young professors and newly trained lawyers streamed out of Ivy League law schools into the expanding federal bureaucracy, where they had a direct hand in shaping legislation. Inspired by the idealism of the New Deal, many of them would devote their lives to public service and the principles of social welfare liberalism.

The Hundred Days

Roosevelt promised "action now," and he kept his promise. The first months of his administration produced a whirlwind of activity in Congress, which was controlled by Democrats elected with Roosevelt in 1932. In a legendary legislative session, known as the "Hundred Days," Congress enacted fifteen major bills. This legislation focused primarily on four major problems—banking failures, agricultural overproduction, the business slump, and soaring unemployment.

The Emergency Banking Act. The president and Congress first addressed the banking crisis. Since the stock market crash, bank failures had cut into the savings of nearly nine million families; to prevent more failures, dozens of states had closed their banks. On March 5, the day following his inauguration, FDR declared a national "bank holiday"—a euphemism for closing all the banks—and called Congress into special session. Four days later Congress passed the Emergency Banking Act—the debate in the House took only thirty-eight minutes—which permitted banks to reopen if a Treasury Department inspection showed they had sufficient cash reserves.

The act worked because Roosevelt convinced the public that it would. In his first Sunday night fireside chat, to a radio audience estimated at 60 million, the president reassured citizens that federal scrutiny would ensure the safety of their deposits. When the banking system reopened on March 13, deposits exceeded withdrawals, restoring stability to one of the nation's prime financial institutions. "Capitalism was saved in eight days," quipped Roosevelt's advisor Raymond Moley. A second banking law of 1933, the Glass-Steagall Act, further restored public confidence; it created the Federal Deposit Insurance Corporation (FDIC), which insured deposits up to $2,500. Four thousand banks had collapsed in the months prior to Roosevelt's inauguration, but only sixty-one closed their doors in all of 1934 (Table 24.1).

The avalanche of legislation now began. Congress created the Home Owners Loan Corporation to refinance home mortgages threatened by foreclosure. It then established the Civilian Conservation Corps (CCC), which mobilized 250,000 young men to do reforestation and conservation work. Two controversial measures also won quick approval. One set up the Tennessee Valley Authority (TVA), a government-owned corporation that would produce cheap hydroelectric power and encourage economic development in the flood-prone river valley (see Map 24.3 on p. 760); critics assailed it as creeping socialism. The second act legalized the sale of beer, offending moral reformers; but full repeal of Prohibition, by constitutional amendment, was already in the works and came eight months later, in December 1933.

The Agricultural Adjustment Act. Because farmers formed more than a quarter of the workforce, Roosevelt considered effective agricultural legislation

TABLE 24.1 American Banks and Bank Failures, 1920–1940

Year	Total Number of Banks	Total Assets ($ billion)	Bank Failures
1920	30,909	53.1	168
1929	25,568	72.3	659
1931	22,242	70.1	2,294
1933	14,771	51.4	4,004
1934	15,913	55.9	61
1940	15,076	79.7	48

SOURCE: *Historical Statistics of the United States: Colonial Times to 1970* (Washington, D.C.: U.S. Government Printing Office, 1975), 1019, 1038–1039.

COMPARING AMERICAN VOICES

Ordinary People Respond to the New Deal

Franklin Roosevelt's fireside chats and his relief programs prompted thousands of ordinary Americans to write directly to the president and his wife Eleanor. Taken together, they offer a vivid portrait of depression-era America and of popular support for, and opposition to, the New Deal.

MRS. M.H.A.

Mrs. M.H.A. worked in the County Court House in Eureka, California.

June 14, 1934
Dear Mrs. Roosevelt:

I know you are overburdened with requests for help and if my plea cannot be recognized, I'll understand it is because you have so many others, all of them worthy. . . .

My husband and I are a young couple of very simple, almost poor families. We married eight years ago on the proverbial shoe-string but with a wealth of love. . . . We managed to build our home and furnish it comfortably. . . . Then came the depression. My work has continued and my salary alone has just been sufficient to make our monthly payments on the house and keep our bills paid. . . . But with the exception of two and one-half months work with the U.S. Coast and Geodetic Survey under the C.W.A. [Civil Works Administration], my husband has not had work since August, 1932.

My salary could continue to keep us going, but I am to have a baby. . . . I can get a leave of absence from my job for a year. But can't you, won't you do something so my husband can have a job, at least during that year? . . .

As I said before, if it were only ourselves, or if there were something we could do about it, we would never ask for help. We have always stood on our own feet and been proud and happy. But you are a mother and you'll understand this crisis.

Very sincerely yours,
Mrs. M. H. A.

UNSIGNED LETTER

This unsigned letter came from a factory worker in Paris, Texas.

November 23, 1936
Dear President,

[N]ow that we have had a land Slide [in the election of 1936] and done just what was best for our country . . . I do believe you Will Strain a point to help the ones who helped you mostly & that is the Working Class of People I am not smart or I would be in a different line of work & better up in ever way yet I will know you are the one & only President that ever helped a Working Class of People. . . .

I am a White Man American age, 47 married wife 2 children in high School am a Finishing room foreman I mean a Working foreman & am in a furniture Factory here in Paris Texas where thaire is 175 to 200 Working & when the NRA [National Recovery Administration] came in I was Proud to See my fellow workmen Rec 30 Per hour in Place of 8 cents to 20 cents Per hour. . . .

I can't see for my life President why a man must toil & work his life out in Such factories 10 long hours ever day except Sunday for a small sum of 15 cents to 35 cents per hour & pay the high cost of honest & deason living expences. . . .

please see if something can be done to help this one Class of Working People the factories are a man killer not venelated or kept up just a bunch of Republickins Grafters 90/100 of them Please help us some way I Pray to God for relief. I am a Christian . . . and a truthful man & have not told you wrong & am for you to the end.

[not signed]

R.A.

R.A. was 69 years old and an architect and builder in Lincoln, Nebraska.

May 19/34
Dear Mrs Roosevelt:

In the Presidents inaugural address delivered from the capitol steps the afternoon of his inauguration he made mention of The Forgotten Man, and I with thousands of others am wondering if the folk who was borned here in America some 60 or 70 years a go are this Forgotten Man, the President had in mind, if we are this Forgotten Man then we are still Forgotten.

We who have tried to be diligent in our support of this most wonderful nation of ours boath social and other wise, we in our younger days tried to do our duty without complaining. . . .

And now a great calamity has come upon us and seemingly no cause of our own it has swept away what little savings we had accumulated and we are left in a condition that is imposible for us to correct, for two very prominent reasons if no more.

First we have grown to what is termed Old Age, this befalls every man.

Second, . . . we are confronted on every hand with the young generation, taking our places, this of corse is what we have looked forward to in training our children. But with the extra ordinary crises which left us helpless and placed us in the position that our fathers did not have to contend with. . . .

We have been honorable citizens all along our journey, calamity and old age has forced its self upon us please do not send us to the Poor Farm but instead allow us the small pension of $40.00 per month. . . .

Mrs. Roosevelt I am asking a personal favor of you as it seems to be the only means through which I may be able to reach the President, some evening very soon, as you and Mr. Roosevelt are having dinner together privately will you ask him to read this. And we American citizens will ever remember your kindness.

Yours very truly.
R. A.

M.A.

M.A. was a woman who held a low-level salaried position in a corporation.

Jan. 18, 1937
[Dear Mrs. Roosevelt:]

I . . . was simply astounded to think that anyone could be nitwit enough to wish to be included in the so called social security act if they could possibly avoid it. Call it by any name you wish it, in my opinion, (and that of many people I know) is nothing but downright stealing. . . .

I am not an "economic royalist," just an ordinary white collar worker at $1600 per [year — about $21,700 in 2007]. Please show this to the president and ask him to remember the wishes of the forgotten man, that is, the one who dared to vote against him. We expect to be tramped on but we do wish the stepping would be a little less hard.

Security at the price of freedom is never desired by intelligent people.
M. A.

M.A.H.

M.A.H. was a widow who ran a small farm in Columbus, Indiana.

December 14, 1937
Mrs. Roosevelt:

I suppose from your point of view the work relief, old age pensions, slum clearance and all the rest seems like a perfect remedy for all the ills of this country, but I would like for you to see the results, as the other half see them.

We have always had a shiftless, never-do-well class of people whose one and only aim in life is to live without work. I have been rubbing elbows with this class for nearly sixty years and have tried to help some of the most promising and have seen others try to help them, but it can't be done. We cannot help those who will not try to help themselves and if they do try a square deal is all they need, . . . let each paddle their own canoe, or sink. . . .

I live alone on a farm and have not raised any crops for the last two years as there was no help to be had. I am feeding the stock and have been cutting the wood to keep my home fires burning. There are several reliefers around here now who have been kicked off relief but they refuse to work unless they can get relief hours and wages, but they are so worthless no one can afford to hire them. . . . They are just a fair sample of the class of people on whom so much of our hard earned tax money is being squandered and on whom so much sympathy is being wasted. . . .

You people who have plenty of this worlds goods and whose money comes easy have no idea of the heart-breaking toil and self-denial which is the lot of the working people who are trying to make an honest living, and then to have to shoulder all these unjust burdens seems like the last straw. . . . No one should have the right to vote theirself a living at the expense of the tax payers.
M. A. H.

SOURCES (IN ORDER): Robert S. McElvaine, *Down and Out in the Great Depression* (Chapel Hill: University of North Carolina Press, 1983), 54–55; Michael P. Johnson, ed., *Reading the American Past*, 3rd ed., 2 vols. (Boston: Bedford/St. Martin's, 2005), 2: 166–167; Robert D. Marcus and David Burner, eds., *America Firsthand*, 7th ed. (Boston: Bedford/St. Martin's, 2007), 184, 182–184.

ANALYZING THE EVIDENCE

- How do you explain the personal, almost intimate, tone of these letters to the Roosevelts?
- How have specific New Deal programs helped or hurt the authors of these letters?
- What are the basic values of the authors? Do they differ between those who support and oppose the New Deal?

"the key to recovery." The federal government had long assisted farmers: through cheap prices for land, the extension services of the Department of Agriculture, and the Federal Farm Loan Act of 1916. But the Agricultural Adjustment Act (AAA), a measure jointly developed by administration officials and major farm organizations, represented a new level of government involvement in the farm economy. To solve the problem of overproduction, which resulted in low prices for farm crops, the AAA set up an allotment system for seven major commodities (wheat, cotton, corn, hogs, rice, tobacco, and dairy products). The act provided cash subsidies to farmers who cut their production of these crops; to pay these subsidies, the act imposed a tax on the processors of these commodities, which they in turn passed on to consumers. New Deal policymakers hoped that farm prices would rise as production (and supply) fell, spurring consumer purchases by farmers and assisting a general economic recovery.

By dumping cash in farmers' hands (a special-interest policy that continues to this day), the AAA stabilized the farm economy. But the act's benefits were not evenly distributed. Subsidies went primarily to the owners of large- and medium-sized farms, who often cut production by reducing the amount of land they rented to tenants and sharecroppers. In the South, where many sharecroppers were black and the landowners and government administrators were white, such practices forced 200,000 black families off the land. Some black farmers tried to protect themselves by joining the Southern Tenant Farmers Union (STFU), a biracial organization founded in 1934. "The same chain that holds you hold my people, too," an elderly black farmer reminded his white colleagues. But landowners had such economic power and such support from local politicians and sheriffs that the STFU could do little. Dispossessed of access to land and denied government aid, hundreds of thousands of black sharecroppers and white smallholders moved to the cities.

The National Recovery Act. The New Deal's initial response to depressed levels of business activity was the National Industrial Recovery Act. The act drew on the regulatory approaches of Bernard Baruch's War Industries Board during World War I and Herbert Hoover's trade associations of the 1920s. It also reflected "corporatist" theories of a government-planned economy popular in Europe and implemented in Italy by Benito Mussolini. The government agency charged with implementing the act, the National Recovery Administration (NRA), established a system of self-government in more than six hundred industries. Each industry — ranging from large businesses such as coal, cotton, and steel to small ones such as dog food and costume jewelry — regulated itself by hammering out a government-approved code of prices and production quotas, similar to those for farm products. These agreements had the force of law and covered workers as well as employers. The codes outlawed child labor and set minimum wages and maximum hours for adult workers. One of the most far-reaching provisions, Section 7(a), guaranteed workers the right to organize and bargain collectively "through representatives of their own choosing." This right to union representation was an important spur to the growth of the labor movement in the 1930s.

In many instances the trade associations set by Hoover in the 1920s, which were controlled by large companies, dominated the code-drafting process. As a result, the NRA solidified the power of large businesses at the expense of smaller enterprises, labor unions, and consumer interests. To sell the program to skeptical consumers and businesspeople, the NRA launched an extensive public relations campaign, complete with plugs in Hollywood films and "Blue Eagle" stickers with the NRA slogan, "We Do Our Part."

Unemployment Legislation. The early New Deal also addressed the critical problem of unemployment and impoverished working families. By 1933, local governments and private charities had exhausted their resources and looked to Washington for assistance. Roosevelt responded reluctantly because he feared a budget deficit. Nonetheless, he asked Congress to fund relief for millions of unemployed Americans. In May, Congress established the Federal Emergency Relief Administration (FERA). Directed by Harry Hopkins, a hard-driving social worker from New York, the FERA provided federal funds to the states for relief programs. In his first two hours in office, Hopkins distributed $5 million. Over the program's two-year existence, FERA spent $1 billion.

Roosevelt and his advisors had strong reservations against the "dole," the popular name for these government welfare payments. As Hopkins worried, "I don't think anybody can go year after year, month after month, accepting relief without affecting his character.... It is probably going to undermine the independence of hundreds of thousands of families." To maintain a commitment to individual initiative, the New Deal tried to put people to work. Early in 1933, Congress appropriated $3.3 billion

Selling the NRA in Chinatown

To mobilize support for its program, the National Recovery Administration (NRA) distributed millions of posters to businesses and families, urging them to display the "Blue Eagle" in shops, factories, and homes. Here Constance King and Mae Chinn of the Chinese Y.M.C.A. affix a poster (and a Chinese translation) to a shop in San Francisco that is complying with the NRA codes. Copyright Bettmann / Corbis.

for the Public Works Administration (PWA), a construction program directed by Secretary of the Interior Harold L. Ickes. However, Ickes's cautious approach to approving public works projects limited the agency's effectiveness in providing jobs or spurring recovery. So in November 1933 Roosevelt established the Civil Works Administration (CWA), named Harry Hopkins as its head, and gave it $400 million in PWA funds. Within thirty days, Hopkins had put 2.6 million men and women to work; at its peak in January 1934, the CWA funded the employment of 4 million Americans in public works' projects: repairing bridges, building highways, constructing public buildings, and setting up community projects. The CWA, a stopgap measure to get the country through the winter of 1933–1934, lapsed the next spring after spending all its funds.

When an exhausted Congress recessed in June 1933, it had accomplished much: banking reform, recovery programs for agriculture and industry, unemployment relief, and a host of other measures. Few presidents had so dominated a legislative session and won the passage of so many measures (the only future president to do so would be Lyndon Baines Johnson in 1965; see Chapter 28). A mass of "alphabet" agencies (the CCC, CWA, FERA, AAA, NRA), as the New Deal programs came to be known, began to flow from Washington. But if the avalanche of new laws and programs halted the downward psychological spiral of the Hoover years, they had yet to break the grip of the depression.

Financial Reform. As Roosevelt waited anxiously for the economy to revive, he turned his attention to the reform of Wall Street, where insider trading, fraud, and reckless speculation had triggered the financial panic of 1929. In 1934, Congress established the Securities and Exchange Commission (SEC) to regulate the stock market. The commission had broad powers to regulate companies that issued stock and bonds to the public, set rules for margin (credit) transactions, and prevent stock sales by those with inside information on corporate plans. The Banking Act of 1935 authorized the president to appoint a new Board of Governors of the Federal Reserve System, placing control of interest rates and other money-market policies at the federal level rather than with regional banks.

The New Deal under Attack

As Congress and the president consolidated the New Deal, their work came under attack from many quarters. Roosevelt saw himself as the savior of the American system of democratic capitalism, declaring simply: "To preserve we had to reform." Many bankers and business executives disagreed. To them, FDR became "That Man," a traitor to his class. In 1934, Republican business leaders joined with conservative Democrats in a "Liberty League" that lobbied against the "reckless spending" and "socialist" reforms of the New Deal. Reflecting their outlook, Herbert Hoover condemned the NRA as a "state-controlled or state-directed social or economic system"; and that, the former president declared, is "tyranny, not liberalism."

The Supreme Court likewise repudiated many New Deal measures. In May 1935, the Court unanimously ruled that the National Industrial Recovery Act represented an unconstitutional delegation of Congress's legislative power to a code-writing agency in the executive branch of the government. The case, *Schechter v. United States,* arose when a firm in Brooklyn, New York, sold diseased chickens to local storekeepers in violation of NRA codes. In addition to the delegation issue, the Court declared that the NRA unconstitutionally extended federal authority to *intrastate* (as opposed to *interstate*) commerce. Roosevelt publicly protested that the Court's narrow interpretation would return the Constitution "to the horse-and-buggy definition of interstate commerce," but he could only watch helplessly as the Court also struck down a raft of New Deal legislation in 1935: the Agricultural Adjustment Act, a Railroad Retirement Act, and the Frazier-Lemke debt relief act.

Challenges from the Left. If business executives and the Supreme Court thought the New Deal had gone too far, other Americans believed it had not gone far enough. Francis Townsend, a Long Beach, California, doctor, spoke for the nation's elderly, most of whom had no pension plans and feared poverty in their old age. In 1933 Townsend proposed the Old Age Revolving Pension Plan, which would give $200 a month (about $3,000 today) to citizens over the age of sixty. To receive payments the elderly would have to retire from their jobs, thus opening their positions to younger workers, and agree to spend the money within a month. Townsend Clubs soon sprang up across the country, particularly in the Far West. These clubs mobilized mass support for old-age pensions and helped win passage of the far less ambitious Social Security Act of 1935 (see p. 746).

Father Charles Coughlin also challenged Roosevelt's leadership and attracted a large following, especially in the Midwest. A priest in a Catholic parish in Detroit, Coughlin had turned to the radio in the mid-1920s to enlarge his pastorate. By 1933, about forty million Americans listened regularly to the Radio Priest's broadcasts. Coughlin initially supported the New Deal but turned against it when Roosevelt refused to nationalize the banking system and expand the money supply. To promote these programs, which resembled the proposals of the Populist Party of the 1890s (see Chapter 19), Coughlin organized the National Union for Social Justice and continued to attack the administration's policies.

The most direct political threat to Roosevelt came from Senator Huey Long. As the Democratic governor of Louisiana, the flamboyant Long had achieved stunning popularity by lowering utility bills, increasing taxes on corporations, and building new highways, bridges, hospitals, and schools. Long's accomplishments came at a price: To push through these measures, he had seized almost dictatorial control of the state government. In 1934, Long broke with the New Deal and, like Townsend and Coughlin, established a national movement. His "Share Our Wealth Society," which boasted over four million followers, argued that the depression did not stem from overproduction but from underconsumption. The unequal distribution of wealth prevented ordinary families from buying goods and stimulating economic activity. To put money in the hands of millions of consumers, the Society advocated a tax of 100 percent of all income over $1 million and all inheritances over $5 million. Long hoped that this program would carry him into the White House.

Although somewhat simplistic, the economic proposals offered by Townsend, Coughlin, and Long were no more radical than the NIRA or the AAA. Like the New Deal measures, they were plausible responses to the depression; in fact, some of them were subsequently endorsed by social welfare liberals. It was the constitutional views of Coughlin and Long that separated them from most politically engaged Americans: Neither man had much respect for representative government. "I'm the Constitution around here," Long declared during his governorship, while Coughlin suggested that dictatorial rule might be necessary to preserve democracy. Voters seemed not to mind. As their policies won increasing popularity, Roosevelt and his advisors feared that Long might join forces with Coughlin and Townsend to form a third party that would appeal to many Democratic voters. This prospect encouraged Republicans, who hoped that a split among between New Dealers and other reformers might return their party, and its ideology of small government and free enterprise, to political power in the 1936 election.

The Kingfish

Huey Long, the Louisiana governor and senator, called himself "the Kingfish" because, he said, "I'm a small fish here in Washington. But I'm the Kingfish to the folks down in Louisiana." An exceptionally charismatic man and a brilliant campaigner, he attracted a significant following with his "Share Our Wealth" plan, which aimed to redistribute the nation's wealth. Democrats worried that he might run for president in 1936 on a third-party ticket, threatening Franklin Roosevelt's reelection. But in September 1935 Long was killed (apparently by his bodyguard) during an assassination attempt by a young doctor over a Louisiana political dispute. Long is seen here shaking hands with a Louisiana supporter.
Louisiana State Museum.

"Big Steel" executives capitulated without a fight in March 1937 and recognized the Steel Workers Organizing Committee (SWOC). Another group of companies, "Little Steel," refused to negotiate, sparking a protest at the Republic Steel Corporation in Chicago that took the lives of ten strikers; only in 1941 did workers in Little Steel win union recognition.

The 1930s constituted one of the most active periods of labor solidarity in American history (Map 24.1). The sit-down tactic spread rapidly and reached a high point in March 1937, when a total of 167,210 workers staged 170 sit-down strikes. Labor unions called nearly 5,000 strikes that year and won favorable terms in 80 percent of them. Large numbers of middle-class Americans opposed the sit-down tactics, which they considered a violation of private property. In 1939, the Supreme Court accepted this argument and upheld a law that banned the sit-down tactic.

The CIO welcomed new groups to the labor movement. Unlike the AFL, which had long excluded or segregated African American workers, the CIO actively organized blacks in the steel and meatpacking industries. In California, its organizers set out to win equal pay for Mexican American women who worked in the canning industry. Corporate giants such as Del Monte, McNeill, and Libby paid women around $2.50 a day, while their male counterparts received $3.50 to $4.50. These differentials shrank following the formation in 1939 of the United Cannery, Agricultural, Packing, and Allied Workers, an unusually democratic union in which women played leading roles. Altogether, some 800,000 women workers joined CIO unions.

Labor's new vitality spilled over into political action. The AFL generally had stood aloof from partisan politics, but the CIO quickly allied itself with the Democratic Party, hoping to persuade the Party to nominate candidates sympathetic to labor. The CIO gave $770,000 (about $12 million today) to Democratic campaigns in 1936, and its Political Action Committee became a major Democratic contributor during the 1940s.

Despite its successes during the 1930s, the labor movement did not develop into a dominant force in American life. Roosevelt never made the growth of the labor movement a high priority, and many workers remained suspicious of unionization, especially as New Deal programs provided unemployment assistance and pension benefits. And while the Wagner Act helped unions to achieve better working conditions for their members, it did not redistribute power in American industry. Managers retained authority over most corporate affairs. In fact, business executives found that unions could be used as a buffer against rank-and-file militancy; likewise, National Labor Relation Board officials, concerned about rising consumer prices, pressed unions to moderate their demands for higher wages and benefits. The road to union power, even with New Deal protection, continued to be a rocky and uncertain one.

Organize

The Steel Workers Organizing Committee was one of the most vital labor organizations contributing to the rise of the CIO during the late 1930s. Note that artist Ben Shahn chose a man who might be of either European or African ancestry to represent the steel workers, part of a conscious effort to build a labor movement across racial and ethnic lines. This iconography also reinforced the notion that the typical worker was male, despite the large number of women who joined the CIO. Library of Congress.

Women and Blacks in the New Deal

Although the New Deal did not directly challenge gender inequities and racial injustice, its programs generally enhanced the welfare of women and African Americans.

Women in Government. Women won the vote in 1920, but only with the New Deal did they enter the higher ranks of government in significant numbers.

MAP 24.1 Popular Protest in the Great Depression, 1933–1939

The depression forced Americans to look closely at their society, and many of them did not like what they saw. Some citizens expressed their discontent through popular movements, and this map suggests the geography of discontent. The industrial Midwest witnessed union movements, strikes, and Radio Priest Charles Coughlin's demands for social reform. Simultaneously, farmers' movements — tenants in the South, smallholders in the agricultural Midwest — engaged in strikes and dumping campaigns, and rallied behind the ideas of progressives in Wisconsin and Huey Long in the South. Protests took diverse forms in California, which was home to strikes by farmworkers, women, and — in San Francisco — all wage workers. The West was also the seedbed of two important reform proposals: Upton Sinclair's "End Poverty in California" movement and Francis Townsend's "Old Age Revolving Pension" clubs.

Frances Perkins, the first woman named to a cabinet post, served as secretary of labor throughout Roosevelt's presidency. Molly Dewson, a social reformer turned politician, headed the Women's Division of the Democratic National Committee, where she pushed an issue-oriented program that supported New Deal reforms. Roosevelt's women appointees also included the first female director of the mint, the head of a major WPA division, and a judge on a circuit court of appeals. Many of those women were close friends as well as professional colleagues and cooperated in an informal network to advance feminist and reform causes.

Eleanor Roosevelt exemplified the growing prominence of women in public life. In the 1920s she had worked closely with other reformers to expand positions for women in political parties, labor unions, and education. During her years in the

A First Lady without Precedent

Reflecting Eleanor Roosevelt's tendency to turn up in odd places, a famous 1933 *New Yorker* cartoon has one coal miner saying to another, "For gosh sakes, here comes Mrs. Roosevelt." Life soon imitated art. In this photograph from 1935, the first lady emerges from a coal mine in Dellaire, Ohio, still carrying her miner's cap in her left hand and talking to mine supervisor Joseph Bainbridge. Wide World Photos, Inc.

White House, Mrs. Roosevelt emerged as an independent and influential public figure. She held press conferences for women journalists, wrote a popular syndicated news column called "My Day," and traveled extensively throughout the country. By descending deep into coal mines to view working conditions and meeting with African American antilynching advocates, she became the conscience of the New Deal, pushing her pragmatically minded husband to do more for the disadvantaged. "I sometimes acted as a spur," Mrs. Roosevelt later reflected, "even though the spurring was not always wanted or welcome." And she knew the limits of her power with the president: "I was one of those who served his purposes."

Without the vocal support of Eleanor Roosevelt, Frances Perkins, and other prominent women, New Deal policymakers might have completely overlooked the needs of women. Despite their efforts, a fourth of the NRA codes set a lower minimum wage for women than for men performing the same jobs; only 7 percent of the workers in the Civil Works Administration were female; and the Civilian Conservation Corps excluded women entirely. Women fared better under the Works Progress Administration; at its peak, 405,000 women were on the job rolls. Still, most policymakers and most Americans viewed the depression primarily as a crisis for male breadwinners and gave priority to their needs. When asked in a 1936 Gallup poll whether wives should work when their husbands had jobs, 82 percent of those interviewed said no. Reflecting such sentiments, many state legislatures enacted laws that prohibited married women from working. Not until the 1970s would women's quest for equal rights begin to be addressed.

Blacks Join the New Deal Coalition. Especially in the South, African Americans remained in the lowest paying jobs and faced harsh social and political discrimination. In a celebrated 1931 case in

Scottsboro, Alabama, nine young black men were accused of rape by two white women who had been riding a freight train. The women's stories contained many inconsistencies, but in interracial matters a southern white woman was usually taken at her word. Within two weeks, a white jury convicted all nine defendants of rape; eight received the death sentence. After the U.S. Supreme Court overturned the sentences on grounds that the defendants had been denied adequate legal counsel, five of the men were again convicted and sentenced to long prison terms. The Scottsboro case received wide coverage in black communities across the country, as did the rise in the number of lynchings; white mobs lynched twenty blacks in 1930 and twenty-four in 1934.

This violence, and the dispossession of sharecroppers by the AAA, prompted a renewal of the "Great Migration" of African Americans to the cities of the North and Midwest. One destination was Harlem, where housing was already at a premium because of the black influx during the 1920s. Because residential segregation kept African Americans from moving to many sections of New York, they had to pay high rents to live in crowded and deteriorating buildings. Jobs were scarce. White-owned stores in Harlem would not employ blacks; elsewhere in New York City hard-pressed whites took over the menial jobs traditionally held by blacks — as waiters, domestic servants, elevator operators, and garbage collectors. Unemployment in Harlem rose to 50 percent, twice the national rate. These conditions triggered a major race riot in March 1935 as blacks went on a rampage. Before order was restored, four rioters were killed and millions of dollars in property was destroyed.

For the majority of white Americans, the events in Scottsboro and Harlem reinforced their beliefs that blacks were a "dangerous class." Consequently, there was little support for federal intervention to secure the civil rights of African Americans. In fact, many New Deal programs reflected prevailing racist attitudes. CCC camps segregated blacks and whites, and many NRA codes did not protect black

Scottsboro Defendants

The 1931 trial in Scottsboro, Alabama, of nine black youths accused of raping two white women became a symbol of the injustices African Americans faced in the South's legal system. Denied access to an attorney, the defendants were found guilty, and eight were sentenced to death. When the U.S. Supreme Court overturned their convictions in 1932, the International Labor Defense organization hired the noted criminal attorney, Samuel Leibowitz, who eventually won the acquittal of four defendants and jail sentences for the rest. This photograph, taken in a Decatur jail, shows Leibowitz conferring with Haywood Patterson, in front of the other eight defendants. Brown Brothers.

Mary McLeod Bethune

This 1943 painting by Betsy Graves Reyneau captures the strength and dignity of one of the twentieth century's most important African Americans. Behind Bethune is a picture of the first building at the Daytona Literary and Industrial School for Training of Negro Girls, which later became Bethune-Cookman College. National Portrait Gallery, Smithsonian Institution / Art Resource, NY.

workers from discrimination. Most tellingly, Franklin Roosevelt repeatedly refused to support legislation to make lynching a federal crime, arguing it would antagonize southern Democrats whose support he needed to pass New Deal measures.

Nevertheless, blacks received significant benefits from New Deal relief programs directed toward poor Americans. Reflecting their poverty, African Americans made up about 18 percent of the WPA's recipients, although they constituted only 10 percent of the population. The Resettlement Administration, established in 1935 to help small farmers and tenants buy land, fought for the rights of black tenant farmers until angry southerners in Congress drastically cut its appropriations. Such help from New Deal agencies, and a belief that the White House—or at least Eleanor Roosevelt—cared about their plight, caused blacks to change their political allegiance. Since the Civil War, African Americans had staunchly supported the party of Abraham Lincoln, the Great Emancipator; even in the dark depression year of 1932, black voters in northern cities overwhelmingly supported Republican candidates. But in 1936 black Americans outside the South (where few blacks were allowed to vote) gave Roosevelt 71 percent of their votes. In Harlem, where state and federal relief dollars increased dramatically in the wake of the 1935 riot, African American support for the president was an extraordinary 81 percent. Black voters have remained strongly Democratic ever since.

Mary McLeod Bethune: Black New Dealer.

African Americans supported the New Deal in part because the Roosevelt administration appointed many blacks to federal office. Among the most important of these was Mary McLeod Bethune. Born in 1875 in South Carolina, Bethune was the child of former slaves who founded a school that eventually became the prestigious Bethune-Cookman College. Becoming an educator herself, Bethune served during the 1920s as president of the National Association of Colored Women (NACW)—a leading black women's organization. In 1935 she organized the National Council of Negro Women (NCNW), a coalition of the major associations of black women.

Bethune joined the New Deal in 1935, serving first as a member of the advisory committee of the National Youth Administration and then as director of the NYA's Division of Negro Affairs. In that position she emerged as the leader of the Federal Council of Negro Affairs, a group of black administrators who met on Sunday nights at her home in Washington. Along with NAACP general secretary Walter White, she had access to the White House and pushed continually, though often without success, for New Deal programs that would directly assist African Americans.

The Indian Reorganization Act.

The New Deal had a greater direct impact on Native Americans. Indian peoples had long made up one of the nation's most disadvantaged and powerless minorities. Their average annual income in 1934 was only $48, and their unemployment rate was three times the national average. The plight of Native Americans won the attention of Secretary of the Interior Harold Ickes and Commissioner of the Bureau of Indian Affairs John Collier. They pushed for an Indian Section of the Civilian Conservation Corps and earmarked FERA and CWA work relief projects for Indian reservations.

More ambitious was the Indian Reorganization Act of 1934, sometimes called the "Indian New Deal." That law reversed the Dawes Act of 1887 by promoting Indian self-government through formal constitutions and democratically elected tribal

A Bitter Harvest

In the early 1930s California was rocked by strikes, and one of the largest was the cotton pickers' strike of 1933. Demanding higher wages and better working conditions, the predominantly Mexican American workforce set up camps for the duration of the strike. While the men stood on the picket line, their wives and daughters took care of the cooking, cleaning, and child care. Bancroft Library, University of California, Berkeley.

councils. A majority of Indian peoples—some 174—accepted the reorganization policy, but 78 refused to participate, primarily because they preferred traditional consensus-seeking methods of making decisions. New Deal administrators accepted their decision. Influenced by academic anthropologists, who celebrated the unique character of native cultures, government officials no long attempted to assimilate Native Americans into mainstream society. Instead, they embraced a policy of **cultural pluralism** and pledged to preserve Indian languages, arts, and traditions.

Migrants and Minorities in the West

Over the course of the late nineteenth and twentieth centuries, the American West—and especially California—grew dramatically in population and wealth (see Chapter 16). During the 1920s and 1930s, agriculture in California became a big business—large scale, intensive, and diversified. Corporate-owned farms produced specialty crops—lettuce, tomatoes, peaches, grapes, and cotton—whose staggered harvests required lots of transient labor during picking seasons. Thousands of workers, initially migrants from Mexico and Asia and later from the midwestern states, trooped from farm to farm harvesting those crops for shipment to eastern markets. Some of these migrants also settled in the rapidly growing cities along the West Coast, especially the sprawling metropolis of Los Angeles. Until the Great Depression, many foreign migrants viewed California as the promised land.

Mexicans and Asians. The economic downturn brought dramatic changes to the lives of thousands of Mexican Americans. The 1930 census reported 617,000 Mexican Americans; by 1940 the number had dropped to 377,000. A formal deportation

A New Deal for Indians

John Collier, the New Deal's commissioner for Indian affairs, was a former social worker who had become interested in Native American tribal cultures in the 1920s. A longtime opponent of the assimilationist policies of the Dawes Act of 1887, Collier led successful efforts to provide Native American peoples with communally controlled lands and self-government. Here, Collier speaks with Chief Richard of the Blackfoot Nation, one of the Indian leaders attending the Four Nation celebration at historic Old Fort Niagara, New York, in 1934. Corbis-Bettmann.

MAP 24.2 The Dust Bowl and Federal Building Projects in the West, 1930–1941

A U.S. Weather Bureau scientist called the drought of the 1930s "the worst in the climatological history of the country." Conditions were especially severe in the southern plains, where farming on marginal land threatened the environment even before the drought struck. As farm families migrated west on U.S. Route 66, the federal government began a series of massive building projects that provided flood control, irrigation, electric power, and transportation facilities to residents of the states of the Far West.

policy for illegal immigrants instituted by the Hoover administration was partly responsible for the decline in numbers, but even more Mexicans left voluntarily in the first years of the depression. Working as migrant laborers, they knew that local officials would ship them back to Mexico rather than support them on relief during the winter.

Under the New Deal, the situation of Mexican Americans improved. Those migrants living in Los Angeles, El Paso, and other cities qualified for relief more easily, and there was more relief to go around. New Deal initiatives supporting labor unions indirectly encouraged the acculturation of Mexican immigrants; joining the CIO was an important stage in becoming Americans for many Mexicans. Other immigrants heeded the call of the Democratic Party to join the New Deal coalition. Los Angeles activist Beatrice Griffith noted, "Franklin D. Roosevelt's name was the spark that started thousands of Spanish-speaking persons to the polls."

The farm union organizer César Chavez grew up in such a family. In 1934, when Chavez was ten, his father lost his farm near Yuma, Arizona, and the family became part of the migrant workforce in California. They experienced continual discrimination, even in restaurants where signs proclaimed "White Trade Only." César's father joined several bitter strikes in the Imperial Valley, part of a wave of job actions across the state. All of the strikes failed, including one in the San Joaquin Valley that mobilized 18,000 cotton pickers. But these strikes set the course for the young Chavez, who founded the United Farm Workers, a successful union of Mexican American workers, in 1962 (see pp. 886–887).

Men and women of Asian descent—mostly from China, Japan, and the Philippines—formed a tiny minority of the American population but were a significant presence in some western cities and towns. Immigrants from Japan and China had long faced discrimination; for example, a California law of 1913 prohibited immigrants from owning land. Japanese farmers, who specialized in fruit and vegetable crops, circumvented this restriction by putting land titles in the names of their American-born children. As farm prices declined during the depression and racial discrimination undermined the prospects of rising generation for nonfarm jobs, about 20 percent of the migrants returned to Japan.

Chinese Americans were even less prosperous than their Japanese counterparts were. Only 3 percent of Chinese Americans worked in professional and technical occupations, and discrimination kept them out of most industrial jobs. In San Francisco, most Chinese worked in small ethnic businesses—restaurants, laundries, and firms that imported textiles and ceramics. In the hard times of the depression, they turned for assistance both to traditional Chinese social organizations such as *huiguan* (district associations) and to local authorities; in 1931, about one-sixth of San Francisco's Chinese population

Drought Refugees
Like the Joad family in John Steinbeck's powerful novel *The Grapes of Wrath* (1939), many thousands of poor people hit hard by the drought, dust, and debt of farm life in the Great Plains loaded their possessions into pickup trucks and hoped for brighter futures in the West. This photograph, shot in 1937 by Dorothea Lange, shows a family of Missouri drought refugees taking a break on Highway 99 near Tracy, California. Library of Congress.

was receiving public welfare aid. Few benefited from the New Deal. Until the repeal of the Chinese Exclusion Act in 1943, Chinese immigrants were classified as "aliens ineligible for citizenship" and therefore excluded from most federal programs.

Because Filipino immigrants came from a U.S. territory, they were not affected by the ban on Asian immigration passed in 1924 (see Chapter 23). During the 1920s their numbers swelled to about 50,000, many of whom worked as laborers on large corporate-owned farms. As the depression cut wages, Filipino immigration slowed to a trickle and was virtually cut off by the Tydings-McDuffie Act of 1934. The act granted independence to the Philippines (which since 1898 had been an American dependency), classified all Filipinos in the United States as aliens, and restricted immigration to fifty persons per year.

Dust Bowl Migration to California. Even as California lost its dazzle for Mexicans and Asians, it became the destination of tens of thousands of displaced farmers from the "dust bowl" of the Great Plains. Between 1930 and 1941, a severe drought afflicted farmers in the semiarid states of Oklahoma, Texas, New Mexico, Colorado, Arkansas, and Kansas. But the dust bowl was primarily a human creation. Farmers had pushed the agricultural frontier beyond its natural limits, stripping the land of its native vegetation and destroying the delicate ecology of the plains (Map 24.2). When the rains dried up and the winds came, nothing remained to hold the soil. Huge clouds of thick dust rolled over the land, turning the day into night.

This ecological disaster prompted a mass exodus. Their crops ruined and their debts unpaid, at least 350,000 "Okies" (so-called whether or not they were from Oklahoma) loaded their meager belongings into beat-up Fords and headed to California. Many were drawn by handbills distributed by commercial farmers that promised good jobs and high wages; instead, they found low wages and terrible living conditions. Before the depression, white native-born workers made up 20 percent of the migratory farm labor force of 175,000; by the late 1930s, Okies accounted for 85 percent of the workers. John Steinbeck's novel *The Grapes of Wrath* (1939) immortalized them and their journey, and New Deal photographer Dorothea Lange's haunting images of migrant camps in California gave a

VOICES FROM ABROAD

Odette Keun

A Foreigner Looks at the Tennessee Valley Authority

In 1936 French writer Odette Keun visited the United States and was so impressed by the Tennessee Valley Authority (TVA) that she wrote a book about it. Keun was struck not only by the vast size of the TVA but also by its imaginative scope. By promoting such projects, she argued, democratic governments could ward off popular support for fascist solutions to the Great Depression.

The vital question before democracy is, therefore, not how to bring back an economic freedom which is irretrievably lost, but how to prevent the intellectual freedom, which is still our heritage, from being submerged. It is already threatened. It will be threatened more and more strongly in the years ahead — and the menace, of course, is dictatorship. But to fight dictatorship it is necessary first to understand in what circumstances it arises, and then to think out the counterattack which democracy can launch against its approaching force.

Dictatorship springs from two very clear causes. One is the total incapacity of parliamentary government: total, as in Germany in 1933 and in Spain in 1935. To such a breakdown neither the democratic nations of Europe nor America have yet been reduced, although everywhere there are very ominous creaks and cracks, and the authority and prestige of parliamentary institutions have greatly and perilously diminished. The other cause, infinitely closer to us and more dynamic, is the failure of the economic machine to function properly, and by functioning properly I mean ensuring a livelihood for the entire population. No system can survive if it cannot procure food and wages for the people who live under it. Man has to get subsistence from his rulers, for the most immediate and the most imperious law of our nature is that the belly must be filled. It is perfectly futile to orate on fine, high, and abstract principles to human beings who are permanently hungry, permanently harassed, permanently uncertain, who hear their wives begging for the rent and their children crying out for nourishment. . . .

One of the main tenets of liberalism — I reiterate this like a gramophone, but I must get it to sink in — is that all necessary overhauling and adjustment ought to be done in a manner which will minimize the shock to the greatest number, and soften as much as possible the unavoidable human suffering which these changes entail. This opposition to extremes, this practice of a graduated change, we can call "the middle of the road in time and space." But it is not nearly enough to conceive it and to bestow upon it a name. We must reach it. It is unutterably foolish to look at the middle of the road, to talk of the middle of the road, to hope for the middle of the road — and never get there.

Now I have tried to show that the middle of the road is already being laid down in America. The Tennessee Valley Authority is laying it down. Handicapped and restricted though it is in all sorts of ways, it is the noblest, the most intelligent, and the best attempt made in this country or in any other democratic country to economize, marshal, and integrate the actual assets of a region, plan its development and future, ameliorate its standards of living, establish it in a more enduring security, and render available to the people the benefits of the wealth of their district, and the results of science, discovery, invention, and disinterested forethought. In its inspiration and its goal there is goodness, for goodness is that which makes for unity of purpose with love, compassion, and respect for every life and every pattern of living. The economic machine, bad though it is, has not been smashed in the Tennessee Watershed; it is being very gradually, very carefully, very equitably reviewed and amended, and the citizens are being taught and directed, but not bullied, not coerced, not regimented, not frightened, within the constitutional frame the nation itself elected to build. It is not while the Tennessee Valley Authority has the valley in its keeping that despair or disintegration can prepare the ground for a dictatorship and the loss of freedom. The immortal contribution of the TVA to liberalism, not only in America but all over the world, is the blueprint it has drawn, and that it is now transforming into a living reality, of the road which liberals believe is the only road mankind should travel.

SOURCE: Odette Keun, "A Foreigner Looks at the TVA," in *This Was America*, ed. Oscar Handlin (Cambridge, MA: Harvard University Press, 1949), 547–549.

ANALYZING THE EVIDENCE

- According to Keun, why has dictatorship come to Germany and Spain? Why might the TVA prevent such an outcome in the United States?

- What does the term *liberalism* mean to Keun, and why does she consider the TVA an example of that ideology?

personal face to some of the worst suffering of the depression.

A New Deal for the Environment

Concern for the land was one of the dominant motifs of the New Deal, and the shaping of the public landscape was among its most visible legacies. Franklin Roosevelt and Interior Secretary Harold Ickes were avid conservationists and used public concern over the drought and devastation in the dust bowl to spread "the gospel of conservation." Their national resources policy stressed scientific management of the land and the often aggressive use of public authority to preserve or improve the natural environment.

The Tennessee Valley Authority. The most extensive New Deal environmental undertaking was the Tennessee Valley Authority (TVA). Since World War I, experts had recommended the building of dams to control severe flooding and erosion in the Tennessee River Basin, a seven-state area with some of the country's heaviest rainfall (Map 24.3). But when progressive reformers in the 1920s proposed a series of flood-control dams that would also generate cheap electricity, private utility companies blocked the project. As governor of New York, FDR had waged a similar unsuccessful battle to develop public power in the Niagara region. So in 1933 he encouraged Congress to fund the Tennessee project. The TVA was the ultimate watershed demonstration area, integrating flood control, reforestation, electricity generation, and agricultural and industrial development, including the production of chemical fertilizers. The dams and their hydroelectric plants provided cheap electric power for homes and industrial plants and ample recreational opportunities for the valley's residents. The project won praise around the world (see Voices from Abroad, "Odette Keun: A Foreigner Looks at the Tennessee Valley Authority," p. 758).

The TVA also contributed to the efforts of the Roosevelt administration to keep farmers on the land by enhancing the quality of rural life. The Rural Electrification Administration (REA), established in 1935, was central to that goal. Fewer than one-tenth of the nation's 6.8 million farms had electricity, and private utilities balked at the expense of running lines to individual farms. The REA addressed this problem by promoting the creation of nonprofit farm cooperatives. For a $5 down payment, local farmers could join the coop and apply for low-interest federal loans covering the cost of installing power lines. By 1940, 40 percent of the nation's farms had electricity; a decade later, 90 percent did.

Electricity brought relief from the drudgery and isolation of farm life. Electric milking machines and water pumps saved hours of manual labor. Electric irons, vacuum cleaners, and washing machines eased women's burdens, and radios enlivened the lives of the entire family. Electric lights extended the time children could read, women could sew, and families could eat their evening meals. One farm woman remembered, "I just turned on the light and kept looking at Paw. It was the first time I'd ever really seen him after dark." Along with the automobile, electricity probably did more than any other technological innovation to break down the barriers between urban and rural life in twentieth-century America.

Still, the dust bowl disaster focused the attention of urban dwellers and government planners on rural issues of land management and ecological balance. Agents from the Soil Conservation Service in the Department of Agriculture taught farmers to prevent soil erosion by tilling hillsides among the contours of the land. Government

The Human Face of the Great Depression

Migrant Mother by Dorothea Lange is one of the most famous documentary photographs of the 1930s. Lange spent only ten minutes in the pea-picker's camp in California where she captured this image and did not even get the name of the woman whose despair and resignation she so powerfully recorded. She was later identified as Florence Thompson, a full-blooded Cherokee from Oklahoma. Library of Congress.

MAP 24.3 **The Tennessee Valley Authority, 1933–1952**

The Tennessee Valley Authority was one of the New Deal's most far-reaching environmental projects. Between 1933 and 1952, the TVA built twenty dams and improved five others, taming the flood-prone Tennessee River and its main tributaries. The cheap hydroelectric power generated by the dams brought electricity to hundreds of thousands of area residents, and artificial lakes provided extensive recreational facilities. Widely praised at the time, the TVA came under attack in the 1970s for its practice of strip mining and the pollution caused by its power plants and chemical factories.

agronomists also tried to remove marginal farms from cultivation. One of their most widely publicized programs was the Shelterbelts, the planting of 220 million trees running north along the ninety-ninth meridian from Abilene, Texas, to the Canadian border. Planted as a windbreak, the trees also prevented soil erosion.

New Deal projects that enhanced people's enjoyment of the natural environment can be seen today throughout the country. CCC and WPA workers built the famous Blue Ridge Parkway, which connects the Shenandoah National Park in Virginia with the Great Smoky Mountain National Park in North Carolina. In the West, government workers built the San Francisco Zoo, Berkeley's Tilden Park, and the canals of San Antonio. The CCC helped to complete the East Coast's Appalachian Trail and the West Coast's Pacific Crest Trail through the Sierra Nevada. In state parks across the country, cabins, shelters, picnic areas, lodges, and observation towers stand as monuments to the New Deal ethos of recreation coexisting with nature.

The New Deal and the Arts

Many American artists redefined their relationship to society in response to the Great Depression, and many became politically engaged. Never had there been a decade, critic Malcolm Cowley noted in 1939, "when literary events followed so closely on the flying coat-tails of social events." Because the New Deal funded many arts projects, the link between politics and the arts was both close and controversial.

Federal Arts Projects. As the economic downturn dried up traditional sources of private patronage, creative artists, like other Americans, turned to Washington. A WPA project known as "Federal One" put unemployed artists, actors, and writers to work, but its spirit and purpose extended far beyond relief. New Deal administrators encouraged artists to create projects of interest to the entire community, not just the cultured elite. "Art for the millions" became a popular New Deal slogan and encouraged the painting of murals in hundreds of public buildings (see Reading American Pictures, "Interpreting the Public Art of the New Deal," p. 761).

The Federal Art Project (FAP) gave work to many young artists who would become the twentieth century's leading painters, muralists, and sculptors. Jackson Pollock, Alice Neel, Willem de Kooning, and Louise Nevelson all received support. The Federal Music Project employed fifteen thousand musicians, and government-sponsored orchestras toured the country, presenting free concerts of both classical and popular music. Like many New Deal programs, the Music Project emphasized American themes. The composer Aaron Copland wrote his ballets *Billy the Kid* (1938) and *Rodeo* (1942) for the WPA, basing the compositions on western folk motifs. The federal government also employed the musicologist Charles Seeger and his wife, the composer Ruth Crawford Seeger, to catalog hundreds of American folk songs.

The Federal Writers' Project (FWP) gave work to five thousand writers and produced more than a thousand publications. It collected the oral histories

READING AMERICAN PICTURES

Interpreting the Public Art of the New Deal

"The Promise of the New Deal," Ben Shahn (1938). Roosevelt Arts Project.

Murals are perhaps the most pervasive artistic legacy of the New Deal. They decorate federal buildings throughout the nation today. The goals of the agencies that commissioned murals were to give employment to artists, bring art to the masses, and celebrate the American people and their nation. All murals were "realistic" in style and many embodied the decade's emphasis on regionalism by depicting the history of a locality and its people at work and play. This image comes from a large, three panel mural by well-known artist Ben Shahn that adorns a public school in Roosevelt, New Jersey.

Originally called the Jersey Homesteads, the town was created by the Farm Security Administration as a planned community for poor immigrant Jewish garment workers from New York City. The first two panels of the mural depict Jewish immigrants and their work. The third panel, pictured here, features in the left corner a teacher instructing workers about the history of unions. Seated at the right are New Deal planners and labor leaders. The figures behind them are the prospective residents of the new community. For the full mural, go to **www.scc.rutgers.edu/njh/homesteads/mural.htm.**

ANALYZING THE EVIDENCE

▶ What does this third panel of Shahn's mural tell us about the character and the goals of the New Deal?

▶ Note the blueprint of the street plan and the houses depicted on the mural (top center). Then turn to the cartoon in Chapter 27 (p. 837) which depicts Levittown, a famous housing development built by a private corporation in the late 1940s. What does a comparison of those two images suggest?

▶ How does this mural fit with the discussion of the documentary impulse discussed in this chapter?

of many Americans, including two thousand narratives by former slaves, and published a set of popular state guidebooks. Young FWP employees who later achieved fame included Saul Bellow, Ralph Ellison, Tillie Olsen, and John Cheever. The black folklorist and novelist Zora Neale Hurston finished three novels while in the Florida FWP, among them *Their Eyes Were Watching God* (1937). And Richard Wright won the 1938 *Story* magazine prize for the best tale by a WPA writer. Wright used his spare time to complete *Native Son* (1940), a novel that took a bitter look at racism.

Of all the New Deal arts programs, the Federal Theatre Project (FTP) was the most ambitious. Under the gifted direction of Hallie Flanagan, the FTP reached an audience of 25 to 30 million people in the four years of its existence. Talented directors, actors, and playwrights, including Orson Welles, John Huston, and Arthur Miller, offered their services. Because many FTP productions took a critical look at American social problems, it was attacked in Congress as sympathetic to communism and its funding was cut off in 1939.

The Documentary Impulse. The WPA arts projects reflected a broad artistic trend called the "documentary impulse." Documentary artists focused on actual events that were relevant to people's lives and presented them in ways that aroused the interest and emotions of the audience. It influenced practically every aspect of American culture—literature, photography, art, music, film, dance, theater, and radio. It is evident in John Steinbeck's *Grapes of Wrath* and in John Dos Passos's *USA* trilogy, which used actual newspaper clippings and headlines in its fictional story. *The March of Time* newsreels, which movie audiences saw before feature films, presented images of world events for a pre-television age. New photojournalism magazines, including *Life* and *Look,* carried this documentary approach into millions of living rooms.

The federal government played a leading role in compiling the documentary record of the 1930s. It sent journalist Lorena Hickok, writer Martha Gellhorn, and many other investigators into the field to report on the conditions of people on relief. And the Historical Section of the Farm Security Administration compiled a remarkable series of photographs of the American scene. Under the direction of Roy Stryker, a talented group of photographers—Dorothea Lange, Walker Evans, Ben Shahn, and Margaret Bourke-White—produced haunting images of sharecroppers, dust bowl migrants, and urban homeless, permanently shaping the image of the Great Depression.

Building the American Future

Margaret Bourke-White's photograph of the Fort Peck Dam in Montana, with the two human figures in the foreground establishing its huge scale, graced the inaugural cover of *Life* magazine in 1936. Fort Peck was one of a series of dams built by the Works Projects Administration to control floods on the Missouri River. *Life*'s first issue also contained a photo essay about the town nearest to the Fort Peck Dam, which was named, appropriately, New Deal, Montana. Margaret Bourke-White, *Life Magazine,* copyright 1936 Time Warner, Inc.

The Legacies of the New Deal

The New Deal did much more than simply reinforce and extend the "regulatory" liberalism of the Progressive era. By creating a powerful national bureaucracy and laying the foundation of a social welfare state, it redefined the meaning of American liberalism. For the first time the federal government became an ongoing part of everyday life. During the 1930s, millions of people began to pay taxes directly to the Social Security Administration and the Internal Revenue Service, and more than a third of the population received direct government assistance from new federal programs, including old-age pensions, unemployment compensation, farm loans, relief work, and mortgage guarantees. Furthermore, the government stood ready to intervene in the economy when private enterprise failed to produce economic stability. New legislation regulated the stock market, reformed the Federal Reserve System, and subjected business corporations to federal regulation.

Like all major social transformations, the New Deal was criticized by those who thought it did too much and those who protested that it did too little. "Classical" liberals, who gave high priority to small government and individual freedom, pointed out that the New Deal state intruded deeply into the personal and financial lives of the citizenry. The Social Security Act, for example, imposed compulsory taxes on workers and forced families to comply with ever more complicated bureaucratic regulations. As one historian has written, the act instigated a "mercantilist regulation of family life not seen since the eighteenth century." Conversely, advocates of social welfare liberalism complained that the New Deal's safety net had many holes, especially in comparison with the far more extensive welfare systems provided by the governments of western Europe. These critics pointed out that there was no provision for a national health-care system; that domestic workers and farm laborers were excluded from most welfare programs; and that, in the many New Deal programs administered by state governments, benefits were often low.

Despite recurring debate about the increased presence of the state in American life, the New Deal set a pattern of government involvement in the life of the society that would persist for the rest of the twentieth century. There was a significant expansion of social welfare programs in the 1960s during the "Great Society" initiative of President Lyndon Johnson, and most of those programs remained intact in the wake of the "Reagan Revolution" of the 1980s (see Chapters 28 and 30).

The New Deal Coalition. Whatever the fate of the depression-era social welfare liberalism, there is no question that it was brilliant politics. The Democratic Party courted and won the allegiance of citizens who benefited from New Deal programs. Organized labor aligned itself with the administration that had made it a legitimate force in modern industrial life. Blacks voted Democratic as economic aid began to flow into their communities. The Women's Division of the Democratic National Committee elicited grassroots political support from 80,000 women who praised what the New Deal had done for their communities. The unemployed also looked kindly on the Roosevelt administration. According to one of the earliest Gallup polls, 84 percent of those on relief voted the Democratic ticket in 1936.

Roosevelt's magnetic personality and the New Deal's farm relief and social security programs also brought millions of middle-class voters into the Democratic fold. Many were first- or second-generation immigrants from southern and central Europe—Italians, Poles, Slovaks, and Jews—who had now found a secure place in American life. The New Deal completed the transformation of the Democratic Party that had begun in the 1920s. Its coalition of ethnic groups, city dwellers, organized labor, blacks, and a broad cross-section of the middle class formed the nucleus of the northern Democratic Party for decades to come, and provided support for additional liberal reforms.

From its inception, the New Deal coalition also contained a potentially fatal contradiction involving the issue of race. Roosevelt and the Democratic Party depended heavily on white voters in the South, who strongly preferred to keep African Americans poor and powerless. Such policies faced increasing opposition not only from northern liberals but also from the increasing number of northern black Democrats. As the struggle over civil rights for African Americans entered the national agenda beginning in the late 1940s, it would gradually destroy the Roosevelt coalition. Even in the late 1930s, southern Democrats refused to support the expansion of federal power, fearing it would undermine white rule in the South. Thanks in part to this southern Democratic opposition, the New Deal, as we have seen, ground to a halt. The darkening international scene was also important. As Europe moved toward war and Japan flexed its muscles in the Far East, Roosevelt became increasingly preoccupied with international relations and pushed domestic reform further and further into the background.

➤ What impact did the New Deal have on organized labor, women, and racial and ethnic minorities?

➤ Under the New Deal, the government's involvement in the environment and in the arts was unprecedented. What were the major components of this new departure?

➤ What were the most significant long-term results of the New Deal? What were its limitations?

SUMMARY

We have seen the ways in which Franklin Delano Roosevelt's First New Deal concentrated on stimulating economic recovery, providing jobs and relief to the unemployed, and reforming banks and other financial institutions. His goal was to restore Americans' confidence in their society and institutions. The Second New Deal was different. Influenced by the persistence of the depression and the popularity of Huey Long's Share Our Wealth Society, FDR promoted social welfare legislation that would provide economic security for American citizens.

We also explored the impact of the New Deal on various groups of citizens, especially blacks, women, and unionized workers. Our survey focused on the depression-era experiences of migrants in the West, particularly the Mexicans, Asians, and Okies who worked in the farms and factories of California. Because New Deal legislation and programs assisted such groups, they gravitated to the Democratic Party. Its coalition of white southerners, ethnic urban workers, farmers, and a cross-section of the middle classes gave the party overwhelming majorities in Congress and provided FDR with a landslide presidential victory in 1936.

Finally, we examined the accomplishments and legacies of the New Deal. In the short run, it pulled the nation out of the crisis of 1933, provided relief, and preserved capitalist economic institutions and a democratic political system. Over the longer run, it expanded the size and power of the federal government and, through the Social Security system, farm subsidy programs, and public works projects, extended its presence into the lives of nearly every American. Great dams and electricity projects sponsored by the Tennessee Valley Authority in the Southeast, the Works Project Administration in the West, and the Rural Electrification Administration made permanent contributions to the quality of national life.

Connections: Economy

As we noted in the essay that opened Part Five (p. 671), between 1914 and 1945 the United States "boasted the world's most productive economic system." But the performance of the American economy varied widely over the decades. In Chapter 22 we saw how spending for military mobilization during World War I invigorated the industrial sector and food shortages in Europe ushered in a boom time for American farmers. But after the war, the farm economy fell into a two-decades-long crisis. As Chapter 23 explained, during the 1920s food surpluses cut farm prices and farm income, and Presidents Coolidge and Hoover vetoed farm relief legislation. Chapter 24 described the farm policies of the New Deal, which both subsidized farm owners and forced many tenant and sharecropping families off the land. As we will see in Chapter 25, new shortages of goods during World War II restored the prosperity of the farm sector, which was now increasingly dominated by the operators of large-scale farms.

The evolution of the industrial economy followed a roughly similar pattern. As we saw in Chapter 23, there was a sharp postwar economic recession in the early 1920s but then a quick recovery, thanks to the demand for new consumer goods: automobiles and many kinds of electrical goods. However, the wages paid to workers were not sufficient to sustain the boom, which collapsed in 1929. As this chapter explained, the various economic policies of the New Deal preserved the capitalist system and demonstrated the crucial importance of government intervention in smoothing out the business cycle and maintaining prosperity. Chapter 25 will show how massive government spending ended the Great Depression and, in the process, confirmed the economic theories of John Maynard Keynes.

CHAPTER REVIEW QUESTIONS

- Some historians have seen the New Deal as an evolution of Progressivism, but others have argued that it represented a revolution in social values and government institutions. What do you think?

- In what ways did Roosevelt's personality, values, and political style affect the policies and programs of the New Deal?

- What changes took place during the depression era with respect to the lives of women, workers, and racial and ethnic minorities? What role did the New Deal play?

TIMELINE

1931–1937	Scottsboro case: trials and appeals
1933	FDR's inaugural address and first fireside chats
	Emergency Banking Act begins the Hundred Days
	Civilian Conservation Corps (CCC) created
	Agricultural Adjustment Act (AAA)
	National Industrial Recovery Act (NIRA)
	Tennessee Valley Authority (TVA) established
	Townsend Clubs promote Old Age Revolving Pension Plan
	Twenty-first Amendment repeals Prohibition
1934	Securities and Exchange Commission (SEC) created
	Southern Tenant Farmers Union (STFU) founded
	Indian Reorganization Act
	Senator Huey Long promotes Share Our Wealth Society
	Father Charles Coughlin founds National Union for Social Justice
1935	Harlem race riot
	Supreme Court voids NRA in *Schechter v. United States*
	National Labor Relations (Wagner) Act
	Social Security Act creates old-age pension system
	Works Progress Administration (WPA) created
	Huey Long assassinated
	Rural Electrification Administration (REA) established
	Supreme Court voids Agricultural Adjustment Act
	Congress of Industrial Organizations (CIO) formed
1936	General Motors sit-down strike
	Landslide reelection of FDR marks peak of New Deal power
1937	FDR's Supreme Court plan fails
1937–1938	"Roosevelt recession" raises unemployment
1938	Fair Labor Standards Act (FLSA)
1939	Federal Theatre Project terminated

FOR FURTHER EXPLORATION

Robert S. McElvaine, *The Great Depression* (1984), provides a general treatment of the New Deal. Blanche Wiesen Cook's *Eleanor Roosevelt* (vol. 1, 1992; vol. 2, 1999) and Katie Loucheim, ed., *The Making of the New Deal: The Insiders Speak* (1983), portray important New Dealers. For popular reaction to Roosevelt's fireside chats, see Lawrence W. Levine and Cornelia R. Levine, *The People and the President* (2002). Robert S. McElvaine's *Down and Out in the Great Depression* (1983) contains letters written by ordinary people, while Studs Terkel's *Hard Times: An Oral History of the Great Depression* (1970) offers their memories. For audio versions of Terkel's interviews, go to the Chicago Historical Society at **www.studsterkel.org/index.html**. James Agee and Walker Evans's *Let Us Now Praise Famous Men* (1941) is a compelling portrait of southern poverty. For a memoir of a depression-era childhood, see Russell Baker's *Growing Up* (1982). John Steinbeck, *The Grapes of Wrath* (1939); Josephine Herbst, *Pity Is Not Enough* (1933); and Richard Wright, *Native Son*, (1940) are classic novels. See also Harvey Swados, *The American Writer and the Great Depression* (1966).

For two extensive collection of 1930s materials, see the "New Deal Network" at **newdeal.feri.org** and "America in the 1930s" at **xroads.virginia.edu/~1930s/home_1.html**, which includes clips of radio programs. See also the University of Utrecht's "American Culture in the 1930s" at **www.let.uu.nl/ams/xroads/1930proj.htm** and the wonderful collection of government-commissioned art at **www.archives.gov/exhibits/new_deal_for_the_arts/index.html**. The Library of Congress has a multimedia presentation, "Voices from the Dust Bowl," at **memory.loc.gov/ammem/afctshtml/tshome.html** and a superb collection of photographs covering the years 1935–1945 at **lcweb2.loc.gov/ammem/fsowhome.html**. For music, listen to **www.authentichistory.com/1930s.html**. The political cartoons of the day are available in the "FDR Cartoon Archive" at **www.nisk.k12.ny.us/fdr**.

For the impact of the depression and the New Deal on African Americans, go to **memory.loc.gov/ammem/aaohtml/exhibit/aopart8.html**. For the "'The Scottsboro Boys' Trials: 1931–1937," log on to **www.law.umkc.edu/faculty/projects/FTrials/scottsboro/scottsb.htm**. For audio reminiscences about racial segregation during this and later decades, listen to "Remembering Jim Crow" at **americanradioworks.publicradio.org/features/remembering**.

TEST YOUR KNOWLEDGE

To assess your command of the material in this chapter, see the Online Study Guide at **bedfordstmartins.com/henretta**.

For Web sites, images, and documents related to topics and places in this chapter, visit **bedfordstmartins.com/makehistory**.

25 The World at War
1939–1945

THE SECOND WORLD WAR WAS "the largest single event in human history, fought across six of the world's seven continents and all of its oceans. It killed fifty million human beings, left hundreds of millions of others wounded in mind or body and materially devastated much of the heartland of civilization" both in Europe and East Asia. So concluded the noted military historian John Keegan, in a grim judgment that still rings true. The war was so vast and so destructive because it was waged both with technologically advanced weapons and with massive armies. The military conflict began in 1939 with a *blitzkrieg* ("lightning war") attack by wonderfully engineered German tanks across the plains of Poland. It ended in 1945 when American planes dropped two atomic bombs, the product of even more breathtaking scientific breakthroughs, on the Japanese cities of Hiroshima and Nagasaki. In between these demonstrations of technological prowess and devastating power, huge armies confronted and destroyed one another on the steppes of Russia, the river valleys of China, and the sandy deserts of North Africa.

Well might soldiers and civilians "jive in the streets" around Times Square in New York City on August 1945, celebrating V-J (Victory over Japan) Day. World War II was finally over. Many American lives had been lost or forever damaged, but the country emerged from the war intact

The Road to War
The Rise of Fascism
Isolationists versus Interventionists
Retreat from Isolationism
The Attack on Pearl Harbor

Organizing for Victory
Financing the War
Mobilizing the American Fighting Force
Workers and the War Effort
Politics in Wartime

Life on the Home Front
"For the Duration"
Migration and Social Conflict
Civil Rights during Wartime

Fighting and Winning the War
Wartime Aims and Tensions
The War in Europe
The War in the Pacific
Planning the Postwar World

Summary
Connections: Government

◀ **One City (and Island) at a Time**

By late 1944, the victory of the United States and its allies was nearly certain, but Japanese and German troops continued to fight with great courage and determination. Many European cities and every Pacific island had to be taken foot by foot. Here, American troops from the 325th Regiment of the 82nd Airborne Division advance slowly through the rubble-filled street of a German city in early 1945. Collection of Jeff Ethell.

and prosperous. As one man told journalist Studs Terkel, "Those who lost nobody at the front had a pretty good time." In fact, many Americans viewed the brutal conflict as the "good war," a successful defense of democratic values from the threat posed by German and Japanese fascism. When evidence of the grim reality of the Jewish Holocaust came to light, U.S. participation in the war seemed even more just.

Although it was not fully apparent at the time, World War II changed the nation's government in fundamental ways. The power of the federal government, which had been increasing since the Progressive era and World War I, grew exponentially during the conflict. Equally important, the government remained powerful after the war ended. Federal laws, rules, and practices put in place during the war—universal taxation of incomes, nationwide antidiscrimination employment standards, a huge military establishment, and multibillion dollar budgets, to name but a few—became part of American life. So too did the active participation of the United States in international politics and diplomacy, a participation all the more important because of the unresolved issues of the wartime alliance with the Soviet Union. A powerful American state, the product of a long "hot" war, would remain in place to fight an even longer, more expensive, and more dangerous Cold War.

The Road to War

The Great Depression disrupted economic life and political life around the world, everywhere endangering traditional institutions. An antidemocratic movement known as fascism, which had developed in Italy during the 1920s, spread to Japan, Germany, and Spain. By the mid-1930s, these states had forsaken their democratic institutions and instituted authoritarian, militaristic governments led by powerful dictators: Adolf Hitler in Nazi Germany, Benito Mussolini in Italy, Francisco Franco in Spain, and, after 1940, Hideki Tojo in Japan. As early as 1936, President Roosevelt warned Americans that other peoples had "sold their heritage of freedom for the illusion of a living" and called on them to work for "the survival of democracy" both at home and abroad. Hampered at first by the pervasive isolationist sentiment in the country, by 1939 FDR was leading the nation toward war against the Fascist powers.

The Rise of Fascism

World War II had its roots in the settlement of World War I (see Chapter 22). Germany deeply resented the harsh terms imposed on it by the Treaty of Versailles, and Japan and Italy revived their dreams of overseas empires that had been thwarted by the treaty makers. The League of Nations, the collective security system established at Versailles, proved unable to maintain the existing international order.

The first challenge came from Japan. In 1930, that small island nation was controlled by a militaristic regime with an expansionist agenda. To become a major industrial power, Japan needed raw materials and overseas markets for its goods. To get them, Japan embarked on a program of military expansion. In 1931, its troops occupied Manchuria, the northernmost province of China, and in 1937 it launched a full-scale invasion of China. In both instances the League of Nations condemned Japan's action but took no action to stop the military invasion.

Hitler

In 1933, Adolph Hitler seized power in Germany, intent on restoring its status as a major power. His ambitions grew steadily: overturning the Versailles treaty, asserting German control of central Europe, dominating Europe and the world. Here, dressed as usual in a military uniform, he salutes army troops and brown-suited members of his National-Socialist German Workers Party (NSDAP or Nazi) at the party's annual meeting in Nuremberg in 1938. Note the swastika — the symbol of his Nazi Party — prominently displayed on the *führer's* sleeve. Time Life Pictures / Getty Images.

Japan's defiance of the League encouraged a fascist dictator half a world away: Italy's Benito Mussolini who had come to power in 1922 and introduced a fascist political system. Fascism in Italy and, later, in Germany rested on an ideology of a powerful state that directed economic and social affairs. It disparaged parliamentary government, independent labor movements, and individual rights and celebrated authoritarian rule; Mussolini called for "a dictatorship of the state over many classes cooperating."

The Italian dictator had long been unhappy with the Versailles treaty, which had not awarded Italy any of the former German or Turkish colonies in Africa or the Middle East. So in 1935 he invaded Ethiopia, one of the few independent countries left in Africa. The Ethiopian emperor, Haile Selassie, appealed to the League of Nations, which condemned the invasion but imposed only limited sanctions. By 1936 the Italians had subjugated Ethiopia and were now an imperial nation.

Hitler and National Socialism. But it was Germany, not Italy, that presented the gravest threat to the world order in the 1930s. There, huge World War I reparation payments, economic depression, fear of communism, labor unrest, and rising unemployment fueled the rise of Adolf Hitler and his National Socialist (Nazi) Party. In 1933 Hitler became chancellor of Germany, and the legislature, the *Reichstag*, granted him dictatorial powers to deal with the crisis. He soon took the title of *führer* (leader) and outlawed other political parties.

Hitler's goal was nothing short of European domination and world power, as he made clear in his book *Mein Kampf* (*My Struggle*). Hitler's plan was to overturn the territorial settlements of the Versailles treaty, unite Germans living throughout central and eastern Europe in a great German fatherland, and annex large areas of eastern Europe. The "inferior races" who lived in these lands—Jews, Gypsies, and Slavs—would be removed or subordinated to the German "master race." A virulent anti-Semite, Hitler had long blamed Jews for Germany's problems. Once in power, he began a sustained and brutal persecution of Jews, which expanded to a campaign of extermination when the war began.

Hitler's strategy for restoring Germany's lost territories and military power was to provoke a series of minor crises—daring Britain and France to go to war to stop him. In 1935, Hitler announced that he planned to rearm the nation in violation of the Versailles treaty. No one stopped him. In 1936 Germany sent troops into the Rhineland, a region that had been declared a demilitarized zone under the treaty; once again, France and Britain took no action. Later that year, Hitler and Mussolini joined forces in the Rome-Berlin Axis, a political and military alliance. Also in 1936, Germany signed an Anti-Comintern Pact with Japan. Its announced purpose was to oppose the Comintern, a Soviet-backed worldwide organization that spread communist ideology, but the pact was really a military alliance between Japan and the Axis Powers.

Isolationists versus Interventionists

While these events were taking place in Europe, the Roosevelt administration focused its energies on restoring the American economy and, diplomatically, on consolidating American influence in the Western Hemisphere. Secretary of State Cordell Hull implemented a Good Neighbor Policy, under which the United States voluntarily renounced the use of military force and armed intervention in Latin America. As part of this effort, in 1934 Congress repealed the Platt Amendment, a relic of the Spanish-American War, which asserted the U.S. right to intervene in Cuba's affairs (see Chapter 21). However, the United States kept (and still maintains) a major naval base at Cuba's Guantanamo Bay, and its diplomats continued to intervene in various Latin American countries on behalf of American business interests there.

Congress and the American public accepted such economic intervention, but they were increasingly resistant to diplomatic initiatives that might result in political entanglements. In part, the growing support for political isolationism reflected disillusionment with American participation in World War I. In 1934 Gerald P. Nye, a progressive Republican senator from North Dakota, began a congressional investigation into the profits of munitions makers during World War I and then widened the investigation to determine their influence (and that of the banks that lent millions to the Allies) on America's decision to declare war. Nye's committee concluded that war profiteers, whom it called "merchants of death," had maneuvered the nation into World War I for financial gain.

Although the Nye committee failed to prove this charge, its factual findings gave momentum to the isolationist movement and resulted in the passage of a series of legislative acts. All were explicitly designed to prevent a recurrence of the events that helped to pull the nation into World War I. Thus, the Neutrality Act of 1935 imposed an embargo on arms trading with countries at war and declared that American citizens traveled on the ships of belligerent nations at their own risk. In 1936 Congress expanded the act to ban loans to belligerents, and in

1937 it adopted a "cash-and-carry" provision: If a country at war wanted to purchase nonmilitary goods from the United States, it had to pay for them in cash and pick them up in its own ships.

The Popular Front. Other Americans, especially writers, intellectuals, and progressive social activists, responded to the rise of fascism in Europe by advocating interventionist policies. Some of them joined the American Communist Party, which had taken the lead in organizing opposition to fascism and which was also gaining supporters as the depression revealed deep flaws in the capitalist system. Between 1935 and 1938, Communist party membership peaked at about 100,000, from a wide range of social groups: African American farmers in Alabama, white electrical workers in New York, union organizers, even a few New Deal administrators. Many intellectuals did not join the party, but considered themselves "fellow travelers." They sympathized with the party's objectives, wrote for the *Daily Worker*, and supported organizations sponsored by the party.

The courting of intellectuals, union members, and liberal organizations reflected a shift in the strategy of the Communist Party. Fearful of German and Japanese aggression, the Soviet Union instructed its followers in western Europe and the United States to join in a Popular Front with other opponents of fascism. The Popular Front strategy became even more urgent with the outbreak of the Spanish Civil War in 1936. Armed forces led by Generalissimo Francisco Franco, strongly supported by the Fascist regimes in Germany and Italy, led a rebellion against Spain's democratically elected Republican government. Backed only by the Soviet Union and Mexico, the Republicans, or Loyalists, relied heavily on military volunteers from other countries, including the 3,200-strong American Abraham Lincoln Brigade. The governments of the United States, Great Britain, and France, despite their Loyalist sympathies, remained neutral — a policy that ensured a Fascist victory. American intellectuals strongly supported the Spanish Loyalists but grew increasingly uneasy with the Popular Front because of the rigidity of their Communist associates and the cynical brutality and political repression of Soviet leader Joseph Stalin.

The Failure of Appeasement. Further encouraged by the passivity of the Allied Powers during the Spanish Civil War, Hitler expanded his aggression in 1938. He sent troops to annex German-speaking Austria, while simultaneously scheming to seize a part of Czechoslovakia. Because Czechoslovakia had an alliance with France, war seemed imminent. But at the Munich Conference in September 1938, Britain and France again capitulated, agreeing to let Germany annex the Sudetenland — the German-speaking border areas of Czechoslovakia — in return for Hitler's pledge to seek no more territory. The agreement, declared British Prime Minister Neville Chamberlain, guaranteed "peace for our time."

Within six months, however, Hitler's forces had overrun the rest of Czechoslovakia and were threatening to march into Poland. Britain and France, realizing that their policy of appeasement had been disastrous, now prepared to take a stand. Then in August 1939 Hitler and Stalin shocked the world by signing a Nonaggression Pact. The pact had advantages for both sides. It protected Russia from a German invasion but only at the cost of destroying the Popular Front and severely weakening support for the Communist Party in western Europe and the United States. For Germany, the results of the pact were all positive. It assured Hitler that he would not have to wage a two-front war. Now protected in the east, on September 1, 1939, Hitler launched a *blitzkrieg* ("lightning war") against Poland; two days later Britain and France declared war on Germany. World War II had begun.

Retreat from Isolationism

Because the United States had become a major world power, its response would affect the course of the European conflict. Two days after the European war started, the United States officially declared its neutrality. Roosevelt made no secret of his sympathies and pointedly rephrased Woodrow Wilson's declaration of 1914 (see p. 675): "This nation will remain a neutral nation, but I cannot ask that every American remain neutral in thought as well." The overwhelming majority of Americans — some 84 percent, according to a poll in 1939 — supported Britain and France rather than Nazi Germany, but most Americans did not want to be drawn into another war.

At first the need for American intervention seemed remote. After the German conquest of Poland in September 1939, a false calm settled over Europe. But then on April 9, 1940, Nazi tanks overran Denmark. Norway fell to the Nazi *blitzkrieg* next, and the Netherlands, Belgium, and Luxembourg followed. Finally, on June 22, 1940, France fell. Britain stood alone against Hitler's plans for domination of Europe.

Support for Intervention Grows. What *Time* magazine would later call America's "thousand-step road to war" had already begun. After a bitter battle in Congress in 1939, Roosevelt won a change in the neutrality laws to allow the Allies to buy arms on a cash-and-carry basis. Interventionists, led by the journalist William Allen White and his Committee to Defend America by Aiding the Allies, became increasingly vocal. In response, isolationists, including the aviator Charles Lindbergh and Senator Gerald Nye, formed the America First Committee to keep the nation out of the war; they attracted strong support in the Midwest and from conservative newspapers.

Despite the efforts of the America Firsters, in 1940 the United States moved closer to involvement in the war. In May Roosevelt created the National Defense Advisory Commission and laid the basis for a bipartisan defense effort by bringing two prominent Republicans, Henry Stimson and Frank Knox, into his cabinet as secretaries of war and the navy, respectively. During the summer, the president traded fifty World War I destroyers to Great Britain in exchange for the right to build military bases on British possessions in the Atlantic, thus circumventing the nation's neutrality law by executive order. In October, a bipartisan vote in Congress approved a large increase in defense spending and instituted the first peacetime draft registration and conscription in American history.

While the war expanded from Europe to its colonial possessions in North Africa and the oil-rich Middle East, the United States was preparing for the 1940 presidential election. The conflict had convinced Roosevelt that he should seek an unprecedented third term. Overcoming strong opposition from conservative Democrats, Roosevelt chose the liberal secretary of agriculture, Henry A. Wallace, as his running mate. The Republicans nominated Wendell Willkie of Indiana, a former Democrat who supported many New Deal policies. The two parties' platforms differed only slightly. Both parties pledged aid to the Allies, and both candidates pledged not to send "one American boy into the shambles of another war," as Willkie put it. Willkie's spirited campaign resulted in a closer election than those of 1932 or 1936; nonetheless, Roosevelt and the Democrats won 55 percent of the popular vote and a lopsided total in the Electoral College.

Lend-Lease and the Atlantic Charter. With the election behind him, Roosevelt concentrated on persuading the American people to increase aid to Britain, whose survival he viewed as the key to American security. In an address to Congress in January 1941, he outlined "four essential freedoms" (freedom of speech and of religion, freedom from want and fear) that he believed it was necessary to protect. Two months later, with Britain no longer able to pay cash for arms, Roosevelt convinced Congress to pass the Lend-Lease Act. The legislation authorized the president to "lease, lend, or otherwise dispose of" arms and other equipment to any country whose defense was considered vital to the security of the United States. When Hitler abandoned his Nonaggression Pact with Stalin and invaded the Soviet Union in June 1941, the United States promptly extended lend-lease to the Soviets, who became part of the Allied coalition. The implementation of lend-lease marked the unofficial entrance of the United States into the European war.

Roosevelt underlined his support for the Allied cause by meeting in August 1941 with Winston Churchill, who had become Britain's prime minister. Their joint press release, which became known as the Atlantic Charter, provided the ideological foundation of the Western cause. Like Wilson's Fourteen Points and Roosevelt's Four Freedoms, the charter called for economic collaboration and guarantees of political stability after the war to ensure that "all men in all the lands may live out their lives in freedom from fear and want." The charter also supported free trade, national self-determination, and the principle of collective security.

As in World War I, when Americans started supplying the Allies, Germany attacked U.S. and Allied ships. By September 1941 Nazi submarines and American vessels were fighting an undeclared naval war in the Atlantic, unknown to the American public (Map 25.1). Without a dramatic enemy attack, however, and with the public reluctant to enter the conflict, Roosevelt hesitated to ask Congress for a declaration of war.

The Attack on Pearl Harbor

The final provocation came not from Germany but from Japan. Throughout the 1930s, Japanese military advances in China had upset the balance of political and economic power in the Pacific, where the United States had long enjoyed the benefits of the open-door policy (see Chapter 21). After Japan's invasion of China in 1937, Roosevelt denounced "the present reign of terror and international lawlessness," suggesting that aggressors be "quarantined" by peace-loving nations. Despite such rhetoric, the United States refused to intervene when Japanese troops sacked the city of Nanking, massacred 300,000 Chinese residents and raped thousands of women, and sank an American gunboat in the Yangtze River.

As Japan pacified coastal areas of China, its imperial ambitions expanded. In 1940 Japan signed a formal military alliance with Germany and Italy, and its troops occupied the northern section of the French colony of Indochina (present-day Vietnam). Its goal was to create and dominate a Greater East

Map 25.1 World War II in the North Atlantic, 1939–1943

After the start of the war in Europe in September 1939, Germany escalated its submarine attacks on Allied and American merchant shipping in the Atlantic. Continued German advances spurred Congress to pass the Lend-Lease Act in March 1941 and President Roosevelt and Prime Minister Churchill to issue the Atlantic Charter in August. A pivotal factor in the Allied victory in Europe would be countering the German submarine threat in the Atlantic. With the establishment of the convoy system — the protection of merchant vessels with destroyers armed with sonar and depth charges — the Atlantic shipping lanes became safer, allowing the transport of troops and materials to Great Britain and North Africa.

Asia Co-Prosperity Sphere stretching from Indonesia to Korea. The United States responded to the invasion of Indochina by restricting trade with Japan, especially aviation-grade gasoline and scrap metal. Roosevelt hoped these economic sanctions would deter Japanese aggression. But in July 1941 Japanese troops occupied the rest of Indochina. Roosevelt now froze Japanese assets in the United States and instituted an embargo on all trade with Japan, including vital oil shipments that accounted for almost 80 percent of Japanese consumption.

In September 1941 the government of Prime Minister Hideki Tojo began secret preparations for war against the United States. By November American military intelligence knew that Japan was planning an attack but did not know where it would come. Early on Sunday morning, December 7, 1941, Japanese bombers attacked Pearl Harbor in Hawaii, killing more than 2,400 Americans. They destroyed or heavily damaged eight battleships, three cruisers, three destroyers, and almost two hundred airplanes.

Pearl Harbor, December 7, 1941
Sailors at the Naval Air Station stare in disbelief as a huge explosion rocks the battleship USS *Arizona*, anchored at Pearl Harbor. The Japanese bombed both the American fleet and the nearby military airfields to prevent a counterattack against the aircraft carriers that had launched the strike. U.S. Naval Historical Foundation.

Although the assault was devastating, it united the American people (as the September 11, 2001, terrorist attacks would do some sixty years later). The next day Roosevelt went before Congress. Calling December 7 "a date which will live in infamy," he asked for a declaration of war against Japan. The Senate voted unanimously for war, and the House concurred by a vote of 388 to 1. The lone dissenter was Jeannette Rankin of Montana, who had also opposed American entry into World War I. Three days later Germany and Italy declared war on the United States, and the United States in turn declared war on those nations.

➤ Compare the impact of the depression on the politics and political institutions of the United States, Italy, and Germany. What are the similarities and differences?

➤ As the world edged toward war in the late 1930s, many Americans were committed to political isolationism. What were the sources of this isolationism, and how was it manifest?

➤ Why did the United States join the fight in World War II? What are the key events leading to America's involvement?

Organizing for Victory

The task of fighting a global war greatly accelerated the influence of the federal government on all aspects of American life. Coordinating the changeover from civilian to war production, raising an army, and assembling the necessary workforce required a vast increase in the scope and size of government agencies. Mobilization on such a scale also demanded close cooperation between business executives in major corporations and political leaders in Washington, solidifying a partnership that had been growing since World War I. But the most dramatic expansion of power occurred at the presidential level when Congress passed the War Powers Act of December 18, 1941, giving President Roosevelt unprecedented authority over all aspects of the conduct of the war. This act marks the beginning of what historians call the Imperial Presidency — the far-reaching use (and abuse) of executive authority during decades of American world dominance, from 1945 to the present.

Financing the War

Defense mobilization definitively ended the Great Depression. In 1940, the gross national product stood at $99.7 billion; in 1945 it reached $211 billion. After-tax profits of American businesses nearly doubled, and farm output grew by a third. Federal spending of $186 billion on war production powered this advance; by late 1943, two-thirds of the economy was directly involved in the war effort (Figure 25.1). The government paid for these military expenditures by raising taxes and borrowing money. The Revenue Act of 1942 dramatically expanded the number of people paying income taxes from 3.9 million to 42.6 million; the annual revenue rose to $35.1 billion, facilitated by a payroll deduction system instituted in 1943. Most citizens willingly paid their income taxes as an expression of patriotism. Thanks to this revolutionary — and apparently permanent — change in government financing, taxes on personal incomes and business profits paid for half the cost of the war, compared with 30 percent of the cost of World War I. The government borrowed the rest, both from wealthy Americans and ordinary citizens, who invested some of their wartime wages in long-term Treasury bonds. The **national debt** grew steadily, topping out at $258.6 billion in 1945.

The war also brought a significant expansion in the federal bureaucracy. The number of civilians employed by the government increased almost fourfold, to 3.8 million — a far more dramatic growth than during the New Deal. Leadership of federal agencies also changed as the Roosevelt administration turned from New Deal reformers to business executives. These executives became known as "dollar-a-year men" because they accepted only a token government salary and remained on the payroll of their corporations. Donald Nelson, a former executive at the Sears, Roebuck Company headed the powerful War Production Board (WPB). The Board awarded defense contracts, evaluated military and civilian requests for scarce resources, and oversaw the conversion of industry to military production. To encourage businesses to convert to war production, the board granted generous tax write-offs for plant construction and approved contracts with "cost-plus" provisions that guaranteed a profit and promised that businesses could keep the new factories after the war.

Henry J. Kaiser: "Miracle Man." In the interest of maximum production, the WPB preferred to deal with major corporations rather than with small businesses. America's fifty-six largest corporations received three-fourths of the war contracts; the top ten received a third. The best-known contractor was Henry J. Kaiser. Already highly successful from building roads in California and the Hoover and Grand Coulee dams, Kaiser turned to industrial production. At his Richmond, California, shipyard, he revolutionized ship construction by applying

Figure 25.1 Government Military and Civilian Spending as a Percentage of GDP, 1920–1980.

Government military spending was about 3 percent of the gross domestic product (GDP) in the 1920s and 1930s, but it ballooned to more than 25 percent during World War II, to 13 percent during the Korean War, and to nearly 10 percent during the Vietnam War. Federal government spending for civilian purposes doubled during the New Deal and has remained at about 17 to 20 percent of GDP ever since.

The Miracle Man

Henry Kaiser knew how to run a business with no-nonsense efficiency. He built towns to house his workers, provided them with superior medical care, and organized them to build ships in record time. Here Kaiser uses an 81-piece, 14-foot-long model to show ship owners and Navy brass how his workers built a 10,400-ton Liberty freighter in the amazing time of 4 days, 15 hours, and 26 minutes. Corbis-Bettmann.

Henry Ford's techniques of mass production. Previously, most shipbuilding had been done by skilled workers who had served lengthy apprenticeships. To meet wartime production schedules, Kaiser broke the work process down into small, specialized tasks that newly trained workers could do quickly. Soon each of his work crews was building a "Liberty Ship," a huge vessel to carry cargo and troops to the war zone, every five days. The press dubbed him the "Miracle Man."

The Kaiser shipyards were also known for their corporate welfare programs, which boosted workers' productivity almost as much as his efficient assembly system. Kaiser offered his workers day care for their children, financial counseling, subsidized housing, and low-cost health care. The Kaiser Permanente Medical Care Program, founded in 1942, provided subsidized, prepaid health care for the shipyard workers and their families (and lives on today, as one of the nation's largest and most successful health maintenance organizations).

Central to all of Kaiser's business miracles was a close relationship with the federal agencies. The government financed the great dams he built during the depression and, through the Reconstruction Finance Corporation, lent him $300 million to build shipyards and manufacturing plants during the war. One historian has aptly called Kaiser a "government entrepreneur," the model for a new breed of business executive that prospered because of government contracts (and continue to do so, today). As Secretary of War Henry Stimson put it, in capitalist countries at war "you had better let business make money out of the process or business won't work."

Working together, American business and government turned out a prodigious supply of military hardware: 86,000 tanks; 296,000 airplanes; 15 million rifles and machine guns; 64,000 landing craft; and 6,500 cargo ships and naval vessels. The system of allotting contracts, along with the suspension of the antitrust prosecutions during the war, hastened the trend toward large corporate structures. In 1940, the largest one hundred companies produced 30 percent of the industrial output; by 1945, their share had soared to 70 percent. These same corporations formed the core of the nation's military-industrial complex of the Cold War era (see Chapters 26 and 27).

Mobilizing the American Fighting Force

Going to war meant mobilizing human resources, both on the battlefield and the home front (see Reading American Pictures, "U.S. Political Propaganda on the Home Front During World War II," p. 776). During World War II, the armed forces of the United States numbered more than 15 million men and women. The draft boards registered about 31 million men between the ages of eighteen and forty-four, but more than half the men failed to meet the physical standards, many because of defective teeth. The military tried to screen out homosexuals but had little success. Once in the services, homosexuals found opportunities to participate in a gay culture more extensive than that in civilian life.

Racial discrimination was part of military life, directed mainly against the approximately 700,000 blacks in uniform. The National Association for the Advancement of Colored People (NAACP) and other civil rights groups chided the government with reminders such as "A Jim Crow army cannot fight for a free world," but the military continued to segregate African Americans and to assign them the most menial duties. In contrast, Native Americans and Mexican Americans were never officially segregated and usually welcomed into combat units.

READING AMERICAN PICTURES

U.S. Political Propaganda on the Homefront during World War II

Why We Fight. National Museum of American Art, Smithsonian Institution, Washington, D.C.

Please Stay Home. Picture Research Consultants & Archives.

In times of war, governments use visual imagery to motivate the public and frame the meaning of the war both at home and abroad. During World War II, as we point out in the text, the United States government made every effort to convince the American people to understand and support the war. But what can visual imagery tell us about the nature of World War II? These two pictures — produced in the U.S. during the war — provide some answers. The first is a 1942 lithograph by two artists, Karl Koehler and Victor Ancona, depicting a Nazi officer. The second is a poster of bus travelers produced by the Office of Defense Transportation.

ANALYZING THE EVIDENCE

▶ How might these images affect a viewer? What visual cues or elements do the image-makers employ to create an impact? List some of these items and compare them across the two images. Is one image more convincing than the other? Why?

▶ What kind of message does each image convey? Are these messages consistent with each other? Can you combine the messages into a larger statement explaining the U.S. perspective on fighting the war?

Approximately 350,000 American women enlisted in the armed services. About 140,000 served as army WACS (Women's Army Corps) and 100,000 as naval WAVES (Women Accepted for Volunteer Emergency Service). One-third of the nation's registered nurses, almost 75,000 overall, volunteered for military duty. In addition, about 1,000 WASPs (Women's Airforce Service Pilots) ferried planes and supplies in noncombat areas. The armed forces limited the types of duty assigned to women, as it did with blacks. Women officers could not command men, and WACS and WAVES were barred from combat duty, although female as well as male nurses served close to the front lines, risking capture or death. Most of the jobs women did in the military—clerical work, communications, and health care—reflected stereotypes of women's roles in civilian life.

Workers and the War Effort

As millions of working age citizens joined the military, the nation faced a critical labor shortage. The backlog of depression-era unemployment quickly disappeared, as defense industries alone provided jobs for about seven million new workers. Substantial numbers of women and blacks joined the industrial workforce; unions, benefiting from the demand for their members, negotiated higher wages and improved conditions for America's workers.

Rosie the Riveter. Government and corporate recruiters drew on patriotism as they urged women to take jobs in defense industries. "Longing won't bring him back sooner... GET A WAR JOB!" one poster beckoned, while the artist Norman Rockwell's famous "Rosie the Riveter" beckoned to women from the cover of the *Saturday Evening Post*. The government directed its publicity at housewives, but many working women gladly abandoned low-paying "women's" jobs as domestic servants or file clerks for higher-paying work in the defense industry. Suddenly the nation's factories were full of women working as airplane riveters, ship welders, and drill-press operators. Women made up 36 percent of the labor force in 1945, compared with 24 percent at the beginning of the war. Women war workers often faced sexual harassment on the job and usually received lower wages than men did. In shipyards women with the most seniority and responsibility earned $6.95 a day, whereas the top men made as much as $22.

When the men came home from war and the nation's plants returned to peacetime operations, Rosie the Riveter was out of a job. But many married women refused to put on aprons and stay home, and women's participation in the labor force rebounded steadily for the rest of the 1940s. The wartime expansion of the female workforce, especially among married women, began a trend that would continue for the rest of the twentieth century and change the character of family life (see Comparing American Voices, "Women in the Wartime Workplace," pp. 778–779).

Organized Labor. Workers used wartime mobilization to extend the gains in unionization and

A Real "Rosie" at Work

Elegant posters by artists J. Howard Miller (1942) and Norman Rockwell (1943) celebrated the work of the six million women who worked in the defense industry during World War II, as did the song that gave them a generic name: Rosie the Riveter. As this photograph suggests, the work itself had more grease and grime than elegance. This young woman operates a high-powered lathe, a boring machine that makes engine parts to precise specifications. Library of Congress.

COMPARING AMERICAN VOICES

Women in the Wartime Workplace

During World War II, millions of men served in the armed forces and millions of women worked in war-related industries. A generation later, some of these women workers recounted their wartime experiences to historians in oral interviews.

EVELYN GOTZION
Becoming a Union Activist

Evelyn Gotzion went to work at Rayovac, a battery company in Madison, Wisconsin, in 1935; she retired in 1978. While at Rayovac, Gotzion and her working husband raised three children.

I had all kinds of jobs. [During the war] we had one line, a big line, where you'd work ten hours and you'd stand in one spot or sit in one spot. It got terrible, all day long. So I suggested to my foreman, the general foreman, that we take turns of learning everybody's job and switching every half hour. Well, they [the management] didn't like it, but we were on the side, every once in a while, learning each other's job and learning how to do it, so eventually most all of us got so we could do all the jobs, [of] which there were probably fifteen or twenty on the line. We could do every job so we could go up and down the line and rotate. And then they found out that that was really a pretty good thing to do because it made the people happier....

I one day I was the steward, and they wouldn't listen to me. They cut our rates, so I shut off the line, and the boss came up and he said, "What are you doing?" I said, "Well, I have asked everybody that I know why we have gotten a cut in pay and why we're doing exactly the same amount of work as we did.... So, anyhow, we wrote up a big grievance and they all signed it and then I called the president of the union and then we had a meeting.... At that point the president decided that I should be added to the bargaining committee so that I would go in and argue our case, because I could do it better than any of the rest of them because I knew what it was.... We finally got it straightened out, and we got our back pay, too. From then on I was on the bargaining committee all the years that I worked at Rayovac.

SOURCE: Michael E. Stevens and Ellen D. Goldlust, eds., *Women Remember the War, 1941–1945* (Madison: State Historical Society of Wisconsin Press, 1993), 26–29.

FANNY CHRISTINA (TINA) HILL
War Work: Social and Racial Mobility

After migrating to California from Texas and working as a domestic servant, Tina Hill, an African American, got a wartime job at North American Aircraft. After time off for a pregnancy in 1945, Hill worked there until 1980.

Most of the men was gone, and ... most of the women was in my bracket, five or six years younger or older. I was twenty-four. There was a black girl that hired in with me. I went to work the next day, sixty cents an hour.... I could see where they made a difference in placing you in certain jobs. They had fifteen or twenty departments, but all the Negroes went to Department 17 because there was nothing but shooting and bucking rivets. You stood on one side of the panel and your partner stood on this side and he would shoot the rivets with a gun and you'd buck them with the bar. That was about the size of it. I just didn't like it ... went over to the union and they told me what to do. I went back inside and they sent me to another department where you did bench work and I liked that much better....

Some weeks I brought home twenty-six dollars ... then it gradually went up to thirty dollars [about $400 in 2007].... Whatever you make you're supposed to save some. I was also getting that fifty dollars a month from my husband and that was just saved right away. I was planning on buying a home and a car.... My husband came back [from the war, and] ... looked for a job in the cleaning and pressing place, which was just plentiful.... That's why he didn't bother to go out to North American. But what we both weren't thinking about was that they [North American] have better benefits because they did have an insurance plan and a union to back you up. Later he did come to work there, in 1951 or 1952....

When North American called me back [after she left to have a baby] was I a happy soul!... It made me live better. It really did. We always say that Lincoln took the bale off of the Negroes. I think there is a statue up there in Washington, D.C., where he's lifting something off the Negro. Well, my sister always said — that's why you can't interview her because she's so radical — "Hitler was the one that got us out of the white folks' kitchen."

SOURCE: Excerpted from Sherna B. Gluck, *Rosie the Riveter Revisited* (Boston: G. K. Hall & Co., 1987), 37–42.

PEGGY TERRY
War: Wider Horizons and Personal Tragedies

Peggy Terry was born in Oklahoma, grew up in Paducah, Kentucky, and worked in defense plants in Kentucky and Michigan before settling in Chicago.

The first work I had after the Depression was at a shell-loading plant in Viola, Kentucky. It is between Paducah and Mayfield. They were large shells: anti-aircraft, incendiaries, and tracers.... We made the fabulous sum of thirty-two dollars a week [about $445 in 2007]. To us it was just an absolute miracle. Before that, we made nothing.

You won't believe how incredibly ignorant I was. I knew vaguely that a war had started, but I had no idea what it meant.... I was eighteen. My husband was nineteen. We were living day to day. When you are involved in stayin' alive, you don't think about big things like a war. It didn't occur to us that we were making these shells to kill people. It never entered my head.... We were just a bunch of hillbilly women laughin' and talkin'....

I worked in building number 11. I pulled a lot of gadgets on a machine. The shell slid under and powder went into it. Another lever you pulled tamped it down. Then it moved on a conveyer belt to another building where the detonator was dropped in. You did this over and over.

Tetryl was one of the ingredients and it turned us orange. Just as orange as an orange. Our hair was streaked orange. Our hands, our face, our neck just turned orange, even our eyeballs. We never questioned. None of us ever asked, What is this? Is this harmful?... The only thing we worried about was other women thinking we had dyed our hair. Back then it was a disgrace if you dyed your hair....

I think of how little we knew of human rights, union rights. We knew Daddy had been a hell-raiser in the mine workers' union, but at that point it hadn't rubbed off on any of us women. Coca-Cola and Dr. Pepper were allowed in every building, but not a drop of water. You could only get a drink of water if you went to the cafeteria, which was about two city blocks away. Of course you couldn't leave your machine long enough to go get a drink....

The war just widened my world. Especially after I came up to Michigan.... We made ninety dollars a week [about $1,000 in 2007]. We did some kind of testing for airplane radios. Ohh, I met all those wonderful Polacks. They were the first people I'd ever known that were any different from me. A whole new world just opened up. I learned to drink beer like crazy with 'em. They were all very union-conscious. I learned a lot of things that I didn't even know existed....

My husband was a paratrooper in the war, in the 101st Airborne Division. He made twenty-six drops in France, North Africa, and Germany.... Until the war he never drank. He never even smoked. When he came back he was an absolute drunkard. And he used to have the most awful nightmares. He'd get up in the middle of the night and start screaming. I'd just sit for hours and hold him while he just shook. We'd go to the movies, and if they'd have films with a lot of shooting in it, he'd just start to shake and have to get up and leave. He started slapping me around and slapped the kids around. He became a brute.

SOURCE: Studs Terkel, *"The Good War": An Oral History of World War II* (New York: Pantheon, 1984), 102–111.

ANALYZING THE EVIDENCE

▶ What common themes appear in the working lives of these three women? For example, how do labor unions affect their conditions of employment?

▶ How did the war change the lives of these women?

▶ These interviews occurred long after the events they describe. How might that long interval have affected the women's accounts of those years?

working conditions made in the New Deal. By 1945 almost 15 million workers belonged to a union, up from 9 million in 1939. These gains stemmed in part from organized labor's embrace of patriotism. In December 1941, representatives of the major unions made a "no-strike" pledge — nonbinding in character — for the duration of the war. In January 1942 Roosevelt set up the National War Labor Board (NWLB), composed of representatives of labor, management, and the public. The NWLB established wages, hours, and working conditions and had the authority to order government seizure of plants that did not comply. Forty plants were seized during the war.

During its tenure the NWLB handled 17,650 disputes affecting 12 million workers. It resolved the controversial issue of mandatory union membership through a compromise. New hires did not have to join a union, but those who already belonged had to maintain their union membership over the life of a contract. Agitation for wage increases caused a more serious disagreement. Because managers wanted to keep production running smoothly and profitably, they were willing to pay higher wages. However, pay raises conflicted with the government's efforts to combat inflation, which drove up prices dramatically in the early war years. Incomes rose as much as 70 percent during the war because workers earned pay for overtime work, which was not covered by wage ceilings and greatly increased output.

Despite higher incomes, many union members felt cheated as they watched corporate profits soar in relation to wages. Dissatisfaction peaked in 1943 when a nationwide railroad strike was narrowly averted. Then, John L. Lewis led more than half a million United Mine Workers out on strike, demanding an increase in wages over that recommended by the NWLB. Lewis's tactics won concessions, but they also alienated many Americans and made him one of the most disliked public figures of the 1940s. Congress responded by passing (over Roosevelt's veto) the Smith-Connally Labor Act of 1943, which required a thirty-day cooling-off period before a strike and prohibited strikes in defense industries. The legacy of this public and congressional hostility would hamper the union movement in the postwar years.

African American and Mexican American Workers. During the war, a new mood of militancy swept through the African American community. "A wind is rising throughout the world of free men everywhere," Eleanor Roosevelt wrote during the war, "and they will not be kept in bondage." Black leaders pointed out parallels between anti-Semitism

Fighting for Freedom at Home and Abroad, 1941
This protester from the Negro Labor Relations League pointedly drew the parallel between blacks serving in the armed forces and winning access to jobs at the Bowman Dairy Company, a Chicago bottler, dried milk producer, and distributor that employed three thousand workers. Library of Congress.

in Germany and racial discrimination in America and pledged themselves to a "Double V" campaign: victory over Nazism abroad and victory over racism and inequality at home.

Even before Pearl Harbor, black labor activism was on the rise. In 1940 only 240 of the nation's 100,000 aircraft workers were black, and most of them were janitors. African American leaders demanded that the government require defense contractors to hire more blacks. When the government took no action, A. Philip Randolph, head of the Brotherhood of Sleeping Car Porters, the largest black union, announced plans for a "March on Washington" in the summer of 1941. Roosevelt was not a strong supporter of civil rights, but he feared the embarrassment of a massive public protest and he worried about a disruption of the nation's war preparations.

In June 1941, in exchange for Randolph's cancellation of the march, Roosevelt issued Executive Order 8802. It prohibited "discrimination in the employment of workers in defense industries or government because of race, creed, color, or national origin," and established the Fair Employment Practices Commission (FEPC). This federal commitment to minority employment rights was both unprecedented and limited: For example, it did not affect segregation in the armed forces, and the FEPC could not require compliance with its orders. Still, the committee resolved about a third of the more than eight thousand complaints it received.

Encouraged by the ideological climate of the war years, the League of United Latin American Citizens (LULAC) — the Latino counterpart to the NAACP — challenged long-standing patterns of discrimination and exclusion. In Texas, where it was still common to see signs reading, "No Dogs or Mexicans Allowed," the organization protested limited job opportunities and the segregation of schools and public facilities. The NAACP itself grew ninefold to 450,000 members by 1945, and in Chicago James Farmer helped to found the Congress of Racial Equality (CORE), a group known nationwide for protesting through direct action, such as rallies and sit-ins. These wartime developments — both federal intervention in the form of the FEPC and resurgent African American militancy — laid the groundwork for the civil rights revolution of the 1960s.

Politics in Wartime

The federal government expanded dramatically during the war years, but there was little attempt to use the state to promote progressive social reform on the home front, as in World War I. Many people, including business leaders, believed that an enlarged federal presence was justified only insofar as it assisted war aims. Moreover, in the 1942 elections Republicans had picked up ten seats in the Senate and forty-seven seats in the House, bolstering conservatives in Congress and cutting back prospects for new social initiatives. As war mobilization brought full employment, Roosevelt ended several popular New Deal programs, such as the Civilian Conservation Corps and the National Youth Administration.

As the war dragged on, Roosevelt began to lay the ideological foundations for new federal social welfare measures. In his State of the Union address in 1944, he called for a second bill of rights, which would guarantee that Americans had jobs, adequate food and clothing, decent homes, medical care, and education. There was some public support for such welfare measures, but Congress was less enthusiastic and extended benefits only to military veterans or GIs (short for "government issue"). The Servicemen's Readjustment Act (1944), popularly known as the "GI Bill of Rights," provided education, job training, medical care, pensions, and mortgage loans for men and women who had served in the armed forces. An extraordinarily influential program, particularly in expanding access to higher education, it distributed almost $4 billion in benefits to nine million veterans between 1944 and 1949; in the 1950s, it was extended to veterans of the Korean War.

The Election of 1944. Roosevelt's call for social legislation was part of a plan to reinvigorate the New Deal political coalition. In the election of 1944, Roosevelt once again headed the Democratic ticket. Party leaders, aware of FDR's health problems and anxious to find a middle-of-the-road successor, dropped Vice President Henry Wallace from the ticket. They feared that Wallace's outspoken support for labor, civil rights, and domestic reform would alienate southern Democrats. In his place they chose Senator Harry S. Truman of Missouri. A direct-speaking, no-nonsense politician, Truman won his seat because of the sponsorship of Thomas Pendergast, the Democratic boss in Kansas City. Truman rose to prominence for heading a Senate investigation of government efficiency in awarding wartime defense contracts.

The Republicans nominated Governor Thomas E. Dewey of New York. Only forty-two years old, Dewey had won fame fighting organized crime as a U.S. attorney. Like drug smuggling today, the bootlegging of liquor during Prohibition generated huge profits and highly organized criminal "families" that subsequently turned to prostitution and the "protection" racket. Dewey took on the mobs in New York and, despite his use of controversial "third-degree" interrogation tactics, won the admiration of many Americans. Because Dewey accepted the general principles of welfare state liberalism domestically and internationalism in foreign affairs, he attracted some of Roosevelt's supporters. But a majority of voters preferred political continuity. Roosevelt received 53.5 percent of the nationwide vote and 60 percent in cities of more than 100,000 people, where ethnic minorities and labor unions strongly supported Democratic candidates. The continuing strength of the New Deal coalition after the economic emergency of the Great Depression had passed indicated that the long era of Republican political dominance (1896–1932) had come to an end.

> - In what ways did World War II contribute to the growth of the federal government? How did it foster what historians now call the "military-industrial complex"?
> - What impact did war mobilization have on women, racial minorities, and organized labor? What legislation or government rules affected their lives as workers, and what effect did it have on their political allegiance?

Life on the Home Front

The United States did not suffer the physical devastation that ravaged much of Europe and East Asia, but the war deeply affected the lives of millions of civilians, in ways good and bad. Americans welcomed the return of prosperity but shuddered every time they saw a Western Union boy on his bicycle, fearing he carried a telegram from the War Department reporting the death of someone's son, husband, or father. Many citizens also grumbled about the annoying government regulations that were a constant fact of life, but accepted that things would be different "for the duration."

"For the Duration"

Just like the soldiers in uniform, people on the home front had jobs to do. They worked on civilian defense committees, recycled old newspapers and scrap material, and served on local rationing and draft boards. About twenty million home "Victory gardens" produced 40 percent of the nation's vegetables. Various federal agencies encouraged these efforts, especially the Office of War Information (OWI), which disseminated news and promoted patriotism. The OWI urged advertising agencies to link their clients' products to the war effort, arguing that patriotic ads would not only sell goods but also "invigorate, instruct and inspire" the citizenry.

Popular Culture. Popular culture, especially the movies, reinforced the connections between the home front and the war effort. Hollywood producers, directors, and actors offered their talent to the War Department. Director Frank Capra created a series of "Why We Fight" documentaries to explain war aims to conscripted soldiers. Movie stars such as John Wayne, Anthony Quinn, and Spencer Tracy portrayed the heroism of American fighting men in many films, including *Wake Island* (1942), *Guadalcanal Diary* (1943), and *Thirty Seconds over Tokyo* (1945). Other movies, such as *Watch on the Rhine* (1943), warned of the danger of fascism at home and abroad, while the Academy Award–winning *Casablanca* (1943) demonstrated the heroism and patriotism of an ordinary American in German-occupied North Africa.

Average weekly movie attendance soared to over 100 million. Demand was so high that many theaters operated around the clock to accommodate defense workers on the swing and night shifts. Many movies had patriotic themes. In the box-office hit *Since You Went Away* (1943), Claudette Colbert starred as a wife who took a defense job after her husband left for war, while Oscar-winning Greer Garson played a courageous British housewife in *Mrs. Miniver* (1942). In this pre-television era, newsreels accompanying the feature films kept the public up-to-date on the war, as did on-the-spot radio broadcasts by Edward R. Murrow and other well-known commentators.

Wartime Prosperity and Rationing. Perhaps the major source of Americans' high morale was wartime prosperity. Federal defense spending had ended the depression, unemployment had disappeared, and per capita income doubled in real terms from $595 in 1939 to $1,237 in 1945. Despite geographical dislocations and shortages of many items, about 70 percent of Americans admitted midway through the war that they had personally experienced "no real sacrifices." A Red Cross worker put it bluntly: "The war was fun for America. I'm not talking about the poor souls who lost sons and daughters. But for the rest of us, the war was a hell of a good time."

For many Americans the major inconveniences of the war were the limitations placed on their consumption. In contrast to the largely voluntaristic approach used during World War I, federal agencies such as the Office of Price Administration subjected almost everything Americans ate, wore, or used during World War II to rationing or regulation. The first major scarcity was rubber. The Japanese conquest of Malaya and the Netherlands Indies cut off 97 percent of America's imports of natural rubber, an essential raw material. An entire new industry, synthetic rubber, was born and by late 1944 was producing 762,000 tons a year. To conserve rubber for the war effort, the government rationed tires, and so many of the nation's thirty million car owners put their cars up on blocks for the duration. As more people walked, they wore out their shoes. In 1944 shoes were rationed to two pairs per person a year, half the prewar average.

The government also rationed fuel oil, so schools and restaurants shorted their hours, and homeowners lowered their thermostats to 65 degrees. To cut domestic gasoline consumption, the government rationed supplies and imposed a nationwide speed limit of 35 miles per hour, which cut highway deaths dramatically. By 1943, the government was regulating the amount of meat, butter, sugar, and other foods Americans could buy. Most people cooperated with the complicated system of rationing points and coupons, but almost a fourth occasionally bought items on the black market, especially meat, gasoline, cigarettes, and nylon stockings. Manufacturers of automobiles, refrigerators, and radios, who had been forced to switch to military production, told consumers to save their money now and buy products once the war ended.

Migration and Social Conflict

The war and government policies determined where many people lived. When men entered the armed services, their families often followed them to training bases or points of debarkation. The lure of high-paying defense jobs encouraged others — Native Americans on reservations, white southerners in the hills of Appalachia, farmers on marginal lands — to move. About fifteen million Americans changed residences during the war years, half of them moving to another state.

As a major center of defense production for the Pacific war, California was affected more than any other state by wartime migration. The state welcomed nearly three million new residents and grew by 53 percent during the war. "The Second Gold Rush Hits the West," headlined the *San Francisco Chronicle* in 1943. A tenth of all federal dollars flowed into California, and the state's factories turned out one-sixth of all war materials. People went where the defense jobs were — to Los Angeles, San Diego, and the San Francisco Bay area. Some towns grew practically overnight: Within two years of the opening of

A Family Effort
After migrating from the Midwest to Portland, Oregon, fifteen members of the family of John R. Brauckmiller (sixth from left) found jobs at Henry Kaiser's Swan Island shipyard. From 1943 to 1945, the shipyard turned out 152 T-2 Tankers, mostly for use by the U.S. Navy to carry fuel oil. A local newspaper pronounced the Brauckmillers as "the shipbuildingest family in America," and because of the importance of shipbuilding to the war effort, *Life* magazine featured the family in its issue of August 16, 1943. Ralph Vincent, *The Journal*, Portland, OR.

Zoot Suit Youth in Los Angeles

During a four-day riot in June 1943, servicemen in Los Angeles attacked young Latino men wearing distinctive "zoot suits," which were widely viewed as emblems of gang membership and a delinquent youth culture. The police response was to arrest scores of zoot-suiters. Here, a group of handcuffed young Latino men is about to board a Los Angeles County Sheriff's bus to make a court appearance. Note the wide-legged pants that taper at the ankle, a hallmark of the zoot suit. Library of Congress.

the huge Kaiser Corporation shipyard in Richmond, California, the town's population had quadrupled.

The growth of war industries prompted the migration of more than a million African Americans from the rural South to California, Illinois, Michigan, Ohio, and Pennsylvania — a continuation of the "Great Migration" earlier in the century (see Chapter 22). As migrant blacks and whites competed for jobs and housing, racial conflicts broke out in forty-seven cities during 1943. The worst violence took place in the Detroit area. In June 1943, a major race riot erupted, with Polish Americans and southern white migrants on one side and African Americans on the other. It left thirty-four people dead and hundreds injured.

Racial conflict struck the West as well. In Los Angeles, male Hispanic teenagers organized *pachuco* (youth) gangs. Many dressed in "zoot suits" — broad-brimmed felt hats, pegged trousers, and clunky shoes; they wore their long hair slicked down and carried pocket knives on gold chains. The young women who partied with them favored long coats, huarache sandals, and pompadour hairdos. Some blacks and working-class white teenagers in Los Angeles and eastern cities took up the zoot suit style to indicate both their group identity and their rejection of white, middle-class values. To many adults, the zoot suit symbolized wartime juvenile delinquency. When rumors circulated in July 1943 that a *pachuco* gang had beaten a white sailor, it set off a four-day riot. White servicemen roamed through Mexican American neighborhoods and attacked zoot-suiters, taking special pleasure in slashing their pegged pants. Some attacks occurred in full view of white police officers, who did nothing to stop the violence.

Civil Rights during Wartime

These outbreaks of social violence were sharp but limited. Unlike World War I, which evoked intense prejudice and widespread harassment of German Americans, the mood on the home front was generally calm in the 1940s. Federal officials interned about five thousand potentially dangerous German and Italian aliens during the war. But leftists and Communists, prime targets of government repression at the end of World War I, experienced few problems, in part because the Soviet Union and the United States were allies in the fight against right-wing fascist nations.

Japanese Internment. The internment of Japanese aliens and Japanese American citizens was a glaring exception to this record of tolerance. Immediately after the attack on Pearl Harbor, the West Coast remained calm. Then, as residents began to fear attacks, spies, and sabotage, California's long history of racial antagonism toward Asian immigrants came into play (see Chapters 16, 21, and 24). Local politicians and newspapers whipped up sentiment against Japanese Americans, who numbered only about 112,000, had no political power, and clustered together in ethnic communities in the three West Coast states.

Early in 1942 Roosevelt responded to West Coast fears by issuing Executive Order 9066. The order, and

Behind Barbed Wire

As part of the forced relocation of 112,000 Japanese Americans, Los Angeles photographer Toyo Miyatake and his family were sent to Manzanar, a camp in the California desert east of the Sierra Nevada. Miyatake secretly began shooting photographs of the camp with a handmade camera. Eventually, Miyatake received permission from the authorities to document life in the camp — its births, weddings, deaths, and high school graduations. To communicate the injustice of internment, he also took staged photographs, such as this image of three young boys behind barbed wire with a watchtower in the distance. For Miyatake, it gave new meaning to the phrase "prisoners of war." *Toyo Miyatake.*

a subsequent act of Congress, gave the War Department the authority to evacuate Japanese Americans from the West Coast and intern them in relocation camps for the rest of the war. Despite the lack of any evidence of disloyalty or sedition activity among the evacuees, few public leaders opposed the plan. "A Jap's a Jap," snapped General John DeWitt, the officer charged with defense of the West Coast. "It makes no difference whether he is an American citizen or not."

The relocation plan shocked Japanese Americans, more than two-thirds of whom were native-born American citizens. (They comprised the Nisei generation, the children of the immigrant Issei generation.) Army officials gave families only a few days to dispose of their property. Businesses that took a lifetime to build were liquidated overnight, and speculators snapped up Japanese real estate for a fraction of its value (see Voices from Abroad, "Monica Itoi Sone: Japanese Relocation," p. 786). The War Relocation Authority moved the internees to hastily built camps in desolate areas in California, Arizona, Utah, Colorado, Wyoming, Idaho, and Arkansas (Map 25.2). Ironically, the Japanese Americans who made up one-third of the population of Hawaii, and presumably posed a greater threat because of their numbers and proximity to Japan,

Map 25.2 Japanese Relocation Camps

In 1942, the government ordered 112,000 Japanese Americans living on the West Coast into internment camps in the nation's interior because of their supposed threat to public safety. Some of the camps were as far away as Arkansas. The federal government rescinded the mass evacuation order in December 1944, but when the war ended in August 1945, 44,000 people still remained in the camps.

VOICES FROM ABROAD

Monica Itoi Sone
Japanese Relocation

As Monica Itoi Sone discovered, her legal status as an American citizen did not keep her from being treated like an unwelcome foreigner. Her autobiography, Nisei Daughter (1953), tells the story of the relocation and internment of Japanese Americans during World War II. In 1942 Sone was a young woman who had been born and raised in Seattle; she saw herself as an "American." In this selection, Sone ponders the question of national identity as she describes the Itoi family's forced evacuation by the U.S. Army. Her family spent the entire war in an internment camp in Idaho, but in 1943 Sone was allowed to attend college in Indiana.

We felt fortunate to be assigned to a room at the end of the barracks because we had just one neighbor to worry about. The partition wall separating the rooms was only seven feet high with an opening of four feet at the top, so at night, Mrs. Funai next door could tell when Sumi was still sitting up in bed in the dark, putting her hair up. "Mah, Sumi-chan," Mrs. Funai would say through the plank wall, "are you curling your hair tonight again? Do you put it up every night?" Sumi would put her hands on her hips and glare defiantly at the wall.

The block monitor, an impressive Nisei who looked like a star tackle with his crouching walk, came around the first night to tell us that we must all be inside our room by nine o'clock every night. At ten o'clock, he rapped at the door again, yelling, "Lights out!" and Mother rushed to turn the light off not a second later.

Throughout the barracks, there were a medley of creaking cots, whimpering infants and explosive night coughs. Our attention was riveted on the intense little wood stove which glowed so violently I feared it would melt right down to the floor. We soon learned that this condition lasted for only a short time, after which it suddenly turned into a deep freeze. Henry and Father took turns at the stove to produce the harrowing blast which all but singed our army blankets, but did not penetrate through them. As it grew quieter in the barracks, I could hear the light patter of rain. Soon I felt the "splat! splat!" of raindrops digging holes into my face. The dampness on my pillow spread like a mortal bleeding, and I finally had to get out and haul my cot toward the center of the room. In a short while Henry was up. "I've got multiple leaks, too. Have to complain to the landlord first thing in the morning."

All through the night I heard people getting up, dragging cots around. I stared at our little window, unable to sleep. I was glad Mother had put up a makeshift curtain on the window for I noticed a powerful beam of light sweeping across it every few seconds. The lights came from high towers placed around the camp where guards with Tommy guns kept a twenty-four hour vigil. I remembered the wire fence encircling us, and a knot of anger tightened in my breast. What was I doing behind a fence like a criminal? If there were accusations to be made, why hadn't I been given a fair trial? Maybe I wasn't considered an American anymore. My citizenship wasn't real, after all. Then what was I? I was certainly not a citizen of Japan as my parents were. On second thought, even Father and Mother were more alien residents of the United States than Japanese nationals for they had little tie with their mother country. In their twenty-five years in America, they had worked and paid their taxes to their adopted government as any other citizen.

Of one thing I was sure. The wire fence was real. I no longer had the right to walk out of it. It was because I had Japanese ancestors. It was also because some people had little faith in the ideas and ideals of democracy. They said that after all these were but words and could not possibly insure loyalty. New laws and camps were surer devices. I finally buried my face in my pillow to wipe out burning thoughts and snatch what sleep I could.

SOURCE: Monica Itoi Sone, *Nisei Daughter* (Boston: Little, Brown & Co., 1953), 176–178.

ANALYZING THE EVIDENCE

- What was the difference between Sone's legal status and that of her parents? Why were they treated the same, given their different legal statuses?

- Based on the information in the text, what answer would the Supreme Court have given to Sone's claim that she deserved a "fair trial" before being imprisoned "like a criminal"?

were not interned. They provided much of the unskilled labor in the island territory and the Hawaiian economy could not function without them.

Cracks soon appeared in the relocation policy. A labor shortage in farming led the government to furlough seasonal agricultural workers from the camps as early as 1942. About 4,300 college students were allowed to resume their education outside the West Coast military zone. Another route out of the camps was enlistment in the armed services. The 442nd Regimental Combat Team, a segregated unit composed almost entirely of Nisei volunteers, served with distinction in Europe.

Gordon Hirabayashi: Constitutional Rights. Nisei Gordon Hirabayashi was among the few Japanese Americans who actively resisted incarceration. A student at the University of Washington, Hirabayashi was a religious pacifist who had registered with his draft board as a conscientious objector. He challenged internment by refusing to register for evacuation; instead, he turned himself in to the FBI. "I wanted to uphold the principles of the Constitution," Hirabayashi later stated, "and the curfew and evacuation orders which singled out a group on the basis of ethnicity violated them." Tried and convicted in 1942, he appealed his case to Supreme Court in *Hirabayashi v. United States* (1943). In that case, and also in *Korematsu v. United States* (1944), the Court allowed the removal of Japanese Americans from the West Coast on the basis of "military necessity," but avoided ruling on the constitutionality of the internment program. But in *Ex Parte Endo* (1944), the Court held that American citizens of undoubted loyalty could not be confined by government authorities.

The Court's refusal to rule directly on the relocation program underscored the fragility of civil liberties in wartime. Although Congress in 1988 issued a public apology and $20,000 in cash to each of the 80,000 surviving Japanese American internees, it once again gave the government sweeping powers of arrest and detention in the PATRIOT Act of 2001 (see Chapter 32).

> What impact did World War II have on everyday life for the majority of Americans?

> What distinguished the internal migration of Americans during World War II from that of the World War I era? Who moved and why?

> How do you explain the decision to intern Americans of Japanese birth or ancestry?

Fighting and Winning the War

World War II was, literally, a war for control of the world. Had the Axis Powers triumphed, Germany would have dominated, either directly or indirectly, all of Europe and much of Africa; Japan would have controlled most of East Asia. To prevent this outcome, which would have crippled democracy worldwide, destroyed the British and French empires, and restricted American power to the Western Hemisphere, the Roosevelt administration took the United States to war. The United States extended aid to the Allied Powers in the late 1930s, resorted to economic warfare against Germany and Japan in 1940 and 1941, and then fully committed its industrial might and armed forces from 1942 to 1945. Its intervention, and that of the Soviet Union, decided the outcome of conflict and shaped the character of the postwar world.

Wartime Aims and Tensions

Great Britain, the United States, and the Soviet Union were the key actors in the Allied coalition. China, France, and other nations played lesser roles. The "Big Three," consisting of President Franklin Roosevelt, Prime Minister Winston Churchill of Great Britain, and Premier Joseph Stalin of the Soviet Union, set military strategy and diplomatic policy. The Atlantic Charter, which Churchill and Roosevelt had drafted in August 1941, set out the Anglo-American vision of the postwar international order. It called for free trade, national self-determination, and collective security. Stalin had not participated in that agreement and disagreed fundamentally with some of its precepts, such as a capitalist-run international trading system. Moreover, he hoped to protect the USSR from invasion from the West by setting up a band of Soviet-controlled buffer states along his border with Germany and western Europe.

The first major conflict among the Allies concerned military strategy and timing. While they agreed that defeating Germany (rather than Japan) was the top military priority, they argued over how best to do it. In 1941 the German army had invaded the Soviet Union and advanced to the outskirts of Leningrad and Moscow before being halted by hard-pressed Russian forces in early 1942. To relieve pressure on the Soviet army, Stalin wanted the British and Americans to attack Germany in western Europe, opening this "second front" with a major invasion through France. Roosevelt informally assured Stalin that the Allies would open a second front in 1942, but the British opposed an early invasion and American war production was not yet sufficient to support it. For the next eighteen months, Stalin's pleas went unanswered, and the Soviet Union bore the brunt of the fighting. Then, at a conference of the "Big Three" in Tehran, Iran, in November 1943, Churchill and Roosevelt agreed to open a second front in France within six months in return for Stalin's promise to join the fight against Japan. Both sides adhered to this agreement, but the long delay in creating a second front angered Stalin, who became increasingly suspicious about American and British intentions.

The War in Europe

Following the attack on Pearl Harbor, the Allies suffered one defeat after another. German armies pushed deep into Soviet territory in the south; advancing through the wheat fields of the Ukraine and the rich oil fields of the Caucasus, they moved toward the major city of Stalingrad. Simultaneously the Germans began an offensive in North Africa aimed at seizing the Suez Canal. In the Atlantic, German submarines relentlessly and successfully damaged American convoys carrying oil and other vital supplies to Britain and the Soviet Union.

The Allied Advance. Then, in the winter of 1942–1943, the tide began to turn in favor of the Allies. In the epic Battle of Stalingrad, Soviet forces decisively halted the German advance, killing or capturing 330,000 German soldiers, and began to push westward (Map 25.3). By early 1944, Stalin's troops had driven the German army out of the

Map 25.3 World War II in Europe, 1941–1943

Hitler's Germany reached its greatest extent in 1942 when Nazi forces had occupied Norway, France, North Africa, central Europe, and much of western Russia. The tide of battle turned in late 1942 when the German advance stalled at Leningrad and Stalingrad. By early 1943, the Soviet army had launched a massive counterattack at Stalingrad, and Allied forces had driven the Germans from North Africa and launched an invasion of Sicily and the Italian mainland.

Map 25.4 World War II in Europe, 1944–1945

By the end of 1943, the Russian army had nearly pushed the Germans out of the Soviet Union, and by June 1944, when the British and Americans finally invaded France, the Russians had liberated eastern Poland and most of southeastern Europe. By the end of 1944, British and American forces were ready to invade Germany from the west, and the Russians were poised to do the same from the east. Germany surrendered on May 8, 1945.

Soviet Union. Meanwhile, the Allies launched a major offensive in North Africa, Churchill's substitute for a second front in France. Between November 1942 and May 1943, Allied troops under the leadership of General Dwight D. Eisenhower and General George S. Patton defeated Germany's *Afrika Korps,* led by General Erwin Rommel.

From Africa, the Allied command followed Churchill's strategy of attacking the Axis through its "soft underbelly": Sicily and the Italian peninsula. Faced with an Allied invasion, the Italian king ousted Benito Mussolini's Fascist regime in July 1943. German troops took control of Italy and bitterly resisted the Allied invasion. American and British troops took Rome only in June 1944 and were still fighting German forces in northern Italy when the European war ended in May 1945 (Map 25.4). Churchill's southern strategy proved a time-consuming and costly failure.

The long-promised invasion of France came on "D-Day," June 6, 1944. That morning, after an agonizing delay caused by bad weather, the largest armada ever assembled moved across the English Channel under the command of General Dwight D. Eisenhower. When American, British, and Canadian soldiers hit the beaches of Normandy, they suffered terrible causalities but secured a beachhead. Over the next few days, more than 1.5 million soldiers and thousands of tons of military supplies and equipment flowed into France. In August Allied troops liberated Paris; by September they had driven the Germans out of most of France and Belgium. Meanwhile, long-range Allied bombers had attacked German cities as well as military and

Hitting the Beach at Normandy

These American soldiers were among the 156,000 Allied troops who stormed the beaches of Normandy, France, on D-Day, June 6, 1944; on that day alone, more than 10,000 were killed or wounded. Within a month, one million Allied troops came ashore. Filmmaker Steven Spielberg recreated the carnage and confusion of the landing in the opening scene of *Saving Private Ryan* (1998). Library of Congress.

industrial targets. The air campaign killed some 305,000 civilians and soldiers and wounded another 780,000.

The Germans were not yet ready to give up, however. In December 1944 they mounted a final offensive in Belgium, the so-called Battle of the Bulge, before being pushed back across the Rhine River into Germany. As American and British troops drove toward Berlin from the west, Soviet troops advanced from the east through Poland. On April 30, as Russian troops massed outside Berlin, Hitler committed suicide; on May 8, Germany formally surrendered.

The Holocaust. As Allied troops advanced into Poland and Germany in the spring of 1945, they came face to face with Adolf Hitler's "final solution of the Jewish question": the extermination camps where six million Jews had been put to death, along with another six million Poles, Slavs, Gypsies, homosexuals, and other "undesirables." Photographs of the Nazi death camps at Buchenwald, Dachau, and Auschwitz showed bodies stacked like cordwood and survivors so emaciated they were barely alive. Quickly published in *Life* and other mass-circulation magazines, the photographs horrified the American public.

The Nazi persecution of German Jews in the 1930s was widely known in the United States. But when Jews began to flee from Germany, the United States refused to relax its strict immigration laws to take them in. American officials, along with those of most other nations, continued this exclusionist policy during World War II, as the Nazi regime extended its control over millions of east European Jews. Among the various factors that combined to inhibit American action, the most important was widespread anti-Semitism: in the State Department, Christian churches, and the public at large. The legacy of the immigration restriction legislation of the 1920s and the isolationist attitudes of the 1930s also discouraged policymakers from assuming responsibility for the fate of the refugees. As later American administrations would learn (as "ethnic cleansing" killed millions in India in the 1940s and Bosnia

The Living Dead

When Allied troops advanced into Germany in the spring of 1945, they came face to face with what had long been rumored — concentration camps, Adolf Hitler's "final solution of the Jewish question." In this picture from Wobbelin concentration camp — liberated by the 82nd Airborne Division of the 9th U.S. Army — emaciated inmates are being taken to a hospital. In the days before the camp was liberated, one thousand of the five thousand prisoners had been allowed to starve to death. U.S. Holocaust Memorial Museum.

and Rwanda in the 1990s), such political considerations often conflict with humanitarian values. Taking a narrow view of the national interest, the State Department allowed only 21,000 Jewish refugees to enter the United States during the war. But the War Refugee Board, established by President Roosevelt in 1944, following a plea by Secretary of the Treasury Henry Morganthau, helped to move 200,000 European Jews to safe havens in various countries.

The War in the Pacific

Winning the war against Japan was as arduous as the campaign against Germany in Europe. After crippling the American battle fleet at Pearl Harbor, the Japanese quickly expanded their military presence in the South Pacific, with seaborne invasions of Hong Kong, Wake Island, and Guam. Japanese forces then advanced into Southeast Asia, conquering the Solomon Islands, Burma, and Malaya and threatening Australia and India. By May 1942, they had forced the surrender of American forces in the Philippine Islands and, in the Bataan "death march," callously allowed the deaths of 10,000 prisoners of war.

At that dire moment, American naval forces scored two crucial victories. In the Battle of the Coral Sea near southern New Guinea in May 1942, they halted the Japanese offensive against Australia. In June, at the Battle of Midway Island, the American navy inflicted serious damage on the Japanese fleet. In both battles dive bombers and fighters launched from American aircraft carriers provided the margin of victory.

The American military command, led by General Douglas MacArthur and Admiral Chester W. Nimitz, then took the offensive in the Pacific (Map 25.5). For the next eighteen months, American forces advanced slowly toward Japan, taking one island after another in the face of bitter Japanese resistance. In October 1944, MacArthur and Nimitz began the reconquest of the Philippines by winning the Battle of Leyte Gulf, a massive naval encounter in which the Japanese lost practically their entire fleet (Map 25.6).

By early 1945, victory over Japan was in sight. Japanese military forces had suffered devastating losses, and American bombing of the Japanese homeland had killed about 330,000 civilians and crippled its economy. But the closer U.S. forces got to the Japanese home islands, the more fiercely the Japanese fought. On the small island of Iwo Jima, 21,000 Japanese soldiers fought to the death, killing 6,000 American marines and wounding 14,000 more. On Okinawa, the American toll reached 7,600 dead and 32,000 wounded. Desperate to halt the American advance and short of ammunition, Japanese pilots flew *kamikaze* (suicidal) missions, crashing their bomb-laden planes into American ships. Based on the fighting on Okinawa and Iwo Jima, American military commanders grimly predicted millions of casualties in the upcoming invasion of Japan.

Planning the Postwar World

As Allied forces moved toward victory in the Pacific and Europe, Roosevelt, Churchill, and Stalin met in February 1945 at Yalta, a resort on the Black Sea. Roosevelt focused on maintaining Allied unity, which he saw as the key to postwar peace and stability. But two sets of issues, the fate of the British and French colonial empires and of central and eastern Europe, threatened to divide

Map 25.5 World War II in the Pacific, 1941–1942

After the attacks on Pearl Harbor in December 1941, the Japanese rapidly extended their domination in the Pacific. The Japanese flag soon flew as far east as the Marshall and Gilbert islands and as far south as the Solomon Islands and parts of New Guinea. Japan also controlled the Philippines, much of Southeast Asia, and parts of China, including Hong Kong. By mid-1942, American naval victories at the Coral Sea and Midway stopped further Japanese expansion.

the Big Three. An independence movement in British India, led by Mahatma Gandhi, had already gathered strength and caused friction between Roosevelt and Churchill. A more serious source of conflict was Stalin's insistence that Russian national security demanded the installation of pro-Soviet governments in central and eastern Europe. Roosevelt pressed for an agreement that guaranteed self-determination and democratic elections in Poland and neighboring countries but, given the presence there of Soviet troops, had to accept a pledge from Stalin to hold "free and unfettered elections" at a future time. The three leaders agreed to divide Germany into four administrative zones, each controlled by one of the four powers (the United States, Great Britain, France, and the Soviet Union) and also to partition the capital city, Berlin, which lay in the middle of the Soviet zone, among the four powers.

Creating the United Nations. To continue and expand their alliance, the Big Three agreed to establish an international body to replace the discredited League of Nations. They decided that the new United Nations organization would have a Security Council composed of the five major Allied powers — the United States, Britain, France, China, and the Soviet Union — and six other nations elected on a rotating basis. They also agreed that the five permanent members of the Security Council should have veto power over decisions of the

Map 25.6 World War II in the Pacific, 1943–1945
Allied forces retook the islands in the central Pacific in 1943 and 1944 and ousted the Japanese from the Philippines early in 1945. The capture of Iwo Jima and Okinawa put American bombers in position to attack Japan itself. As the Soviet army invaded Japanese-occupied Manchuria in August 1945, the United States dropped atomic bombs on Hiroshima and Nagasaki. The Japanese offered to surrender on August 10.

General Assembly, in which all nations would be represented. Roosevelt, Churchill, and Stalin announced that the United Nations would convene in San Francisco on April 25, 1945.

Roosevelt returned to the United States in February, visibly exhausted by his 14,000-mile trip. The sixty-three-year-old president was a sick man, suffering from heart failure and high blood pressure. On April 12, 1945, during a short visit to his vacation home in Warm Springs, Georgia, Roosevelt suffered a cerebral hemorrhage and died.

The Atom Bomb. When Harry S Truman assumed the presidency, he learned for the first time about the top-secret Manhattan Project, charged with developing a new weapon—an atomic bomb. European physicists, many of them Jewish, had achieved the theoretical breakthroughs that foreshadowed the atomic age during the first decades of the twentieth century. By the 1930s scientists knew that the tiny nuclei of atoms could be split into yet smaller particles, a process called fission. They also knew that the fission of highly processed uranium would produce a chain reaction and unleash tremendous amounts of energy. Working at the University of Chicago in December 1942, Enrico Fermi and Leo Szilard, refugees from Fascist Italy and Nazi Germany, produced the first controlled chain reaction. With the aid of Albert Einstein, the greatest theorist of modern physics and a refugee

The Big Three at Yalta

With victory in Europe at hand, Roosevelt journeyed in 1945 to Yalta, on the Black Sea, and met for the final time with Churchill and Stalin. The leaders discussed the important and controversial issues of the treatment of Germany, the status of Poland, the creation of the United Nations, and Russian entry into the war against Japan. The Yalta agreements mirrored a new balance of power and set the stage for the Cold War. Franklin D. Roosevelt Library.

scholar at Princeton, they persuaded Franklin Roosevelt to develop an atomic weapon, warning that German scientists were also working on such nuclear reactions.

The Manhattan Project cost $2 billion, employed 120,000 people, and involved the construction of thirty-seven installations in nineteen states — all of this activity hidden from Congress, the American people, and even Vice President Truman. Directed by General Leslie Graves and scientist Robert Oppenheimer, the nation's top physicists assembled the first bomb in Los Alamos, New Mexico, and successfully tested it on July 16, 1945. Overwhelmed by its frightening power, Oppenheimer recalled the words from the *Bhagavad Gita,* the Hindu bible: "I am become Death, Destroyer of Worlds."

Three weeks later, President Truman ordered the dropping of atomic bombs on two Japanese cities, Hiroshima on August 6 and Nagasaki on August 9. Truman was not a reflective man, and he did not question the morality of using such a revolutionary weapon. Administration officials were convinced that Japan's military leaders would never surrender unless their country was utterly devastated, and they knew that an American invasion would cost hundreds of thousands of lives. Truman may also have hoped that use of the bomb would intimidate Stalin and ease his objections to American plans for the postwar world. Whatever the long-range intention or result, atomic bombs achieved the immediate goal. The deaths of 100,000 people at Hiroshima and 60,000 at Nagasaki prompted the Japanese government to offer to surrender on August 10 and to sign a formal agreement on September 2, 1945.

Hiroshima

This aerial view of Hiroshima after the dropping of an atomic bomb on August 6, 1945, shows the terrible devastation of the city. A U.S. Army report prepared in 1946 describes the bomb exploding "with a blinding flash in the sky, and a great rush of air and a loud rumble of noise extended for many miles around the city; the first blast was soon followed by the sounds of falling buildings and of growing fires, and a great cloud of dust and smoke began to cast a pall of darkness over the city." Except for fifty concrete-reinforced buildings designed to withstand earthquakes, every structure within one mile of the center of the bomb blast was reduced to rubble. The physical destruction was second to the human cost: With a population estimated at between 300,000 and 400,000 people, Hiroshima lost 100,000 in the initial explosion, and many thousands more died slowly of radiation poisoning. U.S. Air Force.

Fascism had been defeated, thanks to a strange alliance between the capitalist nations of the West and the communist government of the Soviet Union. The coming of peace would strain, and then destroy, the victorious coalition.

- Describe the course of the war in Europe and the Pacific. What factors led to the Allied victory in World War II?
- Explain why the United States used atomic weapons in Japan. Why was the Americans' use of these weapons controversial?

SUMMARY

As we have seen, the rise of fascism and expansionism in Germany, Italy, and Japan led to the outbreak of World War II. Initially, the American public preferred a policy of noninvolvement. But by 1940 President Roosevelt had begun mobilizing public opinion for intervention and converting the economy to war production. The Japanese attack on Pearl Harbor on December 7, 1941, brought the nation into World War II, a global conflict that involved massive military campaigns in both Europe and the Pacific.

As with World War I, mobilization led to a dramatic expansion of the size and power of the federal government. It also increased geographical and social mobility as new defense plants in California and elsewhere created job opportunities for women, rural whites, southern blacks, and Mexican Americans. Government intervention in the economy assisted the labor movement to consolidate its gains during the 1930s. In addition, the ideological climate of fighting Nazism aided the cause of civil rights for African Americans. At the same time, religious and racial animosity blocked the admission of Jewish refugees and prompted the forced internment of 112,000 Japanese Americans, a devastating denial of civil liberties.

As our account makes clear, the prospects of an American and Allied victory were bleak during much of 1942. By 1943 the Allies had taken the offensive, thanks to advances by the Soviet army in Europe and the American navy in the Pacific; by the end of 1944 victory was all but certain. Among the major powers, only the United States emerged physically unharmed from the war, and it alone possessed the atomic bomb, the most lethal weapon of mass destruction ever created. But the most vexing result of World War II was the onset of the Cold War between the United States and the Soviet Union. This conflict would dominate American foreign policy for the next four decades.

Connections: Government

The "Rise of the State" has been a central theme of Part Five. As we stated in the essay that opened Part Five (p. 671), "American participation in World War I called forth an unprecedented mobilization of the domestic economy" by government institutions, a process we described in Chapter 22. Chapter 23 then explained how that wartime collaboration continued in the 1920s. Herbert Hoover and other government officials promoted polices of the "associated state" and "welfare capitalism," which encouraged large corporate businesses to assume broad economic and social responsibilities. When the Great Depression revealed the flaws in these policies and ideologies, Franklin Roosevelt's New Deal instituted a variety of new government programs to spur economic recovery and social welfare. As Chapter 24 made clear, the National Recovery Association, the Agricultural Adjustment Act, the Works Project Administration, and similar measures represented unprecedented levels of government supervision of American economic life. Likewise, the ideology of social welfare liberalism and its partial realization in the Social Security Act of 1935 gave the federal government major responsibility for the welfare of a substantial majority of American citizens. As we saw in Chapter 25, these links between the state and its citizenry grew even closer and more pervasive during World War II, with the creation of universal income taxation and the enactment of the GI Bill of Rights. Moreover, as we noted in the Part Opener, "Unlike the experience after World War I, the new state apparatus remained in place when the war ended." In Part Six, which covers the period from 1945 to 1980, we will explain how the federal government grew in size and power as it both armed the nation to fight a Cold War abroad and worked to end poverty and expand prosperity at home.

CHAPTER REVIEW QUESTIONS

- According to the oral historian Studs Terkel, World War II was a "good war." Do you agree with this assessment?
- Overall, what sort of impact — positive or negative — did World War II have on women and minority groups in the United States?
- Why was there tension among the Allies during the war, and what long-term impact did it have?

TIMELINE

1933	Adolf Hitler becomes chancellor of Germany
1935	Italy invades Ethiopia
1935–1937	U.S. Neutrality Acts
1936	Germany reoccupies Rhineland demilitarized zone
	Rome-Berlin Axis established
	Japan and Germany sign Anti-Comintern Pact
1937	Japan invades China
1938	Munich agreement between Germany, Britain, and France
1939	Nazi-Soviet Nonaggression Pact
	Germany invades Poland
	Britain and France declare war on Germany
1940	American conscription reinstated
	Germany, Italy, and Japan sign Tri-Partite Pact
1941	Roosevelt promulgates Four Freedoms
	Germany invades Soviet Union
	Lend-Lease Act passed
	Fair Employment Practices Commission created
	Atlantic Charter promulgated
	Japanese attack Pearl Harbor
1942	Allies suffer severe defeats in Europe and Asia
	Executive Order 9066 leads to Japanese internment camps
	Battles of Coral Sea and Midway halt Japanese advance
	Women recruited for war industries
1942–1945	Rationing of scarce goods
1943	Race riots in Detroit and Los Angeles
	Fascism falls in Italy
1944	D-Day: Allied landing in France
	GI Bill of Rights enacted
	Supreme Court avoids issue of the constitutionality of Japanese American internment
1945	Yalta Conference
	Battles of Iwo Jima and Okinawa
	Germany surrenders
	Harry S Truman becomes president after Roosevelt's death
	United Nations convenes
	Atomic bombs dropped on Hiroshima and Nagasaki
	Japan surrenders

FOR FURTHER EXPLORATION

The standard military history of World War II is Henry Steele Commager, *The Story of World War II*, as expanded and revised by Donald L. Miller (1945; revisions 2001). Fifty-three personal stories of war appear in *War Stories: Remembering World War II* (2002), edited by Elizabeth Mullener. An engaging overview of war on the home front is John Morton Blum, *V Was for Victory* (1976). See also "Cents and Sacrifice" at **www.nauticom.net/www/harts/homefront.html**, a comprehensive site with many links to other valuable resources. The National Archives Administration at **www.archives.gov/exhibit_hall/index.html** has two World War II sites: "A People at War" and "Powers of Persuasion: Poster Art from World War II." An anthology that focuses on popular culture and the wartime experience is Lewis A. Erenberg and Susan E. Hirsch, eds., *The War in American Culture* (1996). Powerful novels inspired by the war include John Hersey, *A Bell for Adano* (1944); James Jones, *From Here to Eternity* (1951); and Norman Mailer, *The Naked and the Dead* (1948).

The Library of Congress exhibit "Women Come to the Front: Journalists, Photographers, and Broadcasters During World War II" at **lcweb.loc.gov/exhibits/wcf/wcf0001.html** and "Rosie Pictures: Select Images Relating to American Women Workers During World War II" at **www.loc.gov/rr/print/list/126_rosi.html** record the contributions of women during World War II. Sherna B. Gluck, *Rosie the Riveter Revisited* (1988), offers compelling accounts by women war workers.

Many sites cover the Japanese internment, including the interesting one at the University of Washington on Seattle's Japanese American community: **www.lib.washington.edu/exhibits/harmony/default.htm**. For interviews with detainees and thousands of images, go to **www.densho.org/densho.asp**. The Library of Congress site "Suffering Under a Great Injustice" at **memory.loc.gov/ammem/aamhtml** presents a haunting exhibition of Ansel Adams's photographs of the Manzanar camp.

For "'Man on the Street Interviews' Following the Attack on Pearl Harbor," go to **lcweb2.loc.gov/ammem/afcphhtml/afcphhome.html**. See also the "Rutgers Oral History Archive of World War II" at **oralhistory.rutgers.edu**.

The decision to drop the bomb remains controversial. An excellent site is Lehigh University Professor Edward J. Gallagher's "*The Enola Gay* Controversy: How Do We Remember a War That We Won?" at **www.lehigh.edu/~ineng/enola**. See also the masterful biography of the bomb's principal architect: Kai Bird and Martin J. Sherwin, *American Prometheus: The Triumph and Tragedy of J. Robert Oppenheimer* (2005).

TEST YOUR KNOWLEDGE

To assess your command of the material in this chapter, see the Online Study Guide at **bedfordstmartins.com/henretta**.

For Web sites, images, and documents related to topics and places in this chapter, visit **bedfordstmartins.com/makehistory**.

PART SIX
The Age of Cold War Liberalism
1945–1980

	DIPLOMACY	POLITICS	ECONOMY	SOCIETY	CULTURE
	The Cold War	**Decline of the Liberal Consensus**	**Ups and Downs of U.S. Economic Dominance**	**Social Movements and Demographic Diversity**	**Consumer Culture and Its Critics**
1945	▸ Truman Doctrine (1947) ▸ Marshall Plan (1948) ▸ Berlin blockade ▸ NATO founded (1949)	▸ Truman's Fair Deal liberalism ▸ Taft-Hartley Act (1947) ▸ Truman reelected (1948)	▸ Reconversion ▸ Strike wave (1946) ▸ Bretton Woods system established: World Bank, IMF	▸ Migration to cities accelerates ▸ Armed forces desegregated (1948)	▸ End of wartime rationing ▸ Rise of television ▸ First Levittown (1947)
1950	▸ Permanent mobilization: NSC-68 (1950) ▸ Korean War (1950–1953) ▸ U.S replaces France in Vietnam	▸ McCarthyism ▸ Eisenhower's modern Republicanism ▸ Warren Court activism	▸ Rise of military-industrial complex ▸ Industrial economy booms ▸ Labor-management accord	▸ *Brown v. Board of Education* (1954) ▸ Montgomery bus boycott (1955) ▸ Urban crisis emerges	▸ Growth of suburbia ▸ Sun Belt emerges ▸ Religious revival ▸ Baby boom ▸ Youth culture develops
1960	▸ Cuban missile crisis (1962) ▸ Vietnam War escalates (1965) ▸ Tet offensive (1968); peace talks begin	▸ Kennedy's New Frontier ▸ Kennedy assassinated ▸ Great Society, War on Poverty ▸ Nixon's election (1968) ushers in conservative era	▸ Kennedy-Johnson tax cut, military expenditures fuel economic growth	▸ March on Washington (1963) ▸ Civil rights legislation (1964, 1965) ▸ Student activism ▸ Black Power	▸ Shopping malls spread ▸ Baby boomers swell college enrollment ▸ Hippie counterculture
1970	▸ Nixon visits China (1972); SALT initiates détente (1972) ▸ Paris Peace accords (1973) end Vietnam War ▸ Carter brokers Camp David accords between Egypt and Israel (1978) ▸ Iranian revolution; hostage crisis	▸ Watergate scandal; Nixon resigns (1974) ▸ Weak presidencies of Ford and Carter	▸ Arab oil embargo (1973–1974); inflation surges, while income stagnates ▸ Onset of deindustrialization	▸ Revival of feminism ▸ *Roe v. Wade* (1973) ▸ New Right urges conservative agenda	▸ Consumer and environmental protection movements ▸ Deepening social divide over ERA and gay rights

"What Rome was to the ancient world," proclaimed the influential journalist Walter Lippmann in 1945, "America is to be for the world of tomorrow." Lippmann's remark captures America's sense of triumphant confidence at the end of World War II. What he underestimated were the challenges, both global and domestic, confronting the United States. In this Part Six, covering the years 1945–1980, we track how the United States fared in its quest to become the Rome of the twentieth century.

DIPLOMACY Hardly had Lippmann penned his triumphant words in 1945 than the Soviet Union challenged America's plans for postwar Europe. The Truman administration responded by crafting the policies and alliances that came to define the Cold War. That struggle spawned two "hot" wars in Korea and Vietnam and fueled a terrifying nuclear arms race. By the early 1970s, as the bi-polar assumptions of the Cold War broke down, the Nixon administration got on better terms with both the Soviet Union and China. The high hopes for détente, however, fell short, and during Carter's tenure Soviet-U.S. relations lapsed into a state of anxious stalemate. The hostage crisis in Iran revealed that, beyond the Cold War, other big challenges, especially from the aggrieved Muslim world, faced the United States.

POLITICS Lippmann's confidence in America's future in part stemmed from his sense of a nation united on the big domestic questions. Except for a brief postwar reaction, which brought forth the Taft-Hartley Act (1947), the liberal consensus prevailed. And while not much headway was made by Truman's Fair Deal, neither did Republicans under Eisenhower attempt any dismantling of the New Deal. Johnson's ambitious Great Society, however, did provoke a conservative response and, beginning with the debacle of the Democratic convention of 1968, the country moved to the right. The interaction of the domestic and global — the links between liberalism and the Cold War — was especially clear at this juncture because it was Vietnam that, more than anything, undermined the Great Society and the liberal consensus. By the end of the 1970s, with a big assist from the Carter administration, the Democrats had lost the grip they had won under FDR as the nation's dominant party.

ECONOMY In no realm did America's supremacy seem so secure in the postwar years as in economics. While the war-torn countries of Europe and Asia were picking through the rubble, the American economy boomed, fed both by the military-industrial complex and by a high-spending consumer culture. Real income grew, and collective bargaining became well entrenched. In the 1950s, no country was competitive with America's economy. By the 1970s, however, American industry had been overtaken, and a sad process of dismantling, of deindustrialization, began. At the same time, the inflationary spiral that had begun during the Vietnam War speeded up under the impact of the oil embargo of 1973. A decade of "stagflation" set in, and with it a suspicion that America's vaunted economic powerhouse had seen its best days.

SOCIETY The victory over Nazism in World War II spurred demands for America to make good on its promise of equality for all. In great waves of protests beginning in the 1950s, African Americans — and then women, Latinos, and other minorities — challenged the status quo. Starting with the Supreme Court's landmark *Brown v. Board of Education* (1954) decision, the country began to outlaw the practices of segregation, discrimination, and disfranchisement that had held minorities down. In the 1970s, however, reaction set in, fueled in part by the growing militancy of blacks and others, in part by the discovery of a resentful "silent majority" by conservative politicians. Achieving equality, it turned out, was easier said than done.

CULTURE America's economic power in the postwar years accelerated the development of a consumer society that cherished the tract house, the car, and television set. As millions of Americans moved into suburban subdivisions, the birth-rate speeded up, spawning a baby boom generation whose social influence would be felt for the next seventy-five years. Under the surface calm of the 1950s, a mood of cultural rebellion took hold. In the 1960s, it would burst forth in the hippie counterculture and the antiwar movement. Although both subsided in the early 1970s, they left a lasting impact on the country's politics, in particular, as fuel that fed the resurgence of American conservatism.

Walter Lippmann died in 1974. He had lived long enough to see his high hopes of 1945 blasted by the Cold War, by economic troubles, and by the collapse of the liberal consensus.

26 Cold War America
1945–1960

ON MAY 1, 1950, THE RESIDENTS OF Mosinee, Wisconsin, staged a mock Communist takeover of their small papermill town. Secret police interrogated citizens. The mayor was carted off to jail. The local paper reappeared as a mini-*Pravda*. And restaurants served only potato soup and black bread. Dreamed up by the American Legion, Mosinee's "Day Under Communism" was a sensational media event that conveyed a chilling message: America's way of life was under siege by the Communist menace.

The Mosinee episode captured a towering irony of the postwar period. Americans in 1945 had indeed been anxious over what would follow victory. But their anxiety was not directed at the Soviet Union. Weren't we all part of the Grand Alliance? No, what worried Americans was closer to home. Defense plants were shutting down, war workers being laid off, and twelve million job-seeking veterans on the way home. Might the country slide back into the Great Depression? In short order, those fears dissipated. Home building picked up. Cars flowed from the assembly lines. Consumers began to spend like crazy the savings they had piled up during the war. The economy was in fact entering the strongest boom in American history. But instead of being able to settle back and enjoy their prosperity, the good people of Mosinee worried about a Soviet coup in their town. They had exchanged one fear — of economic hard times — for another: the Communist menace.

The Cold War
Descent into Cold War, 1945–1946
George Kennan and the Containment Strategy
Containment in Asia

The Truman Era
Reconversion
The Fair Deal
The Great Fear

Modern Republicanism
They Liked Ike
The Hidden-Hand Presidency
Eisenhower and the Cold War
Containment in the Post-Colonial World
Eisenhower's Farewell Address

Summary
Connections: Diplomacy and Politics

◀ **The Perils of the Cold War**
In this detail of a 1948 Pulitzer Prize–winning cartoon, Rube Goldberg depicts the perilous nature of America's postwar peace — one that was based largely on the threat of nuclear annihilation. University of California at Berkeley, Bancroft Library.

The conflict that emerged between the Soviet Union and the United States, while not leading to any direct engagement on the battlefield, inaugurated a long twilight era of international tension — a Cold War — when either side, armed with nuclear weapons, might have tipped the entire world into oblivion.

The impact of the Soviet-American confrontation on domestic affairs was far-reaching. The Cold War fostered a climate of fear and suspicion of "subversives" in government, education, and the media. It boosted military expenditures, fueling a growing arms race between the two superpowers, creating a "military-industrial complex" in the United States, and undergirding an amazing era of economic expansion (see Chapter 27). That prosperity helped to expand federal power, perpetuating the New Deal state in the postwar era. But the Cold War also now held liberal politics hostage because the ability of the New Deal coalition to advance its agenda at home depended on its prowess as a Cold Warrior abroad. In all these ways, the line between the international and the domestic blurred. That was an enduring legacy of the Cold War.

The Cold War

The Cold War began in 1946. It ended forty-five years later with the collapse of the Soviet Union. In that intervening period, a vast amount was written by historians about why the Cold War had happened. By no means did all blame the Soviets. Eventually, indeed, those holding the opposite view — the "revisionist" historians, so-called — often held the upper hand. But in truth, the debate was ultimately inconclusive because the scholarly conditions that prevailed really precluded definitive history. The Soviet archives, for one thing, were completely closed. More important, perhaps, historians were trying to capture an event that was still happening. Only now that it is over can historians look back and gain the perspective needed for understanding why the Cold War occurred.

Descent into Cold War, 1945–1946

World War II itself set the basic conditions for Cold War rivalry. With Germany and Japan defeated and America's British and French allies exhausted, only the two superpowers remained standing in 1945. Even had nothing else divided them, the United States and the USSR would have jostled against each other as they moved to fill the vacuum. But, of course, the two countries *were* divided — by ideology, by history, by geography and strategic interest, even by relative power (with the advantage, both militarily and economically, heavily on the American side). FDR understood that bridging the divide and maintaining the U.S.-Soviet alliance were essential conditions for postwar stability. But he also believed that permanent peace depended on adherence to the Wilsonian principles of collective security, self-determination, and free trade (see Chapter 22). The challenge was to find a way of reconciling Wilsonian principles with U.S.-Soviet power realities.

Yalta. That was what Roosevelt, Churchill, and Stalin had undertaken at the Yalta Conference of February 1945. They agreed there to go forward with the United Nations, committing themselves to a new international forum for resolving future conflicts and fostering world peace. The realist side of that noble arrangement, demanded by the U.S. and the USSR, was that permanent seats with veto rights be reserved for them (and their three major allies) on the Security Council. The paramount problem at Yalta, however, was eastern Europe. Roosevelt and Churchill agreed that Poland and its neighbors would fall under the Soviet "sphere of influence" — thus meeting Stalin's demand for secure western borders. But Yalta also called for "free and unfettered" elections — thus upholding the essential principle of democratic self-determination. Implicit in Yalta's details was an expectation — the nub of the deal — that freely elected governments would consent to Soviet domination.

That actually had happened in Finland and, after Yalta, briefly in Czechoslovakia. It could not happen in Poland. For that, Stalin had himself to blame. With war impending in 1939, he made his infamous secret pact with Hitler for the partition of Poland. When the Nazis invaded, the Soviet Union seized its apportioned share (and reclaimed much of it as sovereign territory when the Nazis retreated in 1944). Then Stalin ordered the execution of the entire Polish officer corps in Russian hands in the Katyn forest, a deed that, when exposed by the Nazis in 1943, caused a rift with the Polish government-in-exile in London. Equally unforgivable was Stalin's betrayal of the Poles of Warsaw late in the war. When they rose against the Germans, the Red Army halted on the outskirts so that any potential anti-Communist opposition could be finished off by the Nazis. Evidently blind to the resentment of his victims, Stalin — American observers reported — was taken aback by the fear and loathing that greeted his approaching armies. So there would be no free elections, a conclusion Stalin had already arrived at before Yalta. He got the puppet regime he required, but never the consent of the Poles, or the Hungarians, Romanians, and other subject peoples of eastern Europe. Stalin's unwillingness — his *inability*, if he was to fulfill his ambitions — to hold free elections was the precipitating event of the Cold War.

Truman Takes Command. Historians doubt that, had he lived, even the resourceful Roosevelt could have preserved the Grand Alliance. With Harry Truman, no such possibility existed. Truman was inexperienced in foreign affairs. As vice president, he had been kept in the dark about Roosevelt's negotiations (or even about the atomic bomb). His blunt instinct was to stand up to Stalin. At a meeting held shortly after he took office, the new president berated the Soviet foreign minister, V. M. Molotov, over the Soviets' failure to honor their Yalta agreements. He abruptly halted lend-lease shipments that the Soviets desperately needed and denied their request for $6 billion in credits. Truman used what he called "tough methods" that July at the Potsdam Conference, which had been called to take up postwar planning. After learning of the successful test of America's atomic bomb, Truman "told the Russians just where they got off and generally bossed the whole meeting," recalled Winston Churchill.

Stalin was not taken by surprise. He had been kept informed by his spy network about the Manhattan Project virtually from its inception in 1942 — far earlier than Truman himself knew about it. Nor was Stalin intimidated. His spies assured him that the small American arsenal posed no immediate threat to the Soviet Union. And his own scientists were on a crash course to producing a Soviet bomb, their efforts much eased by plutonium bomb blueprints stolen from the Manhattan Project. It was a time, as Stalin said, for strong nerves. But the atomic issue did enflame tensions, requiring extra displays of toughness by the Soviets, deepening their suspicions of the West, and, on the American side, encouraging a certain swagger. It was unwise, warned Secretary of War Stimson, for the United States to try to negotiate with "this weapon rather ostentatiously on our hip."

In early 1946, the United States made an effort to head off the impending nuclear race, proposing in the Baruch Plan (after its sponsor, the financier Bernard Baruch) that all weapons-related development and production be placed under the control of a special U.N. atomic agency and that a strict system of inspections and punishments (not subject to Security Council veto) be instituted to prevent violations by individual nations. Once international controls were fully in place, the United States would dispose of its stockpile of atomic bombs. Hot on the trail of their own bomb, the Soviets, although they went through the motions of negotiation, regarded the Baruch Plan as an American trick to dominate them. Its failure foreshadowed a frenzied nuclear arms race between the two superpowers.

By then, Truman's instinctive toughness was being seconded by his more seasoned advisors, a distinguished group known collectively as the Establishment for their elite pedigrees and high-placed public service. Close students of diplomacy, some of them, like Averell Harriman and George F. Kennan, experts on Soviet affairs, concluded that Stalin's actions in eastern Europe were not an aberration, but truly reflective of Stalin's despotic regime. A cogent summary of their views came, ironically, from a former Russian foreign minister, Maxim Litvinoff, who had negotiated America's recognition of the Soviet Union with FDR in 1933. Lamenting the end of wartime cooperation, Litvinoff told a CBS Moscow correspondent that the USSR had returned "to the outmoded concept of security in terms of territory — the more you've got, the safer you are." This was because "the ideological concept prevailing here [is] that conflict between Communist and capitalist worlds is inevitable." The Soviet Union was at that time, in early 1946, expanding its reach, maintaining troops in northern Iran, pressing Turkey for access to the Mediterranean, sponsoring a guerrilla war in Greece. If the current Soviet demands were satisfied, the CBS man asked, what then? "It would lead to the West's being faced, after a more or less short time, with the next set of demands," replied Litvinoff.

George Kennan and the Containment Strategy

Just how the West should respond was crystallized in February 1946 by George F. Kennan in an eight-thousand-word cable, dubbed the "Long Telegram," from his post at the U.S. embassy in Moscow. Kennan argued that the Soviet Union was an "Oriental despotism" and Communism just "the fig-leaf" justifying its crimes. For Soviet leaders, hostility to the West provided the essential excuse "for the dictatorship without which they do not know how to rule." The West had no way of altering this perverse internal dynamic. Its only recourse, Kennan wrote in a famous *Foreign Affairs* article a year later, was to meet the Soviets "with unalterable

George F. Kennan

As a diplomat, foreign policy theorist, and historian, George F. Kennan (1904–2005) enjoyed a long and distinguished career spanning more than seventy years. This portrait by Guy Rowe dates from 1955. National Portrait Gallery, Smithsonian Institution/Art Resource, N.Y.

counter-force at every point where they show signs of encroaching upon the interests of a peaceful and stable world." Kennan called for "long-term, patient but firm and vigilant *containment* of Russian expansive tendencies." Containment, the key word, defined America's evolving strategic stance against the Soviet Union, and Kennan, its author, became one of the most influential advisors in the Truman administration.

On its face, containment seemed a counsel of despair, dooming the United States to a draining, inconclusive struggle without end. In fact, Kennan was more optimistic than that. The Soviet system, he argued with notable foresight, was inherently unstable, and eventually — not in Stalin's time, but eventually — it would collapse. Moreover, the Soviets were not reckless. "If . . . situations can be created in which [conflict] is not to [their] advantage," they would pull back. So it was up to the West to create those situations, avoiding an arms race, picking its fights carefully, exercising patience.

Kennan's attentive readers included Stalin, who had quickly obtained a copy of the classified Long Telegram. To keep things even, Stalin ordered his ambassador in Washington to prepare his own Long Telegram, and got back an eerie mirror image of Kennan's analysis, with the United States cast as imperialist aggressor, driven by the crisis of monopoly capitalism, and spending "colossally" on arms and overseas bases. Like Kennan, the Soviet ambassador was confident of the adversary's instability, only in his case, from a rather shorter-term perspective. America's problem was its British alliance, which was "plagued with great internal contradictions" and bound to explode, probably over differences in the Middle East.

The Truman Doctrine. The alliance, in fact, was in some difficulty, not out of conflicting interests, however, but because of British exhaustion. In February 1947 London informed Truman that it could no longer afford to support the anti-Communists in Greece, where a bitter guerrilla war was going on. If the Communists won in Greece, Truman worried, that would embolden the Communist parties in France and Italy and, of more immediate concern, threaten Soviet domination of the eastern Mediterranean. In response the president announced what

Postwar Devastation

Berlin, Germany, was reduced to rubble during World War II. Allied bombing, followed by brutal fighting in April 1945 when Soviet troops entered Berlin, devastated the once impressive capital city. Here, in a telling statement about the collapse of Hitler's Third Reich, German refugees walk in front of what was once Goebbels's Propaganda Ministry. U.S. policymakers feared that the economic disorder following this type of destruction would make many areas of postwar Europe vulnerable to Communist influence. National Archives.

came to be known as the Truman Doctrine. In a speech to the Republican-controlled Congress on March 12, he asserted an American responsibility "to support free peoples who are resisting attempted subjugation by armed minorities or by outside pressures." To that end, Truman requested large-scale assistance for Greece and Turkey. "If we falter in our leadership, we may endanger the peace of the world," Truman declared, and "we shall surely endanger the welfare of our own nation." Despite the open-endedness of this military commitment, Congress quickly approved Truman's request for $300 million in aid to Greece and $100 million for Turkey.

The Marshall Plan. In the meantime, Europe was sliding into economic chaos. Devastated by the war, it was hit by the worst winter in memory in 1947. People were starving, and European credit was nearing zero. At Secretary of State George C. Marshall's behest, Kennan's small team of advisers came up with a remarkable proposal: a massive infusion of American capital to help get the European economy back on its feet. Speaking at the Harvard commencement in June 1947, Marshall urged the nations of Europe to work out a comprehensive recovery program and then ask the United States for aid, which would be forthcoming.

Truman's pledge of financial aid to European economies met with significant opposition in Congress. Republicans castigated the Marshall Plan as a huge "international W.P.A." But in the midst of the congressional stalemate, on February 25, 1948, came a Communist coup in Czechoslovakia. A stark reminder of Soviet ruthlessness, the coup rallied congressional support for the Marshall Plan. In March 1948 Congress voted overwhelmingly to approve funds for the program. Like most other foreign-policy initiatives of the 1940s and 1950s, the Marshall Plan won bipartisan support.

Over the next four years, the United States contributed nearly $13 billion to a highly successful recovery effort. Western European economies revived, industrial production increased 64 percent, and the appeal of the local Communist parties waned. The Marshall Plan was actually a good deal for the United States, providing stronger markets for American goods and fostering the economic multilateralism and interdependence it wanted to encourage in Europe (see Voices from Abroad, "Jean Monnet: Truman's Generous Proposal," p. 807). And, most notably, the Marshall Plan was a strategic masterstroke. The Soviets had been invited to participate. At first they did, then Stalin, sensing a trap, ordered his delegation home and, on further reflection, ordered the satellite delegations home as well. It was a clumsy performance, placing the onus for dividing Europe on the Soviets and depriving their threadbare partners of assistance they sorely needed.

The Berlin Crisis. The flashpoint for a hot war, if it existed anywhere, was Germany. This was because the stakes were so high for both sides and the German situation initially so fluid. At Yalta, Germany's future had been left undecided, except that it would be made to pay heavy reparations and be permanently demilitarized. For the time being, a defeated Germany would be divided into four zones of occupation controlled by the Soviet Union, the United States, Britain, and France. A similar arrangement later applied to Berlin (Map 26.1). As it happened, Anglo-American

MAP 26.1 Cold War in Europe, 1955

This map vividly shows the Cold War division of Europe as it was in 1955. In green are the NATO countries, allied to the United States; in purple, the Warsaw Pact countries, allied to the USSR. At that point, in 1955, West Germany had just been admitted to NATO, completing Europe's stabilization into two rival camps. But Berlin, Germany's traditional capital, remained divided, and one can see, from its location deep in East Germany, why it was always a flashpoint in Cold War controversies.

VOICES FROM ABROAD

Jean Monnet
Truman's Generous Proposal

Jean Monnet was an eminent French statesman and a tireless promoter of postwar European union. As head of a French postwar planning commission, he helped oversee the dispersal of Marshall Plan funds, the importance of which he describes in his memoirs.

So we had at last concerted our efforts to halt France's economic decline; but now, once more, everything seemed to be at risk. Two years earlier [1947], we thought that we had plumbed the depths of material poverty. Now we were threatened with the loss of even basic essentials.... Our dollar resources were melting away at an alarming rate, because we were having to buy American wheat to replace the crops we had lost during the winter.... A further American loan was soon exhausted.

Nor was this grim situation confined to France. Britain too had come to the end of her resources. In February 1947 she had abruptly cancelled her aid to Greece and Turkey, whose burdens she had seemed able to assume in 1945. Overnight, this abrupt abdication gave the United States direct responsibility for part of Europe. Truman did not hesitate for a moment: with the decisiveness that was to mark his actions as President, he at once asked for credits and arms for both Turkey and Greece.... [Soon after], he announced the Truman Doctrine of March 12, 1947. Its significance was general: it meant that the United States would prevent Europe from becoming a depressed area at the mercy of Communist advance. On the very same day, the Four-Power Conference began in Moscow. There, for a whole month, George Marshall, Ernest Bevin, and Georges Bidault argued with Vyacheslav Molotov about all the problems of the peace, and above all about Germany.

When Marshall returned to Washington, he knew that for a long time there would be no further genuine dialogue with Stalin's Russia. The "Cold War," as it was soon to be known, had begun.... Information from a number of sources convinced Marshall and his Under-Secretary Dean Acheson that once again, as in 1941, the United States had a great historic duty. And once again there took place what I had witnessed in Washington a few years earlier: a small group of men brought to rapid maturity an idea which, when the Executive gave the word, turned into vigorous action. This time, it was done by five or six people, in total secrecy and at lightning speed. Marshall, Acheson, [William] Clayton, Averell Harriman, and George Kennan worked out a proposal of unprecedented scope and generosity. It took us all by surprise when we read the speech that George Marshall made at Harvard on June 5, 1947. Chance had led him to choose the University's Commencement Day to launch something new in international relations: helping others to help themselves.

SOURCE: Jean Monnet, *Memoirs*, trans. Richard Mayne (New York: Doubleday, 1978), 264–266.

ANALYZING THE EVIDENCE

- Why, according to Monnet, did Europe need massive economic assistance, and fast?
- Monnet was writing as an embattled Frenchman about the Marshall Plan. If you compare his account with the textbook's account, what is missing from Monnet's account?
- Can you explain, on the basis of Monnet's account of the Marshall Plan, why the North Atlantic Treaty Organization, which was established the following year, proved so durable?

forces, encountering much less German resistance than did the Soviets, could have occupied virtually all of Germany, including Berlin. Churchill pleaded for this, but Roosevelt said no. Even so, Eisenhower's troops ended up a hundred miles inside the Soviet zone at war's end, only to be withdrawn — again over Churchill's protests — at Truman's order. These goodwill gestures proved of no account as tensions mounted and the two sides jockeyed for advantage in Germany. When no agreement for a unified state was forthcoming in 1947, the western allies consolidated their zones and prepared to establish an independent federal German republic, supported by an infusion of Marshall Plan money.

Some of that money was slated for West Berlin, in hopes of making it a capitalist showplace deep inside the Soviet zone. On its face, of course, the Allied presence in Berlin was anomalous, an accident of interim wartime arrangements, and indefensible against the Soviets. That, at any rate, was the way Stalin saw it. In June 1948 he halted all Allied traffic to West Berlin. Instead of giving way, as he had expected, Truman and the British were galvanized into action. They improvised an airlift. For nearly a year American and British pilots, who had been dropping bombs on Berlin only four years earlier, flew in 2.5 million tons of food and fuel — nearly a ton for each resident. The Berlin crisis was the closest the two sides came to actual war, and probably the closest America came — since it had no other military option at the time — to using the atomic bomb against the USSR. But Stalin backed down. On May 12, 1949, he lifted the blockade. West Berlin became a symbol of resistance to Communism.

The crisis in Berlin persuaded western European nations that they needed a collective security pact with the United States. In April 1949, for the first time since the end of the American Revolution, the United States entered into a peacetime military alliance, the North Atlantic Treaty Organization (NATO). Under the NATO pact, twelve nations — the United States, Canada, Britain, France, Italy, Belgium, the Netherlands, Luxembourg, Denmark, Norway, Portugal, and Iceland — agreed that "an armed attack against one or more of them in Europe or North America shall be considered an attack against them all." In May 1949 those nations also agreed to the creation of the Federal Republic of Germany (West Germany), which joined NATO in 1955. In response, the Soviet Union set up the German Democratic Republic (East Germany) in 1949; an economic association, the Council for Mutual Economic Assistance (COMECON), in 1949; and a military alliance for eastern Europe, the Warsaw Pact, in 1955. In these parallel steps, the two superpowers were institutionalizing the Cold War and thereby translating tense uncertainty into permanent stalemate.

Nuclear Stalemate. The final stage in that process came in September 1949, when American military intelligence detected a rise in radioactivity in the atmosphere — proof that the Soviet Union

The Berlin Airlift

For 321 days American planes like this one flew missions to bring food and other supplies to Berlin after the Soviet Union had blocked all surface routes into the former German capital. The blockade was finally lifted on May 12, 1949, after the Soviets conceded that it had been a failure. AP Images.

Testing the Bomb

After World War II, the development of nuclear weapons went on apace, requiring frequent testing of the more advanced weapons. This photograph shows members of the 11th Airborne division viewing the mushroom cloud from one such A-bomb test at the Atomic Energy Commission's proving grounds at Yucca flats in Nevada, November 1, 1951. Finally acknowledging the dangers to the atmosphere (and the people in the vicinity or downwind), the United States and the Soviet Union signed a treaty in 1963 banning above-ground testing. J. R. Eyerman/Time Life Pictures/Getty Images.

had detonated an atomic bomb. With America's brief tenure as sole nuclear power over, there was a pressing need for a major reassessment of the nation's strategic planning. Truman turned to the National Security Council (NSC), an advisory body established by the National Security Act of 1947 that also created the Department of Defense and the Central Intelligence Agency (CIA). In April 1950 the NSC delivered its report, known as "NSC-68." Bristling with alarmist rhetoric, the document urged a crash program to maintain America's nuclear edge, including stepped-up production of atomic bombs and the development of a hydrogen bomb, a thermonuclear device a thousand times more destructive than the atomic bombs that had destroyed Hiroshima and Nagasaki. What American intelligence did not know was that Soviet scientists, unlike their American counterparts, had been working on both tracks all along and were making headway toward a hydrogen bomb. The United States got there first, exploding its first hydrogen bomb in November 1952; the Soviet Union followed in 1953.

Although he accepted the NSC-68 recommendation, Truman had grave misgivings about the furies he was unleashing. This was apparent in his decision to lodge control over nuclear weapons in a civilian agency, not with the military. Truman did not want nuclear weapons incorporated into military planning and treated as a functional part of the nation's arsenal (as they had been at Hiroshima and Nagasaki). Evidence suggests that Stalin, in fact, had similar misgivings. And with the advent of the hydrogen bomb, the utility of nuclear devices as actual weapons shrank to zero. No political objective could possibly be worth the destructiveness of a thermonuclear exchange. One effect was to reinforce the grudging stalemate that had taken hold in Europe. A "balance of terror" now prevailed.

The other, paradoxically, was to magnify the importance of conventional forces. The United States, having essentially demobilized its wartime army, had relied on the atomic bomb as the equalizer against the vast Soviet army. Now, if it wanted a credible deterrent, the only option was a stronger conventional military. To that end, NSC-68 called for increased taxes to finance "a bold and massive program of rebuilding the West's defensive potential to surpass that of the Soviet world." Truman was reluctant to commit to a major defense buildup, fearing that it would overburden the budget. Two months after NSC-68 was completed, events in Asia took that decision out of his hands.

Containment in Asia

Containment aimed primarily at preventing Soviet expansion in Europe. But as tensions built up in Asia, Cold War doctrines began to influence the American position there as well. At first America's attention centered on Japan. After dismantling Japan's military, American occupation forces under General Douglas MacArthur drafted a democratic constitution and oversaw the rebuilding of the economy, paving the way for the restoration of Japanese sovereignty in 1951. Considering the scorched-earth war just ended, this was a remarkable achievement, thanks partly to the imperious MacArthur, but mainly to the Japanese, who put their militaristic past behind them and embraced peace. Trouble on the mainland then drew America's attention, and the Cold War mentality kicked in.

The "Fall" of China. A civil war had been raging in China since the 1930s, as Communist forces led by Mao Zedong (Mao Tse-tung) contended for power with Nationalist forces under Jiang Jieshi (Chiang Kai-shek). Although dissatisfied with the corrupt Jiang regime, American officials did not see Mao as a good alternative, and they resigned themselves to supporting the Nationalists. Between 1945 and 1949 the United States provided more than $2 billion to Jiang's forces, but in August 1949 the Truman administration gave up on the Nationalists and cut off aid. By then their fate was sealed. The People's Republic of China was formally established under Mao on October 1, 1949, and the remnants of Jiang's forces fled to Taiwan.

Initially, the American response was muted. Both Stalin and Truman expected Mao to take an independent line, as the Communist Tito had recently done in Yugoslavia. Mao, however, aligned himself with the Soviet Union, partly out of exaggerated fears that the United States would rearm the Nationalists and send them back to the mainland. As attitudes hardened, many Americans viewed Mao's success as a defeat for the United States. A pro-Nationalist "China lobby" accused Truman's State Department of being responsible for the "loss" of China. Sensitive to these charges, the Truman administration refused to recognize "Red China," and also blocked China's admission to the United Nations, treating the world's most populous country as an international pariah. But the United States pointedly refused to guarantee Taiwan's independence, and in fact accepted the outcome on the mainland. It had not, however, taken account of a country few Americans had ever heard of, Korea, which had been a part of the Japanese Empire since 1910 and whose future now had to be decided.

The Korean War. In Korea, as in Germany, Cold War confrontation grew out of interim arrangements made at the end of the war. The United States and the Soviet Union, both with troops in Korea, had agreed to occupy the nation jointly, dividing their sectors at the thirty-eighth parallel, pending Korea's unification. As tensions rose in Europe, the thirty-eighth parallel hardened into a permanent demarcation line. The Soviets supported a Communist government, led by Kim Il Sung, in North Korea; the United States backed a long-time Korean nationalist, Syngman Rhee, in South Korea. Both were spoiling for a fight, but neither could launch an all-out offensive without the backing of his sponsor. Washington repeatedly said no, and so did Moscow — until Stalin, reading a speech by Secretary of State Dean Acheson declaring South Korea outside America's "defense perimeter," concluded that the United States would not intervene.

On June 25, 1950, the North Koreans launched a surprise attack across the thirty-eighth parallel (Map 26.2). Truman immediately asked the U.N. Security Council to authorize a "police action" against the invaders. Because the Soviet Union was temporarily boycotting the Security Council to protest China's exclusion from the United Nations, it could not veto Truman's request. With the Security Council's approval of a "peacekeeping force," Truman ordered U.S. troops to Korea.

Though fourteen other non-Communist nations sent troops, the rapidly assembled U.N. army in Korea was overwhelmingly American, with General

Testing the Bomb

After World War II, the development of nuclear weapons went on apace, requiring frequent testing of the more advanced weapons. This photograph shows members of the 11th Airborne division viewing the mushroom cloud from one such A-bomb test at the Atomic Energy Commission's proving grounds at Yucca flats in Nevada, November 1, 1951. Finally acknowledging the dangers to the atmosphere (and the people in the vicinity or downwind), the United States and the Soviet Union signed a treaty in 1963 banning above-ground testing.

J. R. Eyerman/Time Life Pictures/Getty Images.

had detonated an atomic bomb. With America's brief tenure as sole nuclear power over, there was a pressing need for a major reassessment of the nation's strategic planning. Truman turned to the National Security Council (NSC), an advisory body established by the National Security Act of 1947 that also created the Department of Defense and the Central Intelligence Agency (CIA). In April 1950 the NSC delivered its report, known as "NSC-68." Bristling with alarmist rhetoric, the document urged a crash program to maintain America's nuclear edge, including stepped-up production of atomic bombs and the development of a hydrogen bomb, a thermonuclear device a thousand times more destructive than the atomic bombs that had destroyed Hiroshima and Nagasaki. What American intelligence did not know was that Soviet scientists, unlike their American counterparts, had been working on both tracks all along and were making headway toward a hydrogen bomb. The United States got there first, exploding its first hydrogen bomb in November 1952; the Soviet Union followed in 1953.

Although he accepted the NSC-68 recommendation, Truman had grave misgivings about the furies he was unleashing. This was apparent in his decision to lodge control over nuclear weapons in a civilian agency, not with the military. Truman did not want nuclear weapons incorporated into military planning and treated as a functional part of the nation's arsenal (as they had been at Hiroshima and Nagasaki). Evidence suggests that Stalin, in fact, had similar misgivings. And with the advent of the hydrogen bomb, the utility of nuclear devices as actual weapons shrank to zero. No political objective could possibly be worth the destructiveness of a thermonuclear exchange. One effect was to reinforce the grudging stalemate that had taken hold in Europe. A "balance of terror" now prevailed.

The other, paradoxically, was to magnify the importance of conventional forces. The United States, having essentially demobilized its wartime army, had relied on the atomic bomb as the equalizer against the vast Soviet army. Now, if it wanted a credible deterrent, the only option was a stronger conventional military. To that end, NSC-68 called for increased taxes to finance "a bold and massive program of rebuilding the West's defensive potential to surpass that of the Soviet world." Truman was reluctant to commit to a major defense buildup, fearing that it would overburden the budget. Two months after NSC-68 was completed, events in Asia took that decision out of his hands.

Containment in Asia

Containment aimed primarily at preventing Soviet expansion in Europe. But as tensions built up in Asia, Cold War doctrines began to influence the American position there as well. At first America's attention centered on Japan. After dismantling Japan's military, American occupation forces under General Douglas MacArthur drafted a democratic constitution and oversaw the rebuilding of the economy, paving the way for the restoration of Japanese sovereignty in 1951. Considering the scorched-earth war just ended, this was a remarkable achievement, thanks partly to the imperious MacArthur, but mainly to the Japanese, who put their militaristic past behind them and embraced peace. Trouble on the mainland then drew America's attention, and the Cold War mentality kicked in.

The "Fall" of China. A civil war had been raging in China since the 1930s, as Communist forces led by Mao Zedong (Mao Tse-tung) contended for power with Nationalist forces under Jiang Jieshi (Chiang Kai-shek). Although dissatisfied with the corrupt Jiang regime, American officials did not see Mao as a good alternative, and they resigned themselves to supporting the Nationalists. Between 1945 and 1949 the United States provided more than $2 billion to Jiang's forces, but in August 1949 the Truman administration gave up on the Nationalists and cut off aid. By then their fate was sealed. The People's Republic of China was formally established under Mao on October 1, 1949, and the remnants of Jiang's forces fled to Taiwan.

Initially, the American response was muted. Both Stalin and Truman expected Mao to take an independent line, as the Communist Tito had recently done in Yugoslavia. Mao, however, aligned himself with the Soviet Union, partly out of exaggerated fears that the United States would rearm the Nationalists and send them back to the mainland. As attitudes hardened, many Americans viewed Mao's success as a defeat for the United States. A pro-Nationalist "China lobby" accused Truman's State Department of being responsible for the "loss" of China. Sensitive to these charges, the Truman administration refused to recognize "Red China," and also blocked China's admission to the United Nations, treating the world's most populous country as an international pariah. But the United States pointedly refused to guarantee Taiwan's independence, and in fact accepted the outcome on the mainland. It had not, however, taken account of a country few Americans had ever heard of, Korea, which had been a part of the Japanese Empire since 1910 and whose future now had to be decided.

The Korean War. In Korea, as in Germany, Cold War confrontation grew out of interim arrangements made at the end of the war. The United States and the Soviet Union, both with troops in Korea, had agreed to occupy the nation jointly, dividing their sectors at the thirty-eighth parallel, pending Korea's unification. As tensions rose in Europe, the thirty-eighth parallel hardened into a permanent demarcation line. The Soviets supported a Communist government, led by Kim Il Sung, in North Korea; the United States backed a long-time Korean nationalist, Syngman Rhee, in South Korea. Both were spoiling for a fight, but neither could launch an all-out offensive without the backing of his sponsor. Washington repeatedly said no, and so did Moscow — until Stalin, reading a speech by Secretary of State Dean Acheson declaring South Korea outside America's "defense perimeter," concluded that the United States would not intervene.

On June 25, 1950, the North Koreans launched a surprise attack across the thirty-eighth parallel (Map 26.2). Truman immediately asked the U.N. Security Council to authorize a "police action" against the invaders. Because the Soviet Union was temporarily boycotting the Security Council to protest China's exclusion from the United Nations, it could not veto Truman's request. With the Security Council's approval of a "peacekeeping force," Truman ordered U.S. troops to Korea.

Though fourteen other non-Communist nations sent troops, the rapidly assembled U.N. army in Korea was overwhelmingly American, with General

MAP 26.2 The Korean War, 1950–1953

The Korean War, which the United Nations officially deemed a "police action," lasted three years and cost the lives of over 36,000 U.S. troops. South and North Korean deaths were estimated at over 900,000. Although hostilities ceased in 1953, the U.S. military and the North Korean army faced each other across the demilitarized zone for the next fifty years.

Map annotations:

- Chinese troops entered the conflict (4), pushing battle lines back into South Korea (5). United States, United Nations, and South Korean forces quickly regained most of the territory to the 38th parallel. The armistice of July 1953 created a demilitarized zone (DMZ) between the two armies, making the 38th parallel the border separating the two Koreas, a boundary that remains heavily militarized on both sides in 2006.

- Sporadic fighting turned into full-scale war when North Korean troops crossed the 38th parallel (1) the post–World War II boundary between occupation zones. Northern forces pushed until stopped at the defense perimeter around the port of Pusan on the southern tip of the Korean peninsula (2).

- In a surprise move, United States forces under General Douglas MacArthur landed at Inchon, near Seoul (3), threatening to cut off supply routes of the North Koreans. As North Korean forces retreated, South Korean, United States, and United Nations forces pushed them deep into North Korea.

Legend:
- North Korean forces
- U.S. and U.N. forces
- Farthest North Korean advance, Sept. 1950
- Farthest U.S. advance, Oct.–Nov. 1950
- Chinese intervention, Oct. 1950
- Chinese advance, 1951

Douglas MacArthur placed in charge. At first, the North Koreans held an overwhelming advantage, occupying the entire peninsula except for the southeast area around Pusan. But on September 15, 1950, MacArthur launched a surprise amphibious attack at Inchon, far behind the North Korean lines, while U.N. forces staged a breakout from Pusan. Within two weeks the U.N. forces controlled Seoul, the South Korean capital, and almost all the territory up to the thirty-eighth parallel. Although the Chinese government in Beijing warned repeatedly against further incursions, MacArthur's troops crossed the thirty-eighth parallel on October 9, reaching the Chinese border at the Yalu River by the end of the month. Just after Thanksgiving a massive Chinese counterattack of almost 300,000 "volunteers" forced MacArthur's forces into headlong retreat back down the Korean peninsula. On January 4, 1951, Communist troops reoccupied Seoul.

Two months later American forces and their allies counterattacked, regained Seoul, and pushed back to the thirty-eighth parallel. Then stalemate set in. With public support in the United States for a prolonged war waning, Truman and his advisors decided to work for a negotiated peace.

MacArthur disagreed. Arrogant and brilliant, the general fervently believed that America's future lay in Asia, not Europe. In an inflammatory letter to the House minority leader, Republican Joseph J. Martin of Massachusetts, he denounced the Korean stalemate, declaring "There is no substitute for victory." The strategy backfired. On

The Korean War

As a result of Harry Truman's 1948 executive order, for the first time in the nation's history, all troops, such as the men of the Second Infantry Battalion, shown here in Korea in 1950, served in racially integrated combat units (see p. 853). National Archives.

April 11 Truman relieved MacArthur of his command, accusing him of insubordination. Truman's decision was highly unpopular, but he had the last word. After failing to win the Republican presidential nomination in 1952, MacArthur faded from public view.

The war dragged on for more than two years after MacArthur's dismissal. An armistice was not signed until July 1953, leaving Korea divided at the original demarcation line at the thirty-eighth parallel. North Korea remained firmly allied with the Soviet Union; South Korea signed a mutual defense treaty with the United States in 1954.

The Impact of the Korean War. The Korean War had lasting consequences. Truman's decision to commit troops to Korea without congressional approval set a precedent for future undeclared wars. His refusal to unleash atomic bombs, even when American forces were reeling under a massive Chinese attack, set limiting ground rules for Cold War conflict. The war also expanded American involvement in Asia, transforming containment into a truly global policy. Finally, it ended Truman's resistance to a major military buildup. Overall defense expenditures grew from $13 billion in 1950, roughly one-third of the federal budget, to $50 billion in 1953, nearly two-thirds of the budget. Although military expenditures dropped briefly after the Korean War, defense spending remained at over $35 billion annually throughout the 1950s. American foreign policy had become more global, more militarized, and more expensive (Figure 26.1). Even in times of peace, the United States now functioned in a state of permanent mobilization.

➤ Why was the United States unable to avoid entering a Cold War with the Soviet Union?

➤ How are the ideas of George F. Kennan reflected in Truman's Cold War policies?

➤ What was the long-term significance of the Korean War?

FIGURE 26.1 National Defense Spending, 1940–1965

In 1950 the defense budget was $13 billion, less than a third of total federal outlays. In 1961 defense spending reached $47 billion, fully half of the federal budget and almost 10 percent of the gross domestic product.

The Truman Era

Harry Truman never intended to be a caretaker president. On September 16, 1945, just fourteen days after Japan surrendered and six months after FDR's death, Truman staked his claim to domestic leadership with a plan that called for a dramatic expansion of the New Deal. He intended to fulfill the expansive Economic Bill of Rights that Roosevelt had famously proclaimed in his State of the Union Address in 1944. Truman phrased his proposals in just that way, as rights expected by all Americans—to a "useful and remunerative" job, good housing, "adequate medical care," "protection from the economic fears of old age," and a "good education." Truman had no way of foreseeing on V-J day the confounding forces lying in wait. In the end, his high hopes were crushed, and Truman went down in history not, as he hoped, as FDR's worthy successor, but as a Cold Warrior.

Reconversion

No sooner had Truman finished laying out his ambitious domestic program than he was waylaid by cascading problems over converting the wartime economy to peacetime. Left in the dark about the atomic bomb, government planners had assumed that reconversion would be phased in while Japan was being subdued. So when the war suddenly ended, no reconversion plan was in place. The hasty dismantling of the vast wartime machine frustrated liberal planners, who had hoped to give small business a headstart in the peacetime market while the big manufacturers were still in war production. What worried Truman, however, was runaway inflation. He wanted to keep the wartime Office of Price Administration (OPA) in place while domestic production caught up with pent-up demand. His efforts at price control were overwhelmed by consumers impatient to spend money and businesses eager to take it from them, with the result that consumer prices soared by 33 percent in the immediate postwar years.

Postwar Strikes and the Taft-Hartley Act. Organized labor was far stronger than it had ever been. Union membership had swelled to over fourteen million by 1945, including two-thirds of all workers in mining, manufacturing, construction, and transportation. Determined to make up for their wartime sacrifices, workers mounted crippling strikes in the automobile, steel, and coal industries. General strikes effectively brought normal life to a halt in half a dozen cities in 1946.

Truman responded erratically. In some cases, he gave way, as, for example, when he lifted price controls on steel in early 1946 so that the industry could grant the wage demands of the strikers. In other instances, Truman tried to show union leaders who was boss. Faced by a devastating railway strike, he threatened to place the nation's railroad system under federal control and asked Congress for the power to draft striking workers into the army—moves that infuriated union leaders but got the strikers back to work. In November 1946, when coal miners called a strike as winter approached, Truman secured a sweeping court order against the union. When its imperious leader John L. Lewis, having been slapped with a huge fine, tried to negotiate, Truman turned him away. He was not going to have "that son of a bitch" in the White House.

If Truman outraged organized labor, an important partner in the Democratic coalition, his display of toughness did little to placate the Republicans, who, having gained control of both houses of Congress in 1946, moved quickly to curb labor's power. In alliance with conservative southern Democrats, they passed the Taft-Hartley Act (1947), a sweeping overhaul of the 1935 National Labor Relations Act. Some of the new provisions aimed at perceived abuses—the **secondary boycott**, crippling national strikes, unionization of supervisory employees. Ultimately of greater significance, however, were skillfully crafted changes in procedures and language that over time eroded the law's stated purpose of protecting the right of workers to organize and engage in collective bargaining. Unions especially disliked Section 14b, which allowed states to pass "right-to-work" laws prohibiting the **union shop**. Truman issued a ringing veto of the Taft-Hartley bill in June 1947, but Congress easily overrode the veto.

The 1948 Election. By 1947, most observers wouldn't have bet a nickel on Truman's future. His popularity ratings had plummeted, and "To err is Truman" had entered the political language. Democrats would have dumped him for 1948 had they found a better candidate. As it was, the party fell into disarray. The left wing split off and formed the Progressive Party, nominating as its candidate Henry A. Wallace, an avid New Dealer whom Truman had fired as secretary of commerce in 1946 because of his vocal opposition to the Cold War. The right-wing challenge came from the South. When northern liberals such as Mayor Hubert H. Humphrey of Minneapolis pushed through a strong civil rights platform at the Democratic convention, the southern delegations bolted and, calling themselves Dixiecrats, nominated Governor J. Strom Thurmond of South Carolina for president. The Republicans meanwhile renominated Thomas E. Dewey, the politically moderate governor of New York who had run a strong campaign against FDR in 1944.

Truman surprised everyone. He launched a strenuous cross-country speaking tour in which he hammered away at the Republicans for opposing legislation for housing, medical insurance, civil rights, and, in general, for running a "do-nothing" Congress. By combining these issues with attacks on the Soviet menace abroad, Truman began to salvage his troubled campaign. At his rallies enthusiastic listeners shouted, "Give 'em hell, Harry!"

Truman won a remarkable victory, receiving 49.6 percent of the vote to Dewey's 45.1 percent (Map 26.3). The Democrats also regained control of both houses of Congress. Strom Thurmond carried only four southern states, while Henry Wallace failed to win any electoral votes. Truman retained the support of organized labor, Jewish and Catholic voters in the big cities, and black voters in the North. Most important, he appealed effectively to people like himself from the farms, towns, and small cities in the nation's heartland.

Truman Triumphant

In one of the most famous photographs in American political history, Harry S Truman gloats over a headline in the *Chicago Daily Tribune*. Pollsters had predicted an easy victory for Thomas E. Dewey. Their primitive techniques, however, missed the dramatic surge in support for Truman during the last days of the campaign. © Bettmann/Corbis.

MAP 26.3 Presidential Election of 1948

Truman's electoral strategy in 1948 was to concentrate his campaign in areas where the Democrats had their greatest strength. In an election with a low turnout, Truman held onto enough support from Roosevelt's New Deal coalition of blacks, union members, and farmers to defeat Dewey by more than two million votes.

Candidate	Electoral Vote	Popular Vote	Percent of Popular Vote
Harry S Truman (Democrat)	303	24,105,182	49.6
Thomas E. Dewey (Republican)	189	21,970,065	45.1
J. Strom Thurmond (States' Rights)	39	1,169,063	2.5
Henry A. Wallace (Progressive)	—	1,157,326	2.5

The Fair Deal

In his 1949 State of the Union address, Truman rechristened his program the Fair Deal. It incorporated the goals he had set out initially—national health insurance, aid to education, a housing program, expansion of Social Security, a higher minimum wage, and a new agricultural program—but also struck out in some new directions. In its attention to civil rights (see Chapter 27), the Fair Deal reflected the growing importance of African Americans to the Democratic Party's coalition of urban voters. And the desire to raise the living standards of an ever-greater number of citizens reflected a new liberal vision of the role of the state.

Truman was inspired by the renown English economist, John Maynard Keynes, who had argued that government was capable by means of its fiscal powers of preventing economic depressions. In bad times, deficit spending would "prime the pump," re-igniting consumer spending and private investment and restoring prosperity. The Employment Act of 1946, which asserted the government's responsibility and established a Council of Economic Advisers to assist the president, embodied this Keynesian policy. Truman wanted the Employment Act reinforced by raising its goal to "full" employment and by expanding welfare programs that would undergird consumer purchasing power.

Among the opportunities that came and went, most notable, in light of the nation's current health-care crisis, was the proposal for national health insurance. This was a popular idea, with strong backing from organized labor, but it was denounced as "socialized medicine" by the American Medical Association; the insurance industry (which had spotted a new profit center); and big corporations, which (to their everlasting regret) preferred providing health coverage directly to employees. Lobbying groups were equally effective at defeating Truman's agricultural reforms, which aimed at helping small farmers, and federal aid to education. In the end, the only significant breakthrough, other than improvements in the minimum wage and Social Security, was the National Housing Act of 1949, which authorized the construction of 810,000 low-income units.

Despite Democratic majorities, Congress remained a huge stumbling block. The same conservative coalition that had blocked Roosevelt's initiatives in his second term and dismantled or cut New Deal programs during wartime continued the fight against the Fair Deal. On top of this came the Cold War. The outbreak of fighting in Korea in 1950 was especially damaging, diverting national attention and federal funds from domestic affairs. Another potent diversion was the nation's growing paranoia over internal subversion, the most dramatic manifestation of the Cold War's effect on American life.

The Great Fear

Was there any significant Soviet penetration of the American government? Historians had mostly debunked the idea and so, in earlier editions, did this textbook. But we were wrong. Records opened up since 1991—intelligence files in Moscow and, among U.S. sources, most importantly the Venona intercepts of Soviet cables—name among American suppliers of information FDR's assistant secretary of the Treasury Department (Harry Dexter White); FDR's administrative aide (Laughlin Currie); a mid-level, strategically placed group in the State Department (including Alger Hiss, who was with FDR at Yalta); and several hundred more, some identified only by code name, working in a range of government departments and agencies.

What are we to make of this? Many of these enlistees in the Soviet cause were bright young New Dealers in the mid-1930s, when Moscow's Popular Front suggested — to the uninformed, at any rate — that the lines between liberal, progressive, and Communist were blurred and permeable (see Chapter 25). At that time, in the mid-1930s, the United States was not at war, nor ever expected to be. And when war did come, the Soviet Union was an American ally. The flow of stolen documents speeded up and kept Soviet intelligence privy to all aspects of the American war effort. What most interested Stalin was U.S. intentions about a second front and — an obsessive fear of his — a separate deal with Hitler. And, of course, the atomic bomb. Even here, people turned a blind eye to Soviet espionage. Many Los Alamos scientists, indeed, thought it a mistake not to tell the Soviets about the bomb. J. Robert Oppenheimer, the director of the Manhattan Project, was inclined to agree. He just didn't like "the idea of having the [secrets] moved out the back door."

Once the Cold War set in, of course, Oppenheimer's indulgent view of Soviet espionage became utterly inadmissible, and the government moved with great fanfare to crack down. In March 1947 President Truman issued an executive order launching a comprehensive loyalty program for federal employees. Of the activities deemed to be "disloyal," the operative one was membership in any of a list of "subversive" organizations compiled by the attorney general. On that basis, federal loyalty boards mounted witch hunts that wrecked the careers of about ten thousand public servants, not one of whom was ever tried and convicted of espionage.

As for the actual suppliers of information to the Soviets, they seem mostly to have left off spying once the Cold War began. For one thing, the professional apparatus of Soviet agents running them was dismantled or disrupted by stepped-up American counterintelligence work. After the war, moreover, most of these well-connected amateur spies moved on to other careers. The State Department official Alger Hiss, for example, was serving as head of the prestigious Carnegie Endowment for International Peace when he was accused in 1948 by a Communist-turned-informant, Whittaker Chambers, of having passed classified documents to him in the 1930s. Skepticism by historians about internal subversion — that it was insignificant — seems justified if we start in 1947, just when the hue-and-cry about internal subversion was blowing up into a second Red Scare (for the first, see Chapter 22).

HUAC. For this, the Truman administration bore some responsibility. It had legitimized making "disloyalty" the proxy for subversive activity. Others, however, were far more ruthless and adept at this technique, beginning with the House Un-American Activities Committee (HUAC), which Congressman Martin Dies of Texas and other conservatives had launched back in 1938. After the war, HUAC helped spark the Great Fear by holding widely publicized hearings on alleged Communist infiltration in the movie industry. A group of writers and directors, soon dubbed the Hollywood Ten, went to jail for contempt of Congress when they cited the First Amendment while refusing to testify about their past associations. Hundreds of other actors, directors, and writers whose names had been mentioned in the HUAC investigation were unable to get work, victims of an unacknowledged but very real **blacklist** honored by industry executives.

Following Washington's lead, many state and local governments, universities, political organizations, churches, and businesses undertook their own antisubversion campaigns, which often included the requirement that employees take loyalty oaths. In the labor movement, where Communists had been active as organizers in the 1930s, charges of Communist domination led to the expulsion of a number of industrial unions by the CIO in 1949. Civil rights organizations such as the NAACP and the National Urban League also expelled Communists or "fellow travelers" — words used to describe people viewed as Communist sympathizers although not members of the Communist Party. Thus the Great Fear spread from the federal government to the farthest reaches of American associational, cultural, and economic life.

Here, too, however, revelations from the Soviet archives have complicated the picture. Historians have mostly regard the American Communist Party as a "normal" organization, acting in America's home-grown radical tradition and playing by the rules of the game. Soviet archives clearly show otherwise. The American party was taking money and instructions from Moscow. It was in no way independent, so that, when Communists joined other organizations, not only red-baiters found their participation problematic. Consider the expulsion of the Communist-led industrial unions mentioned above. In 1948 the CIO had gone all-out for Truman's reelection, which was the only hope it had of reversing the hated Taft-Hartley Act. The Communist line was to support Wallace's Progressive Party, and that's what the Communist-led unions did, thereby

The Army-McCarthy Hearings

These 1954 hearings contributed to the downfall of Senator Joseph McCarthy by exposing his reckless accusations and bullying tactics to the huge television audience that tuned in each day. Some of the most heated exchanges took place between McCarthy (center) and Joseph Welch (seated, left), the lawyer representing the army. When the gentlemanly Welch finally asked, "Have you no decency left, sir?" he fatally punctured McCarthy's armor. The audience broke into applause because someone had finally had the courage to stand up to the senator from Wisconsin. © Bettmann/Corbis.

demonstrating that they were Communists first, trade unionists second—a cardinal sin for the labor movement. The expulsions left in their wake the wrecked lives of many innocent, high-minded trade unionists, and that was true wherever anti-Communism took hold, whether in universities, school boards, or civil rights organizations.

McCarthyism. The finale of the Great Fear opened with the meteoric rise of Senator Joseph McCarthy of Wisconsin. In February 1950 McCarthy delivered a bombshell during a speech in Wheeling, West Virginia: "I have in my hand 57 cases of individuals who would appear to be either card-carrying members or certainly loyal to the Communist Party, but who nevertheless are still helping to shape our foreign policy [in the State Department]." McCarthy later reduced his numbers, and he never released any names or proof, but he had gained the attention he sought. For the next four years, he was

The 1952 Presidential Campaign

The Republican campaign capitalized on scandals involving bribery and influence-peddling that engulfed the Truman administration's second term and on Dwight Eisenhower's popularity. Everyone knew him as "Ike." They didn't particularly know his running mate Richard M. Nixon as "Dick." That was just thrown in for good measure. Collection of Janice L. and David J. Frent.

the central figure in a virulent smear campaign. Critics who disagreed with him exposed themselves to charges of being "soft" on Communism. Truman called McCarthy's charges "slander, lies, character assassination," but could do nothing to curb them. The Republicans, for their part, refrained from publicly challenging their most outspoken senator and, on the whole, were content to reap the political benefits (see Comparing American Voices, "Hunting Communists and Liberals," pp. 820–821).

In early 1954 McCarthy overreached himself by launching an investigation into possible subversion in the U.S. Army. When lengthy hearings — the first of its kind broadcast on the new medium of television — brought McCarthy's smear tactics into the nation's living rooms, support for him declined. In December 1954 the Senate voted 67 to 22 to censure McCarthy for unbecoming conduct. He died from an alcohol-related illness three years later at the age of forty-eight, his name forever attached to a period of political repression of which he was only the most flagrant manifestation.

> ➤ Why did Harry Truman seem a failure during his first term in the White House?
>
> ➤ How does the Fair Deal differ from the New Deal?

> ➤ Why have historians revised their views about the significance of espionage in American government? Does this make any difference about how we evaluate McCarthyism?

Modern Republicanism

As election day 1952 approached, America seemed ready for change. The question was, How much? With the Republican victory, the country got its answer: Very little. The new president, Dwight D. Eisenhower, set the tone for what his supporters called "modern Republicanism"—an updated GOP approach that aimed at moderating, not dismantling, the New Deal state. Eisenhower and his supporters were—despite themselves—successors of FDR, not Herbert Hoover. Foreign policy revealed a similar continuity. Like their predecessors, Republicans saw the world in Cold War polarities. They embraced the defense buildup begun during the Korean War and pushed containment to the far reaches of the world.

They Liked Ike

The Republicans' problem was that, after twenty years of Democratic rule, they were the minority party. Only one in three registered voters was Republican. The party faithful gave their hearts to Robert A. Taft of Ohio, the Republican leader in the Senate since 1939, but their heads told them that only a moderate, less-well-defined candidate was likely to attract the independent vote. General Eisenhower filled the bill. He was an immensely popular figure, widely admired as the architect of D-Day and victory in Europe. Eisenhower was a man without a political past. Believing that democracy required that the military stand aside, he had never voted. Democrats and Republicans courted him, but it turned out that Eisenhower was a Republican, a believer in balanced budgets and individual responsibility. For regional balance, Eisenhower asked Senator Richard M. Nixon of California to be his running mate. Nixon was youthful, tirelessly partisan, and strongly anti-Communist. He had won his spurs by leading HUAC's investigation of Alger Hiss's espionage past.

The Democrats never seriously considered renominating Harry Truman, who by 1952 was a thoroughly discredited leader, primarily because of the unpopularity of the Korean War, but also because of a series of scandals that Republicans dubbed "the mess in Washington." With a certain relief, the Democrats turned to Governor Adlai E. Stevenson of Illinois, who enjoyed the support of respected liberals, such as Eleanor Roosevelt, and of organized labor. To appease conservative southern voters, the Democrats nominated Senator John A. Sparkman of Alabama for vice president.

Throughout the campaign Stevenson advocated New Deal–Fair Deal policies with an almost literary eloquence. But Eisenhower's artfully unpretentious speeches and "I Like Ike" slogan were more effective with voters. Eager to win the support of the broadest electorate possible, Eisenhower played down specific questions of policy. Instead, he attacked the Democrats with the "K_1C_2" formula — "Korea, Communism, and Corruption."

That November Eisenhower won 55 percent of the popular vote, carrying all the northern and western states and four southern states. His triumph did not translate, however, into a new Republican majority. Republicans regained control of Congress on his coattails, but lost it 1954 and did not recover when Eisenhower easily won reelection over Adlai Stevenson in 1956. For most of his tenure, Eisenhower had to work with a Democratic Congress.

The Hidden-Hand Presidency

Although supremely confident as an international leader, Eisenhower started out a novice in domestic affairs. He did his best to set a quieter national mood after the rancorous Truman years. Disliking confrontation, he was reluctant to speak out against Joe McCarthy, and he was not a leader on civil rights. Yet Eisenhower was no stooge as president. Political scientists have characterized his leadership style as the "hidden-hand presidency." They point out that Eisenhower manuevered deftly behind the scenes while maintaining a public demeanor of being above the fray. If he sometimes seemed inarticulate and bumbling, that was often a studied effect to mask his real intentions. He in fact ran a tight ship and was always in command.

After 1954, when the Democrats took control over Congress, the Eisenhower administration accepted legislation promoting social welfare. Federal outlays for veterans' benefits, housing, and Social Security were increased, and the minimum wage was raised from 75 cents an hour to $1. The creation of the new Department of Health, Education, and Welfare (HEW) in 1953 consolidated government administration of social welfare programs, confirming federal commitments in that area. Welfare expenditures went steadily upward during Eisenhower's tenure, consuming an ever larger share of the federal budget. Like Truman, Eisenhower accepted the government's responsibility for economic performance and, despite his faith in a balanced budget, engaged in deficit spending whenever employment dipped. He intervened even more vigorously when it came to holding in check the inflation sparked by the Korean War.

More striking was the expanded scope of federal activity. In a move that drastically altered America's landscape and driving habits, the National Interstate and Defense Highways Act of 1956 authorized $26 billion over a ten-year period for the construction of a nationally integrated highway system (see Map 27.2, p. 839). To link the Great Lakes with the Atlantic Ocean, the United States and Canada cosponsored in 1959 the construction of the St. Lawrence Seaway. These enormous public works programs surpassed anything undertaken during the New Deal. And when the Soviet Union launched the first satellite, *Sputnik*, in 1957, the startled country went into high gear to catch up in this new Cold War space competition (see Reading American Pictures, "Why a Cold War Space Race?," p. 823). Eisenhower authorized the National Aeronautics and Space Administration (NASA) the following year, and, alarmed that the United States was falling behind in science and technology, he persuaded Congress to appropriate additional money for college scholarships and university research.

Only in the area of natural resources did the Eisenhower administration actually reduce federal activity — turning over offshore oil to the states and private developers, and authorizing privately financed hydroelectric dams on the Snake River. In most other ways — New Deal welfare programs, Keynesian intervention in the economy, new departures in public works, scientific research, higher education — the Eisenhower Republicans had become part of a broad **liberal consensus** in American politics. That was the view of a true conservative, Senator Barry Goldwater of Arizona, who remarked sourly that Ike had run a "Dime Store New Deal."

Eisenhower and the Cold War

Every incoming administration likes to proclaim itself a grand departure from its predecessor.

COMPARING AMERICAN VOICES

Hunting Communists and Liberals

The onset of the Cold War created an opportunity for some conservatives to seize on anti-Communism as a weapon to attack the Truman administration. In Senator McCarthy's case, the charge was that the Truman administration was harboring Soviet spies within the government. There was also a broader, more amorphous attack on people not accused of spying but of having Communist sympathies and thus being "security risks" and unsuitable for government positions. For this targeted group, the basis of suspicion was generally membership in organizations that supported policies that overlapped with or seemed similar to policies supported by the Communist Party.

McCARTHYISM
Senator Joseph McCarthy, Speech Delivered in Wheeling, West Virginia, February 9, 1950

Senator McCarthy was actually late getting on board the anti-Communist rocket ship. This was the speech that launched him into orbit. No one ever saw the piece of paper he waved about with the names of fifty-seven spies in the State Department. Over time, the number fluctuated, and never materialized into a single indictable spy. Still, McCarthy had an extraordinary talent for whipping up anti-Communist hysteria. His downfall came in 1954, when the U.S. Senate formally censured McCarthy for his conduct; three years later, he died of alcoholism at the age of 48.

Today we are engaged in a final, all-out battle between communistic atheism and Christianity. The modern champions of communism have selected this as the time. And, ladies and gentlemen, the chips are down — they are truly down....

The reason why we find ourselves in a position of impotency is not because our only powerful potential enemy has sent men to invade our shores, but rather because of the traitorous actions of those who have been treated so well by this Nation. It has not been the less fortunate or members of minority groups who have been selling this Nation out, but rather those who have had all the benefits that the wealthiest nation on earth has had to offer — the finest homes, the finest college education, and the finest jobs in Government we can give....

I have in my hand 57 cases of individuals who would appear to be either card carrying members or certainly loyal to the Communist Party, but who nevertheless are still helping to shape our foreign policy....

THE ORDEAL OF FRANK P. GRAHAM
Fulton Lewis Jr.'s Radio Address, January 13, 1949

The groundwork for McCarthy's anti-Communist crusade was laid by the House Un-American Activities Committee (HUAC), which had been formed in 1938 by conservative southern Democrats seeking to investigate alleged Communist influence around the country. One of its early targets had been Dr. Frank P. Graham, the distinguished president of the University of North Carolina. A committed southern liberal, Graham was a leading figure in the Southern Conference on Human Welfare, the most prominent southern organization supporting the New Deal, free speech, organized labor, and greater rights for southern blacks — causes that some in the South saw as pathways for Communist subversion. After the war, HUAC stepped up its activities and kept a close eye on Dr. Graham.

Among Dr. Graham's duties, one was to serve as the head of the Oak Ridge Institute of Nuclear Studies, a consortium of fourteen southern universities designed to undertake joint research with the federal government's atomic energy facility at Oak Ridge, Tennessee. To enable him to carry on his duties, the Atomic Energy Commission (AEC) granted Dr. Graham a security clearance, overriding the negative recommendation of the AEC's Security Advisory Board. That was the occasion for the following statement by Fulton Lewis Jr., a conservative radio commentator with a nationwide following.

...About Dr. Frank P. Graham, president of the University of North Carolina, and the action of the Atomic Energy Commission giving him complete clearance for all atomic secrets despite the fact that the security officer of the commission flatly rejected him...

President Truman was asked to comment on the matter today at his press and radio conference, and his reply was that he has complete confidence in Dr. Graham.

... The defenders of Dr. Graham today offered the apology that during the time he joined the various subversive and Communist front organizations [like the Southern Conference for Human Welfare] — organizations so listed by the Attorney General of the United States — this country was a co-belligerent with Soviet Russia, and numerous people joined such groups and causes. That argument is going to sound very thin to most American citizens, because the overwhelming majority of us would have no part of any Communist or Communist front connections at any time....

Frank Porter Graham's Telegram to Fulton Lewis Jr., January 13, 1949

One can imagine Graham's shock at hearing himself pilloried on national radio. (He had not even been aware of the AEC's investigation of him.) Following is his response to Lewis.

... In view of your questions and implications I hope you will use my statement to provide for my answers.... I have always been opposed to Communism and all totalitarian dictatorships. I opposed both Nazi and Communist aggression against Czechoslovakia and the earlier Russian aggression against Finland and later Communist aggression against other countries....

During the period of my active participation, the overwhelming number of members of the Southern Conference were to my knowledge anti-Communists. There were several isolationist stands of the Conference with which I disagreed. The stands which I supported as the main business of the Conference were such as the following: Federal aid to the states for schools; abolition of freight rate discrimination against Southern commerce, agriculture, and industry; anti-poll tax bill; anti-lynching bill; equal right of qualified Negroes to vote in both primaries and general elections; the unhampered lawful right of labor to organize and bargain collectively in our region; ... minimum wages and social security in the Southern and American tradition....

I have been called a Communist by some sincere people. I have been called a spokesman of American capitalism by Communists and repeatedly called a tool of imperialism by the radio from Moscow. I shall simply continue to oppose Ku Kluxism, imperialism, fascism, and Communism whether in America ... or behind the "iron curtain."

HOUSE UN-AMERICAN ACTIVITIES COMMITTEE Report on Frank Graham, February 4, 1949

Because of the controversy, HUAC released this report on Dr. Graham.

A check of the files, records and publications of the Committee on Un-American Activities has revealed the following information:

Letterheads dated September 22, 1939, January 17, 1940, and May 26, 1940, as well as the "Daily Worker" of March 18, 1939, ... reveal that Frank P. Graham was a member of the American Committee for Democracy and Intellectual Freedom.... In Report 2277, dated June 25, 1942, the Special Committee on Un-American Activities found that "the line of the American Committee for Democracy and Intellectual Freedom has fluctuated in complete harmony with the line of the Communist Party." The organization was again cited by the Special Committee ... as a Communist front "which defended Communist teachers." ...

A letterhead of February 7, 1946, a letterhead of June 4, 1947 ... and an announcement of the Third Meeting, April 19–21, 1942, at Nashville, Tennessee, reveal that Frank P. Graham was honorary President of the Southern Conference for Human Welfare....

In a report on the Southern Conference for Human Welfare, dated June 16, 1947, the Committee on Un-American Activities found "the most conclusive proof of Communist domination of the Southern Conference for Human Welfare is to be found in the organization's strict and unvarying conformance to the line of the Communist Party in the field of foreign policy. It is also a clear indication of the fact that the real purpose of the organization was not 'human welfare' in the South, but rather to serve as a convenient vehicle in support of the current Communist Party line." ...

SOURCES: *Congressional Record*, U.S. Senate, 81st Cong., 2d Sess. (Washington, D.C.: GPO, 1950); Frank Porter Graham Papers, University of North Carolina at Chapel Hill Library.

ANALYZING THE EVIDENCE

▶ On what grounds do Fulton Lewis Jr. and HUAC assert that Frank Graham was a security risk? Do they charge that he was a Communist? Is there any evidence in these documents that he might have been a security risk?

▶ How does Graham defend himself? Are you persuaded by his defense?

▶ Do you see any similarity between McCarthy's famous speech at Wheeling, West Virginia, and the suspicions voiced against Dr. Graham by Fulton Lewis Jr. and HUAC a year earlier?

Eisenhower's gesture in this direction was his secretary of state, John Foster Dulles, a lawyer highly experienced in world affairs, but ill-suited by his self-righteous temperament for the craft of diplomacy. Dulles despised "atheistic Communism," and, rather than settling for the status quo, he argued for the "liberation" of the "captive countries" of eastern Europe. This was bombast. The power realities that had called forth containment still applied, as was evident in Eisenhower's first important act as president. Redeeming his campaign pledge to resolve the Korean war, Eisenhower went to Korea. More importantly he stepped up the negotiations that led to an agreement essentially fixing in place the military stalemate at the thirty-eighth parallel.

The Khrushchev Era. Stalin's death in March 1953 precipitated an intraparty struggle in the Soviet Union, which lasted until 1956, when Nikita S. Khrushchev emerged as Stalin's successor. He soon startled Communists around the world by denouncing Stalin and detailing his crimes and blunders. Khrushchev also surprised Westerners by calling for "peaceful coexistence." But any hopes of a thaw evaporated when Hungarians rose up in 1956 and demanded that the country leave the Warsaw Pact. Soviet tanks moved into Budapest and crushed the rebellion — an action the United States condemned but could not realistically resist. Some of the blood was on Dulles's hands because he had emboldened the Hungarians with his rhetoric of "rolling back" the Iron Curtain — a pledge that the reality of nuclear weapons made impossible to fulfill.

With no end to the Cold War in sight, Eisenhower turned his attention to containing the cost of containment. Like Truman before him, he hoped to economize by relying on a nuclear arsenal as an alternative to expensive conventional forces. Nuclear weapons delivered "more bang for the buck," explained Defense Secretary Charles E. Wilson. Under the "New Look" defense policy, the Eisenhower administration stepped up production of the hydrogen bomb, approved extensive atmospheric testing, developed the long-range bombing capabilities of the Strategic Air Command, and installed the Distant Early Warning line of radar stations in Alaska and Canada. The Soviets, however, matched the United States weapon for weapon in an escalating arms race. By 1958 both nations had intercontinental ballistic missiles (ICBMs). When an American nuclear submarine launched an atomic-tipped Polaris missile in 1960, Soviet engineers raced to produce an equivalent weapon.

Eisenhower had second thoughts about a nuclear policy aptly named MAD (Mutually Assured Destruction) — based on the premise of annihilating the enemy even if one's own country was destroyed. Eisenhower tried to negotiate an arms-limitation agreement with the Soviet Union. Progress along those lines was cut short, however, when on May 5, 1960, the Soviets shot down an American U-2 spy plane over their territory. Eisenhower at first denied that the plane was engaged in espionage, but when the Soviet Union produced the captured pilot, Francis Gary Powers, Eisenhower admitted that he had authorized secret flights over the Soviet Union. In the midst of the dispute, a proposed summit meeting with Khrushchev was canceled, and Eisenhower's last chance to negotiate an arms agreement evaporated.

Containment in the Post-Colonial World

Containment policy had been devised in response to Soviet threats in Europe but, as intervention in Korea suggested, it was an infinitely expandable concept. The early Cold War era was a time when new nations were emerging across the **Third World**, inspired by powerful anticolonialist movements that went back before World War II. Between 1947 and 1962 the British, French, Dutch, and Belgian empires in the Middle East, Africa, and Asia all but disintegrated. Committed to national self-determination, FDR had favored these developments, often to the fury of his British and French allies. He expected democracies to emerge, new partners in an American-led, free-market world system. But as the Cold War intensified, that confidence began to wane. Both the Truman and Eisenhower administrations often failed to recognize that indigenous nationalist or socialist movements in emerging nations had their own goals and were not necessarily pawns of the Soviet Union.

Believing that nations had to choose sides, the United States tried to draw them into collective security agreements, with the NATO alliance in Europe as a model. Dulles orchestrated the creation of the Southeast Asia Treaty Organization (SEATO), which in 1954 linked America and its major European allies with Australia, Pakistan, Thailand, New Zealand, and the Philippines. An extensive system of defense alliances eventually tied the United States to more than forty other countries (Map 26.4). The United States also signed

READING AMERICAN PICTURES

Why a Cold War Space Race?

Satellite Space Race. The Michael Barson Collection / Past Perfect.

"Wonder Why We're Not Keeping Pace?" © 1957 by Herblock in *The Washington Post*.

At the center of the Cold War was science—big science, evidenced most dramatically by the continuous development of nuclear weapons and advances in rocket technology. In the 1950s, the physicists who created the first atomic (and then thermonuclear) weapons—Robert Oppenheimer, Edward Teller, and others—became household names and part of the collective face of America's scientific superiority. Then, in 1957, the United States was startled when the Soviets successfully launched *Sputnik*, the first man-made satellite to orbit the earth. Almost overnight, the United States embarked on a "space race" aimed at catching up with and surpassing the Soviet Union, at a cost of billions of dollars and with far-reaching consequences for American education, science, and space exploration. The two illustrations above say something about America's initial reaction to the news about *Sputnik*.

ANALYZING THE EVIDENCE

▶ Few scientific or technological achievements spark a card game, yet *Sputnik* did. Under the rules of the game, anyone dealt the *Sputnik* card lost two turns. What does that tell you?

▶ Herblock was perhaps the most influential and widely syndicated political cartoonist of the Cold War era. What does his cartoon suggest are the reasons the United States didn't beat the Soviets into space?

▶ The Cold War was far more than geopolitical conflict. It was also a competition between rival economic and cultural systems. How is that battle to demonstrate superiority revealed by the *Sputnik* episode? And by the "space race" that followed?

MAP 26.4 American Global Defense Treaties in the Cold War Era

The advent of the Cold War led to a major shift in American foreign policy — the signing of mutual defense treaties. Dating back to George Washington's call "to steer clear of permanent alliances with any portion of the foreign world," the United States had avoided treaty obligations that entailed the defense of other nations. As late as 1919, the U.S. Senate had rejected the principle of "collective security," the centerpiece of the League of Nations established by the Treaty of Versailles that ended World War I. But after World War II, in response to fears of Soviet expansion globally, the United States entered defense alliances with much of the non-Communist world, as this map vividly reveals.

bilateral defense treaties with South Korea and Taiwan, and sponsored a strategically valuable defensive alliance between Iran and Iraq on the southern flank of the Soviet Union.

The Eisenhower administration, less concerned about democracy than stability, tended to support governments, no matter how repressive, that were overtly anti-Communist. Some of America's staunchest allies — the Philippines, Korea, Iran, Cuba, and Nicaragua — were governed by dictatorships or right-wing regimes that lacked broad-based support. Moreover, Dulles often resorted to covert operations against governments that, in his opinion, were too closely aligned with the Soviets.

For such tasks he used the Central Intelligence Agency (CIA), which had moved beyond its original mandate of intelligence-gathering into active, albeit covert, involvement in the internal affairs of foreign countries, even to the extent of overthrowing several governments. When Iran's nationalist premier, Muhammad Mossadegh, seized British oil properties in 1953, CIA agents helped depose him and installed the young Muhammad Reza Pahlavi as Shah of Iran. In 1954 the CIA engineered a coup in Guatemala against the popularly elected Jacobo Arbenz Guzman, who had expropriated land owned by the American-owned United Fruit Company and accepted arms from Czechoslovakia. Eisenhower specifically approved those CIA efforts. "Our traditional ideas of international sportsmanship," he confessed privately, "are scarcely applicable in the morass in which the world now [1955] flounders."

Vietnam. How Eisenhower's confession might entangle America was already unfolding on a distant stage, in a country of no strategic interest and utterly unknown to most Americans. This was Vietnam, part of French Indochina. When the Japanese occupiers surrendered in August 1945, the nationalist movement that had led the resistance, the Vietminh, seized control, with American encouragement. Their leader, Ho Chi Minh, admired the United States, and when he proclaimed an independent republic, he did so with words drawn from the American Declaration of Independence. But Ho was also a Communist, and as the Cold War took hold, being Communist outweighed America's commitment to self-determination. The next year, when France moved to restore its control over the country, Truman rejected Ho's plea for support in the Vietnamese struggle for independence and sided with France.

Eisenhower picked up where Truman left off. If the French failed, Eisenhower argued, the **domino theory**—a notion that would henceforth bedevil American strategic thinking—would one after the next lead to the collapse of all non-Communist governments in the region. Although the United States eventually provided most of the financing, the French still failed to defeat the tenacious Vietminh. After a fifty-six-day siege in early 1954, the French went down to stunning defeat at the huge fortress of Dienbienphu. The result was the 1954 Geneva Accords, which partitioned Vietnam temporarily at the seventeenth parallel (see Map 28.6, p. 877), committed France to withdraw from north of that line, and called for elections within two years that would lead to a unified Vietnam.

The United States rejected the Geneva Accords and immediately set about undermining them. With the help of the CIA, a pro-American government took power in South Vietnam in June 1954. Ngo Dinh Diem, an anti-Communist Catholic residing in the United States, returned as premier. The next year, in a rigged election, Diem became president of an independent South Vietnam. Facing certain defeat by the popular Ho Chi Minh, Diem called off the reunification elections that were scheduled for 1956. As the last French soldiers left in March 1956, the United States took over, with South Vietnam now the front line in the American battle to contain Communism in Southeast Asia. To prop him up, the Eisenhower administration sent Diem an average of $200 million a year in aid and stationed approximately 675 American military advisors in Saigon, the capital. Few Americans, including probably Eisenhower himself, had any inkling where this might lead.

The Middle East. If Vietnam was still of minor concern, the same could not be said for the Middle East, an area rich in oil and complications. The Zionist movement had long encouraged Jews to return to their ancient homeland of Israel (Palestine). After World War II, many survivors of the Nazi extermination camps resettled in Palestine, which

Future Israelis

In 1945 these survivors of the Buchenwald concentration camp, like many other Jewish survivors of Hitler's gas ovens, resettled in Palestine. International guilt over the Holocaust was one of the factors that led the United Nations in 1947 to the acceptance of a Jewish state and to the partition of Palestine making such a state possible. National Archives.

was still controlled by Britain under a World War I mandate (see Chapter 22). On November 29, 1947, the U.N. General Assembly voted to partition Palestine, between Jewish and Arab sectors. When the British mandate ended, Zionist leaders proclaimed the state of Israel. The Arab League nations invaded, but Israel survived. Many Palestinians fled or were driven from their homes during the fighting. The Arab defeat, which meant they could not return, left them permanently stranded in refugee camps. President Truman quickly recognized the new state, winning crucial support from Jewish voters in the 1948 election, but alienating the Arabs.

Long dominant in the Persian Gulf, Britain began a general withdrawal after giving up the mandate in Palestine. Two years after gaining independence from Britain, Egypt in 1954 came under the rule of Gamal Abdel Nasser, who proclaimed a form of pan-Arab socialism that aimed at leading the entire Middle East out of its dependent, colonial relationship with the West. When Nasser obtained promises of help from the Soviet Union in building the Aswan Dam on the Nile, Secretary of State Dulles countered with an offer of American assistance. Nasser refused to distance himself from the Soviets, however, and Dulles abruptly withdrew his offer in July 1956. A week later Nasser retaliated, nationalizing the Suez Canal, through which three-quarters of western Europe's oil was transported. After several months of fruitless negotiation, Britain and France, in alliance with Israel, attacked Egypt and retook the canal. The attack came just as Eisenhower was condemning the Soviet invasion of Hungary. The president demanded that France and Britain pull back. Egypt retook the Suez Canal and built the Aswan Dam with Soviet support.

MAP 26.5 The Military-Industrial Complex

Defense spending gave a big boost to the Cold War economy, but, as the upper map suggests, the benefits were by no means equally distributed. The big winners were the Middle Atlantic states, the industrialized upper Midwest, Washington State (with its aircraft and nuclear plants), and California. The epicenter of California's military-industrial complex was Los Angeles, which, as is evident in the lower map, was studded with military facilities and major defense contractors like Douglas Aircraft, Lockheed, and General Dynamics. There was work a-plenty for engineers and rocket scientists.

The Suez Crisis, 1956

In this photograph, Egyptian President Gamal Abdel Nasser is greeted ecstatically by Cairo crowds after he nationalized the Suez Canal. Nasser's gamble paid off. Thanks to American intervention, military action by Britain, France, and Israel failed, and Nasser emerged the triumphant voice of Arab nationalism across the Middle East. The popular emotions he unleashed against the West survived his death in 1970 and are more potent today than ever, although now expressed more through Islamic fundamentalism than Nasser's brand of secular nationalism. Getty Images.

In early 1957, concerned that the USSR might step into the vacuum left by the British, the president announced the Eisenhower Doctrine, which stated that American forces would assist any nation in the region "requiring such aid, against overt armed aggression from any nation controlled by International Communism." Later that year, Eisenhower invoked the doctrine when he sent the U.S. Sixth Fleet to the Mediterranean Sea to aid King Hussein of Jordan against a Nasser-backed revolt. A year later he landed 14,000 troops to back up a pro-American government in Lebanon. The Eisenhower Doctrine was further proof of the global reach of containment, in this instance, accentuated by the strategic need to protect the West's access to steady supplies of oil.

Eisenhower's Farewell Address

In his final address to the nation, Eisenhower warned against the power of what he called the **"military-industrial complex,"** which by then was employing 3.5 million Americans (Map 26.5). Its pervasive influence, he said, "is felt in every city, every statehouse, every office of the federal government." Even though his administration had fostered this growing defense establishment, Eisenhower was gravely concerned about its implications for a democratic people: "We must guard against the acquisition of unwarranted influence, whether sought or unsought, by the military-industrial complex," he warned. "We must never let the weight of this combination endanger our liberties or democratic processes." With those words Dwight Eisenhower showed how well he understood the impact of the Cold War on American life. Only by vigilance could the democratic values of a free people be preserved in an age of constant global struggle.

- Why do we say that Eisenhower was heir to FDR, not Herbert Hoover?
- Was Eisenhower an adherent to the concept of containment? How so?
- Why was America's deepening involvement in the Third World a phenomenon of the 1950s rather than the 1940s?

SUMMARY

We have seen how the Cold War began as a conflict between the United States and the Soviet Union over eastern Europe. Very early in the conflict the United States adopted a strategy of containment, and although initially intended only for Europe, the strategy quickly expanded to Asia when China was "lost" to Mao's Communists. The first effect of that expansion was the Korean War, after which, under Eisenhower, containment of Communism became America's guiding principle across the Third World. Cold War imperatives meant a major military buildup, a scary nuclear arms race, and unprecedented entanglements across the globe.

We have also seen how, on the domestic front, Truman started out with high hopes for an expanded New Deal, only to be stymied by the problems of reconversion, by resistance from Congress, and by competing spending demands of the Cold War. The greatest Cold War–inspired distraction, however, was a climate of fear over internal subversion by Communists that gave rise to McCarthyism. Truman's successor, Dwight Eisenhower, brought the Republicans back into power. Although personally conservative, Eisenhower actually proved a New Dealer in disguise. He declined to cut back on social welfare programs and broke new ground in federal spending on highways, scientific research, and higher education. When he left office, it seemed that a "liberal consensus" prevailed, with old-fashioned, laissez-faire conservativism mostly marginalized.

Connections: Diplomacy and Politics

In the essay opening Part Six, we started with Walter Lippmann's boast at the close of World War II that "what Rome was to the ancient world...America is to be for the world of tomorrow." His confidence in America's future rested in part on his expectation that the Grand Alliance described in Chapter 25 would be durable. Had he gone further back to World War I (see Chapter 21), Lippmann might not have been so optimistic. Woodrow Wilson's hostile response to the Russian revolution had assumed that the two systems were irreconcilable, a belief that the Soviets fully shared. Once the Cold War began after 1945, it became the dominant event in American diplomatic history for the next half-century. In the case of the liberal consensus, its roots in the New Deal (Chapter 24) are entirely clear. Between 1945 and 1960, the liberal consensus held sway, even during Eisenhower's presidency, but after peaking in the mid-1960s with Johnson's Great Society (Chapter 28), it went into decline. The New Deal structure itself remained durable, despite the reaction against the War on Poverty, but the Democratic Party's grip on the country began to fail, and by the close of the Carter administration, conservatism and the Republican Party were clearly in the ascendancy (Chapter 29).

CHAPTER REVIEW QUESTIONS

- What factors gave rise to the Cold War between the United States and the Soviet Union?
- In what ways were President Truman's and Eisenhower's foreign policies similar? How did they differ?
- What was the domestic impact of the anti-Communist crusade of the late 1940s and 1950s?

TIMELINE

1945	Yalta and Potsdam conferences
	Harry S Truman succeeds Roosevelt
	End of World War II
	Senate approves U.S. participation in United Nations
1946	George Kennan outlines containment policy
	Baruch Plan for international control of atomic weapons fails
	War begins between French and Vietminh over control of Vietnam
1947	Taft-Hartley Act limits union power
	House Un-American Activities Committee (HUAC) investigates film industry
	Truman Doctrine promises aid to governments resisting Communism
	Marshall Plan aids economic recovery in Europe
1948	Communist coup in Czechoslovakia
	Truman signs executive order desegregating armed forces
	State of Israel created
	Stalin blockades West Berlin; Berlin airlift begins
1949	North Atlantic Treaty Organization (NATO) founded
	Soviet Union detonates atomic bomb
	Mao Zedong establishes People's Republic of China
1950–1953	Korean War
1950	Joseph McCarthy's "list" of Communists in government
	NSC-68 calls for permanent mobilization
1952	Dwight D. Eisenhower elected president
1953	Stalin dies
1954	Army-McCarthy hearings on army subversion
	French defeat at Dienbienphu in Vietnam
	Geneva Accords partition Vietnam at seventeenth parallel
1956	Crises in Hungary and at Suez Canal
	Interstate Highway Act
1957	Soviet Union launches *Sputnik*
1958	National Aeronautics and Space Administration (NASA) established
1960	U-2 incident leads to cancellation of U.S.-USSR summit meeting
1961	Eisenhower warns nation against military-industrial complex

FOR FURTHER EXPLORATION

James T. Patterson, *Grand Expectations: The United States, 1945–1974* (1996), offers a detailed, comprehensive account of this period. For a reconsideration of the Cold War from a post–Cold War perspective, see especially John Lewis Gaddis, *We Now Know: Rethinking Cold War History* (1997), and, for a more wide-ranging analysis, *The Cold War: A New History* (2005). On the Fair Deal, the best treatment is Alonso Hamby, *Beyond the New Deal: Harry S. Truman and American Liberalism* (1973). Jennifer Klein, *For All These Rights* (2003), is a probing analysis of why the United States failed to develop a national healthcare system. On McCarthyism, David Oshinsky, *A Conspiracy So Immense: The World of Joe McCarthy* (1983), is excellent. Key books containing documents and analysis of Soviet espionage are John E. Haynes and Harvey Klehr, *The Secret World of American Communism* (1995), and *Venona: Decoding Soviet Espionage in America* (1999). On the 1950s, see J. Ronald Oakley, *God's Country: America in the Fifties* (1986). David Halberstam's *The Fifties* (1993) offers a brief but searing account of CIA covert activities in Iran and Guatemala.

The Woodrow Wilson International Center for Scholars has established the Cold War International History Project at **www.wilsoncenter.org/index.cfm?topic_id=1409&fuseaction=topics.home**, an exceptionally rich Web site offering documents on the Cold War, including materials from former Communist-bloc countries. The Center for the Study of the Pacific Northwest's site, "The Cold War and Red Scare in Washington State," at **www.washington.edu/uwired/outreach/cspn/curcan/main.html**, provides detailed information on how the Great Fear operated in one state. Its bibliography includes books, documents, and videos. Project Whistlestop: Harry Truman at **www.trumanlibrary.org/whistlestop/student_guide.htm**, a program sponsored by the U.S. Department of Education, is a searchable collection of images and documents from the Harry S Truman Presidential Library. The site is organized into categories such as the origins of the Truman Doctrine, the Berlin airlift, the desegregation of the armed forces, and the 1948 presidential campaign. Users can also browse through the president's correspondence. "Korea + 50: No Longer Forgotten" is cosponsored by the Harry S Truman and Dwight D. Eisenhower Presidential Libraries, at **www.trumanlibrary.org/korea**. It offers official documents, oral histories, and photographs connected to the Korean War. It also features an audio recording of President Truman's recollections of his firing of General MacArthur in 1951.

TEST YOUR KNOWLEDGE

To assess your command of the material in this chapter, see the Online Study Guide at **bedfordstmartins.com/henretta**.

For Web sites, images, and documents related to topics and places in this chapter, visit **bedfordstmartins.com/makehistory**.

The Saturday Evening POST

June 4, 1955 — 15¢

America's Mighty Mile: THE SOO

LOOK, MOM—NO WHEELS! The Vehicle That Floats on Land

27 The Age of Affluence
1945–1960

IN 1959, VICE PRESIDENT RICHARD NIXON traveled to Moscow to open the American National Exhibit. It was the height of the Cold War. After sipping Pepsi-Cola, Nixon and Soviet Premier Nikita Khrushchev got into a heated debate about the relative merits of Soviet and American societies. Standing in the kitchen of a model American home, they talked dishwashers, toasters, and televisions, not rockets, submarines, and missiles. Images of the "kitchen debate" flashed across TV screens around the world.

What was so striking about the Moscow exhibition was the way its American planners enlisted affluence and mass consumption in service to Cold War politics. The suburban lifestyle trumpeted at the exhibition symbolized the superiority of capitalism over Communism.

During the postwar era, Americans did enjoy the highest standard of living in the world. But behind the affluence, everything was not as it seemed. The suburban calm masked contradictions in women's lives and cultural rebelliousness among young people. Suburban growth often came at the expense of urban life, sowing the seeds of inner-city decay and exacerbating racial tensions. Nor was prosperity ever as widespread as the Moscow exhibit implied. The suburban lifestyle was beyond the reach of the working poor, Spanish-speaking immigrants, and most African Americans. And in the South, a civil rights revolution was in the making.

Economic Powerhouse
Engines of Economic Growth
The Corporate Order
Labor-Management Accord

The Affluent Society
The Suburban Explosion
The Search for Security
Consumer Culture
The Baby Boom
Contradictions in Women's Lives
Youth Culture
Cultural Dissenters

The Other America
Immigrants and Migrants
The Urban Crisis
The Emerging Civil Rights Struggle

Summary
Connections: Economy

◀ **Life in the Suburbs**
In the 1950s the *Saturday Evening Post* celebrated the suburban ideal: family, leisure, and a nurturing wife and mother. © 1959 SEPS: Licensed by Curtis Publishing Company, Indianapolis, IN. All rights reserved. www.curtispublishing.com.

Economic Powerhouse

The United States enjoyed overwhelming political and economic advantages at the end of World War II. Unlike the Soviet Union, western Europe, and Japan, America emerged physically unscathed from the war and poised to take advantage of the postwar boom. Dominated by giant corporations, the American economy benefited from stable internal markets, heavy investment in research and development, and the rapid diffusion of new technology. For the first time, employers generally accepted collective bargaining, which for workers translated into rising wages, expanding benefits, and a growing rate of home ownership. At the heart of this postwar prosperity lay the involvement of the federal government. Federal outlays for defense and domestic programs gave a huge boost to the economy. Not least, the federal government recognized that prosperity rested on global foundations.

Engines of Economic Growth

By the end of 1945, war-induced prosperity launched the United States into an era of unprecedented economic growth. Pent-up demand after years of wartime mobilization made Americans eager to spend. Business applied scientific and technological innovations developed for military purposes, such as plastics and synthetic fibers, to the production of consumer goods. Over the next two decades, the gross domestic product (GDP) tripled, benefiting a wider segment of society than anyone would have dreamed possible in the dark days of the Depression.

The Bretton Woods System. American global supremacy rested in part on economic institutions created at a United Nations conference at Bretton Woods, New Hampshire, in July 1944. The International Bank for Reconstruction and Development (known commonly as the World Bank) provided private loans for the reconstruction of war-torn Europe as well as for the development of Third World countries. A second institution, the International Monetary Fund (IMF), was set up to stabilize the value of currencies and provide a predictable monetary environment for trade, with the U.S. dollar serving as the benchmark for other currencies. The United States dominated the World Bank and the IMF because it contributed the most capital and the strongest currency. In 1947, multinational trade negotiations resulted in the first General Agreement on Tariffs and Trade (GATT), which led to the establishment of an international body to oversee trade rules and practices.

The World Bank, the IMF, and GATT were the cornerstones of the so-called Bretton Woods system that guided the world economy after the war. These international organizations encouraged stable prices, the reduction of tariffs, flexible domestic markets, and international trade based on fixed exchange rates. The Bretton Woods system effectively served America's conception of the global economy, paralleling America's ambitious diplomatic aims in the Cold War.

The Kitchen Debate

At the Moscow Fair in 1959, the United States put on display the technological wonders of American home life. When Vice President Richard Nixon visited, he and Soviet Premier Nikita Khrushchev got into a heated debate over the relative merits of their rival systems, with the up-to-date American kitchen as a case in point. This photograph shows the debate in progress. Khrushchev is the bald man pointing his finger at Nixon. On the other side of Nixon stands Leonid Brezhnev, who would be Khrushchev's successor. Getty Images.

The Military-Industrial Complex. A second linchpin of postwar prosperity was defense spending. The military-industrial complex that President Eisenhower identified in his 1961 Farewell Address had its roots in the business-government partnerships of the world wars. But unlike after 1918, the massive commitment of government dollars for defense continued after 1945. Even though the country was technically at peace, the economy and the government operated practically on a war footing — in a state of permanent mobilization.

Based at the sprawling Pentagon in Arlington, Virginia, the Defense Department evolved into a massive bureaucracy. Defense-related industries entered into long-term relationships with the Pentagon in the name of national security. Some companies did so much business with the government that they became dependent on Defense Department orders. Over 60 percent of the income of Boeing, General Dynamics, and Raytheon eventually came from military contracts, while Lockheed received 81 percent and Republic Aviation 100 percent. All of them were giant enterprises, made even bigger by the Pentagon's inclination to favor the largest firms.

As permanent mobilization took hold, science, industry, and the federal government became increasingly intertwined. According to the National Science Foundation, federal money underwrote 90 percent of the cost of research on aviation and space, 65 percent of that on electricity and electronics, 42 percent of that on scientific instruments, and 24 percent of that on automobiles. With the government footing part of the bill, corporations transformed new ideas into useful products with amazing speed. After the Pentagon backed IBM's investment in integrated circuits in the 1960s, those new devices, which were crucial to the computer revolution, entered commercial production within three years.

The growth of this military-industrial establishment had a dramatic impact on national priorities. Between 1900 and 1930, excepting World War I, the country spent less than 1 percent of GDP on the military. By the early 1960s the figure had risen to nearly 10 percent. The defense buildup created jobs, and lots of them. Taking into account the indirect benefits (the additional jobs created to serve and support defense workers), perhaps one worker in seven nationally owed his or her job to the military-industrial complex. But increased military spending also limited the resources for domestic social needs. Critics of military spending calculated the trade-offs: The cost of a nuclear aircraft carrier and support ships equaled that of a subway system for Washington, D.C.; the money spent on one Huey helicopter could have built sixty-six units of low-income housing.

FIGURE 27.1 Gross Domestic Product, 1930–1972

After a sharp dip during the Great Depression, the GDP rose steadily in both real and constant dollars in the postwar period.

The Economic Record. America's annual GDP jumped from $213 billion in 1945 to more than $500 billion in 1960; by 1970, it exceeded $1 trillion (see Figure 27.1). To working Americans, this sustained economic growth meant a 25 percent rise in real income between 1946 and 1959. Postwar prosperity also featured low inflation. After the postwar reconversion period, inflation slowed to 2 to 3 percent annually during the 1950s, and it stayed low until the escalation of the Vietnam War in the mid-1960s. Low inflation meant stable and predictable prices. Feeling secure about the present and confident about the future, most Americans rightly felt that they were better off than they had ever been before. In 1940, 43 percent of American families owned their homes; by 1960, 62 percent did. Prosperity, as measured by the rate of income growth at different income levels, was quite equally distributed. Families in the 95th percentile did no better than lower-income families; the fastest rate of income growth, in fact, was at the 60th percentile.

Even so, the picture was not entirely rosy. The distribution of income remained stubbornly skewed, with the top 10 percent of Americans earning more than the bottom 50 percent. Moreover, the economy was plagued by periodic recessions, damaging especially to the most disadvantaged Americans. In *The Affluent Society* (1958) the economist John Kenneth Galbraith argued that the poor were only an "afterthought" in the minds of economists and politicians. Yet, as Galbraith noted, one in thirteen families at the time earned less than $1,000 a year.

The Corporate Order

For over half a century, American enterprise had favored the consolidation of economic power into big corporate firms. That tendency continued—indeed, it accelerated—as domestic and world markets increasingly overlapped after 1945. In 1970 the top four U.S. carmakers produced 91 percent of all motor vehicles sold in the country; the top four in tires produced 72 percent, in cigarettes 84 percent, and in detergents 70 percent. Despite laws restricting branch banking to a single state, in 1970 the four largest banks held 16 percent of the nation's banking assets; the top fifty banks held 48 percent.

The classic, vertically integrated corporation of the early twentieth century had produced a single line of products that served a national market (see Chapter 17). This strategy worked even better in the 1950s, when sophisticated media advertising enabled large corporations to break into hitherto resistant markets, for example, beer, where loyalty to local brews in their infinite variety was legendary. To erode that preference, Anheuser-Busch and other national producers sponsored televised sports, parlaying the aura of championship games into national acceptance of their standardized, "lighter" beers. "Bud, the King of Beers"—just as good for the little guy as for the big-league star. By 1970, big multiplant brewers controlled 70 percent of the beer market.

To this well-honed approach, national firms now added a new strategy of diversification. CBS, for example, hired the Hungarian inventor Peter Goldmark, who perfected color television during the 1940s, long-playing records in the 1950s, and a video recording system in the 1960s. As the head of CBS Laboratories, Goldmark patented more than a hundred new devices and created multiple new markets for his happy employer. Because big outfits like CBS had the deepest pockets, they were the firms best able to diversify through investment in industrial research.

More revolutionary was the sudden rise of the conglomerates, giant enterprises comprised of firms in unrelated industries. Conglomerate-building resulted in the nation's third great merger wave (the first two had taken place in the 1890s and the 1920s). Because of their diverse holdings, conglomerates shielded themselves from instability in any single market and seemed better able to compete globally. International Telephone and Telegraph transformed itself into a conglomerate by acquiring Continental Baking (famous for Wonder Bread), Sheraton Hotels, Avis Rent-a-Car, Levitt and Sons home builders, and Hartford Fire Insurance. Ling-Temco-Vought, another conglomerate, produced steel, built ships, developed real estate, and brought cattle to market.

Expansion into foreign markets also spurred corporate growth. At a time when "made in Japan" still meant shoddy workmanship, U.S. products were considered the best in the world. American firms expanded into foreign markets when domestic demand became saturated or when recessions cut into sales. During the 1950s U.S. exports nearly doubled, giving the nation a trade surplus of close to $5 billion in 1960. By the 1970s, Gillette, IBM, Mobil, and Coca-Cola made more than half their profits from abroad.

In their effort to direct such giant enterprises, managers placed more emphasis on planning. Companies recruited top executives who had business-school training, the ability to manage information, and skills in corporate planning, marketing, and investment. A new generation of corporate chieftains emerged, operating in a complex environment that demanded long-range forecasting and close coordination with investment banks, law firms, the federal government, the World Bank, and the IMF.

The New Managerial Class. To man their bureaucracies, the postwar corporate giants required a huge supply of white-collar foot soldiers. They turned to the universities, which, fueled partly by the GI Bill, grew explosively after 1945. Better educated than their elders, the members of the new managerial class advanced more quickly, and at a younger age, into responsible jobs. As one participant-observer remarked: "If you had a college diploma, a dark suit, and anything between the ears, it was like an escalator; you just stood there and moved up." (He was talking about men; few women gained entrance to the managerial ranks.)

Corporations offered lifetime employment, but they also expected lifetime loyalty. Atlas Van Lines, in the business of moving them, estimated that corporate managers were transferred an average of fourteen times—once every two and a half years—during their careers. Perpetually mobile IBM managers joked that the company's initials stood for "I've Been Moved."

Climbing the corporate ladder rewarded men without hard edges—the "well adjusted." In *The Lonely Crowd* (1950) the sociologist David Reisman contrasted the independent businessmen and professionals of earlier years with the managerial class of the postwar world. He concluded that the new corporate men were "other-directed," more attuned

Organization Men (and a Few Women)

What happened when the 5:57 P.M. discharged commuters in Park Forest, Illinois, a suburb of Chicago? This was the subject of William H. Whyte's *The Organization Man* (1956). Were these hordes of commuters thinking about their stressful workdays at the office or the martinis waiting for them when they walked in the doors of their suburban homes? *Photo by Dan Weiner, Courtesy Sarah Weiner.*

to their associates than driven by their own goals. The sociologist William Whyte painted a somber picture of "organization men" who left the home "spiritually as well as physically to take the vows of organization life." A recurring theme of the 1950s, in fact, was that the conformity demanded of the man in the gray flannel suit (the title of Sloan Wilson's popular novel) was stifling creativity and blighting lives.

Labor-Management Accord

For blue-collar workers, collective bargaining became for the first time the normal means for determining how their labor would be rewarded. Anti-union employers had fought long and hard against collective bargaining, confining organized labor to a narrow band of craft trades and a few industries, primarily coal mining, railroading, and stove manufacture. The power balance shifted during the Great Depression (see Chapter 24), and by the time the dust settled after World War II, labor unions overwhelmingly represented America's industrial work force (Figure 27.2). The question then became: How would labor's power be used?

In late 1945, Walter Reuther of the United Auto Workers (UAW) challenged General Motors in a fundamental way. The youthful Reuther was thinking big, beyond a single company, or even a single industry. He aimed at nothing less than a reshaped, high-employment economy. To jumpstart it, he demanded a 30 percent wage hike with no price increase for GM cars, and when General Motors said no, it couldn't afford that, Reuther demanded that the company "open the books."

General Motors implacably resisted this "opening wedge" into the rights of management. The company took a 113-day strike, rebuffed the government's intervention, and soundly defeated the UAW. Having made its point, General Motors laid out the terms for a durable relationship. It would accept the UAW as its bargaining partner

FIGURE 27.2 Labor Union Strength, 1900–1997

Labor unions reached their peak strength immediately after World War II, when they represented close to 40 percent of the nonfarm workforce. Although there was some decline after the mid 1950s, unions still represented nearly 30 percent in 1973. Thereafter, their decline was precipitous. SOURCE: AFL-CIO Information Bureau, Washington, D.C.

and guarantee GM workers an ever higher living standard. The price was that the UAW abandon its assault on the company's "right to manage." On signing the five-year GM contract of 1950 — the Treaty of Detroit, it was called — Reuther accepted the company's terms.

The Treaty of Detroit opened the way for a more broadly based "labor-management accord" — not industrial peace, because the country still experienced many strikes, but general acceptance of collective bargaining as the method for setting the terms and conditions of employment. For industrial workers, the result was rising real income, from $54.92 a week in 1949 to $71.81 (in 1947–1949 dollars) in 1959. The average worker with three dependents gained 18 percent in spendable real income in that period. In addition, collective bargaining delivered greater leisure (more paid holidays and lengthier vacations) and, in a startling departure, a social safety net.

In postwar Europe, America's allies were constructing welfare states. That was the preference of American unions as well. But having lost the bruising battle in Washington for national health care, the unions turned to the bargaining table. By the end of the 1950s, union contracts commonly provided defined-benefit pension plans (supplementing Social Security); company-paid health insurance; and, for two million workers, mainly in steel and auto, a guaranteed annual wage (via supplementary unemployment benefits). Collective bargaining had become, in effect, the American alternative to the European welfare state.

The sum of these union gains was a new sociological phenomenon, the "affluent" worker — as evidenced by relocation to the suburbs, by homeownership, by increased ownership of cars and other durable goods, and, an infallible sign of rising expectations, by installment buying. For union workers, the contract became, as Reuther boasted, the passport into the middle class. Generally overlooked, however, were the many unorganized workers with no such passport — those consigned to casual labor or low-wage jobs in the service sector. In retrospect, economists recognized that America had developed a two-tiered, inequitable labor system.

The labor-management accord that generated the good life for so many workers seemed in the 1950s absolutely secure. The union rivalries of the 1930s abated. In 1955 the industrial-union and craft-union wings joined together in the AFL-CIO, representing 90 percent of the nation's 17.5 million union members. At its head stood George Meany, a cigar-chomping former New York plumber who, in his blunt way, conveyed the reassuring message that organized labor had matured and was management's fit partner.

The labor-management accord, impressive though it was, never was as durable as it seemed. Vulnerabilities lurked, even in the accord's heyday. For one thing, the sheltered markets — the essential condition for passing on the costs of collective bargaining — were in fact quite fragile. In certain industries, the leading firms were already losing market share — for example, in meatpacking and steel — and nowhere, not even in auto, was their dominance truly secure. A second, more obvious vulnerability, was the non-union South, which, despite a strenuous postwar drive, the unions failed to organize. The South's success at attracting companies pointed to a third, most basic vulnerability, namely, the abiding anti-unionism of American employers. At heart, they regarded the labor-management accord as a negotiated truce, not a permanent peace. It was only a matter of time, and the onset of a more competitive environment, before the scattered anti-union forays of the 1950s turned into a full-scale counteroffensive.

The postwar labor-management accord, it turns out, was a transitory event, not a permanent condition of American economic life. And, in a larger sense, that was true of the postwar boom. It was a transitory event, not a permanent condition.

Lost in Levittown

This 1954 *New Yorker* cartoon humorously reflected what critics saw as the stifling uniformity of the new suburbs. Suburbanites didn't seem to mind. They understood that Levitt's houses were so cheap because he built them all alike. But, admittedly, Mrs. Barnes's confusion was a downside. The New Yorker Collection, 1954, Robert J. Day, from cartoonbank.com. All Rights Reserved.

"I'm Mrs. Edward M. Barnes. Where do I live?"

> - In what ways is the prosperity of the 1950s explained by the Cold War?
> - Why is "the man in the gray flannel suit" the representative businessman of the 1950s?
> - What do we mean by the "labor-management accord"?

The Affluent Society

Prosperity is more easily measured — how much an economy produces, how much people earn — than the good life that prosperity actually buys. For the 1950s, however, the contours of the American good life emerged with exceptional distinctness: a preference for suburban living, a high valuation on consumption, and a devotion to family and domesticity. In this section we ask, why those particular choices? And with what — not necessarily happy — consequences?

The Suburban Explosion

Suburban migration had been ongoing ever since the nineteenth century, but never on the explosive scale that the country experienced after World War II. Within a decade or so, developers filled up farmland on the outskirts of cities with tract housing and shopping malls. Entire counties once rural, like San Mateo, south of San Francisco, or Prince Georges, outside Washington, D.C., were built up. By 1960, more people lived in suburbs than in cities.

The Housing Boom. Home construction had virtually ended during the Great Depression, and returning veterans, dreaming of home and family, faced a critical housing shortage. After the war, construction surged to meet pent-up demand. A fourth of the country's entire housing stock in 1960 had not even existed a decade earlier.

An innovative Long Island building contractor, William J. Levitt, revolutionized the suburban housing market by applying mass-production techniques and turning out new homes at dizzying speed. Levitt's basic four-room house, complete with kitchen appliances, was priced at $7,990 in 1947. Levitt did not need to advertise; word of mouth brought buyers flocking to his developments in New York, Pennsylvania, and New Jersey (all called, naturally, Levittown). Dozens of other developers, including California's shipping magnate Henry J. Kaiser, were soon snapping up cheap farmland and building subdivisions around the country.

Even at $7,990, Levitt's homes were beyond the means of young families, or would have been, had the traditional home-financing standard — half down and ten years to pay off the balance — still prevailed. That's where the Federal Housing Administration (FHA) and the Veterans Administration (VA) came in. After the war, the FHA insured 30-year mortgages with as little as 5 percent down and interest at 2 or 3 percent. The VA was even more lenient, requiring only a token $1 down for qualified ex-GI's. FHA and VA mortgages best explain why, after hovering around 45 percent for the previous half-century, home ownership jumped to 60 percent by 1960.

What purchasers of Levitt's houses got, in addition to a good deal, were homogeneous communities. The developments contained few old people or unmarried adults. Even the trees were young. Owners agreed to cut their lawns once a week and not to hang out laundry on the weekends. Then there was the matter of race. Levitt's houses came with **restrictive covenants** prohibiting occupancy "by members of other than the Caucasian Race." (Covenants often applied to Jews and Catholics as well.)

Levitt, a marketing genius, knew his customers. The UAW learned the hard way. After the war, the CIO union launched an ambitious campaign for open-housing ordinances in the Detroit area. White auto workers rebelled, rebuking the union leadership by voting for racist politicans who promised to keep white neighborhoods white. A leading advocate of racial equality nationally, the UAW quietly shelved the fight at the local level. In *Shelley v. Kraemer* (1948) the Supreme Court outlawed restrictive covenants, but the practice persisted informally long afterward. Among America's bastions of racial segregation, the suburb was probably the last to fall.

The Sun Belt. Suburban living, although a nationwide phenomenon, was most at home in the Sun Belt, where taxes were low, the climate mild, and open space allowed for sprawling subdivisions (Map 27.1). Fueled by World War II, the South and

MAP 27.1 Shifting Population Patterns, 1950–1980

This map shows the two major, somewhat overlapping, patterns of population movement between 1950 and 1980. Most striking is the rapid growth of the Sun Belt states. All the states experiencing increases of over 100 percent in that period are in the Southwest, plus Florida. The second pattern involves the growth of metropolitan areas, defined as a central city or urban area and its suburbs. The central cities were themselves mostly not growing, however. The metropolitan growth shown in this map was accounted for by the expanding suburbs. And because Sun Belt growth was primarily suburban growth, that's where we see the most rapid metropolitan growth, with Los Angeles the clear winner.

West began to boom. Florida added 3.5 million people, many of them retired, between 1940 and 1970. Texas profited from an expanding petrochemical industry and profitable agriculture. Most dramatic was California's growth, spurred especially by lots of work in the state's defense-related aircraft and electronics industries. California's climate and job opportunites acted as magnets pulling people from all parts of the country. By 1970, California contained a tenth of the nation's population and surpassed New York as the most populous state.

Boosters heralded the booming development of the Sun Belt. But growth came at a price. In the arid Southwest, increasing demands for water and energy made for environmental and health problems. As cities competed for scarce water resources, they depleted underground acquifers and dammed scenic rivers. The proliferation of coal-burning power plants increased air pollution, and so did traffic. The West's nuclear industry, while good for the economy, also brought nuclear waste, uranium mines, and atomic test sites. And growth had a way of consuming the easy, uncongested living that attracted people to the Sun Belt in the first place. Still, for folks occupying those ranch-style houses, with their nice lawns, barbecues, and air-conditioning, suburban living seemed at its best in sunny California or Arizona.

Cars and Highways. Without automobiles, suburban growth on such a massive scale would have been impossible. Planners laid out subdivisions on the assumption that everybody would drive. And they did—to get to work, to take the children to Little League, to shop at the mall. With gas plentiful at 15 cents a gallon, no one cared about fuel efficiency, or seemed to mind the elaborate tail fins and chrome detail that weighed down their V-eights. In 1945 Americans owned twenty-five million cars; by 1965 the number had tripled to seventy-five million (see Voices from Abroad, "Hanoch Bartov: Everyone Has a Car," p. 840).

More cars required more highways, and the federal government obliged. In 1947 Congress authorized the construction of 37,000 miles of highways; major new legislation in 1956 increased this commitment by another 42,500 miles (Map 27.2). One of the largest civil-engineering projects in history, the new interstate system linked the entire country, with far-reaching effects on both the cities and the countryside. The interstate highways rerouted traffic away from small towns, bypassed well-traveled main roads like Route 1 on the East Coast and the cross-country Route 66, and cut wide swaths through old neighborhoods in the cities. Excellent mass transit systems, like those of Los Angeles and the San Francisco Bay Area, gave way to freeways. Federal highway funding specifically excluded mass transit, and the auto industry

MAP 27.2 Connecting the Nation: The Interstate Highway System, 1930 and 1970

The 1956 Interstate and Defense Highways Act paved the way for an extensive network of federal highways throughout the nation. The act pleased American drivers and enhanced their love affair with the automobile, and also benefited the petroleum, construction, trucking, real estate, and tourist industries. The new highway system promoted the nation's economic integration, facilitated the growth of suburbs, and contributed to the erosion of America's distinct regional identities.

VOICES FROM ABROAD

Hanoch Bartov
Everyone Has a Car

One of Israel's foremost writers and journalists, Hanoch Bartov spent two years in the United States working as a correspondent for the newspaper Lamerchav. *As a newcomer to Los Angeles in the early 1960s, he was both fascinated and appalled by Americans' love affair with the automobile.*

Our immediate decision to buy a car sprang from healthy instincts. Only later did I learn from bitter experience that in California, death was preferable to living without one. Neither the views from the plane nor the weird excursion that first evening hinted at what I would go through that first week.

Very simple — the nearest supermarket was about half a kilometer south of our apartment, the regional primary school two kilometers east, and my son's kindergarten even farther away. A trip to the post office — an undertaking, to the bank — an ordeal, to work — an impossibility.

Truth be told: the Los Angeles municipality . . . does have public transportation. Buses go once an hour along the city's boulevards and avenues, gathering all the wretched of the earth, the poor and the needy, the old ladies forbidden by their grandchildren to drive, and other eccentric types. But few people can depend on buses, even should they swear never to deviate from the fixed routes. . . . There are no tramways. No one thought of a subway. Railroads — not now and not in the future. Why? Because everyone has a car. A man invited me to his house, saying, "We are neighbors, within ten minutes of each other." After walking for an hour and a half I realized what he meant — "ten minute drive within the speed limit." Simply put, he never thought I might interpret his remark to refer to the walking distance. The moment a baby sees the light of day in Los Angeles, a car is registered in his name in Detroit. . . .

At first perhaps people relished the freedom and independence a car provided. You get in, sit down, and grab the steering wheel, your mobility exceeding that of any other generation. No wonder people refuse to live downtown, where they can hear their neighbors, smell their cooking, and suffer frayed nerves as trains pass by bedroom windows. Instead, they get a piece of the desert, far from town, at half price, drag a water hose, grow grass, flowers, and trees, and build their dream house. . . .

The result? A widely scattered city, its houses far apart, its streets stretched in all directions. Olympic Boulevard from west to east, forty kilometers. Sepulveda Boulevard, from Long Beach in the south to the edge of the desert, forty kilometers. Altogether covering 1,200 square kilometers. As of now.

Why "as of now"? Because greater distances mean more commuting, and more commuting leads to more cars. More cars means problems that push people even farther away from the city, which chases after them.

The urban sprawl is only one side effect. Two, some say three, million cars require an array of services. . . .

. . . Why bother parking, getting out, getting in, getting up and sitting down, when you can simply "drive in"? Mailboxes have their slots facing the road, at the level of the driver's hand. That is how dirty laundry is deposited, electricity and water bills paid. That is how love is made, how children are taken to school. That is how the anniversary wreath is laid on the graves of loved ones. There are drive-in movies. And, yes, we saw it with our own eyes: drive-in churches. Only in death is a man separated from his car and buried alone. . . .

SOURCE: Oscar and Lilian Handlin, eds., *From the Outer World* (Cambridge, MA: Harvard University Press, 1997), 293–296.

ANALYZING THE EVIDENCE

▸ From Bartov's observations, what are the pluses and minuses of America's car culture? In what ways was the automobile changing American society?

▸ Why did Bartov find owning a car was necessary, especially in southern California?

▸ Everyone, of course, didn't have a car. Who, according to Bartov, used public transportation?

City Life Belts

What to do in case of nuclear attack? That was the problem Norbert Wiener, a renown cyberneticist at MIT, was thinking about when he and his colleagues came up with this design for an eight-lane "Life-Belt" around the country's major cities. Citizens who made it out would find safety at camp sites beyond the targeted areas. *Life* magazine, December 18, 1950.

was no friend either. General Motors made it a practice of buying up mass transit systems and scrapping them. By 1960 two-thirds of Americans drove to work each day. In Sun Belt cities like Los Angeles and Phoenix, the proportion came closer to 100 percent.

The postwar suburban explosion was distinctively American. In war-ravaged European cities, home construction was centered on high-density neighborhoods and along mass transit lines. Not until twenty years later did Europeans experiment with low-density suburban housing, and never with the disastrous effect, as in America, of gutting the central cities.

The Search for Security

There was a reason why Congress called the 1956 legislation creating America's modern freeway system the National Interstate and *Defense* Highways Act. The four-lane freeways, used every day by commuters, might some day, in a nuclear war, evacuate them to safety. That captured as well as anything the underside of postwar life, when suburban living abided side by side with the shadow of annihilation.

The Cold War, reaching as it did across the globe, was omnipresent at home as well, permeating domestic politics, intruding on the debate over racial injustice, and creating an atmosphere that stifled dissent. For the first time, America had a peacetime draft. In every previous war, the country had quickly demobilized. But when World War II ended, the draft remained in place. Every neighborhood seemed to have a boy in the armed forces.

Most alarming was the nuclear standoff with the Soviet Union. Bomb shelters and civil defense drills

Duck and Cover
The nation's Civil Defense Agency's efforts to prepare Americans for a nuclear attack extended to children in schools, where repeated drills taught them to "duck and cover" when the alarm went off. Variations of this 1954 scene at Franklin Township School in Quakertown, New Jersey, were repeated all over the nation. Paul F. Kutta. Courtesy *Reminisce Magazine*.

provided a daily reminder of mushroom clouds. In the late 1950s a small but growing number of citizens raised questions about radioactive fallout from above-ground bomb tests. Federal investigators later documented illnesses, deaths, and birth defects among "downwinders"—people who lived near nuclear test sites. The most shocking revelations, however, came in 1993, when the Department of Energy released previously classified documents on human radiation experiments conducted in the late 1940s and 1950s under the auspices of the Atomic Energy Commission and other federal agencies. Many of the experiments were undertaken with little concern for or understanding of the adverse effects on the subjects.

By the late 1950s, public concern over nuclear testing had become a high-profile issue, and new antinuclear groups such as SANE (the National Committee for a Sane Nuclear Policy) and Physicians for Social Responsibility called for an international test ban.

Returning to the Church. In an age of anxiety, Americans yearned for a reaffirmation of faith. Church membership jumped from 49 percent of the population in 1940 and to 70 percent in 1960. People flocked especially into the evangelical Protestant denominations, who benefited from a remarkable new crop of preachers. Most notable was the young Reverend Billy Graham, who made brilliant use of television, radio, and advertising to spread the gospel. The religious reawakening meshed, in a time of Cold War, with Americans' view of themselves as a righteous people opposed to "godless Communism." In 1954 the phrase "under God" was inserted into the Pledge of Allegiance, and after 1956 U.S. coins carried the words, "In God We Trust."

The resurgence of religion, despite its evangelical bent, had a distinctly moderate tone. An ecumenical movement bringing Catholics, Protestants, and Jews together flourished, and so did a concern for the here-and-now. In his popular television program, Catholic Bishop Fulton J. Sheen asked, "Is life worth living?" He and countless others answered that it was. None was more affirmative than Norman Vincent Peale, whose best-selling book *The Power of Positive Thinking* (1952) embodied the trend toward the therapeutic use of religion, an antidote to the stresses of modern life.

Consumer Culture

In some respects, postwar consumerism seemed like a return to the 1920s—an abundance of new gadgets and appliances, more leisure time, the craze for automobiles, and new types of mass media. Yet there was a significant difference. In the 1950s consumption became associated with citizenship. Buying things, once a sign of personal indulgence, now meant fully participating in American society and, moreover, fulfilling a social responsibility. By spending, Americans fueled a high-employment economy. What the suburban family consumed, asserted *Life* magazine in a photo essay featuring one such family, would help assure "full employment

Billy Graham, Evangelist

Billy Graham was the first great revival preacher of the postwar era, a worthy successor to Billy Sunday and Aimee Semple McPherson. In this photograph, the Reverend Graham is preaching to more than thirty thousand people jammed into Wall Street on July 10, 1957. In what he termed the "greatest service" of his New York Crusade, the evangelist gave a twenty-minute extemporaneous sermon from an improvised pulpit on the steps of the Federal Memorial Hall. In the foreground is the foot of the George Washington statue. At rear is the New York Stock Exchange.
© Bettmann/Corbis.

and improved living standards for the rest of the nation."

Advertising. As in the past, product makers sought to stimulate consumer demand through aggressive advertising. More money was spent in 1951 on advertising ($6.5 billion) than on primary and secondary education ($5 billion). The 1950s gave Americans the Marlboro Man; M&Ms that melt in your mouth, not in your hand; Wonder Bread to build strong bodies in twelve ways; and the "does she or doesn't she?" Clairol hair-coloring woman. Motivational research delved into the subconscious to suggest how the messages should be pitched. Like other features of the consumer culture, this one got its share of muckraking condemnation in Vance Packer's best-selling *The Hidden Persuaders* (1957).

Advertising heavily promoted the appliances that began to fill the suburban kitchen, many of them unavailable during the war, others new to the postwar market. In 1946 automatic washing machines replaced the old machines with hand-cranked wringers, and clothes dryers also came on the market. Commercial laundries across the country struggled to stay in business. Another new item was the home freezer, encouraging the dramatic growth of the frozen-food industry. Partly because of all the electrical appliances, consumer use of electricity doubled during the 1950s.

Television. TV's leap to cultural prominence was swift and overpowering. There were only 7,000 sets in American homes in 1947, yet a year later the CBS and NBC radio networks began offering regular programming, and by 1950 Americans owned 7.3 million TV sets. Ten years later, 87 percent of American homes had at least one television set.

Although licensed by the Federal Communications Commission (FCC), television stations, like radio, depended entirely on advertising for profits. Soon television supplanted radio as the chief diffuser of popular culture. Movies, too, lost the cultural dominance they had once enjoyed. Movie attendance shrank throughout the postwar period, and movie studios increasingly relied on overseas distribution to earn a profit.

What Americans saw on television, besides the omnipresent commercials, was an overwhelmingly white, Anglo-Saxon world of nuclear families, suburban homes, and middle-class life. A typical show was *Father Knows Best,* starring Robert Young and Jane Wyatt. Father left home each morning wearing a suit and carrying a briefcase. Mother was a full-time housewife, always tending to her three children, but, as a sterotypical female, prone to bad driving and tears. The children were sometimes rebellious, but family conflicts were invariably resolved. *The Honeymooners,* starring Jackie Gleason as a Brooklyn bus driver, and *Life of Reilly,* a situation comedy featuring a California aircraft worker, were rare in their treatment of working-class lives. Black characters such as Rochester in Jack Benny's comedy show appeared mainly as sidekicks and servants.

The types of television programs developed in the 1950s built on older entertainment genres but also pioneered new ones. Taking its cue from the movies, television offered some thirty westerns by 1959, including *Gunsmoke, Wagon Train,* and

Advertising in the TV Age

Aggressive advertising of new products, such as the color television, helped fuel the surge in consumer spending during the 1950s. Marketing experts emphasized the role of television in promoting family togetherness, while interior designers offered decorating tips that placed the television at the focal point of living rooms and the increasingly popular "family rooms." Here, the family watches a variety program starring singer Dinah Shore, who was the television spokeswoman for Chevrolet cars. Every American probably could hum the tune of the little song she sang in praise of the Chevy. Motorola.

Bonanza. Professional sports became big-time television — far exceeding the potential of radio. Programming geared to children, such as Walt Disney's *Mickey Mouse Club, Howdy Doody,* and *Captain Kangaroo*, created the first generation of children glued to the tube.

Although the new medium did offer some serious programming, notably live theater and documentaries, FCC Commissioner Newton Minow concluded in 1963 that television was "a vast wasteland." But it did what it intended, which was to sell products and fill America's leisure hours with reassuring entertainment.

The Baby Boom

A popular 1945 song was called "Gotta Make Up for Lost Time," and Americans did just that. Two things were noteworthy about the families they formed after World War II. First, marriages were remarkably stable. Not until the mid-1960s did the divorce rate begin to rise sharply. Second, married couples were intent on having babies. Everyone expected to have two or more children — it was part of adulthood, almost a citizen's responsibility. After a century and a half of decline, the birthrate shot up: More babies were born between 1948 and 1953 than were born in the previous thirty years (Figure 27.3).

Among reasons for this baby boom, one was that everyone was having children at the same time. A second was a drop in the marriage age — down to twenty-two for men, twenty for women. Younger parents meant a bumper crop of children. Women who came of age in the 1930s averaged 2.4 children; their counterparts in the 1950s, 3.2 children. The baby boom peaked in 1957 and remained at a high level until the early 1960s. Thereafter, the

FIGURE 27.3 The American Birthrate, 1860–1980

When birthrates are viewed over more than a century, the postwar baby boom is clearly only a temporary reversal of the longterm downward trend in the American birthrate.

birthrate declined, returning to earlier long-term patterns.

"Scientific" Child Rearing. To keep all those baby-boom children healthy and happy, middle-class parents increasingly relied on the advice of experts. Dr. Benjamin Spock's best-selling *Baby and Child Care* sold a million copies a year after its publication in 1946. Spock urged mothers to abandon the rigid feeding and baby-care schedules of an earlier generation. New mothers found Spock's commonsense approach liberating, but it did not totally soothe their insecurities. If mothers were too protective, Spock and others argued, they might hamper their children's preparation for adult life. Mothers who wanted to work outside the home felt guilty because Spock recommended that they be constantly available for their children.

Less subject to fashion were the very real advances in diet, public health, and medical practice that made for healthier children. Serious illness turned routine after the introduction of such "miracle drugs" as penicillin (introduced in 1943), streptomycin (1945), and cortisone (1946). When Dr. Jonas Salk perfected a polio vaccine in 1954, he became a national hero. The free distribution of Salk's vaccine in the nation's schools, followed in 1961 by Dr. Albert Sabin's oral polio vaccine, demonstrated the potential of government-sponsored public health programs. The conquest of polio made the children of the 1950s the healthiest generation ever.

The baby boom had a vast impact on American society. All those babies fueled the economy as families bought food, diapers, toys, and clothing for their expanding broods. The nation's educational system also got a boost. The new middle class, America's first college-educated generation, placed a high value on education. Suburban parents approved 90 percent of proposed school bond issues during the 1950s. By 1970 school expenditures accounted for 7.2 percent of the gross national

Polio Pioneers

These Provo, Utah, children each received a "Polio Pioneer" souvenir button for participating in the trial of the Salk vaccine in 1954. Dr. Jonas Salk's announcement the next year that the vaccine was safe and effective made him a national hero. March of Dimes Birth Defect Foundation.

A Woman's Dilemma in Postwar America

This 1959 cover of the *Saturday Evening Post* depicts the no-win situation facing women in the postwar era. But at least they could dream. Women consigned to low-paid, dead-end jobs in the service sector imagined suburban life with Mr. Wonderful helping do the dishes. In reality, Mr. Wonderful turned out to be that guy settled before the television set while Mrs. Homemaker scoured a dirty frying pan and the baby fussed. But of course Mrs. Homemaker's dream of a nice office job just was just as much an illusion. A no-win situation. 1959 SEPS: Licensed by Curtis Publishing Company, Indianapolis, IN. All rights reserved. www.curtispublishing.com.

product, double the 1950 level. In the 1960s the baby-boom generation swelled college enrollments and, not coincidentally, the ranks of student protesters (see Chapter 28). The passage of time did not diminish the impact of the baby boom. When baby boomers competed for jobs during the 1970s, the labor market became tight. When career-oriented baby boomers belatedly began having children in the 1980s, the birthrate jumped. And in our own time, as baby boomers begin retiring, huge funding problems threaten to engulf Social Security and Medicare. Who would have thought that the intimate decisions of so many couples after World War II would be affecting American life well into the twenty-first century?

Contradictions in Women's Lives

"The suburban housewife was the dream image of the young American woman," the feminist Betty Friedan wrote of the 1950s. "She was healthy, beautiful, educated, concerned only about her husband, her children, and her home." Friedan gave up a psychology fellowship and a career as a journalist to marry, move to the suburbs, and raise three children. "Determined that I find the feminine fulfillment that eluded my mother...I lived the life of a suburban housewife that was everyone's dream at the time," she said.

The Feminine Mystique. The idea that a woman's place was in the home was, of course, not new. What Betty Friedan called the "feminine mystique" of the 1950s — that "the highest value and the only commitment for women is the fulfillment of their own femininity" — bore remarkable similarities to the nineteenth-century's cult of true womanhood.

The updated version drew on new elements of twentieth-century science and culture, even Freudian psychology. Psychologists equated motherhood with "normal" female identity and berated mothers who worked outside the home. Television and film depicted career women as social and sexual misfits, the heavies in movies like *Mildred Pierce*. The postwar consumer culture also emphasized women's domestic role as purchasing agents for home and family. "Love is said in many ways," ran an ad for toilet paper. Another asked, "Can a woman ever feel right cooking on a dirty range?"

Although the feminine mystique held cultural sway, it by no means was as all-encompassing as Friedan implied in her 1963 best-seller, *The Feminine Mystique*. Indeed, Friedan herself resisted the stereotype, doing freelance journalism while at home, and, as a result of that work, stumbling on the subject and writing the book that made her famous. Middle-class wives often found constructive outlets for their energy in the League of Women Voters, the PTA, and the Junior League. As in earlier periods, some women used the rhetoric of domesticity to justify political activism, which in this period involved community improvement, racial integration, and nuclear disarmament. As for working-class women, many of them doubtless would have loved to embrace domesticity, if only they could. The economic needs of their families demanded otherwise.

Women at Work. The feminine mystique notwithstanding, more than one-third of American women in the 1950s held jobs outside the home. As the service sector expanded, so did the demand for workers in jobs traditionally filled by women.

Occupational segmentation still haunted women. Until 1964 the classified sections of most newspapers separated employment ads into "Help Wanted Male" and "Help Wanted Female." More than 80 percent of all employed women did stereotypical "women's work" as salespersons, health-care technicians, waitresses, stewardesses, domestic servants, receptionists, telephone operators, and secretaries. In 1960 women represented only 3.5 percent of lawyers (many top law schools did not admit women at all) and 6.1 percent physicians, but 97 percent nurses, 85 percent librarians, and 57 percent social workers. Along with women's jobs went women's pay, which averaged 60 percent of men's pay in 1963.

What was new was the range of women at work. At the turn of the century, the typical female worker was young and unmarried. By midcentury she was in her forties, married, and with children in school. In 1940 only 15 percent of wives had worked. By 1960, 30 percent did, and by 1970 it was 40 percent.

Married women worked to supplement family income. Even in the prosperous 1950s, the wages of many men could not pay for what middle-class life demanded: cars, houses, vacations, and college educations for the children. Poorer households needed more than one wage earner just to get by.

How could American society so steadfastly uphold the domestic ideal when so many wives and mothers were out of the house and at work? In many ways the contradiction was hidden by the women themselves. Fearing public disapproval, women usually justified their work in family-oriented terms: "Of course I believe a woman's place is at home, but I took this job to save for college for our children." Moreover, when women took jobs outside the home, they still bore full responsibility for child care and household management. As one overburdened woman noted, she now had "two full-time jobs instead of just one—underpaid clerical worker and unpaid housekeeper."

Youth Culture

In 1956, only partly in jest, the CBS radio commentator Eric Sevareid questioned "whether the teenagers will take over the United States lock, stock, living room, and garage." Sevareid was grumbling about American youth culture, a phenomenon first noticed in the 1920s, that had its roots in lengthening years of education, the role of peer groups, and the consumer patterns of teenagers. Like so much else in the 1950s, the youth culture came down to having money.

Market research revealed a distinct teen market to be exploited. A 1951 *Newsweek* story noted with awe that the $3 weekly spending money of the average teenager was enough to buy 190 million candy bars, 130 million soft drinks, and 230 million sticks of gum. In 1956 advertisers projected an adolescent market of $9 billion for transistor radios (first introduced in 1952), 45-rpm records, clothing, and fads such as Silly Putty (1950) and Hula Hoops (1958). Increasingly, advertisers targeted the young, both to capture their spending money and to exploit their influence on family purchases. Note the changing slogans for Pepsi-Cola: "Twice as much for a nickel" (1935), "Be sociable—have a Pepsi" (1948), "Now it's Pepsi for those who think young" (1960), and finally "the Pepsi Generation" (1965).

Hollywood movies played a large role in fostering a teenage culture. At a time when Americans were being lured by television, young people made up the largest audience for motion pictures. Soon Hollywood studios catered to them with films like *The Wild One* (1951), starring Marlon Brando, and *Rebel without a Cause* (1955), starring James Dean. "What are you rebelling against?" a waitress asks Brando in *The Wild One*. "Whattaya got?" he replies.

What really defined this generation, however, was its music. Rejecting the romantic ballads of the 1940s, teenagers discovered rock 'n' roll, an amalgam of white country and western music and black-inspired rhythm and blues. The Cleveland disc jockey Alan Freed played a major role in introducing white America to the black-influenced sound by playing what were called "race" records. "If I could find a white man who had the Negro sound and the Negro feel I could make a billion dollars," said the owner of a record company. The performer fitting that bill was Elvis Presley, who rocketed into instant celebrity in 1956 with his hit records "Hound Dog" and "Heartbreak Hotel." Between 1953 and 1959 record sales increased from $213 million to $603 million, with rock 'n' roll as the driving force.

Many adults were not happy. They saw in rock 'n' roll music, teen movies, and magazines such as *Mad* (introduced in 1952) an invitation to race mixing, rebellion, and disorder. The media featured hundreds of stories on problem teens, and in 1955 a Senate subcommittee headed by Estes Kefauver conducted a high-profile investigation of juvenile delinquency and its origins in the popular media. Denunciations of the new youth culture, if anything, only increased its popularity.

Cultural Dissenters

Youth rebellion was only one aspect of a broader discontent with the conformist culture of the

Elvis Presley

The young Elvis Presley, shown here on the cover of his first album in 1956, embodied cultural rebellion against the drabness of adult life in the 1950s. 1956 BGM Music.

1950s. Artists, jazz musicians, and writers expressed their alienation in a remarkable flowering of intensely personal, introspective art forms. In New York, Jackson Pollock and other painters developed an inventive style that became known as abstract expressionism. Swirling and splattering paint onto giant canvases, Pollock emphasized self-expression in the act of painting.

A similar trend characterized jazz, where black musicians developed a hard-driving improvisational style known as bebop. Whether the "hot" bebop of saxophonist Charlie Parker or the more subdued "cool" West Coast sound of the trumpeter Miles Davis, postwar jazz was cerebral, intimate, and individualistic. As such, it stood in stark contrast to the commercialized, dance-oriented "swing" bands of the 1930s and 1940s.

Black jazz musicians found eager fans not only in the African American community but among young white Beats, a group of writers and poets centered in New York and San Francisco who disdained middle-class conformity and suburban materialism. In his poem "Howl" (1956), which became a manifesto of the Beat generation, Allen Ginsberg lamented: "I saw the best minds of my generation destroyed by madness, starving hysterical naked, dragging themselves through the angry streets at dawn looking for an angry fix." In works such as Jack Kerouac's novel *On the Road* (1957), the Beats glorified spontaneity, sexual adventurism, drug

FIGURE 27.4 Legal Immigration to the United States by Region, 1931–1984

Historically, immigrants to the United States had come primarily from Europe. This figure shows the dramatic shift that began after 1960, as Latinos and Asians began to arrive in increasing numbers. Asians, who represented nearly 50 percent of all immigrants by the 1980s, especially benefited from the liberalization of U.S. immigration laws. SOURCE: Robert W. Gardner, Bryant Robie, and Peter C. Smith, "Asian Americans: Growth, Change, and Diversity," *Population Bulletin* 40, no. 4 (Washington, D.C.: Population Reference Bureau, 1985): 2.

1931–1960: Europe 58%, Canada 21%, Latin America 15%, Asia 5%, Other 1%
1961–1969: Europe 38%, Latin America 38%, Canada 10%, Asia 12%, Other 2%
1970–1979: Latin America 41%, Asia 34%, Europe 19%, Canada 3%, Other 3%
1980–1984: Asia 48%, Latin America 35%, Europe 12%, Canada 2%, Other 3%

use, and spirituality. Like other members of the postwar generation, the Beats were apolitical; their rebellion was strictly cultural. In the 1960s, however, the Beats would inspire a new generation of young rebels angry at both the political and cultural status quo.

> - In what ways does the growth of the Sun Belt reflect key themes of the suburban explosion?
> - What was the relationship between consumer culture and the emphasis on family life in the postwar era?
> - Is it correct to say that the 1950s was exclusively a time of cultural conformity?

The Other America

While middle-class whites flocked to the suburbs, an opposite stream of poor and working-class migrants, many of them southern blacks, moved into the cities. What these urban newcomers inherited was a declining economy and a decaying environment. To those enjoying prosperity, "the Other America"—as the social critic Michael Harrington called it in 1962—remained largely invisible. Only in the South, where African Americans organized to combat segregation, did the stain of social injustice catch the nation's attention.

Immigrants and Migrants

Ever since the passage of the National Origins Act of 1924 (see Chapter 23), U.S. immigration policy had aimed mainly at keeping foreigners out. Anti-immigrant sentiment intensified during the Great Depression, hardly budging even to rescue Jews fleeing Nazi persecution. World War II caused the bar to be lowered slightly, enabling returning servicemen to bring home their war brides and, under the Displaced Persons Act (1948), permitting the entry of approximately 415,000 Europeans, among them former Nazis like Werner von Braun, the rocket scientist. The overt anti-Asian bias of America's immigration laws also became untenable. In a gesture to an important ally, the Chinese Exclusion Act was repealed in 1943. More far-reaching was the 1952 McCarran-Walter Act, which (in addition to barring Communists and other radicals) ended the exclusion under the 1924 act of Japanese, Koreans, and southeast Asians.

Although not many came until later, the immediate impact on Asian immigrant communities was considerable. On the eve of World War II, Chinatowns were populated primarily by men. Although largely married, their wives remained in China. The repeal of the Chinese Exclusion Act, and the granting of naturalization rights, encouraged those men to bring their wives to America. The result was a more normal, family-oriented community, a development also seen in the Filipino American and Japanese American communities. Approximately 135,000 men and 100,000 women of Chinese origin were living in the United States in 1960, mostly in New York State and California (Figure 27.4).

Latino Immigration. After the national-origins quota system went into effect in 1924, Mexico replaced eastern and southern Europe as the nation's labor reservoir. During World War II, the federal government introduced the *bracero* (temporary worker) program to ease wartime labor shortages (see Chapter 25), and then revived the program in 1951, during the Korean War. At its peak in 1959, Mexicans on temporary permits accounted for one-quarter of the nation's seasonal workers. The federal government's ability to control the flow, however, was strictly limited. Mexicans came illegally, and by the time the *bracero* program ended in 1964, many of that group — an estimated 350,000 — had managed to settle in the United States. When unemployment became a problem during the recession of 1953–1954, federal authorities responded by deporting many Mexicans in a program grimly named "Operation Wetback" (because Mexican migrants often waded across the Rio Grande River), but the Mexican population in the country continued to rise nonetheless.

Mostly they settled in to Los Angeles, Long Beach, El Paso, and other southwestern cities, following the crops during the harvest season or working in the expanding service sector. But many also went north, augmenting well-established Mexican American communites in Chicago, Detroit, Kansas City, and Denver. Although still important for American agriculture, more Mexican Americans by 1960 were employed as industrial and service workers.

Another major group of Spanish-speaking migrants came from Puerto Rico. American citizens since 1917, Puerto Ricans enjoyed an unrestricted right to move to the mainland. Migration increased dramatically after World War II, when mechanization of the island's sugarcane industry pushed many Puerto Ricans off the land. Airlines began to offer cheap direct flights between San Juan and New York City. With the fare at about $50, two weeks' wages, Puerto Ricans became America's first immigrants with the luxury of arriving by air.

Most Puerto Ricans went to New York, where they settled first in East ("Spanish") Harlem and then scattered in neighborhoods across the city's five boroughs. This massive migration, which increased the Puerto Rican population to 613,000 by 1960, transformed the ethnic composition of the city. More Puerto Ricans now lived in New York City than in San Juan. They faced conditions common to all recent immigrants: crowded and deteriorating housing, segregation, menial jobs, poor schools, and the problems of a bilingual existence.

Cuban refugees constituted the third largest group of Spanish-speaking immigrants. In the six years after Fidel Castro's seizure of power in 1959 (see Chapter 28), an estimated 180,000 people fled Cuba for the United States. The Cuban refugee community grew so quickly that it turned Miami into a cosmopolitan, bilingual city almost overnight. Unlike other migrants to urban America, Miami's Cubans quickly prospered, in large part because they had arrived with money and middle-class skills.

Indian Relocation. In western cities, an influx of Native Americans also contributed to the rise in the nonwhite urban population. In 1953, Congress passed a resolution authorizing a program to terminate the autonomous status of the Indian tribes and empty the reservations. The Bureau of Indian Affairs encouraged voluntary migration by subsidizing moving costs and establishing relocation centers in San Francisco, Denver, Chicago, and other cities. Despite the program's stated goal of assimilation, the 60,000 Native Americans who migrated to the cities mostly settled together in ghetto neighborhoods, with little prospect of adjusting successfully to an urban environment.

Black Migration. African Americans came in large number to cities from the rural South, continuing the "Great Migration" that had begun during World War I (see Chapter 22). Black migration was hastened by the transformation of southern agriculture. Synthetic fabrics cut into the demand for cotton, while mechanization cut into the demand for farm labor. The mechanical cotton picker, introduced in 1944, effectively destroyed the sharecropper system. Cotton acreage declined from 43 million acres in 1930 to less than 15 million in 1960, while the southern farm population fell from 16.2 million to 5.9 million. Although both whites and blacks left the land, the starkest decline was among blacks. By 1990 only 69,000 black farmers remained nationwide, a tiny fraction of the country's farmers.

Where did these displaced farmfolk go? White southerners from Appalachia moved north to "hillbilly" ghettos, such as Cincinnati's Over the Rhine neighborhood and Chicago's Uptown. As many as 3 million blacks headed to Chicago, New York, Washington, Detroit, Los Angeles, and other cities between 1940 and 1960. Certain sections of Chicago seemed like the Mississippi Delta transplanted, so pervasive were the migrants. By 1960 about half the nation's black population was living outside the South, compared with only 23 percent before World War II.

The Urban Crisis

Migration to American cities, whether from Europe or rural America, had always been attended by hardship — by poverty, slum housing, and cultural dislocation. So severe had these problems seemed

West Side Story

The influx of Puerto Rican immigrants after World War II inspired Leonard Bernstein's 1957 Broadway hit *West Side Story*. The plot recast Shakespeare's *Romeo and Juliet* in a Puerto Rican neighborhood on New York's West Side in the 1950s. Confrontations between members of youth gangs and adult figures of authority, as pictured here in a still from the movie version, were set to highly stylized song and dance routines. The Kobal Collection.

half a century earlier that they had helped spark the reform wave of the Progressive era (see Chapter 20). But hardship then had been temporary, a kind of waystation on the path to a better life. That had been true initially of the post-1941 migration, when blacks had found jobs in defense industry and, in the postwar boom, in Detroit auto plants and Chicago packing houses. Later migrants were not so lucky. By the 1950s, the economy was changing. The manufacturing sector was contracting, and technological advances — what people then called "automation" — hit unskilled and semiskilled jobs especially hard — "jobs in which Negroes are disproportionately concentrated," noted the civil rights activist Bayard Rustin. Black migrants, Rustin warned, were becoming economically superfluous, and in that respect their situation was fundamentally different, far bleaker than anything faced by earlier immigrants.

A second difference involved race. Every immigrant wave — Irish, Italian, Slavic, Jewish — had been greeted by hostility, but none so virulent as that experienced by black migrants. In the 1950s, a more tolerant era, they were spared the race rioting that had afflicted their predecessors. But racism in its more covert forms held them back at every turn — by housing restrictions, by schools increasingly segregated, by an urban infrastructure underfunded and decaying because whites were fleeing to the suburbs.

Racial Segregation, North Carolina, 1950
Until as recently as forty years ago, separate drinking fountains like the ones in this picture could be seen across the South. It was the resulting humiliation visited on blacks every day of their lives that explains why the Greensboro Four finally decided to sit down at that Woolworth's lunch counter in 1959 (see p. 855). Elliot Erwitt/Magnum Photos, Inc.

In the 1950s, the nation's twelve largest cities lost 3.6 million whites while gaining 4.5 million nonwhites.

Urban Renewal. As if joblessness and discrimination were not enough, black ghettoes were hit during the 1950s by a frenzy of urban renewal. Seeking to revitalize city centers, urban planners, politicians, and real-estate developers proposed razing blighted neighborhoods to make way for modern construction projects. Local residents were rarely consulted about whether they wanted their neighborhoods "renewed." In Boston, almost a third of the old city was demolished — including the historic West End, a long-established Italian neighborhood — to make way for a new highway, high-rise housing, and government and commercial buildings. In San Francisco some 4,000 residents of the Western Addition, a predominantly black neighborhood, lost out to an urban renewal program that built luxury housing, a shopping center, and an express boulevard. Between 1949 and 1967 urban renewal demolished almost 400,000 buildings and displaced 1.4 million people.

The urban experts knew what to do with these people. They would be relocated to federally funded housing projects, an outgrowth of New Deal housing policy, now much expanded and combined with generous funding for slum clearance. However well intentioned, these grim projects had a disastrous impact on black community life, destroying neighborhoods and relegating the inhabitants to social isolation. The notorious Robert Taylor Homes in Chicago, a huge complex of 28 sixteen-story buildings and 20,000 residents, almost all black, became a breeding ground for crime and hopelessness.

In 1962, the Swedish sociologist Gunnar Myrdal (author of *An American Dilemma*, a pioneering book about the country's race relations) wondered whether shrinking economic opportunity in the United States might not "trap an 'under-class' of unemployed and, gradually, unemployable and underemployed persons and families at the bottom of a society." Myrdal's term *underclass*— referring to a population permanently mired in poverty and dependency — would figure centrally in future American debates about social policy. In 1962, however, *underclass* was a newly coined word, describing a phenomenon not yet noticed but already well under way in the inner cities of 1950s America.

The Emerging Civil Rights Struggle

In the South, segregation prevailed. In most southern states, blacks could not eat in restaurants patronized by whites or use the same waiting rooms and toilets at bus stations. All forms of public transportation were rigidly segregated by custom or by law. Even drinking fountains were labeled "White" and "Colored."

Blacks understood that segregation would never be abolished without grassroots struggle. But that was not their only weapon. They also had the Bill of Rights and the great Reconstruction amendments to the Constitution. In this respect, fighting segregation was different from fighting poverty. Blacks had no constitutional right not to be poor, but they did have constitutional rights not to be discriminated against, if only these rights could be exercised. The Cold War, moreover, gave civil rights advocates added leverage because America's reputation in the world now counted to America's leaders. So the battle against racial injustice, as it took shape after World War II, proceeded on two tracks — on the ground, where blacks began to stand up for their rights, and in the courts and corridors of power, where words sometimes mattered more than action.

FIGURE 27.4 Legal Immigration to the United States by Region, 1931–1984

Historically, immigrants to the United States had come primarily from Europe. This figure shows the dramatic shift that began after 1960, as Latinos and Asians began to arrive in increasing numbers. Asians, who represented nearly 50 percent of all immigrants by the 1980s, especially benefited from the liberalization of U.S. immigration laws. SOURCE: Robert W. Gardner, Bryant Robie, and Peter C. Smith, "Asian Americans: Growth, Change, and Diversity," *Population Bulletin* 40, no. 4 (Washington, D.C.: Population Reference Bureau, 1985): 2.

1931–1960: Europe 58%, Canada 21%, Latin America 15%, Asia 5%, Other 1%
1961–1969: Europe 38%, Latin America 38%, Asia 12%, Canada 10%, Other 2%
1970–1979: Latin America 41%, Asia 34%, Europe 19%, Canada 3%, Other 3%
1980–1984: Asia 48%, Latin America 35%, Europe 12%, Other 3%, Canada 2%

---

use, and spirituality. Like other members of the postwar generation, the Beats were apolitical; their rebellion was strictly cultural. In the 1960s, however, the Beats would inspire a new generation of young rebels angry at both the political and cultural status quo.

> - In what ways does the growth of the Sun Belt reflect key themes of the suburban explosion?
> - What was the relationship between consumer culture and the emphasis on family life in the postwar era?
> - Is it correct to say that the 1950s was exclusively a time of cultural conformity?

The Other America

While middle-class whites flocked to the suburbs, an opposite stream of poor and working-class migrants, many of them southern blacks, moved into the cities. What these urban newcomers inherited was a declining economy and a decaying environment. To those enjoying prosperity, "the Other America" — as the social critic Michael Harrington called it in 1962 — remained largely invisible. Only in the South, where African Americans organized to combat segregation, did the stain of social injustice catch the nation's attention.

Immigrants and Migrants

Ever since the passage of the National Origins Act of 1924 (see Chapter 23), U.S. immigration policy had aimed mainly at keeping foreigners out. Anti-immigrant sentiment intensified during the Great Depression, hardly budging even to rescue Jews fleeing Nazi persecution. World War II caused the bar to be lowered slightly, enabling returning servicemen to bring home their war brides and, under the Displaced Persons Act (1948), permitting the entry of approximately 415,000 Europeans, among them former Nazis like Werner von Braun, the rocket scientist. The overt anti-Asian bias of America's immigration laws also became untenable. In a gesture to an important ally, the Chinese Exclusion Act was repealed in 1943. More far-reaching was the 1952 McCarran-Walter Act, which (in addition to barring Communists and other radicals) ended the exclusion under the 1924 act of Japanese, Koreans, and southeast Asians.

Although not many came until later, the immediate impact on Asian immigrant communities was considerable. On the eve of World War II, Chinatowns were populated primarily by men. Although largely married, their wives remained in China. The repeal of the Chinese Exclusion Act, and the granting of naturalization rights, encouraged those men to bring their wives to America. The result was a more normal, family-oriented community, a development also seen in the Filipino American and Japanese American communities. Approximately 135,000 men and 100,000 women of Chinese origin were living in the United States in 1960, mostly in New York State and California (Figure 27.4).

Latino Immigration. After the national-origins quota system went into effect in 1924, Mexico replaced eastern and southern Europe as the nation's labor reservoir. During World War II, the federal government introduced the *bracero* (temporary worker) program to ease wartime labor shortages (see Chapter 25), and then revived the program in 1951, during the Korean War. At its peak in 1959, Mexicans on temporary permits accounted for one-quarter of the nation's seasonal workers. The federal government's ability to control the flow, however, was strictly limited. Mexicans came illegally, and by the time the *bracero* program ended in 1964, many of that group — an estimated 350,000 — had managed to settle in the United States. When unemployment became a problem during the recession of 1953–1954, federal authorities responded by deporting many Mexicans in a program grimly named "Operation Wetback" (because Mexican migrants often waded across the Rio Grande River), but the Mexican population in the country continued to rise nonetheless.

Mostly they settled in to Los Angeles, Long Beach, El Paso, and other southwestern cities, following the crops during the harvest season or working in the expanding service sector. But many also went north, augmenting well-established Mexican American communites in Chicago, Detroit, Kansas City, and Denver. Although still important for American agriculture, more Mexican Americans by 1960 were employed as industrial and service workers.

Another major group of Spanish-speaking migrants came from Puerto Rico. American citizens since 1917, Puerto Ricans enjoyed an unrestricted right to move to the mainland. Migration increased dramatically after World War II, when mechanization of the island's sugarcane industry pushed many Puerto Ricans off the land. Airlines began to offer cheap direct flights between San Juan and New York City. With the fare at about $50, two weeks' wages, Puerto Ricans became America's first immigrants with the luxury of arriving by air.

Most Puerto Ricans went to New York, where they settled first in East ("Spanish") Harlem and then scattered in neighborhoods across the city's five boroughs. This massive migration, which increased the Puerto Rican population to 613,000 by 1960, transformed the ethnic composition of the city. More Puerto Ricans now lived in New York City than in San Juan. They faced conditions common to all recent immigrants: crowded and deteriorating housing, segregation, menial jobs, poor schools, and the problems of a bilingual existence.

Cuban refugees constituted the third largest group of Spanish-speaking immigrants. In the six years after Fidel Castro's seizure of power in 1959 (see Chapter 28), an estimated 180,000 people fled Cuba for the United States. The Cuban refugee community grew so quickly that it turned Miami into a cosmopolitan, bilingual city almost overnight. Unlike other migrants to urban America, Miami's Cubans quickly prospered, in large part because they had arrived with money and middle-class skills.

Indian Relocation. In western cities, an influx of Native Americans also contributed to the rise in the nonwhite urban population. In 1953, Congress passed a resolution authorizing a program to terminate the autonomous status of the Indian tribes and empty the reservations. The Bureau of Indian Affairs encouraged voluntary migration by subsidizing moving costs and establishing relocation centers in San Francisco, Denver, Chicago, and other cities. Despite the program's stated goal of assimilation, the 60,000 Native Americans who migrated to the cities mostly settled together in ghetto neighborhoods, with little prospect of adjusting successfully to an urban environment.

Black Migration. African Americans came in large number to cities from the rural South, continuing the "Great Migration" that had begun during World War I (see Chapter 22). Black migration was hastened by the transformation of southern agriculture. Synthetic fabrics cut into the demand for cotton, while mechanization cut into the demand for farm labor. The mechanical cotton picker, introduced in 1944, effectively destroyed the sharecropper system. Cotton acreage declined from 43 million acres in 1930 to less than 15 million in 1960, while the southern farm population fell from 16.2 million to 5.9 million. Although both whites and blacks left the land, the starkest decline was among blacks. By 1990 only 69,000 black farmers remained nationwide, a tiny fraction of the country's farmers.

Where did these displaced farmfolk go? White southerners from Appalachia moved north to "hillbilly" ghettos, such as Cincinnati's Over the Rhine neighborhood and Chicago's Uptown. As many as 3 million blacks headed to Chicago, New York, Washington, Detroit, Los Angeles, and other cities between 1940 and 1960. Certain sections of Chicago seemed like the Mississippi Delta transplanted, so pervasive were the migrants. By 1960 about half the nation's black population was living outside the South, compared with only 23 percent before World War II.

The Urban Crisis

Migration to American cities, whether from Europe or rural America, had always been attended by hardship — by poverty, slum housing, and cultural dislocation. So severe had these problems seemed

West Side Story

The influx of Puerto Rican immigrants after World War II inspired Leonard Bernstein's 1957 Broadway hit *West Side Story*. The plot recast Shakespeare's *Romeo and Juliet* in a Puerto Rican neighborhood on New York's West Side in the 1950s. Confrontations between members of youth gangs and adult figures of authority, as pictured here in a still from the movie version, were set to highly stylized song and dance routines. The Kobal Collection.

half a century earlier that they had helped spark the reform wave of the Progressive era (see Chapter 20). But hardship then had been temporary, a kind of waystation on the path to a better life. That had been true initially of the post-1941 migration, when blacks had found jobs in defense industry and, in the postwar boom, in Detroit auto plants and Chicago packing houses. Later migrants were not so lucky. By the 1950s, the economy was changing. The manufacturing sector was contracting, and technological advances — what people then called "automation" — hit unskilled and semiskilled jobs especially hard — "jobs in which Negroes are disproportionately concentrated," noted the civil rights activist Bayard Rustin. Black migrants, Rustin warned, were becoming economically superfluous, and in that respect their situation was fundamentally different, far bleaker than anything faced by earlier immigrants.

A second difference involved race. Every immigrant wave — Irish, Italian, Slavic, Jewish — had been greeted by hostility, but none so virulent as that experienced by black migrants. In the 1950s, a more tolerant era, they were spared the race rioting that had afflicted their predecessors. But racism in its more covert forms held them back at every turn — by housing restrictions, by schools increasingly segregated, by an urban infrastructure underfunded and decaying because whites were fleeing to the suburbs.

Racial Segregation, North Carolina, 1950

Until as recently as forty years ago, separate drinking fountains like the ones in this picture could be seen across the South. It was the resulting humiliation visited on blacks every day of their lives that explains why the Greensboro Four finally decided to sit down at that Woolworth's lunch counter in 1959 (see p. 855). Elliot Erwitt/Magnum Photos, Inc.

In the 1950s, the nation's twelve largest cities lost 3.6 million whites while gaining 4.5 million nonwhites.

Urban Renewal. As if joblessness and discrimination were not enough, black ghettoes were hit during the 1950s by a frenzy of urban renewal. Seeking to revitalize city centers, urban planners, politicians, and real-estate developers proposed razing blighted neighborhoods to make way for modern construction projects. Local residents were rarely consulted about whether they wanted their neighborhoods "renewed." In Boston, almost a third of the old city was demolished—including the historic West End, a long-established Italian neighborhood—to make way for a new highway, high-rise housing, and government and commercial buildings. In San Francisco some 4,000 residents of the Western Addition, a predominantly black neighborhood, lost out to an urban renewal program that built luxury housing, a shopping center, and an express boulevard. Between 1949 and 1967 urban renewal demolished almost 400,000 buildings and displaced 1.4 million people.

The urban experts knew what to do with these people. They would be relocated to federally funded housing projects, an outgrowth of New Deal housing policy, now much expanded and combined with generous funding for slum clearance. However well intentioned, these grim projects had a disastrous impact on black community life, destroying neighborhoods and relegating the inhabitants to social isolation. The notorious Robert Taylor Homes in Chicago, a huge complex of 28 sixteen-story buildings and 20,000 residents, almost all black, became a breeding ground for crime and hopelessness.

In 1962, the Swedish sociologist Gunnar Myrdal (author of *An American Dilemma*, a pioneering book about the country's race relations) wondered whether shrinking economic opportunity in the United States might not "trap an 'under-class' of unemployed and, gradually, unemployable and underemployed persons and families at the bottom of a society." Myrdal's term *underclass*—referring to a population permanently mired in poverty and dependency—would figure centrally in future American debates about social policy. In 1962, however, *underclass* was a newly coined word, describing a phenomenon not yet noticed but already well under way in the inner cities of 1950s America.

The Emerging Civil Rights Struggle

In the South, segregation prevailed. In most southern states, blacks could not eat in restaurants patronized by whites or use the same waiting rooms and toilets at bus stations. All forms of public transportation were rigidly segregated by custom or by law. Even drinking fountains were labeled "White" and "Colored."

Blacks understood that segregation would never be abolished without grassroots struggle. But that was not their only weapon. They also had the Bill of Rights and the great Reconstruction amendments to the Constitution. In this respect, fighting segregation was different from fighting poverty. Blacks had no constitutional right not to be poor, but they did have constitutional rights not to be discriminated against, if only these rights could be exercised. The Cold War, moreover, gave civil rights advocates added leverage because America's reputation in the world now counted to America's leaders. So the battle against racial injustice, as it took shape after World War II, proceeded on two tracks—on the ground, where blacks began to stand up for their rights, and in the courts and corridors of power, where words sometimes mattered more than action.

Civil Rights under Truman. During World War II, the National Association for the Advancement of Colored People (NAACP) redoubled its efforts to combat discrimination in housing, transportation, and other areas. Black demands for justice continued into the postwar years, spurred by symbolic victories, as when Jackie Robinson broke through the color line in major league baseball by joining the Brooklyn Dodgers in 1947. African American leaders also had hopes for President Truman. Although capable of racist language, Truman supported civil rights on moral grounds. He understood, moreover, the growing importance of the black vote in key northern states, a fact driven home by his surprise 1948 victory. Truman also worried about America's image abroad. It didn't help that the Soviet Union often compared the South's treatment of blacks with the Nazis' treatment of the Jews.

Lacking support in Congress, Truman turned to executive action. In 1946 he appointed a National Civil Rights Commission, whose 1947 report called for robust federal action on behalf of civil rights. In 1948, under pressure from A. Phillip Randolph's Committee Against Jim Crow in Military Service, Truman signed an executive order desegregating the armed forces. And then, with his hand strengthened by the victory for civil rights at the 1948 Democratic convention, Truman went on the offensive, pushing legislation on a variety of fronts, including voting rights and equal employment opportunity. Invariably, his efforts were defeated by filibustering southern Senators.

With Dwight Eisenhower as president, civil rights no longer had a champion in the White House. But in the meantime, NAACP lawyers Thurgood Marshall and William Hastie had been preparing the legal ground in a series of test cases challenging racial discrimination, and in 1954 they hit pay dirt.

Brown v. Board of Education. The case involved Linda Brown, a black pupil in Topeka, Kansas, who had been forced to attend a distant segregated school rather than the nearby white elementary school. The NAACP's chief counsel, Thurgood Marshall, argued that such segregation, mandated by the Topeka Board of Education, was unconstitutional because it denied Linda Brown the "equal protection of the laws" guaranteed by the Fourteenth Amendment. In a unanimous decision on May 17, 1954, the Supreme Court agreed, overturning the "separate but equal" doctrine of *Plessy v. Ferguson* (see Chapter 19). Speaking for the Court, the new Chief Justice Earl Warren wrote:

> To separate Negro children . . . solely because of their race generates a feeling of inferiority as to their status in the community that may affect their hearts and minds in a way unlikely ever to be undone. . . . We conclude that in the field of public education the doctrine of "separate but equal" has no place. Separate educational facilities are inherently unequal.

In an implementing 1955 decision known as *Brown II*, the Court declared simply that integration should proceed "with all deliberate speed."

In the South, however, the call went out for "massive resistance." A Southern Manifesto signed in 1956 by 101 members of Congress denounced the *Brown* decision as "a clear abuse of judicial power" and encouraged their constituents to defy it. That year 500,000 southerners joined White Citizens' Councils dedicated to blocking school integration. Some whites revived the old tactics of violence and intimidation, swelling the ranks of the Ku Klux Klan to levels not seen since the 1920s.

President Eisenhower accepted the *Brown* decision as the law of the land, but he thought it was a mistake and was not happy about committing federal power to enforce it. A crisis in Little Rock, Arkansas, finally forced his hand. In September 1957 nine black students attempted to enroll at the all-white Central High School. Governor Orval Faubus called out the National Guard to bar them. Then the mob took over. Every day the nine students had to run a gauntlet of angry whites chanting "Go back to the jungle." As the vicious scenes played out on television night after night, Eisenhower acted. He sent 1,000 federal troops to Little Rock and nationalized the Arkansas National Guard, ordering them to protect the black students. Eisenhower thus became the first president since Reconstruction to use federal troops to enforce the rights of blacks (see Reading American Pictures, "The Cold War and the Civil Rights Movement," p. 854).

The *Brown* decision validated the NAACP's legal strategy, but white resistance also revealed that winning in court was not enough. Prompted by one small act of defiance, southern black leaders embraced nonviolent protest.

The Montgomery Bus Boycott. On December 1, 1955, Rosa Parks, a seamstress in Montgomery, Alabama, refused to give up her seat on a city bus to a white man. She was arrested and charged with violating a local segregation ordinance. Parks's act was not the spur-of-the-moment decision that it seemed. A woman of sterling reputation and a long-time NAACP member, she had been chosen to play that part. Rosa Parks fit the bill perfectly for the challenge the local NAACP intended against segregated buses.

READING AMERICAN PICTURES

The Cold War and the Civil Rights Movement

"Careful, the Walls Have Ears." *Oakland Tribune,* September 11, 1957.

"Right Into Their Hands." *Arkansas Democrat-Gazette,* September 11, 1957.

In 1957, in the far-off African nation of Mozambique, an official at the U.S. embassy worried that the school desegregation crisis in Little Rock, Arkansas, had "become a symbol of Negro-White relations in the United States." Similar worries about the impact of the Arkansas crisis on the Cold War struggle with the Soviet Union surfaced in many American newspapers and magazines, often in the form of political cartoons. The first cartoon above appeared in the *Oakland Tribune* on September 11, 1957, two weeks before President Eisenhower intervened by federalizing the Arkansas National Guard. The second cartoon appeared on the same day in the local newspaper, the *Arkansas Democrat-Gazette.*

ANALYZING THE EVIDENCE

➤ How has the artist's drawing for the *Arkansas Democrat-Gazette* depicted Little Rock segregationists? Are they the kind of people that the cartoonist thinks should be representing America before the world?

➤ Why do you suppose the *Oakland Tribune's* artist omitted African Americans and depicted the crisis as a battle between two groups of whites? Why is "The Whole Wide World" paying such close attention?

➤ Do both cartoons convey the same message, or do they suggest different perspectives on the issue?

➤ As historical evidence, how useful do you think these cartoons are at explaining why Americans began to take the civil rights struggle seriously in the 1950s?

The Greensboro Four

Pictured here are the four African American students who, entirely on their own, decided to demand service at the Woolworth's whites-only lunch counter in Greensboro, North Carolina, and started a sit-down protest movement across the South. Second from the left is Franklin McCain, whose interview appears in Comparing American Voices, "Challenging White Supremacy," on the following pages. © Bettmann/Corbis.

Once the die was cast, the black community turned for leadership to the Reverend Martin Luther King Jr., the recently appointed pastor of Montgomery's Dexter Street Baptist Church. The son of a prominent black minister in Atlanta, King embraced the teachings of Mahatma Gandhi, whose campaigns of passive resistance had led to India's independence from Britain in 1947. After Rosa Parks's arrest, King endorsed a plan by a local black women's organization to boycott Montgomery's bus system until it was integrated.

For the next 381 days Montgomery blacks formed car pools or walked to work. The bus company neared bankruptcy, and downtown stores complained about the loss of business. But only after the Supreme Court ruled in November 1956 that bus segregation was unconstitutional did the city of Montgomery finally comply. "My feets is tired, but my soul is rested," said one satisfied woman boycotter.

The Montgomery bus boycott catapulted King to national prominence. In 1957, along with the Reverend Ralph Abernathy, he founded the Southern Christian Leadership Conference (SCLC), based in Atlanta. The black church, long the center of African American social and cultural life, now lent its moral and organizational strength to the civil rights movement. Black churchwomen were a tower of strength, transferring the skills honed by years of church work to the fight for civil rights. Soon the SCLC joined the NAACP as one of the main advocacy groups for racial justice.

Greensboro. The battle for civil rights entered a new phase in Greensboro, North Carolina, on February 1, 1960, when four black college students

COMPARING AMERICAN VOICES

Challenging White Supremacy

No problem is more challenging to the historian than figuring out how long-oppressed, ordinary people finally rise up and demand justice. During the 1950s that liberating process was quietly under way among southern blacks, first bursting forth dramatically in the Montgomery bus boycott of 1955 and then, by the end of the decade, emerging across the South. Here we take the testimony of two individuals who stepped forward and took the lead in those struggles.

FRANKLIN McCAIN
Desegregating Lunch Counters

Franklin McCain was one of the four African American students at North Carolina A&T College in Greensboro, North Carolina, who sat down at the Woolworth's lunch counter on February 1, 1960, setting off by that simple act a wave of student sit-ins that rocked the South and helped initiate a national civil rights movement. In the following interview, McCain describes how he and his pals took that momentous step.

The planning process was on a Sunday night, I remember it quite well. I think it was Joseph who said, "It's time that we take some action now. We've been getting together, and we've been, up to this point, still like most people we've talked about for the past few weeks or so — that is, people who talk a lot but, in fact, make very little action." After selecting the technique, then we said, "Let's go down and just ask for service." It certainly wasn't titled a "sit-in" or "sit-down" at that time. "Let's just go down to Woolworth's tomorrow and ask for service, and the tactic is going to be simply this: we'll just stay there."

...Once getting there...we did make purchases of school supplies and took the patience and time to get receipts for our purchases, and Joseph and myself went over to the counter and asked to be served coffee and doughnuts. As anticipated, the reply was, "I'm sorry, we don't serve you here." And of course we said, "We just beg to disagree with you. We've in fact already been served."... The attendant or waitress was a little bit dumbfounded, just didn't know what to say under circumstances like that....

At that point there was a policeman who had walked in off the street, who was pacing the aisle...behind us, where we were seated, with his club in his hand, just sort of knocking it in his hand, and just looking mean and red and a little bit upset and a little bit disgusted. And you had the feeling that he didn't know what the hell to do.... Usually his defense is offense, and we've provoked him, yes, but we haven't provoked outwardly enough for him to resort to violence. And I think this is just killing him; you can see it all over him.

If it's possible to know what it means to have your soul cleansed — I felt pretty clean at that time. I probably felt better on that day than I've ever felt in my life. Seems like a lot of feelings of guilt or what-have-you suddenly left me, and I felt as though I had gained my manhood.... Not Franklin McCain only as an individual, but I felt as though the manhood of a number of other black persons had been restored and had gotten some respect from just that one day.

The movement started out as a movement of nonviolence and a Christian movement.... It was a movement that was seeking justice more than anything else and not a movement to start a war.... We knew that probably the most powerful and potent weapon that people have literally no defense for is love, kindness. That is, whip the enemy with something that he doesn't understand.... The individual who had probably the most influence on us was Gandhi.... Yes, Martin Luther King's name was well-known when the sit-in movement was in effect, but...no, he was not the individual we had upmost in mind when we started the sit-in movement.

SOURCE: Howell Raines, *My Soul Is Rested.* Copyright ©1977 by Howell Raines. Originally published by Penguin Putnam, 1977. Reprinted with permission of PFD, Inc.

JOHN McFERREN
Demanding the Right to Vote

In this interview, given about ten years after the events he describes, John McFerren tells of the battle he undertook in 1959 to gain the vote for the blacks of Fayette County, Tennessee. By the time of the interview, he had risen in life and become a grocery-store owner and property holder, thanks, he says, to the economic boycott imposed on him by angry whites. Unlike Greensboro, the struggle in Fayette County never made national headlines. It was just one of many local struggles that signaled the beginning of a new day in the South.

My name is John McFerren. I'm forty-six years old. I'm a Negro was born and raised in West Tennessee, the county of Fayette, District 1. My foreparents was brought here from North Carolina five years before the Civil War . . . because the rumor got out among the slaveholders that West Tennessee was still goin to be a slaveholdin state. And my people was brought over here and sold. And after the Civil War my people settled in West Tennessee. That's why Fayette and Haywood counties have a great number of Negroes.

Back in 1957 and '58 there was a Negro man accused of killin a deputy sheriff. This was Burton Dodson. He was brought back after he'd been gone twenty years. J. F. Estes was the lawyer defendin him. Myself and him both was in the army together. And the stimulation from the trial got me interested in the way justice was bein used. The only way to bring justice would be through the ballot box.

In 1959 we got out a charter called the Fayette County Civic and Welfare League. Fourteen of us started out in that charter. We tried to support a white liberal candidate that was named L. T. Redfearn in the sheriff election and the local Democrat party refused to let Negroes vote.

We brought a suit against the Democrat party and I went to Washington for a civil-rights hearing. Myself and Estes and Harpman Jameson made the trip. It took us twenty-two hours steady drivin. . . . I was lookin all up—lotsa big, tall buildins. I had never seen old, tall buildins like that before. After talkin to [John Doar] we come on back to the Justice Department building and we sat out in the hall while he had a meetin inside the attorney general's office. And when they come out they told us they was gonna indict the landowners who kept us from voting. . . .

Just after that, in 1960, in January, we organized a thousand Negroes to line up at the courthouse to register to vote. We started pourin in with big numbers—in this county it was 72 percent Negroes—when we started to register to vote to change the situation.

In the followin . . . October and November they started puttin our people offa the land. Once you registered you had to move. Once you registered they took your job. Then after they done that, in November, we had three hundred people forced to live in tents on Shepard Towles's land. And when we started puttin em in tents, then that's when the White Citizens Council and the Ku Klux Klan started shootin in the tents to run us out.

Tent City was parta an economic squeeze. The local merchants run me outa the stores and said I went to Washington and caused this mess to start. . . . They had a blacklist . . . And they had the list sent around to all merchants. Once you registered you couldn't buy for credit or cash. But the best thing in the world was when they run me outa them stores. It started me thinkin for myself. . . .

The southern white has a slogan: "Keep em niggers happy and keep em singin in the schools." And the biggest mistake of the past is that the Negro has not been teached economics and the value of a dollar. . . . Back at one time we had a teacher . . . from Mississippi—and he pulled up and left the county because he was teachin the Negroes to buy land, and own land, and work it for hisself, and the county Board of Education didn't want that taught in the county. And they told him, "Keep em niggers singin and keep em happy and don't teach em nothin."

. . . You cannot be free when you're beggin the man for bread. But when you've got the dollar in your pocket and then got the vote in your pocket, that's the only way to be free. . . . And I have been successful and made good progress because I could see the only way I could survive is to stay independent. . . . The Negro is no longer goin back. He's goin forward.

SOURCE: Stanley I. Kutler, ed., *Looking for America*, 2d ed., 2 vols. (New York: Norton, 1979), 2: 449–453.

ANALYZING THE EVIDENCE

- McCain took a stand on segregated lunch counters. McFerren took a stand on the right to vote. Why did they choose different targets? Does it matter that they did?

- McCain speaks of the sense of "manhood" he felt as he sat at that Woolworth counter. Would that feeling have been enough to satisfy McFerren?

- Almost certainly, McCain and McFerren never met. Suppose they had. What would they have had in common? Would what they had in common have been more important than what separated them?

- McCain speaks knowingly of the figures and ideas that influenced him. Why do you suppose McFerren is silent about such matters? If he had spoken up, do you suppose he would have—or should have—mentioned Booker T. Washington (see Chapter 20)?

took seats at the "whites-only" lunch counter at the local Woolworth's. They were determined to "sit in" until they were served (see Comparing American Voices, "Challenging White Supremacy," pp. 856–857). Although they were arrested, the sit-in tactic worked — the Woolworth lunch counter was desegregated — and sit-ins quickly spread to other southern cities. A few months later Ella Baker, an administrator with the SCLC, helped to organize the Student Non-Violent Coordinating Committee (SNCC, known as "Snick") to facilitate student sit-ins. By the end of the year, about 50,000 people had participated in sit-ins or other demonstrations, and 3,600 of them had been jailed. But in 126 cities across the South blacks were at last able to eat at Woolworth lunch counters.

The victories so far had been limited, but the groundwork had been laid for a civil rights offensive that would transform the nation's race relations.

- What were the most significant migration trends in this era?
- What were the key components of the urban crisis?
- What is the significance of the *Brown v. Board of Education of Topeka* decision?

SUMMARY

We have explored how, at the very time it became mired in the Cold War, the United States entered an unparalleled era of prosperity. Indeed, the Cold War was one of the engines of prosperity. The postwar economy was marked especially by the dominance of big corporations. Corporate dominance in turn helped make possible the labor-management accord that spread the benefits of prosperity to workers beyond the dreams of earlier generations.

After years of depression and war-induced insecurity, Americans turned inward toward religion, home, and family. Postwar couples married young, had several children, and — if they were white and middle class — raised their children in a climate of suburban comfort and consumerism. The profamily orientation of the 1950s celebrated social conformity and traditional gender roles, even though millions of women entered the workforce in those years. Cultural conformity, however, provoked resistance, both by the burgeoning youth culture and by a remarkably inventive generation of painters, musicians, and writers.

Not everyone, moreover, shared the postwar prosperity. Postwar cities increasingly became places of last resort for the nation's poor. Black migrants, unlike earlier immigrants, encountered an urban economy that had little use for them. Without opportunity, and faced by pervasive racism, they were on their way to becoming, many of them, an American underclass. In the South, however, discrimination produced a civil rights uprising that white America could not ignore. Many of the smoldering contradictions of the postwar period — Cold War anxiety in the midst of suburban domesticity, tensions in women's lives, economic and racial inequality — helped spur the protest movements of the 1960s.

Connections: Economy

"In the 1950s," we noted in the essay opening Part Six, "no country was competitive with America's economy." The roots of that supremacy went back into the late nineteenth century when, as we discussed in Chapter 17, heavy industry, mass-production technology, and corporate business structure emerged. In the 1920s (Chapter 23) this industrial economy was refined and, after the hiatus of the Great Depression, became the basis for the post–World War II economic boom. In Chapter 29, we describe the first stages in the decline of this manufacturing economy during the 1970s. The postwar consumer culture had roots that went back into the 1920s (Chapter 23), while the accompanying suburbanization went back even earlier, into the nineteenth century (Chapter 18). Similarly, we can trace back to earlier discussions the migratory patterns (to Chapters 17 and 22) and the decay of the cities (to Chapter 18).

CHAPTER REVIEW QUESTIONS

- How do you acount for the economic prosperity of the postwar era?
- Why did the suburb achieve paramount significance for Americans in the 1950s?
- Who were the people who occupied "the Other America"? Why were they there rather than in mainstream America?

TIMELINE

1944	Bretton Woods economic conference World Bank and International Monetary Fund (IMF) founded
1946	First edition of Dr. Spock's *Baby and Child Care*
1947	First Levittown built Jackie Robinson joins the Brooklyn Dodgers
1948	Beginning of network television
1950	Treaty of Detroit initiates labor-management accord
1953	Operation Wetback
1954	*Brown v. Board of Education of Topeka*
1955	Montgomery bus boycott begins AFL and CIO merge
1956	National Interstate and Defense Highways Act Elvis Presley's breakthrough records
1957	Peak of postwar baby boom Eisenhower sends U.S. troops to enforce integration of Little Rock Central High School Southern Christian Leadership Conference (SCLC) founded
1960	Student sit-ins in Greensboro, North Carolina

FOR FURTHER EXPLORATION

Two engaging introductions to postwar society are Paul Boyer, *Promises to Keep* (1995), and David Halberstam, *The Fifties* (1993). John K. Galbraith, *The Affluent Society* (1958), is a lively and influential contemporary analysis of the postwar economy. Nelson Lichtenstein, *State of the Union: A Century of American Labor* (2002), offers a searching account of the labor-management accord. The best book on the consumer culture, wide-ranging in perspective, is Lizabeth Cohen, *A Consumers' Republic: The Politics of Mass Consumption in Postwar America* (2003). Elaine Tyler May, *Homeward Bound* (1988), is the classic introduction to postwar family life. For insightful essays on the impact of television, see Karal Ann Marling, *As Seen on TV* (1996). An excellent, award-winning memoir of the Beat generation is Joyce Johnson, *Minor Characters* (1983). For youth culture, see William Graebner, *Coming of Age in Buffalo* (1990), and, a classic of the period, Paul Goodman, *Growing Up Absurd* (1960). On the urban crisis, see especially Nicholas Lemann, *The Promised Land: The Great Migration and How It Changed America* (1991), and Thomas J. Sugrue, *The Origins of the Urban Crisis: Race and Inequality in Postwar Detroit* (1996). Taylor Branch's biography of Martin Luther King Jr., *Parting the Waters: America in the King Years, 1954–1963* (1988), while focusing on King's leadership, provides an engaging account of the early civil rights movement.

Literary Kicks: The Beat Generation, at **www.litkicks.com/BeatPages/msg.jsp?what=BeatGen**, is an independent site created by New York writer Levi Asher devoted to the literature of the Beat generation. The site includes writings by Jack Kerouac, Allen Ginsberg, Neal Cassady, and others; material on Beats, music, religion, and film; an extensive bibliography; biographical information; and photographs.

The Arkansas *Democrat Gazette* has compiled materials from two Arkansas newspapers covering the Central High School crisis in Little Rock in 1957 at **www.ardemgaz.com/prev/central**. Editorials and daily news coverage, including photographs, are featured, as well as later commentary by such diverse political figures as former president and Arkansas governor Bill Clinton and former Arkansas governor Orval Faubus.

TEST YOUR KNOWLEDGE

To assess your command of the material in this chapter, see the Online Study Guide at **bedfordstmartins.com/henretta**.

For Web sites, images, and documents related to topics and places in this chapter, visit **bedfordstmartins.com/makehistory**.

28 The Liberal Consensus: Flaming Out
1960–1968

O**N INAUGURATION DAY, 1961, STANDING** bare-headed in the wintry January brightness, the freshly sworn-in president issued a ringing declaration: "Let the word go forth from this time and place, to friend and foe alike, that the torch has passed to a new generation of Americans, born in this century, tempered by war, disciplined by a hard and bitter peace, proud of our ancient heritage." John F. Kennedy challenged Americans everywhere: "Ask not what your country can do for you, ask what you can do for your country." And, more than anyone might have expected, Americans responded. "There's a moral wave building among today's youth," said a civil rights volunteer in 1964, "and I intend to catch it." Kennedy's politics of expectation might have been initially mostly a matter of atmospherics, but over time it built into the greatest burst of liberal reform since the New Deal—landmark civil rights laws, Medicare, the War on Poverty, and much else. All this—the triumph of the liberal consensus—starts with the indelible image of the youthful Kennedy exhorting the country on that Inauguration Day, 1961.

Fast forward to 1968, to the Democratic National Convention in Chicago. Kennedy is dead, assassinated. His civil rights mentor, Martin Luther King Jr., is dead, assassinated. His younger brother and heir apparent, Bobby, is dead, assassinated. And his successor in the White

John F. Kennedy and the Politics of Expectation
The New Politics
The Kennedy Administration
The Civil Rights Movement Stirs
Kennedy, Cold Warrior
The Kennedy Assassination

Lyndon B. Johnson and the Great Society
The Momentum for Civil Rights
Enacting the Liberal Agenda

Into the Quagmire, 1963–1968
Escalation
Public Opinion on Vietnam
Student Activism

Coming Apart
The Counterculture
Beyond Civil Rights

1968: A Year of Shocks
The Politics of Vietnam
Backlash

Summary
Connections: Diplomacy and Politics

◀ **Peace Demonstrators**
Antiwar demonstrators wave a red flag bearing the peace sign near the Washington Monument where thousands gathered for a Moratorium Day rally in Washington, D.C., November 15, 1969. © Bettmann/Corbis.

House, Lyndon B. Johnson, is so discredited that he has withdrawn his name from nomination. On the streets the Chicago police teargassed and clubbed demonstrators, who screamed (as the TV cameras rolled), "The whole world is watching!" Some of them had once been the idealistic young people of Kennedy's exhortation. Now they detested everything that Kennedy's liberalism stood for. Inside the convention hall, the proceedings were chaotic, the atmosphere poisonous, the delegates bitterly divided over Vietnam. As expected, Johnson's vice president, Hubert Humphrey, easily won the nomination, but he hadn't been done any favors. He acknowledged going home feeling not triumphant, but "heartbroken, battered, and defeated." The Chicago convention had been "a disaster."

In this chapter we undertake to explain how Kennedy's stirring Inauguration metamorphosed into the searing Democratic National Convention of 1968. Between those two events, indelible in America's memory, the liberal consensus flamed out.

John F. Kennedy and the Politics of Expectation

Since the days of FDR and the New Deal, Americans had come increasingly to look to Washington and the president for answers to the nation's problems. Few presidents were happier to oblige than John Kennedy. He came to Washington primed for action, promising that his "New Frontier" would get America moving again. The British journalist Henry Fairley called this activist impulse "the politics of expectation." Soon enough, expectation came up against unyielding reality, but Kennedy's can-do style nevertheless left a lasting impression on American politics.

The New Politics

Charisma, style, and personality — these, more than platforms and issues — were hallmarks of a new brand of politics that we associate with John F. Kennedy. With the power of the media in mind, a younger generation of politicians saw in television a new way to reach directly to the voters. Candidates drifted away from traditional party organizations, with their ward bosses, state committees, and party machines that had once delivered the votes on election day. By using the media, campaigns could bypass the party structures and touch, if only with a 30-second commercial, the ordinary citizen.

The new politics was Kennedy's natural environment. A Harvard alumnus, World War II hero, senator from Massachusetts, he had inherited his love of politics from his grandfathers, both colorful Irish-Catholic politicians in Boston. Ambitious, hard-driving, and deeply aware of style, the forty-three-year-old Kennedy made full use of his many

The Kennedy Magnetism

John Kennedy, the Democratic candidate for president in 1960, used his youth and personality to attract voters. Here the Massachusetts senator draws an enthusiastic crowd on a campaign stop in Elgin, Illinois. AP Images.

advantages to become, as novelist Norman Mailer put it, "our leading man." His one disadvantage — that he was Catholic in a country that had never elected a Catholic president — he masterfully neutralized. His family's wealth and his energetic fund-raising financed an exceptionally expensive campaign. And thanks to media advisers and his youthful, attractive personality, he projected a superb television image.

His Republican opponent, Eisenhower's vice president Richard M. Nixon, was a more seasoned politician, but personally awkward and ill-endowed for combat in the new politics. The great innovation of the 1960 campaign was a series of four nationally televised debates. Nixon, less photogenic than Kennedy, looked sallow and unshaven under the intense studio lights. Polls showed that television did sway political perceptions: Voters who heard the first debate on the radio concluded that Nixon had won, but those viewing it on television favored Kennedy.

Despite the edge Kennedy enjoyed in the debates, he won only the narrowest of electoral victories, receiving 49.7 percent of the popular vote to Nixon's 49.5 percent. Kennedy attracted Catholics, black voters, and the labor vote; his vice presidential running mate, Lyndon Johnson from Texas, brought in southern Democrats. Yet only 120,000 votes separated the two candidates, and the shift of a few thousand votes in key states such as Illinois (where Chicago Mayor Richard Daley's machine miraculously generated the needed margin) would have reversed the outcome. Despite his razor-thin margin, Kennedy won 303 electoral votes, compared to Nixon's 219, revealing once again the distorting effect of the electoral college on the people's choice.

The Kennedy Administration

Unlike Eisenhower, Kennedy believed in a federal government that was visibly active and a presidency that set the tone for bold leadership. Kennedy's vigor attracted unusually able and ambitious people, including Robert McNamara, a renowned systems analyst and former head of Ford, at Defense, and C. Douglas Dillon, a highly admired Republican banker, as secretary of the Treasury. A host of trusted advisers and academics — "the best and the brightest," the journalist David Halberstam called them — flocked to Washington to join the New Frontier. Included on the team as attorney-general was Kennedy's kid brother, Robert, a trusted adviser who had made a name as a hard-hitting investigator of organized crime. Not everyone was enchanted.

Kennedy's people "might be every bit as intelligent as you say," House Speaker Sam Rayburn told his old friend Lyndon Johnson, "but I'd feel a whole lot better about them if just one of them had run for sheriff once." Sure enough, the new administration immediately got into hot water.

The Bay of Pigs. In January 1961 Soviet Premier Nikita Khrushchev announced that the USSR intended to support "wars of national liberation" wherever in the world they occurred. Kennedy took Khrushchev's words as a challenge, especially as they applied to Cuba, where in 1959 Fidel Castro had overthrown the dictator Fulgencio Batista and declared a revolution. Determined to keep Cuba out of the Soviet orbit, Kennedy took up plans by the Eisenhower administration to dispatch Cuban exiles from Nicaragua to foment an anti-Castro uprising. The invaders had been trained by the Central Intelligence Agency, but they were ill prepared for their task and betrayed by the CIA's inept planning. Upon landing at Cuba's Bay of Pigs on April 17, the force of 1,400 was apprehended and crushed by Castro's troops. The anticipated rebellion never happened. Kennedy had the good sense to reject CIA pleas for a U.S. air strike. And he was gracious in defeat. He went before the American people and took full responsibility for the fiasco.

Peace Corps, Foreign Aid, Astronauts. Kennedy redeemed himself with a series of bold initiatives. One was the Peace Corps, which embodied his call to public service in his inaugural address. Thousands of men and women agreed to devote two or more years to programs teaching English to Filipino schoolchildren or helping African villagers obtain adequate supplies of water. Exhibiting the idealism of the early 1960s, the Peace Corps was also a Cold War weapon intended to show developing countries of the so-called Third World that there was a better way than Communism (Map 28.1). Also embodying this aim were ambitious programs of economic assistance. The State Department's Agency for International Development coordinated foreign aid for the Third World, and its Food for Peace program distributed surplus agricultural products. In 1961 the president proposed a "ten-year plan for the Americas" called the Alliance for Progress, a $20 billion partnership between the United States and the republics of Latin America, to reverse the cycle of poverty and stimulate economic growth.

Kennedy was also keen on space exploration. Early in his administration, Kennedy proposed that the nation commit itself to landing a man on the

The Peace Corps

The Peace Corps, a New Frontier program initiated in 1961, attracted thousands of idealistic young Americans, including these volunteers who worked in a vaccination program in Bolivia. David S. Boyer/National Geographic Society Image Collection.

moon within the decade. Two weeks later, on May 5, 1961, Alan Shepard became the first American in space (beaten there by the Soviet cosmonaut Yuri Gagarin's 108-hour flight). The following year, John Glenn manned the first space mission to orbit the earth. Capitalizing on America's fascination with space flight, Kennedy persuaded Congress to greatly increase funding for the National Aeronautics and Space Administration (NASA), enabling the United States to pull ahead of the Soviet Union. (Kennedy's men on the moon arrived in 1969.)

Domestic Agenda. Kennedy's most striking domestic achievement — another of his bold moves — was the application of modern economic theory to government **fiscal policy**. New Dealers had lost faith in a balanced budget, turning instead to the Keynesian approach of deliberate deficit spending to stimulate economic growth. Now, in addition to deficit spending, Kennedy and his economic advisers proposed a reduction in income taxes. A tax cut, they argued, would put money in the hands of consumers, thereby generating more demand, more jobs, and ultimately higher tax revenues. Congress balked at this unorthodox proposal, but it made its way through in 1964, marking a milestone in the use of tax cuts to encourage economic growth, an approach later embraced by Republican fiscal conservatives (see Chapter 30).

But Kennedy was less engaged by the more humdrum matters of social policy, notwithstanding that he had given lip service to an ambitious agenda during his presidential campaign. In part, he was stymied by the lack of a strong popular mandate in the election's outcome. He was also a cautious politician, unwilling to expend capital where the odds were against him. Kennedy managed to push through legislation raising the minimum wage and expanding Social Security, but on other emerging issues — federal aid to education, mass transportation, medical insurance for the elderly — he gave up in the face of conservative opposition in Congress.

The Civil Rights Movement Stirs

Kennedy was equally cautious about civil rights. Despite his campaign commitment, in his first two years he failed to deliver on a civil rights bill. The opposition in Congress, where segregationist southern Democrats dominated key committees, just seemed too formidable. But civil rights was not like other domestic issues. Its fate was going to be decided not in the halls of Congress, but on the streets of southern cities.

Freedom Riders. Emboldened by the success of SNCC's sit-in tactics at integrating lunch counters (see Chapter 27), the interracial Congress of Racial Equality (CORE) organized a series of "freedom rides" in 1961 on interstate bus lines throughout the South. The aim was to call attention to blatant violation of recent Supreme Court rulings against segregation in interstate commerce. The activists who signed on, mostly young, both black and white, knew they were taking their lives in their hands. In Anniston, Alabama, club-wielding Klansmen attacked one of the buses with stones and set it on fire. The freedom riders escaped only moments before the bus exploded. Other riders were brutally beaten in Montgomery and Birmingham. State authorities refused to intervene. "I cannot guarantee protection for this bunch of rabble rousers," declared Governor John Patterson. That left it up to Washington. Although Kennedy discouraged the freedom rides, films of beatings and burning buses

MAP 28.1 Decolonization and the Third World, 1943–1990

At the end of World War II, the colonial empires built up over the previous centuries by European countries were still formally intact. After 1945, movements for national self-determination swept across Africa, India, and Southeast Asia. This map shows the many nations carved out of that struggle, all of them parts of the "Third World," a Cold War term designating countries not formally aligned either with the Western or the Soviet blocs. Courted by both the United States and the Soviet Union, some Third World nations like Vietnam and Angola became key battlegrounds of the Cold War, often with disastrous results for the local populations.

MAP 28.2   The Civil Rights Struggle, 1954–1965

In the postwar battle for black civil rights, the first major victory was the NAACP litigation of *Brown v. Board of Education*, which declared public school segregation unconstitutional. As indicated on this map, the struggle then quickly spread, raising other issues and seeding new organizations. Other organizations quickly joined the battle and shifted the focus away from the courts to mass action and organization. The year 1965 marked the high point, when violence against the Selma, Alabama, marchers spurred the passage of the Voting Rights Act (see p. 872).

shown on the nightly news prompted Attorney General Robert Kennedy to dispatch federal marshals. Civil rights activists learned that nonviolent protest could succeed if it provoked violent white resistance (Map 28.2).

Birmingham. This lesson was confirmed in Birmingham, Alabama, when Martin Luther King Jr. called for protests against conditions in what he called "the most segregated city in the United States." In April 1963 thousands of black demonstrators marched downtown to picket Birmingham's department stores. They were met by Eugene ("Bull") Connor, the city's commissioner of public safety, and his police, who used snarling dogs, electric cattle prods, and high-pressure fire hoses to

Racial Violence in Birmingham

When thousands of blacks marched through downtown Birmingham, Alabama, to protest racial segregation in April 1963, they were met with fire hoses and attack dogs unleashed by Police Chief "Bull" Connor. The violence, which was televised on the national evening news, shocked many Americans and helped build sympathy for the civil rights movement among northern whites. AP Images/Bill Hudson.

break up the crowds. Television cameras captured the scene for the evening news.

Outraged by the brutality, President Kennedy decided it was time to step in. On June 11, 1963, after Alabama Governor George Wallace barred two black students from the state university, Kennedy went on television and delivered a passionate speech denouncing racism and announcing a new civil rights bill. Black leaders hailed the speech as a "Second Emancipation Proclamation." That night Medgar Evers, president of the Mississippi chapter of the NAACP, was shot in the back and killed in his driveway in Jackson. The martyrdom of Evers became a spur to further action.

The March on Washington. To marshal support for Kennedy's bill, civil rights leaders adopted a tactic that A. Philip Randolph had first advanced in 1941 (see Chapter 25): a massive demonstration in Washington. Although the planning was not primarily Martin Luther King's, he was truly the public face of the March on Washington on August 28, 1963. It was King's dramatic "I Have a Dream" speech, ending with the exclamation from an old Negro spiritual—"Free at last! Free at last! Thank God Almighty, we are free at last!"—that captured the nation's imagination. The sight of 250,000 blacks and whites marching solemnly together marked the high point of the civil rights movement and confirmed King's position, especially among white liberals, as the leading spokesperson for the black cause.

Although the March on Washington galvanized public opinion, it changed few congressional votes. Southern senators continued to block Kennedy's legislation by threatening a filibuster. In September a Baptist church in Birmingham was bombed and four black Sunday school students were killed,

The March on Washington

The Reverend Martin Luther King Jr. (1929–1968) was the most eloquent advocate of the civil rights movement. For many, his "I Have a Dream" speech of the 1963 March on Washington was the high point of the day, and, for some, of the entire civil rights struggle. The focus on the charismatic King, however, meant that the importance of other civil rights leaders was frequently overlooked. Bob Adelman/Magnum Photos, Inc.

shocking the nation and bringing the civil rights demonstrations to a boiling point.

Kennedy, Cold Warrior

Foreign affairs gave greater scope for Kennedy's fertile mind. A resolute cold warrior, Kennedy took a hard line against Communism. In contrast to Eisenhower, whose cost-saving New Look program had built up the American nuclear arsenal at the expense of conventional weapons, Kennedy proposed a new policy of "flexible response," stating that the nation must be prepared "to deter all wars, general or limited, nuclear or conventional, large or small." Congress quickly granted Kennedy's military requests, and by 1963 the defense budget reached its highest level as a percentage of total federal expenditures in the Cold War era.

Already strained by the Bay of Pigs invasion, U.S.-Soviet relations deteriorated further in June 1961 when Soviet Premier Khrushchev deployed soldiers to isolate Communist-controlled East Berlin from the western sector controlled by West Germany. With congressional approval, Kennedy responded by adding 300,000 troops to the armed forces and promptly dispatching 40,000 of them to Europe. In mid-August, to stop the exodus of East Germans, the Soviets ordered construction of the Berlin Wall, and East German guards began policing the border. Until it was dismantled in 1989, the Berlin Wall remained the supreme symbol of the Cold War.

The climactic confrontation of the Cold War came in October 1962. In a somber televised address, Kennedy revealed that reconnaissance planes had spotted Soviet-built bases for intermediate-range ballistic missiles in Cuba. Some of those weapons had already been installed, and more were on the way. Kennedy announced that the United States would impose a "quarantine on all offensive military equipment" intended for Cuba (Map 28.3). As the two superpowers went on full military alert, people around the world feared an imminent nuclear war. But as the world held its breath, the ships carrying Soviet-made missiles turned back. After a week of tense negotiations, both Kennedy and Khrushchev made concessions: Kennedy pledged not to invade Cuba, and Khrushchev promised to dismantle the missile bases.

The risk of nuclear war, greater during the Cuban missile crisis than at any other time in the postwar period, led to a slight thaw in U.S.-Soviet relations. As national security advisor McGeorge Bundy put it, both sides were chastened by "having come so close to the edge." Kennedy softened his Cold War rhetoric and Soviet leaders, similarly chastened, agreed to talk. In August 1963 the three principal nuclear powers—the United States, the Soviet Union, and Great Britain—announced a ban on the testing of nuclear weapons in the atmosphere, although underground testing was allowed to continue. The new emphasis on peaceful coexistence also led to the establishment of a Washington-Moscow telecommunications "hotline" in 1963 so that leaders could contact each other quickly in a crisis.

But no matter how much American leaders talked about opening channels of communication with Moscow, relations with the Soviet Union

MAP 28.3 The United States and Cuba, 1961–1962

Fidel Castro's takeover in Cuba in 1959 brought Cold War tensions to the Caribbean. In 1961 the United States tried unsuccessfully to overthrow Castro's regime by supporting the Bay of Pigs invasion of Cuban exiles launched from Nicaragua and other points in the Caribbean. In 1962 a major confrontation with the Soviet Union occurred over Soviet construction of nuclear missile sites in Cuba. The Soviets removed the missiles after President Kennedy ordered a naval blockade of the island. Despite the fall of the Soviet Union in 1991 and the official end of the Cold War, the United States continues to view Cuba, still governed in 2006 by Fidel Castro, as an enemy nation.

remained tense, and containment remained the cornerstone of U.S. policy.

The Vietnam Puzzle. When Kennedy became president, he inherited Eisenhower's involvement in Vietnam. Kennedy saw Vietnam in very much the same Cold War terms. But what really grabbed him was the chance to test the counterinsurgency doctrine associated with his "flexible response" military strategy. The army was training U.S. Special Forces, called Green Berets for their distinctive headgear, to engage in unconventional, small-group warfare. Kennedy and his advisers wanted to try out the Green Berets in the Vietnamese jungles.

Despite American aid, the corrupt and repressive Diem regime installed by Eisenhower in 1954 was losing ground (see Chapter 26). By 1961 Diem's opponents, with backing from North Vietnam, had formed a revolutionary movement known as the National Liberation Front (NLF). The NLF's guerrilla forces—the Vietcong—found a receptive audience among peasants alienated by Diem's "strategic hamlet" program, which uprooted whole villages and moved them into barbed-wire compounds. Buddhists charged Diem, a Catholic, with religious persecution. Starting in May 1963, militant Buddhists staged dramatic demonstrations, including several self-immolations recorded by American television crews. Losing patience with Diem, Kennedy let it be known in Saigon that the United States would support a military coup. On November 1, 1963, Diem was overthrown and assassinated—an eventuality evidently not anticipated by Kennedy. At that point, there were about 16,000 American "advisers" (an elastic term that included helicopter crews and Special Forces) in Vietnam.

In a CBS interview, Kennedy had remarked that it was up to the South Vietnamese whether "their war"

The Berlin Wall

A West Berlin resident walks alongside a section of the Berlin Wall in 1962, a year after its construction. Note the two border guards on the East Berlin side, plus the numerous loud speakers, which East German Communists used to broadcast propaganda over the barricade that divided the city. © Bettmann/Corbis.

would be won or lost. Advisers close to the president later argued that, had he run strongly in the 1964 election, he would have felt emboldened to cut America's losses and leave. But that argument downplays the geopolitical issues at stake in Vietnam. The United States was now engaged in a global war against Communism. Giving up in Vietnam would be weakening America's "credibility" in that struggle. And, under the prevailing "domino theory," other pro-American states would topple after Vietnam's loss. Kennedy subscribed to these received Cold War tenets. Whether he might have surmounted them down the road is, like how Lincoln might have handled Reconstruction after the Civil War had he lived, an unanswerable historical question.

The Kennedy Assassination

On November 22, 1963, Kennedy went to Texas on a political trip. As he and his wife, Jacqueline, rode in an open car past the Texas School Book Depository in Dallas, he was shot through the head and neck by a sniper. Kennedy died within the hour. (The accused killer, Lee Harvey Oswald, a twenty-four-year-old loner, was himself killed while in custody a few days later.) Before Air Force One left Dallas to take the president's body back to Washington, a grim-faced Lyndon Johnson was sworn in as president. Kennedy's stunned widow, still wearing her bloodstained pink suit, looked on.

Kennedy's youthful image, the trauma of his assassination, and the nation's sense of loss contributed to a powerful Kennedy mystique. His canonization after death actually capped an extraordinarily successful effort at stage-managing the presidency. An admiring country saw in Jack and Jackie Kennedy an ideal American marriage (he was in fact an obsessive womanizer); in Kennedy the man the epitome of robust good health (although he was actually afflicted by Addison's disease and

Buddhist Protest, 1966

Buddhist nun Thich Nu Thanh Quang burns to death at the Dieu de Pagoda in Hue, South Vietnam, in a ritual act of suicide in protest against the Catholic Saigon regime on May 29, 1966. Its inability to win over the Buddhist population was a major source of weakness for the South Vietnamese government. AP Images.

kept going by potent medications); and in the Kennedy White House a glamorous world of high fashion and celebrity. No presidency ever matched the Kennedy aura of "Camelot"—after the mythical realm of King Arthur in the hit musical of that title—but every president after him embraced the idea, with greater or lesser success, that image mattered as much as reality—maybe more—in conducting a politically effective presidency. In Kennedy's case, the ultimate irony was that his image as martyred leader produced grander legislative results than anything he might have achieved as a live president in the White House.

- Why was Kennedy an effective politican?
- Why did civil rights become a big issue during the Kennedy years?
- What were the results of Kennedy's foreign policy?

Lyndon B. Johnson and the Great Society

Lyndon Johnson was a seasoned politician from Texas, a longtime Senate leader at his best negotiating in the back rooms of power. Compared to Kennedy, Johnson was a rough-edged character who had scrambled his way up, without too many scruples, to wealth and political eminence. But unlike other bootstrap successes, he never forgot his hill-country origins or lost his sympathy for the downtrodden. Johnson was no match for the Kennedy style, but he capitalized on Kennedy's assassination, applying his astonishing energy and negotiating skills to bring to fruition many of Kennedy's stalled programs and more than a few of his own in an ambitious program he called the "Great Society."

The Momentum for Civil Rights

On assuming the presidency, Lyndon Johnson promptly pushed for civil rights legislation as a memorial to his slain predecessor. His motives were a combination of the political and the personal. As a politician, he wanted the Democratic Party to benefit from the national groundswell for civil rights, although he was too shrewd an operative not be aware of the price the party would pay in the South. It was more important to him, as a president from the South, to reach across regional lines and appeal to a broad national audience. Achieving historic civil rights legislation would, he hoped, place his mark on the presidency.

The Civil Rights Act of 1964. Overcoming a southern filibuster, Congress approved in June 1964 the most far-reaching civil rights legislation since Reconstruction. The keystone of the Civil Rights Act, Title VII, outlawed discrimination in employment on the basis of race, religion, national origin, or sex. Another section guaranteed equal access to public accommodations and schools. The law granted new enforcement powers to the U.S. attorney general and established the Equal Employment Opportunity Commission (EEOC) to implement

Freedom Summer, 1964

In the summer of 1964 — "Freedom Summer" — hundreds of civil rights volunteers converged on Mississippi and Alabama to conduct voter registration drives. In this photograph, college students in Oxford, Ohio, sing and hold hands before their departure for Mississippi. They knew that rough days were ahead of them. Shapiro/Black Star/Stockphoto.com.

the prohibition against job discrimination. It was a law with real teeth. But it left untouched obstacles to black voting rights.

Freedom Summer. So protesters went back into the streets. In 1964 black organizations and churches mounted a major civil rights campaign in Mississippi. Known as "Freedom Summer," the effort drew several thousand volunteers from across the country, including many idealistic white college students. Freedom Summer workers established freedom schools, which taught black children traditional subjects as well as their own history; conducted a major voter registration drive; and organized the Mississippi Freedom Democratic Party, a political alternative to the all-white Democratic organization in Mississippi. Some southerners reacted swiftly and violently. Fifteen civil rights workers were murdered; only about 1,200 black voters were registered that summer.

The need for federal action became even clearer in March 1965, when Martin Luther King Jr. and other black leaders called for a massive march from Selma, Alabama, to the state capitol in Montgomery to protest the murder of a voting-rights activist. As soon as the marchers left Selma, mounted state troopers attacked them with tear gas and clubs. The scene was shown on national television that night. Calling the episode "an American tragedy," President Johnson redoubled his efforts to persuade Congress to pass the pending voting-rights legislation.

The Voting Rights Act. The Voting Rights Act, which passed on August 6, 1965, outlawed the literacy tests and other measures most southern states used to prevent blacks from registering to vote and authorized the attorney general to send federal examiners to register voters in any county where less than 50 percent of the voting-age population was registered. Together with the Twenty-fourth Amendment (1964), which outlawed the poll tax in federal elections, the Voting Rights Act enabled millions of blacks to register and vote for the first time since after Reconstruction.

In the South the results were stunning. In 1960 only 20 percent of blacks of voting age had been registered to vote; by 1964 the figure had risen to 39 percent, and by 1971 it was 62 percent (Map 28.4). As Hartman Turnbow, a Mississippi farmer who risked his life to register in 1964, later declared, "It won't never go back where it was."

Enacting the Liberal Agenda

Johnson's success in pushing through the Voting Rights Act had stemmed in part from the 1964 election, when he had faced the Republican Barry Goldwater of Arizona. An arch-conservative, Goldwater ran on a anti-Communist, anti-government platform, offering "a choice, not an echo." There would be no Republican "Dime Store New Deal" this time around. The voters didn't buy it. Johnson and his running mate Hubert H. Humphrey of Minnesota won in a landslide (Map 28.5). In the long run, Goldwater's candidacy marked the beginning of a grassroots conservative revolt that would eventually transform the Republican Party and American politics. In the short run, however, Johnson's sweeping victory enabled him to bring to fruition the legislative programs of the "Great Society."

Like most New Deal liberals, Johnson held an expansive view of the role of government. Now he

MAP 28.4 Black Voter Registration in the South, 1964 and 1975

After passage of the Voting Rights Act of 1965, black registration in the South increased dramatically. The bars on the map show the number of blacks registered in 1964, before the act was passed, and in 1975, after it had been in effect for ten years. States in the Deep South, such as Mississippi, Alabama, and Georgia, had the biggest increases.

had a popular mandate and, equally important, the filibuster-proof majority he needed to push his programs forward (see Table 28.1).

One of Johnson's first successes was breaking the congressional deadlock on aid to education. Passed in April 1965, the Elementary and Secondary Education Act authorized $1 billion in federal funds, sidestepping the religious issue by dispensing aid to public and parochial schools alike on the basis of the number of needy children in attendance. Six months later, Johnson signed the Higher Education Act, providing federal scholarships for college students.

The Eighty-ninth Congress also gave Johnson the votes he needed to achieve some form of national health insurance. Realizing the game was up, the American Medical Association fell back to a demand that services be provided through the existing private system of doctors and hospitals. On that basis, two new programs came forth: Medicare, a health plan for the elderly funded by a surcharge on Social Security payroll taxes, and Medicaid, a health plan for the poor paid for by general tax revenues and administered by the states.

Johnson's programs targeted not only the disadvantaged; the middle class benefited, too. Federal urban renewal and home mortgage assistance helped those who could afford to live in single-family homes or modern apartments. Medicare covered every elderly person eligible for Social Security, regardless of need. Much of the federal aid to education went to the children of the middle class.

And everyone benefited from the Great Society's environmental reforms. President Johnson pressed for expansion of the national park system, improvement of the nation's air and water, protection for endangered species and the wilderness, and stronger land-use planning. At the insistence of his wife, Lady Bird Johnson, he promoted the Highway Beautification Act of 1965. His approach marked a break with past conservation efforts, which had concentrated on husbanding the nation's natural

MAP 28.5 Presidential Election of 1964

This map reveals how one-sided Lyndon Johnson's victory was over Barry Goldwater in 1964. Except for Arizona, his home state, Goldwater won only five states in the deep South — not of much immediate consolation to him, but a sure indicator that the South was cutting its historic ties to the Democratic Party. Moreover, although soundly rejected in 1964, Goldwater's Far Right critique of "big government" laid the foundation for a Republican resurgence in the 1980s.

Candidate	Electoral Vote	Popular Vote	Percent of Popular Vote
Lyndon B. Johnson (Democrat)	486	43,121,085	61.1
Barry M. Goldwater (Republican)	52	27,145,161	38.5

TABLE 28.1 Major Great Society Legislation

Civil Rights

1964	Twenty-fourth Amendment	Outlawed poll tax in federal elections
	Civil Rights Act	Banned discrimination in employment and public accommodations on the basis of race, religion, sex, or national origin
1965	Voting Rights Act	Outlawed literacy tests for voting; provided federal supervision of registration in historically low-registration areas

Social Welfare

1964	Economic Opportunity Act	Created Office of Economic Opportunity (OEO) to administer War on Poverty programs such as Head Start, Job Corps, and Volunteers in Service to America (VISTA)
1965	Medical Care Act	Provided medical care for the poor (Medicaid) and the elderly (Medicare)
1966	Minimum Wage Act	Raised hourly minimum wage from $1.25 to $1.40 and expanded coverage to new groups

Education

1965	Elementary and Secondary Education Act	Granted federal aid for education of poor children
	National Endowment for the Arts and Humanities	Provided federal funding and support for artists and scholars
	Higher Education Act	Provided federal scholarships for postsecondary education

Housing and Urban Development

1964	Urban Mass Transportation Act	Provided federal aid to urban mass transit
	Omnibus Housing Act	Provided federal funds for public housing and rent subsidies for low-income families
1965	Housing and Urban Development Act	Created Department of Housing and Urban Development (HUD)
1966	Metropolitan Area Redevelopment and Demonstration Cities Acts	Designated 150 "model cities" for combined programs of public housing, social services, and job training

Environment

1964	Wilderness Preservation Act	Designated 9.1 million acres of federal lands as "wilderness areas," barring future roads, buildings, or commercial use
1965	Air and Water Quality Acts	Set tougher air quality standards; required states to enforce water quality standards for interstate waters

Miscellaneous

1964	Tax Reduction Act	Reduced personal and corporate income tax rates
1965	Immigration Act	Abandoned national quotas of 1924 law, allowing more non-European immigration
	Appalachian Regional and Development Act	Provided federal funding for roads, health clinics, other public works projects in economically depressed regions

resources. Secretary of the Interior Stewart Udall emphasized quality of life, battling the problem "of vanishing beauty, of increasing ugliness, of shrinking open space, and of an overall environment that is diminished daily by pollution and noise and blight." In a similar vein, the National Endowment for the Arts and the Humanities was established in 1965 to support the work of artists, writers, and scholars.

In the prevailing reform climate, it even became possible to tackle the nation's discriminatory immigration policy, which since 1924 had used a national-origins quota system that favored northern Europeans. The Immigration Act of 1965 abandoned the quota system, replacing it with more equitable numerical limits on immigration from all nations. To promote family reunification, the law also provided that close relatives of individuals already legally resident in the United States could be admitted outside the numerical limits, an exception that especially benefited Asian and Latin American immigrants. The ethnic diversity of our nation today—and of our campuses—goes back to that 1965 Immigration Act.

The War on Poverty. What drove Johnson hardest, however, was his determination to "end poverty in our time." The president called it a national disgrace that, in the midst of plenty, a fifth of all Americans—hidden from sight in Appalachia, in urban ghettos, in migrant labor camps, on Indian reservations—lived in poverty. Many had fallen through the cracks and were not served by New Deal welfare programs.

The "Johnson Treatment"

Lyndon B. Johnson, a shrewd and adroit politician, learned many of his legislative skills while serving as majority leader of the Senate from 1953 to 1960. Here he zeroed in on Senator Theodore Francis Green of Rhode Island. After assuming the presidency, Johnson remarked, "They say Jack Kennedy had style, but I'm the one who got the bills passed." George Tames, *The New York Times*.

So one tactic was shoring up those programs. The Great Society broadened Social Security to include waiters and waitresses, domestic servants, farmworkers, and hospital employees. Social welfare expenditures increased rapidly, especially for Aid to Families with Dependent Children (AFDC), as did public housing and rent subsidy programs. Food stamps, begun in 1964 mainly to stabilize farm prices, grew into a major source of assistance to low-income families.

The Office of Economic Opportunity (OEO), established by the Economic Opportunity Act of 1964, was the Great Society's showcase in the War on Poverty. Built around the twin principles of equal opportunity and community action, OEC advanced programs so numerous and diverse that they recalled the alphabet agencies of the New Deal. Head Start provided free nursery schools to prepare disadvantaged preschoolers for kindergarten. The Job Corps and Upward Bound provided young people with training and jobs. Volunteers in Service to America (VISTA), modeled on the Peace Corps, provided technical assistance to the urban and rural poor. An array of regional development programs aimed, like foreign aid, at spurring economic growth in impoverished areas. The Community Action Program encouraged its clients to demand "maximum feasible participation" in decisions that affected them. Community Action organizers worked closely with lawyers employed by the Legal Services Program to provide the poor with access to the legal system.

The Limits of the Great Society. By the end of 1965, the Johnson administration had compiled the most impressive legislative record since the New Deal and put issues of poverty, justice, and access at the center of national political life. Yet the Great Society never quite measured up to the extravagant promises made for it.

The proportion of Americans living below the poverty line dropped from 20 percent to 13 percent between 1963 and 1968 (Figure 28.1). African Americans did even better. In the 1960s the black poverty rate fell by half as millions of blacks moved into the middle class. Critics, however, credited the decade's booming economy more than government programs. Moreover, distribution of wealth remained highly skewed. In relative terms, the bottom 20 percent remained as far behind as ever.

An inherent problem was the limited funding, which was set at less than $2 billion annually. It also proved impossible to hold together the extraordinarily diverse political coalition first forged by Franklin Roosevelt in the 1930s — middle-class and poor; white and nonwhite; Protestant, Jewish, and Catholic; urban and rural — that Johnson rallied for the Great Society. Inevitably, the demands of certain groups — such as blacks' demands for civil rights and the urban poor's demands for increased political power — conflicted with the interests of other Democrats. In the end Johnson's coalition was not strong enough to withstand a growing challenge by conservatives who resisted expanded civil rights and social welfare benefits.

FIGURE 28.1 Americans in Poverty, 1959–2000

Between 1959 and 1973 the poverty rate among American families dropped by more than half — from 23 percent to 11 percent. There was, however, sharp disagreement about the reasons for that notable decline. Liberals credited the War on Poverty, while conservatives favored the high-performing economy, with the significant poverty dip of 1965–1966 caused by military spending, not Johnson's domestic programs.

Democrats were themselves plagued by disillusionment over the shortcomings of their reforms. In the early 1960s the lofty rhetoric of the New Frontier and the Great Society had raised people's expectations. But competition for federal largesse was keen, and the shortage of funds left many promises unfulfilled, especially after 1965 when the Vietnam War siphoned funding away from domestic programs. In 1966 the government spent $22 billion on the Vietnam War and only $1.2 billion on the War on Poverty. Ultimately, as Martin Luther King Jr. put it, the Great Society was "shot down on the battlefields of Vietnam."

▶ Why, after years of resistance, did Congress pass the great civil rights acts of 1964 and 1965?

▶ What were the key components of the Great Society?

▶ What factors limited the success of the War on Poverty?

Into the Quagmire, 1963–1968

Just as Kennedy inherited Vietnam from Eisenhower, so Lyndon Johnson inherited Vietnam from Kennedy. Only the inheritance was now more burdensome, for it became clear that only massive American intervention could prevent the collapse of South Vietnam (Map 28.6). Johnson was a subscriber, like Kennedy, to the Cold War tenets of global containment—that America's credibility was at stake in Vietnam and that the domino effect would have devastating consequences. But whereas, in Kennedy's case, second thoughts might have prevailed, that was an impossibility with Johnson. "I am not going to lose Vietnam," he vowed upon taking office. "I am not going to be the President who saw Southeast Asia go the way China went."

Escalation

Johnson was unwilling to level with the American people. For one thing, he doubted that they had the

MAP 28.6 The Vietnam War, 1968

The Vietnam War was a guerrilla war, fought in skirmishes rather than set-piece battles. Despite repeated airstrikes, the United States was never able to halt the flow of North Vietnamese troops and supplies down the Ho Chi Minh Trail, which wound through Laos and Cambodia. In January 1968 Vietcong forces launched the Tet offensive, a surprise attack on cities and provincial centers across South Vietnam. Although the attackers were pushed back with heavy losses, the Tet offensive revealed the futility of American efforts to suppress the Vietcong guerrillas and marked a turning point in the war.

now had to face the reality of large-scale public opposition to his policies.

- What difficulties did the United States face in fighting a war against North Vietnam and the Vietcong in South Vietnam?
- Why did President Johnson suffer a "credibility gap" over Vietnam?
- What was the student role in the antiwar movement? How can we explain students' willingness to protest the war?

Coming Apart

In the student protests, in the SDS, and in the Berkeley Free Speech Movement, more obviously was at stake than Vietnam. Indeed, antiwar protest merged into a variegated, broad-based attack on the status quo — "the Movement," to its participants — that not only challenged Cold War assumptions, but blasted America's liberal consensus.

The roots of this assault go back to the 1950s, back to when the Beats denigrated capitalism, teenagers defied their elders, and African American sit-ins protested racial injustice. By the mid-1960s this angry disaffection had broadened into a many-sided attack on mainstream America.

The Counterculture

While the New Left plotted against the political and economic "system," a growing number of young Americans embarked on a general revolution against authority and middle-class respectability. The "hippie" — attired in ragged blue jeans, tie-dyed T-shirts, beads, and army fatigues, with long, unkempt hair — symbolized the new counterculture.

Not surprisingly, given the importance of rock 'n' roll in the 1950s, popular music helped define the counterculture. Folk singer Pete Seeger set the tone for the era's political idealism with songs such as the antiwar ballad "Where Have All the Flowers Gone?" In 1963, the year of the Birmingham demonstrations and President Kennedy's assassination, Bob Dylan's "Blowin' in the Wind" reflected the impatience of people whose faith in America was wearing thin.

Other winds of change in popular music came from the Beatles, four working-class Brits who burst onto the American scene early in 1964. The Beatles' music, by turns lyrical and driving, was remarkably successful, spawning a commercial and cultural phenomenon called "Beatlemania." American youths' eager embrace of the Beatles deepened the generational divide between teenagers and their elders. The Beatles also helped to pave the way for the more rebellious, angrier music of other British groups, notably the Rolling Stones.

Drugs intertwined with music in the rituals of the youth culture. The recreational use of drugs — especially marijuana and the hallucinogenic popularly known as LSD or "acid" — was celebrated in popular music. San Francisco bands such as the Grateful Dead and Jefferson Airplane and musicians like guitarist Jimi Hendrix developed a musical style known as "acid rock," which was characterized by long, heavily amplified guitar solos accompanied by psychedelic lighting effects. In August 1969, 400,000 young people journeyed to Bethel, New York, to "get high" on music, drugs, and sex at the three-day Woodstock Music and Art Fair.

Jimi Hendrix at Woodstock

The three-day outdoor Woodstock concert in August 1969 was a defining moment in the rise of the counterculture. The event attracted 400,000 young people, who journeyed to Bethel, New York, for a weekend of music, drugs, and sex. Jimi Hendrix closed the show early Sunday morning with an electrifying version of "The Star-Spangled Banner." More overtly political than most counterculture music, Hendrix's rendition featured sound effects that seemed to evoke the violence of the Vietnam War. Michael Wadleigh, who directed the documentary *Woodstock*, called Hendrix's performance "his challenge to American foreign policy." Allan Koss/The Image Works.

For a brief time adherents of the counterculture believed a new age was dawning. They experimented in communal living and glorified uninhibited sexuality. In 1967 the "world's first Human Be-In" drew 20,000 people to Golden Gate Park in San Francisco. The Beat poet Allen Ginsberg "purified" the site with a Buddhist ritual, and the LSD advocate Timothy Leary, a former Harvard psychology teacher, urged the gathering to "turn on to the scene, tune in to what is happening, and drop out." That summer—dubbed the "Summer of Love"—San Francisco's Haight-Ashbury, New York's East Village, and Chicago's Uptown neighborhoods swelled with young dropouts, drifters, and teenage runaways dubbed "flower children." Their faith in instant love and peace quickly turned sour, however, as they suffered bad drug trips, sexually transmitted diseases, loneliness, and violence. Although many young people kept their distance, media coverage made it seem as if all of American youth was rejecting the nation's social and cultural norms.

Beyond Civil Rights

Among young blacks, knocking the mainstream meant something else. It meant rejecting the established civil rights leadership, with its faith in the courts and legislative change. It meant an eye-for-an-eye, not Martin Luther King's nonviolence. It meant wondering why blacks wanted to be integrated with whites anyway. Above all, it expressed fury at the poverty of blacks and at white racism that was beyond the reach of civil rights laws.

Malcolm X. Black rage had expressed itself historically in demands for racial separation, espoused in the late nineteenth century by the Back-to-Africa movement and in the 1920s by Marcus Garvey (see

Malcolm X (1925–1965)

Malcolm X has an assistant hold up the picture of a fallen black as he addresses a Harlem rally on May 14, 1963, in support of civil rights demonstrations in Birmingham, Alabama. The photograph was not in fact related to the brutal police attack on Birmingham demonstrators, but it represented what Malcolm X considered to be the norm for how blacks were treated in America. From a Birmingham jail, Martin Luther King Jr. warned that if his appeal for racial justice went unheeded, African Americans would turn to "people who have lost faith in America . . . and who have concluded that the white man is an incurable 'devil.'" He had Malcolm X in mind. © Bettmann/Corbis.

Chapter 23). In the 1960s the leading exponent of black separatism was the Nation of Islam, which fused a rejection of Christianity with a strong dose of self-improvement. Black Muslims, as they were known, adhered to a strict code of personal behavior, with the men always recognizable by their dark suits and white shirts, the women by their long dresses and head coverings. Black Muslims preached an apocalyptic brand of Islam, anticipating the day when Allah would banish the white "devils" and give the black nation justice. Although its full converts numbered only about 10,000, the Nation of Islam had a wide popular following in urban ghettoes.

The most charismatic Black Muslim was Malcolm X (the X stood for his African family name lost under slavery). A spellbinding speaker, Malcolm X preached a philosophy of militant protest and separatism, though he advocated violence only for self-defense. Hostile to the traditional civil rights organizations, he caustically referred to the 1963 March on Washington as the "Farce on Washington." In 1964, after a power struggle with the founder, Elijah Muhammad, Malcolm X broke with the Nation of Islam. While remaining a black nationalist, his anti-white views moderated, and he began to talk in terms of class struggle uniting poor whites and blacks. But he got no further. On February 21, 1965, Malcolm X was assassinated while delivering a speech in Harlem. Three Black Muslims were later convicted of his murder.

Black Power. A more secular brand of black nationalism emerged in 1966 when young black SNCC and CORE activists, following the lead of Stokely Carmichael, began to call for black self-reliance and racial pride under the banner of "Black Power." Amid growing distrust of whites, SNCC declared itself a blacks-only organization and ejected its white members. In the same year Huey Newton and Bobby Seale, two college students in Oakland, California, founded the Black Panthers, a militant self-defense organization dedicated to protecting blacks from police violence. The Panthers' organization quickly spread to other cities, where members undertook a wide range of community organizing projects. Their rhetoric, however, declared their affinity for Third World revolutionary movements and armed struggle.

Among the most significant legacies of Black Power was the assertion of racial pride. Rejecting white society, blacks wore African clothing and hairstyles and awakened interest in black history, art, and literature. By the 1970s many colleges and universities were offering programs in black studies.

Urban Riots. The rage expressed by Black Power boiled over, in inchoate form, in a wave of riots that struck the nation's cities. The first "long hot summer" began in July 1964 in New York City, when police shot a black criminal suspect in Harlem. Angry youths looted and rioted there for a week. Over the next four years, the volatile issue of police brutality set off riots in dozens of cities. In August 1965 the arrest of a young black motorist in the Watts section of Los Angeles sparked six days of rioting that left thirty-four dead. The riots of 1967 were the most serious, engulfing twenty-two cities in July and August. The most devastating outbreaks occurred in Newark and Detroit. Forty-three people were killed in Detroit alone, nearly all of them black, and $50 million worth of property was destroyed.

The Assassination of Martin Luther King Jr. Stirred by this turmoil, and by disappointment with his civil rights achievements, Martin Luther King began to confront the deep-seated problems of poverty and racism facing American blacks. He spoke out eloquently against the Vietnam War and planned a poor people's campaign to fight economic injustice and inequality. In support of that cause, he went to Memphis, Tennessee, to support a strike by predominantly black sanitation workers, and there, on April 4, 1968, he was assassinated. King's death set off a further round of urban rioting, with major violence breaking out in many cities.

Although King died unfulfilled, he had set in motion permanent, indeed revolutionary, changes in American race relations. He had helped end Jim Crow segregation, won federal legislation ensuring black Americans' most basic civil rights, and broke the white monopoly on political power in the South. And not least, his example inspired other oppressed groups in America to enter the struggle for equal rights.

César Chavez and the Chicano Movement. For Mexican Americans, the counterpart to Martin Luther King was César Chavez, although, in Chavez's case, the conversion to economic struggle came much earlier. He and Dolores Huerta had begun in the Community Service Organization, a California group founded in the 1950s to promote Mexican political participation and civil rights. Leaving that organization in 1962, Chavez concentrated on the agricultural region of Delano, California, and with Huerta, organized the United Farm Workers (UFW), a union for migrant workers. While Huerta, a brilliant organizer, was crucial

César Chávez

Mexican American labor leader César Chávez, seen here addressing a rally in Guadalupe, California, won national attention in 1965 during a strike of migrant farmworkers, most of them Mexican Americans, against California grape growers. Drawing on tactics from the civil rights movement, Chávez called for nonviolent action and effectively mobilized nationwide support for a boycott of nonunion table grapes. FPG/Getty Images.

to the movement, it was Chávez, with his deep spirituality and commitment to nonviolent protest, who became the symbol for what was popularly called *La Causa*. A 1965 grape pickers' strike led the UFW to call a nationwide boycott of table grapes, bringing Chávez huge publicity and backing from the AFL-CIO. In a bid for attention to the struggle, Chávez staged a hunger strike in 1968, which ended dramatically after twenty-eight days with Senator Robert F. Kennedy at his side to break the fast. Victory came in 1970 when California grape growers signed contracts recognizing the UFW.

On a parallel track, Mexican Americans had since the 1930s (see Chapter 24) actively worked to surmount the poverty, uncertain legal status, and language barriers that made political mobilization difficult. That situation began to change when the Mexican American Political Association (MAPA) mobilized support for John F. Kennedy. Over the next four years, MAPA and other organizations worked successfully to elect Mexican American candidates such as Edward Roybal of California and Henry González of Texas to Congress.

Younger Mexican Americans grew impatient with MAPA, however. The barrios of Los Angeles and other western cities produced the militant Brown Berets, modeled on the Black Panthers (who wore black berets). Rejecting the assimilationist approach of their elders, 1,500 Mexican American students met in Denver in 1969 to hammer out a new political and cultural agenda. They proclaimed a new term, *Chicano*, to replace Mexican American, and later organized a new political party, La Raza Unida (The United Race), to promote Chicano interests and candidates. In California and other southwestern states, students staged demonstrations

Wounded Knee Revisited

In 1973 members of the American Indian Movement staged a seventy-one-day protest at Wounded Knee, South Dakota, site of the 1890 massacre of two hundred Sioux by U.S. soldiers (see Chapter 16). The takeover was sparked by the murder of a local Sioux by a group of whites but quickly expanded to include demands for basic reforms in federal Indian policy and tribal governance. © Bettmann/Corbis.

to press for bilingual education, the hiring of more Chicano teachers, and the creation of Chicano studies programs. By the 1970s dozens of such programs were offered at universities throughout the region.

The Native American Movement. American Indians also found a model in black struggles for equality. Numbering nearly 800,000 in the 1960s, they were exceedingly diverse, divided by language, tribal history, region, and degree of integration into American life. As a group, they shared a staggering unemployment rate (ten times the national average), the worst housing, the highest disease rates, and the least access to education of any group in the United States.

Since World War II, the National Congress of American Indians had lobbied for reform. In the 1960s the prevailing spirit of protest swept through Indian communities. Young militants, like their counterparts in the black civil rights movement, challenged the accommodationist approach of their elders. Proposing a new name for themselves — Native Americans — they embraced the concept of "Red Power." Beginning in 1968 with the formation of the militant American Indian Movement (AIM), young Native Americans staged escalating protests, occupying the deserted federal penitentiary on Alcatraz Island in San Francisco Bay and sitting-in at the headquarters of the hated Federal Bureau of Indian Affairs in Washington, D.C. In February 1973, a siege at Wounded Knee, South Dakota, the site of the infamous 1890 massacre of the Sioux, ended in a gun battle with the FBI.

Although upsetting to many white onlookers, Native American protest did spur government action on tribal issues.

- What are the elements in the counterculture of the 1960s?
- How do you account for the Black Power movement?
- How do you explain the spillover of the black civil rights struggle into the Mexican American and Native American communities?

1968: A Year of Shocks

By 1968, a sense of crisis gripped the country. Riots in the cities, campus unrest, and a nose-thumbing counterculture seemed on the verge of tearing America apart. What crystallized the crisis was the fact that 1968 was an election year.

The Politics of Vietnam

President Johnson had gambled in 1965 on a quick victory, before the political cost of escalation at home came due. But there was no quick victory. North Vietnamese and Vietcong forces fought on, the South Vietnamese government enjoyed little popular support, and American casualties mounted. By early 1968, the death rate reached several hundred a week. Johnson and his generals kept insisting that there was "light at the end of the tunnel." Facts on the ground showed otherwise.

The Tet Offensive. On January 30, 1968, the Vietcong unleashed a massive, well-coordinated assault in South Vietnam. Timed to coincide with Tet, the lunar Vietnamese new year holiday, the offensive struck thirty-six of the forty-four provincial capitals and five of the six major cities, including Saigon, where Vietcong nearly overran the supposedly impregnable U.S. embassy. In strictly military terms, the Tet offensive was a failure, with very heavy Vietcong losses and the South Vietnamese government still intact. But psychologically, the effect was devastating. Television brought into American homes the shocking images — the American embassy under siege, with a pistol-wielding staff member peering warily from a window, the Saigon police chief placing a pistol to the head of a Vietcong suspect and, live on TV, executing him.

The Tet offensive made a mockery of official pronouncements that the United States was winning the war. Just before, a Gallup poll found that 56 percent of Americans considered themselves "hawks" (supporters of the war), while only 28 percent identified with the "doves" (war opponents). Three months later doves outnumbered hawks 42 to 41 percent. Without embracing the peace movement, many Americans simply concluded that the war was unwinnable (see Reading American Pictures, "War and Its Aftermath: Images of the Vietnam Conflict, 1968 and 1982," p. 890).

So did a growing faction within the Democratic Party. Even before Tet, Senator Eugene J. McCarthy of Minnesota had entered the Democratic primaries as an antiwar candidate. A core of student activists "went clean for Gene" by cutting their hair and putting away their jeans. President Johnson won the early New Hampshire primary, but McCarthy received a stunning 42.2 percent of the vote. To make matters worse for the president, McCarthy's showing propelled Senator Robert Kennedy, a far more formidable opponent, into the race.

Johnson realized that his political support was evaporating. At the end of an otherwise routine televised address on March 31, he stunned the nation by announcing that he would not seek reelection. He also called a partial halt to the bombing and vowed to devote his remaining months in office to the search for peace. On May 10, 1968, preliminary peace talks between the United States and North Vietnam opened in Paris.

Political Turmoil. Just four days after Johnson's withdrawal from the presidential race, Martin Luther King Jr. was assassinated in Memphis. The ensuing riots in cities across the country left forty-three people dead. Soon afterward, students protesting Columbia University's plans for expanding into a neighboring ghetto occupied several campus buildings. The brutal response of the New York City police helped to radicalize even more students.

Then came the final tragedy of the year. On June 5, 1968, as he celebrated his victory in the California primary over Eugene McCarthy, Robert Kennedy was shot dead by a young Palestinian. Robert Kennedy's assassination was a calamity for the Democratic Party because only he had seemed able to surmount the party's Vietnam problem. In his brief but dramatic campaign, Kennedy had reached beyond the antiwar elements to traditional members of the New Deal coalition, including blue-collar workers, who were becoming susceptible to patriotic appeals from the right.

With Kennedy gone, the energy went out of the antiwar Democrats. McCarthy's campaign limped along, while Senator George S. McGovern of South Dakota entered the Democratic race in an effort to keep the Kennedy forces together. Meanwhile, Vice President Hubert H. Humphrey lined up pledges from traditional Democratic constituencies — unions, urban machines, and state political organizations. Democrats found themselves on the verge of nominating not an antiwar candidate but a public figure closely associated with Johnson's war policies.

The Siege of Chicago. At the August Democratic convention, the political divisions generated by the war consumed the party. Most of the drama occurred not in the convention hall but outside on the streets of Chicago. Thousands of protesters descended on the city. The most visible group, led by Jerry Rubin and Abbie Hoffman, a remarkable pair of troublemakers, claimed to represent the Youth International Party. To mock those inside the convention hall, these "Yippies" nominated a pig, Pigasus, for president. Their stunts, geared for maximum media exposure, diverted attention from the more serious, far more numerous activists who had come to Chicago to protest the war.

Richard J. Daley, the Democratic mayor, increasingly angry as protesters disrupted his convention, ordered the police to break up the demonstrations. Several nights of skirmishes between protesters and police culminated on the evening of the nominations. In what an official report later described as a "police riot," police officers attacked protesters with Mace, tear gas, and clubs. As the nominating speeches proceeded, television networks broadcast films of the riot, cementing a popular impression of the Democrats as the party of disorder. Inside the hall the Democrats dispiritedly nominated Hubert

READING AMERICAN PICTURES

War and Its Aftermath: Images of the Vietnam Conflict, 1968 and 1982

America's Longest War. Copyright Tim Page.

The Vietnam Veterans Memorial. Peter Marlow / Magnum Photos, Inc.

The Vietnam War ended in 1975, but it remains a painful and contested event in the American memory. Images of both combat and remembrance continue to shape our understanding not only of the conflict itself, but also of the meaning of U.S. participation in wars abroad today. The first photograph shows the brutal aftermath of a combat operation by U.S. soldiers in Vietnam during the war. The second photo captures a group of U.S. veterans embracing in front of the Vietnam Veterans' Memorial in Washington, D.C. Dedicated in 1982, the monument, designed by architect Maya Ling, contains the names of over 58,000 U.S. servicemen and -women killed in the war.

ANALYZING THE EVIDENCE

- What does the first photo, "America's Longest War," reveal about how the war was fought and experienced by ordinary soldiers?

- Given the political climate of the late 1960s, what effect on their feelings about the war do you think this image of carnage and others like it had on those who viewed it?

- Why are the veterans embracing in front of the memorial? What is the significance of the clothing and items they are wearing?

- Traditionally, war memorials featured statues of combatants or generals in heroic poses; this one has only the names of those killed in combat. Yet the Vietnam monument is widely seen as being emotionally evocative. What does this suggest about the American view of the Vietnam War? See **www.nps.gov/vive** for more information about the memorial.

H. Humphrey, who chose Senator Edmund S. Muskie of Maine as his running mate. The delegates approved a middle-of-the-road platform that endorsed continued fighting in Vietnam while urging a diplomatic solution to the conflict.

Backlash

Political realignments are infrequent in American history. The last one had been 1932, when many Republicans, despairing over the Great Depression, had switched sides and voted for FDR. The year 1968 was another such pivotal moment. Consider a forty-seven-year-old machinist's wife from Dayton, Ohio, described by the social scientists Ben J. Wattenberg and Richard Scammon in their book, *The Real Majority* (1970):

> That lady in Dayton is afraid to walk the streets alone at night . . . she has a mixed view about blacks and civil rights because she lived in a neighborhood that became all black . . . her brother-in-law is a policeman [and] she is deeply distressed that her son is going to a community junior college where LSD was found on campus.

Growing up in the Great Depression, she was likely a great admirer of FDR, maybe with his picture on her living room wall. Such working-class people were the heart and soul of the New Deal democracy. But now, in the sour aftermath of the Chicago convention, their votes were up for grabs. And as always, politicians with their noses to the wind were eager to oblige.

Governor George C. Wallace of Alabama, a third-party candidate, skillfully exploited working-class anxieties over student protests and urban riots. He called for "law and order" in the streets and denounced welfare mothers who, thanks to Johnson's Great Society, were "breeding children as a cash crop." Wallace skewered "overeducated, ivory-towered folks with pointed heads looking down their noses at us." Although no longer overtly a racist, Wallace traded on his fame as the segregationist governor who had stood up to the federal government during the Selma crisis of 1965. His hope was that, by carrying the South, he could deny the major parties an electoral majority and force the 1968 election into the House of Representatives. That strategy failed, and Wallace's political star faded after a near-fatal shooting in 1972 left him paralyzed, but he had defined hot-button issues — liberal elitism, welfare queens, law and order — of immense utility to the next generation of mainstream conservatives.

The Republican candidate, Richard Nixon, offered a more sophisticated version of Wallace's populism. After losing the presidential campaign in 1960, and after losing again in the California gubernatorial race in 1962, Nixon had seemed finished, but he engineered an amazing political comeback and in 1968 won the Republican presidential nomination. As part of what his advisers called the "southern strategy," he chose Spiro Agnew, the conservative governor of Maryland, as his running mate. Nixon hoped to attract southern voters still smarting over Democratic civil rights legislation. Nationally, Nixon appealed to people who came to be known as the "silent majority." He pledged to represent the "quiet voice" of the "great majority of Americans, the forgotten Americans, the nonshouters, the nondemonstrators."

Despite the Democratic debacle in Chicago, the election actually proved to be close. In the last weeks of the campaign, Humphrey rallied by disassociating himself from Johnson's war policies. When on October 31 President Johnson announced a complete halt to the bombing of North Vietnam, Nixon countered by intimating that he had his own plan to end the war (in reality no such plan existed). On election day Nixon received 43.4 percent of the vote to Humphrey's 42.7 percent, defeating him by a scant 500,000 votes out of the 73 million that were cast (Map 28.7). Wallace finished with 13.5 percent of the popular vote.

The closeness of the outcome masked the fact that 1968 really was a pivotal election. Humphrey received almost 12 million fewer votes than had Johnson in 1964. The South, except for Texas, abandoned the Democratic Party, never to return. Nixon's "southern strategy" had worked. In the North, he and Wallace made significant inroads among traditionally Democratic voters. And while party divisions over Vietnam had been briefly patched up, the underlying ideological differences — signified by the rivalry of Hubert Humphrey and George McGovern — persisted, with corrosive effect on the party's effectiveness. New Deal Democrats would never again have the unity of purpose that had served them for thirty years. Assaulted from both left and right, the liberal consensus was coming apart.

➤ What were the critical events of 1968 that have led historians to describe it as a "watershed year"?

➤ Why did the Democrats lose their grip as the majority party in the late 1960s?

MAP 28.7 Presidential Election of 1968

Candidate	Electoral Vote	Popular Vote	Percent of Popular Vote
Richard M. Nixon (Republican)	301	31,770,237	43.4
Hubert H. Humphrey (Democrat)	191	31,270,533	42.7
George C. Wallace (American Independent)	46	9,906,141	13.5
Minor parties	—	239,908	—

With Lyndon B. Johnson's surprise withdrawal and the assassination of the party's most charismatic contender, Robert Kennedy, the Democrats faced the election of 1968 in disarray. Governor George Wallace of Alabama, who left the Democrats to run as a third-party candidate, campaigned on the backlash against the civil rights movement. As late as mid-September Wallace held the support of 21 percent of the voters. But in November he received only 13.5 percent of the vote, winning five southern states. Republican Richard M. Nixon, who like Wallace emphasized "law and order" in his campaign, defeated Hubert H. Humphrey with only 43.4 percent of the popular vote, but it was now clear, given that Wallace's southern support would otherwise have gone to Nixon, that the South had shifted decisively to the Republican side.

SUMMARY

In this chapter, we saw how the liberal consensus—agreement about a New Deal approach to the nation's social and economic ills—peaked in the mid-1960s and then, under the combined pressure of the Vietnam War and cultural conflict, flamed out. John F. Kennedy opened the politics of expectation in the 1960 campaign, although the domestic accomplishments of the New Frontier were limited. Following John Kennedy's assassination in 1963, Lyndon Johnson advanced the most ambitious liberal reform program since the New Deal, securing not only civil rights legislation, but an array of programs in education, medical care, transportation, and, above all, his War on Poverty. But the Great Society fell short of its promise as Johnson escalated the American involvement in Vietnam.

The war bitterly divided Americans. Galvanized by the carnage of war and the draft, the antiwar movement spread rapidly among young people. The spirit of rebellion spilled beyond the antiwar movement. The New Left challenged the corporate dominance of society, while the more apolitical counterculture preached personal liberation through sex, drugs, music, and spirituality. Moving beyond civil rights, the Black Power movement encouraged racial pride and assertiveness, serving also as a model for Mexican Americans and Native Americans.

In 1968, the nation was rocked by the assassinations of Martin Luther King and Robert F. Kennedy and a wave of urban riots, fueling a growing popular desire for law and order. Adding to the national disquiet was a Democratic convention that summer, divided by the Vietnam war and under siege by rioting in the streets. A new wave of conservatism took hold of the country, contributing to the resurgence of the Republican Party under Richard Nixon.

Connections: Diplomacy and Politics

In the Part Six opening essay, we remark that "the interaction of domestic and global—the links between liberalism and the Cold War—was especially clear [in the 1960s] because it was Vietnam that, more than anything else, undermined the Great Society and the liberal consensus." In Chapter 26, we showed how that link between liberalism and the Cold War was forged during the Truman and Eisenhower administrations. Unlike in earlier periods, anti-Communism in its McCarthyite phase was not regarded as an attack on liberal reform. In the wake of Vietnam this changed, and prosecution of the Cold War increasingly became an attack on the liberal consensus, a development that, as we shall see in Chapter 30, culminated under the leadership of Ronald Reagan in the 1980s.

CHAPTER REVIEW QUESTIONS

▶ How do you explain the preeminence of civil rights in the politics of the 1960s?

▶ What are the differences between Kennedy's New Frontier and Johnson's Great Society?

▶ Why is the United States' involvement in the Vietnam War so often called a "quagmire"?

TIMELINE

1960
- John F. Kennedy elected president

1961
- Peace Corps established
- Bay of Pigs invasion
- Berlin Wall erected

1962
- Cuban missile crisis
- Students for a Democratic Society (SDS) founded
- César Chavez and Dolores Huerta organize the United Farm Workers (UFW)

1963
- Betty Friedan's *The Feminine Mystique*
- Civil rights protest in Birmingham, Alabama
- March on Washington
- Nuclear test-ban treaty
- John F. Kennedy assassinated; Lyndon B. Johnson assumes presidency

1964
- Freedom Summer; Civil Rights Act
- Economic Opportunity Act inaugurates War on Poverty
- Free Speech Movement at Berkeley
- Gulf of Tonkin Resolution authorizes military action in Vietnam

1965
- Immigration Act abolishes national quota system
- Voting Rights Act
- Medicare and Medicaid programs established
- Malcolm X assassinated
- Operation Rolling Thunder escalates bombing campaign
- First U.S. combat troops arrive in Vietnam
- Race riot in Watts district of Los Angeles

1966
- Stokely Carmichael proclaims black power

1967
- Hippie counterculture's "Summer of Love"
- 100,000 march in antiwar protest in Washington, D.C.

1968
- Tet offensive dashes American hopes of victory
- Martin Luther King Jr. and Robert F. Kennedy assassinated
- Riot at Democratic National Convention in Chicago
- Richard Nixon elected president
- American Indian Movement (AIM) organized

FOR FURTHER EXPLORATION

Good starting points for understanding Kennedy's presidency are W. J. Rorabaugh, *Kennedy and the Promise of the Sixties* (2002), and David Halberstam, *The Best and the Brightest* (1972). Arthur M. Schlesinger Jr., *A Thousand Days* (1965), offers a detailed insider's account. For Lyndon Johnson, see Robert Dallek, *Flawed Giant* (1998).

Henry Hampton and Steve Fayer's oral history, *Voices of Freedom* (1991), and Harvard Sitkoff, *The Struggle for Black Equality*, 2nd ed. (1993), offer engaging accounts of the civil rights movement. On Martin Luther King Jr., see Taylor Branch's three-part biography, *Parting the Waters: 1954–1963* (1988), *Pillar of Fire: 1963–1965* (1998), and *At Canaan's Edge: 1965–1968* (2005). On Vietnam, the basic history is George Herring, *America's Longest War: The United States and Vietnam* (1986). Vivid accounts of dissent in the 1960s are Todd Gitlin, *The Sixties: Years of Hope, Days of Rage* (1987), and Maurice Isserman and Michael Kazin, *America Divided: The Civil War of the 1960s* (1999).

The period is unusually rich in compelling primary accounts. *Takin' It to the Streets* (1995), edited by Alexander Bloom and Wini Breines, offers an impressive array of documents that encompass the war, counterculture, civil rights, feminism, gay liberation, and other issues. Henry Hampton and Steve Fayer's oral history, *Voices of Freedom* (1991), and *The Autobiography of Malcolm X* (1965), cowritten with Alex Haley, provide insight into black struggle. Memoirs of Vietnam are numerous. Secretary of Defense Robert McNamara offers an insider's view and belated apologia in his *In Retrospect* (1995). Ron Kovic's *Born on the Fourth of July* (1976) is one soldier's powerful account of the war experience and its aftermath.

The John F. Kennedy Library and Museum's site at **www.jfklibrary.org** provides a large collection of records from Kennedy's presidency, including transcripts and recordings of JFK's speeches, a database of his executive orders, and a number of other resources. Civil Rights in Mississippi Digital Archive, at **www.lib.usm.edu/~spcol/crda/oh/index.html**, offers 150 oral histories relating to the civil rights movement in Mississippi. Audio clips are also included, as are short biographies, photographs, newsletters, FBI documents, and arrest records. A useful Vietnam site that includes state papers and official correspondence from 1941 to the fall of Saigon in 1975 is at **www.mtholyoke.edu/acad/intrel/vietnam.htm**.

TEST YOUR KNOWLEDGE

To assess your command of the material in this chapter, see the Online Study Guide at **bedfordstmartins.com/henretta**.

For Web sites, images, and documents related to topics and places in this chapter, visit **bedfordstmartins.com/makehistory**.

Buy it here

NO GAS

29 The 1970s: Toward a Conservative America

"THE UNITED STATES STEEL CORPORATION announced yesterday that it was closing 14 plants and mills in 8 states. About 13,000 production and white-collar workers will lose their jobs." "Weyerhaeuser Co. may trim about 1,000 salaried employees from its 11,000 member workforce over the next year." "Philadelphia: Food Fair Inc. plans to close 89 supermarkets in New York and Connecticut." Imagine a citizen of the 1950s emerging from a time capsule into the 1970s. She is bewildered by these gloomy newspaper headlines. What happened to America's vaunted economic supremacy? Equally bewildering is the sight of the all-powerful United States withdrawing from Vietnam, defeated by a third-tier country this citizen has probably never heard of. And she is utterly stunned, as one whose notion of an American president is Dwight D. Eisenhower, to be told that the current president, charged with obstruction of justice, has resigned in disgrace and left the White House.

Yet it's not all bad news. Who would have imagined Americans, in a time of joblessness and runaway inflation, mounting robust consumer and environmental movements? Yet that's what happened in the 1970s. Or the struggle for civil rights, far from pausing after the strenuous 1960s, intensifying and, in the case of women's and gay rights, breaking

The Nixon Years
Nixon's Domestic Agenda
Détente
Nixon's War
The 1972 Election
Watergate

Battling for Civil Rights: The Second Stage
The Revival of Feminism
Enforcing Civil Rights

Lean Years
Energy Crisis
Environmentalism
Economic Woes

Politics in the Wake of Watergate
Jimmy Carter: The Outsider as President
Carter and the World

Summary
Connections: Society

◀ **No Gas**

During the energy crisis of 1973, American motorists faced widespread gasoline shortages for the first time since World War II. Although gas was not rationed, gas stations were closed on Sundays, and some communities instituted further restrictions such as creating systems by which motorists with license plates ending in even numbers could purchase gas on certain days, with alternate days being reserved for odd numbers. Tom Ebenhoh/Black Star/Stockphoto.com.

new ground? Or a grassroots conservative movement, rising up in the millions in defense of traditional values?

If the historian is hard put making sense of the 1970s, it's because these crosscurrents suggest a country in the throes of change. But with Ronald Reagan's election in 1980, Americans better understood what was happening. They were leaving the liberal America behind and entering an age of political conservatism.

The Nixon Years

Richard Nixon was a master of the subtle art of politics. In the 1968 campaign his "southern strategy" and appeal to the "silent majority" had worked wonders at undermining the New Deal coalition. But Nixon was not, in fact, prepared to offer a genuine alternative. And insofar as he tried, he came up against a Democrat-controlled Congress — itself a stubborn legacy of the liberal age. Like Kennedy, moreover, Nixon much preferred foreign affairs. But here, too, while more adept a strategist, he was enmeshed by his inheritance of Vietnam. So we have to put Nixon down as a transitional figure — with one foot in the liberal past, the other in the conservative future — except in one respect. His departure was not transitional. He left with a big bang.

Nixon's Domestic Agenda

As a Republican candidate, it was incumbent on Nixon to run on an antigovernment platform. He called his approach the "New Federalism," vowing to "reverse the flow of power and resources from the states and communities to Washington and start power and resources flowing back . . . to the people." Nixon's particular take on this pledge was his revenue-sharing program, which distributed a portion of federal tax revenues to the states as block grants to be spent as state officials saw fit — an approach that became a fixture on the Republican agenda. Nixon also scaled back government programs that had grown dramatically during the Johnson administration. War on Poverty programs were reduced and the Office of Economic Opportunity entirely dismantled in 1971. Nixon also refused to spend billions of dollars appropriated by Congress for urban renewal, pollution control, and other environmental initiatives, and vetoed a 1971 bill to establish a comprehensive national child-care system on the grounds that such "communal approaches to child rearing" endangered the American family.

Yet Nixon could be imaginative, even daring, when it came to social welfare. He was much influenced by a key White House adviser, Daniel Moynihan, a Democrat and an independent-minded expert on urban affairs. In 1969 Nixon proposed a Family Assistance Plan, which would guarantee a family of four an income of $1,600 a year, plus $600 in food stamps. The appeal of this proposal lay in its simplicity: It would eliminate multiple layers of bureaucracy and pare down the nation's jerry-built welfare system. Attacked in the Senate both by conservatives and liberals, however, Nixon's plan failed. Welfare reform was postponed for another day. And so was national health insurance, another of Nixon's failed initiatives, in which he proposed a public/private system that would guarantee universal coverage.

No enemy of the major **entitlement programs**, Nixon approved generous advances in Medicare, Medicaid, and Social Security. And his administration expanded the regulatory apparatus of the modern state. New government agencies — the Environmental Protection Agency (EPA) in 1970, the Occupational Safety and Health Administration (OSHA), and the Consumer Products Safety Commission in 1972 — brought the federal government deep into areas hitherto only lightly regulated or not regulated at all.

Nixon's mixed record reflected the political crosscurrents of his time. His conservative base pushed in one direction; the Democratic Congress pushed in another. Consumer and environmental protections loomed large for the middle class. Social Security and Medicare mattered to working-class voters he was appealing to. But Nixon was himself not a laissez-faire conservative, and — what especially distinguished him — he had a zest for experimenting with the mechanics of government.

Détente

Richard Nixon regarded himself a "realist" in foreign affairs. That meant, above all, advancing the national interest. Everything else — commitments to allies, extending democracy abroad, championing human rights — came second, if that. Nixon's realism was fervently seconded by his national security adviser, Henry Kissinger, although Kissinger had arrived at Nixon's view by a more scholarly route. As a Harvard professor, he had closely studied the nineteenth-century diplomat Metternich, who at the Vienna Congress of 1815 crafted a balance-of-power system that stabilized Europe for an entire century.

Conducting foreign affairs Metternich's way, however, required a degree of secrecy that was antithetical to America's constitutional system. Nixon and Kissinger did the best they could. They bypassed Congress, cut out the State Department (including the secretary of state, William Rogers), and established "back channels" to agencies whose expertise they needed. It was a dangerous game, but for a time, a game they played successfully. Nixon and Kissinger were preparing to take advantage of international conditions ripe for change.

For one thing, all the major players faced significant internal unrest. It was not only the United States that was rocked by student protesters. Street rioting almost brought down the French government in May 1968. German universities were hotbeds of protest. On the Communist side, it had taken Russian tanks to put down a reformist challenge — the "Prague Spring" — in Czechoslovakia. But tanks only put down people; they couldn't put down dissident ideas, which seeped even into the Soviet Union. And in China, Mao Zedong's Cultural Revolution had gotten out of hand, with young Red Guards turning on the regime. A shared sense of internal fragility made all the major powers receptive to an easing of international tensions.

Ultimately of greater importance, however, was an upheaval in the original arrangement of the Cold War. The notion of a bipolar world no longer held. Once the Cold War stalemated around 1950, neither superpower found it possible to keep its side in line. In America's case, the most difficult partner was France, which under the imperious Charles de Gaulle, thumbed its nose at the United States and walked away from NATO. That, however, was nothing compared to Soviet relations with China, which by 1969 had deteriorated from eternal friendship into outright border warfare, with the possibility of a nuclear exchange not excluded.

Nixon saw his chance. In 1971 he sent Kissinger secretly to Beijing (Peking) to explore an accommodation. Mao was actually thinking along the same lines. So an arrangement was not difficult to arrive at. The United States would back away from the Chinese Nationalists on Taiwan, permit China's admission to the United Nations (with a permanent seat on the Security Council), and eventually grant recognition (in 1978). In February 1972, President Nixon arrived in Beijing in a blaze of publicity to ratify the deal. This was the man who had clawed his

Nixon in China
When President Nixon arrived in China in February 1972 to ratify détente with Mao Zedong, a required part of the visit was a tour of the Great Wall. In this photograph, Mao is on the president's left, Secretary of State William Rogers on his right. @ Bettmann/Corbis.

way into prominence by railing against the Democrats for "losing" China and hounding Alger Hiss into prison. Nixon's credentials as an anti-Communist were impeccable. That was why he felt free to come to Beijing, he remarked genially to Mao. "Those on the right can do what those on the left only talk about." Mao responded: "I like rightists."

Nixon then turned to the Soviet Union. He had already reached a secret understanding with Leonid Brezhnev, the Soviet premier, about Cuban issues left hanging after the missile crisis of 1962. In exchange for an American promise not to invade, the Soviets agreed to dismantle a submarine base and withhold offensive missiles from Castro. Three months after the Beijing summit, Nixon journeyed in another blaze of publicity to Moscow to sign the first Strategic Arms Limitations Treaty (SALT I) limiting the production and deployment of intercontinental ballistic missiles (ICBMs) and antiballistic missile systems (ABMs). SALT I, while technically modest, was intended only as a first step toward comprehensive arms limitation.

The summits in Beijing and Moscow inaugurated what came to be known as **détente** (in French: "relaxation of tensions"). Although the agreements themselves were quite limited, and rocky times lay ahead, the fact was the Cold War had reached a turning point. Nixon had parlayed a strategic advantage — the dangerous rift in the Communist world — into a new tripartite balance of power. The world had become a less dangerous place. And Nixon hoped for a dividend over Vietnam.

Nixon's War

Vietnam became an American project in the 1950s on the assumption that containing Communism was a global struggle, East against West, with Vietnam on the front line. The concept of a bipolar world, already outmoded in Lyndon Johnson's time, was utterly refuted by Richard Nixon's embrace of détente. Yet, when it came to Vietnam, Nixon picked up where Johnson had left off. Abandoning Vietnam, Nixon insisted, would damage America's "credibility" and make it seem "a pitiful, helpless giant." And, like Johnson, Nixon had himself to consider. He was not going to be the first American president to lose a war. Nixon wanted peace, but only "peace with honor."

The North Vietnamese were not about to oblige him. The only outcome acceptable to them was a unified Vietnam under their control. What remained negotiable were the details, the terms of surrender, and that, plus the wiliness of the North Vietnamese negotiators, enabled the Paris talks begun by Johnson to continue, intermittently. But on the essentials, North Vietnam was immovable. So Nixon fashioned a two-pronged response.

To damp down criticism at home, he began withdrawing American troops while delegating the ground fighting to the South Vietnamese. Under this new policy of "Vietnamization," American troop levels dropped from 543,000 in 1968, to 334,000 in 1971, to barely 24,000 by early 1973. American casualties, and the political liabilities they entailed, dropped correspondingly. But the killing in Vietnam continued. As the U.S. ambassador to Vietnam, Ellsworth Bunker, noted cynically, it was just a matter of changing "the color of the bodies."

The companion policy called for an intensified bombing campaign, concealed from the war-weary American public. To step up the pressure, Nixon in March 1969 ordered secret air attacks on neutral Cambodia, through whose territory the North Vietnamese had been moving supplies and reinforcements. The secret war on Cambodia culminated on April 30, 1970, in an "incursion" into Cambodia to destroy enemy havens there. In late 1971, as American troops withdrew from the region, Communist forces infiltrated back in and stepped up their attacks. The next spring North Vietnamese forces launched a major offensive against South Vietnam. In April, as the fighting intensified, Nixon ordered B-52 bombing raids against North Vietnam, and a month later he approved the mining of North Vietnamese ports, something Johnson had never dared do. Nixon had a freer hand because, in the "spirit" of détente, China no longer threatened to intervene. Nor was Brezhnev deterred from welcoming Nixon in May 1972 at the height of the B-52 bombing onslaught (causing some Soviet casualties). The North Vietnamese might have felt more isolated, but supplies from China and the USSR continued, and they fought on.

At home, Nixon's war exacted a huge toll. Far from abating, the antiwar movement intensified. On November 16, 1969, Mobilization Day brought a record half a million protesters to Washington. A secret war, moreover, could be kept secret only for so long. When news of the invasion of Cambodia came out, American campuses exploded in outrage and, for the first time, students died. On May 4, 1970, at Kent State University in Ohio, panicky National Guardsmen fired into an antiwar rally, killing four students and wounding eleven. At Jackson State College in Mississippi, Guardsmen stormed a dormitory, killing two black students. More than 450 colleges closed in protest; across the country the spring semester was essentially canceled.

Pro-War Rally
Under a sea of American flags, construction workers in New York City march in support of the Vietnam War. Tens of thousands of them wearing "hard hats" jammed Broadway for four blocks opposite City Hall, and the overflow crammed the side streets. Working-class patriotism became a main source of support for Nixon's war. Paul Fusco/Magnum Photos, Inc.

The Vietnam poison infected even the military. In November 1969, the story of the My Lai Massacre broke, revealing the slaughter of 350 Vietnamese villagers by U.S. troops in retaliation for earlier casualties they had taken. The young lieutenant in command, William Calley, was court-martialed, sentenced to life imprisonment, then released to his barracks at Nixon's order, and eventually paroled. As the war dragged on, morale sank. Troops refused to go into combat; thousands deserted or turned to drugs. Many sewed peace symbols on their uniforms. In the heat of battle, overbearing junior officers were sometimes "fragged" — killed or wounded by grenades of their own soldiers. At home, a group called Vietnam Veterans against the War turned in their combat medals at demonstrations outside the U.S. Capitol.

Despite everything, Nixon persevered, hunkering down in the White House, castigating student protesters as "bums," and rallying a potent backlash against them. "Hardhat" became a patriotic symbol after New York construction workers beat demonstrators at a peace rally in May 1970. Slowly, Vietnamization eroded the antiwar opposition. With the army's manpower needs reduced, the draft was cut back (and ended entirely in 1973), deflating the ardor of many antiwar students. And militant groups, like the SDS, splintered and became ineffective, while the SDS's violent offshoot, the Weathermen, were arrested or driven underground. In the end, Nixon outlasted his critics. What he couldn't outlast was North Vietnam.

With the 1972 election approaching, Nixon sent Henry Kissinger back to the Paris peace talks. In a key concession, Kissinger accepted the continued

The Fall of Saigon
After the 1973 U.S. withdrawal from Vietnam, the South Vietnamese government lasted another two years. In March 1975 the North Vietnamese forces launched a final offensive and by April they had surrounded the capital of Saigon. Here, panicked Vietnamese seek sanctuary at the U.S. embassy compound. Nik Wheeler/Sipa Press.

presence of North Vietnamese troops in South Vietnam. North Vietnam then agreed to an interim arrangement whereby the Saigon government would stay in power while a tripartite commission arranged elections and a final settlement. American prisoners of war would be returned, and the remaining U.S. troops withdrawn. With Kissinger's announcement that "peace is at hand," Nixon got the election lift he wanted, but the agreement was then sabotaged by General Nguyen Van Thieu, the South Vietnamese president. So Nixon, in one final spasm of blood-letting, unleashed the two-week "Christmas bombing," the most savage of the entire war. On January 27, 1973, the two sides signed the Paris Peace Accords, essentially restating the cease-fire agreement of the previous October. The United States might have achieved that agreement four years earlier had it been willing to accept North Vietnamese troops in the South.

Nixon hoped that, with massive U.S. aid, the Thieu regime might survive. But Congress was in revolt. It refused appropriations for bombing Cambodia after August 15, 1973, and gradually cut back aid to South Vietnam. In March 1975 North Vietnamese forces launched a final offensive. On television, horrified American viewers watched as South Vietnamese officials and soldiers battled American embassy personnel to board the last helicopters out of Saigon. On April 29, 1975, Vietnam was reunited. Saigon was renamed Ho Chi Minh City, after the founding father of the Communist regime.

Did this sad outcome matter? Yes, certainly, for America's Vietnamese allies, who lost jobs and property, spent years in "re-education" camps, or fled the country. Yes, for next-door Cambodia, where the maniac Khmer Rouge took over, murdered 1.7 million people, and drove the country nearly back to the Stone Age. For the United States, yes, for the wasted lives (58,000 dead, 300,000 wounded), the $150 billion spent, the slow-to-heal internal wounds, the lost confidence in America's political leaders. But in geopolitical terms? Not really. Defeat in South Vietnam did not mean, as successive American administrations had feared, victory for the Communist side because there no longer was a Communist "side." The Hanoi regime called itself Communist, but never intended to be anybody's satellite, least of all China's, an ancient enemy. (Within a few years the two countries fell to fighting over disputed borders.) Today, after twenty years of embargo, America's relations with the People's Republic of Vietnam are normal, with diplomatic recognition granted in 1995. That event would hardly be worth mentioning but for the fact that it is a postscript to America's most disastrous military adventure of the twentieth century.

The 1972 Election

The Democrats had fallen into disarray after 1968. Swept up by reform enthusiasms, followers of George McGovern took over the party, adopting new rules intended to encourage grassroots participation and assure that women, blacks, and young people held delegate seats "in reasonable relation to their presence in the population." Benefiting from these guidelines, McGovern's army of antiwar activists blitzed the precinct-level caucuses, winning delegate commitments far beyond McGovern's actual party support. Fresh faces filled the 1972 convention—38 percent women, 15 percent black, 23 percent under thirty (compared to 2.6 percent in 1968)—bursting with enthusiasm, but mostly innocent of national politics. In the past, an alliance of urban machines, labor unions, and ethnic groups—the heart of the New Deal coalition—would almost certainly have rejected an upstart candidate like McGovern. But few of the party faithful qualified as delegates under the changed rules. The crowning insult came when the convention rejected the credentials of Chicago Mayor Richard Daley and his delegation, seating instead an Illinois delegation led by Jesse Jackson, a firebrand young black minister and former aide of Martin Luther King.

Capturing the party was one thing; winning a national election quite another. McGovern was, in fact, a weak campaigner. He started badly at the convention, which was in bedlam when he finally delivered his acceptance speech at 2:30 A.M. His running mate, Senator Thomas Eagleton of Missouri, turned out to have a history of mental illness and had to be replaced. And McGovern failed to mollify key party backers like the AFL-CIO, which, for the first time in memory, refused to endorse the Democratic ticket.

McGovern was no match for Nixon, who pulled out all the stops. Using the advantages of incumbency, he gave the economy a well-timed lift and proclaimed (prematurely) a cease-fire in Vietnam. Nixon's appeal to the "silent majority"—people who "care about a strong United States, about patriotism, about moral and spiritual values"—was by now well-honed, with added wrinkles about "forced" busing and law and order.

Nixon won in a landslide, receiving nearly 61 percent of the popular vote and carrying every state except Massachusetts and the District of Columbia. The returns revealed how fractured traditional Democratic voting blocs had become. McGovern received only 38 percent of the big-city Catholic vote, and overall lost 42 percent of self-identified Democrats. The 1972 election marks a pivotal moment in the country's shift to the right. The full effect of that shift was delayed, however, by the president's soon-to-be-discovered self-inflicted wounds.

Watergate

On June 17, 1972, a funny thing happened at the Watergate complex in Washington, D.C. Early that morning, five men carrying wiretapping equipment were apprehended breaking into the Democratic National Committee's (DNC) headquarters. The arrest of two accomplices soon followed. Queried by the press, a White House spokesman dismissed the episode as "a third-rate burglary attempt." Wiretap equipment? At the DNC headquarters? Pressed further, Nixon himself denied any White House involvement in "this very bizarre incident."

In fact, the two kingpins, G. Gordon Liddy and E. Howard Hunt, were former FBI and CIA agents currently working for Nixon's Committee to Reelect the President (CREEP). Earlier they had been on the White House payroll, hired in 1971 after the publication by the *New York Times* of the Pentagon Papers, a classified history of American involvement in Vietnam up to 1967, before Nixon's time. Even so, Nixon was enraged at the leak by Daniel Ellsberg, one of Washington's "best and brightest" and a trusted Pentagon insider. In response, the president set up a clandestine squad, known as the "plumbers" because their job was to plug administration leaks and do other nasty jobs. Hunt and Liddy, two of the plumbers, burglarized Ellsberg's psychiatrist's office in an unsuccessful effort to discredit him. Now, as CREEP operatives, they were arranging illegal wiretaps at DNC headquarters, part of a campaign of "dirty tricks" against the Democrats.

The Watergate burglary was no isolated incident. It was part of a broad pattern of illegality and misuse of power by a White House obsessed with the antiwar movement and prepared to fight its critics by any means, fair or foul. That siege mentality best explains why Nixon took a fatal misstep. He could have dissociated himself from the break-in by dismissing his guilty aides, or even just by letting justice take its course. But it was election time, and Nixon hung tough. He arranged hush money for the burglars and instructed the CIA to stop an FBI investigation into the affair. This was obstruction of justice, a criminal offense.

The Wheels of Justice. Nixon kept the lid on until after the election, but then, as the wheels of justice turned, the lid came off. In January 1973, the Watergate burglars were found guilty. One of them, the security chief for CREEP, began to talk. In the meantime, two tenacious reporters at the *Washington Post,* Carl Bernstein and Bob Woodward, uncovered CREEP's illegal "slush fund" and its links to key White House aides. (Their informant, famously known as Deep Throat, was finally revealed in 2005 to be the second-in-command at the FBI, W. Mark Felt.) In May a Senate investigating committee began holding nationally televised hearings, at which Assistant Secretary of Commerce Jeb Magruder confessed his guilt and implicated former Attorney General John Mitchell, White House Counsel John Dean, and others. Dean, in turn, implicated Nixon. Just as startling, a former White House aide revealed that Nixon had installed a secret taping system in the Oval Office.

Citing executive privilege, Nixon refused to surrender his tapes. Under enormous pressure, he eventually released sanitized transcripts and some of the tapes, but with a highly suspicious eighteen-minute gap. Finally, on June 23, 1974, the Supreme Court ordered Nixon to release the unexpurgated tapes. Lawyers were astounded to find in them incontrovertible evidence that the president had ordered the cover-up six days after the break-in. By then, the House Judiciary Committee was already considering articles of impeachment. Certain that he would be convicted by the Senate, on August 9, 1974, Nixon became the first U.S. president to resign his office.

The next day Vice President Gerald Ford was sworn in as president. Ford, the Republican minority leader in the House of Representatives, had replaced Vice President Spiro Agnew, who had himself resigned in 1973 for accepting kickbacks while governor of Maryland. The transfer of power proceeded smoothly. A month later, however, Ford stunned the nation by granting Nixon a "full, free, and absolute" pardon "for all offenses he had committed or might have committed during his presidency." Ford took that action, he said, to spare the country the agony of Nixon's criminal prosecution.

Aftermath. In Moscow, puzzled Kremlin leaders suspected a giant right-wing conspiracy against Nixon. They could not understand, recalled the Soviet ambassador to Washington at the time, "how a powerful president could be forced to resign . . . because of what they saw as a minor breach of conduct. Soviet history knew no parallel." That was one meaning of Watergate — that, in America, the rule of law prevailed (just barely; Nixon likely would have survived had he destroyed the tapes). A second meaning involved the constitutional separation of powers. As commander-in-chief, Nixon asserted unlimited authority, including wiretapping or worse, in the name of national security and, like the Kremlin leaders, he was perplexed at being brought down by a "pigmy-sized" incident like Watergate.

Congress pushed back, passing a raft of laws against the abuses of the Nixon administration — the War Powers Act (1973), reining in the president's ability to deploy U.S. forces without congressional approval; the Freedom of Information Act (1974), protecting privacy and access to federal records; the Fair Campaign Practices Act (1974), limiting and regulating contributions in presidential campaigns; and the Federal Intelligence Surveillance Act (1978), prohibiting domestic wiretapping without a warrant. Only in the short run, however, can it be said that these measures curbed America's tendency to embrace an imperial presidency.

▶ Why is the Nixon presidency considered a transitional one between the liberalism of the preceding decades and the conservatism that emerged in the 1980s?

▶ What do we mean when we say that Nixon was a "realist" in foreign affairs?

▶ Why did it take Nixon four years to reach a settlement with North Vietnam?

▶ How do you account for the Watergate scandal? What was its significance?

Battling for Civil Rights: The Second Stage

In the midst of Nixon's travail, the civil rights struggle continued, now entering a second, more complicated stage. In the first stage, the landmark achievements—*Brown v. Board of Education* (1954), the Civil Rights Act of 1964, and the Voting Rights Act of 1965—had been bitterly resisted, but once those battles ended, the moral atmosphere shifted. In principle, at any rate, Americans no longer defended segregation, or racial discrimination, or the denial of voting rights. But now the time came for enforcing those rights, sometimes, it turned out, at the expense of other Americans—and that meant strife. In the 1970s, moreover, the battle lines shifted from race to gender, as women, and then gays, mobilized and demanded equal rights. For many Americans, that was a great deal harder to handle because equality of the sexes hit closer to home than did racial equality. The effect was galvanizing. If the battle for equal rights had entered a second stage, so did the evolution of the conservative movement, increasingly driven as it now was by moral values and religious faith.

The Revival of Feminism

In the postwar years feminism was a languishing movement, with few advocates and no burning issues. That changed dramatically during the 1960s, initially sparked by the black civil rights movement, and then by the decade's broader social upheaval. But the revival of feminism also sprang from the deeply felt needs of many women at this juncture in their lives.

One spark was Betty Friedan's indictment of suburban domesticity, *The Feminine Mystique*, which appeared in 1963 (see Chapter 27). White, college-educated, middle-class women read Friedan's book and thought, "She's talking about me." *The Feminine Mystique*, after a slow start, became a runaway best seller. It gave women a vocabulary with which to express their dissatisfaction and made them believe that self-realization was attainable through jobs, education, and escape from mind-deadening domesticity.

Paradoxically, *The Feminine Mystique* was a bit out of date by the time it appeared. The domesticity it described was already crumbling. More and more women were working, including married women (40 percent by 1970) and mothers with preschool children (30 percent by 1970). After the postwar baby boom, women were again having fewer children, aided now by the birth control pill, first marketed in 1960, and the intrauterine device (IUD). At the same time the divorce rate, on the rise for the past century, speeded up as the states liberalized divorce laws. Educational levels were also rising; by 1970 women made up 42 percent of the college population. All these changes undermined traditional gender roles and enabled women, as they read *The Feminine Mystique*, to embrace its liberating prescriptions.

Budding feminists also received positive signals from Washington. In 1961, Kennedy appointed a Presidential Commission on the Status of Women, which issued a 1963 report documenting employment and educational discrimination against women. The result was some minor legislation, but, more importantly, a rudimentary network of activist women in public life that had formed in the course of the commission's work. A bigger breakthrough resulted by sheer inadvertence. Hoping to derail the pending Civil Rights Act of 1964, a key conservative, Representative Howard Smith of Virginia, mischievously added "sex" to the categories protected against discrimination under Title VII. The act passed anyway, and, to everyone's surprise, women suddenly had a powerful tool for fighting sex discrimination—provided, of course, that the Equal Employment Opportunity Commission (EEOC) could be prodded into doing its job.

With that objective in mind, Friedan and others founded the National Organization for Women (NOW) in 1966. Modeled on the NAACP, NOW intended to be a civil rights organization for women, with the aim of bringing "women into full participation in . . . American society now, exercising all the privileges and responsibilities thereof in truly equal partnership with men"—a classic statement of feminism. Under Friedan, who served as NOW's first president, membership grew from 1,000 in 1967 to 15,000 in 1971, and NOW became, like the NAACP, a powerful voice for equal rights.

The 1960s spawned another branch of feminists, the women's liberationists, primarily younger, college-educated women who had earned their spurs in the civil rights, New Left, and the antiwar movements. To their chagrin, they discovered that the male leaders of these movements were no better than the frat boys they had known in college. Women who tried to raise feminist issues were shouted off the platform with jeers like "Move on, little girl, we have more important issues to talk about here than women's liberation."

Fed up with this treatment, women radicals broke away and began their own movement. Unlike NOW, women's liberation had little formal structure and was best described as an alliance of loose collectives that had formed in New York, San Francisco, and other big cities. "Women's lib," as it was dubbed by a skeptical media, went public in 1968 at the Miss America pageant. Most eye-catching was a "freedom trash can" into which women were invited to fling false eyelashes, hair curlers, brassieres, and girdles—all

Women's Liberation
Arguing that beauty contests were degrading to women, members of the National Women's Liberation Party staged a protest against the Miss America pageant held in Atlantic City, New Jersey, in September 1968. AP Images.

branded as symbols of female oppression. Women's liberation was a phenomenon of the 1960s, mirroring the identity politics of Black Power activists and the self-dramatization of the counterculture.

An activity more broadly experienced was "consciousness raising"—group sessions in which women shared their experiences. Swapping stories about being passed over for a promotion, needing a husband's signature on a credit card application, or enduring whistles and leers on the streets, participants began to realize that their individual problems were part of a wider pattern of oppression.

Feminism at High Tide. Before 1969 most women heard about NOW and other feminist organizations by word of mouth. After that, the media brought women's issues to a wider audience. New terms such as *sexism* and *male chauvinism* became part of the national vocabulary. As converts flooded in, the two branches of the women's movement began to converge. Radical women realized that key feminist goals—child care, equal pay, and abortion rights—could best be achieved in the political arena. At the same time, more traditional activists developed a broader view of women's oppression. Although still largely white and middle class, feminists began to think of themselves as part of a broad and growing social crusade. Only later did the movement grapple with the fact that as much divided women—race, class, age, sexual preference—as united them.

U.S. Women's Lightweight Crew
Crew was one of those muscle sports from which college women had traditionally been excluded until Title IX came along and opened the sport to women. Some of the best of that first generation of college rowers ended up on the U.S. women's team competing in the Canadian Regatta in 1982, shown at left. The rower in the bow seat (far right) is the daughter of one of the co-authors of this text. Private collection.

Women's opportunities expanded dramatically in higher education. Formerly all-male bastions, such as Yale, Princeton, and the U.S. Military Academy, admitted women undergraduates for the first time. Hundreds of colleges started women's studies programs, and the proportion of women attending graduate and professional schools rose markedly. With the adoption of Title IX in 1972, Congress broadened the 1964 Civil Rights Act to include educational institutions, prohibiting colleges and universities that received federal funds from discriminating on the basis of sex. By requiring comparable funding for sports programs, Title IX made women's athletics a real presence on college campuses.

Women also became increasingly visible in public life. The National Women's Political Caucus, founded in 1971, actively promoted the election of women to public office. Bella Abzug, Elizabeth Holtzman, Shirley Chisholm, Patricia Schroeder, and Geraldine Ferraro served in Congress; Ella T. Grasso became Connecticut's governor in 1974, as did Dixie Lee Ray in Washington State in 1976. Women's political mobilization produced significant legislative and administrative gains. Congress authorized child-care tax deductions for working parents in 1972, and in 1974 passed the Equal Credit Opportunity Act, which enabled married women to get credit, including credit cards and mortgages, in their own names. In 1977, 20,000 women went to Houston for the first National Women's Conference. Their "National Plan of Action" represented a hard-won consensus on topics ranging from violence against women to homemakers' rights, the needs of older women, and, most controversially, abortion and other reproductive issues.

Phyllis Schlafly: The Equal Rights Amendment, Defeated. Buoyed by its successes, the women's movement renewed the fight for an Equal Rights Amendment (ERA) to the Constitution. First introduced in Congress in 1923, the ERA stated in its entirety, "Equality of rights under the law shall not be denied or abridged by the United States or any State on the basis of sex." In the early days, the ERA had split the women's movement, with social reformers fearing that the amendment would jeopardize protective legislation for women. That fear, while not wholly gone, no longer prevented feminists of all varieties from favoring the amendment. As much as anything, the ERA became a symbolic statement of women's equality. Congress enthusiastically adopted the amendment in 1972, and within two years thirty-four states ratified it. But then progress abruptly halted (Map 29.1).

For this, credit goes chiefly to a remarkable woman, Phyllis Schlafly, a lawyer, outspoken anti-Communist, and long-time activist in conservative causes. Despite her own flourishing career, Schlafly advocated traditional roles for women. She liked to bait feminists by opening her speeches with "I'd like to thank my husband for letting me be here tonight." The ERA, she proclaimed, would create an unnatural "unisex society," with women drafted into the army and forced to use single-sex toilets and locker rooms. Her STOP ERA organization galvanized a "silent" population of conservative Americans. Grassroots networks mobilized, showing up at statehouses with home-baked bread and apple pies. As labels on baked goods at one anti-ERA rally expressed it, "My heart and hand went into this dough / For the sake of the family please vote no." It was a message that

Phyllis Schlafly

Phyllis Schlafly, leader of the Stop ERA movement, talks with reporters during a rally at the Illinois State Capitol on March 4, 1975, at a time when the state legislature was considering whether to ratify the Equal Rights Amendment. Schlafly described herself as a housewife and called her strenuous political career a "hobby."
© Bettmann/Corbis.

Map 29.1 States Ratifying the Equal Rights Amendment, 1972–1977

The ratifying process for the Equal Rights Amendment (ERA) went smoothly in 1972 and 1973 but then stalled. The turning point came in 1976, when ERA advocates lobbied extensively, particularly in Florida, North Carolina, and Illinois, but failed to sway the conservative legislatures in those states. After Indiana ratified in 1977, the amendment still lacked three votes toward the three-fourths majority needed for adoption. Efforts to revive the ERA in the 1980s were unsuccessful, and it became a dead issue.

resonated widely, especially among those troubled by the rapid pace of social change (see Comparing American Voices, "Debating the Equal Rights Amendment," pp. 908–909). The ERA never was ratified, despite a congressional extension of the deadline until June 30, 1982.

Gays and Lesbians. Parallel to, and inspired by, the feminist movement, homosexual men and women launched their own protest movement. The crystallizing event was the "Stonewall riot" of 1969 in New York City, when patrons of a gay bar fought back against police harassment. In the assertion of pride that followed, activists began to call themselves *gay* rather than homosexual; founded advocacy groups, newspapers, and political organizations; and offered emotional support to those who "came out" and publicly affirmed their homosexuality. In New York's Greenwich Village, San Francisco's Castro district, and other urban enclaves, vibrant gay communities emerged. In 1973 the National Gay Task Force launched a campaign to make gay men and lesbians a protected group under laws covering employment and housing rights. These efforts succeeded mostly at the local level. During the 1970s Detroit, Boston, Los Angeles, Miami, San Francisco, and other cities passed laws barring discrimination on the basis of sexual preference.

Like the ERA, gay rights came under attack from conservatives. When the Miami city council passed a measure banning discrimination against gay men and lesbians in 1977, the singer Anita Bryant led a campaign to repeal the law by popular referendum. Later that year voters overturned the measure by a two-to-one majority, prompting similar antigay campaigns around the country. Once again, the country was witnessing the clash between equal rights for an oppressed minority and the moral values of a conservative majority.

Enforcing Civil Rights

The Equal Rights Amendment provoked a *political* struggle. Supporters and opponents mobilized and lobbied their legislators. The losing side, bitter though it might be, could not say its voice had been unheard. But to a large degree the civil rights struggle bypassed this democratic process. For one thing, under the American constitutional system fundamental rights trumped majority rule—which was, for example, the basis on which *Brown v. Board of Education* had struck down state-mandated segregated schooling. For another thing, and perhaps more important, *enforcing* civil rights was a judicial and/or executive function. Courts and federal agencies did the heavy lifting. And that—the unaccountability of the key actors—fed the outrage of many Americans already feeling adversely affected by the gains of protected minorities.

Affirmative Action. When Congress banned job discrimination in the Civil Rights Act (1964), all that it intended was that employers hire on a merit basis and without regard to race, religion, ethnicity, or sex. The wave of urban riots made the Johnson administration think again. The Kerner Commission (1968), after investigating the causes behind the rioting, strongly urged a massive federal effort at countering the white racism that held blacks back and deprived them of hope. One result was *affirmative action*—procedures designed to take into account the disadvantaged position of minorities after centuries of discrimination. First advanced by the Labor Department in 1968, affirmative action was refined by a series of court rulings that identified acceptable procedures, including hiring and enrollment goals, special recruitment and training programs, and *set-asides* (specially reserved slots).

Aided by affirmative action, African Americans enrolled in colleges and universities doubled between and 1970 and 1977, to 1.1 million, or 9.3 percent of total student population. Blacks moved into white-collar professions, found new opportunities in civil service, or got better access to union jobs. Latinos did as well, and white women far better.

Affirmative action, however, did not sit well with many whites, who felt the deck was being stacked against them. Complaints began to be heard about "reverse discrimination." Especially troubling were quotas because they were easily abused, tempting employers and college administrators to shoot for the numbers, without too much concern about whether the minorities hired or admitted really merited affirmative action.

In 1978 Allan Bakke, a white man, sued the University of California at Davis Medical School for rejecting him in favor of less qualified minority candidates. The Supreme Court rejected the medical school's quota system, which set aside 16 of 100 places for "disadvantaged" students. The Court ordered Bakke admitted, but indicated that a more flexible approach, in which racial factors could be considered along with other factors, would still pass muster. *Bakke v. University of California* thus upheld affirmative action, but by rejecting straightforward implementation, also called it into question. "Reverse discrimination" had become a rallying cry for conservatives.

Busing. The other main civil rights objective—desegregating the schools—produced far more fireworks. For fifteen years southern states, by a variety of stratagems, had fended off court directives that they move to integration "with all deliberate speed" (see Chapter 27). In 1968, hardly a third of all black children in the South attended schools with whites. At that point, the federal courts got serious and, in a series of stiff decisions, ordered an end to "dual school systems." Where this did not happen, the courts intervened directly. In 1971, in a landmark decision, the Supreme Court imposed a county-wide busing plan on Charlotte-Mecklenberg, North Carolina. In this case, integration went smoothly, and, in fact, the South as a whole essentially gave up the fight. By the mid-1970s, 86 percent of black children were attending school with whites.

But in the North, where segregated schooling was also a fact of life—arising, however, from residential patterns, not legally mandated separation—busing orders sparked intense and sometimes violent opposition. In South Boston, a strongly Irish-Catholic working-class neighborhood, mobs attacked African American students bused in from Roxbury. Armed police were required to keep South Boston High School open.

As a solution to segregation, busing came up against cherished attachments to neighborhood schooling. Busing also had the perverse effect of speeding up "white flight" to the suburbs. The result was egregiously evident in Detroit, where a black city was encircled by white suburbs. To integrate Detroit schools would have required merging city and suburban districts, which in fact was what a lower court ordered in 1971. But in *Milliken v. Bradley* (1974) the Supreme Court overruled the lower court. Thereafter, busing as a means of achieving racial balance fell out of favor. But in the meantime "forced busing," much touted by Nixon in the 1972 campaign, added to the grievances of conservatives, not least by reminding them of how much they hated what they perceived as the arrogance of unelected judges.

COMPARING AMERICAN VOICES

Debating the Equal Rights Amendment

Fifty years after it had first been introduced, Congress in 1972 finally approved the Equal Rights Amendment ("Equality of rights under the law shall not be denied or abridged by the United States or by any State on account of sex") and sent it off to the states for ratification. The amendment set off a furious debate, especially in the South and Midwest. Following are four of the voices in that debate.

J. MARSE GRANT

J. Marse Grant was the editor of the Biblical Recorder *and Chairman of the Baptist State Convention of North Carolina. He delivered these remarks to the Constitutional Amendments Committee of the state legislature.*

Recently I received a letter in which the writer told me to pick up my Bible. . . . He told me to read what God would have me do about ERA. I told him that this is exactly what I had done. And from my Bible I learned long ago that God loves all His children. That He gave them talents and abilities, and that in Him there is no male or female. . . .

The New Testament reveals countless ways in which women are an integral art of Jesus' ministry. He gave them new respect and dignity. He forsook the old traditions of his day—He talked to women in public—He visited in their homes—and it's little wonder, and not just accidentally, in my opinion, that women were the last ones at the cross. They were the first ones at the Resurrection, too. How anyone can distort the teachings of Christ and try to say that Christ was against equality and freedom for all people is hard for me to understand. . . .

It is unfortunate that I am here to apologize today that some here in the church oppose this amendment, but some in the church also opposed the Civil Rights Act in 1964. Some in the church defended slavery and quoted scripture to try to prove it. Some opposed the right of women to vote using many of the fallacious arguments that they are now using against ERA, but they were wrong. Dead wrong.

SOURCE: William A. Link, ed., *The South in the History of the Nation* (Boston: Bedford/St. Martin's, 1999), 293–294.

JERRY FALWELL

Jerry Falwell was a fundamentalist Baptist preacher in Virginia, a television evangelist, and the founder of the Moral Majority (see p. 929 for his photograph).

I believe that at the foundation of the women's liberation movement there is a minority core of women who were once bored with life, whose real problems are spiritual problems. Many women have never accepted their God-given roles. . . . God Almighty created men and women biologically different and with differing needs and roles. He made men and women to complement each other and to love each other. . . . Women who work should be respected and accorded dignity and equal rewards for equal work. But this is not what the present feminist movement and equal rights movement are all about.

The Equal Rights Amendment is a delusion. I believe that women deserve more than equal rights. And, in families and in nations where the Bible is believed, Christian women are honored above men. Only in places where the Bible is believed and practiced do women receive more than equal rights. Men and women have differing strengths. The Equal Rights Amendment can never do for women what needs to be done for them. Women need to know Jesus Christ as their Lord and Savior and be under His Lordship. They need a man who knows Jesus Christ as his Lord and Savior, and they need to be part of a home where their husband is a godly leader and where there is a Christian family. . . . ERA is not merely a political issue, but a moral issue as well. A definite violation of holy Scripture, ERA defies the mandate that "the husband is the head of the wife, even as Christ is the head of the church" (Ep. 5:23). In 1 Peter 3:7 we read that husbands are to give their wives honor as unto the weaker vessel, that they are both heirs together of the grace of life. Because a woman is weaker does mean that she is less important.

SOURCE: Jerry Falwell, *Listen America* (New York: Doubleday, 1980), 150–151.

SAM ERVIN JR.

Sam Ervin Jr. represented North Carolina in the U.S. Senate from 1954 to 1974 and was a key figure in the Watergate investigation. In 1971, he inserted these remarks into the Congressional Record.

Let us consider for a moment whether there be a rational basis for reasonable distinctions between men and women in any of the relationships or undertakings of life.

When He created them, God made physiological and functional differences between men and women. These differences confer upon men a greater capacity to perform arduous and hazardous physical tasks. Some wise people even profess the belief that there may be psychological differences between men and women. To justify their belief, they assert that women possess an intuitive power to distinguish between wisdom and folly, good and evil.

To say these things is not to imply that either sex is superior to the other. It is simply to state the all important truth that men and women complement each other in the relationships and undertakings on which the existence and development of the race depend. . . . The physiological and functional differences between men and women constitute the most important reality. Without them human life could not exist.

For this reason, any country which ignores these differences when it fashions its institutions and makes its laws is woefully lacking in rationality. . . .

The Congress and the legislatures of the various states have enacted certain laws based upon the conviction that the physiological and functional differences between men and women make it advisable to exempt or exclude women from certain arduous and hazardous activities in order to protect their health and safety. . . . Among federal laws of this nature are the Selective Service Act, which confines compulsory military service to men. . . . Among the state laws of this kind are laws which limit hours during which women can work, and bar them from engaging in occupations particularly arduous and hazardous such as mining.

If the Equal Rights Amendment should be interpreted by the Supreme Court to forbid any legal distinctions between men and women, all existing and future laws of this nature would be nullified.

SOURCE: *Congressional Record*, 15 February 1972 (Washington, D.C.: GPO, 1972).

ELIZABETH DUNCAN KOONTZ

Elizabeth Duncan Koontz was a distinguished educator, the first black woman to head the National Education Association and the U.S. Women's Bureau. At the time she made this statement at state legislative hearings on the ERA in 1977, she was assistant state superintendent for public instruction in North Carolina.

A short time ago I had the misfortune to break my foot. . . . The pain . . . did not hurt me as much as when I went into the emergency room and the young woman upon asking me my name, the nature of my ailment, then asked me for my husband's social security number and his hospitalization number. I asked her what did that have to do with my emergency. And she said, "We have to be sure of who is going to pay your bill." I said, "Suppose I'm not married, then." And she said, "Then give me your father's name."

I did not go through that twenty years ago when I was denied the use of that emergency room because of my color. I went through that because there is an underlying assumption that all women in our society are protected, dependent, cared for by somebody who's got a social security number and hospitalization insurance. Never once did she assume I might be a woman who might be caring for my husband, instead of him by me, because of some illness. She did not take into account the fact that one out of almost eight women heading families in poverty today [is] in the same condition as men in families and poverty. . . .

My greater concern is that so many women today . . . oppose the passage of the ERA very sincerely and . . . tell you without batting an eye, "I don't want to see women treated that way." And I speak up, "What way is that?" . . . Women themselves have been a bit misguided. We have mistaken present practice for law, and women have . . . assumed too many times that their present condition cannot change. The rate of divorce, the rate of desertion, the rate of separation, and the death rate of male supporters is enough for us to say: "Let us remove all legal barriers to women and girls making their choices—this state cannot afford it."

SOURCE: Lind & Wheeler, *op cit.*, 295–296.

ANALYZING THE EVIDENCE

▶ J. Marse Grant and Jerry Falwell were both southern Baptists. Both appealed to the Bible in discussing the ERA. Yet they came to opposite conclusions. How do you explain that?

▶ Senator Ervin characterizes his opposition to the ERA as being based on "rational" grounds. What does he mean by that? Would he agree with Falwell that the ERA was "not merely a political issue, but a moral issue as well"?

▶ Falwell speaks of women as "the weaker vessel." Why does Elizabeth Duncan Koontz disagree with that characterization? And what does her disagreement suggest to you about the social divisions underlying the debate over the ERA?

An Antibusing Confrontation in Boston

Tensions over court-ordered busing ran high in Boston in 1976. When a black lawyer tried to cross the city hall plaza during an antibusing demonstration, he became a victim of Boston's climate of racial hatred and violence. This Pulitzer Prize–winning photograph by Stanley Forman for the Boston *Herald American* shows a protester trying to impale the man with a flagpole.
Stanley Forman.

Judicial Activism. The decision that initiated the tumult over busing — *Brown v. Board of Education* (1954) — also triggered a larger judicial revolution. Traditionally, it was liberals, not conservatives, who favored *judicial restraint,* which roughly meant that courts defer to legislatures. After many years, the liberal espousal of judicial restraint finally triumphed in 1937, when the Supreme Court reversed itself and let stand key New Deal laws — to the shock and outrage of conservatives.

That history explains why many respected liberal jurists and legal scholars, while favoring racial equality, objected to the *Brown* decision. They felt it violated principles of judicial restraint they had spent lifetimes defending. What ultimately persuaded them was a shift in the big issues coming before the Court. When property rights had been at stake, conservatives favored activist courts willing to curb antibusiness legislatures. Now that personal rights came to the fore, it was liberals' turn to celebrate activist judges and, preeminently, the man whom President Eisenhower appointed chief justice of the Supreme Court in 1953, Earl Warren. A popular Republican governor of California, Warren surprised many, including Eisenhower, by his robust advocacy of civil rights and civil liberties issues. If conservatives found reason to bewail judicial activism, there was no one they blamed more than Chief Justice Warren.

Consider these landmark Warren Court decisions. On the treatment of criminals: that they had a constitutional right to counsel, including at initial interrogations (1963, 1964), and to be informed by arresting officers of their right to remain silent (1966). On indecency: that pornography was protected by freedom of the press unless shown to be "utterly without redeeming social importance" (1964). On prayers and Bible reading in the schools: that religious ritual of any kind violated the constitutional separation of church and state (1962, 1963). In *Griswold v. Connecticut* (1965), the Supreme Court struck down an 1879 state law prohibiting the purchase and use of contraceptive devices by couples as a violation of their constitutional right of privacy.

Griswold opened the way for *Roe v. Wade* (1973), which declared the anti-abortion laws of Texas and Georgia unconstitutional. Abortions performed during the first trimester were protected by the right of privacy (following *Griswold*). At the time, and afterward, some legal authorities questioned whether the Constitution recognized any such privacy right (which the Court extracted from the Third and Eighth Amendments). Moreover, individual states were already legalizing abortion. Nevertheless, the Supreme Court chose to move forward, translating a policy matter traditionally state-regulated into a national, constitutionally protected right. For the women's movement and liberals generally, *Roe v. Wade* was a great, if unanticipated, victory; for evangelical Christians, Catholics, and conservatives generally, it was a bitter pill. Other rights-creating issues — "coddling" criminals, prohibiting school prayer, protecting pornography — had a polarizing effect. But *Roe v. Wade* was in a class by itself. In 1976 opponents convinced Congress to deny Medicaid funds for abortions, an opening round in a protracted campaign against *Roe* that continues to this day.

- What were the sources of growth for the women's rights movement?
- Why did enforcing civil rights prove more controversial than passing civil rights legislation?
- Why did the conservative/liberal alignment on judicial restraint change after 1954?

Lean Years

On top of everything else, the economy went into a tailspin. Oil supplies suddenly fell short, disrupting industry and sending gas prices sky-high. At the same time the United States found itself challenged by foreign competitors making better and cheaper products. All the economic indicators—inflation, employment, productivity, growth—turned negative. In such times, quality-of-life concerns normally get short shrift. Not in the 1970s, when, along side economic distress, environmental and consumer movements began to flourish.

Energy Crisis

Modern economies run on oil. And if the oil stops, woe follows. Something like that happened to the United States in the 1970s. Once the world's leading producer, the United States by the late 1960s was heavily dependent on imported oil, which mostly came from the Persian Gulf (Figure 29.1). American and European oil companies had discovered and developed the Middle Eastern fields, but control had been wrested away by the emerging Muslim states as they threw off the remnants of European colonialism. Foreign companies still extracted and marketed the oil—only they had the expertise at the time—but under profit-sharing agreements that recognized ownership by the Persian Gulf states. In 1960, they and other oil-rich developing countries formed the Organization of Petroleum Exporting Countries (OPEC). OPEC was a cartel, and had it been a domestic enterprise, it would have been treated as an unlawful conspiracy in restraint of trade. But nothing prevented independent countries from conspiring in restraint of trade. During the 1960s, with the world awash in oil, the OPEC cartel was in fact ineffective.

That changed in 1973, when Egypt and Syria invaded Israel, initiating the Yom Kippur War. Israel prevailed, but only after being resupplied by an emergency American airlift. Already resentful of Western support for Israel (and encouraged by the Soviets), the Arab states declared an oil embargo against the United States, western Europe, and Japan. The effect was devastating, forcing Americans to spend long hours in line at the pumps and pushing gas prices up by 40 percent. Oil had become a political weapon. And the West's vulnerability stood revealed. In 1979, after a second shortage caused by the Iranian revolution, oil prices peaked at $34 a barrel, $31 dollars more than in 1973.

The United States scrambled to meet its energy needs. A national speed limit of 55 miles an hour was imposed to conserve fuel. Americans began to buy smaller, more fuel-efficient cars, only not from Detroit, which was tooled up to produce "gas guzzlers." Pretty soon VWs, Toyotas, and Datsuns (Nissans at a later date) dotted American highways, while sales of American cars slumped. The effect on the economy was considerable because one of every six jobs in the country was generated directly or indirectly by the auto industry. Even worse was the

FIGURE 29.1 U.S. Energy Consumption, 1900–2000

Coal was the nation's primary source of energy until the 1950s, when it was surpassed by oil and natural gas. The revival of coal consumption after 1960 stemmed from new open-pit mining in the West that provided cheaper fuel for power plants. The decline in oil consumption in 1980 reflects the nation's response to the oil crisis of the 1970s, including, most notably, fuel-efficient automobiles. Nuclear energy became an important new fuel source, but after 1990 its contribution leveled off as a result of the safety concerns triggered by the Three Mile Island incident (see pp. 913–914). SOURCE: *World Almanac 2002.*

raging inflation set off by the oil shortage. Worst of all perhaps was the psychic shock to Americans at the discovery that their well-being was hostage to forces beyond their control.

Environmentalism

The energy crisis — and the realization it drove home that the earth's resources were not limitless — gave a huge boost to the environmental movement. In some ways, environmentalism was an offshoot of the 1960s counterculture. Activists talked about the "rights of nature," just as they had about the rights of women or blacks. Civil rights and antiwar activism readily translated into protest tactics against polluters and wilderness destroyers. More fundamentally, however, environmentalism was a feature of America's advanced consumer society. Now that they had the basic necessities, and then some, Americans wanted a quality of life defined by a healthy environment and by access to unspoiled nature.

The modern movement began in 1962 when Rachel Carson published *Silent Spring*, a stunning analysis of the impact of pesticides, most especially DDT, on the food chain. There followed a succession of galvanizing issues — concern over an environmentally destructive Alaskan oil pipeline, a proposed airport in the Florida Everglades, and a huge oil spill in January 1969 off the coast of Santa Barbara, California. Environmentalism became certifiably a mass movement on the first Earth Day, April 22, 1970, when 20 million citizens gathered in communities across the country to express their support for the endangered planet.

Earth Day, 1970

No single event better encapsulated the growing environmental awareness of Americans than the nationwide celebration of the first Earth Day on April 22, 1970. In this photograph, young people in Dallas have just hoisted their placard on a heap of garbage swept up from the city streets. TimeLife Pictures/Getty Images.

Nuclear Energy. The mother of environmental wars in the 1970s was the controversy over nuclear power. Electricity from the atom—what could be better? That was how Americans had greeted the arrival of power-generating nuclear technology in the 1950s. By 1974, utility companies were operating forty-two nuclear power plants, with a hundred more planned. Given the oil crisis, nuclear energy might have seemed a godsend. Besides, unlike coal- or oil-driven plants, nuclear operations produced no air pollutants. But environmentalists saw only the dangers. A meltdown would be catastrophic and so, in slow motion, might be the unsolved problem of radioactive wastes. These fears seemed to be confirmed in March 1979 when the reactor core at a nuclear plant at Three Mile Island near Harrisburg, Pennsylvania, came close to meltdown. A prompt shutdown saved the plant, but the near-catastrophe enabled environmentalists to win the battle over nuclear energy (see Reading American Pictures, "A Near Meltdown at Three Mile Island, 1979," p. 914). After Three Mile Island, the utility industry backed down and stopped building nuclear-powered plants.

The Consumer Movement. Environmentalism helped rekindle a consumer movement that had languished since the Progressive era (see Chapter 20). The key figure was Ralph Nader, a young Harvard-educated lawyer whose book, *Unsafe at Any Speed* (1965), attacked General Motors for putting flashy styling ahead of safety in the engineering of the rear-engine Chevrolet Corvair. Buoyed by his success, Nader in 1969 launched a Washington-based consumer protection organization that spawned a national network of activists fighting everything from consumer fraud to dangerous toys. Staffed largely by student volunteers known as "Nader's Raiders," the organization pioneered such legal tactics as the class-action suit, which enabled lawyers to represent an entire pool of grievants in a single litigation. In Nader's wake, dozens of other groups emerged in the 1970s and afterward to combat the tobacco industry, unethical insurance and credit practices, and a host of other consumer problems.

Environmental Legislation. Environmentalists proved remarkably adept at sparking governmental action. In 1969 Congress passed the National Environmental Policy Act, which required the developers to file environmental impact statements assessing the impact of their projects on particular ecosystems. The next year Nixon established the Environmental Protection Agency (EPA) and signed the Clean Air Act, which established standards for auto emissions that caused air pollution. Following the lead of several states, Congress banned the use of DDT in 1972, and in 1980 created the Superfund to finance the cleanup of toxic waste sites. The Endangered Species Act (1973) expanded the scope of the Endangered Animals Act of 1964, granting species such as snail darters and spotted owls protected status. On the consumer front, a big victory was the establishment of the federal Consumer Products Safety Commission in 1972.

These environmental successes were not, however, universally appreciated. Fuel-economy standards for cars was said to hinder the auto industry as it struggled to keep up with foreign competitors. Corporations resented environmental regulations, but so did many of their workers, who believed that tightened standards threatened their jobs. "IF YOU'RE HUNGRY AND OUT OF WORK, EAT AN ENVIRONMENTALIST" read one labor union's bumper sticker. In a time of rising unemployment, activists clashed head-on with proponents of economic growth and global competitiveness.

Economic Woes

While the energy crisis had dealt a hard blow, the economy was also beset by a host of longer-term problems. The high cost of the Vietnam War and the Great Society contributed to a growing federal deficit and spiraling inflation. In the industrial sector, the country faced growing competition from Germany and Japan. America's share of world trade dropped from 32 percent in 1955 to 18 percent in 1970, and was headed down. As a result, in 1971 the value of the dollar fell to its lowest level since World War II, and the United States posted its first trade deficit in almost a century.

In the 1970s, the country's economic performance turned dismal. Gross domestic product (GDP), which had been increasing at a sizzling 4.1 percent per year in the 1960s, dropped after 1970 to 2.9 percent. In a blow to national pride, nine western European countries surpassed the United States in per capita GDP by 1980. The economy was also characterized by stagnating wages, unemployment, and galloping inflation (Figure 29.2). The devastating combination of unemployment and inflation—*stagflation*, so-called—contradicted a basic principle taught by economists: Prices were not supposed to rise in a stagnant economy. In the 1970s, they did. For ordinary Americans, the reality of

READING AMERICAN PICTURES

A Near Meltdown at Three Mile Island, 1979

Goldsboro, PA. National Archives.

Crisis Management. Jimmy Carter Presidential Library.

Hardly had atomic bombs devastated Japan in 1945 than American leaders began touting the "peaceful" uses of atomic technology, especially the generation of electrical power by nuclear-powered steam turbines. By 1979, nuclear plants were producing 11 percent of the nation's electricity. At that point, dreams of a nuclear-powered America suddenly ended, punctured by a nearly catastrophic accident at the Three Mile Island plant near Harrisburg, Pennsylvania.

On March 28, 1979, the pumps for the Unit 2 reactor shut down, stopping the flow of cooling water and initiating a meltdown of the radioactive core. Had a full meltdown occurred, it would have breached the walls of the containment building and released huge amounts of radiation into the atmosphere. Fortunately, a full meltdown at Three Mile Island was averted. But for several days it was touch-and-go.

ANALYZING THE EVIDENCE

▶ When talk about nuclear energy began, not a lot was said about the fact that the huge plants would have to be placed in somebody's backyard. The first photo shows the neighborhood abutting the Three Mile Island facility. Look carefully at the houses. What sort of people might live there? Would you be happy to live there? What are the social implications of your answer?

▶ The second photograph shows President Carter and his wife Rosalynn inspecting the facility on April 1, 1979, just as the crisis was ending. Carter had been a nuclear engineer. Do you suppose he was there to offer his expertise? If not, what was he doing there?

Nervous Humor. © Batom. North American Syndicate.

▶ The cartoon is a commentary on Carter's visit. What does it portend about the future of nuclear energy in America? What details in the cartoon can you point to that support your answer?

FIGURE 29.2 The Inflation Rate, 1960–2000

The impact of the oil crisis of 1973 on the inflation rate appears all too graphically in Figure 29.2. The dip in 1974 reflects the sharp recession that began that year, after which the inflation rate zoomed up to a staggering 14 percent in 1980. The return to normal levels after 1980 stemmed from very harsh measures by the Federal Reserve Board, which, while they succeeded, came at the cost of a painful slowdown in the economy. SOURCE: *Statistical Abstract of the United States, 2000.*

stagflation was a noticeable decline in the standard of living, as discretionary income per worker dropped 18 percent between 1973 and the early 1980s. Many families were kept afloat only by the second income brought in by working wives.

Deindustrialization. America's economic woes struck hardest in the industrial sector, which suddenly—shockingly—began to be dismantled. Worst hit was the steel industry, which for seventy-five years had been the economy's crown jewel. Its problems were, ironically, partly a product of good fortune. Only the American steel industry had been left unscathed by the devastation of World War II. In the postwar years, that gave U.S. producers an open, hugely profitable field, but it also saddled them with outdated plants and equipment.

When the German and Japanese industries rebuilt—with the aid of American funding and technology—they incorporated the latest and best of everything. Moreover, the American industry's natural advantages were eroding. With its abundant iron-ore reserves exhausted, the industry competed for raw materials on global markets like everyone else. Meanwhile, advances in international shipping deprived it of the comparative advantage of location. Distant from markets and with no natural resources, Japan built a powerhouse of an industry. When Japanese steel flooded in during the 1970s, the American industry was simply overwhelmed. A massive dismantling began, including the entire Pittsburgh district. By the time the smoke cleared in the mid-1980s, the American industry was competitive again, but it was a shadow of its former self.

The steel industry was the prime example of what became known as *deindustrialization*. The country was in the throes of an economic transformation that left it largely stripped of its industrial base. A swath of the Northeast and Midwest, the country's manufacturing heartland, became the nation's "Rust Belt" (Map 29.2), strewn with abandoned plants and dying communities.

Many thousands of blue-collar workers lost well-paid union jobs. What they faced is revealed by the 4,100 steelworkers left jobless by the shutdown of the Campbell Works of the Youngstown Sheet & Tube Co. in 1977. Two years later, a third had retired early, at half pay. Ten percent had moved, mostly to the Sun Belt. Fifteen percent were still jobless, with unemployment benefits long gone. Forty percent had found local work, but mostly in low-paying, service-sector jobs. Most of these Ohio

Map 29.2 From Rust Belt to Sun Belt, 1940–2000

One of the most significant developments of the post–World War II era was the growth of the Sun Belt. Sparked by federal spending for military bases, the defense industry, and the space program, states of the South and Southwest experienced an economic boom in the 1950s (see Map 27.1 on page 838). This growth was further enhanced in the 1970s, as the heavily industrialized regions of the Northeast and Midwest declined, and migrants from what was quickly dubbed the "Rust Belt" headed to the South and West in search of jobs.

steelworkers had fallen from their perch in the middle class.

Organized Labor in Decline. Deindustrialization dealt harshly with the labor movement. In the early 1970s, as inflation hit, the number of strikes surged; 2.4 million workers participated in work stoppages in 1970 alone. Challenged by foreign competition, industry became more resistant to union demands, and labor's bargaining power waned. In these hard years, the much-vaunted labor-management accord of the 1950s went bust. Instead of higher wages, unions now mainly fought to save jobs. In the 1970s union membership dropped sharply, with industrial unions — the Rust Belt unions — especially hard hit. By the end of the 1980s, only 16 percent of American workers were organized (See Figure 27.2, p. 836).

The impact on liberal politics was huge. With labor's decline, a main buttress of the New Deal coalition was coming undone.

Taxpayer Revolts. The economic crisis also hardened anti-tax sentiment, reversing a postwar spirit of generous public investment. The premier example was California, which after World War II created, among other achievements, an unrivaled system of higher education. With stagflation, real estate values rocketed upward, and so did property taxes. Especially hard hit were retirees and others on fixed incomes. Into this dire situation stepped Howard Jarvis, an anti-New Dealer cut to the same cloth as the ERA-hating Phyllis Schlafly and, like her, a genius at mobilizing a grassroots movement. Despite opposition by virtually the entire state establishment, Californians in 1978 voted overwhelmingly

Symbol of the Rust Belt

A padlock on the gate of Youngstown, Ohio's United States Steel mill symbolizes the creation of the Rust Belt in the 1970s. Economic hard times caused widespread plant closures in the industrial areas of the Midwest and Northeast and an exodus to the booming Sun Belt (see Map 29.2). © Bettmann/Corbis.

for Proposition 13, which rolled back property taxes, capped future increases, and harnessed all tax measures, state or local, to a two-thirds voting requirement. As a vehicle for hobbling public spending, Prop 13 was extraordinarily effective. Per capita funding of California public schools plunged from the top tier to the bottom (next to Mississippi). Prop. 13 also pulled off the neat trick of hugely benefiting, under the shelter of California's elderly, wealthy homeowners and businesses (commercial property got the same protection). More broadly, Prop. 13 inspired tax revolts across the country and gave conservatives an enduring issue: No New Taxes.

➤ Why did the United States enter an energy crisis in the 1970s?

➤ What were the major concerns of the environmentalist movement?

➤ What were the causes and effects of deindustrialization?

Politics in the Wake of Watergate

Nixon's resignation in 1974 left American politics in limbo. Popular disdain for politicians, already evident in declining voter turnout, deepened. "Don't vote. It only encourages them," read one bumper stick in 1976. Watergate damaged short-term Republican prospects, but also created an opening for the party's right wing. It was telling that Gerald Ford, in advance of his 1976 reelection bid, dumped his vice president, Nelson Rockefeller, a liberal Republican, for a conservative running mate, Senator Robert Dole of Kansas. As for the Democrats, Watergate granted them a reprieve, a second chance at recapturing their eroding base. But that required leadership, not something the party's freewheeling rules for choosing a candidate could guarantee. Any governor with a nice head of hair, a winning manner, some money in the bank, and a semblance of organization had a shot at the party's nomination.

Jimmy Carter: The Outsider as President

"Jimmy Who?" was how journalists first responded when James E. Carter, governor of Georgia and self-styled peanut farmer, emerged from the pack and went on to win the Democratic nomination. Trading on Watergate, Carter pledged to restore morality to the White House. "I will never lie to you," he promised voters. Carter played up his credentials as a Washington outsider, although he made sure, in selecting Senator Walter F. Mondale of Minnesota, to have a running mate with ties to traditional Democratic voting blocs. Ford, still wounded by his pardon of Nixon and with little to boast about as a caretaker president, was a fairly easy mark. Carter won with 50 percent of the popular vote to Ford's 48 percent.

For a time, Carter got some mileage out of casting himself as an outsider, the common man who walked back to the White House after the Inauguration, delivered fireside chats in a cardigan sweater,

A Framework for Peace

After two weeks of intense personal diplomacy, President Jimmy Carter persuaded President Anwar el-Sadat of Egypt (left) and Prime Minister Menachem Begin of Israel (right) to sign a peace treaty in 1978. The signing of the Camp David Accords marked an important first step in constructing a framework for peace in the Middle East. This was Carter's greatest foreign-policy achievement. David Rubinger/TimeLife Pictures/Getty Images.

and carried his own bags. The fact that he was a born-again Christian also played well. But Carter's inexperience began to tell. His outsider strategy distanced him from established congressional leaders. Shying away from the Democratic establishment, Carter relied heavily on inexperienced advisers and friends from Georgia. And he himself, a prodigious worker, was an inveterate micromanager, exhausting himself over details best left to subordinates.

Economic Policy. On the domestic front, Carter's big challenge was managing the economy. The problems he faced defied easy solution. Most confounding was stagflation. If the government focused on the inflation side — forcing prices down by increasing taxes or raising interest rates — unemployment became worse. If the government tried to stimulate employment, inflation became worse. Seeking to cut through this conundrum, Nixon had imposed price and wage controls in 1971, a brave try, but one that created more problems than it solved.

Carter lacked Nixon's daring. At heart, in fact, he was an economic conservative. He toyed with the idea of an "industrial policy" to bail out the ailing manufacturing sector, but moved instead in a free-market direction by lifting the New Deal–era regulation of the airline, trucking, and railroad industries. **Deregulation** stimulated competition and cut prices, but also drove firms out of business and hurt unionized workers.

Taking office after a sharp mid-1970s downturn, Carter offered a stimulus package that was at cross-purposes with his Federal Reserve Board's program of attacking inflation by raising interest rates. Then turmoil in the Middle East in 1979 curtailed oil supplies, and gas prices jumped again. In a major TV address, Carter lectured Americans about the nation's "crisis of confidence" and "crisis of the spirit." He called energy conservation "the moral equivalent of war" — or, in the media's shorthand, "MEOW," aptly capturing the nation's assessment of Carter's homily. By then, his approval rating had fallen below 30 percent. And no wonder: an inflation rate over 11 percent, failing

VOICES FROM ABROAD

Fei Xiaotong
America's Crisis of Faith

Fei Xiaotong, a Chinese anthropologist and sociologist, wrote influential books on the United States during World War II and the 1950s. Despite his criticism of U.S. foreign policy, his often sympathetic treatment of America contributed to twenty years of political ostracism in China. Regaining prominence in the late 1970s, he joined an official delegation to the United States in 1979. When he returned to China, Fei wrote a series of essays entitled "Glimpses of America." In this passage, he responds to President Jimmy Carter's assertion in his famous "malaise" speech of 1979 that Americans faced a spiritual crisis.

I read in the newspaper that the energy crisis in the United States is getting worse and worse. I hear that after spending several days of quiet thought in his mountain retreat, President Carter decided that America's real problem is not the energy crisis but a "crisis of faith." The way it is told is that vast numbers of people have lost their faith in the present government and in the political system, and do not believe that the people in the government working with current government methods can solve the present series of crises. Even more serious, he believes that the masses have come to have doubts about traditional American values, and if this continues, in his opinion, the future of America is terrible to imagine. He made a sad and worried speech. I have not had an opportunity to read the text of his speech, but if he has truly realized that the present American social system has lost popular support, that should be considered a good thing because at least it shows that the old method of just treating the symptoms will no longer work.

In fact, loss of faith in the present social system on the part of the broad masses of the American people did not begin with the energy crisis. The spectacular advances in science and technology in America in the last decade or two and the unceasing rise in the forces of production are good. But the social system remains unchanged, and the relations of production are basically the same old capitalism. This contradiction between the forces of production and the relations of production has not lessened but become deeper. The ruling class, to be sure, still has the power to keep on finding ways of dealing with the endless series of crises, but the masses of people are coming increasingly to feel that they have fallen unwittingly into a situation where their fate is controlled by others, like a moth in a spiderweb, unable to struggle free. Not only the blacks of Harlem—who are clearly able to earn their own living but still have to rely on welfare to support themselves without dignity—but even well-off families in gardenlike suburban residences worry all day that some accident may suddenly rob them of everything. As the dependence of individuals on others grows heavier and heavier, each person feels in his heart that this society is no longer to be relied on. . . . No wonder people complain that civilization was created by humans, but humans have been enslaved by it. Such a feeling is natural in a society like America's. Carter is right to call this feeling of helplessness a "crisis of faith," for it is a doubting of the present culture. Only he should realize that the present crisis has been long in the making and is already deep. . . .

These "Glimpses of America" essays may be brought to a close here, but to end with the crisis of faith does violence to my original intention. History is a stream that flows on and cannot be stopped. Words must be cut off, but history goes bubbling on. It is inconceivable that America will come to a standstill at any crisis point. I have full faith in the great American people and hope that they will continue to make even greater contributions to the progress of mankind. . . .

SOURCE: R. David Arkush and Leo O. Lee, trans. and eds., *Land Without Ghosts: Chinese Impressions of America from the Mid-Nineteenth Century to the Present* (Berkeley: University of California Press, 1989).

ANALYZING THE EVIDENCE

- Xiaotong is writing about America as someone schooled in Marxist (or Communist) analysis. Can you point to elements in his essay that indicate that perspective?

- Xiaotong agrees with Carter that America's problem is not the energy crisis, but a "crisis of faith." Does that mean he agrees with the president about the nature of the crisis?

- As a historical document, what value, if any, do you think a historian would find in Xiaotong's essay?

Afghanistan, 1980

Afghani fighters stand in triumph on a destroyed Soviet helicopter. The weapon that brought it down might well have been a shoulder-launched missile from the American-supplied arsenal, courtesy of the CIA. When the defeated Soviets left Afghanistan, the CIA congratulated itself on its smart moves, only to experience what experts call "blow back," as empowered mujahaddin such as those depicted here turned on the United States and made Afghanistan under the Taliban a haven for Al Qaeda. As for those shoulder-launched missiles, they have become a major headache for the West in the battle against Islamic terrorism. © Alain DeJean/Sygma/Corbis.

industries, long lines at the pumps. It seemed the worst of all possible economic worlds (see Voices from Abroad, "Fei Xiaotong: America's Crisis of Faith," p. 919).

Carter and the World

In foreign affairs, President Carter had a firmer sense of what he was about. He was the anti-Nixon, a world leader who rejected Kissinger's "realism" in favor of human rights and peacemaking. Carter established the Office of Human Rights in the State Department and withdrew economic and military aid from repressive regimes in Argentina, Uruguay, and Ethiopia, although he was unable to budge equally repressive U.S. allies like the Philippines, South Korea, and South Africa. In Latin America, Carter punctured an enduring symbol of Yankee imperialism by signing a treaty on September 7, 1977, turning control over the Panama Canal to Panama (effective December 31, 1999). Despite a conservative outcry, the Senate narrowly approved the treaty.

President Carter scored his greatest success by tackling the intractable Arab-Israeli conflict. In 1978 he invited Israel's prime minister Menachem Begin and Egyptian president Anwar el-Sadat to Camp David, the presidential retreat in Maryland. For two weeks, Carter kept the discussions going and finally, after promising additional economic aid, persuaded Sadat and Begin to adopt a "framework for peace," under which Egypt recognized Israel and received back the Sinai Peninsula, which Israel had occupied since 1967.

Though deploring "inordinate fear of Communism," Carter's efforts at improving relations with the Soviet Union foundered. He caused resentment by criticizing the Kremlin's record on

American Hostages in Iran

Images of blindfolded, handcuffed American hostages seized by Iranian militants at the American embassy in Tehran in November 1979 shocked the nation and created a foreign-policy crisis that eventually cost President Carter his chance for reelection. Alain Mingam/Gamma Press Images.

human rights. Negotiations for arms reductions went slowly, and when the SALT II agreement limiting bombers and missiles was finally signed in 1979, Senate hawks objected. Hopes for Senate ratification collapsed when the Soviet Union invaded Afghanistan that December. Treating the invasion as a major crisis, Carter placed an embargo on wheat shipments to the USSR, called for increased defense spending, and declared an American boycott of the 1980 summer Olympics in Moscow (in return the USSR boycotted the 1984 games in Los Angeles). In a fateful decision, Carter began providing covert assistance to anti-Soviet fighters in Afghanistan, some of whom metamorphosed into anti-American Islamic radicals in later years.

Carter's undoing, however, came in Iran. The Shah, Muhammad Reza Pahlavi, was an American client, installed by the CIA in 1953 (see Chapter 26) to prevent the nationalization of Iran's oil industry. Thereafter, the United States counted Iran as a faithful ally, a bulwark in the troubled Middle East, and a steady source of oil. Notwithstanding his fine words, Carter followed the same path as his Cold War predecessors, overlooking the crimes of Iran's CIA-trained secret police, SAVAK, the growing fragility of the Shah's regime, and mounting popular enmity toward the United States. Early in 1979, the Shah was driven into exile, overthrown by an Iranian revolution that brought the Shiite cleric Ayatollah Ruhollah Khomeini to power.

In October 1979, the United States admitted the deposed Shah, who was suffering from cancer, for medical treatment. In response, Iranian students seized the U.S. embassy in Teheran, taking sixty-six Americans hostage. The captors demanded that the Shah be returned to Iran for trial, but the United States refused. Instead, President Carter suspended arms sales to Iran and froze Iranian assets in American banks.

For the next fourteen months, the hostage crisis paralyzed Jimmy Carter's presidency. Night after night, humiliating pictures of blindfolded hostages appeared on television newscasts. An attempt to mount a military rescue in April 1980 had to be aborted because of equipment failures in the desert. During the withdrawal, one of the helicopters collided with a transport plane, setting off ammunition explosions and causing multiple American casualties. After this fiasco, the torturous negotiations, simplified by the Shah's death, finally succeeded. As a parting shot, the Iranians waited until the day Carter left office to deliver the hostages.

Every war president in the twentieth century — Wilson, FDR, Truman, Johnson — had been a Democrat. So Carter performed a remarkable feat. Single-handedly, he marked the Democrats indelibly

PART SEVEN
Entering a New Era: Conservatism, Globalization, Terrorism
1980–2006

	DIPLOMACY	GOVERNMENT	ECONOMY	SOCIETY	TECHNOLOGY AND SCIENCE
	Beyond the Cold War	**Conservative Ascendancy**	**Uneven Affluence and Globalization**	**Demographic Change and Culture Wars**	**Media and the Information Revolution**
1980	▶ Reagan begins arms buildup ▶ Intermediate Nuclear Forces Treaty (1988) ▶ Berlin Wall falls (1989)	▶ New Right and evangelical Christians help to elect Ronald Reagan president ▶ Reagan cuts taxes and federal regulatory system	▶ Reaganomics; budget and trade deficits soar ▶ Labor union membership declines	▶ Rise of "Yuppies" ▶ Rise in Latino and Asian immigration ▶ Crime and drug crises in the cities ▶ AIDS epidemic	▶ Cable News Network (CNN) founded (1980) ▶ Television industry deregulation ▶ Compact discs and cell phones invented
1990	▶ Persian Gulf War (1990) ▶ USSR collapses; end of the Cold War ▶ U.S. peacekeeping forces in Bosnia	▶ Republican "Contract with America" (1994) ▶ Bill Clinton advances moderate Democratic policies; wins welfare reform ▶ Clinton impeached and acquitted (1998–1999)	▶ New technology prompts productivity rise ▶ Global competition cuts U.S. manufacturing; jobs outsourced overseas	▶ Los Angeles race riots (1992) ▶ "Culture Wars" over affirmative action, feminism, abortion, and gay rights	▶ Dramatic growth of the Internet and World Wide Web ▶ America Online rises and declines ▶ Biotech revolution
2000–	▶ Radical Muslim attacks on Twin Towers and the Pentagon (2001) ▶ U.S. and allies oust Taliban in Afghanistan ▶ United States invades Iraq (2003) ▶ North Korea tests a nuclear weapon (2006); stalemate with Iran over its nuclear program	▶ George W. Bush narrowly elected president (2000) ▶ Bush pushes Faith-Based Initiatives and No Child Left Behind ▶ USA PATRIOT Act passed (2002) ▶ *Hamdan v. Rumsfeld* (2006) overturns administration's policies on the treatment of detainees	▶ Bush tax cuts ▶ Huge trade deficits with China and Asia ▶ Rising budget deficits ▶ Illegal immigration boosts low-wage work ▶ Stock market and hedge fund boom ▶ Fall in value of dollar	▶ Many states ban gay marriages ▶ "Minutemen" patrol Mexican border; immigration changes proposed ▶ Baby boomers begin to retire; new federal drug benefits for elderly	▶ Broadband access grows ▶ "Blogging" increases ▶ "Creation Science" controversy ▶ Bush limits on stem-cell research challenged ▶ Global warming increases

In a 1972 interview, President Richard M. Nixon remarked, "History is never worth reading until it's fifty years old. It takes fifty years before you're able to come back and evaluate a man or a period of time." Nixon's comments remind us that writing recent history poses a particular challenge; not knowing the future course of events, we can't say for certain which present-day trends will prove to be the most important. Part Seven is therefore a work-in-progress; its perspective will change as events unfold. At this point, it focuses on five broad themes: the ascendancy in American politics of the New Right, the impact of economic globalization, social conflicts stemming from cultural diversity, the revolution in information technology, and the end of the Cold War and the rise of Muslim terrorism.

DIPLOMACY In a surprising development in the late 1980s, the Soviet Union and its satellite Communist regimes in Eastern European suddenly collapsed. The Soviet demise produced, in the words of President George H. W. Bush, a "new world order" and left the United States as the only military superpower. Accepting that role, the United States worked to counter civil wars, terrorist activities, and military aggression in many parts of the world and especially in the Middle East. In 1991, it fought the Persian Gulf War in response to Iraq's invasion of Kuwait and, in the late 1990s, led military action and peacekeeping efforts in Serbia and Bosnia. In 2001, in response to terrorist attacks on New York and Washington by the radical Islamic group Al Qaeda, President George W. Bush attacked Al Qaeda's bases in Afghanistan. He then ordered an invasion of Iraq in 2003 that quickly toppled the regime of dictator Saddam Hussein but triggered civil chaos and a violent insurgency that is still ongoing.

GOVERNMENT With Ronald Reagan's election in 1980, "New Right" conservatism began its ascendancy. The conservative agenda was to roll back the social welfare state created by liberal Democrats during the New Deal and the Great Society. Presidents Reagan, George H. W. Bush, and George W. Bush cut taxes, limited the regulatory activities of federal agencies, transferred some powers and resources to state governments, and appointed conservative-minded judges to the federal courts. The most important change in the federal welfare system, however, came during the Clinton administration in 1996, with new legislation designed to shift families from dependency on welfare payments to employment in the labor market. Evangelical Christians and conservative lawmakers brought abortion, gay rights, and other cultural issues into the political arena, setting off controversies that revealed sharp divisions among the American people.

ECONOMY The American economy grew substantially during the quarter century beginning in 1980, thanks to the increased productivity of workers and the controversial tax and spending policies of the federal government. Tax cuts spurred investment and government spending for military purposes boosted production; these policies also created huge budget deficits, a dramatic increase in the national debt, and a widening gap between rich and poor Americans. Equally significant, the end of Cold War allowed the spread of capitalist enterprise around the globe. As multinational corporations set up manufacturing facilities in China and other low-wage countries, they undercut industrial production and wage rates in the United States and helped to create a massive American trade deficit. Because of the trade and budget deficits, American prosperity rested on an increasingly shaky foundation.

SOCIETY The increasing heterogeneity of American society — in demographic composition and in cultural values — was yet another characteristic of life in the first decade of the twenty-first century. Increased immigration from Latin America and Asia added to cultural tensions and produced a new nativist movement. Continuing battles over affirmative action, abortion, sexual standards, homosexuality, feminism, and religion in public life took on an increasingly passionate character, inhibiting the quest for politically negotiated solutions.

TECHNOLOGY AND SCIENCE One effect of faith-based politics was a significant challenge to scientific evidence and research, most especially against the claims of evolution and the advent of stem-cell research. Even the dramatic changes in technology, which boosted economic productivity and provided easy access to information and entertainment, posed new challenges. Would cable technology, with its multitude of choices, further erode a common American culture? Would the World Wide Web facilitate the outsourcing of American middle-class jobs? Would computer technology allow corporations — and government agencies — to track the lives and limit the freedom of American citizens? Like any revolution, the innovations in computer technology had an increasingly significant impact on many spheres of American life.

A "new world order," a New Right ascendancy, a new global economy, massive new immigration, and a technological revolution: We live in a time of rapid political and social changes and continuing diplomatic and technological challenges that will test the resiliency of American society and the creativity of American leaders.

30 The Reagan Revolution and the End of the Cold War

1980–2001

O<small>N NOVEMBER 9, 1989, MILLIONS</small> of television viewers worldwide watched jubilant Germans knock down the Berlin Wall. The wall, which had divided the city since 1961, was a vivid symbol of Communist repression and the Cold War division of Europe. More than four hundred East Germans had lost their lives trying to escape to freedom on the other side. Now East and West Berliners, young and old, danced on the remains of the forbidding wall. Two years later, in 1991, the Soviet Union itself dissolved, ending the Cold War. A new world order was in the making.

The end of the Cold War was the result, in part, of a dramatic change in American political life. The election of President Ronald Reagan began a conservative political ascendancy that continues to the present. Supported by the Republican Party's New Right, Reagan declared political war against both the Soviet Union and the liberal ideology that had informed American public policy since the New Deal of Franklin D. Roosevelt (1933–1945). However, the Republicans' domestic agenda was complicated by a split between religious conservatives, who demanded strong government action to implement their faith-based agenda, and economic conservatives, who favored limited government and free markets. Moreover, the Democratic Party remained a potent—and flexible—political force. Acknowledging the rightward shift in the country's mood,

The Rise of Conservatism
Reagan and the Emergence of the New Right
The Election of 1980

The Reagan Presidency, 1981–1989
Reaganomics
Reagan's Second Term

Defeating Communism and Creating a New World Order
The End of the Cold War
The Presidency of George H. W. Bush
Reagan, Bush, and the Middle East, 1980–1991

The Clinton Presidency, 1993–2001
Clinton's Early Record
The Republican Resurgence
Clinton's Impeachment
Foreign Policy at the End of the Twentieth Century

Summary
Connections: Government and Politics

◀ **The Wall Comes Down**
As the Communist government of East Germany collapsed, West Berliners showed their contempt for the wall dividing the city by defacing it with graffiti. Then, in November 1989, East and West Berliners destroyed huge sections of the wall with sledgehammers, an act of psychic liberation that symbolized the end of the Cold War. Alexandria Avakian / Woodfin Camp & Associates.

Democrat Bill Clinton trod a centrist path that led him to the White House in 1992 and again in 1996. "The era of big government is over," Clinton declared. At home as well as abroad, a new order emerged during the last decades of the century.

The Rise of Conservatism

The Great Depression of the 1930s and World War II had discredited the traditional conservative program of limited government at home and an isolationist-oriented foreign policy. Although the conservatives' crusade against communism revived their political fortunes during the height of the Cold War in the 1950s, they failed to articulate an ideology and a set of policies that would command the support of a majority of American voters. Then, in the late 1970s, conservative Republicans took advantage of serious blunders by liberal Democrats and built a formidable political coalition.

Reagan and the Emergence of the New Right

The personal odyssey of Ronald Reagan embodies the story of "New Right" Republican conservatism. Before World War II, Reagan was a well-known movie actor—and a New Deal Democrat and admirer of Franklin Roosevelt. He turned away from the New Deal partly out of self-interest (he disliked paying high taxes) and partly out of principle. As head of the Screen Actors Guild from 1947 to 1952, he had to deal with communist union organizers—the left wing of the liberal New Deal. Dismayed by their hard-line tactics and goals, he became a militant anti-communist and a conservative. Giving up his fading movie career, Reagan became a well-known spokesperson for the General Electric Corporation. By the early 1960s, he had become a Republican and threw himself into California politics, speaking for conservative causes and candidates.

Ronald Reagan came to national prominence in 1964. Speaking to the Republican convention on national television, he delivered a powerful speech supporting the presidential nomination of arch-conservative Barry Goldwater (see Chapter 28). Just as the "Cross of Gold" speech elevated William Jennings Bryan to fame in 1896, so Reagan's address—titled "A Time for Choosing" and delivered again and again throughout the mid-1960s—secured his political future. With the financial backing of wealthy southern California business interests, he won the governorship of California in 1968 and again in 1972. His impassioned rhetoric supporting limited government, low taxation, and law and order won broad support among citizens of the most populous state and made him a force in national politics. Narrowly defeated in his bid for the Republican presidential nomination in 1976, Reagan counted on his growing popularity to make him the party's candidate in 1980.

Liberal Decline and Conservative Resurgence. In 1964, the conservative message preached by Ronald Reagan and Barry Goldwater appealed to few American voters. Then came the series of events that mobilized opposition to the Democratic Party and its liberal agenda: a stagnating economy, the failed war in Vietnam, African American riots, a judiciary that legalized abortion and enforced school busing, and an expanded federal regulatory state. By the mid-1970s, conservatism commanded greater popular support. In the South, long a Democratic stronghold, whites hostile to federal support of civil rights for African Americans voted Republican in increasing numbers. Simultaneously, middle-class suburbanites and migrants to the Sun Belt states endorsed the conservative agenda of combating crime, limiting social welfare spending, and increasing expenditures on military defense.

Strong "New Right" grassroots organizations spread the message. In 1964, 3.9 million volunteers had campaigned for Barry Goldwater, twice as many as worked for Lyndon B. Johnson; in the late 1970s, they swung their support to Ronald Reagan. Skilled conservative political operatives such as Richard Viguerie, a Louisiana-born Catholic and antiabortion activist, applied new computer technology to political campaigning. They used computerized mailing lists to solicit campaign funds, drum up support for conservative causes and candidates, and get out the vote on election day.

Other organizational support for the New Right came from think tanks funded by wealthy conservatives. The Heritage Foundation, American Enterprise Institute, and the Cato Institute issued policy proposals and persistently attacked both liberal social policy and the permissive culture they claimed it spawned. These organizations blended the traditional conservative themes of unrestrained individualism and a free-market economy with the hot-button "social issues" of affirmative action, the welfare state, and changing gender and sexual values. They also fostered the growth of a cadre of conservative intellectuals. For decades, William F. Buckley, the founder and editor of the *National*

Review, and Milton Friedman, the Nobel Prize–winning laissez-faire economist at the University of Chicago, were virtually the only prominent conservative intellectuals. Now they were joined on the public stage by the so-called neoconservatives—well-known intellectuals such as Jeane Kirkpatrick, Nathan Glazer, and Norman Podhoretz, editor of *Commentary* magazine. Many neoconservatives had once advocated radical and liberal causes; vehemently recanting their former views, they provided intellectual respectability to the Republican Right. As liberal New York Senator Daniel Moynihan remarked, suddenly "the GOP has become a party of ideas."

The Religious Right. The most striking new entry into the conservative coalition was the Religious Right. Drawing its membership from conservative Catholics and Protestant evangelicals, the Religious Right condemned growing public acceptance of divorce, abortion, premarital sex, and feminism. Charismatic television evangelists, such as Pat Robertson, the son of a U.S. senator, and Jerry Falwell, the founder of the Moral Majority, emerged as the champions of a faith-based political agenda. As these cultural and moral conservatives attacked Democratic liberals for supporting lenient punishments for criminals, permissive sexuality, and welfare payments to unmarried mothers with multiple children, economic conservatives called for cuts in taxes and government regulations. Ronald Reagan endorsed the programs of both groups and, with their support, captured the Republican nomination for president in 1980 (see Comparing American Voices, "Christianity and Public Life," pp. 930–931). To win the votes of more moderate Republicans, Reagan chose former CIA director George H. W. Bush as his running mate.

The Election of 1980

In the election of 1980, President Jimmy Carter's sinking popularity virtually doomed his campaign. When the Democrats renominated him over his liberal challenger, Edward (Ted) Kennedy of Massachusetts, Carter's approval rating was stunningly low—a mere 21 percent of Americans believed he was an effective president. The reasons were readily apparent. Economically, millions of citizens were feeling the pinch from stagnant wages, high inflation, crippling mortgage rates, and an unemployment rate of nearly 8 percent (see Chapter 29). Diplomatically, the nation blamed Carter for failing to respond strongly to Soviet expansion and to the Iranian hostage crisis.

Jerry Falwell

The resurgence of evangelical religion in the 1970s was accompanied by a conservative movement in politics known as the New Right or the Christian Right. Founded in 1979 by televangelist Jerry Falwell, the Moral Majority was one of the earliest New Right groups, committed to promoting "family values" and (as the title to the record album suggests) patriotism in American society and politics. Wally McNamee/Corbis.

The incumbent president found himself constantly on the defensive, while Reagan remained upbeat and decisive. "This is the greatest country in the world," Reagan reassured the nation in his warm baritone voice, "we have the talent, we have the drive.... All we need is the leadership." To emphasize his intention to be a formidable international leader, Reagan hinted that he would take strong action to win the hostages' return. To signal a rejection of the Democrats' liberalism, the California governor declared his opposition to affirmative action and forced busing, and promised to get "the government off our backs." Most important, Reagan effectively appealed to the many Americans who felt financially insecure. In a televised debate between the candidates, Reagan emphasized the economic plight of working- and middle-class Americans in an era of "stagflation"—stagnant wages amidst rapidly rising prices. He posed the rhetorical question, "Are you better off today than you were four years ago?"

COMPARING AMERICAN VOICES

Christianity and Public Life

Modern social welfare liberalism embodies an ethic of moral pluralism and favors the separation of church and state. Conservative Christians challenge the legitimacy of pluralism and secularism and seek, through political agitation and legal action, to make religion an integral part of public life.

PRESIDENT RONALD REAGAN
"The Rule of Law under God"

Reagan's candidacy was strongly supported by Christian conservatives. He delivered these remarks to the National Association of American Evangelicals in 1983.

I want you to know that this administration is motivated by a political philosophy that sees the greatness of America in you, her people, and in your families, churches, neighborhoods, communities — the institutions that foster and nourish values like concern for others and respect for the rule of law under God.

Now, I don't have to tell you that this puts us in opposition to, or at least out of step with, a prevailing attitude of many who have turned to a modern-day secularism, discarding the tried and time-tested values upon which our very civilization is based. No matter how well intentioned, their value system is radically different from that of most Americans. And while they proclaim that they're freeing us from superstitions of the past, they've taken upon themselves the job of superintending us by government rule and regulation. Sometimes their voices are louder than ours, but they are not yet a majority....

Freedom prospers when religion is vibrant and the rule of law under God is acknowledged. When our Founding Fathers passed the First Amendment, they sought to protect churches from government interference. They never intended to construct a wall of hostility between government and the concept of religious belief itself.

Last year, I sent the Congress a constitutional amendment to restore prayer to public schools. Already this session, there's growing bipartisan support for the amendment, and I am calling on the Congress to act speedily to pass it and to let our children pray....

SOURCE: Ronald Reagan, *Speaking My Mind: Selected Speeches* (New York: Simon & Schuster, 1989), 169–180.

DONALD E. WILDMON
Network Television as a Moral Danger

Wildmon is a Christian minister and a grassroots religious activist. This selection comes from The Home Invaders *(1985).*

One night during the Christmas holidays of 1976, I decided to watch television with my family.... Not far into the program was a scene of adultery. I reacted to the situation in the manner as I had been taught. I asked one of the children to change channels. Getting involved in the second program, we were shocked with some crude profanity....

As I sat in my den that night, I became angry. I had been disturbed by the deterioration of morals I had witnessed in the media and society during the previous twenty-five years. This was accompanied by a dramatic rise in crime, a proliferation of pornography, increasingly explicit sexual lyrics in music, increasing numbers of broken homes, a rise in drug and alcohol use among the youth, and various other negative factors. I had managed to avoid those unpleasant changes to a large degree by staying away, turning my head, justifying my actions with the reasons most commonly expressed: freedom of speech, pluralism, tolerance....

Realizing that these changes were being brought into the sanctity of my home, I decided I could and would no longer remain silent.... Out of that decision came the National Federation for Decency (and out of the NFD came the Coalition for Better Television).... But the more I dealt with the problems, the more I realized that I was dealing only with symptoms not the disease....

This great struggle is one of values, particularly which ones will be the standard for our society and a base for our system of justice in the years to come. For 200 years our country has based its morals, its sense of right and wrong, on the Christian view of man. The Ten Commandments and the Sermon on the Mount have been our solid foundation ... the most perfect system ever devised in the history of mankind.

Television is the most pervasive and persuasive medium we have. At times it is larger than life. It is our only true national medium. Network television is the greatest educator we have.... It is teaching that adultery is an acceptable and approved lifestyle.... It is teaching that hardly anyone goes to church, that very few people in our society are Christian or live by Christian principles. How? By simply censoring Christian characters, Christian values, and Christian culture from the programs.

If within the next five years we fail to turn the tide of this humanist value system which seeks to replace our Christian heritage, then we have ... lost the battle.

SOURCE: Donald E. Wildmon, *The Home Invaders* (Elgin, IL: Victor Books, 1985), 3–7.

A. BARTLETT GIAMATTI
The Moral Majority as a Threat to Liberty

A. Bartlett Giamatti was the president of Yale University (1978–1986) and subsequently president of the National (Baseball) League. He offered these remarks to the entering class of Yale undergraduates in 1981.

A self-proclaimed "Moral Majority," and its satellite or client groups, cunning in the use of a native blend of old intimidation and new technology, threaten the values [of pluralism and freedom]. . . .

From the maw of this "morality" come those who presume to know what justice for all is; come those who presume to know which books are fit to read, which television programs are fit to watch. . . . From the maw of this "morality" rise the tax-exempt Savonarolas who believe they, and they alone, possess the "truth." There is no debate, no discussion, no dissent. They know. . . . What nonsense.

What dangerous, malicious nonsense. . . .

We should be concerned that so much of our political and religious leadership acts intimidated for the moment and will not say with clarity that this most recent denial of the legitimacy of differentness is a radical assault on the very pluralism of peoples, political beliefs, values, forms of merit and systems of religion our country was founded to welcome and foster.

Liberty protects the person from unwarranted government intrusions into a dwelling or other private places. In our tradition the State is not omnipresent in the home. And there are other spheres of our lives and existence, outside the home, where the State should not be a dominant presence. Freedom extends beyond spatial bounds. Liberty presumes an autonomy of self that includes freedom of thought, belief, expression, and certain intimate conduct.

SOURCE: Yale University Archives.

ANTHONY KENNEDY
The Constitution Protects Privacy

Kennedy, a Roman Catholic, was named to the Supreme Court by Ronald Reagan in 1988. In Lawrence v. Texas *(2003), he wrote the opinion for five of the six justices in the majority; Sandra Day O'Connor wrote a concurring opinion.*

The question before the Court is the validity of a Texas statute making it a crime for two persons of the same sex to engage in certain intimate sexual conduct.

In Houston, Texas, officers of the Harris County Police Department were dispatched to a private residence in response to a reported weapons disturbance. They entered an apartment where one of the petitioners, John Geddes Lawrence, resided. . . . The officers observed Lawrence and another man, Tyron Garner, engaging in a sexual act. The two petitioners were arrested, held in custody over night, and charged and convicted before a Justice of the Peace.

The complaints described their crime as "deviate sexual intercourse, namely anal sex, with a member of the same sex (man)." . . .

We conclude the case should be resolved by determining whether the petitioners were free as adults to engage in the private conduct in the exercise of their liberty under the Due Process Clause of the Fourteenth Amendment to the Constitution.

[The Texas statute in question seeks] to control a personal relationship that, whether or not entitled to formal recognition in the law, is within the liberty of persons to choose without being punished as criminals. . . . The liberty protected by the Constitution allows homosexual persons the right to make this choice. . . .

The present case does not involve minors. It does not involve persons who might be injured or coerced or who are situated in relationships where consent might not easily be refused. It does not involve public conduct or prostitution. It does not involve whether the government must give formal recognition to any relationship that homosexual persons seek to enter. The case does involve two adults who, with full and mutual consent from each other, engaged in sexual practices common to a homosexual lifestyle. The petitioners are entitled to respect for their private lives. The State cannot demean their existence or control their destiny by making their private sexual conduct a crime. Their right to liberty under the Due Process Clause gives them the full right to engage in their conduct without intervention of the government. "It is a promise of the Constitution that there is a realm of personal liberty which the government may not enter."

SOURCE: *Lawrence v. Texas*, 539 U.S. 558, 562–563, 567, 571, 579 (2003).

ANALYZING THE EVIDENCE

- What would Ronald Reagan think of the opinion written by Justice Kennedy, his appointee? Would Reagan agree with it, given his condemnation of those who are intent on "subordinating us to government rule and regulation"?
- According to Wildmon and Giamatti, what should be shown on television, and who should make those decisions?
- When should the government police private conduct? Consider the criteria outlined in the final paragraph of Justice Kennedy's opinion.

MAP 30.1 Presidential Election of 1980

Ronald Reagan easily defeated Democratic incumbent Jimmy Carter, taking 51 percent of the popular vote to Carter's 41 percent and winning the electoral vote in all but six states and the District of Columbia. Reagan cut deeply into the traditional Democratic coalition by wooing many southern whites, urban ethnics, and blue-collar workers. More than five million Americans expressed their discontent with Carter's ineffectiveness and Reagan's conservatism by voting for Independent candidate John Anderson, a longtime Republican member of the House of Representatives.

Candidate	Electoral Vote	Popular Vote	Percent of Popular Vote
Ronald Reagan (Republican)	489	43,899,248	50.7
Jimmy Carter (Democrat)	49	35,481,435	41.0
John B. Anderson (Independent)	—	5,719,437	6.6
Minor parties	—	1,395,558	—

In November, the voters gave a clear answer. They repudiated Carter, giving him only 41 percent of the vote. Independent candidate John Anderson garnered 7 percent, and Reagan won easily, with 51 percent of the popular vote nationwide and higher percentages in the South (Map 30.1). Equally important, the Republicans elected thirty-three new members of the House of Representatives and twelve new senators, which gave them control of the U.S. Senate for the first time since 1954.

Superior financial resources contributed to the Republican success: Two-thirds of all corporate donations to political action committees went to conservative Republican candidates. While the Demo-cratic Party saw its key constituency — organized labor — dwindle in size and influence, the GOP used its ample funds to reach voters through a sophisticated campaign of television and direct-mail advertisements. "Madison Avenue" advertising techniques — long used to sell commercial products — had begun to shape political campaigns in the 1960s. Now they became the primary means of trumpeting the virtues of a political candidate and attacking the credentials of his or her opponent.

Political Realignment. This aggressive campaigning continued the realignment of the American electorate that had begun during the 1970s. The core of the Republican Party remained the relatively affluent, white, Protestant voters who supported balanced budgets, opposed government activism, feared crime and communism, and believed in a strong national defense. But "Reagan Democrats" had now joined the Republican cause; prominent among these formerly Democratic voters were southern whites, who opposed civil rights legislation, and Catholic blue-collar workers, who were alarmed by antiwar protestors, feminist demands, and welfare expenditures. Reagan Republicanism also struck a responsive note among young voters, who increasingly identified themselves as "moderates" or "conservatives," and among the socially mobile residents of rapidly growing suburban communities in Texas, Arizona, and California.

The Religious Right was another significant contributor to the Republican victory. The Moral Majority claimed that it registered two million new voters for the 1980 election, and the Republican Party's platform reflected its influence. The platform called for a constitutional ban on abortion, voluntary prayer in public schools, and a mandatory death penalty for certain crimes. The Republicans also demanded an end to court-mandated busing and, for the first time in forty years, opposed the Equal Rights Amendment. Within the Republican Party, conservatism had triumphed.

Reagan's victory led some observers to predict a long-lasting alteration in American voting patterns. As *U.S. News & World Report* proclaimed, "A Massive Shift . . . Right." Other commentators offered more cautious assessments. They noted that Reagan won a bare majority of the votes cast and that turnout was unusually low because many working-class voters — disillusioned Democrats — stayed home. Rather than an endorsement of conservatism, one analyst called the election a "landslide vote of no confidence in an incompetent administration." Whatever the verdict, Ronald Reagan's victory raised the possibility of a dramatic shift in government policies and priorities. As he entered office, the new president claimed the American public had given him a mandate for sweeping change. His success — or failure — would determine the significance of the election and the New Right.

- What were the key groups of the new Republican coalition? Were their goals complementary? Contradictory?
- What factors led to Ronald Reagan's election in 1980?

The Reagan Presidency, 1981–1989

Ronald Reagan's personality was as important as his policies. Frayed by the cultural turmoil of the 1960s and the economic malaise of the 1970s, the majority of voters embraced the former movie actor's optimistic message of national pride and purpose. Even when major scandals threatened his administration, Reagan maintained his popularity, leading critics to dub him "the Teflon president" since nothing damaging seemed to stick. More sympathetic observers called him "the Great Communicator"; they praised his ability to address the anxieties of Americans and to win support for the Republicans' conservative economic and cultural agenda.

Reaganomics

First elected at age sixty-nine, Ronald Reagan was the oldest man ever to serve as president. His appearance and demeanor belied his age. Concerned since his acting days with his physical fitness, the president conveyed a sense of vigor and purpose (see Reading American Pictures, "Image Warfare: Fighting to Define the Reagan Presidency," p. 934). His folksy humor endeared him to millions, who overlooked his frequent misstatements and indifference to details of public policy. He kept his political message clear and simple. "Government is not the solution to our problem," Reagan declared. "Government is the problem."

In his first year of office, Reagan and his chief advisor, James A. Baker III, moved quickly to set new government priorities. To roll back the expanded liberal state, they launched a coordinated three-pronged assault on federal taxes, social welfare spending, and the regulatory bureaucracy. To win the Cold War, they advocated a vast increase in defense spending. And, to match the resurgent economies of Germany and Japan, whom the United States had defeated in World War II and then helped to rebuild, they set out to restore American leadership of the world's capitalist societies.

"Supply-Side" Theory. To achieve this goal, the new administration advanced a new set of economic and tax policies. Quickly dubbed "Reaganomics," these policies sought to boost the economy by increasing the supply of goods. The theory underlying "supply-side economics," as this approach was called, emphasized the need to increase investment in productive enterprises. According to George Gilder, a major supply-side theorist, the best way to bolster investment was to reduce the taxes paid by business corporations and wealthy Americans, who could then use these funds to expand production. Supply-siders maintained that the resulting economic expansion would increase government revenues and offset the loss of tax dollars stemming from the original tax cuts.

Taking advantage of Republican control of the Senate and his personal popularity following a failed assassination attempt, Reagan won congressional approval of the Economic Recovery Tax Act (ERTA). The act reduced income tax rates paid by most Americans by 23 percent over three years. For the wealthiest Americans — those with millions to invest — the highest marginal tax rate dropped from 70 to 50 percent. The act also slashed estate taxes, the levies on inheritances instituted around 1900 to prevent the transmission of huge fortunes from one generation to the next. Finally, the new legislation trimmed the taxes paid by business corporations by $150 billion over a period of five years. As a result of ERTA, by 1986 the annual revenue of the federal government had been cut by $200 billion.

Shifts in Spending. David Stockman, Reagan's budget director, hoped to match this sizable reduction in tax revenue with a comparable cutback in federal expenditures. To meet this ambitious goal, he proposed substantial cuts in Social Security and Medicare. But Congress — and the president — rejected such efforts because they were not willing to antagonize middle-class and elderly voters who viewed these government entitlements as sacrosanct. As neoconservative columnist George Will noted ironically, "Americans are conservative. What they want to conserve is the New Deal." This contradiction between Republican ideology and practical politics would frustrate the GOP into the twenty-first century.

In a futile attempt to balance the budget, Stockman advocated spending cuts on programs for food stamps, unemployment compensation, and welfare assistance such as Aid to Families with Dependent Children (AFDC). In the administration's view, these programs represented the worst features of Lyndon Johnson's Great Society — a huge

READING AMERICAN PICTURES

Image Warfare: Fighting to Define the Reagan Presidency

As might be expected, U.S. presidents and their staffs attempt to project a positive image of the chief executive and the administration's policies. But contradictions often arise between the image and values cultivated by a president and the actual policies pursued by the White House. The presidency of Ronald Reagan is a case in point. As the text points out, Reagan helped to stimulate a conservative movement in American politics and society during the 1980s. Images of Reagan quickly became vital for the White House to deliver its message of conservative reform to the American people. As the cartoon published by the *Arkansas Gazette* illustrates, powerful imagery could also be wielded by Reagan's political opponents.

ANALYZING THE EVIDENCE

- Examine the photo of Reagan at his ranch in California. This image was taken by a White House photographer. What message does the image convey about Reagan as a person? How does this message reinforce the policies created by Reagan that you read about in the text?

- What message does the cartoon convey about Reagan policies? How does this differ from the official White House message expressed in the photo of Reagan?

- Together, what do these two images tell us about the image and reality of the Reagan presidency? Do you think that cartoons or photographs are a more accurate source of information for understanding the historical meaning of a particular president and his administration? Why or why not?

President Reagan at His Ranch in Southern California. Ronald Reagan Presidential Library.

Presidential Landscaping. Courtesy *Arkansas Gazette*, 1984.

FIGURE 30.1 The Annual Federal Budget Deficit (or Surplus), 1940–2005

During World War II, the federal government incurred an enormous budget deficit. But between 1946 and 1965, it ran either an annual budget surplus or incurred a relatively small debt. As measured in 2005 dollars, the accumulated national debt increased by about $50 billion during that twenty-year period or about $2.5 billion a year. The annual deficits rose significantly during the Vietnam War and the stagflation of the 1970s, but they really exploded between 1982 and 1994, in the budgets devised by the Ronald Reagan and George H. W. Bush administrations, and again between 2002 and 2005, in those prepared by George W. Bush. The Republican presidents increased military spending while cutting taxes, an "enjoy-it-now" philosophy that transferred the cost to future generations of Americans.

SOURCE: National Priorities Project. See also *U.S. Budget for Fiscal Year 2007*, Historical Tables, Table 15.6.

---

handout to economic drones at the expense of hardworking taxpayers. Congress approved some cutbacks but preserved most of these welfare programs because of their importance; in 1980, some 21 million people relied on the food stamp program. It likewise continued to lavish huge subsidies and tariff protection on wealthy farmers and business corporations — "welfare for the rich," as some critics put it. As the administration's spending cuts fell far short of its goal, the federal budget deficit increased dramatically.

Military spending accounted for the bulk of the growing federal deficit, and President Reagan was its strongest supporter. "Defense is not a budget item," he declared, "you spend what you need." To "make America number one again," Reagan and Defense Secretary Caspar Weinberger pushed through Congress a five-year, $1.2 trillion military spending program that accelerated an arms buildup begun in 1978 by President Carter after the emergence of a pro-Soviet government in Afghanistan. The administration revived the B-1 bomber, which Carter had canceled because of its great expense and limited usefulness, and continued development of the MX, a new missile system approved by Carter. Reagan's most ambitious and controversial weapons plan, proposed in 1983, was the Strategic Defense Initiative (SDI). Popularly known as "Star Wars" because of its science-fiction-like features, SDI would consist of a system of laser-equipped satellites that would detect and destroy incoming ballistic missiles carrying atomic weapons. Would it work? Most scientists were dubious; Secretary of State George Shultz thought it was "lunacy," and even Weinberger, who liked every weapons system he saw, dismissed the idea. Nonetheless, Congress approved initial funding for the controversial — and enormously expensive — project. During Reagan's presidency military spending accounted for nearly one-fourth of all federal expenditures.

The combination of lower taxes and higher defense spending led to a skyrocketing national debt (Figure 30.1). By the time Reagan left office, the federal deficit had tripled — rising from $930 billion in 1981 to $2.8 trillion in 1989. Every American citizen — from small baby to senior citizen — now owed a hidden debt of $11,000.

Regulatory Cutbacks. Advocates of Reaganomics also asserted that excessive regulation by federal government agencies impeded economic growth. Some of these bureaucracies, such as the U.S. Department of Labor, had risen to prominence during the New Deal; others, such as the Environmental Protection Agency (EPA) and the Occupational Safety and Health Administration (OSHA), were created by Democratic Congresses during the Great Society and the Nixon administration (see Chapters 24, 28, and 29). Although these agencies provided many services to business corporations, they also increased their costs — by assisting labor unions to organize, ordering safety improvements in factories, and requiring expensive equipment to limit the release of toxic chemicals into the environment. To reduce the reach of federal regulatory agencies, the Reagan administration cut their budgets — by an average of 12 percent. And, invoking the idea of the "New Federalism" advocated by President Nixon, it began to transfer regulatory responsibilities to the state governments.

The Reagan administration also limited the regulatory efforts of federal agencies by staffing them with leaders who were hostile to their mission. James Watt, an outspoken conservative who headed up the Department of the Interior, explicitly attacked environmentalists as "a left-wing cult." Acting on his free-enterprise principles, Watt opened public lands for use by private businesses — oil and coal corporations, large-scale ranchers, timber companies. Already under heavy criticism for these economic give-aways, Watt was forced to resign in 1983 when he dismissively characterized members of a public commission as "a black, a woman, two Jews, and a cripple." Anne Gorsuch Buford, whom Reagan appointed to head the EPA, likewise resigned when she was implicated in a money scandal and was cited for contempt of Congress for refusing to provide documents regarding the Superfund program, which cleans up toxic waste sites.

The Sierra Club and other environmental groups roused enough public outrage about these appointees and their policies that the administration changed its position. During President Reagan's second term, he significantly increased the EPA's budget, created new wildlife preserves, and added acreage to the National Wilderness Preservation System and animals and plants to the endangered species lists.

Reaganomics Stalled. Ultimately, politics in a democracy is "the art of the possible," and savvy politicians know when to advance and when to retreat. Having attained two of his prime goals — a major tax cut and a dramatic increase in defense spending — Reagan did not carry through on his promises to scale back big government and the welfare state. When Reagan left office in 1989, federal spending stood at 22.1 percent of the gross domestic product (GDP) and federal taxes at 19 percent of GDP, both virtually the same as in 1981. In the meantime, the federal deficit had tripled in size, and the number of civilian government workers had increased from 2.9 to 3.1 million. This outcome — so different from the president's lofty rhetoric — elicited harsh criticism from conservative commentators. As one of them angrily charged, there was no "Reagan Revolution."

That verdict was too narrow. Despite its failed promises, the presidency of Ronald Reagan set the nation on a new political and ideological path. Social welfare liberalism, ascendant since 1933, was now thoroughly on the defensive. Moreover, the Reagan presidency restored popular belief that America — and individual Americans — could enjoy increasing prosperity.

Reagan's Second Term

As Ronald Reagan campaigned in 1984 for a second term in the White House, he claimed credit for a resurgent economy. On coming into office in 1981, he had supported the "tight" money policy implemented by the Federal Reserve Board headed by Paul Volker. By raising interest rates to the extraordinarily high level of 18 percent, Volker had quickly cut the high inflation rates of the Carter years. But this deflationary policy caused an economic recession that put some ten million Americans out of work. President Reagan's approval rating plummeted, and in the elections of 1982, Democrats picked up twenty-six seats in the House of Representatives and seven state governorships.

The economy — and the president's popularity — quickly revived. During the 1984 election campaign, Reagan hailed his tax cuts as the reason for the economic resurgence. His campaign theme, "It's Morning in America," suggested that a new day of prosperity and pride had dawned. The Democrats nominated former vice president Walter Mondale of Minnesota. With strong ties to labor unions, ethnic groups, and party leaders, Mondale epitomized the New Deal coalition that had dominated the Democratic Party since Franklin Roosevelt. To appeal to women voters, Mondale selected Representative Geraldine Ferraro of New York as his running mate — the first woman to run on the presidential ticket of a major political party. Neither Ferraro's presence nor Mondale's credentials made a difference. The incumbent president carried the entire nation except for Minnesota and the District of Columbia and won a landslide victory. Still, Democrats retained their majority in House and, in 1986, regained control of the Senate.

The Iran-Contra Affair. A major scandal marred Reagan's second term. Early in 1986 news leaked out that the administration had negotiated an "arms-for-hostages" deal with the revolutionary Islamic government of Iran. For years the president had denounced Iran as an "outlaw state" and a supporter of terrorism. Now he wanted its help. To win Iran's assistance in freeing some American hostages held by Hezbollah, a pro-Iranian Shiite terrorist group in Lebanon, the administration covertly sold arms to the "outlaw state." While this secret Iranian arms deal was diplomatically suspect and politically controversial, the use of resulting profits in

Nicaragua was patently illegal. In 1981, the Reagan administration had suspended aid to the Sandinista government of Nicaragua. It charged that the Sandinistas, a left-wing movement that had overthrown dictator Anastasio Somoza Debayle, were pursuing socialist policies detrimental to American interests, forming a military alliance with Fidel Castro in Cuba, and supporting a leftist rebellion in neighboring El Salvador (Map 30.2). To overthrow the Sandinista government, President Reagan ordered the Central Intelligence Agency (CIA) to aid an armed Nicaraguan opposition group called the Contras. Although Reagan praised the Contras as "freedom fighters," Congress worried that the president and other executive branch agencies were assuming war-making powers that the Constitution reserved to the legislature. In 1984 it strengthened the Boland Amendment, thereby banning the CIA and other government officials from providing any military support to the Contras.

Oliver North, a lieutenant colonel in the U.S. Marines and an aide to the National Security Council, consciously defied that ban. With the tacit or explicit consent of high-ranking administration officials, including the president, he used the profits from the Iranian arms deal to assist the Contras. When asked if he knew of North's illegal actions, Reagan replied, "I don't remember." Still swayed by

MAP 30.2 U.S. Involvement in Latin America and the Caribbean, 1954–2000

Ever since the Monroe Doctrine (1823), the United States has claimed a special interest in Latin America. During the Cold War, U.S. foreign policy throughout Latin America focused on containing instability and the appeal of communism in a region plagued by poverty and military dictatorships. Providing foreign aid was one approach to addressing social and economic needs, but the United States frequently intervened with military forces (or by supporting military coups) to remove unfriendly or socialist governments. The Reagan administration's support of the Contra rebels in Nicaragua, some of which was contrary to U.S. law, was one of those interventions.

Reagan's charm, the public accepted this convenient loss of memory. Nonetheless, the Iran-Contra affair resulted in the prosecution of Colonel North and several other officials and jeopardized the president's historical reputation. It was not only that administration officials (as Lawrence Walsh, the special prosecutor appointed to investigate the scandal, concluded) carried out "two programs contrary to congressional policy and contrary to national policy [and] . . . broke the law," but also that President Reagan — of all people — had bribed terrorists. Most Americans were shocked by Reagan's dealings with Iran and its terrorist allies.

The Reagan Legacy. Deeply stung by the Iran-Contra scandal, Reagan proposed no bold domestic policy initiatives in his last two years in office. He had entered office promising to limit the federal government and to give free-market forces freer rein. His success was only partial. Although he reordered the priorities of the federal government, he failed to reduce its size or scope. Social Security and other entitlement programs remained untouched, and the enormous military buildup outweighed cuts in other programs. Concerned to unite the country, Reagan did not actively advocate the agenda of the Religious Right. The president called for tax credits for private religious schools, restrictions on abortions, and a constitutional amendment to permit prayer in public schools, but refused to expend his political capital to secure these measures.

Perhaps Reagan's most significant institutional legacy was his judicial appointments. During his two terms, he appointed 368 federal court judges, many of them with conservative credentials, and three Supreme Court justices, Sandra Day O'Connor, Antonin Scalia, and Anthony Kennedy. O'Connor became the first woman to serve on the Supreme Court and wrote an important decision supporting a woman's right to an abortion. Both she and Kennedy won a reputation as judicial moderates, leaving Scalia as Reagan's only genuinely conservative appointee. But Reagan also elevated Justice William Rehnquist, a conservative Nixon appointee, to the position of chief justice. Under Rehnquist's conservative leadership (1986–2005), an often-divided court watered down, but did not usually overturn, the liberal rulings of the Warren Court (1954–1967) with respect to individual liberties, abortion rights, affirmative action, and the rights of criminal defendants.

Reagan failed to roll back the social welfare and regulatory state of the New Deal-Great Society era, but he did change the dynamic of American politics.

Another Barrier Falls

In 1981, Sandra Day O'Connor, shown here with Chief Justice Warren Burger, was appointed to the Supreme Court by President Ronald Reagan, the first woman to serve on that body. In 1993, she was joined by Ruth Bader Ginsburg, an appointee of President Bill Clinton. O'Connor emerged as a leader of the "moderate" bloc on the Court during the 1990s; she retired in 2006. Fred Ward/Black Star/Stockphoto.com.

His antigovernment rhetoric won many adherents, as did his bold and fiscally dangerous tax cuts. As one historian has summed up Reagan's domestic legacy, "For the next twenty years at least, American policies would focus on retrenchment and cost-savings, budget cuts and tax cuts, deregulation and policy redefinitions."

- ➤ What were the key elements of Reagan's domestic policy?
- ➤ What limits did Reagan face in promoting conservative goals? What successes did he achieve?

Defeating Communism and Creating a New World Order

Ronald Reagan entered office determined to confront the Soviet Union diplomatically and militarily. Backed by Republican hard-liners, Reagan unleashed some of the harshest Cold War rhetoric since

Reagan and Gorbachev: Fellow Political Revolutionaries

Both Ronald Reagan and Mikhail Gorbachev changed the political outlook of their nations. As Reagan undermined social welfare liberalism in the United States, Gorbachev challenged the rigidity of the Communist Party and state socialism in the Soviet Union. Although they remained ideological adversaries, by the mid-1980s the two leaders had established a personal rapport, which helped to facilitate agreement on a series of arms reduction measures. © Bettmann/Corbis.

the 1950s, labeling the Soviet Union an "evil empire" and vowing to make certain it ended up "on the ash heap of history." By his second term Reagan had decided that this goal was best achieved by actively cooperating with Mikhail Gorbachev, its young and reform-minded leader. The collapse of the Soviet Union in 1991 ended the nearly fifty-year-long Cold War, but a new set of foreign challenges quickly appeared: the creation of a viable new world order (see Voices from Abroad, "Zhu Shida: China and the United States: A Unique Relationship," p. 940).

The End of the Cold War

The collapse of the Soviet Union and the end of the Cold War were the most dramatic developments in foreign affairs during the 1980s and early 1990s. The fall of the Soviet regime was the result of external pressure from the United States and the internal weaknesses of the Communist economy and society. To defeat the Soviets, the administration pursued a two-pronged strategy. First, it abandoned the policy of "détente" and set about to rearm America. This buildup in American military strength, reasoned Secretary of Defense Caspar Weinberger, a determined hard-liner, would force the Soviets into an arms race that would strain their economy and undermine support for the Communist regime. Second, the president supported the policy of CIA Director William Casey to fund guerrillas who were trying to overthrow pro-Communist governments in Angola, Mozambique, Afghanistan, and Central America—and thereby roll back Soviet influence in the Third World.

The Weaknesses of the Soviet Union. These strategies succeeded because they exploited the internal weaknesses and policy mistakes of the Communist regime. Its system of state socialism and central economic planning had transformed Russia

VOICES FROM ABROAD

Zhu Shida

China and the United States: A Unique Relationship

To understand the dynamics of American society and American foreign policy, the government-funded Chinese Academy of Social Sciences created an Institute of American Studies. Zhu Shida is a research associate at the Institute; in 2002, he published this piece on a semiofficial Chinese government Web site.

The relationship between China, one of the oldest civilizations with the biggest population, and the United States, one of the youngest civilizations with the strongest economy, is significant not only for the two peoples but also for the future of the whole world.

The factors influencing the Sino-US relationship include economic, strategic, diplomatic and cultural elements. Undoubtedly, among them the economic factor is the most important one. Economic interests are at the heart of China-US relations. In 2001, trade volume between the two nations hit US $8.4 billion, 8.1 percent higher than the previous year. Tempted by the colossal Chinese market, the US has become China's biggest investor with an investment of US $4.8 billion in 2001 and an accumulated investment of US $35.5 billion. . . .

Strategically, China and the US have common interests. The White House needs China's assistance and influence to handle North Korea and non-proliferation issues. America also needs China's cooperation in fighting terrorism. On the Taiwan question that remains the most sensitive issue, China asks the United States to abide by the three joint communiqués and pursue the one-China policy. . . .

To handle the Sino-US relationship appropriately, both sides should realize the necessity to further understanding and respect for each other's cultures, which, unfortunately, often has been neglected.

The origins of American culture lie in a combination of Puritanism, liberalism, individualism and republicanism. Reflected in politics, American culture takes the form of hegemonism with a strong religious flavor and labeled by its self-defined freedom, democracy and human rights standard. . . . Beginning with the original immigrating Puritans, Americans have regarded themselves as the chosen people, superior to any other peoples in the world. Meanwhile, in free and open America, there is no room for the strict consensus system characteristic of traditional societies. Therefore, without a unified attitude and consistent account in all fields of its political culture, discordant voices can be heard from time to time in American society, which is unimaginable and almost impossible in China.

The essence of Chinese culture is family affection and attachment. Any individual behavior damaging national dignity and group honor is not encouraged in Chinese society that thinks highly of collective benefits and reputation, which is beyond the understanding of American people.

In addition to the cultural differences between the two nations, we also need to realize the inherent discrepancies in American culture that influence American politics and foreign policies frequently. On the one hand, in terms of Puritanism, one of the origins of the American culture, since the earliest Puritans came to the New World due to the religious persecutions they suffered in England, the freedom and right for individuals to pursue welfare have occupied a special position in Puritanism. Naturally, Puritans harbor religious fervor for human rights. On the other, the protracted existence of racial discrimination and segregation did not change until after the Civil Rights movement during the 1950s and 1960s. Even today, the deep-rooted barrier between whites and minorities is still hard to be removed completely in the United States. The cultural contradictions are the source of America's double standards on the human rights issue.

The aggressive American culture with a short history of a little more than 200 years is built on the basis of individualism and liberalism, while the introversive Chinese culture with a 5000 years' tradition lays stress on collectivism and cultural consensus at the expense of individual voices. Obviously, the essences of these two cultures are contradictory. This cultural contradiction is the main reason for the constant Sino-US clashes. Nevertheless, mutual complementarities in economy magnetize the two nations, forcing them to compromise for their cultural discrepancies.

SOURCE: China Internet Information Center, www.china.org.cn/english/2002/Mar/29138.htm.

ANALYZING THE EVIDENCE

- Ronald Reagan frequently evoked Puritan John Winthrop's image of America as a shining "city on a hill" and a beacon for mankind. How does Zhu Shida interpret the impact of Puritan ways of thinking on American foreign policy? Based on your reading in this textbook, how accurate is his understanding of American culture?

- Given the institutional status of the writer and the essay's place of publication, how should we interpret it?

- According to the author, what factors pull China and the United States together? Which ones push them apart?

Pope John Paul II in Poland, 1979
Polish-born Karol Joseph Wojtyla (1920–2005) was named a cardinal of the Roman Catholic Church in 1967 and was selected as pope in 1978. The following year he visited Poland, where he reiterated his opposition to Communist rule. His visit sparked the formation of the Solidarity workers' movement and, as its founder Lech Walesa put it, "started this chain of events that led to the end of communism." © Bettmann/Corbis.

from an agricultural to an industrial society. But it had done so very inefficiently; lacking the discipline and opportunities of a market economy, most enterprises hoarded raw materials, employed too many workers, and did not develop new products. Except in military weaponry and space technology, the Russian economy fell farther and farther behind those of capitalist societies in the post–World War II years, and most people in the Soviet bloc endured a low standard of living. Moreover, the Soviet invasion of Afghanistan, like the American war in Vietnam, turned out to be major blunder — an unwinnable war that cost vast amounts of money, destroyed military morale, and undermined popular support of the Communist government.

Mikhail Gorbachev, a younger Russian leader who became general secretary of the Communist Party in 1985, recognized the need for internal economic reform, technological progress, and an end to the Afghanistan war. His policies of *glasnost* (openness) and *perestroika* (economic restructuring) spurred widespread criticism of the rigid institutions and authoritarian controls of the Communist regime. To lessen tensions with the United States, Gorbachev met with Reagan in 1985, and the two leaders established a warm personal rapport. By 1987, they agreed to eliminate all intermediate-range nuclear missiles based in Europe. A year later, Gorbachev ordered Soviet troops out of Afghanistan, and Reagan replaced many of his hard-line advisors with policymakers who favored a renewal of détente.

The Collapse of Communism in Europe. As Gorbachev's reforms revealed the flaws of the Soviet system, the peoples of eastern and central Europe demanded the ouster of their Communist governments. In Poland, the Roman Catholic Church and its pope — Polish-born John Paul II — joined with Solidarity, the trade union movement led by Lech Walesa, to push for the overthrow of the pro-Soviet regime. In 1956, 1964, and 1968, Russian troops had quashed popular uprisings in Hungary, East Germany, and Czechoslovakia. Now they did not intervene, and a series of peaceful uprisings — "Velvet Revolutions" — created a new political order throughout the region. The destruction of the Berlin Wall in November 1989 symbolized the end of the Communist rule in central Europe. Two years later, the Soviet Union collapsed. Alarmed by Gorbachev's reforms, Soviet military leaders seized the premier in August 1991. But widespread popular opposition led by Boris Yeltsin, the president of the Russian Republic, thwarted their efforts to oust him from office. Their failure broke the dominance of the Communist Party. On December 25, 1991, the Union of Soviet Socialist Republics formally dissolved to make way for an eleven-member Commonwealth of Independent States (CIS). The Russian Republic assumed leadership of the CIS, but the USSR was no more (Map 30.3).

In 1956 Nikita Khrushchev had told the United States, "We will bury you," but now the tombstone read, "The Soviet Union, 1917–1991." For more than forty years the United States fought a bitter economic and ideological battle against its Communist foe, a struggle that had an enormous impact on American society. By linking the campaign for African American rights to the diplomatic competition with the Soviet Union in the Third World, liberal politicians advanced the cause of racial equality in the United States; conversely, by labeling social welfare legislation as "communistic," conservative politicians limited its extent, as did the staggering cost of Cold War. American taxpayers spent some *$4 trillion* on nuclear weapons and trillions more on conventional arms. The physical and psychological costs were equally high: radiation from atomic weapons tests, anti-Communist witch-hunts, and — most pervasive of all — a constant fear of nuclear annihilation. "Nobody — no country, no party, no person — 'won' the cold war," concluded George Kennan, the architect in 1947 of the American policy of "containment," because both sides paid such a heavy price to wage the war and both benefited greatly from its end. Of course, many

MAP 30.3 The Collapse of the Soviet Union and the Creation of Independent States, 1989–1991

The collapse of Soviet Communism dramatically altered the political landscape of central Europe and central Asia. The Warsaw Pact, the USSR's answer to NATO, vanished. West and East Germany reunited, and the nations created by the Versailles Treaty of 1919 — Estonia, Latvia, Lithuania, Poland, Czechoslovakia, Hungary, and Yugoslavia — reasserted their independence or split into smaller ethnically defined nations. The Soviet republics bordering Russia, from Belarus in the west to Kyrgyzstan in the east, also became independent states, while remaining loosely bound with Russia in the Commonwealth of Independent States (CIS).

Americans had no qualms about proclaiming victory, and advocates of free-market capitalism, particularly conservative Republicans, celebrated the outcome. The collapse of Communism in Eastern Europe and the disintegration of the USSR itself, they argued, demonstrated that they had been right all along. Thus, Ronald Reagan's role in facilitating the end of the Cold War, for reasons both international and domestic, was his most important achievement.

The Presidency of George H. W. Bush

George H. W. Bush, Reagan's vice president and successor, was a man of intelligence, courage, and ambition. Born to wealth and high status, he served with great distinction as a naval aviator during World War II and then graduated Phi Beta Kappa from Yale University. Bush prospered as a Texas oil developer and Member of Congress, and then served, under Richard Nixon, as ambassador to the United Nations and head of the CIA. Although Bush lacked Reagan's extraordinary charisma and commanding presence, he had many other strengths that his predecessor lacked.

George Bush won the Republican nomination in 1988 and chose as the vice presidential candidate a young conservative Indiana senator, Dan Quayle. In the Democratic primaries, Governor Michael Dukakis of Massachusetts easily outpolled the charismatic civil rights leader Jesse Jackson, whose populist Rainbow Coalition brought together minority and liberal groups within the party. Dukakis chose Senator Lloyd Bentsen of Texas as his running mate.

The election campaign had a harsh tone as brief television "attack ads" took precedence over a thoughtful discussion of policy issues. The Republican's mantra was "Read My Lips: No New Taxes," a sound bite drawn from a Bush speech. The Bush campaign charged that Dukakis was "a card-carrying member" of the American Civil Liberties Union and was "soft on crime." Bush supporters repeatedly ran TV ads focused on Willie Horton, a convicted African American murderer who had raped a woman while on furlough from a prison in Dukakis's state of Massachusetts. Placed on the defensive by these attacks, Dukakis failed to unify the liberal and moderate factions within Democratic Party and to mount an effective campaign. Bush carried thirty-eight states, winning the popular vote by 53.4 percent to 45.6 percent, but Democrats retained control of the House of Representatives and the Senate.

Democratic Legislative Initiatives. Faced with a Democratic Congress and personally interested in foreign affairs, George H. W. Bush proposed few distinctive domestic initiatives. Rather, congressional Democrats took the lead. They enacted legislation allowing workers to take leave for family and medical emergencies, a measure that Bush vetoed. Then, over the president's opposition, they secured legislation enlarging the rights of workers who claimed discrimination because of their race or gender. With the president's support, congressional liberals also won approval of the Americans with Disabilities Act, a major piece of legislation that significantly enhanced the legal rights of physically disabled people in employment, public transportation, and housing.

Activist Republican Judges. As Democratic politicians seized the initiative in Congress, conservative Republican judges made their presence known in the courts. In *Webster v. Reproductive Health Services* (1989), the Supreme Court upheld the authority of state governments to limit the use of public funds and facilities for abortions. The following year, the justices approved a regulation that prevented federally funded health clinics from discussing abortion with their clients. Then, in the important case of *Planned Parenthood of Southeastern Pennsylvania v. Casey* (1992), the court upheld a Pennsylvania law requiring a twenty-four-hour waiting period prior to an abortion. Surveying these and other decisions, a reporter suggested that 1989 was "The Year the Court Turned Right," with a conservative majority ready and willing to limit or invalidate liberal legislation and legal precedents.

This observation was only partly correct. While the Court was no longer a bastion of liberal jurisprudence, it was not yet firmly conservative in character. Although the *Casey* decision, written by Reagan appointee Sandra Day O'Connor, upheld certain restrictions on abortions, it affirmed the "essential holding" in *Roe v. Wade* that women had a constitutional right to control their bodies. Justice David Souter, appointed to the Court by Bush in 1990, voted with O'Connor to uphold *Roe* and, like her, emerged as an ideologically "moderate" justice on a range of issues.

Bush's other appointment to the Court was Clarence Thomas, an African American conservative with little judicial experience or legal expertise. Thomas's nomination proved controversial; he was opposed by leading black organizations, such as the NAACP and the Urban League, and accused of sexual harassment by Anita Hill, a black law professor. Hill told the all-male Senate Judiciary Committee that Thomas had sexually harassed her when they were colleagues at a federal agency. Despite these charges, Republicans in the Senate won Thomas's

Anita Hill Challenges a Supreme Court Nominee
University of Oklahoma law professor Anita Hill accused Clarence Thomas, an African American nominated to the Supreme Court by President George H. W. Bush, of sexual harassment. Hill's charges sparked controversy during Thomas's confirmation hearings, but the Senate, voting largely on party lines, narrowly approved his appointment by a vote of 52 to 48. Subsequently, women's rights activists embarked on a campaign to elect more women to Congress. Brad Markel/Getty Images.

confirmation by a narrow margin. Once on the bench, Thomas took his cues from his conservative colleagues, Chief Justice William Rehnquist and Justice Antonin Scalia.

"Read My Lips." The controversy over Clarence Thomas hurt Bush at the polls. Politically minded women accused Republicans of ignoring sexual harassment—an issue of concern to many men and women—and vowed to mobilize voters. In the election of 1992, the number of women, mostly Democrats, elected to the Senate increased from three to seven, and in the House it increased from thirty to forty-eight.

Bush's main political problems stemmed from the huge budget deficit bequeathed to his administration by Ronald Reagan. In 1985 Congress had enacted the Gramm-Rudman Act, which mandated automatic cuts in government programs in 1991 if the budget remained wildly out of balance. That moment had now come. Unless Congress and the president acted, there would be a shutdown of all nonessential government departments and the lay-off of thousands of employees. To resolve the crisis, Congress enacted legislation that cut spending and significantly increased taxes. Abandoning his pledge of "No New Taxes," Bush signed the legislation, earning the enmity of conservative Republicans and diminishing his chances for reelection in 1992.

Bush also struggled with an economic recession that began in 1990 and stretched into the middle of 1991. As unemployment mounted, the president could do little because the funding for many federal programs—including housing, public works, and social services—had been shifted to state and local governments during the Reagan administration. The states faced problems of their own because the economic slowdown sharply eroded their tax revenues. Indeed, to balance their budgets, as required by their constitutions, they laid off workers and cut social spending. The combination of the tax increase, which alienated Republican conservatives, and a tepid federal response to the recession, which turned independent voters against the administration, became crucial factors in denying George H. W. Bush reelection in 1992.

Reagan, Bush, and the Middle East, 1980–1991

The end of the Cold War left the United States as the only military superpower and raised the prospect of a "new world order" dominated by the United States and its European and Asian allies. But there were problems. American diplomats now confronted an array of regional, religious, and ethnic conflicts that defied easy solutions. Those in the Middle East—the oil-rich lands stretching between Afghanistan and Morocco—remained the most pressing and the most threatening to American interests.

Israel and the Palestinians. Like previous presidents, Ronald Reagan had little success in resolving the conflicts between the Jewish state of Israel and its Muslim Arab neighbors. In 1982 the Reagan administration initially supported Israel's invasion of Lebanon to attack forces of the Palestine Liberation Organization (PLO), which had taken over part of that country. As the violence escalated in 1984, the administration urged an Israeli withdrawal and dispatched an American military force as "peacekeepers," a decision it quickly regretted. Lebanese Muslim militants, angered by U.S. support for Israel, targeted American marines with a truck bomb, killing 241 soldiers; rather than confront the bombers, the administration withdrew American forces. Three years later, Palestinians in the Gaza

Men — and Women — at War

Women played visible roles in the Persian Gulf War, comprising approximately 10 percent of the American troops. In the last decades of the twentieth century, increasing numbers of women chose military careers and, although prohibited from most fighting roles, were increasingly assigned to combat zones. Luc Delahaye/Sipa Press.

Strip and along the West Bank of the Jordan River — territories occupied by Israel since 1967 — mounted an *intifada*, a civilian uprising against Israeli authority. In response, American diplomats stepped up their efforts to persuade the PLO and Arab nations to accept the legitimacy of Israel and to convince the Israelis to allow the creation of a Palestinian state. Neither initiative met with much success.

Iran and Iraq. American policymakers faced a second set of problems in the oil-rich nations of Iran and Iraq. In September 1980 the revolutionary Islamic government of Iran, headed by Ayatollah Khomeini, found itself at war with Iraq, a secular state headed by the ruthless dictator Saddam Hussein and his Sunni Muslim followers. The war started over a series of boundary disputes, in particular, access to deep water ports in the Persian Gulf essential to shipping oil. Fighting quickly escalated into a war of attrition that claimed a million casualties. The Reagan administration ignored Hussein's brutal repression of his political opponents in Iraq and the murder (using poison gas) of tens of thousands of Iraqi Kurds and Shiite Muslims. Anxious to preserve a balance of power in the Middle East, the administration provided Hussein with military intelligence and other aid. Finally, in 1988, an armistice ended the inconclusive war, with both sides still claiming the territory that sparked the conflict.

The Gulf War, 1990–1991. Two years later, in August 1990, Saddam Hussein again went to war to expand Iraq's boundaries. His troops quickly conquered Kuwait, Iraq's small oil-rich neighbor and threatened Saudi Arabia, the site of one-fifth of the world's known oil reserves and an informal ally of the United States. In response, President George H. W. Bush quickly sponsored a series of resolutions in the United Nations Security Council condemning Iraq, calling for its withdrawal from Kuwait, and imposing an embargo and trade sanctions. When Hussein refused to withdraw, Bush successfully prodded the UN to authorize the use of force against "the butcher of Baghdad" if Iraq did not withdraw by January 15. Demonstrating great diplomatic finesse, the president organized a military coalition of thirty-four nations. The House of Representatives authorized American participation by a vote of 252 to 182; dividing mostly along party lines, the Senate voted for war by the close vote of 52 to 47.

The war for the "liberation of Kuwait" was quickly won by the coalition forces led by the United States. A month of American air strikes crushed the communication network of the Iraqi army, destroyed its air forces, and weakened the morale of its soldiers. A land offensive then quickly forced the withdrawal of Iraqi forces from Kuwait (see Map 32.2, p. 1001). To avoid a protracted war and retain French and Russian support for the UN coalition, President Bush did not try to occupy Iraq and remove Saddam Hussein from power. Instead, he won the passage of United Nations Resolution 687, which imposed economic sanctions against Iraq unless it allowed unfettered inspection of its weapons systems, destroyed all biological and chemical arms, and unconditionally pledged not to develop nuclear weapons.

The military victory, low incidence of American casualties, and quick withdrawal produced a euphoric reaction at home. "By God, we've kicked the Vietnam syndrome once and for all," Bush gloated, as his approval rating shot up precipitously. The president spoke too soon. Throughout the 1990s, Saddam Hussein would remain a problem for American policymakers. Indeed, his secretive policies were one factor that, in March 2003, caused Bush's son, President George W. Bush, to initiate another war in Iraq — one that was much more protracted, expensive, and bloody for Americans and Iraqis alike (see Chapter 32).

Thus, the end of the Cold War resulted not in an era of peace but rather two very hot wars in the Middle East. For half a century, the United States and the USSR had tried to divide the world into two rival commercial and ideological blocs — Communist and capitalist. The next half century promised a new set of struggles, one of them between a Western-led agenda of economic and cultural globalization and an anti-Western ideology of Muslim and Arab regionalism.

- ▶ What factors led to the end of the Cold War?
- ▶ How did the composition and decisions of the Supreme Court change during the Reagan-Bush administrations?
- ▶ Why did the United States intervene in the conflicts between Iraq and Iran and Iraq and Kuwait? What were American goals in each case?

The Clinton Presidency, 1993–2001

The election of 1992 brought a Democrat, Arkansas Governor Bill Clinton, to the White House. A profound admirer of John F. Kennedy, Clinton hoped to rekindle the idealistic vision of the slain president. Like Kennedy, Clinton was a political pragmatist; distancing himself from party liberals and special-interest groups, he styled himself as a "New Democrat" who would bring "Reagan Democrats" and middle-class voters back to the party.

Clinton's Early Record

Raised in Hope, Arkansas, by an alcoholic stepfather who abused his mother, Clinton left home to study at Georgetown University. He won a Rhodes scholarship to Oxford and earned a law degree at Yale, where he married a classmate, Hillary Rodham. Returning to Arkansas, he entered politics and won election to six 2-year terms as governor. In 1991 at age forty-five, he was energetic, ambitious, and a policy "wonk" — extraordinarily well informed about political issues.

The Election of 1992. Clinton became the Democratic candidate, but only after surviving charges that he dodged the draft to avoid service in Vietnam, smoked marijuana, and cheated repeatedly on his wife. Although all of those stories had an element of truth, Clinton adroitly talked his way into the presidential nomination — he had charisma and a way with words. For his running mate he chose Al Gore, a second-term senator from Tennessee. At age forty-four, Gore was about the same age as Clinton, making them the first baby-boom national ticket, as well as the first all-southern ticket.

President Bush easily won renomination over his lone opponent, the conservative columnist Pat Buchanan. But Bush allowed the Religious Right to dominate the Republican convention and write a conservative platform that alienated many political moderates. The Bush campaign also suffered from the independent candidacy of Texas billionaire H. Ross Perot, whose condemnation of the rising federal deficit and the influence of corporate lobbyists on Congress appealed to many middle-class voters.

The Democrats mounted an aggressive campaign that focused on Clinton's domestic agenda: He promised a tax cut for the middle classes, universal health insurance, and a reduction of the huge Republican budget deficit. Freed from the demands of the Cold War, Democrats hoped that an emphasis on domestic issues where they traditionally ran strong would sweep them to victory. They were right. On election day, Bush could not overcome voters' discontent over the weak economy and conservatives' disgust at his tax hikes. He received only 37 percent of the popular vote, as millions of Republicans cast their ballots for Ross Perot, who won more votes (19 percent) than any independent candidate since Theodore Roosevelt in 1912. With 44 percent of the vote, Clinton won the election handily (Map 30.4). Moreover, the Democratic Party retained control of both houses of Congress, ending twelve years of divided government. Still, even as

MAP 30.4 Presidential Election of 1992

The first national election after the end of the Cold War focused on the economy, which had fallen into a recession in 1991. The first-ever all-southern Democratic ticket of Bill Clinton (Arkansas) and Al Gore (Tennessee) won support across the country but won the election with only 44 percent of the popular vote. The Republican candidate, Vice President George H. W. Bush, ran strongly in his home state of Texas and the South, an emerging Republican stronghold. Independent candidate H. Ross Perot, a wealthy technology entrepreneur, polled an impressive 19 percent of the popular vote by capitalizing on voter dissatisfaction with the huge federal deficits of the Reagan-Bush administrations.

the sun again shown on the Democrats, dark clouds appeared on the horizon. Bill Clinton entered the White House supported by a minority of voters and opposed by political enemies who considered him "a pot-smoking, philandering, draft-dodger" unqualified for the highest office in the land. He would need great political skills and more than a little good fortune to lead the country successfully, especially since he longed to go down in history as a great president.

The Failure of Health-Care Legislation. Clinton's ambition exceeded his abilities. The first year of his administration was riddled by mistakes — failed nominations of two attorney generals, embarrassing patronage revelations about the White House travel office, and an unsuccessful attempt to end a ban on homosexuals in the military. The president looked like a political amateur, out of his depth. He compounded these minor errors by selecting health reform, an enduring liberal cause since the Truman administration but also an enormously complex issue, as the major objective of his first year in office.

Clinton's goal was to provide a system of health care that would cover all Americans. Though the United States spent a higher percentage of its GNP on medical care than any other nation, it was the only major industrialized country that did not provide government-guaranteed health insurance to all citizens. With medical costs and insurance premiums spiraling out of control, the president designated his wife, attorney Hillary Rodham Clinton, to head a task force to draft new legislation. This appointment was controversial because no First Lady had ever played a formal role in policymaking, but it also suited the times: In many American families, both husbands and wives held responsible positions in the workforce.

The recommendations of the task force were even more controversial. Recognizing the potency of Reagan's attack on "big government," the task force proposed a system of "managed competition": Market forces and private insurance companies, not government bureaucrats, would control health-care costs. The cost of the new system would fall heavily on employers, who had to pay 80 percent of their workers' health benefits, and many smaller businesses and insurance companies campaigned strongly against it. By September 1994, congressional Democratic leaders admitted that the Clintons' liberal health-care proposal was dead. Its failure left about forty million Americans, or 15 percent of the population, without health coverage.

Addressing other concerns of social welfare Democrats, Clinton appointed two pro-choice liberal jurists, Ruth Bader Ginsburg and Stephen Breyer, to the Supreme Court. He also placed women and racial minorities in cabinet positions. Janet Reno became attorney general, the first woman to head the Department of Justice; Donna E. Shalala headed the Department of Health and Human Services; and, in Clinton's second term, Madeleine Albright served as secretary of state. Clinton chose an African American, Ron Brown, as secretary of commerce, and two Latinos, Henry Cisneros and Frederico Peña, to head the Department of Housing and Urban Development (HUD) and the Department of Transportation, respectively.

The Clinton administration's policies toward social welfare, abortion, and crime likewise appealed to liberal Democrats. In 1993, Clinton signed the Family and Medical Leave Act, which had twice been

A Forceful and Controversial First Lady and Senator

Drawing inspiration from Eleanor Roosevelt, Hillary Rodham Clinton hoped the country was ready for a First Lady who actively shaped policy. It wasn't, or at least it wasn't ready for her health-care plan. Subsequently, Hillary Rodham Clinton assumed a less visible role in administration policymaking. In 2000, and again in 2006, she won election to the U.S. Senate from New York.
Robert Trippet/Sipa Press.

vetoed by President Bush, and the Clinic Entrance Act, which made it a federal crime to obstruct people entering hospitals or abortion clinics. Clinton's administration also won approval of two gun-control measures, on handguns and assault weapons, though neither had much affect on gun sales or the murder rate. To counter criticism from conservatives, Clinton "got tough on crime" and included funding in this legislation for 100,000 new police officers in local communities across the nation.

Clinton's Centrist Agenda. The president was more successful with the "centrist" New Democrat elements of his political agenda. Shortly before he left office, George H. W. Bush had signed the North American Free Trade Agreement (NAFTA), an arrangement among the United States, Canada, and Mexico to create a free-trade zone covering all of North America. The Clinton administration presided over Congress's consideration of the agreement, which was bitterly fought. Manufacturers looking for new markets or hoping to move their plants to Mexico, where workers' wages were much lower, strongly supported NAFTA. Labor unions — a traditional Democratic constituency — opposed the agreement because it cut American jobs. Environmentalists likewise condemned the pact because antipollution laws were weak (and even more weakly enforced) south of the border. However, the Clinton administration was filled with advocates of free trade, including Treasury Secretary Lloyd Bentsen, Labor Secretary Robert Reich, and Economic Policy adviser Robert Rubin. With Clinton's support, they pushed NAFTA through Congress by assembling a coalition of free-trade Democrats and Republicans.

More important, Clinton took meaningful action to reduce the budget deficits of the Reagan-Bush presidencies. In 1993 Clinton secured a five-year budget package that would reduce the federal deficit by $500 billion. Republicans unanimously opposed the proposal because it raised taxes on corporations and individuals with high incomes, and liberal Democrats complained because it limited social spending. Clinton also paid a price because he had to abandon his campaign promise to lower taxes for the middle class. But shared sacrifice led to shared rewards. By 1998, Clinton's fiscal policies had balanced the federal budget and had begun to pay down the federal debt — at a rate of $156 billion a year between 1999 and 2001. As fiscal sanity returned to Washington, the economy boomed, thanks in part to the low interest rates stemming from deficit reduction. Ready access to cheap oil between 1986 and 2001 also fueled the growing economy. During Clinton's two terms in office, unemployment fell from 6 to 4 percent, the GNP increased at an annual rate of 3 percent (twice that of Japan), the stock market more than doubled in value, and home ownership rose to an all-time high.

The Republican Resurgence

The failure of health reform and the passage of NAFTA discouraged liberal Democrats even as Clinton's policies on homosexuals, guns, and abortion energized conservative Republicans in Congress and throughout the country. "Clinton-haters" — those who denied his fitness to be president — hammered away at his conduct as governor, and his participation in an allegedly fraudulent Arkansas real estate deal that became known as "Whitewater." Hoping to prove that the president and Hillary Clinton were free from any taint of fraud, the Clinton administration appointed an independent prosecutor to investigate the case.

In the meantime, the midterm election of 1994 became a referendum on Clinton and his presidency, and its results transformed the political

A Bipartisan Balanced Budget

Throughout his time in the White House, Bill Clinton worked to reduce federal deficits by increasing taxes and restraining spending. On August 5, 1997, a smiling President Clinton signed a balanced budget bill, surrounded by congressional leaders including Republican John Kasich of Ohio (front row, far right), Chair of the House Budget Committee, and Republican Newt Gingrich of Georgia (front row, second from right), the Speaker of the House. Also looking on with satisfaction was Vice President Al Gore, who already had hopes for the presidency in 2000. Ron Edmonds/AP Images.

landscape. In a well-organized and well-funded campaign strongly supported by the National Rifle Association and the Religious Right, Republicans gained 52 seats in the House of Representatives, giving them control for the first time in forty years; they also retook control of the Senate and captured eleven governorships.

The "Contract with America." Leading the Republican charge was Representative Newt Gingrich, an intellectually aggressive conservative from Georgia, who became the new Speaker of the House. During the campaign, Gingrich announced a Republican "Contract with America," a list of proposals that he vowed would be voted on in the first one hundred days of the new session. The contract included constitutional amendments to balance the budget and term limits for members of Congress. It also promised significant tax cuts, reductions in welfare and other entitlement programs, anticrime initiatives, and cutbacks in federal regulations. These initiatives, and Republican control of Congress after 1994, represented the completion of the conservative-backed Reagan Revolution of 1980. The president and the Democrats were now on the defensive. In his State of the Union message of 1996, Clinton suggested that "the era of big government is over." For the rest of his presidency, he eschewed expansive liberal social welfare policies and sought Republican support for a centrist, New Democrat program.

The Budget Struggle and Welfare Reform. Despite Clinton's acceptance of governmental restraint, the Republican-dominated Congress failed to make significant reductions in the size of the federal budget. Most big-budget items were politically or economically untouchable. The Treasury had to pay interest on the national debt; the military budget had to be met; the Social Security system had to be funded. When Republicans passed a government funding act in 1995 that included tax cuts to the wealthy and less money for Medicare, Clinton vetoed the legislation, thereby shutting down many government offices for three weeks. Depicted by Democrats and many independent observers as heartless opponents of aid for senior citizens, the Republicans admitted defeat and gave the president a bill he would sign.

Republicans had greater success in reforming the welfare system, a measure that saved relatively little money but carried a big ideological message. The program for Aid to Families with Dependent Children (AFDC) provided annual payments (including food stamps) to families earning less than $7,740, well below the established poverty line. Still, many taxpaying Americans believed, with some justification, that the AFDC program perpetuated poverty by encouraging women recipients to bear children and to remain on welfare rather than to seek productive employment. Various state legislatures — both Democrat- and Republican-run — had already imposed work requirements and denied benefits for additional children born to women who were already on AFDC. In August 1996, the federal government did the same. After vetoing two Republican-authored bills, President Clinton signed the Personal Responsibility and Work Opportunity Act. This historic overhaul of federal entitlements ended the guarantee of cash assistance by abolishing AFDC, required most adult recipients to find work within two years, and gave states wide discretion in running their welfare programs.

The 1996 Election. The Republican takeover of Congress had one unintended consequence: It united the usually fractious Democrats behind the president. Unopposed in the 1996 primaries, Clinton burnished his image as a moderate by endorsing welfare reform. He also benefited from the continuing strength of the economy. The Republicans settled on Senate Majority Leader Bob Dole of Kansas as their presidential candidate. A veteran of World War II, in which he lost the use of an arm, Dole was a safe but uninspiring candidate, lacking both personal charisma and innovative policies. He called for a 15 percent tax cut *and* a balanced budget, a fiscal combination that few Americans believed possible. On election day, Clinton took 49 percent of the popular vote to 41 percent for Dole. Ross Perot, who failed to build his independent movement of 1992 into a coherent political party, received 8 percent. By dint of great effort — dozens of risky vetoes, centrist initiatives, determined fund-raising — Clinton had staged a heroic comeback from the electoral disaster of 1994. Still, Republicans remained in control of Congress and, angry at Clinton's reelection, returned to Washington eager to engage in partisan combat.

Clinton's Impeachment

Clinton's hopes for a distinguished place in history unraveled halfway through his second term when a sex scandal led to his impeachment. The impeachment charges stemmed from Clinton's sworn testimony in a lawsuit filed by Paula Jones, a former Arkansas state employee. In that testimony and later on national television, Clinton denied having sexually harassed Jones during his governorship. These denials may well have been truthful. But during the testimony Clinton also denied having a sexual affair with Monica Lewinsky, a former White House intern — a charge that was undoubtedly true. Kenneth Starr, a conservative Republican who had taken over as independent counsel in the Arkansas Whitewater land deal, now widened his probe to include the Jones affair. Starr's report of September 1998 concluded that Clinton had lied under oath regarding Lewinsky and obstructed justice, and that these actions were grounds for impeachment.

Viewed historically, Americans have usually defined "high crimes and misdemeanors" — the constitutional standard for impeachment — as involving a serious abuse of public trust that threatened the integrity of the republic. In 1998, many conservative Republicans favored a much lower standard because they had never accepted "Slick Willy" Clinton's legitimacy as president. In reply to the question, "Why do you hate Clinton so much?",

The Politics of Impeachment

As this cartoon shows, the Republicans caught President Clinton with his pants down. But they failed to persuade a majority of Americans that Clinton's sexual escapades with White House intern Monica Lewinsky (and his lies about it while under oath) were "high crimes and misdemeanors" that merited his removal from office. The episode is best seen as an expression of the harsh ideological politics of the 1990s and, in retrospect, as an unnecessary and dangerous diversion of the nation's energies away from the looming threat of terrorism.

Auth ©1998 *The Philadelphia Inquirer*. Reprinted with permission Universal Press Syndicate. All Rights Reserved.

one conservative declared, "I hate him because he's a womanizing, Elvis-loving, non-inhaling, truth-shading, war-protesting, draft-dodging, abortion-protecting, gay-promoting, gun-hating baby boomer. That's why." Seeing Clinton as an exemplar of the permissive social values of the 1960s, conservative Republicans vowed to use the sex scandal to oust him from office. On December 19 the House of Representatives narrowly approved two articles of impeachment against Clinton: one for perjury for lying to a grand jury about his liaison with Lewinsky, and a second for obstruction of justice by encouraging others to lie on his behalf. Most Americans did not applaud the House's action; according to a CBS news poll, 38 percent supported impeachment while 58 percent opposed it.

Lacking public support, Republicans in the Senate fell well short of the two-thirds majority they needed to remove the president. Like Andrew Johnson, the only other president to be tried by the Senate (see Chapter 15), Bill Clinton paid a high price for this victory. The president spent so much time in his defense that he was unable to fashion a coherent Democratic alternative to the Republicans' conservative domestic agenda and, equally important, to address important problems of foreign policy.

Foreign Policy at the End of the Twentieth Century

Unlike George H. W. Bush, Clinton claimed no expertise in international affairs and did not desire to develop one. "Foreign policy is not what I came here to do," he lamented as he faced a series of minor international crises. Neither of his main advisors, Secretary of State Warren Christopher and Secretary of Defense Les Aspin, had a strategic vision of America's role in the post–Cold War world. Consequently, Clinton pursued a cautious diplomatic policy. Unless important American interests were directly threatened, the president avoided a commitment of U.S. influence and troops.

"Peacekeeping" in Somalia and Haiti. Clinton's caution stemmed in part from a harrowing episode in the east African country of Somalia, where ethnic warfare had created political chaos and massive famine. President Bush had approved American participation in a UN peacekeeping force, and Clinton had added additional troops. When bloody fighting in October 1993 killed eighteen American soldiers and wounded eighty-four, Clinton gradually withdrew the troops. The United States had few economic and diplomatic interests in Somalia, and even a sizeable peacekeeping force would be unable to quell the factional violence and restore national unity. For similar reasons, Clinton refused in 1994 to dispatch American forces to the central African nation of Rwanda, where ethnic conflict had escalated to genocide — the killing by Hutu extremists of at least 800,000 people, mostly ethnic Tutsis.

The Caribbean was much closer to home, and Clinton consequently gave it closer attention. In 1991 a military coup in Haiti had deposed Jean-Bertrand Aristide, the democratically elected president. Then a candidate for president, Clinton had criticized President Bush's refusal to grant asylum to refugees from the oppressive new Haitian regime. Once in the White House, Clinton reversed his stance: To thwart a massive influx of impoverished Haitian "boat people" who would strain welfare services and increase racial tension, the new president called for Aristide's return to power. Threatening a U.S. invasion, Clinton forced Haiti's military rulers to step down. American troops maintained Aristide in power until March 1995, when the United Nations took over responsibility for keeping the peace.

Intervention in the Balkans. An even more intractable set of internal conflicts — based on ethnicity, religion, and nationality — led to the disintegration of the Communist nation of Yugoslavia in 1991. Initially, the Roman Catholic regions of Slovenia and Croatia declared independence from Yugoslavia, which was dominated by Russian Orthodox Serbians. In 1992, the heavily Muslim province of Bosnia and Herzegovina declared its independence, but its substantial Serbian population refused to live in a Muslim-run multiethnic state. Supported financially and militarily by Slobodan Milosevic, the uncompromisingly nationalistic leader of Yugoslavia, they formed their own breakaway state and, to make it an all-Serbian society, launched a ruthless campaign of "ethnic cleansing." They drove tens of thousands of Bosnian Muslims and Croats from their homes, executed tens of thousands of men, raped equal numbers of women, and forced the survivors into crowded refugee camps.

America's European allies, particularly Germany, had long-standing economic ties to the Balkans, and the United States had taken an active role in its affairs during the Cold War. However, both Clinton and NATO leaders feared that military action against the Serbs would result in a Vietnam-like quagmire. Finally, in November 1995, Clinton organized a NATO-led bombing campaign and peacekeeping effort, backed by twenty thousand American troops, that ended the Serbs' vicious expansionist drive. Four years later a new crisis emerged in Kosovo, another province of the Serbian-dominated Federal Republic of Yugoslavia. Most Kosovo residents were ethnic Albanian Muslims, whom the Russian Orthodox Serbs vowed to drive out of the region. Again led by the United States, NATO intervened with aircraft strikes and military forces to preserve Kosovo's autonomy (Map 30.5). While always acting prudently in defense of American interests, the Clinton administration had slowly developed a policy of active "engagement" in nations beset with internal conflict.

Islamic Radicalism. In the Middle East, Clinton was as unsuccessful as previous presidents in mediating the long-standing conflict between Jews and Arabs. In 1994 he arranged a meeting in Washington

MAP 30.5 Ethnic Conflict in the Balkans: The Breakup of Yugoslavia, 1991–1992

The collapse of the Soviet Union spurred the disintegration of the independent Communist state of Yugoslavia, a multiethnic and multireligious state held together after 1945 by the near-dictatorial authority of Josip Broz Tito (1892–1980). Fanned by ethnic and religious hatreds, Yugoslavia splintered into warring states. Slovenia and Macedonia won their independence in 1991, but Russian Orthodox Serbia, headed by president Slobodan Milosevic, tried to rule the rest of the Balkan peoples. Roman Catholic Croatia freed itself from Serb rule in 1995, and, after ruthless Serbian aggression against Muslims in Bosnia and later in Kosovo, the United States and NATO intervened militarily to create the separate states of Bosnia-Herzegovina (1995) and Montenegro (2006) and the autonomous Muslim province of Kosovo (1999).

between Israeli prime minister Yitzhak Rabin and Yasir Arafat, chairman of the Palestine Liberation Organization. Urged on by Clinton, they negotiated an agreement that allowed limited Palestinian self-rule in the Gaza Strip and Jericho. The hope that this breakthrough would lead to a general peace settlement was short lived. In 1995, a Jewish religious fanatic assassinated Rabin, and the new prime minister, Benjamin Netanyahu of the religious Likud Party, reverted to a hard-line policy against the Palestinians. Despite Clinton's continuing efforts, the "peace process" failed to produce substantial progress.

Terrorists Bomb USS *Cole*

On October 12, 2000, a radical Muslim group with ties to Al Qaeda detonated a powerful bomb near the USS *Cole*, which was refueling in the port of Aden in Yemen. The explosion killed seventeen American sailors and injured thirty-seven others. After repairs costing $250 million, the USS *Cole* returned to active duty in April 2002. © Bettmann/Corbis.

Indeed, the rise of radical Muslim organizations undermined the prospects of a Middle Eastern peace and challenged security and stability throughout the world. During the 1990s, radical Islamic movements staged armed insurgencies in parts of Russia and China and threatened existing governments in the Muslim states of Algeria, Egypt, Pakistan, and Indonesia. These terrorist groups likewise mounted a series of attacks against the United States, which they condemned as the main agent of economic globalization and cultural imperialism. In 1993 radical Muslim immigrants set off a bomb in the World Trade Center in New York City. Five years later, Muslim terrorists used truck bombs to blow up the American embassies in Kenya and Tanzania, and in 2000 they bombed an American warship, the USS *Cole*, in the port of Aden in Yemen. The Clinton administration knew these attacks were the work of Al Qaeda, a network of terrorists organized by the wealthy Saudi exile Osama bin Laden, but no one — in the State Department, CIA, or Pentagon — had yet figured out how to deal with these Islamic extremists (see Chapter 32).

As the Soviet Union collapsed in 1991, the director of the CIA had seen little cause to celebrate. "We have slain a large dragon," he admitted, "but we live now in a jungle filled with a bewildering variety of poisonous snakes. And in many ways, the dragon was easier to keep track of." As the century ended, his assessment rang true. The Balkan and African crises, the Middle Eastern morass, and radical Islamic terrorist groups served as potent reminders of a world in conflict and the limits of American power. If not quite as dangerous as the Cold War era, the "new world order" was no less problematic.

▶ In what ways did Clinton's administration suggest that he was a "New Democrat"?

▶ What was the goal of the Republicans' "Contract with America"?

▶ What foreign policy challenges did Clinton face, and how did he address them?

SUMMARY

As we have seen, the concluding decades of the twentieth century were a time of momentous change. In the international arena, the collapse of the Soviet Union and the end of the Cold War diminished the prospect of nuclear war. Nonetheless, regional and ethnic conflicts continued to pose a serious challenge to U.S. foreign policy. Militarily dominant, the United States found its economy challenged by strong competitors in Europe and Asia and its security endangered by ruthless terrorist groups.

The shifting economic fortunes of the nation affected domestic politics. The "stagflation" of the 1970s helped to ensure the electoral triumph of Ronald Reagan in 1980, and his administration's massive expenditures on defense boosted the domestic economy while creating an enormous federal deficit. Rather than getting "the government off our backs," Reagan simply used its power in different ways. "Reaganomics" shifted wealth into the hands of military planners and affluent Americans, mostly at the expense of the poor. Middle-class Americans—the majority of the population—generally prospered during the 1980s but divided ever more sharply over cultural issues. Influenced by the powerful lobby of the Religious Right, the Republican Party vigorously attacked the welfare state and the liberal cultural values that it represented.

These economic and cultural issues played out in the politics of the 1990s. The economic recession of 1991 assisted the election of Bill Clinton in 1992, as did his centrist, "New Democrat" policies that reflected the conservative movement's call for limited government. The Republican congressional landslide of 1994 limited Clinton's options, as did his sexual misconduct, which in 1998 led to his impeachment and loss of political effectiveness. As the century ended, American society was experiencing a massive technological revolution that promised to transform many aspects of life.

Connections: Government and Politics

Far into the future historians will debate Ronald Reagan's personal impact on the two great events presented in this chapter—the triumph of the conservative movement in America and the end of the Cold War. Still, there is no doubt, as we observed in the opening essay for Part Seven (p. 925), that President Ronald Reagan and his conservative successors were determined to carry out a governmental revolution:

The conservatives' agenda was to roll back the social welfare state created by liberal Democrats during the New Deal and the Great Society. Presidents Reagan, George H. W. Bush, and George W. Bush cut taxes, reduced spending on social welfare programs, and limited the regulatory activities of federal agencies.

In previous chapters, we have watched the slow construction of the governmental system that the conservatives attacked. Although prefigured in the regulatory legislation of the Progressive era (Chapter 20), it had its origins in the New Deal of Franklin Roosevelt. As we saw in Chapter 24, in response to the Great Depression the Roosevelt administration created a phalanx of federal agencies to oversee the American economy and, in the Social Security Act of 1935, laid the groundwork of a system to ensure the welfare of all Americans. But the powerful federal government of today is also the product of World War II and the Cold War. Those conflicts, as we saw in Chapters 25 and 26, brought a massive increase in government spending, taxes, and employees, as well as an influential "military-industrial complex" of private corporations. In fact, as our discussion of the decades since 1945 suggests, many private-interest groups have become reliant on favorable legislation or outright government subsidies. Because the modern state is so deeply implicated in the social and economic welfare of the American people as well as in their military defense, conservative politicians—as we explained in this chapter—have been unable to shrink substantially the size or scope of governmental activity.

CHAPTER REVIEW QUESTIONS

- How did the domestic policies of Presidents Reagan, Bush, and Clinton reflect the rise of conservatism in American politics?

- What comparisons can you make between the Iran-Contra scandal of Ronald Reagan's administration and the impeachment crisis of Bill Clinton's?

- What new challenges did the end of the Cold War bring to American foreign policy?

TIMELINE

1970s	Rise of the New Right
1981	Ronald Reagan becomes president; Republicans win control of Senate
	Economic Recovery Tax Act (ERTA) cuts taxes
	Military expenditures increase sharply
	Reagan cuts budgets of regulatory agencies
	Sandra Day O'Connor appointed to the Supreme Court
1981–1989	National debt triples
	Emergence of New Right think tanks: Heritage Foundation, American Enterprise Institute, and the Cato Institute
	U.S. assists Iraq in war against Iran (1980–1988)
1983	Strategic Defense Initiative (Star Wars)
1985	Gramm-Rudman Budget Act
	Mikhail Gorbachev takes power in Soviet Union
1986	Iran-Contra scandal weakens Reagan presidency
	William Rehnquist named chief justice
1987	United States and USSR agree to limit missiles in Europe
1988	George H. W. Bush elected president
1989	Destruction of Berlin Wall; "Velvet Revolutions" in eastern Europe
	Webster v. Reproductive Health Services limits abortion services
1990–1991	Persian Gulf War
	Americans with Disabilities Act
1991	Dissolution of Soviet Union ends Cold War
	Clarence Thomas named to the Supreme Court
1992	Democratic moderate Bill Clinton elected president in three-way race
	Planned Parenthood of Southeastern Pennsylvania v. Casey upholds *Roe v. Wade*
1993	Congress passes Family and Medical Leave Act
	North American Free Trade Agreement (NAFTA)
1994	Clinton fails to win health insurance but reduces budget deficit and national debt
	Republicans gain control of Congress
1995	U.S. troops enforce peace in Bosnia
1996	Personal Responsibility and Work Opportunity Act reforms welfare system
1998–1999	Bill Clinton impeached and acquitted
	American intervention in Bosnia and Serbia
	Rise of radical Muslim movements and Al Qaeda terrorists

FOR FURTHER EXPLORATION

James T. Patterson, *Restless Giant: The United States from Watergate to Bush v. Gore* (2005), provides a solid analysis of the 1980s and 1990s. For evangelical politics, see Frances FitzGerald, *Cities on a Hill* (1986), which has a section on Jerry Falwell and the Moral Majority; William Martin, *With God on Our Side: The Rise of the Religious Right in America* (1996); and Lisa McGerr, *Suburban Warriors: The Origins of the New American Right* (2001). Two valuable overviews of the Reagan presidency are Lou Cannon, *President Reagan: The Role of a Lifetime* (2000), and Haynes Johnson, *Sleepwalking through History: America in the Reagan Years* (1992). John Greene, *The Presidency of George Bush* (2000), discusses the policies of the senior Bush.

On foreign policy, consult Richard A. Melanson, *American Foreign Policy since the Vietnam War* (2005), which covers the years from 1970 to 2000, and Raymond Garthoff, *The Great Transition: Russian-American Politics and the End of the Cold War* (1994). Two fine Web sites that document various Cold War incidents are The National Security Archive, at **www.gwu.edu/~nsarchiv**, and The Cold War International History Project, at **www.wilsoncenter.org/index.cfm?fuseaction= topics.home&topic_id=1409**. For the Gulf War, see Michael Gordon and Bernard Trainor, *The Generals' War: The Inside Story of the Conflict in the Gulf* (1995), and **www.pbs.org/ wgbh/pages/frontline/gulf**, a site with maps, documents, and interviews with decision makers and soldiers.

For the Clinton years, consult William Berman, *From the Center to the Edge: The Politics and Policies of the Clinton Presidency* (2001), and Joe Klein, *The Natural: The Misunderstood Presidency of Bill Clinton* (2002). Richard A. Posner, *An Affair of State: The Investigation, Impeachment, and Trial of President Clinton* (1999), probes the legal aspects of that affair. For online materials on Clinton's impeachment, consult Jurist, the Law Professors' Network, at **jurist.law.pitt.edu/impeach.htm**.

Other interesting political studies include Steven Gillon, *"That's Not What We Meant to Do": Reform and Its Unintended Consequences in Twentieth Century America* (2001); Fred Greenstein, *The Presidential Difference: Leadership Style from FDR to Clinton* (2000); and Ted Halstead and Michael Lind, *The Radical Center: The Future of American Politics* (2001). Information on all U.S. presidents is available at **www.ipl.org/div/potus**.

TEST YOUR KNOWLEDGE

To assess your command of the material in this chapter, see the Online Study Guide at **bedfordstmartins.com/henretta**.

For Web sites, images, and documents related to topics and places in this chapter, visit **bedfordstmartins.com/makehistory**.

31 A Dynamic Economy, A Divided People
1980–2000

America in the Global Economy and Society
The Economic Challenge
A Turn to Prosperity
Globalization

The New Technology
The Computer Revolution
Technology and the Control of Popular Culture

Culture Wars
An Increasingly Pluralistic Society
Conflicting Values: Women's and Gay Rights

Summary
Connections: Society and Technology

As 1999 came to a close, a technological disaster threatened millions of computers around the world. For decades programmers had used a two-digit field to describe dates, recording 1950 as simply "50." What would happen when the clock flashed to "Y2K"—shorthand for the year 2000? Would millions of personal, corporate, and government computers clock it as 1900, magically shifting the world a century back in time? Or would the computers crash and wipe out the data of millions of users? As it turned out, the great "Y2K" fear proved unfounded, as thousands of software programmers managed to patch the world's computer systems and avoid a disaster.

The moment was nonetheless symbolic. As the world entered the third millennium of the Christian era, the fates of its many peoples were directly tied to one another electronically and in many other ways. In centuries past, periodic waves of epidemical diseases—the Black Death, cholera, and influenza—had joined the peoples of the world, and then only in death. Now millions of people across the globe were linked together on a daily basis—working in export-oriented factories, watching television programs created in distant nations, flying thousands of miles in jet planes to other continents, and—perhaps most amazing of all—having pictures of their towns and fields snapped by satellite cameras

◂ **www.TimBerners-Lee**

Nothing represents the globalization of the world's economy and culture better than the World Wide Web, which allows instant access to Web sites around the globe. The technology behind the Web was invented between 1989 and 1991 by Tim Berners-Lee, an English computer scientist working at the time at CERN, the European Particle Physics Laboratory in Geneva, Switzerland. This photomosaic picture of Berners-Lee, who presently teaches at MIT, is composed of 2,304 Web sites. Tim Berners-Lee.

high in the stratosphere and beamed instantly around the world. The globe was growing smaller.

But not necessarily more harmonious. "Globalization"—the movement of goods, ideas, and organizations across political boundaries—created as many conflicts as it solved. Likewise, increased contact among Americans through modern means of communications made them more conscious of their differences—racial, ethnic, religious, ideological—and sharpened cultural conflict at home. In particular, New Right conservatives, who had come into their own in the Reagan-Bush years, squared off against social welfare liberals, who adhered to many of the social values that had flourished from the 1930s through the 1960s. The resulting "culture wars" strained social harmony as the twentieth century drew to a close.

America in the Global Economy and Society

When Bill Clinton ran for president in 1992, a large sign in his campaign "war room" underlined the main issue: "THE ECONOMY, STUPID." Throughout the last quarter of the century, bread-and-butter issues loomed large in the minds of many Americans. The abrupt rise in global oil prices in the 1970s had triggered a corrosive "stagflation" that had heaped hardship on the poor, shrunk middle-class expectations, and shaken the confidence of policymakers and business executives. It would take time, ingenuity, and a bit of luck to restore America's self-confidence.

The Economic Challenge

The 1980s began on a depressing economic note. Unemployment remained above 7 percent, and the cost of living continued to soar at a rate of 8 percent a year. When the Federal Reserve jacked up interest rates (to nearly 20 percent) to combat inflation (see Chapter 30), the nation experienced a sharp recession in 1981–1982, with nearly 10 percent of the workforce without jobs.

However, the economy quickly revived and turned the rest of the decade into one of relative prosperity. The wealthiest one-fifth of Americans, the primary beneficiaries of President Reagan's tax

FIGURE 31.1 Productivity, Family Income, and Wages, 1970–2004

This chart tells a complex and not altogether happy story. The median hourly wages of American workers (adjusted for inflation) stagnated between 1970 and 1995. The rise in median family income reflected the increasing proportion of two-earner families, as more married women entered the workforce. The dramatic increases in productivity did not lead to higher wages for workers. Rather, businesses used those gains either to cut prices to compete in the global marketplace or to reward owners, shareholders, and, particularly, corporate executives.

Akio Morita and the Sony Corporation

In 1946 Akio Morita and Masaru Ibuka founded the Tokyo Telecommunications Engineering Corporation, which evolved into the Sony Corporation. Its first great sales success came in the mid-1950s with a pocket-sized transistor radio. Other innovative products followed in subsequent decades: in the 1960s, the popular Trinitron TV; in the 1970s, the Betamax video recorder and the Walkman radio; in the 1980s, the compact disc, the three-and-a-half inch diskette, and, shown here in a picture of Morita in 1985, the Handycam. In the 1990s, Sony devised the PlayStation, the memory stick, and many more electronic products. In 2005, Sony employed 150,000 workers and sold goods worth $18 billion in the United States and $67 billion worldwide. Photo by Bill Pierce/Time Life Pictures/Getty Images.

cuts and economic policies, did especially well. Many middle-class Americans also enjoyed a modest affluence, but the real wages of manufacturing and retail workers continued to stagnate (Figure 31.1). The poor — the thirty million citizens below the poverty line — struggled to survive.

Domestic Affluence and Foreign Debts. The fate of the poor was of little concern to the well-educated "baby boom" children who entered the labor force in the early 1980s. Many took high-paying jobs in the rapidly growing professional and technology sectors of the economy. These young urban professionals — the Yuppies, as they were called — set the tone for a strikingly materialistic culture. Yuppies (and Buppies, their black counterparts) dined at gourmet restaurants, enjoyed vacations at elaborate resorts, and lived in large suburban houses filled with expensive consumer goods. Their example shaped the outlook of the next generation. Surveys reported that 80 percent of college students in the 1980s placed a high value on individual economic success while only 40 percent gave importance to enlightened social values — an exact reversal of student attitudes during the 1960s. The majority of Americans who could not afford the new luxuries experienced them vicariously by watching *Lifestyles of the Rich and Famous*, a popular TV series that debuted in 1984. Every week, host Robin Leach took audiences into the mansions of people who enjoyed "champagne wishes and caviar dreams."

Tempering this enthusiasm, commentators warned of the nation's economic decline. Until the 1970s the United States had been the world's leading exporter of agricultural products, manufactured goods, and investment capital. Then, American exports began to fall, undercut in world markets by cheaper and often better designed products from Germany and Japan (see Chapter 29). By 1985, for the first time since 1915, the United States registered a negative balance of international payments. It now imported more goods than it exported, a trade deficit fueled by soaring imports of foreign oil, which increased between 1960 and 2000 from two to twelve million barrels per day. Moreover, America's earnings from foreign investments did not offset the imbalance in trade. The United States had become a debtor (rather than a creditor) nation; each year, it had to borrow money, in the form of credit or investment capital, to maintain the standard of living many Americans had come to expect.

Japan's Rise, America's Decline. The rapid ascent of the Japanese economy to the second largest in the world was a key factor in this historic reversal. Japan's Nikkei stock index tripled in value between 1965 and 1975, and then tripled again by 1985. Now more than a third of the American annual trade deficit of $138 billion was with Japan, whose corporations exported huge quantities of electronic goods (TVs, VCRs, microwave ovens) and other consumer products. Indeed, Japanese auto companies accounted for nearly a quarter of all cars bought in the United States. Using the profits of these sales, Japanese businesses bought up prime pieces of real estate, such as New York City's Rockefeller Center, and took over well-known American corporations. The purchase by Japan's Sony Corporation of two American icons, Columbia Pictures and CBS Records, frightened politicians and ordinary citizens. The post-1945 economic primacy of the United States was in rapid decline.

While Japan and Germany prospered, American businesses grappled with a worrisome decline in productivity. Between 1973 and 1992, the productivity of American workers grew at the meager rate of 1 percent a year, a far cry from the post–World War II rate of 3 percent annually. As a consequence, the wages of most employees stagnated and the number of high-paying, union-protected manufacturing jobs shrank. Unemployed industrial workers took whatever jobs they could find, usually minimum-wage positions as sales "associates" in fast-food franchises or in big-box stores, such as Wal-Mart or Home Depot. By 1985, more people in the United States worked for McDonald's slinging Big Macs than labored in the nation's steel industry, rolling out rails, girders, and sheet steel. Middle-class Americans — baby boomers included — also found themselves with less economic security. To remain competitive internationally, corporations reduced the number of middle-level managers and back-office accountants. Most laid-off middle managers eventually found new jobs, but many had to take sizeable cuts in pay.

As middle-class families struggled to make ends meet, poor Americans just held their own. The number remained stable, at about 31 million, and despite the Reagan-era budget cuts, Americans entitled to Medicare, food stamps, and Aid to Families with Dependent Children received about the same level of benefits in 1990 than they had in 1980. Still, the number of homeless citizens doubled. A Community Services Society report movingly described how thousands of people found themselves without a place to live: "Something happens — a job is lost, unemployment benefits run out, creditors and banks move in to foreclose, eviction proceedings begin — and quite suddenly the respectable poor find themselves among the disreputable homeless."

The Impact on Family Life. Challenging economic times accelerated changes already underway in family life and gender roles. As early as the 1960s, married women entered the paid workforce in increasing numbers, both to exercise their talents and to bolster their families' income (Figure 31.2). As men's wages stagnated during the 1970s, women increasingly sought paid employment — even though their pay averaged only about 70 percent of that paid to men. By 1994, 58 percent of adult women were in the labor force, up from 38 percent in 1962. Many women, especially those with young children, did double duty; as one working mother remarked, "You're on duty at work. You come home, and you're on duty" again.

Some women entered male-dominated fields, such as medicine, law, skilled trades, law enforce-

FIGURE 31.2 The Increase in Two-Worker Families

In 1968, about 43 percent of married couples sent both the husband and the wife into the workforce; thirty years later, 60 percent were two-earner families. The percentage of families in which the wife alone worked doubled (from 3 percent to 5 percent) during these years, while those with no earners (welfare recipients and, increasingly, retired couples) rose from 8 percent to 13 percent. Because these figures do not include unmarried persons and most illegal immigrants, they do not give a complete picture of the American workplace. But there is no doubt that women now play a major role in the workforce.

Barbie Goes to Work

Since 1959, the shapely Barbie doll has symbolized the "feminine mystique," the female as sexual object, and diffused this view of American womanhood around the nation and the globe. More than 500 million Barbies have been sold in 140 countries. But Barbie moves with the times. In 1985, she got her first computer, and in 1999, this doll and CD set transformed Barbie into a working woman, earning her own bread in the corporate workplace and, perhaps, with something intelligent to say! © Mattel.

ment, and the military, but the majority still labored in traditional fields, such as teaching, nursing, and sales work. In fact, one in five women held a clerical or secretarial job, the same proportion as in 1950. Still, as women flooded the labor force, cultural expectations and ideals began to change. Men learned to accept women as coworkers — and even as their bosses — and took responsibility for more household tasks. By the 1990s, only about 15 percent of U.S. households conformed to the model of the ideal American family depicted by the Hollywood script writers of the 1950s: employed father, homemaker wife, and young children.

The Turn to Prosperity

Between 1985 and 1990, American corporate executives and workers learned how to compete against their German and Japanese rivals. One key was technology and especially the use of information processing, which had been pioneered by Microsoft, Cisco, Sun, and other American companies. As corporations fitted out their plants and offices with computers, robots, and other "smart" machines, the productivity of the workforce rose. Bethlehem Steel, which invested $6 billion to modernize its operations during the late 1980s, soon doubled its productivity. Other firms retooled their corporate vision. Between 1980 and 1981, the Ford Motor Company lost $2.5 billion because of high expenses and stagnating sales. Responding to this desperate situation, Ford made fundamental reforms that improved the quality of its cars, enhanced the morale of assembly-line workers, and cut costs by adopting the Japanese system of rapid inventory resupply.

The stock market quickly reflected these initiatives, as ambitious and aggressive baby-boom brokers took control of Wall Street and government policy encouraged private investors. Prompted by the deregulation policies of the Carter administration, the Securities and Exchange Commission enacted new rules that made the financial industry more open and competitive (see Chapter 29). These measures encouraged the creation of discount brokerage firms, whose low fees prompted more small-scale investors to enter the stock market. Between 1980 and 2000, the percentage of American families owning some stock quadrupled from 13 to 51 percent. As the economic expansion gathered steam, stock prices spurted upward. In a six-month period in 1986, the value of stocks rose $400 billion. Even a major financial scandal in the savings and loan industry (which eventually cost taxpayers $132 billion) and a startling Wall Street crash in October 1987, in which stocks lost a fourth of their value, did not deter investors. Within two years, the market had regained its former level and continued to rise.

Goats and Heroes of the 1980s: Ivan Boesky, Lee Iacocca, and Donald Trump. The rise in stock values unleashed a wave of corporate mergers, as companies used stock to buy up competitors. As these deals multiplied, so too did the number of traders who profited illegally from insider knowledge. The most notorious of the white-collar criminals was Ivan Boesky, who acquired a fortune—and a reputation as an astute financier—as he arranged takeovers and buyouts. Invited to deliver the commencement address to graduates of the Business School at the University of California at Berkeley, Boesky said, "I think greed is healthy. You can be greedy and still feel good about yourself." At least until scandal strikes! Convicted of illegal trading, Boesky was sentenced to three-and-a-half years in prison (he served two years) and had to disgorge $50 million from his illicit profits and another $50 million in fines.

While sleazy financiers like Boesky gave corporate millionaires a bad name, successful business executives basked in the Reagan administration's adulation of wealth. When the president christened self-made entrepreneurs "the heroes for the eighties," he probably had Lee Iacocca in mind. The son of Italian immigrants, Iacocca personified the American Dream. Trained as an engineer, he rose through the ranks to become president of the Ford Motor Corporation; resigning from that position in 1978, he took over the ailing Chrysler auto company. Over the next decade, Iacocca turned Chrysler into a profitable company—securing a crucial $1.5 billion loan from the U.S. government and pushing the

An Automated Assembly Line
Most basic manufacturing is now done by machines, like these robotic welders on an automobile assembly line. The use of these machines increases productivity, in part by eliminating the jobs traditionally done by welders. But this advance in technology also creates new jobs in making and servicing the robots and other automated machines. © Bettmann/Corbis.

development of new cars. To encourage Americans to buy improved Chrysler models, Iacocca starred in TV advertisements and echoed Reagan's rhetoric: "Let's make American mean something again."

Simultaneously, real estate entrepreneur Donald Trump revived the morale of many aspiring residents of New York City, whose government had long teetered on the brink of bankruptcy. In 1983, the flamboyant Trump built the equally flamboyant Trump Towers. At the entrance of the $200 million apartment building stood two enormous bronze "T's," a display of self-promotion reinforced by the media. Calling him "The Donald," a nickname used by his first wife, TV reporters and magazines commented relentlessly on his marriages and divorces and the extravagant lifestyle that his $3 billion real estate empire made possible.

Trump personified the materialistic values of the Reagan era. Accustomed to the elegance and extravagance of Hollywood, Ronald and Nancy Reagan created an affluent atmosphere in the White House that contrasted sharply with the austerity of the 1970s and Jimmy and Rosalynn Carter's subdued lifestyle. At Carter's inauguration in 1977, the Carter family dressed simply, walked to the ceremony, and led an evening of restrained merrymaking; four years later, Reagan and his wealthy Republican supporters racked up inauguration expenses of $16 million. Critics lambasted the extravagance of Trump and the Reagans, but many Americans joined with them in celebrating the return of American prosperity and promise.

The Boom Years of the 1990s. The economic resurgence of the late 1980s did not restore America's once dominant position in the international economy. The nation's heavy industries — steel, autos, chemicals — continued to lose market share, both because of weak executive leadership and because of the relatively high wages paid to American workers. Nonetheless, during the 1990s the economy of the United States grew at the impressive average rate of 3 percent per year. Moreover, its main international competitors were now struggling. In Germany, France, and other European industrial nations, high taxes and high wages stifled economic growth, while in Japan spectacular busts in the speculative-driven real estate and stock markets in 1989 crippled the economy. Its banking system burdened by billions of yen in bad debts, Japan limped though the 1990s with a meager growth rate of 1.1 percent a year.

Meanwhile, boom times came to the United States. During Bill Clinton's two terms in the White House (1993–2001), the stock market value of American companies nearly tripled. This boom, which was fueled by the flow of funds into high-tech and e-commerce firms, enriched American citizens and their governments. Middle-income families who were covered by pension plans saw their retirement savings suddenly double and felt good about the future. Simultaneously, the taxes collected on stock sales and profits provided a windfall for the state and federal governments. By 2000, the Clinton administration had paid off half of the enormous national debt created during the Reagan and Bush presidencies and was sending balanced budgets to Congress. Indeed, on the basis of recent events, the Congressional Budget Office projected an astonishing surplus of $4.6 trillion in governmental revenue during the coming decade.

As was the case during the Reagan era, the prosperity of the Clinton years was not equally distributed. By 1998 the income of the wealthiest 13,000 families in the United States was greater than the poorest 20 *million* families. Moreover, the good times did not last. A spectacular "bust" hit the over-inflated stock market in late 2000; within two years stock values fell about 40 percent (Figure 31.3). Their savings suddenly worth less, older Americans delayed their retirements. Faced by falling tax revenues, state governments cut services to balance their budgets, and the federal government again spent billions more than it collected.

Donald Trump

Some people are larger than life, and Donald Trump is certainly one of them. The beneficiary of an inheritance of $200 million from his father, "The Donald" built a series of spectacular hotels and condominiums, first in New York City and later in Atlantic City and Palm Beach. Trump's grandiose vision — of himself and his projects — has often placed him in vulnerable personal and financial situations. But neither a bitter divorce nor brushes with bankruptcy have dented his ego and ambition. He is pictured here in 1989 in the atrium of the Trump Tower in New York City. Photo by Ted Thai/Time Life Pictures/Getty Images.

Globalization

As Americans sought economic security, they recognized that their success depended in part on developments in the world economy. In one sense, this situation was not new. Over the centuries, Americans had depended on foreign markets for their tobacco, cotton, wheat, and industrial goods, and they had long received manufactures and millions of immigrants from other countries. But the *intensity* of international exchange varied over time, and it was again on the upswing. The end of the Cold War had shattered the political barriers that had restrained international trade and impeded capitalist development of vast areas of the world. Moreover, new communication systems — satellites, fiber optic cables, global positioning networks — would shrink

"McWorld" and Globalization in Saudi Arabia
Many of the leading multinational corporations transforming the world's economy are purveyors of American-style consumer goods like Nike and Disney products. So successful was McDonald's in extending its international markets with 13,000 foreign outlets that many critics refer to the results of globalization in general as "McWorld." AP Images.

others—hired English-speaking Indians to staff consumer call centers; and many American firms hired electrical engineers and computer technicians in Bangalore and other Indian high-tech centers.

From the standpoint of corporate profits, outsourcing made sense. In 2005 an American graduate of the California Institute of Technology could expect a starting salary of $56,000, while a graduate of the Indian Institute of Technology commanded only one-third as much. Viewed from a national economic perspective, the outsourcing of skilled American jobs seemed more problematic. Unlike the "brain drain" that brought tens of thousands of foreign-born doctors, engineers, scientists, and technicians to the United States, where they enriched its society, outsourcing undermined the wages of American workers and threatened the long-term vitality of its economy.

Outsourcing had a cultural as well as an economic impact. One of Nike's advertising campaigns, focused on American basketball superstar Michael Jordan, sold millions of pairs of shoes and made Jordan an international celebrity. It also spread American entrepreneurial values as Nike's ads urged people around the world to "Just Do It." Some of them took up the challenge. Yao Ming, a 7′6″ basketball star in China, joined the Houston Rockets, one of a dozen or more players from European and Asian countries who now played in the National Basketball Association. In professional sports, as in other businesses, owners now drew their employees from around the world. In the pursuit of productivity and profit in the new global economy, the political boundaries of nation-states became increasingly irrelevant.

Disease and Death in an Interconnected World.
An exponential growth in the movement of people and ideas across borders was yet another marker of a shrinking world. On any given day in the late twentieth century, an estimated two million travelers and immigrants crossed an international border. Ideas moved even faster. Communications satellites transmitted phone conversations, television programs, and business data through the air, while fiber optic cables instantaneously connected e-mail users and World Wide Web servers in distant continents.

As the globe shrank in size, certain dangers increased in magnitude. In 1918 and 1919, soldiers from distant lands spread a killer flu virus from the battlefields of Europe to most of the world (see Chapter 22). That vicious pandemic killed fifty million people. An equally deadly disease, the human immunodeficiency virus (HIV), spread from Africa to the United States during the 1970s. In 1981 American physicians recognized HIV as a new disease, one that was killing hundreds of gay males, who had become its main carriers. Within two decades HIV, which causes AIDS (acquired immune deficiency syndrome), had spread worldwide, infected over fifty million people of both sexes, and killed more than twenty million.

Within the United States, AIDS took thousands of lives—more than died in the Korean and Vietnam wars combined. Then, between 1995 and 1999, American deaths from HIV dropped 30 percent. This decline—the result of new treatment strategies using a combination of drugs, or a "cocktail"—led to cautious optimism about controlling the disease, for which there is no cure. The high cost of

A Nike Factory in China

In 2005, Nike produced its shoes and sportswear at 124 plants in China; additional factories were located in other low-wage countries. Most of the Chinese plants are run by subcontractors, who house the workers — mostly women between the ages of sixteen to twenty-five — in crowded dormitories. The wages are low, about $3 a day, but more than the women could earn if they remained in their rural villages. AP Images.

these drugs limited their availability, particularly in poor nations. In sub-Saharan Africa, the HIV crisis has reached epidemic proportions, with 30 million infections. South and Southeast Asia, as well as countries of the former Soviet Union, also have millions of infected people — five million in India alone.

Other life-threatening diseases have the potential to spread around the world in days. In February 2003, a viral respiratory illness called SARS (severe acute respiratory syndrome) appeared in China. Within a few months, the disease spread to more than two dozen countries in North America, South America, Europe, and Asia. Despite elaborate public health measures, the virus infected over eight thousand people and killed almost eight hundred of them. And in 2006 a bird virus infected — and killed — a few dozen people and raised the prospect of a new pandemic, if the bird virus mutates to a form that easily spreads among humans.

The Endangered Environment. The expanding global economy also threatened the health of the world's peoples by polluting the environment. In some countries, the rapid rise in the number of mines, factories, and power plants destroyed irreplaceable natural resources or rendered them unusable. During the last three decades in Brazil, land-hungry peasants, lumber companies, and agribusinesses have cut down roughly a third of the region's ancient rain forests. In Taiwan and China, waste products from new industries and farms have polluted nearly every river — killing fish and rendering the water unsafe to drink.

The industrialized nations also threatened the environment. As millions of cars and thousands of

AIDS in Africa

AIDS (acquired immune deficiency syndrome) originated in Africa, where a chimpanzee virus jumped to humans in the 1960s, and it has taken its greatest toll on that continent. This man, from the Rakai province in southern Uganda, is dying — slowly wasting away — and is completely dependent for support on his twelve-year-old daughter. The Uganda government has implemented an AIDS-prevention program in Rakai and elsewhere and has reported a decline in the prevalence of HIV, the virus that causes AIDS. But it appears that the decline in the number of HIV-infected people is primarily the result of the deaths of many of them. In 2002 in Rakai, 200 people with long-standing HIV infections died, and 125 people became newly infected. Photo by Michael Jensen/www.world-photo.dk.

power plants in Europe and North America burned coal, oil, and other hydrocarbons, they raised the temperature of the atmosphere and the acidity of the oceans — a "greenhouse" effect with potentially momentous consequences. Similarly, the decades-long release into the atmosphere of chlorofluorocarbons (CFCs) — compounds used in industrial cleaning agents, refrigerators, and aerosol cans — significantly depleted the layer of ozone that protects humans from the sun's dangerous ultraviolet rays.

These dangers prompted thousands of Americans to join environmental-protection organizations, such as the Sierra Club and the Nature Conservatory. These groups, and officials of the Environmental Protection Agency, successfully curtailed some pollution. But they were unable to alter government policy on major issues or to convince their fellow citizens of the wisdom of conservation. Ignoring warnings of tightening of oil supplies, the Reagan and Bush administrations refused to support legislation raising mileage requirements for car manufacturers. General Motors and Ford likewise rejected such warnings because they wanted to sell more high-profit gas-guzzling SUV's and small trucks. Nor would most American consumers voluntarily change their lifestyles to reduce energy consumption and cut pollution.

Still, the United States supported a few environmental initiatives. In 1987 the United States was one of thirty-four nations that signed the Montreal Protocol, which banned the production of ozone-damaging CFCs by 1999. The American government likewise joined sixty-three other countries in the Basel Convention of 1994, which ended the export of hazardous wastes to developing countries. Still, American businesses and their political allies resisted efforts to prevent global warming. Although President Clinton signed the Kyoto Treaty of 1998, which committed industrialized countries to reduce greenhouse-gas emissions, the U.S. Senate refused to ratify the agreement. In 2001, the administration of George W. Bush rejected the Kyoto accord, both because it did not apply to underdeveloped countries — which were some of the worst polluters — and because it would restrict or raise the cost of American economic production.

Globalization and Its Critics. President George W. Bush has celebrated globalization as "the triumph of human liberty stretching across national borders ... [and holding] the promise of delivering billions of the world's citizens from disease and hunger and want." Critics are less optimistic. Some see globalization as a new form of imperialism, whereby the industrialized nations exploit the peoples and natural resources of the rest of the world. Giving political form to these criticisms, Lori Wallach founded Public Citizens' Global Watch, an organization whose goal was to promote "democracy by challenging corporate globalization." Condemning multinational corporations for their failure to protect workers or the environment, Global Watch spearheaded a massive protest at the World Trade Organization meeting in Seattle in 1999. Thousands of activists, including union organizers, environmentalists, and concerned students, disrupted the city and prevented the WTO from convening. As one protestor explained, people "can't go to the

WTO Demonstration, Seattle, 1999

In November 1999, an estimated 75,000 people from many states and foreign nations staged an effective protest at a World Trade Organization (WTO) meeting in Seattle. The goals of the protesters were diffuse; many feared that the trend toward a system of free (capitalist-run) trade would primarily benefit multinational corporations and would hurt both developing nations and the working classes in the industrialized world. Protests have continued at subsequent meetings of the WTO and the World Bank. Hector Mata/AFP/Getty Images.

polls and talk to these big conglomerates. So they had to take to the streets and talk to them." Similar protests against globalization have occurred at meetings of the World Bank, International Monetary Fund, and the G-8 nations.

Indeed, on the occasion of a G-8 meeting in Scotland in 2005, critics mounted a worldwide protest against the financial impact of globalization on poor countries. "Live-8" assembled an international cast of music stars who gave free concerts at ten venues — stretching from London to Tokyo and from Philadelphia to Johannesburg. Broadcast on television and the World Wide Web, the concerts reached a huge audience. Although the concerts helped to persuade the G-8 nations to forgive billions of dollars of debts owned by African nations, they did little to address the internal corruption that has gravely hindered those countries' development. Still, by using the communication infrastructure of the global world, critics had forced a discussion of its effects.

- What were the sources of the American economic recovery of the 1980s and 1990s? Who were its heroes, and what were its shortcomings?
- What factors promoted "globalization"?
- Outline the arguments for and against globalization. Who is making these arguments? Why?

The New Technology

The technological advances that enabled Live-8 had already changed the character of everyday life for millions of Americans. Computers, cell phones, the Internet, and other electronic-based devices altered work, leisure, and access to knowledge in stunning ways.

The Computer Revolution

Scientists devised the first computers — information-processing machines that stored and manipulated data — for military purposes during World War II. Subsequently, the federal government funded computer research as part of the drive for American military superiority during the Cold War. Using this research, private companies began to build large "main frame" computers. In 1952, CBS News used UNIVAC (Universal Automatic Computer), the first commercial computer system, to predict the outcome of the presidential election.

Innovation and Miniaturization. The first computers were cumbersome and finicky machines. They used heat-emitting vacuum tubes for computation power and punched cards for writing programs and analyzing data. UNIVAC and other main-frame computers occupied an entire air-conditioned room, and programming them took several days. In 1947, scientists at Bell Labs invented the transistor, a tiny silicon device that amplifies a signal or opens or closes a circuit many times each second. The transistor revolutionized the electronics industry and allowed technicians to build a second generation of computers — smaller, more powerful, and much cheaper to manufacture. Then in 1959, scientists invented the integrated circuit — a silicon microchip composed of large numbers of interconnected transistors — and ushered in the third computer generation.

Progress continued at an unrelenting pace, as computer wizards devised smaller and more sophisticated chips. A great breakthrough came in 1971 with the development of the microprocessor, which placed the entire central processing unit (CPU) of a computer on a single silicon chip about the size of the letter "O" on this page. By the mid-1970s, a few chips provided as much processing power as a World War II–era computer.

The day of the personal computer (PC) had arrived. In 1977, the Apple Corporation offered a personal computer for $1,195 (about $3,300 today), a price middle-class Americans could afford. When the Apple II became a runaway success, other companies scrambled to get into the market. International Business Machines (IBM) offered its first personal computer in 1981. In three decades, the computer had moved from a few military research centers, to thousands of corporate offices, and then to millions of people's homes. In the process, it created huge entrepreneurial opportunities and a host of overnight millionaires.

Bill Gates and Microsoft. Making computers user-friendly was the major challenge of the PC revolution. In the early 1970s, two former high-school classmates, Bill Gates, aged nineteen, and Paul Allen, twenty-one, set a goal of putting "a personal computer on every desk and in every home." They perceived that the key was "software," the programs that would tell the electronic components (the "hardware") what to do. In 1975 they founded the Microsoft Corporation, which soon dominated the software industry. The phenomenal success of Microsoft's MS-DOS and Windows operating systems stemmed primarily from the company's ability to anticipate industry trends, develop products

Triumph of the Geeks: Microsoft Employees, 1978
This group portrait shows eleven of Microsoft's thirteen employees as the company was about to relocate from Albuquerque, New Mexico, to Seattle, Washington. The oldest member was Paul Allen (front row, far right), age twenty-five; Bill Gates (front row, far left) was twenty-three. A quarter of a century later, Allen was worth $20 billion, Gates was worth nearly $100 billion, and Microsoft had more than fifty thousand employees. Courtesy, Bob Wallace.

quickly, and market them relentlessly. As a Microsoft veteran described the corporate strategy: "See where everybody's headed, then catch up and go past them." And pass them it did. By 2000, the company's products ran nine out of every ten personal computers in the United States and a majority of those around the world. Bill Gates became a billionaire, and Microsoft exploded into a huge company with 57,000 employees and annual revenue of $38 billion. Indeed, Microsoft's near-monopoly of basic computer operating systems prompted government regulators in the United States and the European Union to lodge antitrust suits against the company and force changes in its business practices.

The Impact of the Internet. During the 1990s, personal computers grew even more significant with the spread of the Internet and the World Wide Web. Like the computer itself, the Internet was the product of military-based research. During the 1970s, the Pentagon set up a system of hundreds of computers (or "servers") that were widely dispersed across the United States and connected to each other by copper wires (and now by fiber optic cables). Designed to preserve military communications in the event of a Soviet nuclear attack, the system was soon used by government scientists, academic specialists, and military contractors to exchange text-based e-mail messages via their computers.

The debut in 1991 of the graphics-based World Wide Web, a vast collection of interconnected documents, enhanced the popular appeal and commercial possibilities of the Internet. By 2006, nearly 70 percent of all Americans and slightly more than one billion people worldwide used the Internet to send messages or to view material on the Web. The Web allowed companies, organizations, and individuals to create their own "home pages," incorporating visual, audio, and textual information. Businesses used the Internet to sell their products and services; the volume of e-commerce transactions grew steadily, to $114 billion in 2003 and $172 billion in 2005. During his unsuccessful bid for the 2004 Democratic presidential nomination, Governor Howard Dean of Vermont demonstrated the political potential of the Internet, by using it to raise money and mobilize grassroots support for his campaign. Other politicians and social activists have followed his lead, using the Internet and the Web in ever more creative ways.

Already thousands of businesses were using networked computers—creating the modern electronic office. Small companies kept their records and did all their correspondence and billing on a few desktop machines; large corporations set up linked computers that shared a common database. Some employees no longer came physically to the office; some days they worked as "telecommuters" with their home computers and fax machines connected to the office network by telephone lines, fiber optic cables, and wireless relay systems.

Computers and the Internet transformed leisure as well as work. Millions of Americans took advantage of e-mail to stay in close touch with family and friends. More anonymously, they joined online chat rooms, dating services, and interactive games. Those with broadband connections to the Internet watched "streaming videos" of news events and downloaded music videos and feature films. Interestingly—and importantly—millions of users tried to persuade others to see the world as they do. In 1997 a few people began personal online diaries called Web logs or "blogs"; by 2004, the number of bloggers had grown to eight million, and they offered their authors' perspectives on a wide range of issues: politics, diplomacy, and consumer affairs.

More profoundly, the Web empowered people by providing easy access to knowledge. For nearly two centuries, local public libraries had served that function; now, much of the content of a library was instantly available in a home or office. Using powerful "search engines" such as Google and Yahoo!, people easily located information—some wonderfully accurate and some distressingly problematic—on nearly every subject under the sun. Millions of Americans regularly read newspapers online and used the Web to acquire medical information about diet, drugs, and disease. Students and scholars mined the Web's digital archives and online journals; lawyers used Lexis-Nexis programs for immediate access to hundreds of cases on specific legal issues. Many things that libraries did well, the Web did wonderfully.

Small Electronics. Advances in electronic technology fostered the rapid creation of new leisure and business products. The 1980s saw the introduction of videocassette recorders (VCRs), compact disc (CD) players, cellular telephones, and inexpensive fax machines. Hand-held video camcorders joined film-based cameras as instruments for preserving family memories; parents video-taped their children's lives—sports achievements, graduations, and marriages—and played them on the home television screen. By 2000, cameras took digital pictures that could be stored and transmitted on computers, digital video discs (DVDs) became the newest technology for viewing movies, and TiVo (a direct video recording system) gave television viewers enormous flexibility in watching programs. At the same time, higher resolution television sets, flat plasma screens, and home theater setups became more affordable and widely disseminated.

Wireless telephones (or cell phones), which became available in the 1980s, presaged a communications revolution. By 2003, two-thirds of American adults carried these portable devices, and people under thirty used them in an increasing variety of ways—to take pictures, play games, connect to the Internet, and send text messages. Building on wireless technology for computers, prosperous families created a home network of telephones, computers, and media/entertainment systems. In 2001, Apple Computer revolutionized the pop music industry with the iPod, a hand-sized unit that stored up to 5,000 songs, and iTunes, a system for downloading music from the Web. By 2006, iPods could store and play video. This revolution in technology, like the cultural revolution of the 1960s, was increasingly the work of the young, who dragged their parents into the new information age.

Legal, Ethical, and Social Issues. Like all new technologies, the computers-Internet-electronics revolution raised a host of social issues and legal conflicts. Many disputes involved the "pirating" of intellectual property through the illegal reproduction of a computer program or a content file. Microsoft and other software companies devised a variety of technical and legal stratagems to protect their copyrighted products, which usually cost millions of dollars to develop. Similarly, the recording industry used lawsuits to shut down the NAPSTER program, which allowed music buffs to share songs through the Internet and burn their own CDs for virtually no cost. Yet intellectual piracy continues, both because of the refusal of governments in China and elsewhere to protect copyrights and because of the decentralized character of the new technology. Just as the Defense Department's system of hundreds of servers would "work around" a Soviet attack, so the existence of millions of personal computers (and skilled operators) has thwarted efforts to police their use.

Computers empowered scientists as well as citizens. Researchers in many scientific disciplines used powerful "supercomputers" to analyze complex natural and human phenomena ranging from economic forecasting to nuclear fusion to human genetics. In 1990, officials at the National Science Foundation allocated $350 million for the Human Genome Project. The Project's goal was to map the human genetic code and unravel the mysteries of DNA (deoxyribonucleic acid), the basic building block of all living things. In 1998, Celera Genomics, a private company backed by pharmaceutical corporations, launched a competing project in hopes of developing profitable drugs. Eventually the two groups pooled their efforts and, by 2003, had built a map of every human gene and posted it, free of charge, on the Web.

As scientists used computers and other technological innovations to probe the mysteries of life, they revived long-standing moral debates. Should employers or insurance companies be permitted to use genetic testing for purposes of hiring or healthcare coverage? Should the stem cells from aborted (or in vitro produced) fetuses be used in the search for cures for Alzheimer's, AIDS, and other debilitating diseases (see Chapter 32)? As commentators debated these biomedical issues, other observers worried about the negative impact of the new computer-based technology. Would the use of automatic telephone menus, bank ATMs, and scanners in retail stores gradually create a machine-driven world in which people had little contact with each other? Would the use of the Web by children and

The Biotech Revolution

In 1953, scientists James Watson, Francis Crick, and Roslyn Franklin discovered the double helix structure of DNA (deoxyribonucleic acid), the molecule that carries the distinct genetic blueprint of specific living things. Once DNA's structure was understood, it became theoretically possible to isolate the genetic codes that control nearly every human characteristic — from height and hair color to inherited diseases and certain cancers. But the process would be enormously complicated, given that there are nearly three billion nucleic acid base pairs in just one set of human chromosomes. With the assistance of computer-linked, automated gene-sequencing machines (like these at the Whitehead Institute at MIT), scientists produced a genetic blueprint of the human species in 2003. The medical payoffs are still to come. © Sam Ogden, Photo Researchers.

youths expose them to sexual abuse? Could personal and financial privacy be preserved in a digital world in which businesses and governments could easily create an electronic "profile" of people's lives and hack into their computers?

Political questions were equally challenging. What were the implications of the Patriot Act of 2001 (see Chapter 32), which permits the federal government to monitor electronically citizens' telephone, e-mail, Web, and library usage? Is the loss of civil privacy and liberty an acceptable price to pay for increased security from terrorists? Such questions, debated throughout the twentieth century, acquired increased urgency in the electronic age.

Finally, would a "digital divide" accentuate existing class and racial divisions? Would affluent Americans who could afford computers and Internet access race ahead of poorer citizens? The evidence was contradictory. In 2005, fewer than half of the families with incomes of $30,000 or less had home access to the Internet. Yet most poorer children and adults had access to the new technology and the global communications network because the local, state, and federal governments have connected computers in schools and public libraries to the Internet and the Web.

Technology and the Control of Popular Culture

Americans have reveled in mass-consumer culture ever since the 1920s, when the spread of automobiles, electric appliances, movies, and radio enhanced the quality of everyday life and leisure. By exposing citizens to the same movies and radio programs, the new communication technologies also helped to forge a homogeneous national popular culture. During the 1950s, the spread of television — and its domination by three networks: ABC, CBS, and NBC — likewise encouraged the emergence of a uniform perspective among a majority of middle-class Americans.

Fragmentation in the Television Industry. During the 1970s, new technological developments reshaped the television industry and the cultural landscape. The advent of cable and satellite broadcasting brought more specialized networks and programs into American living rooms. People now got news round-the-clock from Ted Turner's CNN (Cable News Network), watched myriad sports events on the ESPN channels, and tuned into the Fox network for innovative entertainment. By the 1990s, millions of viewers had access to scores, sometimes hundreds, of specialized channels. They could watch old or new movies, golf tournaments, and cooking classes; view religious or African American or Hispanic programming; and buy goods on home-shopping channels. By 1998, such specialized programming had captured 53 percent of the prime-time TV audience.

One of the most successful niche channels was MTV (Music TV), which debuted in 1981. Initially, its main offerings were slickly made videos featuring popular vocalists, who sang and acted out the words of their songs. Essentially advertisements for CDs, these videos were extremely popular among teenagers, who often watched the channel for two hours a day. With its flashy colors, creative choreography, and rapid cuts, MTV popularized singers such as Michael Jackson and Madonna and pushed forward the creation of a culture based on visual and aural "stimulation."

As television became more competitive, network and cable programmers increasingly laced their shows with sexual stimulation. As a television executive explained, "In a cluttering environment where there are so many more media, you have to be more explicit and daring to stand out." In the 1980s network stations began to feature steamier plots on daytime and evening soaps, like *Dallas* and *Dynasty*, while in the 1990s cable shows, such as Home Box Office's (HBO) *Sex in the City*, aired partial nudity and explicit discussion of sexual relations. Talk-show hosts, ranging from the respectable Oprah Winfrey to the shocking Jerry Springer, recruited ordinary Americans to share the secrets of their personal lives — which often involved sexuality, drug abuse, and domestic violence. As the American pop-artist Andy Warhol had predicted, ordinary people eagerly embraced the opportunity to expose their lives and to be "world-famous for 15 minutes."

As TV became more "stimulating" and "reality" oriented, critics argued that it negatively shaped people's outlooks and actions. For evidence they cited violent television dramas, such as HBO's critically acclaimed series *The Sopranos*, which interweaved the personal lives of a Mafia family with the amoral and

Oprah Winfrey

Oprah Winfrey is an American success story. She was born in 1954 to unwed parents, lived first with her grandmother in rural Mississippi and then with her mother in Milwaukee and her father in Nashville. After graduating from Tennessee State University, she became a radio broadcaster and hit the big time in the mid-1980s, with a successful debut as a movie actress and as a national television daytime talk show host. Presently the *Oprah Winfrey Show* boasts a weekly audience of 21 million in 105 countries. Here she chats with author Toni Morrison, whose prize-winning novels Oprah has publicized on her Book Club. © Reuters / Corbis.

relentless violence of their business deals. Did the impact of the dozens of such violence-focused dramas, combined with the widespread availability of guns, increase the already high American murder rate? Did it play a role in a series of shootings by high school students, which culminated in 1991 with the murder of twelve students and one teacher at Columbine High School in Littleton, Colorado? Some lawmakers thought so. In a half-hearted effort to thwart youthful violence, Congress stipulated in the Telecommunication Reform Act of 1996 that manufacturers include a "V-chip" in new TV sets to allow parents to block specific programs.

Deregulation and Media Giants: Warner-AOL and Rupert Murdoch. As the controversy over TV violence indicates, technology never operates in a social and political vacuum. The expansion of cable television and specialized programming stemmed in part from policies set by the Federal Communications Commission (FCC) during the Reagan administration. Mark Fowler, the FCC chair, shared the president's disdain for government regulation of business. "Television is just another appliance.... It's a toaster with pictures," Fowler suggested, as the FCC eliminated requirements that stations provide extensive news programming and allow full debate on controversial political issues. Freed from such "public service" responsibilities, TV newscasts increasingly shunned serious coverage of political and economic events and focused on lurid events, such as floods, fires, murders, and scandals connected to celebrities. The troubled marriage and divorce of Prince Charles of England and Lady Diana—and her subsequent death—saturated the airwaves, and the distinction between news and entertainment became blurred.

Fowler's FCC also minimized controls over children's programming. Soon cartoon programs such as *G.I. Joe* and *Care Bears* became extended advertisements for licensed replicas of their main characters. Even the characters of the Public Broadcasting Service's popular *Sesame Street* joined the parade of licensed replicas, as consumer culture extended into the lives of the youngest Americans. Responding to complaints from parents and children's advocates, Congress enacted the Children's Television Act of 1990, which reinstated some restrictions, but the commercialization of virtually every aspect of childhood proceeded nonetheless.

Whatever the programming, the television stations that carried them were increasingly owned by a handful of large companies. In 1985, Congress raised the number of television stations a company could own from seven to twelve. Subsequent regulations promoted even more concentration in media ownership; by 2003, one company owned eight radio stations and three television stations in a single city, in addition to a newspaper and a TV cable system. On the national level, there was a similar trend toward monopolization. In 1990 Warner Communications merged with Time/Life to create an enormous entertainment corporation that included the Warner Brothers film studio, HBO, TNT, Six Flags, the Atlanta Braves, Atlantic Records, and the magazines of Time, Inc. (*Time, Fortune, Sports Illustrated,* and *People*). In 1995, the company brought in $21 billion in revenues. Subsequently, Warner Communications merged with America Online (renamed simply "AOL" in 2006), the largest provider of Internet access. Although this merger turned out to be a poor business decision, it testified to the growing cultural influence of a few giant corporations.

Australian-born entrepreneur Rupert Murdoch stands as the exemplar of concentrated media ownership in the new global economy. As of 2004, Murdoch owned satellite TV companies in five countries and a worldwide total of 175 newspapers; in the United States, his holdings included Direct TV, the Fox TV Network, the Twentieth Century Fox Studio, the *New York Post*, and thirty-five television stations. A conservative ideologue as well as an entrepreneur, Murdoch has used his news empire to promote his political views. His career indicates not only the technological dimensions of globalization but also the influence of conservative individuals, institutions, and ideas at the beginning of the twenty-first century.

▶ What are the most important aspects of the computer revolution? What are the social consequences of this changing technology?

▶ How is the computer revolution related to globalization?

▶ How did the television industry change after 1980? Why does it matter?

Culture Wars

Times of economic affluence, like the 1950s, often encourage social harmony by damping down class conflict. Such was not the case in the 1980s and 1990s, a prosperous era that was marked by unrelenting warfare over cultural issues. Rooted in the social divisions of the 1960s, these "culture wars" generally pitted religious conservatives against secular liberals. Often instigated by politicians to advance their candidacies, they focused primarily on issues of racial and ethnic pluralism, on challenges to traditional "family values," and on the

FIGURE 31.4 American Immigration, 1920–2000

Legislation inspired by nativism slowed the influx of immigrants after 1920, as did the dislocations brought on by economic depression and war in the 1930s and 1940s. Note the high rate of non-European immigration since the 1970s, the result of new eligibility rules in the Immigration Act of 1965 (see Chapters 27 and 28). The dramatic increase since 1980 in the number of migrants from Latin America and Asia reflects American economic prosperity, traditionally a magnet for migrants, and the rapid acceleration of illegal immigration.

rights of sexual minorities, especially gay men and women.

An Increasingly Pluralistic Society

In 1992, Republican presidential hopeful Patrick Buchanan warned Americans that their country was "undergoing the greatest invasion in its history, a migration of millions of illegal aliens a year from Mexico." A sharp-tongued cultural warrior, Buchanan exaggerated — but not by much. According to the Census Bureau, the population of the United States grew from 203 million people in 1970 to 280 million in 2000 (and topped 300 million in October 2006). Of that increase of 77 million, immigrants accounted for 28 million, with legal migrants numbering about 21 million and illegal entrants adding another 7 million (Figure 31.4). Relatively few migrants — legal or illegal — came from Europe (2 million), Africa (about 600,000), and Canada (250,000), the historical homelands of most American citizens. The overwhelming majority, some 25 million, came either from East Asia (9 million) or Latin America (16 million).

These immigrants and their children profoundly altered the demography of various states and the entire nation. By 2000, 27 percent of California's population was foreign-born; and Asians, Latinos, and native-born blacks constituted a majority of the residents. Nationally, there were now more Latinos (about 35 million) than African Americans (34 million), and Asians numbered over 12 million. Based on present rates of immigration and births, demographers predicted that by 2050 Americans of European descent would be a minority of the population. As Buchanan had pointed out, a "great invasion" was indeed changing the character — and the color — of American society. Small wonder that ethnic and racial diversity, long a source of conflict in American society, emerged as a prominent theme of the culture wars.

Latino and Asian Immigration. The massive inflow of *legal* immigrants was the unintended result of the Immigration Act of 1965, which allowed family members to join migrants already in the United States. Spanish-speaking Latinos took advantage of this provision; millions of Mexicans came to the United States, and hundreds of thousands arrived

MAP 31.2 Hispanic and Asian Populations, 2000

In 2000, people of Hispanic descent made up more than 11 percent of the American population, and now outnumber African Americans as the largest minority group. Asian Americans accounted for an additional 4 percent of the population. Demographers predict that by the year 2050 only about half of the U.S. population will be composed of non-Hispanic whites. Note the high percentage of Hispanics and Asians in California and certain other states.

from El Salvador, Guatemala, and the Dominican Republic. Historically, most Latinos had lived in California, Texas, and New Mexico; now they settled in cities throughout the country — numbering 16 percent of the population in Florida and New York (see Map 31.2).

Most Latinos were poor men and women seeking a better life in the United States. They willingly worked for low wages — cleaning homes, tending lawns, servicing hotel rooms, painting houses, working construction. Many labored "for cash, no questions asked"; as members of the "underground" economy, they did not pay income or Social Security taxes. Instead, many immigrants regularly sent funds to their families back home and urged them to migrate — legally or illegally. Their hopes lay in the future, especially in their American-born children, who could claim the rights of U.S. citizens (see Comparing American Voices, "Cheap Labor: Immigration and Globalization," pp. 978–979).

COMPARING AMERICAN VOICES

Cheap Labor: Immigration and Globalization

Immigrants populated the United States and they continue to remake it. But for whose benefit? Under what conditions? And at whose expense? Those are three of the questions raised by these testimonials from men and women employed in the labor-intensive industries of garment manufacturing and agricultural production.

GEORGE STITH AND JUANITA GARCIA
"Local farm workers could not get jobs at all"

George Stith and Juanita Garcia were farmworkers and union members. In 1952, they testified before a congressional committee considering whether to expand or restrict the Mexican "guest worker" (braceros) program.

STITH: Mr. Chairman and members of the committee, My name is George Stith. My address is Star Route Box 5, Gould, Ark. All my life I have worked on cotton plantations. When I was 4 years old my family moved to southern Illinois, near Cairo. We picked cotton in southeast Missouri, and west Tennessee nearly every year. We later moved across the river into Missouri and share-cropped. In 1930 we moved back to Arkansas. I don't know whether I am a migratory worker or not, but we certainly did a lot of migrating.

In 1936 when I was share cropping in Woodruff County, Ark. I joined the union which was then called the Southern Tenant Farmers Union. It is now the National Farm Labor Union, A. F. of L. I have been a member of the union ever since....

For a long time I had heard about labor shortages in the West and how Mexican workers were being imported. I was sure that no people would be imported from Mexico to work on farms in Arkansas. There were too many people living in the little towns and cities who go out to chop and pick cotton....

The importation of Mexican nationals into Arkansas did not begin until the fall of 1949. Cotton-picking wages in my section were good. We were getting $4 per 100 pounds for picking. As soon as the Mexicans were brought in the wages started falling. Wages were cut to $3.25 and $3 per 100 pounds. In many cases local farm workers could not get jobs at all.... The cotton plantation owners kept the Mexicans at work and would not employ Negro and white pickers....

GARCIA: My name is Juanita Garcia. I live in Brawley, Calif. I work in the field and in the packing sheds. I lost my job in a packing shed about 2 weeks ago. I was fired because I belonged to the National Farm Labor Union.... My father, my brothers, and sisters also work on the farms. For poor people like us who are field laborers, making a living has always been hard. Why? Because the ranchers and companies have always taken over....

In the Imperial Valley we have a hard time. It so happens that the local people who are American citizens cannot get work.... The wetbacks [illegal immigrants] and nationals from Mexico have the whole Imperial Valley.... The nationals and wetbacks take any wages the ranchers offer to pay them. The wages get worse every year....

Last year they fired some people from the shed because they had nationals to take their jobs. There was a strike.... They took the nationals from the camps to break our strike. They had 5,000 scabs that were nationals. We told the Mexican consul about this. We told the Labor Department. They were supposed to take the nationals out of the strike. They never did take them away.

SOURCE: Migratory Labor, Hearings before Subcommittee on Labor and Labor-Management Relations, 82nd Congress, 2nd Session (Washington, D.C., Government Printing Office, 1952), 89–90, 93–94.

TRONG AND THANH NGUYEN
"We're political refugees.... We spend our money here."

Trong and Thanh Nguyen fled from Communist Vietnam in the mid-1970s.

TRONG: When my wife and I came to Chicago, our major concern was to feed our five small children. We had Vietnamese pride and did not want to take public aid. We wanted the American community and authorities to respect us.

Just trying to begin a new life here, we had so many difficulties. When I worked as a janitor at Water Tower Place, a co-worker told me, "Trong, do you know that America is overpopulated? We have more than two hundred million people. We don't need you. Go back where you belong." I was shocked to hear people trying to chase us out....

THANH: When we first came to Chicago, I cried a lot. In the factory where I worked, there weren't many Americans. Most were Mexicans, some legal, but also many illegal aliens.... They cursed our people. Some Mexicans said, "You come here and take our jobs. Go back wherever you came from.".... "You come here to make money, then go back home and live like kings." That was too much. I couldn't hold it in any more.

I told them in a very soft voice, "We are Vietnamese people. You don't have enough education to know where our country is. Vietnam is a small country, but we did not come to America to look for jobs. We're political refugees. We can't go back home." I didn't call them bad names or anything, but I said, "You are the ones who come here to make money to bring back to your country. We spend our money here." After that, they didn't bother us very much.

SOURCE: Paul S. Boyer, ed., *Enduring Voices*, 3rd ed. (Boston: Houghton Mifflin, 1996), 408–409.

PETRA MATA AND FEIYI CHEN
"Garment workers ... made a decent living before free trade"

Petra Mata and Feiyi Chen are immigrants from low-wage countries who were "insourced"; on coming to the United States they worked as low-paid garment workers. Then, their jobs were "outsourced"—sent abroad to even lower-paid workers as a result of free trade and globalization.

MATA: My name is Petra Mata. I was born in Mexico. I have completed no more than the sixth grade in school. In 1969, my husband and I came to the U.S. believing we would find better opportunities for our children and ourselves. We first arrived without documents, then became legal, and finally became citizens. For years I moved from job to job until I was employed in 1976 by the most popular company in the market, Levi Strauss & Company. I earned $9.73 an hour and also had vacation and sick leave. Levi's provided me and my family with a stable situation, and in return I was a loyal employee and worked there for fourteen years.

On January 16, 1990, Levi's closed its plant in San Antonio, Texas, where I had been working, leaving 1,150 workers unemployed, a majority of whom were Mexican-American women. The company moved its factory to Costa Rica....

As a result of being laid off, I personally lost my house, my method of transportation, and the tranquility of my home. My family and I had to face new problems. My husband was forced to look for a second job on top of the one he already had. He worked from seven in the morning to six at night. Our reality was very difficult. At that time, I had not the slightest idea what free trade was or meant....

Our governments make agreements behind closed doors without participation from the working persons who are most affected by these decisions—decisions that to my knowledge only benefit large corporations and those in positions of power....

CHEN: My name is Feiyi Chen. I immigrated to the United States in December 1998 from China. I began my working career as a seamstress in a garment factory because I did not speak English and the garment manufacturing industry was one of the few employment opportunities available to me. I typically worked ten hours a day, six days a week, at a backbreaking pace. Most garment bosses know that new immigrants have few choices when it comes to work and so they take advantage by paying workers less than the minimum wage with no overtime pay.... I learned from some of the older garment workers that garment workers in San Francisco actually made a decent living before free trade lured many of the better-paying garment factories over to other countries and forced the smaller and rule-abiding factories to shut down because they could not compete with the low cost of production from neighboring countries....

Working as a seamstress and an assembly worker has always been hard, but with so many of the factories leaving the country in search of cheaper labor, life for immigrant workers like myself is getting worse. For example, many garment workers who were paid one dollar for sewing a piece of clothing are now only making fifty cents for the same amount of work. There are a lot of garment workers who still work ten hours a day but make less than thirty dollars a day.

SOURCE: Christine Ahn, *Shafted: Free Trade and America's Working Poor* (Oakland, CA: Food First Books, 2003), 32–38.

ANALYZING THE EVIDENCE

▶ Describe the experiences of the workers as related in their statements. What generalizations can you make about the impact of immigration on wages? On the relations among ethnic groups in the United States?

▶ How does "globalization," a major focus of this chapter, affect the lives of these workers? Provide some specific examples from the documents that show its impact.

▶ What role would these workers like the federal government to play? According to the discussion in this chapter, what is American policy with respect to globalization?

▶ Consider the questions raised in the introduction: Who benefits from immigration, legal or illegal? How does it affect working conditions? Is there a cost, and who pays it?

New Immigrants

In the 1980s, many Korean immigrants opened small grocery and fruit stores in urban neighborhoods. Their economic success was hard won — the result of disciplined saving and long hours of work — and often led to conflicts with poor blacks and Hispanics, who resented their rapid economic mobility. Kay Chernush.

Most Asian migrants came from China, the Philippines, South Korea, India, and Pakistan. In addition, 700,000 refugees migrated to the United States from Indochina (Vietnam, Laos, and Cambodia) after the Vietnam War. Some of these Asians were well educated or entrepreneurial; they adapted quickly and successfully to life in their new homeland. But a majority lacked professional or vocational skills and took low-paying jobs.

As in the past, the immigrants congregated in ethnic conclaves. In Los Angeles, Koreans created the thriving community of "Koreatown"; in Brooklyn, New York, Russian Jews settled in "Little Odessa"; Latino migrants took over entire sections of Chicago, the District of Columbia, Dallas, and Houston. As the number of immigrants grew, ethnic entrepreneurs catered to their tastes — establishing restaurants, food stores, clothing shops, and native-language newspapers — while mainstream department stores, car dealers, and politicians vied for their dollars and votes. Although many migrants worked and shopped outside their ethnic enclaves, they usually socialized, attended church, and married within the community.

Anti-immigrant Sentiment. While some native-born Americans celebrated this renewal of the nation's ethnic pluralism, many others worried about its massive size. Similar concerns had fueled nativist opposition to Irish Catholic immigrants in the 1840s and to Jews and Catholics from eastern and southern Europe around 1900. As in the past, critics argued that immigrants assimilated slowly, depressed wages for all workers, and raised crime rates (see Voices from Abroad, "Janet Daley: A U.S. Epidemic," p. 981). They also sounded new and potent themes: that the rapidly rising population endangered the environment and burdened governments with millions of dollars in costs for schools, hospitals, police, and social services. Responding to such concerns, the Welfare Reform Act of 1996 curtailed the access of legal immigrants to food stamps and other welfare benefits.

The most far-reaching challenges to mass immigration emerged at the state level. In 1986, California voters overwhelmingly supported Proposition 63, which established English as the state's "official language," and seventeen other states followed suit. Eight years later, Californians approved Proposition 187, a ballot initiative forthrightly named "Save Our State," which barred illegal aliens from public schools, nonemergency care at public health clinics, and all other state social services. The initiative also required law enforcement officers, school administrators, and social workers to report suspected illegal immigrants to the Immigration and Naturalization Service. When a federal judge ruled that Proposition 187 was unconstitutional, supporters of the measure demanded that Congress take action to curtail legal migration and expel illegal entrants.

An unlikely coalition of politicians prevented the passage of such federal legislation. Heeding the pleas of business owners and large-scale farmers, who wanted a plentiful supply of low-wage workers, conservative Republicans refused to restrict immigration. Liberal Democrats also opposed such legislation because they supported ethnic pluralism and cultural diversity. Indeed, in 1986 Congress enacted (and President Reagan signed) a measure that granted amnesty to nearly two million illegal aliens and, in its lack of rigorous enforcement provisions, ensured that the flood of illegal migrants would continue, as indeed it has. By 2006, Congress was again debating this contentious issue.

African Americans. The dramatic increase in Asians and Latinos brought some benefits to African Americans. As immigrant workers took the lowest paid jobs in the construction, manufacturing, and hotel service industries, many blacks used their experience and facility in English to move into supervisory positions. Some of these African Americans joined the ranks of the middle classes and moved to better lives in the suburbs. Yet the poorer blacks who remained in the inner cities now paid more for housing because the demand from

VOICES FROM ABROAD

Janet Daley

A U.S. Epidemic

Around 8:30 p.m. on April 19, 1989, marauding gangs of youths began to beat up joggers and bicyclists in New York City's Central Park. About the same time, Trisha Meilli, a twenty-nine-year-old American investment banker of Italian descent, was brutally raped, beaten, and left for dead in the park. In a coma for twelve days, Meilli did not remember any details of the attack. Five black and Latino young men from Harlem, arrested initially because of the gang attacks, confessed to the assault and served prison terms of seven to eleven years. In 2002, long after Daley's article appeared in an English newspaper, *The Independent*, DNA tests pinned the attack on Matias Reyes, a convicted serial rapist and murderer. Reyes, who was born in Puerto Rico, told prison officials that he alone raped and beat the jogger.

[London, August 29, 1990] THE TRIAL in New York of the Central Park rapists has brought into focus two tacit assumptions that underpin conventional wisdom about America and the prognosis for our own [English] future.

The first is that everything wrong with American society is a result of its "system" (that is, its political and economic organisation). The second is that as our "system" becomes more like that of the United States (more free-market based), we shall inevitably suffer the same problems of a mindlessly violent underclass....

Both of these contentions seem to me wrong. To begin with, the notion that a country's social mores and attitudes are brought about entirely by the form of its government and economy is a bit of Marxist theoretical baggage that ought to be thrown out. ... It is an absurd idea that whatever is wrong with our social relations, or even our family lives, must be accounted for by the structure of our national institutions. Juvenile crime is a plague in communist China and alcoholism—a more traditional kind of drug abuse—is endemic in the Soviet Union.

Many of the worst instances of anarchic violence in America—such as the attack on the Central Park jogger—do not arise from the underclass in the proper economic sense at all. These boys were not notably poor, or from families without aspirations.

Those aspects of American life that are most repugnant—its lunatic viciousness and criminality—can be accounted for by purely historical circumstances which the political system could influence in only the most marginal way. The United States is an enormous continental landmass which was settled in an ad hoc, opportunist fashion by disparate groups of people with different motivations and lifestyles. This Babel-like chaos was governed in the most minimal way.... Each immigrant group created its own cohesiveness. The Irish, the East Europeans, the Jews all had their communities which gave them some sense of security. And when the geographical communities began to disperse, there were still networks of tribal feeling and attachment.

Into this mix early this century came a great wave of Sicilians who brought with them their own family industry. The Mafia gained a hold in America at a time when law enforcement was nominal and social insecurity was universal. Having had its roots in the Little Italy of New York, it now runs the gambling, prostitution and drug empires of America. It has had deep connections with whole swathes of the transport industry through its connections with certain unions....

This pervasive influence of organised crime which arose through a historical coincidence—the arrival of a particular subculture in a loosely organised country which, for separate historical reasons, had committed itself constitutionally to the citizen's right to bear arms—is more central to the current problems of the US than its capitalist economy or its political ideology.

To describe Britain as inevitably on the same road is simple historical ignorance. For a stable and deeply conservative society to come to grips with immigrant groups may present us with a challenge, but it can never lead to the conditions with which America is faced, and which are the result of attempting to build a society from scratch out of a diverse and discordant collection of peoples.

The oppressive conformity and intolerance of American life arise from this compulsion to create a homogeneous culture out of ethnic chaos. A society without a central historical axis breeds chronic anxiety.

SOURCE: *The Independent* (London), August 29, 1990, p. 18.

ANALYZING THE EVIDENCE

- According to Daley, why is violence so widespread in the United States? How convincing is her analysis?
- Does Daley's argument provide insight into the rape of the Central Park jogger?
- What are we to make of Daley's conclusion, given the bombing of the London subway system in 2005 by four Muslim youth, three of whom were born in England of Pakistani descent?

immigrants drove up rents. Massive immigration also adversely affected many inner-city black children because overcrowded and underfunded schools diverted scarce resources to bilingual education for Spanish- and Chinese-speaking students.

Still, government policy continued to provide African Americans (and Latinos and white women) with preferential treatment in areas such as hiring for public sector jobs, "set-aside" programs for minority-owned businesses, and university admissions. Conservatives had long argued that such programs were deeply flawed because they amounted to intrusive governmental "social engineering," promoted "reverse discrimination" against white men, and resulted in the selection and promotion of less-qualified applicants. During the 1990s, conservatives—along with many Americans who believed in "equal opportunity"—demanded an end to such legal privileges.

Once again, California stood at the center of the debate. In 1995, under pressure from the Republican governor, Pete Wilson, the regents of the University of California voted to scrap its twenty-year-old policy of affirmative action. A year later, California voters approved Proposition 209, which banished affirmative action privileges in state employment and public education. When the number of Latino and African Americans admitted to the flagship Berkeley campus of the University of California plummeted, conservatives hailed the result as proving that the previous admissions policy had lowered intellectual standards. Avoiding a direct reply to that charge, liberals maintained that state universities should educate potential leaders of all ethnic and racial groups.

Affirmative action remained controversial. In 2001, the California Regents devised a new admissions plan to assist minority applicants; two years later the U.S. Supreme Court invalidated an affirmative action plan at the University of Michigan, but allowed racial-preference policies that promoted a "diverse" student body. In the face of growing public and judicial opposition, the future of such programs was uncertain.

Race and Crime: Rodney King and O. J. Simpson. While affirmative action programs assisted some African Americans to rise into the middle classes, they did not address the social problems of poorer blacks. Millions of African Americans lived in households headed by wage-earning single mothers, who had neither the time nor the energy to supervise their children's lives. Many of their daughters bore babies at an early age, while their sons ran with street gangs and dealt in illegal drugs. To address drug use and the crimes that it generated, the Reagan administration urged young people to "Just Say No." This campaign had some success in cutting drug use among middle-class black and white teenagers, but did not staunch the dangerous flow of crack cocaine into poor African American neighborhoods. "The police are losing the war against crack," *Newsweek* noted grimly in 1986, "and the war is turning the ghettos of major cities into something like a domestic Vietnam." Indeed, the murderous competition among black drug dealers took the lives of thousands of young African American men, and police efforts to stop drug use and trafficking brought the arrest and imprisonment of tens of thousands more.

In April 1992, this seething underworld of crime and urban impoverishment erupted in five days of race riots in Los Angeles. The worst civil disorder since the 1960s, the violence took sixty lives and caused $850 million in damage. The riot was set off by the acquittal (on all but one charge) of four white Los Angeles police officers accused of using excessive force in arresting a black motorist, Rodney King, who had led them on a wild car chase. A graphic amateur video showing the policemen kicking and clubbing King did not sway the predominantly white jury, even as it highlighted police brutality and the harassment of minorities.

The riot exposed the fragility of urban America and acute rifts between urban blacks and their immigrant neighbors. Many Los Angeles blacks resented recent immigrants from Korea, who had set up successful small retail businesses. When they

To Live and Die in L.A.

As rioters looted stores in South-Central Los Angeles and burned over one thousand buildings, the devastation recalled that caused by the African American riots in Watts in 1965. But Los Angeles was now a much more diverse community. More than 40 percent of those arrested in 1992 were Hispanic, and the rioters attacked Koreans and other Asians as well as whites. Silvie Kreiss/Liason.

tried to loot and burn these businesses during the riot, the Koreans fought them off with guns. Frustrated by high unemployment and crowded housing conditions, Latinos joined in the rioting and accounted for more than half of those arrested and a third of those killed. The riots represented both an expression of black rage at white injustice and the class-based looting of property by poor African Americans and immigrant Latinos.

In 1995, Los Angeles police worried about another black-led riot as the trial of O. J. Simpson neared its end. A renowned African American college and professional football player and a well-paid representative for Hertz Rental Cars, Simpson was accused of the brutal murder of his ex-wife, Nicole Brown Simpson, a white woman. The prosecution produced damning evidence of Simpson's guilt, but black defense attorney Johnnie Cochran argued that a police detective tampered with the evidence. More important, Cochran played the "race card," encouraging the predominately black jury to view Simpson as a victim of racial prejudice and to acquit him. Although a substantial majority of whites, in Los Angeles and the nation, believed that Simpson was guilty, they peacefully accepted the jury's verdict of "not guilty." In the 1990s, unlike the 1920s and 1940s, whites no longer resorted to racial riots to suppress or take revenge against blacks. Now it was African Americans who took to the streets.

Multiculturalism. For most of the twentieth century, supporters of civil rights for African Americans and other ethnic groups advocated their "integration" into the wider society and culture. Integration had been the dream of Martin Luther King Jr. and César Chavez (see Chapter 28). Beginning in the 1970s, some blacks (and Latinos) rejected integration in favor of "multiculturalism" and set out to win political support for the creation of racially and ethnically distinct institutions. Some liberals supported this multicultural agenda, but Arthur Schlesinger Jr. (a well-known historian and advisor to President Kennedy) and many others opposed such separatist schemes. Conservative commentators, such as George F. Will, William Bennett, and Patrick Buchanan, uniformly condemned multiculturalism as a threat to core American values. Fearing the "balkanization," or fragmentation, of American culture, they opposed classroom instruction of immigrant children in their native languages and revisions of university curricula that deemphasized the importance of European culture.

This warfare over culture issues extended into Congress. Believing that the programs aired on public television and the grants awarded by the National Endowments for the Arts and the Humanities promoted multiculturalism, conservative lawmakers tried to cut off their funding. When that effort failed, they drastically reduced the organizations' budgets. Conservatives also took aim at the antiracist and antisexist regulations and speech codes that had been adopted by many colleges. Demanding the protection of the First Amendment right of free speech, conservatives (along with liberals in the American Civil Liberties Union) opposed attempts to regulate "hate" speech.

Conflicting Values: Women's and Gay Rights

Conservatives were equally worried about the state of American families. They pointed to the 40 percent rate of divorce among whites and the 70 percent rate of out-of-wedlock pregnancies among blacks. The "abrasive experiments of two liberal decades," they charged, had eroded respect for marriage and family values. To members of the Religious Right, there were a wide range of culprits: legislators who enacted liberal divorce laws, funded child care, and allowed welfare payments to unmarried mothers, and judges who banished religious instruction from public schools. While their celebration of "traditional family values" evoked all these issues, religious conservatives were particularly intent on resisting the new freedoms and rights claimed by women and homosexuals.

Feminists, the Religious Right, and Abortion. In the 1980s, public opinion polls showed strong support for many feminist demands, including equal pay in the workplace, an equitable sharing of household and child-care responsibilities, and personal control of reproductive decisions. But in *Backlash: The Undeclared War on American Women* (1991), journalist Susan Faludi warned that conservative social groups had launched an all-out campaign against the feminist movement and its agenda of civic equality for women. To resist this conservative onslaught, the National Organization of Women (NOW) expanded its membership and agenda to include "Third Wave" feminists. These new feminists adopted a multicultural perspective and advanced the distinctive concerns of women of color, lesbians, and working women. Younger feminist women also felt more secure of their sexuality; many of them identified with the pop music star Madonna, whose outrageous sexualized style seemed to empower her rather than make her a sex object.

Abortion became a central issue in the cultural warfare between feminists and religious conservatives, and also a defining issue between Democrats and Republicans. Feminists viewed the issue from the perspective of the pregnant woman; they argued that the right to a legal, safe abortion was crucial to her control over her life. Conversely, religious conservatives maintained that legalized abortion improperly gave a higher value to the woman's individual rights than to her sacred vocation of motherhood. They also viewed abortion from the perspective of the unborn fetus — claiming that its rights trumped those of the living mother. Indeed, in cases of a difficult childbirth, some conservatives would sacrifice the life of the mother to save that of the fetus. To dramatize the larger issues at stake, the antiabortion movement christened itself as "pro-life," while proponents of abortion rights described themselves as "pro-choice." Both ideologies had roots in the American commitment to "life, liberty, and the pursuit of happiness." The question remained: Whose life? Whose liberty? Whose definition of happiness?

The hierarchy of the Catholic Church gave its answer to these questions in 1971, when it sponsored the formation of the National Right to Life Committee. Church leaders launched a sophisticated media campaign to build popular support for its antiabortion stance, distributing films of late-term fetuses in utero and photographs of tiny fetal hands. By the 1980s, fundamentalist Protestants assumed leadership of the antiabortion movement, which became increasingly confrontational and politically powerful.

Pressed by antiabortion interest groups, state legislatures passed laws that regulated the provision of abortion services. These laws required underage girls to obtain parental permission for abortions, denied public funding for abortions for poor women, and mandated waiting periods and elaborate counseling. These laws navigated between conflicting conservative beliefs. Religious conservatives demanded laws prohibiting abortions; "free enterprise" conservatives responded that abortion decisions were private matters and, like businesses, should be immune from government control. However, both groups of conservatives agreed that parents — and not the state — had the right to make important decisions for their minor children. As we saw in Chapter 30, in two decisions, *Webster v. Reproductive Health Services* (1989) and *Planned Parenthood of Southeastern Pennsylvania v. Casey* (1992), the Supreme Court accepted the constitutionality of many of these restrictions. But the federal courts continued to overturn state laws that prohibited late-term abortions when the life of the mother was in danger.

The debate over abortion stirred deep emotions (see Reading American Pictures, "The Abortion Debate Hits the Streets," p. 985). During the 1990s, evangelical Protestant activists mounted protests outside abortion clinics and harassed their staffs and clients. Pro-life extremists advocated killing the doctors and nurses who performed abortions, and a few carried out their threats. In 1994, an antiabortion activist killed a worker at two Massachusetts abortion clinics and wounded five others; other religiously motivated extremists murdered doctors in Florida and New York. Cultural warfare had turned deadly — resorting to terror to achieve its ends.

The Controversy over Gay Rights. The issue of homosexuality stirred equally deep feelings on both sides. As more gay men and women "came out of the closet" in the years after Stonewall (see Chapter 29), they formed groups that demanded a variety of protections and privileges. Defining themselves as a "minority" group, gays sought legislation that protected them from discrimination in housing, education, public accommodations, and employment. Public opinion initially opposed such initiatives, but by the 1990s, many cities and states banned discrimination on the basis of sexual orientation.

This legislation did not end the conflict. Gay groups asserted that civic equality included extensive legal rights for same-sex couples, such as eligibility for workplace health-care coverage on the same basis as married heterosexuals. Indeed, many homosexuals wanted their partnerships recognized as legal marriages and treated identically to opposite-sex unions. Proposals for gay marriage roused widespread opposition because they confounded traditional practices and would have immense implications for the American family system.

The Religious Right had long condemned homosexuality as morally wrong and a major threat to the traditional family. Pat Robertson, North Carolina senator Jesse Helms, and other conservatives campaigned vigorously against antidiscrimination measures for gays. Their arguments that such laws amounted to undeserved "special rights" struck a responsive chord in Colorado. In 1992, Colorado voters amended the state constitution to bar local jurisdictions from passing ordinances protecting gays and lesbians, a measure subsequently overturned as unconstitutional by the Supreme Court. In 1998, Congress entered the fray by enacting the Defense of Marriage Act, which allowed states to refuse to recognize gay marriages or civil unions formed in other jurisdictions. However, in *Lawrence v. Texas* (2003), the Supreme Court ruled that states may not prohibit private homosexual activity between consenting adults (see Chapter 30, Comparing American Voices, pp. 930–931). As the new century began, the debate over legal rights for gays and lesbians rivaled in fervor and importance those over immigration restriction, abortion, and affirmative action. Increasingly, these cultural issues shaped the dynamics of American politics.

READING AMERICAN PICTURES

The Abortion Debate Hits the Streets

Divided Women, Divided Public: Protesting in Washington, D.C., 2004. Declan McCullagh.

Few issues in U.S. history divided late-twentieth-century Americans as profoundly as abortion. Since the Supreme Court's *Roe v. Wade* decision (1973), protests and counterprotests have grown. As the text suggests, the issue intrudes constantly into the social, cultural, and political history of recent decades (see Chapters 29, 30, and 32). Because the battle involves a seemingly irreconcilable difference between conflicting moral principles, finding common ground for compromise has been difficult. Antiabortion activists sometimes compare their fight with that of the abolitionists in the pre–Civil War era (who argued that slavery was immoral) and liken *Roe v. Wade* to *Dred Scott*—the 1857 Supreme Court decision that protected slave property. Those who support abortion often stake their ground on the rights of the individual—a woman's right to control her life and her body—and invoke the Constitution's protection of individual freedom and privacy. The photograph above suggests the character of the resulting political confrontation. What do you see?

ANALYZING THE EVIDENCE

▶ Describe the people marching in the street. Who is protesting on the sidewalk? What does the composition of the two groups say about the abortion controversy?

▶ Next, look at how the police are positioned. From what you've read in the narrative, why might this sort of police deployment be necessary?

▶ Finally, look at the signs both groups are holding up. What messages do they convey? How do the slogans frame the debate? What principles do they invoke?

▶ Abortion was a significant political issue in the mid-nineteenth century, when many states first outlawed the practice, and again in the 1960s, when five states repealed antiabortion laws and eleven others reformed their restrictive legislation. Since the late 1970s, abortion has become an important issue in national politics and often divides Democrats and Republicans. From what you've read in the text and see in this picture, how can you explain the political importance of this issue?

- Who were the new immigrants? What were the sources of hostility to them?
- How do you account for the cultural conflict over issues relating to women and homosexuals? Who are the sides in conflict?

SUMMARY

As we have seen, a number of factors contributed to the revival of the American economy between 1980 and 2000. The defense buildup and the Reagan tax cuts poured billions of dollars into the economy, and American corporations invested heavily in research and new technologies. As the Japanese and German economies faltered, the United States reasserted its leading role in the global economy. The increase in the number of multinational firms, many of them U.S.-based, pushed forward the process of globalization. While nation-states remained immensely important, people, goods, and investment capital moved easily across political boundaries.

Technological innovations strengthened the American economy and transformed daily life. The computer revolution and the spread of the Internet changed the ways in which Americans shopped, worked, learned, and stayed in touch with family and friends. Technology likewise altered the character of television programming and viewing, as cable and satellite technology, along with government deregulation, provided Americans with a wider variety of entertainment choices.

As our account has suggested, globalization and technological change accentuated various cultural conflicts within the United States. Advances in biomedical science revived old moral debates, and globalization facilitated the immigration of millions of Asians and Latin Americans. The new immigrants increased the anxieties of many citizens about ethnic diversity and multiculturalism, while the poverty and crime that characterized the inner cities highlighted the nation's class and racial problems. Conservatives spoke out strongly, and with increasing effectiveness, against what they viewed as serious threats to "family values." Debates over women's rights, access to abortion, affirmative action, and the legal rights of homosexuals intensified. As the nation entered the twenty-first century, its people were sharply divided by cultural values as well as by economic class and racial identity.

Connections: Society and Technology

Cultural conflict has been a significant feature of recent American life. As we noted in the essay that opened Part Seven (p. 925):

> Increased immigration from Latin America and Asia added to cultural tensions and produced a new nativist movement. Continuing battles over affirmative action, abortion, sexual standards, homosexuality, feminism, and religion in public life took on an increasingly passionate character.

Neither set of issues was new. During the 1920s, as we explained in Chapter 23, powerful nativist sentiment forced the passage of a National Origins Act that severely restricted immigration from many countries. That decade also witnessed nationwide Prohibition, a failed attempt to impose a moral code by force of law. Both immigration and moral issues came to the fore again in the 1960s, but with a far different result. As we saw in Chapter 28, the Immigration Act of 1965 opened the way for a more diverse and more numerous flow of migrants, while the countercultural revolution challenged traditional social strictures and moral values and overthrew many of them. The battle was far from over, as we have discovered in Chapter 31. Beginning in the 1970s and gaining force in subsequent decades, moral and sexual conservatives launched a cultural offensive intended to encourage and, if possible, to legislate a return to the social arrangements and values that were dominant in the first half of the twentieth century.

That attempt at cultural control will take place in a world shaped by the technology of the computer chip and the Internet. In assessing possible outcomes, we might look back at earlier technological revolutions — the impact of electricity and the telephone in Chapter 18, of the radio and automobiles in Chapter 23, and of television in Chapter 27 — all of which expanded the range of people's knowledge and choices. In such ways does technology influence, but not determine, cultural outcomes.

CHAPTER REVIEW QUESTIONS

- In what ways did the new technology affect the American economy? What was its relation to globalization?
- What was the outcome of the various cultural wars of the 1980s and 1990s?

TIMELINE

1980s	Rise of "Yuppies" (young urban professionals)
	Japan emerges as major economic power
	Women enter workforce in increasing numbers
	Lee Iacocca revives Chrysler Corporation
	Bill Gates builds Microsoft as computer use spreads
	Immigration of Latinos and Asians expands
	Conservatives challenge affirmative action programs
1981	Reagan crushes air traffic controllers' strike
	AIDS epidemic identified; begins worldwide spread
1985	United States becomes debtor nation
1987	Montreal environmental protocol cuts ozone loss
1989	Savings and loan scandals and crises
1990s	Stock market boom continues after 1987 crash
	Globalization intensifies; American jobs outsourced
	Wal-Mart emerges as major economic force
	Decline of labor unions continues
	Personal computer and small electronics revolution
	Spread of World Wide Web (WWW)
	Human Genome Project unravels structure of DNA
	Deregulation of television industry; concentration of media ownership
	Opposition to immigration and multiculturalism grows
1991	European Union formed
1992	Los Angeles race riots
1993	North American Free Trade Agreement (NAFTA)
1995	World Trade Organization (WTO) created
1998	Battles over abortion, gay rights intensify; Congress passes Defense of Marriage Act
1999	Protests against WTO policies begin
2001	George W. Bush administration rejects Kyoto environmental treaty

FOR FURTHER EXPLORATION

Alfred Eckes Jr. and Thomas Zeilin, *Globalization and the American Century* (2003), link American prosperity during the twentieth century to participation in the global economy. For insight into the dynamics and character of American social classes, see David Brooks, *Bobos in Paradise: The New Upper Class and How They Got There* (2000); Barbara Ehrenreich, *Fear of Falling: The Inner Life of the Middle Class* (1989); and Nelson Lichtenstein, *State of the Union: A Century of American Labor* (2002). In *More Equal Than Others* (2004), Godfrey Hodgson points to increasing social inequality as a central theme of the United States in the late twentieth century. Two other authors put greater emphasis on ideological demands for equality: John Skrentny, *The Minority Rights Revolution* (2002), and Samuel Walker, *The Rights Revolution: Rights and Community in Modem America* (1998). Two fine studies of family life are Stephanie Coontz, *The Way We Never Were: American Families and the Nostalgia Trap* (1992), and Arlie Hochschild, *The Second Shift: Working Parents and the Revolution at Home* (2002). See also Susan Faludi, *Backlash: The Undeclared War against American Women* (1991).

Provocative studies of technology include Howard Segal, *Future Imperfect: The Mixed Blessings of Technology in America* (1994), and Edward Tenner, *Why Things Bite Back: Technology and the Revenge of Unintended Consequences* (1996). Mary Ann Watson, *Defining Visions: Television and the American Experience Since 1945* (1998), surveys the changing character of the TV era, while Leonard Downie Jr. and Robert G. Kaiser, *The News about the News: American Journalism in Peril* (2002), point to its impact on the press. For a discussion of environmental issues, consult Adam Rose, *The Bulldozer in the Countryside: Suburban Sprawl and the Rise of American Environmentalism* (2001). The course of the AIDS epidemic can be followed in the *New York Times*—go to **www.nytimes.com/ref/health/25years-aids.html**.

On the culture wars, see Gertrude Himmelfarb, *One Nation, Two Cultures* (1999), and James Hunter, *Culture Wars: The Struggle to Define America* (1991). For race relations, consult Terry Anderson, *The Pursuit of Fairness: A History of Affirmative Action* (2004), and Jennifer Hochschild, *Facing Up to the American Dream: Race, Class, and the Soul of America* (1996). In *Debating Immigration, 1882–Present* (2001), Roger Daniels and Otis Graham offer a historical perspective on a contemporary issue. For discussions of recent arrivals, consult Nicolaus Mills, ed., *Arguing Immigration* (1994) and "The New Americans" at **www.pbs.org/independentlens/newamericans**.

TEST YOUR KNOWLEDGE

To assess your command of the material in this chapter, see the Online Study Guide at **bedfordstmartins.com/henretta**.

For Web sites, images, and documents related to topics and places in this chapter, visit **bedfordstmartins.com/makehistory**.

32 Into the Twenty-First Century

JUST AS MEMORIES DEFINE INDIVIDUALS, so collective memories shape a nation. Few Americans ever forgot the moment when they learned of the Japanese attack on Pearl Harbor on December 7, 1941. "You wake up on a Sunday morning," one later reflected, "and the world as you know it ends." Sixty years later, on the bright morning of September 11, 2001, Americans felt exactly the same way as they watched live on television the collapse of the two 110-story towers of New York City's World Trade Center. They knew that the nation had at arrived another defining moment.

The attack by Al Qaeda terrorists, like that of the Japanese on Hawaii, caught the nation by surprise, and for good reason. As the world's only superpower, the United States faced significant challenges in many places: North Korea, Bosnia, Iraq, Iran, and Russia. Only in retrospect did the Al Qaeda threat come sharply into focus. Yes, Osama bin Laden, its wealthy Saudi-born leader, had called in 1998 for a *jihad*, a holy war, against America. Al Qaeda operatives had bombed American embassies in Kenya and Tanzania in 1998 and the USS *Cole*, an American warship visiting Yemen, in 2000. But no one, not the CIA, nor the Pentagon, nor Presidents Bill Clinton and George W. Bush, imagined suicidal terrorists ramming commercial jets into the World Trade Center and

The Advent of George W. Bush
The Contested Election of 2000
The Bush Agenda

American Hegemony Challenged
September 11, 2001
The War on Terror: Iraq
The Election of 2004

Unfinished Business
The President's Travails
What Kind of America?
What Kind of World?

◀ **A Poignant Symbol**

This striking photograph captures one of the nation's most revered symbols, the Statue of Liberty, against a backdrop of smoke from New York City's World Trade Center following the terrorist attacks of September 11, 2001. Daniel Hulshizer/AP Images.

Pentagon. Al Qaeda's brutal audacity simply exceeded American experience.

Once a minor annoyance, this band of terrorists became defined — no doubt to Osama bin Laden's great satisfaction — as an existential threat, on a par with the Nazis of 1941 and the nuclear-armed Soviets of 1950. America's global mission became the War on Terror. The cost of that effort, which is not finished, has been high — wars in Afghanistan and Iraq, $300 billion expended (as of 2006), tens of thousands of dead and wounded American soldiers and Iraqis, civil liberties in the United States at risk. However the War on Terror turns out, it has already left its mark on America. Gone are the high hopes inspired by victory in the Cold War. Instead, the United States enters the twenty-first century off its stride, somehow ill-equipped, despite its military and economic preeminence, for the challenges it now faces.

The Advent of George W. Bush

Less than a year before 9/11, Americans lived through a different kind of traumatic event. So closely contested was the presidential election of November 2000 that for a month the outcome remained in doubt. Only in mid-December, when the Supreme Court intervened, did Republican candidate George W. Bush's victory become certain. Having lost the popular vote, the new president might have been expected to govern in a moderate, bipartisan fashion. But, in fact, he proceeded as if he had won a popular mandate. In the process, he redefined conservatism. Traditionally, Republicans stood for limits on federal powers, balanced budgets, and individual rights. Now, these principles mostly went by the boards. The Bush administration tried simultaneously to cut taxes, expand entitlements, federalize public education, please the Religious Right, and expand America's global power. Where the Bush presidency stood on the political spectrum became an open question.

The Contested Election of 2000

George W. Bush's adversary was Al Gore, vice president in the Clinton administration. Both candidates came from privileged backgrounds. After a childhood in Midland, Texas, where his family had moved from Connecticut, Bush attended an elite New England private school and Yale University. Gore went to Harvard. Both men boasted impressive political pedigrees. Gore's father, a senator from Tennessee, had long groomed his son for the presidency. Bush's paternal grandfather was a Connecticut senator and his father, George H. W. Bush, had recently served as president.

The Candidates. There the resemblance stopped. Where Al Gore was a straight arrow — divinity student, journalist, elected to Congress at the age of twenty-eight — Bush was at that age a bit of a hell-raiser, going through what he himself described as a "nomadic" period of "irresponsible youth." Still, Karl Rove, his future political guru, saw something special even then in the happy-go-lucky Bush and became a steadfast ally. Bush became a Texas oil man, unsuccessfully, and ran for the House of Representatives in 1978, unsuccessfully, but he remained active in politics, mostly working for his father. After the elder Bush became president, George W. finally made it in business as managing partner of the Texas Rangers baseball franchise. In 1994, with Rove at his side, he was elected Texas governor and was on his way.

On the campaign trail against Gore, Bush presented himself as the genuine article, a regular guy. Unburdened by political baggage, he was free to position himself as he chose, and he chose the center. He ran as an outsider, deploring Washington partisanship and casting himself as a "uniter, not a divider," and promising to restore "honor and dignity" to the White House after the Clinton scandals. On domestic policy, he stood for "compassionate conservatism." Bush's campaign was orchestrated by Karl Rove, a supremely gifted strategist and political in-fighter. One of Rove's maxims was to find the right message and stick to it. That was George W. Bush, always "on message."

Al Gore, by contrast, never settled on a message. Vacillating between Clinton's centrism and his own liberalism, he gave the unfortunate impression of a man without fixed principles. His professorial demeanor — although well earned — came off badly against Bush's affability. If Bush was the superior campaigner, Vice President Gore was the beneficiary of the prosperity of the Clinton years. Affronted by the White House scandals, however, Gore distanced himself from Clinton — a decision that cost him crucial votes. Gore's real nemesis, however, was Ralph Nader, whose Green Party candidacy drew away the votes that certainly would have carried him to victory. As it was, Gore won the popular vote, amassing 50.9 million votes to 50.4 million for Bush, only to fall short in the Electoral College, 267 to 271.

The Mess in Florida. The Democrats immediately challenged the tally in Florida. In the heavily

The Contested Vote in Florida, 2000

When the vote recount got under way in Palm Beach, both sides brought out supporters to demonstrate outside the Supervisor of Elections Office, in hopes of influencing the officials doing the counting. In this photograph, supporters of George W. Bush and Al Gore clash after a rally on November 13, 2000, that had been addressed by Jesse Jackson, the dominant African American figure in the Democratic Party. ©Reuters/Corbis.

Democratic Miami area, confusing "butterfly" ballots caused elderly Gore supporters mistakenly to vote for Patrick Buchanan, the candidate of the conservative Reform Party. Elsewhere, election officials had to decide whether to count partially punched ballots registered by antiquated voting machines.

These problematic ballots turned the election into a partisan brawl. When Gore's campaign demanded hand recounts in several counties, Florida's Republican secretary of state halted the process and declared Governor Bush the winner. On appeal by the vice president's lawyers, Florida's Supreme Court ordered the recount to proceed. The Bush campaign immediately went to the U.S. Supreme Court. On December 12, the Court ruled, by a margin of 5 to 4, that recounting ballots in only selected counties violated the rights of other Floridians under the Fourteenth Amendment's equal protection clause. As if acknowledging the fragility of that argument, the Court declared *Bush v. Gore* a one-shot deal, not to be regarded as precedent in any future case. It surprised many legal experts that the Supreme Court had even accepted the case. The likeliest explanation for why it did was that cutting short the controversy seemed preferable to having it thrust into a bitterly divided U.S. House of Representatives, with unforeseeable consequences. But by making a transparently political decision, warned dissenting Justice Stephen G. Breyer, the majority was running "the risk of undermining the public's confidence in the Court itself." Still, the Court's ruling stuck. Gore had always played by the rules, and did so now, conceding the election to his Republican opponent.

The Bush Agenda

Although George Bush had positioned himself as a moderate, counter-tendencies drove his administration from the start. Foremost was the man he had chosen as his running mate, Richard Cheney, an uncompromising, conservative Republican. Ordinarily, the politics of vice presidents don't matter much, but Cheney was not an ordinary vice president. Offsetting the president's inexperience, the older Cheney was a seasoned Washington veteran, and, with Bush's consent, he became virtually a dual president, backed by a big staff and granted wide policymaking latitude. Equally determining was Bush's decision to bring his campaign advisor, Karl Rove, into the White House. Rove made a key strategic decision that Bush's political future required playing to the party's conservative base, foreclosing the easy-going centrism of Bush the campaigner.

On Capitol Hill, Rove's hard line was reinforced by Tom DeLay, the Republican whip and, after 2002, House majority leader. As Newt Gingrich's second-in-command in 1995, DeLay declared "all-out war" on the Democrats, and he was as good as his word. He masterminded the K Street Project (after the street housing Washington's lobbyists) that achieved a Republican lock on the big-money lobbying firms. Everything then fell into place. Lobbyists got access; House members got campaign funding; and, as paymaster, DeLay got a disciplined rank-and-file. Some of that money ended up underwriting a Republican takeover of the Texas legislature, which then gerrymandered five extra

Republican congressional districts. With that cushion, DeLay had a safe House majority, and no need to deal with Democrats. The Senate, although more collegial, went through a similar hardening process. After 2002, with Republicans in control of both Congress and the White House, any pretense of bipartisan lawmaking ended.

Out of these disparate elements — Bush's compassionate conservatism, Rove's political calculations, exceptionally combative allies — there emerged a hybrid brand of conservatism that defies easy classification.

Faith-Based Politics. After his wayward early years George W. Bush became, at the hands of the Rev. Billy Graham, a born-again Christian, the first to be president since Jimmy Carter. Bush let it be known that a prayer opened cabinet meetings and that a Bible study class met at the White House. On his first day in office, he banned foreign-aid funding for family-planning programs that offered abortion counseling.

As a sign of his commitment, Bush launched his "faith-based initiative" for federal support of church-related social-service programs. To this end, he created a special office in the White House, channeled federal money to a new Compassion Capital Fund, and persuaded Congress to authorize a Community-Based Abstinence Education program. Federal money began to flow to religiously based centers, many of them focusing on pregnancy services for unwed mothers and sexual abstinence for teenagers. Challenged that his faith-based initiative violated the constitutional separation of church and state, Bush took a page from the playbook of civil rights advocates. The First Amendment, he argued, did not require "discriminating against religious institutions simply because they are religious." He was similarly audacious about discriminatory issues posed by his faith-based initiative. A 2002 executive order exempted religious groups receiving federal grants from the civil rights prohibition against hiring on the basis of religious affiliation.

Although the money involved was modest — a small fraction of total federal funding of social-service agencies — Bush's faith-based initiative demonstrated concretely his commitment to the Religious Right. To a unique degree, evangelical leaders had an ally in the White House, a true believer in their moral agenda.

The Politics of Inclusiveness. Bush's campaign had been blessedly free of Republican race-mongering, such as — to take a paternal example — his father's Willie Horton ad (featuring a black murderer) in the 1988 race against the hapless Michael Dukakis (see Chapter 30). By contrast, George W. was determinedly inclusive. Black speakers and entertainers featured prominently at the Republican convention, and of those most prominently featured, General Colin Powell, a former chair of the Joint Chiefs of Staff, became secretary of state, and Condoleezza Rice, a Stanford foreign-policy expert, became national security advisor and then, after Powell's retirement, secretary of state. Mexican Americans also

Colin Powell and Condoleezza Rice

Colin Powell, a distinguished army general, and Condoleezza Rice, a former Stanford academic, were leading figures in the Bush administration and powerful symbols of Bush's efforts at racial inclusiveness. Powell was secretary of state, and Rice national security advisor. Here they are seated side by side, attending a state dinner at the Grand Palace in Bangkok, Thailand, October 19, 2003. Paul J. Richards/AFP/Getty Images.

No Child Left Behind

President Bush was tireless at getting out into the country to drum up support for his programs. Here he chats with fourth graders on a visit to the Pierre Laclede Elementary School in St. Louis, Missouri, on January 5, 2004. The sign on the blackboard tells us why he was there. © Jason Reed/Reuters/Corbis.

figured prominently, and Bush, on easy terms with Texas's Latino community, was committed to finding a middle ground for resolving the increasingly contentious crisis over illegal immigrants.

On civil rights, the new administration hewed to a traditionally conservative line, routinely opposing affirmative action in cases coming before the courts. But when it came to equal opportunity, Bush was a crusader. He spoke feelingly of "the soft prejudice of low expectations," and that arresting phrase launched him into the thickets of educational reform.

No Child Left Behind. Fulfilling a campaign pledge, Bush in 2001 proposed the No Child Left Behind Act, which increased federal funding for primary and secondary education and funneled money to schools with a high percentage of students from disadvantaged backgrounds. Conservatives who favored school choice could take satisfaction from the provision that allowed students in underperforming schools to transfer to better institutions. But the main thrust of the law was hardly conservative. No civic responsibility in America was more distinctively local than the public schools, funded as they were by property taxes and controlled by locally elected school boards. No Child Left Behind overrode this precious autonomy, imposing federal standards for student performance as a means of disciplining a lagging educational system.

Local and state officials fought back. They argued that, because of inadequate congressional funding, the mandated programs ate into local budgets; that the emphasis on testing distorted good educational practice; and that a program emanating from Washington was bound to have unintended consequences (tempting school districts, for example, to encourage low-scoring students to drop out). By 2005 state governments were challenging the act in the courts.

Whatever its ultimate fate, there can be no denying the vaulting ambition of No Child Left Behind, or the degree to which it departed from conservative canons of states' rights and federal restraint.

Health Care. Equally confounding to conservative principles was Bush's response to the nation's festering health-care crisis. Despite hand-wringing by fiscal conservatives, the president did little to contain Medicare costs, which jumped from $433 billion to $627 billion during his first five years in office. What did grab his attention was a gaping hole in Medicare benefits. Without drug coverage, desperate seniors were surfing the Web and turning to Canada for more cheaply priced medicines. Preempting the Democrats, the Bush administration in 2003 muscled through Congress a drug-benefit bill that would cost $385 billion over the first five years. The conservative side of it was in the particulars: first, no negotiating by Medicare for bulk purchases, although that was how Canada and America's own Veterans Administration had cut drug costs; second, no direct provision by Medicare, but only via private insurers, who would compete for Medicare customers; and, third, substantial copayments, topping out at $3,600 for beneficiaries with big drug bills. In its solicitude for private business, market competition, and individual responsibility, Bush's drug program was soundly conservative, but with the government picking up the tab. No wonder that traditional conservatives were bewildered or that it had taken extraordinary steps by Tom DeLay's machine to wring out the final Republican votes to pass the bill in the House.

Included in the law was a provision enabling people to set up tax-free health savings accounts to pay for ordinary medical expenses. The central idea, generated by conservative think tanks, was to foster an "ownership society," in which individuals, rather than the state, took primary responsibility for their own welfare.

By 2005, the time seemed ripe to strike a bigger blow for Bush's ownership society. In the name of "reforming" Social Security, he proposed the diversion of a portion of its revenues into individual retirement accounts that account holders could invest in stocks and bonds. Despite a strenuous sales campaign and much support from conservatives, Bush's plan fell flat. It seemed that Americans preferred the comfort of the existing Social Security system to the adventure of an ownership society.

Embracing Business. The concern for private insurers and the drug companies shown in the Medicare drug bill faithfully reflected the administration's embrace of American business. As if to signal what was to come, Vice President Cheney — himself the former head of the oil-equipment giant Halliburton — met with oil men as soon as the new administration was installed and hammered out an energy policy that, among other things, called for oil drilling in Alaska's Arctic National Wildlife Refuge and generous subsidies for Gulf of Mexico oil and gas operators (Map 32.1). In the case of electric utilities, the problem was the huge fines they faced for evading the requirement by the Clean Air Act that new or upgraded coal-burning equipment meet high air-quality standards. The Environmental Protection Agency (EPA), now run by Bush appointees, came to the rescue by issuing more accommodating rules (the most important of which exempted upgrades costing less than 20 percent of the replacement cost of the equipment). Better, the administration argued, to achieve regulatory goals voluntarily, a task best achieved, as with the EPA, by appointing industry people to do the regulating.

Life involved trade-offs, the administration argued: cheaper electricity or cleaner air? And, indeed, a whole host of issues — fuel economy standards for oversized SUVs, snowmobiles in Yellowstone, logging in the national forests — involved trade-offs. What struck Bush's critics was how consistently he came

Map 32.1 Proposed Oil Development in the Arctic National Wildlife Refuge (ANWR)

Environmentalists fought the Bush administration to a standstill over the issue of opening Alaska's Arctic National Wildlife Refuge to oil exploration. This map shows the contested area, as well as the north slope of Alaska already producing oil and the pipeline bringing it to market.

down on the side of business. The president could speak with emotion about companies hit by the huge injury awards in cases involving medical malpractice and defective products. For him, legislation limiting company liability constituted a major achievement. He also supported a Republican-sponsored bill strongly advocated by credit card operators that tightened bankruptcy laws against delinquent borrowers. Bush kept a lower profile on organized labor, but his actions as employer — which, for the federal bureaucracy, he ultimately was — spoke loud and clear. He was adamant that the collective-bargaining rights of public employees not be applied to the new Department of Homeland Security. Adverse decisions by his appointees to the Labor Department and NLRB also began to have a cumulatively damaging effect on the labor movement.

Complicating the president's efforts was a cascade of corporate scandals triggered by the Wall Street plunge of 2000. Most spectacular was the collapse of Enron, a Houston-based energy giant and a big player in Republican politics. The first sign of trouble was a mysterious roiling of the California energy market, with sudden power shortages, rolling blackouts, and price spikes. When state officials appealed to Washington, they were rebuffed. Let the free market operate, said the administration. In fact, it was market rigging at work, and guilty traders eventually went to jail and disgorged illegal profits. For Enron, a major player, the scam was the least of its troubles. Enron fell into bankruptcy, a victim of astounding accounting frauds and insider dealing. Thousands of employees lost their jobs and retirement savings. The scandal spread to New York investment banks, which had turned a blind eye while marketing Enron securities, and to its auditing firm, Arthur Andersen, which was driven out of business. Similar misconduct destroyed WorldCom, a major provider of telephone and telecommunications services; Global Crossing, a fiber optic cable company; and Adelphia Communications, a cable television conglomerate. As in the 1980s (see Chapter 31), these scandals cast a cloud over corporate America, with some of the nation's vaunted CEOs facing prison and business under heightened regulatory scrutiny.

Cutting Taxes. The domestic issue that most engaged President Bush, as it had Ronald Reagan, was taxes. Like Reagan, Bush acted immediately on taking office. His Economic Growth and Tax Relief Act of 2001 had something for everyone. It slashed income tax rates, extended the earned income credit for the poor, and phased out the estate tax by 2010 (when it would resume, unless Congress acted, at the original high rate). A second round of cuts in 2003 targeted dividend income and capital gains. By sheer magnitude, Bush's tax cuts exceeded Reagan's.

Bush denied Democratic accusations that his tax cuts favored the wealthy. If one looked at the rate of decline in a household's *tax bill*, the president was correct. The average low-income family got a whopping tax savings of 48 percent. But if measured by the effect on family *income*, Bush's cuts clearly favored the rich. His signature cuts — those favoring big estates and well-to-do owners of stocks and bonds — especially skewed the distribution upwards. Overall, low-income families (averaging $19,521 annually) got a tax break of $435; middle-income families (averaging $70,096) got

The Fall of Enron

Enron was an iconic corporation of the booming 1990s, widely touted as an example of how inspired business leadership could transform a stodgy company into a world leader — in Enron's case, as a trader in energy and other commodities. Its business turned out to be largely smoke and mirrors, kept aloft by fake accounting and financial manipulation. When the entire edifice came crashing down in 2001, Enron was overnight transformed from icon to villain. Symbolic of its fall from grace was the change in the name of the Houston Astros' baseball stadium — from Enron Field to **Minute Maid Park.** Brett Coomer/AP Images.

TABLE 32.1	Impact of the Bush Tax Cuts, 2001–2003					
Income in 2003	Taxpayers	Gross Income	Total Tax Cut	% Change in Tax Bill	Tax Bill	Tax Rate
Less than $50,000	92,093,452	$19,521	$435	−48%	$474	2%
$50,000 to 100,000	26,915,091	70,096	1,656	−21	6,417	9
$100,000 to 200,000	8,878,643	131,797	3,625	−17	18,281	14
$200,000 to 500,000	1,999,061	288,296	7,088	−10	60,464	21
$500,000 to 1,000,000	356,140	677,294	22,479	−12	169,074	25
$1,000,000 to 10,000,000	175,157	2,146,100	84,666	−13	554,286	26
$10,000,000 or more	6,126	25,975,532	1,019,369	−15	5,780,926	22

SOURCE: *New York Times,* April 5, 2006.

$1,656; and the very wealthy (averaging $2,146,100) got $84,666 (Table 32.1). Nor did everyone benefit equally. Taxpayers at the bottom and middle gained only 60 percent of the relative benefit—the ratio of money saved to income—enjoyed by those at the top.

No matter, the president suggested, because the main thing was that everyone benefited from the boost to the economy. Critics warned that because so little of the federal budget was discretionary, Bush's tax cuts were bound to plunge the federal government into debt. Bush was unperturbed. He was, in fact, not of the conservative school that favored tax cuts as a means of shrinking the government—"starving the beast," as Reaganites had called it—because, as it turned out, he was himself a champion spender. By 2006, federal expenditures had jumped 33 percent, at a faster clip than under any president since Lyndon Johnson. There followed a swift reversal of fiscal fortunes, with the Clinton-inherited federal surplus transformed into bulging deficits—estimated at over $300 billion for 2006. Over 60 percent of that shortfall was attributable to reduced tax revenues (see Reading American Pictures, "Conservatism at a Crossroads," p. 997).

Midway through Bush's second term the national debt stood at over $8 trillion, much of it owned by foreign investors, who also financed the nation's huge trade deficit. On top of that, staggering Social Security and Medicare obligations were coming due with the looming retirement of the baby boomers. It seemed that these burdens—in per capita terms, the national debt currently stands at $28,000 for every man, woman, and child—would be passed on to future generations.

How Bush's presidency might have fared in normal times is another of those unanswerable questions of history. In making his case as a candidate in 2000, George W. Bush had said little about foreign policy. He had assumed that his administration would rise or fall on the appeal of his domestic program. With 9/11, an altogether different political scenario unfolded.

▶ Explain why, if Bush lost the popular vote in 2000, he nevertheless became president.

▶ In what ways did Bush's policies depart from traditional conservatism?

▶ What were the main issues in the debate over tax cuts?

American Hegemony Challenged

The dictionary defines *hegemony* as "predominant influence exercised by one state over others." That was the United States in 2001, the hegemonic power in the world, unrivaled now that the Soviet Union was gone. It was therefore incumbent on the United States, George W. Bush often said, to be "humble" in its relations with other states. "If we're an arrogant nation," he warned, other peoples will "resent us." Bush's campaign words, however, bore little relation to his true bent. Once in office, he was much more inclined to take a muscular approach to foreign affairs. In this, Bush was heartily seconded by his vice president, a Cold Warrior of many years' standing. Cheney's key ally was the new secretary of defense, Donald Rumsfeld, who brought in a high-powered team of neoconservatives led by his deputy, Paul Wolfowitz. The neocons

READING AMERICAN PICTURES

Conservativism at a Crossroads

Since the New Deal of the 1930s, conservatives agreed on one thing—government needed to be small for American liberty to thrive. Small government meant, above all, fiscal restraint and minimal federal regulation, especially of the economy. The Republican Party won national power in 1980 by rejecting liberal Democratic programs and heeding Ronald Reagan's call to "get the government off our backs" (see Chapter 30). What do we make of conservatism today? Many conservatives today find themselves divided—whether to support the initiatives of the Bush administration or remain true to their core values. Throughout this text the authors have used political cartoons to illuminate where the American people stand on many different issues and, once again, the cartoonists haven't let us down.

ANALYZING THE EVIDENCE

▶ What does the first cartoon, published in the *St. Louis Post-Dispatch*, suggest are the causes of Uncle Sam's expanding waistline?

▶ In what ways does the second cartoon, from the *National Review*, offer a different explanation for the government's spending spree? Hint: The word "pork" for Washington insiders means spending bills favoring special interests or the pet projects of individual congressmen or senators.

▶ The *National Review* is a leading conservative journal, while the *St. Louis Dispatch* is generally regarded as a liberal newspaper. Can you tell that one is conservative and the other liberal from these two cartoons published in their pages? In what ways?

Weighing the Return of Big Government. © Matson / *St. Louis Post-Dispatch* / caglecartoons.com.

A National Shopping Spree. By permission of Gary Varvel / *The Indianapolis Star* / and Creator's Syndicate, Inc. This appeared in the *National Review*, May 22, 2006, p. 49.

disdained the idea of a "humble" foreign policy. On the contrary, they championed "benevolent hegemony"—the untrammeled use of America's power, military power if need be, to fashion a better, more democratic world.

In a striking display of unilateralism, the new administration walked away from an array of completed or pending diplomatic agreements. It repudiated the International Criminal Court and a UN convention banning biological weapons, and backed away from nuclear test bans, weapons reduction, and antiballistics missiles treaties. Most startling was its withdrawal from the Kyoto Protocol on global warming. When participating countries met in Bonn, Germany, in July 2001 to refine the Protocol and satisfy America's objections, the U.S. representative was instructed not to participate. All too soon, the United States would be looking for the world's support.

September 11, 2001

On that bright morning, nineteen Al Qaeda terrorists hijacked four commercial jets and flew two of them into New York City's World Trade Center, destroying its twin towers and killing over 2,600 people. A third plane plowed into the Pentagon, near Washington, D.C., and killed almost 200 passengers and Defense Department employees; the fourth, presumably headed for the White House, crashed in Pennsylvania when the passengers fought back and thwarted the hijackers.

How could it have happened? No fully satisfying answer was ever forthcoming, not even when the blue-ribbon 9/11 Commission issued its final report three years later. It was not as if the attack was unprecedented—the World Trade Center itself had been the target of an earlier truck bombing in 1993—or even that the plot had gone wholly undetected. While attending flight schools, a few of the hijackers had drawn suspicions, and one suspect, Zacarias Moussoaui, had actually been taken into custody. Two of the hijackers had been flagged by the CIA, but it neglected to inform the FBI that they were in the country. The failure was not so much one of intelligence gathering, the 9/11 Commission concluded, but of an inability to "connect the dots"—much like the conclusion of the Senate committee that had looked into the Pearl Harbor attack of 1941. Although the incoming administration had been slow developing a counterterrorism program, the new president escaped blame for the disaster because the country's attention had turned to war.

On September 14, as soon as he got his bearings, President Bush headed for the World Trade Center ground zero, embraced rescue workers standing in the rubble, picked up a bullhorn and stirred the nation. As an outburst of patriotism swept the United States, Bush proclaimed a "War on Terror" and vowed to carry the battle to Al Qaeda.

Operating out of Afghanistan, where they had been given haven by the fundamentalist Taliban

September 11, 2001

Cameramen photographing the scene after a plane crashed into the north tower of New York City's World Trade Center found themselves recording a defining moment in the nation's history. When a second airliner approached and then slammed into the building's south tower at 9:03 A.M., the nation knew this was no accident. The United States was under attack. Of the 2,843 people killed on September 11, 2,617 died at the World Trade Center.
Robert Clark / AURORA.

Americans, Think!

While incomprehensible to Americans, the murderous attacks of 9/11 were greeted with satisfaction by many in the Muslim world. Their anti-Americanism was based in part on U.S. support for Israel, but also stemmed from their resentment of American wealth and power and of the corrosive effects that they felt Western capitalism and modernity exerted on their societies. Here, Pakistanis demonstrate at an anti-American rally in Islamabad on September 15, 2001. B.K. Bangash / AP Images.

regime, the elusive Al Qaeda at this moment offered a clear target. When the Taliban refused to turn over mastermind Osama bin Laden, the United States attacked, not with conventional forces, but by deploying military advisers, supplies, and special forces that bolstered anti-Taliban rebel forces. While Afghani allies carried the ground war, American planes and missiles rained destruction on the enemy. By early 2002, this lethal combination had ousted the Taliban government, destroyed the Al Qaeda training camps, and killed or captured many of its operatives. Bin Laden retreated to a mountain redoubt. Inexplicably, U.S. Special Forces failed to press the attack. Bin Laden evidently bought off the local war lords and escaped over the border into Pakistan.

The War on Terror: Iraq

At this point, the Bush administration could have declared victory and relegated the unfinished business—tracking down the Al Qaeda remnants, stabilizing Afghanistan, and shaking up the nation's security agencies—to a post-victory operational phase. President Bush had no such inclination. For him and his advisers, the War on Terror was not a metaphor, but the real thing, an open-ended war that required putting aside business-as-usual.

On the domestic side, Bush declared the terrorist threat too big to be contained by ordinary law-enforcement means. He wanted the government's powers of domestic surveillance placed on a wartime footing. With no hearings and little debate, Congress passed by virtual acclamation the USA PATRIOT Act (Uniting and Strengthening America by Providing Appropriate Tools Required to Intercept and Obstruct Terrorism), and, true to its title, the Patriot Act granted the administration sweeping authority to monitor citizens and apprehend suspected terrorists.

On the international front, the War on Terror called forth a policy of preventive war. International law recognized a nation's right to strike first if faced by an imminent threat from another state. The so-called Bush doctrine lowered the bar, declaring that the United States reserved the right to attack dangerous states even absent any imminent threat. Secretary of Defense Rumsfeld called it "anticipatory self-defense." In his State of the Union address in January 2002, President Bush singled out Iran, North Korea, and Iraq—"an axis of evil"—as the states most threatening to the United States.

Of the three, Iraq seemed the easiest mark, a pushover for Secretary Rumsfeld's lean, high-tech military. Neoconservatives in the Pentagon regarded Iraq as unfinished business, left over from the Gulf War of 1991 (see Chapter 30). They believed the elder Bush had been wrong, first, not to press on to Baghdad and, second, to have encouraged the Shiites, who constituted the Iraqi majority, to rise up against the tyrant Saddam Hussein and then to abandon them. Deputy Secretary of Defense Paul Wolfowitz, who had flown over the devastated rebel areas, vowed that there would be a reckoning. On a larger scale, Iraq represented for neoconservatives like Wolfowitz a chance to unveil the American mission to democratize the world. Iraqis would surely embrace democracy if given half a chance, and the democratizing effect would

The Search for Al Qaeda

After the terrorist attacks of 9/11, the United States succeeded in marshaling a multinational force to invade Afghanistan, where the Taliban regime harbored key elements of the Al Qaeda network. Here, Canadian infantrymen board a U.S. Army Chinook helicopter in the Shahi Kot mountains of Afghanistan in March 2002. By then, Taliban and Al Qaeda had mostly been cleared out of the country, but the Taliban regrouped in northern Pakistan and by 2006 had staged a comeback in the remote southern provinces of Afghanistan. © Jim Hollander / AFP / Corbis.

spread across the Middle East, reforming other unpopular Arab regimes and stabilizing the region. That in turn would secure the Middle East's oil supply, whose fragility Saddam's invasion of Kuwait in 1990 had made all too clear. And it was the oil, of course, that was of vital interest to the United States (Map 32.2).

None of these considerations, either singly or together, met Bush's declared threshold for preventive war. The administration, moreover, was sharply divided. The secretary of state, Colin Powell, although less influential than the Department of Defense hawks, was nevertheless a formidable voice. Powell and others, including America's anxious European allies, persuaded a reluctant President Bush that he needed international approval for any military action, and that meant going to the UN Security Council. The framework was already in place: Resolution 687 (and a succession of supporting resolutions) ordered Iraq after the Gulf War to halt all work on weapons of mass destruction (WMD). UN inspectors had rooted out chemical and biological stockpiles and an unexpectedly advanced nuclear program, but in 1998 Iraq expelled the inspectors, and no one could be certain whether the WMD programs had resumed. At Secretary of State Powell's behest, the Security Council approved Resolution 1441, which demanded that Saddam Hussein allow the return of the UN weapons inspectors. Unexpectedly, he agreed.

Most of the nations supporting Resolution 1441 saw it as means of defusing the crisis: The main thing was to keep talking. The Bush administration saw Resolution 1441 as a prelude to war: The main thing was to get on with the invasion. Naturally, the diplomatic parrying became rancorous. Most mysterious was Saddam, who actually had no WMDs but by his obstructive efforts acted as if he did. Since he didn't, the UN inspectors came up empty-handed. Intelligence experts, both U.S.

Map 32.2 U.S. Involvement in the Middle East, 1979–2006

The United States has long played an active role in the Middle East, driven by the strategic importance of that region and, most importantly, by America's need to ensure a reliable supply of oil from the Persian Gulf states. This map shows the highlights of that troubled involvement, from the Tehran embassy hostage-taking in 1979 to the invasion and current occupation of Iraq.

and European, were flummoxed. It seemed incredible that their estimates could be totally wrong. The Bush administration, gearing up for war, made the best intelligence case it could that Iraq constituted a "grave and gathering danger" and forged ahead.

Unable to secure a second Security Council resolution, the United States declared previous UN resolutions sufficient and invaded Iraq in March 2003. Its one major ally was Great Britain. A handful of other governments joined "the coalition of the willing," braving popular opposition at home to do so. Relations with France and Germany became poisonous. Even neighboring Mexico and Canada condemned the invasion, and Turkey, a key military ally, refused transit permission, ruining the army's plan for a northern thrust into Iraq. As for the Arab world, it exploded in anti-American demonstrations.

As in Afghanistan, the war began with massive air attacks intended to "shock and awe." *Time* magazine reported that targets around the capital city of Baghdad "got pulverized"; 130,000 U.S. and 30,000 British troops entered southern and central Iraq, accompanied by dozens of "embedded" reporters who broadcast events as they occurred. Within three weeks, the troops had taken Baghdad. The Iraqi regime collapsed, and its leaders went into hiding (Saddam Hussein was captured nine months later). On May 1, President Bush flew onto the aircraft carrier *Abraham Lincoln* in a Navy jet dressed in fighter pilot's togs. Framed by a "Mission Accomplished" banner, Bush declared victory. But in fact the battle in Iraq had not ended; it was just beginning.

Despite meticulous preparations, the Pentagon had paid little attention to what the military called Phase IV, post-conflict operations. Pentagon planners simply assumed an easy transition, with a quick draw-down of forces by September. Early in the assault, however, Saddam's paramilitary — the *fedayeen* — began mounting attacks behind the lines. Field commanders wanted a pause so that the fedayeen could be dealt with. Rumsfeld ordered the advance onward, refusing to acknowledge that, as army commanders immediately recognized, the fedayeen signified an insurgency in the making. An opportunity to nip it in the bud was lost. The secretary of defense was similarly dismissive of the many well-respected, knowledgeable voices warning that the Iraqi occupation was going to be no picnic. So when, as the coalition forces arrived, the Iraqi police and civil authorities simply dissolved, the American military had no contingency plans and not enough troops to maintain order.

Thousands of poor Iraqis looted everything they could get their hands on — stores, shops, museums, industrial plants, government offices, and

Abu Ghraib

This is an image obtained by the Associated Press showing a detainee bent over with his hands on the bars of a cell while being watched by a comfortably seated soldier at the Abu Ghraib prison in late 2003. Although displaying one of the milder forms of torture, this Abu Ghraib photograph captured all too vividly the humiliating treatment of detainees that outraged the Muslim world. AP Images.

military arsenals filled with guns and tons of deadly explosives. The looting shattered the infrastructure of Baghdad and other Iraqi cities, leaving them without reliable supplies of electricity and water. In the midst of this turmoil, the insurgency got started, sparked by Sunni Muslims who had dominated Iraq under Saddam's Baathist regime. In a decision afterward regretted, the Coalition Provisional Authority disbanded the Iraqi army, turning loose thousands of armed, well-trained Baathists with nothing better to do than fight Americans. Insurgents began mounting daily attacks, employing increasingly effective IEDs (improvised explosive devices) to blow up Humvees and other troop carriers. On the Shiite side, the radical cleric Moqtada al-Sadr demanded immediate American withdrawal and twice unleashed his armed militia against U.S. forces. With the borders unguarded, Al Qaeda supporters flocked into Iraq from all over the Middle East, eager to do battle with the infidel Americans, bringing along a *jihadi* specialty, the suicide bomber (see Voices from Abroad, "Abu Musab al-Zarqawi: A Strategy for the Iraq Insurgency," p. 1003).

Popular insurgencies are a problem from hell for superpowers. Lyndon Johnson discovered this in Vietnam. Leonid Brezhnev discovered it in Afghanistan. And George W. Bush rediscovered it in Iraq. The intractable fact is that the superpower's troops are invaders. Although hard for Americans to believe, that was how Iraqis of all stripes viewed the U.S. troops — as an occupation army. From this, a dilemma followed. If the occupying forces cracked down hard, the civilian population suffered and became hostile. If the occupying forces relented, insurgents became bolder and took control as, for example, at the Sunni strongholds of Al Ramadi and Falluja (see Map 32.3, p. 1016). The one proven alternative was to pacify and hold insurgent areas, denying the guerrillas a base of support and forcing them to seek a political solution. But that required far more soldiers than the occupation authority had available, thanks to Rumsfeld's insistence on a lean military. Nor did planners reckon with the fact that, in a war against insurgents, no occupation force comes out with clean hands. In Iraq, that painful truth burst forth graphically in photographs showing American guards at Baghdad's Abu Ghraib prison abusing and torturing suspected insurgents. The ghastly images shocked the world. For Muslims, they offered final proof of American perfidy.

At that low point, in 2004, the United States had spent upwards of $100 billion. A thousand American soldiers had died, and ten thousand more had been wounded, many maimed for life. But if the U.S. pulled out, Iraq would descend into chaos. So, as Bush took to saying, the United States had to "stay the course."

The Election of 2004

The president had emerged from the 9/11 crisis looking invincible, with an approval rating approaching 90 percent. For party strategists, this was like money in the bank, only it proved to be a depleting resource, steadily drawn down as bad news from Iraq accumulated. Once the fruitless scouring for Iraqi WMDs ended, the administration came under relentless questioning. How had the United States gotten into this war? Was it a case of faulty intelligence? Or had the president misled the

VOICES FROM ABROAD

Abu Musab al-Zarqawi
A Strategy for the Iraq Insurgency

From 2004 to June 2006, when he was killed by American forces, Abu Musab al-Zarqawi led the Al Qaeda–linked insurgency in Iraq. Born in Jordan in 1966, al-Zarqawi spent his youth as a petty criminal. During the 1980s, he fought as an Islamic jihadist against the Soviet occupation of Afghanistan. Al-Zarqawi then returned to Jordan, where he was imprisoned for seven years for conspiring to overthrow the monarchy and establish an Islamic caliphate. In this effort he was bent on expelling all Western influences from the Islamic world. But al-Zarqawi was also engaged in a struggle inside the Islamic world. He was Sunni, and he regarded the other main branch of Islam, the Shi'ite, as a heretical enemy as vile as the hated West. Early in 2004, as he was taking up his struggle in Iraq, al-Zarqawi wrote the following letter, which outlined the deadly strategy of bombings and sectarian violence he proposed to follow. The letter should be read for what it reveals of the mind of the figure who, until his death, was more responsible than any other for plunging Iraq into chaos.

God favored the [Islamic] nation with jihad on His behalf in the land of Mesopotamia [the ancient name for Iraq].... The Americans, as you know well, entered Iraq on a contractual basis to create the State of Greater Israel from the Nile to the Euphrates and that this Zionized American Administration believes that accelerating the creation of the State of [Greater] Israel will accelerate the emergence of the Messiah. It came to Iraq with all its people, pride, and haughtiness toward God and his Prophet. It thought that the matter would be somewhat easy.... But it collided with a completely different reality. The operations of the brother mujahidin [fighters] began from the first moment.... This forced the Americans to conclude a deal with the Shi'a, the most evil of mankind. The deal was concluded on [the basis that] the Shi'a would get two-thirds of the booty for having stood in the ranks of the Crusaders against the mujahidin.

[The Shi'a are] the insurmountable obstacle, the lurking snake, the crafty and malicious scorpion, the spying enemy, and the penetrating venom.... Shi'ism is the looming danger and the true challenge. "They are the enemy. Beware of them. Fight them. By God, they lie." History's message is validated by the testimony of the current situation, which informs most clearly that Shi'ism is a religion that has nothing in common with Islam....

[Among the Sunni mujahidin,] jihad here unfortunately [takes the form of] mines planted, rockets launched, and mortars shelling from afar. The Iraqi brothers still prefer safety and returning to the arms of their wives, where nothing frightens them. Sometimes the groups have boasted among themselves that not one of them has been killed or captured. We have told them in our many sessions with them that safety and victory are incompatible... that the [Islamic] nation cannot live without the aroma of martyrdom.

America did not come to leave, and it will not leave no matter how numerous its wounds become and how much of its blood is spilled. It is looking to the near future, when it hopes to disappear into its bases secure and at ease and put the battlefields of Iraq into the hands of the foundling government with an army and police that will bring [the terror] of Saddam ... back to the people. There is no doubt that the space in which we can move has begun to shrink and that the grip around the throats of the [Arab and Sunni] mujahidin has begun to tighten. With the deployment of soldiers and police, the future has become frightening....

The Shi'a ... in our opinion are the key to change. I mean that targeting and hitting them in [their] religious, political, and military depth will provoke them to show the Sunnis their rabies ... and bare the teeth of the hidden rancor working in their breasts. If we succeed in dragging them into the arena of sectarian war, it will become possible to awaken the inattentive Sunnis as they feel imminent danger and annihilating death at the hands of these [Shi'a]....

I come back and again say that the only solution is for us to strike the religious, military, and other cadres among the Shi'a with blow after blow until they bend to the Sunnis.... God's religion is more precious than lives and souls. When the overwhelming majority stands in the ranks of truth, there has to be sacrifice for this religion. Let blood be spilled....

SOURCE: Documents on Terrorist Abu Musab al-Zarqawi, 2004, www-personal.umich.edu/~jrcole/zarqawi/zarqawi.htm.

ANALYZING THE EVIDENCE

- According to al-Zarqawi, the Americans invaded Iraq "to create the State of Greater Israel from the Nile to the Euphrates." Why would he make a fantastic claim like that?

- If the Americans are the occupiers, why is his letter mostly about the Shi'ites? Why are they his primary target?

- Al-Zarqawi wrote this letter in early 2004. By mid-2006, at the time he was killed, how successful, based on your reading of the text, do you think he was in fulfilling the letter's aims?

presidential powers, he had slowed it a bit. At a critical moment, six weeks before the election, the recently installed Iraqi prime minister, Ayad Allawi, had visited the White House to say how well things were going in Iraq. But the problems kept coming. If the insurgency was bad news, civil war was worse. By 2006 Sunnis and Shiites were at each other's throats, and it became a race between insurgent efforts at fomenting civil war and American efforts at establishing a stable Iraqi government.

With no end in sight, recriminations over the Iraqi tangle kept bubbling up. In April 2006, half a dozen retired generals broke the military code of silence and called for Secretary Rumsfeld's resignation. "The commitment of our forces in this fight," charged Marine Lieutenant General Gregory Newbold in one widely quoted article, "was done with a casualness and swagger that are the special province of those who have never had to execute these missions — or bury the results." By the time General Newbold penned those searing words, 2,300 troops had died in Iraq, $300 billion had been spent, and public opinion had shifted decisively: 57 percent of Americans thought the war a mistake.

The political toll on Bush was enormous. His approval rating sank below 40 percent, and his committed base — those "strongly" approving — shrank calamitously to 20 percent. In effect, Bush had exhausted his windfall from the War on Terror; he would henceforth be governing from a position of political weakness.

Bush's vulnerability was revealed most graphically when he approved a contract for a Dubai-owned company to operate American seaports. So vociferous was the congressional opposition that the president backed down and scrapped the deal. Increasingly, he came under attack from his own base: from Christian conservatives who felt betrayed by Bush's post-election silence on the gay-marriage amendment, and from right wingers who, when serious debate began in mid-2006, preferred a punitive solution to the problem of illegal immigrants. Bush's biggest asset, his can-do aura, was punctured by his administration's slow response to Hurricane Katrina, which devastated New Orleans in August 2005, and then by the confused start of the Medicare drug benefit that left many elderly bewildered and without medication.

Meanwhile, Tom DeLay's K Street Project imploded. The lobbying scandals that brought it down cast a shadow on DeLay. Already under indictment for his role in the Texas gerrymandering scheme, he resigned from the House. His crony, the ace lobbyist Jack Abramoff, fingered other senior Republicans before heading off to jail and, to top things off, a sex scandal hit Capitol Hill in October 2006. Republican Congressman Mark Foley, a champion of family values, turned out to be a closeted gay who had harassed teenage Congressional pages. Foley immediately resigned, but damaging questions were raised about negligent oversight by the Republican leadership. As Democratic charges of a "culture of corruption" sank in, the approval ratings for the Republican-dominated Congress sank to record lows.

The bill came due in the midterm elections on November 7, 2006. The Democrats regained control of the House of Representatives and against all odds — they needed to take five out of six contested Republican seats — captured the Senate by a single seat. Gone was the heady talk sparked by the 2004 victory of a permanent Republican majority. Karl Rove's strategy, although it worked as intended, turned out not to be foolproof. The Republican base remained steadfast, comparable to 2004. The party's vaunted get-out-the-vote machinery did its job. And computer-aided redistricting gave Republican incumbents a big advantage. But the Democratic surge overwhelmed these defenses in key red states. Of the total votes cast in House races, Democrats won 55 percent, far exceeding Bush's winning margin in 2004. It was a dramatic shift in the independent vote — something like 25 percent of independents who had gone for Bush in 2004 voted Democratic in 2006 — that did the trick. Moreover, Republicans lost control of six governorships and ten state legislatures, putting at risk their gerrymandered advantage in those states.

Only time will tell whether 2006 was a critical election, presaging a new political realignment, or just a temporary setback for the Republicans. Whatever the long-term consequences, the immediate impact on the political environment was evident, even before the returns were in. The Democrats, spooked by Iraq in 2004, had pressed the issue aggressively, and effectively made the midterm elections a referendum on the Iraq war. Finally acknowledging its unpopularity, President Bush began to give ground. He officially retired the phrase, "stay the course," lowered his sights from a democratic to a stable Iraq, and indicated that he was open to suggestions. The day after the election, Secretary of Defense Rumsfeld resigned. Bush was bowing to a new reality: The opposition party controlled Congress.

In the American political system, however, it is the president, not Congress, who bestrides the

Hurricane Katrina

When Hurricane Katrina bore down on New Orleans on August 29, 2005, officials thought at first that the city had avoided the brunt of the storm, but the impact was great enough to breach the surrounding earthen dams and flood New Orleans, hitting hardest the lower-lying neighborhoods where poor blacks lived. Two days later, the people on the roof of this apartment house were still stranded and desperately awaiting rescue. Images like this one of suffering ghetto-dwellers brought home a truth that many Americans had forgotten — that a black underclass still exists in this country. © Smiley N. Pool / Dallas Morning News / Corbis.

country. Presidents like Franklin D. Roosevelt and Ronald Reagan make a huge difference, indelibly marking and perhaps even redefining the country. But even the least of incumbents, because of the power of the office, leave the historian with a lot to think about, including, most notably, what has been left unresolved. Six years into his presidency, that seems likely to be a big part of George W. Bush's legacy — lots of unfinished business.

What Kind of America?

Terri Schiavo's tragedy could have happened in any family. She was a young woman who had fallen into a deep coma after a heart seizure. When her husband asked that her feeding tube be removed, her devoutly Catholic parents filed a lawsuit to stop him. On appeal, the Florida courts eventually ruled in the husband's favor. That normally would have concluded this family tragedy. Instead, conservative Republicans intervened, transforming Schiavo's plight into a right-to-life crusade. Senate Majority Leader Bill Frist, a surgeon in private life, opined after viewing a videotape that Schiavo was alert. With much fanfare, Congress enacted emergency legislation on March 21, 2005, transferring the case to the Federal Courts, but to no avail. The Supreme Court turned down a final appeal, and Schiavo was allowed to die. An autopsy confirmed that she had indeed been in an irreversible vegetative state.

Faith against Science. What was essentially symbolic in the Schiavo case became hugely consequential in the controversy over stem-cell research. Medical researchers perceived in stem cells, the embryonic cells that develop into a baby's specialized body-building cells, the potential for regenerating damaged organs, offering hope for victims of heart attacks, spine injuries, and a host of degenerative diseases. The research requires a supply of stem

COMPARING AMERICAN VOICES

The Stem-Cell Research Controversy

When George W. Bush took office in 2001, the country was bitterly divided over whether or not the federal government should fund stem-cell research using frozen embryos. The following selections illuminate that debate and trace its course over the next five years.

GEORGE W. BUSH
"Human life is a sacred gift from our creator"

Himself a born-again Christian and politically aligned with the pro-life voter, President Bush sought a policy that would satisfy both opponents and advocates of stem-cell research. In a television address in August 2001, he presented the following rationale for his position.

My administration must decide whether to allow federal funds, your tax dollars, to be used for scientific research on stem cells derived from human embryos. A large number of these embryos already exist. They are the product of a process called in-vitro fertilization, which helps so many couples conceive children. When doctors match sperm and egg to create life outside the womb, they usually produce more embryos than are implanted in the mother. Once a couple successfully has children or if they are unsuccessful, the additional embryos remain frozen in laboratories. . . . A number have been donated to science and used to create privately funded stem-cell lines.

Based on preliminary work that has been privately funded, scientists believe further research using stem cells offers great promise that could help improve the lives of those who suffer from many terrible diseases, from juvenile diabetes to Alzheimer's, from Parkinson's to spinal cord injuries. . . .

Scientists further believe that rapid progress in this research will come only with federal funds. Federal dollars help attract the best and brightest scientists. They ensure new discoveries are widely shared at the largest number of research facilities. . . .

[But] research on embryonic stem cells raises profound ethical questions, because extracting the stem cell destroys the embryo, and thus destroys its potential for life.

As I thought through this issue I kept returning to two fundamental questions. First, are these frozen embryos human life and therefore something precious to be protected? And second, if they're going to be destroyed anyway, shouldn't they be used for a greater good, for research that has the potential to save and improve other lives? . . .

I've asked those questions and others of scientists, scholars, bioethicists, religious leaders, doctors, researchers, members of Congress, my Cabinet and my friends . . . and I have found widespread disagreement. I . . . believe human life is a sacred gift from our creator. I worry about a culture that devalues life, and believe as your president I have an important obligation to foster and encourage respect for life in America and throughout the world. . . .

As a result of private research, more than 60 genetically diverse stem cell lines already exist. They were created from embryos that have already been destroyed, and they have the ability to regenerate themselves indefinitely, creating ongoing opportunities for research.

I have concluded that we should allow federal funds to be used for research on these existing stem cell lines, where the life-and-death decision has already been made. . . .

This allows us to explore the promise and potential of stem-cell research without crossing a fundamental moral line by providing taxpayer funding that would sanction or encourage further destruction of human embryos that have at least the potential for life.

SOURCE: The White House, Office of the Press Secretary, "President Discusses Stem Cell Research," August 9, 2001, press release, www.whitehouse.gov/news/releases/2001/08/20010809-2.html.

CANDI CUSHMAN
"Uncommon Moms"

By 2004, public sentiment seemed to be tilting toward embryonic stem-cell research, with polls showing 60 percent of Americans in favor. In Congress, even some pro-life Republicans began to advocate overturning the restrictions President Bush had placed on federal funding. In this article, we see one element of the counterattack, described in the magazine of Focus on the Family, the leading conservative organization supporting the president's position.

Most credible scientists will admit that an embryo is a human being, with all of the DNA and chromosomes that a human being will ever need from birth to death. . . .

It might be easy for pro-life citizens who don't want their tax dollars supporting the destruction of human life to feel discouraged as this debate unfolds. Because it may seem difficult for embryos that look like microscopic masses to compete with emotionally compelling people pleading for cures.

They can take heart, however, because pro-life moms are walking the halls of Congress. And they're cutting through all that emotional hype by showing politicians the faces of the embryos they're proposing to kill.

One of those faces belongs to Mikayla Tesdall, a bouncy 3-year-old girl with blond pigtails who loves to sing worship songs to whoever will listen.

Mikayla is a Snowflake — the name given to six dozen adopted babies who began life as frozen embryos. Not too long ago, these crawling, talking toddlers were stored in the freezers of in-vitro fertilization clinics across the country. They were labeled by many politicians as mere "excess," worthy of destruction, until the Nightlight Christian Adoptions agency in California devised a way to rescue them by allowing infertile married couples to adopt them. Thus began an amazing process, in which Mikayla's adoptive mother, Sharon, had the little girl implanted in her womb as an embryo. . . .

And that personal experience has transformed Tesdall and other formerly apolitical moms into passionate pro-life warriors. They've been surprisingly effective, gaining access to places even some of the slickest lobbyists can't get into, like the White House. . . . They had a singular mission in mind: presenting Democrats and Republicans alike with undeniable proof that a human being is sacred and worth protecting at any stage — whether an embryo or a fully developed baby. . . .

And that's how, on the muggy morning of Sept. 22 [2004], Tesdall and Mikayla found themselves behind a podium in a U.S. House press room.

"I am two," Mikayla boldly announced to a roomful of reporters and legislators before her mother had a chance to speak. It was an unplanned moment, but no matter. The audience got the point: Mikayla is fully human and already full of self-will. As the little girl played at the foot of the podium with a princess tiara and plastic dolls, Tesdall told the room:

"No one questions that she is fully human today, so how can anyone disagree that she was fully human in her embryonic stage of development? After all, what did any of us adoptive moms, who have given birth to Snowflake babies, add to them? We added nothing — except love, nutrients, and a warm place to grow."

SOURCE: Candi Cushman, "Uncommon Moms," *Citizen Magazine*. Copyright © 2004 Focus on the Family, www.family.org/cforum/citizenmag/features/a0035021.cfm.

MICHAEL CHOROST
"The Promised Land"

Born in 1964, Michael Chorost was always hard of hearing; by his thirties, he was completely deaf. A writer and author, Chorost had a computer installed in his brain in 2001, which allowed him to hear again. In a blog posted on the Scientist *in February 2006, he suggests why millions of people with degenerative diseases support this research.*

I'm an obvious beneficiary of medical technology. Without the computer surgically embedded in my skull, I'd be totally deaf. The device, called a "cochlear implant," routes past my damaged inner ear by triggering my auditory nerves with sixteen tiny electrodes coiled up inside my cochlea.

It's not a cure, though, any more than glasses cure vision loss. It's a prosthesis, a workaround. Compared to the extraordinary delicacy and precision of naturally evolved organs, it's clumsy. . . .

But someday scientists may learn to coax the body into repairing its own damaged parts instead of creating technological fixes that require a constant supply of batteries. That's what makes stem-cell research so exciting. Forget prostheses. How about a cure? . . .

What makes stem cells exciting is that they are pluripotent: With the appropriate chemical triggers and physical nudges and pushes, they'll turn into any kind of cell there is. Several panelists noted that with the help of stem cells, the body is constantly remaking itself — skin, intestines, red blood cells. In many cases, the body degenerates and ages not because it has lost the ability to create stem cells, but because it has lost the ability to trigger the stem cells it has. Find those triggers, learn how to activate them, *et voila* [and there you have it].

SOURCE: Michael Chorost, "Risky Enough Business?" *The Scientist*, February 8, 2006, blog posting, www.thescientist.com/blog/display/23094.

ANALYZING THE EVIDENCE

▶ How would you characterize President Bush's stand on embryonic stem-cell research?

▶ Why is the two-year-old Mikayla Tesdall an important person for the opponents of embryonic stem-cell research? How about Michael Chorost? Is he the equivalent for the proponents?

▶ When many of his Republican allies in Congress changed their minds and voted in 2006 to lift the funding restrictions on stem-cell research, President Bush vetoed the measure. Can his veto — the very first of his administration — be explained by the documents you have read?

Cheney and Secretary of Defense Rumsfeld, both once Nixon appointees—believed had been lost after Watergate (see Chapter 29).

As time passed, concern over the rise of an imperial presidency became more palpable and bipartisan. The libertarian Cato Institute, a pillar of the conservative establishment, concluded, after surveying the record, that "far from defending the Constitution, President Bush has repeatedly sought to strip out the limits the document places on federal power." The question arose, as the ranking Democrat on intelligence in the House, Jane Harman, put it, whether violating the law for the sake of security "gives away the very values we are fighting for."

In the early summer of 2006, the answer to that question began to emerge. The defining issue involved the treatment of Al Qaeda and Taliban detainees at Guantanamo and other overseas sites. The administration had declared that, as "unlawful combatants," such detainees were not entitled to the rights either of prisoners of war or criminals under American law. Their treatment was strictly a matter of executive privilege and, indeed, in devising a policy, the administration acted irregularly, bypassing its own normal channels and delegating the task to a few lawyers operating out of the vice president's office. The abuses that crept in—of which Abu Ghraib was only the most notorious—blackened America's reputation abroad, while at home the detainee program became entangled in ever-mounting legal challenges.

On June 29, 2006, in the landmark *Hamdan v. Rumsfeld* decision, the Supreme Court struck down the military tribunals set up to try the Guantanamo detainees. The Court declared that international law on war prisoners applied to the detainees and that the tribunals fell far short of the Geneva Convention requirement that prisoners of war "receive all the judicial guarantees which are recognized as indispensable by all civilized peoples." Equally important, the Court ruled that such tribunals could not be established without congressional authorization. In declaring that President Bush did not have a "blank check," the Court went beyond the question of military tribunals. It potentially challenged the basic presumption underlying the administration's NSA eavesdropping program and other such secret antiterrorist activities. Faced with *Hamdan v. Rumsfeld*, the White House backed down, rescinding the executive order denying detainees Geneva Convention protections and entering hard bargaining with Congress about an appropriate judicial program for them.

In the short term, the president mostly prevailed. The legislation he signed on October 16, 2006 granted him the Congressional approval he needed, with only limited procedural protections for defendants before military tribunals and a good deal of flexibility left in interrogating suspects. But there were certain to be further court challenges—especially over the denial of habeas corpus rights to foreign detainees—and the constitutional issues remained far from resolved.

Attorney General Gonzales was correct when he argued that other wartime presidents had also invoked the plenary powers that George Bush claimed after 9/11. It had usually taken the return of peace, but eventually all those prior wartime excesses had been followed by bitter regrets. The United States is still wiping out the stain of Japanese American internment in World War II (see Chapter 25). But, of course, the War on Terror was different from other wars. It had, as the president was fond of saying, no discernable end. So the country cannot wait for peace to restore constitutional protections. How Americans strike the balance between security and individual rights remains an open question in an unending War on Terror.

What Kind of World?

It has been said that no military strategy survives the first battle of war. The same might be said of diplomacy, certainly of President Bush's diplomacy. At the outset he operated on the presumption of America's world primacy: The United States would call the tune; everyone else would dance to it. Iraq swiftly exposed one fallacy. As an instrument of foreign policy, America's military power proved sorely wanting; it was a better diplomatic weapon held in reserve than unleashed. More fundamental, however, the administration overestimated its post–Cold War supremacy. Being the sole superpower, it turned out, was no picnic. Other nations did not submit gladly, and had they been so inclined, Bush's early unilateralism—his actions on global warming, arms reductions treaties, and Iraq—finished off that possibility. By the time he realized his mistake, in mid-2003, the harm had been done. Thereafter, the administration scrambled to rebuild coalitions, enlist the UN, and manage diplomatically problems once thought resolvable by force or bluster. In the realm of foreign affairs, the nation's unfinished business had mainly to do with a chastened superpower struggling to catch up with events that had spun out of its control.

A Multi-Polar World. Beyond anyone's expectations, the end of the Cold War altered the world's diplomatic landscape. The European Union (EU) expanded to the east, integrating the nations of central Europe into its ranks. The Communist government of China turned toward capitalism, seized the opportunities of globalization, and challenged Japan for the leadership of East Asia. Oil-rich Muslim nations, stretching across the Middle East to Kazakhstan and south to Indonesia, grew increasingly conscious of their wealth, religious identity, and potential geopolitical power. The old categories of the Cold War — Free World, Communist World, Third World — broke down and, despite America's military supremacy, a new multi-polar system was emerging.

The European Union now embraced twenty-five countries and 450 million people, with the third largest population in the world, behind China and India (see Map 31.1, p. 965). Because it included some of the world's most advanced economies, the EU accounted for a fifth of all global imports and exports. Its money — the euro — emerged as one of the world's preferred currencies for international exchange. Thanks to the euro, the American dollar was no longer supreme. The EU, however, was far from becoming a European version of the United States. Internal tensions ran deep — that became clear in the splintered response to Iraq — and resistance to a supranational EU authority in Brussels was, if anything, intensifying. The EU, moreover, preferred generous social programs to armies, and was militarily no challenge to the United States. Even so, the old commonality of interest was gone, and, on a variety of issues, Europe was as much a rival as an ally of the United States.

In China's case, the tilt was emphatically toward rivalry. A vast nation of 1.3 billion people, China became the fastest growing economy in the world. The Bush administration welcomed China's embrace of capitalism, and American consumers were beneficiaries of its cheap exports. But the economic tensions were many — over the enormous trade imbalance ($170 billion in 2004), over millions of American jobs lost, over an undervalued renminbi (the Chinese currency) that made Chinese goods artificially cheap, over rampant pirating of American intellectual property. China remained a one-party state, and that produced tension over human rights. And as China flexed its muscles, it threatened America's interests in East Asia and worldwide became an increasingly formidable rival.

As China's economy grew, so did its appetite for oil, and so, consequently, did an oil shortage that pushed up world oil prices. While American consumers grumbled about paying $3.50 a gallon for gasoline, policymakers worried about the empowering of oil-producing countries. This was most evident in the case of Russia, which, after reeling economically in the 1990s, revived on a surge of oil revenues. George Bush said he had looked into President Vladimir Putin's heart and found he was a good guy. That was when Russia was down. Putin turned out not to be such a good guy when Russia got back on its feet. He took authoritarian control at home, threatened neighboring former Soviet republics, and, in various ways, stood up to the United States. He was, with some success, reasserting Russia's place in the world. In a lesser way, oil money emboldened Iran and even a bloc of South American countries led by rabidly anti-Yankee Hugo Chavez of Venezuela. For the United States, higher oil prices meant less global leverage.

Nuclear Proliferation. Where its weakened leverage counted most was in America's uphill struggle to contain the spread of atomic weapons. During the Cold War, only the Big Five — the United States, Britain, France, the Soviet Union, and China — plus Israel possessed nuclear arms. Most nations adhered to the Nuclear Non-Proliferation Treaty of 1968, which was policed by the International Atomic Energy Agency (IAEA).

Two of the nonsignatories, India and Pakistan, spurred by their bitter rivalry over Kashmir, secretly developed nuclear weapons during the 1990s. The Pakistani nuclear scientist Dr. A. Q. Khan, undoubtedly with the knowledge of high government officials, sold two other Muslim states, Libya and Iran, nuclear designs and equipment. The Pakistanis also traded the technology to Communist North Korea in exchange for missiles that could be used against India.

North Korea, a desperately poor, Stalinist country, bet the house on nuclear-weapons development, which it used variously as blackmail to extract aid and as insurance against real and imagined enemies. In 1994, the Clinton administration struck a deal, offering food, oil, and an advanced nuclear-power plant for an end to North Korea's atomic weapons program. In the late 1990s, the agreement broke down, amid bitter recriminations and well-founded charges of North Korean cheating. The Bush administration wanted to crack down, but, having failed to bring along China, Russia, and South Korea, it had to settle for ultimately fruitless negotiations. Evidently seeing the U.S. invasion of Iraq as an object lesson, North Korea rushed ahead with its nuclear program and early in 2005 announced that it possessed atomic bombs. In October 2006, it carried out an underground test of a nuclear device.

Iran played a more devious game. A signatory of the Non-Proliferation Treaty, Iran took the position that, while it did not want nuclear weapons, it intended to exercise its rights under the treaty to develop the technology for peaceful nuclear energy. Learning how to enrich plant-grade uranium, however, opens the path to producing weapons-grade

North Korea

Troops parade in Pyongyang, North Korea, in celebration of the seventieth anniversary of the founding of the Korean People's Army. One would have imagined that a country capable of fielding so splendid a military display would have been bursting with resources and wealth, but in fact North Korea was the most threadbare country in all of Asia, incapable of feeding its own people and held together by an extraordinarily dictatorial regime. No country was more nettlesome for the Bush administration as the United States struggled to keep nuclear proliferation in check. KOREAN NEWS SERVICE / AFP / Getty Images.

uranium. In 2002, dissidents alerted the IAEA to secret nuclear sites and, while Iranians adamantly denied it, everyone else concluded that they were bent on building atomic bombs. As with North Korea, the Bush administration took a tough line, including, until it became entangled in Iraq, a credible military threat. Since then, while refusing to take that threat "off the table," the United States has been reduced to playing a diplomatic game, which it appears to be losing because, as with North Korea, it cannot count on the support of other key nations. Its efforts at the UN Security Council have been frustrated by Russia and China, both with economic stakes in Iran. Meanwhile, Iranian elections unexpectedly produced a hard-line Islamic president, Mahmoud Ahmadinejad, who regularly threatened Israel's destruction. In April 2006, Ahmadinejad triumphantly announced that Iran had mastered the enrichment process for plant-grade uranium.

In a multi-polar world, the United States seemed impotent against the spread of nuclear weapons, even to an apocalyptic country like Iran.

Militant Islam. In Iran's case, at least, there was a state to hold responsible. Utterly beyond America's experience was the amorphous Islamic extremism that had no address. After 9/11, the global manhunt largely dismantled the Al Qaeda network. Thereafter, Osama bin Laden served far more as a symbolic than as an operational figure. But as a symbolic figure, he inspired the Muslim world. In its terrorist incarnation, Al Qaeda metastasized into amorphous cells, unknown in number, operating more or less independently but with equally murderous intent. Al Qaeda–inspired suicide bombings have taken a heavy toll in Madrid, London, Bali, and, increasingly, in Muslim countries. This violence was only the cutting edge of anti-Western rage that permeated the Muslim world, a fact brought shockingly home to Europeans in early 2006 in widespread rioting against mocking cartoons of the prophet Muhammad printed in a Danish newspaper.

In the past the United States had regarded Islamic extremism as an internal problem of its Middle Eastern allies. Earlier American administrations supported authoritarian regimes like that of the Shah in Iran (see Chapters 26 and 29) and generally turned a blind eye to their brutal repression of Islamic dissidents. In his second inaugural address, President Bush signaled a major policy shift. The United States, he proclaimed, was committed to ending tyranny around the world. In so doing, Bush was evoking the Wilsonian strain in American foreign policy — the conviction that the country's democratic principles should govern its dealings with the rest of the world — but with a harder edge than President Wilson had ever imagined when he had called for a League of Nations after World War I (see Chapter 22).

Convinced that democracy was the answer to Islamic radicalism, Bush pressed for political reform in the Middle East. But when, as a result, Egypt's regime eased up in the 2005 elections, the militant Muslim Brotherhood gained strength, prompting another government crackdown. More shocking, early in 2006 Palestinians voted into power the hard-line Hamas, which the United States regarded as a terrorist organization. Hamas took office, but refused to disband its fighters or integrate them into the regular Palestinian military. In Lebanon, Hezbollah pursued a similar double-breasted strategy, participating in elections and

Chaos in Iraq

No figure was more adept at inciting chaos in Iraq than the young radical Shi'ite cleric Moqtada al-Sadr, who had a huge following among the Shi'ite poor, especially in the Baghdad slums. Here, he is pictured in the poster held aloft by a supporter celebrating the burning of a U.S. Army truck after an American action in the Shula neighborhood of Baghdad. Initially, al-Sadr aimed his ire at the invading Americans, but with the intensification of sectarian strife, he turned his death squads loose on the Sunnis, while also becoming in 2006 a powerful behind-the-scenes player in the new Iraqi government. Al-Sadr was emblematic of the subterranean complexities of Iraqi society that flummoxed the Bush administration when it undertook to bring democracy to Iraq.
© Ceerwan Aziz / Reuters / Corbis.

MAP 32.3 Ethnoreligious Groups in Iraq, 2006

Like other Middle Eastern countries, Iraq did not have a homogenous population. It was divided along religious lines between Sunni and Shi'ite Muslims (plus some Christians and, until they fled to Israel after 1948, many Jews) and ethnically among Arabs, Kurds, and Turkomen. When Iraq had been created under a League of Nations mandate after World War I, the British, who were in charge, installed the minority Sunni as the dominant political element, an arrangement that persisted until the United States toppled Saddam Hussein in 2003. The bitter internal strife that ensued stems from long-standing enthnoreligious divisions in Iraq and, among the possible outcomes, one is a de facto division of the country into autonomous Shiite, Sunni, and Kurdish regions.

joining the central government, but maintaining armed control of its own region. Hezbollah did not consult with the Beirut government in July 2006 before abducting two Israeli soldiers and precipitating a savage Israeli response that devastated much of Lebanon. Participating in elections, it seemed, was no antidote to Islamic extremism.

In Egypt, Palestine, and Lebanon, of course, the administration was just an anxious bystander. Iraq, however, was Bush's democratic project. Under American prodding, Iraqis held two national elections, wrote a constitution, established a parliament, and, in May 2006, after much wrangling, installed a prime minister. Beneath the formalities, however, Iraqi politics ran strictly along ethnic and sectarian lines. The dominant Shiite parties answered to their respective mullahs and, as with Hamas and Hezbollah, maintained their private militias, even while participating in the new government. Incessant insurgent attacks, capped by the bombing of a revered Samarra mosque in February 2006, finally pushed the Shiites over the edge. Their militias began in earnest to retaliate against Sunnis, utilizing death squads hardly distinguishable from the official police. As the carnage spread, a de facto partitioning began, with mass migrations from mixed Sunni-Shiite areas, and civil war became a real possibility (Map 32.3). That was the grim U.S. official finding three years after the Iraq invasion.

It remained unclear whether the warring sides would step back from the abyss of civil war. Or whether, if they did, the government would take hold. Or whether, if it did, the U.S-created Iraqi army could defeat the insurgency. Even if all these good things happened, if against the odds Iraq held together, in global terms America would still have failed because, in Islamic eyes, the Iraqi involvement had fatally tainted Western-style democracy. It had undercut Bush's global strategy for turning the tide against Islamic militancy, harmed America's leadership role in the world, and complicated its battle against nuclear proliferation. And if, as seemed evermore likely, Iraq went badly, the entire Middle East could go up in flames. The awful realization began to dawn that, beyond the cost in blood and treasure, Iraq had exacted a heavy toll on America's strategic interests in the world.

In an unguarded moment, President Bush remarked that Iraq would be a problem for the next administration. His admission is an apt epitaph for the Iraq involvement. Six months, and out. That was what the Pentagon hawks had expected. They never imagined that this sideshow—a quick victory on the way to bigger and better things—would bog down the Bush administration and become its defining, main event. They had misread the nature of global politics: Problems that force was meant to solve could turn around and bite you back.

TIMELINE

2000 — George W. Bush wins contested presidential election

2001
- September 11, Al Queda terrorists attack the World Trade Center and the Pentagon
- Military operations against the Taliban in Afghanistan begin
- Enron declares bankruptcy
- Congress passes the USA PATRIOT Act

2002
- No Child Left Behind Act becomes law
- The United States defeats the Taliban in Afghanistan
- President Bush declares Iran, North Korea, and Iraq "an axis of evil"

2003
- The United States invades Iraq in March; Iraqi regime quickly collapses
- The Bush administration promotes an "ownership society"

2004
- Torture at the Abu Ghraib prison becomes public
- President Bush wins reelection

2005
- Hurricane Katrina devastates the Gulf Coast
- John G. Roberts, Jr. is sworn in as Chief Justice of the United States
- The *New York Times* publishes reports about a domestic NSA eavesdropping program

2006
- Samuel A. Alito is sworn in as an Associate Justice of the United States Supreme Court
- Congress reauthorizes the USA PATRIOT Act
- President Bush vetoes a stem-cell research bill passed by Congress
- North Korea tests a nuclear device
- Democratic Party regains control of Congress
- Continued sectarian violence in Iraq

FOR FURTHER EXPLORATION

A good starting point for learning about President Bush's background is Bill Minutaglia, *First Son: George W. Bush and the Bush Family Dynasty* (1999). Cass R. Sunstein and Richard A. Epstein, eds., *The Vote: Bush, Gore, and the Supreme Court* (2001), is an assessment by a range of legal scholars of the Supreme Court's decision resolving the disputed presidential election of 2000. Two sympathetic accounts of President Bush's style of leadership are David Frum, *The Right Man: The Surprise Presidency of George W. Bush* (2003), and Fred Barnes, *Rebel-in-Chief: Inside the Bold and Controversial Presidency of George W. Bush* (2006). Bush's domestic record is treated less kindly by Bruce Bartlett, *Impostor: How George W. Bush Bankrupted America and Betrayed the Reagan Administration* (2006); Douglas Brinkley, *The Great Deluge: Hurricane Katrina, New Orleans, and the Mississippi Gulf Coast* (2006); and Ron Suskind, *The Price of Loyalty: George W. Bush, the White House, and the Education of Paul O'Neill* (2004). O'Neill was Bush's first secretary of the Treasury.

On the administration's response to 9/11, see Richard A. Clarke, *Against All Enemies: Inside America's War on Terror* (2004); Seymour M. Hersh, *Chain of Command: The Road from 9/11 to Abu Ghraib* (2004); George Packer, *The Assassins' Gate: America in Iraq* (2004); and James Risen, *State of War: The Secret History of the CIA and Bush Administration* (2006). Especially informative about the prosecution of the war in Iraq is Michael R. Gordon and Bernard R. Trainor, *Cobra II: The Inside Story of the Invasion and Occupation of Iraq* (2006). Joseph Margulies, *Guantanamo and the Abuse of Presidential Power* (2006), is by a lawyer for one of the Guantanamo detainees. A scholarly treatment of critical constitutional issues facing the country is Bruce Ackerman, *Before the Next Attack: Preserving Civil Liberties in an Age of Terrorism* (2006).

The September 11 Digital Archive at **www.911digitalarchive.org** offers firsthand responses of Americans to the terrorist attack of September 11, 2001. The site includes oral histories, video and still images, and a valuable guide to Web sites on the topic.

On the Iraqi insurgency, **www.pbs.org/frontline/insurgency** contains interviews with U.S. military commanders and insurgency leaders, analysis by experts, and access to the *Frontline* documentary "Insurgency."

TEST YOUR KNOWLEDGE

To assess your command of the material in this chapter, see the Online Study Guide at **bedfordstmartins.com/henretta**.

For Web sites, images, and documents related to topics and places in this chapter, visit **bedfordstmartins.com/makehistory**.

The Declaration of Independence

**In Congress, July 4, 1776,
The Unanimous Declaration of the
Thirteen United States of America**

When in the Course of human events, it becomes necessary for one people to dissolve the political bands which have connected them with another, and to assume among the Powers of the earth, the separate and equal station to which the Laws of Nature and of Nature's God entitle them, a decent respect to the opinions of mankind requires that they should declare the causes which impel them to the separation.

We hold these truths to be self-evident, that all men are created equal, that they are endowed by their Creator with certain unalienable rights, that among these are Life, Liberty, and the pursuit of Happiness. That to secure these rights, Governments are instituted among Men, deriving their just powers from the consent of the governed. That whenever any Form of Government becomes destructive of these ends, it is the Right of the People to alter or to abolish it, and to institute new Government, laying its foundation on such principles and organizing its powers in such form, as to them shall seem most likely to effect their Safety and Happiness. Prudence, indeed, will dictate that Governments long established should not be changed for light and transient causes; and accordingly all experience hath shown, that mankind are more disposed to suffer, while evils are sufferable, than to right themselves by abolishing the forms to which they are accustomed. But when a long train of abuses and usurpations, pursuing invariably the same Object evinces a design to reduce them under absolute Despotism, it is their right, it is their duty, to throw off such Government, and to provide new Guards for their future security. — Such has been the patient sufferance of these Colonies; and such is now the necessity which constrains them to alter their former Systems of Government. The history of the present King of Great Britain is a history of repeated injuries and usurpations, all having in direct object the establishment of an absolute Tyranny over these States. To prove this, let Facts be submitted to a candid world.

He has refused his Assent to Laws, the most wholesome and necessary for the public good.

He has forbidden his Governors to pass Laws of immediate and pressing importance, unless suspended in their operation till his Assent should be obtained; and, when so suspended, he has utterly neglected to attend to them.

He has refused to pass other Laws for the accommodation of large districts of people, unless those people would relinquish the right of Representation in the Legislature, a right inestimable to them and formidable to tyrants only.

He has called together legislative bodies at places unusual, uncomfortable, and distant from the depository of their public Records, for the sole purpose of fatiguing them into compliance with his measures.

He has dissolved Representative Houses repeatedly, for opposing with manly firmness his invasions on the rights of the people.

He has refused for a long time, after such dissolutions, to cause others to be elected; whereby the Legislative powers, incapable of Annihilation, have returned to the People at large for their exercise; the State remaining in the mean time exposed to all the dangers of invasion from without and convulsions within.

He has endeavoured to prevent the population of these States; for that purpose obstructing the Laws of Naturalization of Foreigners; refusing to pass others to encourage their migrations hither, and raising the conditions of new Appropriations of Lands.

He has obstructed the Administration of Justice, by refusing his Assent to Laws for establishing Judiciary powers.

He has made Judges dependent on his Will alone, for the tenure of their offices, and the amount and payment of their salaries.

He has erected a multitude of New Offices, and sent hither swarms of Officers to harass our People, and eat out their substance.

He has kept among us, in times of peace, Standing Armies without the Consent of our legislature.

He has combined with others to subject us to a jurisdiction foreign to our constitution, and unacknowledged by our laws; giving his Assent to their Acts of pretended Legislation:

For quartering large bodies of armed troops among us:

For protecting them, by a mock Trial, from Punishment for any Murders which they should commit on the Inhabitants of these States:

For cutting off our Trade with all parts of the world:

For imposing taxes on us without our Consent:

For depriving us, in many cases, of the benefits of Trial by jury:

For transporting us beyond Seas to be tried for pretended offences:

For abolishing the free System of English Laws in a neighbouring Province, establishing therein an Arbitrary government, and enlarging its Boundaries so as to render it at once an example and fit instrument for introducing the same absolute rule into these Colonies:

For taking away our Charters, abolishing our most valuable Laws, and altering fundamentally the Forms of our Governments:

For suspending our own Legislatures, and declaring themselves invested with Power to legislate for us in all cases whatsoever.

He has abdicated Government here, by declaring us out of his Protection and waging War against us.

He has plundered our seas, ravaged our Coasts, burnt our towns, and destroyed the lives of our people.

He is at this time transporting large armies of foreign mercenaries to compleat the works of death, desolation, and tyranny, already begun with circumstances of Cruelty & perfidy scarcely paralleled in the most barbarous ages, and totally unworthy the Head of a civilized nation.

He has constrained our fellow Citizens taken Captive on the high Seas to bear Arms against their Country, to become the executioners of their friends and Brethren, or to fall themselves by their Hands.

He has excited domestic insurrections amongst us, and has endeavoured to bring on the inhabitants of our frontiers, the merciless Indian Savages, whose known rule of warfare, is an undistinguished destruction of all ages, sexes, and conditions.

In every stage of these Oppressions We have Petitioned for Redress in the most humble terms: Our repeated Petitions have been answered only by repeated injury. A Prince, whose character is thus marked by every act which may define a Tyrant, is unfit to be the ruler of a free people.

Nor have We been wanting in attention to our British brethren. We have warned them from time to time of attempts by their legislature to extend an unwarrantable jurisdiction over us. We have reminded them of the circumstances of our emigration and settlement here. We have appealed to their native justice and magnanimity, and we have conjured them by the ties of our common kindred to disavow these usurpations, which would inevitably interrupt our connections and correspondence. They too have been deaf to the voice of justice and of consanguinity. We must, therefore, acquiesce in the necessity, which denounces our Separation, and hold them, as we hold the rest of mankind, Enemies in War, in Peace Friends.

We, therefore, the Representatives of the United States of America, in General Congress, Assembled, appealing to the Supreme Judge of the world for the rectitude of our intentions, do, in the Name, and by Authority of the good People of these Colonies, solemnly publish and declare, That these United Colonies are, and of Right ought to be FREE AND INDEPENDENT STATES; that they are Absolved from all Allegiance to the British Crown, and that all political connection between them and the State of Great Britain, is and ought to be totally dissolved; and that as Free and Independent States, they have full Power to levy War, conclude Peace, contract Alliances, establish Commerce, and to do all other Acts and Things which Independent States may of right do. And for the support of this Declaration, with a firm reliance on the Protection of Divine Providence, we mutually pledge to each other our Lives, our Fortunes, and our sacred Honor.

John Hancock

Button Gwinnett	George Wythe	James Wilson	Josiah Bartlett
Lyman Hall	Richard Henry Lee	Geo. Ross	Wm. Whipple
Geo. Walton	Th. Jefferson	Caesar Rodney	Matthew Thornton
Wm. Hooper	Benja. Harrison	Geo. Read	Saml. Adams
Joseph Hewes	Thos. Nelson, Jr.	Thos. M'Kean	John Adams
John Penn	Francis Lightfoot Lee	Wm. Floyd	Robt. Treat Paine
Edward Rutledge	Carter Braxton	Phil. Livingston	Elbridge Gerry
Thos. Heyward, Junr.	Robt. Morris	Frans. Lewis	Step. Hopkins
Thomas Lynch, Junr.	Benjamin Rush	Lewis Morris	William Ellery
Arthur Middleton	Benja. Franklin	Richd. Stockton	Roger Sherman
Samuel Chase	John Morton	John Witherspoon	Sam'el Huntington
Wm. Paca	Geo. Clymer	Fras. Hopkinson	Wm. Williams
Thos. Stone	Jas. Smith	John Hart	Oliver Wolcott
Charles Carroll of Carrollton	Geo. Taylor	Abra. Clark	

The Articles of Confederation and Perpetual Union

Agreed to in Congress, November 15, 1777; Ratified March 1781

BETWEEN THE STATES OF NEW HAMPSHIRE, MASSACHUSETTS BAY, RHODE ISLAND AND PROVIDENCE PLANTATIONS, CONNECTICUT, NEW YORK, NEW JERSEY, PENNSYLVANIA, DELAWARE, MARYLAND, VIRGINIA, NORTH CAROLINA, SOUTH CAROLINA, GEORGIA.*

Article 1

The stile of this confederacy shall be "The United States of America."

Article 2

Each State retains its sovereignty, freedom and independence, and every power, jurisdiction, and right, which is not by this confederation expressly delegated to the United States, in Congress assembled.

Article 3

The said states hereby severally enter into a firm league of friendship with each other for their common defence, the security of their liberties and their mutual and general welfare; binding themselves to assist each other against all force offered to, or attacks made upon them, or any of them, on account of religion, sovereignty, trade, or any other pretence whatever.

Article 4

The better to secure and perpetuate mutual friendship and intercourse among the people of the different states in this union, the free inhabitants of each of these states, paupers, vagabonds, and fugitives from justice excepted, shall be entitled to all privileges and immunities of free citizens in the several states; and the people of each State shall have free ingress and regress to and from any other State, and shall enjoy therein all the privileges of trade and commerce, subject to the same duties, impositions, and restrictions, as the inhabitants thereof respectively; provided, that such restrictions shall not extend so far as to prevent the removal of property, imported into any State, to any other State of which the owner is an inhabitant; provided also, that no imposition, duties, or restriction, shall be laid by any State on the property of the United States, or either of them.

If any person guilty of, or charged with treason, felony, or other high misdemeanor in any State, shall flee from justice and be found in any of the United States, he shall, upon demand of the governor or executive power of the State from which he fled, be delivered up and removed to the State having jurisdiction of his offence.

Full faith and credit shall be given in each of these states to the records, acts, and judicial proceedings of the courts and magistrates of every other State.

Article 5

For the more convenient management of the general interests of the United States, delegates shall be annually appointed, in such manner as the legislature of each State shall direct, to meet in Congress, on the 1st Monday in November in every year, with a power reserved to each State to recall its delegates, or any of them, at any time within the year, and to send others in their stead for the remainder of the year.

No State shall be represented in Congress by less than two, nor by more than seven members; and no person shall be capable of being a delegate for more than three years in any term of six years; nor shall any person, being a delegate, be capable of holding any office under the United States, for which he, or any other for his benefit, receives any salary, fees, or emolument of any kind.

Each State shall maintain its own delegates in a meeting of the states, and while they act as members of the committee of the states.

In determining questions in the United States, in Congress assembled, each State shall have one vote.

Freedom of speech and debate in Congress shall not be impeached or questioned in any court or place out of Congress: and the members of Congress shall be protected in their

---

*This copy of the final draft of the Articles of Confederation is taken from the *Journals*, 9:907-25, November 15, 1777.

persons from arrests and imprisonments, during the time of their going to and from, and attendance on Congress, except for treason, felony, or breach of the peace.

Article 6

No State, without the consent of the United States, in Congress assembled, shall send any embassy to, or receive any embassy from, or enter into any conference, agreement, alliance, or treaty with any king, prince, or state; nor shall any person, holding any office of profit or trust under the United States, or any of them, accept of any present, emolument, office or title, of any kind whatever, from any king, prince, or foreign state; nor shall the United States, in Congress assembled, or any of them, grant any title of nobility.

No two or more states shall enter into any treaty, confederation, or alliance, whatever, between them, without the consent of the United States, in Congress assembled, specifying accurately the purposes for which the same is to be entered into, and how long it shall continue.

No state shall lay any imposts or duties which may interfere with any stipulations in treaties entered into by the United States, in Congress assembled, with any king, prince, or state, in pursuance of any treaties already proposed by Congress to the courts of France and Spain.

No vessels of war shall be kept up in time of peace by any State, except such number only as shall be deemed necessary by the United States, in Congress assembled, for the defence of such State or its trade; nor shall any body of forces be kept up by any State, in time of peace, except such number only as, in the judgment of the United States, in Congress assembled, shall be deemed requisite to garrison the forts necessary for the defence of such State; but every State shall always keep up a well regulated and disciplined militia, sufficiently armed and accoutred, and shall provide, and constantly have ready for use, in public stores, a due number of field pieces and tents, and a proper quantity of arms, ammunition and camp equipage.

No State shall engage in any war without the consent of the United States, in Congress assembled, unless such State be actually invaded by enemies, or shall have received certain advice of a resolution being formed by some nation of Indians to invade such State, and the danger is so imminent as not to admit of a delay till the United States, in Congress assembled, can be consulted; nor shall any State grant commissions to any ships or vessels of war, nor letters of marque or reprisal, except it be after a declaration of war by the United States, in Congress assembled, and then only against the kingdom or state, and the subjects thereof, against which war has been so declared, and under such regulations as shall be established by the United States, in Congress assembled, unless such State be infested by pirates, in which case vessels of war may be fitted out for that occasion, and kept so long as the danger shall continue, or until the United States, in Congress assembled, shall determine otherwise.

Article 7

When land forces are raised by any State for the common defence, all officers of or under the rank of colonel, shall be appointed by the legislature of each State respectively, by whom such forces shall be raised, or in such manner as such State shall direct; and all vacancies shall be filled up by the State which first made the appointment.

Article 8

All charges of war and all other expences, that shall be incurred for the common defence or general welfare, and allowed by the United States, in Congress assembled, shall be defrayed out of a common treasury, which shall be supplied by the several states, in proportion to the value of all land within each State, granted to or surveyed for any person, as such land and the buildings and improvements thereon shall be estimated according to such mode as the United States, in Congress assembled, shall, from time to time, direct and appoint.

The taxes for paying that proportion shall be laid and levied by the authority and direction of the legislatures of the several states, within the time agreed upon by the United States, in Congress assembled.

Article 9

The United States, in Congress assembled, shall have the sole and exclusive right and power of determining on peace and war, except in the cases mentioned in the 6th article; of sending and receiving ambassadors; entering into treaties and alliances, provided that no treaty of commerce shall be made, whereby the legislative power of the respective states shall be restrained from imposing such imposts and duties on foreigners as their own people are subjected to, or from prohibiting the exportation or importation of any species of goods or commodities whatsoever; of establishing rules for deciding, in all cases, what captures on land or water shall be legal, and in what manner prizes, taken by land or naval forces in the service of the United States, shall be divided or appropriated; of granting letters of marque and reprisal in times of peace; appointing courts for the trial of piracies and felonies committed on the high seas, and establishing courts for receiving and determining, finally, appeals in all cases of captures; provided, that no member of Congress shall be appointed a judge of any of the said courts.

The United States, in Congress assembled, shall also be the last resort on appeal in all disputes and differences now subsisting, or that hereafter may arise between two or more states concerning boundary, jurisdiction or any other cause whatever; which authority shall always be exercised in the manner following: whenever the legislative or executive authority, or lawful agent of any State, in controversy with another, shall present a petition to Congress, stating the matter in question, and praying for a hearing, notice thereof shall be given, by order of Congress, to the legislative or executive authority of the other State in controversy, and a day assigned for the appearance of the parties by their lawful agents, who shall then be directed to appoint, by joint consent, commissioners or judges to constitute a court for hearing and determining the matter in question; but, if they cannot agree, Congress shall name three persons out of each of the United States, and from the list of such persons each party shall alternately strike out one, the petitioners beginning, until the number shall be reduced to thirteen; and from that number not less than seven, nor more than nine names, as Congress shall direct, shall, in the presence of Congress, be drawn out by lot; and the persons whose names shall be so drawn, or any five of them, shall be commissioners or judges to hear and finally determine the controversy, so always as a major part of the judges who shall hear the cause shall agree in the determination; and if either party shall neglect to attend at the day appointed, without shewing reasons which Congress shall judge sufficient, or, being present, shall refuse to strike, the Congress shall proceed to nominate three persons out of each State, and the secretary of Congress shall strike in behalf of such party absent or refusing; and the judgment and sentence of the court to be appointed, in the manner before prescribed, shall be final and conclusive; and if any of the parties shall refuse to submit to the authority of such court, or to appear or defend their claim or cause, the court shall nevertheless proceed to pronounce sentence or judgment, which shall, in like manner, be final and decisive, the judgment or sentence and other proceedings begin, in either case, transmitted to Congress, and lodged among the acts of Congress for the security of the parties concerned: provided, that every commissioner, before he sits in judgment, shall take an oath, to be administered by one of the judges of the supreme or superior court of the State where the cause shall be tried, "well and truly to hear and determine the matter in question, according to the best of his judgment, without favour, affection, or hope of reward:" provided, also, that no State shall be deprived of territory for the benefit of the United States.

All controversies concerning the private right of soil, claimed under different grants of two or more states, whose jurisdictions, as they may respect such lands and the states which passed such grants, are adjusted, the said grants, or either of them, being at the same time claimed to have originated antecedent to such settlement of jurisdiction, shall, on the petition of either party to the Congress of the United States, be finally determined, as near as may be, in the same manner as is before prescribed for deciding disputes respecting territorial jurisdiction between different states.

The United States, in Congress assembled, shall also have the sole and exclusive right and power of regulating the alloy and value of coin struck by their own authority, or by that of the respective states; fixing the standard of weights and measures throughout the United States; regulating the trade and managing all affairs with the Indians not members of any of the states; provided that the legislative right of any State within its own limits be not infringed or violated; establishing and regulating post offices from one State to another throughout all the United States, and exacting such postage on the papers passing through the same as may be requisite to defray the expences of the said office; appointing all officers of the land forces in the service of the United States, excepting regimental officers; appointing all the officers of the naval forces, and commissioning all officers whatever in the service of the United States; making rules for the government and regulation of the said land and naval forces, and directing their operations.

The United States, in Congress assembled, shall have authority to appoint a committee to sit in the recess of Congress, to be denominated "a Committee of the States," and to consist of one delegate from each State, and to appoint such other committees and civil officers as may be necessary for managing the general affairs of the United States, under their direction; to appoint one of their number to preside; provided that no person be allowed to serve in the office of president more than one year in any term of three years; to ascertain the necessary sums of money to be raised for the service of the United States, and to appropriate and apply the same for defraying the public expences; to borrow money or emit bills on the credit of the United States, transmitting, every half year, to the respective states, an account of the sums of money so borrowed or emitted; to build and equip a navy; to agree upon the number of land forces, and to make requisitions from each State for its quota, in proportion to the number of white inhabitants in such State; which requisitions shall be binding; and thereupon, the legislature of each State shall appoint the regimental officers, raise the men, and cloathe, arm, and equip them in a soldier-like manner, at the expence of the United States; and the officers and men so cloathed, armed, and equipped, shall march to the place appointed and within the time agreed on by the United States, in Congress assembled; but if the United States, in Congress assembled, shall, on consideration of circumstances, judge proper that any State should not raise men, or should raise a smaller number than its quota, and that any other State should raise a greater number of men than the quota thereof, such extra number shall be raised, officered, cloathed, armed, and equipped in the same manner as the quota of such State, unless the legislature of such State shall judge that such extra number cannot be safely spared out of the same, in which case they shall raise, officer, cloathe, arm, and equip as many of such extra number as they judge can be safely spared. And the officers and men so cloathed, armed, and equipped, shall march to the place appointed and within the time agreed on by the United States, in Congress assembled.

The United States, in Congress assembled, shall never engage in a war, nor grant letters of marque and reprisal in time of peace, nor enter into any treaties or alliances, nor coin money, nor regulate the value thereof, nor ascertain the sums and expences necessary for the defence and welfare of the United States, or any of them: nor emit bills, nor borrow money on the credit of the United States, nor appropriate money, nor agree upon the number of vessels of war to be built or purchased, or the number of land or sea forces to be raised, nor appoint a commander in chief of the army or navy, unless nine states assent to the same; nor shall a question on any other point, except for adjourning from day to day, be determined, unless by the votes of a majority of the United States, in Congress assembled.

The Congress of the United States shall have power to adjourn to any time within the year, and to any place within the United States, so that no period of adjournment be for a longer duration than the space of six months, and shall publish the journal of their proceedings monthly, except such parts thereof, relating to treaties, alliances or military operations, as, in their judgment, require secrecy; and the yeas and nays of the delegates of each State on any question shall be entered on the journal, when it is desired by any delegate; and the delegates of a State, or any of them, at his, or their request, shall be furnished with a transcript of the said journal, except such parts as are above excepted, to lay before the legislatures of the several states.

Article 10

The committee of the states, or any nine of them, shall be authorized to execute, in the recess of Congress, such of the powers of Congress as the United States, in Congress assembled, by the consent of nine states, shall, from time to time, think expedient to vest them with; provided, that no power be delegated to the said committee, for the exercise of which, by the articles of confederation, the voice of nine states, in the Congress of the United States assembled, is requisite.

Article 11

Canada acceding to this confederation, and joining in the measures of the United States, shall be admitted into and entitled to all the advantages of this union; but no other colony shall be admitted into the same, unless such admission be agreed to by nine states.

The Constitution of the United States of America

Agreed to by Philadelphia Convention, September 17, 1787
Implemented March 4, 1789

We the People of the United States, in Order to form a more perfect Union, establish Justice, insure domestic Tranquility, provide for the common defence, promote the general Welfare, and secure the Blessings of Liberty to ourselves and our Posterity, do ordain and establish this Constitution for the United States of America.

Article I

Section 1. All legislative Powers herein granted shall be vested in a Congress of the United States, which shall consist of a Senate and a House of Representatives.

Section 2. The House of Representatives shall be composed of Members chosen every second Year by the People of the several States, and the Electors in each State shall have the Qualifications requisite for Electors of the most numerous Branch of the State Legislature.

No Person shall be a Representative who shall not have attained to the Age of twenty-five Years, and been seven Years a Citizen of the United States, and who shall not, when elected, be an Inhabitant of that State in which he shall be chosen.

Representatives and direct Taxes shall be apportioned among the several States which may be included within this Union, according to their respective Numbers, *which shall be determined by adding to the whole Number of free Persons, including those bound to Service for a Term of Years, and excluding Indians not taxed, three fifths of all other Persons.** The actual Enumeration shall be made within three Years after the first Meeting of the Congress of the United States, and within every subsequent Term of ten Years, in such Manner as they shall by Law direct. The Number of Representatives shall not exceed one for every thirty Thousand, but each State shall have at Least one Representative; and *until such enumeration shall be made, the State of New Hampshire shall be entitled to chuse three, Massachusetts eight, Rhode Island and Providence Plantations one, Connecticut five, New York six, New Jersey four, Pennsylvania eight, Delaware one, Maryland six, Virginia ten, North Carolina five, South Carolina five, and Georgia three.*

When vacancies happen in the Representation from any State, the Executive Authority thereof shall issue Writs of Election to fill such Vacancies.

The House of Representatives shall chuse their Speaker and other Officers; and shall have the sole Power of Impeachment.

Section 3. The Senate of the United States shall be composed of two Senators from each State, *chosen by the Legislature thereof,*† for six Years; and each Senator shall have one Vote.

Immediately after they shall be assembled in Consequence of the first Election, they shall be divided as equally as may be into three Classes. The Seats of the Senators of the first Class shall be vacated at the Expiration of the second Year, of the second Class at the Expiration of the fourth Year, and of the third Class at the Expiration of the sixth Year, so that one-third may be chosen every second Year; and if Vacancies happen by Resignation, or otherwise, during the Recess of the Legislature of any State, the Executive thereof may make temporary Appointments until the next Meeting of the Legislature, which shall then fill such Vacancies.‡

No person shall be a Senator who shall not have attained to the Age of thirty Years, and been nine Years a Citizen of the United States, and who shall not, when elected, be an Inhabitant of that State for which he shall be chosen.

The Vice President of the United States shall be President of the Senate, but shall have no Vote, unless they be equally divided.

The Senate shall chuse their other Officers, and also a President pro tempore, in the absence of the Vice President, or when he shall exercise the Office of President of the United States.

The Senate shall have the sole Power to try all Impeachments. When sitting for that Purpose, they shall be on Oath or Affirmation. When the President of the United States is tried, the Chief Justice shall preside: And no Person shall be convicted without the Concurrence of two-thirds of the Members present.

Note: The Constitution became effective March 4, 1789. Provisions in italics are no longer relevant or have been changed by constitutional amendment.
*Changed by Section 2 of the Fourteenth Amendment.
†Changed by Section 1 of the Seventeenth Amendment.
‡Changed by Section 2 of the Seventeenth Amendment.

Judgment in Cases of Impeachment shall not extend further than to removal from Office, and disqualification to hold and enjoy any Office of honor, Trust or Profit under the United States: but the Party convicted shall nevertheless be liable and subject to Indictment, Trial, Judgment and Punishment, according to Law.

Section 4. The Times, Places and Manner of holding Elections for Senators and Representatives, shall be prescribed in each State by the Legislature thereof; but the Congress may at any time by Law make or alter such Regulations, except as to the Places of Chusing Senators.

The Congress shall assemble at least once in every Year, and such Meeting *shall be on the first Monday in December, unless they shall by Law appoint a different Day.**

Section 5. Each House shall be the Judge of the Elections, Returns and Qualifications of its own Members, and a Majority of each shall constitute a Quorum to do Business; but a smaller number may adjourn from day to day, and may be authorized to compel the Attendance of absent Members, in such Manner, and under such Penalties, as each House may provide.

Each House may determine the Rules of its Proceedings, punish its Members for disorderly Behavior, and, with the Concurrence of two-thirds, expel a Member.

Each House shall keep a Journal of its Proceedings, and from time to time publish the same, excepting such Parts as may in their Judgment require Secrecy; and the Yeas and Nays of the Members of either House on any question shall, at the Desire of one-fifth of those Present, be entered on the Journal.

Neither House, during the Session of Congress, shall, without the Consent of the other, adjourn for more than three days, nor to any other Place than that in which the two Houses shall be sitting.

Section 6. The Senators and Representatives shall receive a Compensation for their Services, to be ascertained by Law, and paid out of the Treasury of the United States. They shall in all Cases, except Treason, Felony and Breach of the Peace, be privileged from Arrest during their Attendance at the Session of their respective Houses, and in going to and returning from the same; and for any Speech or Debate in either House, they shall not be questioned in any other Place.

No Senator or Representative shall, during the Time for which he was elected, be appointed to any civil Office under the Authority of the United States, which shall have been created, or the Emoluments whereof shall have been increased, during such time; and no Person holding any Office under the United States, shall be a Member of either House during his Continuance in Office.

---

*Changed by Section 2 of the Twentieth Amendment.

Section 7. All Bills for raising Revenue shall originate in the House of Representatives; but the Senate may propose or concur with Amendments as on other Bills.

Every Bill which shall have passed the House of Representatives and the Senate, shall, before it becomes a Law, be presented to the President of the United States; If he approve he shall sign it, but if not he shall return it, with his Objections to that House in which it shall have originated, who shall enter the Objections at large on their Journal, and proceed to reconsider it. If after such Reconsideration two-thirds of that House shall agree to pass the Bill, it shall be sent, together with the Objections, to the other House, by which it shall likewise be reconsidered, and if approved by two-thirds of that House, it shall become a Law. But in all such Cases the Votes of both Houses shall be determined by Yeas and Nays, and the Names of the Persons voting for and against the Bill shall be entered on the Journal of each House respectively. If any Bill shall not be returned by the President within ten Days (Sundays excepted) after it shall have been presented to him, the Same shall be a Law, in like Manner as if he had signed it, unless the Congress by their Adjournment prevent its Return, in which Case it shall not be a Law.

Every Order, Resolution, or Vote to which the Concurrence of the Senate and the House of Representatives may be necessary (except on a question of Adjournment) shall be presented to the President of the United States; and before the Same shall take Effect, shall be approved by him, or being disapproved by him, shall be repassed by two-thirds of the Senate and House of Representatives, according to the Rules and Limitations prescribed in the Case of a Bill.

Section 8. The Congress shall have Power To lay and collect Taxes, Duties, Imposts and Excises, to pay the Debts and provide for the common Defence and general Welfare of the United States; but all Duties, Imposts and Excises shall be uniform throughout the United States;

To borrow money on the credit of the United States;

To regulate Commerce with foreign Nations, and among the several States, and with the Indian Tribes;

To establish an uniform Rule of Naturalization, and uniform Laws on the subject of Bankruptcies throughout the United States;

To coin Money, regulate the Value thereof, and of foreign Coin, and fix the Standard of Weights and Measures;

To provide for the Punishment of counterfeiting the Securities and current Coin of the United States;

To establish Post Offices and post Roads;

To promote the Progress of Science and useful Arts, by securing for limited Times to Authors and Inventors the exclusive Right to their respective Writings and Discoveries;

To constitute Tribunals inferior to the supreme Court;

To define and punish Piracies and Felonies committed on the high Seas, and Offenses against the Law of Nations;

To declare War, grant Letters of Marque and Reprisal, and make Rules concerning Captures on Land and Water;

To raise and support Armies, but no Appropriation of Money to that Use shall be for a longer Term than two Years;

To provide and maintain a Navy;

To make Rules for the Government and Regulation of the land and naval Forces;

To provide for calling forth the Militia to execute the Laws of the Union, suppress Insurrections and repel Invasions;

To provide for organizing, arming, and disciplining the Militia, and for governing such Part of them as may be employed in the Service of the United States, reserving to the States respectively, the Appointment of the Officers, and the Authority of training the Militia according to the discipline prescribed by Congress;

To exercise exclusive Legislation in all Cases whatsoever, over such District (not exceeding ten Miles square) as may, by Cession of particular States, and the acceptance of Congress, become the Seat of Government of the United States, and to exercise like Authority over all Places purchased by the Consent of the Legislature of the State in which the Same shall be, for the Erection of Forts, Magazines, Arsenals, dock-Yards, and other needful Buildings;—And

To make all Laws which shall be necessary and proper for carrying into Execution the foregoing Powers, and all other Powers vested by this Constitution in the Government of the United States, or in any Department or Officer thereof.

Section 9. The Migration or Importation of such Persons as any of the States now existing shall think proper to admit, shall not be prohibited by the Congress prior to the Year one thousand eight hundred and eight but a tax or duty may be imposed on such Importation, not exceeding ten dollars for each Person.

The privilege of the Writ of Habeas Corpus shall not be suspended, unless when in Cases of Rebellion or Invasion the public Safety may require it.

No Bill of Attainder or ex post facto Law shall be passed.

No capitation, or other direct, Tax shall be laid, unless in Proportion to the Census or Enumeration herein before directed to be taken.*

No Tax or Duty shall be laid on Articles exported from any State.

No Preference shall be given by any Regulation of Commerce or Revenue to the Ports of one State over those of another: nor shall Vessels bound to, or from, one State, be obliged to enter, clear, or pay Duties in another.

No Money shall be drawn from the Treasury, but in Consequence of Appropriations made by law; and a regular Statement and Account of the Receipts and Expenditures of all public Money shall be published from time to time.

No Title of Nobility shall be granted by the United States: And no Person holding any Office of Profit or Trust under them, shall, without the Consent of the Congress, accept of any present, Emolument, Office, or Title, of any kind whatever, from any King, Prince, or foreign State.

---

*Changed by the Sixteenth Amendment.

Section 10. No State shall enter into any Treaty, Alliance, or Confederation; grant Letters of Marque and Reprisal; coin Money; emit Bills of Credit; make any Thing but gold and silver Coin a Tender in Payment of Debts; pass any Bill of Attainder, ex post facto Law, or Law impairing the Obligation of Contracts, or grant any Title of Nobility.

No State shall, without the Consent of the Congress, lay any Imposts or Duties on Imports or Exports, except what may be absolutely necessary for executing its inspection Laws: and the net Produce of all Duties and Imposts, laid by any State on Imports or Exports, shall be for the Use of the Treasury of the United States; and all such Laws shall be subject to the Revision and Control of the Congress.

No State shall, without the Consent of the Congress, lay any duty of Tonnage, keep Troops, or Ships of War in time of Peace, enter into any Agreement or Compact with another State, or with a foreign Power, or engage in War, unless actually invaded, or in such imminent Danger as will not admit of delay.

Article II

Section 1. The executive Power shall be vested in a President of the United States of America. He shall hold his Office during the Term of four Years, and, together with the Vice President, chosen for the same Term, be elected, as follows:

Each State shall appoint, in such Manner as the Legislature thereof may direct, a Number of Electors, equal to the whole Number of Senators and Representatives to which the State may be entitled in the Congress; but no Senator or Representative, or Person holding an Office of Trust or Profit under the United States, shall be appointed an Elector.

The Electors shall meet in their respective States, and vote by Ballot for two Persons, of whom one at least shall not be an Inhabitant of the same State with themselves. And they shall make a List of all the Persons voted for, and of the Number of Votes for each; which List they shall sign and certify, and transmit sealed to the Seat of the Government of the United States, directed to the President of the Senate. The President of the Senate shall, in the Presence of the Senate and House of Representatives, open all the Certificates, and the Votes shall then be counted. The Person having the greatest Number of Votes shall be the President, if such Number be a Majority of the whole Number of Electors appointed; and if there be more than one who have such Majority, and have an equal Number of Votes, then the House of Representatives shall immediately chuse by Ballot one of them for President; and if no Person have a Majority, then from the five highest on the List the said House shall in like Manner chuse the President. But in chusing the President, the Votes shall be taken by States, the Representation from each State having one Vote; a quorum for this Purpose shall consist of a Member or Members from two thirds of the States, and a Majority of all the States shall be necessary to a Choice. In every Case, after the Choice of the President, the Person having the greatest Number of Votes of the

Electors shall be the Vice President. But if there should remain two or more who have equal Votes, the Senate shall chuse from them by Ballot the Vice President.*

The Congress may determine the Time of chusing the Electors, and the Day on which they shall give their Votes; which Day shall be the same throughout the United States.

No Person except a natural born Citizen, or a Citizen of the United States, at the time of the Adoption of this Constitution, shall be eligible to the Office of President; neither shall any Person be eligible to that Office who shall not have attained to the Age of thirty five Years, and been fourteen Years a Resident within the United States.

In Case of the Removal of the President from Office, or of his Death, Resignation, or Inability to discharge the Powers and Duties of the said Office, the same shall devolve on the Vice President, *and the Congress may by Law provide for the Case of Removal, Death, Resignation, or Inability, both of the President and Vice President, declaring what Officer shall then act as President, and such Officer shall act accordingly, until the Disability be removed, or a President shall be elected.*†

The President shall, at stated Times, receive for his Services a Compensation, which shall neither be increased nor diminished during the Period for which he shall have been elected, and he shall not receive within that Period any other Emolument from the United States, or any of them.

Before he enter on the Execution of his Office, he shall take the following Oath or Affirmation:—"I do solemnly swear (or affirm) that I will faithfully execute the Office of President of the United States, and will to the best of my Ability, preserve, protect and defend the Constitution of the United States."

Section 2. The President shall be Commander in Chief of the Army and Navy of the United States, and of the Militia of the several States, when called into the actual Service of the United States; he may require the Opinion, in writing, of the principal Officer in each of the executive Departments, upon any Subject relating to the Duties of their respective Offices, and he shall have Power to Grant Reprieves and Pardons for Offences against the United States, except in Cases of Impeachment.

He shall have Power, by and with the Advice and Consent of the Senate, to make Treaties, provided two thirds of the Senators present concur; and he shall nominate, and by and with the Advice and Consent of the Senate, shall appoint Ambassadors, other public Ministers and Consuls, Judges of the supreme Court, and all other Officers of the United States, whose Appointments are not herein otherwise provided for, and which shall be established by Law: but the Congress may by Law vest the Appointment of such inferior Officers, as they think proper, in the President alone, in the Courts of Law, or in the Heads of Departments.

The President shall have Power to fill up all Vacancies that may happen during the Recess of the Senate, by granting Commissions which shall expire at the End of their next Session.

Section 3. He shall from time to time give to the Congress Information of the State of the Union, and recommend to their Consideration such Measures as he shall judge necessary and expedient; he may, on extraordinary Occasions, convene both Houses, or either of them, and in Case of Disagreement between them, with Respect to the Time of Adjournment, he may adjourn them to such Time as he shall think proper; he shall receive Ambassadors and other public Ministers; he shall take Care that the Laws be faithfully executed, and shall Commission all the Officers of the United States.

Section 4. The President, Vice President and all civil Officers of the United States, shall be removed from Office on Impeachment for, and Conviction of, Treason, Bribery, or other high Crimes and Misdemeanors.

Article III

Section 1. The judicial Power of the United States, shall be vested in one supreme Court, and in such inferior Courts as the Congress may from time to time ordain and establish. The Judges, both of the supreme and inferior Courts, shall hold their Offices during good Behaviour, and shall, at stated Times, receive for their Services a Compensation, which shall not be diminished during their Continuance in Office.

Section 2. The judicial Power shall extend to all Cases, in Law and Equity, arising under this Constitution, the Laws of the United States, and Treaties made, or which shall be made, under their Authority;—to all Cases affecting Ambassadors, other public Ministers and Consuls;—to all Cases of admiralty and maritime Jurisdiction;—to Controversies to which the United States shall be a Party;—to Controversies between two or more States;—*between a State and Citizens of another State;*‡—between Citizens of different States;—between Citizens of the same State claiming Lands under Grants of different States, and between a State, or the Citizens thereof, and foreign States, Citizens or Subjects.

In all Cases affecting Ambassadors, other public Ministers and Consuls, and those in which a State shall be Party, the supreme Court shall have original Jurisdiction. In all the other Cases before mentioned, the supreme Court shall have appellate Jurisdiction, both as to Law and Fact, with such Exceptions, and under such Regulations as the Congress shall make.

---

*Superseded by the Twelfth Amendment.
†Modified by the Twenty-fifth Amendment.

‡Restricted by the Eleventh Amendment.

The trial of all Crimes, except in Cases of Impeachment, shall be by Jury; and such Trial shall be held in the State where said Crimes shall have been committed; but when not committed within any State, the Trial shall be at such Place or Places as the Congress may by Law have directed.

Section 3. Treason against the United States, shall consist only in levying War against them, or in adhering to their Enemies, giving them Aid and Comfort. No Person shall be convicted of Treason unless on the Testimony of two Witnesses to the same overt Act, or on Confession in open Court.

The Congress shall have Power to declare the Punishment of Treason, but no Attainder of Treason shall work Corruption of Blood, or Forefeiture except during the Life of the Person attainted.

Article IV

Section 1. Full Faith and Credit shall be given in each State to the public Acts, Records, and judicial Proceedings of every other State. And the Congress may by general Laws prescribe the Manner in which such Acts, Records, and Proceedings shall be proved, and the Effect thereof.

Section 2. The Citizens of each State shall be entitled to all Privileges and Immunities of Citizens in the several States.

A Person charged in any State with Treason, Felony, or other Crime, who shall flee from Justice, and be found in another State, shall on demand of the executive Authority of the State from which he fled, be delivered up, to be removed to the State having Jurisdiction of the Crime.

No Person held to Service or Labour in one State, under the Laws thereof, escaping into another, shall, in Consequence of any Law or Regulation therein, be discharged from such Service or Labour, but shall be delivered up on Claim of the Party to whom such Service or Labour may be due.*

Section 3. New States may be admitted by the Congress into this Union; but no new State shall be formed or erected within the Jurisdiction of any other State; nor any State be formed by the Junction of two or more States, or parts of States, without the Consent of the Legislatures of the States concerned as well as of the Congress.

The Congress shall have Power to dispose of and make all needful Rules and Regulations respecting the Territory or other Property belonging to the United States; and nothing in this Constitution shall be so construed as to Prejudice any Claims of the United States, or of any particular State.

Section 4. The United States shall guarantee to every State in this Union a Republican Form of Government, and shall protect each of them against Invasion; and on Application of the Legislature, or of the Executive (when the Legislature cannot be convened) against domestic Violence.

Article V

The Congress, whenever two-thirds of both Houses shall deem it necessary, shall propose Amendments to this Constitution, or, on the Application of the Legislatures of two-thirds of the several States, shall call a Convention for proposing Amendments, which, in either Case, shall be valid to all Intents and Purposes, as Part of this Constitution, when ratified by the Legislatures of three-fourths of the several States, or by Conventions in three-fourths thereof, as the one or the other Mode of Ratification may be proposed by the Congress; Provided that no Amendment which may be made prior to the Year One thousand eight hundred and eight shall in any Manner affect the first and fourth Clauses in the Ninth Section of the first Article; and that no State, without its Consent, shall be deprived of its equal Suffrage in the Senate.

Article VI

All Debts contracted and Engagements entered into, before the Adoption of this Constitution, shall be as valid against the United States under this Constitution, as under the Confederation.

This Constitution, and the Laws of the United States which shall be made in Pursuance thereof; and all Treaties made, or which shall be made, under the Authority of the United States, shall be the supreme Law of the Land; and the Judges in every State shall be bound thereby, any Thing in the Constitution or Laws of any State to the Contrary notwithstanding.

The Senators and Representatives before mentioned, and the Members of the several State Legislatures, and all executive and judicial Officers, both of the United States and of the several States, shall be bound by Oath or Affirmation, to support this Constitution; but no religious Test shall ever be required as a Qualification to any Office or public Trust under the United States.

Article VII

The Ratification of the Conventions of nine States shall be sufficient for the Establishment of this Constitution between the States so ratifying the Same.

Done in Convention by the Unanimous Consent of the States present the Seventeenth Day of September in the Year of our Lord one thousand seven hundred and Eighty seven and of the Independence of the United States of America the Twelfth. In Witness whereof We have hereunto subscribed our Names.

---

*Superseded by the Thirteenth Amendment.

Go. Washington
President and deputy from Virginia

New Hampshire
John Langdon
Nicholas Gilman

Massachusetts
Nathaniel Gorham
Rufus King

Connecticut
Wm. Saml. Johnson
Roger Sherman

New York
Alexander Hamilton

New Jersey
Wil. Livingston
David Brearley
Wm. Paterson
Jona. Dayton

Pennsylvania
B. Franklin
Thomas Mifflin
Robt. Morris
Geo. Clymer
Thos. FitzSimons
Jared Ingersoll
James Wilson
Gouv. Morris

Delaware
Geo. Read
Gunning Bedford jun
John Dickinson
Richard Bassett
Jaco. Broom

Maryland
James McHenry
Dan. of St. Thos. Jenifer
Danl. Carroll

Virginia
John Blair
James Madison, Jr.

North Carolina
Wm. Blount
Richd. Dobbs Spaight
Hu Williamson

South Carolina
J. Rutledge
Charles Cotesworth Pinckney
Pierce Butler

Georgia
William Few
Abr. Baldwin

Amendments to the Constitution with Annotations (Including the Six Unratified Amendments)

In their effort to gain Antifederalists' support for the Constitution, Federalists frequently pointed to the inclusion of Article 5, which provides an orderly method of amending the Constitution. In contrast, the Articles of Confederation, which were universally recognized as seriously flawed, offered no means of amendment. For their part, Antifederalists argued that the amendment process was so "intricate" that one might as easily roll "sixes an hundred times in succession" as change the Constitution.

The system for amendment laid out in the Constitution requires that two-thirds of both houses of Congress agree to a proposed amendment, which must then be ratified by three-quarters of the legislatures of the states. Alternatively, an amendment may be proposed by a convention called by the legislatures of two-thirds of the states. Since 1789, members of Congress have proposed thousands of amendments. Besides the seventeen amendments added since 1791, only the six "unratified" ones included here were approved by two-thirds of both houses but not ratified by the states.

Among the many amendments that never made it out of Congress have been proposals to declare dueling, divorce, and interracial marriage unconstitutional as well as proposals to establish a national university, to acknowledge the sovereignty of Jesus Christ, and to prohibit any person from possessing wealth in excess of $10 million.*

Among the issues facing Americans today that might lead to constitutional amendment are efforts to balance the federal budget, to limit the number of terms elected officials may serve, to limit access to or prohibit abortion, to establish English as the official language of the United States, and to prohibit flag burning. None of these proposed amendments has yet garnered enough support in Congress to be sent to the states for ratification.

Although the first ten amendments to the Constitution are commonly known as the Bill of Rights, only Amendments 1 through 8 provide guarantees of individual rights. Amendments 9 and 10 deal with the structure of power within the constitutional system. The Bill of Rights was promised to appease Antifederalists who refused to ratify the Constitution without guarantees of individual liberties and limitations to federal power. After studying more than two hundred amendments recommended by the ratifying conventions of the states, Federalist James Madison presented a list of seventeen to Congress, which used Madison's list as the foundation for the twelve amendments that were sent to the states for ratification. Ten of the twelve were adopted in 1791. The first on the list of twelve, known as the Reapportionment Amendment, was never adopted (p. D-16). The second proposed amendment was adopted in 1992 as Amendment 27 (p. D-24).

Amendment I [1791][†]

Congress shall make no law respecting an establishment of religion, or prohibiting the free exercise thereof; or abridging the freedom of speech, or of the press; or the right of the people peaceably to assemble, and to petition the Government for a redress of grievances.

• • •

The First Amendment is a potent symbol for many Americans. Most are well aware of their rights to free speech, freedom of the press, and freedom of religion and their rights to assemble and to petition, even if they cannot cite the exact words of this amendment.

The First Amendment guarantee of freedom of religion has two clauses: the "free exercise clause," which allows individuals to practice or not practice any religion, and the "establishment clause," which prevents the federal government from discriminating against or favoring any particular religion. This clause was designed to create what Thomas Jefferson referred to as "a wall of separation between church and state." In the 1960s the Supreme Court ruled that the First Amendment prohibits prayer and Bible reading in public schools.

Although the rights to free speech and freedom of the press are established in the First Amendment, it was not until the twentieth century that the Supreme Court began to explore the full meaning of these guarantees. In 1919 the Court ruled in Schenck v. United States *that the government could suppress free expression only where it could cite a "clear and present danger." In a decision that continues to raise controversies, the Court ruled in 1990, in* Texas v. Johnson, *that flag burning is a form of symbolic speech protected by the First Amendment.*

---

*Richard B. Bernstein, *Amending America* (New York: Times Books, 1993), 177–81.

[†]The dates in brackets indicate when the amendment was ratified.

Amendment II [1791]

A well regulated Militia, being necessary to the security of a free State, the right of the people to keep and bear Arms shall not be infringed.

. . .

Fear of a standing army under the control of a hostile government made the Second Amendment an important part of the Bill of Rights. Advocates of gun ownership claim that the amendment prevents the government from regulating firearms. Proponents of gun control argue that the amendment is designed only to protect the right of the states to maintain militia units.

In 1939 the Supreme Court ruled in United States v. Miller that the Second Amendment did not protect the right of an individual to own a sawed-off shotgun, which it argued was not ordinary militia equipment. Since then, the Supreme Court has refused to hear Second Amendment cases, whereas lower courts have upheld firearm regulations. Several justices currently on the bench seem to favor a broader interpretation of the Second Amendment, which would affect gun-control legislation. The controversy over the impact of the Second Amendment on gun owners and gun-control legislation will certainly continue.

Amendment III [1791]

No Soldier shall, in time of peace, be quartered in any house, without the consent of the Owner, nor in time of war, but in a manner to be prescribed by law.

. . .

The Third Amendment was extremely important to the framers of the Constitution, but today it is nearly forgotten. American colonists were especially outraged that they were forced to quarter British troops in the years before and during the American Revolution. The philosophy of the Third Amendment has been viewed by some justices and scholars as the foundation of the modern constitutional right to privacy.

Amendment IV [1791]

The right of the people to be secure in their persons, houses, papers, and effects, against unreasonable searches and seizures, shall not be violated, and no Warrants shall issue, but upon probable cause, supported by Oath or affirmation, and particularly describing the place to be searched, and the persons or things to be seized.

. . .

In the years before the Revolution, the houses, barns, stores, and warehouses of American colonists were ransacked by British authorities under "writs of assistance" or general warrants. The British, thus empowered, searched for seditious material or smuggled goods that could then be used as evidence against colonists who were charged with a crime only after the items were found.

The first part of the Fourth Amendment protects citizens from "unreasonable" searches and seizures. The Supreme Court has interpreted this protection as well as the words search and seizure in different ways at different times. At one time, the Court did not recognize electronic eavesdropping as a form of search and seizure, although it does today. At times, an "unreasonable" search has been almost any search carried out without a warrant, but in the two decades before 1969 the Court sometimes sanctioned warrantless searches that it considered reasonable based on "the total atmosphere of the case."

The second part of the Fourth Amendment defines the procedure for issuing a search warrant and states the requirement of "probable cause," which is generally viewed as evidence indicating that a suspect has committed an offense.

In Weeks v. U.S. (1994) and Mapp v. Ohio (1962), the Court excluded evidence seized in violation of constitutional standards. The justification is that excluding such evidence deters violations of the amendment, but doing so may allow a guilty person to escape punishment.

Amendment V [1791]

No person shall be held to answer for a capital or otherwise infamous crime, unless on a presentment or indictment of a Grand Jury, except in cases arising in the land or naval forces, or in the Militia, when in actual service in time of War or public danger; nor shall any person be subject for the same offence to be twice put in jeopardy of life or limb; nor shall be compelled in any criminal case to be a witness against himself, nor be deprived of life, liberty, or property, without due process of law; nor shall private property be taken for public use, without just compensation.

. . .

The Fifth Amendment protects people against government authority in the prosecution of criminal offenses. It prohibits the state, first, from charging a person with a serious crime without a grand-jury hearing to decide whether there is sufficient evidence to support the charge and, second, from charging a person with the same crime twice. The best-known aspect of the Fifth Amendment is that it prevents a person from being "compelled . . . to be a witness against himself." The last clause, the "takings clause," limits the power of the government to seize property.

Although invoking the Fifth Amendment is popularly viewed as a confession of guilt, a person may be innocent yet still fear prosecution. For example, during the cold war era of the late 1940s and 1950s, many people who had participated in legal activities that were associated with the Communist Party claimed the Fifth Amendment privilege rather than testify before the House Un-American Activities Committee because the mood of the times cast those activities in a negative light. Because "taking the Fifth" was viewed as an admission of guilt, those people often lost their jobs or became unemployable. Nonetheless, the right to protect oneself against self-incrimination plays an important role in guarding against the collective power of the state.

Amendment VI [1791]

In all criminal prosecutions, the accused shall enjoy the right to a speedy and public trial, by an impartial jury of the State and district wherein the crime shall have been committed, which district shall have been previously ascertained by law, and to be informed of the nature and cause of the accusation; to be confronted with the witnesses against him; to have compulsory process for obtaining witnesses in his favor, and to have the Assistance of Counsel for his defence.

• • •

The original Constitution put few limits on the government's power to investigate, prosecute, and punish crime. This process was of great concern to many Antifederalists, and of the twenty-eight rights specified in the first eight amendments, fifteen have to do with it. Seven rights are specified in the Sixth Amendment. These include the right to a speedy trial, a public trial, a jury trial, a notice of accusation, confrontation of opposing witnesses, testimony by favorable witnesses, and the assistance of counsel.

Amendment VII [1791]

In suits at common law, where the value in controversy shall exceed twenty dollars, the right of trial by jury shall be preserved, and no fact tried by a jury, shall be otherwise reexamined in any Court of the United States, than according to the Rules of the common law.

• • •

This amendment guarantees people the same right to a trial by jury as was guaranteed by English common law in 1791. Under common law, in civil trials (those involving money damages) the role of the judge was to settle questions of law and that of the jury was to settle questions of fact. The amendment does not specify the size of the jury or its role in a trial, however. The Supreme Court has generally held that those issues be determined by English common law of 1791, which stated that a jury consists of twelve people, that a trial must be conducted before a judge who instructs the jury on the law and advises it on facts, and that a verdict must be unanimous.

Amendment VIII [1791]

Excessive bail shall not be required, nor excessive fines imposed, nor cruel and unusual punishments inflicted.

• • •

The language used to guarantee the three rights in this amendment was inspired by the English Bill of Rights of 1689. The Supreme Court has not had a lot to say about "excessive fines." In recent years it has agreed that despite the provision against "excessive bail," persons who are believed to be dangerous to others can be held without bail even before they have been convicted.

Although opponents of the death penalty have not succeeded in using the Eighth Amendment to achieve the end of capital punishment, the clause regarding "cruel and unusual punishments" has been used to prohibit capital punishment in certain cases, such as minors and the mentally retarded.

Amendment IX [1791]

The enumeration in the Constitution, of certain rights, shall not be construed to deny or disparage others retained by the people.

• • •

Some Federalists feared that inclusion of the Bill of Rights in the Constitution would allow later generations of interpreters to claim that the people had surrendered all rights not specifically enumerated there. To guard against this, James Madison added language that became the Ninth Amendment. Interest in this heretofore largely ignored amendment revived in 1965 when it was used in a concurring opinion in Griswold v. Connecticut *(1965). While Justice William O. Douglas called on the Third Amendment to support the right to privacy in deciding that case, Justice Arthur Goldberg, in the concurring opinion, argued that the right to privacy regarding contraception was an unenumerated right that was protected by the Ninth Amendment.*

In 1980 the Court ruled that the right of the press to attend a public trial was protected by the Ninth Amendment. Although some scholars argue that modern judges cannot identify the unenumerated rights that the framers were trying to protect, others argue that the Ninth Amendment should be read as providing a constitutional "presumption of liberty" that allows people to act in any way that does not violate the rights of others.

Amendment X [1791]

The powers not delegated to the United States by the Constitution, nor prohibited by it to the States, are reserved to the States respectively, or to the people.

• • •

The Antifederalists were especially eager to see a "reserved powers clause" explicitly guaranteeing the states control over their internal affairs. Not surprisingly, the Tenth Amendment has been a frequent battleground in the struggle over states' rights and federal supremacy. Prior to the Civil War, the Jeffersonian Republican Party and Jacksonian Democrats invoked the Tenth

Amendment to prohibit the federal government from making decisions about whether people in individual states could own slaves. The Tenth Amendment was virtually suspended during Reconstruction following the Civil War. In 1883, however, the Supreme Court declared the Civil Rights Act of 1875 unconstitutional on the grounds that it violated the Tenth Amendment. Business interests also called on the amendment to block efforts at federal regulation.

The Court was inconsistent over the next several decades as it attempted to resolve the tension between the restrictions of the Tenth Amendment and the powers the Constitution granted to Congress to regulate interstate commerce and levy taxes. The Court upheld the Pure Food and Drug Act (1906), the Meat Inspection Acts (1906 and 1907), and the White Slave Traffic Act (1910), all of which affected the states, but it struck down an act prohibiting interstate shipment of goods produced through child labor. Between 1934 and 1935 a number of New Deal programs created by Franklin D. Roosevelt were declared unconstitutional on the grounds that they violated the Tenth Amendment. As Roosevelt appointees changed the composition of the Court, the Tenth Amendment was declared to have no substantive meaning. Generally, the amendment is held to protect the rights of states to regulate internal matters such as local government, education, commerce, labor, and business as well as matters involving families such as marriage, divorce, and inheritance within the state.

Unratified Amendment

Reapportionment Amendment (proposed by Congress September 25, 1789, along with the Bill of Rights)

After the first enumeration required by the first article of the Constitution, there shall be one Representative for every thirty thousand, until the number shall amount to one hundred, after which the proportion shall be so regulated by Congress, that there shall be not less than one hundred Representatives, nor less than one Representative for every forty thousand persons, until the number of Representatives shall amount to two hundred; after which the proportion shall be so regulated by Congress, that there shall not be less than two hundred Representatives, nor more than one Representative for every fifty thousand persons.

. . .

If the Reapportionment Amendment had passed and remained in effect, the House of Representatives today would have more than 7,000 members rather than 435 to reflect the current U.S. population.

Amendment XI [1798]

The Judicial power of the United States shall not be construed to extend to any suit in law or equity, commenced or prosecuted against one of the United States by Citizens of another State, or by Citizens or subjects of any foreign state.

. . .

In 1793 the Supreme Court ruled in favor of Alexander Chisholm, executor of the estate of a deceased South Carolina merchant. Chisholm was suing the state of Georgia because the merchant had never been paid for provisions he had supplied during the Revolution. Many regarded this Court decision as an error that violated the intent of the Constitution.

Antifederalists and many other Americans feared a powerful federal court system because they worried that it would become like the British courts of this period, which were accountable only to the monarch. Furthermore, Chisholm v. Georgia prompted a series of suits against state governments by creditors and suppliers who had made loans during the war.

In addition, state legislators and Congress feared that the shaky economies of the new states, as well as the country as a whole, would be destroyed, especially if Loyalists who had fled to other countries sought reimbursement for land and property that had been seized. The day after the Supreme Court announced its decision, a resolution proposing the Eleventh Amendment, which overturned the decision in Chisholm v. Georgia, *was introduced in the U.S. Senate.*

Amendment XII [1804]

The Electors shall meet in their respective States and vote by ballot for President and Vice-President, one of whom, at least, shall not be an inhabitant of the same State with themselves; they shall name in their ballots the person voted for as President, and in distinct ballots the person voted for as Vice-President, and they shall make distinct lists of all persons voted for as President, and of all persons voted for as Vice-President, and of the number of votes for each, which lists they shall sign and certify, and transmit sealed to the seat of government of the United States, directed to the President of the Senate;—the President of the Senate shall, in the presence of the Senate and House of Representatives, open all the certificates and the votes shall then be counted;—The person having the greatest number of votes for President, shall be the President, if such number be a majority of the whole number of Electors appointed; and if no person have such majority, then from the persons having the highest numbers not exceeding three on the list of those voted for as President, the House of Representatives shall choose immediately, by ballot, the President. But in choosing the President, the votes shall be taken by States, the representation from each State having one vote; a quorum for this purpose shall consist of a member or members from two-thirds of the States, and a majority of all the States shall be necessary to a choice. And if the House of Representatives shall not choose a President whenever the right of choice shall devolve upon them, before *the fourth day of March* next following, then the Vice-President shall act as

President, as in the case of the death or other constitutional disability of the President.*— The person having the greatest number of votes as Vice-President, shall be the Vice-President, if such number be a majority of the whole number of Electors appointed; and if no person have a majority, then from the two highest numbers on the list, the Senate shall choose the Vice-President; a quorum for the purpose shall consist of two-thirds of the whole number of Senators, and a majority of the whole number shall be necessary to a choice. But no person constitutionally ineligible to the office of President shall be eligible to that of Vice-President of the United States.

• • •

The framers of the Constitution disliked political parties and assumed that none would ever form. Under the original system, electors chosen by the states would each vote for two candidates. The candidate who won the most votes would become president, and the person who won the second-highest number of votes would become vice president. Rivalries between Federalists and Republicans led to the formation of political parties, however, even before George Washington had left office. In 1796 Federalist John Adams was chosen as president, and his great rival, Thomas Jefferson (whose party was called the Republican Party), became his vice president. In 1800 all the electors cast their two votes as one of two party blocs. Jefferson and his fellow Republican nominee, Aaron Burr, were tied with seventy-three votes each. The contest went to the House of Representatives, which finally elected Jefferson after thirty-six ballots. The Twelfth Amendment prevents these problems by requiring electors to vote separately for the president and vice president.

Unratified Amendment

Titles of Nobility Amendment
(proposed by Congress May 1, 1810)

If any citizen of the United States shall accept, claim, receive or retain any title of nobility or honor or shall, without the consent of Congress, accept and retain any present, pension, office or emolument of any kind whatever, from any emperor, king, prince or foreign power, such person shall cease to be a citizen of the United States, and shall be incapable of holding any office of trust or profit under them, or either of them.

• • •

This amendment would have extended Article I, Section 9, Clause 8 of the Constitution, which prevents the awarding of titles by the United States and the acceptance of such awards from foreign powers without congressional consent. Historians speculate that general nervousness about the power of the Emperor Napoleon, who was at that time extending France's empire throughout Europe, may have prompted the proposal. Though it

___
*Superseded by Section 3 of the Twentieth Amendment.

fell one vote short of ratification, Congress and the American people thought the proposal had been ratified, and it was included in many nineteenth-century editions of the Constitution.

The Civil War and Reconstruction Amendments (Thirteenth, Fourteenth, and Fifteenth Amendments)

In the four months between the election of Abraham Lincoln and his inauguration, more than two hundred proposed constitutional amendments were presented to Congress as part of a desperate attempt to hold the rapidly dissolving Union together. Most of these were efforts to appease the southern states by protecting the right to own slaves or by disfranchising African Americans through constitutional amendment. None were able to win the votes required from Congress to send them to the states. Ultimately, the Corwin Amendment seemed to be the only hope for preserving the Union by amending the Constitution.

The northern victors in the Civil War tried to restructure the Constitution just as the war had restructured the nation. Yet they were often divided in their goals. Some wanted to end slavery; others hoped for social and economic equality regardless of race; others hoped that extending the power of the ballot box to former slaves would help create a new political order. The debates over the Thirteenth, Fourteenth, and Fifteenth Amendments were bitter. Few of those who fought for these changes were satisfied with the amendments themselves; fewer still were satisfied with their interpretation. Although the amendments put an end to the legal status of slavery, it was nearly a hundred years after the amendments' passage before most of the descendants of former slaves could begin to experience the economic, social, and political equality the amendments were intended to provide.

Unratified Amendment

Corwin Amendment
(proposed by Congress March 2, 1861)

No amendment shall be made to the Constitution which will authorize or give to Congress the power to abolish or interfere, within any State, with the domestic institutions thereof, including that of persons held to labor or service by the laws of said State.

• • •

Following the election of Abraham Lincoln, Congress scrambled to try to prevent the secession of the slaveholding states. House member Thomas Corwin of Ohio proposed the "unamendable" amendment in the hope that by protecting slavery where it existed, Congress would keep the southern states in the Union. Lincoln indicated his support for the proposed amendment in his first inaugural address. Only Ohio and Maryland ratified the Corwin Amendment before the war caused it to be forgotten.

Amendment XIII [1865]

Section 1. Neither slavery nor involuntary servitude, except as a punishment for crime whereof the party shall have been duly convicted, shall exist within the United States, or any place subject to their jurisdiction.

Section 2. Congress shall have power to enforce this article by appropriate legislation.

. . .

Because the Emancipation Proclamation of 1863 abolished slavery only in the parts of the Confederacy still in rebellion, Republicans proposed a Thirteenth Amendment that would extend abolition to the entire South. In February 1865, when the proposal was approved by the House, the gallery of the House was newly opened to black Americans who had a chance at last to see their government at work. Passage of the proposal was greeted by wild cheers from the gallery as well as tears on the House floor, where congressional representatives openly embraced one another.

The problem of ratification remained, however. The Union position was that the Confederate states were part of the country of thirty-six states. Therefore, twenty-seven states were needed to ratify the amendment. When Kentucky and Delaware rejected it, backers realized that without approval from at least four former Confederate states, the amendment would fail. Lincoln's successor, President Andrew Johnson, made ratification of the Thirteenth Amendment a condition for southern states to rejoin the Union. Under those terms, all the former Confederate states except Mississippi accepted the Thirteenth Amendment, and by the end of 1865 the amendment had become part of the Constitution and slavery had been prohibited in the United States.

Amendment XIV [1868]

Section 1. All persons born or naturalized in the United States, and subject to the jurisdiction thereof, are citizens of the United States and of the State wherein they reside. No State shall make or enforce any law which shall abridge the privileges or immunities of citizens of the United States; nor shall any State deprive any person of life, liberty, or property, without due process of law; nor deny to any person within its jurisdiction the equal protection of the laws.

Section 2. Representatives shall be apportioned among the several States according to their respective numbers, counting the whole number of persons in each State, excluding Indians not taxed. But when the right to vote at any election for the choice of electors for President and Vice-President of the United States, Representatives in Congress, the Executive and Judicial officers of a State, or the members of the Legislature thereof, is denied to any of the male inhabitants of such State, being twenty-one years of age and citizens of the United States, or in any way abridged, except for participation in rebellion, or other crime, the basis of representation therein shall be reduced in the proportion which the number of such male citizens shall bear to the whole number of male citizens twenty-one years of age in such State.

Section 3. No person shall be a Senator or Representative in Congress, or Elector of President and Vice-President, or hold any office, civil or military, under the United States, or under any State, who, having previously taken an oath, as a member of Congress, or as an officer of the United States, or as a member of any State legislature, or as an executive or judicial officer of any State, to support the Constitution of the United States, shall have engaged in insurrection or rebellion against the same, or given aid or comfort to the enemies thereof. Congress may, by a vote of two-thirds of each house, remove such disability.

Section 4. The validity of the public debt of the United States, authorized by law, including debts incurred for payment of pensions and bounties for services in suppressing insurrection or rebellion, shall not be questioned. But neither the United States nor any State shall assume or pay any debt or obligation incurred in aid of insurrection or rebellion against the United States, or any claim for the loss or emancipation of any slave; but all such debts, obligations, and claims shall be held illegal and void.

Section 5. The Congress shall have power to enforce, by appropriate legislation, the provisions of this article.

. . .

Less than a year after Lincoln's assassination, Andrew Johnson was ready to bring the former Confederate states back into the Union and Confederate leaders back into Congress. Anxious Republicans drafted the Fourteenth Amendment to prevent that from happening. Moreover, most Southern states had enacted "Black Codes" that restricted the legal, political, and civil rights of former slaves. The most important provisions of this complex amendment made all native-born or naturalized persons American citizens and prohibited states from abridging the "privileges or immunities" of citizens; depriving them of "life, liberty, or property, without due process of law"; and denying them "equal protection of the laws." In essence, it made all former slaves citizens and protected the rights of all citizens against violation by their own state governments.

As occurred in the case of the Thirteenth Amendment, former Confederate states were forced to ratify the amendment as a condition of representation in the House and the Senate. The intentions of the Fourteenth Amendment, and how those intentions should be enforced, have been the most debated point of constitutional history. The terms due process *and* equal protection *have been especially troublesome. Was the amendment* designed to outlaw racial segregation? Or was the goal simply to prevent the leaders of the rebellious South from gaining political power?

The framers of the Fourteenth Amendment hoped Section 2 would produce black voters who would increase the power of the Republican Party. The federal government, however, never used its power to punish states for denying blacks their right to vote. Although the Fourteenth Amendment had an immediate impact in giving black Americans citizenship, it did nothing to protect blacks from the vengeance of whites once Reconstruction ended. In the late nineteenth and early twentieth centuries, Section 1 of the Fourteenth Amendment was often used to protect business interests and strike down laws protecting workers on the grounds that the rights of "persons," that is, corporations, were protected by "due process." More recently, the Fourteenth Amendment has been used to justify school desegregation and affirmative action programs, as well as to dismantle such programs.

Amendment XV [1870]

Section 1. The right of citizens of the United States to vote shall not be denied or abridged by the United States or by any State on account of race, color, or previous condition of servitude—

Section 2. The Congress shall have power to enforce this article by appropriate legislation.

• • •

The Fifteenth Amendment was the last major piece of Reconstruction legislation. Although earlier Reconstruction acts had already required black suffrage in the South, the Fifteenth Amendment extended black voting rights to the entire nation. Some Republicans felt morally obligated to do away with the double standard between the North and South because many northern states had stubbornly refused to enfranchise blacks. Others believed that the freedman's ballot required the extra protection of a constitutional amendment to shield it from white counterattack in the South. But partisan advantage also played an important role in the amendment's passage because Republicans hoped that by giving the ballot to blacks, they could lessen their party's political vulnerability.

Many women's rights advocates had fought for the amendment. They had felt betrayed by the inclusion of the word *male* in Section 2 of the Fourteenth Amendment and were further angered when the proposed Fifteenth Amendment failed to prohibit denial of the right to vote on the grounds of sex as well as "race, color, or previous condition of servitude." In this amendment, for the first time, the federal government exerted its power to regulate the franchise, or vote. It was also the first time the Constitution placed limits on the power of the states to regulate access to the franchise. Although ratified in 1870, the amendment was not enforced until the twentieth century.

The Progressive Amendments (Sixteenth–Nineteenth Amendments)

No amendments were added to the Constitution between the Civil War and the Progressive Era. America was changing, however, in fundamental ways. The rapid industrialization of the United States after the Civil War led to many social and economic problems. Hundreds of amendments were proposed, but none received enough support in Congress to be sent to the states. Some scholars believe that regional differences and rivalries were so strong during this period that it was almost impossible to gain a consensus on a constitutional amendment. During the Progressive Era, however, the Constitution was amended four times in seven years.

Amendment XVI [1913]

The Congress shall have power to lay and collect taxes on incomes, from whatever source derived, without apportionment among the several States, and without regard to any census or enumeration.

• • •

Until passage of the Sixteenth Amendment, most of the money used to run the federal government came from customs duties and taxes on specific items, such as liquor. During the Civil War the federal government taxed incomes as an emergency measure. Pressure to enact an income tax came from those who were concerned about the growing gap between rich and poor in the United States. The Populist Party began campaigning for a graduated income tax in 1892, and support continued to grow. By 1909 thirty-three proposed income tax amendments had been presented in Congress, but lobbying by corporate and other special interests had defeated them all. In June 1909 the growing pressure for an income tax, which had been endorsed by presidents Roosevelt and Taft, finally pushed an amendment through the Senate. The required thirty-six states had ratified the amendment by February 1913.

Amendment XVII [1913]

Section 1. The Senate of the United States shall be composed of two Senators from each State, elected by the people thereof, for six years; and each Senator shall have one vote. The electors in each State shall have the qualifications requisite for electors of [voters for] the most numerous branch of the State legislatures.

Section 2. When vacancies happen in the representation of any State in the Senate, the executive authority of such State shall issue writs of election to fill such vacancies: Provided, that the Legislature of any State may empower the executive thereof to make temporary appointments until the people fill the vacancies by election as the Legislature may direct.

Section 3. This amendment shall not be so construed as to affect the election or term of any Senator chosen before it becomes valid as part of the Constitution.

. . .

The framers of the Constitution saw the members of the House as the representatives of the people and the members of the Senate as the representatives of the states. Originally, senators were to be chosen by the state legislators. According to reform advocates, however, the growth of private industry and transportation conglomerates during the late nineteenth century had created a network of corruption in which wealth and power were exchanged for influence and votes in the Senate. Senator Nelson Aldrich, who represented Rhode Island in this period, for example, was known as "the senator from Standard Oil" because of his open support of special business interests.

Efforts to amend the Constitution to allow direct election of senators had begun in 1826, but because any proposal had to be approved by the Senate, reform seemed impossible. Progressives tried to gain influence in the Senate by instituting party caucuses and primary elections, which gave citizens the chance to express their choice of a senator who could then be officially elected by the state legislature. By 1910 fourteen of the country's thirty senators received popular votes through a state primary before the state legislature made its selection. Despairing of getting a proposal through the Senate, supporters of a direct-election amendment had begun in 1893 to seek a convention of representatives from two-thirds of the states to propose an amendment that could then be ratified. By 1905 thirty-one of forty-five states had endorsed such an amendment. Finally, in 1911, despite extraordinary opposition, a proposed amendment passed the Senate; by 1913 it had been ratified.

Amendment XVIII [1919; repealed 1933 by Amendment XXI]

Section 1. After one year from the ratification of this article the manufacture, sale, or transportation of intoxicating liquors within, the importation thereof into, or the exportation thereof from the United States and all territory subject to the jurisdiction thereof, for beverage purposes, is hereby prohibited.

Section 2. The Congress and the several States shall have concurrent power to enforce this article by appropriate legislation.

Section 3. This article shall be inoperative unless it shall have been ratified as an amendment to the Constitution by the legislatures of the several States, as provided by the Constitution, within seven years from the date of the submission thereof to the States by the Congress.

. . .

The Prohibition Party, formed in 1869, began calling for a constitutional amendment to outlaw alcoholic beverages in 1872. A prohibition amendment was first proposed in the Senate in 1876 and was revived eighteen times before 1913. Between 1913 and 1919 another thirty-nine attempts were made to prohibit liquor in the United States through a constitutional amendment. Prohibition became a key element of the Progressive agenda as reformers linked alcohol and drunkenness to numerous social problems, including the corruption of immigrant voters. Whereas opponents of such an amendment argued that it was undemocratic, supporters claimed that their efforts had widespread public support. The admission of twelve "dry" western states to the Union in the early twentieth century and the spirit of sacrifice during World War I laid the groundwork for passage and ratification of the Eighteenth Amendment in 1919. Opponents added a time limit to the amendment in the hope that they could thereby block ratification, but this effort failed. (See also Amendment XXI.)

Amendment XIX [1920]

Section 1. The right of citizens of the United States to vote shall not be denied or abridged by the United States or by any State on account of sex.

Section 2. Congress shall have the power to enforce this article by appropriate legislation.

. . .

Advocates of women's rights tried and failed to link woman suffrage to the Fourteenth and Fifteenth Amendments. Nonetheless, the effort for woman suffrage continued. Between 1878 and 1912 at least one and sometimes as many as four proposed amendments were introduced in Congress each year to grant women the right to vote. Although over time women won very limited voting rights in some states, at both the state and federal levels opposition to an amendment for woman suffrage remained very strong. President Woodrow Wilson and other officials felt that the federal government should not interfere with the power of the states in this matter. And many people were concerned that giving women the vote would result in their abandoning traditional gender roles. In 1919, following a protracted and often bitter campaign of protest in which women went on hunger strikes and chained themselves to fences, an amendment was introduced with the backing of President Wilson. It narrowly passed the Senate (after efforts to limit the suffrage to white women failed) and was adopted in 1920 after Tennessee became the thirty-sixth state to ratify it.

Unratified Amendment

Child Labor Amendment
(proposed by Congress June 2, 1924)

Section 1. The Congress shall have power to limit, regulate, and prohibit the labor of persons under eighteen years of age.

Section 2. The power of the several States is unimpaired by this article except that the operation of State laws shall be suspended to the extent necessary to give effect to legislation enacted by Congress.

. . .

Throughout the late nineteenth and early twentieth centuries, alarm over the condition of child workers grew. Opponents of child labor argued that children worked in dangerous and unhealthy conditions, that they took jobs from adult workers, that they depressed wages in certain industries, and that states that allowed child labor had an economic advantage over those that did not. Defenders of child labor claimed that children provided needed income in many families, that working at a young age helped to develop character, and that the effort to prohibit the practice constituted an invasion of family privacy.

In 1916 Congress passed a law that made it illegal to sell through interstate commerce goods made by children. The Supreme Court, however, ruled that the law violated the limits on the power of Congress to regulate interstate commerce. Congress then tried to penalize industries that used child labor by taxing such goods. This measure was also thrown out by the courts. In response, reformers set out to amend the Constitution. The proposed amendment was ratified by twenty-eight states, but by 1925 thirteen states had rejected it. Passage of the Fair Labor Standards Act in 1938, which was upheld by the Supreme Court in 1941, made the amendment irrelevant.

Amendment XX [1933]

Section 1. The terms of the President and Vice-President shall end at noon on the 20th day of January, and the terms of Senators and Representatives at noon on the 3rd day of January, of the years in which such terms would have ended if this article had not been ratified; and the terms of their successors shall then begin.

Section 2. The Congress shall assemble at least once in every year, and such meeting shall begin at noon on the 3rd day of January, unless they shall by law appoint a different day.

Section 3. If, at the time fixed for the beginning of the term of the President, the President-elect shall have died, the Vice-President-elect shall become President. If a President shall not have been chosen before the time fixed for the beginning of his term, or if the President-elect shall have failed to qualify, then the Vice-President-elect shall act as President until a President shall have qualified; and the Congress may by law provide for the case wherein neither a President-elect nor a Vice-President-elect shall have qualified, declaring who shall then act as President, or the manner in which one who is to act shall be selected, and such person shall act accordingly until a President or Vice-President shall have qualified.

Section 4. The Congress may by law provide for the case of the death of any of the persons from whom the House of Representatives may choose a President whenever the right of choice shall have devolved upon them, and for the case of the death of any of the persons from whom the Senate may choose a Vice-President whenever the right of choice shall have devolved upon them.

Section 5. Sections 1 and 2 shall take effect on the 15th day of October following the ratification of this article.

Section 6. This article shall be inoperative unless it shall have been ratified as an amendment to the Constitution by the Legislatures of three-fourths of the several States within seven years from the date of its submission.

. . .

Until 1933, presidents took office on March 4. Because elections are held in early November and electoral votes are counted in mid-December, this meant that more than three months passed between the time a new president was elected and when he took office. Moving the inauguration to January shortened the transition period and allowed Congress to begin its term closer to the time of the president's inauguration. Although this seems like a minor change, an amendment was required because the Constitution specifies terms of office. This amendment also deals with questions of succession in the event that a president- or vice-president-elect dies before assuming office. Section 3 also clarifies a method for resolving a deadlock in the electoral college.

Amendment XXI [1933]

Section 1. The eighteenth article of amendment to the Constitution of the United States is hereby repealed.

Section 2. The transportation or importation into any State, Territory, or Possession of the United States for delivery or use therein of intoxicating liquors, in violation of the laws thereof, is hereby prohibited.

Section 3. This article shall be inoperative unless it shall have been ratified as an amendment to the Constitution by conventions in the several States, as provided in the Constitution, within seven years from the date of the submission thereof to the States by the Congress.

. . .

Widespread violation of the Volstead Act, the law enacted to enforce prohibition, made the United States a nation of lawbreakers. Prohibition caused more problems than it solved by encouraging crime, bribery, and corruption. Further, a coalition of liquor and beer manufacturers, personal liberty advocates, and constitutional scholars joined forces to challenge the amendment. By 1929 thirty proposed repeal amendments had been introduced in Congress, and the Democratic Party made repeal part of its platform in the 1932 presidential campaign. The Twenty-first Amendment was proposed in February 1933 and ratified less than a year later. The failure of the effort to enforce prohibition through a constitutional amendment has often been cited by opponents of subsequent efforts to shape public virtue and private morality.

Amendment XXII [1951]

Section 1. No person shall be elected to the office of the President more than twice, and no person who has held the office of President, or acted as President, for more than two years of a term to which some other person was elected President shall be elected to the office of President more than once. But this article shall not apply to any person holding the office of President when this Article was proposed by the Congress, and shall not prevent any person who may be holding the office of President, or acting as President, during the term within which this Article becomes operative from holding the office of President or acting as President during the remainder of such term.

Section 2. This article shall be inoperative unless it shall have been ratified as an amendment to the Constitution by the legislatures of three-fourths of the several States within seven years from the date of its submission to the States by the Congress.

. . .

George Washington's refusal to seek a third term of office set a precedent that stood until 1912, when former president Theodore Roosevelt sought, without success, another term as an independent candidate. Democrat Franklin Roosevelt was the only president to seek and win a fourth term, though he did so amid great controversy. Roosevelt died in April 1945, a few months after the beginning of his fourth term. In 1946 Republicans won control of the House and the Senate, and early in 1947 a proposal for an amendment to limit future presidents to two four-year terms was offered to the states for ratification. Democratic critics of the Twenty-second Amendment charged that it was a partisan posthumous jab at Roosevelt.

Since the Twenty-second Amendment was adopted, two of the three presidents who might have been able to seek a third term, had it not existed, were Republicans Dwight Eisenhower and Ronald Reagan. Since 1826, Congress has entertained 160 proposed amendments to limit the president to one six-year term. Such amendments have been backed by fifteen presidents, including Gerald Ford and Jimmy Carter.

Amendment XXIII [1961]

Section 1. The District constituting the seat of Government of the United States shall appoint in such manner as the Congress may direct: A number of electors of President and Vice-President equal to the whole number of Senators and Representatives in Congress to which the District would be entitled if it were a State, but in no event more than the least populous State; they shall be in addition to those appointed by the States, but they shall be considered for the purposes of the election of President and Vice-President, to be electors appointed by a State; and they shall meet in the District and perform such duties as provided by the twelfth article of amendment.

Section 2. The Congress shall have the power to enforce this article by appropriate legislation.

. . .

When Washington, D.C., was established as a federal district, no one expected that a significant number of people would make it their permanent and primary residence. A proposal to allow citizens of the district to vote in presidential elections was approved by Congress in June 1960 and was ratified on March 29, 1961.

Amendment XXIV [1964]

Section 1. The right of citizens of the United States to vote in any primary or other election for President or Vice-President, for electors for President or Vice-President, or for Senator or Representative in Congress, shall not be denied or abridged by the United States or any State by reason of failure to pay any poll tax or other tax.

Section 2. The Congress shall have the power to enforce this article by appropriate legislation.

. . .

In the colonial and Revolutionary eras, financial independence was seen as necessary to political independence, and the poll tax was used as a requirement for voting. By the twentieth century, however, the poll tax was used mostly to bar poor people, especially southern blacks, from voting. Although conservatives complained that the amendment interfered with states' rights, liberals thought that the amendment did not go far enough because it barred the poll tax only in national elections and not in state or local elections. The amendment was ratified in 1964, however, and two years later the Supreme Court ruled that poll taxes in state and local elections also violated the equal protection clause of the Fourteenth Amendment.

Amendment XXV [1967]

Section 1. In case of the removal of the President from office or of his death or resignation, the Vice-President shall become President.

Section 2. Whenever there is a vacancy in the office of the Vice-President, the President shall nominate a Vice-President who shall take office upon confirmation by a majority vote of both Houses of Congress.

Section 3. Whenever the President transmits to the President pro tempore of the Senate and the Speaker of the House of Representatives his written declaration that he is unable to discharge the powers and duties of his office, and until he transmits to them a written declaration to the contrary, such powers and duties shall be discharged by the Vice-President as Acting President.

Section 4. Whenever the Vice-President and a majority of either the principal officers of the executive departments or of such other body as Congress may by law provide, transmit to the President pro tempore of the Senate and the Speaker of the House of Representatives their written declaration that the President is unable to discharge the powers and duties of his office, the Vice-President shall immediately assume the powers and duties of the office as Acting President.

Thereafter, when the President transmits to the President pro tempore of the Senate and the Speaker of the House of Representatives his written declaration that no inability exists, he shall resume the powers and duties of his office unless the Vice-President and a majority of either the principal officers of the executive department[s] or of such other body as Congress may by law provide, transmit within four days to the President pro tempore of the Senate and the Speaker of the House of Representatives their written declaration that the President is unable to discharge the powers and duties of his office. Thereupon Congress shall decide the issue, assembling within forty-eight hours for that purpose if not in session. If the Congress, within twenty-one days after receipt of the latter written declaration, or, if Congress is not in session, within twenty-one days after Congress is required to assemble, determines by two-thirds vote of both Houses that the President is unable to discharge the powers and duties of his office, the Vice-President shall continue to discharge the same as Acting President; otherwise, the President shall resume the powers and duties of his office.

. . .

The framers of the Constitution established the office of vice president because someone was needed to preside over the Senate. The first president to die in office was William Henry Harrison, in 1841. Vice President John Tyler had himself sworn in as president, setting a precedent that was followed when seven later presidents died in office. The assassination of President James A. Garfield in 1881 posed a new problem, however. After he was shot, the president was incapacitated for two months before he died; he was unable to lead the country, and his vice president, Chester A. Arthur, was unable to assume leadership. Efforts to resolve questions of succession in the event of a presidential disability thus began with the death of Garfield.

In 1963 the assassination of President John F. Kennedy galvanized Congress to action. Vice President Lyndon Johnson was a chain-smoker with a history of heart trouble. According to the 1947 Presidential Succession Act, the two men who stood in line to succeed him were the seventy-two-year-old Speaker of the House and the eighty-six-year-old president of the Senate. There were serious concerns that any of these men might become incapacitated while serving as chief executive. The first time the Twenty-fifth Amendment was used, however, was not in the case of presidential death or illness, but during the Watergate crisis. When Vice President Spiro T. Agnew was forced to resign following allegations of bribery and tax violations, President Richard M. Nixon appointed House Minority Leader Gerald R. Ford vice president. Ford became president following Nixon's resignation eight months later and named Nelson A. Rockefeller as his vice president. Thus, for more than two years, the two highest offices in the country were held by people who had not been elected to them.

Amendment XXVI [1971]

Section 1. The right of citizens of the United States, who are eighteen years of age or older, to vote shall not be denied or abridged by the United States or by any State on account of age.

Section 2. The Congress shall have power to enforce this article by appropriate legislation.

. . .

Efforts to lower the voting age from twenty-one to eighteen began during World War II. Recognizing that those who were old enough to fight a war should have some say in the government policies that involved them in the war, Presidents Eisenhower, Johnson, and Nixon endorsed the idea. In 1970 the combined pressure of the antiwar movement and the demographic pressure of the baby-boom generation led to a Voting Rights Act lowering the voting age in federal, state, and local elections.

In Oregon v. Mitchell (1970), the state of Oregon challenged the right of Congress to determine the age at which people could vote in state or local elections. The Supreme Court agreed with Oregon. Because the Voting Rights Act was ruled unconstitutional, the Constitution had to be amended to allow passage of a law that would lower the voting age. The amendment was ratified in a little more than three months, making it the most rapidly ratified amendment in U.S. history.

Unratified Amendment

Equal Rights Amendment (proposed by Congress March 22, 1972; seven-year deadline for ratification extended to June 30, 1982)

Section 1. Equality of rights under the law shall not be denied or abridged by the United States or by any State on account of sex.

Section 2. The Congress shall have the power to enforce, by appropriate legislation, the provisions of this article.

Section 3. This amendment shall take effect two years after the date of ratification.

. . .

In 1923, soon after women had won the right to vote, Alice Paul, a leading activist in the woman suffrage movement, proposed an amendment requiring equal treatment of men and women. Opponents of the proposal argued that such an amendment would invalidate laws that protected women and would make women subject to the military draft. After the 1964 Civil Rights Act was adopted, protective workplace legislation was partially removed.

The renewal of the women's movement, as a by-product of the civil rights and antiwar movements, led to a revival of the Equal Rights Amendment (ERA) in Congress. Disagreements over language held up congressional passage of the proposed amendment, but on March 22, 1972, the Senate approved the ERA by a vote of 84 to 8, and it was sent to the states. Six states ratified the amendment within two days, and by the middle of 1973 the amendment seemed well on its way to adoption, with thirty of the needed thirty-eight states having ratified it. In the mid-1970s, however, a powerful "Stop ERA" campaign developed. The campaign portrayed the ERA as a threat to "family values" and traditional relationships between men and women. Although thirty-five states ratified the ERA, five of those state legislatures voted to rescind ratification, and the amendment was never adopted.

Unratified Amendment

D.C. Statehood Amendment
(proposed by Congress August 22, 1978)

Section 1. For purposes of representation in the Congress, election of the President and Vice President, and article V of this Constitution, the District constituting the seat of government of the United States shall be treated as though it were a State.

Section 2. The exercise of the rights and powers conferred under this article shall be by the people of the District constituting the seat of government, and as shall be provided by Congress.

Section 3. The twenty-third article of amendment to the Constitution of the United States is hereby repealed.

Section 4. This article shall be inoperative, unless it shall have been ratified as an amendment to the Constitution by the legislatures of three-fourths of the several states within seven years from the date of its submission.

. . .

The 1961 ratification of the Twenty-third Amendment, giving residents of the District of Columbia the right to vote for a president and vice president, inspired an effort to give residents of the district full voting rights. In 1966 President Lyndon Johnson appointed a mayor and city council; in 1971 D.C. residents were allowed to name a nonvoting delegate to the House; and in 1981 residents were allowed to elect the mayor and city council. Congress retained the right to overrule laws that might affect commuters, the height of District buildings, and selection of judges and prosecutors. The district's nonvoting delegate to Congress, Walter Fauntroy, lobbied fiercely for a congressional amendment granting statehood to the district. In 1978 a proposed amendment was approved and sent to the states. A number of states quickly ratified the amendment, but, like the ERA, the D.C. Statehood Amendment ran into trouble. Opponents argued that Section 2 created a separate category of "nominal" statehood. They argued that the federal district should be eliminated and that the territory should be reabsorbed into the state of Maryland. Most scholars believe that the fears of Republicans that the predominantly black population of the city would consistently elect Democratic senators constituted a major factor leading to the defeat of the amendment.

Amendment XXVII [1992]

No law varying the compensation for the services of the Senators and Representatives, shall take effect, until an election of Representatives shall have intervened.

. . .

Whereas the Twenty-sixth Amendment was the most rapidly ratified amendment in U.S. history, the Twenty-seventh Amendment had the longest journey to ratification. First proposed by James Madison in 1789 as part of the package that included the Bill of Rights, this amendment had been ratified by only six states by 1791. In 1873, however, it was ratified by Ohio to protest a massive retroactive salary increase by the federal government. Unlike later proposed amendments, this one came with no time limit on ratification. In the early 1980s Gregory D. Watson, a University of Texas economics major, discovered the "lost" amendment and began a single-handed campaign to get state legislators to introduce it for ratification. In 1983 it was accepted by Maine. In 1984 it passed the Colorado legislature. Ratifications trickled in slowly until May 1992, when Michigan and New Jersey became the thirty-eighth and thirty-ninth states, respectively, to ratify. This amendment prevents members of Congress from raising their own salaries without giving voters a chance to vote them out of office before they can benefit from the raises.

APPENDIX

The American Nation

Admission of States into the Union

State	Date of Admission	State	Date of Admission	State	Date of Admission
1. Delaware	December 7, 1787	18. Louisiana	April 30, 1812	35. West Virginia	June 20, 1863
2. Pennsylvania	December 12, 1787	19. Indiana	December 11, 1816	36. Nevada	October 31, 1864
3. New Jersey	December 18, 1787	20. Mississippi	December 10, 1817	37. Nebraska	March 1, 1867
4. Georgia	January 2, 1788	21. Illinois	December 3, 1818	38. Colorado	August 1, 1876
5. Connecticut	January 9, 1788	22. Alabama	December 14, 1819	39. North Dakota	November 2, 1889
6. Massachusetts	February 6, 1788	23. Maine	March 15, 1820	40. South Dakota	November 2, 1889
7. Maryland	April 28, 1788	24. Missouri	August 10, 1821	41. Montana	November 8, 1889
8. South Carolina	May 23, 1788	25. Arkansas	June 15, 1836	42. Washington	November 11, 1889
9. New Hampshire	June 21, 1788	26. Michigan	January 26, 1837	43. Idaho	July 3, 1890
10. Virginia	June 25, 1788	27. Florida	March 3, 1845	44. Wyoming	July 10, 1890
11. New York	July 26, 1788	28. Texas	December 29, 1845	45. Utah	January 4, 1896
12. North Carolina	November 21, 1789	29. Iowa	December 28, 1846	46. Oklahoma	November 16, 1907
13. Rhode Island	May 29, 1790	30. Wisconsin	May 29, 1848	47. New Mexico	January 6, 1912
14. Vermont	March 4, 1791	31. California	September 9, 1850	48. Arizona	February 14, 1912
15. Kentucky	June 1, 1792	32. Minnesota	May 11, 1858	49. Alaska	January 3, 1959
16. Tennessee	June 1, 1796	33. Oregon	February 14, 1859	50. Hawaii	August 21, 1959
17. Ohio	March 1, 1803	34. Kansas	January 29, 1861		

Territorial Expansion

Territory	Date Acquired	Square Miles	How Acquired
Original states and territories	1783	888,685	Treaty of Paris
Louisiana Purchase	1803	827,192	Purchased from France
Florida	1819	72,003	Adams-Onís Treaty
Texas	1845	390,143	Annexation of independent country
Oregon	1846	285,580	Oregon Boundary Treaty
Mexican cession	1848	529,017	Treaty of Guadalupe Hidalgo
Gadsden Purchase	1853	29,640	Purchased from Mexico
Midway Islands	1867	2	Annexation of uninhabited islands
Alaska	1867	589,757	Purchased from Russia
Hawaii	1898	6,450	Annexation of independent country
Wake Island	1898	3	Annexation of uninhabited island
Puerto Rico	1899	3,435	Treaty of Paris
Guam	1899	212	Treaty of Paris
The Philippines	1899–1946	115,600	Treaty of Paris; granted independence
American Samoa	1900	76	Treaty with Germany and Great Britain
Panama Canal Zone	1904–1978	553	Hay–Bunau-Varilla Treaty
U.S. Virgin Islands	1917	133	Purchased from Denmark
Trust Territory of the Pacific Islands*	1947	717	United Nations Trusteeship

*A number of these islands have been granted independence: Federated States of Micronesia, 1990; Marshall Islands, 1991; Palau, 1994.

Presidential Elections

Year	Candidates	Parties	Percentage of Popular Vote	Electoral Vote	Percentage of Voter Participation
1789	**George Washington**	No party designations	*	69	
	John Adams†			34	
	Other candidates			35	
1792	**George Washington**	No party designations		132	
	John Adams			77	
	George Clinton			50	
	Other candidates			5	
1796	**John Adams**	Federalist		71	
	Thomas Jefferson	Democratic-Republican		68	
	Thomas Pinckney	Federalist		59	
	Aaron Burr	Democratic-Republican		30	
	Other candidates			48	
1800	**Thomas Jefferson**	Democratic-Republican		73	
	Aaron Burr	Democratic-Republican		73	
	John Adams	Federalist		65	
	Charles C. Pinckney	Federalist		64	
	John Jay	Federalist		1	
1804	**Thomas Jefferson**	Democratic-Republican		162	
	Charles C. Pinckney	Federalist		14	
1808	**James Madison**	Democratic-Republican		122	
	Charles C. Pinckney	Federalist		47	
	George Clinton	Democratic-Republican		6	
1812	**James Madison**	Democratic-Republican		128	
	De Witt Clinton	Federalist		89	
1816	**James Monroe**	Democratic-Republican		183	
	Rufus King	Federalist		34	
1820	**James Monroe**	Democratic-Republican		231	
	John Quincy Adams	Independent Republican		1	
1824	**John Quincy Adams**	Democratic-Republican	30.5	84	26.9
	Andrew Jackson	Democratic-Republican	43.1	99	
	Henry Clay	Democratic-Republican	13.2	37	
	William H. Crawford	Democratic-Republican	13.1	41	
1828	**Andrew Jackson**	Democratic	56.0	178	57.6
	John Quincy Adams	National Republican	44.0	83	
1832	**Andrew Jackson**	Democratic	54.5	219	55.4
	Henry Clay	National Republican	37.5	49	
	William Wirt	Anti-Masonic	8.0	7	
	John Floyd	Democratic	‡	11	
1836	**Martin Van Buren**	Democratic	50.9	170	57.8
	William H. Harrison	Whig		73	
	Hugh L. White	Whig		26	
	Daniel Webster	Whig	49.1	14	
	W. P. Mangum	Whig		11	
1840	**William H. Harrison**	Whig	53.1	234	80.2
	Martin Van Buren	Democratic	46.9	60	
1844	**James K. Polk**	Democratic	49.6	170	78.9
	Henry Clay	Whig	48.1	105	
	James G. Birney	Liberty	2.3		

Year	Candidates	Parties	Percentage of Popular Vote	Electoral Vote	Percentage of Voter Participation
1848	**Zachary Taylor**	Whig	47.4	163	72.7
	Lewis Cass	Democratic	42.5	127	
	Martin Van Buren	Free Soil	10.1		
1852	**Franklin Pierce**	Democratic	50.9	254	69.6
	Winfield Scott	Whig	44.1	42	
	John P. Hale	Free Soil	5.0		
1856	**James Buchanan**	Democratic	45.3	174	78.9
	John C. Frémont	Republican	33.1	114	
	Millard Fillmore	American	21.6	8	
1860	**Abraham Lincoln**	Republican	39.8	180	81.2
	Stephen A. Douglas	Democratic	29.5	12	
	John C. Breckinridge	Democratic	18.1	72	
	John Bell	Constitutional Union	12.6	39	
1864	**Abraham Lincoln**	Republican	55.0	212	73.8
	George B. McClellan	Democratic	45.0	21	
1868	**Ulysses S. Grant**	Republican	52.7	214	78.1
	Horatio Seymour	Democratic	47.3	80	
1872	**Ulysses S. Grant**	Republican	55.6	286	71.3
	Horace Greeley	Democratic	43.9		
1876	**Rutherford B. Hayes**	Republican	48.0	185	81.8
	Samuel J. Tilden	Democratic	51.0	184	
1880	**James A. Garfield**	Republican	48.5	214	79.4
	Winfield S. Hancock	Democratic	48.1	155	
	James B. Weaver	Greenback-Labor	3.4		
1884	**Grover Cleveland**	Democratic	48.5	219	77.5
	James G. Blaine	Republican	48.2	182	
1888	**Benjamin Harrison**	Republican	47.9	233	79.3
	Grover Cleveland	Democratic	48.6	168	
1892	**Grover Cleveland**	Democratic	46.1	277	74.7
	Benjamin Harrison	Republican	43.0	145	
	James B. Weaver	People's	8.5	22	
1896	**William McKinley**	Republican	51.1	271	79.3
	William J. Bryan	Democratic	47.7	176	
1900	**William McKinley**	Republican	51.7	292	73.2
	William J. Bryan	Democratic; Populist	45.5	155	
1904	**Theodore Roosevelt**	Republican	57.4	336	65.2
	Alton B. Parker	Democratic	37.6	140	
	Eugene V. Debs	Socialist	3.0		
1908	**William H. Taft**	Republican	51.6	321	65.4
	William J. Bryan	Democratic	43.1	162	
	Eugene V. Debs	Socialist	2.8		
1912	**Woodrow Wilson**	Democratic	41.9	435	58.8
	Theodore Roosevelt	Progressive	27.4	88	
	William H. Taft	Republican	23.2	8	
	Eugene V. Debs	Socialist	6.0		
1916	**Woodrow Wilson**	Democratic	49.4	277	61.6
	Charles E. Hughes	Republican	46.2	254	
	A. L. Benson	Socialist	3.2		

Year	Candidates	Parties	Percentage of Popular Vote	Electoral Vote	Percentage of Voter Participation
1920	**Warren G. Harding**	Republican	60.4	404	49.2
	James M. Cox	Democratic	34.2	127	
	Eugene V. Debs	Socialist	3.4		
1924	**Calvin Coolidge**	Republican	54.0	382	48.9
	John W. Davis	Democratic	28.8	136	
	Robert M. La Follette	Progressive	16.6	13	
1928	**Herbert C. Hoover**	Republican	58.2	444	56.9
	Alfred E. Smith	Democratic	40.9	87	
1932	**Franklin D. Roosevelt**	Democratic	57.4	472	56.9
	Herbert C. Hoover	Republican	39.7	59	
1936	**Franklin D. Roosevelt**	Democratic	60.8	523	61.0
	Alfred M. Landon	Republican	36.5	8	
1940	**Franklin D. Roosevelt**	Democratic	54.8	449	62.5
	Wendell L. Willkie	Republican	44.8	82	
1944	**Franklin D. Roosevelt**	Democratic	53.5	432	55.9
	Thomas E. Dewey	Republican	46.0	99	
1948	**Harry S Truman**	Democratic	49.6	303	53.0
	Thomas E. Dewey	Republican	45.1	189	
1952	**Dwight D. Eisenhower**	Republican	55.1	442	63.3
	Adlai E. Stevenson	Democratic	44.4	89	
1956	**Dwight D. Eisenhower**	Republican	57.6	457	60.6
	Adlai E. Stevenson	Democratic	42.1	73	
1960	**John F. Kennedy**	Democratic	49.7	303	64.0
	Richard M. Nixon	Republican	49.5	219	
1964	**Lyndon B. Johnson**	Democratic	61.1	486	61.7
	Barry M. Goldwater	Republican	38.5	52	
1968	**Richard M. Nixon**	Republican	43.4	301	60.6
	Hubert H. Humphrey	Democratic	42.7	191	
	George C. Wallace	American Independent	13.5	46	
1972	**Richard M. Nixon**	Republican	60.7	520	55.5
	George S. McGovern	Democratic	37.5	17	
1976	**Jimmy Carter**	Democratic	50.1	297	54.3
	Gerald R. Ford	Republican	48.0	240	
1980	**Ronald W. Reagan**	Republican	50.7	489	53.0
	Jimmy Carter	Democratic	41.0	49	
	John B. Anderson	Independent	6.6	0	
1984	**Ronald W. Reagan**	Republican	58.4	525	52.9
	Walter F. Mondale	Democratic	41.6	13	
1988	**George H. W. Bush**	Republican	53.4	426	50.3
	Michael Dukakis	Democratic	45.6	111**	
1992	**Bill Clinton**	Democratic	43.7	370	55.1
	George H. W. Bush	Republican	38.0	168	
	H. Ross Perot	Independent	19.0	0	
1996	**Bill Clinton**	Democratic	49	379	49.0
	Robert J. Dole	Republican	41	159	
	H. Ross Perot	Reform	8	0	
2000	**George W. Bush**	Republican	47.8	271	51.3
	Albert Gore	Democratic	48.4	267	
	Ralph Nader	Green	0.4	0	
2004	**George W. Bush**	Republican	50.7	286	60.3
	John Kerry	Democratic	48.3	252	
	Ralph Nader	Independent	.38	0	

*Prior to 1824, most presidential electors were chosen by state legislators rather than by popular vote.
†Before the Twelfth Amendment was passed in 1804, the Electoral College voted for two presidential candidates; the runner-up became vice president.
‡Percentages below 2.5 have been omitted. Hence the percentage of popular vote might not total 100 percent.
**One Dukakis elector cast a vote for Lloyd Bentsen.

Supreme Court Justices

Name	Terms of Service	Appointed by	Name	Terms of Service	Appointed by
John Jay,* N.Y.	1789–1795	Washington	Samuel Blatchford, N.Y.	1882–1893	Arthur
James Wilson, Pa.	1789–1798	Washington	Lucius Q. C. Lamar, Miss.	1888–1893	Cleveland
John Rutledge, S.C.	1790–1791	Washington	**Melville W. Fuller**, Ill.	1888–1910	Cleveland
William Cushing, Mass.	1790–1810	Washington	David J. Brewer, Kan.	1890–1910	B. Harrison
John Blair, Va.	1790–1796	Washington	Henry B. Brown, Mich.	1891–1906	B. Harrison
James Iredell, N.C.	1790–1799	Washington	George Shiras Jr., Pa.	1892–1903	B. Harrison
Thomas Johnson, Md.	1792–1793	Washington	Howell E. Jackson, Tenn.	1893–1895	B. Harrison
William Paterson, N.J.	1793–1806	Washington	Edward D. White, La.	1894–1910	Cleveland
John Rutledge, S.C.	1795	Washington	Rufus W. Peckham, N.Y.	1896–1909	Cleveland
Samuel Chase, Md.	1796–1811	Washington	Joseph McKenna, Cal.	1898–1925	McKinley
Oliver Ellsworth, Conn.	1796–1800	Washington	Oliver W. Holmes, Mass.	1902–1932	T. Roosevelt
Bushrod Washington, Va.	1799–1829	J. Adams	William R. Day, Ohio	1903–1922	T. Roosevelt
Alfred Moore, N.C.	1800–1804	J. Adams	William H. Moody, Mass.	1906–1910	T. Roosevelt
John Marshall, Va.	1801–1835	J. Adams	Horace H. Lurton, Tenn.	1910–1914	Taft
William Johnson, S.C.	1804–1834	Jefferson	Charles E. Hughes, N.Y.	1910–1916	Taft
Brockholst Livingston, N.Y.	1807–1823	Jefferson	**Edward D. White**, La.	1910–1921	Taft
Thomas Todd, Ky.	1807–1826	Jefferson	Willis Van Devanter, Wy.	1911–1937	Taft
Gabriel Duvall, Md.	1811–1835	Madison	Joseph R. Lamar, Ga.	1911–1916	Taft
Joseph Story, Mass.	1812–1845	Madison	Mahlon Pitney, N.J.	1912–1922	Taft
Smith Thompson, N.Y.	1823–1843	Monroe	James C. McReynolds, Tenn.	1914–1941	Wilson
Robert Trimble, Ky.	1826–1828	J. Q. Adams	Louis D. Brandeis, Mass.	1916–1939	Wilson
John McLean, Ohio	1830–1861	Jackson	John H. Clarke, Ohio	1916–1922	Wilson
Henry Baldwin, Pa.	1830–1844	Jackson	**William H. Taft**, Conn.	1921–1930	Harding
James M. Wayne, Ga.	1835–1867	Jackson	George Sutherland, Utah	1922–1938	Harding
Roger B. Taney, Md.	1836–1864	Jackson	Pierce Butler, Minn.	1923–1939	Harding
Philip P. Barbour, Va.	1836–1841	Jackson	Edward T. Sanford, Tenn.	1923–1930	Harding
John Cartron, Tenn.	1837–1865	Van Buren	Harlan F. Stone, N.Y.	1925–1941	Coolidge
John McKinley, Ala.	1838–1852	Van Buren	**Charles E. Hughes**, N.Y.	1930–1941	Hoover
Peter V. Daniel, Va.	1842–1860	Van Buren	Owen J. Roberts, Pa.	1930–1945	Hoover
Samuel Nelson, N.Y.	1845–1872	Tyler	Benjamin N. Cardozo, N.Y.	1932–1938	Hoover
Levi Woodbury, N.H.	1845–1851	Polk	Hugo L. Black, Ala.	1937–1971	F. Roosevelt
Robert C. Grier, Pa.	1846–1870	Polk	Stanley F. Reed, Ky.	1938–1957	F. Roosevelt
Benjamin R. Curtis, Mass.	1851–1857	Fillmore	Felix Frankfurter, Mass.	1939–1962	F. Roosevelt
John A. Campbell, Ala.	1853–1861	Pierce	William O. Douglas, Conn.	1939–1975	F. Roosevelt
Nathan Clifford, Me.	1858–1881	Buchanan	Frank Murphy, Mich.	1940–1949	F. Roosevelt
Noah H. Swayne, Ohio	1862–1881	Lincoln	**Harlan F. Stone**, N.Y.	1941–1946	F. Roosevelt
Samuel F. Miller, Iowa	1862–1890	Lincoln	James R. Byrnes, S.C.	1941–1942	F. Roosevelt
David Davis, Ill.	1862–1877	Lincoln	Robert H. Jackson, N.Y.	1941–1954	F. Roosevelt
Stephen J. Field, Cal.	1863–1897	Lincoln	Wiley B. Rutledge, Iowa	1943–1949	F. Roosevelt
Salmon P. Chase, Ohio	1864–1873	Lincoln	Harold H. Burton, Ohio	1945–1958	Truman
William Strong, Pa.	1870–1880	Grant	**Frederick M. Vinson**, Ky.	1946–1953	Truman
Joseph P. Bradley, N.J.	1870–1892	Grant	Tom C. Clark, Texas	1949–1967	Truman
Ward Hunt, N.Y.	1873–1882	Grant	Sherman Minton, Ind.	1949–1956	Truman
Morrison R. Waite, Ohio	1874–1888	Grant	**Earl Warren**, Cal.	1953–1969	Eisenhower
John M. Harlan, Ky.	1877–1911	Hayes	John Marshall Harlan, N.Y.	1955–1971	Eisenhower
William B. Woods, Ga.	1881–1887	Hayes	William J. Brennan Jr., N.J.	1956–1990	Eisenhower
Stanley Matthews, Ohio	1881–1889	Garfield	Charles E. Whittaker, Mo.	1957–1962	Eisenhower
Horace Gray, Mass.	1882–1902	Arthur	Potter Stewart, Ohio	1958–1981	Eisenhower

Name	Terms of Service	Appointed by	Name	Terms of Service	Appointed by
Bryon R. White, Colo.	1962–1993	Kennedy	Antonin Scalia, Va.	1986–	Reagan
Arthur J. Goldberg, Ill.	1962–1965	Kennedy	Anthony M. Kennedy, Cal.	1988–	Reagan
Abe Fortas, Tenn.	1965–1969	Johnson	David H. Souter, N.H.	1990–	Bush, G. H. W.
Thurgood Marshall, Md.	1967–1991	Johnson	Clarence Thomas, Ga.	1991–	Bush, G. H. W.
Warren E. Burger, Minn.	1969–1986	Nixon	Ruth Bader Ginsburg, N.Y.	1993–	Clinton
Harry A. Blackmun, Minn.	1970–1994	Nixon	Stephen G. Breyer, Mass.	1994–	Clinton
Lewis F. Powell Jr., Va.	1971–1987	Nixon	**John G. Roberts, Jr.**, Md.	2005–	Bush, G. W.
William H. Rehnquist, Ill.	1971–1986	Nixon	Samuel A. Alito Jr., N.J.	2006–	Bush, G. W.
John Paul Stevens, Ill.	1975–	Ford			
Sandra Day O'Connor, Ariz.	1981–2006	Reagan			
William H. Rehnquist, Va.	1986–2005	Reagan			

*Chief Justices are printed in bold type.

The American People: a Demographic Survey

A Demographic Profile of the American People

	Life Expectancy from Birth		Average Age at First Marriage		Number of Children Under 5 (per 1,000 Women Aged 22–24)	Percentage of Persons in Paid Employment		Percentage of Paid Workers Who Are Women
Year	White	Black	Men	Women		Men	Women	
1820					1,295		6.2	7.3
1830					1,145		6.4	7.4
1840					1,085		8.4	9.6
1850					923		10.1	10.8
1860					929		9.7	10.2
1870					839		13.7	14.8
1880					822		14.7	15.2
1890			26.1	22.0	716	84.3	18.2	17.0
1900	47.6	33.0	25.9	21.9	688	85.7	20.0	18.1
1910	50.3	35.6	25.1	21.6	643	85.1	24.8	20.0
1920	54.9	45.3	24.6	21.2	604	84.6	22.7	20.4
1930	61.4	48.1	24.3	21.3	511	82.1	23.6	21.9
1940	64.2	53.1	24.3	21.5	429	79.1	25.8	24.6
1950	69.1	60.8	22.8	20.3	589	81.6	29.9	27.8
1960	70.6	63.6	22.8	20.3	737	80.4	35.7	32.3
1970	71.7	65.3	22.5	20.6	530	79.7	41.4	38.0
1980	74.4	68.1	24.7	22.0	440	77.4	51.5	42.6
1990	76.1	69.1	26.1	23.9	377	76.4	57.4	45.2
2000	77.6	71.7	26.7	25.1	365	74.8	58.9	46.3
2004	78.2	73.4	27.4	25.8		73.3	59.2	46.5

SOURCE: U.S. Bureau of the Census, *Historical Statistics of the United States, Colonial Times to 1970* (1975); *Statistical Abstract of the United States, 2001*; *Statistical Abstract of the United States, 2006*.

American Population

Year	Population	Percentage Increase	Year	Population	Percentage Increase
1610	350	—	1820	9,638,453	33.1
1620	2,300	557.1	1830	12,866,020	33.5
1630	4,600	100.0	1840	17,069,453	32.7
1640	26,600	478.3	1850	23,191,876	35.9
1650	50,400	90.8	1860	31,443,321	35.6
1660	75,100	49.0	1870	39,818,449	26.6
1670	111,900	49.0	1880	50,155,783	26.0
1680	151,500	35.4	1890	62,947,714	25.5
1690	210,400	38.9	1900	75,994,575	20.7
1700	250,900	19.2	1910	91,972,266	21.0
1710	331,700	32.2	1920	105,710,620	14.9
1720	466,200	40.5	1930	122,775,046	16.1
1730	629,400	35.0	1940	131,669,275	7.2
1740	905,600	43.9	1950	150,697,361	14.5
1750	1,170,800	29.3	1960	179,323,175	19.0
1760	1,593,600	36.1	1970	203,235,298	13.3
1770	2,148,100	34.8	1980	226,545,805	11.5
1780	2,780,400	29.4	1990	248,709,873	9.8
1790	3,929,214	41.3	2000	281,421,906	13.2
1800	5,308,483	35.1	2005	296,410,404	5.0
1810	7,239,881	36.4			

Note: These figures largely ignore the Native American population. Census takers never made any effort to count the Native American population that lived outside their reserved political areas and compiled only casual and incomplete enumerations of those living within their jurisdictions until 1890. In that year the federal government attempted a full count of the Indian population: The Census found 125,719 Indians in 1890, compared with only 12,543 in 1870 and 33,985 in 1880.

SOURCES: U.S. Bureau of the Census, *Historical Statistics of the United States, Colonial Times to 1970* (1975); *Statistical Abstract of the United States, 2001;* U.S. Bureau of the Census, Population Finder, http://factfinder.census.gov.

White/Nonwhite Population

Urban/Rural Population

The Ten Largest Cities by Population, 1700–2000

Year	Rank	City	Population	Year	Rank	City	Population
1700	1.	Boston	6,700	1930	1.	New York	6,930,446
	2.	New York	4,937*		2.	Chicago	3,376,438
	3.	Philadelphia	4,400†		3.	Philadelphia	1,950,961
1790	1.	Philadelphia	42,520		4.	Detroit	1,568,662
	2.	New York	33,131		5.	Los Angeles	1,238,048
	3.	Boston	18,038		6.	Cleveland	900,429
	4.	Charleston, S.C.	16,359		7.	St. Louis	821,960
	5.	Baltimore	13,503		8.	Baltimore	804,874
	6.	Salem, Mass.	7,921		9.	Boston	781,188
	7.	Newport, R.I.	6,716		10.	Pittsburgh	669,817
	8.	Providence, R.I.	6,380	1950	1.	New York	7,891,957
	9.	Marblehead, Mass.	5,661		2.	Chicago	3,620,962
	10.	Portsmouth, N.H.	4,720		3.	Philadelphia	2,071,605
1830	1.	New York	197,112		4.	Los Angeles	1,970,358
	2.	Philadelphia	161,410		5.	Detroit	1,849,568
	3.	Baltimore	80,620		6.	Baltimore	949,708
	4.	Boston	61,392		7.	Cleveland	914,808
	5.	Charleston, S.C.	30,289		8.	St. Louis	856,796
	6.	New Orleans	29,737		9.	Washington, D.C.	802,178
	7.	Cincinnati	24,831		10.	Boston	801,444
	8.	Albany, N.Y.	24,209	1970	1.	New York	7,895,563
	9.	Brooklyn, N.Y.	20,535		2.	Chicago	3,369,357
	10.	Washington, D.C.	18,826		3.	Los Angeles	2,811,801
1850	1.	New York	515,547		4.	Philadelphia	1,949,996
	2.	Philadelphia	340,045		5.	Detroit	1,514,063
	3.	Baltimore	169,054		6.	Houston	1,233,535
	4.	Boston	136,881		7.	Baltimore	905,787
	5.	New Orleans	116,375		8.	Dallas	844,401
	6.	Cincinnati	115,435		9.	Washington, D.C.	756,668
	7.	Brooklyn, N.Y.	96,838		10.	Cleveland	750,879
	8.	St. Louis	77,860	1990	1.	New York	7,322,564
	9.	Albany, N.Y.	50,763		2.	Los Angeles	3,485,398
	10.	Pittsburgh	46,601		3.	Chicago	2,783,726
1870	1.	New York	942,292		4.	Houston	1,630,553
	2.	Philadelphia	674,022		5.	Philadelphia	1,585,577
	3.	Brooklyn, N.Y.	419,921‡		6.	San Diego	1,110,549
	4.	St. Louis	310,864		7.	Detroit	1,027,974
	5.	Chicago	298,977		8.	Dallas	1,006,877
	6.	Baltimore	267,354		9.	Phoenix	983,403
	7.	Boston	250,526		10.	San Antonio	935,933
	8.	Cincinnati	216,239	2000	1.	New York	8,008,278
	9.	New Orleans	191,418		2.	Los Angeles	3,694,820
	10.	San Francisco	149,473		3.	Chicago	2,896,016
1910	1.	New York	4,766,883		4.	Houston	1,953,631
	2.	Chicago	2,185,283		5.	Philadelphia	1,517,550
	3.	Philadelphia	1,549,008		6.	Phoenix	1,321,045
	4.	St. Louis	687,029		7.	San Diego	1,223,400
	5.	Boston	670,585		8.	Dallas	1,188,580
	6.	Cleveland	560,663		9.	San Antonio	1,144,646
	7.	Baltimore	558,485		10.	Detroit	951,270
	8.	Pittsburgh	533,905				
	9.	Detroit	465,766				
	10.	Buffalo	423,715				

*Figure from a census taken in 1698.
†Philadelphia figures include suburbs.
‡Annexed to New York in 1898.
SOURCE: U.S. Census data.

Immigration by Decade

Year	Number	Percentage of Total Population	Year	Number	Percentage of Total Population
1821–1830	151,824	1.6	1921–1930	4,107,209	3.9
1831–1840	599,125	4.6	1931–1940	528,431	0.4
1841–1850	1,713,251	10.0	1941–1950	1,035,039	0.7
1851–1860	2,598,214	11.2	1951–1960	2,515,479	1.6
1861–1870	2,314,824	7.4	1961–1970	3,321,677	1.8
1871–1880	2,812,191	7.1	1971–1980	4,493,000	2.2
1881–1890	5,246,613	10.5	1981–1990	7,338,000	3.0
1891–1900	3,687,546	5.8	1991–2000	9,095,083	3.7
1901–1910	8,795,386	11.6	Total	32,433,918	
1911–1920	5,735,811	6.2			
Total	33,654,785		1821–2000 GRAND TOTAL	66,088,703	

SOURCES: U.S. Bureau of the Census, *Historical Statistics of the United States, Colonial Times to 1970* (1975), part 1, 105–106; *Statistical Abstract of the United States*, 2001.

Regional Origins

[Stacked bar chart showing number of immigrants per decade (in millions) from 1820 to 2000, broken down by region: African, Asian, Western Hemisphere[a], South and Central European[b], North and West European[c].]

[a] Canada and all countries in South America and Central America.
[b] Italy, Spain, Portugal, Greece, Germany (Austria included, 1938–1945), Poland, Czechoslovakia (since 1920), Yugoslavia (since 1920), Hungary (since 1861), Austria (since 1861, except 1938–1945), former USSR (excludes Asian USSR between 1931 and 1963), Latvia, Estonia, Lithuania, Finland, Romania, Bulgaria, Turkey (in Europe), and other European countries not classified elsewhere.
[c] Great Britain, Ireland, Norway, Sweden, Denmark, Iceland, Netherlands, Belgium, Luxembourg, Switzerland, France.

SOURCES: Stephan Thernstrom, ed., *Harvard Encyclopedia of American Ethnic Groups* (1980), 480; U.S. Bureau of the Census, *Statistical Abstract of the United States*, 1991; U.S. Immigration and Naturalization Service, *Statistical Yearbook*, 2000.

The Labor Force (Thousands of Workers)

Year	Agriculture	Mining	Manufacturing	Construction	Trade	Other	Total
1810	1,950	11	75	—	—	294	2,330
1840	3,570	32	500	290	350	918	5,660
1850	4,520	102	1,200	410	530	1,488	8,250
1860	5,880	176	1,530	520	890	2,114	11,110
1870	6,790	180	2,470	780	1,310	1,400	12,930
1880	8,920	280	3,290	900	1,930	2,070	17,390
1890	9,960	440	4,390	1,510	2,960	4,060	23,320
1900	11,680	637	5,895	1,665	3,970	5,223	29,070
1910	11,770	1,068	8,332	1,949	5,320	9,041	37,480
1920	10,790	1,180	11,190	1,233	5,845	11,372	41,610
1930	10,560	1,009	9,884	1,988	8,122	17,267	48,830
1940	9,575	925	11,309	1,876	9,328	23,277	56,290
1950	7,870	901	15,648	3,029	12,152	25,870	65,470
1960	5,970	709	17,145	3,640	14,051	32,545	74,060
1970	3,463	516	20,746	4,818	15,008	34,127	78,678
1980	3,364	979	21,942	6,215	20,191	46,612	99,303
1990	3,223	724	21,346	7,764	24,622	60,849	118,793
2000	2,464	475	19,644	9,931	15,763	88,260	136,891

SOURCES: U.S. Bureau of the Census, *Historical Statistics of the United States, Colonial Times to 1970* (1975), 139; *Statistical Abstract of the United States, 1998*, table 675; *Statistical Abstract of the United States, 2006.*

Changing Labor Patterns

SOURCES: U.S. Bureau of the Census, *Historical Statistics of the United States, Colonial Times to 1970* (1975), 139; *Statistical Abstract of the United States, 1998*, table 675.

Birth Rate, 1820–2000

Births per thousand Americans

- 1820: 55
- 1840: 52
- 1860: 44
- 1880: 40
- 1900: 32
- 1920: 28
- 1940: 19
- 1950: 24 (Baby Boom)
- 1980: 16
- 1990: 17
- 2000: 14.4

SOURCES: Data from U.S. Bureau of the Census, *Historical Statistics of the United States, Colonial Times to 1970* (1975); *Statistical Abstract of the United States, 2001*; *Vital Statistics of the United States, 2000*.

Death Rate, 1900–2000

Deaths per thousand Americans

- 1900: 17.2
- 1920: 13.0
- 1940: 10.8
- 1960: 9.5
- 1980: 8.8
- 1990: 8.6
- 2000: 8.5 (Projected)

SOURCES: Data from U.S. Bureau of the Census, *Historical Statistics of the United States, Colonial Times to 1970* (1975); *Statistical Abstract of the United States, 1998*; *National Vital Statistics Reports*, vol. 54, no. 16, April 19, 2006, table 1.

Life Expectancy (at birth), 1900–2000

Year	Women	Men
1900	48	46
1920	55	54
1940	65	61
1960	73	67
1980	77	70
1990	79	72
2000	79.5	74.1

SOURCES: Data from U.S. Bureau of the Census, *Historical Statistics of the United States, Colonial Times to 1970* (1975); *Statistical Abstract of the United States, 1998*; *United States Life Tables*, 2000 NVSR.

The Aging of the U.S. Population, 1850–2000

SOURCES: U.S. Bureau of the Census, *Historical Statistics of the United States, Colonial Times to 1970* (1975), 139; *Statistical Abstract of the United States, 2001*.

The American Government and Economy

The Growth of the Federal Government

	Employees (millions)		Receipts and Outlays ($ millions)	
Year	Civilian	Military	Receipts	Outlays
1900	0.23	0.12	567	521
1910	0.38	0.13	676	694
1920	0.65	0.34	6,649	6,358
1930	0.61	0.25	4,058	3,320
1940	1.04	0.45	6,900	9,600
1950	1.96	1.46	40,900	43,100
1960	2.38	2.47	92,500	92,200
1970	3.00	3.06	193,700	196,600
1980	2.99	2.05	517,112	590,920
1990	3.13	2.07	1,031,321	1,252,705
2000	2.88	1.38	2,025,200	1,788,800

SOURCES: *Statistical Profile of the United States, 1900–1980; Statistical Abstract of the United States, 2001.*

Gross Domestic Product, 1840–2000

Note: GDP values have not been adjusted for inflation or deflation. GDP is plotted here on a logarithmic scale.
SOURCES: *Statistical Abstract of the United States, 2001.*

GDP per Capita, 1840–2000

Note: GDP values have not been adjusted for inflation or deflation. GDP is plotted here on a logarithmic scale.

Main Sectors of the U.S. Economy: 1849, 1899, 1950, 1990, and 2001

1849
- Mining 1.4
- Construction 7.9
- Manufacturing 32.1
- Agriculture 59.3

1899
- Mining 4.6
- Construction 12.6
- Agriculture 33.3
- Manufacturing 49.3

1950
- Gas, electricity, sanitation 1.9
- Government 8.3
- Trade 18.0
- Services 8.5
- Communication 1.6
- Transportation 5.6
- Finance, real estate, insurance 10.7
- Mining 3.2
- Construction 4.4
- Manufacturing 29.5
- Agriculture 7.3

1990
- Gas, electricity, sanitation 3.3
- Government 10.5
- Trade 17.2
- Services 15.2
- Communication 2.6
- Transportation 3.7
- Finance, real estate, insurance 14.5
- Mining 3.0
- Construction 4.3
- Manufacturing 23.0
- Agriculture 2.3

2001
- Gas, electricity, sanitation 2.2
- Government 12.2
- Trade 15.9
- Services 21.4
- Communication 2.9
- Transportation 3.1
- Finance, real estate, insurance 19.8
- Mining 1.3
- Construction 4.6
- Manufacturing 15.3
- Agriculture 1.3

SOURCES: Data from U.S. Bureau of the Census, *Historical Statistics of the United States, Colonial Times to 1970* (1975); *Statistical Abstract of the United States, 1998*; U.S. Bureau of Economic Analysis, *Industry Accounts Data, 2001*.

Consumer Price Index

$100 in the year	1790 is equivalent to	$2,204 in 2005
	1800	1,605
	1810	1,640
	1820	1,720
	1830	2,185
	1840	2,330
	1850	2,580
Civil War Inflation	1860	2,425
	1870	1,540
	1880	1,970
$100 in the year	1890 is equivalent to	2,210 in 2005
	1900	2,400
World War I Inflation	1910	2,120
	1920	975
	1930	1,170
Post World War II Inflation	1940	1,400
	1950	810
	1960	660
	1970	500
	1980	240
$100 in the year	1990 is equivalent to	150 in 2005
	2000	115

This index provides a very rough guide to the purchasing power of $100 in various periods of American history. For example, in the early 1830s, day laborers earned about $1 a day or about $300 a year. This sum is the equivalent of about $6,555 a year in 2005 (3 × $2,185 = $6,555) or sixty percent of the gross income of a worker earing the federal government-designated minimum wage of $5.15 per hour.

SOURCE: Lawrece H. Officer and Samuel H. Williamson, "Purchasing Power of Money...1774–2005," MeasuringWorth.com, August 2006. www.measuringworth.com/calculators/ppowerus/

GLOSSARY

anarchism The advocacy of a stateless society achieved by revolutionary means. Feared for their views, anarchists became the scapegoats for the 1886 Haymarket Square bombing. (p. 543)

Anglo-Saxonism A theory widely held in the late nineteenth century that the English-speaking peoples were racially superior and, for that reason, justified in colonizing and dominating the peoples of less-developed areas of the world. Combined with Social Darwinism, Anglo-Saxonism fueled American expansionism in the late nineteenth century. (p. 647)

armistice A temporary cession of military hostilities. World War I ended when the armistice of November 1918 simply continued because both sides had lost their will to fight further. (p. 679)

Black Codes Laws passed by southern states after the Civil War denying ex-slaves the civil rights enjoyed by whites and intended to force blacks back to the plantations. (p. 459)

blacklist Procedure used by employers throughout the nineteenth century to label and identify workers affiliated with unions. In the 1950s, blacklists were utilized to exclude alleged Communists from jobs in government service, the motion picture business, and many industries and unions.(p. 322)

business cycle The periodic rise and decline of business activity characteristic of capitalist-run, market economies. A quest for profit stimulates a level of production that exceeds demand and prompts a decline in output. In the United States, major periods of expansion (1802–1818, 1824–1836, 1846–1856, 1865–1873, 1896–1914, and 1922–1928) were followed by either relatively short financial panics (1819–1822 and 1857–1860) or extended depressions (1837–1843, 1873–1896, and 1929–1939). Since 1945, government intervention (through tax cuts, increased spending, interest rate hikes, etc.) has moderated the swings of the business cycle. (p. 239)

capitalism A system of economic production based on the private ownership of property and the contractual exchange for profit of goods, labor, and money (capital). Although some elements of capitalism existed in the United States before 1820, a full-scale capitalist economy — and society — emerged only with the Market Revolution (1820–1850) and reached its pinnacle during the final decades fo the century. *See* Market Revolution. (p. 520)

carpetbaggers A derisive name given by Southerners to Northerners who moved to the South during Reconstruction. Former Confederates despised these Northerners as transient exploiters. Carpetbaggers actually were a varied group, including Union veterans who had served in the South, reformers eager to help the ex-slaves, and others looking for business opportunities. (p. 470)

classical liberalism The political ideology, dominant in England and the United States during the nineteenth century, that celebrated individual liberty, private property, a competitive merket economy, free trade, and limited government. In the late twentieth-century United States, many economic conservatives embrace, the principles of classical liberalism (and oppose, the principles of social welfare liberalism). (p. 738)

closed shop Workplace in which a job seeker had to be a union member to gain employment. In the nineteenth century, the closed shop was favored by craft unions as a method of keeping out incompetent and lower-wage workers and of strengthening the unions' bargaining position with employers. (p. 540)

collective bargaining A process of negotiation between labor unions and employers, particularly favored by the American Federation of Labor (AFL). Led by Samuel Gompers, the AFL accepted the new industrial order, but fought for a bigger share of the profits for the workers. (p. 540)

common law Centuries-old body of English law based on custom and judicial interpretation, not legislation, and evolving case by case on the basis of precedent. The common law was transmitted to America along with English settlement and became the foundation of American law at the state and local levels. In the United States, even more than in Britain, the common law gave the courts supremacy over the legislatures in many areas of law. (p. 622)

conservationist Advocacy for the protection of the natural environment for sustained use. As applied by Theodore Roosevelt at the start of the twentieth century, conservation accepted development of public lands, provided this was in the public interest and not wastefully destructive. In contrast, preservationists valued wilderness in its natural state and were more broadly opposed to development. (p. 629)

cultural pluralism A term coined in 1924 that posits that diversity, especially religious and ethnic diversity, can be a source of strength in a democratic nation and that cultural differences should be respected and valued. (p. 755)

deficit spending High government spending in excess of tax revenues based on the ideas of British economist John Maynard Keynes, who proposed in the 1930s that governments should be prepared to go into debt to stimulate a stagnant economy. (p. 748)

deflation The sustained decline of prices, generally accompanying an economic depression, but in the United States after the Civil War, the result of rapidly rising productivity, market competition, and a tight money supply. (p. 604)

deregulation Process of removing or limiting federal regulatory mechanisms, justified on the basis of promoting competition and streamlining government bureaucracy. President Carter began deregulation in the 1970s, starting with the airline, banking, and communications industries. The process continued under subsequent administrations. (p. 918)

détente From the French word for "a relaxation of tension," this term was used to signify the new foreign policy of President Nixon, which sought a reduction of tension and hostility between the United States and the Soviet Union and China in the early 1970s. (p. 898)

direct primary The selection of party candidates by a popular vote rather than by the party convention, this progressive reform was especially pressed by Robert La Follette, who viewed it as an instrument for breaking the grip of machines on the political parties. In the South, where it was limited to whites, the primary was a means of disfranchising blacks. (p. 624)

dollar diplomacy Policy adopted by President Taft emphasizing the connection between America's economic and political interests overseas. The benefits would flow in both directions. Business would gain from diplomatic efforts in its behalf, while the strengthened American economic presence overseas would give added leverage to American diplomacy. (p. 664)

domino theory An American Cold War concept associated with the containment policy that posited that in areas of East-West conflict, the loss of one country to communism would lead to the toppling of other non-communist regimes. The term was first used by President Eisenhower, who warned of "falling dominos" in Southeast Asia if Vietnam became Communist. (p. 825)

entitlement programs Government programs that provide financial benefits to which recipients are entitled by law. Examples include Social Security, Medicare, unemployment compensation, and agricultural price supports. (p. 896)

ethnocultural Refers to the distinctive social characteristics of immigrants and religious groups, especially in determining their party loyalties and stance on political issues touching personal behavior and public morality. (p. 590)

feminism, feminist Doctrine advanced in the early twentieth century by women activists that women should be equal to men in all areas of life. Earlier women activists and suffragists had accepted the notion of separate spheres for men and women, but feminists sought to overcome all barriers to equality and full personal development. (p. 617)

fiscal policy The range of decisions involving the finances of the federal government. These decisions include how much to tax, how much to spend, and what level of resulting deficit or surplus is acceptable. Such decisions—fiscal policy—have a big effect on a nation's allocation of economic resources, the distribution of income, and the level of economic activity. (p. 864)

Fourteen Points President Wilson proposed these principles as a basis for peace negotiations at Versailles in 1919. Included in the points were open diplomacy, freedom of the seas, free trade, territorial integrity, arms reduction, national self-determination, and establishment of the League of Nations. (p. 694)

fundamentalism, fundamentalist Any religious movement that adopts a "pure" and rigid belief system. In the United States, it usually refers to evangelical Protestants who interpret the Bible literally. In the 1920s, fundamentalists opposed modernist Protestants, who tried to reconcile Christianity with Darwin's theory of evolution by natural selection and other scientific discoveries. Fundamentalists' promotion of anti-evolution laws for public schools led to the famous Scopes trial of 1925; in recent decades, fundamentalists have strongly supported legislation to prohibit abortions and gay marriages. (p. 721)

gang-labor system A system of work discipline used on southern cotton plantations in the mid-nineteenth century. White overseers or black drivers constantly supervised gangs of enslaved laborers to enforce work norms and secure greater productivity. (p. 464)

general strike A strike that draws in all the workers in a society, with the intention of shutting down the entire system. Radical groups like the Industrial Workers of the World (IWW), in the early twentieth century, saw the general strike as the means for initiating a social revolution. (p. 546)

gerrymander The political strategy (named after the early nineteenth-century politician Elbridge Gerry) of changing the boundaries of voting districts to give the dominant party an advantage. (p. 596)

ghetto Term describing an urban neighborhood composed of the poor, and occasionally used to describe any tight-knit community containing a single ethnic or class group. Ghettos came into being in the nineteenth century, in tandem with the enormous influx of immigrants to American cities. (p. 566)

Great American Desert The name given to the drought-stricken Great Plains by Euro-Americans in the early nineteenth century. Believing the region was unfit for cultivation or agriculture, Congress designated the Great Plains as permanent Indian country in 1834. (p. 488)

greenbacks Paper money issued by the U.S. Treasury during the Civil War to finance the war effort. Greenbacks had the status of legal tender in all public and private transactions. Because they were issued in large amounts and were not backed by gold or silver, the value of a greenback dollar fell during the war to 40 cents (but much less than the notes issued during the Revolutionary War, which became virtually worthless) and recovered only as the Union government won the war and proceeded to reduce its war-related debt. (p. 604)

habeas corpus Latin for "bring forth the body," a legal writ forcing government authorities ot justify their arrest and detention of an individual, Rooted in English common law, habeas corpus was given the status of a formal privilege in the U.S. Constitution (Article 1, Section 9), which also allows its suspension in cases of invasion or in-surrection, During the Civil War, Lincoln suspended habeas corpus to stop protests against the draft and other anti-Union activities. The USA PATRIOT Act (2001) likewise suspends this privilege in cases of suspected terrorism, but the constitutional legitimacy of this and other provisions of the act have yet to be decided by the courts. (p. 1012)

home rule A rallying cry used by southern Democrats painting Reconstruction governments as illegitimate—imposed on the South—and themselves as the only party capable of restoring the South to "home rule." By 1876, northern Republicans were inclined to accept this claim. (p. 480)

ideology A systematic philosophy or political theory that purports to explain the character of the social world or to prescribe a set of values or beliefs. (p. 587)

impeachment First step in the constitutional process for removing the president from office, in which charges of wrongdoing (articles of impeachment) are passed by the House of Representatives. A trial is then conducted by the Senate to determine whether the impeached president is guilty of the charges. (p. 468)

indenture, indentured servants A seventeenth-century labor contract that required service for a period of time in return for passage to North America. Indentures were typically for a term of four or five years, provided room and board in exchange for labor, and granted free status at the end of the contract period. (p. 511)

industrial union A group of workers in a single industry (for example, automobile, railroad, or mining) organized into a single association, regardless of skill, rather than into separate craft-based associations. The American Railway Union, formed in the 1880s, was one of the first industrial unions in the nation. (p. 544)

isolationism, isolationist A foreign-policy stance supporting the withdrawal of the United States from involvement with other nations, especially an avoidance of entangling diplomatic relations. The common view of post–World War I U.S. foreign policy is that it was isolationist, but in fact the United States played an active role in world affairs, particularly in trade and finance. (p. 712)

Jim Crow A term first heard in antebellum minstrel shows to designate black behavior and used in the age of segregation to designate facilities restricted to blacks, such as Jim Crow railway cars. (p. 598)

jingoism This term came to refer to the super-patriotism that took hold in the mid-1890s during the American dispute with Spain over Cuba. Jingoes were enthusiastic about a military solution as a way of showing the nation's mettle and, when diplomacy failed, they got their wish with the Spanish-American War of 1898. (p. 648)

Keynesian economics The theory, developed by British economist John Maynard Keynes in the 1930s, that purposeful government intention into the economy (through lowering or raising taxes, interest rates, and government spending) can affect the level of overall economic activity and thereby prevent severe depressions and runaway inflation. (p. 748)

laissez-faire The doctrine, based on economic theory, that government should not interfere in business or the economy. Laissez-faire ideas guided American government policy in the late nineteenth century and conservative politics in the twentieth. Business interests that supported laissez-faire in the late nineteenth century accepted government interference when it took the form of tariffs or subsidies that worked to their benefit. Broader uses of the term refer to the simple philosophy of abstaining from all government interference. (p. 587)

liberal, liberalism The ideology of individual rights and private property outlined by John Locke (circa 1690) and embodied in many American constitutions, bills of rights, and institutions of government. *See also* classical liberalism *and* social welfare liberalism. (p. 479)

liberal consensus Refers to widespread agreement among Americans in the decades after World War II that the pro-government policies of the New Deal were desirable and should be continued. In politics, the liberal consensus was reflected in the relatively small differences on economic and social policies between Republicans and Democrats until the advent of Ronald Reagan. (p. 819)

lien (crop lien) A legal device enabling a creditor to take possession of the property of a borrower, including the right to have it sold in payment of the debt. Furnishing merchants took such liens on cotton crops as collateral for supplies advanced to sharecroppers during the growing season. This system trapped farmers in a cycle of debt and made them vulnerable to exploitation by the furnishing merchant. (p. 474)

literacy test The requirement that an ability to read be demonstrated as a qualification for the right to vote. It was a device easily used by registrars to prevent blacks from voting, whether they could read or not, and was widely adopted across the South beginning with Mississippi in 1890. (p. 594)

machine tools Cutting, boring, and drilling machines used to produce standardized metal parts that were assembled into products like sewing machines. The development of machine tools by American inventors in the early nineteenth century facilitated the rapid spread of the Industrial Revolution. (p. 528)

mass production A system of factory production that often combines sophisticated machinery, a disciplined labor force, and assembly lines to turn out vast quantities of identical goods at low cost. In the nineteenth century, the textile and meatpacking industries pioneered mass production, which eventually became the standard mode for making consumer goods from cigarettes to automobiles, to telephones, radios, televisions, and computers. (p. 538)

military-industrial complex A term first used by President Eisenhower in his farewell address in 1961, it refers to the interlinkage of the military and the defense industry that emerged with the arms buildup of the Cold War. Eisenhower particularly warned against the "unwarranted influence" that the military-industrial complex might exert on public policy. (p. 827)

muckrakers Journalists in the early twentieth century whose stock-in-trade was exposure of the corruption of big business and government. Theodore Roosevelt gave them the name as a term of reproach. The term comes from a character in *Pilgrim's Progress*, a religious allegory by John Bunyan. (p. 614)

national debt The financial obligations of the U.S. government for money borrowed from its citizens and foreign investors. Alexander Hamilton wanted wealthy American to invest in the national debt so that they would support the new national government. In recent decades, that same thinking has led the United States to encourage individuals and institutions in crucial foreign nations—Saudi Arabia and Japan, for example—to invest billions of dollars in the American national debt. (p. 774)

national self-determination This concept holds that nations have the right to be sovereign states with political and economic autonomy. A central component of Woodrow Wilson's Fourteen Points for a World War I peace treaty, this concept challenged the existing colonial empires. The right of national self-determination continues to be invoked by nationalist, usually ethnic, groups, such as the Basques in Spain, the Kurds in Turkey and Iraq, and the Palestinians in Israel. (p. 695)

nationalize, nationalization Government seizure and ownership of a business or natural resource. In the 1890s the Populist Party demanded nationalization of American railroads; in the 1950s the seizure by Cuba of American-owned sugar plantations and gambling casinos sparked a long-lasting diplomatic conflict. (p. 712)

nativist, nativism Antiforeign sentiment in the United States that fueled drives against the immigration of Irish and Germans in the 1840s and 1850s, the Chinese and Japanese in the 1880s and 1890s, migrants from eastern and southern Europe in the 1910s and 1920s, and Mexicans in the 1990s and 2000s. Nativism prompted the Chinese Exclusion Act of 1882, the Immigration Restriction Act of 1924, and the interment of Japanese Americans during World War II. (p. 718)

oligopoly In economics, the situation in which a given industry (steel making, automobile manufacturing) is dominated by a small number of large-scale companies. (p. 709)

patronage The power of elected officials to grant government jobs. Beginning in the early nineteenth century, politicians systematically used—and abused—patronage to create and maintain strong party loyalties. After 1870, political reformers gradually introduced merit-based civil service systems in the federal and state governments. (p. 584)

peonage (debt peonage) As cotton prices declined during the 1870s, many sharecroppers fell into permanent debt. Merchants often conspired with landowners to make the debt a pretext for forced labor, or peonage. (p. 474)

pocket veto Presidential way to kill a piece of legislation without issuing a formal veto. When congressional Republicans passed the Wade-Davis Bill in 1864, a harsher alternative to President Lincoln's restoration plan, Lincoln used this method to kill it by simply not signing the bill and letting it expire after Congress adjourned. (p. 458)

political machines Nineteenth-century term for highly organized groups operating within and intending to control political parties. Machines were regarded as antidemocratic by political reformers and were the target especially of Progressive era leaders such as Robert La Follette. The direct primary was the factored antimachine instrument because it made the selection of party candidates the product of a popular ballot rather than conventions that were susceptible to machine control. (p. 569)

poll taxes A tax paid for the privilege of voting, used in the South beginning during Reconstruction to disfranchise freedmen. Nationally, the northern states used poll taxes to keep immigrants and others deemed unworthy from the polls. (p. 469)

pragmatism Philosophical doctrine developed primarily by William James that denied the existence of absolute truths and argued that ideas should be judged by their practical consequences. Problem solving, not ultimate ends, was the proper concern of philosophy, in James's view. Pragmatism provided a key intellectual foundation for progressivism. (p. 613)

preservationist, preservation Early-twentieth-century activists, like John Muir, who fought to protect the natural environment from commercial exploitation, particularly in the American West. (p. 629)

Prohibition Law dictated by the Eighteenth Amendment of the Constitution that banned the manufacture and sale of alcoholic beverages. Prohibition took effect in January of 1920, but public resistance was intense. "Speakeasies" (illegal saloons) sprang up around the country and bootleggers (illegal providers) supplied alcoholic beverages smuggled from Canada and Mexico. Organized crime invested heavily in bootlegging and gang-war slayings generated much publicity. Public pressure led to the repeal of prohibition by the Twenty-First Amendment in 1933. (p. 688)

pump priming Term first used during the Great Depression of the 1930s to describe the practice of increased government spending in the hope that it would generate additional economic activity throughout the system. It is the beginning of a process that is supposed to lead to significant economic recovery. (p. 730)

residual powers The constitutional principle that powers not explicitly granted to the federal government belong to the states. (p. 588)

restrictive covenants Limiting clauses in real estate transactions intended to prevent the sale or rental of properties to classes of the population considered "undesirable," such as African Americans, Jews, or Asians. Such clauses were declared unenforcable by the Supreme Court decision in *Shelley v. Kraemer* (1948), but continued to be instituted informally in spite of the ruling. (p. 838)

rural ideal Concept advanced by the landscape architect Andrew Jackson Downing urging the benefits of rural life, it was especially influential among middle-class Americans making their livings in cities but attracted to the suburbs. (p. 557)

scalawags Southern whites who joined the Republicans during Reconstruction and were ridiculed by ex-Confederates as worthless traitors. They included ex-Whigs and yeomen farmers who had not supported the Confederacy and who believed that an alliance with the Republicans was the best way to attract northern capital and rebuild the South. (p. 470)

scientific management A system of organizing work, developed by Frederick W. Taylor in the late nineteenth century, designed to get the maximum output from the individual worker and reduce the cost of production, using methods such as the time-and-motion study to determine how factory work should be organized. The system was never applied in its totality in any industry, but it contributed to the rise of the "efficiency expert" and the field of industrial psychology. (p. 538)

secondary boycott (secondary labor boycott) Technique used by unions in labor disputes to exert pressure on an employer involved in the dispute by targeting other parties not involved but having a relationship to the employer, for example, as a supplier or as a customer. A secondary labor boycott was used in the Great Pullman Boycott of 1894 and failed when the government intervened. (p.544)

secret ballot Before 1890, most Americans voted in "public." That is, voters either announced their vote to a clerk or handed in a ballot that had been printed by—and so was recognizable as the work of—a political party. Voting in "private" or in "secret" was first used on a wide scale in Australia. When the practice was adopted in the United States, it was known as the Australian ballot. (p. 594)

self-made man The nineteenth-century ideal that celebrated men who rose to wealth or social prominence from humble origins through self-discipline, hard work, and temperate habits. (p. 289)

separation of powers The constitutional arrangement that gives the three governmental branches—executive, legislative, and judicial—independent standing, thereby diffusing the federal government's overall power and reducing the chances that it might turn tyrannical and threaten the liberties of the people. (p. 458)

severalty Individual ownership of land. The term applied to the Dawes Severalty Act of 1890, which undertook to end tribal ownership and grant Indians deeds to individual holdings, i.e., severalty. (p. 503)

sharecropping The labor system by which freedmen agreed to exchange a portion of their harvested crops with the landowner for use of the land, a house, and tools. A compromise between freedmen and white landowners, this system developed in the cash-strapped South because the freedmen wanted to work their own land but lacked the money to buy it, while white landowners needed agricultural laborers but did not have money to pay wages. (p. 473)

Social Darwinism The application of Charles Darwin's biological theory of evolution by natural selection to the development of society, this late-nineteenth-century principle encouraged the notion that societies progress as a result of competition and the "survival of the fittest." Intervention by the state in this process was counterproductive because it impeded healthy progress. Social Darwinists justified the increasing inequality of late-nineteenth-century, industrial American society as natural. (p. 588)

"social welfare" liberalism The liberal ideology implemented in the United States during the New Deal of the 1930s and the Great Society of the 1960s. It uses the financial and bureaucratic resources of the state and federal governments to provide economic and social security to individual citizens, interest groups, and corporate enterprises. Social welfare programs include old age pensions, unemployment compensation, subsidies to farmers, mortgage guarantees, and tax breaks for corporations. (p. 738)

spoils system The widespread award of public jobs to political supporters following an electoral victory. Underlying this practice was the view that in a democracy rotation in office was preferable to a permanent class of officeholders. In 1829 Andrew Jackson began this practice on the national level, and it became a central, and corrupting, feature of American political life. (p. 584)

states' rights An interpretation of the Constitution that exalts the sovereignty of the states and circumscribes the authority of the national government. Expressed first by Antifederalists in the debate over the Constitution, and then in the Virginia and Kentucky resolutions of 1798, the ideology of states' rights became especially important in the South. It informed white southerners' resistance to the high tariffs of the 1820s and 1830s, to legislation to limit the spread of slavery, and to attempts by the national government in the mid-twentieth century to end Jim Crow practices. (p. 585)

subtreasury system A scheme deriving from the Texas Exchange, a cooperative in the 1880s, through which cotton farmers received cheap loans and marketed their crops. When the Texas Exchange failed in 1891, Populists proposed that the federal government take over these functions on a national basis through a "subtreasury," which would have the added benefit of increasing the stock of money in the country and thus push up prices. (p. 602)

suburbanization The movement of the upper and middle classes beyond city limits to less crowded areas with larger homes that are connected to city centers by streetcar or subway lines. By 1910, 25 percent of the population lived in these new communities. The 1990 census revealed that the majority of Americans lived in the suburbs. (p. 560)

suffrage The right to vote. In the early national period suffrage was limited by property restrictions. Gradually state constitutions gave the vote to all white men over the age of twenty-one. Over the course of American history, suffrage has expanded as barriers of race, gender, and age have fallen. In the late nineteenth and early twentieth centuries, women activists on behalf of the vote were known as "suffragists." (p. 466)

syndicalism A revolutionary movement that, like socialism, believed in the Marxist principle of class struggle and advocated the organization of society on the basis of industrial unionism. This approach was advocated by the Industrial Workers of the World (IWW) at the start of the twentieth century. (p. 546)

tariff A tax on imports, which has two purposes: raising revenue for the government and protecting domestic products from foreign competition. A hot political issue throughout much of American history, in the late nineteenth century the tariff became particularly controversial as protection-minded Republicans and pro-free-trade Democrats made the tariff the centerpiece of their political campaigns. (p. 585)

temperance, temperance movement A long-term series of activities by reform organizations to encourage individuals and governments to limit the consumption of alcoholic beverages. Leading temperance groups include the American Temperance Society of the 1830s, the Washingtonian Association of the 1840s, the Women's Christian Temperance Union of the late nineteenth century, and Alcoholics Anonymous, which was founded in the 1930s. (p. 692)

Third World This term came into use in the post-World War II era to describe developing or ex-colonial nations that were not aligned with either the Western capitalist countries led by the United States or the socialist states of eastern Europe led by the Soviet Union. It referred to developing countries in Asia, Africa, Latin America, and the Middle East. (p. 822)

trusts A term originally applied to a specific form of business organization enabling participating firms to assign the operation of their properties to a board of trustees, but by the early twentieth century, the term applied more generally to corporate mergers and business combinations that exerted monopoly power over an industry. It was in this latter sense that progressives referred to firms like United States Steel and Standard Oil as trusts. (p. 627)

union shop The requirement that, after gaining employment, a worker must join a union, as distinct from the closed shop, which requires union membership *before* gaining employment. (p. 814)

vaudeville A professional stage show composed of singing, dancing, and comedy routines that changed live entertainment from its seedier predecessors like minstrel shows to family entertainment for the urban masses. Vaudeville became popular in the 1880s and 1890s, the years just before the introduction of movies. (p. 574)

voluntarism The view that citizens should themselves improve their lives, rather than rely on the efforts of state. Especially favored by Samuel Gompers, voluntarism was a key idea within the labor movement, but one gradually abandoned in the course of the twentieth century. (p. 622)

war of attrition A military strategy of small-scale attacks used, usually by the weaker side, to sap the resources and morale of the stronger side. Examples include the attacks carried out by Patriot militias in the South during the War of Independence, and the guerrilla tactics of the Vietcong and North Vietnamese during the Vietnam War. (p. 679)

welfare capitalism A system of labor relations that stresses management's responsibility for employees' well-being. Originating in the 1920s, welfare capitalism offered such benefits as stock plans, health care, and old-age pensions and was designed to maintain a stable workforce and undercut the growth of trade unions. (p. 710)

welfare state A nation that provides for the basic needs of its citizens, including such provisions as old-age pensions, unemployment compensation, child-care facilities, education, and other social programs. Major European countries began to provide such programs around 1900; the New Deal of the 1930s brought them to the United States. In the early twenty-first century, aging populations and the emergence of a global economy (the transfer of jobs to low-wage countries) threatens the economic foundation of the European and American welfare systems. (p. 615)

white-collar Middle-class professionals who are salaried workers as opposed to business owners or wage laborers; they first appeared in large numbers during the industrial expansion in the late nineteenth century. Their ranks were composed of lawyers, engineers, and chemists, as well as salesmen, accountants, and advertising managers. (p. 529)

yellow-dog contract An agreement by a worker, as a condition of employment, not to join a union. Employers in the late nineteenth century used this along with the blacklist and violent strikebreaking to fight unionization of their workforces. (p. 543)

yellow journalism Term that refers to newspapers that specialize in sensationalistic reporting. The name came from the ink used in Hearst's *New York Journal* to print the first comic strip to appear in color in 1895 and is generally associated with the inflammatory reporting leading up to the Spanish-American War of 1898. (p. 577)

CREDITS

Chapter 15
Voices from Abroad: David Macrae. "The Devasted South." From *America Through British Eyes*, edited by Allan Nevins. Copyright © 1968 by Allan Nevins. Reprinted by permission of Peter Smith Publisher, Gloucester, MA.

Comparing American Voices: Edward Barnell Heyward. From *Looking for America* Second Edition, Volume 1, by Stanley I. Kutler, editor. Copyright © 1979, 1976 by Stanley I. Kutler. Used by permission of W.W. Norton & Company, Inc.

Comparing American Voices: Jordan Anderson. From *Looking for America*, Second Edition, Volume 1 by Stanley I. Kutler, editor. Copyright © 1979, 1976 by Stanley I. Kutler. Used by W. W. Norton & Company, Inc.

Chapter 16
Voices from Abroad: Baron Joseph Alexander von Hubner. "A Western Boom Town." From *This Was America*, edited by Oscar Handlin. Copyright © 1949 by Harvard University Press. © 1960 by Oscar Handlin. Reprinted with the permission of the author.

Chapter 17
Voices From Abroad: Count Vay de Vaya und Luskod. "Pittsburgh Inferno" From *This Was America* edited by Oscar Handlin. Copyright © 1949 by Harvard University Press. © 1960 by Oscar Handlin. Reprinted with the permission of the author.

Comparing American Voices: "Wives in the Mills: A Debate." From *We Will Rise in Our Might: Workingwomen's Voices from Nineteenth-Century New England* by Mary H. Blewett. Copyright © 1991 by Cornell University. Used by permission of the publisher, Cornell University Press.

Chapter 18
Voices From Abroad: José Marti. Coney Island, 1881. From *The America of José Marti: Selected Writings by José Marti*, and translated by Juan de Onis. Copyright © 1954 by Joan de Onis. Published by Noonday Press. Reprinted with permission.

Chapter 19
Voices from Abroad: Ernst Below: "Beer and German-American Politics." From *This Was America*, edited by Oscar Handlin. Copyright © 1949 by Harvard University Press. © 1960 by Oscar Handlin. Reprinted with the permission of the author.

Comparing American Voices: Tom Watson. "Speech of the Honorable Thomas E. Watson, 1904." From Thomas E. Watson Papers #752. Southern Historical Collection, Wilson Library, University of North Carolina at Chapel Hill. Reprinted with permission.

Chapter 20
Comparing American Voices: William G. Shepard, Reporter. From *Out of the Sweatshop*, edited by Leon Stein. Copyright © 1977 by Leon Stein. Reprinted with permission.

Comparing American Voices: Stephen S. Wise, Rabbi. From *Out of the Sweatshop*, edited by Leon Stein. Copyright © 1977 by Leon Stein. Reprinted with permission.

Comparing American Voices: Rose Schneiderman, Trade Unionist. From *Out of the Sweatshop* edited by Leon Stein. Copyright © 1977 by Leon Stein. Reprinted with permission.

Comparing American Voices: Max D. Steuer, Lawyer. From *Out of the Sweatshop*, edited by Leon Stein. Copyright © 1977 by Leon Stein. Reprinted with permission.

Voices From Abroad: James Bryce, America in 1905: "Business is King." From *America Through British Eyes*, edited by Allan Nevins. Copyright 1968 by Allan Nevins. Reprinted by permission of Peter Smith, Publisher, Gloucester, MA.

Fig. 20.1. "The Federal Bureaucracy, 1890–1917." From p. 41 in *The Federal Government Service*, edited by W.S. Sayre. The American Assembly, Prentice-Hall, Englewood Cliffs, NJ.

Chapter 21
Voices from Abroad: Robin Dario. "To Roosevelt." From *Selected Poems of Ruben Dario by Ruben Dario*. Translated by Lysander Kemp. Copyright © 1965, renewed 1993. By permission of the University of Texas Press.

Chapter 23
Comparing American Voices: John Roach Straton. From "The Most Sinister Movement in the United States," in *American Fundamentalist* 26, December 1925: 8–9. Reprinted in *Preachers, Pedagogues, and Politicians: The Evolution Controversy in North Carolina* by Willard B. Gatewood, Jr. Copyright © 1966 by the University of North Carolina at Chapel Hill. Used by permission of the publisher.

Voices from Abroad: Mary Agnes Hamilton. "Breadlines and Beggers." From *America Through British Eyes*, edited by Allan Nevins. Copyright © 1968 by Allan Nevins. Reprinted with permission of Peter Smith, publisher, Gloucester, MA.

Chapter 24
Voices From Abroad: Odette Keun. "A Foreigner Looks at the Tennessee Valley Authority." From *This Was America*, edited by Oscar Handlin. Copyright © 1949 by Harvard University Press. © 1960 by Oscar Handlin. Reprinted with the permission of the author.

Chapter 25

Comparing American Voices: Evelyn Gotzion. From *Women Remember the War 1941–1945*, by Michael E. Stevens and Ellen D. Goldlust, editors. Copyright © 1993 by Michael E. Stevens and Ellen D. Goldlust. Reprinted with the permission of the Wisconsin Historical Society.

Comparing American Voices: Fanny Christina Hill. Excerpted from interview on pp. 37–42 in *Rosie the Riveter Revisited* by Sherna Berger Gluck. Copyright © 1987 by Sherna B. Gluck. Reprinted with permission of the author.

Comparing American Voices: Peggy Terry. Excerpt from *The Good War* by Studs Terkel. Copyright 1984 by Studs Terkel. Reprinted by permission of Donadio & Olson, Inc.

Voices from Abroad: Monica Itoi Sone. "Japanese Relocation." From *Nisei Daughter* by Monica Sone. Copyright © 1953 by Monica Sone. Copyright © renewed 1981 by Monica Sone. By permission of Little, Brown, and Company, Inc.

Chapter 26

Voices from Abroad: Jean Monnet: Truman's Generous Proposal. Excerpt from *Memoirs* by Jean Monnet, translated by Richard Mayne. Translation copyright © 1978 by Doubleday, a division of Bantam, Doubleday Dell, a division of Random House, Inc.

Comparing American Voices: Fulton Lewis, Jr's Radio Address, January 13, 1949. Manuscript Sept CB# 3926 Frank Porter Graham Papers #1819. Manuscript CB #3926 Wilson Library. Southern Historical Collection, University of North Carolina at Chapel Hill. Reprinted with permission.

Comparing American Voices: Frank Porter Graham's Telegram to Fulton Lewis Jr, January 13, 1949. Frank Porter Graham Papers #1819. Manuscript #3926 Wilson Library. Southern Historical Collection, Southern Historical Collection, Wilson Library, University of North Carolina at Chapel Hill. Reprinted with permission.

Comparing American Voices: House Un-American Activities Committee Report on Frank Graham. Frank Porter Graham Papers #1819. Manuscript Sept CB#3926 Wilson Library, University at Chapel Hill. Reprinted with permission.

Chapter 27

Voices from Abroad: Hanoch Bartov. "Everyone Has a Car." From *Arbaah Isrealim Vekhol America (Four Israelis and the Whole of America)* by Hanoch Bartov. Copyright © Hanoch Bartov, Acum House, Israel. Reprinted by permission of the author and Acum House.

Comparing American Voices: Franklin McCain. "Desegrating Lunch Counters." From *My Soul Is Rested: Movement Days in the Deep South Remembered*, by Howell Raines. Copyright © 1977 by Howell Raines. Originally published by Penguin Putnam, 1977. Reprinted with permission of PFD, Inc.

Comparing American Voices: John McFerren: "Demanding the Right to Vote." From *Looking for America*, Second Edition, Volume 1 by Stanley I. Kutler, editor. Copyright © 1979, 1976 by Stanley I. Kutler. Used by permission of W.W. Norton & Company, Inc.

Chapter 28

Comparing America Voices: James R. Wilson. Excerpts from *Landing Zones: Southern Veterans Remember Vietnam* by James R. Wilson. Copyright © 1990 Duke University Press. All rights reserved. Used by permission of the publisher.

Comparing American Voices: Arthur E. Woodley. Excerpt from *Bloods: An Oral History of the Vietnam War by Black Veterans* by Wallace Terry. Copyright © 1984 by Wallace Terry. Used by permission of Random House, Inc.

Comparing American Voices: Gayle Smith. Excerpt from *Everything We Had* by Albert Santoli. Copyright © 1981 by Albert Santoli and Vietnam Veterans of America. Used by permission of Random House.

Voices from Abroad: Che Guevara: "Vietnam and the World Freedom Struggle." From "Message to the Tricontinental" from *Che Guevara Speaks* by Ernesto Che Guevara. Copyright © 1967, 2000 by Pathfinder Press. Reprinted by permission.

Voices from Abroad: Fei Xiaotong. America's Crisis of Faith. From *Land Without Ghosts* by David Arkrush. Copyright © 1989 by the University of California Press Books. Reprinted by the permission of the California University of PressBooks in the format Textbook via Copyright Clearance Center.

Chapter 30

Comparing American Voices: Ronald Reagan. "The Rule of Law Under God." From *Speaking My Mind* by Ronald Reagan. Copyright © 1989 by Ronald Reagan. Reprinted with the permission of Simon & Schuster Adult Publishing Group.

Comparing American Voices: Donald E. Wildmon. "Network Television as a Moral Danger." Excerpt from *The Home Invaders* by Donald E. Wildmon. Copyright © 1985 by Donald E. Wildmon. Reprinted with permission.

Voices from Abroad.: Zhu Shida. "Chaina and the United States: A Unique Relationship." From the China Internet Information Center. Reprinted with permission. www.china.org.en/english/2002/mar/29138.

Chapter 31

Comparing American Voices: Trong and Thanh Nguyen. "We're Political Refugees.... We Spend Our Money Here." Excerpt from *Enduring Voices*, volume II. Copyright © 1966 by D.C. Heath and Company. Used with permission of Houghton Mifflin.

Comparing American Voices: Petra Mata and Feiyi Chen: "Garmet Workers made a decent living before free trade." From *Shafted: Free Trade and America's Working Poor* edited by Christine Ahn. Copyright © 2003 Food First/Institute for Food and Development Policy. Oakland, CA. Reprinted with permission.

Voices from Abroad : Janet Daley. A US Epidemic. From *The Independent*, August 29, 1990. Copyright 1990. Reprinted with permission of Independent Newspapers, A Division of Independent News & Media Ltd. Theindependentsyndication@independent.co.uk.

Chapter 32

Voices From Abroad.: Abu Musab al-Zarqawi. "A Strategy for the Iraq Insurgency." Reprinted by permission of Juan R.I. Cole. Jrcole@mich.edu.

Comparing American Voices: "The Promised Land." Reprinted with permission of Michael Chorost.

INDEX

A note about the index: Names of individuals appear in boldface; biographical dates are included for major historical figures. Letters in parentheses following pages refer to: *(f)* figures, including charts and graphs; *(i)* illustrations, including photographs and artifacts; *(m)* maps; and *(t)* tables.

AAA. *See* Agricultural Adjustment Act; American Automobile Association
Abbott, Grace, 746
Abbott, Jacob, 564
Abernathy, Ralph, 855
Abilene, Kansas, 492
abolitionism, Douglass and, 624
abortion, 564, 924, 947–948, 955, 987
　opposition to, 910
　Roe v. Wade and, 910, 943, 985(i), 1008
　Supreme Court on, 985, 1008
Abramoff, Jack, 1006
abstract expressionism, 848
"The Absurd Attempt to Make the World Over" (Sumner), 588
Abu Ghraib prison, 1002, 1002(i), 1017
Abzug, Bella, 904
accommodationism, 624
Acheson, Dean, 807, 812
ADA. *See* Americans with Disabilities Act
Adams, Brooks, 647
Adams, Charles Francis, 654
Adams, Charles Francis, Jr., 592
Adams, Samuel Hopkins, 631
Adamson eight-hour law for railroad workers, 637
Addams, Jane, 612–615, 615(i), 654
Adelphia Communications, 995
adolescence, 564, 580. *See also* juvenile delinquency; youth
advertising
　automobile and, 714
　brand names and, 527, 527(i)
　consumer culture and, 670, 713–714, 734
　corporate growth and, 834
　of Kansas, 495(i)
　mass marketing and, 527, 527(i)
　New Deal and, 742
　in 1920s, 713–714
　political campaigns and, 932
　postwar, 843
　presidential campaign of 2004 and, 1005
　radio and, 717, 737(i)
　by railroads, 495, 513

　religion and, 842
　television and, 844(i)
　of Wild West Show, 494(i)
　youth culture and, 847
AFDC. *See* Aid to Families with Dependent Children
affirmative action, 907, 924, 928, 982, 987, 993
affluent society (1950s), 831–859
The Affluent Society (Galbraith), 833
Afghanistan, 939, 990, 998, 1000(i)
　Al Qaeda in, 925
　insurgencies in, 1002
　Soviet invasion of, 920(i), 921, 941
　Taliban in, 924
　U.S. aid to, 921
　U.S. attack on, 999, 1001(m), 1017
　U.S. invasion of Iraq and, 1001
AFL. *See* American Federation of Labor
AFL-CIO, 836, 838, 887, 901. *See also* American Federation of Labor; Congress of Industrial Organizations
Africa
　African American migration to, 726
　AIDS in, 967
　debts of, 970
　foreign trade and, 728
　North, 788(m), 789
　post-WWI colonialism in, 696–697
　WWI and, 674
African Americans. *See also* civil rights movement; desegregation; free blacks; racism; segregation; slavery; slaves
　affirmative action and, 907
　in Armed Forces, 681–683
　Back-to-Africa movement, 599
　Black Power and, 886, 892, 904
　as buffalo soldiers, 502
　Bush (George W.) and, 992–993
　in cattle industry, 493(i)
　changing demographics and, 976, 977(m), 980, 982
　churches of, 472
　civil rights movement and, 853–858, 879, 885–888, 892
　as cowboys, 492–493, 493(i)
　Democratic Party and, 754, 763
　Dred Scott and, 985(i)
　education of, 472(i)
　election of 1936 and, 747
　election of 1972 and, 901
　equality of, 597–599

　as Exodusters, 496, 496(i), 517
　Fifteenth Amendment and, 595–596, 598, 598(i)
　Fourteenth Amendment and, 588, 595–596, 598
　German propaganda toward, 682
　Great Migration of, 685–687, 690(m), 703
　Great Society and, 876
　Harlem Renaissance and, 723(i), 723–726
　Hurricane Katrina and, 1007(i)
　immigrant workers and, 980, 982
　in industrial jobs, 699
　jazz and, 716(i), 716–717, 848
　JFK and, 863
　Korean immigrants and, 980(i)
　labor unions and, 542–543, 750
　LBJ and, 871
　leadership of, 470–471
　legal system and, 753, 753(i)
　lynchings of, 599, 599(i), 698
　militancy of, 734, 885–886, 892
　in military, 652, 652(i), 681–683
　music of, 848
　Muslim, 886
　New Deal and, 742
　in New South, 529–530, 595–599, 608
　1920s and, 708
　nominating process and, 624
　northward migration of, 567, 625, 685–687, 690(m), 703
　as percent of population, 567
　post-WWI, 698(i), 698–699
　racial equality and, 946
　Republican Party and, 470–471, 585
　resettlement in Africa of, 599
　rights of. *See* civil rights
　riots by, 982(i), 982–983
　rock 'n' roll and, 847–848
　in Spanish-American War, 652, 652(i)
　on television, 843
　urban, 567–568, 572(i), 815
　urban migration of, 742, 753, 850–851
　urban rioting of, 886, 892. *See also* race riots
　Vietnam War (1961-1975) and, 882
　violence against, 476–478, 867
　voting by, 465(i), 470
　voting rights and, 586, 597(m), 597–599, 598(i), 608
　War on Poverty and, 876
　welfare system and, 747
　white supremacy movement and, 597–599, 608

I-1

African Americans (*continued*)
  women, 708, 750
  working women among, 533
  WWI and, 676
  WWII and, 777, 780–781, 784
African Methodist Episcopal Church (AME), 472
Afrika Korps, 789
Agency for International Development, 863
Agent Orange, 879, 882
Agnew, Spiro, 891, 902
Agricultural Adjustment Act (AAA), 739–742, 745, 747(*t*), 765
agriculture. *See also* corn; cotton; farmers; grain; sugar; tobacco; wheat; yeoman farmers
  in California, 511–514
  capital for, 498
  drought and, 757
  dry-farming, 497
  Granger movement and, 498, 602
  on Great Plains, 488(*m*), 488–489, 495–498
  immigrants and, 978–979
  irrigation for, 497, 515
  labor shortage in, 787
  migrant labor and, 511–512
  New Deal and, 742, 755–756
  in 1920s, 706, 710, 727
  orchards and, 512–513
  prices for, 602, 607
  in the South, 529, 529(*m*), 530, 530(*i*), 685, 850
  subtreasury system and, 602
  technology for, 497
  in Texas, 587
  TVA and, 759–760
  WWII and, 774
Aguinaldo, Emilio, 653, 653(*i*), 654
Ahmadinejad, Mahmoud, 1014
AIDS (acquired immune deficiency syndrome), 924, 966–967, 968(*i*), 987
Aid to Dependent Children (ADC), 747, 876
Aid to Families with Dependent Children (AFDC), 747, 876, 933, 950, 960
Air and Water Quality Acts (1965), 874(*t*)
airline industry, 850. *See also* commercial aviation
air traffic controller strike, 965, 987
Alabama
  black registered voters in, 470
  coal mining in, 521
  iron industry in, 530
Alabama (Confederate warship), 642
Alaska, 643, 912
  Arctic National Wildlife Refuge in, 994, 994(*m*)
Albright, Madeline, 947
alcohol
  blue laws and, 590, 592
  prohibition, 691–692
  prohibition of, 590, 592, 594–595, 595(*i*). *See also* Prohibition
  taxes on, 585
Aldrich, Nelson W., 632
Alger, Horatio, 587, 587(*i*)
Algeria, radical Islamic movements in, 953
Aliquippa, Pennsylvania, 552
Alito, Samuel A., Jr., 1008, 1009(*i*), 1017
Allawi, Ayad, 1006
Allen, Paul, 970, 971(*i*)
Allen, Thomas, 471
Alliance for Progress, 863
Allied Powers (WWII), 674–675, 675(*i*), 678–680, 683, 695, 697, 771, 787–791, 796–797
  wartime debts and, 711
Al Qaeda, 925, 953, 989–990, 998–999, 1000(*i*), 1001(*m*), 1002, 1014
  in Iraq, 1003
America First Committee, 771
American Automobile Association (AAA), 714
American Civil Liberties Union (ACLU), Scopes trial and, 721, 724
The American Commonwealth (Bryce), 583, 628
American Communist Party, 816–817
An American Dilemma (Myrdal), 852
American Enterprise Institute, 928, 955
American Expeditionary Force (AEF), 678–679, 681, 683
American Federation of Labor (AFL), 542–543, 548, 622, 685, 749–750, 836, 901
American Federation of Teachers, 724–725
American fever, 496
American Indian Movement (AIM), 888
American Indians, National Council of, 888
Americanization campaign, 693–694
American Legion, 683
American Medical Association (AMA), 815, 873
American Peace Society, 666
American Plan, meaning of, 711
American Protective League, 693
American Railway Union (ARU), 544
The Americans at Home (Macrae), 460
Americans with Disabilities Act (ADA; 1990–1991), 955
An American Tragedy (Dreiser), 723
American Union against Militarism, 676
The American Woman's Home (Beecher), 561
American Woman Suffrage Association, 469
America Online, 924
Ames, Adelbert, 478
amnesty
  for Confederates, 458
  for illegal aliens, 980
  for Southerners, 459
Amos 'n' Andy (radio program), 717
amusement parks, 574(*i*), 575
anarchism, 543
Ancona, Victor, 776
Anderson, John, 932
Anderson, Jourdon, 462–463
Angel's Camp, California, 513
Angelus Temple, 721(*i*)
Anglo-Saxonism, 647
Angola, West Africa, 939
Anheuser-Busch, 834
Anschutz, Thomas P., 537(*i*)
antelope, 489
Anthony, Susan B. (1820–1906), 469, 594
antiballistic missile systems (ABMs), 898
anticipatory self-defense, 999
Anti-Comintern Pact, 769, 797
anticommunism, 815–819, 828. *See also* **McCarthy, Joseph R.**
Antigua, 474
Anti-Imperialist Leagues, 654
Anti-Saloon League, 622
anti-Semitism, 838
  Holocaust and, 790
  racism and, 780
antitrust laws, 635–636, 707
  Microsoft Corporation, 971
  Sherman Antitrust Act (1890), 629, 632, 635–636
  wartime suspension of, 684
antiwar movement (Vietnam War), 879–884, 892, 901
  backlash against, 891, 899
  Chicago Democratic convention (1968), 889, 891
  decline of, 899
  draft and, 882–883, 892
  hardhat protest and, 899, 899(*i*)
  Kent State and, 898
  student protests and, 882–884, 892
ANZUS (Australia, New Zealand, United States; 1951), 824(*m*)
AP. *See* Associated Press
A&P, 527, 713
Apache Indians, 498–499, 499(*m*)
Appalachia, 729(*m*), 874(*t*), 875
  migration from, 850
  War on Poverty and, 875
Appalachian Regional Development Act (1965), 874(*t*)
Appalachian Trail, 760
appeasement (WWII), 770
Apple Corporation, 970, 972
appliances, household, 843
Appomattox Court House, Virginia, 466
Arab League, 826
Arabs. *See also* Middle East; Muslims
  Islamic fundamentalism and, 944–945
  U.S. invasion of Iraq and, 1001
Arafat, Yasir, 952
Arapaho Indians, 498, 499(*m*)

arbitration, WWI and, 675
Arctic National Wildlife Refuge, 994(m)
Argentina, 728, 920
Arikara Indians, 489, 499(m)
Aristide, Jean-Bertrand, 951–952
Arizona
    Hispanic settlement in, 508
    Japanese internment in, 785, 785(i)
    Mexican Americans in, 685
    mining in, 510(i)
Arkansas, Japanese internment in, 785, 785(i)
Arkansas Democrat-Gazette, 854, 854(i)
Armistice (1918), 679, 685, 703
Armour & Co., 525
arms control, 939. *See also* weapons of mass destruction
    Carter and, 921
    nuclear test ban treaty (1963), 868
    SALT I, 898
    SALT II, 921
    Washington Naval Arms Conference (1921), 713
arms race, 803. *See also* atomic bomb; nuclear weapons
    nuclear, 802–803, 841–842, 898
    nuclear proliferation and, 841–842
Armstrong, Louis, 717
Army, U.S., 641, 701
    conscription for, 678–679
    in Germany, 767(i)
    Indian wars and, 499(m), 502–504
    in Philippines, 654
    in Pullman boycott, 545(i)
    racial segregation in, 681–683
    racial violence in, 681
    Special Forces of, 869
Army Corps of Engineers, U.S., 661
art
    cultural dissent and, 848
    New Deal and, 737(i), 760–762
    in 1920s, 710(i)
Arthur, Chester A. (1829–1886), as president (1881-1885), 583, 642
Arthur Andersen, 995
artisans. *See also* mechanics
    in industrial age, 520, 531, 537(i)
    Reconstruction and, 470
    trade unionism and, 540–541
art museums, 578
Ashcroft, John D., 1009
Asia. *See also* particular countries
    European empires in, 642, 645–646, 663, 663(m)
    foreign powers in (1898–1910), 663(m)
    immigrants from, 849(f), 976(f)
    Nike in, 965
Asian Americans, 643(i)
    discrimination against, 838, 849
    New Deal and, 756–757
    population increase of, 977(m)

Asian immigrants
    in California, 784
    race riots by, 982(i)
Aspin, Les, 951
assembly lines, 539(i), 714. *See also* mass production
    for automobiles, 962(i)
Associated Press (AP), 717
associated state, 706–707
Aswan Dam, 826
Atkinson, Edward, 587
Atkins v. Children's Hospital, 711
Atlanta, Georgia, Ku Klux Klan in, 708(m)
Atlanta Journal (newspaper), 686
Atlantic Charter (1941), 771, 772(m), 787, 797
Atlantic City, New Jersey, real estate in, 963(i)
Atlantic Monthly, 579
Atlas Van Lines, 834
atomic bomb, 796, 802, 808–810, 812, 816. *See also* nuclear power; nuclear weapons
    use of, 670, 767, 793(m), 794, 795(i), 797
Atomic Energy Commission (AEC), 842
Auschwitz concentration camp, 790
Australia, 643
    Chinese immigration to, 511
    gold rush in, 505
    secret ballot from, 594
    WWII and, 791
Austria, 696, 770
Austria-Hungary, 674
automobile
    culture of, 706, 709, 714, 836, 839–841
    foreign, 911
    fuel-efficient, 911(f)
    Great Depression and, 727
    interstate highways and, 839(m)
    1950s culture and, 840
    rural life and, 714
    suburbs and, 839–841
automobile industry
    assembly lines in, 962(i)
    consolidation in, 834
    energy crisis and, 911
    environmentalism and, 913
    international economy and, 963
    labor unions and, 749
    market share of U.S., 834, 836
    mass production in, 538, 539(i), 548
    mass transit systems and, 841
    in 1920s, 735
    quality in, 961
Axis, Rome-Berlin (WWII), 769, 787, 797
axis of evil (Iran, Iraq, and North Korea), 999, 1017
Ayres, Thomas A., 487(i)

Baathist regime, 1002
Babbitt (Lewis), 723
Babcock, Orville, 479

Baby and Child Care (Spock), 845
baby-boom generation, 844–849, 924, 946, 959, 996
Backlash: The Undeclared War on American Women (Faludi), 983
Back-to-Africa movement, 599
Baghdad, Iraq
    looting in, 1001–1002
    Persian Gulf War and, 999
    slums of, 1015(i)
    U.S. invasion of Iraq and, 1001
Bainbridge, Joseph, 752(i)
Baker, Ella, 858
Baker, Ray Stannard, 693
Bakke, Allan, 907
Bakke v. University of California (1978), 907
balance of power, 659, 663, 896, 898
Bali, Islamic terrorist bombing in, 1014
balkanization, 983
Balkans, 666, 674, 698, 952
Ballinger, Richard A., 633
Baltic provinces, 679, 696–697
Baltimore, Maryland, population of, 552(t)
bananas, 712(i)
bandits, 510
Banking Act (1863), 604
Banking Act (1935), 744, 747(t)
bankruptcy
    of Enron, 995
    of farmers, 730
    holding company pyramid and, 706
    of Northern Pacific Railroad, 479
    of railroads, 549, 727
bankruptcy laws, 995
banks
    consolidation of, 834
    corporate coordination with, 834
    economic expansion and (1920s), 709–711
    failure of, 479
    failures of, 727–728, 739, 739(t)
    gold standard and, 604–607, 606(i)
    Great Depression and, 733
    National Banking Acts and, 604
    New Deal and, 744
    postwar, 832
    reform of, 635
Baptists
    African American, 567–568
    National Convention of, 472
    prohibition and, 692
Barbados (West Indies), 474
barbed wire, 497
Barbie dolls, 961(i)
Barnum, P. T., 578
Barrow Plantation, 473(m)
Barry, Leonora M., 542
Bartov, Hanoch, 840
Baruch, Bernard, 684, 684(i), 739, 742, 803
Baruch Plan, 803
baseball, 576–577, 577(i)

Basel Convention (1994), 969
Bataan death march, 791
Batista, Fulgencio, 863
Bayard, Thomas F., 642
Bayer, 694
Bay of Pigs invasion (1961), 863, 869(m)
Beall, Lester, 737(i)
the Beatles, 884
Beats, 848–849, 884
beauty pageants, 903–904, 904(i)
bebop, 848
Beecher, Catharine, 561
Beecher, Henry Ward, 573, 579
beer, 834
    German immigrants and, 688(i)
    Prohibition and, 722(i)
    prohibition and, 692
Begin, Menachem, 918(i), 920
Belgium, 674, 770, 790
Bell, Alexander Graham, 555
Belleau Wood, Battle of, 679(m)
Bellow, Saul, 762
Below, Ernst, 593
benevolent hegemony, 998
Bennett, James Gordon, 577
Bennett, William, 983
Bentsen, Lloyd, 948
Berger, Victor, 619, 694
Berkman, Alexander, 700
Berle, Adolph A., Jr., 739
Berlin, Germany, 790, 805(i), 806, 808
    division of, 792, 806, 808
    JFK and, 868
Berlin Airlift, 808, 808(i)
Berlin Conference (1884), 645
Berlin Wall, 868, 870(i)
    fall of, 924, 927, 942, 955
Berners-Lee, Tim, 957(i)
Bernstein, Carl, 902
Bernstein, Leonard, 851(i)
Bessemer, Henry, 520
Bessemer furnace, 520–521, 521(i)
Betamax video recorder, 959(i)
Bethlehem Steel, 521(i), 961
Bethune, Mary McLeod, 754(i), 754–755
Bethune-Cookman College, 754, 754(i)
Beveridge, Alfred J., 648
Bevin, Ernest, 807
Bible, evolution and, 721–722
Bidault, Georges, 807
Big Foot, Chief of Sioux, 504
Big Four, 696
Big Three, 787–788
Billy the Kid (Copland), 760
bin Laden, Osama, 953, 989–990, 999, 1014
bintel brief, 570
biotechnology, 924, 973(i)
bipolar world system, 897–898
Bird, Caroline, 728
bird flu, 967

Birmingham, Alabama, 866–867, 867(i)
birth control, 910
    declining birth rate and, 903
    rhythm method of, 564
Birth of a Nation (film), 721
birth rate. *See also* population
    declining, 903
    increasing, 524
    in 1950s, 844, 845(f)
Black, Hugo, 748
black churches, 472, 568. *See also particular denominations* under African Americans
    in New York, 567–568
Black Codes, 459, 471, 481
Black Elk, Sioux holy man, 504(i)
Blackfeet Indians, 489, 499(m)
Blackfoot Indians, 755(i)
Black Hills, South Dakota, 502, 505
blacklist, 816, 828
black market, during WWII, 783
Black Muslims, 886
Black Panthers, 886–887
Black Star Line steamship company, 726
"Black Thursday" (Oct. 24, 1929), 727
"Black Tuesday" (Oct. 29, 1929), 727
Blaine, James G., 586, 586(m), 592, 643
Bland-Allison Act (1878), 604
blitzkrieg, 767, 770
blogging, 924
blogs, meaning of, 971–972
bloody shirt, the, 585–586
blue laws, 590, 592
Blue Ridge Parkway, 760
Boesky, Ivan, 962
Boland Amendment, 937
Bolivia, 643
Bolshevik Revolution (1917), 679, 700
Bolshevism, 674, 679, 700, 703. *See also* communism
Bonanza (television show), 844
Bonaparte, Charles J., 618
Bonn, Germany, 998
Bonnin, Gertrude Simmons (Zitkala-ša), 501
Bonsack, James A., 530
Bonus Army (1932), 731, 735
boodle, 572
boomer movement, 503
Booth, John Wilkes, 457–458
Borah, William E., 697
Bosnia, 674, 924–925, 952, 952(m), 955
Boston, Massachusetts
    art museum in, 578
    elite in, 558–559
    immigrants in, 566
    population of, 552(t)
    school busing in, 907, 910(i)
    suburbs of, 560
    urban renewal in, 852
Boston Guardian, 625

Bourke-White, Margaret, 762, 762(i)
Bourne, Rudolph, 692
Bow, Clara, 715(i), 715–716
Bowery, New York, 576
Bowman Dairy Company, 780(i)
Boxer rebellion (China; 1900), 663, 663(m)
Boyce, Ed, 546
boycotts
    by Atlanta African Americans, 599
    of California grapes, 887
    civil rights movement and, 879
    Pullman, 544, 545(i), 605, 611
    secondary, 544, 813–814
braceros program, 850, 978
Bradford, Perry, 716(i)
Bradley, Joseph P., 481
Brandeis, Louis D., 613, 615, 617, 635
Brando, Marlon, 847
Brauckmiller, John R., 783(i)
Brazil, 967
    foreign trade and, 728
    land distribution in, 474
breadlines, 731(i), 732
breaker boys, 536(i)
Brest-Litovsk, Treaty of, 679
Bretton Woods system, 832
breweries
    prohibition and, 692
    Volstead Act and, 722(i)
Breyer, Stephen G., 947, 991, 1009(i)
Brezhnev, Leonid, 832(i), 898, 1002
Briand, Aristide, 713
Britain. *See* Great Britain
British Caribbean, land distribution in, 474
British Columbia, gold in, 505
British Guiana, 474
broadband connections, 924, 971
brokerage firms, 962
Brooklyn, New York, 552(t)
Brooks, Phillips, 573
Brotherhood of Sleeping Car Porters, 780
Brown, Ron, 947
Brown Berets, 887
Brownlow, William G., 477
Brown v. Board of Education (1954), 853, 903, 907, 910
Bruce, Blanche K., 471
Bruce, William, 718
Brush, Charles F., 554, 555(i)
Brussels, 965(m)
Bryan, William Jennings, 605–607, 606(i), 607(m), 632, 654, 666–667, 722, 726, 928
Bryant, Anita, 906
Bryce, James, 583–584, 587, 592
    on America, 628
    on diplomacy, 644
Buchanan, Patrick, 946, 976, 983, 991
Buchenwald concentration camp, 790
Buckley, William F., 928

buffalo, 489, 492, 492(i)
Buffalo Bill, the King of the Border Men (Buntling), 494
buffalo soldiers, 502
Buford (vessel), 700
Buford, Anne Gorsuch, 936
Bulgaria, WWI and, 674
Bulge, Battle of, 790
Bulkley, William Lewis, 625
Bull Moose Party, 633
Bundy, McGeorge, 868
Bunker, Ellsworth, 898
Buntline, Ned, 494
Bunyan, John, 614
Burger, Warren, 910, 938(i)
Burgess, John W., 624
Burkitt, Frank, 597
Burma, 791
Burroughs, Edgar Rice, 563
Bush, George H. W. (1924-), 924–925, 929, 947(i), 955
    automobile mileage requirements and, 968
    Persian Gulf War and, 999
    as president (1989-1993), 943–946, 993(i)
    signing of NAFTA and, 948
Bush, George W. (1946-), 925, 946
    Air National Guard and, 1005
    approval ratings of, 1002, 1004, 1006
    dressed up as fighter pilot, 1001
    election of 2000 and, 990–991, 991(i), 1002, 1004–1005
    election of 2004 and, 1002, 1004–1005, 1017
    Enron and, 995
    favoritism to business by, 994–995
    globalization and, 969
    homeland security and, 995, 1004(i)
    Kyoto Treaty and, 969, 987, 998
    as president (2001-), 990–1017
    rollback of federal government and, 954, 996
    scandals during administration of, 995
    second term of, 1005–1016
    September 11 attacks and, 998
    State of the Union address of 2002, 999, 1009(i)
    stem cell research veto by, 1007–1008, 1010, 1017
    unilateralism of, 1012
Bush doctrine, 999
Bushnell, Horace, 579
Bush v. Gore (2000), 991
business. *See also* corporations
    Bush (George W.) and, 994–995
    Cheney and, 994
    consolidation of, 709–710
    energy industry and, 995(i)
    failures in, 728(f)
    government cooperation with, 706–713
    mobilization for war and, 774–777
    modern management and, 537, 548
    New Deal and, 742, 763
    in 1920s, 709–711
    productivity decline in, 959–960
    U.S. interventions and, 937(m)
business cycles, 710, 727
busing, school, 907, 910(i)
butterfly ballots, 991
Byrnes, James F., 748

Cable New Network (CNN), 924
cable television, 973–975
Cahan, Abraham, 573
California
    affirmative action in, 907, 982
    agriculture in, 511–512
    Catholic missions in, 513
    Chinese immigrants in, 511
    climate of, 505, 513
    culture of, 512–513, 515
    Enron scam and, 995
    European immigrants in, 510
    gold rush (1849–1857) in, 517
    Hispanic settlement, 509
    immigration to, 976
    internal migration to, 491, 755–756, 783, 838(m), 839
    Japanese internment in, 785, 785(i)
    Latino immigrants in, 850
    Mexican Americans in, 685
    as mining frontier, 505–508, 506(m), 508(i), 515
    movie industry in, 714
    national parks in, 514
    Native Americans in, 509
    prohibition and, 691
    Proposition 13 in, 916–917
    racial antagonism in, 784
    racism in, 511–512
    Reagan and, 928
    settlement of, 489
    stem-cell research in, 1008
California, University of, Free Speech Movement and, 882, 882(i)
Californios, 509
Calley, William, 899
Cambodia
    Khmer Rouge in, 900
    Vietnam War and, 877(m), 878, 899–900
Camp David accords (1978), 918(i), 920
Canada, 642, 968, 987
    medication prices in, 993
    NAFTA and, 948, 964
    settlement of boundaries with, 659
    Sioux Indians in, 502
    U.S. invasion of Iraq and, 1001
    war on terrorism and, 1000(i)
Canby, Henry Seidel, 561
cancer, genetic codes and, 973(i)
Cannon, "Uncle Joe", 633

capital goods, 520
capitalism, 999(i)
    automobiles and, 713–714
    business cycles in, 710, 727
    corporate, 709–711, 832
    election of 1932 and, 733(m)
    free-market, 943
    industrialization and, 519–549
    New Deal and, 739
    in 1950s, 831
    postwar liberalism and, 832
    pyramid of holding companies and, 706
    robber barons and, 522–523
    Social Darwinism and, 588
    vs. communism, 831
    welfare, 710–711, 781, 796
    WWI and, 684
    WWII and, 787
Capra, Frank, 782
Caribbean Islands (West Indies)
    Asian migration to, 511
    expansionist foreign policy and, 655(m), 668
    military interventions in, 711
    U.S. as power in, 649
    U.S. intervention in, 937(m), 951–952
Caribbean Sea, 646–647, 655(m), 668
    "policing" of, 661–662, 662(m)
Carmichael, Stokely, 886
Carnegie, Andrew, 519(i), 520–521, 522(i), 526, 543, 549, 578–579, 587, 654, 676
Carolinas. *See* North Carolina; South Carolina
carpetbaggers, 470, 478
Carranza, Venustiano, 664–666
Carroll, James, 892
Carson, Rachel, 912
Carter, Jimmy (James E.; 1924-), 922, 963
    Camp David accords and, 918(i), 920
    defeat of, 929, 932, 932(m)
    defense spending of, 935
    as president (1977-1981), 917–922
cartoons, political, 523(i), 546(i), 584(i)
Cartwright, Alexander, 576
Casablanca (film), 782
Cascades mountains, 505
Casey, William, 939
caste labor system, 512
Castro, Fidel, 850, 863, 869(m), 898, 937
Caterpillar Tractors, 965
Catholicism
    Americanism and, 572–573
    election of 1928 and, 726
    ethnic identity and, 573
    of Mexican Americans, 685
    presidential elections and, 863, 901
    rhetoric against, 586
Catholics
    abortion and, 984
    California missions and, 513
    Democratic party and, 590, 590(f), 592
    immigration restriction and, 718

Catholics (continued)
    Irish, 573
    JFK and, 863
    Ku Klux Klan and, 719(i), 721
    in 1920s, 718, 726
    in 1950s, 842
    opposition to, 980
    in Poland, 941
    Religious Right and, 928
    in the Southwest, 509
Cato Institute, 928, 955, 1012
Catt, Carrie Chapman, 617, 688, 709(i)
cattle industry, 525, 525(m). See also meat packing industry; ranching
    African Americans in, 493, 493(i)
    on Great Plains, 492–493
    Hispanics in, 493, 493(i), 509
    and Long Drive, 493, 517
CBS Laboratories, 834
CBS News, 970
CBS Records, 959
"The Celebrated Jumping Frog of Calaveras County" (Twain), 513
Celera Genomics, 972
cellular telephones, 924, 972
CENTO. See Central Treaty Organization
Central America
    immigrants from, 976–977
    U.S. intervention in, 939
Central Asia, 942(m)
Central Europe, immigration from, 976(f)
Central Intelligence Agency (CIA)
    Afghanistan and, 921
    covert operations of, 824–825, 937
    creation of, 809
    Cuba and, 863
    Iran and, 921
    Nixon's dirty tricks and, 901–902
Central Pacific Railroad, 507
    building of, 492, 517
    Chinese labor for, 511, 512(i)
Central Park rapists, 981
Central Powers, 674–675, 675(i), 676, 679–680, 697
Central Treaty Organization (CENTO), 824(m)
centrist agenda, 948, 950
A Century of Dishonor (Jackson), 500, 503
CERN, 957(i)
Cervera, Pascual, 650, 652
CFC. See chlorofluorocarbons
Chamberlain, Neville, 770
Chambers, Whittaker, 816
Chaplin, Charlie, 713, 715
charitable activities
    Great Depression and, 729, 729(m), 733
    New Deal and, 742
Charles, Prince of England, 975
Chase, Salmon P., 468
Chase Manhattan Bank, 965

Chateau-Thierry, Battle of, 679, 679(m)
Chatel-Chehery, Battle of, 680
Chautauqua, New York, 578
Chavez, César, 756, 886–887, 887(i), 983
Chavez, Hugo, 1013
checks and balances, 468
Cheever, John, 762
chemical industry, 963
Chen, Feiyi, 979
Cheney, Richard, 991, 996, 1012
Chernobyl meltdown, 914
Cherokee Indians, 499, 499(m), 759(i)
Cherry family, 569(i)
Cheyenne, Wyoming, 492
Cheyenne Indians, 489, 498, 499(m), 502
Chiang Kai-shek (Jiang Jieshi), 810
Chicago, Burlington, and Quincy Railroad, 522
Chicago, Illinois, 551–553
    African Americans in, 567, 687
    art museum in, 578
    Berlin and, 558
    as center of meat industry, 498, 525, 525(m)
    expansion in, 554(m)
    fire of 1871, 556
    Haymarket bombing in, 549
    immigrants in, 566
    jazz and, 716
    Ku Klux Klan in, 708(m)
    mass transit in, 553(i)
    migration to, 718, 850
    population of, 552(t)
    race riots in, 698(i), 698–699, 703
    Robert Taylor Homes, 852
    Scopes trial and, 722
    skyline of, 554
    transportation and, 498
Chicago, University of, 793
Chicago Columbian Exposition (1893), 557
Chicago Commission on Race Relations, 686
Chicago Defender (newspaper), 686
Chicago Democratic Convention (1968), 889, 891
Chicago Rapid Transit Company, 706
Chicago school of architecture, 553
Chicago Urban League, 686
Chicanos. See Mexican Americans
Chickasaw Indians, 499, 499(m)
Child, Lydia Maria, 469
child care programs, 896, 905
child labor, 536, 536(i)
    New Deal and, 742, 748
children
    attitudes toward, 564, 566
    inner-city, 982
    labor of, 536, 536(i)
    of Native Americans, 503
    in 1950s culture, 844–846
    Sheppard-Towner Act and, 709
    television regulation and, 975
Children's Television Act (1990), 975

Chile, 643, 965
China. See also People's Republic of China; Taiwan
    Boxer rebellion in, 663, 663(m)
    capitalism and, 1012
    civil war in, 810
    copyright issues and, 972
    Cultural Revolution in, 897
    European spheres of influence in, 645, 651, 662–664, 663(m), 668
    foreign trade and, 728
    immigrants from, 756–757
    Japanese invasion of, 768, 797
    lobby for, 810
    multinational corporations and, 925
    Nationalist, 664, 810, 812, 897–898
    Nike and, 967(i)
    Nixon in, 897(i), 897–898
    pollution in, 967
    radical Islamic movements in, 953
    trade with, 645, 662–664
    U.S. relations with, 940
    WWI and, 674
    WWII and, 787, 792(m)
Chinatown, 511, 743(t)
Chinese Exclusion Act (1882), 511, 517, 849
Chinese immigrants, 510–512, 517, 849
    discrimination against, 505, 511, 517
    immigration restriction and, 511, 718, 849
    in the West, 510–512, 512(i), 515, 517
Chinn, Mae, 743(t)
chips. See silicone microchips
Chisholm, Shirley, 905
Chloe and Sam (Hovenden), 457(i)
chlorofluorocarbons (CFC), 968
Choctaw Indians, 499, 499(m)
Chorost, Michael, 1011
Christianity. See also evangelism; revivalism; *particular denominations*
    African-American, 568
    muscular, 574
    public life and, 930
    Reconstruction and, 478
    revivalism and, 574
    Social Gospel and, 612
Christopher, Warren, 951
Chrysler, 962
church and state, separation of, 573, 930, 992
Churchill, Winston
    Atlantic Charter and, 772(m), 787
    on division of Germany, 808
    at Potsdam Conference, 803
    United Nations and, 793
    wartime planning and, 771, 789
    at Yalta Conference, 791–792, 794(i), 802
Church of Jesus Christ of Latter-day Saints. See Mormons
Cincinnati, Ohio, 558–559
    migration to, 850
    population of, 552(t)

CIO. *See* Congress of Industrial Organizations
CIS. *See* Commonwealth of Independent States
Cisco, 961
Cisneros, Henry, 947
cities. *See also* urbanization
  African American migration to, 742, 753, 850
  American *vs.* European, 553
  amusements in, 574–578
  in art and literature, 579
  crime increases in, 924
  decaying inner, 849–852
  drug crises in, 924
  election of 1928 and, 727(*i*)
  election of 1932 and, 733
  flapper in, 716
  gay communities in, 906
  growth of, 551–552, 552(*m*), 580, 838(*m*)
  high culture in, 578–580
  immigrants in, 551, 551(*i*), 566
  industrialization and, 487
  Korean immigrants in, 980, 980(*i*)
  Ku Klux Klan in, 708(*m*)
  life belts around, 841(*i*)
  life in, 566–580
  lighting of, 554–555
  mass media and, 718
  move to suburbs from, 831, 837–838
  population growth and, 551, 552(*t*), 735, 849–850
  private/public, 555–558
  Protestantism in, 573–574
  race riots in, 698(*i*), 698–699, 703, 886, 892, 982–983
  riots in, 797, 886
  skyscrapers in, 553–554
  sprawl of, 840
  Summer of Love (1967) in, 885
  in Sun Belt, 839
  ten largest U.S., 552(*t*)
  transportation in, 553, 553(*i*), 580
  urban development and, 873, 874(*t*)
  urban renewal and, 852, 896
City Beautiful movement, 556
Civil Defense Agency, 842(*i*)
Civilian Conservation Corps (CCC), 739, 747(*t*), 752–754, 765
civil liberty, 817(*i*)
civil rights
  Bush (George W.) and, 993
  conservative opposition to, 875
  Eisenhower and, 853
  federal government and, 831
  Fifteenth Amendment and, 468(*t*), 469, 477, 595–596, 598, 598(*i*), 624
  of former slaves, 459, 474
  Fourteenth Amendment and, 465–466, 468(*t*), 477, 588, 595–596, 598

  for homosexuals, 903, 906
  integration and, 983
  JFK and, 861, 864
  LBJ and, 871–872
  legislation on, 874(*t*)
  for Mexican Americans, 886–888, 892
  for Native Americans, 888, 892
  in 1970s, 922
  Nixon and, 896
  nonviolent protest and, 853, 855
  Truman and, 853
  for women, 903–906
  WWII and, 780(*i*), 784–787
Civil Rights Act (1866), 459, 465, 468(*t*), 478, 483
Civil Rights Act (1964), 871–872, 874(*t*), 903
  Title IX and, 905
  women and, 903, 905
Civil Rights Bill (1870), 478
Civil Rights Commission, National, 853
civil rights movement, 852(*i*), 852–858, 855(*i*), 855(*m*), 879, 885–888
  African Americans and, 853–858, 879, 885–886, 892
  anticommunism and, 816
  Cold War and, 814–815, 852–858
  conflicts within, 858
  federal government and, 828, 864, 866
  feminism and, 903–906
  gay rights and, 906
  Harlem Renaissance and, 726
  in 1970s, 902–910
  sit-ins and, 855–858
  television and, 867, 872
  violence against, 858
  WWII and, 781
Civil Service Commission, 584
civil service reform, 479, 584–585, 624
civil unions, 984
civil war
  in Iraq, 1006, 1016
  in Russia, 679
Civil War (1861–1865)
  financing of, 604
  party loyalty and, 590
  Reconstruction and, 474
  roles of France and Britain in, 642
  warships of, 642
Civil Works Administration (CWA), 743–744, 747(*t*)
  Native Americans and, 754
  women and, 743, 752
Clark, Champ, 634(*i*)
class. *See* social structure
class-action suits, 913
class distinctions
  Hurricane Katrina and, 1007(*i*)
  World War I and, 674
Clayton Antitrust Act (1914), 635–637
Clean Air Act (1970), 913, 994

Clemenceau, Georges, 695(*i*), 696
Clemens, Samuel. *See* **Twain, Mark**
Cleveland, Grover (1837–1908), 629
  election of 1884 and, 586, 592
  election of 1888 and, 582(*i*)
  as passive president (1885-1889), 584(*i*)
  as president (1885–1889; 1893–1897), 584(*i*), 584–587, 589(*i*), 592, 602, 605, 643, 648–649
  Pullman boycott and, 544, 549, 605
  as reformer, 586
Cleveland, Ohio
  African Americans in, 567
  oil refining in, 526
Clinic Entrance Act (1993), 948
Clinton, Bill (William Jefferson; 1946-)
  balanced budget and, 948, 949(*i*), 996
  big government and, 928, 950
  economy and, 958, 963
  first term of, 955
  impeachment of, 924, 950–951, 951(*i*), 954–955
  Kyoto Treaty and, 969
  nuclear power and, 1013
  as president (1993–2001), 946–953
Clinton, Hillary Rodham, 946–948, 948(*i*)
clothing industry. *See* textile industry
Coalition Provisional Authority, 1002
coal mining, 521–522, 531, 536, 546, 622
  breaker boys and, 536, 536(*i*)
  decline of (1920s), 710, 727
  increase in, 911(*f*)
  in New South, 529(*m*)
  strikes and, 637
  strikes in, 813
coal shortages, 684
Coca-Cola, 834
Cochran, Johnnie, 983
Cody, William F. (Buffalo Bill), 493–494, 494(*i*)
Cohan, George M., 678
Colbert, Claudette, 782
Cold War, 801–829, 897–898
  affluent society and, 831
  arms race in, 868
  beginning of, 807
  Berlin Wall and, 868, 870(*i*)
  civil rights movement and, 814–815, 852–858
  Cuba in, 863, 869(*m*)
  détente and, 897
  domino effect and, 877
  end of, 925, 927, 939, 954–955, 1012
  in Europe, 805–806, 806(*m*)
  impact of, 841–842
  Iran and, 921
  mainframe computers and, 970
  in Middle East, 825–827
  nuclear test ban treaties and, 868
  Peace Corps and, 863

Cold War (continued)
    staggering cost of, 942
    Third World and, 865(m)
    Vietnam War and, 877–884
    WWII and, 768, 775, 796
    Yalta and, 794(i)
Cole, U.S.S., attack on, 953, 953(i), 989, 1001(m)
collective bargaining, 540, 749
collective security, 771, 802, 822, 824
Collier, John, 754, 755(i)
Collier's magazine, 613, 631
Colombia, 659
colonialism, 822
colonization
    end of, 865(m)
    by Spain, 505
Colorado
    Chinese in, 511
    gay rights legislation in, 984
    Japanese internment in, 785, 785(i)
    migration to, 510
    mining in, 505, 511, 607
Colorado Coal Company v. United Mine Workers, 711
Colorado plateau, 505
Colored Farmers' Alliance, 596–597
Colored Women, National Association of (NACW), 754
Colored Women's Clubs, National Association of, 625
Colored Women's League of Washington, D.C., 626(i)
Columbia Broadcasting Service (CBS), 717
Columbia Pictures, 959
Columbia plateau, 505
Columbia University, 889
Columbine High School, 975
Comanche Indians, 489, 499(m)
Comintern, 700, 769, 797
commercial aviation, WWI and, 681
Commission on Industrial Relations, 637
Committee Against Jim Crow in Military Service, 853
Committee on Public Information, 693, 703
Committee to Defend America by Aiding the Allies, 771
Committee to Re-Elect the President (CREEP), 901
common law, 622
Commonwealth Edison Company, 706
Commonwealth of Independent States (CIS), 942, 942(m)
communication systems, globalization and, 963–964, 966
communism
    Carter and, 921
    in China, 964
    Chinese, 877, 897–898
    Cold War and, 831, 832(i), 877–879, 892, 897–898

collapse of, 938–943, 941(i), 942(m)
conservatives and, 928
containment of, 804, 809–810
European economy and, 805–806
Federal Theatre Project and, 762
in Germany, 769
godless, 842
Great Fear of, 815–818
Greece and, 804–805
international, 822
Iran and, 921
JFK and, 863, 870
in Latin America, 937(m)
Nixon and, 897–898
Peace Corps and, 863
Soviet, 815–816, 898, 939
U.S. interventions and, 937(m)
Vietnam War and, 892, 901
vs. capitalism, 831
in Yugoslavia, 952
Communist Labor Party, 700
Communist Party, 770
    election of 1932 and, 733, 733(m)
    in Great Depression, 731, 735
    popular protests and, 751(m)
    in Russia, 679, 697, 700
    in Soviet Union, 941–942
    U.S., 700
Community Action Program, 876
compact discs (CD), 924, 959(i), 972, 974
compassionate conservatism, 990, 992
Compromise of 1877, 481, 483
computers
    millennium fears and, 957
    revolution, 987
computer technology, 970–972
Comstock, Anthony, 564
Comstock Lode (1859), 506
concentration camps, 791(i)
Coney Island, 575
Confederate States of America. *See also* Civil War; secession
    radical Reconstruction of, 467(m)
conglomerates, rise of, 834
Congregationalism, politics of, 590(f)
Congress, U.S. *See also* House of Representatives, U.S.; Senate, U.S.
    civil rights movement and, 867
    declaration of war and, 678, 697, 771, 773
    Democratic control of, 814, 896, 901, 946–947
    drug benefit bill in, 993–994
    FDR and, 748, 759
    Federal Theatre Project and, 762
    Great Depression and, 730
    Gulf of Tonkin Resolution (1964), 878
    illegal aliens and, 980
    immigration restriction and, 718–719
    Japanese internments and, 787

labor unions and, 780
Latin American countries and, 769
Medicare cuts and, 933
military veterans and, 781
Native Americans and, 850
New Deal and, 739, 742, 744, 748
Republicans in, 932, 949–950
Roosevelt recession and, 749
scheduled meeting of, 458–459
Schiavo case and, 1007
Supreme Court and, 708
television regulation and, 975
welfare programs and, 935
women in, 709, 944(i)
Congress of Industrial Organizations (CIO), 670, 749–750, 750(i), 756, 765, 836, 838, 887, 901
Congress of Racial Equality (CORE), 781, 864, 886
Conkling, Roscoe, 478, 585, 587
Connor, Eugene ("Bull"), 866, 867(i)
conscientious objectors, 678
consciousness raising, 904
conscription, 678–679, 770–771, 797. *See also* draft, military
conservation, 968–969. *See also* environment; pollution
    Carter on, 918, 920
    LBJ and, 873, 875
    New Deal and, 759–760
    Roosevelt (Theodore) and, 629, 631
conservationists, 629
conservatism, 934, 983, 986, 990, 992
    creationism and, 1008
    election of 1980 and, 932(m)
    gay rights and, 906
    Great Society and, 875
    in 1970s, 895–896, 901, 907, 910, 922
    political cartoons about, 997(i)
    resurgence of, 891–892
    rise of, 928–932
    small government and, 997
    stem-cell research and, 1008
    vs. feminism, 905–906
Constitution, U.S.
    acquired territories and, 654
    amendments to, 684. *See also particular amendments*
    electoral college and, 481
    Japanese internments and, 787
    New Deal and, 748
    secession and, 458, 467
constitutions, state, 471, 511
construction industry, 520, 728(f)
consumerism
    installment buying and, 836
    interstate highways and, 839
    in 1950s, 831, 840
    women and, 847
consumer price index (CPI), 728

Consumer Products Safety Commission, 896, 913
consumers
   protection of, 631–632
   rights of, 913
Consumers' League, National, 615
consumer spending
   economic development and, 844
   postwar, 836
   television and, 844(i)
containment policy, 804, 822–827, 942
   in Asia, 810–814, 822, 825
   Eisenhower Doctrine and, 827
   LBJ and, 877
   meaning of, 804
   militarization of (NSC=68), 809–810
   Third World and, 822, 824–825
   in Truman administration, 822, 828
Contras, 937, 937(m)
Conwell, Russell H., 561, 587
Cooke, Jay, 479, 492
Coolidge, Calvin (1882–1933), 699
   ethics of, 707(i)
   as president (1923-1929), 707–708, 710, 718, 735
   as vice-presidential candidate, 706
Cooperstown, New York, 576
Copland, Aaron, 760
copper mines, 506
copyright issues, 972
Coral Sea, Battle of, 791, 792(m), 797
CORE. *See* Congress of Racial Equality
Corinne, Utah, 507
corn. *See also* grain
   price supports for, 710
corporate capitalism, 684
corporate executives, salaries of, 958(f)
corporate welfare programs, 775
corporations. *See also* business
   capitalism and, 709–711, 728
   computer networks and, 971
   conglomerates, 834
   consolidation of, 613, 709–710, 834
   consumer rights movement and, 913
   foreign competition and, 915–916
   foreign purchases of, 959
   information processing in, 961
   managerial class in, 834–835
   multinational, 925
   multinationalization of, 965–966, 966(i), 969
   outsourcing and, 965–966, 987
   political action committees and, 932
   power of, 613, 635–637
   radio and, 717
   rise of, 522
   scandals in, 995
   tariff protection for, 935
   taxation of, 684
   vertically integrated, 834

Corrigan, Michael A., 573
corruption
   in Harding administration, 707
   in Nixon administration, 901–902
   political, 471, 479, 613
cotton
   former slaves and, 464(i)
   prices for, 602
   price supports for, 710
   production of, 474
   sharecropping and, 473–474, 476
   in the South, 529(m), 530, 530(i)
   strikes and, 755(i), 756
   in Texas, 530(i), 598, 602
Coughlin, Charles, 744–745, 748, 751(m), 765
Council for Mutual Economic Assistance (COMECON), 808
counterculture
   drugs and, 884–885
   of 1950s, 847–849
   of 1960s, 879, 882, 884–885
   1970s activism and, 912
counterinsurgency, 863
courtship, parental control and, 576
court system. *See also* judiciary; Supreme Court
   conservative federal judges and, 925
covert interventions, meaning of, 824
cowboys, 492–493, 493(i)
Cowley, Malcolm, 760
Cox, James M., 706
Coxey, Jacob S., 605
craftsmen. *See* artisans
Crane, Stephen, 497, 579
Crazy Horse, 502
creationism, 924, 1008
credit. *See also* debt
   consumer, 836, 913
   Great Depression and, 728
Creek Indians, 499, 499(m)
Creel, George, 693
creeping socialism, 739
Crick, Francis, 973(i)
The Crisis, 625, 723(i)
Croatia, 952
Croats, 952(m)
Crocker, Charles, 511
cronyism, 479
crop-lien laws, 474, 476
crops. *See* agriculture
"Cross of Gold" speech, 928
Crow Indians, 489, 499(m)
Cruikshank, United States v., 478
Cuba
   Bay of Pigs in, 863, 868, 869(m)
   expansionism and, 642
   independence of, 652
   JFK and, 863, 870
   land distribution in, 474
   military alliance with, 937

   Nixon and, 898
   refugees from, 850
   sensationalist journalism and, 648, 649(i), 649–650
   Spanish "reconcentration" camps in, 648–649, 651
   U.S. relations with, 661–662, 662(m), 769
   vs. Spain, 647–655
Cuban missile crisis (1962), 863, 868, 869(m)
Cullen, Countee, 723
cultural assimilation, Native Americans and, 850
cultural pluralism, 755
cultural values
   automobile and, 706
   conflict and, 718
culture. *See also* multiculturalism; popular culture
   automobile, 836, 839–841
   of California, 512–513, 515
   in cities, 578–579
   conflict, 958
   of corruption, 1006
   dissent and, 847–849
   fragmentation of, 983
   modern American (1920s), 733–734
   national, 706, 713–718
   of Native Americans, 513
   of 1950s, 847–849
   popular, 782
   technology and, 973–975
culture wars, 726, 924–925, 975–985
Cummins, Albert B., 624
currency. *See also* specie
   euro, 1013
   free silver and, 604, 606(i)
   renminbi, 1013
   U.S. as dominant, 832
Currie, Laughlin, 815
Cushman, Candi, 1010
Custer, George Armstrong, 502
Czechoslovakia, 696, 802, 805, 825, 942, 942(m)
   German invasion of, 770
   Prague Spring in, 897
Czolgosz, Leon F., 627

Dachau concentration camp, 790
Daily Worker (newspaper), 770
Dakota territory
   homesteaders in, 497
   Indian reservations in, 498–504, 499(m), 502(m)
   Scandinavian migration to, 496
Daley, Janet, 981
Daley, Richard J., 863, 889, 901
Dallas (TV program), 974
Damrosch, Leopold, 578
Dario, Ruben, 660
Darrow, Clarence, 722

Darwin, Charles, 588, 647, 721–722
Darwinism, 1008
Davis, David, 481
Davis, John W., 708
Davis, Miles, 848
Dawes, Charles G., 711
Dawes Plan (1924), 670, 711, 735
Dawes Severalty Act (1887), 503, 517, 754, 755(*i*)
Day, William R., 652–653
day care, corporations and, 775
"Day Under Communism" (Mosinee, Wisconsin), 801
D-Day (June 6, 1944), 789, 790(*i*), 797
DDT, 912–913
Dean, Howard, 971, 1004–1005
Dean, John, 902
death squads, 1016
Debayle, Anastasio Somoza, 937
Debs, Eugene, 544–545, 546(*i*), 548–549, 619, 635(*m*), 676, 694, 703
debt
    Asian migrants and, 511
    consumer, 710, 727–728
    farmers and, 474
    foreign, 711, 728, 959
    national, 774, 935, 948, 950, 955, 996. *See also* deficit spending
    of states, 471
    tax cuts and, 996
    of U.S., 963, 987
    during WWI, 683–684
decolonization, 865(*m*), 911
defense industry, women in, 777
Defense of Marriage Act (1998), 984, 987
defense spending, 774(*f*), 812, 813(*f*)
    economy and, 916(*m*)
    Eisenhower and, 863
    JFK and, 863
    postwar development and, 839
    Reagan and, 935–936, 954
    WWII, 774–775
deficit spending, 748, 913. *See also* debt
    economy and, 911, 925, 936
    in New Deal, 864
    by Nixon, 911
    Reaganomics and, 935, 935(*f*), 954
deflation, 604, 936
de Gaulle, Charles, 897
deindustrialization, 915–916, 917(*i*)
"De Kid Wot Works at Night" (Hard), 613
de Kooning, Willem, 760
DeLay, Tom, 991–993, 1006
De Leon, Daniel, 545
De Lesseps, Ferdinand, 642–643
Dellaire, Ohio, 752(*i*)
Dell Computer, 965
Del Monte, 750
de Lome, Dupuy, 649

democracy
    direct, 624
    Great Depression and, 732
    in Iraq, 999, 1015(*i*)
    militant Muslims and, 1015–1016
    New Deal and, 744
Democracy in America (Tocqueville), 583
Democratic National Committee, Women's Bureau of, 677(*i*), 751, 763
Democratic Party. *See also* elections; presidential elections
    African Americans and, 754, 763
    Catholics and, 590, 590(*f*), 592
    Chicago convention of (1968), 889, 891
    coalition of, 763, 863, 875, 917, 932(*m*), 948
    in Congress, 902
    control of Congress by, 814, 896, 902
    in 1870s, 479
    election of 1912 and, 635, 635(*m*)
    election of 1924 and, 707
    election of 1928 and, 726, 727(*i*)
    election of 1932 and, 733
    election of 1936 and, 747–748
    election of 1964 and, 873(*m*)
    election of 1972 and, 901
    election of 1980 and, 932, 932(*m*)
    election of 1982 and, 936
    election of 1992 and, 946
    election of 2004 and, 1004–1005
    FDR and, 748–749
    free trade and, 585
    Ku Klux Klan and, 476–477
    labor and, 622, 637, 750
    LBJ and, 871
    liberalism and, 892, 928
    "Lost Cause" and, 596
    Mexican Americans and, 756
    National Committee of, 677(*i*), 751, 763, 901
    New Deal and, 748, 889
    in New South, 596–599
    Nixon's dirty tricks and, 901
    organized labor and, 813
    progressive politics and, 612, 633
    Reagan and, 925, 928, 932
    Redeemers, 476, 478, 482
    in the South, 745(*i*)
    Southern, 814, 864
    split in (1948), 814
    states' rights and, 585
    urban liberalism and, 622
    women in, 751, 763
    during WWI, 684
    in WWII, 781
demographics
    African Americans and, 977(*m*), 980–981
    immigration and, 976–980
Dempsey, Jack, 718
Denmark, 770

depressions. *See also* Great Depression; Panics; recessions
    of 1873, 479
    of 1890s, 611, 629
deregulation, 918, 986
    of television industry, 924, 975, 987
desegregation, 871–872, 886, 907, 910(*i*)
detainees
    Abu Ghraib prison, 1002, 1002(*i*)
    at Guantanamo, 1012, 1017
    Muslim immigrants as, 1009
détente, 896–898, 939, 941
Detroit, Michigan
    busing in, 907
    Ku Klux Klan in, 708(*m*)
    riots in, 797, 886
Dewey, George, 650–651, 651(*m*), 655
Dewey, John, 692–693
Dewey, Thomas E., 781, 814
DeWitt, John, 785
Dewson, Molly, 751
Diana, 975
Díaz, Porfirio, 664–665
Dickinson, G. Lowes, 579
Diem, Ngo Dinh, 825, 869
Dies, Martin, 816
digital cameras, 972
Dillon, C. Douglas, 863
diplomacy
    Carter and, 920–922
    Clinton and, 951
    dollar, 664
    economic, 645–646
    isolationism and, 670
    in Latin America, 642–643
    military power as, 1012
    Senate and, 642
    U.S. expansion and, 642–644
discount brokerage firms, 962
discrimination. *See also* racism
    affirmative action and, 907
    against African Americans, 505, 530, 595–599, 752–754, 775
    against Chinese, 505, 511
    in employment, 768
    against gays, 984
    against Hispanics, 505, 510
    against Mexican Americans, 756
    in military, 775
    reverse, 907, 982
    against women, 902–906
    against women in military, 945(*i*)
    against women in workforce, 777
disease. *See also* influenza; smallpox
    epidemic, 681(*i*)
    globalization and, 966–967
    influenza, 682(*i*)
    malaria, 661, 661(*i*)
    Native Americans and, 489
diskettes, 959(*i*)

Displaced Persons Act, 849
Distant Early Warning line, 822
diversity. *See also* ethnic diversity
    Armed Forces and, 681–683
    cultural, 925
divorce, 905
Dixiecrats. *See* States' Rights Party
DNA (deoxyribonucleic acid), 972, 973(i)
Doar, John, 857
documentary impulse, 762
Dodge City, Kansas, 492
Dodson, Burton, 857
the dole, 742. *See also* welfare
Dole, Robert J. (Bob), 917, 950
dollar-a-year men, meaning of, 774
dollar diplomacy, 664
domestic servants
    African Americans as, 753
    Social Security and, 746, 763
    women as, 533
    WWII and, 777
Dominican Republic, 662, 712, 735
domino theory, 825, 870, 877
Dorr, Retha Childe, 594
Dos Passos, John, 723, 762
Doubleday, Abner, 576
Double V campaign, 780
doughboys, 678
Douglas, William O., 748
Douglass, Frederick (1818–1895), 469, 624
    home of, 626(i)
Dover, Pennsylvania, 1008
Dow Chemical Company, 882
Downing, Andrew Jackson, 560
draft, military, 678
    first in U.S., 770
    peacetime, 841
    Vietnam War and, 882, 892, 899
    WWII and, 775
Drake, Edwin L., 526
Dred Scott decision (*Dred Scott v. Sandford*; 1857), 985(i)
Dreiser, Theodore, 551, 559, 723
drought
    conservation and, 757
    federal building projects and, 756(m)
    on Great Plains, 488, 497, 517
    migration and, 757, 757(i)
    in Texas, 587
Droughty Kansas (Worrall), 495(i)
drug abuse, 982
drug benefits, for baby-boom generation, 924
drug use, 576
dry-farming methods, 497
Du Bois, W.E.B., 625, 625(i), 723, 723(i)
Dukakis, Michael, 992
Duke, James B., 530
Dulles, John Foster, 822, 824, 826
Dust Bowl (Oklahoma, Texas, New Mexico, Colorado, Arkansas, Kansas)

    conservation and, 670, 757
    federal building projects in, 756(m)
Dutch Republic. *See* Netherlands
DVD (digital video discs), 972
Dylan, Bob, 884
Dynasty (TV program), 974

Earth Day, 912, 912(i)
the East, Native American rights and, 503
Eastern Airlines, 681, 965
Eastern Europe, 803, 822, 828, 965(m)
    end of Cold War and, 941–943, 942(m)
    immigration from, 976(f)
Eastern Front (WWI), 674, 679
East Germany. *See* German Democratic Republic
East St. Louis, Illinois, 698, 703
eavesdropping program, 1009, 1017
Economic Bill of Rights, 813
economic development. *See also* agriculture; industrialization; manufacturing; mining; ranching
    capital goods and, 520
    consumer spending and, 844
    fear of communism and, 801
    government spending and, 815
    industrial capitalism and, 519–549
    military-industrial complex in, 802
    in Sun Belt, 838–839
    tax cuts and, 864
    Whig program for, 585
Economic Growth and Tax Relief Act (2001), 995
Economic Opportunity, Office of (OEO), 876, 896
Economic Opportunity Act (1964), 874(t)
Economic Recovery Tax Act (ERTA; 1981), 933, 955
economic rights of women, 533–536
economic theory
    Keynesian, 748
    supply-side, 933
    tax cuts and, 864
economic transformations, Atlantic Charter and, 771, 787
economy. *See also* business; capitalism; depressions; inflation; market economy; Panics; recessions; trade, foreign
    agricultural, 473–474, 529, 529(m), 530, 530(i)
    balanced budget and, 864, 948, 949(i)
    budget deficits and, 925, 934(i), 935(f), 936, 944, 946, 947(m), 996
    business cycles in, 710, 727
    of China, 1013
    concentration of, 627, 629
    of diminished expectations, 911
    downsizing and, 895
    election of 1972 and, 902
    expansionism and, 643–646

    federal role in, 469, 739, 742, 762
    Ford and, 917
    free-market, 928, 938
    Great Deflation and, 520
    Great Depression and, 670–671
    industrial, 613
    international, 711, 911, 916
    laissez-faire, 587, 603–604, 608, 613
    mass-consumption, 706
    Nixon and, 896
    postwar, 832–837
    productivity in, 960, 960(f)
    prohibition and, 692
    Reagan and, 954
    reconversion of, after Korean War, 813–815
    in the Southwest, 510
    in Soviet Union, 941
    tax cuts and, 996
    U.S. dominance of international, 911
    West German, 807–808
    women's rights and, 905
    WWI and, 683–685
    WWII and, 768, 774
Edison, Thomas A., 553, 555, 705
education
    about sexually transmitted diseases, 691
    affirmative action in, 907, 993
    of African Americans, 472(i)
    bilingual, 982
    child-care, 615, 615(i)
    in cities, 982
    federal aid to, 815, 831
    Freedmen's School, 472(i)
    GI Bill and, 781, 796–797, 834
    high school graduates, 565(t)
    JFK and, 864
    LBJ and, 873
    legislation on, 874(t)
    managerial class and, 834–835
    of Native American children, 503
    in 1950s, 845–846
    parochial, 592
    prayer in public schools and, 910
    public, 471–472
    school segregation and, 595–596, 886
    women and, 564, 903, 905
Educational Amendments Act (1972), 905
Egypt, 826–827
    Bush (George W.) and, 1016
    Camp David accords and, 918(i), 920
    invasion of Israel by, 911
    radical Islamic movements in, 953
Eighteenth Amendment (Prohibition; 1920), 693(m), 703, 722(i), 722–723, 735
Eighth Amendment, 910
eight-hour day, 479. *See also* work day
Einstein, Albert, 793
Eisenhower, Dwight D. (1890–1969), 895
    civil rights and, 853
    communism and, 822, 824

Eisenhower, Dwight D. (*continued*)
   covert intervention and, 824
   Cuba and, 863
   defense spending and, 827–828, 863, 868
   domino theory and, 825
   Korea and, 822
   McCarthy and, 819
   on military-industrial complex, 827–828, 833
   New Look in foreign policy of, 822, 868
   as president (1953–1961), 818–819, 822, 824, 828
   Suez crisis and, 826–827
   U-2 spy plane and, 822
   Vietnam and, 825, 869
   in WWII, 789, 808
Eisenhower Doctrine, 827
elections. *See also* presidential elections
   of 1866, 465
   of 1868, 468–469
   of 1872, 479
   of 1876, 480–481
   of 1896, 611
   of 1916, 677–678
   of 1940, 771
   of 1942, 781
   of 1944, 781
   of 1982, 936
   of 1992, 946–947, 947(*i*)
   of 1994, 948–949
   of 2006, 1006
   voter turnout for, 590(*i*), 708
electoral college, 479, 481
   election of 1940 and, 771
   election of 1928 and, 726, 727(*i*)
   election of 1932 and, 733(*m*)
   election of 2000 and, 990
   election of 2004 and, 1005
   Wilson and, 678
electricity, 522
electric utility companies, 706, 708
electrification, 747(*t*)
   rural, 737(*i*)
   TVA and, 739, 759, 760(*m*)
electronic products
   imports of, 959
   inventions of, 959(*i*), 970, 972
Elementary and Secondary Education Act (1965), 873–874
elevators, 553
Eliot, T. S., 723, 735
elite. *See also* middle class; social structure
   national, 559
   urban, 558–559, 580
Elk Hills, California, 707
Elkins Act (1903), 629
Ellington, Edward "Duke", 717
Ellison, Ralph, 762
Ellsberg, Daniel, 901
Ellsworth, Kansas, 492

el-Mokri, El-Hadj, 667(*i*)
El Paso, Texas, 508, 850
El Salvador, 937
embedded reporters, 1001
Emergency Banking Act (1933), 739, 747(*t*), 765
Emerson, Ralph Waldo (1803–1882), on children, 564
employment. *See also* unemployment
   equal opportunity in, 852
   gay rights and, 906
Endangered Animals Act (1964), 913
Endangered Species Act (1973), 913
End Poverty in California (EPIC), 751(*m*)
energy. *See also* oil industry
   alternative sources of, 913
   coal as, 727
   consumption of, 911(*f*)
   electrical, 522, 747(*t*), 759
   for manufacturing, 521–522
   nuclear, 839, 911(*f*), 913
   in Sun Belt, 838–839
energy crisis (1973–1974), 894(*i*), 911–913, 917
enforcement laws, 477
England. *See* Great Britain
English Channel, 789
English language, 980
Enron Corporation, 995, 995(*i*), 1017
entitlement programs, 896
entrepreneurs
   corporate economy and, 706
   gold rush and, 506
   sports complexes and, 718
   WWII and, 775
environment, 514, 839. *See also* national parks
   effects of mining on, 508(*i*)
   globalization and, 967–969
   of Great Plains, 488, 488(*m*), 497
   immigrants and, 980
   LBJ and, 873, 875
   legislation on, 873, 874(*t*), 913
   NAFTA and, 948
   Nixon and, 896
   Tennessee Valley Authority and, 760(*m*)
   urban, 556–558, 580
environmentalism, 514–515, 936
   in 1970s, 896, 912–913, 922
   Sierra Club and, 514
Environmental Policy Act, National (1969), 913
Environmental Protection Agency (EPA), 896, 913, 935–936, 968, 994
EPA. *See* Environmental Protection Agency
epidemics. *See also* disease
   influenza, 680(*i*)
   Native Americans and, 489
Equal Credit Opportunity Act (1974), 905
Equal Employment Opportunity Commission (EEOC), 903
equality

   of African Americans, 597–599
   before the law, 465
equal opportunity, 852, 982
Equal Rights Amendment (ERA), 905(*i*), 905–906, 906(*m*), 908–909
   election of 1980 and, 932
   opposition to, 908–909
Equal Rights Association, 469
Erdman Mediation Act (1898), 611
Erickson, Norman, 710(*i*)
Erie Railroad, 523, 523(*i*), 527
ERTA. *See* Economic Recovery Tax Act
Ervin, Sam, Jr., 908–909
Espionage Act (1917), 694, 703
Estonia, 696
Ethiopia, 769, 797, 920
ethnic cleansing, 790–791, 945, 952
ethnic conflict, 983. *See also* race riots
   in the Balkans, 952, 952(*m*)
   in Somalia, 951
ethnic diversity
   in 19th-century America, 530–531, 590(*f*)
   politics and, 589–592, 590(*f*), 606–607
ethnicity, 566, 568, 573. *See also* race
   Prohibition and, 722
ethnic minorities
   employment for, 674
   prohibition and, 692
ethnocultural conflict, 590, 592
EU. *See* European Union
Europe. *See also* migration
   Chinese spheres of influence and, 645, 651, 662–664, 663(*m*), 668
   economic recovery of, 965(*i*)
   growth of industrial regions in, 553
   immigration from, 510, 849(*f*), 976(*f*)
   jazz and, 717
   mass transit in, 558
   19th century alliances in, 666
   oil embargo *vs.*, 911
   radio in, 717
   urban development in, 553
   vs. postwar U.S., 832
   welfare system in, 746
   WWI and, 674–675, 694–698, 696(*m*)
   WWII in, 788(*m*)
European Recovery Program. *See* Marshall Plan
European Union (EU), 964, 965(*i*), 987, 1012–1013
evangelism, 573, 721, 721(*i*). *See also* Protestantism; revivalism
   abortion and, 984
   Bush (George W.) and, 992
   election of 2004 and, 1005
   in 1950s, 842
   in 1970s, 908–909
   in 1980s, 924–925
   Religious Right and, 928

Evans, Walker, 762
Evers, Medgar, 867
"evil empire," 939
evolution, 587–588, 721–722, 1008
Executive Order 8802 (minority employment rights), 781
Executive Order 9066 (Japanese internment), 784–785, 797
Exodusters, 496, 496(i), 517
expansionism, 655, 655(m)
  economy of, 644–646
  as foreign policy, 642–644
  ideology of, 647
  Manifest Destiny and, 647–648
  opposition to, 654
  roots of, 641–644
Ex Parte Endo (1944), 787
exports, 644–645. See also trade
  decline of, 959
  Great Depression and, 728
  during WWI, 684

factory system. See also industrialization; manufacturing; mills
  assembly line and, 539(i)
  industrialization and, 487
Fairbanks, Douglas, 715
Fair Campaign Practices Act (1974), 902
Fair Deal, 815, 819, 828
Fair Employment Practices Commission (FEPC), 781, 797
Fair Labor Standards Act (FLSA; 1938), 747(t), 748, 765
Fairley, Henry, 862
faith-based initiatives, 924–925, 929
faith-based politics, 992, 1008
Fall, Albert, 707
Faludi, Susan, 983
Falwell, Jerry, 908, 929, 929(i)
families, 561–566. See also birth control; children; women
  desertion of, 570
  feminism and, 905
  gay rights and, 984
  of immigrants, 976
  immigration and, 570–571
  income of, 958(f), 960(f)
  in 1950s, 844–846
  sharecropping and, 474
  television and, 844(i)
  wages and, 960–961
  wartime assistance for, 691
  women in workforce and, 777
  working-class, 529, 532–536
Family and Medical Leave Act (1993), 947, 955
Family Assistance Plan (Nixon), 896
family values, 908–909, 929(i), 975–976, 983, 986
  gay rights and, 984
A Farewell to Arms (Hemingway), 723, 735

Farmer, James, 781
farmers. See also agriculture; tenant farmers; yeoman farmers
  African American, 754
  drought and, 757
  economic problems of, 728
  election of 1936 and, 747
  as homesteaders, 495–498
  in Kansas, 495(i)
  Native Americans as, 503–504
  New Deal and, 742, 754, 762
  1920s and, 710, 727, 734
  Populism and, 602–604
  protests by, 751(m)
  rural electrification and, 737(i), 759
  socialism and, 545
  Social Security and, 746, 763
  subsidies for, 935
  War on Poverty and, 876
  during WWI, 684–685
Farmers' Alliance of the Northwest, 602
Farm Holiday Association, 730, 735, 751(m)
farming. See agriculture; farmers
Farm Loan Act (1916), 742
Farm Security Administration (FSA), 747(t), 762
Farnham, Dwight Thompson, 687
the Far West, 487, 505–515
fascism, 768–769, 782, 784, 796–797. See also Nazi (National Socialist) Party
Father Knows Best (TV program), 843
Faubus, Orval, 853
Fauset, Jessie, 723
fax (facsimile) machines, 972
FBI. See Federal Bureau of Investigation
FCC. See Federal Communications Commission
fedayeen, 1001
Federal Art Project (WPA), 760
Federal Bureau of Indian Affairs, 888
Federal Bureau of Investigation (FBI), 700, 901–902
Federal Communications Commission (FCC), 843–844, 975
Federal Deposit Insurance Corporation (FDIC), 739
Federal Emergency Relief Administration (FERA), 729(m), 742, 747(t), 754
Federal Farm Loan Act (1916), 637
federal government, 673
  activism of, 861, 875
  as broker state, 763
  bureaucracy of, 637, 637(f), 749, 762, 774, 896, 917
  Carter and, 917
  civil rights movement and, 828, 864, 867
  economy and, 815
  environmental legislation and, 913
  expansion of, 749, 768, 781, 876

  highways and, 839, 841
  housing and, 837–838
  LBJ and, 872–873, 875–876
  mining interests and, 546
  New Deal and, 739–749, 762
  in 1970s, 922
  Nixon and, 896
  photography and, 762
  public cynicism and, 896, 918
  railroads and, 522, 544, 588
  Reagan and, 924, 936, 996
  Republican Party and, 896
  shrinking of, 936, 954, 996
  states and, 896
  wartime propaganda of, 685, 693
  welfare capitalism and, 710–711
  WWII and, 781
Federal Housing Administration (FHA), 837–838
Federal Intelligence Surveillance Act (1978), 902
Federal Music Project, 760
Federal Reserve Act (1913), 635
Federal Reserve system, 918
  inflation and, 936, 959
  New Deal and, 744, 763
  1970s recessions and, 915(f)
  Roosevelt recession and, 748
  tariff reform and, 635
Federal Theatre Project (FTP), 762, 765
Federal Trade Commission (FTC), 636, 707
Federal Writers' Project (FWP), 760–762
Fei Xiaotong, 919
fellow travelers, 770, 816
Felt, W. Mark, 902
The Feminine Mystique (Friedan), 846, 903
feminism, 904(i), 924
  in 1970s, 903–906, 922
  opposition to, 905–906, 908–909, 983
  revival of, 903–906
  rise of, 617–618, 638
  third-wave, 983
Fermi, Enrico, 793
Ferraro, Geraldine, 905, 936
Field, Stephen J., 588–589
Fifteenth Amendment, 468(t), 469, 477, 483, 595–596, 598, 598(i)
  African Americans and, 624
  enforcement laws, 477–478
fifties. See affluent society (1950s)
Filipinos, wartime treatment of, 654. See also Philippines
films. See movies
"final solution," 791(i)
Finland, 696, 802, 965
fireside chats, 738–740, 765
First Amendment, 816, 910, 983
First World War. See World War I
Fiske, John, 647
Fitzgerald, F. Scott, 723, 735
Flanagan, Hallie, 762

flappers, 715–716
Fleetwood, Sara Iredell, 626(i)
Fleming, Alexander, 692(i)
flexible response policy, 868–869
"flexible specialization," 528
Florida
    abortion clinic murders in, 984
    black registered voters in, 470
    election fiasco in, 990–991
    election of 2000 in, 991(i)
    migration to, 838(m), 839
    Reconstruction in, 467(m), 469–470
    Republican government in, 478, 480–481
    Schiavo case in, 1007
Foch, Ferdinand, 679
Foley, Mark, 1006
folk songs, 760
Food Administration (WWI), 684
Food and Drug Administration (FDA), 632
food conservation, 673, 673(i), 683(i)
Food for Peace program, 863
food rationing, 673(i)
food stamps, 876, 935, 950, 960
Foote, Edward Bliss, 564
Forbes, John Murray, 523
Ford, Gerald R. (1913–2006), 902, 922
    as president (1974–1977), 917
Ford, Henry, 538, 676, 685, 706, 710
Ford Model T, consumer culture and, 713–714
Ford Motor Company, 644, 731, 961–962, 968
Fordney-McCumber Tariff (1922), 711
Ford's Theatre, 457
Foreign Affairs, 803–804
foreign aid, 863, 937(m)
foreign policy. *See also* international relations
    acquisition of territories and, 654–655
    anti-imperialism in, 654
    in Asia, 662–664
    bipartisan, 814
    Bush (George H. W.), 944–946
    Bush (George W.), 996, 1012, 1015
    in Caribbean, 655(m), 668
    Carter, 920–922
    Clinton, 951–953
    Cold War and, 812, 892
    Eisenhower, 822, 824
    expansionist, 642–644, 655(m), 668
    Ford, 917
    globalization and, 646, 655
    imperial experiment in, 652–655
    JFK, 863, 871
    lack of purpose in, 642–644, 668
    "large," 646, 649
    neoconservatives and, 998
    in 1920s, 712–713
    Nixon, 896–898
    nonalignment, 642
    Reagan, 927, 936–943

    trade and, 645–646, 662
    Venezuela and, 647
    Wilson's philosophy of reform and, 664, 693
Forman, Stanley, 910(i)
Forrest, Nathan Bedford, 476(i), 476–477
Fort Buford, Montana, 502
Fort Hall, 491
Fortounescere, Vito, 568
Fort Peck Dam, 762(i)
Fort Pillow, Tennessee, massacre at, 476
Fort Worth, Texas, 525, 525(m)
"forty-niners," 513. *See also* gold rush
Foster, William Z., 733
The Four Hundred, 559
four-minute men, 693
Four-Power Conference (1947), 807
Four Square Gospel Church, 721(i)
Fourteenth Amendment (1868), 465–467, 468(t), 477–478, 483, 588, 595–596, 598, 853
    abortion rights and, 910
    enforcement laws, 477–478
Fowler, Mark, 975
France, 770. *See also* Paris, Treaty of; Versailles, Treaty of
    appeasement and, 770
    Germany and, 769–770
    Great Depression and, 728
    in Indochina, 825
    jazz and, 717
    liberation of, 789(i)
    NATO and, 897
    Suez Canal and, 826
    U.S. invasion of Iraq and, 1001
    Washington Naval Arms Conference and, 713
    WWI and, 674, 679–680, 696–697
    WWII role of, 787, 789
Franco, Francisco, 768, 770
Franco-Prussian War (1870), 666
Frankfurter, Felix, 613, 700, 739, 748
Franklin, Roslyn, 973(i)
Franz Ferdinand, Archduke of Austria, assassination of (1914), 674
Frazer-Lemke debt relief act, 744
free blacks
    black churches and, 472
    economic independence and, 461
    education of, 472(i)
    labor of, 464(i), 474
    Reconstruction and, 459, 461–464, 470–471
    sharecropping and, 473–476
    terrorism against, 476–478
    voting rights for, 469
    wage labor and, 461, 464, 473, 479
    women, 474
Freed, Alan, 847
Freedman's Savings and Trust Company, 479
Freedmen's Bureau, 459, 461, 464, 471, 473, 483

Freedom of Information Act, 902
freedom of speech, 694, 882, 882(i)
Freedom Riders, 864, 866
Freedom Summer (1964), 872, 872(i), 882
free-market capitalism, 943
free-market economy, 928, 938
free silver, 611, 633
free speech, Scopes trial and, 721–722, 735
Free Speech Movement (FSM), 882, 882(i)
Frick, Henry Clay, 543–544, 579
Friedan, Betty, 846, 903
Friedman, Milton, 929
Friends. *See* Quakers
Frist, Bill, 1007
frontier
    concept of, 647–648
    end of, 515, 517
    mythic, 487(i), 493–494
Fuel Administration, 684
Fujita, Jun, 698(i)
Fulbright, J. William, 879
fundamentalism
    abortion and, 984
    Scopes trial and, 721–722
    Taliban and, 998
F.W. Woolworth Company, 527

G-7 nations, 964
G-8 nations, 964, 970
Gagarin, Yuri, 864
Galbraith, John Kenneth, 833
Gandhi, Mahatma, 792, 855
gang-labor system, 464, 464(i), 474
gangs
    African Americans in, 982
    zoot suits and, 784, 784(i)
Garcia, Juanita, 978
Garfield, James A. (1831–1881), 584–585
Garland, Hamlin, 496, 566
garment industry, 537, 545, 978–979
Garson, Greer, 782
Garvey, Marcus, 726, 885–886
Gary, Elbert H., 629, 699
Gary, Indiana, 710(i)
gasoline prices, 1013
Gates, Bill, 970–971, 971(i), 987
Gatling machine guns, 502
GATT. *See* General Agreement on Tariffs and Trade
gay rights, 903, 924
    conflicting values and, 984
    marriage and, 1005–1006
    in military, 947
    in 1970s, 922
    opposition to, 975, 987
Gay Task Force, National, 906
Gaza Strip, 944–945, 952, 1001(m)
GDP. *See* gross domestic product
Gellhorn, Martha, 762

gender roles, 928–929. *See also* men; women
  conservative view of, 908–909
  farming and, 496
  feminism and, 905–906
  of free blacks, 461, 464
  homesteaders and, 496
  in 1950s, 846–847
  sex-typing and, 532–533
  on television, 843
  wives and, 561–562
General Agreement on Tariffs and Trade (GATT), 832, 964
General Assembly (UN), 793, 826
General Electric (GE), 711, 713, 965
General Motors (GM), 711, 835–836, 841, 968
  sit-down strike and, 749, 765
general strike, 546
genetic codes, 973(i)
genetic testing, 972
Geneva Accords (1954), 825
Gentle Measures in the Management and Training of the Young (Abbott), 564
Gentlemen's Agreement (1907), 664
George, David Lloyd, 695(i), 696–697
George, Henry, 511
Georgia
  Barrow Plantation in, 473(m)
  Democratic Party in, 477
  sharecroppers in, 473(m), 475(i)
German Democratic Republic (East Germany), 808, 942
German immigrants, 496, 530–531, 675–676, 688(i), 693–694
  nativism and, 718
  political activism of, 543, 545, 590(f), 591
  prohibition and, 692
  unionism of, 540
Germany. *See also* Berlin; Berlin Wall; German Democratic Republic
  anti-Semitism in, 769
  automobile industry in, 911
  Balkans and, 952
  defeat of, 806
  division of, 792
  domination by, 787
  fascism in, 768–770
  Great Depression and, 728
  imports from, 959–960
  invasion of Poland by, 767, 797
  Japan and, 771
  Nazi, 768(i)
  propaganda and, 682, 693–694, 700
  reunification of, 942(m)
  Soviet Union and, 787, 789(i)
  surrender of, 790, 797
  U-boats and, 677–678
  U.S. invasion of Iraq and, 1001
  war reparations of, 696–697, 711, 735, 768–769
  welfare system in, 746

  in WWI, 674–675, 677–679
  in WWII, 767(i), 788–789(i), 789, 791
  zones of occupation in, 806
Germany, Federal Republic of (West Germany), 808
Geronimo, Chief, 502
gerrymandering, 991–992, 1006
ghettoes, 566–567, 572, 572(i). *See also* cities
  urban renewal and, 852
ghost dance, 504
ghost towns, 506
Giamatti, A. Bartlett, 931
GI Bill of Rights (Servicemen's Readjustment Act; 1944), 781, 796–797, 834–835
Gibson, Charles Dana, 564, 566
Gibson girl, 564, 566
Gilbert Islands, 792(m)
Gilded Age (late 19th century), 579, 613, 627, 642–644
The Gilded Age (Warner), 579
Gilder, George, 933
Gillette, 834
Gilman, Charlotte Perkins, 617
Gingrich, Newt, 949, 949(i), 991
Ginsberg, Allen, 848, 885
Ginsburg, Ruth Bader, 938(i), 947
glasnost, meaning of, 941
Glass-Steagall Banking Act (1932), 739, 747(t)
Glazer, Nathan, 929
Glenn, John, 864
Global Crossing, 995
globalization, 925, 958, 963–970, 986. *See also* economy: international
  China and, 1013
  computers and, 973
  corporations and, 834
  endangered environment and, 967–969
  foreign policy and, 646, 655
  outsourcing and, 965–966, 987
  terrorism and, 954
Godkin, Edwin L., 558–559
Goethals, George W., 661(i)
gold, monetary system and, 604–607, 606(i)
Goldberg, Rube, 800(i)
Goldman, Emma, 700
Goldmark, Pauline, 681
Goldmark, Peter, 834
gold mining, 505(m), 505–506, 508(i), 607
  in California, 505, 515
  Chinese in, 510–511
gold rush (1849–1857), 505–506, 510, 517
gold standard, 604–607, 606(i), 728
Goldwater, Barry, 819, 872, 873(m), 928
Goldwyn, Samuel, 716
Gompers, Samuel, 542, 542(i), 622, 654, 685
Gonzales, Alberto, 1009
González, Henry, 887
Good Housekeeping (magazine), 561, 717
Good Neighbor Policy, 670, 769

Gorbachev, Mikhail, 939, 939(i), 941–942, 955
Gore, Albert (Al), Jr., 946, 947(i), 949(i), 990–991, 991(i)
Gorgas, William C., 661(i)
Gorson, Aaron Henry, 519(i)
Gotzion, Evelyn, 778
Gould, Jay, 523, 542
government
  in America, 924, 954
  federal, 673
  limited, 479, 683, 685, 928, 936, 938, 954
  New Deal and, 737–738, 742, 745, 749
  partnership with business and, 706–713
  radio licenses and, 717
  women in, 750–752, 763
graft, in ward politics, 572
Graham, Billy, 842, 843(i), 992
Graham, Frank P., 820–821
grain. *See also* corn; rice; wheat
  prohibition and, 692
  during WWI, 684
Gramm-Rudman Act (1985), 944, 955
Grand Alliance, 801, 803
grandfather clauses, 597
Granger movement, 498, 517, 602
Grant, J. Marse, 908
Grant, Ulysses S. (1822–1885), 480(i)
  1868 election and, 468–469, 483
  1872 election and, 479, 483
  Ku Klux Klan Act of 1871 and, 478
  as president (1869–1877), 478–479, 592, 642
  Reconstruction and, 467, 478, 481–482
  scandals during administration of, 479
The Grapes of Wrath (Steinbeck), 757, 757(i), 762
grasslands, 488(m), 488–489, 497
Grasso, Ella T., 905
Grateful Dead, 884
Graves, Leslie, 794
Great American Desert, 488, 488(m), 489, 495. *See also* Great Plains
Great Atlantic and Pacific Tea Company (A&P), 527, 713
Great Basin, 505
Great Britain, 647
  alliances of, 666
  appeasement and, 770
  Germany and, 769
  Great Depression and, 728
  invasion of Iraq and, 1001
  naval blockade by, 676
  neutrality of, 770–771
  nuclear test ban treaties and, 868
  Palestine and, 826
  steel production and, 487
  Suez Canal and, 826
  U.S. relations with, 659, 668, 771
  Washington Naval Arms Conference and, 713

Great Britain (*continued*)
   welfare system in, 746
   WWI and, 674–675, 696–697
   WWII role of, 787
Great Deflation (19th century), 520
Great Depression, 622–623, 670–671, 719, 727–733, 729(f)
   beginning of, 706, 727–728
   causes of, 710
   conservatives and, 928, 954
   Hoover and, 726
   human face of, 759(i), 762
   labor unions in, 835
   popular protests in, 751(m)
   Prohibition and, 723
   WWII and, 768, 777, 781
Greater East Asia Co-Prosperity Sphere, 771–772
The Great Gatsby (Fitzgerald), 723, 735
Great Lakes, iron ore in, 521
Great Migration, 685–687, 690(m), 703, 753
   WWII and, 784
Great Moments in History (radio program), 713
Great Northern Railroad, 522–523
Great Plains
   climate of, 488(m), 488–489, 495, 497, 517
   ecosystem of, 488(m), 488–489
   as Great American Desert, 488(m), 495
   homesteaders on, 495–498, 496(i), 497, 505, 515
   as Indian country, 489
   marketing of, 491–492, 495(i)5463(i)
   railroads and, 491(m), 491–492
   ranching on, 492–493
   settlement of, 488–504, 515
   sod houses on, 496(i), 497
Great Salt Lake, 497, 505
Great Smoky Mountain National Park, 760
Great Society, 871–877, 884, 892, 925, 933, 935
   declining economy and, 911–912
   funding for, 876–877
   legislation of, 874(t)
Great Strike of 1877, 519–520
Great War. *See* World War I
Greece, 803, 805, 807
Greeley, Horace, 479, 488, 491
Green, Theodore Francis, 875(i)
greenbacks, 604. *See also* currency
Green Berets, 869
Greeneville, Tennessee, 458
greenhouse effect, 968–969
Green Party, 990
Greensboro Four, 852(i), 855(i)
Gresham, Walter Q., 646
Griffith, Beatrice, 756
Griffith, E. H., 692(i)
Grimes County, Texas, 598–599
Griswold v. Connecticut (1965), 910

gross domestic product (GDP), 644
   during 1920s, 710, 727
   postwar, 832, 833(f), 913
   under Reagan, 936
gross national product (GNP)
   under Clinton, 948
   decline of, 911
   defense spending and, 774, 774(f)
   globalization and, 964
   health care and, 947
   postwar, 833, 833(f)
   Roosevelt recession and, 748
   during WWI, 683
Group of Eight nations, 964, 970
Group of Seven nations, 964
Guadalcanal Diary (film), 782
Guam, 651–652, 655, 655(m), 791
Guantanamo Bay, Cuba, 653, 655(m), 661, 662(m), 1012, 1017
Guatemala, 643, 825
guest worker program, 978
Guevara, Che (Ernesto C.), 883
Guggenheim, Harry, 705(i)
Guiteau, Charles, 584
Gulf of Tonkin Resolution (1964), 878
gun control, 948–949
guns
   Rifle Clubs, 478
   during WWI, 674–675, 683
Gunsmoke, 843
Guthrie, Oklahoma, 503
Guy, Seymour J., 560(i)
Guzman, Jacobo Arbenz, 825
Gypsies, Holocaust and, 790

Hague Peace Conference (1899), 666
Haiti, 642, 662, 951–952
   land distribution in, 474
   U.S. military intervention in, 712
Halberstam, David, 863
Hall, G. Stanley, 563
Halliburton, 994
Hamas, 1015–1017
Hamdan v. Rumsfield (2006), 924, 1012, 1017
Hamilton, Mary Agnes, 732
Hancock, Winfield, 586(m)
Handlin, Oscar, 593
Handycam, 959(i)
Hanna, Mark, 606, 611
Hard, William, 614
Harding, Warren G. (1865–1923)
   corruption and, 707(i)
   death of, 707, 735
   as president (1921–1923), 706, 735
hardware, meaning of, 970
Harlan County, Kentucky, 735
Harlem, New York City, 567, 753–754, 765
Harlem Renaissance, 723(i), 723–726
Harman, Jane, 1012

Harper, Frances, 469
Harper's Weekly (journal), 465(i), 537(i), 634(i)
Harriman, Averell, 803, 807
Harrington, Michael, 849
Harrison, Benjamin (1833–1901)
   election of 1892 and, 584, 584(i), 607(m)
   as president (1889-1893), 589, 589(i), 602, 646
   on protective tariffs, 585
Harrison, William Henry (1773–1841), 584(i)
Harte, Bret, 513
Harvey, George, 634(i)
Hastie, William, 853
hat-in-the-ring squadron, 681(i)
hatters, 536, 540
Hawaii. *See also* Pearl Harbor, attack on
   annexation of, 651, 655, 655(m)
   Chinese immigration to, 511
   Japanese internment and, 785, 787
   strategic importance of, 646, 655(m)
   sugarcane in, 643, 643(i)
Hawley-Smoot Tariff (1930), 711, 728, 735
Hay, John, 663
Hayden, Tom, 882
Hayes, Rutherford B. (1822–1893)
   election of 1876 and, 584
   nomination of, 480
   as president (1877–1881), 481, 483
   Strike of 1877 and, 519–520
Haymarket affair, 543, 549
Hay-Pauncefote Agreement (1901), 659
Haywood, "Big Bill", 546
A Hazard of New Fortunes (Howells), 579
Head Start, 876
Health, Education, and Welfare, Department of (HEW), 819
health care
   attempts to reform, 947–948, 948(i)
   baby boom improvements in, 845
   biotechnology and, 972
   Bush (George W.) and, 993–994
   federal government and, 836
   gay rights and, 984
   illegal aliens and, 980
   JFK and, 861
   in shipbuilding industry, 774
   socialized, 815
health insurance, 622
   JFK and, 864
   labor unions and, 836
   national, 746, 815, 947–948, 955
   Social Security and, 746, 763
   welfare capitalism and, 709, 711
health savings accounts, 994
Hearst, William Randolph, 577–578, 578(i), 648–649, 732
hegemony, meaning of, 996
Helms, Jesse, 984
Hemingway, Ernest, 723, 735

Hendrix, Jimi, 884, 884(i)
Henry Street Settlement, 612
Hepburn Railway Act (1906), 629
Hereford cattle, 493
Heritage Foundation, 928, 955
Her Wedding Night (film), 715(i)
Herzegovina, 674, 952
Hess, Jean, 660
Hetch Hetchy Valley, 515
HEW. *See* Health, Education, and Welfare, Department of
Heyward, Edward Barnell, 462
Hezbollah, *versus* Israel, 1015–1017
Hickok, Lorena, 762
Hicks, Clarence J., 623
The Hidden Persuaders (Packer), 843
high crimes and misdemeanors, 466, 951
Higher Education Act (1965), 873–874, 874(t)
high school shootings, 975
Highway Act, National Interstate and Defense (1956), 839(m), 841
Highway Beautification Act (1965), 873
highways
  automobile and, 714
  Interstate, 819, 839(m)
  move to suburbs and, 839, 841
  1950s culture and, 839, 841
  postwar growth of, 819, 839(m)
Hill, Anita, 943, 944(i)
Hill, Fanny Christina (Tina), 778
Hill, James J., 522–523
Hine, Lewis, 622(i)
hippies, 884. *See also* counterculture
Hirabashi, Gordon, 787
Hirabayashi v. United States (1943), 787
Hiroshima, 767, 793(m), 794, 795(i), 797, 809
Hispanics. *See also* Latinos
  in cattle industry, 493, 493(i)
  as cowboys, 492–493, 493(i)
  culture of, 512
  in the Far West, 508–510
  Korean immigrants and, 980, 980(i)
  migratory work and, 510
  population increase of, 977(m)
  race riots by, 982(i)
  as shepherds, 493
  in the Southwest, 505, 508–510
  welfare system and, 747
Hiss, Alger, 815–816, 818, 898
"The History of the Standard Oil Company" (Tarbell), 614(i)
Hitler, Adolph, 748, 768, 768(i), 769–771, 790, 797
  Holocaust and, 790, 791(i), 825(i)
HIV infection. *See also* AIDS
  AIDS and, 968(i)
  globalization and, 966–967
Hoar, George F., 654
Höbner, Joseph Alexander von, 507

Ho Chi Minh, 697, 825
Hoffman, Abbie, 889
Hohenberg, Duchess of, 674
Holland. *See* Netherlands
Hollywood, California, 714, 715(i), 742. *See also* Los Angeles, California; movies
Hollywood films, venereal diseases, 692(i)
Hollywood Ten, 816
Holmes, Oliver Wendell, Jr., 613, 694
Holocaust, 768, 790–791, 791(i), 825(i)
  homosexuals and, 790
Holtzman, Elizabeth, 905
Home Depot, 960
home front, during WWI, 683–694, 702
Home Insurance Building, 554
Homeland Security, Department of, 995, 1004(i)
homelessness (1990s), 960
Home Owners Loan Corporation, 739
home pages, meaning of, 971
home rule, 480
Homestead Act (1862), 495, 503, 517
homesteaders, 495–498, 496(i)–497(i), 505, 515
Homestead steel strike (1892), 487, 543–544
homosexuals, 983, 986. *See also* gay rights; lesbians
  civil rights for, 903, 906
  gay liberation movement and, 906
  Holocaust and, 790
  in military, 775
  in New York City, 576
The Honeymooners (TV program), 843
Hong Kong, 791, 792(m)
Hoover, Herbert (1874–1964), 684
  at Department of Commerce, 706–707, 733
  election of 1928 and, 726, 735
  election of 1932 and, 733(m)
  Great Depression and, 728–730, 738
  illegal immigrants and, 756
  New Deal and, 742, 744
  as president (1929–1933), 728–730, 734
Hoover, J. Edgar, 700
Hoovervilles, 730, 730(i)
Hopkins, Harry, 742–743
Horton, Willie, 992
House, Edward, 677
House Committee on Un-American Activities (HUAC), 816–818, 820–821
House of Representatives, U.S. *See also* Congress, U.S.; Senate, U.S.
  Clinton impeachment and, 951
  Democratic control of, 936, 1006
  Gulf War and, 945
  Republican gains in, 932, 949
  woman suffrage and, 691
  women in, 944(i)

housing
  in cities, 851–852
  discrimination in, 838, 852
  gay rights and, 906
  LBJ and, 873
  legislation on, 747(t), 815, 819, 874(t)
  postwar boom in, 837–838
  public, 876
  suburban, 560–561
  tenements, 556–557, 556(f), 569, 572(i)
  wartime migration and, 784
Housing and Urban Development, Department of (HUD), 947
Houston, Texas, 530(i), 681
Houston Astros, 995(i)
Hovenden, Thomas, 457(i)
Howard, Oliver O., 461
Howe, Frederic, 605
Howe, Julia Ward, 469
Howe, Marie Jenny, 617
Howells, William Dean, 579
"Howl" (Ginsberg), 848
HUAC. *See* House Committee on Un-American Activities
HUD. *See* Housing and Urban Development, Department of
Huerta, Victoriano, 664–665
Hughes, Charles Evans, 677, 706, 713
Hughes, Langston, 723
Hughes, Robert P., 657
Hull, Cordell, 769
Hull House, 612, 615, 615(i)
Human Genome Project, 987
human resources, WWII and, 775–777
human rights
  Carter and, 920, 922
  in China, 1013
Human Rights, Office of, 920
Humphrey, Hubert H., 814, 863
  election of 1968 and, 889, 891, 892(m)
Hundred Days (New Deal), 739–744
Hungarian immigrants, 531–532
Hungary, 674, 696, 803, 822, 826, 942
hunger marches, 735
hunger strikes, 690
Hunt, E. Howard, 901
Hurricane Katrina (2005), 1006, 1007(i), 1017
Hurston, Zora Neale, 723, 762
Huston, John, 762
Hussein, King of Jordan, 827
Hussein, Saddam, 925, 945–946, 999–1001, 1004, 1016(m)
Hutu extremists, 951
hydrogen bomb, 809, 822. *See also* nuclear weapons

Iacocca, Lee, 962, 987
IAEA. *See* International Atomic Energy Agency
IBM. *See* International Business Machines
Ibuka, Masaru, 959(i)

Ickes, Harold, 739, 743, 754, 759
Idaho
    Chinese in, 511
    Japanese internment in, 785, 785(i)
    mining in, 511, 546
idealism, 863
    progressive, 613
identity, in California, 512
identity politics, 904
ideology, 587
IED. *See* improvised explosive devices
illegal immigrants, 976, 980
    Bush (George W.) and, 993, 1006
Illinois
    prohibition and, 691
    wheat in, 498
illness. *See* disease
IMF. *See* International Monetary Fund
immigrants, 638. *See also* Chinese immigrants; German immigrants; immigration; Irish immigrants; migration
    Americanization of, 681, 693–694
    Asian, 849(f), 875, 924, 976–980
    Catholic, 573
    as cheap labor, 530–531, 548
    in cities, 551, 551(i), 566–568, 570–572
    Democratic Party and, 590–592, 590(f), 707
    deportation of, 850
    discrimination against, 734–735, 875
    disease and, 966
    Eastern European, 875
    European, 531, 531(f), 549, 567(m), 849(f)
    Filipino, 849
    German, 530–531, 540, 543, 545, 675–676, 688(i), 693–694
    hostility to, 987
    Hungarian, 531–532
    Irish, 530–531, 537, 675, 692
    Italian, 530–531, 566, 567(i)
    Japanese, 718, 849
    Jewish, 716
    Korean, 849, 980
    Latino, 849–850, 924, 976–980
    legal, 849(f)
    Mexican, 924, 976
    newspapers and, 566
    in New York City, 552
    Norwegian, 496
    politics and, 735
    Puerto Rican, 850
    Scandinavian, 530–531
    South American, 850, 875
    Southeast Asian, 849
    Swedish, 496
    U.S. fear of anarchy and, 700–701
immigration
    of Asians, 987
    of Latinos, 987
    legislation on, 874(t), 875
    in 1920s, 718
    in 1950s, 847, 849–850
    restrictions on, 622, 718–721
    trends in, 976(f)
Immigration Act (1965), 875, 976, 986
Immigration and Naturalization Service (INS), 980
immigration laws, 719, 849(f)
    LBJ and, 875
    in 1950s, 849–850
Immigration Restriction League, 622
impeachment
    of Adelbert Ames, 478
    Clinton, 950–951, 951(i), 954
    Johnson, 467–468, 483, 951
    Nixon, 902
imperialism, U.S., 641–642, 652–655, 658(i)
    globalization and, 969
    opposition to, 654, 656–657, 660, 668
Imperial Presidency, 774
imports. *See* trade, foreign
improvised explosive devices (IED), 1002
inclusiveness, politics of, 992–993
income. *See also* wages
    of families, 958(f), 960(f)
    of farmers, 727
    of immigrants, 977–979
    of Native Americans, 754
    unequal distribution of, 713, 727
income taxes, 684–685
indentured servants
    Asians as, 511
    in Caribbean, 474
    laws against, 511
India, 1013
    McDonald's in, 965
    nuclear power and, 1013
    outsourcing and, 965–966
    WWII and, 791
Indiana
    Ku Klux Klan in, 721
Indian Affairs, Bureau of, 850
Indian Affairs, Office of, 499, 502–503
Indian Education (Morgan), 500
Indian Reorganization Act (1934), 754, 765
Indian reservations. *See* Native Americans: reservation system and
Indian Rights Association, 503
Indian Territory
    of Oklahoma, 503
individualism, 628, 928
    election of 1928 and, 726
    Great Depression and, 732
    ideology of, 587–588
    Lindbergh and, 705
individual rights, New Deal and, 737–738
Indochina, 771–772, 822. *See also* Cambodia; Vietnam
Indonesia, 1013
    foreign trade and, 728
    radical Islamic movements in, 953

industrialization. *See also* factory system; manufacturing; mills
    accumulation of wealth and, 587–589
    capitalism and, 519–549
    environmental pollution and, 519(i)
    immigrant labor and, 530–531, 548
    integrated systems within, 521, 525(m), 526, 528
    large-scale enterprise and, 524–528
    in late 19th century, 487, 519(i), 519–538
    middle class and, 560–561
    mining and, 506
    in New South, 529(m), 529–530
    railroads and, 519–520, 522–524, 524(m)
    reversal of, 915–916
    robber barons and, 522–523
    skills for, 531
    urbanization and, 551–552, 580, 638
Industrial Revolution, in Great Britain, 520
industrial unionism, 544, 749. *See also* labor unions
Industrial Workers of the World (IWW; Wobblies), 546–547, 549, 637, 694, 700
industry
    automobiles and, 714
    decline of, 915–916
    development of, 628, 837
    employment in, 835–836
    foreign policy and, 827
    growth of, 642, 668
    interstate highways and, 839(m)
    managerial revolution and, 709
    new techniques in, 709
    postwar, 835–837
    during WWI, 683–685
infant mortality, 709
inflation
    after WWI, 699
    Carter and, 918, 920
    energy crisis and, 911–912
    interest rates and, 958
    in 1920s, 710
    in 1970s, 913, 915, 915(f), 922
    postwar, 833
    Roosevelt recession and, 748
    Vietnam War and, 879
    WWII and, 780
The Influence of Seapower upon History (Mahan), 646
influenza
    1918–1919 epidemic of, 680(i)
    wartime propaganda and, 693–694
information age, 972
information technology, 925
In His Steps (Sheldon), 574
In Our Time (Hemingway), 723
In Re Jacobs (1885), 588
insider knowledge, 962
installment plans, 713. *See also* credit
Insull, Samuel, 705–706

insurgencies
    in Iraq, 1002–1003, 1006, 1016
    in Vietnam, 1002
intellectual property rights, 964, 972
"intelligent design," 1008
Inter-American Treaty of Reciprocal Assistance (Rio Treaty; 1947), 824(m)
intercontinental ballistic missiles (ICBMs), 868, 898
Intermediate Nuclear Forces Treaty (1988), 924
Internal Revenue Service (IRS), 762. See also taxation
International Atomic Energy Agency (IAEA), 1013–1014
International Bank for Reconstruction and Development (World Bank), 832
International Business Machines (IBM), 834, 970
International Criminal Court, 998
International Harvester, 710
internationalism, 832. See also globalization; isolationism
International Monetary Fund (IMF), 832, 834, 964, 970
international relations
    Cold War, 822, 824(m), 824–827
    overseas bases and, 646, 668
    U.S. dominance in, 659–662
    before WWI, 674
International Telephone and Telegraph Corporation, 834
International Typographical Union (1852), 541
Internet, 924, 971–973
Interstate Commerce Commission (ICC), 629
Interstate Highway Act (1956), 819, 839, 839(m), 841
interventionism, 769–770
intifada, meaning of, 945
iPod, 972
Iran, 803, 825
    dictatorship in, 824
    nuclear power and, 1013–1014
    oil production in, 911, 921
    revolution in, 911, 921, 945
    Shah of, 921
    uranium enrichment by, 1017
Iran-Contra affair, 936–938, 937(m), 955
Iranian hostage crisis, 921, 921(i), 922, 929, 1001(m)
Iraq, 696(m)
    creation of, 1016(i)
    dead soldiers in, 990
    insurgencies in, 1002–1003, 1006
    invasion of Kuwait by, 925, 945
    oil production in, 911
    Persian Gulf War and (1990–1991), 945–946, 1001(m)
    al-Sadr in, 1015(i)
    U.S. invasion of, 924–925, 999–1002, 1016–1017
Ireland, famine in, 530
Ireland, John, 572
Irish Home Rule, 675
Irish immigrants, 675
    Democratic Party and, 590, 590(f)
    machine politics and, 572
    nativism and, 718
    19th-century, 530–531, 537
    opposition to, 980
    prohibition and, 692
iron industry, 537, 537(i), 540
    coal in, 552
    in Great Britain, 487
    mining in, 529(m)
    pig iron in, 520
    steel and, 520
    wrought iron in, 520
"Ironworkers-Noontime" (painting), 537(i)
irreconcilables, 697
irrigation
    Mormons and, 497
    water resources and, 515
Islam. See also Muslims; Shiite Muslims; Sunni Muslims
    African American, 886
    fundamentalist, 921, 1001(m)
    militant terrorists, 1014–1016
    radicalism, 952–953
Islamic extremism, 1014–1016
isolationism, 642, 644, 666, 670, 697
    opposition to, 769–770
    retreat from, 770–771
    WWI and, 712
    WWII and, 790
Israel, 999(i), 1014
    Camp David accords and, 918(i), 920
    in international politics, 911
    oil embargo and, 911
    Palestinians and, 825–826, 944–945, 1001(m)
    versus Hezbollah, 1017
Italy, 674, 696
    fascism in, 768–770, 797
    immigration from, 530–531, 566, 567(i)
    invasion of Ethiopia by, 769, 797
    Japan and, 771
    Washington Naval Arms Conference and, 713
    WWII and, 788(m), 789
Iwo Jima, 791, 793(m), 797
IWW. See Industrial Workers of the World

Jackson, Helen Hunt, 500, 503, 513, 517
Jackson, Jesse, 901, 991(i)
Jackson, William Henry, 553(i)
Jackson State College, killing at, 898
James, Henry, 579

James, William, 613, 654
Japan, 645–646
    automobile industry in, 911
    defeat of, 813
    domination by, 787
    economic growth and, 963
    as economic power, 959–960, 987
    fascism in, 768–769
    Germany and, 767(i)
    immigrants from, 512, 756
    imports from, 959–960
    Indochina (Vietnam) and, 771–772
    invasion of China by, 768–769, 771, 797
    invasion of Manchuria by, 768
    oil embargo *vs.*, 911
    Pearl Harbor and, 772–773, 773(i), 796–797
    quality of products from, 834
    surrender of, 794, 797
    U.S. relations with, 663–664, 668
    war with Russia (1905) and, 675
    Washington Naval Arms Conference and, 713
    WWI and, 674, 697
    WWII and, 782, 791
Japanese Americans
    internment of, 670, 784–787, 785(i)
    Nisei (second-generation), 785, 787
Jarvis, Howard, 916
jazz, 716(i), 716–717, 848
Jazz Age (1920s), 718, 726
The Jazz Singer (film), 716
Jefferson Airplane, 884
Jenney, William Le Baron, 554
Jericho, Israel, 952
Jewish Daily Forward, 566, 570–571
Jews
    Arabs and, 952
    discrimination against, 838
    election of 1936 and, 747
    Holocaust and, 790–791
    immigration restrictions and, 718
    Ku Klux Klan and, 721
    movie studios and, 716
    Nazi view of, 769
    in 1950s, 842
    in Soviet Union, 920–921
    Yiddish theater and, 566
Jiang Jieshi (Chiang Kai-shek), 810
jihad, meaning of, 989
jihadi bomber, meaning of, 1002
Jim Crow laws, 597–599, 624, 721, 886
jingoism, 648–650
Job Corps, 876
Joffre, Joseph, 678
John Paul II, Pope (1920–2005), 941, 941(i)
Johnson, Andrew (1808–1875), 458(i)
    impeachment of, 467–468, 483, 951
    as president (1865-1869), 458–466, 483

Johnson, Andrew (*continued*)
  Reconstruction plan of, 458(*i*), 458–459, 461, 473, 481, 483
  veto of civil rights bill by, 464
  veto of Reconstruction Act by, 467
Johnson, Hiram W., 618, 697
Johnson, Lady Bird, 873
Johnson, Lyndon B. (1908–1973), 744, 862, 928, 996, 1002
  affirmative action and, 907
  civil rights movement and, 872
  credibility gap of, 879
  Great Society of, 871–877, 884, 892
  as president (1963–1969), 871–877
  Vietnam policy of, 877–878, 878(*f*), 884, 891–892
Jolson, Al, 716
Jones, Bobby, 718
Jones, Paula, 952
Jones Act (1916; 1917), 654
Jones and Laughlin steel works (Pittsburgh), 531
Jordan, 827, 1003
Joseph, Chief of Nez Percé, 502
journalism. *See also* mass media
  national culture and, 717–718
  reform, 613–614
  sensationalist, 648–649, 649(*i*)
  women in, 752
  yellow, 577–578
Journal of Negro History, 686
judicial restraint, 910
judiciary. *See also* common law; court system; law; Supreme Court
  Ku Klux Klan and, 478
  on rights of private property, 588
  supremacy of in late 19th century, 588–589
Julian, George, 466
The Jungle (Sinclair), 632
the Junta (Cuban exiles), 648
juvenile delinquency
  music and, 847
  WWII and, 784

Kaiser, Henry J., 774–775, 775(*i*), 783(*i*), 837
Kaiser Corporation, 784
Kaiser Permanente Medical Care Program, 775
kamikaze missions, 791
Kansas
  advertising, 495(*i*)
  African American exodus to, 496, 496(*i*)
  Apache Indians in, 502
  creationism and, 1008
  farmers in, 495(*i*), 498
  Long Drive and, 492
  prohibition and, 693(*m*)
Kansas City, Missouri, 492, 557–558
  jazz and, 716
  stockyard centers in, 525, 525(*m*)
Kansas Pacific Railroad, 492(*i*)

Kashmir, 1013
Kasich, John, 949(*i*)
Kazakhstan, 1013
Kearney, Denis, 511
Keaton, Buster, 715
Keegan, John, 767
Kefauver, Estes, 847
Kelley, Florence, 615
Kelley, Oliver H., 498
Kellogg, Frank, 713
Kellogg-Briand Peace Pact (1928), 713, 735
Kennan, George F., 803–804, 804(*i*), 807
  containment theory of, 804, 942
Kennedy, Anthony, 931, 938
Kennedy, Edward (Ted), 929
Kennedy, Jacqueline, 870
Kennedy, John Fitzgerald (1917–1963), 862(*i*)
  assassination of, 870–871, 884, 892
  civil rights and, 867
  domestic policies of, 864
  foreign policy of, 863
  Mexican Americans and, 887
  as president (1961–1963), 861–871
  Vietnam policy and, 877–878, 892
Kennedy, Robert F., 863, 887
  assassination of, 861, 889, 892, 892(*m*)
  civil rights and, 866
Kent State University, killings at, 898
Kentucky, strikes in, 735
Kenya, 953, 989
Kerner Commission (1968), 907
Kerouac, Jack, 848
Kerry, John, 1004(*i*), 1004–1005
Keun, Odette, 758
Keynes, John Maynard, 748, 815
Khan, A.Q., 1013
Khomeini, Ayatollah Ruhollah, 921, 945
Khrushchev, Nikita S., 822, 832(*i*), 863, 868, 942
Kim Il Sung, 810
King, Constance, 743(*t*)
King, Martin Luther, Jr. (1929–1968), 855–856, 866–867, 868(*i*), 872, 876, 983
  assassination of, 861, 886, 889, 892
  Jesse Jackson and, 901
King, Rodney, 982
Kingfish. *See* **Long, Huey**
King's Canyon National Park, 514
King's College. *See* Columbia University
Kiowa Indians, 489, 499(*m*)
Kirkpatrick, Jeane, 929
Kissinger, Henry, 896–897, 899–900
"kitchen debate" (Nixon-Khrushchev), 831, 832(*i*)
Knickerbocker Trust Company, 635
Knights of Labor, 540, 541(*i*), 542–543, 548–549, 595
Knox, Frank, 771
Kodak, 644
Koehler, Karl, 776

Koontz, Elizabeth Duncan, 909
Korea, 772. *See also* North Korea; South Korea
  dictatorship in, 824
  immigrants from, 849, 980, 980(*i*)
  Japanese and Chinese claims to, 646, 664
  thirty-eighth parallel in, 811(*m*), 812–813
Koreans, race riots by, 982(*i*), 983
Korean War (1950–1953), 810–812, 811(*m*), 812(*i*)
  beginning of, 810, 815
  defense spending and, 774(*f*)
  end of, 812
  impact of, 812, 818
  public support in U.S. for, 811, 819
Korematsu v. United States (1944), 787
Kosovo, 952(*m*)
K Street Project, 991, 1006
Kuhn, Loeb & Co., 524
Ku Klux Klan, 476(*i*)–477(*i*), 477–478, 483, 598(*i*), 670, 853, 857
  civil rights movement and, 872
  Democratic Party and, 477, 707
  leader of, 476–477
  revival of, 708(*m*), 734–735
  women in, 719(*i*)
Ku Klux Klan Act (1871), 468(*t*), 477–478
Kurds, 945, 1016(*i*)
Kuwait
  Iraq's invasion of, 925, 945, 1000
  oil production in, 911
  Persian Gulf War and, 1001(*m*)
Kyoto Treaty (1997), 969, 987, 998

labor. *See also* indentured servants; labor unions; slavery
  Adamson eight-hour law for, 637
  antiunion movement and, 699
  autonomous, 536–538
  capital and, 519–549
  free black, 461, 464, 464(*i*)
  gang, 464, 464(*i*), 474
  shortage of, 777
  Southern, 529–530
  systematic control of, 537–538
  wage, 464(*i*), 473, 479
  work day and, 685
  work week and, 677(*i*), 710, 718
  yellow-dog contracts and, 543
Labor, U.S. Department of, 935
laborers
  factory, 622
  Jewish garment, 537, 545
  migrant, 719, 849–850, 886–887
  railroad, 637
labor force
  aristocracy of, 537
  changes in, 528–536, 528(*f*)
  children in, 536, 536(*i*)
  for manufacturing, 528–538
  for mining, 536(*i*)

sex-typing and, 532–533
white-collar workers in, 529
women in, 531, 533–537, 545
Labor Relations Act. *See* Wagner Act
labor unions, 538–548, 622. *See also* strikes
African Americans and, 542–543, 750
Amalgamated Association of Iron and Steel Workers, 543
anti-unionism and, 636–637
Brotherhood of Locomotive Firemen, 544
Bush (George W.) damage to, 995
communism and, 816
decline of, 924, 987
Democratic Party and, 901
election of 1936 and, 747
emergence of, 540, 542–543, 670
immigration and, 718
industrial unions and, 544
Mexican Americans and, 886–887
in mining industry, 506
NAFTA and, 948, 966
need for, 538, 540
New Deal and, 742, 749–750, 756
organized shops and, 814
Populist Party and, 603
postwar strikes and, 813
post-WWI antiunion movement and, 685, 699, 699(i)
pure-and-simple unionism, 542–543
reform and, 540–542, 613
Seattle strike and, 699, 699(i)
seniority systems in, 749
steel industry and, 749–750, 750(i)
strength of, 835–836, 836(f)
in Sun Belt, 916
trade unionism and, 540–542
wages and, 780
welfare capitalism and, 711
women in, 541–544
working hours and, 543, 637
WWII and, 777, 780
Ladies' Home Journal (magazine), 561, 717
La Follette, Robert M., 613, 623–624, 627, 638, 676, 697, 708
laissez-faire principle, 896
Lakin, Kansas, 497(i)
Lakota. *See* Sioux Indians
land
livestock and, 509–510
Native Americans and, 755(i)
ownership of, 472–476, 478
sharecroppers and, 742
land grants
for railroads, 491, 495, 522
from Spain, 509–510
in Virginia, 489
Lange, Dorothea, 757, 757(i), 759(i), 762
languages
in California, 980
Catholic immigrants and, 573

English, 980
German, 676, 693
immigrants and, 983
Latino immigrants and, 976
of Native Americans, 755
Yiddish, 570, 572, 574
Laos, Vietnam War and, 877(m), 878, 900
Laredo, Texas, 720(i)
Latin America
immigration from, 719, 976, 976(f)
interventionism and, 769
military interventions in, 711
U.S. involvement in, 937(m)
Latinos. *See also* Hispanics
affirmative action and, 907
Bush (George W.) and, 993
employment discrimination and, 781
migration to cities of, 850
race riots and, 983
on television, 843
youth gangs of, 784, 784(i)
Latter-day Saints, Church of Jesus Christ of. *See* Mormons
Latvia, 696
law, 876. *See also* common law; court system; immigration laws; judiciary; Supreme Court
antitrust, 629, 635–636, 684
blue, 590, 592
child labor, 615, 633, 637
eight-hour, 637
equality before, 465
experience and, 613
Jim Crow, 597–599, 721, 886
minimum wage, 615, 617–618, 633, 815, 819
right-to-work, 814
on women's civil rights, 903, 905
The Law of Civilization and Decay (B. Adams), 647
Lawrence, William, 587
Lawrence v. Texas (2003), 931, 984
lawyers, 605
Leach, Robin, 959
lead mines, 506
League of Nations, 695, 696(m), 697, 702
U.S. and, 703, 706
WWII and, 768–769, 792
League of United Latin American Citizens (LULAC), 781
League of Women Voters, 708, 709(i)
Leary, Timothy, 885
Lease, Mary Elizabeth, 603, 603(i)
Lebanon, 696(m), 827, 944, 1016
Legal Services Program, 876
Leibowitz, Samuel, 753(i)
leisure
automobile and, 714
consumerism and, 714
labor unions and, 836
in 1920s, 714, 718

Lemke, William, 748
Lend-Lease Act (1941), 771, 772(m), 797
Lenin, Vladimir Ilych, 679
Leningrad, Soviet Union, 787, 788(m)
lesbians, 906
Leslie's Illustrated Weekly Newspaper, 673(i)
Le Temps (newspaper), 655, 659
Levitt, Arthur, 837(i), 837–838
Levittown, Long Island, 837(i), 837–838
Lewinsky, Monica, 950–951, 951(i)
Lewis, John L., 749, 780, 813
Lewis, Sinclair, 723
Lexis-Nexis programs, 972
Leyte Gulf, Battle of, 791
liability, limited, 522
Libby, 750
liberal consensus, 819
liberalism, 892
Fair Deal, 815
New Deal and, 737–738, 758, 762
postwar coalition of, 819
role of the state and, 815
urban, 618–626, 638
Liberal Republican Party, 479
Liberty League, 744
liberty of contract, 613
Liberty ships, 775, 775(i)
libraries
establishment of, 578–579
Internet and, 972
Liddy, G. Gordon, 901
liens, sharecropping and, 474, 476
Life (magazine), 658(i), 762, 762(i), 783(i), 790, 842
life belts, around cities, 841(i)
Life of Reilly (TV program), 843
Lifestyles of the Rich and Famous (TV program), 959
lightning war. *See* blitzkrieg
Likud Party (Israel), 952
Liliuokalani, Queen of Hawaii (r. 1891–1893), 643
limited liability, 522
Lincoln, Abraham (1809–1865), 754. *See also* Civil War
assassination of, 458, 483
paper money and, 604
Reconstruction and, 458, 870
second inaugural address of, 457
speeches of, 457
tariffs under, 585
Ten Percent Plan, 458, 483
Lincoln Brigade, American, 770
Lindbergh, Charles (1902–1974), 705, 705(i), 735, 771
Ling, Maya, 890
Ling-Temco-Vought, 834
Lippmann, Walter, 637, 828
literacy, voting rights and, 872
literacy tests, 593, 597

mills (continued)
    steel, 519(i), 520–522, 521(i)
    textile, 529(m), 529–530
Milosevic, Slobodan, 952, 952(m)
miltary tribunals, Guantanamo and, 1012, 1017
minimum wage
    JFK and, 864
    laws on, 615, 617–618, 633, 815, 819
    New Deal and, 742
    Supreme Court on, 748
    vs. unemployment, 960
    for women, 633, 750
    women and, 711
Minimum Wage Act (1966), 874(t)
mining
    in Arizona, 510(i)
    Chinese labor for, 510–511
    coal, 521–522, 531, 536
    copper, 506
    environmental pollution of, 508(i)
    in the Far West, 505–506
    free silver and, 604
    gold, 505(m), 505–506, 508(i), 607. *See also* gold rush
    labor force for, 531, 536(i)
    migrant labor and, 510, 531
    silver, 505(m), 605
    strikes against, 603
    strikes in, 546, 547(i)
    technology for, 508(i)
    zinc, 506
mining camps, 513
Minneapolis, Minnesota, 555(i)
Minneconjou Indians, 504
Minnesota, 496, 498
minorities. *See also* particular groups
    consumer culture and, 734
    1950s culture and, 847
    rights of, 906–907
    women, 750, 763
Minow, Newton, 844
Minutemen border patrols, 924
Miss America pageant, 903, 904(i)
missiles
    intercontinental ballistic (ICBMs), 822
    Polaris, 822
    "Star Wars" and, 955
"Mission Accomplished" banner, 1001
Mississippi, 478
    black registered voters in, 470
    Ku Klux Klan in, 478
Mississippi Freedom Democratic Party, 872
Missouri, stem-cell research in, 1008
Missouri Pacific Railroad, 492, 523
Missouri River, 762(i)
Mitchell, John, 902
Miyatake, Toyo, 785(i)
Mobil, 834

mobs. *See also* race riots; riots
    in San Francisco, 511
A Modern Instance (Howells), 579
modernism, Protestant, 721
Moley, Raymond, 739
Molotov, Vyacheslav, 803, 807
Mondale, Walter F., 917, 936
monkey trial. *See* Scopes ("monkey") trial
Monnet, Jean, 807
monopolies, 526
    computer operating systems, 971
    mining and, 506
    on nuclear weapons, 803
    railroads and, 498
    Standard Oil Company, 614, 614(i)
    television regulation and, 975
Monroe Doctrine (1823), 647, 937(m)
    Roosevelt Corollary to, 662
Montana
    gold in, 505
    mining in, 511
    Sioux Indians in, 502
Montgomery, Alabama, 853, 855
Montgomery Ward, 498, 527
Montreal environmental protocol, 987
Montreal protocol (1987), 968
Moody, Dwight L., 574
Moore, John Bassett, 655
Moral Majority, 908, 929, 929(i)
moral reform, after WWI, 691–692
Morgan, J. P., 578, 605, 627(i)
Morgan, Thomas J., 499–500
J.P. Morgan & Co., 524
Morgenthau, Henry, Jr., 739
Morita, Akio, 959(i)
Mormons, 505, 507
    as farmers, 497
    prohibition and, 692
Moroccan crisis, 666
Morrison, Tony, 974(i)
Morton, Ferdinand "Jelly Roll", 717
Morton, Oliver, 466
Moscow, 787
Mosinee, Wisconsin, mock Communist takeover, 801
Mossadegh, Muhammad, 825
motels, forerunners to, 714
Moussoaui, Zacarias, 998
movies, 574
    mass culture and, 670, 714–716
    "talkies," 715(i), 716, 735
    youth culture and, 847
movie theaters, 782
Moynihan, Daniel Patrick, 896, 929
Mozambique, 854, 939
Mrs. Miniver (film), 782
muckrakers, 613–614, 622
Mugwumps, 592, 594, 654
Muhammad, Elijah, 886
Muir, John, 514(i), 514–515, 629

Mulberry Street, New York City, 551(i)
Muller v. Oregon (1908), 615, 616(t), 617
multiculturalism, 983, 987. *See also* ethnic diversity
multi-polar world, 1012–1014
Munich Conference (1938), 770, 797
Murdoch, Rupert, 975
Murrow, Edward R., 782
museums, in cities, 578
music
    African American, 847–848
    the Beatles, 884
    bebop, 848
    of counterculture, 884, 892
    cultural dissent and, 848
    folk, 884
    jazz, 716(i), 716–717
    New Deal and, 760
    rhythm and blues, 847
    rock 'n' roll, 884
    of youth culture, 847–848
Muskie, Edmund S., 891
Muslims, 952, 952(m). *See also* Arabs; Islam
    African American, 886
    in Europe, 1017
    fundamentalist, 921, 1001(m)
    hatred of America by, 999(i)
    humiliating treatment of, 1002, 1002(i)
    militant, 1014–1016
    racial profiling and, 1009
    radical, 924, 944–945, 952–953, 953(i), 955
Muslim terrorism, rise of, 925, 953
Mussolini, Benito, 742, 748, 768, 789
My Lai massacre, 899
Myrdal, Gunnar, 852

NAACP. *See* National Association for the Advancement of Colored People
Nader, Ralph, 913, 990
NAFTA. *See* North American Free Trade Agreement
Nagasaki, 767, 793(m), 794, 797, 809
Nanking, sack of (1937), 771
NAPSTER, 972
NASA. *See* National Aeronautics and Space Administration
NASDAQ Exchange, 964(i)
Nasser, Gamal Abdel, 826–827, 827(i)
Nast, Thomas, 477(i)
National Advisory Commission (Kerner Commission; 1968), 907
National Aeronautics and Space Administration (NASA), 819, 864
National American Woman Suffrage Association, 709(i)
National Association for the Advancement of Colored People (NAACP), 638, 723(i), 853, 903
    Communists and, 816

formation of (1909), 625
segregation and, 853, 855
on segregation in military, 775
in WWII, 781
National Basketball Association, 966
National Broadcasting Company (NBC), 717
National Consumer's League, 681
National Defense Advisory Commission, 685, 771
National Endowment for the Arts (NEA), 874(t), 875
National Endowment for the Arts and the Humanities, 983
National Endowment for the Humanities (NEH), 874(t), 875
National Environmental Policy Act (1969), 913
National Gay Task Force, 906
National Grange of the Patrons of Husbandry, 498, 517
National Guard, 882
National Housing Acts
of 1937, 747(t), 748
of 1949, 815
National Industrial Recovery Act (NIRA; 1933), 742, 745, 747(t), 749, 765
nationalism, 911
Arab, 826–827
jingoistic, 648–650
New, 633, 638
nationalization, Mexican government and, 711
National Labor Relations Board (NLRB), 747(t), 750
National Labor Union, 479
national liberation, wars of, 863
National Liberation Front (NLF), 869
National Organization for Women (NOW), 903, 905, 983
National Origins Act (1924), 670, 719, 721, 849, 986
national parks, 514–515, 631(m), 760, 873
National Recovery Administration (NRA), 742, 743(i), 744, 753
National Review (periodical), 928–929
National Rifle Association, 949
National Science Foundation, 833, 972
National Security Act (1947), 809
National Security Agency, eavesdropping program of, 1009, 1017
National Security Council (NSC), 809
National Union for Social Justice, 744
National Union Party, 465
national unity, WWI and, 692–694
National Urban League, 625, 638, 816
National War Labor Board (NWLB), 685, 780
National Wilderness Preservation System, 936
National Woman's Party (NWP), 617, 690, 691(i)
National Woman Suffrage Association, 469, 470(i)

National Women's Conference (1977), 905
National Women's Liberation Party, 904(i)
National Women's Political Caucus, 905
National Women's Trade Union League, 615
National Youth Administration (NYA), 755
Nation of Islam, 886
Native Americans, 647. *See also individual peoples/tribes*
in Armed Forces, 681–683
assimilation of, 755
civil rights of, 888, 892
culture of, 513
education of, 500–501, 503, 503(i), 888
on Great Plains, 488(m), 489, 498, 515
migration to cities of, 850
in military, 775
mission life and, 513
mythic West and, 494
New Deal and, 755, 755(i)
religions of, 489
reservation system and, 498–504, 499(m), 502(m), 517, 850
termination policy and, 888
unemployment among, 888
War on Poverty and, 875
wars with, 487, 499(m)
Native Son (Wright), 762
nativism, 718–721
NATO. *See* North Atlantic Treaty Organization
natural resources. *See* environment
natural selection, 588
Nature Conservancy, 968
Navajo Indians, 499, 499(m), 509
naval blockades, during WWI, 676
naval power. *See* Navy, U.S.
Naval War College, 642
Navy, U.S., 641–642, 678–679
battleships and, 640(i), 668
building of, 647, 659
power of, 646–647, 659, 664, 668
strategy of, 652–653
NAWSA. *See* Woman Suffrage Association, National American
Nazi movement, in America, 721
Nazi (National Socialist) Party, 768(i), 769, 796
Nebraska, 497–498
Neel, Alice, 760
Negro Labor Relations League, 780(i)
Negro National League, 718
Negro Women, National Council of (NCNW), 754
Negro World, 726
Nelson, Donald, 774
neoconservatives, 929, 933, 996, 998–999, 1004
nesters, 493
Netanyahu, Benjamin, 952
Netherlands, German invasion of, 770
neutrality, 670, 675–678

Neutrality Acts, 797
of 1935, 769
of 1937, 770
Nevada, 505, 513
Nevelson, Louise, 760
Newark, New Jersey, rioting in, 886
Newbold, Gregory, 1006
New Deal (1933–1939), 548, 673, 691, 726, 729(m), 730, 765, 813, 819, 927
African Americans and, 752–754
anticommunism and, 816
banks and, 739
capitalism and, 739
coalition of, 875
Cold War and, 802
conservation and, 757, 759–760
conservatism *vs.*, 896
deficit spending and, 864
election of 1932 and, 733
first (1933-1935), 738, 747(t)
first Hundred Days of, 739–744
Great Society and, 872, 875
legacies of, 814
legislation of, 739, 747(t)
Native Americans and, 755
postwar programs and, 832
Republican Party and, 814
rollback of, 819, 828
second (1935–1938), 746–749
Supreme Court on, 748, 750
vs. Truman's Fair Deal, 815
women and, 750, 763
WWII and, 771, 774, 781
New Democrats, 946, 950, 954
New England, textile industry in, 529
New Federalism, 896
New Freedom, 634, 637–638
New Frontier, 862–864, 892
New Guinea, 791, 792(m)
New Jersey, rioting in, 886
Newlands Reclamation Act, 631
New Left, 882, 892, 903. *See also* Students for a Democratic Society (SDS)
New Look, 868
New Mexico
Hispanic culture in, 508–509
Mexican Americans in, 685
mining in, 510(i)
Native Americans in, 509
New Nationalism, 633–635, 638
New Orleans, Louisiana
Hurricane Katrina and, 1006, 1007(i)
population of, 552(t)
railroad connections to, 492
New Right, 924–925, 927–928, 929(i), 954, 958
New Spain, 505, 508
newspapers, 655, 659. *See also* journalism
African American, 686
baseball and, 577

newspapers (*continued*)
   circulation of, 577(*t*)
   globalization and, 975
   immigrants and, 566
   mass culture and, 717
   New York, 576–577, 648–649
   propaganda and, 693
   Red Scare and, 700
   in San Francisco, 513
   Treaty of Versailles and, 697
   yellow journalism in, 577
newsreels, 762, 782
Newsweek, 847
Newton, Huey, 886
new world order, 944, 953
New York
   abortion clinic murders in, 984
   progressive reform in, 709
   prohibition and, 691
New York Central Railroad, 522–523
New York City, 551(*i*), 552. *See also* Wall Street
   African American migration to, 723
   art museum in, 578
   the Bowery in, 576, 576(*i*)
   as financial capital, 709
   gay rights movement in, 906
   Great Depression in, 730(*i*), 732
   Henry Street Settlement, 612
   high society in, 559
   homosexuals in, 576
   housing in, 753
   immigrants in, 552, 566, 568(*i*)
   jazz and, 716
   Lower East Side in, 568(*m*)
   Metropolitan Opera in, 560(*i*)
   migration to, 718
   population of, 552(*t*)
   Prohibition in, 722
   prostitution in, 576
   real estate in, 962, 963(*i*)
   skyscrapers in, 554
   subway in, 553
   tenements in, 556–557, 569, 572(*i*)
   V-J Day and, 767
New York Herald (newspaper), 576–577
New York Journal (newspaper), 648–649
New York Sun (newspaper), 577
New York Times (newspaper), 902, 1009, 1017
New York Tribune, 471, 479
New York World, 577, 648
Nez Percé Indians, 499(*m*), 502
Nguyen, Thanh, 978
Nguyen, Trong, 978
Niagara Movement, 625
Nicaragua, 662, 824
   Contras in, 936–937, 937(*m*)
   U.S. intervention in, 712
Nicholas II, Tsar, 679
nickelodeons, 574, 714
Nightlight Christian Adoptions, 1008

Nike, 965–966, 966(*i*)–967(*i*)
Nikkei stock index, 959
Nimitz, Chester W., 791
Nineteenth Amendment, 670, 691, 709(*i*)
NIRA. *See* National Industrial Recovery Act
Nisei (second-generation Japanese Americans), 785, 787
Nisei Daughter (Sone), 786
Nixon, Richard M. (1913–1994), 831, 832(*i*), 896–902, 897(*i*), 922, 925, 935, 943
   Alger Hiss and, 898
   antiwar movement and, 898–899, 902
   as Eisenhower's running mate, 818, 818(*i*)
   election of 1968 and, 891, 892(*m*)
   election of 1972 and, 901
   environment and, 913
   pardon of, 917
   as president (1969–1974), 896–902
   recognition of China, 897–898
   on television, 863
   Vietnamization and, 878(*f*), 898, 900
   Vietnam War and, 892
   Watergate and, 895, 901–902
noble experiment. *See* Prohibition
No Child Left Behind, 924
No Child Left Behind Act (2002), 993, 993(*i*), 1017
Nonaggression Pact, Nazi-Soviet (1939), 770–771, 797
nonviolent civil disobedience, 690
Normandy, France, D-Day (June 6, 1944) in, 789, 790(*i*), 797
Norris, George, 676
the North
   African American migration to, 567, 685–687, 690(*m*), 703
   election of 1928 and, 727(*i*)
   racist propaganda in, 478
   Reconstruction and, 476
North, Oliver, 937–938
North Africa, WWII in, 788(*m*), 789
North American Free Trade Agreement (NAFTA), 948, 955, 964, 987
North Atlantic Treaty Organization (NATO), 806(*m*), 822, 824(*m*)
   creation of (1949), 808
   France's departure from, 897
   Kosovo and, 952, 952(*m*)
   peacekeeping forces of, 952
North Carolina
   Democratic Party in, 477
   election of 1928 and, 726
   freedmen in, 461
North Dakota
   farmers in, 498
   homesteaders in, 497
   prohibition and, 693(*m*)
   Scandinavian migration to, 496
Northern Pacific Railroad, 479, 492

North Korea, 810–812, 822, 1013–1014, 1014(*i*), 1017
   nuclear weapons and, 924
Norton, Charles Eliot, 654
Norway
   German invasion of, 770, 788(*i*)
   homesteaders from, 496
Norwood (Beecher), 579
NRA. *See* National Recovery Administration
NSC-68 (report of National Security Council), 809–810
Nuclear Non-Proliferation Treaty (1968), 1013
nuclear power, 839, 911(*f*)
   Chernobyl and, 914
   environmentalism and, 913
   Three Mile Island and, 913–914
nuclear weapons, 800(*i*), 808–810, 822, 868. *See also* atomic bomb
   city life belts and, 841(*i*)
   Cold War and, 942
   Great Fear and, 816
   interstate highways and, 841
   in Iraq, 1000
   Iraq and, 946
   in North Korea, 1013–1014
   North Korea and, 1014(*i*), 1017
   radioactive fallout from, 842
   testing of, 809(*i*), 842
   U.S. monopoly of, 803
Nuremberg, Nazi Party in, 768(*i*)
nurses, in military, 777
NWLB. *See* National War Labor Board
NWP. *See* National Woman's Party
Nye, Gerald P., 769–770

Oakland Tribune (newspaper), 854, 854(*i*)
Oakley, Annie, 494
Occupational Safety and Health Administration (OSHA), 896, 935
occupation army, U.S. troops as, 1002
O'Connor, Sandra Day, 931, 938, 938(*i*), 943, 955, 1008
Office of Economic Opportunity (OEO), 876
Office of Price Administration (OPA), 813
Ohio
   electoral college and, 481
   same-sex marriage and, 1005
   unemployment in, 733
oil industry
   energy consumption and, 911(*f*)
   energy crisis and, 894(*i*), 911
   environmentalism and, 913
   gasoline prices and, 1013
   in Middle East, 1001(*m*), 1013
   in Pennsylvania, 526
   in Persian Gulf, 911, 1000
   pipeline and, 994(*m*)
   prices of, 918
   refineries in, 526
   in Sun Belt, 915

Okies, 757. *See also* Dust Bowl
Okinawa, 791, 793(*m*), 797
Oklahoma
 Indian reservations in, 498–504, 499(*m*)
 Ku Klux Klan in, 721
 white settlement, 503–504, 517
Old Age Revolving Pension Plan, 765
oligopoly, 526, 709
Olmsted, Frederick Law, 557–558
Olney, Richard, 544, 611, 647
Olsen, George, 880
Olsen, Tillie, 762
Olympics, boycotts of, 921
Omaha, Nebraska, 492, 525, 525(*m*)
Omnibus Housing Act, 874(*t*)
On the Origin of Species (Darwin), 588
On the Road (Kerouac), 848
OPA. *See* Price Administration, Office of
OPEC. *See* Organization of Petroleum Exporting Countries
open-door policy, 663, 771
Operation Rolling Thunder, 878–879
Operation Wetback, 850
Oppenheimer, J. Robert, 794, 816, 823
oral histories, 760–762
Oregon, 505
 economy of, 506
 Ku Klux Klan in, 721
 migration to, 783(*i*)
 Native American march to, 502
 settlement of, 489, 505–506
Oregon Trail, 491
The Organization Man (Whyte), 835(*i*)
Organization of Petroleum Exporting Countries (OPEC), 911
organized crime, 723, 781
Orlando, Vittorio, 696
Orpen, William, 695(*i*)
Oswald, Lee Harvey, 870
Ottoman Empire, 666, 674, 696(*m*)
"The Outcasts of Poker Flat" (Harte), 513
outsourcing, 965–966, 987
overland freight lines, 491
"Over There" (Cohen), 678
Ovington, Mary White, 625
Owen, Reba, 610(*i*)
Owens Valley, California, 515
ownership society, 994, 1017
Oxford, Ohio, 872(*i*)
ozone, 987

pachuco (youth) gangs, 784
Pacific Crest Trail, 760
Pacific Mail Steamship Company, 511
Pacific region
 strategic importance of, 655(*m*)
 U.S. in, 643–644, 651–655, 661–662, 663(*m*)
 WWII in, 791
Pacific slope, 506, 508, 509(*m*)

pacifism, Vietnam War and, 879
Packer, Vance, 843
Pago Pago (Samoa), 643
Pahlavi, Muhammad Reza, shah of Iran, 825, 921
Paiute Indians, 499(*m*)
Pakistan, 999, 999(*i*)
 Afghanistan and, 921
 nuclear power and, 1013
 radical Islamic movements in, 953
 Taliban in, 1000(*i*)
Palestine, 696(*m*), 825–826, 1015, 1017
Palestine Liberation Organization (PLO), 944–945, 952
Palestinian-Israeli conflict, 944–945, 1001(*m*)
Palm Beach, Florida, 963(*i*), 991(*i*)
Palmer, A. Mitchell, 700
Palmer raids (1919–1920), 699(*i*), 700, 703, 706
Panama (Isthmus of Darien), 642–643
Panama Canal, 626, 655(*m*), 659, 661, 668
 Colombia and, 659
 design of, 662(*m*)
 malaria at, 661, 661(*i*)
 U.S. return of, 920
Pan-American Union, 643
Panics. *See also* depressions
 of 1873, 479, 483, 492, 519, 549
 of 1893, 523, 544, 549, 602, 604, 646
Pankhurst, Christabel, 690
paper money. *See* currency
paper sons, 511
Paramount, 716
Paris, France, 679
Paris, Treaty of (1899), 654
Paris Peace Accords (1973), 900
Parker, Alton B., 629
Parker, Charlie, 848
Parks, Rosa, 853, 855
The Passion of Saco and Vanzetti (Shahn), 701(*i*)
PATRIOT Act (2001), 787, 973
PATRIOT Act (2002), 924, 999, 1009, 1017
patriotism
 defense industries and, 777
 election of 2004 and, 1005
 ground zero and, 998
 labor unions and, 780
 New Right and, 929(*i*)
 Southern, 476
 taxation and, 774
 during WWI, 673–674
patronage
 after WWI, 699
 politics and, 584–585
 Republican Party and, 592
Patrons of Husbandry. *See* Granger movement
Patterson, Haywood, 753(*i*)

Patterson, John, 864
Patterson, Thomas, 656–657
Patton, George S., 789
Paul, Alice, 616–617, 688, 690, 691(*i*)
Pawnee Indians, 489, 499(*m*)
Payne-Aldrich Tariff Act (1909), 633
payroll deductions, 774
PC. *See* personal computers
Peace Corps, 863, 864(*i*)
peaceful coexistence, meaning of, 822
peacekeepers
 Reagan and, 944–945
 in Somalia, 951–952
peace movement, 666. *See also* antiwar movement
peace process, Clinton and, 952
peace ship, 676
Peale, Norman Vincent, 842
Pearce, Charles H., 472
Pearl Harbor, attack on (December 7, 1941), 643, 771–773, 773(*i*), 791, 796–797, 998
peasants, in New Mexico, 509–510
Peña, Frederico, 947
Pendergast, Thomas, 781
Pendleton Act (1883), 584
penicillin, 692(*i*), 845
Pennsylvania
 abortion and, 943
 coal mining in, 521, 536
 creationism in, 1008
 hijacked airplane crash in, 998
 oil industry in, 526
 railroads in, 519, 521
 steel production in, 519(*i*), 521, 531–532
Pennsylvania Railroad, 519, 521
penny arcades, 574
pension plans, 836
pensions, 710–711, 744, 746–747, 762, 765
Pentagon, 833
 attack on, 998
 radical Muslim attack on, 924
 U.S. attack on Iraq and, 1001
Pentagon Papers, 902
peonage, meaning of, 474
People's (Populist) Party, 602–604
People's Republic of China, 810–811
 U.S. recognition of, 897–898
perestroika, meaning of, 941
Perkins, Frances, 619, 739, 746, 751–752
Perot, H. Ross, 946, 947(*i*), 950
Pershing, John J., 665(*i*), 666, 678–679
Persia. *See* Iran
Persian Gulf, 911, 1001(*m*)
Persian Gulf War (1990–1991), 924–925, 945, 955, 999, 1001(*m*)
 women in, 945(*i*)
personal computers (PC), 970–972
Personal Responsibility and Work Opportunity Act (1996), 950, 955
Peru, 643

petrochemical industry, 839
petroleum industry. *See* oil industry
Philadelphia, Pennsylvania, 551, 552(t)
    department stores in, 549
    industrial development in, 553
    population of, 552(t)
philanthropy, 578–579
Philippines, 651–655. *See also* Filipinos
    acquisition from Spain of, 653–654, 668
    dictatorship in, 824
    human rights in, 920
    immigrants from, 756–757, 849
    Senate hearings on, 656–657
    Spanish-American War in, 651, 651(m), 652–655
    vs. United States, 654–655
    in WWII, 791, 792(m)–793(m)
Phillips, David Graham, 614
phonograph, 717
photography, 762
photojournalism, 762
Physicians for Social Responsibility, 842
Pickford, Mary, 715
Pietism, 590
pig iron, 520
Pike, James M., 478
Pike's Peak, Colorado, 505
Pilgrim's Progress (Bunyan), 614
Pinchot, Gifford, 631
Pinckney, Thomas, 461
Pine Bluff, Arkansas, 464
Pinkerton Detective Agency, 543
pirates, 972, 1013
Pittsburgh, Pennsylvania, 556
    Catholic church in, 573(i)
    radio station in, 717
    railroad strike and, 519
    steel production in, 519(i), 521, 531–532
Plain Home Talk on Love, Marriage, and Parentage (Foote), 564
Plame, Valerie, 1004
Planned Parenthood of Southeastern Pennsylvania v. Casey (1992), 943, 955, 984, 1008
plantations. *See also* the South
    impact of sharecropping on, 473(m), 476
    Reconstruction and, 478
Platt, Orville, 644
Platt Amendment, 661, 769
PlayStation, 959(i)
Pledge of Allegiance, 842
Plessy v. Ferguson (1896), 598, 853
PLO. *See* Palestine Liberation Organization
plumbers, Watergate, 901
Plunkitt, George Washington, 569
pluralism. *See also* ethnic diversity
    cultural, 619, 622, 930, 975–976
    ethnic, 975, 980, 983
pocket veto, 458
Podhoretz, Norman, 929

los pogres, 510
Poland, 679, 696, 790, 802
    German invasion of, 767, 770, 797
    Holocaust in, 790
    papal visit to, 941(i)
    Yalta and, 791–792, 794(i), 802–803, 815
police action, meaning of, 810, 811(m)
police brutality, 982
polio vaccine, 845
The Polish Peasant in Europe and America (Thomas; Znaniecki), 570
Political Action Committees (PAC), 750
political campaigns
    fundraising for, 902
    presidential, 818(i), 818–819, 971
    television and, 862–863
political cartoons
    about conservatism, 997(i)
    Grant and, 480(i)
    impeachment, 951(i)
    Muslim riots and, 1015, 1017
    racial equality and, 477(i)
political machines, 568–569, 572
political parties. *See also* elections; *particular parties*
    loyalty to, 590
    political machines and, 592, 608, 623
    priorities of, 585–586
politics
    African Americans in, 567
    computer revolution and, 973
    conservatism and, 929(i)
    corruption in, 471, 479, 611, 613
    culture wars and, 984
    direct primary in, 624
    energy crisis and, 911
    of expectation, 862–871
    faith-based, 992
    free labor and, 479
    government-business cooperation in, 706–713
    of inclusiveness, 992–993
    initiative and recall in, 624
    international, 911
    international trade and, 963
    Ku Klux Klan and, 721
    labor unions in, 750
    of late nineteenth century, 582–609
    machine, 592, 608, 611, 613, 618–619, 638
    new, 862–863
    patronage and, 584–585
    post-Watergate, 917–922
    power, 624
    race and, 595–599
    reform in, 608, 623–624
    of resentment, 917
    television regulation and, 975
    ward, 568–569
    women in, 905–906
    in WWII, 768, 781

Pollock, Jackson, 760, 848
poll taxes, 598(i), 872
pollution, 967–969. *See also* environmentalism
    highways and, 839
    industrial, 519(i)
    from mining, 508(i)
    in Sun Belt, 839
    TVA and, 760(m)
Pony Express, 491
popular culture. *See also* advertising; mass media; movies; television
    in 1990s, 973–975
    WWII and, 782
Popular Front, 770
population
    of African Americans in armed forces, 681
    of African Americans in industrial heartland, 685
    in California, 756
    changes in, 977(m)
    of Chinese immigrants, 510–511
    in cities, 551, 552(t)
    in the Far West, 505–506
    growth in, 976
    of Hiroshima, 795(i)
    immigration and, 524
    in Iraq, 1016(i)
    life expectancy and, 846
    in Los Angeles, 688(i)
    migratory labor force, 757
    of Native Americans in armed forces, 681
    of radio owners, 717, 717(i)
    shifting patterns in, 838(m)
    shift to cities, 718, 735
    in the West, 509(m)
Populism, 602–604, 607(m)
    African Americans and, 600–601
    of American West, 602(m), 607
    among farmers, 602–603, 603(i)
    Father Coughlin and, 744
    one party rule and, 596–597, 602, 608
    women's rights and, 603, 603(i)
Populist Party, 603–604
pornography, 910
Portland, Oregon, 506
posters, 673, 693
    of steel mills, 710(i)
    during WWII, 777(i)
Potsdam Conference, 803
Pound, Roscoe, 613
poverty, 876(f)
    in 1980s, 959
    Asian migration and, 511
    in California, 751(m)
    election of 1928 and, 726
    Hoover on, 726
    LBJ's war on, 875–876
    New Deal and, 744, 747, 754
    in 1950s, 849–850

in 1990s, 950, 960
of women, 950
Powderly, Terence V., 540, 541(*i*), 541–542
Powder River, 517
Powell, Colin, 992, 992(*i*), 1000
The Power of Positive Thinking (Peale), 842
Powers, Francis Gary, 822
POWs. *See* prisoners of war
pragmatism, 613
Prague Spring, 897
prairies, 488, 488(*m*)
Presbyterians, Republican Party and, 590, 592
preservationists, 629
Presidential Commission on the Status of Women (1963), 903
presidential elections
    Arthur, Chester A. (1880), 586(*m*), 642
    Bush, George H.W. (1988), 935(*i*)
    Bush, George W. (2000), 947(*m*), 954–955, 990–991, 991(*i*), 1017
    Bush, George W. (2004), 1002, 1004–1005
    Cleveland, Grover (1884), 585–586, 586(*m*), 592, 643
    Cleveland, Grover (1888), 586(*m*)
    Cleveland, Grover (1892), 584, 584(*i*), 585, 607(*m*)
    Clinton, William Jefferson (1992), 946–947, 947(*m*), 954–955
    Clinton, William Jefferson (1996), 950
    computer systems and, 970
    Coolidge, Calvin (1924), 707–708
    Eisenhower, Dwight D. (1952), 818(*i*), 818–819, 822
    Garfield, James A. (1880), 586
    Grant, Ulysses S. (1868), 468–469
    Grant, Ulysses S. (1872), 479, 592
    Harding, Warren G. (1920), 706, 735
    Harrison, Benjamin (1888), 582(*i*), 585, 586(*m*), 589(*i*), 602, 647
    Hayes, Rutherford B. (1876), 481, 584
    Hoover, Herbert (1928), 726, 727(*m*)
    Johnson, Lyndon B. (1964), 872, 873(*m*), 878
    Kennedy, John F. (1960), 862–863
    McKinley, William (1896), 606–607, 607(*i*), 607(*m*), 632(*i*), 649
    McKinley, William (1900), 654
    Nixon, Richard M. (1968), 891, 892(*m*), 896
    Nixon, Richard M. (1972), 899–900, 901
    Reagan, Ronald (1980), 925, 932(*m*), 955
    Roosevelt, Franklin D. (1932), 731–733, 733(*m*)
    Roosevelt, Franklin D. (1936), 745, 747–748
    Roosevelt, Franklin D. (1940), 771
    Roosevelt, Franklin D. (1944), 781
    Roosevelt, Theodore (1904), 632, 632(*i*)
    Taft, William Howard (1908), 664
    Truman, Harry (1948), 814, 814(*m*)
    Watson, Tom (1904), 600–601
    Wilson, Woodrow (1912), 635(*m*), 664
presidential powers, terrorism and, 1009, 1012
Presley, Elvis, 847, 848(*i*)
preventive war policy, 999–1000
Price Administration, Office of (OPA), 782
prices. *See also* consumer price index
    agricultural, 602
    controls on, 707, 709–710, 896, 911
    of oil, 918
    WWII and, 782
Princip, Gavrilo, 674
prisoner abuse, 1002
prisoners of war (POWs)
    Bataan death march and, 791
    Japanese internment and, 785(*i*)
    in Vietnam War, 879
Progressive Era (1890–1914), 579, 610–639, 815
    academic expertise in, 613
    consumer rights and, 913
    end of, 706, 726
    New Deal and, 737, 762
    shift from Republican dominance in, 622
Progressive Party, 632
    new, 633, 814, 816
progressivism
    definition of, 612
    fracturing of Republican, 632–633
    national politics and, 634–638
    of 1970s, 913
    Prohibition and, 691–692
    reform and, 692–693, 695
    science and, 613
    white supremacy and, 625
    women and, 612, 692
    in WWI, 678, 683–684
Prohibition, 594–595, 622, 670, 718, 722–723, 986
    Al Smith on, 726
    Democratic Party and, 707
    Eighteenth Amendment on, 692, 693(*m*), 703, 722–723, 735
    organized crime and, 781
    progressive reform and, 691–692
    repeal of (1933), 723, 739, 765
    rural areas *vs.* cities in, 691–692, 693(*m*)
    WWI impetus for, 691–692, 701
Prohibitionist Party, 595, 606
"The Promise of the New Deal" (Shahn), 761(*i*)
Promontory Point, Utah, 492
propaganda
    German, 682
    in the North, 478
    Reagan presidency, 937
    wartime, 685, 693, 695
    during WWII, 776
property. *See* land
prospectors, 505–506
prostitution, 506
    after WWI, 691
    Asian migration and, 511
    in cities, 576
    in New York City, 576
    shelters for, 573
The Prostrate South (Pike), 478
protectionism, 585. *See also* tariffs: protective
Protestantism. *See also* evangelism; *individual denominations*
    abortion and, 984
    accumulation of wealth and, 587
    in cities, 573–574
    immigration restriction and, 718
    Ku Klux Klan and, 719
    middle class and, 707
    in 1950s, 842
    Prohibition and, 692
    Religious Right and, 928
    Republican Party, 590, 590(*f*), 592
    social reform and, 619, 622
    temperance and, 594–595
    work ethic and, 706
psychology, advertising and, 713
public assistance. *See* welfare
Public Citizens' Global Watch, 969
public health system, 682(*i*)
Public Lands Commission, 631
public opinion, on civil rights, 867
public works
    Great Depression and, 729
    in New Deal, 743–744, 747(*t*)
    War on Poverty and, 876
Public Works Administration (PWA), 743, 747(*t*)
Puck, 480(*i*)
Pueblo Indians, 499(*m*), 509
Puerto Rico
    annexation of, 652, 655, 655(*m*)
    immigrants from, 850, 851(*i*)
Puget Sound, 689(*i*)
Pulaski, Tennessee, 477
Pulitzer, Joseph, 577–578, 648
Pullman, George M., 544
Pullman boycott (1894), 544, 545(*i*), 605, 611–612
pump priming, meaning of, 730
pure-and-simple unionism, 542–543
Pure Food and Drug Act, 632
Putin, Vladimir, 1013

Quaker Oats Company, 527(*i*)
Quakers (Society of Friends), women and, 690
Quang, Thich Nu Thanh, 871(*i*)
Quinn, Anthony, 782

Rabin, Yitzhak, 952
race. *See also* ethnicity; *particular groups*
    Democratic coalition and, 763

race (*continued*)
   equal rights and, 946
   feminism and, 904
   in Haiti, 952
   lynchings and, 698
race riots
   African Americans and, 886, 892
   in Chicago, 698–699, 703
   in Harlem, 753–754, 765
   in Harlem (1935), 726, 734
   in Los Angeles, 924, 982(i), 982–983, 987
   police brutality and, 982
   post-WWI, 698–699
   Springfield (1908), 625
   WWII and, 797
racial profiling, 1009
racism. *See also* lynching; segregation
   anti-Asian, 663–664
   anti-Semitism and, 780
   in Armed Forces, 681–683
   in California, 511–512
   in cities, 567, 572, 851–852
   immigration restriction and, 664, 718
   Jim Crow laws and, 597–599, 886
   Ku Klux Klan and, 707
   in literature, 762
   in military, 775
   in New South, 595–599, 599(i)
   in 1920s, 707
   opposition to, 885–888, 892
   Philippine annexation and, 654
   post-WWI, 688, 698(i), 698–699
   race riots and, 982–983
   reform and, 624–626
   in the South, 595–596, 608, 886
   in Spanish-American War, 652, 652(i)
   in suburbs, 838
   in WWI, 674
radar, 822
radiation poisoning, in Hiroshima, 795(i)
radical Islamic terrorist groups, 953
radicalism, 544–548, 604
   fear of, 699–700
   in the West, 546, 547(i), 602(m), 607
Radical Republicans, 459, 466, 470–471, 481
radio
   clear-channel stations, 717(i)
   Father Coughlin on, 744
   FDR and, 738–739
   first commercial broadcast, 717, 735
   in Great Depression, 717(m)
   JFK-Nixon debates on, 863
   music and, 847
   national culture and, 713–714, 717–718
   religion and, 842
   rural electrification and, 737(i)
radioactive fallout, 842
Railroad Retirement Act, 744
railroads, 522–524, 529(m), 548. *See also individual railroads*
   Adamson eight-hour law and, 637
   advertising by, 495
   Baltimore and Ohio Railroad, 519, 549
   bankruptcy of, 602
   Brotherhood of Locomotive Firemen, 544
   Chinese labor and, 511
   Chinese workers and, 511
   completion of transcontinental (1869), 491–492
   development of California and, 511
   elevated, 553, 553(i)
   expansion of, 552
   federal government and, 522, 544, 588
   freight rates for, 498, 513, 523
   government support for, 522, 544, 585, 588
   Great Depression and, 727
   in Great Plains, 491(m), 491–493, 498
   industrialization and, 519–520, 522–524, 524(m)
   investment in, 522
   labor unions and, 544, 611
   land grants for, 491, 522
   managerial revolution and, 527–528
   mining and, 506
   nationalization of, 708
   Native Americans and, 498
   Pullman boycott (1894) of, 544, 545(i), 605, 611
   regulation of, 584–585, 629
   segregation laws and, 596, 598–599, 599(i)
   strikes against, 519, 544, 545(i), 549, 603, 813
   technology for, 523
   transcontinental, 491(m), 491–492, 512(i), 517
   Wall Street and, 524
   western expansion and, 522–523, 524(m)
   Western Trunk lines, 491(m)
Railroad War Board, 684
Ramona (Jackson), 513, 517
ranching
   barbed wire and, 497
   on Great Plains, 493, 515
   in Texas, 492
Randolph, A. Philip, 676, 780, 853, 867
Rankin, Jeannette, 678, 773
rape, of slaves, 461
rationing, WWII, 670, 782–783, 797
Rauschenbush, Walter, 612
Ray, Dixie Lee, 904
Rayburn, Sam, 863
La Raza Unida (The United Race), 887
Readers Digest (magazine), 713
Reagan, Nancy, 934(i), 963
Reagan, Ronald (1911–2004), 934(i), 939(i), 947, 995
   air traffic controllers and, 965, 987
   automobile mileage regulations and, 968
   Christianity and, 930
   conservatism and, 896
   extravagance of, 963
   Iran-Contra Affair and, 937(m)
   Just Say No campaign of, 982
   as president (1981–1989), 924–925, 927–973
   rollback of federal power and, 954, 997, 997(i)
   scandals in administration of, 936
   Star Wars of, 935, 955
Reagan Democrats, 932
Reaganomics, 924, 933
   budget deficits and, 935(f), 936, 947(m), 954
Reagan Revolution, 936
real estate boom, in California, 513
realism, legal, 613
The Real Majority (Wattenberg, Scammon), 891
recessions. *See also* depressions
   of FDR, 748–749
   migrant workers and, 850
   of 1920-1921, 710, 735
   of 1975-1976, 918, 920
   of 1990s, 944
   of Reagan (1981-1982), 937, 954, 958
   vs. Great Depression, 727
Reconstruction (1865–1877), 457–483, 624
   end of, 481
   end of (1877), 596, 608
   Fourteenth Amendment and, 588
   Presidential, 458–466, 481
   Radical, 466–476, 467(m)
   Republicans and, 457, 585
   undoing of, 476–481
Reconstruction Act (1867), 466, 468(t), 483
Reconstruction Finance Corporation (RFC), 730, 735
Red Baron, 681
Red Cloud, Chief of the Sioux, 498
Redeemers, 476, 478, 482, 596, 599
Redfearn, L. T., 857
Red River Valley, North Dakota, 497
Red River Valley, Texas, 502
Red Scare, 670, 700, 703, 721. *See also* anti-communism
Red Shirts, 478
reform, 611, 613, 638. *See also* social reform
   labor, 618–619
   moral, 592, 608, 691–692
   municipal, 624
   party, 624
   progressive, 708–709
   racism and, 624–626
   Republican Party and, 632–633
   tariff, 635
Reform Party, 991
refugees
   Cuban, 850

Holocaust and, 790–791
in 1950s, 849
regionalism, 839(m)
regulation. See also deregulation
    public, 613
    of railroads, 584–585, 629
Rehnquist, William, 938, 944, 955, 1008, 1017
Reich, Robert, 948
Reisman, David, 834–835
relief. See welfare
religion. See also evangelism; revivalism; *particular denominations*
    African-American, 567
    conservative social values and, 927, 975, 992
    cultural conflict and, 718
    extremism in, 1014–1016
    Native American, 489
    in 1920s, 718
    in 1950s, 842
    parochial schools and, 592
    prayer in public schools and, 910, 938
    prohibition and, 692
    same-sex marriage and, 1005
    separation of church and state, 573, 930, 992
    social meaning and, 574
religious factions. See Native Americans
Religious Right
    Bush (George W.) and, 992
    cultural values and, 927, 938, 949, 954
    election of 1980 and, 929
    election of 1992 and, 946
    family values and, 983
"Remember the Maine," 649(i)
rent riots, 731
Reorganized Church of Jesus Christ of Latter-day Saints. See Mormons
republicanism
    modern, 818–819
Republican Party, 677, 699
    affluence and, 932
    African Americans and, 754
    anti-communism and, 816
    on big government, 873(m)
    candidates of, 990
    in Congress, 933
    conservatism of, 891, 892(m)
    "Contract with America" and, 924, 949–950
    domestic policies of, 896
    election of 1924 and, 708
    election of 1928 and, 726, 727(i)
    election of 1932 and, 731–733
    election of 1936 and, 747–748
    election of 2004 and, 1005
    free silver and, 611
    Halfbreeds in, 585
    JFK and, 868
    Ku Klux Klan and, 477–478
    law and order campaign of, 891–892, 892(m)

    liberal, 479
    as majority party, 466, 469, 707, 733, 932(m), 955, 991–992
    modern, 818–819
    Mugwumps and, 590, 592
    New Deal and, 744, 814
    in 1920s, 706
    organized labor and, 813–814
    pietism and, 590
    presidency and, 706
    progressive politics and, 612
    protectionism and, 585
    Protestants and, 590, 590(f), 592
    Reconstruction and, 457, 466, 478, 481
    reform and, 632–633
    Schiavo case and, 1007
    in Senate, 933
    silent majority and, 891
    small government and, 997
    in the South, 469–472, 481, 896
    Stalwarts in, 585
    stem-cell research and, 1008
    Theodore Roosevelt and, 627, 635
    veterans' benefits and, 585
    white supremacy and, 624
    women's rights groups and, 469
    in WWII, 781
Republic Steel Corporation, 750
reservations
    of Dakota territory, 498–504, 499(m), 502(m), 504, 517, 850
    of Oklahoma territory, 499(m), 504, 517
Reserve Officer Training Corps (ROTC), 882
Resettlement Administration, 754
restrictive covenants, 838
Reuther, Walter, 835–836
Revels, Hiram, 471(i)
Revenue Acts
    of 1916, 703
    of 1935, 747(t)
    tax cuts and, 729
revenue-sharing program, 896
reverse discrimination, 907, 982
revisionist historians, 802
revivalism, 574, 721. See also evangelism
Reyes, Matias, 981
Reyneau, Betsy Graves, 754(i)
Rhee, Syngman, 810
Rhineland, 769, 797
Rhode Island
    election of 1928 and, 726
    election of 1928 and, 727(i)
    prohibition and, 691
Rice, Condoleeza, 992, 992(i)
rice, price supports for, 710
Richmond, California, 784
Richmond, Virginia, trolley cars in, 553
Richtofen, Manfred von (Red Baron), 681
Rickenbacker, Eddie, 680–681, 681(i)
Rifle Clubs, 478

Riis, Jacob, 557(i)
Rio Grande Valley, Hispanic settlement in, 508, 510
Rio Treaty (Inter-American Treaty of Reciprocal Assistance; 1947), 824(m)
riots. See also mobs
    anti-U.S., 643
    armory construction and, 520
    in China, 897
    in Detroit, 797, 886
    in Europe, 897
    in Harlem, 726, 734
    in Los Angeles, 784, 784(i), 797, 886, 982(i), 982–983, 987
    in Memphis, 465
    by Muslims, 1017
    in Newark, 886
    rent, 731
    in San Francisco, 517
    school busing and, 907, 910(i)
    urban, 886, 892
The Rise of David Levinsky (Cahan), 573
The Rise of Silas Lapham (Howells), 579
Roaring Twenties, 718, 722
Roberts, John, 1008, 1009(i), 1017
Robertson, Pat, 929, 984
Robert Taylor Homes, 852
Robinson, Jackie, 853
Rockefeller, John D., 526, 547, 614(i)
Rockefeller, Nelson, 917
Rockefeller Center, 959
rock 'n' roll, 847, 884
Rockwell, Norman, 777, 777(i)
Rocky Mountains, 488, 505
Rodeo (Copland), 760
Roe v. Wade (1973), 910, 943, 955, 1008
Rogers, William, 896, 897(i)
Rolling Stones, 884
Roman Catholic church. See Catholicism
Roman Catholics. See Catholics
Romania, 803
Rommel, Erwin, 789
Roosevelt, Eleanor, 733, 740, 751–752, 752(i)
    African Americans and, 754
    civil rights and, 780
    Stevenson and, 819
Roosevelt, Franklin Delano (1882–1945), 670, 684, 738(i). See also New Deal
    Alger Hiss and, 815
    Atlantic Charter and, 772(m), 787
    conservation and, 759
    death of, 793, 797, 803
    declaration of war and, 787
    election of 1932 and, 733, 735
    Four Freedoms of, 797, 771
    Great Depression and, 729(m), 891
    Imperial Presidency and, 774
    isolationism and, 769
    labor unions and, 780
    New Deal of, 813, 862, 927–928

Roosevelt, Franklin Delano (*continued*)
   on Pearl Harbor, 773, 796
   popularity of, 738
   as president (1933–1945), 734, 737–763, 765, 770–794
   second term of, 815
   on self-determination, 822
   Soviet Union and, 802
   Stalin and, 802
   Supreme Court and, 748
   third term of, 771
   trade with Japan and, 771–772
   United Nations and, 793
   as vice-presidential candidate, 706
   wartime planning and, 771
   WWII and, 774, 780, 794, 796
   at Yalta, 791–792, 794(*i*)
Roosevelt, Theodore (1858–1919), 563, 594, 614(*i*), 627–632, 636, 675, 677, 733
   as assistant secretary of the navy, 646, 650
   attack on legal system, 633
   balance of power philosophy of, 659
   conservation and, 629, 631
   Japanese immigration and, 718
   Moroccan intervention by, 666–667, 667(*i*)
   popular vote of, 943
   as president (1901-1909), 659, 663–664
   presidential powers and, 739
   as rancher, 493
   as "Rough Rider," 650, 652
   Spanish-American War and, 647, 650, 652
   Square Deal of, 632, 632(*i*), 638
   Taft and, 632
   trust-busting and, 629, 632
   Wall Street Giants and, 630(*i*)
Roosevelt Corollary (to Monroe Doctrine), 662
Root, Elihu, 661, 666
Root-Takahira Agreement (1908), 664
Rosie the Riveter, 777, 777(*i*)
Ross, Edward A., 622
Rough Riders, 650, 652
Rove, Karl, 990–992, 1005–1006
Rowe, Guy, 804(*i*)
Roybal, Edward, 887
rubber scarcity, 782
Rubin, Robert, 948
Ruef, Abe, 618
Rumsfeld, Donald, 924, 996, 999, 1001–1002, 1006, 1012, 1017
Rural Electrification Administration, 759, 765
rural ideal, 557
rural life
   automobile and, 714
   electrification and, 759
   Prohibition and, 691–692, 693(*m*)
   urbanization and, 718
Russia. *See also* Soviet Union
   Bush (George W.) and, 1013
   claims on China of, 646
   Communist Party in, 679, 695–697
   1917 revolution in, 679, 700
   radical Islamic movements in, 953
   war with Japan (1905) and, 675
   in WWI, 674, 703
   during WWII, 770, 789(*i*)
Russo-Japanese War (1904–1905), 663, 663(*m*)
Rust Belt, 915–916, 916(*m*)
Rustin, Bayard, 851
Ruth, Babe, 718
Rwanda, 951

Sabin, Albert, 845
Sacco, Nicola, 700–701, 701(*i*), 703
Sacco-Vanzetti case, 700–701, 703
Sackville-West, Lionel, 641
Sacramento, California, 492, 509(*m*)
al-Sadat, Anwar, 918(*i*), 920
al-Sadr, Moqtada, 1002, 1015(*i*)
safe for democracy, 678, 691
Safeway, 713
Saigon, Vietnam, 825, 869, 879, 889, 900, 900(*i*)
St. Louis, Missouri
   Bush in, 993(*i*)
   population of, 552(*t*)
St. Louis Post-Dispatch, 577
St. Mihiel, 679
St. Paul, Minnesota, 492
Salk, Jonas, 845
saloons, 595, 595(*i*)
SALT I (Strategic Arms Limitations Treaty), 898
SALT II (Strategic Arms Limitation Treaty), 921
Salvation Army, 573
Samoa, 643, 655
San Diego, California, 509(*m*), 513, 783
Sandinistas, 937
SANE (National Committee for a Sane Nuclear Policy), 842, 879
San Francisco, California
   Anglo migration to, 509
   anti-Chinese riots in, 517
   Chinatown in, 511
   Chinese businesses in, 756
   earthquake (1906) in, 556
   Eastern connections of, 508
   as economic hub of the West, 508
   elite in, 559
   gay rights movement in, 906
   gold rush and, 559
   growth of, 505, 509, 509(*m*), 515
   NRA codes and, 743(*i*)
   population of, 552(*t*)
   United Nations and, 793
   urban renewal in, 852
   wartime migration to, 783
San Francisco Chronicle (newspaper), 783
San Francisco Examiner (newspaper), 577
sanitary zone, 697
San Juan Hill, Battle of (1898), 627, 652, 652(*i*)
Santa Fe, New Mexico, 505, 508, 513
Santa Fe Railroad, 492, 513
Santanella, Zeno, 738(*i*)
Santiago (Cuba), 652
Santiago de Cuba, Battle of (1898), 640(*i*)
Santo Domingo, 642
Sarajevo, Serbia, 674
SARS. *See* severe acute respiratory syndrome
satellite television, 973–974
Saturday Evening Post (magazine), 717, 777, 846(*i*)
Saudi Arabia, 911, 921, 945, 966(*i*)
Savage, Augusta, 723
Saving Private Ryan (film), 790(*i*)
savings and loan scandals, 962, 987
Savio, Mario, 882
scalawags, 470
Scalia, Antonin, 938, 944
Scammon, Richard, 891
Schechter v. United States, 744, 765
Schenck, Charles T., 694
Schenck v. United States (1919), 694, 703
Schiavo, Terri, 1007
Schlafly, Phyllis, 905(*i*), 905–906, 916
Schlesinger, Arthur, Jr., 983
Schneiderman, Rose, 615–616, 620–621
Schroeder, Patricia, 905
Schurz, Carl, 592, 654
science, 924–925
   art and, 579
   management and, 538, 548, 613, 710
   progressivism and, 613
SCLC. *See* Southern Christian Leadership Conference
Scopes, John T., 721–722
Scopes ("monkey") trial (1925), 724–725, 735
Scotland, Live-8 concert in, 970
Scott, Emmett J., 686
Scottsboro, Alabama, 753, 753(*i*)
Screen Actors Guild, 928
Scudder, Vida, 562
Seale, Bobby, 886
Seamen's Act (1916), 637
Sears, Roebuck, 527
SEATO. *See* Southeast Asia Treaty Organization
Seattle, Washington, 506, 509(*m*), 689(*i*)
   Microsoft in, 971(*i*)
   strike in, 699, 699(*i*)
   WTO meeting in, 969(*i*)
SEC. *See* Securities and Exchange Commission
secession
   champions of, 476
   Constitution and, 458, 467
Second World War. *See* World War II
secret ballot, 594

secularism, 930
Securities and Exchange Commission (SEC), 744, 747(t), 765, 962
Security Council (UN), 792, 803, 810, 897, 1000–1001, 1014
Sedalia, Missouri, 492
Sedition Act (1918), 694
Seeger, Charles, 760
Seeger, Pete, 884
Seeger, Ruth Crawford, 760
segregation, 852(i), 907. See also busing, school; desegregation
    anti-Asian sentiment and, 664
    in Armed Forces, 681–683
    Jim Crow and, 598–599, 886
    laws supporting, 596, 598, 608
    in military, 775
    opposition to, 853–859
    school, 851, 907, 910(i)
    of transportation, 867
Selassie, Haile, 769
Selective Service, 882
Selective Service Act (1917), 678, 703
self-determination, national, 802, 825
    Atlantic Charter and, 771, 787
    movements for, 865(m)
    Yalta and, 792
self-determination principle, 695, 696(m), 696–697, 699
self-made man ideal, 731
Selle River (France), 678
Selma, Alabama, 872
Seminole Indians, 499, 499(m)
Semple, Robert, 721(i)
Senate, U.S. See also Congress, U.S.; House of Representatives, U.S.
    Clinton impeachment and, 951
    conduct of diplomacy and, 642
    Democratic Party control of, 936, 1006
    Gulf War and, 945
    hearings on the Philippines, 656–657
    Kyoto Treaty and, 969
    Republican control of, 932(m), 949
    Treaty of Versailles and, 697, 701
    Watergate Committee of, 902
    woman suffrage and, 691
    women in, 944(i)
Seneca Falls convention (1848), 691
Seoul, South Korea, 811
separation of church and state, 573, 930, 992
separation of powers, 458, 902. See also checks and balances
September 11, 2001, terrorist attacks, 924–925, 989(i), 998(i), 998–999, 1001(m), 1017
Sequoia National Park, 514
Serbia, 674, 925, 952, 952(m), 955
Servicemen's Readjustment Act (GI Bill; 1944), 781, 796–797
Sesame Street (TV program), 975

set-asides, 907
settlement houses, 610(i), 612, 614–615, 615(i), 625, 690
Sevareid, Eric, 847
severe acute respiratory syndrome (SARS), 967
Seward, William H., 642
Sex in the City (TV program), 974
sexual harassment, 777, 944, 944(i)
sexuality
    automobile and, 714
    changing views of, 563–564, 580
    disease and, 691
    jazz and, 716
    music and, 847
    rock 'n' roll and, 847
    women's rights and, 906
sexual values, 928–929
Seymour, Horatio, 468
Shahn, Ben, 701(i), 750(i), 761(i), 762
Shakespeare, William, 579
Shalala, Donna E., 947
sharecropping, 473–476, 475(i), 742. See also agriculture; tenant farmers
Share Our Wealth Society, 745, 745(i), 751(m), 765
Sheen, Bishop Fulton, 842
sheep raising, 493, 497, 509
Sheldon, Charles M., 574
Shelley v. Kraemer (1948), 838
shell shock, 646(i)
Shelterbelts, 760
Shenandoah National Park, 760
Shepard, Alan, 864
Shepard, William G., 620
Sheppard-Towner Act (1921), 709, 709(i), 735
Sheridan, Philip H., 492, 642
Sherman, William Tecumseh (1820–1891), 481
    land for liberated slaves and, 461
Sherman Antitrust Act (1890), 629, 632–633, 636
Sherman Silver Purchase Act (1890), 604–605
Shiite Muslims, 945, 999, 1002–1003, 1006, 1016, 1016(m)
Shiloh, Battle of, 476
shipbuilding industry
    Kaiser and, 774–775, 775(i), 783(i)
    wartime migration and, 783(i)
"shock and awe," 1001
Shore, Dinah, 844(i)
Shores, Jerry, 497(i)
Shultz, George, 935
Sicily, WWII in, 788(m), 789
sickness. See disease
Sierra Club, 514, 936, 968
Sierra Nevada mountains, 492, 505, 511, 514

"The Significance of the Frontier in American History" (Turner), 648
silent majority, 896
Silent Sentinels, 690
Silent Spring (Carson), 912
silicone microchips, 970
Simpson, Nicole Brown, 983
Simpson, O. J., 982–983
Sinai Peninsula, 920
Since You Went Away (film), 782
Sinclair, Upton, 632, 751(m)
Singer Sewing Machine Company, 527, 644, 644(i)
Sino-Japanese War (1894–1895), 646, 663–664
Sioux Indians, 498–499, 499(m), 502, 502(m), 504, 517
    AIM and, 888, 888(i)
    Battle of Little Big Horn and, 502, 517
    religion of, 489
    wars with, 494
    Wounded Knee massacre and, 487, 499(m), 504, 504(i), 517
Sister Carrie (Dreiser), 551
sit-ins, civil rights movement and, 781, 855–858
Sitting Bull, Chief of Sioux, 494, 502
Six Companies, 511
Sixteenth Amendment, 684
skyscrapers, 553–554
slackers, 678
slavery. See also cotton; plantations; the South
    anti-slavery movement and. See abolitionism
    white south and, 596
slaves
    former, 459, 464(i)
    labor gang system and, 464, 464(i), 474
Slavs, Holocaust and, 790
Sloan, John, 619(i)
Slovenia, 952
smallpox, 489
Smith, Adam, 709
Smith, Alfred E. (Al), 619, 708–709, 726, 727(i)
Smith, Bessie, 717
Smith, Gayle, 881
Smith, Howard, 903
Smith, Mamie, 716(i)
Smith-Connally Labor Act (1943), 780
smuggling, 722–723
SNCC. See Student Non-Violent Coordinating Committee
soap operas, radio and, 737(i)
Social Darwinism, 587–588, 613, 647, 668
Social Gospel, 612
social identity, in California, 512
social insurance, 622–623. See also health insurance; welfare
socialism, 544–547

suffrage
    for African Americans, 466–467
    after Reconstruction, 470(i), 474
    universal, 479
    for women, 469, 470(i)
suffrage movement, 608, 618(m), 688–691, 691(i), 702, 709(i). *See also* voting rights
    activists in, 594–595, 617, 617(i), 638
    American politics and, 617–618, 638
    Mugwumps and, 592, 594
    organizations in, 469, 594, 617, 703
    revival of, 615–617
sugar
    Asian laborers and, 643(i)
    plantations and, 643, 643(i), 648
    Puerto Rican immigrants and, 849
    U.S. foreign investment in, 711
sugarcane farming, 643(i)
suicide bombings, 1014
Sullivan, Louis, 554
Sumner, Charles, 466, 469, 478
Sumner, Willliam Graham, 588
Sun, 961
The Sun Also Rises (Hemingway), 723
Sun Belt, 838–839, 915, 916(m)
Sun Dance, 489
Sunday, Billy, 574, 721
Sunni Muslims, 945, 1002–1003, 1006, 1015(i), 1016, 1016(m)
supercomputers, 972
Superfund program, 913, 936
Supreme Court. *See also individual decisions*
    in 2006, 1009(i)
    on abortion, 984–985
    abortion rights and, 910. *See also Roe v. Wade*
    on affirmative action, 907
    affirmative action and, 982
    antitrust laws and, 707
    Bush (George W.) and, 1008
    Congress and, 708
    constitutionality of Civil Rights Bill (1870) and, 478
    decisions of, 616(t)
    election of 2000 and, 991
    FDR and, 748, 765
    gay rights and, 984
    on housing discrimination, 838
    on Japanese internment, 787, 797
    judicial restraint and, 910
    Ku Klux Klan and, 478
    New Deal and, 744
    on New York subway, 556
    on prayer in public schools, 910
    school busing and, 907
    strikes and, 750
    war prisoners and, 1012
    welfare capitalism and, 711
Sutter's Mill, discovery of gold (1848) at, 506
Swan Island, Oregon, 783(i)

swastika, 768(i)
Sweden, 496
Swift, Gustavus F., 524–527, 547, 549
Swift Boat controversy, 1005
symphony orchestras, 578
syndicalism, 546
synthetic rubber, 782
Syria, 696(m)
    invasion of Israel by, 911
Szilard, Leo, 793

Taft, William Howard (1857–1930), 624, 632–633, 636
    as Philippines governor-general, 654
    as president (1909–1913), 664, 666, 707
    Roosevelt and, 632–633
Taft-Hartley Act, 813–814, 816
Taiwan, 812, 897, 967
Taliban, 921, 924, 998–999, 1000(i), 1001(m), 1017
Tammany Hall, 569, 572, 619, 726
Tanzania, 953, 989
Taos, New Mexico, 513
Tarbell, Ida, 614, 614(i), 693
Tardieu, Andre, 667
tariffs
    McKinley and, 602, 605, 611, 643
    protective, 585, 602, 605, 632–633
Tarzan of the Apes (Burroughs), 563
taxation
    on agricultural commodities, 742
    under Bush (George W.), 944, 995–996, 996(i)
    in Cold War, 810
    decay of inner cities and, 851–852
    estates, 933
    excess-profits, 684
    excise levies and, 585
    federal surplus and, 585
    for highway construction, 714
    income, 933
    on income, 588, 684, 774
    legislation on, 874(t)
    poll tax, 598(i), 872
    property, 471
    radical Republicans and, 471
    Reaganomics and, 933, 936, 954
    reductions in, 728, 864, 916–917, 924–925, 936, 949, 954–955, 986, 995–996, 996(i)
    for Social Security, 746, 763
    taxpayers' revolts against, 916–917
    WWII and, 768
Tax Reduction Act (1964), 864
Taylor, Frederick W., 538, 548–549, 613, 710
Teapot Dome scandal (1924), 707, 735
technology. *See also* machinery
    in agriculture, 497, 511
    alternative, 913
    capitalism and, 918

    computer, 928, 957, 970–972
    economic growth and, 986, 961–962
    in mining, 508(i)
    popular culture and, 973–975
    postwar development and, 839
    in railroad system, 523
    in steel production, 520–522, 521(i)
    U.S. Army and, 502
    WWII and, 767
teenagers. *See* adolescence; youth
Tehran, Iran, 788
Tejanos, 510
Telecommunications Reform Act (1996), 975
telecommuters, 971
telegrams, reports of death by, 782
telegraph, 491, 642
telephone
    cellular, 924, 972
    company, 533(i), 834
television
    civil rights movement and, 867, 872
    color, 834
    documentaries on, 844
    JFK-Nixon debates on, 863
    JFK's election and, 862–863
    1950s culture and, 843–844
    proliferation of channels, 973–974
    religion and, 842
    sitcoms on, 843
    as "vast wasteland," 844
    V-chips in, 975
Teller, Henry M., 650
temperance movement, Prohibition and, 594–595, 595(i), 691–692
tenant farmers. *See also* sharecropping
    Populist party and, 596
Tenderloin, New York City, 576
Tenement House Law (1901; New York), 556–557
tenements, 556–557
    dumbbell, 556(f)
    in New York City, 569, 572(i)
Tennessee
    Ku Klux Klan in, 477
    public education in, 471
    Reconstruction and, 465, 476–477
    Scopes trial in, 721–722, 724–725
    Thirteenth Amendment and, 459
Tennessee Coal and Iron Company, 633
Tennessee Valley Authority (TVA), 670, 739, 747(t), 758–760, 760(m), 765
    Supreme Court on, 748
Ten Percent Plan, 458, 483
Tenure of Office Act (1867), 467–468, 468(t), 483
Terkel, Studs, 768
terrorism, 955
    abortion clinic murders and, 984
    against blacks, 478

fears about, 973, 1004(i)
  in Middle East, 1001(m)
  Muslims and, 953
  in 1980s, 954–955
  1993 World Trade Center bombing, 998
  presidential powers and, 1009, 1012
  Red Scare and, 700
  September 11, 2001, 989(i), 989–990, 998(i), 998–999, 1001(m), 1017
  U.S.S. *Cole* attack, 953, 953(i), 989, 1001(m)
Terry, Peggy, 779
Tet offensive, 877(m), 889
Texas
  cattle ranching in, 492, 509–510, 517
  cotton in, 496, 530(i), 598
  election of 1928 and, 726
  farming in, 509
  gay rights and, 984
  gerrymandering, 991–992, 1006
  Hispanics in, 493, 508–510
  Latino immigrants in, 850
  Mexican Americans in, 685
  migration to, 839
  segregation in, 781
Texas Rangers, 990
textile industry
  decline of, 710
  Jewish garment workers in, 537, 545
  in the South, 529(m), 529–530
  strikes in, 637
  women in, 533
Thailand, 992(i)
Thayer, Webster, 700, 701(i)
theater
  in New Deal, 762
  vaudeville, 574
  Yiddish, 566
Their Eyes Were Watching God (Hurston), 762
Thieu, Nguyen Van, 900
think tanks, New Right and, 928, 955
Third Amendment, 910
Third International, 700
Third World
  Cold War and, 822, 828
  meaning of, 865(m)
Thirteenth Amendment, 458–459, 468(t)
Thirty Seconds over Tokyo (film), 782
Thomas, Clarence, 943–944, 944(i), 955, 1009(i)
Thomas, Norman, 733
Thomas, Theodore, 578
Thomas, William I., 570
Thompson, Florence, 759(i)
Thompson, LaMarcus, 574(i)
Thoughts for the Young Men of America (Alger), 587
Three Mile Island, Pennsylvania, 911(f), 913–914
The Three Soldiers (Dos Passos), 723
Thurman, A.G., 582(i)

Thurmond, J. Strom, 814
tides of commerce, 626
Tilden, Samuel J., 480
Tilden Park, 760
Tillman, Ben, 598
Time (magazine), 705, 735, 770
time-and-motion study, 538
Time/Life, 975
time zones, 549
The Titan (Dreiser), 559
Title IX, Educational Amendments Act (1972), 904(i), 905
Titusville, Pennsylvania, 526
TiVo system, 972
tobacco, 834
  duties on, 585
  price supports for, 710
  Southern production of, 529(m)
Tocqueville, Alexis de, 583
Tojo, Hideki, 768, 772
Tokyo Telecommunications Engineering Corporation, 959(i)
Toomer, Jean, 723
torture, Abu Ghraib prison, 1002, 1002(i), 1017
Towles, Shepard, 857
Townsend, Francis, 744–746, 748, 751(m)
Townsend Clubs, 744, 765
Tracy, Benjamin F., 647
Tracy, Spencer, 782
trade. *See also* exports; *particular commodities*
  European domination of, 674
  free, 771, 787, 802
  with Japan, 772
  multi-polar world and, 1013
  restraint of, 635–636
  of Sioux Indians, 489
  during WWI, 676, 683
trade, foreign, 664, 959
  automobile and, 911
  balance of, 644–645, 645(f), 832, 911. *See also* trade deficits
  corporations and, 834
  Great Depression and, 728
  postwar, 832
  recessions and, 832
  restrictions on, 728
  surpluses in, 832
trade associations, 742
trade deficits, 911, 918, 924–925, 959
  under Bush (George W.), 996
  Reaganomics and, 924, 936, 947(m)
trade unionism, 479, 540–542, 622. *See also* labor unions
Trans-Alaska Pipeline, 994(m)
transistor, invention of, 970
transistor radio, 959(i)
Trans-Missouri case (1897), 629
Transportation, Department of, 947

transportation system. *See also* airline industry; highways; railroads
  cattle drives and, 493
  freight lines and, 491
  JFK and, 864
  legislation on, 874(t)
  public, 840
  segregation of, 867
  water, 521–522
  during WWI, 684
Treasury bonds, 774
treaties. *See also* arms control; *particular treaties by name*
  with Great Plains Indians, 498–499, 502
  mutual defense, 824(m)
  nuclear test ban, 868
Treitschke, Heinrich von, 558
trench warfare, 646(i)
Triangle Shirtwaist factory fire, 618–619, 619(i), 620–621
Trinitron TV, 959(i)
Tri-Partite Pact (Germany, Japan, Italy; 1940), 797
Triple Alliance, 666, 674
Triple Entente, 666, 674
Triumphant Democracy (Carnegie), 587
Trotter, William Monroe, 625
True Story (magazine), 713
Truman, Harry S (1884–1972), 781, 797, 818–819
  atom bomb and, 793–795
  civil rights and, 815, 853
  Cold War and, 892
  communism and, 810, 825, 828
  death of Roosevelt and, 803
  desegregation of armed forces, 853
  election of 1948 and, 814, 814(i)
  Fair Deal of, 815, 819, 828
  George Kennan and, 803–804
  Korean War and, 810–812
  loyalty program of, 816
  Marshall Plan and, 805–807
  McCarthy and, 817–818
Truman, Harry S
  postwar price controls and, 813
  at Potsdam, 803
  as president (1945–1953), 803–819
  railroad strike and, 813
  recognition of Israel, 826
  Soviet Union and, 803
Truman Doctrine (1947), 804
Trumbull, Lyman, 459, 464
Trump, Donald, 962–963, 963(i)
trust-busting, 629. *See also* antitrust laws
trusts, 627, 629
Truth, Sojourner, 469
Tucson, Arizona, 509
Tugwell, Rexford, 739
turbine, 522
Turkey, 674, 803, 805, 1001

Turnbow, Hartman, 872
Turner, Frederick Jackson, 648
Turner, Henry M., 461
Tutsi, genocide of, 951
Twain, Mark (Samuel Clemens), 513, 555, 566, 579, 592, 594
Tweed, William Marcy "Boss", 572
"Tweed Days in St. Louis" (Steffens), 614
Twentieth Amendment (1933), 733
Twenty-first Amendment (1933), 692, 723, 765
Twenty-fourth Amendment (1964), 872, 874(t)
Twin Towers, radical Muslim attack on, 924
Tydings-McDuffie Act (1934), 757
Tyler, James G., 640(i)
Typographical Union (1852), 541

Udall, Stewart, 875
Uganda, 968(i)
Ukraine, 679, 788
Underwood Tariff Act (1913), 635
unemployment
   compensation for, 622, 746, 762, 819
   decay of inner cities and, 851–852
   decline of, 948
   declining economy and, 911
   environmentalism and, 913
   in Germany, 769
   Great Depression and, 729, 729(f), 731
   in late 19th century, 602
   migrant workers and, 849
   Native American, 888
   New Deal and, 742–744, 746–747
   in 1920s, 710, 728
   postwar, 835
   race riots and, 983
   rise in, 929, 944, 959–960
   Roosevelt recession and, 748, 765
   in Rust Belt, 916
   workers' compensation and, 622
   WWII and, 777
unemployment compensation, spending cuts for, 933
Union. *See* Civil War
Union Army, African Americans in, 471(i)
Union Pacific Railroad, 492, 507, 517, 523
Union Party, 748
unions. *See* labor unions
United Artists, 716
United Automobile Workers (UAW), 749, 835–836, 838
United Cannery, Agricultural, Packing, and Allied Workers, 750
United Farm Workers (UFW), 756, 886–887
United Fruit Company, 711, 712(i)
United Mine Workers (UMW), 749, 780
United Nations (UN), 794(i), 802–803
   Bush (George W.) and, 998
   China and, 810–811, 897

   founding of, 670, 792–793, 797
   General Assembly of, 793, 826
   Gulf War and, 945–946
   Haiti and, 952
   Korean War and, 810–812
   peacekeeping forces of, 810–811
   Persian Gulf War and, 1001(m)
   Security Council, 792, 803, 810, 897, 1000–1001, 1014
   weapons inspectors from, 1000
United States Border Patrol, 720(i)
United States Steel Corporation, 629, 633, 707, 710(i), 749–750, 895
United States v. Cruikshank, 478
UNIVAC computer, 970
Universal Negro Improvement Association (UNIA), 726
Unsafe at Any Speed (Nader), 913
Upward Bound, 876
urbanization, 551–581. *See also* cities
   industrialization and, 552, 580, 638
Urban Mass Transportation Act, 874(t)
U'Ren, Harold, 624
Uruguay, 920
U.S. News & World Report (magazine), 932
USA trilogy (Dos Passos), 762
USS *Abraham Lincoln,* 1001
USS *Arizona,* 773(i)
Utah, 505
   Japanese internment in, 785, 785(i)
Ute Indians, 499, 499(m)

Valparaiso (Chile), anti-U.S. riot in, 643
Vanderbilt, Cornelius, 522–523, 560(i), 579
Vanderbilt, George W., 579
Vanderbilt, William H., 560(i)
Van Kleek, Mary, 681
Vanzetti, Bartolomeo, 700–701, 701(i), 703
vaudeville, 574
Vaya, Count Vay de, 531–532
VCR (videocassette recorders), 972
Velvet Revolutions, 942, 955
venereal diseases, 692(i)
Venezuela, 642, 647, 1013
Verdun, 675, 679
Vermont, election of 1936 and, 748
Versailles, Treaty of (1919), 684(i), 694–698, 695(i), 703, 824(m)
   Hitler and, 768(i), 769
   Senate refusal to ratify, 670, 697, 702
   states created by, 942(m)
   WWII and, 768–769
vertical integration, 525(m), 526, 528, 834
veterans, benefits for, 622–623, 819
Veterans Administration, 837–838
victory gardens, 782
video recording, invention of, 834
Vienna Congress (1815), 896
Vietcong, 869, 878–879, 889

Vietnam
   communism in, 825
   insurgencies in, 1002
Vietnam Veterans Memorial, 890, 890(i)
Vietnam War (1961–1975), 877–884. *See also* antiwar movement
   aftermath of, 890
   Agent Orange and, 879, 882
   bombing campaigns in, 878–879, 889, 898, 900
   Buddhist opposition to, 869, 871(i)
   Cambodian attacks and, 898–900
   credibility gap in, 879
   defense spending and, 774(f)
   détente and, 898
   economy and, 833, 879
   Eisenhower administration and, 877, 892
   election of 1968 and, 888, 892(m)
   election of 1972 and, 899–900
   fall of Saigon and, 900, 900(i)
   firsthand accounts of, 880–881
   Great Society and, 877
   guerrilla tactics in, 877(m), 879
   Gulf of Tonkin resolution and, 878
   Johnson administration and, 877–884, 878(f), 882, 884, 892
   Kennedy administration and, 877, 892
   legacy of, 890
   mass media and, 879, 889, 900
   My Lai massacre and, 899
   Nixon administration and, 878(f), 892, 898–901
   Operation Rolling Thunder and, 878–879
   opposition to, 879–884, 898. *See also* antiwar movement
   Paris peace talks and, 898–900
   Persian Gulf War and, 946
   poverty and, 876, 876(f)
   prisoners of war in, 879
   Tet offensive and, 877(i)
   troops in, 878(i), 878–879, 878(f)
   Vietnamization policy in, 878(i), 898–899
vigilantes, Ku Klux Klan as, 708(m)
Viguerie, Richard, 928
Villa, Pancho, 665(i), 665–666, 678
Virginia
   election of 1928 and, 726
   freed blacks in, 470
   Reconstruction in, 467(m), 469
Virginia City, Nevada, 506
The Virginian (Wister), 563
Volker, Paul, 936
Volstead Act (1919), 722(i)
voluntarism
   Hoover and, 728
   trade unions and, 622
   in WWI, 683–684
voluntary sacrifice, 673(i), 684
Volunteers in Service to America (VISTA), 876

voting rights, 461, 465(i). See also Fifteenth Amendment
   African Americans and, 466–467, 476, 595–599, 597(m), 598(i), 872
   civil rights movement and, 872
   federal protection of, 853
   literacy tests and, 593, 597, 598(i), 599
   poll tax and, 598(i)
   in the South, 873(m)
   universal suffrage, 479
   women, 691(i)
   for women, 469. See also suffrage movement
Voting Rights Act (1965), 872, 873(m), 874(t), 903

Wabash Railroad, 523
WACs (Women's Army Corps), 777
Wade, Benjamin F., 468
Wade-Davis Bill (1864), 458, 483
Wadleigh, Michael, 884(i)
wage differentials, 750, 752
wages. See also minimum wage
   controls on, 717
   gender gap in, 533–536, 983
   immigrants and, 977–979
   labor for, 461, 464, 464(i), 473, 479
   multinational corporations and, 925
   productivity and, 958(f), 960, 960(f)
   in the South, 529–530, 596
   welfare capitalism and, 710–711
wageworkers, Hispanics as, 510
Wagner, Robert F., 619, 709
Wagner Act (Labor Relations Act; 1935), 747(t), 748–750, 765, 813 0–814
Wagon Train (TV show), 843
wagon trains, 489, 491, 505
Wake Island, 791
Wake Island (film), 782
Walesa, Lech, 941, 941(i)
Walkman radio, 959(i)
Wallace, George C., 867, 891–892, 892(m)
Wallace, Henry A., 739, 771, 781, 814
Wallace, Henry C., 706
Wallach, Lori, 969
Wall Street, New York City, 524, 605, 709, 744. See also stock market
Wal-Mart, 960, 965, 987
Wanamaker, John, 527, 549
War Brides Act (1945), 849
ward politics, 568–569
War Finance Corporation, 730
Warhol, Andy, 974
War Industries Board, 742
War Information, Office of (OWI), 782
Warm Springs, Georgia, 793
Warner, Charles Dudley, 579
Warner Brothers, 716
Warner Communications, 975
War on Poverty, 875–876, 892, 896

War on Terror, 990, 998–1002, 1006
War Powers Act (1941), 774
War Powers Act (1973), 902
War Production Board (WPB), 774
War Refugee Board, 791
War Relocation Authority, 785
Warren, Earl, 853, 910, 938
War Revenue Bills (1917), 684
War Risk Insurance Act (1917), 691, 703
Warsaw Pact, 806(m), 808, 822
Wartime Industries Board, 684(i), 684–685, 703
war to end all wars, 694
Washington, Booker T., 624–625
Washington, George (1732–1799), on foreign alliances, 824(m)
Washington Naval Arms Conference (1921), 670, 713, 735
Washington Post (newspaper), Watergate and, 902
Washington state, 505
WASPs (Women Airforce Service Pilots), 777
The Waste Land (Eliot), 723, 735
Watch on the Rhine (film), 782
Watergate scandal, 895, 901–902, 922, 1012
water power, manufacturing and, 521–522
water resources
   agriculture and, 497, 515
   preservation of, 874(t)
   in Sun Belt, 839
   transportation and, 521–522
Watson, James, 973(i)
Watson, Tom, 596–598, 600–601
Watt, James, 936
Wattenberg, Ben J., 891
WAVES (Women Accepted for Volunteer Emergency Service), 777
Wayne, John, 782
wealth. See also economy
   creed of individualism and, 587
   distribution of, 875, 963
   increase of, 627, 629
   per capita income and, 520, 782
   Reagan administration and, 962
   taxation and, 670, 995–996
   tax cuts and, 925, 935, 958–959
   unequal distribution of, 727, 745, 745(i)
   during WWI, 684
weapons of mass destruction (WMD), 1000, 1001(m), 1002. See also atomic bomb; nuclear weapons
The Weary Blues (Hughes), 723
Weathermen, 899
Weaver, James B., 602, 602(m), 607(m)
Web. See World Wide Web
Web logs. See blogs
Webster v. Reproductive Health Service (1989), 943, 955, 984
Weinberger, Caspar, 935, 939
Welch, Joseph, 817(i)

welfare, 691, 748, 756–757, 928
   during 1990s, 960
   collective bargaining as, 836
   conservativism and, 875, 916, 942
   cuts for, 933, 936, 939(i)
   in Europe, 747
   federal involvement with, 819, 896
   Great Depression and, 729(m), 733
   legislation on, 874(t)
   maternalist, 615
   New Deal and, 742–744, 747, 762–763
   Nixon and, 896
   reform of, 896, 924–925, 947, 950, 955, 958
   resentment of, 916
   Truman and, 815
   War on Poverty and, 876
   women and, 638
   WWII and, 781
welfare capitalism, 670, 710–711, 781, 796
Welfare Reform Act (1996), 980
Welles, Orson, 762
Wells, David A., 524
Wells, Ida B., 599, 599(i)
the West. See also migration
   closing of frontier in, 647
   economic growth of, 916, 916(m)
   election of 1928 and, 727(i)
   Kaiser and, 774–775
   Ku Klux Klan in, 708(m), 721
   migration to, 755–759, 757(i), 838–839, 850, 915, 916(m)
   pension plans in, 744
   settlement of, 487–517
   transmountain, 487(i), 487–517. See also California; Pacific slope
West Bank, 945, 1001(m)
Western Federation of Miners (WFM), 546
Western Front (WWI), 674–675, 675(m), 679, 679(m)
Western Trail (periodical), 495
Western Union, 523
West Germany. See Germany, Federal Republic of
West Indies. See also Caribbean Islands
   exports to, 987
Westinghouse, George, 523
West Side Story, 851(i)
westward expansion. See migration
Weyl, Walter, 613
Weyler, Valeriano, 648–649
Wharton, Edith, 559
wheat
   in California, 511, 513
   on Great Plains, 497–498
   prices of, 602, 710
   during WWI, 684
Whiskey Ring, 479, 483
White, Harry Dexter, 815
White, Walter, 755

I-40 ■ INDEX

White, William Allen, 589, 771
White Citizens' Councils, 853
White Man's Union, 599
white supremacy, 464, 481, 597–599, 608, 624–626. *See also* Ku Klux Klan; racism
Whitewater investigation, 948, 950
Whitfield, Donald L., 880
Whitlock, Brand, 590, 619
wholesale prices, 520(f)
Whyte, William, 835, 835(i)
"Why We Fight" documentaries, 782
Wickersham, George, 633
Wiener, Norbert, 841(i)
Wilderness Preservation Act (1964), 874(t)
Wildmon, Donald E., 930
The Wild One, 847
Wild West Show, 494, 494(i)
Wilhelm II, Emperor of Germany (r. 1888–1918), 666
Will, George F., 933, 983
Willamette Valley, Oregon, 491, 505–506
Willard, Frances, 594–595
Williams, Charles, 682
Williams v. Mississippi (1898), 598
Willkie, Wendell, 771
Wilson, Charles E., 822
Wilson, Edith Bolling Galt, 697
Wilson, Joseph C., 1004
Wilson, Pete, 982
Wilson, Sloan, 835
Wilson, Woodrow (1856–1924), 624, 635, 706, 802, 1015
    on congressional government, 585
    as Democratic Party nominee, 634(i), 634–635
    "Fourteen Points" of, 670, 694–696, 703, 771
    isolationism and, 770
    neutrality in WWI and, 674–675, 677
    the New Freedom and, 633–638
    as president (1913–1921), 664–666, 668, 673, 677(i), 677–678, 683, 684(i), 684–685, 691, 693, 695(i), 697, 700, 702–703
    presidential powers and, 739
    social program of, 636–637
    suffragists and, 617(i)
    trusts and, 635–636
Wilson-Gorman Tariff (1894), 605
Winfrey, Oprah, 974, 974(i)
The Winning of the West (T. Roosevelt), 647
Wisconsin, wheat in, 498
Wise, Stephen S., 620
Wissler, Clark, 489
Wister, Owen, 563
WMD. *See* weapons of mass destruction
Wobbelin concentration camp, 791(i)
Wobblies. *See* Industrial Workers of the World
Wojtyla, Karol Joseph (1920–2005), 941(i)

Wolfowitz, Paul, 996, 999
Woman's Christian Temperance Union (WCTU), 594–595, 595(i)
Woman Suffrage Association, National American (NAWSA), 594, 617, 688–691
women. *See also* children; marriage
    advertising to, 843
    African American, 474
    Asian migration and, 511
    birth rates and, 903
    in breadlines, 731(i)
    in cabinet positions, 947
    changing roles of, 905
    in China, 967(i)
    in Congress, 678
    consumer culture and, 714
    discrimination against, 903–906
    divorce and, 903
    as domestic servants, 533
    education of, 564
    employment of, 674, 685, 688, 689(i)
    feminist movement and, 903–906
    free black, 464, 474
    in Hispanic culture, 510
    Homestead Act and, 496
    jazz and, 716, 716(i)
    Ku Klux Klan and, 719(i), 721
    in labor force, 531, 533(i), 533–537, 545
    labor unions and, 541–544, 750
    legal status of married, 564
    middle-class, 714
    in military, 777, 945(i)
    minimum wage for, 617–618, 633, 750, 752
    New Deal and, 763
    in 1920s, 708–709, 709(i), 711, 714
    in 1950s, 846(i), 846–847
    opportunities for, 852
    in politics, 708–709
    popular protests and, 751(m)
    Progressivism and, 612, 614–618
    Radical Reconstruction program and, 469, 471
    rural electrification and, 759
    sexual harassment of, 944
    as sexual objects, 961(i)
    sharecropping and, 474
    social reform and, 545
    Social Security Act and, 763
    in textile industry, 533
    voter turnout and, 708
    wage gap and, 533–536
    War on Poverty and, 876
    in wartime jobs, 685, 688, 689(i)
    welfare and, 638
    westward migration and, 496–497
    in workforce, 778–779, 835(i), 846(i), 846–847, 905, 958(f), 960–961, 960(f), 987
    WWI and, 684–685, 688–692
    WWII and, 777–779, 797

Women's Christian Temperance Union (WCTU), 594–595, 595(i)
Women's Division of Democratic National Committee, 677(i), 751, 763
Women's Joint Congressional Committee, 708
Women's Land Army, 689(i)
Women's Peace Party, 676
women's rights, 603. *See also* feminism; suffrage movement
    conflicting values and, 983–984
    economic, 533–536
    equal, 721
    feminist movement and, 903–906
    in labor force, 545
    media and, 905
    movement for, 541–542, 594–595, 603, 603(i)
    radical Republicans and, 471
    sex-typing and, 532–533
    Title IX and, 905
    Title VII and, 903, 905
    voting, 469, 470(i), 594–595, 691(i)
    women's liberation and, 903, 904(i), 905
Woodley, Arthur E., Jr., 880–881
Woodstock, rock concert at, 884, 884(i)
Woodward, Bob, 902
Woolworth Building, 554
Woolworths, 713
work day, length, 479, 685
workers. *See* labor; labor force
workers' compensation programs, 709
working class. *See also* laborers
    conservatism of, 916
    feminism and, 904
    movie industry and, 715
    in 1950s, 849
    Nixon and, 896, 899
    prohibition and, 692
    school busing and, 907
    strikes and, 699
    on television, 843
    Vietnam War and, 899
    women, 846–847
    during WWI, 688
Working Men's Party, 511
Works Progress Administration (WPA), 747, 747(t), 752, 762(i), 765
    African Americans and, 754
    Federal One of, 760
    Roosevelt recession and, 748
World Bank (International Bank for Reconstruction and Development), 832, 834, 964, 970
WorldCom, 995
World's Work (periodical), 698
World Trade Center, 989, 989(i), 998, 998(i). *See also* September 11, 2001 terrorist attacks
    1993 bombing of, 953, 998

World Trade Organization (WTO), 964, 969(i), 969–970, 987
World War I (WWI; 1914–1918), 674–694, 703, 824(m)
  domestic efforts during, 673(i)
  Eastern Front, 674, 679
  liberty bonds of, 673, 683(i), 684
  Lusitania and, 677, 703
  progressive reforms and, 691–692
  Prohibition and, 703
  propaganda in, 682, 685, 693
  Red Scare after, 815–818
  reparations for, 735
  social reform and, 781
  trench warfare in, 646(i)
  U-boats in, 677–678
  U.S. involvement in, 703
  Western Front, 674–675, 675(m), 679, 679(m)
  women and, 685, 688–692, 689(i)
  WWII and, 768
World War II (WWII; 1939–1945), 767–797
  budget deficits in, 935(f)
  casualties in, 767, 789–791
  causes of, 713
  decolonization and, 865(m)
  defense spending and, 774(f)
  in Europe (1941–1943), 788(m), 788–789(m)
  government spending and, 749
  in North Atlantic, 772(m)
  in Pacific, 792–793(m)
  reparations and, 806
  second front in, 787
  women during, 777, 777(i), 778–779
  WWI and, 768
World Wide Web, 924, 957(i), 966, 970–972, 987. *See also* Internet
Worrall, Henry, 495(i)
Wounded Knee, South Dakota
  massacre at, 487, 499(m), 504, 504(i), 517
  occupation of (1973), 888, 888(i)
Wovoka, Indian holy man, 503–504
Wright, Richard, 762
WTO. *See* World Trade Organization
WWI. *See* World War I
WWII. *See* World War II
Wyoming, 505, 785, 785(i)

Yalta meeting (1945), 791–792, 794(i), 797, 802–803, 815
Yalu River, 811
Yao Ming, 966
Yellow Bird, Sioux medicine man, 504, 504(i)
yellow-dog contracts, 543
yellow journalism, 577–578
The Yellow Kid (comic strip), 578
Yeltsin, Boris, 942
Yemen, 953(i), 989
yeoman farmers, 470
yippies, 889
YMCA. *See* Young Men's Christian Association

Yom Kippur War (1973), 911
York, Alvin, 680
Yosemite National Park, 515
Yosemite Valley, 487(i), 514, 517
Young Men's Christian Association (YMCA), 573, 593, 691
Young Women's Christian Association (YWCA), 573, 691
youth, 564, 580, 876. *See also* National Youth Administration
  WWII and, 784
youth culture, 564. *See also* counterculture
  music of, 847–848
  in 1950s, 847
Ypres, 675
Y2K fears, 957
Yugoslavia, 697, 942(m), 952, 952(m)
Yuppies, 924, 959, 987
YWCA. *See* Young Women's Christian Association

al-Zarqawi, Abu Musab, 1003
Zhu Shida, 940
Zimmerman, Arthur, 678
zinc mines, 506
Zionism, 825–826
Zitkala-Ša (Gertrude Simmons Bonnin), 501
Znaniecki, Florian, 570
Zola, Emile, 660
zoot suits, 784(i)

Abbreviations	
ALB.	ALBANIA
AUS.	AUSTRIA
BEL.	BELGIUM
B.H.	BOSNIA AND HERZEGOVINA
CR.	CROATIA
CZ. REP.	CZECH REPUBLIC
DEN.	DENMARK
HUNG.	HUNGARY
LUX.	LUXEMBOURG
MAC.	MACEDONIA
NETH.	NETHERLANDS
S.M.	SERBIA AND MONTENEGRO
SLK.	SLOVAKIA
SLN.	SLOVENIA
SWITZ.	SWITZERLAND

Understanding History through Maps

Working with maps deepens your understanding of the basic issues of geography and how they relate to historical studies. Understanding these five themes — location, place, region, movement, and interaction — will enrich your readings of maps and the historical situation they depict.

Location "When?" and "where?" are the first questions asked by historians and cartographers. Every event happens somewhere and at some point in time, and maps are the best devices to show a particular location at a particular time.

Place Human activity creates places. Locations exist on their own without the presence of people, but they become places when people use the spots in some way. As human enterprise thickens and generation after generation use a place, it accumulates artifacts, develops layers of remains, and generates a variety of associations held in a society's history and memory.

Region A region highlights common elements, tying certain places together as a group distinguishable from other places. Perceiving regional ties helps the reader of historical maps because they suggest the forces binding individual interests together and encouraging people to act in common.

Movement All historical change involves movement. People move in their daily activities, in seasonal patterns, and in migration to new places of residence. To understand a map fully, the reader must always envision it as one part of a sequence, not unlike a "still" excerpted from a motion picture.

Interaction The interaction between people and the environment goes both ways. On the one hand, people change their environment to suit their needs. Human ingenuity has found ways to put almost all places to some use. On the other hand, climate and topography present constraints on how people use the land and force people to change their behavior and culture as they adapt to their natural surroundings.